October 7–12, 2012
Tampere, Finland

Association for Computing Machinery

Advancing Computing as a Science & Profession

CODES+ISSS'12

Proceedings of the Tenth ACM International Conference on

Hardware/Software-Codesign and System Synthesis

(co-located with ESWEEK)

Sponsored by:

ACM SIGMICRO, ACM SIGBED, and ACM SIGDA

Technical Supporters:

IEEE Computer Society, IEEE Circuits and Systems Society, and IEEE Council on Electronic Design Automation

Supporters:

IFIP, IEEE Finland Section, and Federation of Finnish Learned Societies

Association for
Computing Machinery

Advancing Computing as a Science & Profession

The Association for Computing Machinery
2 Penn Plaza, Suite 701
New York, New York 10121-0701

Notice to Past Authors of ACM-Published Articles
ACM intends to create a complete electronic archive of all articles and/or other material previously published by ACM. If you have written a work that has been previously published by ACM in any journal or conference proceedings prior to 1978, or any SIG Newsletter at any time, and you do NOT want this work to appear in the ACM Digital Library, please inform permissions@acm.org, stating the title of the work, the author(s), and where and when published.

ISBN: 978-1-4503-1423-7 (Digital)

ISBN: 978-1-4503-1426-8 (Print)

Additional copies may be ordered prepaid from:

ACM Order Department
PO Box 30777
New York, NY 10087-0777, USA

Phone: 1-800-342-6626 (USA and Canada)
+1-212-626-0500 (Global)
Fax: +1-212-944-1318
E-mail: acmhelp@acm.org
Hours of Operation: 8:30 am – 4:30 pm ET

ACM Order Number: 618122

Printed in the USA

Welcome Message

On behalf of the Organizing Committee and the committees of our participating conferences - CASES, CODES+ISSS, and EMSOFT - we would like to welcome you to Embedded Systems Week - ESWEEK 2012 - in Tampere, Finland. 2012 marks the 8th edition of ESWEEK. Earlier meetings were held in Jersey City, Seoul, Salzburg, Atlanta, Grenoble, Scottsdale and Taipei. This meeting has grown from two conferences and a handful of workshops to three conferences and ten workshops and symposia. ESWEEK is now widely recognized as the premier technical event in embedded computing.

The combined programme of the three conferences will offer three plenary keynotes, an industry day, and over 100 technical paper presentations. ESWEEK will also offer a number of half-day tutorials that cover hot topics of general interest to the embedded systems community. Additionally, this year, the International Symposium on System-on-Chip (SoC) will be co-located with ESWEEK. First of all, special thanks go to the technical programme chairs of the three conferences: Vincent Mooney, Rodric Rabbah, Franco Fummi, Naehyuck Chang, Florence Maraninchi, and John Regehr. This year, Embedded Systems Week includes ten workshops featuring outstanding contributions on specific topics. We especially wish to thank the workshop organisers: Aviral Shrivastava, Wolfgang Ecker, Wolfgang Mueller, Shahrokh Daijavad, Sumedh Sathaye, Seraphin Calo, Dimitrios Serpanos, Jian-Jia Chen, Maurizio Palesi, Nikil Dutt, Jason Xue, Jeff Jackson, Peter Marwedel, Kenneth Ricks, Fabiano Hessel, Jérôme Hugues, Frédéric Rousseau, Rolf Ernst and Alberto Sangiovanni-Vincentelli.

A complex event such as ESWEEK is a team effort that requires a dedicated group of volunteers to manage the success of the conference's growth in scale and offerings. We wish to thank every member of the organizing committee for their dedicated efforts in making the event a success. In particular, special thanks go to the following people for managing critical aspects of the conference organization: Jari Nurmi and Irmeli Lehto for local organization; David Atienza for finances; Suzanne Lesecq for publications; Francescantonio Della Rosa and Aviral Shrivastava for the conference website; Edward Chu and Frédéric Pétrot for electronic media and the paper submission system; Sungjoo Yoo, Tapani Ahonen and Yuan Xie for industry liaison; Gabriela Nicolescu, Jian-Jia Chen and Roberto Airoldi for workshops; Saddek Bensalem for tutorials; Henri-Pierre Charles, Xiaobo Sharon Hu and Hamaguchi Kiyoharu for publicity; Enrico Macii for coordinating the best paper award selections; Rolf Ernst for panels and special sessions; Hiroto Yasuura and Hiroyuki Tomiyama for handling the Asia liaison; Luigi Carro and Fabiano Hessel for handling Latin America liaison; Rajesh Gupta, Alex Orailoglu, Marilyn Wolf, Naehyuck Chang and Donald Thomas for professional society liaisons.

We also thank the Steering Committee members and the Technical Programme Committee members of each conference and workshop for selecting papers of the highest quality. Finally, we thank our sponsoring societies: ACM (SIGBED, SIGDA, SIGMICRO), IEEE (CAS, Computer, CEDA), and the cooperation with IFIP.

Tampere – the SoC city – is situated in the heart of beautiful Finnish Lakeland. The banks of the Tammerkoski rapids still feature old traditional industrial buildings which have now been converted to house pleasant restaurants, pubs or high-tech companies. Tampere is also a city of theatres, arts, sciences, sport and modern industrial culture. We therefore invite you to attend ESWEEK 2012 to learn about the latest in embedded system technologies, and also discover the beauty, culture and technological miracles of Finland.

Ahmed Jerraya
ESWeek 2012 General Chair
CEA, France

Luca Carloni
ESWeek 2012 General co-Chair
Columbia University, USA

CODES+ISSS Technical Program Co-Chair Welcome Message

On behalf of the IEEE/ACM International Conference on Hardware/Software-Codesign and System Synthesis (CODES+ISSS) Technical Program Committee, we would like to welcome you to the 10th CODES+ISSS. The CODES+ISSS is the premier conference for system-level synthesis and design ranging from embedded systems to large-scale systems and beyond, systems of systems, with a focus on the design of hardware, software, and tools. In 2012, we continue the tradition of maintaining a high-quality forum for active discussion on current and innovative topics on system synthesis and design that bring together the latest in academic and industrial research and development.

We carried out a rigorous review process and a face-to-face Technical Program Committee meeting and selected 48 papers among 163 submissions with an acceptance rate of 29%. The Technical Program Committee carefully reviewed all papers with an average of 4 reviews per paper. The entire review process strictly obeyed the blind review policy, and the Technical Program Committee meeting was carefully conducted considering conflict of interest of the Technical Program Committee members. The Technical Program Committee members selected the a part of high-quality papers, and a part of high-quality papers were not accepted because this year CODES+ISSS paper selection was highly competitive. As interaction between presenters and other conference attendees is extremely important in CODES+ISSS, we organize poster sessions during the last 30 minutes of every session to encourage extensive interaction among the speakers and audiences.

The CODES+ISSS is part of the growing Embedded Systems Week (ESWEEK) that has been positioned as the premier international event in embedded systems research and development. The CODES+ISSS is complemented by two other flagship sister conferences: EMSOFT (International Conference on Embedded Software) and CASES (International Conference on Compliers, Architecture and Synthesis for Embedded Systems). Registrants to ESWEEK may attend sessions in any of the three conferences. The technical programs of the three conferences, including keynotes, special sessions, panels, tutorials and workshops, have been carefully planned to avoid major overlaps and complement each other.

In 2012, the CODES+ISSS Technical Program Committee compose 16 regular sessions, one of which is a joint session with the CASES Program Committee, two special sessions, and three tutorials. We implemented a two-stage selection process of the special sessions again in 2012. Special session proposals have been submitted to the Program Committee, presented and evaluated at the Program Committee meeting. We selected the best two proposals such as TLM verification and system-level design consisting of five contributions each. The special session paper presentation will be followed by a panel discussion with the special sessions organizers. In addition, the CODES+ISSS Technical Program is completed by two tutorials organized in the context of ESWeek.

The high technical quality of the CODES+ISSS program is a direct result of the dedicated efforts of the Steering Committee, Organizing Committee, Technical Program Committee and numerous reviewers who contributed their time and expertise, as well as the authors who submitted their work to the conference. We are grateful to all of them for their efforts and thank them whole heartedly. We would also like to thank our sponsoring societies: ACM Special Interest Group on

Embedded Systems (SIGBED), Special Interest Group on Design Automation (SIGDA), Special Interest Group on Microarchitecture (SIGMICRO), IEEE Circuits and Systems Society (CAS), Computer Society (CS), and the Council of Electronic Design Automation (CEDA).

In 2012, the CODES-ISSS is held in Tampere, Finland. We hope the conference and its proceedings prove useful to you, and that you enjoy attending.

Naehyuck Chang	**Franco Fummi**
CODES+ISSS	*CODES+ISSS*
Technical Program Co-Chairs	*Technical Program Co-Chairs*

Table of Contents

Session 2A: Managing Parallelism in Multi-core Systems

Session 2B: NOC and Memory Performance Analysis and Mapping

Session 3A: Efficient Simulation Techniques

Session 3B: Routing Algorithms and NoC Architectures for Next-Generation 2D/3D SoCs

Session 5B: Enabling Hardware Design in System Context

Session Chair: Jarmo Takala *(Tampere University of Technology)*

Session 6A: Special Session Testbenches for Advanced TLM Verification

Session Chair: Wolfgang Mueller *(C-LAB)*

Session 6B: Power-Efficient Mobile Computing

Session Chair: William Fornaciari *(Politecnico di Milano)*

Session 6C: System-level Synthesis and Optimization

Session Chair: Brett Meyer *(McGill University)*

Session 8B: Special Session Synthesis of Executable Extra-Functional System-Level Models for Timing and Power Exploration

Session Chair: Kim Grüttner *(OFFIS Institute for Information Technology)*

Tutorial

ESWEEK 2012 Organizing Committee

General Chairs:	Ahmed Jerraya *(CEA-Leti, France)* Luca Carloni *(Columbia University, USA)*
Conference Programme Chairs:	CASES Vincent Mooney *(Georgia Institute of Technology, USA)* Rodric Rabbah *(IBM, USA)* CODES+ISSS Franco Fummi *(University of Verona, Italy)* Naehyuck Chang *(Seoul National University, Korea)* EMSOFT Florence Maraninchi *(Grenoble INP, France)* John Regehr *(School of Computing, University of Utah, USA)*
Finance Chair:	David Atienza *(EPFL, Switzerland)*
Local Arrangements Chairs:	Jari Nurmi *(Tampere University of Technology, Finland)* Irmeli Lehto *(Tampere University of Technology, Finland)*
Workshop Chairs:	Gabriela Nicolescu *(Polytechnique Montréal, Canada)* Jian-Jia Chen *(Karlsruhe Institute of Technology, Germany)* Roberto Airoldi *(Tampere University of Technology, Finland)*
Publication Chair:	Suzanne Lesecq *(CEA-Leti, France)*
Awards Chair:	Enrico Macii *(Politecnico di Torino, Italy)*
Tutorials Chair:	Saddek Bensalem *(Université Joseph Fourier, France)*
Panels & Special Sessions Chair:	Rolf Ernst *(TU Braunschweig, Germany)*
Web Chairs:	Aviral Shrivastava *(Arizona State University, USA)* Francescantonio Della Rosa *(Tampere University of Technology, Finland)*
Electronic Media Chairs:	Edward Chu *(National Yunlin University of Science and Technology, Taiwan)* Frederic Pétrot *(Grenoble INP, France)*
Publicity Chair Europe:	Henri-Pierre Charles *(CEA-List, France)*
Publicity Chair North America:	Xiaobo Sharon Hu *(University of Notre Dame, USA)*

Publicity Chair Asia Pacific: Hamaguchi Kiyoharu *(Osaka University, Japan)*

Industry Liaison Asia Pacific: Sungjoo Yoo *(Postech, Korea)*

Industry Liaison Europe: Tapani Ahonen *(Tampere University of Technology)*

Industry Liaison North America: Yuan Xie *(Pennsylvania State University, USA)*

Latin America Liaison Chairs: Luigi Carro *(Federal University of Rio Grande do Sul, Brasil)*
Fabiano Hessel *(PUCRS, Brasil)*

Asia Liaison: Hiroto Yasuura *(Kyushu University, Japan)*
Hiroyuki Tomiyama *(Ritsumeikan University, Japan)*

IEEE CEDA/CAS Liaison: Rajesh Gupta *(University of California, San Diego, USA)*

IEEE CS Liaison: Alex Orailoglu *(University of California, San Diego, USA)*

IFIP Liaison: Marilyn Wolf *(Georgia Tech, USA)*

ACM SIGDA Liaison: Naehyuck Chang *(Seoul National University, Korea)*

ACM SIGBED Liaison: Donald Thomas *(Carnegie Mellon University, USA)*

Steering Committee: CASES
Joerg Henkel *(Karlsruhe Institute of Technology, Germany)*
Vinod Kathail *(Xilinx, Synfora, USA)*

CODES+ISSS
Reinaldo Bergamaschi *(Odysci, USA)*
Don Thomas *(Carnegie Mellon University, USA)*

EMSOFT
Insup Lee *(University of Pennsylvania, USA)*
Lothar Thiele *(ETH Zurich, Switzerland)*

CODES+ISSS 2012 Organization

Program Co-Chair: Naehyuck Chang *(Seoul National University, Korea)*
Franco Fummi *(University of Verona, Italy)*

Program Committee: Bashir Al-Hashimi *(University of Southampton)*
Sudarshan Banerjee *(University of California, Irvine)*
Lars Bauer *(Karlsruhe Institute of Technology)*
Luca Benini *(University of Bologna)*
Reinaldo Bergamaschi *(University of California, Berkeley)*
Yiran Chen *(University of Pittsburgh)*
Kiyoung Choi *(Seoul National University)*
Alessandro Cimatti *(FBK)*
Robert Dick *(University of Michigan)*
Rainer Doemer *(University of California, Irvine)*
Adam Donlin *(University of Edinburgh)*
Nikil Dutt *(University of California, Irvine)*
Petru Eles *(Linköping University)*
Rolf Ernst *(Technical University of Braunschweig)*
Fabrizio Ferrandi *(Politecnico di Milano)*
Catherine Gebotys *(University of Waterloo)*
Andreas Gerstlauer *(University of Texas at Austin)*
Tony Givargis *(University of California, Irvine)*
Kees Goossens *(Eindhoven University of Technology)*
Ann Gordon-Ross *(University of Florida)*
Soonhoi Ha *(Seoul National University)*
Frank Hannig *(University of Erlangen-Nuremberg)*
Christian Haubelt *(University of Rostock)*
Jörg Henkel *(Karlsruhe Institute of Technology)*
Roman Hermida *(Complutense University)*
Pao-Ann Hsiung *(National Chung Cheng University)*
Shi-Yu Huang *(National Tsing Hua University)*
Tohru Ishihara *(Kyoto University)*
Fadi J. Kurdahi *(University of California, Irvine)*
Axel Jantsch *(Royal Institute of Technology, Stockholm)*
Ahmed Jerraya *(CEA-LETI, MINATEC, France)*
Niraj Jha *(Princeton University)*
Alex Jones *(University of Pittsburgh)*
Per Kjeldsberg *(Norwegian University of Science and Technology)*
Erwin Kock *(Philips Research, Netherlands)*
Wido Kruijtzer *(Philips Research Laboratories, Netherlands)*
Tei-Wei Kuo *(National Taiwan University)*
Luciano Lavagno *(Politecnico di Torino)*
Chang-Gun Lee *(Seoul National University)*
Jenq-Kuen Lee *(National Tsing Hua University)*

Program Committee (continued):

Youn-Long Lin *(National Tsing Hua University)*
Roman Lysecky *(University of Arizona)*
Susan Lysecky *(University of Arizona)*
Enrico Macii *(Politecnico di Torino)*
Jan Madsen *(Technical University of Denmark)*
Radu Marculescu *(Carnegie Mellon University)*
Grant Martin *(Tensilica Inc.,)*
Peter Marwedel *(Technical University of Dortmund)*
Brett Meyer *(McGill University)*
Prabhat Mishra *(University of Florida)*
Wolfgang Mueller *(University of Paderborn)*
Hyunok Oh *(Hanyang University)*
Alex Orailoglu *(University of California, San Diego)*
Maurizio Palesi *(Kore university)*
Preeti Panda *(IIT Delhi)*
Sri Parameswaran *(The University of New South Wales)*
Sudeep Pasricha *(Colorado State University)*
JoAnn Paul *(Virginia Tech)*
Andy Pimentel *(University of Amsterdam)*
Massimo Poncino *(Politecnico di Torino)*
Graziano Pravadelli *(University of Verona)*
Martin Radetzki *(University of Stuttgart)*
Praveen Raghavan *(Catholic University of Leuven)*
Vijay Raghunathan *(Purdue University)*
Karamvir S. Chatha *(Arizona State University)*
Marco Santambrogio *(Massachusetts Institute of Technology)*
Gunar Schirner *(Northeastern University)*
Donatella Sciuto *(Politecnico di Milano)*
Dimitrios Serpanos *(University of Patras)*
Edwin Sha *(University of Texas at Dallas)*
Zili Shao *(Hong Kong Polytechnic University)*
Aviral Shrivastava *(Arizona State University)*
Frank Slomka *(The University of Ulm)*
Todor Stefanov *(Leiden University)*
Greg Stitt *(University of Florida)*
Jürgen Teich *(University of Erlangen-Nuremberg)*
Donald Thomas *(Carnegie-Mellon University)*
Hiroyuki Tomiyama *(Ritsumeikan University)*
Frank Vahid *(University of California)*
Kazutoshi Wakabayashi *(NEC)*
Yuan Xie *(Pennsylvania State University)*
Jiang Xu *(The Hong Kong University)*
Jason Xue *(City University of Hong Kong)*
Chia-Lin Yang *(National Taiwan University)*
Mark Zwolinski *(University of Southampton)*

ESWEEK 2012 Sponsors & Supporters

Sponsors:

Technical Supporters:

Supporters:

ESWEEK 2012 Keynote Talk

Wireless Innovations for Smartphones

Hannu Kauppinen
Nokia Research Center,
Helsinki, Finland
hannu.kauppinen@nokia.com

ABSTRACT

The ever increasing demand for fast mobile internet connectivity continues to set challenges for research in radio communications. On one hand the capacity demand can be served by offloading data traffic to local networks. On the other hand using more bandwidth, and possibly dynamically allocating spectrum in a flexible way, will improve the usage of the available spectrum. The future of wireless access continues to be defined by the 3GPP and IEEE standards setting bodies. Radios can also provide innovative features that offer new functionalities for consumers, such as ultra-fast local connectivity, sensing and positioning. This talk will present examples of various radio, sensing and multimedia innovations for smartphones.

Categories and Subject Descriptors

H.4.3 [**Information Systems Applications**]: Communications Applications

General Terms

Design.

Keywords

Radio connectivity, mobile internet connectivity, dynamic spectrum allocation.

BIOGRAPHY

Dr. Hannu Kauppinen is currently holding the position of Vice President, Head of Nokia Research Center. In this capacity he is responsible for the long term research of mobile technologies that will secure product differentiation and long-term profitable growth for Nokia. Hannu Kauppinen has a strong track record in bringing research innovations to products.

Hannu Kauppinen joined Nokia Research Center in 1997 has since then held key leadership positions in Nokia's wireless research. He has contributed to and overseen research in cognitive radio systems, cellular systems, wireless local connectivity, networking technologies, software defined radios, RF and antenna design, as well as sensing and positioning radios. During 2007-2008 and 2010-2011 Hannu Kauppinen was the Director of the Radio Systems Laboratory in Nokia Research Center. He was responsible for the research for 3GPP and IEEE radio standards as well as the research for cognitive and sensor radios to ensure innovativeness and competitiveness of wireless communication solutions in Nokia's products.

Hannu Kauppinen holds a PhD degree in Physics from the Helsinki University of Technology (1997) and an Executive MBA from the Helsinki School of Economics (2007).

ESWEEK 2012 Special Presentation
CASES'12, CODES+ISSS'12, EMSOFT'12,
Oct. 7–12, 2012, Tampere, Finland.
ACM 978-1-4503-1424-4 & 978-1-4503-1426-8
& 978-1-4503-1425-1/12/09.

ESWEEK 2012 Keynote Talk

Computing Without Processors

Satnam Singh
Technical Infrastructure division,
Google
1600 Amphitheatre Parkway
Mountain View, CA 94043
s.singh@acm.org

ABSTRACT

The duopoly of computing has up until now been delimited by drawing a line in the sand that defines the instruction set architecture as the hard division between software and hardware. On one side of this contract Intel improved the design of processors and on the other side of this line Microsoft developed ever more sophisticated software. This cozy relationship is now over as the distinction between hardware and software is blurred due to relentless pressure for performance and reduction in latency and energy consumption. Increasingly we will be forced to compute with architectures and machines which do not resemble regular processors with a fixed memory hierarchy based on heuristic caching schemes. Other ways to bake all that sand will include the evolution of GPUs and FPGAs to form heterogeneous computing resources which are much better suited to meeting our computing needs than racks of multicore processors. This presentation will highlight some of the programming challenges we face when trying to develop for heterogeneous architectures and a few promising lines of attack are identified.

Categories and Subject Descriptors

D.1.0 [**Programming Techniques**]: General

General Terms

Algorithms, Design.

Keywords

HW/SW frontier, programming, heterogeneous architecture.

BIOGRAPHY

Prof. Singh works in the Technical Infrastructure division of Google in Mountain View, California and focuses on the configuration management of Google's data-center services. Previously Prof. Singh worked on the design of heterogeneous systems at Microsoft Research in Cambridge UK and on parallel programming techniques at Microsoft's Developer Division in Redmond USA. He has also worked on re-configurable computing and formal verification at Xilinx in San Jose, California and as an academic at the University of Glasgow. He also currently holds a part-time position as the Chair of Reconfigurable Systems at the University of Birmingham.

ESWEEK 2012 Special Presentation
CASES'12, CODES+ISSS'12, EMSOFT'12,
Oct. 7–12, 2012, Tampere, Finland.
ACM 978-1-4503-1424-4 & 978-1-4503-1426-8
& 978-1-4503-1425-1/12/09.

ESWEEK 2012 Keynote Talk

A Standards-Based, Fully-Open Software Platform for Smart Embedded Systems

Jong-Deok Choi
Samsung Electronics
Suwon, Gyeonggi-Do, Korea
jd11.choi@samsung.com

ABSTRACT

There has been an explosion of smart mobile devices over the last few years. These smart devices, such as smartphones and tablets, have changed many aspects of modern life. They have also enabled whole new industries to grow up that develop and manufacture "companion products" of the smart devices. These companion products, however, are mostly built around the smart devices, instead of being tightly integrated into them, and fail to utilize the full capabilities of the smart devices. The main cause for their failure is that the software platforms these smart devices are built on are not fully open. This hinders efforts by device manufacturers or software developers to create innovative new products or product categories based on those software platforms.

In this talk, we present Tizen (www.tizen.org), which is a "fully open" software platform for embedded systems. Tizen allows for everyone involved in building and using devices built on it to freely define, invent, add new features or business models, or create new device categories. Tizen offers an industry leading HTML5-based application APIs, the preferred development environment for apps and services for the future. The HTML5-based APIs make it easy for developers to create applications that run across various categories of devices such as mobile, in-vehicle infotainment (IVI), Digital TV, netbooks, health and medical devices, etc. In this talk we also present Tizen's optimization technologies that enable HTML5-based applications to enjoy performance comparable to that of native applications. We also describe how Tizen balances the trade-offs between performance and power consumption, which is of extreme importance for mobile devices.

Categories and Subject Descriptors

D.3.3 [**Programming Languages**]: Language Constructs and Features – *frameworks.*

General Terms

Languages.

Keywords

Tizen, HTML5, smart device, software platform.

BIOGRAPHY

Dr. Jong-Deok Choi is an Executive Vice President at Samsung Electronics in Korea, and is currently in charge of the Software Platform Team within Samsung's Software Research Center. Before joining Samsung Electronics, he worked at IBM T. J. Watson Research Center as a Research Staff Member and Manager.

While working at IBM Research, he contributed to optimizing Java Webservices applications, the JikesRVM open-source Java virtual machine (JVM), the PTRAN parallelizing-compiler project, and others.

Dr. Choi has published over 50 technical papers in top journals and conferences on various fields in computer science, and holds over 20 US patents. He has served as a program (co-)chair, conference steering-committee member, and program-committee member for numerous technical conferences.

Dr. Choi received his Ph.D. and M.S. in Computer Sciences from University of Wisconsin - Madison, USA, in 1989 and 1985, respectively; M.S. in Electrical Engineering from KAIST, Korea, in 1981; and B.S. in Electronic Engineering from Seoul National University (SNU), Korea, in 1979.

ESWEEK 2012 Special Presentation
CASES'12, CODES+ISSS'12, EMSOFT'12,
Oct. 7–12, 2012, Tampere, Finland.
ACM 978-1-4503-1424-4 & 978-1-4503-1426-8
& 978-1-4503-1425-1/12/09.

Internet-of-Energy: Combining Embedded Computing and Communication for the Smart Grid

Randolf Mock
Siemens AG
Munich, Germany

Moritz Neukirchner, Rolf Ernst
TU Braunschweig
Braunschweig, Germany

Ruud Wijtvliet
Centrosolar Group
Hamburg, Germany

Michael Huetwohl
Lantiq GmbH
Munich, Germany

Pascal Urard
ST Microelectronics
Crolles, France

Ovidiu Vermesan *(organizer)*
Sintef ICT
Oslo, Norway
Ovidiu.Vermesan@sintef.no

ABSTRACT
Driven by increasing cost of energy and by the inclusion of renewable but time variant sources of energy on the production side, and by new requirements from electromobility, building and home automation on the consumption side, the energy grid has moved in the focus of research, industry and infrastructure development. One of the key challenges is the interaction of the numerous em-bedded systems controlling energy producing and consuming devices using an "internet of energy."

This session will provide different views on this development towards a smart energy grid. The first talk given by a leading provider of energy grid equipment will give an overview on the new developments and challenges in modeling and simulating local grid behavior. The second talk discusses building energy management at the interface between home automation and the smart grid, both from the application and the embedded platform perspective. The third talk addresses home automation which serves many objectives, besides being a terminal network of the smart grind. Last not least, the fourth talk presents new development in wireless sensor devices as an important component of future home and energy networks.

Categories and Subject Descriptors
J.7 [**Computer Applications**]: COMPUTERS IN OTHER SYSTEMS – *Command and control; Process control; Real time.*

Keywords
Design, Measurement, Performance, Reliability, Verification, Smart Energy, Smart Grid.

1. Interactions of Large Scale EV Mobility and Smart Grids - Chances and Challenges of Grid Infrastructure Simulations
Randolf Mock, Siemens, Germany

The complex interactions between electric mobility on a large scale with the electric distribution grid constitute a considerable challenge regarding the feasibility, the efficiency and the stability of smart electric distribution grids. Grid infrastructure simulations which take into account the details of these interactions and which are backed by comprehensive demonstrators may help to shed light on crucial aspects of both energy and information exchange between the traffic and the electric energy infrastructure regime. This will be highlighted by selected topics which intend to shed light on the scope and the challenges inherent in this area of simulation.

2. Reliable Building Energy Management in the Smart Grid
Moritz Neukirchner, Rolf Ernst, TU Braunschweig; Ruud Wijtvliet, Centrosolar, Germany

Reliable building energy management must guarantee a variety of services, support of local network control for grid stability and optimization, access for remote device maintenance and diagnosis, tamperfree metering, security against attacks targeting the building or network operations. The talk discusses applications, derives embedded platform requirements, and shows first solutions based on virtualization and self-protection.

3. Home Networks for the Smart Grid and Other Future Applications
Michael Huetwohl, Lantiq, Germany

The number of connected devices in our daily live has significantly increased. And it will continue to further increase x-fold in the near future. IPv6 is the key enabler. The huge social-economic challenges like the transition to renewable energy sources or the aging society are the drivers for this development. The devices and related applications will have a wide spread of different requirements: data rates from kbit/s to Gbit/s, Qualtity of Service, security and reliability will be of significant importance. In order to support these requirements a powerful Home Network and smart, easy-to-use, interoperable communication devices will be needed. The current status of Home Networks is not adequate and needs improvement.

4. Wireless Sensor Components (Draft title)
Pascal Urard, ST Microelectronics, France

Abstract not available at time of publication.

ESWEEK 2012 Special Presentation
CASES'12, CODES+ISSS'12, EMSOFT'12,
Oct. 7–12, 2012, Tampere, Finland.
ACM 978-1-4503-1424-4 & 978-1-4503-1426-8
& 978-1-4503-1425-1/12/09.

Trends in Automotive Embedded Systems

Dan Gunnarsson
BMW Group
Munich, Germany

Stefan Kuntz
Continental Corp.
Regensburg, Germany

Glenn Farrall
Infineon
Bristol, UK

Akihiko Iwai
Denso Corp.
Kariya-shi, Japan

Rolf Ernst *(organizer)*
Technische Universität Braunschweig
Braunschweig, Germany
r.ernst@tu-bs.de

ABSTRACT

Automotive embedded systems have developed from single controllers to networked embedded systems integrating an ever growing variety of distributed applications. New features for driving assistance, improved safety, motor and energy management, and infotainment lead to shorter innovation cycles for software architectures, network technologies, and hardware architectures. While, e.g., the new FlexRay bus standard has just been introduced, next generation Ethernet is already at the edge of introduction. The 4 talks in this session present OEM, 1st tier supplier and semiconductor vendor views from leading automotive companies and suppliers.

Categories and Subject Descriptors

C.3 [**Computer Systems Organization**]: Real-time and embedded systems.

Keywordss

Design, Economics, Performance, Reliability, Security, Verification, Automotive electronics.

1. Trends and new Challenges in Automotive E/E Architectures

Dan Gunnarsson, BMW, Germany

Over the last decades integrated systems, where functions are partitioned on several ECUs, connected with data communication networks has evolved. During this development new communication methods and principal have been introduced, starting with system with low to moderate complexity moving to highly complex systems. Current requirements on the E/E Architecture are increasingly complex e.g. through the introduction of new and more advanced driver assistance systems where new use-cases like transmission of video streams with real-time requirements are becoming more common. To meet these requirements Ethernet is currently being introduced as an automotive network. This means that new challenges with regard to gateways and the transition between different protocols and networks have to be mastered. To cope with these increasingly complex tasks new modeling and analysis capabilities are needed.

ESWEEK 2012 Special Presentation
CASES'12, CODES+ISSS'12, EMSOFT'12,
Oct. 7–12, 2012, Tampere, Finland.
ACM 978-1-4503-1424-4 & 978-1-4503-1426-8
& 978-1-4503-1425-1/12/09.

2. New Challenges in HW and SW Integration

Stefan Kuntz, Continental, Germany

The continuing increase in/of functionality and density of functions in embedded distributed real-time systems within the automotive industry, as well as the importance of satisfying safety and security requirements in such systems require new approaches in managing the resulting complexities. Namely the integration of hardware and software is a concern and faces new challenges with the advent of multicore and manycore systems in the automotive domain. This presentation identifies the main challenges and sketches out some directions to tackle those challenges utilizing model based development and methodologies.

3. Virtualisation Support for an Embedded Automotive Environment

Glenn Farrall, Infineon, UK

Virtualisation is now a well established and relied upon technology for many environments - servers, cloud computing and even some environments that can be considered embedded. There is a difference however between soft-real time or multimedia embedded environments and systems in the safety and the hard-real time application space. This presentation covers some of the differences in the Automotive arena making the problem both easier and harder in various aspects and some of the features and solutions provided in the AURIX(r) multicore devices to address these issues.

4. Software Engineering for the next-generation automotive systems

Akihiko Iwai, Denso, Japan

Nowadays automotive E/E systems are getting large and complex due to its growing needs for new functionalities. The source of such new functionalities include active safety applications using vehicle to infrastructure communication, telematics services cooperating with services on cloud, vehicle to grid/home energy management applications. In this talk, while introducing some cooperative works in Japanese embedded systems industries, we will talk about current works and some technical issues of automotive software development.

Research Issues in Smart Phones, Notepads and Related Services

Petri Liuha
Nokia
Finland

Kari Pehkonen
Renesas Mobile
Finland

Juhani Rummukainen
ST-Ericsson
Finland

Veli-Pekka Vatula
Intel
Finland

Tatu Koljonen *(organizer)*
VTT
Finland
Tatu.Koljonen@vtt.fi

ABSTRACT

Networked embedded systems are building intelligence to everyplace. There are more and more incentives to open proprietary data and interfaces for free to third party service developers. This development called "ubiquitous communication" or "internet of things" requires new dominant design for user interfaces, interoperability and contextuality. In the user interface design, for example, we have witnessed the growth of the smartphone display, which today is at about 5 inches. Developing the new dominant designs is part of the "ecosystem war", where the most attractive platforms are getting the most developer, users and profits. The four speakers of today represent companies that have entered the competition with different platforms, assets and strategies and hence have different research challenges to be solved..

Categories and Subject Descriptors

C.3 [**Computer Systems Organization**]: Real-time and embedded systems.

General Terms

Design, Economics, Performance, Reliability, Security, Verification.

ESWEEK 2012 Special Presentation
CASES'12, CODES+ISSS'12, EMSOFT'12,
Oct. 7–12, 2012, Tampere, Finland.
ACM 978-1-4503-1424-4 & 978-1-4503-1426-8
& 978-1-4503-1425-1/12/09.

1. Challenges in Building Smart Spaces (Draft title)

Petri Liuha, Nokia, Finland

2. Role of Wireless in Networked Embedded Systems (Draft title)

Kari Pehkonen, Renesas Mobile, Finland

3. Enable Coolest, Richest, Affordable Devices (Draft title)

Juhani Rummukainen, ST-Ericsson, Finland

4. Expanding from Chips to Handset (Draft title)

Veli-Pekka Vatula, Intel, Finland

Lifetime Improvement through Runtime Wear-based Task Mapping

Adam S. Hartman
ahartman@ece.cmu.edu

Donald E. Thomas
thomas@ece.cmu.edu

Department of Electrical and Computer Engineering
Carnegie Mellon University
5000 Forbes Ave.
412-268-3545
Pittsburgh, PA 15217

ABSTRACT

As transistors continue to become smaller, they become exponentially susceptible to permanent wearout faults. Without mitigation, these types of faults will render systems useless within unacceptably short time periods. Our work presents the design for a runtime task mapping subsystem which mitigates these faults using a wear-based heuristic. We compare our wear-based heuristic to power- and temperature-based heuristics used within the same system framework. Using a wide range of synthetic and real-world benchmarks, we show that our wear-based heuristic is able to improve total system lifetime by an average of 7.1% over temperature-based heuristics. Additionally, we show that our wear-based heuristic can be used to drastically improve the time to the first component failure (TTFF) of a system. TTFF is a metric that is of interest to designers who wish to avoid the design and verification difficulties of systems which are expected to recover after a component failure. Our wear-based heuristic improves TTFF by an average of 14.6% over temperature-based heuristics across all of our benchmarks. Our observations lead us to conclude that runtime, wear-based task mapping must be incorporated into systems for which lifetime is a primary design goal.

Categories and Subject Descriptors

B.8.1 [**Performance and Reliability**]: Reliability, Testing, and Fault Tolerance

General Terms

Reliability, Design, Algorithms, Measurement

Keywords

Task mapping, wear, runtime, lifetime

1. INTRODUCTION

The ITRS has identified reliability as a growing challenge for users and designers of all types of integrated circuits [3]. In particular, wearout faults are expected to increase exponentially as feature sizes scale past 65nm [16]. By acknowledging the importance of these faults and the failures caused by them, designers can take steps to improve the expected lifetime of the system. Many system-level techniques, such as communication architecture design and slack allocation, are capable of improving embedded chip multiprocessor lifetime. Task mapping is another system-level technique that can enhance the lifetime of the system and is especially attractive since it can be changed at runtime to adapt to the current state of the system. Further, the task mapping process can use information about the amounts of wear accumulated by the components in the system to directly focus on system lifetime. In this paper, we present the design of a runtime wear-based task mapping subsystem which is capable of significantly extending the usable lifetime of an embedded chip multiprocessor.

Figure 1 shows how our task mapping subsystem fits into the overall design of a network-on-chip (NoC) based embedded chip multiprocessor. The red boxes represent processors and the blue circles represent switches. Though Figure 1 shows four processors connected by a simple mesh network, our methods are compatible with arbitrary network sizes and topologies. We assume that each processor has a wear sensor, similar to the delay-based design for measuring time-dependent dielectric breakdown in [6], and these are depicted as white boxes inside the processors. Existing research on these sensors is discussed in Section 7.

Our task mapping subsystem only determines the set of tasks mapped to each component; the underlying operating system schedules those tasks at runtime. The task mapping subsystem collects data from the sensors on each processor and gets information from the operating system about the application being run on the system and the capabilities of the hardware. Based on this information, the task mapping subsystem computes a task mapping which will extend the lifetime of the system. Task mappings can be computed only when required (i.e, when a component fails), or they can be computed at regular intervals. Once computed, the task mapping is communicated to the operating system and applied to the system.

In a wear-based task mapping heuristic, components which have smaller amounts of accumulated wear are favored dur-

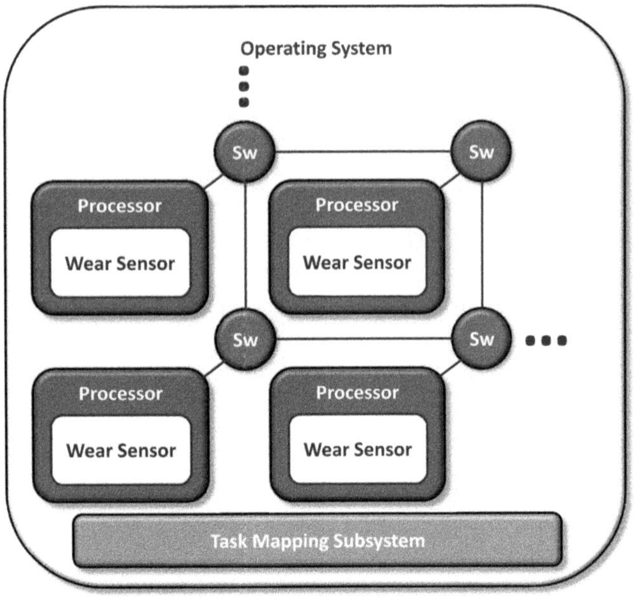

Figure 1: NoC-based embedded chip multiprocessor system overview.

ing the task mapping process. This type of heuristic minimizes the accumulation of wear on components, thereby directly extending their lifetime. In turn, the lifetime of the system as a whole is also extended. Since the current amount of wear on a component is simply the sum of all the wear that was accumulated prior to the current time, this single measurement inherently captures all of the past wear-related state of a component. Thus, wear can be contrasted with component temperature or power dissipation, which only capture the current state of the system.

We evaluate our wear-based task mapping approach by comparing it to approaches which use other types of information to select a task mapping. Both temperature and power information have been used in other task mapping approaches, and these approaches can potentially improve system lifetime. The lifetime of each component in the system is related to its temperature, and consequently, its power dissipation. It then follows that task mappings which optimize temperature or power will also affect the lifetime of the system in some way. However, temperature and power do not directly affect lifetime to the extent that wear does, and temperature and power measurements lack information about prior state. Our results support this reasoning and show that while temperature- and power-based task mapping strategies have a positive, but indirect, effect on lifetime, they cannot produce results as good as those of our wear-based heuristic which directly targets system lifetime.

The main contribution of this paper is the design of a runtime task mapping subsystem which improves system lifetime through the use of component wear information and its ability to continually adapt to the current state of the system. Ours is the first approach to dynamically manage the lifetime of embedded chip multiprocessors at runtime through the use of task mapping. By definition, runtime task mapping allows us to account for variations in the applications or system that would otherwise be impossible to address at design time. We will demonstrate that the systems being tested have a significantly longer lifetime when using our task mapping subsystem as compared to power- or temperature-based task mapping. Ultimately, we will be able to conclude that runtime wear-based task mapping is a requirement for systems in which lifetime is an important characteristic.

2. TASK MAPPING AND SYSTEM LIFETIME

Power-, temperature-, and wear-based task mapping affect system lifetime in different ways due to the relationship between power, temperature, and wear. The power cost of executing a task on a system with heterogeneous components depends on which component executes the task and the path taken through the network by the task's traffic. A power-based task mapping heuristic attempts to minimize the total power dissipation of the system by using information about the components in the system and their locations relative to each other. Therefore, the different amounts of total power dissipation which result from different task mappings will lead to different system lifetimes. While system lifetime can be improved to some degree by these task mappings, power can be thought of as two levels of indirection below wear when attempting to optimize system lifetime. These levels of indirection, along with the fact that power dissipation only captures the current state of the system, cause a power-based task mapping heuristic to be inferior for lifetime optimization.

Temperature-based task mapping heuristics function at a higher level than power-based heuristics in that they consider the component temperatures which result from a set of power dissipation values. By basing task mapping decisions on temperatures rather than power dissipation, temperature-based task mapping can take a more global view of task mapping since a component's temperature will affect the temperatures of neighboring components. Power-based task mapping is less global since the power dissipation of a component does not significantly affect the power dissipation of neighboring components. Task mappings which minimize temperature will increase system lifetime since the time at which a component will fail due to wear-out is related to the temperature of the component. Similar to power dissipation, optimizing temperature does not directly optimize system lifetime since it is still one level of indirection below wear. Also like power dissipation, component temperature does not indicate anything about the past state of the system. Wear-based task mapping heuristics can extend system lifetime better than either power- or temperature-based heuristics since they directly optimize the metric most closely related to system lifetime.

Regardless of the way in which the task mapping is selected, we must precisely define the metrics used to evaluate the task mapping heuristics. The word "lifetime" can mean different things to different people depending on how the system was designed. Our first interpretation of "lifetime" is mean time to failure (MTTF), and we define this as the amount of time starting when the system is first turned on and ending when the number of component failures leaves the system with insufficient resources to execute its application. Existing work [13] has shown that adding slack to a system (i.e, sizing resources beyond what is needed to support the application being executed) allows it to continue to function as components begin to fail. This work assumes that either the operating system or some hardware resource is able to detect component failures and reconfigure various parts of the system, such as routing tables, in order to keep the system functional. While it is feasible to build systems which conform to these assumptions, the design and verification tasks are difficult since the number of combinations of component failures that must be validated increases superlinearly with the number of components in the system. Despite these difficulties, MTTF is still an important metric in system design.

Our second interpretation of "lifetime" is time to first failure (TTFF), and we define this as the amount of time starting when the system is first turned on and ending when one component in the system fails. In order to simplify the design and verification of their systems, some designers only want to consider their systems usable while no components in the system have failed. While the system may still have the resources to continue functioning after the first component has failed, the system is no longer used because the resulting scenarios were not validated at design time. Notably, our results show that slack is still a useful notion under this definition of lifetime since certain task mapping algorithms are able to use the slack to significantly increase TTFF.

3. LIFETIME EVALUATION

In order to determine the MTTF and TTFF of a system, we must model the changes a system goes through during its lifetime. System lifetime is modeled by simulating sequences of component failures and determining how long performance constraints are satisfiable. Our systems are comprised of processors, memories, and switches that execute fixed applications which are comprised of processing tasks and memory arrays. Monte Carlo simulation is used to sample many random systems from which an average lifetime can be determined. In this section, we discuss our general assumptions about the system and its components along with the details of the lifetime evaluation algorithm.

We must make several assumptions about how components in the system fail and when these failures cause the overall system to fail in order to better define our problem. Individual processors and switches within a system may fail over the course of its lifetime. We assume that memories are not susceptible to permanent failure, as they can be covered by simple row and column redundancy, but they can become inaccessible when the switches to which they are attached fail. That said, our approach could be easily adapted to account for situations in which memories are susceptible to permanent failure by treating them in the same manner as processors during task mapping. We assume that systems can automatically detect component failure (for example, using [15]), at which point the operating system signals our task mapping algorithm to execute. In addition to this method of computing task mappings reactively (i.e, only when necessary), our task mapping algorithm can also be triggered at pre-defined time intervals in an effort to proactively address system lifetime. The task mapping algorithm is responsible for remapping tasks and data from failed resources to those with slack, re-routing the affected traffic, and improving the lifetime of the system through decisions made during this process. As long as a valid task mapping exists, the system can satisfy its performance constraints and continue to function [11, 20].

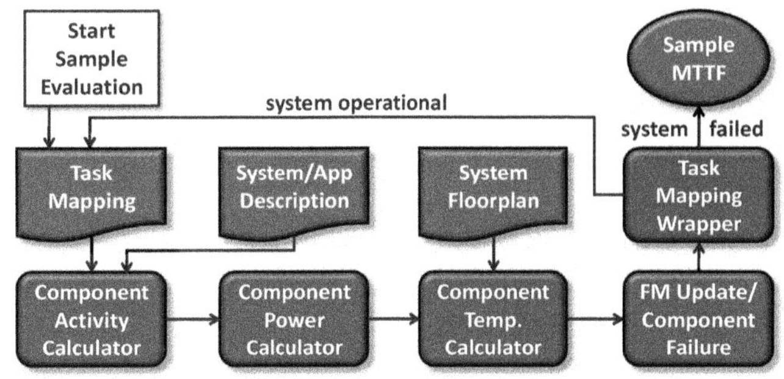

Figure 2: System lifetime evaluation process for a single Monte Carlo sample.

To accurately estimate the distribution of permanent component failures due to wear-out, we adopted a lognormal failure distribution model for each of three temperature-dependent failure mechanisms [17]: electromigration, time-dependent dielectric breakdown, and thermal cycling. Each failure mechanism is normalized so that its MTTF is 30 years for a characterization temperature of 345 K [10]. This normalization equalizes the effect of the three failure mechanisms on a given component.

Figure 2 gives an overview of our lifetime evaluation process for a single Monte Carlo sample. We use an initial task mapping that minimizes power dissipation regardless of the task mapping heuristic that will be used later. We cannot use temperature or wear information to determine the initial task mapping since components have neither a temperature nor an amount of wear associated with them yet. The utilization of each component is first calculated based on that task mapping and given information about the system and the application (Component Activity Calculator block in Figure 2). Given component activity, component power dissipation can be derived using data sheet values for processors [1], CACTI [2] for memories, and ORION [18] for switches (Component Power Calculator block in Figure 2). Using the floorplan and per-component power dissipation data, steady-state temperatures for each component are calculated using Hotspot [14] (Component Temperature Calculator block in Figure 2). Our temperature modeling assumptions (range, average value, etc.) are designed to match previously published temperature modeling assumptions for the same types of systems [8]. These component temperatures are then used to shape the failure distribution for each failure mechanism.

For each Monte Carlo sample, failure times are randomly selected from the initial failure distributions of each failure mechanism of each component (processors and switches). The failure distribution for each failure mechanism of a component is based on that component's temperature, which is derived from the current task mapping. Once the failure distributions are computed, we determine which component in the system has the earliest failure time based on the amount of wear that has been accumulated so far (FM Update/Component Failure block in Figure 2). In addition to their place in the simulation, we use the time to failure and accumulated wear values that are calculated in this step as "outputs" from the wear sensors we assume to exist on chip, and these values are used as input to our wear-based task mapping heuristic. We mark this component as failed

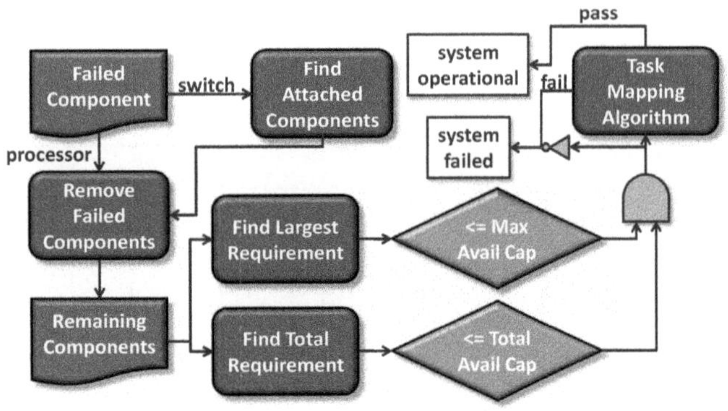

Figure 3: Generalized task mapping process.

and proceed to the task mapping process (Task Mapping Wrapper block in Figure 2). If we are able to find a valid task mapping, the "system operational" path is taken, and the simulation loop begins another iteration. If a valid task mapping does not exist, the "system failed" path is taken, and we record the current simulation time as the failure time for the sample system. Section 4 details the task mapping process and the heuristics we use in it.

4. TASK MAPPING HEURISTICS

We use the lifetime evaluation process discussed in Section 3 to compare a number of task mapping heuristics. The purpose of the task mapping process is to determine whether or not a component failure can be survived through remapping or if the system is no longer able to satisfy performance constraints. The task mapping process is successful if every task can be assigned to a single component without violating any capacity or communication constraints. Tasks cannot be split into pieces, and so they must be mapped to a single component; a single component can accommodate as many tasks as its capacity allows. Communication between tasks is routed through the network and is subject to the communication constraints of the routers. The exception to this rule is when two communicating tasks are mapped to the same resource, and in this case, no network traffic is generated. If a mapping has been created without violating any capacity or communication constraints, we assume that the operating system will be able to create a valid schedule for the tasks mapped to each resource, and this process is outside the scope of our work.

All of our task mapping heuristics are based on the same underlying algorithm, and they differ in which system values are used to make decisions. The outer layer of the task mapping algorithm is shown in Figure 3 and corresponds to the Task Mapping Wrapper block in Figure 2. The task mapping process begins by identifying the type of the failed component. If the failed component is a switch, we assume that all processors and memories connected directly to it become inaccessible, and consequently failed. After identifying the set of failed components, we consider the remainder of the components as candidates for the new task mapping. Our task mapping process considers all tasks in the task graph when it is invoked rather than just the tasks that are orphaned by failed and inaccessible components. We found that considering all tasks led to an increase in system lifetime when using the heuristics discussed below without a significant increase in the runtime of the task mapping algorithm.

Algorithm 1 Task mapping algorithm

```
1: bool taskMapping(tasks, components)
2: mapping.clear()
3: tasks = sort(tasks,largeToSmall)
4: for all t in tasks do
5:     candidates.clear()
6:     for all c in components do
7:         if c.availableCapacity() ≥ t.requirement() then
8:             candidates.add(c)
9:         end if
10:    end for
11:    if candidates.empty() = true then
12:        return usePreviousSolution()
13:    end if
14:    minPow = findMinPow(candidates)
15:    minCap = findMinCap(candidates,t)
16:    minTemp = findMinTemp(candidates)
17:    maxTTF = findMaxTTF(candidates)
18:    minWear = findMinWear(candidates)
19:    maxScore = 0
20:    for all c in candidates do
21:        powScore = powWt * maxPow/c.getPow()
22:        capScore = capWt * minCap/c.getCap()
23:        tempScore = tempWt * minTemp/c.getTemp()
24:        ttfScore = ttfWt * c.getTTF()/maxTTF
25:        wearScore = wearWt * minWear/c.getWear()
26:        totScore = powScore + capScore + tempScore +
   ttfScore + wearScore
27:        if totScore ≥ maxScore then
28:            maxScore = totScore
29:            bestComp = c
30:        end if
31:    end for
32:    mapping.add(t,bestComp)
33:    bestComp.availableCapacity() -= t.requirement()
34: end for
35: return route(mapping)
```

To short-circuit the task mapping process when possible, we perform a capacity check to compare the requirements of the application to the remaining resources in the system. The capacity check begins by computing the total processing and memory requirements for all tasks and arrays and the largest processing and memory requirements of any single task or array. These total and largest single requirements are compared to the total amount of remaining resources and largest single resource in the system. If either of these simple checks fails, we know that task mapping will be impossible for this scenario and end the sample ("system failed" box in Figure 3). The "system failed" and "system operational" boxes in Figure 3 correspond to the paths of the same name in Figure 2. If both of the above capacity checks pass, we know that finding a task mapping may be possible.

In the case that a task mapping may be possible, we use a weighted scoring function, detailed in Algorithm 1, to map each task to a component. The algorithm is discussed below and corresponds to the "Task Mapping Algorithm" block in Figure 3. The tasks are first sorted by their requirements, and are run through the scoring function from largest to smallest (line 3). We performed some experimentation with different task orderings, but found that the order of descending requirements generally produced the best results. An in-depth analysis of the effects of task ordering in our task mapping algorithm is the subject of future research.

Given a task, the scoring function only considers components which currently have the available capacity to execute the task (lines 5-10). The score for a task/component pair is the weighted sum (lines 21-26), where the sum of the weights is always 1.0, of a number of individual scores that are each normalized to 1.0 (normalization values found on lines 14-18). Therefore, the highest total score that any task/component pair can receive is 1.0. The given task is mapped to the component with the highest score, and the available capacity for that component is reduced by an amount equal to the requirement of the task (lines 32-33). We consider each unique set of weights to be a different task mapping heuristic that is used within the larger framework of our task mapping algorithm.

The individual scores in the weighted sum are based on power, available capacity, temperature, time to failure, and wear. The power score for a task/component pair is based on the amount of power dissipated by the component per unit of work, and lower amounts of power dissipation per unit of work receive higher scores (line 21). This definition implies that the power score is dependent only on the characteristics of the component and is task independent.

The available capacity score for a task/component pair is based on the difference between the component's available capacity and the requirement of the task, and smaller differences generate higher scores (line 22). As an alternative to this definition of the available capacity score, we tested a method which was only based on the available capacity of the component, but this method produced inferior results.

The temperature score for a task/component pair is based on the current temperature of the component, and higher scores are given to components with lower temperatures (line 23). We assume that each component on the chip has a temperature sensor which reports the maximum temperature observed within the area of that component.

The time to failure (TTF) score is based on the amount of time before the component will fail due to a wearout fault, and higher scores correspond with higher times (line 24). The wear score is based on the wear accumulated by the component as a percentage of the amount of wear which will cause the component to fail (line 25). Components with a lower percentage of accumulated wear are favored by this score, and this wear score offers a slightly different interpretation of the data available from wear sensors than the TTF score. Our assumptions about the capabilities of wear sensors are supported by existing research that is discussed in Section 7. Like the power score, the temperature, TTF, and wear scores are all independent of the task requirement.

We implement different task mapping heuristics by changing the weights that are used in lines 21 through 24 of Algorithm 1. We tested numerous combinations of weights, and we chose a subset of the best performing combinations to show in our results. The combinations of weights we used to create different heuristics are shown in Table 1. Each column in 1 corresponds to one of the weights used in Algorithm 1, and each row corresponds to one class of task mapping heuristics. While each heuristic uses a significant power weight, power cannot be used by itself to create a good task mapping heuristic.

Table 1: Task mapping scoring weights used to create task mapping heuristics.

Heur.	powWt	capWt	tempWt	ttfWt	wearWt
Power	0.5	0.5	0.0	0.0	0.0
Temp	0.75	0.0	0.25	0.0	0.0
TTF	0.75	0.0	0.0	0.25	0.0
Wear	0.75	0.0	0.0	0.0	0.25

We tested a combination of weights in which the power weight was set to 1.0 and all other weights were set to 0.0, and the resulting heuristic did not perform as well as any of the other heuristics we discuss in this paper. The reason for this result is that many of the components dissipate the same amount of power per unit of work, and some other measurement is needed to intelligently break those ties. The heuristics are named according to the weight that is used in addition to the power weight.

Once all processing tasks have been mapped as described above, we employ a simple, greedy task mapping strategy for memory arrays. This strategy maps memory arrays from largest requirement to smallest requirement and favors memories whose available capacity matches that of the array being mapped. We chose not to employ our more sophisticated mapping heuristics for memory arrays due to our other assumption that memories cannot fail, and so the mapping of arrays to memories will not significantly impact lifetime.

If the task mapping process reaches a point where there are no valid candidate components for a task or memory array, the process temporarily fails (lines 11-13). We found that some combinations of system state (power, available capacity, temperature, TTF, wear) prevent a task mapping from being found by our task mapping process even though one was previously found for the same set of failed components and a different system state. When we encounter these cases, we simply apply the previously found task mapping, even though it was "optimal" for a different system state. If no task mappings exist given the current set of failed components, then our task mapping algorithm fails ("fail" path in Figure 3).

The final step in the task mapping algorithm is traffic routing, which we perform via a basic implementation of Dijkstra's algorithm (line 32). After traffic routing, the amount of bandwidth placed on each link is compared to the maximum allowed bandwidth for that link. If any links exceed their maximum allowed bandwidth after the traffic routing process, our task mapping algorithm fails ("fail" path in Figure 3). Assuming no link bandwidth violations are found, component utilization and temperature are then re-calculated so that component failure times may be updated accordingly [10] ("pass" path in Figure 3).

When there are no feasible task mappings for the current combination of remaining components, we record the time at which the sample system fails. We also record the time of the first component failure in each sample system, although it may be equal to the system failure time depending on the amount of slack in the system. When enough sample systems have been simulated, system MTTF is estimated by computing the mean of all system failure times, and system TTFF is estimated by computing the mean of all first component failure times. We found that 10000 samples were

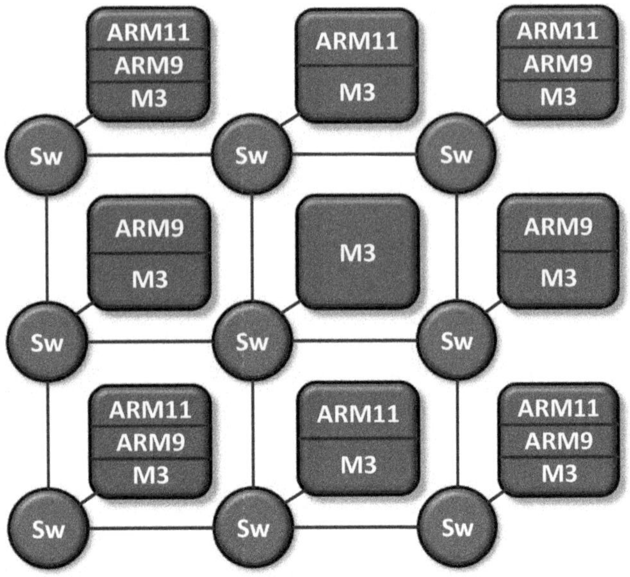

Figure 4: 9-s mesh hardware architecture.

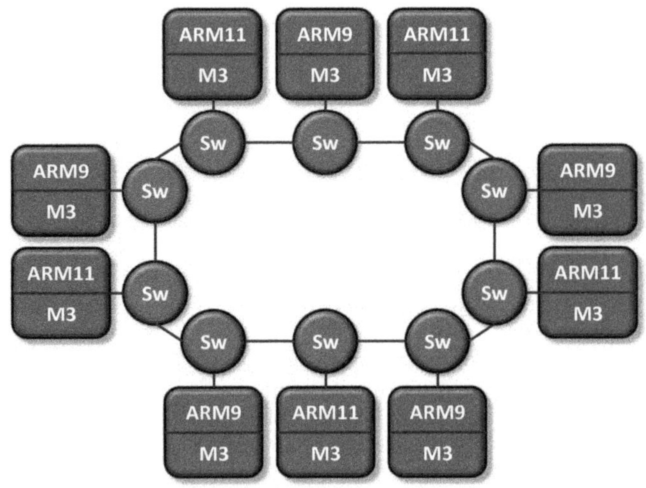

Figure 5: 10-s ring hardware architecture.

enough to estimate system MTTF/TTFF with a 95% confidence interval of 1% or less of the system MTTF/TTFF.

5. BENCHMARKS

We have tested all of the heuristics in Section 4 using a suite of benchmarks. Each of our benchmarks consists of a hardware architecture and a task graph that must be mapped, and remapped as components fail, to it. The components used to construct the architectures include 4- and 5-port switches, three types of ARM processors, and memories of various sizes. The computational capabilities of the processors range from 125 to 500 MIPS, and the memory sizes range from 64KB to 512KB. Each processor or memory must be connected to exactly one switch, and each switch may connect to any combination of processors, memories, or other switches so long as its port limit is observed. We assume that components are connected via links with a maximum bandwidth of 256MB/s. BloBB [7] is used to create floorplans for all of our designs.

Our benchmarks can be divided into two groups. The benchmarks in the first group are related by a common hardware architecture while the benchmarks in the second group are related by a common task graph. Details about these benchmark groups are covered in the following subsections.

5.1 Single Architecture, Multiple Applications

For our first set of benchmarks, we selected a hardware architecture similar to one found commonly in academic examples and in industry: a mesh. This architecture contains nine switches (9-s) arranged in a mesh topology, and each switch contains a 5x5 crossbar which allows it to connect to five other components. The ports on each switch that are not used to connect to other switches are connected to processors. Nine M3 processors, six ARM9 processors, and six ARM11 processors are connected to the switches, and their arrangement is detailed in Figure 4. Although multiple processors are shown in a single red box with a single link to the switch, each processor in the box is actually independent of the others and has its own link to the switch. This simplification is also used in Figure 5.

We used Task Graphs for Free (TGFF) [9] to generate nine random applications for the mesh architecture. The generated applications contain a random number of tasks in the range of 45 to 55, and the computational requirements for each task are also randomly generated. We parametrized TGFF such that a complete task graph would use about 80% of the resources of the system on average. While communication rates between tasks are also selected randomly by TGFF, we set the parameters for their generation such that they would fall well below the bandwidth limit of the links. Consequently, bandwidth limits are unlikely to restrict the set of feasible task mappings for this set of benchmarks.

To further expand this set of benchmarks, we used the same set of generated applications that were described above in conjunction with a second hardware architecture. The second architecture contains ten 4-port switches (10-s) arranged in a ring. Thus, each switch is connected to two other switches and two processors. A total of ten M3 processors, five ARM9 processors, and five ARM11 processors are used in this architecture, which is detailed in Figure 5. The 9-s mesh and 10-s ring architectures do not contain memories.

5.2 Single Application, Multiple Architectures

Our second set of benchmarks is based on an implementation of an MPEG Core Profile Level 1 decoder. The task graph for this application contains 17 processing tasks and five memory arrays. While this task graph is somewhat smaller than the randomly generated task graphs, it provides valuable data about how the various task mapping heuristics deal with a real-world system.

The MPEG task graph is combined with several different hardware architectures to create the second set of benchmarks, and all of those architectures are built around five switches arranged in a ring. We create different hardware architectures by varying the types of processors and memories connected to the switches. The first design point in this set of benchmarks contains just enough resources to execute the task graph, and additional design points are created by replacing the baseline components with those having greater computation or storage abilities. By varying the types of components, we are able to see how the task mapping heuristics use slack to affect the lifetime of the system.

We duplicate the MPEG task graph in a second part of this group of benchmarks in order to create another large-scale example and to see how the task mapping heuristics handle the mapping of two, independent task graphs. The hardware architectures are doubled in size, by doubling the number of components, to accommodate the addition of the second instance of the task graph. The doubled hardware architectures contain two rings of five switches each which are connected to each other through switches with previously unconnected ports. Thus, while the two instances of the task graph do not communicate, the underlying tasks can be mapped to any component in the system since there is a path between any two components. We also assume that components are able to simultaneously accommodate tasks from the two task graphs if resource constraints are met.

6. RESULTS

We use the benchmarks from Section 5 to compare the effects of the task mapping heuristics described in Section 4 on system MTTF and TTFF. We break down our results by benchmark set in the same manner as Section 5.

6.1 Single Architecture, Multiple Applications

This section covers the results of the experiments we ran using the benchmarks in Section 5.1. Figure 6 depicts the system MTTFs that were obtained when several task mapping heuristics were applied to the nine task graphs on the 9-s mesh architecture. The x-axis in the figure is a category axis in which each group represents the MTTFs resulting from the task mapping heuristics for one of the task graphs. The y-axis shows the MTTF, as measured in years, when a particular task mapping heuristic is used to map a particular task graph. Each group of bars is organized from left to right as follows: power (red), temperature (blue), TTF (green), and wear (orange). For the temperature-, TTF-, and wear-based heuristics, we show the results when using the heuristic at two different intervals with two different shades of the same color. The color used to represent each heuristic remains consistent throughout the remainder of the paper. The interval time (i.e, amount of time between triggering of the task mapping subsystem) is prefixed by a "-" in the name of the data set and is measured in years. When the power-based heuristic is used, new task mappings are only generated when a component fails since the amount of power a component dissipates per unit of work does not change over time. Thus, the power-based heuristic is listed without a task mapping interval time in the legend.

In all task graphs, the power-based heuristic yields the lowest MTTF. The temperature-based heuristics produce higher MTTF than the power-based heuristic, and this is further improved upon by the TTF- and wear-based heuristics. The TTF- and wear-based heuristics produce similar results for many of the task graphs, but there are a few cases in which the wear-based heuristics produce the best results by a measurable margin. Since the task graphs are not listed on the x-axis in any particular order, there is no observable trend in MTTF influenced by the characteristics of the task graph. Analyzing the relationship between task

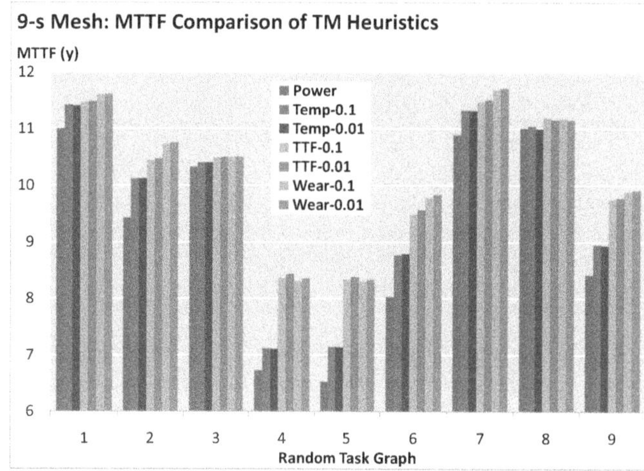

Figure 6: 9-s mesh MTTF results.

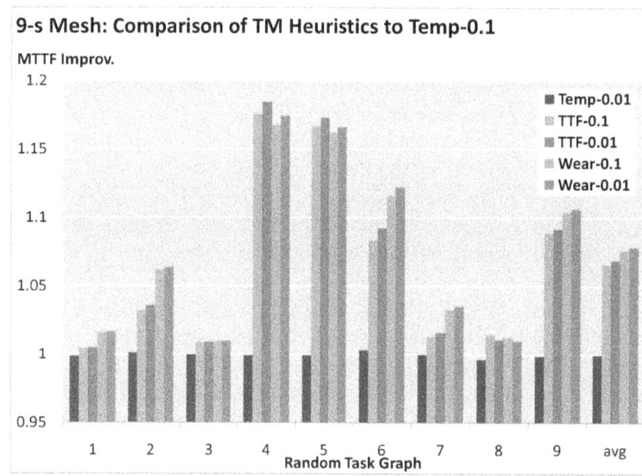

Figure 7: 9-s mesh MTTF improvement.

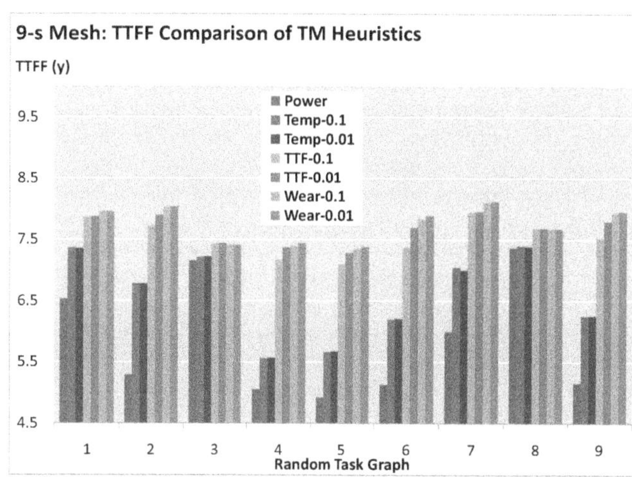

Figure 8: 9-s mesh TTFF results.

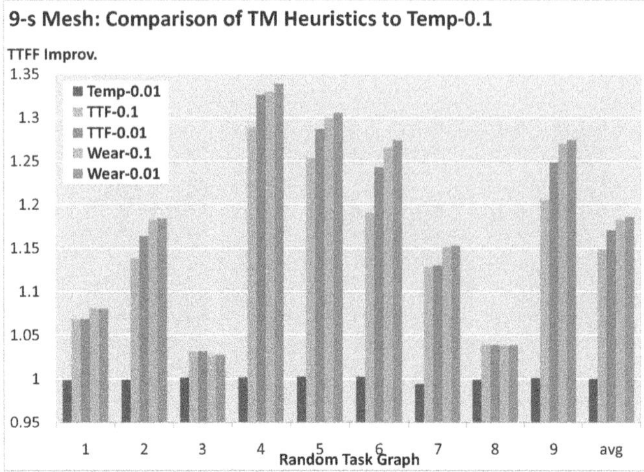

Figure 9: 9-s mesh TTFF improvement.

graph properties and system MTTF is outside of the scope of this paper and is left for future work.

Figure 7 shows the same data as in Figure 6, but all data has been normalized to the results of the temperature-based heuristic using an interval of 0.1 years. The x-axis remains a category axis representing the different task graphs, and it includes an "avg" group which shows the average improvement in lifetime across the nine task graphs that each heuristic achieved. The y-axis shows the percent improvement in MTTF that a particular heuristic was able to achieve over the Temp-0.1 heuristic. For example, the value of the Wear-0.01 heuristic for task graph 1 is shown to be 1.016, or a 1.6% improvement. We arrive at this value by dividing the MTTF which results from using that heuristic (11.61 years) by the MTTF which results from using the Temp-0.1 heuristic (11.42 years). The results for the power-based heuristic are not shown in this figure since they are always worse than those of the Temp-0.1 heuristic. This figure shows that the Wear-0.01 heuristic usually produces the greatest improvement over the Temp-0.1 heuristic with an average MTTF improvement of 7.8% and a maximum MTTF improvement of 17.4%. These MTTF improvement results are mirrored in the "Wear-0.01" row of Table 2 by the values of 1.078 and 1.174 in the "9-s Mesh/Avg" and "9-s Mesh/Max" columns.

Figure 8 is set up in the same manner as Figure 6 with the exception that the y-axis shows TTFF as measured in years. All measurements shown in Figure 8 are less than or equal to the corresponding measurements in Figure 6 since the systems have enough slack to continue functioning after the first component failure. The same patterns observed in the MTTF data also apply to this TTFF data: the wear-based heuristic performs the best, followed by the TTF-, temperature-, and power-based heuristics. Figure 9 shows the TTFF improvement over the Temp-0.1 heuristic corresponding to the data in Figure 8, and it is set up in the same manner as Figure 7. Once again, the Wear-0.01 heuristic shows the greatest improvement in TTFF across all of the task graphs with an average improvement of 18.6% and a maximum improvement of 33.9%. These values for average and maximum improvement can also be found in the "Wear-0.01" row of Table 3 as the values 1.186 and 1.339 in the "9-s Mesh/Avg" and "9-s Mesh/Max" columns.

Table 2 summarizes the improvements in MTTF yielded by each heuristic for all of our benchmark sets. Each row in the table corresponds to one of the heuristics we tested in our task mapping subsystem, and each of the four major columns corresponds to one of our four benchmark sets. Under each benchmark set name, there are two subcolumns named "Avg" and "Max" which denote the average and maximum results across all benchmarks in a benchmark set. Each entry in the table represents a factor of improvement that is measured according to the description of Figure 7 above. These factors of improvement show how well a particular heuristic does compared to the Temp-0.1 heuristic. Values below 1.0 indicate that a heuristic did not perform as well as the Temp-0.1 heuristic, while values above 1.0 indicate that a heuristic performed better than the Temp-0.1 heuristic. The entire row for the Temp-0.1 heuristic contains entries of 1.0 to show that all results in the table are normalized to this heuristic. Table 3 is set up in the same manner as described above, except that it summarizes improvements in TTFF yielded by each heuristic.

Our second set of experiments involved mapping the nine random task graphs to the 10-s ring architecture, and a summary of these results can be found in the second major column of Tables 2 and 3. In this set of experiments, the TTF-0.01 heuristic performed as well, on average, as the Wear-0.01 heuristic in regard to MTTF. Both heuristics managed to improve MTTF by an average of 6% over the Temp-0.1 heuristic. The Wear-0.01 heuristic does show marginal improvement over the TTF-0.01 heuristic in regard to average TTFF improvement. Thus, the Wear-0.01 heuristic is again the best heuristic of the ones we tested.

6.2 Single Application, Multiple Architectures

The results from our experiments with the MPEG decoder application can be found in the third and fourth major columns of Tables 2 and 3. The Wear-0.01 heuristic again leads to the greatest average improvement in MTTF in both the single- and double-sized MPEG benchmark sets. In the single-sized MPEG benchmark set, the Wear-0.01 heuristic improves lifetime by up to 11.5% over the Temp-0.1 heuristic, and that maximum improvement jumps to 15.4% in the double-sized MPEG benchmark set. Similar to the results in the synthetic benchmark sets, the Wear-0.01 and TTF-0.01 heuristics perform similarly with respect to improvement in TTFF. On average, the Wear-0.01 heuristic improves TTFF by 11.1% in the single-sized MPEG benchmark set and by 17.7% in the double-sized MPEG benchmark set. The maximum TTFF improvements achieved by the Wear-0.01 heuristic are even greater: 15.7% in the case of the single-size MPEG benchmark set and 27.9% in the case of the double-size MPEG benchmark. These results indicate that our wear-based task mapping heuristic performs well across the benchmarks we tested, and the improvements in TTFF scale with the number of tasks in the application.

7. RELATED WORK

The work we present in this paper relies on the existence of on-chip wear sensors to provide data to some of the task mapping heuristics. The design and performance of wear sensors is discussed in several pieces of existing work. [6] presents a method for creating a wear sensor which tracks TDDB via critical path delay and is able to accurately predict when microarchitectural components fail with a small

Table 2: Improvement in MTTF by task mapping heuristic and benchmark set.

Heuristic	9-s Mesh		10-s Ring		MPEG		MPEG (double)	
	Avg	Max	Avg	Max	Avg	Max	Avg	Max
Power	0.951	0.997	0.975	1.026	0.947	0.980	0.974	1.014
Temp-1.0	1.000	1.011	0.999	1.005	1.000	1.011	1.002	1.004
Temp-0.1	1.000	1.000	1.000	1.000	1.000	1.000	1.000	1.000
Temp-0.01	0.999	1.003	1.002	1.007	1.000	1.007	1.000	1.005
TTF-1.0	1.054	1.151	1.046	1.102	1.041	1.105	1.046	1.136
TTF-0.1	1.065	1.176	1.057	1.127	1.052	1.134	1.050	1.165
TTF-0.01	1.068	1.184	1.061	1.137	1.055	1.134	1.050	1.169
Wear-1.0	1.062	1.141	1.044	1.091	1.051	1.094	1.045	1.121
Wear-0.1	1.076	1.167	1.057	1.113	1.061	1.116	1.053	1.156
Wear-0.01	1.078	1.174	1.060	1.123	1.062	1.115	1.053	1.154

Table 3: Improvement in TTFF by task mapping heuristic and benchmark set.

Heuristic	9-s Mesh		10-s Ring		MPEG		MPEG (double)	
	Avg	Max	Avg	Max	Avg	Max	Avg	Max
Power	0.882	0.996	0.913	1.038	0.883	0.971	0.885	1.009
Temp-1.0	1.011	1.033	1.004	1.030	1.001	1.009	1.001	1.010
Temp-0.1	1.000	1.000	1.000	1.000	1.000	1.000	1.000	1.000
Temp-0.01	1.000	1.002	1.002	1.007	1.001	1.008	0.998	1.005
TTF-1.0	1.108	1.245	1.071	1.156	1.070	1.105	1.117	1.218
TTF-0.1	1.149	1.289	1.095	1.173	1.100	1.134	1.157	1.261
TTF-0.01	1.170	1.326	1.105	1.190	1.104	1.133	1.177	1.288
Wear-1.0	1.154	1.265	1.089	1.152	1.095	1.130	1.141	1.210
Wear-0.1	1.182	1.329	1.103	1.184	1.109	1.153	1.175	1.275
Wear-0.01	1.186	1.339	1.108	1.193	1.111	1.157	1.177	1.279

overhead cost. [4] discusses wear sensors which can be placed inside of flip-flops to track system wear due to negative bias temperature instability (NBTI), and although we do not model the effects of NBTI in this paper, our framework allows us to include it in the future. [19] details a slightly different method for sensors which track wear caused by NBTI. Finally, [5] explains how circuitry can be added to SRAM cells in order to track accumulated wear in memories.

To the best of our knowledge, [12] is the only other work which discusses task mapping for lifetime optimization. The major difference between our work and [12] is that we apply out task mapping methods at runtime while [12] applies them at design time. We assume that the task mapping may be changed while the system is running, while [12] assumes that a single task mapping and schedule are used until one component in the system fails. Another difference between our work and [12] is that we account for the existence of slack and memories in the system, and we simulate the use of slack to extend system lifetime beyond the failure of the first component. This simulation allows us to see how task mapping heuristics influence system MTTF, while [12] is only able to observe the effects on TTFF. Finally, our work uses lognormal distributions for increased accuracy of the failure mechanism models, and we are able to model changes in the rate of wear as component temperatures change. [12] uses Weibull distributions to model failure mechanisms and is only capable of modeling a constant rate of wear.

8. CONCLUSIONS

We presented the design for a runtime task mapping subsystem which extends system lifetime by using a wear-based heuristic. We assume the existence of on-chip wear sensors and use data from them to modify the task mapping as the system runs to adapt to the changing wear patterns in the system. Basing task mapping decisions on a combination of wear and power data gives us a direct path to system lifetime optimization in contrast with using power by itself, or a combination of temperature and power, as proxies for lifetime. Also, using wear data is elegant and concise since it captures all relevant, previous system state in a single value. Temperature and power information only show the current state of the system by default and would require more complicated heuristics to capture and utilize prior values.

Our results showed that our wear-based task mapping heuristic performed well across a wide range of benchmarks. When testing large, random task graphs on a mesh architecture, we improved TTFF by an average of 18.6% and MTTF by an average of 7.8% over a temperature-based heuristic. We then used the same set of task graphs on a different hardware architecture, a ring, to show that our results were not dependent on a mesh architecture. Our wear-based task mapping heuristic improved TTFF by 10.8% and MTTF by 6.0% over a temperature-based heuristic when the ring architecture was used.

We based a second set of benchmarks on a real-world MPEG decoder application with a corresponding hardware architecture and a variety of slack allocations. We were able to improve TTFF and MTTF by averages of 11.1% and 6.2%, respectively, over a temperature-based heuristic. In order to see how our heuristics scaled with system size, we composed another set of benchmarks by combining two instances of the MPEG application with double-sized hardware architectures. In these benchmarks, we improve TTFF by an average of 17.7% and MTTF by an average of 5.3% over a temperature-based heuristic.

Our data also led to two interesting secondary results. First, we showed that the addition of slack to the system can improve both TTFF and MTTF when our wear-based task mapping heuristic is used. Thus, we can conclude that task mapping and slack allocation are important considerations in designs where lifetime is a design goal, even if those systems are not meant to be used after the failure of any components. Second, we found that there are diminishing returns in lifetime improvement with regard to how often task mapping is performed. When decreasing the task mapping interval from one year to 0.1 years in both the wear- and temperature-based heuristic, a reasonable improvement in lifetime is seen in all benchmarks. As the task mapping interval is moved from 0.1 years to 0.01 years, we observed a much smaller improvement in lifetime. This observation means that designers must choose an appropriate task mapping interval depending on the overhead required to change the task mapping to obtain a good tradeoff between that overhead and lifetime improvement. This observation also points to the fact that the time required to compute the task mapping, which is on the order of seconds, is significantly shorter than the amount of time between the computation of task mappings, which is on the order of tens of days.

9. ACKNOWLEDGMENTS

This work was supported by the National Science Foundation through Grant CCF-1116856. Any opinions, findings, and conclusions or recommendations expressed in this material are those of the authors and do not necessarily reflect the views of the NSF.

10. REFERENCES

[1] http://www.arm.com/products/processors/index.php.

[2] Cacti 5.3. http://www.hpl.hp.com/research/cacti.

[3] International technology roadmap for semiconductors, 2011 edition: Process integration, devices, and structures. http://www.itrs.net/Links/2011ITRS/2011Chapters/2011PIDS.pdf.

[4] M. Agarwal, V. Balakrishnan, A. Bhuyan, K. Kim, B. C. Paul, W. Wang, B. Yang, Y. Cao, and S. Mitra. Self-calibrating online wearout detection. In *Test Conference (ITC), 2008 IEEE International*, pages 1–10, October 2008.

[5] F. Ahmed and L. Milor. Analysis and on-chip monitoring of gate oxide breakdown in sram cells. *Very Large Scale Integration (VLSI) Systems, IEEE Transactions on*, PP(99):1–11, 2011.

[6] J. Blome, S. Feng, S. Gupta, and S. Mahlke. Self-calibrating online wearout detection. In *Microarchitecture (MICRO), 40th Annual IEEE/ACM International Symposium on*, pages 109–122, December 2007.

[7] H. H. Chan and I. L. Markov. Practical slicing and non-slicing block-packing without simulated annealing. In *VLSI (GLSVLSI), 2004 Great Lakes Symposium on*, pages 282–287, April 2004.

[8] A. K. Coskun, T. S. Rosing, and K. Whisnant. Temperature aware task scheduling in mpsocs. In *Design, Automation Test in Europe Conference and Exhibition (DATE), 2007*, pages 1–6, April 2007.

[9] R. P. Dick, D. L. Rhodes, and W. Wolf. Tgff: Task graphs for free. In *Hardware/Software Codesign (CODES+CASHE), 1998 Sixth International Workshop on*, pages 97–101, March 1998.

[10] Z. Gu, C. Zhu, L. Shang, and R. P. Dick. Application-specific mpsoc reliability optimization. *Very Large Scale Integration (VLSI) Systems, IEEE Transactions on*, 16(5):603–608, 2008.

[11] A. S. Hartman, D. E. Thomas, and B. H. Meyer. A case for lifetime aware task mapping in embedded chip multiprocessors. In *Hardware/Software Codesign and System Synthesis (CODES+ISSS), 2010 IEEE/ACM/IFIP International Conference on*, pages 145–154, October 2010.

[12] L. Huang, F. Yuan, and Q. Xu. Lifetime reliability-aware task allocation and scheduling for mpsoc platforms. In *Design, Automation Test in Europe Conference and Exhibition (DATE), 2009*, pages 51–56, April 2009.

[13] B. H. Meyer, A. S. Hartman, and D. E. Thomas. Cost-effective slack allocation for lifetime improvement in noc-based mpsocs. In *Design, Automation Test in Europe Conference and Exhibition (DATE), 2010*, pages 1596–1601, March 2010.

[14] K. Skadron, M. R. Stan, W. Huang, S. Velusamy, K. Sankaranarayanan, and D. Tarjan. Temperature-aware microarchitecture. In *Computer Architecture (ISCA), 30th Annual International Symposium on*, pages 2–13, June 2003.

[15] J. C. Smolens, B. T. Gold, J. C. Hoe, B. Falsafi, and K. Mai. Detecting emerging wearout faults. In *Silicon Errors in Logic - System Effects (SELSE-3), 2007 IEEE Workshop on*, pages 0–0, April 2007.

[16] J. Srinivasan, S. V. Adve, P. Bose, and J. A. Rivers. The impace of technology scaling on lifetime reliability. In *Dependable Systems and Networks (DSN), 2004 International Conference on*, pages 177–186, June 2004.

[17] J. Srinivasan, S. V. Adve, P. Bose, and J. A. Rivers. Exploiting structural duplication for lifetime reliability enhancement. In *Computer Architecture (ISCA), 32nd Annual International Symposium on*, pages 520–531, June 2005.

[18] H.-S. Wang, L.-S. Peh, and S. Malik. A power model for routers: Modeling alpha 21364 and infiniband routers. *Micro, IEEE*, 23(1):26–35, 2003.

[19] B. Zandian, W. Dweik, S. H. Kang, T. Punihaole, and M. Annavaram. Wearmon: Reliability monitoring using adaptive critical path testing. In *Dependable Systems and Networks (DSN), 2010 IEEE/IFIP International Conference on*, pages 151–160, July 2010.

[20] C. Zhu, Z. Gu, R. P. Dick, and L. Shang. Reliable multiprocessor system-on-chip synthesis. In *Hardware/Software Codesign and System Synthesis (CODES+ISSS), 2007 IEEE/ACM/IFIP International Conference on*, pages 239–244, October 2007.

A Real-Time, Energy-Efficient System Software Suite for Heterogeneous Multicore Platforms

Shih-Hao Hung[1,2], Chi-Sheng Shih[1,2], Tei-Wei Kuo[1,2], Chia-Heng Tu[1] and Che-Wei Chang[2]

[1]Graduate Institute of Networking and Multimedia

[2]Department of Computer Science and Information Engineering

National Taiwan University, Taipei 106, Taiwan

{hungsh, cshih, ktw, d94944008, f95093}@csie.ntu.edu.tw

ABSTRACT

Heterogeneous multicore systems have become the trend for the embedded market due to its advantage of power/performance over traditional designs. However, monitoring the workload, scheduling the tasks, and managing the energy consumption to enable energy-efficient, real-time applications are increasingly challenging on such systems as both the applications and systems become complex. In this paper, we introduce a comprehensive approach to address the key problems and accelerate the design of a heterogeneous multicore embedded system by providing a suite of energy-aware system software with tightly coupled real-time support and performance/power modeling facilities. We start with a rapid full system modeling/simulation framework to characterize the application workload, design energy-saving algorithms, and verify if performance requirements are met by hardware specifications during the early design stage. With special considerations on today's multicore embedded systems, we developed several key components and integrated them as a system software suite: a portable, efficient library to support inter-core communications and multicore programming, a lightweight kernel for dynamically monitoring and sharing the workload among the processor cores, and a dynamic voltage and frequency scaling scheme to adjust the setting of the processors to save energy. The system software has been implemented on the PAC Duo system as a case study, with experimental results to demonstrate the effectiveness of the proposed approach. This paper discusses the novel techniques included in this system software and shares the lessons that we have learned from this work.[1]

Categories and Subject Descriptors: D.2.2 [Software Engineering]: Design Tools and Techniques.

Keywords: Multicore emulator, inter-core communication library, load sharing kernel, energy saving algorithm.

[1]This work was supported by grants from the National Science Council (99-2220-E-002-028 and 101-2219-E-002-002) and from the Ministry of Economic Affairs (99-EC-17-A-01-S1-034).

CODES+ISSS'12, October 7 - 12, 2012, Tampere, Finland.

1. INTRODUCTION

Today, by mixing general-purpose cores and specialized cores, *heterogeneous* multicore systems generally offer higher power/performance and area efficiency than traditional systems for embedded applications [4]. A modern heterogeneous multicore system contain one or more general-purpose cores as the *main application processor unit* for executing the main application. Specialized cores in the form of *digital signal processor* (DSP), *graphics processing unit* (GPU), *I/O processors* (IOP), and *fixed-function accelerators* are often dedicated to specific tasks, such as encoding, compression, cryptographic operations, and network protocols. DSPs and GPUs are specialized architectures with dedicated instructions to accelerate the processing of signals and multimedia data streams with relatively low energy consumptions.

To produce a cost-effective, energy-efficient multicore embedded system and fulfill the application requirements at the same time is a challenging task, as the applications become more and more complex [27]. The main issues that we are trying to address in this paper are the following:

- *Workflow for Hardware-Software Co-Design:* In practice, it is usually difficult for hardware designers and application developers to collaborate closely to optimize the system design. Besides the fact that hardware and software designers may not speak the same language, it is hard for hardware designers to gauge the requirements of the application to support the application. On the other hand, software designers cannot start developing applications until the actual hardware arrives, which prolongs the time to market.

- *Multicore Systems and Programming:* Multicore systems and multicore programming are both hard topics. Especially, heterogeneous multicore systems are evolving rapidly and are relatively new to many developers. The community demands better development environments, including algorithms, libraries and performance tools, to facilitate the debugging, workload monitoring, and performance analysis on such systems.

In a typical workflow, as shown in Figure 1, the designers often need to accomplish a few challenging tasks to produce an energy-efficient real-time system. To improve the design process, we provide a systematic framework, which offers an effective, friendly workflow and a suite of energy-aware system software with tightly coupled real-time support and performance/power modeling facilities, as shown in Figure 2.

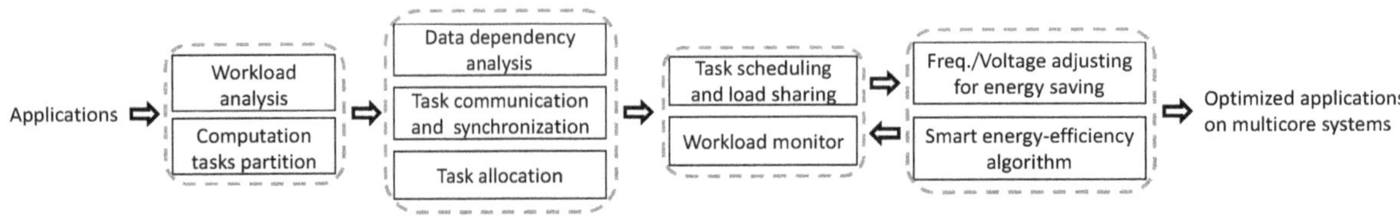

Figure 1: An typical workflow for developing applications on heterogeneous multicore systems.

The following briefly describes how our software suite helps to accelerate the design flow and the optimization process:

1. *Analysis and partitioning of the computational tasks* in the application usually requires the actual hardware. We proposed the *MCEmu* (MultiCore Emulator) framework for a system developer to quickly build an execution environment and model a full-blown heterogeneous multicore system by specifying the hardware configuration of the system and integrating existing simulators of MPU and specialized cores. We have also developed new simulation and profiling techniques to model the performance and power of the systems with a sufficient speed to carry out complex applications.

2. *Analysis of the data dependencies, orchestration of communication and synchronization, and task allocation* often need to be considered simultaneously to optimize the resource utilization for real-time applications. For that, we include *MSG* [18] as a unified application programming interface (API) for orchestrating the tasks on multiple cores. MSG is also intended for the development of cross-platform applications, as it can be easily ported to new platforms with its efficient message operations optimized for code-size, performance, and scalability. Combined with MCEmu, cross-platform multicore applications can be developed and simulated with or without the actual system in place.

3. *Task scheduling and load sharing* are critical for applications with dynamic workload. Runtime workload monitoring is needed to ensure if real-time constraints are met and to detect inefficient resource utilization. We developed a light-weight OS, called *nanoKernel*, to support dynamic scheduling and workload sharing schemes on specialized cores for real-time applications. The code of nanoKernel is designed to run efficiently on specialized cores with little memories, and the load balancer within nanoKernel allows multiple specialized cores to share the workload and dynamically migrate the tasks to fulfill the deadlines of the tasks.

4. *Design of an energy-saving scheme* is often beyond the ability of average developers. The saving of energy can be achieved by dynamically adjusting the working voltages and frequencies of the MPU and the specialized cores, based on the type of workload, the utilization of resource, and the real-time constraints. Such power management facilities should better be built into the system with a variety of smart energy-efficiency algorithms to automatically save system energy for real-time applications without performance loss. For that, we include the dynamic voltage and frequency scaling (DVFS) facilities [39] working with nanoKernel to manage the power consumption of the specialized cores.

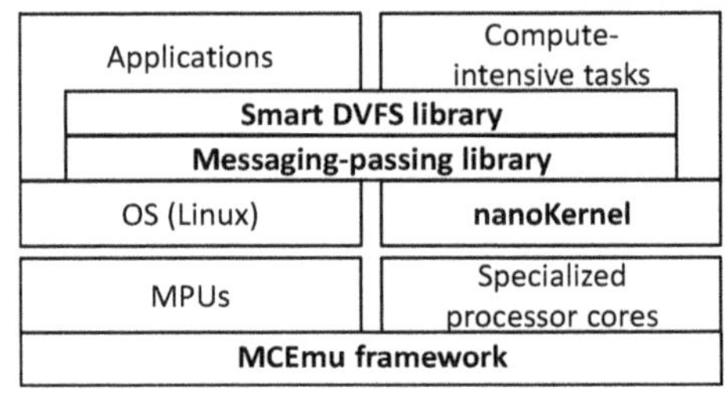

Figure 2: Overview of the proposed framework.

Although there may have been many previous works to solve the individual challenges mentioned above, our framework aims to provide a comprehensive approach to tackling these challenging issues systematically. By developing a practical, portable, integrated framework, we can accelerate the design workflow for real-time applications on new heterogeneous multicore systems in our experience.

The rest of this paper is organized as the following. In the Section 2, we mention some of the related work and discuss the state of the start. Section 3 introduces the MCEmu framework which we use to facilitate the workflow for debugging and performance analysis of multicore applications during the early design stage. The system software suite, i.e. MSG, nanoKernel, and DVFS library, are discussed individually in Section 4. Section 5 illustrates how the integral use of the suite and tools help address the challenges in system development. Finally, Section 6 concludes this paper.

2. BACKGROUND AND RELATED WORK

As the proposed work involves several areas, this section is further divided into four subsections to describe the background and related work in each of these areas.

2.1 Full System Simulation

There have been numerous works focusing on full system emulation [3] [28], which virtualizes the target system to run on host machines and enables software development on existing or hypothetical hardware platforms and system-level performance studies before building actual systems. With the recent advance of *dynamic binary translation* techniques, full system emulators, such as *QEMU* [3], achieve even higher speed via translating blocks of target instructions into optimized sequences of native instructions. Methods for concatenating the functional simulation with the timing simulation, e.g., *FAST* [11] and *FaCSim* [24], were also proposed to deliver fast and accurate simulation results. More recent works, e.g. *virtual timing device* [16] and the *pQEMU* [15], added performance/energy models to a full system emulator to estimate the performance and energy consumption on the target system at the speed of several hundred of million instructions per second.

To simulate a multicore system with a reasonable speed, researchers started to parallelize simulators and execute them on multicore hosts [23, 37, 38]. *COREMU* [38] used multiple instances of QEMU to emulate a homogeneous multicore system in parallel. However, the simulation of *heterogeneous* multicore systems is more complicated. One of the few examples is *SystemSim* [19], for simulating the *IBM Cell* architecture [22]. However, SystemSim is not parallelized and is very slow, which affects its applicability in practice. In comparison, *MCEmu* allows the simulator for each core to be performed by one thread, so the overall simulation speed can be scaled on a multicore host. In addition to software testing and debugging, MCEmu allows the user to quickly build a performance analysis environment, a functionality which we have not yet seen before.

2.2 Multicore Programming

Two major parallel programming models are widely used: *shared-memory* and *message-passing*. Message-passing programming is more portable than shared-memory programming in practice since it does not require the physical shared memory. *MPI* [26] is the standard for developing high performance computing parallel applications, but it is far too large to fit in embedded systems. For embedded multicore platforms, many of the advanced functions in MPI should be eliminated to save the memory usage. While *MCAPI* [29] attempts to keep its footprint small enough to fit in an embedded system, it also introduces some new functions which do not exist in MPI. The adoption of MCAPI has been very slow, with support for x86 and PowerPC-based symmetric shared memory architectures. While data parallel is an abstract, high-level programming model for parallel data processing, with languages such as CUDA [30], and OpenCL [21], an inter-core communication scheme is still needed from the system software to transfer the data among processors.

For heterogeneous multicore systems, vendors offer their own programming models. For example, Texas Instruments provides DSP/BIOS bridge [31] for its DaVinci series, and IBM provides a programming language for the CELL processor [20]. Since we believe that portability and efficiency are the two most important issues to real-time embedded systems, we integrate MSG [18], a lightweight message-passing library designed for portability across heterogeneous multicore systems, into our work. MSG is small enough to fit in the specialized cores of a modern multicore system and provides the basic inter-core communication and synchronization mechanisms for us to build applications and support data parallel programming if needed.

2.3 Load Sharing and Resource Allocation

Existing operating systems on the DSP cores usually support limited features, compared to full-blown embedded real-time operating systems, and lack of certain critical features for embedded real-time applications. For example, VSPWorks by Wind River provides preemptive multitasking and high-speed interrupt support on a range of DSP and ASIC core processors. VSPWorks follows a virtual single-processor model where data objects and tasks can be moved from core to core transparently; the RTOS on MPU handles all the underlying inter-processor communication. DSP/BIOS by Texas Instruments does not support nested interrupts, and the programmers need to write assemble code to handle the nested interrupts. VisualDSP++ by Analog Devices supports nested interrupts on each DSP core but does not support task/thread migration among the cores.

In the nanoKernel, we introduce priority interrupt handling and load sharing among the DSP cores with acceptable overhead on the resource limited processing units. To handle interrupts on multicore platforms, processor affiliation is the widely adopted approach. Foong and Fung [13] redirect interrupts to dedicated processors to improve TCP performance for up to 25%. Combined thread affinity and interrupt affinity can achieve gains of 30%. Boyd-Wickizer and Chen propose *Corey* [5] in which kernel services including interrupt handling are executed on dedicated processors. Applications and daemons run on other processors and can control inter-core sharing. The result shows it scales better on multicore platforms.

Resource reservation approaches [1, 6, 33] guarantee certain amount of computation time for each task in every replenish period. They are created to support applications with a variety of different time constraints.

2.4 Energy-Efficient Designs

Different from personal computers and servers, the design issues of embedded systems are further complicated by their restrictive resource supports and limited battery energy supply. With the modern VLSI circuit designs, numerous processors now support the functionalities of Dynamic Voltage and Frequency Scaling (DVFS) and Dynamic Power Management (DPM). Distinct from the past work, we are interested in energy-efficient real-time job scheduling over multiple DSPs, where a MPU and multiple DSPs work together in energy-efficient real-time scheduling. When the characteristics of multimedia applications are considered, excellent research results were proposed for energy-efficient designs, such as those in [34, 2, 8, 35]. Although there are very good results for energy-efficient task scheduling for multimedia applications over single-core platforms [8, 35], few research results consider multi-core platforms.

In order to efficiently utilize multiple DSPs in a system, functional and data partitioning schemes are two approaches to exploit the parallelism in the executions of multimedia tasks [36]. In this paper, the data-partitioning-based approach [39] is used for energy-efficient real-time task scheduling, where data partitioning provides flexible and scalable alternatives in parallelizing multimedia workload processing. Under the performance constraints, we would propose an algorithm in Section 4.3 to derive a proper duration and subjob assignment over cores for the execution of each job in a multimedia task. Section 5.5 further shows that the proposed algorithm and implementation could help application programmers to efficiently reduce the energy consumption of multimedia applications without looking into the hardware architecture and system implementation.

3. SOFTWARE DEVELOPMENT BASED ON SIMULATORS

We developed the MCEmu (short for *MultiCore Emulator*) framework to create a multicore system emulator from existing emulators, as illustrated in Figure 3. In this example, QEMU [3] provides the functionality for emulating the behavior of MPU(s), main memory, and I/O devices, while the data processor emulators execute the programs compiled for the specialized data processing (DP) cores. MCEmu offers the facilities needed for connecting the MPU emulator and DP emulators, i.e. Virtual Processor Controller and Data Processor Controller, as well as the timing models and performance monitors to support profiling and tracing. Using this simulation environment, we were able to model the ITRI PAC Duo system [7], develop its system software and applications, and project the performance of a planned PAC-8 chip with 8 DP cores. The simulation environment supports the Linux OS and executes ARM9 instructions at up to 200 million instructions per second (MIPS) on a PC with a 2.6GHz Intel Core i7 processor.

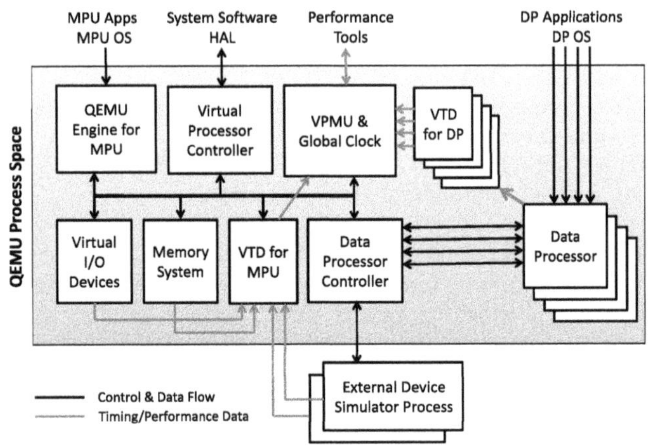

Figure 3: A multicore simulator based on MCEmu.

In addition to providing the facilities for building a heterogeneous multicore simulator, MCEmu allows each component simulator to run as a separate thread in parallel to take advantage of the multiple cores on the host machine. For that, we developed a lazy synchronization strategy to avoid excessive amount of synchronization overhead that would destroy the benefit of parallel simulation. Furthermore, MCEmu may work with external simulators (e.g. a Verilog simulator for an FPGA device) running as separate processes to utilize existing simulators without their source codes.

Software Development on Multicore Platforms.

We developed a *MultiCore Board Support Package* (MCBSP) for multicore system to enable the development of multicore applications on MCEmu, with functions to coordinate parallel execution across heterogeneous processor cores on Linux, such as workload distribution functions, synchronization primitives, and inter-core communication functions.

The system configuration is handled by the *Virtual Processor Controller* (VPC), which provides the system information (e.g. keeping track of the data accelerators and the memory modules) and interacts with system software on resource management. During the hardware initialization stage, the system configuration is stored into the VPC and can be retrieved later by OS and applications. In addition, whenever the OS or an application starts, the MCBSP sends important software information to the VPC, such as symbol table for the kernel, the application binary interface (ABI) and ELF program information for kernel and user applications, to support debugging and tracing in the simulated environment.

The *Data Processor Controller* (DPC) provides a set of interfaces and the protocols for the MCEmu to manage the external simulators. By conforming the interfaces, all of the accelerator simulators can be run in parallel to the full system simulator and synchronized whenever needed as specified by the protocol. Via the interfaces, the QEMU-based MPU emulation can communicate and synchronize with the emulators/simulators of the accelerators. For example, DPC is involved when an application or the OS calls MCBSP to create, pause, and terminate the program on a DP.

The *Data Processors* (DP) are simulators for specialized cores. To perform the emulation of a DP as a thread in the QEMU process space, the emulator must be packaged as a thread-safe function which does not modify global variables. Otherwise, the emulation needs to be performed externally as a standalone process, which could slow down the emulation of the entire system.

Performance Estimation for the Emulated System.

Each processor emulator must have a *timing model* to advance its local clock. However, since a functional emulator like the QEMU does not model the internals of the processor, MCEmu includes a set of timing models for ARM9 cores and allows the users to create their own timing models.

The *Virtual Performance Monitoring Unit* (VPMU) offers a set of ABI for each component emulator/simulator to count the performance-related event. The elapsed time for a core is estimated by its *Virtual Timing Device* (VTD) based on the data recorded in the counter of VPMU. We place counters within QEMU to monitor I/O events, memory accesses, TLB misses, cache misses, executed instructions, etc., and estimate the execution for a block of MPU instructions. For the DP's or external simulators, there is one VTD corresponding to each of them to keep track of the local clocks.

Virtual Power-metering Devices (VPD) are used to derive the power consumption for the emulated system [17] by monitoring the power state of the hardware components in the system, such as MPU, DP, memory module, LCD panel, and Wi-Fi module. Each VTD/VPD runs independently for most of the time and uses a dedicated set of counters to avoid race conditions and serialization. VPMU has a software interface which resembles the interface of the performance monitoring unit (PMU) on ARM processors, and MCBSP includes a driver for VPMU to support existing performance tools.

To evaluate the global clock, MCEmu has the local clocks synchronized only when an inter-core synchronization/communication event occurs, which significantly improves the speed of simulation. At the occurrence of a *software synchronization event*, such as barrier, lock acquisition, and thread creation, MCEmu would have faster simulators wait for slower simulators to complete the synchronization event. MCEmu also forces the simulators to synchronize periodically to keep the simulators execute programs at a similar pace. Accesses to shared resources, such as bus, shared memories, and I/O devices, can also cause resource contention and affect the system performance, so it is important to monitor the utilization of these resources. For frequently accessed shared resource, MCEmu cannot afford to synchronize the component simulators on each access. Alternatively,

MCEmu detects potential bus and memory contention by checking the total access counts periodically and adjusts the affected local clocks.

Support for Performance Analysis.
As the software interface of VPMU is identical to the interface of PMU in an ARM9 processor, existing performance tools, e.g. Oprofile [25] and Perfctr [32], work immediately for profiling Linux kernel and applications. In addition, MCEmu provides an innovative, user-friendly facility to enable non-intrusive event tracing and profiling within the emulator. Via a graphical interface, the user simply selects the functions or data structures for the MCEmu to analyze. Since the analysis is done within the simulator, MCEmu can exclude the overhead of profiling/tracing and eliminate the pollution from a performance tool itself. MCEmu can also visualize system-wide performance statistics for the user via *sampling-based performance analysis*, which records the data in VPMU periodically and reveals the changes between consecutive sample points graphically.

4. THE ENERGY-EFFICIENT REAL-TIME SYSTEM SOFTWARE SUITE

For heterogeneous multicore systems to support real-time applications, our system software suite provides: (1) an efficient, lightweight inter-core communication library, (2) resource allocation and load sharing schemes to accomplish real-time tasks on small cores with limited memory, and (3) dynamic power management schemes to support real-time applications. We will discuss how we design our system software suite to meet these demands in this section.

4.1 Inter-Core Communications

The MSG library [18] provides a unified API and offers the basic message passing functions on a variety of embedded heterogeneous multicore platforms. To ease the effort of creating the MSG library for a new system, MSG adapts a three-layer modular design to separate its implementation into platform-independent functions, architecture-specific functions, and platform-dependent functions:

- The *application layer* provides the management functions, point-to-point message operations, one-sided operations, and collective message operations, which were selected to effectively support the communication patterns that are commonly found on existing message-passing libraries and benchmark suites, such as MPI [14] and MCAPI [29]. For small systems, the one-sided functions can be removed to reduce the footprint, but the inclusion of one-sided functions allows the application to benefit from shared memory and/or DMA engines if available.

- The *core layer* contains two components. The resource management module contains the functions and the data structures for exchanging control messages, handling request queues, and managing buffer pools. The internal protocol module implements the communication protocols for the message-passing functions defined in the application layer with shared memory operations and/or communication primitives provided by the system. This design allows the user to build a version of MSG for a system with or without shared memory while the core layer remains mostly the same.

- To port MSG to a new platform, the library builder needs to implement the two modules in the *porting layer*. The OS-dependent module is required to provide memory management services for shared/distributed memory architectures, and the platform-dependent module handles the transmission of the messages. The implementation calls for the most efficient mechanisms provided by the OS and the platform.

4.2 Load-Sharing NanoKernel

The targeted platform of this work is a multicore heterogeneous SoC platform modeled in Section 3, where DSP cores and HW accelerators receive the requests from user applications running on MPU and send the computation results back to the user applications. The software architecture on the platform is illustrated on Figure 4. On the MPU, a general purpose operating system such as Linux is deployed to manage its local resources, and global resources on the platform including shared memory, storage devices, and network interfaces. On the DSP cores, nanoKernel, an SMP micro-kernel, is deployed to manage the local resources of DSP cores such as local memory, thread scheduling, and interrupts. We assume that the operating systems on both MPU and DSP cores are priority-based and support preemptive scheduling. There are two distinguish components in nanoKernel: *hybrid interrupt handling framework* and *pipeline scheduler with load sharing*. The design and implementation of these two components follow.

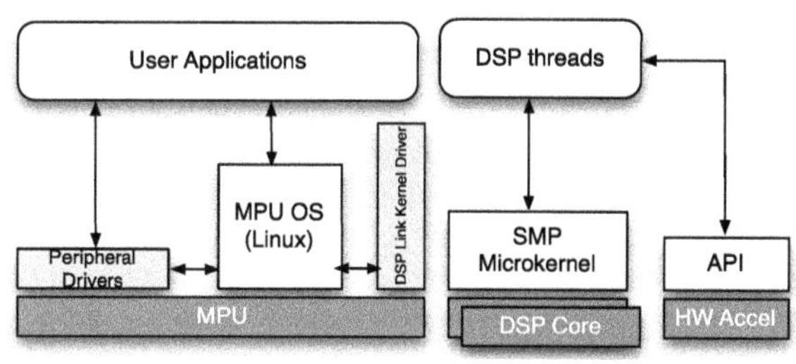

Figure 4: Framework of nanoKernel.

Hybrid Interrupt Handling Framework.
This framework is designed to shorten the jitter of interrupt latency by executing interrupt service routines (ISR) as threads and configuring hardware interrupt masks on demand. There are four major components in the framework: *unified scheduler, quick execution mode, just-in time interrupt masking* and *interrupt priority boost.* Figure 5 shows the control flow of hybrid interrupt handling framework. When an interrupt is triggered, just-in time interrupt masking mechanism checks hardware interrupt masks to decide if the interrupt should be delivered to the scheduler.

Without loss of generality, an activity refers to a sequence of computing operations, which can be the execution of either user thread, kernel thread, or ISRs. When an interrupt is delivered, it turns on interrupt's flag, acknowledges the interrupt controller, and clears the source IRQ line. Then, priority-driven scheduling is triggered to select the next activity. If the next activity is an ISR, the ISR will be dispatched and executed in the quick execution component.

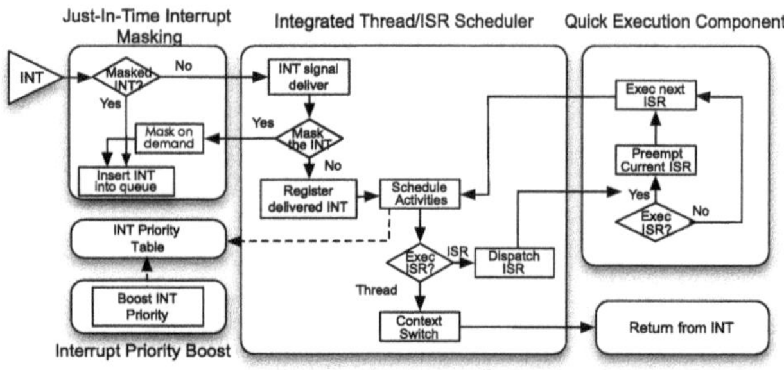

Figure 5: The Control Flow of Hybrid Interrupt Handling Framework.

Otherwise, a context switch takes place to execute the user or kernel thread.

Quick execution component is designed to shorten the blocking time of interrupt latency for high priority thread and support ISR preemption. When the current activity is not serving an ISR, the component executes the ISR in the current context to shorten the interrupt latency. On the other hand, when the current activity is serving a low priority ISR, the component suspends the lower priority ISR, creates a new ISR thread, attaches the lower priority ISR to the new ISR thread, and executes the high priority ISR in current context. The ISR thread will be scheduled later according to its priority level.

Interrupt priority boost component takes advantage of precedence dependencies between threads and interrupts to manage the priority of interrupts. In most operating systems, the priority of interrupts are static. Although this approach is easy to implement and efficient, a high priority thread will be blocked by the execution of a high priority ISR which is triggered by a low priority thread. To avoid such blocking, nanoKernel adopts the priority inheritance protocol to adjust the priority of ISR threads. The priority of an ISR thread inherits that of the dependent user/kernel thread. Therefore, the corresponding ISRs would be scheduled with higher priority and the blocking time of high priority thread is shorten.

The hybrid interrupt handling framework is designed to shorten the interrupt latency and to support priority interrupts. Given this framework, nanoKernel can limit the block for high priority interrupt for at most once but eliminate the overhead of physically masking low priority interrupts.

Thread Migration Mechanism.

Migrating threads among non-MMU cores consists of two steps. In the first step, the kernel selects the overrun thread and its destination core. Second, the kernel assures that the memory stack is well protected and, then, migrates the overrun thread from source core to destination core.

Multi-core Load Sharing Policy (MCLSP) is a distributed load sharing mechanism to select the thread and the destination core to migrate. The algorithm is distributed in the sense that idle cores volunteer to share the load from other cores and the migration is conducted between the source core and destination core. One core is elected as a *broker core* to pair the cores for load sharing and migration.

To keep track of the available computation time on each core, nanoKernel maintains the slack budget for each core. When the slack budget of one core is greater than zero, the core is able to share the load from the others. When the slack budget of one core is less than or equal to zero, the core is not able to share the load. The slack budget on all the cores are reset to zero for a constant interval, which is called a *stage*. The concept of stage is borrowed from hardware/software pipeline scheduling on multicore platforms [12]. The schedules are divided into stages and the schedules on all the cores are synchronized at the boundary of stages.

In nanoKernel, we assumed that each thread has an expected execution time, which can be the average execution time or worst case execution time of a thread. When the thread is time-critical, one can set the expected execution time to the worst case execution time of the task. Otherwise, one can set the expected execution time to the average execution time of the task to enhance resource utilization. NanoKernel provides two slack time accumulation mechanisms: *non-preemptive static schedule* (NPSC) and *constant-bandwidth server* (CBS). In NPSC mechanism, the execution of each thread is non-preemptive until the end of the a stage. When one thread completes before its expected execution time, the difference is added to the slack budget. Otherwise, the difference is deducted from the budget. As a result, under NPSC mechanism, the slack budget of a core may be negative when some threads take longer time to complete. Under CBS mechanism, all threads are allowed to execute up to its expected execution time. When a thread completes before its expected execution time, the difference is added to the slack budget. When a thread does not complete at its expected execution time, it will be suspended and is inserted into its local overrun queue and the slack budget remains unchanged. Under CBS mechanism, the slack budget is no less than zero. The slack budget of each core is sent to the broker core whenever an update occurs.

The broker and other cores communicate to each other via core signals. When any thread overruns, nanoKernel sends an *overrun signal* to the broker core and to ask for load sharing; when all the scheduled threads complete and the slack budget is greater than 0, nanoKernel sends a *idle core signal* to the broker core and to offer for load sharing. The broker core selects the overrun threads and destination core according to the received signals. Upon receiving an overrun signal, the broker core checks if any cores have slack budget. If none of the cores have slack budget, the overrun signal is queued. Otherwise, the broker core selects a core with sufficient slack time to be the destination core and notifies both core to start the migration process. Upon receiving an idle core signal, the broker core checks if there is any queued overrun signal. If the queue is empty, the idle core signal is queued. Otherwise, the broker core selects an overrun thread whose priority is the highest and whose migration overhead is less than the slack budget of the destination core. After the broker core selects the overrun thread to migrate and the destination core, the broker core informs both destination and source cores to start the migration. The first phase of the mechanism is Initialization Phase. In this phase, both cores transit from normal state to halt state, in which the interrupts are disabled. The second phase of the mechanism is Execution Phase. In this phase, at first the source core copies the memory stack of the migrated thread to the destination core. Then, the destination core sets program counter register and stack pointer register for the migrated thread. In the End Phase, both cores transit from the halt state to the normal state and continue to execute.

4.3 Energy-Efficient System Designs

As the MSG library and the nanoKernel are developed and analyzed in previous sections, this section aims at the demonstrating of a multi-core energy-saving strategy over our system software supports. We include an algorithm in [39] with DVFS support for a case study, in which a data-partitioning-based approach is adopted to balance the workloads of multiple cores.

Processor and Task Models for Energy Saving.

For the energy-saving designs, we consider a multi-core platform consisting of M identical cores which support the DVFS capability. An example is the DSP cores of ITRI PAC Duo. The power consumption function of a core with a processing speed s is denoted as $P(s) = C \cdot s^{\alpha} + \beta$, where C, β and α are hardware-dependent constants [10]. In this work, we consider the support of discrete speeds over the cores for the dynamically frequency scaling.

In order to minimize the energy consumption of multimedia applications with our system software, a multimedia application is abstracted as the following task model. We abstract an application as a task set $\mathbf{T}$ which consists of a sequence of tasks that must be sequentially executed with a dispatching period p. We then set p as the reciprocal of the frame rate of the multimedia application in our experiments and in the following discussion. Therefore, if each task is completed before the end of the corresponding period, the scheduling result can meet the quality requirement of the multimedia application.

Problem Formulation.

A multimedia application would include a set of sequential tasks $\mathbf{T} = \tau_1, \tau_2, ..., \tau_N$ (such as the decodings of the pictures in a video clip), where each task could be further partitioned into multiple independent (but with the same deadline) subtasks. The energy-efficient real-time scheduling algorithm would derive a subtask assignment set $\mathbf{G}$ and a frequency configuration set $\mathbf{S}$ of a multimedia application over M cores such that the energy consumption is minimized, and no deadline is violated. For the subtask assignment set $\mathbf{G} = (\mathbf{x}_1, \mathbf{x}_2, \ldots, \mathbf{x}_N)$, each $\mathbf{g}_{i,j}$ in a subtask assignment $\mathbf{x}_i = (\mathbf{g}_{i,1}, \mathbf{g}_{i,2}, \ldots, \mathbf{g}_{i,n_i})$ denotes the subset of the subtasks of τ_i that are assigned to the j_{th} core, where n_i is the number of subtasks of τ_i. For the frequency configuration set $\mathbf{S} = (\mathbf{s}_1, \mathbf{s}_2, \ldots, \mathbf{s}_N)$, each $f_{i,j}$ in a frequency configuration $\mathbf{s}_i = (f_{i,1}, f_{i,2}, \ldots, f_{i,M})$ denotes the frequency of the j_{th} core in running all of the subtasks in $\mathbf{g}_{i,j}$, where M is the number of cores. In the rest of this section, a solution is said to be *feasible* if all tasks meet the relative deadlines by using the subtask assignments and the frequency configurations of the solution. A solution is said to be *optimal* if it is feasible and minimizes the total energy consumption. Therefore, we have the following target problem: *Given a multimedia application with task set* $\mathbf{T}$ *over* M *identical DSP cores and a limited buffer size, the objective is to derive a feasible schedule with the minimum energy consumption.*

An Energy-Efficient Multimedia Scheduling Algorithm.

For the target problem, we introduce an energy-efficient multi-core scheduling algorithm in [39] with our system software supports to minimize the total energy consumption. For a given time point t, assume there are p pending tasks which are $\{\tau_i, \tau_{i+1}, \cdots, \tau_{i+p-1}\}$. Let $w_{k,j}$ denote the number of the total workload (the total execution cycles of the subtasks) assigned to the j_{th} core for the execution of task τ_k. If the time slot reserved for the execution of τ_k is Δ_k, the energy consumption of the j_{th} core for the execution of τ_k can be derived as $P(\frac{w_{k,j}}{\Delta_k})\Delta_k$ before we round up the derived frequency $\frac{w_{k,j}}{\Delta_k}$ to an available frequency level. If the subtask assignment of each pending task is fixed, the ideal minimum energy consumption (with continuous frequencies of cores) is the minimum value of $\sum_{k=i}^{i+p-1}\sum_{j=1}^{M} P(\frac{w_{k,j}}{\Delta_k})\Delta_k$, when all tasks meet their relative deadlines. Such a minimization problem forms a Linear-Programming problem and could be solved by the Lagrange multiplier method [39] by polynomial time. Such a result provides a **lowerbound** of the energy consumption for each fixed assignment of subtasks in the given pending tasks.

In the algorithm, the time slot Δ_i reserved to execute τ_i is set as $\min\{\frac{C_i}{\sum_{k=i}^{r} C_k}(d_r - t) : i \le r \le i+b-1\}$, where C_k is the total number of the execution cycles of τ_k. Considering all pending tasks, the rationale behind the time-slot setting is to explore the potential for minimizing the total energy consumption by reducing the variances of the DSP-core frequencies without any deadline missing. With the time slot Δ_i for the execution of each target task τ_i, the algorithm then derives the subtask assignment and frequency configuration of τ_i. The *Largest-Workload-First* (LWF) strategy is adopted to assign subtasks onto cores since the LWF strategy is with a 1.13-approximation bound for the frame-based task assignment (such as the assignment of the subtasks of a given task) for DSP cores with continuous frequencies. The basic idea for proving this claim is to show that the derived result of the algorithm is no more than 1.13 times of the lower bound of any feasible assignment of subtasks. For the details of the proof, we refer readers to a study of the frame-based scheduling in [9]. With above observation, the algorithm sorts the subtasks of a task in a non-increasing order by their required execution cycles and then assign them to the core with the currently minimum utilization sequentially. With the derived subtask assignment, the frequency of the j_{th} core is configured as the lowest available frequency which is no less than $\frac{w_{i,j}}{\Delta_i}$.

ALGORITHM 1: LWF STRATEGY

Input: pending tasks $\tau_i, \tau_{i+1}, \ldots, \tau_{i+b-1}$ in the buffer.

```
g_{i,j} ← ∅ and w_{i,j} ← 0 for j = 1, 2, ..., M;
Δ_i ← min{ C_i / (Σ_{k=i}^{r} C_k) (d_r − t) : i ≤ r ≤ i + b − 1 };
re-index subtasks of τ_i such that c_(i,p) ≥ c_(i,q) if p < q;
forall the subtasks τ_(i,k) belong to τ_i do
    find the core with currently minimum workload w_{i,m};
    g_{i,m} ← g_{i,m} ∪ {τ_(i,k)} and w_{i,m} ← w_{i,m} + c_(i,k);
set f_{i,j} as the lowest frequency no less than w_{i,j}/Δ_i for each core j;
return x_i, s_i;
```

For the pending tasks in the buffer, Algorithm 1 can derive approximate solutions when we assume that the DSP cores are with continues frequencies. Such a good property could be used to dynamically reduce the energy consumption of an online multimedia application with our DVFS system modules and nanoKernel. Ideally, the energy consumption of the schedule derived by Algorithm 1 is no more than 1.13 times of that of the optimal schedule when any required frequencies are available. For the our implementation, the derived frequencies have to be rounded up to the discrete frequencies of the DSP cores, where the experimental results and analysis are illustrated in Section 5.

5. EXPERIMENTAL RESULTS

In this section, we present a case study to illustrate the use of our framework to produce a simulation environment and show how our system software suite helps optimize applications on an embedded heterogeneous multicore platform.

5.1 Multicore Platform and MCEmu

In this case study, we used the PAC Duo SoC [7], which was recently developed by the Industry Technology Research Institute (ITRI) of Taiwan. It consists of an ARM926EJ-S core as the MPU and the two PAC DSP cores as the DP cores for accelerating signal processing and multimedia applications for mobile devices, as shown in Figure 6.

When we started working on this case, there were only a couple of early-stage evaluation boards without system software to support the duo DSP cores. It was relatively painful for software developers to work on this project as the evaluation boards crashed frequently in this stage. To overcome this problem, we first used MCEmu to create a simulation environment and used it to port, develop, and optimize the system software for this platform. Beyond that, MCEmu was also instrumental for us to identify program hotspots and analyze the performance of this multicore system.

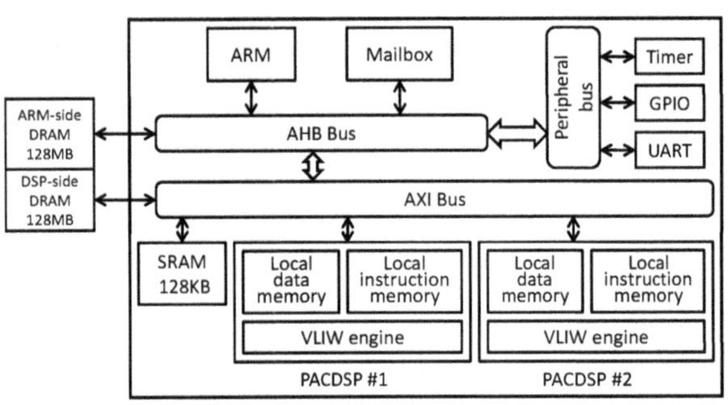

Figure 6: Block diagram of the PAC Duo platform.

5.2 Overview of the Application Study

We used a stream media player as our application study. As shown in Figure 7, a video server sent an encrypted and encoded video stream to the client device. Initially, the tasks on the client side, including network transmission (Linux's network stack), data decryption, decode of images, and placing images in the frame buffer, were performed by the MPU.

We experimented with video streams of 640x480 pixels in each picture frame. We applied two different quality settings of JPEG encoder on the server side: one with 75% image quality and average size of 38KB, and one with 90-100% quality and average size of 172KB. The different encoding settings would result in different workload on the client side and ultimately required us to adopt different task partitioning/power-saving strategies.

Without the MCEmu simulation environment, it was difficult for us to analyze the application performance and evaluate the partitioning strategies. After our performance analysis, we parallelize the application by partitioning the tasks and having the tasks migrated from the MPU to the DSP cores with the communication functions provided by the MSG library. Then, we used the load-sharing mechanism provided by nanoKernel to schedule the tasks dynamically on the DSP cores, since the type of encryption and encoding schemes depend on the server and may vary during the runtime, static partitioning and scheduling would not be appropriate for this application. Finally, the DVFS algorithms included in our system software used nanoKernel's runtime monitors to adjust the voltages and frequencies of the DSP cores to save energy under the application's real-time constraints.

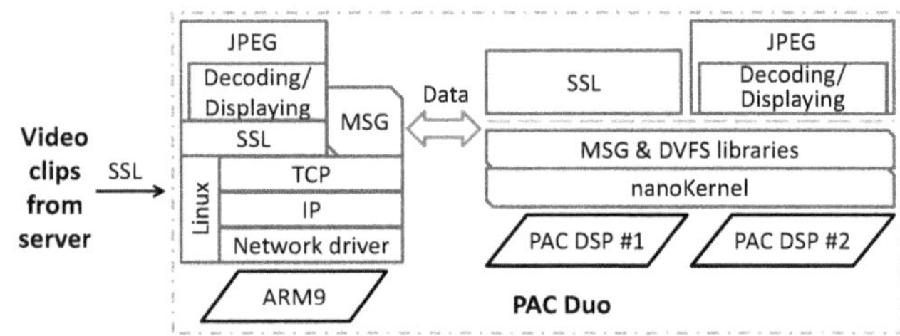

Figure 7: The software components involved in the case study.

5.3 Application Analysis and Parallelization

The MCEmu generated call graphs and the profiles to reveal the flow of the application and the hotspots on the MPU. These charts were useful for deriving and optimizing parallelization schemes. As shown in Figure 8, most of the time was spent on the *JPEG*. Only about 8% of time was consumed by the *Network* and *SSL* for receiving and decrypting data (with AES and SHA1 algorithms) form the server. With the MPU performing all tasks, the system produced only 2.2 frames per second (FPS) even for the low-quality image setting.

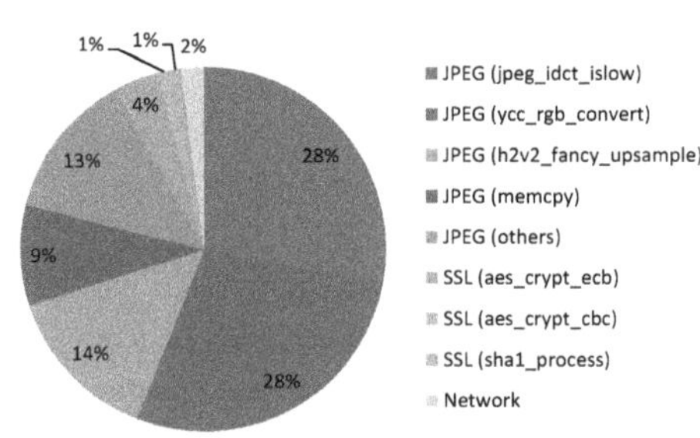

Figure 8: The execution time profile on the ARM core for low-quality images.

To accelerate the frame rate to an acceptable level, we consider move *JPEG* and *SSL* to the DSP cores. The decision was not obvious since the benefit of executing these tasks on the DSP cores could be destroyed by the overhead of communications. MCEmu was again useful in helping us extracting the amount of communications and modeling the impact of the communication overhead.

Configuration	ARM	DSP1	DSP2	FPS for 38KB	FPS for 172KB
I. Solo ARM	T+S+J			2.2	1.2
II. Offloading JPEG only	T+S	J	J	19.1	4.4
III. Offloading SSL/JPEG in pipeline	T	S	J	14.6	5.1
IV. Offloading both SSL and JPEG	T	S+J	S+J	19.5	5.1

T: Network, S: SSL, and J: JPEG

Figure 9: The frame rate under different task offloading schemes.

To parallelize the application, we placed the JPEG and SSL codes on the DSP cores, and used MSG point-to-point functions to connect the functions on MPU and the two DSP cores. Note that the total code size and the memory footprint was crucial to the task running on the DSP cores, since each DSP core has small (64KB) local instruction and data memories. The MSG library only consumed ~14KB of instruction memory and required 1KB data memory from each DSP core. As shown in Figure 9, we attempted several static task offloading schemes on the DSP cores, including offloading merely JPEG, having JPEG and SSL performed separately by two DSP cores in a pipelined fashion, and distributing both JPEG and SSL together onto two DSP cores. The frame rate produced by the system depended on the quality setting of the images and the offloading scheme. While Configuration IV resulted the best performance for both quality settings, it used more instruction/data memory on both DSP cores, which could be an issue for smaller cores. Instead, Configuration II performed well for low-quality images, and Configuration III offered identical frame rate as Configuration IV for high-quality images.

The workflow of *Configuration IV* can be revealed by the tracing/visualization tool in MCEmu, as shown Figure 10. The workflow shows the computation tasks and communication operations (data movement) over time, which is helpful to the design of task scheduling and power saving strategies mentioned in the following subsections.

5.4 Dynamic Load-Sharing

While the aforementioned static task allocation and schedule can achieve good frame rates, for this real-time application, we would like to additionally consider the jitter problem that might occur during the runtime due to the asynchronous rate of producing the image frame. Figure 10 illustrates how the jitter occurred in Configuration IV, when the JPEG function produced images at non-even pace. The interval between the 1st and 2nd images was 34ms, but the interval between 2nd and 3rd images was 68ms. As the jitter problem would cause the LCD panel to flicker, we used the real-time scheduling support in nanoKernel to resolve the issues, as shown in Figure 11, and result in a jitter-free schedule. The nanoKernel solved the issue by dividing the task schedule into stages and finishing (synchronizing) the tasks at the boundary of stages. The task J_1 is not finished at the beginning of the second stage where the nanoKernel was waked up, added the overrun task into the overrun queue, and re-schedule the task according the the mechanism described in Section 4.2.

To utilize the real-time support from nanoKernel, the user declares specific tasks on the DSP cores as real-time modules by describing the dependencies among the tasks, and nanoKernel scheduler will map the tasks to the available processor cores according to the description. The nanoKernel offers a systematic approach for the user to design real-time applications on small data processing cores without having to fine-tune the task schedule manually for the applications.

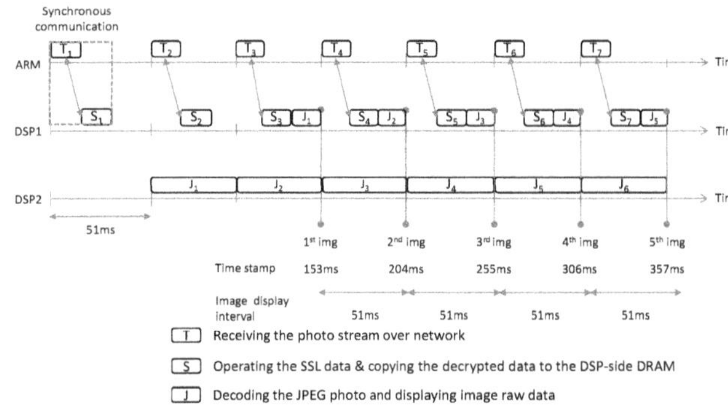

Figure 11: Synchronous frame rate with nanoKernel.

5.5 Energy-Efficient Scheduling

As mentioned in the previous subsection, the real-time constraints in our case study were already described to nanoKernel by the stage by the user. With that information, the DVFS algorithms in our software suite automatically minimized the energy consumption by adjusting the voltage/frequency settings for the MPU and DSP cores, while the real-time constrains of the tasks were satisfied. Figure 12 shows the effect of the DVFS scheme on Configuration III. Our energy-saving module reduced the energy consumption by 8% even for when FPS was set to 14 . When the workload was light, e.g. FPS=2 or FPS=4, one of the two DSP cores was turned off in the *DVFS-DPM* scheme to further save the power consumption. The measurement covered the entire PAC Duo chip, but as far as the DSP cores were concerned, the DVFS-DPM scheme was able save over 63% of the energy consumed by the DSP cores at 2 FPS.

FPS	2	4	6	8	10	12	14
Baseline	222	223	225	226	228	229	230
DVFS	156	159	170	180	191	202	213
DVFS+DPM	145	154	170	180	191	202	213

Unit: Energy per frame (mJ/frame)

Figure 12: The energy consumption under different power management schemes.

6. CONCLUSION

In this paper, we proposed a framework to address the challenges that real-time application developers and multicore system vendors constantly faced, especially in a complicated hardware-software co-design projects. We hope to share our experiences and tools to assist the research and development works in the real-time embedded system community. As many new heterogeneous multicore designs become the mainstream, we envision that the integration of development environment, system software and performance tools will be increasingly important in the future.

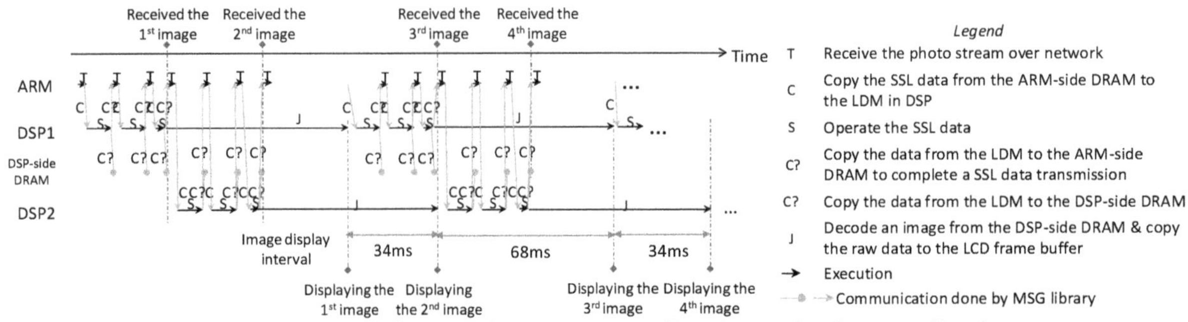

Figure 10: The workflow of the stream media player for low-quality images.

7. REFERENCES

[1] L. Abeni, G. Buttazzo, S. Superiore, and S. Anna. Integrating multimedia applications in hard real-time systems. In *RTSS*, 1998.

[2] M. A. Baker, V. Parameswaran, K. S. Chatha, and B. Li. Power reduction via macroblock prioritization for power aware h.264 video applications. In *CODES+ISSS*, pages 261–266, 2008.

[3] F. Bellard. QEMU, a fast and portable dynamic translator. In *USENIX Technical Conference*, pages 41–46, 2005.

[4] G. Blake, R. G. Dreslinski, and T. Mudge. A survey of multicore processors. *IEEE Signal Processing Magazine*, 26(6):26–37, 2009.

[5] S. Boyd-Wickizer, H. Chen, R. Chen, Y. Mao, F. Kaashoek, R. Morris, A. Pesterev, L. Stein, M. Wu, Y. Dai, Y. Zhang, and Z. Zhang. Corey: an operating system for many cores. In *OSDI*, pages 43–57, 2008.

[6] S. A. Brandt, S. Banachowski, C. Lin, and T. Bisson. Dynamic integrated scheduling of hard real-time, soft real-time and non-real-time processes. In *RTSS*, 2003.

[7] D. C. Chang, T. Lin, C. Wu, J. Lee, Y. Chu, and A. Wu. Parallel Architecture Core (PAC) - the first multicore application processor SoC in Taiwan part I: Hardware architecture & software development tools. *Journal of Signal Processing Systems*, 62(3):373–382, 2011.

[8] C.-W. Chen, C.-Y. Yang, T.-W. Kuo, and M.-W. Chang. Energy-efficient real-time co-scheduling of multimedia DSP jobs. In *SUTC*, pages 225–232, 2008.

[9] J.-J. Chen, H.-R. Hsu, K.-H. Chuang, C.-L. Yang, A.-C. Pang, and T.-W. Kuo. Multiprocessor energy-efficient scheduling with task migration considerations. In *ECRTS*, pages 101–108, 2004.

[10] J.-J. Chen, H.-R. Hsu, and T.-W. Kuo. Leakage-aware energy-efficient scheduling of real-time tasks in multiprocessor systems. In *RTAS*, pages 408–417, 2006.

[11] D. Chiou, D. Sunwoo, J. Kim, N. A. Patil, W. Reinhart, D. E. Johnson, J. Keefe, and H. Angepat. FPGA-accelerated simulation technologies (FAST): Fast, full-system, cycle-accurate simulators. In *MICRO*, pages 249–261, 2007.

[12] Y.-S. Chiu, C.-S. Shih, and S.-H. Hung. Pipeline schedule synthesis for real-time streaming tasks with inter/intra-instance precedence constraints. In *DATE*, pages 1 –6, 2011.

[13] A. Foong, J. Fung, D. Newell, S. Abraham, P. Irelan, and A. Lopez-Estrada. Architectural characterization of processor affinity in network processing. In *ISPASS*, pages 207 –218, 2005.

[14] W. Gropp, E. Lusk, N. Doss, and A. Skjellum. A high-performance, portable implementation of the MPI message passing interface standard. *Parallel Comput.*, 22:789–828, September 1996.

[15] V. Hirvisalo and J. Knuuttila. pQEMU - profiling with an ISA emulator. Technical Report ESG-pQEMU-1, Aalto University, 2010.

[16] W. Hsu, S. Hung, and C. Tu. A virtual timing device for program performance analysis. In *ICCIT*, pages 2255–2260, 2010.

[17] S.-H. Hung, T.-W. Kuo, C.-S. Shih, and C.-H. Tu. System-wide profiling and optimization with virtual machines. In *ASP-DAC*, 2012.

[18] S.-H. Hung, C.-H. Tu, and W.-L. Yang. A portable, efficient inter-core communication scheme for embedded multicore platforms. *Journal of Systems Architecture - Embedded Systems Design*, 57(2):193–205, 2011.

[19] IBM Corp. Performance Analysis with the IBM Full-System Simulator, 2007.

[20] IBM Corp. Data communication and synchronization library programmer's guide and API reference, 2008.

[21] Khronos Group. OpenCL - The open standard for parallel programming of heterogeneous systems. http://www.khronos.org/opencl/, 2012.

[22] M. Kistler, M. Perrone, and F. Petrini. Cell multiprocessor communication network: Built for speed. *IEEE Micro*, 26(3):10–23, 2006.

[23] R. E. Lantz. Fast functional simulation with parallel embra. In *Proceedings of the 4th Annual Workshop on Modeling, Benchmarking and Simulation*, June 2008.

[24] J. Lee, J. Kim, C. Jang, S. Kim, B. Egger, K. Kim, and S. Han. FaCSim: a fast and cycle-accurate architecture simulator for embedded systems. In *LCTES*, pages 89–100, 2008.

[25] J. Levon and P. Elie. OProfile: A system profiler for Linux. http://oprofile.sourceforge.net/, 2011.

[26] E. Lusk, N. Doss, and A. Skjellum. A high-performance, portable implementation of the MPI message passing interface standard. *Parallel Computing*, 22:789–828, 1996.

[27] Machine-to-Machine (M2M) Communications. http://www.mobilein.com/M2M.htm, 2012.

[28] P. Magnusson, M. Christensson, J. Eskilson, D. Forsgren, G. Hallberg, J. Hogberg, F. Larsson, A. Moestedt, and B. Werner. Simics: A full system simulation platform. *Computer*, 35(2):50 –58, feb 2002.

[29] Multicore Association. Multicore communication API specification. http://www.multicore-association.org/workgroup/mcapi.php, 2008.

[30] NVIDIA Corp. CUDA parallel programming made easy. http://www.nvidia.com/object/ cuda_home_new.html, 2012.

[31] OMAPpedia. DSPBridge project. http://omappedia.org/wiki/DSPBridge_Project, 2012.

[32] M. Pettersson. Perfctr: Linux performance monitoring counters kernel extension. http://user.it.uu.se/ mikpe/linux/perfctr/, 2011.

[33] R. Rajkumar, K. Juvva, A. Molano, and S. Oikawa. Resource kernels: A resource-centric approach to real-time and multimedia systems. In *MMCN*, pages 150–164, 1998.

[34] H. Shikano, M. Ito, K. Uchiyama, T. Odaka, A. Hayashi, T. Masuura, M. Mase, J. Shirako, Y. Wada, K. Kimura, and H. Kasahara. Software-cooperative power-efficient heterogeneous multi-core for media processing. In *ASP-DAC*, pages 736–741, 2008.

[35] Y. Tan, P. Malani, Q. Qiu, and Q. Wu. Workload prediction and dynamic voltage scaling for mpeg decoding. In *ASP-DAC*, pages 911–916, 2006.

[36] E. B. V. D. Tol, E. G. T. Jaspers, and R. H. Gelderblom. Mapping of h.264 decoding on a multiprocessor architecture. In *IVCP*, volume 5022, pages 707–718, 2003.

[37] K. Wang, Y. Zhang, H. Wang, and X. Shen. Parallelization of ibm mambo system simulator in functional modes. *SIGOPS Oper. Syst. Rev.*, 42(1):71–76, 2008.

[38] Z. Wang, R. Liu, Y. Chen, X. Wu, H. Chen, W. Zhang, and B. Zang. COREMU: A scalable and portable parallel full-system emulator. In *PPoPP*, page 213–222, 2011.

[39] Y.-H. Wei, C.-Y. Yang, T.-W. Kuo, S.-H. Hung, and Y.-H. Chu. Energy-efficient real-time scheduling of multimedia tasks on multi-core processors. In *SAC*, pages 258–262, 2010.

ViPZonE: OS-Level Memory Variability-Driven Physical Address Zoning for Energy Savings

Luis Angel D. Bathen, Nikil Dutt, Alex Nicolau
Donald Bren School of Information and Computer Science
University of California, Irvine
{lbathen, dutt, nicolau}@ics.uci.edu

Mark Gottscho, Puneet Gupta
Electrical Engineering Department
University of California, Los Angeles
mgottscho@ucla.edu, puneet@ee.ucla.edu

ABSTRACT

ITRS predicts that over the next decade, hardware power variation will increase at alarming rates. As a result, designers must build software that can adapt to and exploit these variations to reduce power consumption and improve system performance. This paper presents ViPZonE, a system-level solution that opportunistically exploits DRAM power variation through physical address zoning. ViPZonE is composed of a variability-aware software stack that allows developers to indicate to the OS the expected dominant usage patterns (write or read) as well as level of utilization (high, medium, or low) through high-level APIs. ViPZonE's variability-aware page allocator, implemented in the Linux kernel, is responsible for interpreting these high-level requests for memory and transparently mapping them to physical address zones with different power consumption. Our experimental results across various configurations running PARSEC workloads show an average of 13.1% memory power consumption savings at the cost of a modest 1.03% increase in execution time over a typical Linux virtual memory allocator.

Categories and Subject Descriptors

B.3 [**Design Styles**]: Virtual Memory; D.4.2 [**Storage Management**]: Allocation/deallocation strategies

General Terms

Design, Experimentation, Management

Keywords

power; variability; memory management; DRAM

1. INTRODUCTION

Over the past decade, inter-die and intra-die process variations have become more significant [11, 8, 12]. The ITRS predicts that over the next decade, both performance and power consumption variation will increase by up to 66%, and 100%, respectively [23]. Variations can stem from semiconductor manufacturing processes, ambient conditions, device wear out, and in case of multi-sourced systems, vendors. Despite considerable hardware variability, the software stack assumes homogeneity in both frequency and power dissipation for a given hardware specification. Device manufacturers have partially masked the presence of variability by guardbanding systems, leading to over-design with less than optimal power and performance. For example, the device community has resorted to binning processors by operating frequencies to reduce the impact of inter-die variation. However, even with guardbanding, binning, and dynamic voltage and frequency scaling, variability is inherently present in any set of identically specified chips. Furthermore, with the emergence of multi-core technology, intra-die variation has also become an issue [21]. To minimize the overheads of guardbanding, recent efforts have shown that exploiting the inherent variation in devices [19, 42, 14, 39] yields significant improvements in both the energy-delay product and overall system performance.

Memory subsystems also suffer from power and timing variations. Off-chip DRAM memory may consume as much power as the processor in a server-class system [25, 47, 22, 49], and this problem may worsen for future many-core platforms (e.g., Tilera's TILEPro64 [41], Intel's Single Chip Cloud Computer (SCC) [20]). A recent study observed up to approximately 20% power variation in an off-the-shelf set of nineteen 1 GB DDR3 DIMMs [17]. On-chip memory designers have tried to create process variation-aware memory subsystems [32, 27, 40, 4] to address this issue, and multiple efforts have been made to minimize off-chip memory accesses via caching [43, 24, 38, 18], OS-level [50, 15, 22], and DRAM-level power management [13, 30, 22]. However, these designs required changes to existing memory configurations. As a result, we should adapt existing DRAM power management schemes in software to account for these variations in power consumption. Moreover, this layer should be flexible enough to deal with a predicted increase in power variation for current [23] and emerging [51, 2] memory technologies (e.g., phase-change memory).

In this work, we present ViPZonE (OS-Level Memory *V*ariability-Driven *P*hysical Address *Z*oning for *E*nergy Savings), a system-level variability-aware solution that adapts to the power variability inherent in a set of DRAM memory modules. Although our approach focuses on harnessing variability in DDR3 memory at the DIMM modular level, our approach could be generalized to work at finer granularities of memory, if variability data and hardware support are available. Our experimental results across various configurations running PARSEC workloads show an average of 13.1%

CODES+ISSS'12, October 7-12, 2012, Tampere, Finland.

memory power consumption savings at the cost of a modest 1.03% increase in execution time over a typical Linux virtual memory allocator, running on a simulated high-end PC platform. The key contributions of this work are as follows:

- An application annotation scheme complemented by a modified GLIBC library for power-aware memory allocations
- A power variation-aware physical address zoning and page allocation scheme implemented inside the kernel
- A study of the challenges traditional systems will face as variation in power consumption reaches 100% and beyond

To the best of our knowledge, ViPZonE is the first OS-level, pure-software, and portable solution to exploit DRAM power variation through memory zone partitioning.

This paper is organized as follows. We begin with a summary of related work and how our approach is novel in Sec. 2, followed by a brief background section discussing memory system terminology and the Linux kernel physical page allocator zoning scheme in Sec. 3. In Sec. 4, we describe our target platform and assumptions, and then move to a discussion of the ViPZonE system architecture and implementation of both the front-end and back-end. Sec. 5 discusses the results of our simulations, and we summarize this work and discuss future research in Sec. 6.

2. RELATED WORK

Most efforts dealing with variation have focused on exploiting frequency variation in processors [42, 21, 14, 39, 35] and process variations (due to voltage scaling) in on-chip memory [32, 27, 40, 4]. Hanson et al. [19] measured the power consumption across identical Intel M processors and found between 3%-10% variation and up to 2x active power variation across various DRAMs. Wanner et al. [44] found over 5x sleep power variation across various Cortex M3 processors and proposed a variability-aware duty cycle scheduling algorithm [45]. Sartori et al. [39] looked at frequency variation across processing cores. Pant et al. [35] proposed hardware signatures to adapt the software stack to deal with performance variation in the underlying hardware in the context of media applications. Pan et al. [34] has proposed a selective wordline voltage boosting for caches to manage yield under process variations. Mutyam et al. [32, 33] and Sasan et al. [40] proposed process variation-aware cache architectures (traditional and NUCA). Bennaser et al. [7] proposed a variable-cycle-latency cache architecture to mitigate the impact of process variations on access latency. Liang et al. [27] proposed replacing 6T SRAM with 3T1D DRAM for caches to address physical device variation. Zhao et al. [48] proposed cache migration schemes that utilizes fast banks while limiting the cost due to migration to address access latency variations in a 3D DRAM stacked non-uniform cache. Meng et al. [31] proposed way prioritization to minimize cache leakage to address within-die leakage variation. Li [26] proposed repairing only important bits to address process variations.

Traditional main memory management has focused primarily on minimizing accesses to main memory through smart caching schemes (hardware) or compiler/OS optimizations (software), yet none of these methods have taken memory variability into account. Sartor et al. [38] and Gu et al. [18] proposed exploiting program hints for optimal cache management to minimize off-chip memory accesses. Wang et al. [43] proposed a DSP partitioning scheme and instruction scheduler to minimize energy in multi-bank memories. Kandemir et al. [24] explored the impact of data transformations on memory bank locality. Hur et al. [22] and Felter et al. [15] exploited throttling at the memory controller level to reduce DRAM power consumption. Delaluz et al. [13] predicted the idle duration of various memory devices (at the controller level) to control the use of low power mode. Zheng et al. [49] proposed the concept of mini-banks to significantly reduce memory power consumption with minimum performance overheads (within 10%). Memory access scheduling has also been explored to increase performance and minimize power consumption [30]. Zhou et al. [50] designed a hardware monitor to track cache misses to improve system performance. Ahn et al. [1] proposed an energy efficient memory module that divides DIMMs into separate virtual entities, improving energy efficiency with minimal performance overheads. Finally, Bathen et al. [5] proposed the introduction of a hardware engine to virtualize on-chip and off-chip memory space to exploit the variation in the memory subsystem.

Our approach is different from the related works, as it specifically optimizes for inter-device variability in memory power, although it may be complemented by other memory management schemes. Compiler-level and directed-cache techniques [43, 24, 38, 18] could exploit our custom APIs (e.g., GLIBC) to define low/high DRAM power consumption zones and map their data to their preferred zones to minimize power consumption. Similarly, OS-level schemes [30, 50] could exploit our variation-aware allocator to map pages with highest cache miss ratio to low power space to minimize power consumption. Our approach can complement [5]; however, we do not need to modify existing architectures to support our physical zoning strategy (our scheme is portable and could be exploited by any system running a Linux kernel, if power data is available). Moreover, our scheme can differentiate between low read and write-power zones, if they happen to be different. Similarly, our scheme can complement [1] by prioritizing among virtual zones within the various DIMMs. Finally, with hardware monitoring support such as [50], our scheme could perform variation-aware page migration with negligible performance/energy overheads.

3. BACKGROUND

3.1 Memory System Architecture

When discussing memory systems and devices, terminology often becomes confusing and is misinterpreted by readers. To avoid this, we will briefly define relevant terms in the memory system. In this work, we use DDR3 DRAM memory technology.

In a typical server, desktop, or notebook system, the memory controller accesses DRAM-based main memory through one or more memory *channels*. Each channel may have one or two *DIMMs*, which is a user-serviceable memory module. Each DIMM may have one or two *ranks* which are typically on opposing sides of the module. Each rank is independently accessible by the memory controller, and is composed of several DRAM devices (Figure 1 shows non-ECC with 8 devices). Inside each DRAM are multiple *banks*, where each bank has an independent memory *array* composed of *rows* and *columns*. A memory location is a single combination

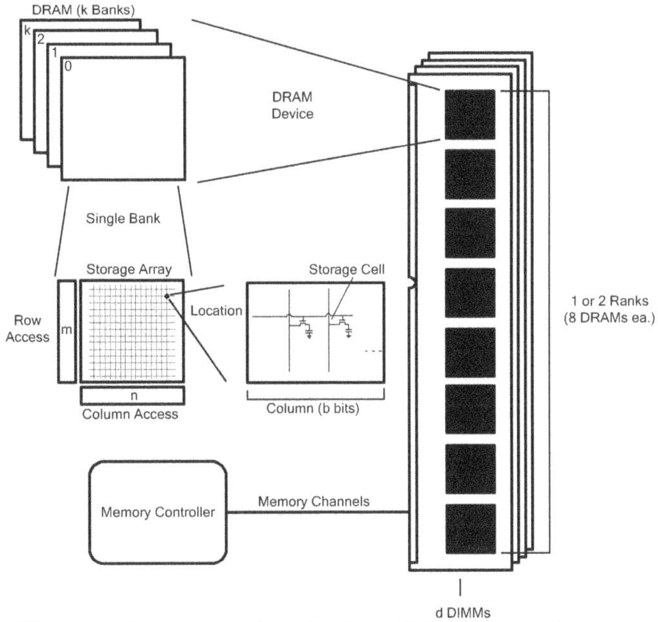

Figure 1: Components in a Typical DRAM Memory System

of rank, bank, row, and column in the main memory system, where an access is issued in parallel to all DRAMs in the selected rank. This hierarchy is depicted in Fig. 1. In this work, we are optimizing for variability measured at the DIMM level. However, our approach can be adapted for finer granularities, as previously mentioned.

3.1.1 Zoning in the Traditional Linux x86-64 Kernel

In order to understand our ViPZonE back-end implementation, we now discuss how the traditional Linux kernel partitions physical memory space. At the core of the Linux kernel memory management subsystem is the physical page allocator. When faced with an allocation request for one or more pages with certain constraints, the system tries to find the most suitable allocation in the least amount of time. The kernel may pass through multiple stages during an allocation attempt, with greater performance penalties as it tries harder to find suitable memory.

The page allocator relies on several important constructs, including, but not limited to: page structures, memory zones, page freelists, and constraint bitmasks [29]. The kernel utilizes several zones to group regions of contiguous physical memory (see Fig. 2a), required for legacy hardware support [29]. In direct memory access (DMA), devices talk directly with physical memory, bypassing the CPU. However, many legacy devices can only address the lowest 16 MB of memory, and must be able to receive page allocations in this region. The kernel, if configured to support DMA, needs to reserve this space accordingly. There are also newer devices that are capable of addressing up to 4 GB of memory, and the kernel must be able to accomodate these DMA32 devices as well, albeit with more headroom.

The kernel does this by representing these spaces with physically contiguous and adjacent DMA and DMA32 memory zones, each of which tracks pages in its space independently of other zones [29, 28]. This allows for separate bookkeeping for each zone as well, such as low-memory watermarks, buddy system page groups, performance metrics, etc. Thus, if both are supported, the DMA zone occupies the first 16 MB of memory, while the DMA32 zone spans 16 MB to 4096 MB. This means that for 64-bit systems with less than 4 GB of memory, all of memory will be in DMA or DMA32-capable zones.

The rest of the memory space not claimed by DMA or DMA32 is left to the "Normal" zone[1]. On x86-64, this will contain all memory above DMA and DMA32. Because the kernel cannot split allocations across multiple zones [29], each allocation must come from a single zone. Thus, each zone maintains its own page freelists, least-recently-used lists, and other metrics for its space.

The kernel tries to fulfill page allocation requests in the most suitable zone first, but it can fall back to other zones if required [29, 28]. For example, a user application will typically have its memory allocated in the normal zone. However, if memory there is low, it will try DMA32 next, and DMA only as a last resort (see Fig. 4a for a simplified decision flow). The kernel can also employ other techniques if required and permitted by the allocation constraints (if the request cannot allow I/O, filesystem use, or blocking, they may not apply) [29, 28]. However, the reverse is not true. If a device driver needs DMA space, it must come from the DMA zone or the allocation will fail. For this reason, the kernel does its best to reserve these restricted spaces for these situations [29].

4. VIPZONE: EXPLOITING OFF-CHIP MEMORY POWER VARIATION

ViPZonE is composed of several different components in the software stack which work together to achieve power savings in the presence of DIMM variability. We refer to these separate components by the "back-end" and the "front-end" and describe them in Sec. 4.2 and Sec. 4.3, respectively. ViPZonE uses source code annotations at the application level[2], which work together with a modified GLIBC library to generate special memory allocation requests which indicate the expected use patterns (write or read dominance, and high-/medium/low utilization) to the OS. Inside the back-end Linux kernel memory management system, ViPZonE can make intelligent physical allocation decisions with this information to reduce DRAM power consumption. By choosing this approach, we are able to keep overheads in the OS a minimum, as we place most of the burden of power-aware memory requests to the application programmer. With our approach, no special hardware support is required beyond available power data or sensors that are software-accessible to the kernel.

An alternative approach could avoid requiring a modified GLIBC library and application-level source annotations, while still utilizing the ViPZonE physical page allocator. However, such an approach would place the burden of smarter page allocations on the kernel. This would likely cause a significant performance and memory overhead, as the kernel would be required to monitor applications' memory access behaviors with hardware support from the mem-

[1]The "HighMem" zone present in x86 32-bit systems is not used in the x86-64 Linux implementation.

[2]Our scheme does not currently support kernel memory allocations (e.g., kmalloc()). The goal of this paper is to provide programmers with the means to opportunistically exploit off-chip memory power variation. We are considering additional support for both kernel-level power variation-aware allocation (requires major changes to the kernel), as well as per-process allocation of memory space to the different zones through compile-time hints.

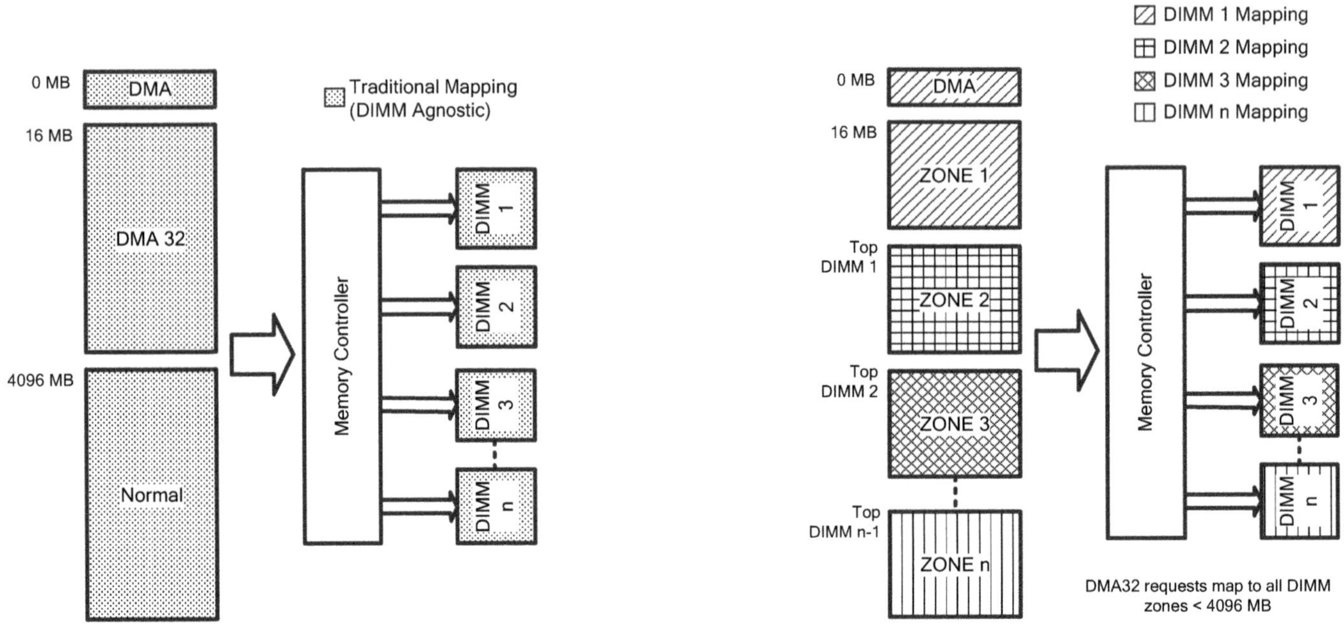

(a) Typical (b) ViPZonE

Figure 2: Typical vs. ViPZonE Physical Address Space Partitioning (Zoning) in Linux x86-64

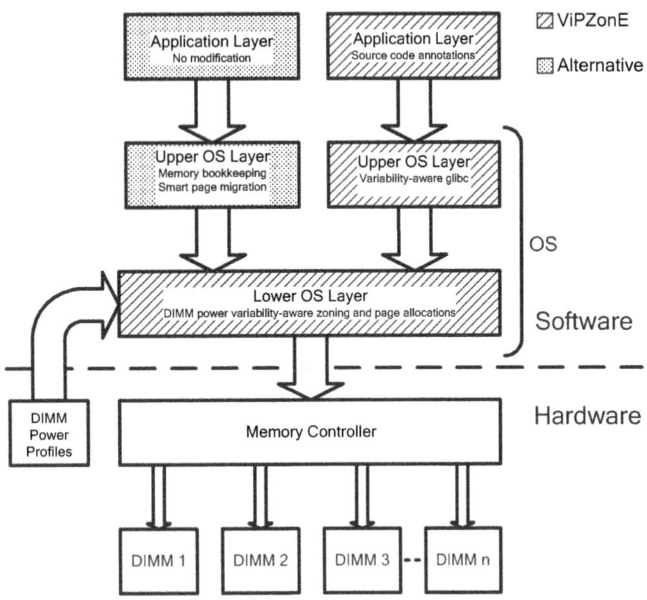

Figure 3: Layered Architecture of ViPZonE With Alternative OS-Level Scheme

ory controller. We leave the second approach as future work, and focus primarily on the use of zoning with application programmer support. The two approaches can be compared in Fig. 3.

4.1 Target Platform and Assumptions

We target generic x86-64 PC and server platforms, that run on a Linux kernel and have access to two or more DIMMs (the more DIMMs, the greater the potential benefit of this work). If device-level power variation is available, then this approach could be adapted to finer granularities, depending on the memory architecture. We make the following assumptions:

- ViPZonE's page allocator has prior knowledge of the approximate write and read power of each DIMM (for an identical workload). We could detect off-chip memory power variation, obtained by one of the following methods: (1) via embedded power data in each DIMM, measured and set at fabrication time, or (2) through embedded or auxiliary power sensors sampled during the startup procedure.
- As DIMM-to-DIMM power variability is mostly fixed post-manufacturing [17], there is little need for real-time monitoring of memory power use for each module. However, if power variation changes (e.g., due to aging and wear-out), we assume these changes can be detected through power sensors in each module (left as future work).
- We can perform direct mapping of the address space (e.g., select which DIMM each read/write request goes through). This is achieved by disabling rank and channel interleaving (though our method should work in a multi-channel system with some minor adaptations). It should be possible to overcome any overheads due to this by deploying multiple memory controllers as in [41, 37, 46].
- There is programmer application-level support through the use of our power-variability enhanced GLIBC library.

4.2 Back-End: ViPZonE Implementation in the Linux Kernel

We will begin the discussion of the back-end implementation of ViPZonE by describing how the generic Linux kernel handles the physical part of page allocation requests, and how it divides the physical address space into multiple contiguous zones for this purpose. We then discuss the implementation of the ViPZonE address partitioning scheme and

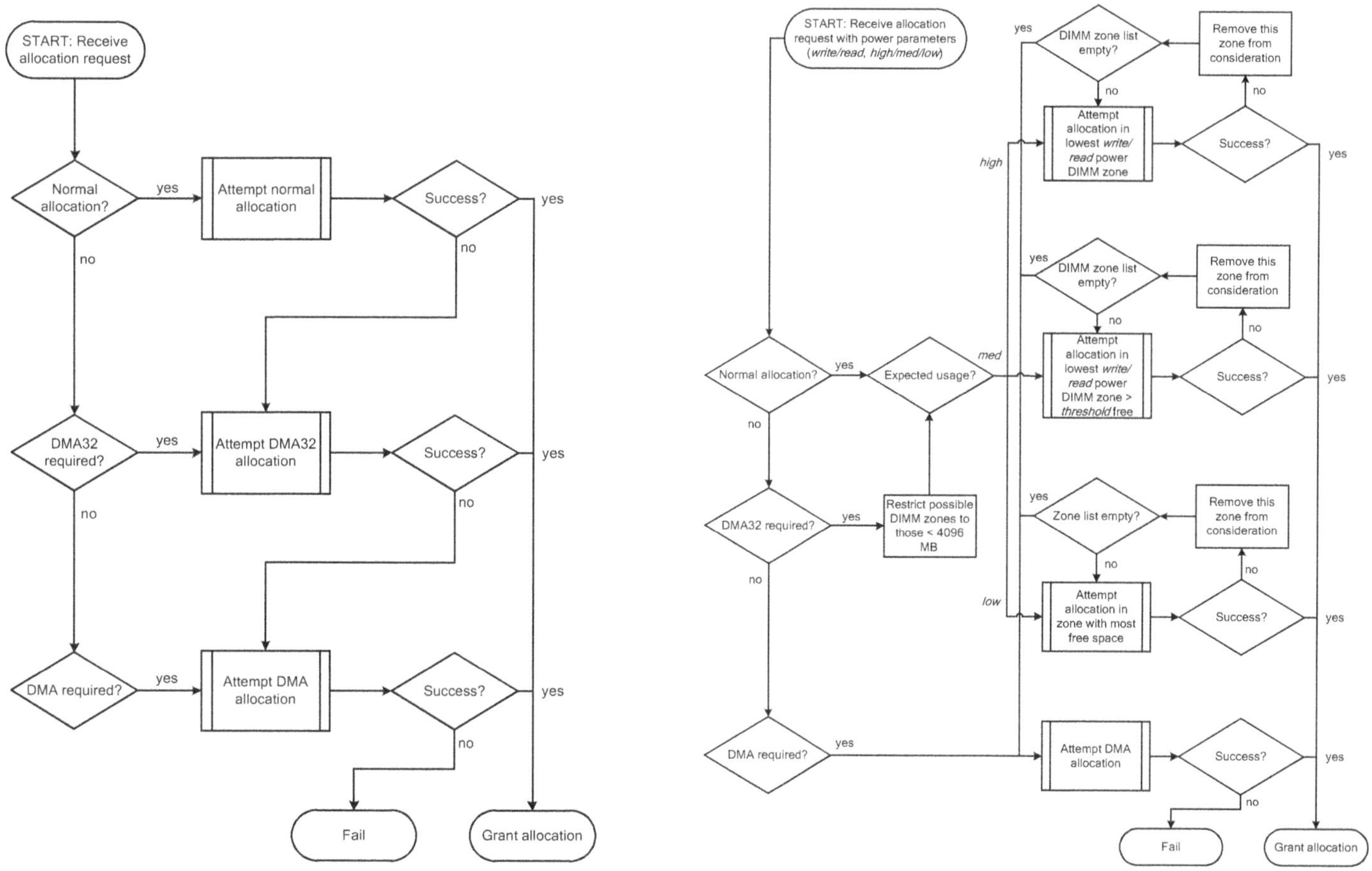

(a) Typical (b) ViPZonE

Figure 4: Typical vs. ViPZonE Memory Allocation Flow in Linux x86-64 (Simplified)

allocation approach. Our implementation is based on the Linux 3.2.14 kernel [28].

4.2.1 Enhancing Physical Memory Zoning to Exploit Variability in ViPZonE Linux x86-64

In order to support memory variability-awareness, the kernel must be able to distinguish between physical regions of different power consumption. If the kernel has knowledge of these power profiles, it can construct separate physical address zones corresponding to each region of different power characteristics. The kernel can then serve allocation requests using the suggestions defined by the front-end of ViPZonE (see Section 4.3).

In the ViPZonE kernel on an x86-64 platform, we have explicitly removed the Normal and DMA32 zones, while still allowing for DMA32 allocation support. Regular DMA-able space is retained. Instead, zones are added for each physical DIMM in the system (Zone 1, Zone 2, etc.), with page ranges corresponding to the actual physical space on each DIMM. Allocations requesting DMA32-capable memory are translated to using certain DIMMs that use the equivalent memory space. Fig. 2b depicts our revised memory zoning scheme for the ViPZonE back-end. For example, in an Linux x86-64 system supporting DMA and DMA32, with 8 GB of memory located on four DIMMs (4x2 GB), the ViPZonE back-end would divide the memory space into zones as follows:

1. *DMA zone*: 0-16 MB, located on DIMM 1 physically.
2. *Zone 1*: 16-2048 MB, located on DIMM 1 physically.
3. *Zone 2*: 2048-4096 MB, located on DIMM 2 physically.
4. *Zone 3*: 4096-6144 MB, located on DIMM 3 physically.
5. *Zone 4*: 6144-8192 MB, located on DIMM 4 physically.

4.2.2 Modifying the Physical Page Allocation Algorithm in ViPZonE Linux x86-64

With this scheme, the ViPZonE back-end now has the ability to control allocations to lower power DIMMs, compared to the traditional kernel, which makes no distinction. With zones set up for each DIMM, the kernel has the essential tools it needs to make power variability-aware page allocations. The modified allocation decision flow is depicted in Fig. 4b. For example, in a system with four DIMMs, each with 2 GB of space, the ViPZonE kernel would make allocation decisions as follows:

1. *Request for DMA-capable space*: Grant in DMA zone.
2. *Request for DMA32-capable space (DMA subset implicit)*: Grant in Zone 2 or Zone 1, with the order determined by DIMM power consumption and usage hints (*write/read* dominance, and *high/med/low* utilization) passed from the front-end (see Sec. 4.3), or DMA zone (as a last resort).

3. *Request for Normal space*: Grant in Zone 4, Zone 3, Zone 2, or Zone 1, with the order determined by DIMM power consumption and usage hints (*write/read* dominance, and *high/med/low* utilization) passed from the front-end (see Sec. 4.3). Again, the DMA zone is only used as a last resort.

4.3 Front-End: High-Level APIs

The other major component of ViPZonE is implemented as the front-end, in the form of upper layer OS functionality in conjunction with annotations to application code. The front-end allows the programmer to make suggestions regarding intended use for memory allocations, so that the kernel can prioritize low power zones for frequently written or read pages.

4.3.1 Modified C-Library

We took the GNU C library (GLIBC [16]) and implemented our power variation enhanced allocation/de-allocation methods as part of the standard library (available at [3]). We will briefly describe the methods and their use. For more details please refer to our technical report [6].

Table 1: Enhanced GLIBC Methods

Function	Parameter	Type	Return Type
*void * vip_malloc*	__size	size_t	Request size
	__vflag	size_t	Bitmap flag used by ViPZonE back-end page allocator
void vip_free	__ptr	void *	Pointer to block to be freed
*void * vip_mmap*	__addr	void *	Address to be mapped (best effort mapping)
	__length	size_t	Size to be allocated
	__prot	int	PROT_READ l PROT_WRITE
	__flags	int	MAP_PRIVATE | __vflag
	__fd	int	MAP_ANONYMOUS
	__offset	off_t	
int munmap	__addr	void *	Address to be freed
	__length	size_t	Size to be allocated

There are two key functions shown in Table 1, which are exposed to the programmer and allow him/her to tell the memory manager to allocate the object in low power memory space. We implement *vip_malloc* and *vip_free* as separate calls to allow the use of custom *mmap* and *munmap* system calls (*vip_mmap* and *munmap*) that serve as hooks into the kernel. We used the kernel's *mmap/unmap* functions defined in the kernel's memory manager (mm) as templates. Furthermore, the kernel consists of *ViPZonE* helper functions that allow us to pass down the flags from the upper layers in the software stack down to the lower levels, from custom *do_vip_mmap_pgoff*, *vip_mmap_region* down to the page allocator (*__alloc_pages_nodemask*). For this purpose, we reserved the four most significant bits in the __flags field to contain the flags passed down from the upper levels of the software stack (__vflags).

Because [17] showed that there is a significant difference between read and write power consumption for the various DIMMs tested, our *vip_malloc* exploits the notion of memory pooling to construct a two-region low power memory space (high-read and high-write utilization) for a given process. These pools are constructed on the first call to *vip_malloc* via the *vip_mmap* function (which then makes the call to the kernel's virtual memory allocator – going all the way to the ViPZonE back-end physical page allocator). These pools are used to serve small requests to minimize the number of system calls (*vip_mmap*). When the pool space is exhausted or the pool space is insufficient to serve a memory allocation request, *vip_malloc* makes a call to *vip_mmap* to serve the request. These pools are managed separate from the memory pools managed by traditional *malloc*, which typically use *sbrk* to grow the heap. The *vip_free* function is used to free low power space. If the space is small enough, it is added back to the read/write pool it belongs to. If the memory space is large enough, it is freed via the *munmap* function.

Because we know that low power memory space is precious, we try to give as much space back to the OS as possible (via *munmap*) when the application no longer needs it. As a result, we prefer the use of *mmap* over traditional *sbrk*, which assumes the heap grows contiguously, and often memory is not really freed (e.g., given back to the OS) until a large amount of contiguous virtual address space is found.

The size of the low power pools is tunable as it depends upon the domain in which the GLIBC library is deployed. In embedded systems, the memory footprint tends to be smaller than the desktop domain, and much smaller than the server domain, thus the pools may range from a few KBs (at least 4 KB) of space to MBs (multiples of the page size, e.g., 4 KB) of space. One key issue is memory fragmentation. To minimize fragmentation due to many *mmap* calls, we can exploit existing patches that re-arrange the virtual address space where the *mmap* area grows from the stack downward, while the heap grows upward as normal [3].

```
1  int lame_encode_buffer_interleaved(
2     lame_global_flags *gfp,
3     short int buffer[], int nsamples,
4     char *mp3buf, int mp3buf_size)
5  {
6    static int frame_buffered=0;
7    int mp3size=0,ret,i,ch,mf_needed;
8    ...
9
10   if (gfp->resample_ratio!=1)  {
11     short int *buffer_l;
12     short int *buffer_r;
13
14     /* Create two read/modify buffers with
15            medium utilization in low power
16            memory space
17     */
18     buffer_l=vip_malloc(
19        sizeof(short int)*nsamples,
20        READ | MED_UTIL);
21     buffer_r=vip_malloc(
22        sizeof(short int)*nsamples,
23        READ | MED_UTIL);
24     if (buffer_l==NULL||buffer_r==NULL) {
25       return -1;
26     }
27     ...
28
29    ret = lame_encode_buffer(gfp,buffer_l,
30       buffer_r,nsamples,mp3buf,mp3buf_size);
31    ...
32    /* Free up the low power memory space */
33    vip_free(buffer_l);
34    vip_free(buffer_r);
35
36    return ret;
37   }
38 }
```

Function 1: Sample Annotated Source Code from LAME Library

4.3.2 User Annotations/Programming Model

Table 2 shows the sample set of flags supported by our GLIBC functions, passed down to the ViPZonE back-end kernel to allocate pages from the preferred zone. Function 1 shows sample code from the LAME Codec library and how to use them via our *vip_malloc* function (underlined red functions in Lines 18-23). The (*READ, WRITE*) flags tell the

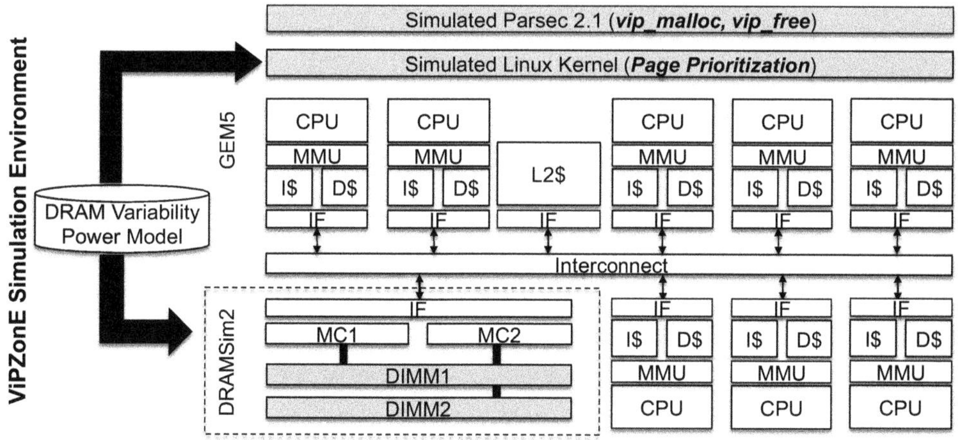

Figure 5: ViPZonE Simulation Framework

Table 2: ViPZonE Supported Flags

Parameter	Flag	Description
Access Type	WRITE	The memory space will have high write to read ratio
	READ	The memory space will have high read to write ratio
Utilization	LOW_UTIL	Low utilization
	MED_UTIL	Medium utilization
	HIGH_UTIL	High utilization

allocator that the expected workload is heavily read or write intensive. If neither write nor read is dominant, the choice of flag is left to the developer[3].

These are used to decide whether to allocate space from the read or write pools (if there is enough space) or from DIMMs with low read power or low write power. Similarly, the utilization flags (*LOW_UTIL, MED_UTIL, HIGH_UTIL*) are used to prioritize among pages from low power memory space. We decided to support these flags (only two bits) rather than using a different metric (e.g., measured utilization), since keeping track of page utilization would require higher storage and logic overheads. To free up the low power memory space, programmers would need to invoke our *vip_free* function (Function 1 Lines 33-34). As shown by this example, the necessary programming changes to exploit our variability-aware memory allocation scheme are minimal.

5. EXPERIMENTAL EVALUATION

5.1 Experimental Setup and Goals

Our goal is to show that ViPZonE is capable of reducing power consumption with minimal (almost negligible) performance overheads. In this section we will investigate the overheads of 1) ViPZonE's software stack (Sec. 5.2) and 2) direct address mapping versus interleaved address mapping at the memory controller level (Sec. 5.3). Next, we will investigate the benefits of our approach in terms of energy savings in two scenarios: a small platform (Table 3) and a large platform (Table 3). Sec. 5.4 will investigate ViPZonE's power savings due to zone prioritization (the ideal case), then ViPZonE's power savings due to zone prioritization and selective page allocation (with the help of program annotations). Sec. 5.4 will conclude with a what-if study that investigates the effect of variation on power consumption as it reaches 100% as predicted by ITRS.

The experimental setup consists of two parts: 1) A real Linux-based ViPZonE implementation to test for execution time overheads and 2) a simulation environment to test the overheads of our direct address mapping (DIMM selection), and the benefits of our allocation mechanisms in the presence of power variation. Figure 5 shows our simulation environment, which consists of interfacing and modifying GEM5 [10] with DRAMSim2 [36] to simulate our page allocation. We simulated two DDR3 1 GB DIMMs (a total of 2 GB physical address space), each DIMM with different power consumption (due to variation). Our DRAM memory variation models are obtained from [17] and used to do realistic simulations and a what-if analysis. Table 3 shows the different platform configurations we used and their workloads, the *Sim2Core* platform has lower resources than the *Sim8Core* platform, as a result, we expect higher main memory utilization.

5.2 ViPZonE Performance Overheads

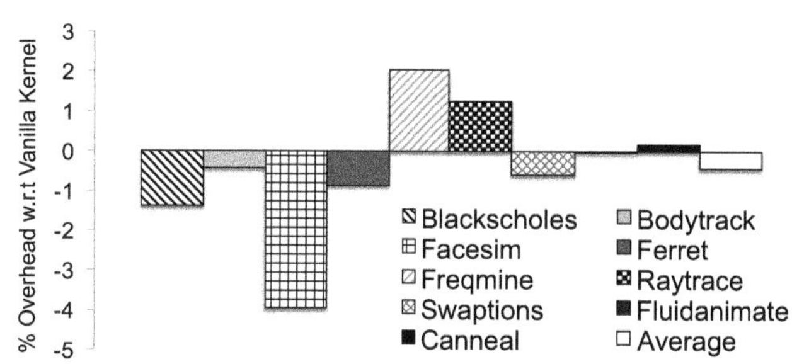

Figure 6: ViPZonE Execution Time Overheads With Respect to Typical Linux Kernel

We have implemented ViPZonE's front-end by modifying GLIBC 2.15 [16] and the Linux 3.2.14 kernel [28]. We then ran PARSEC 2.1 benchmarks [9] with simlarge workloads to estimate the performance overheads of the software stack on a real-system (*Native* configuration in Table 3, running Ubuntu 10.04 on a VirtualBox VM with 2 virtual CPUs).

As we can see from Figure 6, performance overheads due

[3]Some algorithms may allocate a common space for both write and read intensive operation, such as a buffer used in streaming applications. In these cases, the usage of vip_malloc() is left to the application programmer (e.g. he/she might split the buffer in two if possible, or arbitrarily pick write or read priority for a single space).

Table 3: ViPZonE Platform Configurations

Configuration	Cores	Threads	L1 Caches (I/D)	L2 Cache	Workload	Frequency
Sim2Core	2	4	24kB/32KB	1MB	simsmall	1.8GHz
Sim8Core	8	8	32kB/32KB	4MB	simsmall	2.0GHz
Native (i5-540M)	2 Virtual	4	-	-	simlarge	2.53GHz

to ViPZonE's zone prioritization are minimal. On average, we observe a slight performance improvement (less than 0.5%), which is in the noise. The main point is that ViPZonE's performance overheads are minimal and should not have a major effect on system performance, as the virtual page allocator is best effort. In order to effectively exploit the power variation in the memory subsystem we must support physical address mapping, i.e., we must be able to prioritize physical accesses to a particular DIMM based on how frequently a virtual page is accessed (see Sec. 5.3).

5.3 Direct Address Mapping Vs. Interleaved Address Mapping

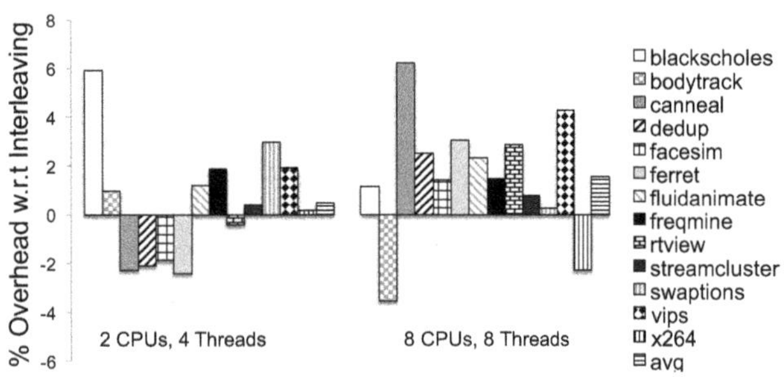

Figure 7: Execution Time Overheads of Non-Interleaved DIMM Accesses

In order to truly test the overheads of DIMM page access prioritization, we need to change the way the virtual to physical address mapping works. Typical mapping assumes rank interleaving to improve performance. As a result, in a typical system, with n DIMMs, it is possible that all DIMMs/ranks are accessed in a pipeline fashion. While one rank is opening a row, another rank may be accessed, thus hiding row access latencies. In order to address the variation of the system, we must disable this interleaving and rely on direct address mapping, i.e., each page is mapped to a single DIMM rank physically. To investigate these overheads, we explored two mappings in GEM5's memory controller and ran PARSEC benchmarks on top of two different simulation configurations (*Sim2Core* and *Sim8Core* in Table 3).

Fig. 7 shows the performance overheads due to direct versus interleaved mapping. We observe an average 1.6% performance overhead for the *Sim8Core* configuration and less than 0.5% for the *Sim2Core* configuration, which gives us a total of 1.03% execution time overhead across all benchmarks with respect to the interleaved mapping. Though a maximum of 6.2% has been observed for the single channel configuration, this overhead might increase for multi-channel configurations. To address this issue, we could exploit multiple memory controllers as shown in [41, 37, 46].

5.4 Power Savings through DIMM Prioritization

ViPZonE's goal is to save power consumption by prioritizing accesses to the low power DIMMs via zoning as discussed in Sec. 4.2.1. In order to show the true benefits of DIMM access prioritization (zoning), we simulated an ideal case

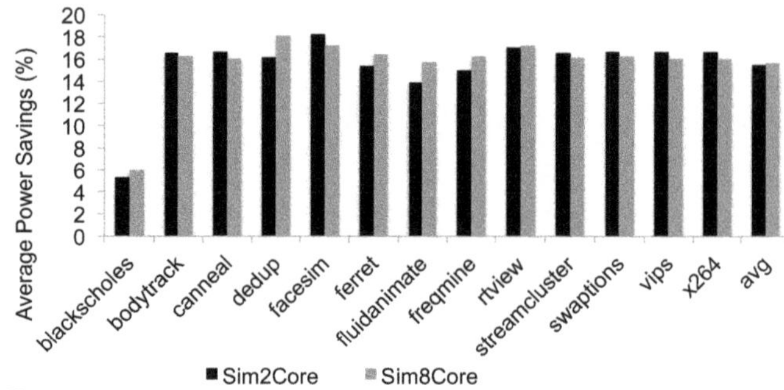

Figure 8: Average Power Savings (%) - Mapping All Data to the Ideal Zone vs. Typical Linux Kernel

Table 4: ViPZonE Maximum Physical Space

Benchmark	Required (MB)	Allocated (MB)
blackscholes	34	16
bodytrack	42	32
canneal	78	64
dedup	107	64
facesim	341	256
ferret	57	32
fluidanimate	52	32
freqmine	83	64
rtview	127	64
streamcluster	32	16
swaptions	32	16
vips	32	16
x264	32	16

where all applications had unlimited space to the low-power zone. In this configuration we mapped all pages used by the PARSEC benchmarks to the low-power DIMM modeled in DRAMSim2, while the second DIMM remained idle. In this experiment, we have one memory controller per DIMM. The base case for comparison in the next set of experiments (Sec. 5.4-5.6) is the typical scheme where a single memory controller interleaves physical pages across the two DIMMs modeled in the system and the virtual memory allocator is unaware of the power variation in the memory subsystem. We will refer to this scheme as *Typical* scheme.

Figure 8 shows the ideal savings with respect to the typical case (no DIMM prioritization and interleaving enabled). As we can observe, we see an average of 15.4% average power consumption savings for the *Sim2Core* configuration and 15.6% savings for the *Sim8Core* configuration with respect to the *Typical* scheme. The average power consumption reflects the total power consumed by the system over the entire execution time of the given workload, so it takes into account any overheads due to direct mapping with respect to interleaved mapping.

5.5 Power Savings through Annotations and Zone Prioritization

Section 5.4 discussed the power consumption savings in an ideal scenario. However, we cannot dedicate the entire physical memory space to a single application since the low power memory space is precious. Moreover, as memory utilization grows past the DIMM capacity, we will be unable to map virtual pages to the low power DIMM(s). As a result, we must prioritize access to the low power memory space in order to minimize the power consumption of the system.

Table 4 shows the total physical space given to each of the PARSEC benchmarks we tested in our system. Some of the benchmarks have smaller footprints as the workloads we simulated were small (*streamcluster-x264*). That is, even if we ran 4 to 8 threads (*Sim2Core* and *Sim8Core*), the maximum physical low power address space will be limited to the amount shown in Table 4 for each application. We simulate the annotation behavior by letting our page allocator know the expected usage of individual virtual pages, the page allocator then decided where to map these virtual pages, be it low power memory space (e.g., low power zone/DIMM) or high power memory space. These annotations are hints, as the allocator will enforce them with best-effort given that the memory power variations will also vary among systems.

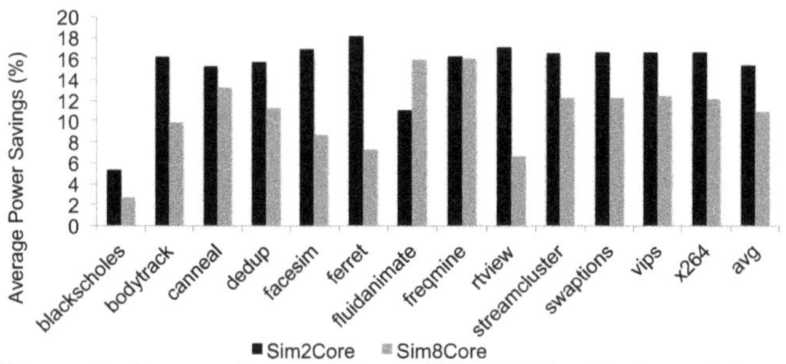

Figure 9: Average Power Savings (%) - ViPZonE's Page Prioritization vs. Typical Linux Kernel

Like Sec. 5.4, the *Sim8Core* configuration had lower DIMM utilization than the *Sim2Core* configuration due to the larger amount of on-chip memory resources. Figure 9 shows the savings due to page prioritization with respect to the traditional case (no prioritization, rank interleaving enabled). We observe an average of 15.3% power consumption savings for the *Sim2Core* configuration and 10.8% savings for the *Sim8Core* configuration (an average 13.1% across both configurations) with respect to the *Typical* scheme. The savings will grow as the memory utilization grows. As memory utilization shrinks, idle power takes over, and ViPZone will perform as good as typical memory allocators (e.g., traditional Linux memory management).

5.6 What-if Scenario: As Power Variation Reaches 100%

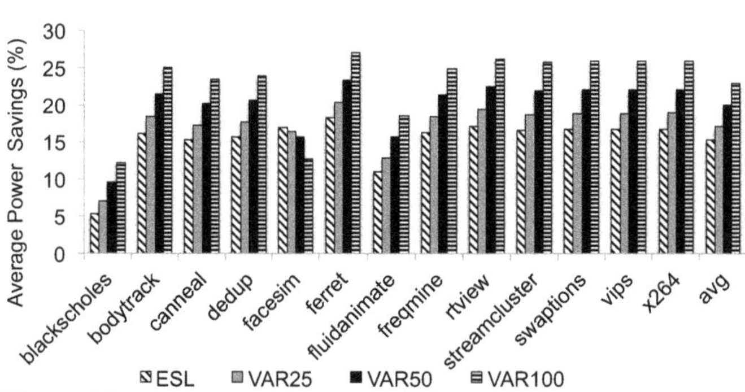

Figure 10: Average Power Savings (%) As Variation Increases - ViPZonE's Page Prioritization vs. Typical Linux Kernel

The experimental results thus far have been based on realistic variation models. In this section, we will investigate

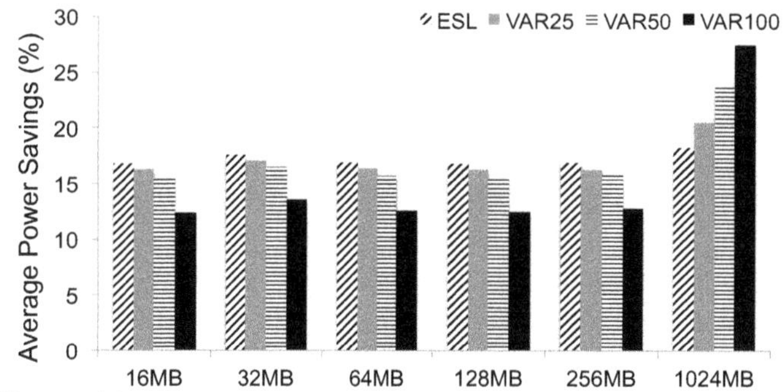

Figure 11: Average Power Savings (%) As Dedicated Memory Space Increases - ViPZonE's Page Prioritization vs. Typical Linux Kernel

the effects of increased variation in average power consumption. Notice that like Sections 5.4 and 5.5, the benefits of our scheme are directly proportional to the main memory utilization. For this experiment, we limited the available physical low power space to the same amounts for each benchmark as in Sec. 5.5.

Figure 10 shows the savings due to page prioritization with respect to the traditional case (no prioritization, rank interleaving enabled) as variation reaches 100% for the *Sim2Core* configuration. Here the *ESL* label refers to the variation reported in [17], while *VAR25-VAR100* refer to variation increases of 25%, 50%, and 100% respectively. As expected, the applications with the highest memory utilization (e.g., the enterprise based benchmark *dedup*) see larger average power savings. Over all benchmarks we see up to 26% average power savings as variation increases by 100%, with an average of 22.8%.

The reason *facesim* does not see the upward improvement in average power savings the other applications see (as shown in Figure 10) is that its memory requirement is higher. Figure 11 shows the average power savings of *facesim* with respect to the *Typical* scheme as the dedicated physical space increases for the different projections (*ESL-VAR100* running the *Sim2Core* configuration. Though the average power consumption savings increase with more dedicated memory, the true benefits of our scheme are more noticeable as we dedicate more space to the *facesim*. In the cases of 16 MB to 256 MB, we notice that though most accessed pages are mapped to low-power DIMM, the second DIMM consumes much more power due to the variation. Since idle power is dominant, it will grow equally for both the *Typical* scheme and our scheme, which leads to the behavior seen in Figures 10 and 11.

6. CONCLUSION AND FUTURE WORK

In this paper we presented ViPZonE (OS-Level Memory *V*ariability-Driven *P*hysical Address *Z*oning for *E*nergy Savings), a system-level variability-aware solution that adapts to the power variability inherent in a set of DRAM memory modules. ViPZonE is portable enough to be deployed in any environment running Linux (from laptops to high-end servers). Our experimental results across various configurations running PARSEC workloads show an average of 13.1% memory power consumption savings at the cost of a modest 1.03% increase in execution time over a typical Linux virtual memory allocator. Our ongoing and future work includes: 1) The complete deployment of our software prototype on an Atom-board and an Intel i7 board to truly evaluate the benefits of our scheme (with support for more than 4 DIMMs). 2) The adoption of server- and scientific-based workloads. 4) Bookkeeping and power variability-aware dynamic page migration between zones. 5) Kernel-space and compiler-driven per-process zone prioritization. 6) Possibly exploring and exploiting memory power variation in mobile platforms (e.g., Android OS). 7) If the data is available, intra-DIMM power variation.

Acknowledgment

This work was partially supported by NSF Variability Expedition Grant Numbers CCF-1029783 and CCF-1029030.

7. REFERENCES

[1] J. Ahn et al. Multicore DIMM: an energy efficient memory module with independently controlled DRAMs. *IEEE Computer Architecture Letters*, 2008.

[2] C. Augustine et al. Spin-transfer torque mrams for low power memories: Perspective and prospective. *Sensors Journal, IEEE*, 2012.

[3] Bathen and Gottscho. ViPZonE: Memory Power Variation-aware Software Stack. *http://vipzone.sourceforge.net*, 2012.

[4] L. Bathen et al. E-RoC: Embedded RAIDs-on-Chip for low power distributed dynamically managed reliable memories. In *DATE*, 2011.

[5] L. Bathen et al. VaMV: Variability-aware Memory Virtualization. In *DATE*, 2012.

[6] L. Bathen et al. A variability-aware software stack for linux-based system. *UCI Center for Embedded Computer Systems TR*, 2012.

[7] M. Bennaser et al. Designing memory subsystems resilient to process variations. In *ISVLSI*, 2007.

[8] S. Bhardwaj et al. Modeling of intra-die process variations for accurate analysis and optimization of nano-scale circuits. In *DAC*, 2006.

[9] C. Bienia et al. The parsec benchmark suite: characterization and architectural implications. In *PACT*, 2008.

[10] N. Binkert et al. The gem5 simulator. *SIGARCH Comput. Archit. News*, 2011.

[11] S. Borkar et al. Parameter variations and impact on circuits and microarchitecture. In *DAC*, 2003.

[12] K. Bowman et al. Impact of die-to-die and within-die parameter variations on the throughput distribution of multi-core processors. In *ISLPED*, 2007.

[13] V. Delaluz et al. Scheduler-based dram energy management. In *DAC*, 2002.

[14] J. Dong et al. Variation-aware scheduling for chip multiprocessors with thread level redundancy. In *PRDC*, 2009.

[15] W. Felter et al. A performance-conserving approach for reducing peak power consumption in server systems. In *ICS*, 2005.

[16] GNU. Glibc, the gnu c library. *http://www.gnu.org/software/libc/*, 2012.

[17] M. Gottscho et al. Power variability in contemporary DRAMs. *IEEE Embedded Systems Letters*, 2012.

[18] X. Gu et al. P-opt: Program-directed optimal cache management. In J. N. Amaral, editor, *LCPC*. 2008.

[19] H. Hanson et al. Benchmarking for power and performance. *2007 SPEC Workshop*, 2007.

[20] J. Howard et al. A 48-core ia-32 message-passing processor with dvfs in 45nm cmos. In *ISSCC*, 2010.

[21] E. Humenay et al. Impact of process variations on multicore performance symmetry. In *DATE*, 2007.

[22] I. Hur et al. A comprehensive approach to dram power management. In *HPCA*, 2008.

[23] ITRS. *http://www.itrs.net/*.

[24] M. Kandemir. Impact of data transformations on memory bank locality. In *DATE*, pages 10506–, 2004.

[25] C. Lefurgy et al. Energy management for commercial servers. *Computer*, 2003.

[26] X. Li. Rethinking memory redundancy: optimal bit cell repair for maximum-information storage. In *DAC '11*, 2011.

[27] X. Liang et al. Process variation tolerant 3t1d-based cache architectures. In *MICRO '07*, 2007.

[28] Linux. Kernel 3.2.14. *http://www.kernel.org/*, 2012.

[29] R. Love. *Linux Kernel Development*. Pearson Education, Inc., 3 edition, 2010.

[30] C.-G. Lyuh et al. Memory access scheduling and binding considering energy minimization in multi-bank memory systems. In *DAC*, DAC '04, 2004.

[31] K. Meng et al. Process variation aware cache leakage management. In *ISLPED '06*, 2006.

[32] M. Mutyam et al. Working with process variation aware caches. In *DATE '07*, 2007.

[33] M. Mutyam et al. Process-variation-aware adaptive cache architecture and management. *IEEE Trans. Comput.*, 2009.

[34] Y. Pan et al. Selective wordline voltage boosting for caches to manage yield under process variations. In *DAC*, 2009.

[35] A. Pant et al. Software adaptation in quality sensitive applications to deal with hardware variability. In *GLSVLSI '10*, 2010.

[36] P. Rosenfeld et al. Dramsim2: A cycle accurate memory system simulator. *Computer Architecture Letters*, 2011.

[37] J. Sancho et al. Analyzing the trade-off between multiple memory controllers and memory channels on multi-core processor performance. In *IPDPSW*, 2010.

[38] J. Sartor et al. Cooperative caching with keep-me and evict-me. In *INTERACT*, 2005.

[39] J. Sartori et al. Variation-aware speed binning of multi-core processors. In *ISQED*, 2010.

[40] A. Sasan et al. Process variation aware sram/cache for aggressive voltage-frequency scaling. In *DATE*, 2009.

[41] Tilera. Tilepro 64. *http://www.tilera.com/*, 2010.

[42] F. Wang et al. Variation-aware task allocation and scheduling for mpsoc. In *ICCAD*, 2007.

[43] Z. Wang et al. Power aware variable partitioning and instruction scheduling for multiple memory banks. In *DATE*, 2004.

[44] L. Wanner et al. A case for opportunistic embedded sensing in presence of hardware power variability. In *HotPower'10*, 2010.

[45] L. Wanner et al. Variability-aware duty cycle scheduling in long running embedded sensing systems. In *DATE '11*, 2011.

[46] T. Xu et al. Optimal memory controller placement for chip multiprocessor. In *CODES+ISSS*, 2011.

[47] J. Yue et al. Evaluating memory energy efficiency in parallel i/o workloads. In *CLUSTER*, 2007.

[48] B. Zhao et al. Variation-tolerant non-uniform 3d cache management in die stacked multicore processor. In *MICRO*, 2009.

[49] H. Zheng et al. Mini-rank: Adaptive dram architecture for improving memory power efficiency. In *MICRO*, 2008.

[50] P. Zhou et al. Dynamic tracking of page miss ratio curve for memory management. In *ASPLOS*, 2004.

[51] P. Zhou et al. A durable and energy efficient main memory using phase change memory technology. In *ISCA '09*, 2009.

Dynamic Transient Fault Detection and Recovery for Embedded Processor Datapaths

Garo Bournoutian
University of California, San Diego
9500 Gilman Dr. #0404
La Jolla, CA 92093-0404
garo@cs.ucsd.edu

Alex Orailoglu
University of California, San Diego
9500 Gilman Dr. #0404
La Jolla, CA 92093-0404
alex@cs.ucsd.edu

ABSTRACT

As microprocessors continue to evolve and grow in functionality, the use of smaller nanometer technology scaling coupled with high clock frequencies and exponentially increasing transistor counts dramatically increases the susceptibility of transient faults. However, the correct and reliable operation of these processors is often compulsory, both in terms of consumer experience and for high-risk embedded domains such as medical and transportation systems. Thus, economical fault detection and recovery becomes essential to meet all necessary market requirements. This paper explores the efficient leveraging of superscalar, out-of-order architectures to enable multi-cycle transient fault-tolerance throughout the datapath in a novel manner. By using dynamic instruction execution redundancy, soft errors within the datapath are both detected and recovered. The proposed microarchitecture selectively reevaluates corrupted instructions, reducing the recovery impact by preserving completed instructions unaffected by the fault. The additional computational workload is dynamically staggered to leverage the out-of-order nature of the architecture and minimize resource conflicts and delays.

Categories and Subject Descriptors

B.8.1 [**Performance and Reliability**]: Reliability, Testing, and Fault-Tolerance

General Terms

Design, Reliability

Keywords

fault tolerance, soft errors, reliability, embedded, datapath

1. INTRODUCTION

As today's embedded processors continue Moore's perpetual trend of exponentially increasing transistor counts, the issue of transient hardware faults will become more prevalent. This is exacerbated by the smaller feature sizes, high clock frequencies, and reduced voltage levels and noise margins being utilized to meet market demands. External events such as cosmic rays or ambient radiation can more easily alter voltage levels and the data represented by those levels [1]. This can lead to temporary inaccuracies within the data computations occurring within the processor, often termed single-event upsets (SEU), transient faults, or soft errors. In the past, the frequency of such transient faults was low, making fault-tolerant computers attractive only for high-risk, mission-critical domains such as medical devices, space programs, and ground and air transportation. However, future microprocessors will be more and more susceptible to transient faults as designs continue to grow in complexity and shrink in size [2, 3, 4]. As we begin to embark on 22nm technology designs, the impact of soft errors will become a significant factor in correct device operation and in the delivery of a positive consumer experience.

Furthermore, a glance into the future of embedded microprocessors will reveal an impending upheaval of present device technologies. Diminishing transistor-speed scaling and practical energy limits of current Silicon CMOS technology will soon compel a transition to a new technology scaling regime. Many arenas are currently under exploration, including carbon nanotubes, graphene, and quantum electronics. Such ground-breaking technologies will provide immensely higher device densities, but will also lead to substantially higher transient fault rates due to quantum effects, increased sensitivity to noise, and decreased fabrication tolerance [5].

As these next-generation processors are deployed into more ubiquitous arenas, such as automotive, industrial, and medical devices, the criticality of accurate computation becomes paramount. For example, a seemingly minute transient fault within a car's anti-lock braking system may result in a fatal accident. Indeed, the emergent domain of *dependable* microprocessors, such as the ARM Cortex-R series, can attest to the growing need for error-resistant processors even in the embedded domain.

Additionally, while fulfilling the goal of providing this fault tolerance, care must be taken in order to ensure that any associated overhead in terms of cost, performance, area, and power are not overly prohibitive. Simply duplicating or triplicating the entire system would indeed achieve resilience, but that would be quite inefficient. In order to remain competitive, a more intelligent and frugal approach to fault detection and recovery is necessitated. It has been shown that the soft error rate (SER) for SRAM cells decreases with decreasing technology size, and that the SER of latches remains relatively constant [6]. On the other hand, the SER of combinational logic within the processor increases quite rapidly as the feature size is reduced [6] and

CODES+ISSS'12, October 7–12, 2012, Tampere, Finland.

as voltage is decreased [4]. Thus, given that memory arrays can affordably be hardened using parity, Hamming codes, or ECC since the cost of the coding logic is amortized over the array, focusing on hardening the combinational logic and state throughout the datapath will become the primary challenge.

This paper proposes a novel approach to leveraging a conventional superscalar, out-of-order architecture to efficiently enable fault-tolerance throughout the datapath, including multi-cycle SEUs. Redundancy is achieved by dynamically duplicating and independently executing each instruction within the datapath. The final result of each instruction pair is compared to detect soft errors occurring within the datapath. Upon fault detection, only the erroneous portion of the instruction chain (e.g. those instructions that were poisoned by the faulty computation) is selectively discarded. Other completed instructions that are independent and unaffected by the fault are preserved in order to reduce unnecessary re-computation time and energy. The duplicated instructions are dynamically staggered in order to leverage the out-of-order nature of the architecture and minimize resource conflicts and performance delays. This helps reduce structural hazards within the functional units, and allows for higher functional unit utilization and overall instruction throughput. We show the implementation of this architecture and provide experimental data taken over a general sample of complex, real-world benchmark applications to show the benefits of such an approach. The simulation results show full soft error recovery, while incurring only an 11% to 26% reduction in processor performance.

2. RELATED WORK

Prior research has investigated the inherent hardware redundancy provided by simultaneous multithreading (SMT) architectures. The AR-SMT architecture proposed duplicating an application into two instruction threads, one leading (A) and one trailing (R) [7]. Each instruction pair is compared and validated. Information from the leading thread is also used to assist the trailing thread with control and data predictions to reduce the performance penalty. Similarly, the authors in [8] leverage the SMT architecture, but relax the coupling between the two threads by only comparing those instructions that produce side-effects visible outside the processor core. In both these cases, fault detection is the primary contribution, with fault recovery involving much overhead.

From the perspective of chip multiprocessors (CMP), [9] proposed executing two duplicate application threads on different processor cores. In comparison to the SMT proposals, leveraging completely separate hardware in different cores obviates the possibility of a transient fault persisting long enough within a common hardware block to corrupt both threads. On the other hand, the inter-process communication to maintain and compare information across cores is costly. Similarly, the authors in [10] proposed executing two duplicate applications on different processor cores, but instead relied on the cache memory interface as the point of comparison and checkpointing to help alleviate the overheads of processor-to-processor communication.

Superscalar out-of-order (OOO) architectures have provided another appealing foundation for fault tolerance. The authors in [11] proposed duplicating instruction execution within the OOO processor, leveraging two adjacent re-order buffer (ROB) entries per instruction. Upon both copies completing execution, they are compared and, if identical, committed. On the other hand, if the pair differs then all the ROB entries that have not been committed are discarded and execution is restarted from the last committed PC value. In this manner, the inherent rewind capability of the OOO processor allows fault recovery at no additional hardware cost. In a similar vein, the O3RS architecture proposed duplicating instruction execution, but removed the requirement of using two ROB entries per instruction [12]. Instead, they employ temporal redundancy by adding a differentiating state of *first* versus *second* execution to the ROB entries. In order to be committed, instructions must go from the *first* state to the *second* state and then be compared. If they differ, the state is moved back to *first* and subsequent ROB entries are also invalidated. Additionally, the idea of staggering the two computational threads was introduced in [13] in order to handle resource hazards, and showed improvement in the performance overhead.

Hybrid approaches of using an OOO processor coupled with an in-order redundancy pipeline have also been proposed. The DIVA architecture consists of a prototypical OOO processor, plus a very simple in-order *checker* processor [14]. Before instructions in the OOO pipeline can be retired, it must be compared with the result found from the in-order *checker*. While this improves the throughput (since the *checker* closely matches the throughput of the OOO processor), it requires separate functional units to be employed within the in-order *checker* which increases hardware overhead. The authors in [13] reduced this hardware overhead by allowing their in-order SHREC checker to share the same pool of functional units as the main OOO processor.

3. MOTIVATION

As mentioned in the introduction, combinational logic within the processor will increasingly become the victim of soft errors [6]. In particular, hardening the datapath of the processor is challenging due to the irregularity of the combinational logic used for computation. Whereas common fault-tolerance techniques, such as ECC, can be employed for uniform, array-like processor structures, the datapath poses additional complexity.

When discussing faults within the combinational logic of a circuit, it is important to observe that not every transient glitch will result in an SEU. The momentary voltage or current fluctuations that occur within the circuit are instead termed single-event transients (SETs). Only if the SET propagates through the circuit and results in an incorrect value being latched into a storage element does it become an SEU. Thus, the timing and longevity of the transient glitch can affect whether or not it manifests as an actual soft error or gets attenuated away. Because of this, the probability that momentary glitches will be captured as valid data in combinational logic increases linearly with frequency because the occurrence of clock edges increases [15, 16, 17].

Thus, the combination of ultra deep submicron scaling, high clock frequencies, and reduced voltage levels and noise margins all contribute to greatly increase the probability of transient glitches manifesting into SEUs within the processor datapath. Indeed, [18] reports the alpha-particle soft error rate (SER) measured increases of ≈2-3x when reducing voltage from 0.95V to 0.75V in a 32nm circuit, while [4] reports a doubling in SER when reducing voltage from 0.7V to 0.5V in 28nm. Furthermore, the rate of propagation of a glitch through the circuit is dependent on the linear energy transfer (LET) of the particle strike. LETs as low as 3 $MeV \cdot cm^2/mg$ are capable of generating sizable transients, and an LET of 70 $MeV \cdot cm^2/mg$ can cause durations exceeding 1ns [17]. Since many high-end embedded systems operate in multi-gigahertz frequencies, this implies that some SETs can last *more than one cycle* when induced by a particle with large enough LET. Given this, the consideration of guarding against multi-cycle faults within the datapath is also essential.

Fault tolerance requires both fault detection, as well as fault recovery once the fault is detected. There are numerous hardware techniques to detect whether a transient fault has occurred within a system. For example, one can simply create two duplicate systems and run them side-by-side, verifying the results at each time interval. Any differences would indicate the presence of a transient fault. While this approach would not degrade performance, the area and material cost of having two complete copies of the system is prohibitive. Furthermore, to enable fault recovery, a third system would typically be required. On the other hand, one can take a single system and execute the target application multiple times (whether in serial or in parallel), checking for differences. This temporal approach does not incur the area costs of hardware replication, yet the performance of such an approach would be poor. For embedded processors, the sensitivity to such area or performance overheads is often more pronounced and efficiency within the fault tolerant design is paramount.

In particular, there are three primary goals one should strive to attain to deliver robust and economic fault tolerance. First, given that the majority of the computations will not encounter a soft error, it is critical to minimize the performance impact of the fault detection logic for these non-faulty cases. Second, given the increased likelihood of soft errors occurring more frequently in ultra deep submicron feature sizes [2, 4], reducing the overhead of recovering from these faults is also important, both in terms of performance and scalability. Lastly, the assumption that transient faults only affect a single cycle is no longer true, necessitating the ability to handle multi-cycle faults. A novel architecture is proposed that will simultaneously achieve these three goals, intelligently leveraging a number of different design techniques to accomplish frugal multi-cycle transient fault tolerance within the datapath. An overview of this proposed architecture is discussed in the next section.

4. PROPOSED ARCHITECTURE

As previously mentioned, fault tolerant proposals often involve some form of spatial or temporal redundancy in order to detect and recover from faults. Such redundancy often incurs degradation in terms of area or performance. However, many of the inherent design properties of superscalar out-of-order (OOO) processors can be leveraged to help bridge this gap. In essence, these systems provide some duplication of hardware structures (functional units) and allow for multiple independent stream execution to occur in parallel. In order to detect transient faults, instruction redundancy can be leveraged within the OOO processor datapath. Instructions can be dynamically duplicated and independently executed. In this manner, fault detection within the datapath will simply become a matter of comparing the resulting values of the two instructions for differences. But, unlike full processor replication, many of the other hardware storage structures, such as the instruction queue, register file, caches, and TLBs, can remain shared and be hardened via other common techniques such as ECC or Hamming codes. Figure 1 shows the sphere of replication wherein the computation is duplicated. Only the computational datapath is replicated, greatly reducing the cost and area overhead of the fault detection. Furthermore, the same mechanisms in

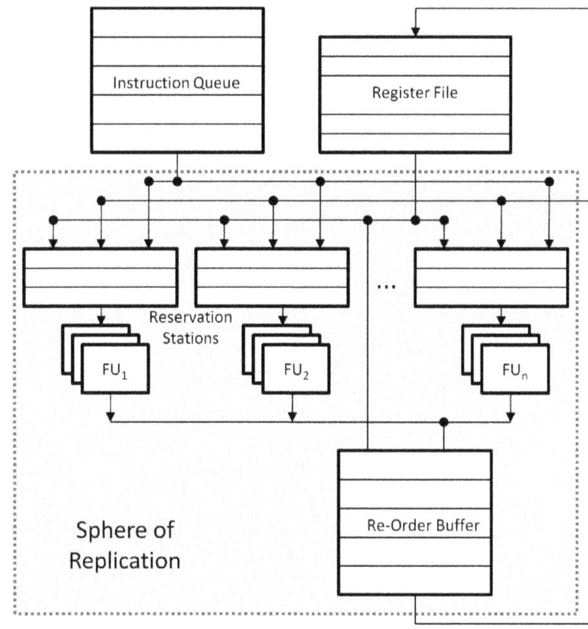

Figure 1: Generic Tomasulo Architecture Showing Sphere of Replication

place for speculative out-of-order execution can be employed to enable fault recovery by simply causing a soft exception to occur and rewind the execution back to a valid prior state. Building on this speculative OOO architecture, the fulfillment of the three primary design goals is described in the following subsections.

4.1 Improving Non-Faulty Performance

One major concern about introducing fault tolerance is the associated performance penalty incurred regardless of whether faults occur. Simplistically in a processor that is 100% utilized, if every instruction is duplicated, then the performance would degrade to 50% of the non-duplicating baseline. However, all computational resources of a processor are rarely utilized 100% continuously. In reality, many functional units may be idle at any given time. In order to reduce the impact of instruction duplication, one would ideally wish to have the duplicated instructions execute on idle functional units, and thus avoid elongating the time of the primary instruction thread.

Yet, if one simply creates two duplicate, independent execution threads, the functional unit access patterns will be identical. This will lower the likelihood of being able to perfectly interleave the secondary thread's hardware needs with that of the first's. The differing lengths of time each functional unit class takes (e.g. floating-point divide vs. integer add) will prevent a solution of simply offsetting the secondary thread by a fixed period of time. Furthermore, once the secondary thread begins, it may then occupy a resource that is also needed by the primary thread, which will elongate the overall time. An example of this is shown in Figure 2(a). The primary thread (shown in blue) and the secondary thread (shown in red) are independent. Assume there is only one functional unit of type A and it takes two cycles to complete, while there are two functional units of type B and they take one cycle to complete. As one can see,

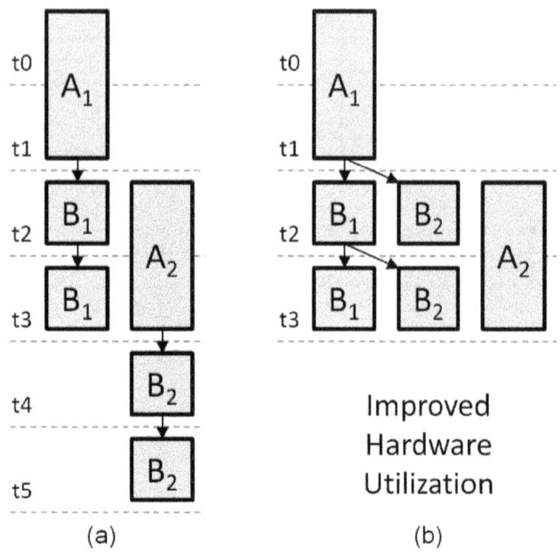

Figure 2: Duplicate Instruction Thread Decoupling Improves Performance

this would force both threads to be sequential, causing the overall time to take 6 cycles.

To rectify this inefficiency, a decoupling of the secondary thread is proposed. Duplicate secondary instructions are still created, but the source operands for each secondary instruction are connected to the corresponding primary instruction(s). Figure 2(b) shows this proposed modification. As one can see, because of this extra degree of freedom, the processor can complete these same six instructions in four cycles instead of six. The hardware utilization is improved, since the additional B-type functional units are now leveraged instead of waiting idly. In this fashion, one can ameliorate and amortize the performance overhead of instruction duplication (regardless of the presence of faults) by decoupling the secondary instructions and allowing them to execute at a lower priority in any functional units that may be available.

4.2 Improving Faulty Performance

As fault rates increase, the importance of optimizing the fault recovery aspect of the proposed architecture becomes more important. Assuming a transient fault has been detected, the most basic recovery approach for a speculative out-of-order processor would be to rewind the state to just before the offending instruction executes, and then restart execution from that point. This effectively throws away all computation that occurred after the offending instruction. This behavior can be quite wasteful if the number of subsequent instructions computed after the instruction in question is large, and those computed instructions are *unaffected* by the offending instruction.

Instead, upon fault detection, only the erroneous portion of the instruction chain (e.g. those instructions that were poisoned by the faulty computation) should be selectively discarded. Other completed instructions that are independent and unaffected by the fault are preserved in order to reduce unnecessary re-computation overhead. This not only abates resource contention within the system, but also enjoys the added benefit of reducing power consumption. Furthermore, as the occurrence of transient faults increases, the proposed architecture will be able to more robustly handle recovery without becoming overwhelmed and unable to resolve faults faster than they occur. Thus, this approach will be able to scale with increases in soft error frequency.

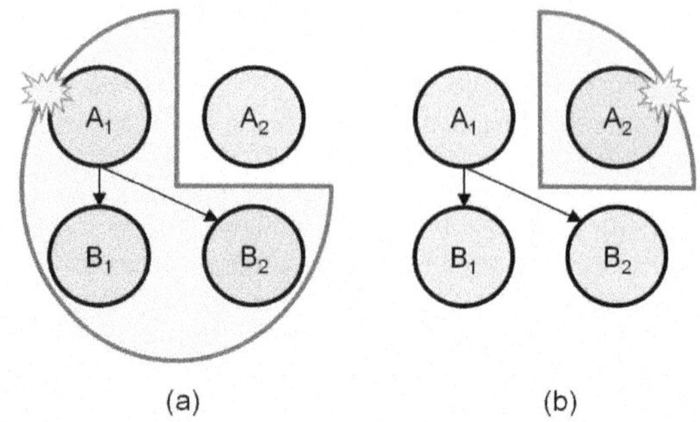

Figure 3: Impact of Uniformly Distributed Fault Results in Balanced Average Re-Computation Effort

In addition to employing poison bits to localize the re-computation effort and avoid invalidating unaffected work, a further optimization is proposed to try and recuperate potentially poisoned work. Given that there are two differing copies of the offending instruction, but no knowledge of which one is valid, a third computation of the offending instruction is initiated and the result of that computation acts as a vote in favor of one of the other two copies. In this manner, the third computation can select which of the two original copies is the correct one, and preserve the valid computational work that was performed in subsequent instructions. The erroneous copy of the instruction is discarded, as well as any subsequent instructions that had the corresponding poison bits.

Assuming a uniform fault distribution, a fault could occur within a primary or secondary instruction with equal probability. Yet, if the fault occurred in the primary instruction, the poison bit setup would impact both the dependent primary instructions, as well as the dependent secondary instructions. On the other hand, if the fault occurred in the secondary instruction, only that single instruction would be affected (since all secondary instructions pull their source operands from primary instructions). As one can observe, probabilistically these two cases balance out. Half of the time, the fault will be in a primary instruction, which would impact the entire dependency chain and require those instructions to be re-computed, as shown in Figure 3(a). The other half of the time, it will occur in the secondary instruction and that single instruction can just be discarded at that point, as shown in Figure 3(b).

4.3 Handling Multi-Cycle Faults

The main concern with multi-cycle faults is the condition where both the primary and secondary instructions are executed on the same functional unit while that unit is being perturbed by the multi-cycle fault. In this situation, both copies of the instruction may match, but both may be incorrect. Thus, the fault detection capability of the system becomes undermined. In order to rectify this situation, each functional unit must guard against being selected to compute an instruction that had the complement instruction previously executed on it. This will ensure the same functional unit will not be used by both copies of the same instruction. One challenge is if the system only has a single functional unit, as may be the case for more infrequent and expensive calculations such as floating-point division (FDIV). In these cases, since there is only a single functional unit, it must be utilized by both the primary and secondary instructions. As will be shown in Section 6, a temporal factor will be included in the guard logic to allow a single functional unit to be shared by both the primary and secondary instructions.

5. DESIGN DECISIONS

While early OOO implementations had a central register update unit (RUU) for bookkeeping, most modern implementations decentralize the information and have a separate reservation station, ROB, and register file to improve throughput in the presence of speculation. This latter class of speculative out-of-order architectures is derived from the Tomasulo design [19], and is the foundation of our proposed fault tolerant implementation. Furthermore, this proposal focuses on the datapath of the processor, which is more challenging to protect due to its irregularity when compared to array-like storage structures. The other processor components, such as cache memories, register files, and TLBs, are assumed to be hardened against faults using existing solutions, such as ECC, and will not be discussed further.

While the original Tomasulo architecture only scheduled instructions via the issue queue read from instruction memory, enabling faulty instructions to re-execute will require a mechanism to reintroduce a completed instruction back into the execution engine. The detailed modifications that are done to implement this are discussed in the next section.

Instructions that cause external side-effects, such as loads, stores, and conditional branch instructions will not be fully duplicated. Allowing two copies of such instructions to execute can cause serious performance and correctness issues within the pipeline. For example, having a load instruction duplicated may cause undesirable cache implications, such as evicting other entries that were also active. Additionally, the bandwidth of the memory subsystem is often a limiting factor and unnecessary congestion should be avoided. Thus, instead of fully duplicating memory instructions, only the effective address calculation is hardened via this proposed duplication scheme, but the actual memory access operation occurs only once. This avoids memory consistency issues and possible performance degradation due to cache sensitivities. As modern architectures typically harden the memory via ECC or similar safeguards, it can be assumed that correct values are retrieved from or stored into memory cells with no additional effort. Similarly, having two copies of a conditional branch instruction that may be divergent will cause many issues. Given this, branch instructions are also not fully duplicated. Rather, only the conditional computation within the datapath is duplicated, but the actual modification of the program-counter is only done once. Again, it is presumed that storage elements providing the target address are hardened against faults using typical memory-array fault tolerance techniques.

6. IMPLEMENTATION

The typical reservation station entry contains the following fields:

- *OpCode* - operation to be performed
- V_j - value of operand 1
- V_k - value of operand 2
- Q_j - ROB # of operand 1 (0 if already available)
- Q_k - ROB # of operand 2 (0 if already available)
- *Dest* - destination ROB #
- *A* - effective address for load/store
- *Busy* - indicates entry and corresponding FU occupied

Reservation Station Entry

OpCode	V_j	V_k	Q_j	Q_k	Dest	A	Busy	Type
6 bits	32 bits	32 bits	8 bits	8 bits	8 bits	32 bits	1 bit	2 bits

Figure 4: Modifications to Reservation Station Entries

Reorder Buffer Entry (Original)

InstType	Dest	Value	Ready
2 bits	32 bits	32 bits	1 bit

OpCode	Dest	Poison	Q_j	Q_k	Value0	Value1	Ready0	Ready1
6 bits	32 bits	256 bits	8 bits	8 bits	32 bits	32 bits	1 bit	1 bit

Reorder Buffer Entry (Modified)

Figure 5: Modifications to Reservation Station Entries

For this proposal, an additional 2-bit field is needed per reservation station entry:

- *Type* - indicates if this is *primary*(0), *secondary*(1), or *tertiary*(2) instruction

The necessary modifications to the reservation station entries are shown in Figure 4, highlighted in red. Moreover, the typical ROB entry contains four fields:

- *InstructionType* - branch, store, or ALU/load
- *Dest* - register or memory address
- *Value* - value of instruction result
- *Ready* - indicates if *Value* is ready

However, in order to enable this proposal each ROB entry will instead contain:

- *OpCode* - operation to be performed
- *Dest* - register or memory address
- *Poison* - bit-vector of progenitor ROB entries
- Q_j - ROB or RF # of operand 1
- Q_k - ROB or RF # of operand 2
- *Value*[2] - value of instruction result
- *Ready*[2] - indicates if *Value* is ready

The necessary modifications for each ROB entry are shown in Figure 5, again highlighted in red. The bit numbers shown assume an ROB size of 256 entries, and can be adjusted accordingly.

The instruction stream will dynamically be duplicated within the computational datapath, running independently on the available hardware. Figure 1 shows the sphere of replication wherein the computation is duplicated. Once an instruction is issued, two independent computations will exist for that instruction. Subsequent dependent instructions that are also duplicated will receive both of their operands from only the primary thread (or the register file, if already committed). In this manner, the additional computation overhead of the second instruction can be decoupled and executed whenever there are idle computation resources available. The pair of instructions will occupy a single ROB

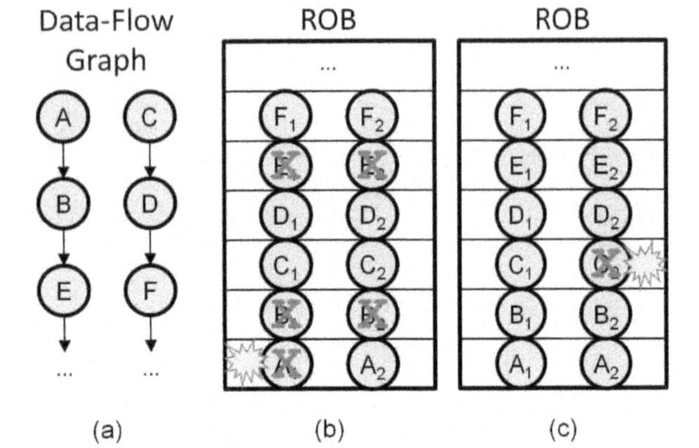

Figure 6: Example of Selective Poisoning in Both Primary and Secondary Threads

entry, but will account for two reservation station entries. Within a given ROB entry, the new *Poison* field that is added will indicate all the other ROB entries that, if erroneous, may potentially pollute this entry's source operands and cause an error. The *Value* and *Ready* fields are duplicated to hold the results of both the *primary* and *secondary* instruction results received from a functional unit. When a functional unit completes its computation, it will send the result value along with the destination ROB # and whether it was a *primary* or *secondary* instruction, allowing the correct ROB entry *Value* field to be updated.

Once both copies of the instruction are completed (e.g. both *Ready* fields in the ROB entry are true), they are compared to detect if a transient fault has occurred. If they match, the instruction is ready to be committed by writing the computed value (either from the *primary* or *secondary* *Value* field within the ROB) into the destination register. This commit will only occur once the ROB entry reaches the *head* of the buffer (to ensure in-order commit, as normally expected). Once the commit occurs, any other ROB entries that refer to the committed entry in their Q_j or Q_k fields will update their index to instead point to the register file destination that was committed by the ROB. In this manner, if a subsequent ROB entry needs to be re-executed (due to a mismatch within itself or from one of its progenitor instructions), the Q_j and Q_k values will be used to correctly repopulate a reservation station entry to allow for the re-execution of that particular ROB entry.

On the other hand, if the two values mismatch, a fault has been detected. In this situation, a third, independent copy of the mismatched instruction will be submitted as a new entry into the reservation station, utilizing the information stored locally within the ROB fields. The reservation station will treat this tertiary instruction as the highest priority, assigning it into the first available functional unit that is able to service the computation. Once the result is computed, it will be compared against both existing *Value* fields in the ROB for a match. If neither matches, another third copy will be submitted and the process recurs until the resulting value matches one of the two existing *Value* fields. An optional maximum retry limit can be added to account for the case of an unrecoverable fault.

Once a match against the third thread is found, that thread (be it *primary* or *secondary*) will be considered correct and the other thread invalid. If it is the *primary* thread that is deemed invalid, then the offending ROB entry will broadcast its ROB # to the other ROB entries. The others will perform a simple bitwise *AND* against their *Poison* field to detect if they may have been poisoned by the fault. The offending ROB entry and all those ROB entries that were poisoned will clear their *Ready* fields and resubmit a new pair of entries into the reservation station for both *primary* and *secondary* instructions, utilizing the information stored locally within the ROB fields. If it is the *secondary* thread that is deemed invalid, no extra work is incurred and the ROB entry is now ready to be committed. The superiority of this approach can be appreciated in that statistically half of the times that a mismatch occurs, the ROB entries are preserved and do not need to be re-computed, reducing the performance and power overhead of fault recovery (since the erroneous entry was the *secondary* instruction). To illustrate this concept, Figure 6 shows (a) an example data-flow graph (DFG) of six instructions, (b) the case of a fault occurring in a *primary* instruction resulting in the poisoning of data-dependent instructions, and (c) the case of a fault occurring in a *secondary* instruction which does not effect data-dependent instructions.

The reservation station functional unit allocation algorithm is modified to allow it to service instructions in a fixed-priority fashion. *Tertiary* instructions (those that have been spawned in order to vote on the correctness of either the *primary* or *secondary* instruction) are considered the highest priority. *Primary* instructions are considered the next highest priority, and *secondary* instructions are considered the lowest priority. The reservation station will try to assign the highest priority instruction it can find that has both of its operand values ready into the next available functional unit. If multiple equivalent-priority instructions are ready to be executed, one is selected at random. An important observation is that this priority-based allocation scheme avoids deadlock. While *secondary* instructions may be likely to get stuck waiting for a functional unit if there are many *primary* instructions continuously occupying the functional units, the general structure of the ROB imposes a dampener on this resource starvation. No new instructions can be issued into the ROB if all the ROB entries are full. If *secondary* instructions are being held in the reservation stations, they preclude the retirement of their corresponding ROB entries. Thus, at some point the ROB will be full and no new *primary* instructions will be issued. This will cause the stream of *primary* instructions to wane and allow the awaiting *secondary* instructions to execute. Once the *secondary* instructions finish and the ROB entries start to commit, then new ROB entries will become available and the system can continue to move forward.

The existence of multi-cycle faults necessitates some additional intelligence in the reservation stations. Utilizing the same exact functional unit for the complement pair of instructions can allow multi-cycle faults to undermine the fault tolerance of the system. To rectify this, the reservation station must ensure both the *primary* and *secondary* instruction do not execute on the same functional unit, or at least not within a certain time period. This is accomplished by having a small table within the reservation station that keeps track of the last N instructions that were executed on each functional unit. The value of N can be determined by the likelihood of a multi-cycle fault lasting longer than N functional unit calculations. For example, if it is infeasible for a fault to last longer than 2 functional unit calculations (e.g. SUB or FDIV), then the table will contain just two entries. The entries will just need to hold the ROB # plus the 2-bits of *Type* to determine which type of instruction it was (*primary*, *secondary*, or *tertiary*). Additionally, to sup-

Table 1: Hardware Config 1

ROB Entries	256
Reservation Station Entries	32 per FU type
LSQ Entries	64
Instruction L1 cache	64 KB, 2-way set-associative
Data L1 cache	32 KB, 2-way set-associative
Unified L2 cache	512KB, 4-way set-associative
Functional Unit Mix	4 IALU (1), 2 IMUL/IDIV (3/19), 2 FALU (2), 2 FMUL/FDIV (4/12)

Table 2: Hardware Config 2

ROB Entries	128
Reservation Station Entries	16 per FU type
LSQ Entries	64
Instruction L1 cache	64 KB, 2-way set-associative
Data L1 cache	32 KB, 2-way set-associative
Unified L2 cache	512KB, 4-way set-associative
Functional Unit Mix	4 IALU (1), 2 IMUL/IDIV (3/19), 2 FALU (2), 1 FMUL/FDIV (4/12)

port the case of a single functional unit (e.g. for FDIV), a time-based decay is added to remove the table entries after a period of inactivity greater than the anticipated multi-cycle fault length. In this manner, full fault tolerance against multi-cycle faults is accomplished, while incurring minimal overhead in the regular operation of the entire datapath.

Based on the proposed architectural modifications, each reservation station would need 2 bits per entry in addition to the preexisting 127 bits. Similarly, each ROB entry would require an additional 309 bits on top of the preexisting 67 bits. Given an architecture with 256 ROB entries and 128 total reservation station entries (for all types of functional units), this would amount to approximately 9.7KB of additional storage elements. While this amount of data is not trivial, it is quite a reasonable price to pay to enable transient fault detection and recovery throughout the processor datapath and demonstrates the frugality of the proposed fault tolerant design.

7. EXPERIMENTAL RESULTS

In order to assess the benefit from this proposed architectural design, we utilized the SimpleScalar framework [20]. The stock code initially utilized a basic register update unit (RUU) structure, combining the reorder buffer (ROB) and reservation stations and provided no register renaming. In order to fully exploit possible parallelism and instruction throughput, we greatly modified the default *sim-outorder* simulator to implement a full speculative Tomasulo architecture [19], including register renaming and decentralized reservation stations. This will allow hardware instruction scheduling to cross basic block boundaries and implicitly reduces register pressure, both of which will help improve IPC (instructions per cycle). Furthermore, the simulator is augmented with the fault detection and recovery scheme presented in this paper. When operating in fault-tolerant mode, all datapath instructions will be replicated and validated. For instructions with side-effects, such as memory accesses and control flow operations, only the numerical computation (e.g. effective memory address calculation or branch condition comparison) will be replicated; the actual modification of the LSQ (load/store queue) or program counter will only be permitted from the primary instruction. This behavior ensures program validity; if a fault does occur the precise exception handling of the speculative Tomasulo implementation will be able to correctly rewind the system state.

A random fault injection routine was added to the simulator, allowing a configurable rate at which to randomly corrupt instructions during execution. As each instruction begins execution within a functional unit, the fault injection routine is queried to determine if that instruction should be forced to be corrupted. If so, the resulting value from the function unit is *XOR*ed with -1, effectively flipping all the bits. Furthermore, 20% of the instances where the fault injection routine triggers a fault, it will also mark the corresponding functional unit as faulty for 2 instructions, simulating a multi-cycle fault. In these cases, the next instruction that enters the functional unit will also be corrupted in the exact same fashion.

We chose two representative superscalar out-of-order system configurations to demonstrate our proposal. Table 1 defines *Config 1*, which is a more aggressive system employing a 256-entry ROB and 32-entry reservation stations for each functional unit type. Table 2 defines *Config 2*, which is more conservative and has half the number of ROB and reservation station entries, and also only a single floating-point multiplier and divider (FMUL/FDIV). Both configurations have pipelined functional units (except for the IDIV and FDIV units). The number of cycles each functional unit type consumes is listed within the parentheses in each table.

The complete SPEC CPU2000 benchmark suite [21] is used, providing 12 integer and 14 floating-point real-world applications. A listing of these benchmarks and their respective descriptions are provided in Table 3. The benchmarks are cross-compiled for the PISA instruction set using the highest level of optimization available for the language-specific compiler. The reference inputs are used for each benchmark, with each benchmark executed in its entirety from start to finish.

In order to assess our proposed architecture, we simulated the benchmarks on four different processor models: *Baseline*, *FT No Faults*, *FT 1E-4 Fault Rate*, and *FT 1E-1 Fault Rate*. The *Baseline* processor model is a plain speculative Tomasulo architecture [19], with no instruction replication or fault tolerance enabled. The *FT No Faults* processor model enables instruction replication and fault tolerance

Table 3: Description of Benchmarks

	Benchmark	Description
INTEGER	bzip2	Memory-based compression algorithm
	crafty	High-performance chess playing game
	eon	Probabilistic ray tracer visualization
	gap	Group theory interpreter
	gcc	GNU C compiler
	gzip	LZ77 compression algorithm
	mcf	Vehicle scheduling combinatorial optimization
	parser	Dictionary-based word processing
	perlbmk	Perl programming language interpreter
	twolf	CAD place-and-route simulation
	vortex	Object-oriented database transactions
	vpr	FPGA circuit placement and routing
FLOATING POINT	ammp	Computational chemistry
	applu	Parabolic partial differential equations
	apsi	Meteorology pollutant distribution
	art	Image recognition / neural networks
	equake	Seismic wave propagation simulation
	facerec	Face recognition image processing
	fma3d	Finite-element crash simulation
	galgel	Computational fluid dynamics
	lucas	Number theory / primality testing
	mesa	3D graphics library
	mgrid	Multi-grid 3D potential field solver
	sixtrack	High energy nuclear physics accelerator
	swim	Shallow water modeling
	wupwise	Physics / quantum chromodynamics

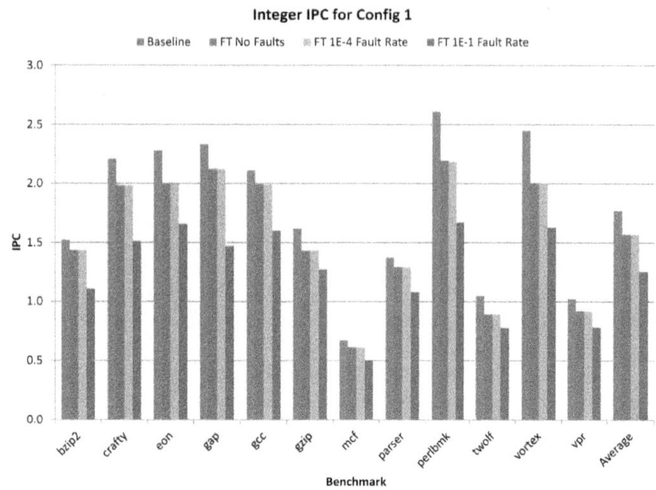

Figure 7: Performance Impact of Fault Tolerance on Integer Benchmarks using *Config 1*

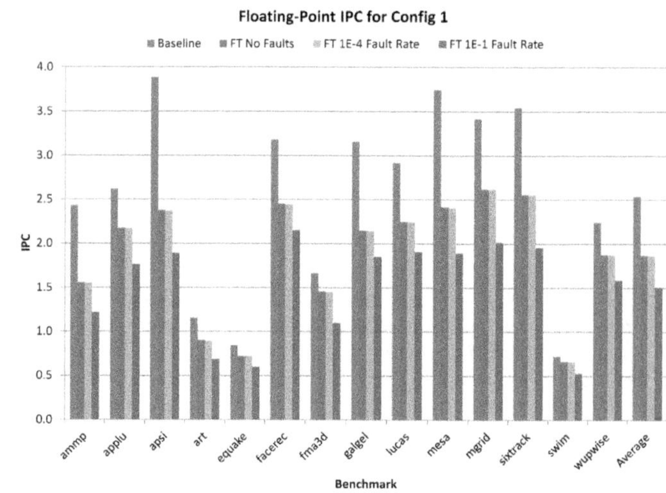

Figure 8: Performance Impact of Fault Tolerance on Floating-Point Benchmarks using *Config 1*

checking, but will not inject any faults. This will demonstrate the overhead of our proposed fault tolerance scheme without the additional cost of recovering from faults. The *FT 1E-4 Fault Rate* and *FT 1E-1 Fault Rate* processor models also enable the fault tolerance scheme, but will inject faults at the rate of 0.01% and 10%, respectively. The experiment range is selected broadly so as to demonstrate the effectiveness of our design in enduring a variety of fault rates, including high ones.

Figure 7 compares the IPC of the four processor models using *Config 1* for each of the 12 integer benchmarks. As one can see, the Baseline attained an average IPC of approximately 1.77. When we enable the fault tolerance datapath replication, the average IPC falls to 1.57, which is a reduction of about 11%. Given that every computational instruction is being executed twice, such a low reduction in IPC is quite impressive. Indeed, if every functional unit was continuously utilized throughout the lifetime of the program, such instruction duplication would amount to an IPC reduction of at least 50%. However, due to the intelligent and efficient implementation of our system, the duplicated instructions are able to dynamically recuperate idle hardware resources and achieve improved overall IPC while doing double the number of computations.

Furthermore, the introduction of a 0.01% fault rate does not cause any noticeable decline in IPC. In fact, the overhead of recovering these faults is quite minimal due to the selective fault chaining that was implemented. When the *primary* and *secondary* instructions mismatch and the *tertiary* voter instruction determines which of the two is incorrect, then only the erroneous instruction and those instructions that were poisoned by it will be thrown away and re-computed. This allows for many independent instructions that were executed in between to be preserved, as opposed to just rewinding the entire ROB back to the offending instruction and starting over. Furthermore, even the re-computation of the poisoned chain is something that will be avoided 50% of the time; if the fault is determined to have occurred in the *secondary* instruction, no re-computation is necessary. This not only helps reduce the performance overhead of fault recovery, but also helps curb unnecessary power consumption.

This efficiency becomes even more apparent as the fault rate goes up to 10%. In the *FT 1E-1 Fault Rate* model, we can still see the system is able to make forward progress, even though about 1 out of every 10 instruction executions was faulty, plus 2 of those times the fault was multi-cycle and corrupted the next instruction. While it may seem like an extreme case to have such a high fault rate, it is important to demonstrate the ability of the system to adeptly handle high rates of failure.

Figure 8 compares the IPC for the same four processor models using *Config 1* across the floating-point benchmarks. In general, the floating-point benchmarks are able to achieve a higher IPC, as their diversity of additional floating-point instructions helps reduce the demands on the other functional units. The average IPC for the Baseline in this case was 2.54, while the *FT No Faults* model achieved 1.87. This reflects a reduction in IPC of approximately 26%. As one can see, the IPC reduction is more pronounced in the floating-point benchmarks. This is due to the smaller number and longer execution time of floating-point functional units, which can become a bottleneck as two copies of each instruction need to be computed. The overhead is quite low, considering the doubling in the computational work that is taking place.

Similar to the integer benchmarks, introducing a modest amount of faults does not significantly reduce the average IPC for floating-point applications. One is able to achieve complete datapath fault tolerance, while only incurring a 26% reduction in performance. Furthermore, the system is still able to handle the high level of faults of the *FT 1E-1 Fault Rate* processor, demonstrating that even in the face of extreme fault occurrence the system is able to make forward progress and eventually provide correct values.

Figure 9 and Figure 10 show the same IPC information for both integer and floating-point applications, respectively, but using the more conservative *Config 2*. In these cases, the number of ROB entries and reservation stations is reduced by 50%. This will reduce the amount of inherent IPC by constraining the amount of instructions that can be in-flight, and also shrinking the effective window of how far the *primary* instruction thread can run ahead of the *secondary* instructions before having to wait for the *secondary* instructions to catch up. These resource limitations will also

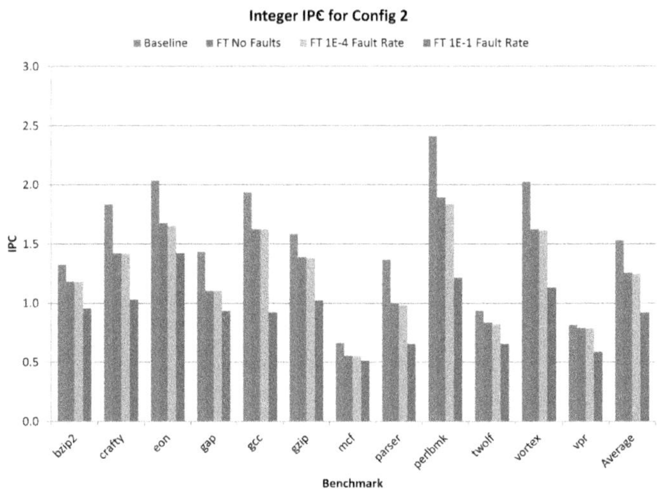

Figure 9: Performance Impact of Fault Tolerance on Integer Benchmarks using *Config 2*

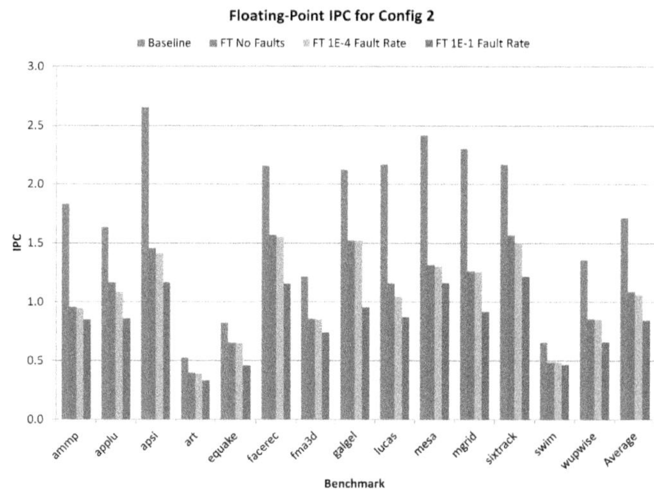

Figure 10: Performance Impact of Fault Tolerance on Floating-Point Benchmarks using *Config 2*

further degrade the performance when instruction replication is enabled, since the available slack in the system is more constrained and the availability of empty reservation station entries is diminished.

As one can see, the *Baseline* IPC for integer and floating-point benchmarks using *Config 2* was 1.53 and 1.72, respectively. When instruction replication is enabled without any faults, the IPC values are reduced by about 18% and 37% to become 1.26 and 1.09, respectively. Once fault injection is enabled, the IPC does slightly degrade as would be expected due to the instruction re-computation overhead. Furthermore, there may be an additional delay in sending the *tertiary* instruction to the reservation station for execution if all entries in the smaller reservation station are already occupied.

Additionally, *Config 2* demonstrates the effectiveness of our proposal in situations where only a single functional unit may exist. In this configuration, only a single FMUL and FDIV functional unit is available. In the case where a multi-cycle fault occurs during an FDIV computation of a *primary* instruction, the system must be smart enough to guard against the corresponding *secondary* instruction running immediately afterward. If that situation were allowed to happen, the *secondary* instruction would be corrupted in an identical fashion, and the fault detection would fail to cover that case. In executing the various benchmarks on *Config 2*, we were able to verify that the architecture properly guarded against this situation, and only allowed a corresponding instruction to execute on the same functional unit after the necessary delay period to ensure the multi-cycle fault would be over.

In addition to the aforementioned IPC values computed for the two fault rates of 1E-4 and 1E-1, we were interested to see the impact on IPC as a result of increasing fault rates. We chose 15 different fault rates, ranging from 1E-6 to 1E-1 to examine how rapidly IPC degrades as the fault rate increases. Obviously, at some point the fault rate will outpace the ability of the system to recover, causing faults faster than they can be re-computed. As this point is approached, one would expect to see an exponential drop-off in IPC. A group of six benchmarks were chosen to explore this behavior: *perlbmk*, *gap*, and *crafty* from the integer suite, and *sixtrack*, *apsi*, and *applu* from the floating-point suite. Using the *Config 1* setup, these benchmarks were executed while varying the fault rate.

Figure 11 presents the interaction of the increasing fault rate on the IPC for the three integer benchmarks. As one can see, the IPC remains somewhat stable with fault rates below 1E-3 (about 1 instruction every 1,000 instructions executed). As the fault rate increases beyond that level, the degradation of IPC becomes more pronounced and eventually begins to rapidly plunge as the fault rate becomes increasingly frequent. When the fault rate reaches 1E-1 (about 1 instruction every 10 instructions executed), the IPC is on a sharp trajectory to soon become stalled and unable to move forward due to overwhelming faults.

Figure 12 presents the same interaction of IPC versus fault rate, but using the three floating-point benchmarks. Similar to the integer data, the IPC remains about the same until reaching 1E-3. At that point, the IPC decays exponentially and eventually will result in the same livelock situation where faults occur faster than they can be recovered from.

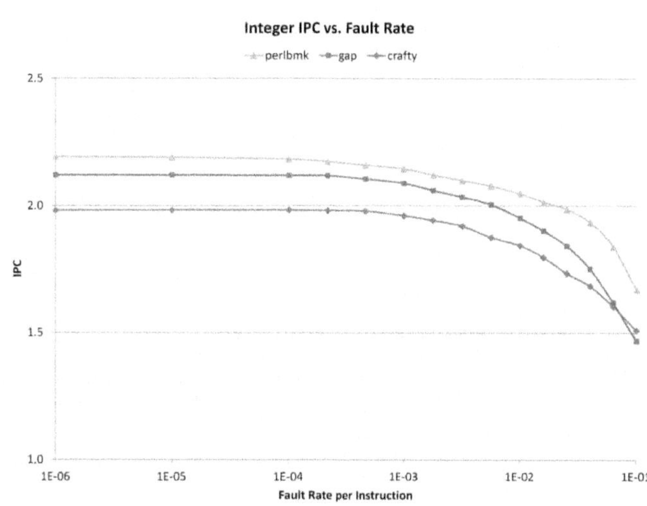

Figure 11: Integer IPC versus Fault Rate

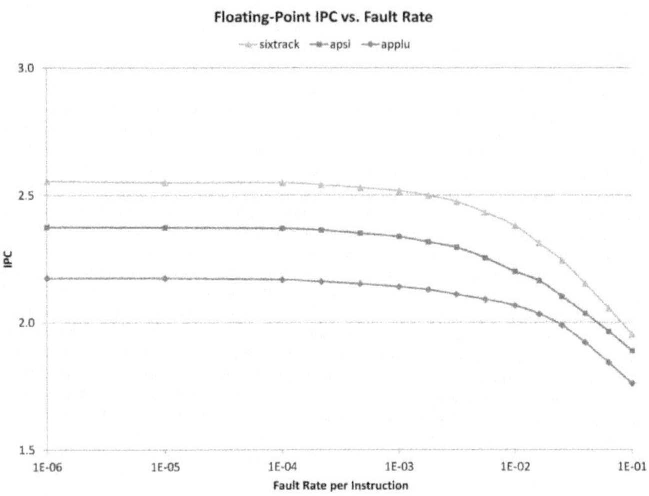

Figure 12: Floating-Point IPC versus Fault Rate

8. CONCLUSIONS

As the feature size and operating voltages of high-end embedded processors continue to shrink to satisfy consumer's insatiable demand for greater functionality and less power consumption, sensitivity to soft errors increases dramatically. In the upcoming generation of 22nm devices and below, the transient fault rate in high-performance processors will increase noticeably. Given this, the correct and reliable operation of these microprocessors will become a more prominent objective in order to satisfy consumer experience levels. Furthermore, as these next-generation processors are deployed into more ubiquitous arenas, such as automotive, industrial, and medical devices, the criticality of accurate computation becomes paramount. Moreover, it has been shown that the combinational logic of the datapath will become a major contributor of soft errors, and an efficient solution to provide fault tolerance is necessary.

In this paper, we have presented a novel and frugal fault tolerance framework for current superscalar out-of-order architectures. In particular, the system is able to account for multi-cycle SEUs, which many existing approaches do not guard against. Furthermore, by leveraging most of the existing hardware structures of the out-of-order machine, the entire datapath can be hardened against transient faults with minimal additional hardware costs. Redundancy is achieved by dynamically duplicating and independently executing each instruction within the datapath's out-of-order infrastructure. Each pair of instructions is compared to detect soft errors, and recovery is accomplished by selectively re-executing only the necessary instructions that were poisoned by the fault. A key optimization is that other completed instructions that were independent and unaffected by the fault are preserved in order to reduce unnecessary recomputation overhead. Furthermore, in order to maximize the IPC during non-faulty operation, the duplicated instructions are allowed to be dynamically staggered and utilize idle hardware functional units in an out-of-order fashion to reduce resource conflicts and improve IPC.

Extensive experimental results are provided to validate the correct operation of the architecture. Complete fault detection and recovery is achieved within the processor datapath, while only incurring moderate reductions of IPC of 11% to 26% in order to handle the replicated computations. Furthermore, the system is able to withstand very high rates of soft errors, and only begins to significantly degrade performance as the fault rate reaches 10% of instructions executed.

9. REFERENCES

[1] R. Baumann. Soft errors in advanced computer systems. *IEEE Design and Test of Computers*, 22(3):258–266, 2005.

[2] K. Lee, A. Shrivastava, M. Kim, N. Dutt, and N. Venkatasubramanian. Mitigating the impact of hardware defects on multimedia applications: A cross-layer approach. In *Proc. Intl. Conf. on Multimedia*, pages 319–328, 2008.

[3] N. Seifert, V. Ambrose, B. Gill, Q. Shi, R. Allmon, C. Recchia, S. Mukherjee, N. Nassif, J. Krause, J. Pickholtz, and A. Balasubramanian. On the radiation-induced soft error performance of hardened sequential elements in advanced bulk cmos technologies. In *Proc. Intl. Reliability Physics Symp.*, pages 188–197, 2010.

[4] A. Dixit and A. Wood. The impact of new technology on soft error rates. In *Proc. Intl. Reliability Physics Symp.*, pages 486–492, 2011.

[5] J. Han, J. Gao, P. Jonker, Q. Yan, and J. A. B. Fortes. Toward hardware-redundant, fault-tolerant logic for nanoelectronics. *IEEE Design and Test of Computer*, 22(4):328–339, 2005.

[6] P. Shivakumar, M. Kistler, S. W. Keckler, D. Burger, and L. Alvisi. Modeling the effect of technology trends on the soft error rate of combinational logic. In *Proc. Intl. Conf. on Dependable Systems and Networks*, pages 389–398, 2002.

[7] E. Rotenberg. AR-SMT: A microarchitectural approach to fault tolerance in microprocessors. In *Proc. 29th Intl. Symp. on Fault-Tolerant Computing*, pages 84–91, 1999.

[8] S. K. Reinhardt and S. S. Mukherjee. Transient fault detection via simultaneous multithreading. In *Proc. 27th Intl. Symp. on Computer Architecture*, pages 25–36, 2000.

[9] M. Gomaa, C. Scarbrough, T. N. Vijaykumar, and I. Pomeranz. Transient-fault recovery for chip multiprocessors. In *Proc. 30th Intl. Symp. on Computer Architecture*, pages 98–109, 2003.

[10] C. Yang and A. Orailoglu. A light-weight cache-based fault detection and checkpointing scheme for MPSoCs enabling relaxed execution synchronization. In *Proc. Intl. Conf. on Compilers, Architectures and Synthesis for Embedded Systems*, pages 11–20, 2008.

[11] J. Ray, J. C. Hoe, and B. Falsafi. Dual use of superscalar datapath for transient-fault detection and recovery. In *Proc. 34th Intl. Symp. on Microarchitecture*, pages 214–224, 2001.

[12] A. Mendelson and N. Suri. Designing high-performance & reliable superscalar architectures: The out of order reliable superscalar (O3RS) approach. In *Proc. Intl. Conf. on Dependable Systems and Networks*, pages 473–481, 2000.

[13] J. C. Smolens, J. Kim, J. C. Hoe, and B. Falsafi. Efficient resource sharing in concurrent error detecting superscalar microarchitectures. In *Proc. 37th Intl. Symp. on Microarchitecture*, pages 257–268, 2004.

[14] T. M. Austin. Diva: A reliable substrate for deep submicron microarchitecture design. In *Proc. 32nd Intl. Symp. on Microarchitecture*, pages 196–207, 1999.

[15] S. Buchner, M. Baze, D. Brown, D. McMorrow, and J. Melinger. Comparison of error rates in combinational and sequential logic. *IEEE Transactions on Nuclear Science*, 44(6):2209–2216, 1997.

[16] L. Anghel and M. Nicolaidis. Cost reduction and evaluation of temporary faults detecting technique. In *Proc. Intl. Conf. on Design, Automation and Test in Europe*, pages 591–598, 2000.

[17] P. E. Dodd, M. R. Shaneyfelt, J. A. Felix, and J. R. Schwank. Production and propagation of single-event transients in high-speed digital logic ICs. *IEEE Transactions on Nuclear Science*, 51(6):3278–3284, 2004.

[18] B. Gill, N. Seifert, and V. Zia. Comparison of alpha-particle and neutron-induced combinational and sequential logic error rates at the 32nm technology node. In *Proc. 47th Intl. Symp. on Reliability Physics*, pages 199–205, 2009.

[19] J. Hennessy and D. Patterson. *Computer Architecture: A Quantitative Approach.* Morgan Kaufmann Publishers, Fifth Edition, 2011.

[20] Todd Austin, Eric Larson, and Dan Ernst. SimpleScalar: An infrastructure for computer system modeling. *Computer*, pages 59–67, 2002.

[21] SPEC CPU2000 Benchmarks. http://www.spec.org/cpu/.

SPI-SNOOPER: A Hardware-Software Approach for Transparent Network Monitoring in Wireless Sensor Networks

Mohammad Sajjad Hossain*
Google Inc.
Mountain View, CA, USA
sajjad@google.com

Woo Suk Lee
Purdue University
West Lafayette, IN, USA
lee992@purdue.edu

Vijay Raghunathan
Purdue University
West Lafayette, IN, USA
vr@purdue.edu

ABSTRACT

The lack of post-deployment visibility into system operation is one of the major challenges in ensuring reliable operation of remotely-deployed embedded systems such as wireless sensor nodes. Over the years, many software-based solutions (in the form of debugging tools and protocols) have been proposed for in-situ system monitoring. However, all of them share the trait that the monitoring functionality is implemented as software executing on the same embedded processor that the main application executes on. This is a poor design choice from a reliability perspective. This paper makes the case for a joint hardware-software solution to this problem and advocates the use of a dedicated reliability co-processor that is tasked with monitoring the operation of the embedded system. As an embodiment of this design principle, this paper presents SPI-SNOOPER, a co-processor augmented hardware platform specifically designed for network monitoring. SPI-SNOOPER is completely cross-compatible with the TELOS wireless sensor nodes from an operational standpoint and is based on a novel hardware architecture that enables transparent snooping of the communication bus between the main processor and the radio of the wireless embedded system. The accompanying software architecture provides a powerful tool for monitoring, logging, and even controlling all the communication that takes place between the main processor and the radio. We present a rigorous evaluation of our prototype and demonstrate its utility using a variety of usage scenarios.

Categories and Subject Descriptors

C.2.1 [**Network Architecture and Design**]: Wireless communication, Distributed networks; C.2.3 [**Network Operations**]: Network monitoring

General Terms

Design, Experimentation, Reliability

Keywords

Wireless sensor networks, reliability, hardware-software co-design, co-processor, monitoring, snooping

*This was performed when the author was at Purdue University.

CODES+ISSS'12, October 7-12, 2012, Tampere, Finland.

1. INTRODUCTION

As networked embedded systems transition from lab-scale research prototypes to large-scale commercial deployments, providing reliable and dependable system operation becomes absolutely crucial to ensuring widespread adoption and commercial success. Due to the fact that sensor nodes operate in dynamic and unpredictable physical environments that cannot be recreated in a lab setting, it is now generally accepted that pre-deployment testing alone (using simulators, emulators, *etc.*) is not sufficient to guarantee reliability and that *in-situ monitoring of nodes after deployment is a must*. In accordance with this belief, a number of techniques have been proposed for post-deployment node-monitoring and control ([10, 13, 26, 27] are a few examples). However, all of them share the common trait that the node-monitoring functionality is implemented as software executing on the same embedded processor that the application executes on.

From a reliability perspective, this is a poor design choice due to several reasons. First, the monitoring software shares (and competes for) resources such as CPU cycles and memory space with the main application software, further depriving the application of these already-scarce resources. Second, the presence of this additional software can perturb the timing behavior of the application, possibly suppressing some subtle bugs, or causing a large slowdown in application execution. Third, such an architecture inherently has a single point of failure; *e.g.*, if the processor hangs or freezes (possibly due to a bug in the main application code), the monitoring software is rendered essentially useless.

We believe that a joint hardware-software approach is both required and ideal to address the problem of post-deployment node monitoring and control. Particularly, we advocate a rethinking of the hardware architecture of sensor nodes to include an additional (low-cost and low-power) component that we call the *reliability co-processor*, which is responsible for monitoring the operation of the sensor node. As we will show, logically and physically separating the monitoring functionality from both the application software and the main processor in this manner allows the monitoring to be conducted in a decoupled, non-intrusive, and transparent manner, enhancing reliability. This paper presents an embodiment of the above design principle in the form of SPI-SNOOPER, a co-processor augmented hardware architecture specifically designed for network monitoring. We select network monitoring because, as we will demonstrate, carefully monitoring the bi-directional communication activity in a sensor node can reveal a significant amount of information about its operation. However, our design (and more generally, any reliability co-processor augmented design) is certainly not limited to network monitoring alone and can be used for a variety of other scenarios as well. Specifically, this paper makes the following contributions:

- We present SPI-SNOOPER, the first wireless sensor node platform that integrates a reliability co-processor into its hardware architecture. SPI-SNOOPER provides many novel hardware features: (a) the reliability co-processor can passively monitor (*i.e.*, snoop) all the transactions on the Serial-Peripheral Interface (SPI) bus that connects the main processor and the radio on our sensor node. This enables the co-processor to have complete visibility into all the information transmitted and received by the node. The snooping is fully transparent in the sense that the main processor and radio are not aware that the bus is being monitored, (b) in addition to passively monitoring processor-radio communication, the co-processor also has the ability to disconnect the main processor from the SPI bus and take control of the bus. In addition to cutting off a processor that exhibits faulty behavior, this also allows the co-processor to independently transmit and receive packets to/from other nodes, (c) the reliability co-processor can also access other hardware components on the sensor node, (*e.g.*, read various sensors). This allows the co-processor to possibly (independently) validate the behavior of the main application software, and (d) the co-processor can reset/reboot the main processor if desired (*e.g.*, if it detects that the main processor has hung or is operating using corrupted state information).
- SPI-SNOOPER features a lightweight, yet powerful software architecture that allows it to exploit the unique hardware features in an accurate, reliable, and transparent manner.
- We design, implement, and evaluate several usage scenarios for the SPI-SNOOPER platform and demonstrate how it can be used to significantly enhance the level of post-deployment visibility and control that network designers have over remotely deployed wireless sensor nodes.

The remainder of this paper is organized as follows. Section 2 and 3 present the novel hardware and software architecture and implementation of SPI-SNOOPER respectively. Section 4 describes a rigorous evaluation that we performed on SPI-SNOOPER and the various usage scenarios that we implemented to demonstrate the utility and capability of the SPI-SNOOPER architecture. Section 5 describes related work and Section 6 concludes the paper with some discussion and avenues for future work.

2. SPI-SNOOPER HARDWARE DESIGN

As mentioned in Section 1, SPI-SNOOPER features a reliability co-processor augmented hardware architecture that enables it to monitor and control network communication in a manner that is transparent to the main-processor. This section describes the SPI-SNOOPER hardware architecture and its implementation in detail.

For compatibility reasons, we decided to base our hardware architecture around an existing wireless sensor node platform. Although there are numerous such platforms available [1], we picked the TELOS mote due to its widespread adoption and use in the wireless sensor network research community. Because, in the TELOS design, main processor and radio IC are placed separately and communicate with each other via SPI bus which is exposed as a trace on PCB, it is possible to physically tap into the bus without modifying the original hardware architecture of the TELOS mote. However, physical access to the SPI interface of an off-the-shelf TELOS mote seems impossible in practice due to the delicate and narrow traces on the compact form factor PCB. Therefore, we built our own PCB implementation of SPI-SNOOPER, which was based on the existing TELOS schematics [3], suitably enhanced with the co-processor and the additional logic required for monitoring and controlling the SPI bus that connects the main processor and the radio.

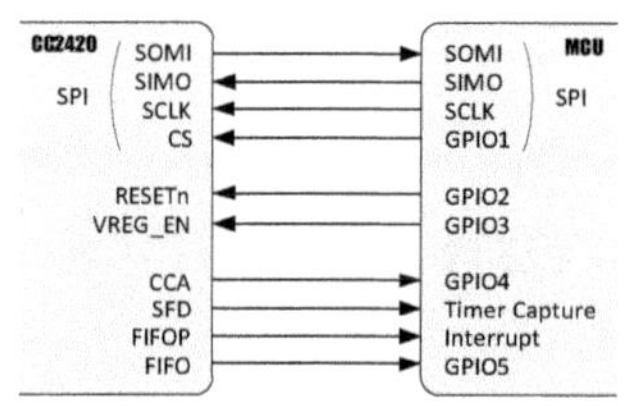

Figure 1: The interface between the CC2420 radio and the main processor on the TELOS mote. In all, ten lines are used.

2.1 The TELOS Mote

The TELOS [19] mote is a popular, open-source platform that features a Texas Instruments (TI) MSP430F1611 microcontroller as the main processor and an IEEE 802.15.4 compliant TI CC2420 radio transceiver. It also has on-board temperature, humidity, and light sensors and 1MB of external flash for data logging.

The hardware interface between the main processor and the radio on the TELOS is depicted in Figure 1. As shown in the figure, the main processor and the radio utilize a total of ten data and control lines for interfacing. They exchange data over an SPI bus using four pins (`SIMO`, `SOMI`, `SCLK`, and `CSn`). SPI is a full-duplex synchronous serial data link standard that supports communication between devices in a master/slave configuration. In the case of the TELOS mote, the processor acts as the master and initiates all bus transactions, while the CC2420 radio acts as the slave. Although the CC2420 radio cannot initiate bus transfers, it utilizes four other control lines (`SFD`, `CCA`, `FIFOP`, and `FIFO`) for reporting events that occurred in the radio. For example, `FIFO`, `FIFOP`, and `SFD` pins are used to notify the main processor of a received packet. In addition, the main processor can reset the radio and control the voltage regulator inside the radio via the `RESETn` and `VREG_EN` pins.

2.2 SPI-SNOOPER Hardware Architecture

As shown in Figure 2 and Figure 3, the SPI-SNOOPER hardware platform consists of four major components: main processor, reliability co-processor, radio, and crossover logic. The main processor is a TI MSP430F1611 that is connected to subsidiary components such as a data flash chip, serial ID chip, LEDs, switches, and sensors in an identical manner as the TELOS mote. For the radio, we utilize an off-the-shelf evaluation module (CC2420EMK from TI) in order to avoid the intricacies of sensitive radio-frequency circuit design. The crossover logic (described further in Section 2.5) is physically located between the main processor and the radio and splits the SPI bus connecting them into two segments. However, if the crossover logic is appropriately configured to simply act as a pass-through, the main processor gets connected to the radio module and becomes functionally identical to the TELOS platform. The dashed line in Figure 2 and Figure 3 represents the circuitry designed directly based on the TELOS mote's schematic [3] (except for a part of the crossover logic that also lies inside this area).

The rest of the SPI-SNOOPER board mainly houses the reliability co-processor and its related peripherals. The additional peripherals, including some LEDs, switches, USB, and JTAG, are mainly used for convenient programming, testing, and debugging of the reliability co-processor. The co-processor can also control the reset line of the main processor, which gives it the ability to reboot the main processor if desired. In addition, the co-processor can independently access the light sensors present on the board through wire traces branched from the sensors. The SPI-SNOOPER board use a nominal supply voltage of 3V and can be powered by either the MSP-FET430UIF [23], or two AA batteries, or the USB port similar to how the TELOS mote can be powered.

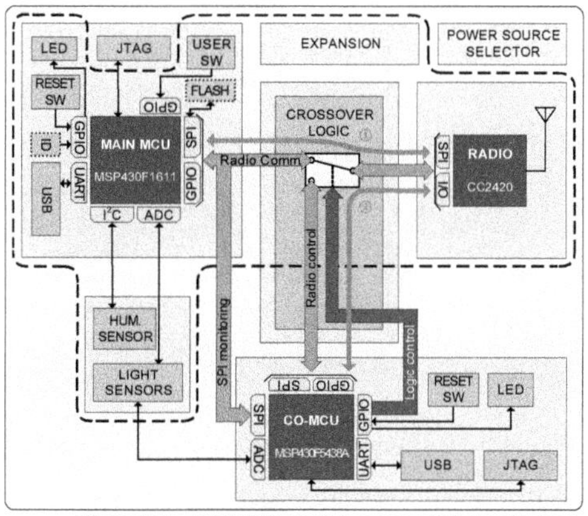

* Flash, serial ID and two 1.5V AA battery holders are placed at the back of the board

Figure 2: Block diagram of the SPI-SNOOPER platform.

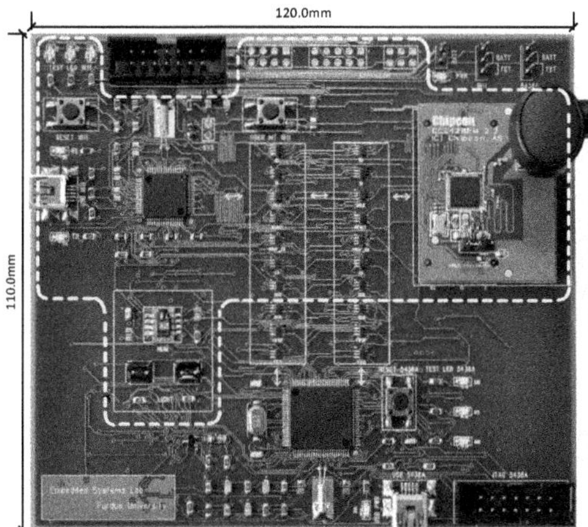

* Flash, serial ID and two 1.5V AA battery holders are placed at the back of the board

Figure 3: Image of an actual SPI-SNOOPER board. The dashed yellow border (roughly) encloses the components found on the TELOS mote.

2.3 Reliability co-processor: MSP430F5438A

The main considerations in selecting which microcontroller to use as the reliability co-processor are that it should be low-cost, low-power, provide sufficient computational resources, be easy to integrate into a larger design with minimal complexity, be easy to program, and have all the peripherals required to support the snooping of the SPI bus. After a survey of the several off-the-shelf MCUs, we selected the TI MSP430F5438A as the reliability co-processor for SPI-SNOOPER as it meets all the requirements above.

The MSP430F5438A is a 16-bit microcontroller that can run at a maximum frequency of 25MHz. It has three 16-bit timers, a 12-bit analog-to-digital (A/D) converter, up to four universal serial communication interfaces (USCI), and up to 87 general purpose IO pins [24]. The generous USCI and GPIO count are particularly crucial requirements, as we will see shortly. An added advantage of selecting this microcontroller is that it uses the same MSP430 instruction set architecture as the main processor on the TELOS, which eases programmer effort (*e.g.*, the same software toolchain can be used for both processors). It is also more power efficient than the main processor, *e.g.*, the MSP430F5438A consumes 350μA at 1MHz with 3V supply voltage in the active mode (AM), whereas the MSP430F1611 consumes 500μA under the same condition [24, 22]. The power consumption of SPI-SNOOPER will further be analyzed in section 4.1.5.

It should be noted that a microcontroller used as a reliability

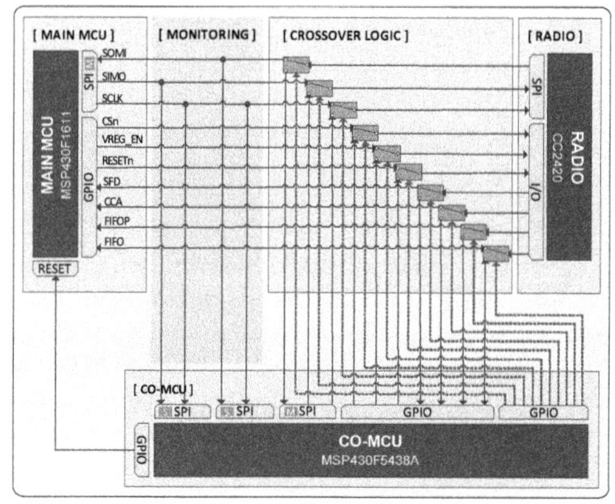

* Connections between 7 control signals (CSn through FIFO) and I/O of the CO-MCU are omitted due to space constraint

Figure 4: Monitoring and crossover logic configuration.

co-processor is not necessarily the MSP430F5438A. Although the MSP430F5438A was chosen due to its adequate performance, any microcontrollers which are able to run at over 20MHz would be a proper choice because the maximum SPI clock frequency of the CC2420 radio is 10MHz.

2.4 Monitoring the Processor-Radio SPI Bus

As mentioned earlier, one of the key features of the SPI-SNOOPER hardware is that it enables the monitoring of the bidirectional communication between the main processor and the radio by transparently snooping the SPI communication bus interface between the main processor and the radio. To do this, the SPI bus lines are forked to two independent SPI interfaces of the reliability co-processor, each of which is configured to act as an SPI slave. One SPI interface on the co-processor (let us call this interface `CoProc_SPI_1`) is dedicated to monitoring the `SIMO` line of the main SPI bus. `SIMO`, in this context, stands for Slave Input Master Output. As the name implies, this line contains a serial bitstream of the data that the main processor (*i.e.*, the bus master) sends to the radio (*i.e.*, the bus slave). This line is connected to the `SIMO` pin of `CoProc_SPI_1`. Now, at each transition of the SPI clock, `CoProc_SPI_1` also receives the data bit that was being sent to the radio. The second SPI interface on the co-processor (let us call this interface `CoProc_SPI_2`) is dedicated to monitoring the `SOMI` line of the main SPI bus. `SOMI`, in this context, stands for Slave Output Master Input. As the name implies, this line contains a serial bitstream of the data that the radio sends to the main processor. This line is connected to the `SIMO` pin of `CoProc_SPI_2`. Now, at each transition of the SPI clock, `CoProc_SPI_2` also receives the data bit that was being received by the main processor from the radio. The other control signals shown in Figure 1 are forked off and connected to GPIO pins of the co-processor. The area marked with "Monitoring" in Figure 4 shows how the processor-radio SPI bus is branched out to the co-processor. `CoProc_SPI_1`, `CoProc_SPI_2`, and the relevant GPIO pins on the co-processor are configured as interrupt-enabled peripherals, thereby allowing the the co-processor to efficiently monitor all the traffic on the SPI bus.

2.5 Crossover Logic

In addition to the bus monitoring ability described above, the reliability co-processor on the SPI-SNOOPER board also has the capability of disconnecting the main processor from the radio and assuming control of the SPI bus itself to communicate directly with the radio. The key component that enables this functionality is

Component	Count	Cost (USD)	
		Unit	Total
MCU	1	4.55	4.55
USB	1	2.95	2.95
SPDT Switch	10	0.13	1.30
PCB	1	8.50	8.50
Misc	-	-	5.00
Total	-	-	22.30

Table 1: Additional cost of one SPI-SNOOPER board (not including components found on the TELOS mote) in quantities of 1000.

the crossover logic on the SPI-SNOOPER board. The crossover logic consists of 10 SN74LVC1G3157 single-pole double-throw (SPDT) switches from TI. The SN74LVC1G3157 SPDT switch provides sufficient switching speed (typically 0.5ns) and operates using a wide supply voltage range (1.65V to 5.5V), while consuming 0.05μA (typical) for maintaining its status regardless of specific supply voltage level [12]. These SPDT switches are controlled by the reliability co-processor, as illustrated in Figure 4. Depending on the control input to the SPDT switches, the switches bridge the radio's SPI and control lines either to the main processor (this mode of operation is illustrated as *Route 1* in Figure 2) or to the co-processor (this mode of operation is illustrated as *Route 1* in Figure 2). The SPI port on the co-processor is configured to be in master mode so that it can initiate bus transfers to the radio if the radio is connected to it.

Note that the reliability co-processor can decide to re-configure the SPDT switches and take control of the radio under various conditions. One common scenario is for the co-processor to make this decision based on the outgoing/incoming data that it sees during passive SPI bus snooping. In such a scenario, perhaps the reception of a specific type of packet (*e.g.*, a special command from the base station) can trigger the co-processor to takeover the radio and communicate directly with the base station.

2.6 Cost Analysis

Table 1 shows the cost of the additional components on the SPI-SNOOPER board, except for the ones included in the TELOS platform, assuming the production of 1,000 boards.

Although SPI-SNOOPER employs additional peripherals such as LEDs and USB for debugging and testing purposes, the co-processor and SPDT switches are the only essential components required for SPI-SNOOPER functionality. According to TI's website, possibly because of the product lineup shift, the reliability co-processor MSP430F5438A costs \$4.55 per unit for 1,000 units while the main processor MSP430F1611 costs \$8.25 per unit for the same amount (as of March 2012). Thus, the added component cost of transforming a platform such as the TELOS mote in a co-processor augmented one is minimal, further justifying this approach.

3. SPI-SNOOPER SOFTWARE ARCHITECTURE

In order to maintain the transparent nature of SPI-SNOOPER, we make absolutely no modification to the software that runs on the main processor. The only information we need is the type of the operating system it runs. The reason is that different operating systems configure the SPI bus and the CC2420 radio differently (more on this in Section 3.3). Rather than porting an OS, we developed the software that runs on the co-processor from scratch in C to keep it lightweight and efficient. Figure 5 shows the key components of the SPI-SNOOPER software architecture.

SPI-SNOOPER can operate in two different modes:

- *Passive Mode:* In this mode, the co-processor listens to all SPI communication as a slave (Section 2.4) The main purpose of this mode is logging the communication that takes place through the SPI bus. In this mode, the co-processor can also access the sensors for checking the integrity of certain types of data that the main processor sends to other nodes. Based on certain types of events (*e.g.*, if the rate of transmission exceeds a threshold) or commands received from other nodes (*e.g.*, the base station), SPI-SNOOPER can switch to the *active mode*.
- *Active Mode:* In this mode, the co-processor works as a master of the SPI bus. It uses the crossover logic (Section 2.5) to assume the control of the bus and the radio. It can then use the CC2420 radio to communicate with other devices in the network. It can also route packets to maintain connectivity of the network, if necessary.

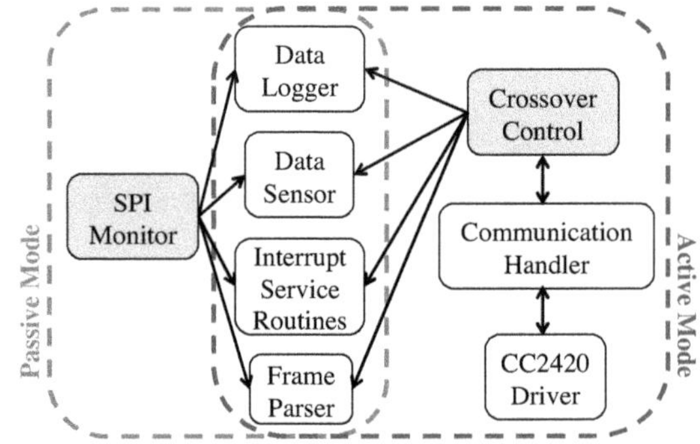

Figure 5: SPI-SNOOPER software architecture

Now, we describe some of the key components of the SPI-SNOOPER software as shown in Figure 5.

- *SPI Monitor:* In passive mode, the co-processor snoops into the SPI bus of the TELOS mote as a slave. The main purpose of this is to be able to identify and record the incoming and the outgoing packets in a mote. This module performs the necessary detection and recording. The details of the detection mechanism is presented in Section 3.2. It can make use of other components in the software stack as well. For example, it often uses the *Data Logger* to log the intercepted bytes to the flash or to the serial port.
- *Crossover Control:* The hardware in SPI-SNOOPER allows the co-processor to assume full control of the SPI bus in TELOS and operate as a master. This control may be necessary in certain situations. For example, if the co-processor suspects malicious behavior by the main processor. This module is used when SPI-SNOOPER operates in active mode. Like the SPI Monitor, it also uses other components of the SPI-SNOOPER software. For example, it may use the *Communication Handler* to communicate with other nodes in the network.
- *Communication Handler:* In active mode, the co-processor is able to and may need to communicate with other nodes. *Communication Handler* performs this task. In our implementation, a CC2420 driver (Figure 5) is provided for the low level communication. It also maintains a routing table if it has to route packets to other nodes.
- *Data Logger:* Sometimes it is expensive or impossible to send the data collected by the co-processor using the CC2420 radio, especially in passive mode. Data Logger uses the onboard flash storage in MSP430F5438A to store the data locally, mostly in meta-data format, which can be retrieved later (Section 4.2). It can also forward the logs to the serial port during run-time. In order to reduce the logging overhead (*e.g.*, write time to the flash), it often logs data in batches.

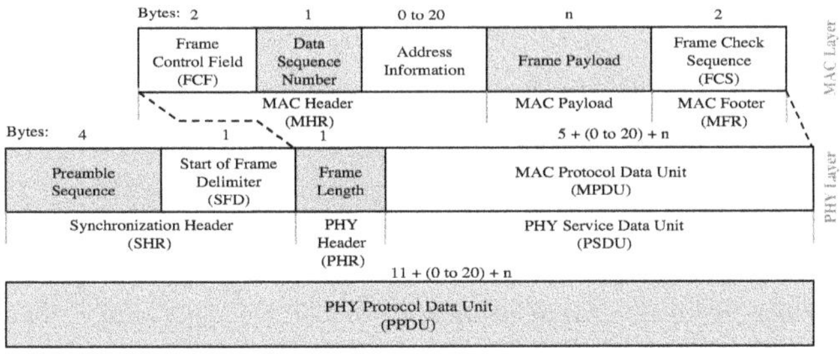

Figure 6: Schematic view of the IEEE 802.15.4 Frame Format

- *Data Sensor:* This module helps to use the onboard sensors in TELOS to be accessed by the co-processor. The samples collected from those sensors can be used to verify the integrity of the data that the main processor is sending (*e.g.*, locally collected light data).
- *Applications:* These are the actual applications (*e.g.*, network logger) that run on the co-processor. As marked with the dotted lines in the Figure 5, an application can work in both active mode and passive mode.

There are also some additional components in the SPI-SNOOPER software architecture, for example, *Frame Parser*, *Interrupt Service Routines*, *etc.* We implemented the SPI-SNOOPER software for TELOS motes running the Contiki [8] operating system.

3.1 Contiki

Contiki [8] is a lightweight operating system developed for resource limited networked embedded systems like wireless sensor networks (WSNs). Contiki contains two communication stacks: uIP [7] and Rime [9]. uIP is a TCP/IP stack for communication using IP and Rime is a lightweight communication stack designed for low-power radios.

3.2 Monitoring Network Communication

The co-processor in SPI-SNOOPER can listen to all communication between the main processor and the radio in TELOS motes. In this section, we will describe how we identify incoming or outgoing packets within the co-processor in SPI-SNOOPER when the main processor is running Contiki.

Detecting Incoming Packets:

Among the pins used for interfacing CC2420 (see section 2.1), The pin `FIFOP` is used to interrupt the microcontroller when a complete frame has been received. As soon as this interrupt is received, co-processor starts recording the bytes that are passed from CC2420 to the main processor (*i.e.*, from `SOMI` in CC2420 to `SOMI` in the main processor). This recording continues until the receive buffer at CC2420 is empty, which can be identified by monitoring the `FIFO` pin. Even though the `FIFOP` pin generated the interrupt when the frame was received at the radio, the main processor may delay the receiving process by few cycles. As a result, just by observing the status of those two pins, we cannot deterministically identify the presence of a packet in the SPI bus. When the processor is ready to receive a packet, it writes `CC2420_RXFIFO | 0x40` (*i.e.*, `0x7F`) to the SPI bus. Henceforth, we refer to this byte as `START_READING`. As a result, whenever the co-processor detects a packet has arrived at the radio, it starts tracking the bytes that are being sent by the main processor. Location of the `START_READING` byte helps us to reliably identify the exact starting point of an incoming packet. Figure 7 shows an example sequence of bytes read by the main processor running Contiki while receiving a packet. As shown there, a packet is read in three parts: the length (red), the payload (green) and the footer (blue). Reading of each part is initiated by sending the `START_READING` byte to the radio.

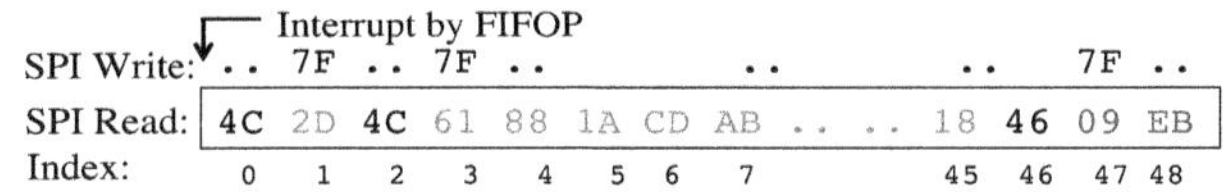

Figure 7: Example of a byte sequence read from the SPI bus while receiving a packet

Detecting Outgoing Packets:

In the previous section, we have shown how two of the pins in CC2420, namely `FIFOP` and `FIFO`, help us to recognize any incoming packets. But for outgoing packets, pins in CC2420 are not very helpful since their statuses are meaningful only when data is available in the radio buffer. That is why we continuously record the bytes written to the SPI bus by the main processor. Before we explain how we detect outgoing packet transmission by monitoring the SPI bus, it is important to understand the high level overview of how Contiki sends a packet using the CC2420 radio. The sending process takes place in two steps: *Prepare* and *Transmit*. During *Prepare*, the MAC header and the MAC payload (Figure 6) are loaded to the radio's transmit buffer. The MAC footer is added by the radio hardware itself. In Contiki, at the beginning of *Prepare*, the processor sends a strobe signal (`CC2420_SFLUSHTX` or `0x09`) to the radio. After that, the packet is sent in two steps: *1)* the frame length (one byte) and *2)* MAC header and the MAC payload (Figure 6). If CRC check is enabled, a two bytes checksum value of the payload is also sent in a third step. Before each step, the address (`CC2420_TXFIFO` or `0x3E`) of the CC2420 transfer buffer is written to the SPI bus. From this, it is easy to recognize that each packet loading should start with the following byte pattern: `0x09 0x3E frame_length 0x3E`. We continuously monitor the outgoing byte stream and as soon as we identify the above pattern, we conclude it as the beginning of a new packet sending process. However, detecting a packet while it was being loaded to the radio's transmit buffer does not indicate that the packet was actually sent from the radio. The actual sending process takes place during the next step: *Transmit*.

During *Transmit*, the processor instructs the radio to start the actual transmission, which may or may not be successful based of the status of the radio. The sequence of bytes that are written to the SPI bus during this phase depends on the configuration of the radio. If the radio is configured to send a packet with *clear channel assessment (CCA)*, the main processor sends two strobe signals: `CC2420_SRXON` (`0x03`) and `CC2420_STXONCCA` (`0x05`). If CCA is not enabled, it only sends `CC2420_STXON` (`0x04`). An arbitrary number of `CC2420_SNOP`s (`0x00`) may also be sent in between the aforementioned signals. To resend an already loaded packet (*e.g.*, if re-transmission is enabled), the processor just needs to issue the above strobe signals again. Thus, multiple *Transmit* steps may follow a single *Prepare* step. After detecting a packet during *Prepare*, SPI-SNOOPER also records the number of times the packet was attempted to send by recording the signals transmitted during one or more occurrences of *Transmit*. Figure 8 shows the sequence of bytes that was sent through the SPI bus while transmitting a packet twice. Please note that the payload length is 43 even though the frame length is 45 (2D in hex). This is because the CC2420 hardware adds two bytes of Frame Control Sequence (Figure 6) before sending a packet.

3.3 SPI-SNOOPER in Other Operating Systems

Fundamentally, the SPI-SNOOPER hardware is capable of working in any sensor network OS, not only Contiki (*e.g.*, TinyOS [4]). But

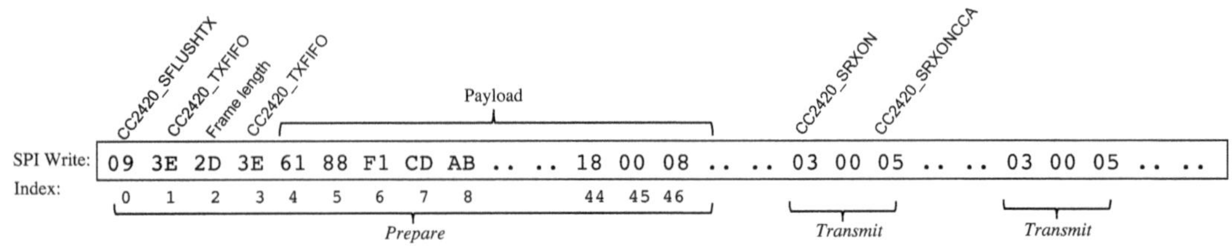

Figure 8: Example of a byte sequence written to the SPI bus while sending a packet

Program	Memory Usage (bytes)	
	RAM	ROM
Contiki (Hello World)	5,396	23,254
monitoring + no logging + no crossover	617	2,448
monitoring + flash logging + no crossover	905	3,124
monitoring + serial logging + no crossover	903	3,180
monitoring + serial logging + crossover	1,210	5,084

Table 2: Memory footprint of Spi-Snooper

the same software may not be compatible across different types of operating systems. The reason is that different operating systems handle CC2420 radio communication differently. One example is how incoming packets are handled in TinyOS, where it follows a different configuration than Contiki. In Section 3.2, we explained how we detect incoming packets using the interrupts generated by the `FIFOP` pin in CC2420. By default, `FIFOP` is an active high pin. But in TinyOS, it is configured to be an active low pin. Thus, the same detection mechanism will not work for TinyOS. We can overcome such issues by modifying the detection mechanisms in Spi-Snooper software and without modifying anything in the underlying hardware. This is true for other operating systems as well. In this paper, we demonstrate Spi-Snooper using the Contiki operating system.

4. EVALUATION

We evaluated Spi-Snooper using a set of microbenchmarking experiments and a set of applications. The accuracy of the methods that Spi-Snooper uses to detect incoming and outgoing packets along with some other things (*e.g.*, sensing, logging, *etc.*) is shown using these experiments. We demonstrate four use cases where Spi-Snooper can be used for transparent monitoring and control of the network communication. The first experiment demonstrates how network communication can be logged and later be used using Spi-Snooper. The second application shows that with prior knowledge of the application packets, Spi-Snooper can verify the integrity of the sensor readings that are being sent from a mote. In our third application, we use Spi-Snooper to detect abnormal behavior of the main processor and take control of the SPI bus to maintain network connectivity. Finally, the fourth example demonstrates how Spi-Snooper can open up an emergency backdoor in a mote for communicating with others in the network. All our motes were Telos with Contiki 2.5 installed. We used the Rime communication stack [9] for network communication.

4.1 Microbenchmarking

The experiments that were used to microbenchmark Spi-Snooper are presented in this section.

4.1.1 *Memory Footprint of* Spi-Snooper

Table 2 shows the memory footprint of Spi-Snooper software in different configurations. With all the features enabled (*e.g.*, crossover logic, sensing) and the ability to log using the serial port, the Spi-Snooper software only incurs around 5KB of ROM usage. The RAM footprint also is very small. For the sake of comparison, we also included the memory usage of a basic Contiki program compiled using the default configuration.

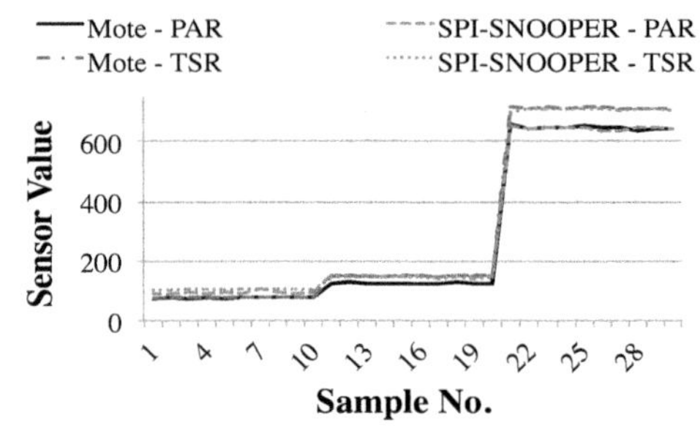

Figure 9: Comparison of the samples collected from the light sensors (PAR and TSR) by Spi-Snooper and the associated mote

4.1.2 *Accuracy of Intercepting Communication*

Since consecutive bytes of a packet are sent using the SPI bus at a fast speed (*e.g.*, CC2420 supports up to 10MHz SPI clock speed), the co-processor has to operate faster than this speed. This is because it not only has to be able to detect each individual bytes, but it may also have to do some additional processing (*e.g.*, storing the data) between consecutive bytes. Hence, the co-processor is set to operate in a fully interrupt-driven manner while running at maximum speed (25MHz).

We used two Telos motes broadcasting 802.15.4 packets. Most of the radio settings were left to the defaults (*e.g.*, transmission power and channel) except we used `nullrdc` for the radio duty cycling (RDC) layer in order to avoid packet re-transmissions. In future experiments, we will show that Spi-Snooper also works properly with other RDC layer protocols, such as, `contikimac`. In the first set of experiments, we used the Telos mote that was being monitored by Spi-Snooper for periodically broadcasting packets that contained the word `Hello`. We varied the packet-sending rate from 1-packet/10 seconds to 128 packets/second. In all cases, we were able to detect 100% of the packets as they were being sent. We also varied the packet sizes by changing the payload and achieved the same level of accuracy. In our next set of experiments, we used the other Telos mote to broadcast similar packets while leaving the mote equipped with Spi-Snooper in receive-only mode. We varied the transmission rates similarly and in all cases, we were able to detect all the packets that were received by the mote. In all experiments, we logged the entire packet to the flash along with some additional information (more on this in the next section). The accuracy was determined in a post-processing phase, where we read the logs and checked the data sequence numbers of the packets.

4.1.3 *Accuracy of Sensing by* Spi-Snooper

Telos contains two optional light sensors: `PHOTOSYNTHETIC` (PAR) and `TOTAL_SOLAR` (TSR). In our hardware design, we allow Spi-Snooper to access the sensors in a transparent way. Since, both

Byte #:	1	2-43	44-47	48
	Length	MAC Protocol Data Unit	Direction and Time Stamp	Frequency

(a) Log format for logging the entire contents of a packet

Byte #:	1	2	3	4-7	8
	Length	Source	Destination	Direction and Time Stamp	Frequency

(b) Log format for logging the metadata of a packet

Figure 10: Possible log formats in SPI-SNOOPER

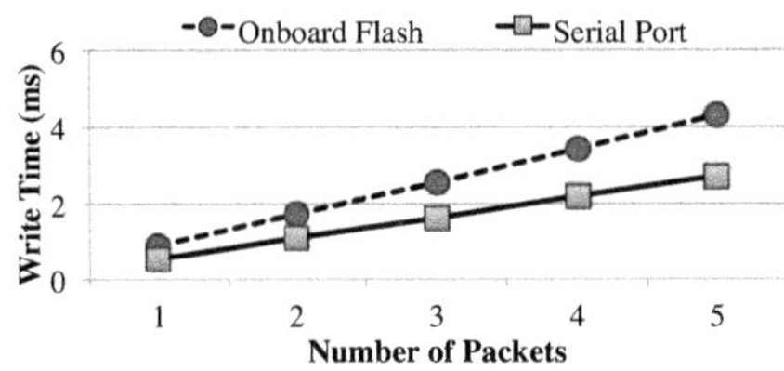

Figure 11: Time needed to log communication to flash and serial port

the main processor and SPI-SNOOPER use the same physical sensors, it is important to verify that the readings they provide are similar and accurate. Figure 9 shows samples collected in three different light conditions by the main processor and SPI-SNOOPER simultaneously (1-sample/5 seconds). As can be seen in the figure, values collected by both of them were similar. Later on, we also show that the values collected by the mote equipped with SPI-SNOOPER are similar to those collected by the regular motes (Section 4.3).

4.1.4 Overhead of Logging in SPI-SNOOPER

As we mentioned earlier, SPI-SNOOPER allows us to log the monitored information to the onboard flash of the co-processor. While data is being written to the flash, all interrupts are disabled. In order to reduce the interruption, we write logs in batches. For example, we logged the entire packet contents for the experiments in Section 4.1.2 in batches of 5 logs. Figure 10(a) shows the format of a log entry used in our experiments. Each log entry was 48 bytes long. Besides containing the MAC protocol data unit of a packet (Figure 6), it also contained the length, direction (incoming or outgoing) and timestamp of the packet. The first bit of byte 44 was used to indicate the direction of a packet. Moreover, we also recorded the number of times a packet was transmitted (for outgoing packets) in the last byte of a log entry. This is useful when re-transmissions are enabled. To make the flash writing process efficient, we used the *Block Write* mode [2]. If we have 256K of flash storage available for logging, we can store 5,461 logs using the format shown in Figure 10(a). If we use the more compact format shown in Figure 10(b), we can store up to 32,768 logs.

Figure 11 shows the time needed to perform the log writing operation. As the number of packets increases in a batch, the time required also increases linearly, as shown in the figure. For the sake of comparison, it also shows the timer required to forward logs to the serial port.

4.1.5 Power consumption

As we mentioned, the SPI-SNOOPER board also contains components specific to a TELOS mote. Hence, it is difficult to measure the power consumption of only the components that are required for the co-processor to function properly. So, we measured the power consumption of an off-the-shelf TELOS mote and a SPI-SNOOPER board separately. For both cases, the main processor was running the same application that broadcasts 10 packets for 0.5 seconds. Except for that, all the functionality for the SPI-SNOOPER board, such as monitoring and logging, was enabled. As can be seen in the figure 13, the average current consumption was around 18.15 mA for a regular TELOS mote and around 22.75mA for the SPI-SNOOPER board. In all cases, the supply voltage was 3.0 V. It should be noted that the additional current consumption was not only due to the co-processor, but also due to other peripherals such as a number of LEDs and USB ports, which were placed on the SPI-SNOOPER prototype board for testing and debugging convenience. It is possible to reduce the overall power consumption of the SPI-SNOOPER board significantly by removing the non-essential components and putting the co-processor in a low power mode whenever the main processor is in low power mode.

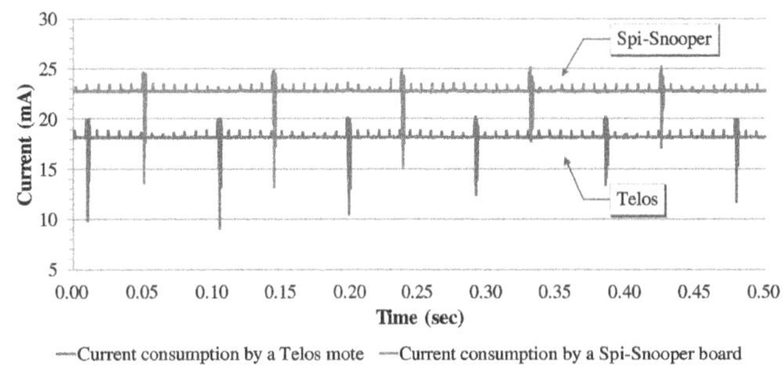

Figure 13: Current consumption by TELOS and SPI-SNOOPER

4.2 Logging Network Communication

We have already shown how SPI-SNOOPER can be used to log SPI bus communication using the onboard flash or serial port. In this experiment, we show how this information can later be used for analyzing the communication that took place in a mote. We used a network topology similar to the one shown in Figure 12(a) except that the base station (node 1) was equipped with SPI-SNOOPER. The TELOS motes were sending packets to the base station using the mesh routing protocol with the Rime communication stack. Packets were being sent periodically with a random interval of 4 – 6 seconds. We also had `contikimac` in the RDC layer with packet acknowledgements and re-transmissions enabled. Each data packet and acknowledgement packet had a size of 45 bytes and 5 bytes respectively (physical layer). Whenever the base station received a packet, it sent a packet back to the original sender. We logged the entire contents of all incoming and outgoing packets to the flash using the format shown in Figure 10(a). Later on, we retrieved the stored logs from the flash and re-constructed the trace of incoming and outgoing packets to and from node 1. Figure 14(a) shows the timeline for all the packets received. This includes both the data packets and the acknowledgements. We constructed this timeline from the timestamps generated by SPI-SNOOPER. Figure 14(b) shows similar traces for the outgoing packets. A point in the graph means an attempt to send a packet that is already in the buffer of the radio was made (Section 3.2). Note that only outgoing data packets are shown since the radio was configured to send acknowledgements for incoming packets automatically. Since re-transmissions were enabled, multiple attempts were made to send a packet until acknowledgements were received or timeouts occurred. Figure 14(c) shows the frequency of such attempts to send each packet from the base station.

In Figure 15, we show a trace produced from the logs generated by SPI-SNOOPER, where two motes were broadcasting packets with extremely high frequency (64 packets/second). Only one mote was equipped with SPI-SNOOPER. Each packet was of size 21 bytes in the physical layer. Since each log was time stamped by SPI-SNOOPER,

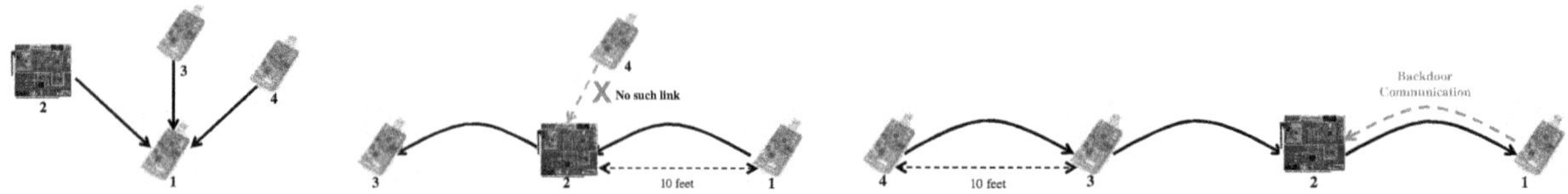

(a) Integrity verification (b) Handling abnormal behavior (c) Providing an emergency backdoor

Figure 12: Topologies used for the experiments

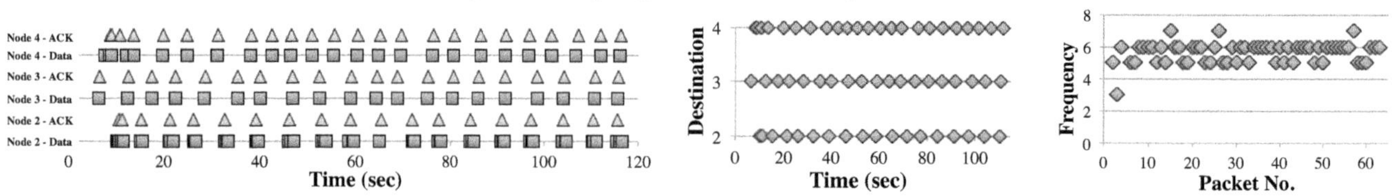

(a) Incoming data packets and acknowledgements (b) Outgoing data packets (c) Frequency of outgoing packets

Figure 14: Trace of incoming and outgoing packets generated from the logs collected by Spi-Snooper

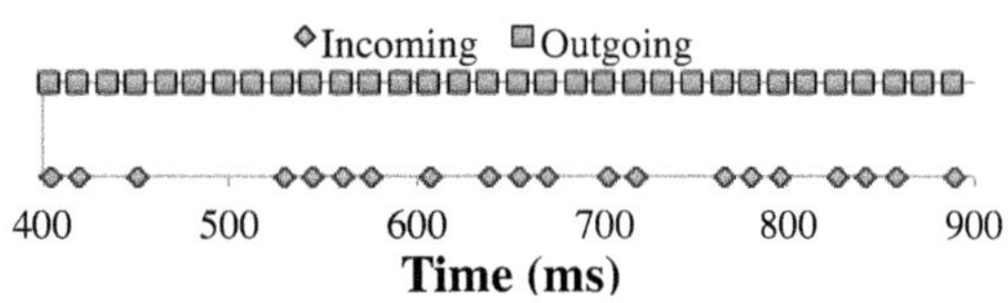

Figure 15: Trace generated from logs generated by Spi-Snooper for high frequency packet transmission between two nodes

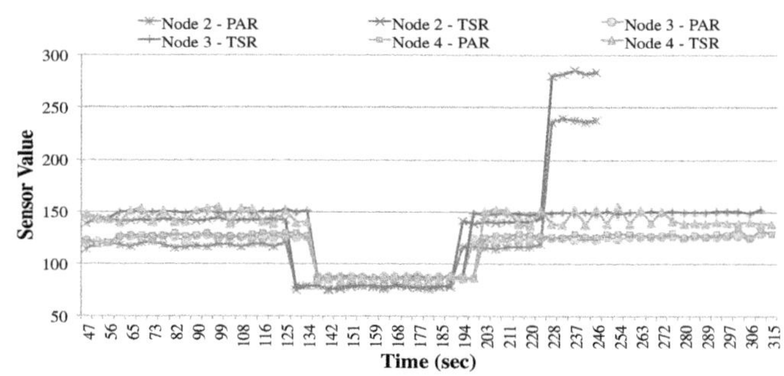

Figure 16: Average light intensity values received by the base station in the experiment described in Section 4.3

we were able to draw this timeline with this high resolution. The figure shows that the number of incoming packets was less than the number of outgoing transmission attempts. The reason was that many packets did not arrive due to high rate of collision. These experiments demonstrate how low-level details about communication can be gathered because of the level of visibility Spi-Snooper provides which otherwise would have been difficult to generate.

4.3 Integrity Verification

With prior knowledge of the application data packets, Spi-Snooper can be used to verify the integrity of the sent data. For this experiment, we used the setup shown in Figure 12(a). Motes were running `sky-collect`, a program that comes with the standard Contiki distribution. Motes running this program periodically collect some sensor data (*e.g.*, light, temperature, *etc.*) and forward them to the base station (node 1) using a tree routing protocol. In this experiment, we set the period to 4 – 6 seconds and used `nullmac` in the RDC layer. Each application packet was of size 101 bytes (physical layer). As we have mentioned earlier, Spi-Snooper has access to the two light sensors (PAR and TSR) present in a Telos mote. In this experiment, we equipped node 2 with Spi-Snooper. Hence, Spi-Snooper could analyze the outgoing packets of node 2; check the values of the light sensors independently by accessing the same set of sensors that the mote used to collect the values. We maintained a history (in this case, the last 5 values for each sensor) of the recently sent values and compared them with the values that were collected by Spi-Snooper. If all values sent within a window differed by more than 20% from their corresponding values collected by Spi-Snooper, we concluded that the Telos was malfunctioning and we disconnected it from the radio. We assumed that the sensors were working properly. To emulate this behavior, we intentionally programmed node 2 in such a way that after some time, it started multiplying the collected values by 2 before sending them. As can be seen in Figure 16, motes started sending the sensed values for the two light sensors in normal indoor light condition. We kept our lights off for the time period of 125 – 190 second. The sensed values from all motes in Figure 16 also corroborate that. Around the 220th second, mote 2 started sending values that were significantly higher than the other motes even though all motes were nearby. Spi-Snooper was able to determine that these values were different than the actual sensor values. After some time, the main processor in node 2 was disconnected from the radio. In the next experiment, we show how Spi-Snooper can keep the communication alive with other motes in the network even after the main processor is disconnected. In this case, we could have used Spi-Snooper to keep sending sensor values even after detecting the erroneous readings from the main processor.

4.4 Handling Abnormal Behavior

Spi-Snooper can analyze incoming and outgoing packets and determine certain types of malicious/buggy activities by the main processor. We demonstrate one such example here. The experimental setup is shown in Figure 12(b). Node 1 was sending packets to node 3 every 4 – 6 seconds using mesh routing protocol from the Rime communication stack. Since there was no direct connection between them, packets were being routed through node 2, which was equipped with Spi-Snooper. As shown in Figure 17, after some time node 3 started receiving packets originating from node 4. However, there were no incoming packets from node 4 to node 2. Hence, this could be due to a bug in node 2 or a malicious behavior (*e.g.*, a wormhole attack) by that node. Spi-Snooper noticed that no packets were received by node 2 from node 4, but still it was forwarding packets that seemed to have originated from there. After monitoring this behavior for some time (in this case, after detecting 5 such incidents), it took control of the SPI bus using the

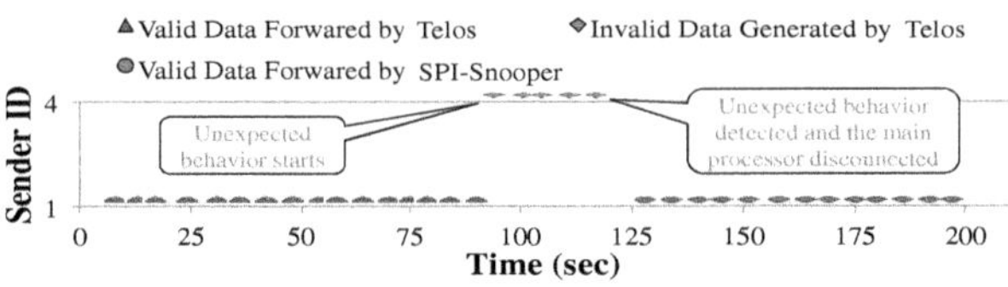

Figure 17: Packets received by node 3 in the Figure 12(b)

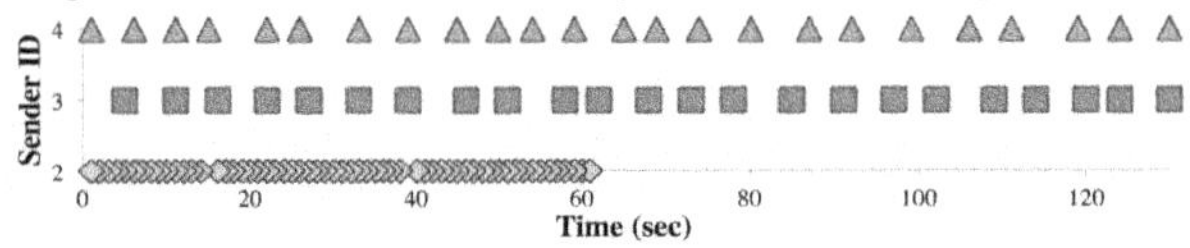

Figure 18: Packets received at the base station in Figure 12(c)

crossover logic (Section 2.5). However, to maintain connectivity of the network, the co-processor kept forwarding the packets that were being received by the radio in node 2 and was not addressed to itself. Before forwarding, the sender address was changed to node 2. Also, it kept a history of packet forwarding by the main processor. Hence, it had a similar routing table available that was used to set the immediate destination address of a packet. Some other information (*e.g.*, hop count) were updated as well. For this, SPI-SNOOPER needed to know what RDC layer protocols were being used in the network as different protocols use different MAC payload header formats. In this case, we used `nullrdc`. Thus, SPI-SNOOPER not only prevented other nodes from the malicious or buggy activity of node 2, but also kept providing services that were essential to maintain the connectivity of the network. Figure 17 shows how node 3 kept receiving packets from node 1 without any interruption. This experiment demonstrates how SPI-SNOOPER can provide emergency services even when the main processor is unavailable or disconnected.

4.5 Providing an Emergency Backdoor

SPI-SNOOPER provides a convenient way to communicate with itself from the rest of the network. Such a backdoor allows other motes, for example, the base station, to send commands or queries to SPI-SNOOPER. We demonstrate one such use case here. We used the network topology in Figure 12(c). As shown there, motes were sending packets to the base station (node 1) using the mesh routing protocol from the Rime communication stack. We used `nullrdc` for the RDC layer. Node 2 was equipped with SPI-SNOOPER. As shown in Figure 18, packets from mote 3 and 4 were being sent with a period of 4 – 6 seconds. Node 2 was sending packet at a much faster rate (1 packet/second). After about a minute, the base station decided not to receive any packet from node 2. It then sent an instruction to disconnect the main processor in node 2 but to keep forwarding packets from the other motes just like the previous example. SPI-SNOOPER responded to the request by disconnecting the main processor from the radio at node 2. As shown in the figure, no more packets from node 2 were delivered to the base station. But, the base station still kept receiving packets from the other motes. We used the regular application packet to send the "disconnect and forward" instruction to SPI-SNOOPER. However, we may have multiple nodes equipped with SPI-SNOOPER. To address the right SPI-SNOOPER in the right mote, we set the original source address of the application packet containing the instruction to the address of the target mote and added an offset to this. For example, in this case, we added 100. SPI-SNOOPER at node 2 detected a packet coming from 102 and understood that it was a packet addressed to itself containing some instructions from the base station. The assumption was that there was no node in the network with the address 102. We can set the offset to a large number to ensure this. Thus, SPI-SNOOPER provided a backdoor entry to node 2 for the base station. In this approach, the application at node 2 also received the command packet since it was a regular application packet. For communicating using Rime, this is the best way to avoid unnecessary flooding in the network. We can encrypt the packets that contain such commands so that the application running at the mote will not be able to understand the actual meaning of the packet. We can further enhance the solution by using uIP [7] and use a dedicated port number for such communications. That way, the regular applications will not receive these packets anymore.

5. RELATED WORK

The concept of using co-processors or watchdog processors has been prevalent in the traditional computers and high-performance systems for decades [18, 17, 14]. Most of the time, they are used to provide more efficiency (*e.g.*, a graphics co-processor) or an additional layer of security (*e.g.*, a cryptographic co-processor) to the main processor(s). [16] is a survey of concurrent system-level error detection techniques using a watchdog processor in the context of traditional PC based systems. None of these solutions were designed to work with networked embedded systems like WSNs. There are few works that are applicable for WSNs. FlashBox [6] is a hybrid hardware-software solution where an additional MCU is used to log the interrupts that take place in the main processor. For logging to work, applications have to be compiled using a modified version of `avr-gcc`. A more recent work, Aveksha [21], is another hardware-software approach that allows tmonitoring and recording of the internal state of the processor in TELOS motes using the on-chip debug module. However, unlike Aveksha, which only monitors and records the internal states of the processor, SPI-SNOOPER not only passively monitors network communication but can also actively monitor the health status of other components of the node using the information gathered through network monitoring, sensor data integrity checking, *etc.*, to enable reliable and robust operation.

There are few other works [20, 25, 15, 5] that aim to record or log certain types of events at run time and replay them later on. Most of them are either software-only approaches or require pre- or post-processing of the gathered execution trace. For example, LiveNet [10] suggested the concept of a Deployment Support Network (DSN), where the authors just connected two individual TELOS nodes (target node and monitoring node) via wires in order to communicate and implicitly exchange certain data of interest by using software routines that reside on both the target node and the monitoring node. Therefore, LiveNet is not transparent and efficient in terms of energy and cost.

Our solution, SPI-SNOOPER, uses a co-processor based design that enables monitoring the SPI bus of resource constrained wireless sensor devices. Moreover, using the crossover logic, SPI-SNOOPER enables the co-processor to assume the control of the network communication, thus providing reliability and fault tolerance.

6. CONCLUSIONS AND FUTURE WORK

In this paper, we have presented SPI-SNOOPER, a co-processor augmented hardware-software approach that can monitor and control the SPI bus communication between the main processor and the radio in a mote. We have designed and developed a prototype for TELOS [19] motes running Contiki [8] and demonstrated how it works in the real world. In principle, it is not confined to TELOS and applicable to any other wireless sensor node platforms regardless of the type of the main processor because the proposed scheme is nothing to do with certain type of the main processor and only related to the exposedness of SPI bus between the processor and the radio. In addition, it works with any other operating systems that uses SPI bus for communication between the main processor and the radio. SPI-SNOOPER works in a transparent manner without the knowledge of the processor or applications that run on the accompanying mote. It provides an added layer of in-situ visibility, which enables fine-grained monitoring of the behavior of a mote from the point of view of network communication. Such visibilities are crucial for successful deployment and debugging of networked embedded systems like WSNs. In our experiments, we have shown that SPI-SNOOPER can detect incoming and outgoing packets with 100% accuracy even when communication takes place at a very high rate. With prior knowledge of the application packets, SPI-SNOOPER is capable of verifying the integrity of outgoing packets containing certain types of data (*e.g.*, sensor readings), thanks to its ability to access the TELOS sensors independently. We have also demonstrated how SPI-SNOOPER can provide emergency services, for example, packet forwarding, in the event when the main processor needs to be disconnected. However, there are still scopes of improvement in our design. We have shown how the snooped information can be logged using the 256KB onboard flash of the MSP430F5438A processor. We are exploring the option of adding an additional external and removable flash with much higher capacity. This will significantly increase the flexibility of using the logging feature of SPI-SNOOPER. We are also working on adding a new feature to SPI-SNOOPER, which will allow us to re-program the associated mote using a golden image or a firmware received over-the-air. This will be extremely useful to perform recovery and diagnosis, if necessary. In our current implementation, the co-processor in SPI-SNOOPER has access to the two light sensors present in TELOS. In future, we would like to add the capability of monitoring and accessing other types of sensors and peripherals. We have shown how SPI-SNOOPER can take control of the SPI bus and keep communicating with the other motes in the network. In addition to this, we are interested in emulating the behavior of a radio using the co-processor. This will allow us to implement a true traffic gatekeeping solution like [11], but with more transparency and no dependency on the main processor of the mote.

7. ACKNOWLEDGMENTS

This work was supported in part by the National Science Foundation (NSF) under grants CNS-0953468 and ECCS-0925851.

8. REFERENCES

[1] List of wireless sensor nodes (Wikipedia). http://en.wikipedia.org/wiki/List_of_wireless_sensor_nodes.

[2] MSP430x5xx/MSP430x6xx Family User's Guide. Texas Instruments.

[3] Telos (Rev. B) Schematics. http://webs.cs.berkeley.edu/tos/hardware/telos/telos-revb-2004-09-27.pdf.

[4] TinyOS. http://www.tinyos.net.

[5] B. Chen, G. Peterson, G. Mainland, and M. Welsh. Livenet: Using passive monitoring to reconstruct sensor network dynamics. *Distributed Computing in Sensor Systems*, pages 79–98, 2008.

[6] S. Choudhuri and T. Givargis. FlashBox: a system for logging non-deterministic events in deployed embedded systems. In *SAC*, pages 1676–1682, 2009.

[7] A. Dunkels. Full TCP/IP for 8 Bit Architectures. In *MobiSys*, May 2003.

[8] A. Dunkels, B. Gronvall, and T. Voigt. Contiki-a lightweight and flexible operating system for tiny networked sensors. In *EmNets '04*, 2004.

[9] A. Dunkels, F. Österlind, and Z. He. An adaptive communication architecture for wireless sensor networks. In *SenSys*, pages 335–349, 2007.

[10] M. Dyer, J. Beutel, T. Kalt, P. Oehen, L. Thiele, K. Martin, and P. Blum. Deployment support network. *Wireless Sensor Networks*, pages 195–211, 2007.

[11] M. Hossain and V. Raghunathan. Aegis: A lightweight firewall for wireless sensor networks. In *DCOSS*, pages 258–272, 2010.

[12] T. Instruments. SN74LVC1G3157; Single- Pole Double-Throw Analog Switch (Rev. G). http://www.ti.com/lit/ds/symlink/sn74lvc1g3157.pdf, 2008.

[13] N. Kothari, K. Nagaraja, V. Raghunathan, F. Sultan, and S. Chakradhar. HERMES: A Software Architecture for Visibility and Control in Wireless Sensor Network Deployments. In *IPSN*, pages 395–406, 2008.

[14] D. Lu. Watchdog processors and structural integrity checking. *IEEE Transactions on Computers*, 100(7):681–685, 1982.

[15] L. Luo, T. He, G. Zhou, L. Gu, T. Abdelzaher, and J. Stankovic. Achieving repeatability of asynchronous events in wireless sensor networks with envirolog. In *INFOCOM*, pages 1–14, 2006.

[16] A. Mahmood and E. McCluskey. Concurrent error detection using watchdog processors– a survey. *IEEE Transactions on Computers*, pages 160–174, 1988.

[17] I. Majzik, W. Hohl, A. Pataricza, and V. Sieh. Multiprocessor checking using watchdog processors. *Computer Systems Science and Engineering*, 11(5):301–310, 1996.

[18] A. Pataricza, I. Majzik, W. Hohl, and J. Hönig. Watchdog processors in parallel systems. *Microprocessing and Microprogramming*, 39(2-5):69–74, 1993.

[19] J. Polastre, R. Szewczyk, and D. Culler. Telos: enabling ultra-low power wireless research. In *IPSN*, pages 48–es, 2005.

[20] V. Sundaram, P. Eugster, and X. Zhang. Efficient diagnostic tracing for wireless sensor networks. In *SenSys*, pages 169–182, 2010.

[21] M. Tancreti, M. S. Hossain, S. Bagchi, and V. Raghunathan. Aveksha: A hardware-software approach for non-intrusive tracing and profiling of wireless embedded systems. In *SenSys*, 2011.

[22] Texas Instruments. MSP430F15x, MSP430F16x, MSP430F161x Mixed Signal Microcontroller (Rev. G) . http://www.ti.com/lit/ds/symlink/msp430f1611.pdf.

[23] Texas Instruments. MSP430 Hardware Tools User's Guide. http://www.ti.com/lit/ug/slau278h/slau278h.pdf, 2010.

[24] Texas Instruments. MSP430F543xA, MSP430F541xA Mixed Signal Microcontroller (Rev. B). http://www.ti.com/lit/ds/symlink/msp430f5438a.pdf, 2010.

[25] H. Thane, D. Sundmark, J. Huselius, and A. Pettersson. Replay debugging of real-time systems using time machines. In *IPDPS*, pages 8–pp. IEEE, 2003.

[26] K. Whitehouse and et al. Marionette: Using RPC for Interactive Development and Debugging of Wireless Embedded Networks. In *IPSN*, 2006.

[27] J. Yang, M. Soffa, L. Selavo, and K. Whitehouse. Clairvoyant: a comprehensive source-level debugger for wireless sensor networks. In *SenSys*, pages 189–203, 2007.

A Novel NoC–Based Design for Fault-Tolerance of Last-Level Caches in CMPs

Abbas BanaiyanMofrad, Nikil Dutt
Center for Embedded Computer Systems
University of California, Irvine
Irvine, CA, USA
{abanaiya, dutt}@uci.edu

Gustavo Girão
Federal University of Rio Grande do Sul
Institute of Informatics
Porto Alegre, Brazil
ggbsilva@inf.ufrgs.br

ABSTRACT

Advances in technology scaling, coupled with aggressive voltage scaling results in significant reliability challenges for emerging Chip Multiprocessor (CMP) platforms, where error-prone caches continue to dominate the chip area. Network-on-Chip (NoC) fabrics are increasingly used to manage the scalability of these CMPs. We present a novel fault-tolerant scheme for Last Level Cache (LLC) in CMP architectures that leverages the interconnection network to protect the LLC cache banks against permanent faults. During a LLC access to a faulty area, the network detects and corrects the faults, returning the fault-free data to the requesting core. By leveraging the NoC interconnection fabric, we can implement any cache fault-tolerant scheme in an efficient, modular, and scalable manner. We perform extensive design space exploration on NoC benchmarks to demonstrate the utility and efficacy of our approach. The overheads of leveraging the NoC fabric are minimal: on an 8-core, 16-cache-bank CMP we demonstrate reliable access to LLCs with additional overheads of less than 3% in area and less than 7% in power.

Categories and Subject Descriptors

B.3.2 [**Design Styles**]: Cache Memories; B.3.4 [**Reliability, Testing, and Fault-Tolerance**]: Error checking, Redundant design; C.1.2 [**Multiple Data Stream Architectures (Multiprocessors)**]: Interconnection architectures.

General Terms

Algorithms, Design, Reliability

Keywords

Reliability, Fault-tolerant Cache, Network-on-Chip, Chip Multiprocessor, Remapping

1. INTRODUCTION

As processor manufacturing continues to follow Moore's Law, we continue to see more, and smaller devices on each generation of chips. Technology scaling, process variation, aging, and thermal problems are severely degrading the reliability of Chip Multiprocessors. Moreover, to reduce power consumption, aggressive voltage scaling is one of the most common schemes which exponentially increases the impact of process variation on memory cells and degrades the memory reliability. With increasing amount of area being devoted to building both off-chip and on-chip memories, reliable and fault-tolerant memories can significantly improve the overall reliability of a CMP system. There are different challenges in design of fault-tolerant on-chip memories. On one hand, many fault-tolerant methods attempt to improve the reliability of various on-chip memories and caches by adding redundancy and increasing overhead. On the other hand, there are multiple methods (such as aggressive voltage scaling) that attempt to save the power by degrading the reliability but tolerating it. All of these methods demonstrate a clear trade-off between reliability, power, performance, and the area overhead of the fault-tolerance scheme. As the number of cores, cache layers and memory banks increase, there is a critical need to develop efficient, scalable, and modular fault-tolerant schemes to cope with the resultant errors.

Although there is a large body of previous work on fault-tolerant design of cache memories, they have mostly focused on either single bank or multi-bank caches with uniform access latency in a single core architecture [11][12][13][14][15][16]. Such schemes face severe limitations with the increasing the number of cores and cache banks in emerging NoC-based multi-core/many-core architectures. On one hand, most of the current fault-tolerant schemes are not efficient, modular, and scalable enough to be leveraged for protection of shared caches with non-uniform access latency and distributed banks in such architectures. Since CMP architectures have more than one core that can access one or different distributed banks simultaneously, fault mapping and protection need to be scalable and distributed. Furthermore, existing fault-tolerant techniques typically use a single fault map and a centralized fault protection scheme which cannot be scaled for large CMP architectures: as a result each access needs to go through the fault map first, and no parallel cache accesses are allowed. On the other hand, these schemes miss the opportunity to leverage the scalable interconnection network (e.g., NoC fabric) to achieve fault-tolerance of the caches in these emerging multi/many-core architectures.

Many research efforts have already investigated fault-tolerant schemes for NoC fabrics, mostly in the areas of fault-aware routing, reliable communication, and fault-tolerant routers [4][5][6][7][8]. However, research on coupling memory and NoC reliability is still in its infancy [3]. Indeed, there are few works studying the reliability of on-chip memories at the network level [1][2]. Angiolini et al. [1] modified the network interface of cores to protect critical data of on-chip memories in a NoC-based

MPSoC. Wang et al. [2] proposed a utility-driven address remapping technique to tackle the capacity loss in NUCA cache of NoC-based CMP architectures. However, to the best of our knowledge, there have been no previous efforts at leveraging the NoC fabric to achieve scalable fault-tolerance of caches.

In this paper, we present a novel solution at the on-chip network level for fault-tolerant design of LLC in CMP architectures. We leverage the network to implement a fault-tolerant scheme to protect the LLC cache banks against permanent faults. During a LLC access to a faulty area, the network detects and corrects the faults, and returns the fault-free data to the corresponding core.

The main contributions of this paper are that we: 1) present a novel NoC-based solution that can be leveraged for fault-tolerant cache design in NoC-based CMPs; 2) propose three policies for implementing a remapping-based fault-tolerant scheme based on the NoC architecture; and 3) quantify the efficacy of the proposed architecture by exploring a design space in 45nm. To the best of our knowledge, this is the first work that leverages the on-chip network to facilitate fault-tolerant design of shared LLC in CMPs.

2. BASIC IDEA AND BASELINE ARCHITECTURE

Unlike traditional fault-tolerant cache schemes that perform all the bookkeeping in the cores, our approach migrates all of the fault-tolerant bookkeeping from the cores to the NoC fabric, by modifying the network routers to perform all the required tasks of a fault-tolerant scheme. As an exemplar of a fault-tolerant scheme, we use a remapping-based technique to demonstrate the effectiveness of our proposed approach. Remapping-based schemes address permanent faults by remapping faulty blocks to other faulty/non-faulty blocks, thereby ensuring delivery of fault-free blocks. We propose three policies to configure the NoC, implement the fault-tolerant scheme, and based on each policy we add a fault map and a multiplexing layer to some of the NoC components. The fault map keeps information about the location of permanent faults and remapping data in the local cache bank of each router. The multiplexing layer performs the fault matching.

Using the NoC interconnection paradigm enables us to implement any fault-tolerant method in an efficient, modular, and scalable manner for several reasons. First, it supports modular and scalable implementation of fault-tolerant methods for emerging multi/many-core architectures. Different policies and configurations are possible with the minimum overhead and design change. Second, using the NoC paradigm, it is easy to control access and management of redundancy resources. Also, redundancy for fault tolerance can be provided easily via the available interconnection network for any entity in the NoC. Third, adaptive and dynamic fault-tolerance of memory banks can be supported via NoC components. Since, the routers have a key role in communication and management of data between all core and cache nodes in a NoC-based CMP architecture, by using their network information and modifying their routing algorithm, we can easily provide adaptive fault-tolerance of cache banks.

We now present our baseline architecture to demonstrate our approach.

2.1 CMP and NUCA LLC

We consider a non-tiled CMP architecture as our baseline which is composed of 8 cores and 16 shared LLC banks. Cores and cache banks are interconnected as a 2-D mesh via a Network-on-Chip (NoC) architecture as shown in Figure 1. Each core is composed of a processing element and private L1 data and instruction caches. Based on our cache organization, each LLC bank is a portion of a larger distributed shared LLC cache.

The baseline design assumes a Non-Uniform Cache Architecture (NUCA) [9] LLC cache. With multiple banks within the LLC cache, we have the choice of either always putting a block into a designated bank (static mapping) or allowing a block to reside in one of multiple banks (dynamic mapping). We consider static mapping in our baseline design and model static NUCA policy for CMP architectures (CMP-SNUCA) [17]. Similar to the original proposal (S-NUCA for uni-core processors in [9]), CMP-SNUCA statically partitions the address space across cache banks connected via a 2D mesh interconnection network.

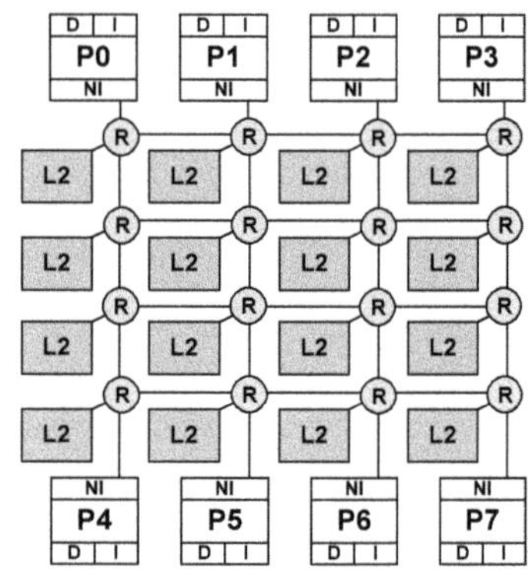

Figure 1. Baseline Architecture.

In static mapping, a fixed hash function uses the lower bits of a block address to select the target bank. LLC access latency is proportional to the distance from the issuing L1 cache to the LLC cache bank. By allowing non-uniform hit latencies, static mapping reduces hit latencies of traditional monolithic cache designs, which fix the latency to the longest path [10]. Because a block can be placed into only one bank, the LLC access latency is essentially decided by the accessing block address.

2.2 NoC Architecture

Network-on-chips are based on conventional computer networks, and have emerged as an alternative to buses to deal with the issues of scalability and regularity. Indeed, because of their regular architecture, NoCs are very suitable for platform-based design.

The NoC exemplar used in this work is a cycle-accurate SystemC implementation based on SoCIN (SoC Interconnection Network) [18]. SoCIN is a Mesh-topology scalable network based on a parametric router architecture conceived with the goal of being in low-cost NoC. The main modules of this implementation of the SoCIN router are the input buffers, the arbiter, the crossbar, and the links as depicted in Figure 2.

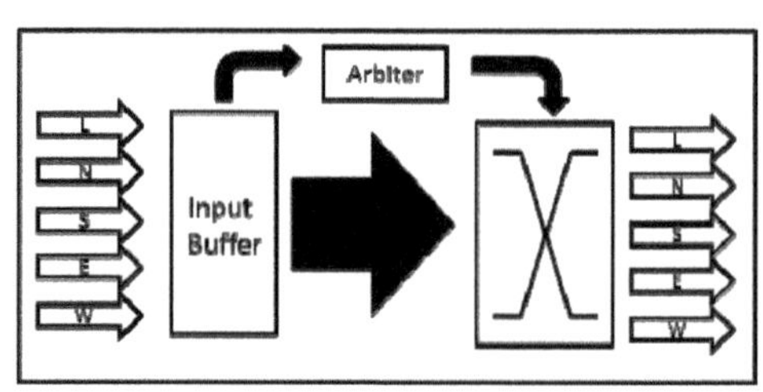

Figure 2. SoCIN router.

SoCIN is a wormhole packet switched network, where each packet is divided into small units called flits (flow control unit). Each flit contains n + 2 bits where n is the payload and the 2 bits are flags for *begin of packet* (bop) and *end of packet* (eop). When a flit arrives in the router it is stored in the input buffer. Once the arbiter reads the first flit (identified by the bop flag) it can determine through which output port the packet must go. This information is passed to the crossbar. If the crossbar determines that the output request is available, it begins to transmit the packet. The condition that defines the availability of the output is that the input buffer of the router connected to it needs to have enough space for at least one flit.

SoCIN implements a deterministic XY routing that avoids deadlocks. The routing is determined by the NoC address of the destination specified in the very first flit of the packet (the n/2 most significant bits are the destination NoC address and the n/2 less significant are the source NoC address). Once the first flit is routed through an output, the handshake protocol between the routers defines when there is enough space in the input buffer to send the next flit. This happens until the flit with the eop flag is routed. Therefore, all flits are routed in a pipeline fashion. Figure 3 shows the packet format in SoCIN.

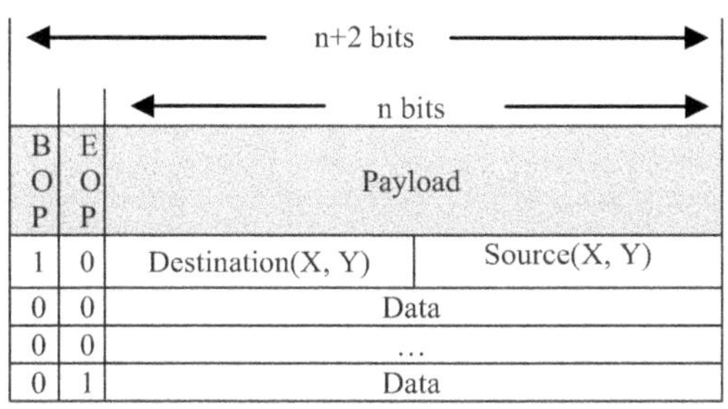

Figure 3. SoCIN Packet format.

The flow control in SoCIN is handshake based. When the sender writes the data on the link, it signals a valid (*val*) bit. When the receiver is ready to read the data it activates the *ack* signal. Figure 4 depicts the Link structure with two unidirectional channels (to send and receive) each one of them has n+2 bits and *val* and *ack* signals.

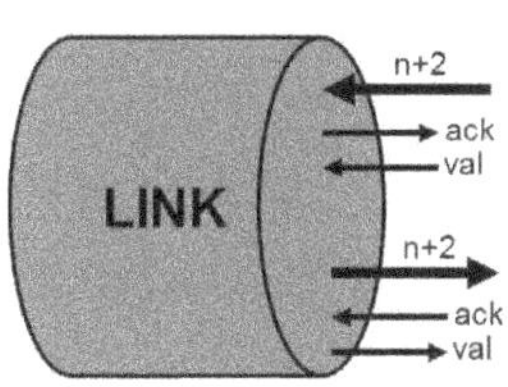

Figure 4. SoCIN link signals.

2.3 Base Fault-tolerant Method

In general, all fault-tolerant schemes leverage some form of redundancy to tolerate the faulty components. As an exemplar for fault-tolerant caches, we consider remapping-based techniques as our base fault-tolerant method from the work in [16]. This method leverages a portion of faulty blocks as redundancy to mask faults in other blocks in cache memories. Here, we present a brief description of this fault-tolerant method. This method uses a BIST module during boot up to detect permanent faults (Hard Errors) in cache blocks and keeps the information of the location of faulty blocks in a fault map. Then based on this information, it configures the address remapping for faulty blocks. This method divides each block of the cache into multiple subblocks that define the granularity at which failures are identified and remapped. A sub-block is labeled faulty if it has at least one faulty bit, as determined by BIST analysis. If two blocks have faults in the same subblock, it means they have conflict and one cannot be used to mask faults in the other. During the configuration process if a block is labeled as faulty, the system attempts to remap faulty portions of that block (Host block) to another block (called the Target block) that has already been marked as faulty and does not conflict with the host block. It then sacrifices and disables the target block to replicate all faulty sub-blocks of the host block. Thus, the fault-free block can be reconstructed from a combination of the two blocks; i.e., the host block together with the target block via leveraging a multiplexing layer.

In many cases, a good choice of the target is another block in the same set (referred to as a local target block), so both host and target blocks can be read in a single access. Barring this case, we should always select target blocks from a different bank (a target bank), so that both blocks can be read without two serialized accesses to the same bank. We refer to this target block as a remote target block. Note that the target block can be selected from any bank in the LLC address space. Here, for each bank we limit the remapping policy to select target blocks from the adjacent banks that are within a one hop distance in the NoC.

3. PROPOSED NOC ARCHITECTURE

We extend the base fault-tolerant method to be leveraged for a shared multi-bank NUCA cache in a CMP architecture using the NoC backbone. Recall that the basic idea is that we distribute the fault map and multiplexing layer over routers of the NoC architecture. There exists one entry in a fault map for each set. We divide each entry to two sections: map of faulty subblocks and remapping data. The first section keeps the map of faulty subblocks in the set. The second section represents the remapping data of all blocks in the set. We keep the fault map of each bank in two separate blocks. We keep the first section of the fault map in a Fault Map Block (FMB). The second block composed of the remapping data of fault map which named Remapping Data Block (RDB). RDB includes one bit that indicates the faulty status of each block. We need the FMB data only to configure the address remapping and initialize the RDB. Therefore, there is no need to access this FMB data during the operation of the system, and we can keep it in main memory or the hard drive. We only need to keep the RDB data at the cache level. Note that we employ a reliable 8T SRAM cell [32] to protect RDB and also tag arrays.

To implement our approach, we perform three modifications to cache access algorithm, the NoC routers, and cache banks to support the fault-tolerant method, as described in the next sections.

3.1 Fault-tolerant Cache Access

We modify the LLC access algorithm to support the fault-tolerant method. In our fault-tolerant cache architecture, each LLC access first accesses the RDB of fault map. Based on the fault status bit of the accessed block, if it is a faulty block it needs to have an extra access to a target block. The target block can be a local one within the same set or may be accessed from another bank (in case of a remote target block). Then based on the location of target block retrieved from the RDB, one or two levels of multiplexing is used to compose a fault free block by choosing appropriate subblocks from both host and target blocks.

Based on our modified cache access, we define a fault-tolerant LLC access in three phases:

1. **Issue**: send access to both host and target blocks
2. **Receive**: wait until receive both host and target blocks
3. **Match**: match both host and target blocks via a multiplexing layer to tolerate faulty subblocks

Figure 5 represents three stages of a fault-tolerant LLC access in our scheme.

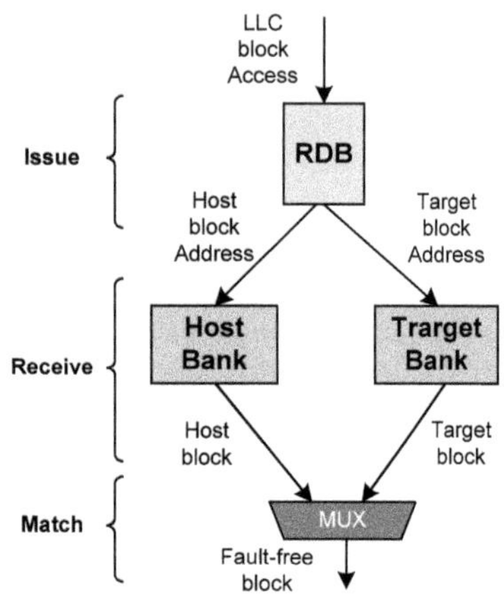

Figure 5. Three phases of a fault-tolerant LLC access.

Since the proposed fault-tolerant cache architecture increases the number of accesses to the LLC banks, it has a direct impact not only on network traffic but also on the LLC network access latency. In fact, efficient implementation of a fault-tolerant cache architecture needs to consider its impact on both network traffic and latency while trying to minimize its performance and cost overheads. Considering such design tradeoffs, we propose three policies to implement a fault-tolerant cache architecture based on a NoC paradigm.

We define an entity as a NoC component (core, router, or cache bank) that can perform a phase of the fault-tolerant LLC access. Based on this definition each one of the cores, routers, or cache banks can be an entity. Therefore, different phases of a fault-tolerant LLC access can be performed by different components (entities) in the NoC architecture. Based on the type and location of entities that perform different phases of a fault-tolerant LLC access, we can have different policies. However, in this architecture we assume all phases of a fault-tolerant LLC access are done in one entity (**Issue entity**) and based on this assumption we define three policies:

1. **Core-Based:** This is the base policy, where all three phases of a fault-tolerant LLC access are done by the core which sends an access to the LLC bank. In this policy, we don't perform any changes to the NoC architecture. The NoC architecture is used to send access to both host and target banks and return the host and target blocks to the issuer core. One advantage of this policy is that it potentially minimizes the network latency by sending access to both host and target block in parallel.
2. **Parallel Issue:** In this policy, the local router of the core performs all three phases of Issue, Receive, and Match. In this policy, we don't change the cores. Only the local routers of the cores are changed. One advantage of this policy is that only a section of routers have to be modified. Also, it reduces the traffic between cores and NoC routers in comparison to the base policy.
3. **Host-Centric:** In this policy, the local router of the host bank performs all three phases of Issue, Receive, and Match and then sends the final fault-free block back to the requester core. One advantage of this policy is that it minimizes the network traffic in comparison with other policies. However, its network latency highly depends on the distance between the host and target banks.

Figure 6 represents different policies based on the Issue entity and shows the differences between them.

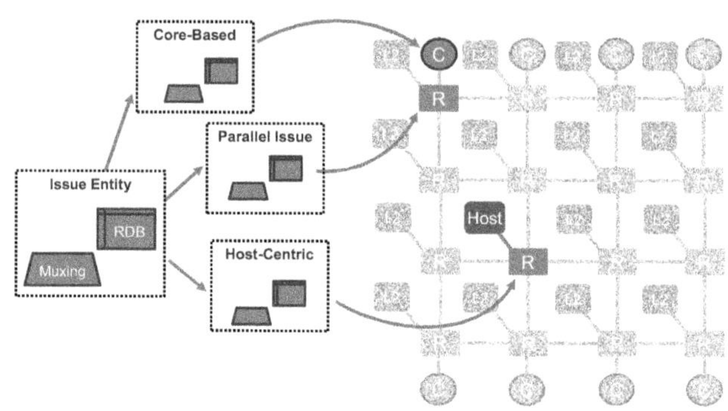

Figure 6. A general view of the NoC with different policies.

3.2 Fault-Aware Router

As mentioned earlier in Section 2.2, the router has the arbiter that reads from the input buffer in order to determine the direction to which the packet must go (namely, north, south, east, west or local). Then it informs the crossbar which input buffer it must read from. This process is depicted in Figure 7(a).

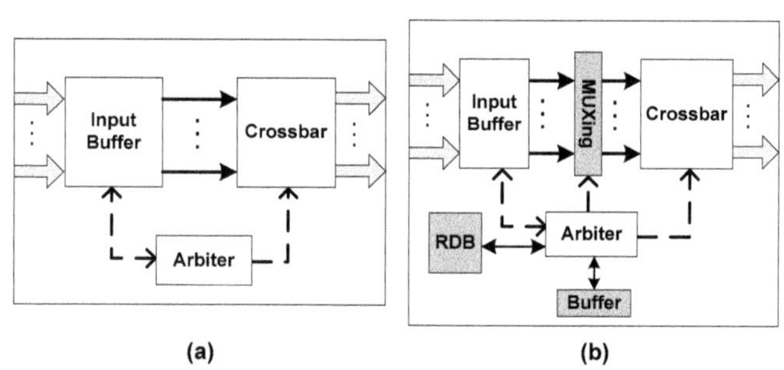

Figure 7. (a) Conventional Router; (b) Fault-aware Router.

In order to support the fault-tolerant LLC access and the Parallel-Issue and Host-centric policies presented in the previous section, we need to change the router. So, we propose a novel fault-aware router to support our fault-tolerant LLC access via the NoC architecture, which is detailed in Figure 7(b). This new router has new components like an RDB, an extra buffer and a multiplexing layer.

In a situation where a data request arrives, the arbiter verifies (using the RDB) if that particular address is a faulty access (access to a faulty block). In case of a faulty access, it checks if the target block is local (within the same set) or remote (another set in another bank). In case of local target block, the cache bank handles the local remapping (more details in next section). In case of a remote target block, the arbiter itself generates another request packet to be sent to the target bank. It keeps 3 pieces of information after that: 1) A flag that indicates that a matching operation is pending; 2) The direction from which the host and target blocks are expected; and 3) The address of the core that originally requested the data.

When a reply packet arrives, the arbiter checks whether this is an expected packet, as part of the original data (host block) request that is pending. If so, it stores the block in the extra buffer. When the target data packet arrives, the arbiter sends it and also the contents of the extra buffer to the multiplexing layer for fault matching. The output of the multiplexing layer will be the final fault-free data packet (block) to be sent to the core that requested the data. It is important to note that for regular non-faulty data requests, the multiplexing layer is bypassed.

Note that based on different policies, we replace none, some, or all of the NoC routers with the new fault-aware one to implement the fault-tolerant method. In case of Core-Based policy, there is no need to use fault-aware router and all of the process mentioned above are performed inside of the cores. For Parallel-Issue policy, we replace all local routers of the cores (the routers directly connected to the cores) by the proposed fault-aware router. In case of Host-centric, since every router in the NoC can be an Issue entity, we replace all of the routers by the fault-aware router.

3.3 Fault-tolerant Cache Banks

We perform some changes in the LLC banks to support our fault-tolerant method. As mentioned earlier in Section 2.3, we divide each block into multiple, equally-sized subblocks. Since our LLC is a set-associative cache, each bank already has a large block-level multiplexer. We replace that multiplexer with a set of smaller ones with subblock size scale. Figure 8 shows a conventional 4-way set associative and the modified one with 3 subblocks in each way. The number of required multiplexers in each bank is equal to the number of subblocks per block.

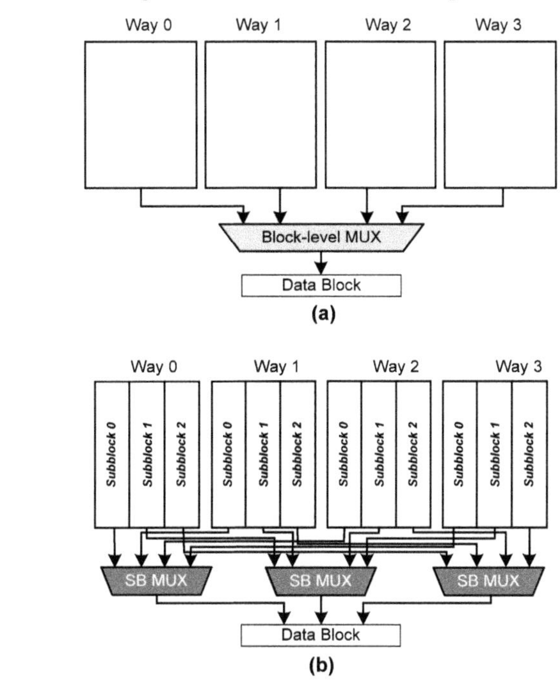

Figure 8. (a) A conventional 4-way set associative cache bank; (b) Modified cache bank with 3 subblocks in each way.

4. LATENCY AND TRAFFIC ANALYSIS

In this section we study latency and network analysis of our proposed policies. The goal is to establish the theoretical components responsible for the latency and traffic in each case.

4.1 Latency Analysis

In this analysis we consider latency as the time between issuing a LLC request and receiving it. Accordingly, we divided the timing into the following components:

- $\mathbf{T_{issue}}$: Time spent sending the request packet(s) from core to issue entity;
- $\mathbf{T_{RDB}}$: Time spent finding where the host and target block are (RDB access time);
- $\mathbf{T_{host}}$: Network latency to send the request packet from the issue entity to the host block and receive it back;
- $\mathbf{T_{target}}$: Network latency to send the request packet from the issue entity to the target block and receive it back;
- $\mathbf{T_{match}}$: Time spent matching the blocks;
- $\mathbf{T_{return}}$: Time spent getting the final block from issue entity to the core;

Overall the Latency of a policy will be given by:

$$T = T_{issue} + T_{access} + T_{return} \quad (1)$$

$$T_{access} = T_{RDB} + MAX(T_{host} + T_{target}) + T_{match} \quad (2)$$

T_{RDB} can easily be obtained based on the size of RDB which, in the worst case, has as many entries as the number of faulty lines. Also, we can obtain T_{host} and T_{target} based on the size of the NoC and the latency per hop. There should be also an extra latency to be added due to network contention. However, it is almost impossible to determine this kind of component beforehand. In addition, T_{match} is given by the critical path of the multiplexing layer. Comparing all three policies we conclude that T_{RDB} and T_{match} are constant and remain the same for different policies. The other timing components are changed in different policies because they relate to the location of Issue Entity which changes in different policies. Figure 9 represents timing components of a fault-tolerant access. Note that as depicted in this figure, T_{issue} is equal to T_{return} independent of the kind of policy because all phases of a fault-tolerant LLC access are performed in a single issue entity.

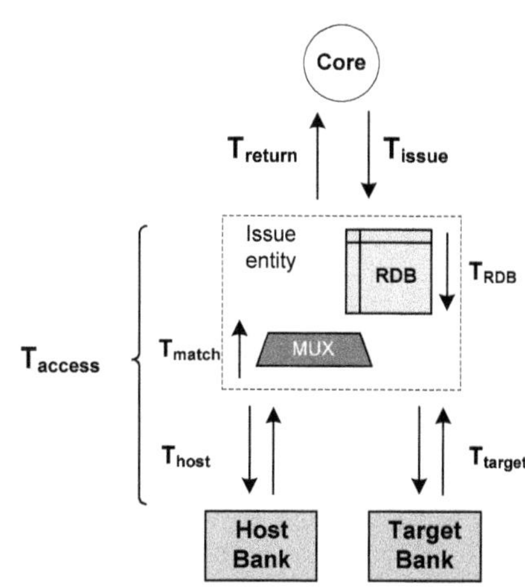

Figure 9. Timing details of a fault-tolerant access.

Regarding the Core-Based and Parallel-Issue policies, T_{host} and T_{target} are changed depending on the location of the host and target block, respectively. For Host-Centric Policy, T_{host} equals the time to fetch the data from the local LLC bank, which we consider it as one hop latency. T_{target} equals to the time of accessing the target block from the host router. Note that for this policy T_{host} is always dominated by the T_{target}.

The summary of our timing analysis is depicted in Table 1. The Core-Based and Parallel-Issue policies have almost the same latency. However, Host-Centric policy could have higher number of hops because in the worst case, the packet would travel through the longest minimum path 3 times. This can be avoided by limiting the amount of hops between the host and target banks.

Note that there are other issues that can affect the latency, such as network contention and cache coherence side-effects. For sake of simplicity, we do not consider them in our timing analysis.

Table 1. Timing analysis for latency of each policy

Latency	Core-Based	Parallel Issue	Host-Centric
$T_{issue} = T_{return}$	0	1 hop	M hops
T_{host}	(M+1) hops	M hops	1 hop
T_{target}	(N+1) hops	N hops	(L+1) hops

M= Number of hops from the core to the host router
N= Number of hops from the core to the target router
L=Number of hops from the host router to the target router

4.2 Traffic Analysis

Essentially, traffic will be the amount of transferring packets in the network. This means that we should not only consider the amount of data but also the number of hops through which the data passes. This is important because the chances of congestion caused by a packet are proportional to the amount of routers that it passes through. The packets can either be LLC access request packet or data packets. It is obvious that if the matching between host and target blocks happening sooner, it leads to a lower traffic. Listed below are the components of the traffic for one fault-tolerant LLC access:

- R_{CB}: Amount of traffic in Core-Based policy
- R_{PI}: Amount of traffic in Parallel-Issue policy
- R_{HC}: Amount of traffic in Host-centric policy
- R_{local}: Amount of traffic between the core and its local router
- R_{host}: Amount of traffic between the core node and the host node
- R_{target}: Amount of traffic between the core node and the target node
- $R_{local\text{-}host}$: Amount of traffic between the local router and the host node
- $R_{local\text{-}target}$: Amount of traffic between the local router and the target node
- $R_{host\text{-}target}$: Amount of traffic between the host node and the target node

In Core-Based policy, there are two concurrent paths to host node and target node from the core. Here, traffic of one LLC access includes two access packets from core node to the host and target nodes and two data packets from host and target nodes to the core.

$$R_{CB} = R_{host} + R_{target} \quad (3)$$

In Parallel-Issue policy, there is a single path between the core node and its local router and then from that point there are two parallel paths to the host and target nodes. Here, traffic of one LLC access includes one access packet from core to the local router node, two access packets from local node to the target and host nodes, two data packets from host and target nodes to the local node, and one data packet from the local node to the core.

$$R_{PI} = R_{local} + R_{local\text{-}host} + R_{local\text{-}target} \quad (4)$$

In Host-Centric policy the requests are serialized and the matching occurs sooner than the Core-Based and Parallel-Issue policies. Here, traffic of one LLC access includes one access packet from core to the host node, one access packet from host to the target node, one data packet from target to the host, and one data packet from the host node to the core.

$$R_{HC} = R_{host} + R_{host\text{-}target} \quad (5)$$

5. EVALUATIONS

This section describes the methodology used to obtain relevant results in order to evaluate the impact of different policies of the proposed fault-tolerant LLC approach on performance, energy, and network metrics.

5.1 Methodology

We use a cycle-accurate SystemC model of a NoC used in previous works [19][20] which is a Mesh based implementation that uses an XY routing and Wormhole switching with a 4-phit buffer size. Each router of this NoC is connected to a 1MB L2 cache bank. All L2 cache banks share the same address space of 16 MB. Additionally, for each router in the first and last rows, there is a module generating data and instruction requests based on memory traces obtained from a Simics [21] simulation using 8 sparcV8 as cores. Table 2 summarizes the experimental setup of our architecture.

Table 2. Experimental Setup

Processor Cores	8 SPARC V8
L1 Instruction/Data Cache	2 Banks, 32KB each, 4-Way, 32B Block Size, 2 cycle
L2 Cache (shared LLC)	16 Banks, 1MB each, 8-Way, 64B Block Size, 10 cycle
Memory Latency	250 cycles
Interconnect	NoC of 2D mesh (4x4 for 16 banks) 32-byte links (2 flits per memory access), 1-cycle link latency, 2-cycle router, XY routing, Wormhole Switching, 4 phit buffer size
Frequency	1.0 GHz
Integrated Technology	45 nm

A workload of parallel programs with very distinct behaviors is created using benchmarks from the well-known SPLASH2 [22], PARSEC [23] and a parallel version of MiBench [24] suites. Table 3 presents a brief description for each one of them. Using the Simics simulator, we extract all memory requests (data and instructions) by executing these applications, one at a time, with 8 threads each. With these memory traces as input of our framework, we are able to extract performance, and energy results. The performance results are the total number of cycles to execute all 8 threads and the energy results are obtained from Cacti 6.5 [25] for the memory subsystem and from Orion 2.0 [26] for the network-on-chip. For the sake of this study, faulty LLC banks are modeled randomly since SRAM cell faults occur as random events. These random faults are due to the major contribution of the random dopant fluctuation to the process variation [11].

Table 3. Benchmarks description

Benchmark Suite	Application	Description
SPLASH	FFT	A complex 1-D version of a six-step FFT algorithm
	LU	Factors a dense matrix in the equivalent lower-upper matrix multiplication
MiBench	Patricia	A data structure used to represent routing tables in network applications
	Susan_corners	An image recognition package. It was developed for recognizing corners and edges in Magnetic Resonance Images of the brain
	Susan_edges	
	Susan_smoothing	
PARSEC	Swaptions	Monte Carlo simulation is used to price a portfolio of swaptions

5.2 Design Space Exploration

We run the simulation process for our three proposed policies running different applications. Additionally, we consider a baseline case based on the original NoC with a simple fault tolerance support that disables faulty blocks. In this scheme, any request to access a faulty block is considered as miss and generates an off-chip memory request. The policies results are all normalized according to the baseline. We evaluate the impact of the proposed NoC based fault-tolerant approach on performance, energy, and network latency and traffic.

We consider the network latency as the amount of cycles spent between issue of the data request packet and receiving the data packet from the L2 cache bank. Network traffic, as defined in section 4.2, is the amount of data that passes through the network taking into account the amount of time that the data spends travelling through the NoC. The idea here is to quantify the influence of the packets on creating possible contention situations. In order to have this notion, we present the traffic as the average buffer occupancy. This kind of result increases as more packets are sent and also increases as more packets flow through more routers in the network. Our performance metric is the number of Instructions per Cycle (IPC). Our energy metrics include the LLC total energy and the energy-delay product. The LLC total energy reflects the total amount of static and dynamic energy from the L2 cache banks and NoC (routers and links) throughout the execution of all traces. The energy-delay product is the product between the energy and the total execution delay for each application.

5.3 Results

5.3.1 Network Latency and Traffic

Figure 10 shows network latency with the baseline and our three proposed policy. As expected, due to the analysis presented in section 4, the Core-Based and Parallel-Issue policies present very similar results. This happens because of the difference between these two policies in terms of traversing the NoC. In the Core-Based policy, the packet must pass through one hop more than in the case of the Parallel-Issue policy. The Host-Centric policy in contrast with our expectation, presents less latency than the other two policies.

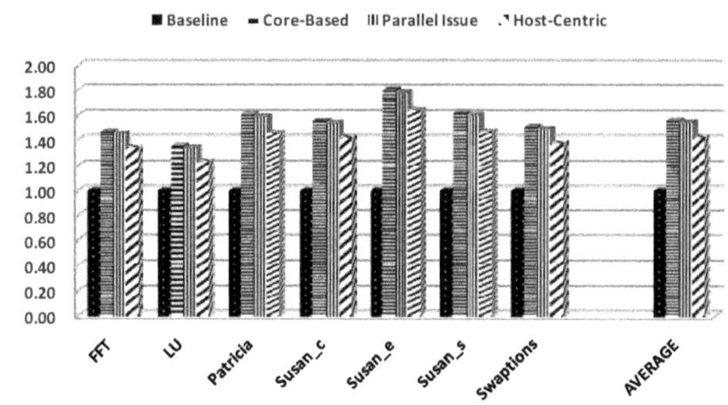

Figure 10. Network latency of the benchmarks normalized to that of Baseline.

These results can be non-intuitive since the Host-Centric policy, essentially, requests the host and the target blocks sequentially, differently from the other two policies. However, it is important to note that the RDB configuration plays a key role in these results, especially for the Host-Centric policy. In this study, by managing the allocation of host lines and target lines in such a way that they be placed in cache banks only at most 1-hop apart each other, we create a situation where the serialization of requests in Host-Centric policy does not affect the latency nor degrade the performance at all. Additionally as shown in Table 4, the RDB configuration generated for these experiments favors the Host-Centric policy since the majority of the target banks are 1-hop apart from their respective host banks. This means that because of XY routing in NoC, in most cases, cache access request and response packets in the Core-Based and Parallel-Issue policies flow through the network using the almost same set of routers as the Host-Centric policy. This affects directly the major advantage of these policies, which is the parallel use of the network.

Table 4. RDB remapping results.

Global Targets	17702 (54.02%)
Lines remapped in 1-hop banks	17092 (96.55%)
Average number of hops to target banks	0.96

In order to verify the impact of each policy on the NoC traffic, we analyze the average buffer occupancy in each case as presented in Figure 11. The results show not only the amount of data packets in each case but also how long they stay in the NoC. In the end, these results show the potential to generate contentions that each policy may have. Since Core-Based and Parallel-Issue policies only perform the multiplexing between the host and target lines in the last node and router of return path, respectively, the network becomes more busy and therefore they have higher average buffer occupancy. On the other hand, the Host-Centric policy matches the lines at the host node and, because of that, it causes less traffic and less possible contention in the network overall.

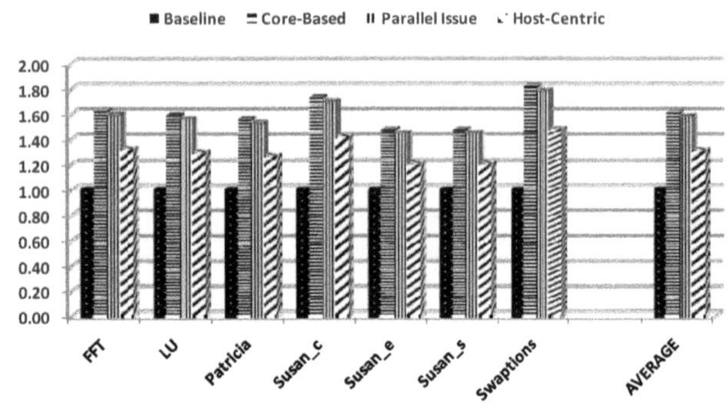

Figure 11. Average Buffer occupancy of different policies normalized to the Baseline.

5.3.2 Performance

Figure 12 represents the IPC results for different policies. It shows that with small variations in different applications, the Host-Centric policy has the best results overall. Core-Based and Parallel-Issue policies have almost the same IPC. This outcome is expected because of the similar trends observed in network latency and average buffer occupancy results.

As shown in the network latency results, some applications benefit more from the fault tolerant method than others. This happens because some memory accesses to faulty lines not necessarily generate L2 misses. Now some of this memory requests will generate L2 hits thanks to the remapping method. With that in mind, we can see that applications like FFT and LU have higher IPC, because they have lower network latency as shown in Figure 10. Also, the amount of off-chip requests due to L2 misses harms the performance of the baseline more than the proposed policies.

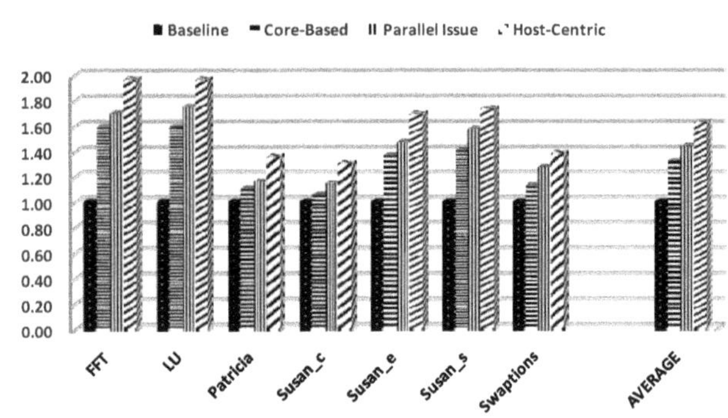

Figure 12. IPC of different policies normalized to the Baseline.

5.3.3 Energy Results

Figure 13 shows the total LLC energy for different policies. As a direct consequence of less access to an off-chip memory, all policies present better energy results than the Baseline. In the case of Core-Based and Parallel-Issue policies, this advantage is smaller than the Host-Centric policy because of the network energy. The fact that the host and target traverse through the network for more hops makes it more energy consuming in case of Core-Based and Parallel-Issue policies, especially for more activity in their router buffers. Also, due to reasons explained before, the network latency for these two policies is higher, which affects their energy consumption as shown in Figure 13.

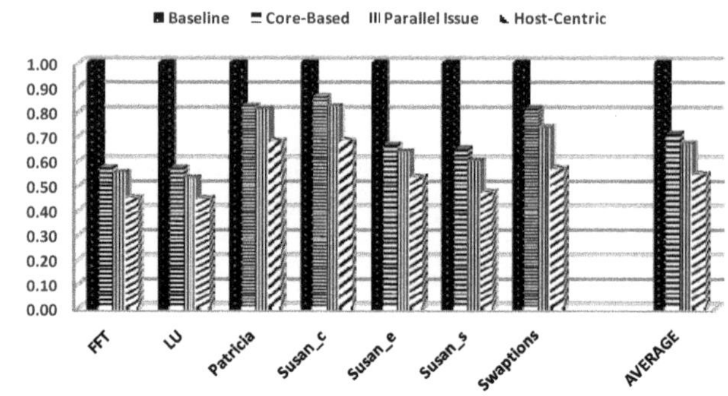

Figure 13. Energy of different policies normalized to the Baseline.

Figure 14 shows energy-delay product (EDP), which summarizes the results presented so far. As we expected, Host-centric policy gains the best EDP because of less amount of off-chip memory access, the lower amount of buffer occupancy, better performance, and lower energy in comparison with other policies.

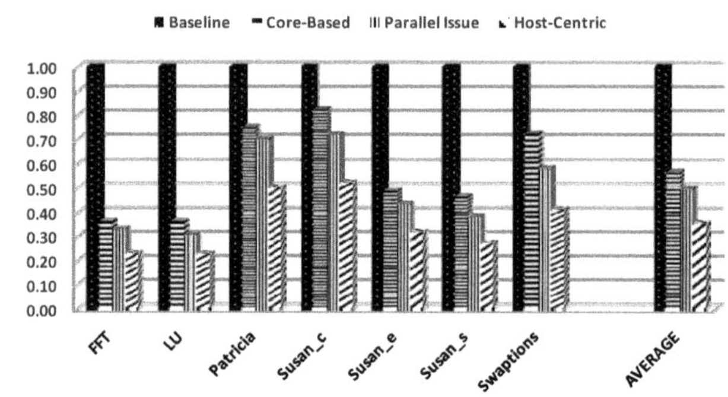

Figure 14. Energy-Delay Product of different polices normalized to the Baseline.

5.3.4 Overhead Results

Since each policy requires some minor architectural changes, the solution presents some area and power overhead caused by the addition of extra components in the router as explained in Section 3.2. Table 5 summarizes the area and power overheads of the proposed architecture for different policies. We consider the overhead of the RDB, the extra buffer, the multiplexing layer, and miscellaneous logic in the issue entities. The RDB is the major contributor to area and static power overhead. In addition, in order to protect the RDB and the tag arrays, we use reliable 8T SRAM cell [32] which has about 33% area overhead for these relatively small arrays in comparison with 6T SRAM data cells.

In the case of the Core-Based and Parallel-Issue policies, each entity must have a full RDB (with entries for every line in the LLC). This is necessary since there is no limitation on which data request will arrive in the entity. Each core can access any line in any bank since they form the same address space. However, the Host-Centric is a different case. Since the issue entity is the router directly connected to the host bank, the data to be requested can only be one of the lines in that host bank. Therefore, the RDB in each router can have only the entries of the lines that the host bank holds. Hence, the overhead in all routers of the Host-Centric policy is equal to the size of one full RDB, while the overhead in the Core-Based and Parallel-Issue policies equals eight times (one per core) the size of a full RDB. Overall, the overhead of all policies in the proposed fault-tolerance solution is minimal (less than 3% area and less than 7% power overhead), demonstrating the viability of our approach.

Table 5. Power and Area overhead results.

Overhead	Core-Based	Parallel Issue	Host-Centric
Area	2.46%	2.46%	0.41%
Static power	5.53%	5.53%	0.81%
Dynamic power	1.05%	1.05%	0.40%

6. RELATED WORK

6.1 Fault-Tolerant Cache Design

Several fault-tolerant solutions have been proposed previously to improve the reliability and yield of cache memories. A number of these works use circuit-level techniques to improve the reliability of each SRAM cell. Apart from the familiar 6T SRAM cell, 8T SRAM cell and 10T SRAM cell [32] have been proposed. Most of these designs have a large area overhead which poses a significant limitation for performance and power consumption of caches.

At the system level, a wide range of Error Detection Code (EDC) and Error Correcting codes (ECC) have been used [33]. ECC is proven as an effective mechanism for handling soft errors [34]. However, in a high-failure rate situation, most coding schemes are not practical because of the strict bound on the number of tolerable faults in each protected data chunk. In addition, using ECC codes incurs a high overhead in terms of storage for the correction code, large latency, slow and complex decoding [35].

Several architectural techniques have also been proposed to improve reliability of on-chip caches. Earlier works on fault-tolerant cache design use simple techniques using redundancy by adding redundant rows/columns to the cache [36] or applying cache down-sizing techniques by disabling a faulty line or block of cache [12]. Agarwal et al. [11] proposed a fault tolerant cache architecture in which the column multiplexers are programmed to select a non-faulty block in the same row, if the accessed block is faulty. In [13] two schemes called Word-disable (WDIS) and Bit-fix (BFIX) have been proposed. Both techniques make use of some cache lines to repair other ones. Roberts et al. [37] proposed a block grouping (pairing) scheme to form a new, fully working logical block. Ansari et al. [15] proposed Archipelago, a fault-tolerant cache that groups faulty cache sets together and sacrifices a different cache set to recover the failures. In [16], a flexible defect map is proposed to configure the cache architecture using a portion of faulty cache blocks as to tolerate other faulty caches blocks. In sum, most of these techniques are designed for a single-core processor with one or two cache banks and uniform cache access (UCA) organization.

A recent work by Wang et al. [2] addresses fault-tolerance of NUCA cache in NoC-based CMPs. They proposed a utility-driven address remapping technique to tackle the capacity loss in NUCA cache of NoC-based CMP architectures. However, their address remapping technique is at the bank-level, and they have not leveraged the NoC fabric for fault-tolerance of the cache.

6.2 Fault-tolerant NoC design

Reliability and fault-tolerance are outstanding research challenges in NoC design [3], and there are many efforts investigating fault-tolerance of NoCs, mostly in the areas of routing algorithms [5][6], communication infrastructure [4][7], or micro-architecture [1][8]. Manolache et al. [38] propose a fault-aware communication mapping. They address the problem of transient link failures by means of temporally and spatially redundant transmission of messages. A stochastic communication paradigm is proposed in [4] to provide a fault-tolerant communication. This approach is based on probabilistic broadcast where packets are forwarded randomly to the neighboring nodes. Similarly, the works in [5] and [6] explore how NoC routing algorithms can route around faults and sustain network functionality in presence of faults. In [38], the authors deploy some error correcting schemes to achieve combined energy minimization and reliability optimization design goals. Angiolini et al. [1] presented a mechanism to maintain a reliable integrated memory subsystem for a NoC-based system. The idea is to have a reliable backup memory (in addition to the main memory) to store all the critical data. The Network Interfaces are responsible for redirecting the critical data access in case of a failure in the main memory. Although, this scenario does provide some amount of reliability to the memory, it has drawbacks like redundancy of data and not being transparent to the programmer.

6.3 NoC on-chip memory Challenges

Several works regarding memory hierarchy in NoC architectures have been developed. In such systems, the massive communication parallelism may lead to different side effects due to the memory hierarchy. Marescaux et al. [27] show a comparison between caches and scratchpads in an NoC-based MPSoC using a distributed shared memory model. In this environment, the use of six DSPs with local L1 caches and a shared L2 cache is considered. Experiments with two NoCs with different QoS methods are presented. The results show that scratchpads have a better performance than caches. Monchinero et al. [28] explore the use of a distributed shared memory in an NoC-based MPSoC. It is shown that by increasing the number of distributed shared banks the performance also increases but only up to some point where the NoC size leads to a greater latency. It is also shown that the energy consumption drops as the number of distributed shared banks increases. Enright-Jerger et al. [29] propose a new cache coherence solution for multi-core architectures. The Virtual Tree Coherence (VTC) relies on a virtually ordered interconnection that keeps track of sharers of a coarse grain region. Other Memory-Centric NoC designs [30][31] can be found but none of them tries to solve fault-tolerant issues on the memory sub-system.

7. CONCLUSION

The move to deep sub-micron technologies and aggressive voltage scaling for low power poses challenges for the reliability of CMP architectures. A major challenge for the design of a reliable CMP is protection of large shared cache blocks against various faults. In this work, we proposed a novel NoC-based architecture for efficient fault-tolerance of NUCA LLCs in CMP architectures. Our design is based on modular extension of NoC routers to support fault-tolerant schemes that also scale with increasing CMP sizes. Our experimental results show that leveraging the on-chip interconnect paradigm in design and implementation of a fault-tolerant scheme for shared LLC banks in a CMP architecture, is an efficient solution that comes with a small overhead (less than 3% area and less than 7% power overhead). We studied the effects of different fault-tolerant policies on the

NoC, and showed that the parallelism of communication affects directly the results. Also, it is very important to consider the effect of fault-tolerant method configuration on NoC parameters. In the cases presented here, the remapping of the fault-tolerant method should consider the distance between the host and target LLC banks in the NoC. On the other hand, perhaps the use of different routing algorithms depending on the fault-tolerant policy adopted could generate better results. Future works include proposing more flexible policies, performing more sensitivity analysis for different NoC parameters, and examining more fault-tolerant methods as case studies.

8. ACKNOWLEDGMENTS

This research was partially supported by NSF Variability Expedition Grant Number CCF-1029783. Also, this work was partially supported by CNPq Brazilian agency.

9. REFERENCES

[1] F. Angiolini, D. Atienza, S. Murali, L. Benini, and G. De Micheli. Reliability Support for On-Chip Memories Using Networks-on-Chip. In *Proc. ICCD*, 2006.

[2] Y. Wang, L. Zhang, Y. Han, H. Li, and X. Li. Address Remapping for Static NUCA in NoC-Based Degradable Chip-Multiprocessors. In *Proc. PRDC*, 2010.

[3] R. Marculescu, et al. Outstanding Research Problems in NoC Design: System. Microarchitecture, and Circuit Perspectives," *IEEE Transactions on CAD*, vol. 28, no. 1, pp. 3-21, Jan. 2009.

[4] P. Bogdan, T. Dumitras, and R. Marculescu. Stochastic communication: A new paradigm for fault-tolerant networks-on-chip. In *Proc. VLSI Design*, Feb. 2007.

[5] V. Puente, J. A. Gregorio, F. Vallejo, and R. Beivide. Immunet: A cheap and robust fault-tolerant packet routing mechanism. In *Proc. ISCA*, Jun. 2004.

[6] M. Pirretti, G. M. Link, R. R. Brooks, N. Vijaykrishnan, M. Kandemir, andM. J. Irwin. Fault tolerant algorithms for network-on-chip interconnect. In *Proc. IEEE Symp. VLSI*, Feb. 2004.

[7] W. Tsai, D. Zheng, S. Chen, and Y.H. Hu. A fault-tolerant NoC scheme using bidirectional channel. In *Proc. DAC*, 2011.

[8] J. Kim, C. Nicopoulos, and D. Park. A Gracefully Degrading and Energy-Efficient Modular Router Architecture for On-Chip Networks. In *Proc. ISCA,* 2006.

[9] C. Kim, D. Burger, and S. W. Keckler. An adaptive, non-uniform cache structure for wire-delay dominated on-chip caches. In *Proc. ASPLOS*, 2002.

[10] N. Aggarwal, et al. Configurable isolation: building high availability systems with commodity multi-core processors. In *Proc. ISCA*, 2007.

[11] A. Agarwal, B. C. Paul, H. Mahmoodi-Meimand, A. Datta, and K. Roy. A process-tolerant cache architecture for improved yield in nanoscale technologies. *IEEE Trans. VLSI Syst.*, 13(1):27–38, 2005.

[12] S. Ozdemir, D. Sinha, G. Memik, J. Adams, and H. Zhou. Yield-aware cache architectures. In *Proc. MICRO*, 2006.

[13] C. Wilkerson, H. Gao, et al. Trading off Cache Capacity for Reliability to Enable Low Voltage Operation. In *Proc. ISCA*, 2008.

[14] C. K. Koh, W. F. Wong, Y. Chen, and H. Li. Tolerating process variations in large, set associative caches: The buddy cache. *ACM TACO*, 6(2):1–34, Jun 2009.

[15] A. Ansari, et al. Archipelago: A polymorphic cache design for enabling robust near-threshold operation. In *Proc. HPCA*, 2011.

[16] A. BanaiyanMofrad, Houman Homayoun, and Nikil Dutt. FFT-Cache: A Flexible Fault-Tolerant Cache Architecture for Ultra Low Voltage Operation. In *Proc. CASES*, 2011.

[17] B. M. Beckmann and D. A. Wood. Managing wire delay in large chip-multiprocessor caches. In *Proc. MICRO*, 2004.

[18] C.A. Zeferino and A.A. Susin. SoCIN: A Parametric and Scalable Network-on-Chip. In *Proc. SBCCI*. 2003.

[19] G. Girao, D. Barcelos, and F.R. Wagner. Performance and Energy Evaluation of Memory Organizations in NoC-Based MPSoCs under Latency and Task Migration. In *Proc. VLSI-SoC*, 2009.

[20] L. Kunz, G. Girao, and F.R. Wagner. Improving the efficiency of a hardware transactional memory on an NoC-based MPSoC. In *Proc. DATE,* 2011.

[21] P.S. Magnusson, et al. Simics: A Full System Simulation Platform. *IEEE Computer*, 35(2): 50-58, 2002.

[22] S.C. Woo, et al. The SPLASH-2 Programs: Characterization and Methodological Considerations. In *Proc. ISCA,* 1995.

[23] C. Bienia, S. Kumar, J.P. Singh, and K. Li. The PARSEC benchmark suite: characterization and architectural implications. In *Proc. PACT,* 2008.

[24] S.M.Z. Iqbal, Y. Liang, H. Grahn. ParMiBench: An Open Source Benchmark for Embedded Multiprocessor Systems. In *Proc. Computer Architecture Letters*, 2010.

[25] N. Muralimanohar, R. Balasubramonian, and N. Jouppi. Cacti 6.5. *In HP Laboratories*, Technical Report, 2009.

[26] A.B. Kahng, B. Li, L.S. Peh, and K. Samadi. ORION 2.0: a fast and accurate NoC power and area model for early-stage design space exploration. In *Proc. DATE*, 2009.

[27] T.Marescaux, E. Brockmeyer, and H. Corporaal. The Impact of Higher Communication Layers on NoC Supported MPSoCs. In *Proc. NOCS*, May 2007.

[28] M. Monchiero, G. Palermo, C. Silvano, and O. Villa. Exploration of Distributed Shared Memory Architectures for NoC-based Multiprocessors. In *Proc. IC-SAMOS*, July 2006.

[29] N. Enright-Jerger, L.-S. Peh, and M. Lipasti. Virtual Tree Coherence: Leveraging Regions and In-Network Multicast Trees for Scalable Cache Coherence. In *Proc. MICRO*, Nov 2008.

[30] A.G. Wassal, H.H. Sarhan, A. ElSherief. Novel 3D memory-centric NoC architecture for transaction-based SoC applications. In *Proc. SIECPC*, 2011.

[31] Donghyun Kim, et al. Solutions for Real Chip Implementation Issues of NoC and Their Application to Memory-Centric NoC. In *Proc. NOCS,* 2007.

[32] B. Calhoun and A. Chandrakasan. A 256 kb sub-threshold sram in 65nm cmos. In *Proc. ISSCC*, 2006.

[33] C. Chen and M. Hsiao. Error-correcting codes for semiconductor memory applications: A state of the art review. *IBM Journal of Research and Development*, 28(2):124–134, 1984.

[34] C. Wilkerson, et al. Reducing Cache Power with Low-Cost, Multi-Bit Error-Correcting Codes. In *Proc. ISCA*, June 2010.

[35] J. Kim, et al. Multi-bit Error Tolerant Caches Using Two-Dimensional Error Coding. In *Proc. MICRO*, 2007.

[36] T. Thomas and B. Anthony. Area, Performance, and Yield Implications of Redundancy in On-Chip Caches. In *Proc. ICCD*, Feb. 1999.

[37] D. Roberts, N. S. Kim, and T. Mudge. On-chip cache device scaling limits and effective fault repair techniques in future nanoscale technology. In *Proc. DSD*, 2007.

[38] S. Manolache, P. Eles, and Z. Peng. Fault and energy-aware communication mapping with guaranteed latency for applications implemented on NoC. In *Proc. DAC*, Jul. 2005.

[39] D. Bertozzi, L. Benini, and G. De Micheli. Error control schemes for on-chip communication links: The energy–reliability tradeoff. *IEEE TCAD*, 24(6): 818–831, Jun. 2000.

Automatic Extraction of Multi-Objective Aware Pipeline Parallelism Using Genetic Algorithms

Daniel Cordes, Michael Engel, Peter Marwedel
TU Dortmund University
Dortmund, Germany
firstname.lastname@tu-dortmund.de

Olaf Neugebauer
Informatik Centrum Dortmund e.V.
Dortmund, Germany
neugebauer@icd.de

ABSTRACT

The development of automatic parallelization techniques has been fascinating researchers for decades. This has resulted in a significant amount of tools, which should relieve the designer from the burden of manually parallelizing an application. However, most of these tools only focus on minimizing execution time which drastically reduces their applicability to embedded devices. It is essential to find good trade-offs between different objectives like, e.g., execution time, energy consumption, or communication overhead, if applications should be parallelized for embedded multiprocessor system-on-chip (MPSoC) devices. Another important aspect which has to be taken into account is the streaming-based structure found in many embedded applications such as multimedia and network services. The best way to parallelize these applications is to extract pipeline parallelism. Therefore, this paper presents the first multi-objective aware approach exploiting pipeline parallelism automatically to make it most suitable for resource-restricted embedded devices. We have compared the new pipeline parallelization approach to an existing task-level extraction technique. The evaluation has shown that the new approach extracts very efficient multi-objective aware parallelism. In addition, the two approaches have been combined and it could be shown that both approaches perfectly complement each other.

Categories and Subject Descriptors

D3.4 [**Programming Languages**]: Processors—*Compilers*; D.1.3 [**Programming Techniques**]: Concurrent Programming—*Parallel Programming*

General Terms

Algorithms, Design, Languages, Performance

Keywords

Automatic Parallelization, Embedded Software, Genetic Algorithms, Multi-Objective, Pipeline Parallelism, Energy

CODES+ISSS'12, October 7-12, 2012, Tampere, Finland.

1. INTRODUCTION

As a result of continuously increasing demands imposed on modern embedded systems, today the market share of multiprocessor system-on-chip (MPSoC) devices is growing at a tremendous rate in different application areas. Higher frequencies of single processing units are no longer achievable due to physical limitations. By using multiple cores in one MPSoC system it is possible to increase the performance of the platform or to execute the same work with reduced CPU frequencies, compared to a single-core platform. Unfortunately, these benefits do not come for free. Nowadays, most embedded applications are written in sequential ANSI-C code and have to be partitioned manually into concurrently executed tasks to take advantage of the additional processing units of an MPSoC. Since manual parallelization tends to be very error-prone and time-consuming, many (semi-) automatic parallelization tools have been invented in the last decades, but most of them are not well applicable to resource-restricted embedded systems.

This is not surprising, since most of these tools were developed to extract parallelism for desktop or even high-performance architectures. For these systems, the minimization of the execution time is very often the only objective, since a huge amount of computational power and – seen from an embedded systems perspective – an almost inexhaustible amount of energy are available. The situation changes if one is looking at embedded devices. Most of them have, e.g., only a very limited amount of computational power, small memories, and are obtaining their energy from a small battery. Thus, multiple objectives have to be considered at the same time during parallelization for resource-restricted systems. For example, it might be a good idea to reduce the amount of extracted parallelism if a given timing criterion is still met, instead of extracting as much parallelism as possible like done by most existing parallelization tools. If less parallelism is extracted, some of the cores can be switched into idle mode and a platform with less cores can be used which saves a significant amount of energy.

In addition to the fact that software for embedded devices should be parallelized using multi-objective aware techniques, special characteristics of embedded software should also be taken into account. By analyzing these applications it is noticeable that many of them have a streaming-based structure. Examples include applications in the domain of network services, voice- and image-processing as well as multimedia tasks like video decoding. To efficiently parallelize these applications, different pipeline stages should be extracted from a (nested) loop body, which execute different iterations of these stages in an interleaved way. Unfortunately, simple loop-level parallelism which is just executing different iterations of a loop in parallel can often not be applied, due to frequently occurring complex dependencies in embedded software. Thus, parallelization tools tailored towards special requirements of embedded devices should be able to extract so-called pipeline parallelism to generate efficient code for MPSoCs. Up to now, all previously published pipeline parallelization approaches are only optimizing a single-objective which limits their applicability to embedded devices.

Therefore, to the best of our knowledge, this paper presents the first multi-objective aware parallelization approach which is able to extract pipeline parallelism from sequential embedded applications. The new approach is based on genetic algorithms and has been compared against the previously published multi-objective aware task-level parallelization approach presented in [7]. The evaluation has shown that the new approach extracts very efficient parallelism for embedded real-world applications. In addition, the two approaches have been combined into one framework and it could be shown that both perfectly complement each other.

The main contributions of this paper are as follows:

1. To the best of our knowledge, this is the first automatic multi-objective aware parallelization approach which uses genetic algorithms to extract pipeline parallelism from sequential applications.

2. In contrast to high-performance computing, this framework focuses on requirements of constraint-driven embedded devices.

3. We use high-level models to evaluate different objectives without re-simulating the application, which drastically decreases the optimization time.

4. We combine this new approach with an existing task-level parallelism extraction technique and show how well both approaches complement each other to extract very efficient parallelism from embedded applications.

The rest of this paper is organized as follows: Section 2 gives a survey of related work, followed by a motivating example in Section 3. Afterwards, Section 4 gives a short explanation of the program dependence graph which is employed as intermediate representation. Section 5 then describes the multi-objective aware approach which is able to extract pipeline parallelism. The integration of this approach into an existing parallelization framework is described in Section 6, before the effectiveness and efficiency of the approach are evaluated in Section 7. Finally, Section 8 summarizes this paper and gives directions for future work.

2. RELATED WORK

In the last decades, many semi- and fully automatic techniques have been published that try to simplify the task of parallelizing a given sequential embedded application. While earlier publications on instruction-level parallelism (see, e.g., [29] and [13]) were targeting VLIW processors, recent multicore architectures rely on the extraction of more coarse-grained software-based parallelism. The latter one can be grouped into at least the three categories of *task-level-*, *loop-level-* and *pipeline parallelism* which are discussed in the following paragraphs.

A representative work of the first category, namely *task-level parallelism*, was presented by Hall et al. [11]. The authors present a technique which automatically extracts task-level parallelism as part of the SUIF Parallelizing and Optimizing Compiler framework [12]. Their approach is based on an interprocedural analysis and is not limited to function boundaries. Ceng et al. developed a semi-automatic parallelization assistant [3]. The application code is transformed into a weighted statement control data flow graph which is subsequently processed by a heuristical clustering algorithm, generating tasks after several iterations. The approach proposed by Ceng requires a user feedback loop to steer the granularity of the parallelized program.

More recent work on automatic extraction of task-level parallelism was presented in our previous publications [8] and [7] describing two techniques based on Integer Linear Programming (ILP) and genetic algorithms. While the ILP-based approach in [8] is only able to optimize the execution time, the second work in [7] is able to extract task-level parallelism in a multi-objective aware manner. However, the potential of parallelizing loops with task-level parallelism is very limited, especially of those with loop-carried dependencies. Therefore, the approach presented in this paper extracts pipeline parallelism to provide a remedy for this restriction.

Other frameworks which extract task-level parallelism were presented by, e.g., Verdoolaege et al. [26], Nikolov et al. [17], Sarkar [22], and Ottoni [18].

Representative publications of the second category, fine-grained *loop-level parallelism*, were developed by Franke et al. [9] and Chandra et al. [4]. Franke describes an approach which automatically extracts loop-level parallelism from C applications for DSP architectures with multiple address spaces. This approach also applies program code recovery techniques which, e.g., replace pointer arithmetic with array accesses to enable more precise data analysis. Chandra parallelizes loops of sequential applications for CC-NUMA (cache-coherent non-uniform memory access) architectures.

Another popular technique to extract fine-grained data-level parallelism from sequential applications is the use of polytope models. Here, loops are transformed into polytopes, which describe the iteration space and dependencies of nested loops by linear inequalities spanning a geometric object in an n-dimensional space. Those approaches have the drawback that they can only analyze affine loops so that already existing applications can, in general, not be parallelized without manually adapting the source code. Papers by Lengauer [15] and Bondhugula et al. [2] are representative publications in this area.

The last mentioned category, *pipeline parallelism*, is most relevant for this work, since the presented approach of this paper aims at the extraction of this kind of parallelism. Raman et al. [20], Tournavitis et al. [24], [25], and our previous work in [6] presented different approaches to achieve this. They are able to automatically split loops into different pipeline stages and further increase the application's performance by splitting pipeline stages into additional tasks. While our approach in [6] uses a mathematical problem description based on Integer Linear Programming, Raman and Tournavitis lack detailed cost models and only use heuristic clustering approaches. However, in contrast to the work of this publication, all those approaches aim at the minimization of the execution time as the only optimization objective.

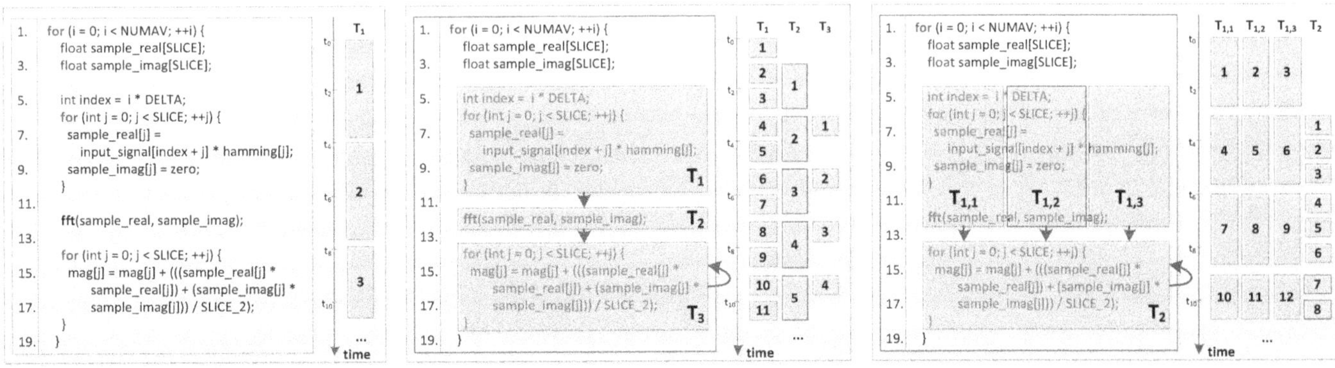

(a) Sequential code (b) Horizontal loop split (c) Horizontal and vertical loop split

Figure 1: Pipelining-based Loop Level Parallelization - Motivating Example

Additional approaches in this area were presented by Liu et al. [16] which eliminate loop-carried dependencies by retiming the execution of statements in a loop. They are moving executions of statements to earlier iterations of the loop. Thus, dependencies may change which creates the opportunity to parallelize different iterations of the loops.

Gordon et al. [10] present a compiler framework which combines the extraction of task, data, and pipeline parallelism for applications written in the programming language StreamIt [23]. The designer has to extract tasks manually by defining independent actors connected by explicit data channels. The algorithms described in [10] search for parallelism in the given task structure.

All aforementioned approaches, with the exception of our previous publication in [7], which extracts a different type of parallelism, have in common that the minimization of the execution time is the only considered objective. Thus, their applicability to resource-restricted embedded devices is very limited. However, some more recent publications try to optimize the energy consumption of parallelized applications. Qiu et al. [19] propose an energy-aware loop parallelization method. This method optimizes performance and energy consumption while parallelizing an application. The approach follows a two-phase strategy. First, it parallelizes loops to optimize the performance of the application. Afterwards, it tries to decrease the energy consumption of the system based on the previously parallelized application. Due to the decoupled phases, this might lead to sub-optimal results. Wang et al. [27] also implement a two-phase strategy to parallelize streaming applications. Cho et al. [5] present theoretical formulas which describe the interplay of program performance and energy consumption of a parallelized application.

Thus, to the best of our knowledge, the work presented in this paper is the first one extracting pipeline parallelism, which is very efficient for many embedded applications, in a multi-objective aware manner.

3. MOTIVATING EXAMPLE

The extraction of coarse-grained task-level parallelism is a very efficient technique to parallelize large independent blocks of an application such as function calls which can be executed concurrently. However, those approaches lack the possibility to extract parallelism from loops, especially from those with loop-carried dependencies. Thus, the new approach presented in this paper extracts pipeline parallelism in a multi-objective aware manner.

Before the extraction algorithm is described, a small motivating example should demonstrate the potential of pipeline parallelism for an embedded real-world application. The code snippet depicted in Figure 1(a-c) represents the main computation loop of the spectral benchmark [14]. On the left-hand side of each figure, the application's source code and the way how the statements are partitioned into concurrently executed tasks are shown. The right-hand side shows the time at which the iterations of the tasks are executed.

Simple loop-level parallelism which is just executing different iterations of the whole outer loop in parallel cannot be applied here, due to a loop-carried dependency of the second inner loop starting in line 14 of Figure 1(a-c). There, the content of the mag-array ($mag[j]$) generated in the previous iteration of the outer loop is consumed which serializes the execution of loop iterations. One way to provide a remedy is the extraction of pipeline parallelism which splits the loop horizontally and vertically into concurrently executed tasks. While horizontal splits distribute the statements of the loop body into disjunctive tasks which are executed in a pipelined manner, vertical splits further partition the different loop iterations of the created tasks into additional sub-tasks.

An example where horizontal splits are applied to the spectral application is depicted in Figure 1(b). There, the loop body of the outer loop is divided into three tasks T_1, T_2, and T_3. The benefit of such a parallelization can be seen on the right-hand side of Figure 1(b). As soon as the first iteration of task T_1 has completed its work, the required data is sent to T_2. Now, T_1's second and third iteration can be executed in parallel to the first iteration of task T_2. Afterwards, T_2 sends its data to T_3, so that all three tasks are executing their work in a pipelined manner.

As can be seen, this example is not well balanced, since T_3 has to wait for data of task T_2 after each iteration. To circumvent this problem, different loop iterations of the created tasks can be executed in parallel, generated by so-called vertical splits. The extracted parallelism in Figure 1(c) combines horizontal and vertical splits and is much more efficient (at least regarding execution time) than the solution which is only generating pipelined tasks, shown in Figure 1(b). Tasks T_1 and T_2 of Figure 1(b) are joined in this solution, but this new task is now vertically divided into three subtasks. These tasks are now executing the first, second and third loop iteration of the statements assigned to this task

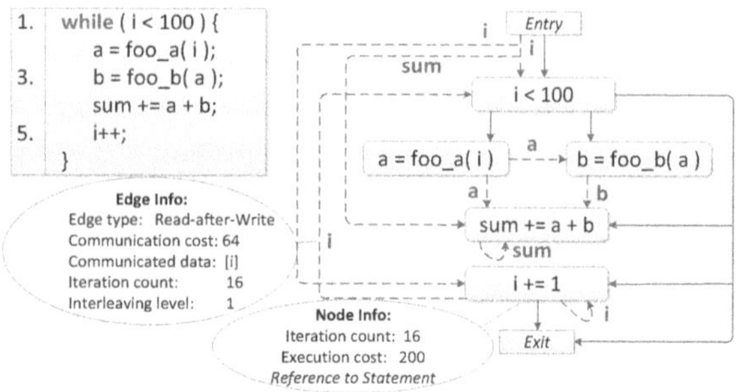

Figure 2: Program Dependence Graph

in parallel. As soon as all tasks have communicated their data to the consuming task T_2, the iterations four, five and six are executed in parallel to the first three iterations of task T_2 and so on. By combining both kinds of splits, the work-load is optimally balanced.

The extraction of this kind of parallelism has already been studied before, e.g., in [6] and [20]. However, in contrast to these earlier approaches, the one presented in this paper is able to consider multiple objectives at the same time while extracting pipeline parallelism. The solution in Figure 1(c) is very efficient regarding execution time, since all tasks execute their work in parallel without any delays. Nevertheless, four processing units are running at maximum speed, which consumes a significant amount of energy. In addition, a large amount of data has to be communicated concurrently which causes high bus contention and may block the execution of the tasks. Even if the solution shown in Figure 1(b) seems to be less efficient, a platform with fewer cores can be used to execute this solution which may save a huge amount of energy. Thus, if timing criteria are still met, solutions with less extracted parallelism may also be beneficial for other objectives.

4. PROGRAM DEPENDENCE GRAPH

The multi-objective aware pipeline parallelization approach presented in this paper employs an intermediate representation called augmented program dependence graph (PDG). The PDG is extracted for each loop of the application and combines both, control- and data-dependencies which makes it most suitable for our purposes. An example is given in Figure 2. The graph contains one entry, one exit and one node for each statement of the considered loop's body. Control flow dependencies are visualized by solid directed edges while data dependencies are represented by dashed arrows. Even for this small example many dependencies exist which makes it nontrivial to detect pipeline parallelism based on the graphical representation.

The presented parallelization approach of this paper uses high-level models to evaluate the benefit of a parallelized solution candidate of the considered loop in a very efficient way (c.f. Section 5.2). These models are used to determine the influence of a newly extracted task for all considered objectives, because task creation overhead and communication costs may prohibit efficient parallel execution. Therefore, necessary information like, e.g., estimated execution costs and the iteration count of the attached statement are annotated to the nodes of the graph (cf. *Node Info* in Figure 2). In addition, the edge type, communication costs, the communicated data, the iteration count and the interleaving level – describing the minimal amount of loop iterations which can be executed before the data is consumed by the target node – are annotated at the edges of the graph (cf. *Edge Info* in Figure 2). By combining the graphical representation with the additional cost information, all necessary information is available to extract well-balanced, efficient pipeline parallelism. The data is automatically extracted by the framework described in Section 6.

5. MULTI-OBJECTIVE AWARE EXTRACTION OF PIPELINE PARALLELISM

The parallelization algorithm presented in this paper is able to extract pipeline parallelism from loops of sequential ANSI-C applications in a multi-objective aware manner. Therefore, each loop(-nest) is transformed into an augmented program dependence graph and processed by a genetic algorithm presented in this section. As a result, a front of Pareto-optimal solutions representing parallelized versions of the considered loop is returned. The method to combine the different solutions of all loops to a global result is presented hereafter in Section 6.

5.1 Chromosome Representation

Genetic algorithms are favored for solving optimization problems in a multi-objective aware manner. They start with an initial population consisting of individuals representing possible solution candidates for the optimization problem. Each individual is characterized by a gene sequence called chromosome which describes the configuration of the optimization values. In each optimization step, some promising individuals are chosen to be mutated or recombined with other individuals to create a new population. This process is then repeated until a pre-defined termination criterion, e.g., a maximum number of generated populations, is met.

The challenge of using genetic algorithms is to map the optimization problem to genes of the individuals' chromosomes in such a way that they can be efficiently evaluated for different objectives. In the case of a genetic pipeline parallelization approach, disjunct pipeline stages of a loop(-nest) which are executed in an interleaved way, like shown in the example of Section 3, should be extracted. This can be achieved by horizontally splitting the loop's body. To further increase the application's performance, the genetic algorithm should also be able to vertically split these pipeline stages so that different loop iterations of the stage can be executed concurrently. Thus, both splits have to be part of each individual's chromosome, like depicted in Figure 3. As can be seen, the structure of the chromosomes is divided into two parts. The mapping of PDG nodes, representing statements of the loop's body, to tasks is shown on the left-hand side. Here, each node is mapped to exactly one task which represents one of the extracted pipeline stages due to horizontal splits. On the right-hand side, an integer variable declares how often each task, i.e., pipeline stage, is split into sub-tasks which are executing different loop iterations of the stage in parallel. In the example of Figure 3, the statements represented by nodes N_1 and N_2 are mapped to task (or pipeline stage) T_1, while node N_3 is mapped to task T_2. The first pipeline stage T_1 is split S_1 times, T_2 is split S_2 times, and so on. Each chromosome can be represented by an array of integers. The size of this array is as large as the number of statements contained in the loop's body plus the

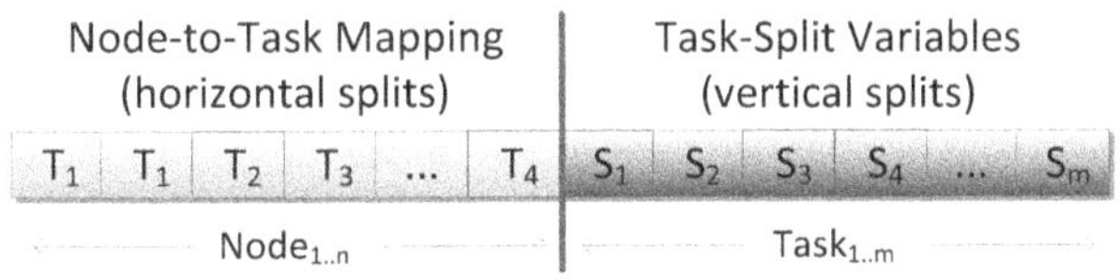

Figure 3: Structure of Chromosomes

number of maximal pipeline stages to generate. Thus, each chromosome can be decoded very efficiently which enables the generation of a huge amount of individuals.

The impact of a chromosome's configuration is visualized in more detail in Figure 4. As can be seen in the top part of the figure, nodes N_1 and N_2 are mapped to the first pipeline stage (T_1), N_4 and N_5 are mapped to stage T_3, while N_3 and N_6 are mapped to stages T_2 and T_4. Thus, T_1 starts with the execution of the first iteration of nodes N_1 and N_2. Afterwards, the generated data is sent to pipeline stages T_2 and T_3 so that the next iteration of T_1 is executed concurrently to the first iteration of T_2 and T_3, analogously to the example of Section 3. The dependencies between the different extracted pipeline stages rely on the node to task (i.e. node to pipeline stage) mapping. Thus, if one node is moved from one task to another, e.g., by mutating an individual, the dependencies between the stages may change which also influences the execution order of the tasks. If, e.g., node N_2 would be moved from T_1 to T_2, a new edge has to be added between the stages of tasks T_2 and T_3 which has to be taken into account while mutating and recombining individuals. Thus, even small changes in the mutation steps may have big influences for the evaluation of different objectives.

The genes of the vertical splits are shown in the bottom-left part of Figure 4. Here, the pipeline stages T_1 and T_3 are split once, resulting in two sub-tasks for both pipeline stages. Stages T_2 and T_4 are not split in this example so that each iteration of these stages is executed sequentially. The timing which belongs to the chromosome's configuration is visualized in the bottom-right corner of Figure 4. Due to the split of stage T_1, the first two iterations of this stage are executed concurrently. As soon as the results are available, the data is communicated to T_2 and both instances of task T_3. In the next time frame, iterations 3 and 4 are executed in parallel to the first and second iterations of T_2 and both sub-tasks of T_3. After four time slots, all six tasks are concurrently executing the statements assigned to their pipeline stage. Depending on task creation and communication costs, this configuration of the genes' values might represent a good solution candidate for the given example regarding executing time. Nevertheless, six tasks are executed in parallel so that many processing units have to execute their work concurrently which consumes significantly more energy if voltage scaling is not applied. Thus, other allocations of the chromosome's decision values might lead to solutions which reduce other limited resources as well.

5.2 Evaluation of Objectives

Since the quality of the final Pareto-optimal solutions returned by a genetic algorithm primarily depends on the population sizes used and the number of generated populations, the configuration of an individual's chromosome must be evaluated very efficiently. Thus, simulating each solution candidate which is generated by the genetic algorithm on the target platform is not an option since it would be too time

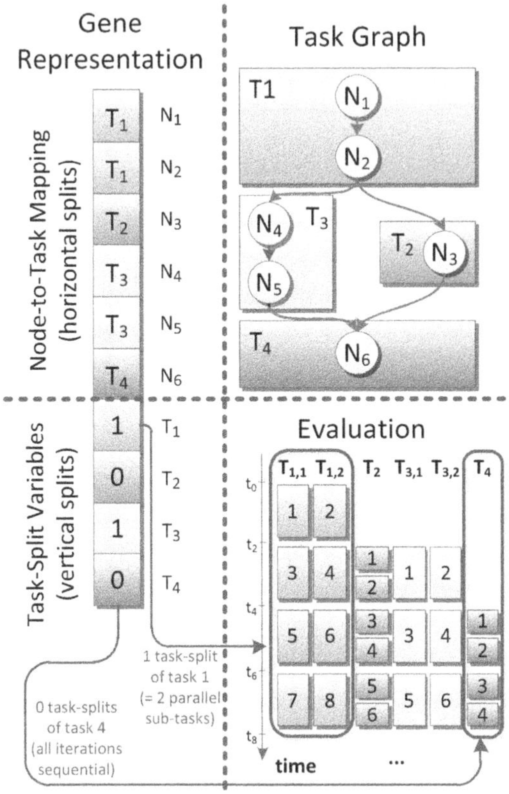

Figure 4: Impact of Genes' Configuration

consuming. Instead, the employed genetic parallelization algorithm uses high-level models to evaluate the different objectives. Here, we adapted the high-level models presented in [7] since these models can be evaluated very efficiently. In addition, the paper has also shown that the results of the objective values generated by the models are comparable to the ones extracted by the MPARM simulator [1], which is also used as target platform in this paper. The current implementation of our framework provides models for the objectives *execution time*, *energy consumption*, and the amount of *communicated data*. These models are described in the following.

Since different iterations of the same task may or may not depend on each other, the loop iterations are virtually unrolled for the calculation within these models. Like depicted in the right part of Figure 4, two circumstances can create dependencies between different tasks and their iterations. First, one iteration of task T_i depends on an iteration of task T_k, if data- or control-dependencies between two statements with the matching interleaving level of these task exist, like shown in the top right part of Figure 4. Second, different iterations of a task T_i may depend on each other controlled by the number of splits (see bottom-right part of Figure 4). Since task T_1 is split into two sub-tasks, iteration one and two of Task T_1 can be executed concurrently, while the third and fourth iteration depend on iteration one and two, respectively. If task T_1 would not be split, all iterations of this task would depend on each other. Thus, the variable T_i^j denotes the jth iteration of task i in the following.

Constants like, e.g., a constant task creation overhead or a communication multiplier can be adjusted in our framework to support different target architectures. In addition, values like execution time or the amount of communicated data are extracted automatically by pre-processing tools of our framework and are annotated to the augmented program dependence graph of the loop to parallelize.

5.2.1 Objective 1: Execution time

To evaluate the objective value representing the execution time of a parallelized loop, high-level models based on the linear models of Sarkar [21] and our previous publication in [7] are used. Both models were developed to evaluate task-level parallelism so that we had to extend them to correctly handle different loop iterations and their dependencies for pipeline parallelism. The returned value of our proposed model is equal to the cycles of the longest (or most critical) execution path of the loop to parallelize. The following equations will describe the evaluation in a formal way.

The first component which is necessary to calculate the overall execution time of the parallelized loop is the execution time of task T_i in iteration j. In our model, the execution time of a task T_i is uniformly dispersed over all loop iterations of the task. Thus, the execution time $ET(T_i^j)$ of task T_i in iteration j is equal to the sum of the execution times $ETN(n)$ of the nodes n which are mapped to T_i, divided by the number of loop iterations LI:

$$ET(T_i^j) = \sum_{n \in Nodes(T_i)} \frac{ETN(n)}{LI}$$

Based on the execution time of one iteration of a task, path costs can be calculated which denote the time until the jth iteration of a task T_i is executed, including all iterations of its predecessors. The path costs $PC(T_i^j)$ of a task T_i in its jth iteration are equal to the sum of T_i's execution costs of the iteration $ET(T_i^j)$ and the path costs of the most expensive predecessor tasks T_ℓ^k including the costs of the communication $CC(T_\ell^k, T_i^j)$ between T_ℓ^k and T_i^j. The communication costs can be adapted to different architectures using a platform-dependent communication overhead. Due to the recursive structure of this formula, the costs of all indirect predecessors are also included:

$$\begin{aligned} PC(T_i^j) &= ET(T_i^j) + \\ &\quad \max\{PC(T_\ell^k) + CC(T_\ell^k, T_i^j) | T_\ell^k \in Pred(T_i^j)\} \end{aligned}$$

The overall execution costs are composed of the platform-dependent configurable task creation costs TCO, multiplied by the number of created tasks NT plus the most expensive path costs $PC(T_i^{LI})$ of all tasks T_i in their last iterations LI:

$$OverallET = TCO * NT + \max\{PC(T_i^{LI}) | \forall T_i \in Tasks\}$$

The changes made to the original model presented in [7] are mainly that the execution time of a task T_i is now dispersed over its loop iterations j and that each iteration is considered on its own to make the models applicable for pipeline parallelism. In addition, the task creation overhead is now added once before the extracted tasks are executed.

5.2.2 Objective 2: Energy consumption

The objective value describing the energy consumption consists of energy costs produced by task creation, communication overhead and the execution costs of statements which are mapped to the tasks.

The incoming communication energy costs $ICE(T_i^j)$ for task i in iteration j are equal to the sum of a constant incoming communication energy overhead $ICEO$ plus the number of transferred bytes $\#Bytes(d)$ multiplied by a platform-dependent communication energy factor ICM:

$$ICE(T_i^j) = \sum_{d \in InData(T_i^j)} ICEO + \#Bytes(d) * ICM$$

The outgoing communication energy $OCE(T_i^j)$ is calculated analogously to $ICE(T_i^j)$:

$$OCE(T_i^j) = \sum_{d \in OutData(T_i^j)} OCEO + \#Bytes(d) * OCM$$

The energy $E(T_i^j)$ which is necessary to execute iteration j of task i contains both, the incoming ($ICE(T_i^j)$) and outgoing ($OCE(T_i^j)$) communication energy costs, increased by the energy $EN(n)$ which is necessary to execute the statements mapped to task T_i. The energy consumption is also dispersed in equal parts over all loop iterations of the task:

$$E(T_i^j) = ICE(T_i^j) + OCE(T_i^j) + \sum_{n \in Nodes(T_i)} \frac{EN(n)}{LI}$$

Finally, the overall energy consumption $OverallEnergy$ includes a constant energy overhead for task creation TCE multiplied with the number of created tasks, increased by the energy which is consumed by all tasks $E(T_i^j)$ in each iteration:

$$OverallEnergy = TCE * NT + \sum_{i \in Tasks} \sum_{j \in \{0..LI\}} E(T_i^j)$$

Here, the main difference to the original model from [7] is that the energy consumption is modeled for each loop iteration separately.

5.2.3 Objective 3: Communication Overhead

The evaluation of the communication overhead is the simplest one and is identical to the original model presented in [7]. Here, all communicated data is summed up and multiplied with a platform-dependent communication factor:

$$CommOverhead = \sum_{d \in Comm} \#Bytes(d) * Costs$$

5.3 Mutation and Recombination

Genetic algorithms generate new solution candidates (i.e. new individuals) by modifying values of the genes of existing individuals. This is done by a combination of mutation and recombination. In the first case, one gene of the chromosome is modified with a given probability. In our case, one statement is moved from one task to another – in case of a horizontal-cut change – or the number of splits of a newly created task is modified. Thus, dependencies between different tasks or at least between different iterations of one task may change in such a mutation step which has to be considered for the evaluation of the solution candidates.

In the second case, the recombination of individuals, also known as cross-over, cuts the chromosomes of two individuals at a random position to combine the left-hand side of the first chromosome with the right-hand side of the other side and vice versa. This operation simulates the combination of profitable individuals to new solution candidates.

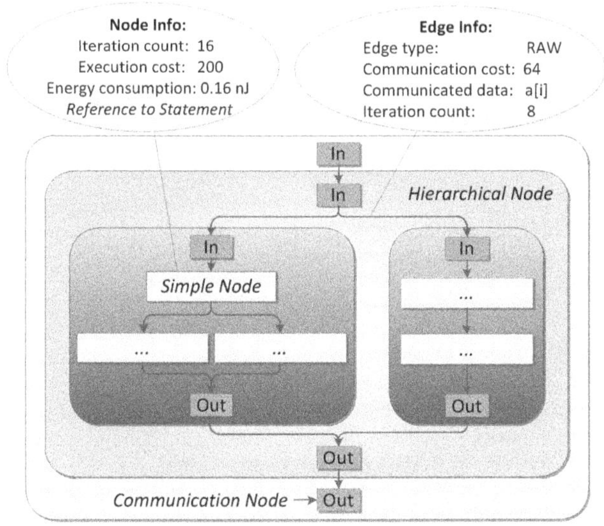

Figure 5: Hierarchical Task Graph

Both, mutation and recombination are processed until a given number of populations are evaluated so that a front of Pareto-optimal solutions of the parallelized loop is returned.

6. FRAMEWORK INTEGRATION

The task-level parallelization approach presented in [7] is the first framework that extracts parallelism in a multi-objective aware manner. The framework is able to automatically extract dependencies and additional information like, e.g., estimated execution times of statements of the application which are necessary to define our high-level models. In addition, our new multi-objective aware pipeline parallelization approach perfectly complements the approach presented in [7], since the older approach has only very limited support to parallelize loops of embedded applications.

The approach presented in [7] employs an annotated hierarchical task graph as intermediate representation like shown in Figure 5. The hierarchical structure of the graph is based on the hierarchical structure of the application's source code. Thus, e.g., function bodies, loops, or conditional statements create new hierarchical levels which can be parallelized in isolation. Unfortunately, the hierarchical task graph hides loop-carried dependencies which makes it unsuitable for the extraction of pipeline parallelism. The approach starts to extract task-level parallelism in a bottom-up search strategy which means that it starts to parallelize the inner-most hierarchical node. Each node is processed by a genetic algorithm which extracts a front of Pareto-optimal solutions which are added as solution candidates for the parallelized node. As soon as all nodes on the same level of the hierarchy are processed, the algorithm moves upwards in the hierarchy knowing that a Pareto-front of solution candidates is attached to each child node. At the next hierarchical level, the algorithm has the possibility to extract new tasks and to recombine this solution with parallel solutions which were found deeper in the hierarchy.

This encapsulated parallelization technique is the key which enables to integrate different parallelization approaches into one framework. Each approach is executed to return solution candidates representing beneficial parallelized versions of the statement represented by the node. The only requirement is that each solution can be evaluated for all considered objectives. Thus, a front of Pareto-optimal points from different approaches can be combined to be used in the following parallelization steps upwards in the hierarchy of the graph.

Here, we combined the multi-objective aware pipeline parallelization approach with the existing task-level technique. While the task-level parallelization approach can be applied to each hierarchical node of the graph, the pipeline parallelization approach is limited to loops. Thus, as soon as a node representing a loop is reached in the parallelization process, the corresponding program dependence graph is extracted and the genetic pipeline parallelization approach is executed. Afterwards, the results are added to the Pareto front. Due to the encapsulated technique, it is also possible to use only a subset of the parallelization approaches offered, like, e.g., only the pipeline parallelization approach.

As soon as the top node of the hierarchical graph is reached, the final front of Pareto-optimal solutions is returned to the application designer, who can choose the solution which represents the best trade-off for the given application scenario.

7. EXPERIMENTAL RESULTS

To evaluate the efficiency of our multi-objective aware parallelization framework we present results achieved from the UTDSP benchmark suite [14] containing representative real-world embedded applications. In addition, we also evaluated other meaningful embedded applications like, e.g., a JPEG encoder. As target platform we used the cycle-accurate MPARM simulator [1] which provides up to four single-core ARM processors. The simulator is also equipped with a detailed energy model called MEMSIM [28] which makes it most suitable for our purposes.

Figure 6(a-d) shows detailed results for four of the considered benchmarks. As explained in Section 5.2, our current framework is optimizing for the three objectives of speedup (execution time), energy consumption of the system and the communication overhead introduced by the extracted parallelism. These objectives are arranged on the x-, y- and z-axes in three dimensional diagrams. All axes are relative to the sequential solution which is located at the bottom-left point of the diagrams with a speedup of $1\times$, 100% energy consumption and zero communication overhead. For better readability we projected the points of the 3D-diagrams to the x-y-plane. Thus, the communication overhead of different solutions can be compared by the height of the vertical bars. Each diagram contains both, Pareto-optimal and Pareto-dominated points of the final solutions generated by our framework. Of course, only the Pareto-optimal ones are returned to the application designer. To compare the efficiency of the new multi-objective aware pipeline parallelization approach presented in this paper with the previously published multi-objective aware task-level parallelization technique contained in the framework presented in Section 6, different shapes are used for both types. In addition, the diagram also shows points which contain some parallel sections produced by task-level and some sections produced by pipeline parallelism. Thus, these points are produced by a combination of both approaches and are labeled as a MIXED solution.

By analyzing the results for the different benchmarks one can see that the number of Pareto-optimal solutions re-

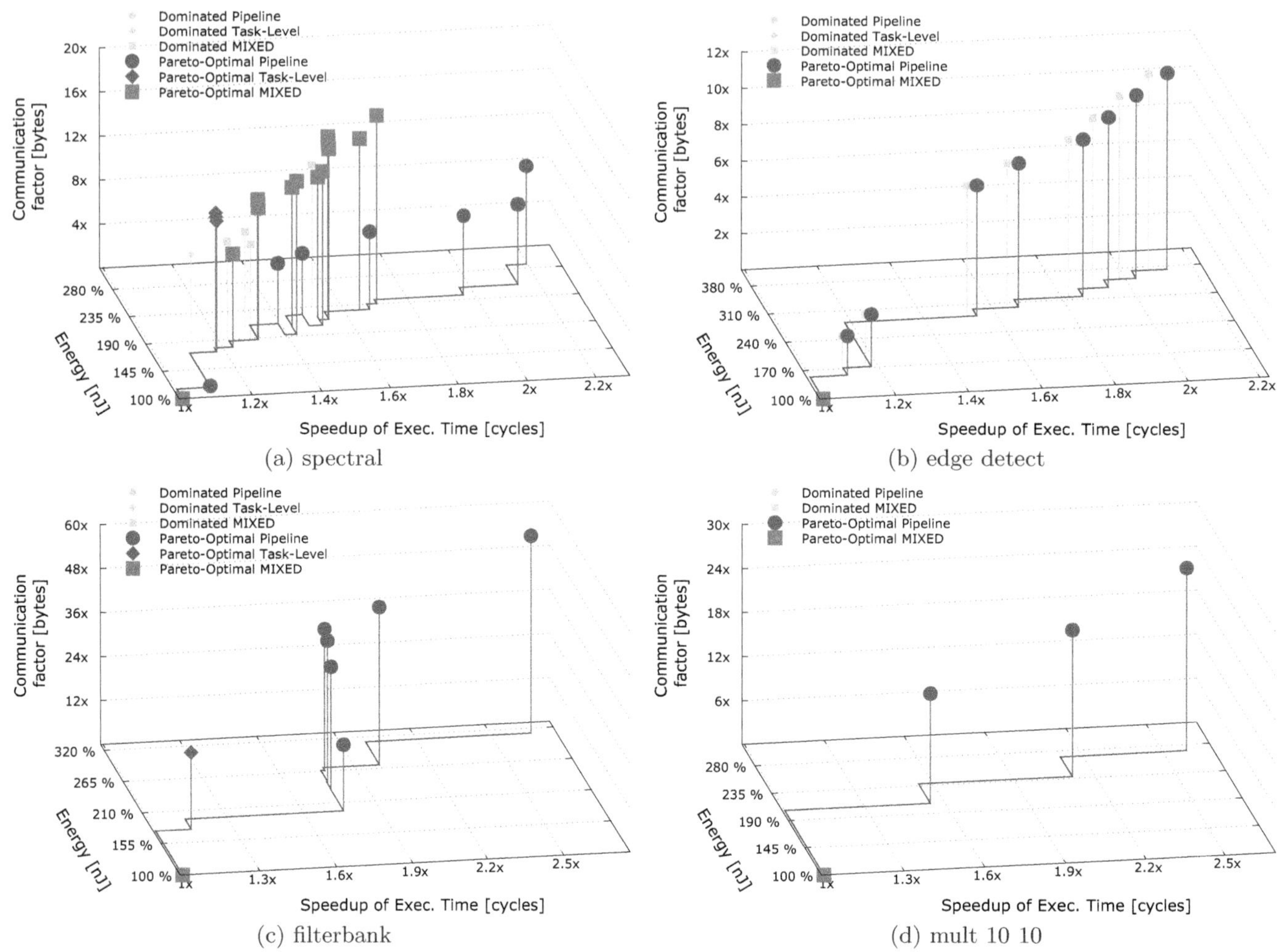

Figure 6: Final parallel solutions returned by the parallelization framework

turned to the application designer ranges from 4 up to 25 solutions which show huge optimization potential for different objectives. The solution with the highest speedup for, e.g., the filterbank benchmark (cf. Figure 6(c)) reduces the execution time by a factor of nearly 2.7×. Even if this solution drastically reduces the execution time of the application, it requires the highest communication overhead. In addition, all cores of the platform are executing threads in parallel which increases the energy consumption of the system to around 320% compared to the sequential solution. If the application designer knows that, e.g., a speedup of 1.9× is sufficient to meet his timing requirements he can choose a solution with less extracted parallelism. Thus, some of the cores can be switched into idle mode for some time and a platform with less processing units can be chosen. This reduces the energy consumption to less than 270% for this solution of the filterbank benchmark which is very efficient compared to 320% energy consumption for the solution with the highest speedup. In addition, the amount of inserted communication is also reduced. The solution with a speedup of 1.7× even reduces the energy consumption to less than 200% which highlights the optimization potential of our multi-objective aware approach. These observations can be made for the other evaluated benchmarks as well.

As already observed in [6], pipeline parallelism is able to generate solutions with a higher speedup compared to solutions which are extracted by task-level parallelism for many embedded applications. When looking at the results of our multi-objective aware framework, this observation is also confirmed, here. The solutions of Figure 6(a-d), which are extracting the highest speedup for the considered applications, are always generated by pure pipeline parallelism. However, these solutions also consume the highest amount of energy. This trade-off can be seen best in Figure 6(a) which shows the solutions of the spectral benchmark. This application was also used as the motiving example in Section 3. Here, 3 of 4 solutions with a speedup of less than 1.2x are generated by the already published coarse-grained task-level extraction approach. Even if the speedup is not as high as the speedup of the other approaches, only a small increase in energy consumption was observed. Nevertheless, a high amount of communication has to be inserted for this kind of parallelism depending on the structure of the application. 14 solutions with speedups between 1.2× and 1.7× are created by a combination of task-level and pipeline parallelism. Thus, the energy consumption is slightly increased but is at least lower than for solutions generated by pure pipeline parallelism. Finally, the solution candidates with more than 1.7× speedup are extracted by the pipeline parallelization approach presented in this paper. As can be

Benchmark	Time[1]	#N	#Pop	#Ind	#Mut	#Cross	#S(TL,PL,MI)
adpcm encoder	01:04	36	1,520	151,049	28,154	98,766	5(2,2,1)
boundary value	01:11	12	644	83,331	15,804	54,032	4(0,3,1)
compress	14:31	336	10,444	821,854	161,617	608,250	5(0,4,1)
edge detect	04:48	105	2,872	196,720	38,125	137,788	9(0,8,1)
filterbank	02:39	7	412	51,035	15,005	136,485	8(1,6,1)
fir 256	00:39	13	388	29,607	5,863	22,317	4(0,3,1)
h264_ldecode_block	01:40	115	3,520	251,166	49,943	179,088	6(5,0,1)
h264_ldecode_macroblock	02:30	51	2,168	238,007	45,870	170,351	5(2,1,2)
iir 4	14:35	13	852	103,294	21,298	92,830	4(0,3,1)
jpeg2000	04:49	62	2,868	313,047	62,630	231,390	45(0,27,18)
latnrm 32	01:34	17	636	53,462	11,931	46,358	4(0,3,1)
mult 10 10	02:45	36	1,060	70,442	14,984	60,399	4(0,3,1)
spectral	03:04	51	2,260	211,023	41,667	160,477	25(3,7,15)

Table 1: Evaluation of Genetic Parallelization Algorithm

seen in the figure, other Pareto-dominated solutions with task-level parallelism, pipeline parallelism and also a mixture of both techniques were generated but not returned to the application designer. Other benchmarks like, e.g., the edge detect benchmark in Figure 6(b) or the matrix multiplication application (mult 10 10) in Figure 6(d) profit even more from the new pipeline parallelization approach.

7.1 Genetic Algorithm Statistics

Due to limited space it is not possible to give results for all evaluated benchmarks in a graphical representation. Therefore, we sum up the results and statistics of the genetic algorithm of the other evaluated benchmarks in Table 1. The columns contain information about the time in minutes[1] which was necessary to parallelize the applications with the combination of the task-level and pipeline parallelization approach (*Time*), the number of processed nodes (*#N*), the number of generated populations (*#Pop*), the overall number of generated and evaluated individuals (*#Ind*), the number of mutated (*#Mut*) and recombined (*#Cross*) individuals and the number of offered Pareto-optimal solutions (*#S*) returned to the designer. The numbers shown in brackets in the last column show how many Pareto-optimal solutions were generated by the task-level- (*TL*) and pipeline parallelization (*PL*) approach as well as the number of solutions generated by combining both approaches (*MI*). The number of individuals and populations used to parallelize a node is determined dynamically, based on the number of child nodes. Thus, nodes with a smaller search space are processed much faster. The numbers of populations, individuals, mutations, etc., shown are summed up over all parallelized nodes and may marginally differ between different tool flow executions due to random decisions taken by genetic algorithms.

As can be seen in the last column of Table 1, most Pareto-optimal solutions are created by the new multi-objective aware pipeline parallelization approach presented in this paper. Nevertheless, some benchmarks also profit from the previously published task-level parallelization approach and also from the combination of both approaches. For example, 25 Pareto-optimal solutions are returned to the application designer for the spectral benchmark, which was used in the motivating example in Section 3. Three of these 25 solutions were generated by the task-level approach, while 7 solutions are purely based on extracted pipeline parallelism. Nevertheless, 15 solutions were generated by the combined approach containing parallel sections with both, task-level and pipeline parallelism. Thus, both approaches and also their combination are adding meaningful solutions which optimize at least one dimension of the Pareto-space. There are also benchmarks which profit either from the task-level parallelization approach, like, e.g., the block decoding of the h264 decoder, or from the pipeline parallelization approach, like, e.g., the latnrm benchmark. However, most benchmarks have shown that they profit from both approaches and their combination.

The table also presents some statistics of the genetic algorithm and the time which was necessary to parallelize the application. For the jpeg2000 application, for example, more than 300,000 individuals were created by mutation and recombination of old solutions. The whole parallelization approach took less than 5 minutes which correlates to less than a microsecond to mutate or recombine and also evaluate one of the individuals. Otherwise it would not be possible to generate a huge amount of solution candidates which would drastically reduce the quality of the solutions generated by the genetic algorithm.

7.2 Summary

To summarize, the following results could be confirmed by the evaluation:

1. A huge optimization potential exists if multiple objectives are considered at the same time in the parallelization process.
2. The new multi-objective aware pipeline parallelization approach presented in this paper extracts, in general, the most efficient parallelism regarding speedup of execution time for the considered embedded applications.
3. Solutions generated by the task-level parallelization approach are less efficient regarding speedup for many embedded applications, but they use less energy at the expense of more communication overhead.
4. The combination of task-level and pipeline parallelism produces highly beneficial solutions which find a good trade-off between the high speedup of pipeline parallelism and less energy consumption of task-level parallelism.

Thus, the results have shown that the multi-objective aware extraction of pipeline parallelism highly improves the quality of the solutions returned by the existing framework. In addition, the combination with task-level parallelism also extends the space of Pareto-optimal solutions.

[1]Measured on a system with two AMD Opteron quad-cores running at 2.4GHz

8. CONCLUSIONS AND FUTURE WORK

To the best of our knowledge, this paper presents the first pipeline parallelization approach which uses genetic algorithms to divide loops of embedded applications horizontally and vertically into concurrently executed tasks in a multi-objective aware manner. In addition, we combined this approach with an existing multi-objective aware task-level parallelization technique to benefit from both types of parallelism. The evaluation was performed using real-world embedded applications and it could be shown that each approach and also their combination are able to add Pareto-optimal solution candidates to the final results. Compared to the state-of-the-art, our framework enables the possibility to select the parallel solution which perfectly matches to a specific application scenario instead of just returning the solution with the highest speedup on cost of other resources.

In the future, we would like to extend our framework and the models used to be aware of static or dynamic voltage frequency scaling to further optimize the energy consumption of the embedded device. Even if this might lead to a decrease of the application's speedup, the trade-off can be perfectly integrated into our framework. In addition, we would also like to evaluate the influence of other objectives (e.g., code size) and adapt the tool flow to be also aware of heterogeneous architectures.

9. REFERENCES

[1] L. Benini, D. Bertozzi, A. Bogliolo, et al. MPARM: Exploring the Multi-Processor SoC Design Space with SystemC. *Journal of VLSI Signal Processing Systems*, 2005.

[2] U. Bondhugula, A. Hartono, J. Ramanujam, et al. A practical automatic polyhedral parallelizer and locality optimizer. In *Proc. of PLDI*, 2008.

[3] J. Ceng, J. Castrillon, W. Sheng, et al. MAPS: an integrated framework for MPSoC application parallelization. In *Proc. of DAC*, 2008.

[4] R. Chandra, D.-K. Chen, et al. Data distribution support on distributed shared memory multiprocessors. *ACM SIGPLAN Notices*, 1997.

[5] S. Cho and R. G. Melhem. On the Interplay of Parallelization, Program Performance, and Energy Consumption. *IEEE Trans. Parallel Distrib. Syst.*, 2010.

[6] D. Cordes, A. Heinig, P. Marwedel, et al. Automatic Extraction of Pipeline Parallelism for Embedded Software Using Linear Programming. In *Proc. of ICPADS*, 2011.

[7] D. Cordes and P. Marwedel. Multi-Objective Aware Extraction of Task-Level Parallelism Using Genetic Algorithms. In *Proc. of DATE*, 2012.

[8] D. Cordes, P. Marwedel, and A. Mallik. Automatic parallelization of embedded software using hierarchical task graphs and integer linear programming. In *Proc. of CODES/ISSS*. ACM, 2010.

[9] B. Franke and M. O'Boyle. Compiler parallelization of C programs for multi-core DSPs with multiple address spaces. In *Proc. of CODES+ISSS*. ACM, 2003.

[10] M. I. Gordon, W. Thies, and S. Amarasinghe. Exploiting coarse-grained task, data, and pipeline parallelism in stream programs. In *Proc. of ASPLOS-XII*. ACM, 2006.

[11] M. H. Hall, S. P. Amarasinghe, B. R. Murphy, et al. Detecting coarse-grain parallelism using an interprocedural parallelizing compiler. In *Proc. of Supercomputing*, 1995.

[12] M. W. Hall, J. M. Anderson, S. P. Amarasinghe, et al. Maximizing Multiprocessor Performance with the SUIF Compiler. *IEEE Computer*, 29(12), 1996.

[13] M. S. Lam and R. P. Wilson. Limits of Control Flow on Parallelism. In *ISCA*, 1992.

[14] C. G. Lee. UTDSP Benchmark Suite. http://www.eecg.toronto.edu/ ~corinna/DSP/infrastructure/UTDSP.html, April 2012.

[15] C. Lengauer. Loop Parallelization in the Polytope Model. In *CONCUR '93, Lecture Notes in Computer Science 715*. Springer-Verlag, 1993.

[16] D. Liu, Z. Shao, M. Wang, et al. Optimal loop parallelization for maximizing iteration-level parallelism. In *Proc. of CASES*, 2009.

[17] H. Nikolov, M. Thompson, T. Stefanov, et al. Daedalus: Toward composable multimedia MP-SoC design. In *Proc. of DAC*, 2008.

[18] G. Ottoni, R. Rangan, A. Stoler, et al. Automatic Thread Extraction with Decoupled Software Pipelining. In *Proc. of MICRO 38*, 2005.

[19] M. Qiu, J.-W. Niu, L. T. Yang, et al. Energy-Aware Loop Parallelism Maximization for Multi-core DSP Architectures. In *Proc. of GreenCom*, 2010.

[20] E. Raman, G. Ottoni, A. Raman, et al. Parallel-stage decoupled software pipelining. In *Proc. of CGO*. ACM, 2008.

[21] V. Sarkar. *Partitioning and Scheduling Parallel Programs for Multiprocessors*. MIT Press, 1989.

[22] V. Sarkar. Automatic partitioning of a program dependence graph into parallel tasks. *IBM Journal of Research and Development*, 1991.

[23] W. Thies, M. Karczmarek, and S. P. Amarasinghe. StreamIt: A Language for Streaming Applications. In *Proc. of CC*. Springer, 2002.

[24] G. Tournavitis and B. Franke. Semi-automatic extraction and exploitation of hierarchical pipeline parallelism using profiling information. In *Proc. of PACT*. ACM, 2010.

[25] G. Tournavitis, Z. Wang, B. Franke, et al. Towards a holistic approach to auto-parallelization: integrating profile-driven parallelism detection and machine-learning based mapping. In *Proc. of PLDI*, 2009.

[26] S. Verdoolaege, H. Nikolov, and T. Stefanov. pn: A Tool for Improved Derivation of Process Networks. *EURASIP Journal on Embedded Systems*, 2007.

[27] Y. Wang, H. Liu, D. Liu, et al. Overhead-aware energy optimization for real-time streaming applications on multiprocessor System-on-Chip. *ACM Trans. Des. Autom. Electron. Syst.*, 16, 2011.

[28] L. Wehmeyer and P. Marwedel. *Fast, Efficient and Predictable Memory Accesses*. Springer-Verlag New York, Inc., 2006.

[29] M. E. Wolf and M. S. Lam. A Loop Transformation Theory and an Algorithm to Maximize Parallelism. *IEEE Trans. Parallel Distrib. Syst.*, 2(4), 1991.

Managing Latency in Embedded Streaming Applications under Hard-Real-Time Scheduling

Mohamed A. Bamakhrama
mohamed@liacs.nl

Todor Stefanov
stefanov@liacs.nl

Leiden Institute of Advanced Computer Science
Leiden University, Leiden, The Netherlands

ABSTRACT

In this paper, we consider the problem of hard-real-time scheduling of embedded streaming applications, modeled using dataflow graphs, while minimizing the application latency. Recently, it has been shown that the actors in an acyclic Cyclo-Static Dataflow (CSDF) graph can be scheduled as a set of implicit-deadline periodic tasks. Such scheduling approach has been shown to yield the maximum achievable throughput for a large set of graphs, called matched I/O rates graphs. We show that scheduling the graph actors as implicit-deadline periodic tasks increases the latency significantly for a class of graphs called unbalanced graphs. To alleviate this problem, we propose a new task-set representation for the actors in which the actors are scheduled as a set of constrained-deadline periodic tasks. We prove that scheduling the actors as constrained-deadline periodic tasks delivers optimal throughput (i.e., rate) and latency for graphs with repetition vector equal to $\vec{1}$. Furthermore, we evaluate the constrained-deadline representation using a set of 19 real-life applications and show that it is capable of achieving the minimum achievable latency for more than 70% of the applications, and even if the application has a repetition vector not equal to $\vec{1}$. We show that choosing the task deadline involves a trade-off between the latency and the resources requirements. Finally, we propose a decision tree to assist the designer in choosing the appropriate real-time periodic task model for scheduling acyclic CSDF graphs.

Categories and Subject Descriptors

C.3 [**Special-Purpose and Application-Based Systems**]: [Real-time and embedded systems]; D.4.7 [**Operating Systems**]: Organization and Design—*Real-time systems and embedded systems*

General Terms

Algorithms, Design, Performance

Keywords

Real-time multiprocessor scheduling, streaming applications

1. INTRODUCTION

Embedded streaming systems have grown in complexity to the point that many of them require hard-real-time (HRT) execution of applications on multiprocessor platforms [11]. Additionally, some of these systems require support for dynamic (i.e., run-time) addition/removal of applications. To cope with such requirements, the system must use fast resource management and scheduling solutions which provide guaranteed services. To this end, algorithms from the hard-real-time multiprocessor scheduling theory represent an attractive solution approach. These algorithms provide many nice properties such as timing guarantees for each application, temporal isolation, and fast admission control of new incoming applications.

Recently, it has been shown that acyclic CSDF graphs with periodic input streams can be scheduled as asynchronous sets of implicit-deadline periodic tasks [3]. An implicit deadline periodic (IDP) task τ_i is defined by a 3-tuple $\tau_i = (S_i, C_i, T_i)$. The interpretation is as follows: τ_i is invoked (i.e., released) at time instants $t = S_i + kT_i$ and it has to execute for C_i time-units before time $t = S_i + (k+1)T_i$ for all $k \in \mathbb{N}_0$, where S_i is the start time of τ_i and T_i is the task period. Such scheduling approach is called strictly periodic scheduling (SPS). In [3], the authors considered the impact of strictly periodic scheduling (SPS) on the throughput and processor requirements of the applications. They showed that scheduling the graph actors as implicit-deadline periodic tasks yields the maximum achievable throughput (i.e., rate) for a large set of graphs, called matched I/O rates graphs. One advantage of using the IDP model is the low complexity of the schedulability test. However, the authors of [3] did not investigate the latency of the applications when scheduled using the IDP model. Generally speaking, latency is defined as the elapsed time between the arrival of a sample to an application and the output of the processed sample by the application. For many embedded streaming applications, latency is the primary performance metric rather than throughput.

In this paper, we show that the IDP model increases the latency significantly for a class of graphs called unbalanced graphs. A balanced graph is the one where the product of actor execution time and repetition is the same for all actors (see Definition 6 in Section 4.1). In contrast, an unbalanced graph is the one where such product differs between actors.

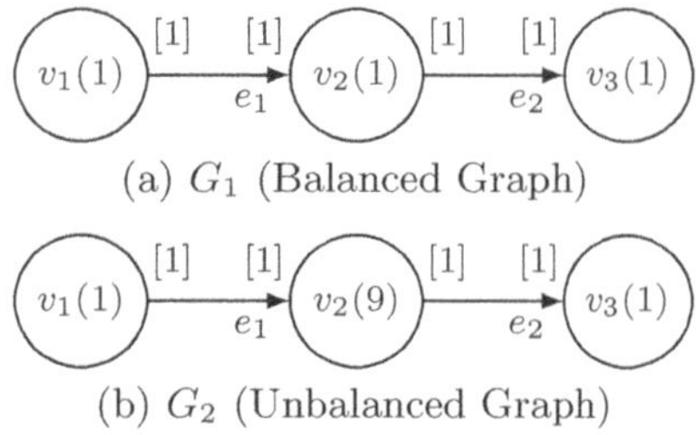

Figure 1: Example of balanced and unbalanced graphs

Table 1: Throughput and latency metrics for G_1 and G_2 under different scheduling schemes

	STS			IDP			CDP		
	R	L	M	R	L	M	R	L	M
G_1	1/1	3	3	1/1	3	3	1/1	3	3
G_2	1/9	11	2	1/9	27	2	1/9	11	2

To illustrate the impact of the IDP model on the latency, we present the following motivational example.

1.1 Motivational Example

In Figure 1, we show two graphs: G_1 and G_2. A schedule consists of an infinitely repeated finite sequence of actor firings. A repetition vector represents the number of actor firings in such finite sequence. Both graphs in Figure 1 have a repetition vector equal to $\vec{1}$. The execution time of each actor is shown next to its name between round brackets (e.g., 9 for v_2 in G_2). G_1 (Figure 1(a)) is an example of a balanced graph since the product of actor execution time and repetition is the same for all actors – 1 in this case. On the other hand, G_2 (Figure 1(b)) is an example of unbalanced graphs.

Let R, L, and M denote the throughput (i.e., rate), latency, and minimum processor requirements of a graph G, respectively. It has been shown that the maximum achievable throughput and minimum achievable latency of a dataflow graph are the ones achieved under self-timed scheduling (STS) [9,17]. Thus, the maximum throughput and minimum latency for both graphs is the one shown under the STS column in Table 1. The throughput and latency resulting from scheduling the actors of both graphs as IDP tasks is shown under the IDP column in Table 1. We see that the IDP model yields the maximum throughput for both graphs, however, it pays a high price in terms of increased latency for the unbalanced graph (up to 2.5x for G_2). Instead, if the actors are to be scheduled as constrained-deadline periodic (CDP) tasks, then it is possible to achieve the optimal throughput and latency (i.e., maximum throughput and minimum latency) as shown under the CDP column in Table 1. In terms of resource usage, we see that the CDP model achieves optimal throughput and latency for G_2 using the same number of processors needed by IDP and STS – 2 processors. Thus, in this example, the CDP model is equally good to the STS in terms of throughput, latency, and resources usage.

1.2 Problem Statement

Given an application modeled as an acyclic CSDF graph:

1. derive its latency when its actors are scheduled as implicit-deadline periodic tasks, and
2. derive a task-set representation for the actors, based on the constrained-deadline model, that minimizes the latency compared to the implicit-deadline model.

1.3 Paper Contributions

We identify two classes of CSDF graphs called balanced and unbalanced graphs. For balanced graphs, we show that the latency of the graph when its actors are scheduled as IDP tasks is equal to the minimum achievable latency. For unbalanced graphs, we devise a task-set representation based on the constrained-deadline model to reduce the latency. We prove that the proposed CDP representation achieves optimal throughput and latency for graphs with repetition vector equal to $\vec{1}$. Furthermore, we evaluate the proposed CDP representation using a set of 19 real-life applications and show that it is capable of achieving the minimum achievable latency for 70% of the applications, and even if the application has a repetition vector not equal to $\vec{1}$. Finally, we propose a decision tree to assist the designer in choosing the appropriate real-time periodic task model for scheduling acyclic CSDF graphs.

The remainder of this paper is organized as follows: Section 2 gives an overview of the related work. Section 3 introduces the background material needed for understanding the contributions of this paper. Section 4 presents the proposed task-set representation. Section 5 presents the evaluation of the proposed task-set representation. Finally, Section 6 ends the paper with conclusions.

2. RELATED WORK

In [17], it is shown that the minimum achievable latency of a Homogeneous Synchronous Dataflow (HSDF, [12]) graph is the one achieved under self-timed scheduling. This minimum latency is equal to the sum of execution times along the critical path in the graph. In [9], Ghamarian et al. extended this result to general Synchronous Dataflow (SDF, [12]) graphs and provided an algorithm to determine the minimum achievable latency. In contrast, our work analyzes the latency of CSDF graphs under strictly periodic scheduling considering different models of periodic tasks, i.e., IDP and CDP. Moreover, our analysis considers CSDF graphs which are more expressive model than SDF/HSDF.

In [10], Goddard studied applying real-time scheduling to dataflow programs modeled using the processing graphs method (PGM). He used a task model called rate-based execution (RBE) in which a real-time task τ_i is characterized by a 4-tuple $\tau_i = (x_i, y_i, d_i, c_i)$. The interpretation is as follows: τ_i executes x_i times in time period y_i with a relative deadline d_i per job release and c_i execution time per job release. Goddard analyzed the latency of PGM graphs scheduled using the RBE model and identified two sources of latency: 1) *inherit latency* which is the latency due to different production and consumption rates in the PGM graph assuming zero execution time for the actors, and 2) *imposed latency* which is the latency when non-zero execution times are imposed on the actors. In contrast, our approach uses CSDF graphs which are more expressive model than PGM graphs in that PGM supports only a *constant* production/consumption rate on edges (same as SDF), whereas CSDF supports *varying* (but predefined) production/consumption rates. As a result, the analysis technique in [10] is not applicable to CSDF graphs.

In [14], Moreira and Bekooij analyzed the latency of SDF graphs under self-timed scheduling and provided bounds on the maximum latency for applications with periodic, sporadic, and bursty sources, together with a technique to check latency requirements. In [15], they proposed algorithms to find combined Time-Division-Multiplexing (TDM)/static order schedules that guarantee a requested minimum throughput and maximum latency, while minimizing the usage of processing resources. Our approach differs from [14, 15] in: 1) we consider the periodic task models which allow applying a variety of proven hard-real-time scheduling algorithms for multiprocessors, and 2) we use the CSDF model which is more expressive than SDF graphs.

3. BACKGROUND

In this section, we provide an overview of the considered dataflow and real-time models. This overview is necessary for understanding the contributions in Section 4.

3.1 Cyclo-Static Dataflow (CSDF)

In [6], the CSDF model is defined as a directed graph $G = \langle V, E \rangle$, where V is a set of actors and $E \subseteq V \times V$ is a set of communication channels. Actors represent functions that transform incoming data streams into outgoing data streams. The communication channels carry streams of data, and an atomic data object is called a *token*. A channel $e_u \in E$ is a first-in, first-out (FIFO) queue with unbounded capacity defined by a tuple $e_u = (v_i, v_j)$. The tuple means that e_u is directed from v_i (called source) to v_j (called destination). The number of actors in a graph G is denoted by $N = |V|$. An actor receiving an input stream of the application is called *input actor*, and an actor producing an output stream of the application is called *output actor*. A path $w_{a \rightsquigarrow z}$ between actors v_a and v_z is an ordered sequence of channels defined as $w_{a \rightsquigarrow z} = \{(v_a, v_b), (v_b, v_c), \cdots, (v_y, v_z)\}$. A path $w_{i \rightsquigarrow j}$ is called *output path* if v_i is an input actor and v_j is an output actor. $\mathcal{W}$ denotes the set of all output paths in G. In this work, we consider only acyclic CSDF graphs. An acyclic graph G has a number of levels, denoted by $\mathcal{L}$, which is given by Algorithm 1. An actor v_i that belongs to set A_j in Algorithm 1 has a level index $\sigma_i = j$. Each actor $v_i \in V$ is associated with two sets of channels and two sets of actors. The sets of channels are the input channels set, denoted by $\mathsf{inp}(v_i)$, which consists of all the input channels to v_i, and the output channels set, denoted by $\mathsf{out}(v_i)$, which consists of all the output channels from v_i. The sets of actors are the successors set, denoted by $\mathsf{succ}(v_i)$, and the predecessors set, denoted by $\mathsf{prec}(v_i)$. They are given by:

$$\mathsf{succ}(v_i) = \{v_j \in V : \exists e_u = (v_i, v_j) \in E\} \quad (1)$$

$$\mathsf{prec}(v_i) = \{v_j \in V : \exists e_u = (v_j, v_i) \in E\} \quad (2)$$

Algorithm 1 LEVELS(G)

Require: Acyclic CSDF graph $G = \langle V, E \rangle$
```
i ← 1
while V ≠ ∅ do
    A_i ← {v_j ∈ V : prec(v_j) = ∅}
    Z_i ← {e_u ∈ E : ∃v_k ∈ A_i that is the source of e_u}
    V ← V \ A_i
    E ← E \ Z_i
    i ← i + 1
end while
L ← i − 1
return L disjoint sets A_1, A_2, ..., A_L, where ⋃_{i=1}^{L} A_i = V
```

Every actor $v_j \in V$ has an execution sequence $[f_j(1), f_j(2), \cdots, f_j(P_j)]$ of length P_j. The interpretation of this sequence is: The nth time that actor v_j is fired, it executes the code of function $f_j(((n-1) \bmod P_j) + 1)$. Similarly, production and consumption of tokens are also sequences of length P_j in CSDF. The token production of actor v_j on channel e_u is represented as a sequence of constant integers $[x_j^u(1), x_j^u(2), \cdots, x_j^u(P_j)]$. The nth time that actor v_j is fired, it produces $x_j^u(((n-1) \bmod P_j) + 1)$ tokens on channel e_u. The consumption of actor v_k is completely analogous; the token consumption of actor v_k from a channel e_u is represented as a sequence $[y_k^u(1), y_k^u(2), \cdots, y_k^u(P_j)]$. The firing rule of a CSDF actor v_k is evaluated as "true" for its nth firing iff all its input channels contain at least $y_k^u(((n-1) \bmod P_j)+1)$ tokens. The total number of tokens produced by actor v_j on channel e_u during the first n invocations, denoted by $X_j^u(n)$, is given by $X_j^u(n) = \sum_{l=1}^{n} x_j^u(l)$. Similarly, the total number of tokens consumed by actor v_k from channel e_u during the first n invocations, denoted by $Y_k^u(n)$, is given by $Y_k^u(n) = \sum_{l=1}^{n} y_k^u(l)$

An important property of the CSDF model is its decidability, which is the ability to derive at compile-time a schedule for the actors. This is formulated in the following definitions and results from [6].

Definition 1. Given a connected CSDF graph G, a *valid static schedule* for G is a *finite sequence of actors invocations* that can be repeated infinitely on the incoming sample stream while the amount of data in the buffers remains bounded. A vector $\vec{q} = [q_1, q_2, \cdots, q_N]^T$, where $q_j > 0$, is a *repetition vector* of G if each q_j represents the number of invocations of an actor v_j in a valid static schedule for G. The repetition vector of G in which all the elements are relatively prime[1] is called the *basic repetition vector* of G, denoted by $\dot{\vec{q}}$. G is *consistent* if there exists a repetition vector. If a deadlock-free schedule can be found, G is said to be *live*. Both consistency and liveness are required for the existence of a valid static schedule.

THEOREM 1 (FROM [6]). *In a CSDF graph G, a repetition vector $\vec{q} = [q_1, q_2, \cdots, q_N]^T$ is given by*

$$\vec{q} = \mathbf{P} \cdot \vec{r}, \qquad \text{with} \qquad P_{jk} = \begin{cases} P_j & \text{if } j = k \\ 0 & \text{otherwise} \end{cases} \quad (3)$$

where $\vec{r} = [r_1, r_2, \cdots, r_N]^T$ is a positive integer solution of the balance equation

$$\mathbf{\Gamma} \cdot \vec{r} = \vec{0} \quad (4)$$

and where the topology matrix $\mathbf{\Gamma} \in \mathbb{Z}^{|E| \times |V|}$ *is defined by*

$$\Gamma_{uj} = \begin{cases} X_j^u(P_j) & \text{if actor } v_j \text{ produces on ch. } e_u \\ -Y_j^u(P_j) & \text{if actor } v_j \text{ consumes from ch. } e_u \\ 0 & \text{Otherwise.} \end{cases} \quad (5)$$

Definition 2. For a consistent and live CSDF graph G, an *actor iteration* is the invocation of an actor $v_i \in V$ for q_i times, and a *graph iteration* is the invocation of *every* actor $v_i \in V$ for q_i times, where $q_i \in \vec{q}$.

Example 1. Figure 2 shows an example of a CSDF graph. The graph has a number of levels $\mathcal{L} = 3$. It also has three

[1] i.e., $\gcd\{q_1, q_2, \cdots, q_N\} = 1$.

output paths given by $\mathcal{W}= \{w_1 = \{(v_1, v_2), (v_2, v_4)\}, w_2 = \{(v_1, v_3), (v_3, v_4)\}, w_3 = \{(v_1, v_4)\}\}$. The repetition vector is $\vec{q} = [3, 2, 1, 3]^T$.

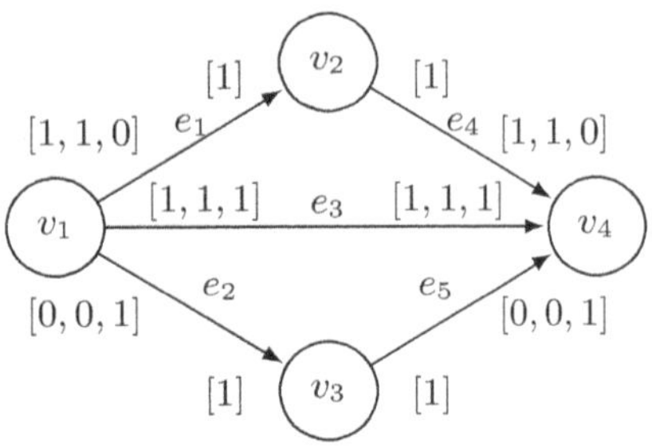

Figure 2: Example of a CSDF graph

3.2 System Model and Scheduling Algorithms

In this section, we introduce the system model and the related schedulability results.

3.2.1 System Model

A system Π consists of a set $\pi = \{\pi_1, \pi_2, \cdots, \pi_m\}$ of m homogeneous processors. The processors execute a task set $\tau = \{\tau_1, \tau_2, \cdots, \tau_n\}$ of n periodic tasks, and a task may be preempted at any time. A periodic task $\tau_i \in \tau$ is defined by a 4-tuple $\tau_i = (S_i, C_i, T_i, D_i)$, where $S_i \geq 0$ is the start time of τ_i, $C_i > 0$ is the worst-case execution time of τ_i, $T_i \geq C_i$ is the task period, and D_i, where $C_i \leq D_i \leq T_i$, is the relative deadline of τ_i. A periodic task τ_i is invoked (i.e., *released*) at time instants $t = S_i + kT_i$ for all $k \in \mathbb{N}_0$. Upon invocation, τ_i executes for C_i time-units. The relative deadline D_i is interpreted as follows: τ_i has to finish executing its kth invocation before time $t = S_i + kT_i + D_i$ for all $k \in \mathbb{N}_0$. If $D_i = T_i$, then τ_i is said to have *implicit-deadline*. If $D_i < T_i$, then τ_i is said to have *constrained-deadline*. If all the tasks in a task-set τ have the same start time, then τ is said to be *synchronous*. Otherwise, τ is said to be *asynchronous*.

The utilization of a task τ_i is $U_i = C_i/T_i$. For a task set τ, the total utilization of τ is $U_{\text{sum}} = \sum_{\tau_i \in \tau} U_i$ and the maximum utilization factor of τ is $U_{\max} = \max_{\tau_i \in \tau} U_i$. Similarly, the density of a task τ_i is $\delta_i = C_i/\min(D_i, T_i)$, the total density of τ is $\delta_{\text{sum}} = \sum_{\tau_i \in \tau} \delta_i$, and the maximum density of τ is $\delta_{\max} = \max_{\tau_i \in \tau} \delta_i$. Note that the density is equivalent to the utilization for implicit-deadline tasks.

Given a system Π and a task set τ, a *valid schedule* is one that allocates a processor to a task $\tau_i \in \tau$ for exactly C_i time-units in the interval $[S_i + kT_i, S_i + kT_i + D_i)$ for all $k \in \mathbb{N}_0$ with the restriction that a task may not execute on more than one processor at the same time.

Based on whether a task can migrate between processors upon preemption, scheduling algorithms are classified into:

- *Partitioned*: Each task is allocated to a processor and no migration is permitted
- *Global*: Migration is permitted for all tasks
- *Hybrid*: Hybrid algorithms mix partitioned and global approaches and they can be further classified to:
  1. Semi-partitioned: Most tasks are allocated to processors and few tasks are allowed to migrate
  2. Clustered: Processors are grouped into clusters and the tasks that are allocated to one cluster are scheduled by a global scheduler

Since we will use both of the implicit and constrained deadline periodic task models, we present below the schedulability analysis results for both models on multiprocessor systems.

3.2.2 Schedulability Analysis

A necessary and sufficient (i.e., exact) condition for an asynchronous set of implicit-deadline periodic tasks τ to be scheduled on m processors to meet all the deadlines (i.e., τ is *feasible*) is:

$$U_{\text{sum}} \leq m \tag{6}$$

A scheduling algorithm $\mathcal{A}$ is said to be *optimal* iff it can schedule any feasible task set τ on Π. Several global and hybrid algorithms were proven optimal for scheduling asynchronous sets of implicit-deadline periodic tasks [7]. In contrast, partitioned scheduling is known to be non-optimal.

For constrained-deadline periodic tasks, we need first to introduce some concepts that are essential for its schedulability analysis.

Definition 3. The *processor demand* of a task τ_i over the time interval $[t_1, t_2]$, denoted by $\text{DBF}(\tau_i, t_1, t_2)$, is the total computation time of all the instances of τ_i having activation time and deadline within $[t_1, t_2]$.

According to [5], $\text{DBF}(\tau_i, t_1, t_2)$ is given by:

$$\text{DBF}(\tau_i, t_1, t_2) = \zeta(\tau_i, t_1, t_2)C_i \tag{7}$$

where $\zeta(\tau_i, t_1, t_2)$ is the total number of τ_i instances that are activated in the interval $[t_1, t_2]$ and have a deadline within the interval $[t_1, t_2]$. The authors in [5] showed that $\zeta(\tau_i, t_1, t_2)$ is given by:

$$\zeta(\tau_i, t_1, t_2) = \max\{0, \left\lfloor \frac{t_2 - S_i - D_i}{T_i} \right\rfloor - \max\{0, \left\lceil \frac{t_1 - S_i}{T_i} \right\rceil\} + 1\} \tag{8}$$

For the whole task-set τ, the processor demand of τ in the interval $[t_1, t_2]$, denoted by $\text{DBF}(\tau, t_1, t_2)$, is given by:

$$\text{DBF}(\tau, t_1, t_2) = \sum_{\tau_i \in \tau} \text{DBF}(\tau_i, t_1, t_2) \tag{9}$$

For uniprocessor systems, an exact schedulability test for constrained-deadline periodic task-sets is stated in the following lemma:

LEMMA 1 (FROM [5]). *A periodic task-set τ is feasible on one processor iff $U_{sum} \leq 1$ and $\text{DBF}(\tau, t_1, t_2) \leq (t_2 - t_1)$ for all $0 \leq t_1 < t_2 < s + 2p$, where $s = \max\{S_1, \cdots, S_n\}$ and $p = \text{lcm}\{T_1, \cdots, T_n\}$ (lcm denotes the least-common-multiple operator).*

For multiprocessor systems, a sufficient schedulability test is obtained by replacing U_{sum} in Equation 6 with δ_{sum} [2]. Hence, a task-set τ is feasible on m processors if:

$$\delta_{\text{sum}} \leq m \tag{10}$$

The exact test in Lemma 1 is known to be co-NP-hard in the strong sense [5], while the sufficient test in Equation 10 is known to be pessimistic. As a result, several tests with less complexity than the exact test and better accuracy than the test in Equation 10 have been proposed in the literature (e.g., [1, 4, 8, 13, 16]).

4. MANAGING LATENCY

In this section, we first introduce the assumptions and definitions needed for our analysis of the latency. Then, we analyze the latency of applications, modeled as CSDF graphs, when their actors are scheduled as implicit-deadline periodic (IDP) tasks. Finally, we propose a new latency minimized task-set representation for the applications based on the constrained-deadline periodic (CDP) model.

4.1 Assumptions and Definitions

In the remainder of this paper, a graph G refers to an acyclic consistent CSDF graph. We base our analysis on the following assumptions:

A1 A graph G has a set $I = \{I_1, I_2, \cdots, I_{\mathcal{K}}\}$ of $\mathcal{K}$ periodic input streams connected to the input actors of G. These streams satisfy the following:

1. The set of input streams connected to an actor v_i is disjoint from all the other sets of input streams connected to other actors. That is, there are no two actors sharing the same input stream.
2. The first samples of all the streams arrive prior to or at the same time when the actors of G start executing.
3. Each input stream I_j is characterized by a constant inter-arrival time of the samples (also called period). This period is assumed to be equal to the period of the input actor which receives I_j. This assumption indicates that the period for input streams can be controlled by the designer to match the periods of the actors.

A2 An actor v_i consumes its input data immediately when it starts its firing and produces its output data just before it finishes its firing.

Now, we introduce the following definitions and results.

Definition 4. For a graph G, the *execution time vector* of G, denoted by $\vec{\mu} \in \mathbb{N}^N$, is a vector such that $\mu_i \in \vec{\mu}$ is the worst-case execution time (WCET) of actor $v_i \in V$.

We assume that the worst-case execution time of an actor includes the worst-case times needed for reading and writing the tokens. That is, the communication cost is included in μ_i.

Let $\eta = \max_{v_i \in V}(\mu_i q_i)$ and $Q = \mathsf{lcm}\{q_1, q_2, \cdots, q_N\}$. Now, we give the following definition:

Definition 5. A graph G is said to be *matched input and output (I/O) rates graph* iff:

$$\eta \bmod Q = 0 \tag{11}$$

If Equation 11 does not hold, then G is said to be *mismatched input/output (I/O) rates graph.*

If $\eta \bmod Q = 0$, then there exists at least a single actor in the graph which is fully utilizing the processor on which it runs. This allows the graph to achieve optimal throughput. On the other hand, if $\eta \bmod Q \neq 0$, then there exist idle durations in the period of each actor which results in sub-optimal throughput.

Definition 6. A graph G is called *balanced* iff:

$$q_1\mu_1 = q_2\mu_2 = \cdots = q_N\mu_N \tag{12}$$

where $q_i \in \vec{q}$ is the repetition of actor $v_i \in V$. If Equation 12 does not hold, then the graph is called *unbalanced.*

Definition 7. Let $w_{a\rightsquigarrow z} = \{(v_a, v_b), \cdots, (v_y, v_z)\}$ be an output path in a graph G. The *latency* of $w_{a\rightsquigarrow z}$ under periodic input streams, denoted by $L(w_{a\rightsquigarrow z})$, is the elapsed time between the start of the first firing of v_a which produces data to (v_a, v_b) and the finish of the first firing of v_z which consumes data from (v_y, v_z).

Consequently, we define the maximum latency of G as follows:

Definition 8. For a graph G, the *maximum latency* of G under periodic input streams, denoted by $L(G)$, is given by:

$$L(G) = \max_{w_{i\rightsquigarrow j} \in \mathcal{W}} L(w_{i\rightsquigarrow j}) \tag{13}$$

Definition 9. A *self-timed schedule* (STS) is one where all the actors are fired as soon as their input data are available.

A self-timed schedule does not impose any extra latency (e.g., by the scheduler) on the actors. This leads us to the following result proven in [17] for HSDF graphs and extended in [9] to SDF graphs.

THEOREM 2 (FROM [9, 17]). *For a graph G, the minimum achievable latency and the maximum achievable throughput are obtained when the actors of G are scheduled using self-timed scheduling policy.*

Theorem 2 applies to CSDF graphs since any CSDF graph can be converted to an equivalent SDF graph.

The authors of [3] proved that it is possible to schedule a graph G actors as implicit-deadline periodic tasks using periods given by the following definition:

Definition 10. For a graph G, a *period vector* $\vec{\lambda}$, where $\vec{\lambda} \in \mathbb{N}^N$, represents the periods, measured in time-units, of the actors in G. $\lambda_j \in \vec{\lambda}$ is the period of actor $v_j \in V$. $\vec{\lambda}$ is given by the solution to both

$$q_1\lambda_1 = q_2\lambda_2 = \cdots = q_{N-1}\lambda_{N-1} = q_N\lambda_N \tag{14}$$

and

$$\vec{\lambda} - \vec{\mu} \geq \vec{0}, \tag{15}$$

where $q_j \in \vec{q}$ (The basic repetition vector of G).

The minimum solution to both Equations 14 and 15 is given by the following lemma:

LEMMA 2 (FROM [3]). *The minimum period vector of G, denoted by $\vec{\lambda}^{min} \in \mathbb{N}^N$, is given by*

$$\lambda_i^{min} = \frac{Q}{q_i}\left\lceil \frac{\eta}{Q} \right\rceil \text{ for } v_i \in V, \tag{16}$$

where $q_i \in \vec{q}$ is the repetition of actor v_i.

Definition 10 implies an equal iteration period for all the actors. This common iteration period is formulated in the following definition:

Definition 11. For G, the *iteration period* under strictly periodic scheduling, denoted by α, is given by:

$$\alpha = q_i\lambda_i \text{ for any } v_i \in V \tag{17}$$

where λ_i is the period of v_i given by Definition 10.

In order to facilitate computing the latency, we introduce the following definitions:

Definition 12. The *cumulative production function* of an actor v_i producing into a channel e_u during the interval $[t_s, t_e)$, denoted by $\mathsf{prd}_{[t_s,t_e)}(v_i, e_u)$, is the sum of the number of tokens produced by v_i into e_u during the interval $[t_s, t_e)$.

Similarly, we define the cumulative consumption function as follows:

Definition 13. The *cumulative consumption function* of an actor v_i consuming from a channel e_u over the interval $[t_s, t_e]$, denoted by $\mathsf{cns}_{[t_s,t_e]}(v_i, e_u)$, is the sum of the number of tokens consumed by v_i from e_u during the interval $[t_s, t_e]$.

Now, we proceed to the latency analysis of CSDF when it is scheduled using the IDP model.

4.2 Latency Analysis under the IDP Model

Let ϕ_i be the earliest start time of an actor $v_i \in V$. Then, according to Definitions 7 and 8, the graph latency $L(G)$ is given by:

$$L(G) = \max_{w_{i \rightsquigarrow j} \in \mathcal{W}} (\phi_j + \hat{y}^u_j \lambda_j + D_j - (\phi_i + \hat{x}^r_i \lambda_i)) \qquad (18)$$

where ϕ_j and ϕ_i are the earliest start times of the output actor v_j and the input actor v_i, respectively, λ_j and λ_i are the periods of v_j and v_i, D_j is the deadline of v_j, and $\hat{y}^u_j$ and $\hat{x}^r_i$ are two constants, such that for an output path $w_{i \rightsquigarrow j}$ in which e_r is the first channel and e_u is the last channel, $\hat{x}^r_i$ and $\hat{y}^u_j$ are given by:

$$\hat{x}^r_i = \min\{k \in \mathbb{N} : x^r_i(k) > 0\} - 1 \qquad (19)$$

$$\hat{y}^u_j = \min\{k \in \mathbb{N} : y^u_j(k) > 0\} - 1 \qquad (20)$$

Under the IDP model, Equation 18 becomes:

$$L(G) = \max_{w_{i \rightsquigarrow j} \in \mathcal{W}} (\phi_j + (\hat{y}^u_j + 1)\lambda_j - (\phi_i + \hat{x}^r_i \lambda_i)) \qquad (21)$$

The earliest start time of actors under the IDP model is given by the following lemma.

LEMMA 3. *For a graph G, the earliest start time of an actor $v_j \in V$, denoted by ϕ_j, under a strictly periodic schedule is given by*

$$\phi_j = \begin{cases} 0 & \text{if } \mathsf{prec}(v_j) = \emptyset \\ \max\limits_{v_i \in \mathsf{prec}(v_j)} (\phi_{i \to j}) & \text{if } \mathsf{prec}(v_j) \neq \emptyset \end{cases} \qquad (22)$$

where

$$\phi_{i \to j} = \min_{t \in [0, \phi_i + \alpha]} \{t : \mathsf{prd}_{[\phi_i, \max(\phi_i, t)+k)}(v_i, e_u) \geq \mathsf{cns}_{[t, \max(\phi_i, t)+k]}(v_j, e_u) \quad \forall k = 0, 1, \cdots, \alpha\} \qquad (23)$$

In case of implicit-deadline periodic tasks, $\mathsf{prd}_{[t_s,t_e)}(v_i, e_u)$ is given by:

$$\mathsf{prd}_{[t_s,t_e)}(v_i, e_u) = \begin{cases} X^u_i\left(\left\lfloor \frac{t_e - t_s}{\lambda_i} \right\rfloor\right) & \text{if } (t_e - t_s) \geq \lambda_i \\ 0 & \text{if } (t_e - t_s) < \lambda_i \end{cases} \qquad (24)$$

Similar to Equation 24, $\mathsf{cns}_{[t_s,t_e]}(v_i, e_u)$ is given by:

$$\mathsf{cns}_{[t_s,t_e]}(v_i, e_u) = \begin{cases} 0 & \text{if } t_e < t_s \\ Y^u_i(\lceil \frac{t_e - t_s}{\lambda_i} \rceil + 1) & \text{if } (t_e - t_s) \bmod \lambda_i = 0 \\ Y^u_i(\lceil \frac{t_e - t_s}{\lambda_i} \rceil) & \text{if } (t_e - t_s) \bmod \lambda_i \neq 0 \end{cases} \qquad (25)$$

Using Equation 21, it is possible to compute the latency under the IDP model for any acyclic CSDF graph.

Example 2. For the graph shown in Figure 2, recall that the repetition vector is $\vec{q} = [3, 2, 1, 3]^T$. Now, assume that the execution time vector is $\vec{\mu} = [5, 8, 24, 4]^T$. It follows that $\eta = \max_{v_i \in V}(\mu_i q_i) = 24$, $Q = \mathsf{lcm}\{q_1, q_2, q_3, q_4\} = 6$, and $\alpha = 24$. Based on that, we compute the minimum period vector $\vec{\lambda}^{\min} = [8, 12, 24, 8]^T$. To compute the earliest start time, we first find the cumulative production/consumption functions. For example, for v_1 on e_1, $\mathsf{prd}_{[t_s,t_e)}(v_1, e_1)$ is:

$$\mathsf{prd}_{[t_s,t_e)}(v_1, e_1) = \begin{cases} X^1_1\left(\left\lfloor \frac{t_e - t_s}{8} \right\rfloor\right) & \text{if } (t_e - t_s) \geq 8 \\ 0 & \text{if } (t_e - t_s) < 8 \end{cases}$$

If we set $[t_s, t_e)$, for example, to $[0, 16)$, then $\mathsf{prd}_{[0,16)}(v_1, e_1) = 2$. Computing ϕ_2 results in:

$$\phi_2 = \max_{v_i \in \mathsf{prec}(v_2)} (\phi_{i \to 2}) = \phi_{1 \to 2}$$

Using (23) to compute $\phi_{1 \to 2}$ gives:

$$\phi_{1 \to 2} = \min_{t \in [0, 24]} \{t : \mathsf{prd}_{[0, \max(0,t)+k)}(v_1, e_1) \geq \mathsf{cns}_{[t, \max(0,t)+k]}(v_2, e_1) \quad \forall k = 0, ..., 24\} = 8$$

Similarly, we compute the earliest start time under the IDP model for each actor which results in $\vec{\phi} = [0, 8, 24, 32]^T$. Using (21), we can compute the latency of the individual output paths as follows:

$$L(w_1) = 32 + (0 + 1) \times 8 - (0 + 0 \times 8) = 40$$
$$L(w_2) = 32 + (2 + 1) \times 8 - (0 + 2 \times 8) = 40$$
$$L(w_3) = 32 + (0 + 1) \times 8 - (0 + 0 \times 8) = 40$$

Therefore, the graph maximum latency is given by

$$L_{\mathsf{IDP}}(G) = \max_{w_{i \rightsquigarrow j} \in \mathcal{W}} L(w_{i \rightsquigarrow j}) = 40$$

Now, we show that for two sub-classes of CSDF graphs, we can derive a simpler expression for the latency. These two classes are: 1) balanced graphs, and 2) graphs where $\vec{q} = \vec{1}$.

THEOREM 3. *The minimum achievable latency of a balanced graph G when its actors are scheduled as implicit-deadline periodic tasks is equal to its minimum achievable latency under self-timed scheduling.*

PROOF. By Definitions 6 and 10, a balanced graph has a period vector in which each actor has a period equal to its execution time (i.e., $\lambda_i = \mu_i$). Therefore, each actor requires execution on a dedicated processor (since $U_i = \mu_i/\lambda_i = 1$). In this case, the actor utilizes fully the processor on which it executes. Hence, there is no idle time or latency imposed by the scheduler and the actors execute in a way that emulates self-timed execution. As a result, the graph has the same latency as if it is executed in a self-timed way. □

Theorem 3 implies that a balanced graph scheduled to achieve the minimum achievable latency requires a number of processors $M = N$, where N is the number of actors in the graph. In such a case, the system has "one-to-one" mapping (i.e., one task per processor). Hence, the type of scheduler is irrelevant since each task requires a dedicated processor, which is fully utilized, in order to achieve the minimum achievable latency.

THEOREM 4. *The minimum achievable latency of a graph G with basic repetition vector $\vec{q} = \vec{1}$, when its actors are scheduled as implicit-deadline periodic tasks, is $L_{\mathsf{IDP}}(G) = \mathcal{L}\max_{v_i \in V} \mu_i$.*

PROOF. Based on Lemma 2, a CSDF graph with basic repetition vector $\vec{q} = \vec{1}$ will have a period vector in which all the periods are the same and equal to $\max_{v_i \in V} \mu_i$. Thus, the latency of the graph is the sum of the periods along the longest output path. By Algorithm 1, the longest output path has $\mathcal{L}$ actors in it. Thus, the graph latency is $L(G) = \mathcal{L}\max_{v_i \in V} \mu_i$. □

Theorem 4 is illustrated in the motivational example in Section 1.1 for G_2 when scheduled using the IDP model. $\mathcal{L}$ for G_2 is equal to 3 and $\max_{v_i \in V}(\mu_i q_i) = 9$. Thus, $L_{\mathsf{IDP}}(G_2) = 3 \times 9 = 27$.

4.3 Latency Minimized Scheduling using the CDP model

For an actor v_j, $\phi_{i \to j}$ depends on the time at which the predecessors have generated enough data to ensure periodic execution of v_j once it starts. Under the IDP model, such time is always constrained to be at the end of a predecessor actor period. Now, let v_m be the predecessor actor that has the maximum $\phi_{i \to j}$. The idea is to set the deadline of v_m to be less than λ_m. The exact value is determined by the designer using a deadline factor $d_m \in [0, 1]$, such that $D_m = \mu_m + d_m(\lambda_m - \mu_m)$. Consequently, the definition of $\mathsf{prd}_{[t_s,t_e)}(v_i, e_u)$ becomes:

$$\underset{[t_s,t_e)}{\mathsf{prd}}(v_i, e_u) = \begin{cases} 0 & \text{if } (t_e - t_s) < \lambda_i \\ X_i^u(\lfloor \frac{t_e - t_s}{\lambda_i} \rfloor + 1) & \text{if } \frac{(t_e - t_s) \bmod \lambda_i}{D_i} \geq 1 \\ X_i^u(\lfloor \frac{t_e - t_s}{\lambda_i} \rfloor) & \text{if } \frac{(t_e - t_s) \bmod \lambda_i}{D_i} < 1 \end{cases} \tag{26}$$

Based on the new definition of $\mathsf{prd}_{[t_s,t_e)}(v_i, e_u)$ in Equation 26, the predecessor v_m generates enough tokens to guarantee periodic execution of v_j earlier. Thus, we reduce $\phi_{m \to j}$. However, reducing $\phi_{m \to j}$ might cause another actor (e.g., v_k) to have a larger $\phi_{k \to j}$ than $\phi_{m \to j}$. Thus, the deadline reduction is repeated until no other actor v_k with larger $\phi_{k \to j}$ is found. The whole procedure is described in Algorithm 2. We assume that the input actors are the ones with no incoming edges (i.e., level-1 actors), and the output actors are the ones with no outgoing edges. Note that Algorithm 2 assumes that $\mathsf{prd}_{[t_s,t_e)}(v_i, e_u)$ is given by Equation 26 rather than Equation 24.

Now, we define the task-set representation of G as follows:

Definition 14. For a graph G, $\tau_{\mathsf{CDP}}(G)$ is the constrained deadline periodic task-set representation of the actors in G such that $\tau_i \in \tau_{\mathsf{CDP}}(G)$ corresponds to actor $v_i \in V$. τ_i is given by

$$\tau_i = (S_i, C_i, T_i, D_i) \tag{27}$$

where:

Algorithm 2 SET-START-TIME-AND-DEADLINE$(G, \vec{d})$

Require: Acyclic CSDF graph $G = \langle V, E \rangle$
Require: Deadline factors $\vec{d}$
1: **for all** $v_j \in V$ **do**
2: **if** $\mathsf{prec}(v_j) = \emptyset$ **then**
3: $\phi_j \leftarrow 0$
4: **else**
5: Initialize the deadline of each actor $v_i \in \mathsf{prec}(v_j)$ to its period (i.e., $D_i = \lambda_i$)
6: Find $v_m \in \mathsf{prec}(v_j)$ such that $\phi_{m \to j} = \max_{v_i \in \mathsf{prec}(v_j)} \phi_{i \to j}$
7: Set the deadline of v_m to $D_m = \mu_m + d_m(\lambda_m - \mu_m)$
8: Find $\phi_j = \max_{v_i \in \mathsf{prec}(v_j)} \phi_{i \to j}$ with the new deadline of v_m
9: Find $v_k \in \mathsf{prec}(v_j)$ such that $\phi_{k \to j} = \max_{v_i \in \mathsf{prec}(v_j)} \phi_{i \to j}$
10: **if** $v_k \neq v_m$ **then**
11: Repeat lines 6 to 9 {A new actor v_k is the bottleneck}
12: **else**
13: $\phi_j \leftarrow \max_{v_i \in \mathsf{prec}(v_j)} \phi_{i \to j}$ {v_m remains the bottleneck even after reducing its deadline}
14: **end if**
15: **end if**
16: **end for**
17: Set the deadline of each output actor v_o to $D_o = \mu_o + d_o(\lambda_o - \mu_o)$
18: **return** $\vec{\phi}$, where $\phi_i \in \vec{\phi}$ is the start time of actor v_i, and $\vec{D}$, where $D_i \in \vec{D}$ is the deadline of actor v_i

- $S_i = \phi_i$ obtained by Algorithm 2
- $C_i = \mu_i$,
- $T_i = \lambda_i$ given by Lemma 2,
- $D_i = D_i$ obtained by Algorithm 2

THEOREM 5. *$\tau_{\mathsf{CDP}}(G)$ is schedulable.*

PROOF. Theorems 2 and 3 in [3] prove the existence of a strictly periodic schedule for the actors of G when: 1) the start time of a level-k actor v_i is equal to ϕ_i given by Equation 22 assuming $\mathsf{prd}_{[t_s,t_e)}(v_i, e_u)$ is given by Equation 24, and 2) the deadline D_i is equal to λ_i. Thus, we need to show that changing ϕ_i and D_i according to Algorithm 2 does not affect the strict periodicity of the actors. According to the CDP model (see Section 3.2.1), changing the deadline does not affect the periodicity. Similarly, the changes to the start time by Algorithm 2 do not affect the periodicity. This is due to the fact that $\phi_{i \to j}$ given by Equation 23 guarantees that an actor starts only if it has enough tokens to continue executing in a strictly periodic way. Thus, any reduction in the start time is guaranteed to not break the strictly periodic execution requirement. □

Example 3. Going back to the graph shown in Figure 2, we compute now the cumulative production function for v_1 on e_1 under the CDP model assuming deadline factors equal to zero. This results in:

$$\underset{[t_s,t_e)}{\mathsf{prd}}(v_1, e_1) = \begin{cases} 0 & \text{if } (t_e - t_s) < 8 \\ X_1^1(\lfloor \frac{t_e - t_s}{8} \rfloor + 1) & \text{if } \frac{(t_e - t_s) \bmod 8}{5} \geq 1 \\ X_1^1(\lfloor \frac{t_e - t_s}{8} \rfloor) & \text{if } \frac{(t_e - t_s) \bmod 8}{5} < 1 \end{cases} \tag{28}$$

Now, applying Algorithm 2 assuming that $\vec{d} = \vec{0}$ results in $\vec{\phi} = [0, 5, 21, 29]^T$, $\vec{D} = [5, 12, 24, 4]^T$, and $L_{\mathsf{CDP}}(G) = 33$.

To compute the buffer sizes under the CDP model, we provide the following lemma.

LEMMA 4. *For a graph G, the minimum bounded buffer size b_u of a communication channel $e_u \in E$ connecting a source actor v_i with start time ϕ_i, and a destination actor v_j with start time ϕ_j, where $v_i, v_j \in V$, under a strictly periodic schedule is given by*

$$b_u = \max_{k\in[0,1,\cdots,\alpha]} \{ \mathsf{prd}_{[\phi_i,\max(\phi_i,\phi_j)+k)}(v_i, e_u) - \mathsf{cns}_{[\phi_j,\max(\phi_i,\phi_j)+k)}(v_j, e_u)\} \quad (29)$$

Note that under the CDP model, Equation 29 should be computed using $\mathsf{prd}_{[t_s,t_e)}(v_i, e_u)$ given by Equation 26.

Now, we prove the following theorem regarding the latency of graphs with $\vec{q} = \vec{1}$ under the CDP model.

THEOREM 6. *The minimum achievable latency of a graph G with basic repetition vector $\vec{q} = \vec{1}$, when the actors of G are scheduled as constrained-deadline periodic (CDP) tasks, denoted by $L^{min}_{\mathsf{CDP}}(G)$, is equal to its minimum achievable latency under self-timed scheduling.*

PROOF. When the actors of G are scheduled as CDP tasks with $\vec{d} = \vec{0}$, an actor $v_i \in V$ is started immediately after all its predecessors have finished one firing. Hence, the latency encountered by the first sample is equal to the sum of actors' execution times along the output path with the largest sum of actors' execution times. This is equivalent to the latency under self-timed scheduling. □

Theorem 6 states that the CDP model achieves optimal latency and rate (i.e., minimum achievable latency and maximum achievable throughput) for graphs with $\vec{q} = \vec{1}$.

5. EVALUATION

We evaluate the constrained-deadline periodic representation proposed in Section 4 by performing an experiment on a set of 19 real-life streaming applications. The objective of the experiment is to compare the latency of streaming applications under the constrained-deadline periodic scheduling model to their minimum achievable latency obtained via self-timed scheduling.

5.1 Benchmarks

The streaming applications used in the experiment are the same as the ones used in [3]. In total, 19 applications are considered as shown in Table 2. The graphs are a mixture of CSDF and SDF graphs. The third column (N) shows the number of actors in each application , and the fourth column (Q) shows the least-common-multiple of the repetition vector elements (i.e., $Q = \mathsf{lcm}\{q_1, \cdots, q_N\}$). The fifth column ($R^{\max}_{\mathsf{SPS}}/R_{\mathsf{STS}}$) shows the ratio of the maximum throughput under strictly periodic scheduling (i.e., $R^{\max}_{\mathsf{SPS}}$) to the maximum achievable throughput of the application (i.e., R_{STS}).

We use the SDF^3 tool-set [18] for computing the minimum latency of SDF graphs. SDF^3 is a powerful analysis tool-set for analyzing CSDF/SDF graphs and is capable of computing several metrics like repetition vector, maximum achievable throughput, etc. For SDF graphs, SDF^3 is capable as well of computing the minimum achievable latency. Thus, we use this capability to compute the minimum achievable latency of a graph and use it as a reference point for comparing the latency under the IDP and CDP models. For CSDF graphs, we construct the self-timed schedule manually and use it to compute the latency.

Table 2: Benchmarks used for evaluation

Domain	Application	N	Q	$R^{\max}_{\mathsf{SPS}}/R_{\mathsf{STS}}$
Signal Processing	Multi-channel beamformer	57	1	1.0
	Discrete cosine transform (DCT)	8	1	1.0
	Fast Fourier transform (FFT) kernel	17	1	1.0
	Filterbank for multirate signal processing	85	1	1.0
	Time delay equalization (TDE)	29	1	1.0
Cryptography	Data Encryption Standard (DES)	53	1	1.0
	Serpent	120	1	1.0
Sorting	Bitonic Parallel Sorting	40	1	1.0
Video processing	MPEG2 video	23	1	1.0
	H.263 video decoder	4	594	1.0
Audio processing	MP3 audio decoder	14	2	1.0
	CD-to-DAT rate converter (SDF)	6	23520	0.04
	CD-to-DAT converter (CSDF)	6	658560	0.05
	Vocoder	114	1	1.0
Communication	Software FM radio with equalizer	43	1	1.0
	Data modem	6	16	1.0
	Satellite receiver	22	5280	0.2
	Digital Radio Mondiale receiver	4	288000	1.0
Medical	Heart pacemaker	4	320	1.0

Table 3: Configurations used for latency comparison

Configuration	Deadline Factor (d_i)	Deadline (D_i)
O_1	1	T_i
O_2	0.75	$C_i + 3(T_i - C_i)/4$
O_3	0.5	$C_i + (T_i - C_i)/2$
O_4	0.25	$C_i + (T_i - C_i)/4$
O_5	0	C_i

5.2 Experiment: Latency Comparison

In this experiment, we compare the latency resulting from the constrained-deadline periodic scheduling to the minimum achievable latency of a streaming application. The minimum achievable latency of a streaming application modeled as a CSDF graph is its latency under self-timed scheduling as mentioned in Section 4. In Algorithm 2, we do not specify an explicit value for the deadline factors vector $\vec{d}$. Thus, we evaluate the effect of the deadline factors values on the latency and resource requirements. This is accomplished by using five configurations with equal periods and different deadline factors. The used periods are the minimum ones given by Lemma 2, while the deadline factors are the ones outlined in Table 3. The first configuration, called O_1, is the one obtained by setting the deadline factor equal to 1 (i.e., $D_i = T_i$). Thus, O_1 results in the implicit-deadline representation. The last configuration O_5 is the one obtained by setting the deadline factor equal to 0 (i.e., $D_i = C_i$). O_2 till O_4 represent intermediate values of the deadline factor. The STS latency is computed using the `sdf3analysis` tool from SDF^3 using the `latency(min_st)` algorithm with auto-concurrency disabled and unbounded FIFO channels sizes.

Figure 3 shows the ratio of the latency of three configurations (O_1, O_3, and O_5) to the minimum achievable latency (i.e., STS latency). A ratio equal to 1.0 means that the CDP latency is equal to the STS latency. We see that the CDP model with $d_i = 0$ (i.e., configuration O_5) achieves the minimum achievable latency for 14 graphs, and even if the basic repetition vector of the graph is not equal to $\vec{1}$. We also see that the mis-matched I/O rates applications (i.e., CD2DAT-(S,C) and Satellite) have higher latency under strictly periodic scheduling. The only matched I/O rates applications with higher latency under strictly periodic scheduling are

Receiver and Pacemaker. They have higher latency because their execution times have large variations between firings. Such variation is captured under self-timed scheduling, while our strictly periodic scheduling assumes always the WCET. It is evident that the IDP model (i.e., configuration O_1) increases the latency on average by 5x compared to the STS latency. O_3 shows approximately a 36% average reduction in latency compared to O_1 and an average 3.2x increase in latency compared to the STS latency.

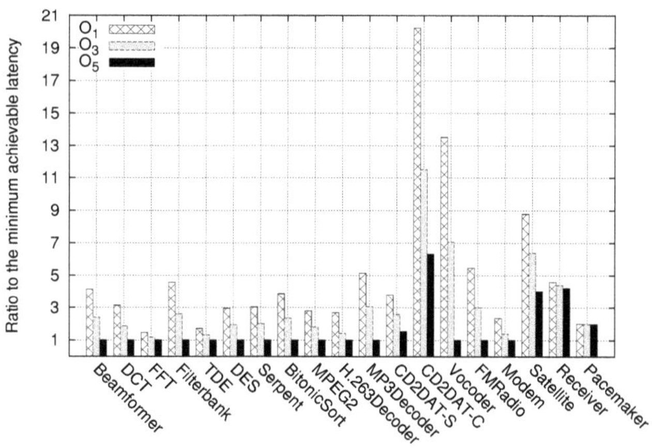

Figure 3: Ratios of the latency under configurations O_1, O_3, and O_5 from Table 3 to the STS latency

Now, we evaluate the same three configurations (i.e., O_1, O_3, and O_5) in terms of resource usage as shown in Figure 4. We do that by computing the minimum number of processors needed to schedule an application. For O_1, this is accomplished by using Equation 6. For O_3 and O_5, we use the sufficient test in Equation 10. We see that the minimum latency achieved by O_5 in most cases comes at a price of significant increase in resource requirements. In O_5, the total density δ_{sum} is equal to the number of actors (i.e., N in Table 2) for 16 applications. If achieving the minimum achievable latency is a requirement, then the designer can use a more accurate schedulablility test to reduce the number of processors (see Section 3.2.2). We also see that increasing the deadline increases the latency but reduces the resource requirements and vice versa. Thus, when the designer has flexibility over the desired latency, he/she might make a trade-off between latency and resources. Such a trade-off is illustrated in Figure 5. In Figure 5, the average ratios of the latency and the number of processors are shown as functions of the configuration. O_1-O_5 are the configurations shown in Table 3, while O_{STS} represents the self-timed schedule constructed using one-to-one mapping (i.e., one task per processor). The latency ratio for the jth configuration is given by

$$\Omega_j(L) = \frac{\sum_{G_i \in \mathcal{G}} (L_{O_j}(G_i)/L_{O_{STS}}(G_i))}{|\mathcal{G}|} \tag{30}$$

where $\mathcal{G}$ is the set of applications in Table 2 and G_i is the ith application. Similarly, the resource usage ratio for the jth configuration is given by

$$\Omega_j(M) = \frac{\sum_{G_i \in \mathcal{G}} (M_{O_j}(G_i)/M_{O_1}(G_i))}{|\mathcal{G}|} \tag{31}$$

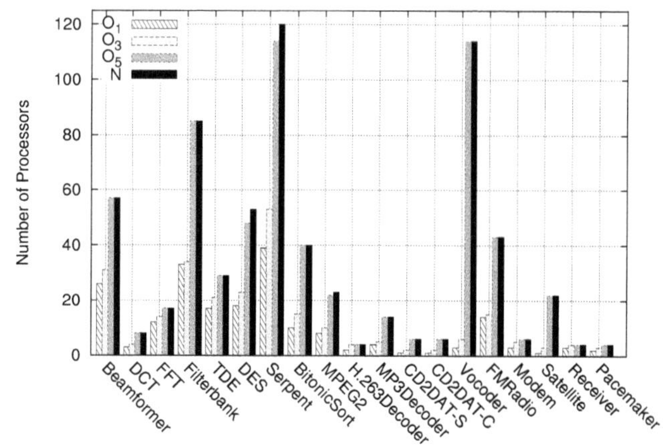

Figure 4: Resource usage for configurations O_1, O_3, and O_5 from Table 3

We see clearly that the latency decreases almost linearly as we decrease the deadline. However, we see that the number of processors increases non-linearly as we decrease the deadline. A "compromise" value for the deadline would be around O_4 where we see a latency of 2.4x compared to the STS latency achieved using around 1.7x the number of processors needed by O_1.

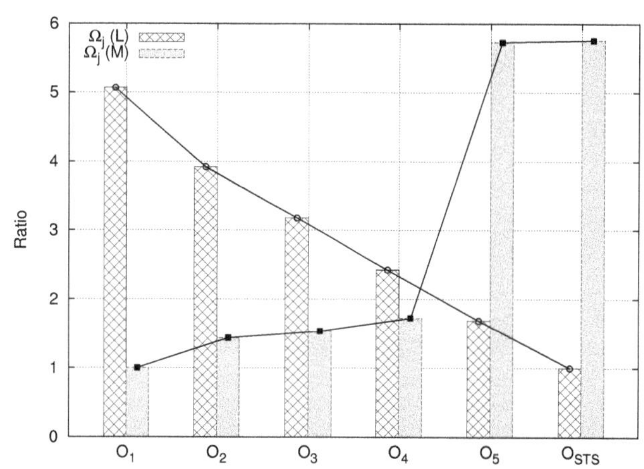

Figure 5: Average ratios of latency and number of processors as functions of the configuration

5.3 Decision Tree for Real-Time Scheduling of CSDF

Based on the results proven in Section 4 and the evaluation results in Section 5.2, we present a decision tree for selecting the real-time periodic task model for scheduling CSDF graphs. The decision tree is illustrated in Figure 6. The first decision is to determine whether the graph is matched I/O rates or not. It is proven in [3] that the periodic task model achieves the maximum achievable throughput for matched I/O rates graphs. If the graph is matched I/O rates and balanced, then the IDP model is *latency and rate optimal (LRO)*. If the graph is matched I/O but unbalanced, then the CDP model helps in reducing the latency. For certain

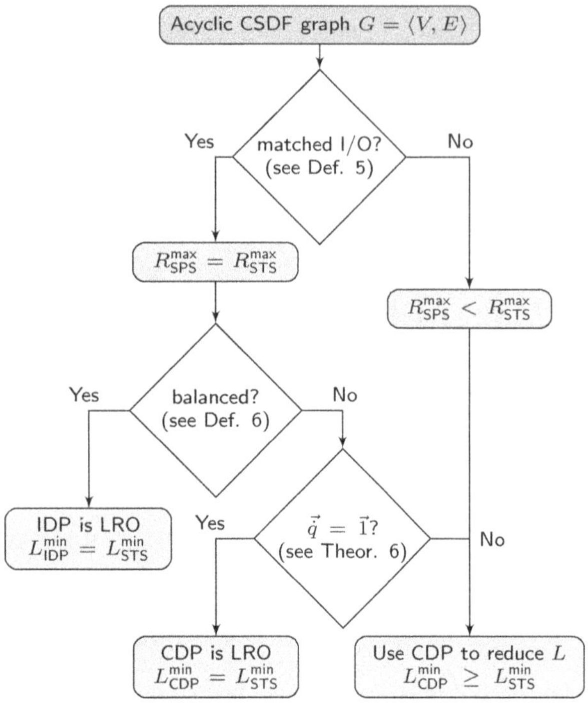

Figure 6: Decision tree for scheduling CSDF actors as real-time periodic tasks. $L^{\min}_{\mathsf{IDP}}$ and $L^{\min}_{\mathsf{CDP}}$ refer to the latency when $\vec{\lambda} = \vec{\lambda}^{\min}$ and $\vec{d} = \vec{0}$ (for the CDP case)

class of graphs (e.g., graphs with $\vec{q} = \vec{1}$), the CDP model is also latency and rate optimal. For mis-matched I/O graphs, the CDP helps in reducing the latency if the throughput achieved under strictly periodic scheduling is acceptable.

6. CONCLUSIONS

We analyze the latency of acyclic CSDF graphs when scheduled using the implicit-deadline periodic (IDP) model. We show that the IDP model achieves the minimum achievable latency for a class of graphs called balanced graphs, however, it increases the latency significantly for unbalanced graphs. To alleviate this problem, we propose an alternative task representation for unbalanced graphs actors based on the constrained-deadline periodic (CDP) model. We prove that the CDP representation achieves the minimum achievable latency for graphs with basic repetition vector equal to $\vec{1}$. Based on empirical evaluations, we show that the CDP representation delivers the minimum achievable latency even for graphs with basic repetition vector different from $\vec{1}$. We summarize our results in the form of a decision tree to assist the designer in choosing the appropriate real-time periodic task model for scheduling acyclic CSDF graphs.

7. ACKNOWLEDGMENTS

This work has been supported by CATRENE/MEDEA+ project number 2A718 (TSAR: Tera-scale multicore processor architecture).

8. REFERENCES

[1] K. Albers and F. Slomka. Efficient feasibility analysis for real-time systems with EDF scheduling. In *Proc. DATE*, pages 492–497, 2005.

[2] T. Baker and S. Baruah. Schedulability Analysis of Multiprocessor Sporadic Task Systems. In I. Lee et al., editors, *Handbook of Real-Time and Embedded Systems*. Chapman & Hall/CRC, Boca Raton, FL, 1st edition, 2007.

[3] M. Bamakhrama and T. Stefanov. Hard-real-time scheduling of data-dependent tasks in embedded streaming applications. In *Proc. EMSOFT*, pages 195–204, 2011.

[4] S. Baruah and N. Fisher. The partitioned multiprocessor scheduling of deadline-constrained sporadic task systems. *IEEE Trans. Comput.*, 55(7):918–923, 2006.

[5] S. Baruah, L. Rosier, and R. Howell. Algorithms and complexity concerning the preemptive scheduling of periodic, real-time tasks on one processor. *Real-Time Syst.*, 2:301–324, 1990.

[6] G. Bilsen et al. Cyclo-static dataflow. *IEEE Trans. Signal Process.*, 44(2):397–408, 1996.

[7] R. Davis and A. Burns. A survey of hard real-time scheduling for multiprocessor systems. *ACM Comput. Surv.*, 43(4):35:1–35:44, 2011.

[8] U. Devi. An improved schedulability test for uniprocessor periodic task systems. In *Proc. ECRTS*, pages 23–30, 2003.

[9] A. Ghamarian et al. Latency Minimization for Synchronous Data Flow Graphs. In *Proc. DSD*, pages 189–196, 2007.

[10] S. Goddard. *On the Management of Latency in the Synthesis of Real-Time Signal Processing Systems from Processing Graphs.* PhD thesis, University of North Carolina at Chapel Hill, 1998.

[11] L. Karam et al. Trends in multicore DSP platforms. *IEEE Signal Process. Mag.*, 26(6):38–49, 2009.

[12] E. Lee and D. Messerschmitt. Synchronous data flow. *Proc. IEEE*, 75(9):1235–1245, 1987.

[13] A. Masrur, S. Chakraborty, and G. Färber. Constant-Time Admission Control for Partitioned EDF. In *Proc. ECRTS*, pages 34–43, 2010.

[14] O. Moreira and M. Bekooij. Self-Timed Scheduling Analysis for Real-Time Applications. *EURASIP J. Adv. Signal Process.*, 2007:1–15, 2007.

[15] O. Moreira, F. Valente, and M. Bekooij. Scheduling multiple independent hard-real-time jobs on a heterogeneous multiprocessor. In *Proc. EMSOFT*, pages 57–66, 2007.

[16] R. Pellizzoni and G. Lipari. A new sufficient feasibility test for asynchronous real-time periodic task sets. In *Proc. ECRTS*, pages 204–211, 2004.

[17] S. Sriram and S. Bhattacharyya. *Embedded Multiprocessors: Scheduling and Synchronization.* CRC Press, Boca Raton, FL, 2nd edition, 2009.

[18] S. Stuijk, M. Geilen, and T. Basten. SDF^3: SDF For Free. In *Proc. ACSD*, pages 276–278, 2006.

Dynamic Scheduling of Stream Programs on Embedded Multi-core Processors

Haeseung Lee, Weijia Che and Karam S. Chatha,
Faculty of Computer Science and Engineering
Arizona State University, Tempe, AZ 85287
{hlee133, weijia.che, kchatha}@asu.edu

ABSTRACT

Stream computing has emerged as an important model of computation for embedded system applications particularly in the multimedia and network processing domains. In recent past several programming languages and embedded multicore processors have been proposed for streaming applications. This paper examines the execution and dynamic scheduling of stream programs on embedded multi-core processors. The paper addresses the problem in the context of a multi-tasking environment with a time varying allocation of processing elements for a particular streaming application. As a solution the paper proposes a two step approach where the stream program is first compiled to gather key application information, and to generate re-targetable code. A light weight dynamic scheduler incorporates the second stage of the approach. The dynamic scheduler utilizes the static information and available resources to assign or partition the application across the multi-core architecture. The objective of the dynamic scheduler is to maximize the throughput of the application, and it is sensitive to the resource (processing elements, scratch-pad memory, DMA bandwidth) constraints imposed by the target architecture. We evaluate the proposed approach by compiling and scheduling benchmark stream programs on a representative embedded multi-core processor. We present experimental results that evaluate the quality of the solutions generated by the proposed approach by comparisons with existing techniques.

Categories and Subject Descriptors

D.1.3 [**Software**]: Programming TechniquesConcurrent Programming[Parallel programming]

General Terms

Design, Performance

Keywords

Dynamic scheduling, Embedded systems, Multi-core architectures, Stream programming

CODES+ISSS'12, October 7-12, 2012, Tampere, Finland.

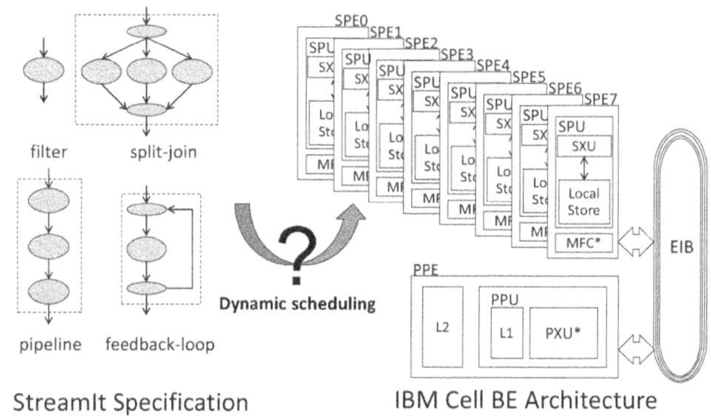

Figure 1: Problem addressed by the paper

1. INTRODUCTION

Stream computing has emerged as an important programming model for high performance compute intensive embedded system workloads. Examples of such workloads include network processing, multimedia and signal processing and computer vision. Stream programs are typically specified as a set of actors or filters communicating with each other through FIFOs. In each execution an actor consumes a fixed amount of tokens or data items on its input FIFO(s) and produces a fixed amount of tokens on its output FIFO(s). Thus, a stream program specification exposes the task and data level parallelism of the application. A number of stream programming languages have also emerged in recent past for specifying such applications. CUDA [15], Peakstream [18], Rapidmind [14], TStreams [11], OpenCL [19], StreamIt [20], and CAL [6] are examples of commercial and academic stream programming languages. Typically, stream applications exhibit stable actor execution sequence and memory access patterns. Consequently, stream applications can be aggressively analyzed statically to generate highly optimized implementations.

Processor architectures specifically aimed at stream programming workloads have also emerged concomitantly with stream computing and programming languages. Such processor architectures are also called as stream processors and they incorporate specialized architectural features. As stream computing workloads are characterized by high computation requirements, stream processors are implemented by multicore architectures. Specifically, stream processors are implemented as heterogeneous multi-core architecture where control plane processor(s) implements the more mundane workloads (such as OS, JVM and so on) and a multi-core data plane sub-system implements the streaming workloads.

The data plane sub-system typically consists of an array of homogeneous processor cores that may incorporate specialized instructions based on the target domain. More importantly as stream programs permit extensive static analysis, the data plane processors incorporate scratch pad memories (or SPM) instead of caches. SPM requires the programmer or compiler to manage the code execution and scheduling along with data communication. Although, there is a greater burden on the static (manual or automated) design phase with SPM, the generated designs exhibit higher performance and lower power consumption in comparison to cache based architectures. Finally, the data plane processors do not host an OS. Rather, the OS or scheduler executing on the control plane processor is responsible for overall orchestration of application execution on the data plane. Examples of commercial stream processors include IBM Cell Broadband Engine (BE) [9], Nvidia GeForce series [10], Ageia's PhysX [22], TI TMS320C6472 [21] and many DSPs.

A key challenge in implementing stream programs on associated stream processor architectures is the partitioning or parallelization of the application across the multi-core data plane. As the data plane processors incorporate an SPM the programmer or compiler is burdened with the task of also partitioning the limited SPM for code and data, and initiating transfers of code from external DRAM memory, and data to/from external DRAM and SPMs of other cores. The programmer or compiler must balance computation with communication overheads to maximize the throughput of the application. To the best of our knowledge there are no commercial tool chains that can effectively perform all the design trade-offs for implementing an application on stream processor architectures. However, several compiler techniques and optimizations have been proposed in recent past in academia.

A key drawback of the static compilation approaches is that it produces a single executable code implementation. For example if the target processor architecture has 8 cores, the compiler will optimize the application to utilize all the 8 cores (or fewer if specified). However, the number of cores available to execute an application vary in a typical multitasking embedded system. For example it is quite possible that 4 cores are initially available to run an application, after some time 8 cores are available, and next 2 cores are available. In other words the number of cores available to execute a stream application may vary over time. Existing compiler approaches do not permit dynamic variation in the available number of cores for a streaming application. *This paper addresses the problem of dynamic scheduling of streaming applications on embedded multi-core architectures (see Figure 1).* Specifically, we present a two stage approach consisting of retargetable code generation at compile time, and its dynamic scheduling at run time. The proposed dynamic scheduling approach is able to assign actors to processing cores at runtime while effectively balancing the limited SPM memory and communication overheads. We present experimental results that compare the proposed approach against other existing dynamic scheduling techniques, and static compilation approaches.

2. PREVIOUS WORK

Pino et al. [17] addressed the problem of scheduling SDF specifications on multi-core processors. Chen et al. [5] and Ostler et al. [16] proposed approaches for mapping networking applications on multi-core network processors. Liao et al. [13] proposed techniques for parallelizing Brook language specifications on general purpose processors. Gordon et al. [7] developed a heuristic approach to generate multi-threaded code for RAW processor architecture. Kudlur et al. [12] proposed an integer linear programming (ILP) based approach for mapping StreamIt applications on IBM Cell BE. Che et al. [4] proposed an ILP and heuristic technique for mapping StreamIt specifications on Cell BE that accounted for the on-chip memory constraints. They improved upon their previous work by addressing cyclical dependencies in the StreamIt specification [3]. All of these approaches generate one parallelized implementation for the input specification based on the available cores in the target architecture. If the available number of cores that are available on the target architecture are reduced the implementation cannot be utilized. Thus, the compiled executables are not able to address dynamic variations in available resources.

Wiggers et al. [23] made a case for runtime scheduling and noticed that for dataflow based applications runtime scheduling can be managed at high level of abstraction. Zhang et al. [24] proposed a dynamic scheduling scheme for IBM Cell BE that utilizes a operating system like ready queue based approach which ignores the overall structure of the application. Blagojevic et al. [2] presented a multi-grain parallel scheduling (MGPS) approach for IBM Cell BE that uses message passing interface (MPI) protocol and aims to combine task and loop parallelization schemes. The approach relies upon a fixed task to SPE assignment and therefore cannot effectively adopt to variations in number of available cores.

Flexstream proposed by Hormati et al. [8] is one of the two existing approaches whose problem focus closely matches ours. Flexstream utilizes a compile time ILP optimization to generate a maximal parallel implementation of the StreamIt specification on the IBM Cell like architecture. The parallel implementation is then adopted to address variations in available number of cores at run time. Baker et al. [1] also proposed an approach to dynamic scheduling of StreamIt specification on IBM Cell BE. They utilize compile time heuristic approach to generate a periodic admissible sequential schedule (or PASS) of the StreamIt specification that is dynamically parallelized at run time. Our static compile time approach is similar to Baker et al. However, we also describe schemes for generation of re-targetable code and its implementation at run-time. Our dynamic scheduler is distinguished from both Flexstream and Baker et al. by its structured unrolling approach to achieve highly optimized implementations through fusion and fission. Further, in comparison to Baker et al. the computational complexity of our algorithm is linear for a fixed number of cores. The experimental results demonstrate the superior performance of the proposed approach against both Flexstream and Baker et al., and establish the contribution of the paper.

3. PRELIMINARIES

3.1 Stream program

We consider stream programs that are specified using StreamIt [20]. In StreamIt a filter, also called an actor in the paper, is the smallest unit of computation (see Figure 1). An actor can be composed by container classes into a split-join construct to specify task level parallelism, a pipeline construct to specify data level parallelism, and feedback construct. A filter communicates with other filters through FIFOs. A filter in each execution or firing consumes a fixed number of tokens or data items from its input FIFOs and produces a fixed number of tokens on its output FIFOs. An actor can fire as long as there are enough tokens on its input FIFOs and the output FIFOs have sufficient space to hold the data tokens. As such the StreamIt execution semantics closely follow synchronous dataflow (SDF) model of computation, and the intermediate representation (IR) used by our approach is based on SDF.

3.2 Embedded multi-core architecture

We consider the IBM Cell BE [9] as a representative stream processor architecture (see Figure 1). The Cell BE is a 32-bit architecture composed of a Power processor element (PPE) that acts as the control plane processor, and eight synergistic processing elements (SPEs) that form the data plane subsystem. Each SPE has 256 KB SPM that must be managed by the programmer for hosting both code and data. Each SPE is also equipped with a DMA engine for communicating both code and data to/from DRAM and other SPMs. The 9 processing cores are connected with each other and the DRAM controller through the element interconnect bus (EIB). The DMA overhead for sending data over the EIB has been characterized as $(0.21 + 0.075 \times d)\mu s$ where d is the size of data in KB that is being communicated [3].

3.3 Problem description

Given:

- An SDF based description of the StreamIt specification as $G(V, E)$ where V is the set of actors and E is the set of FIFOs. For each $u \in V$, $t(v)$ describes the run time of the actor on a single SPE and $s(v)$ describes the code size in KB. Similarly for each $e(u, v) \in E$, $p(e)$ denotes the number of tokens produced by u, $c(e)$ gives the number of tokens consumed by v, $s(e)$ gives the size of each token in KB of each token produced by u, and $d(e)$ gives the initial number of tokens on an edge (relevant in the case of cycles).

- An embedded multi-core processor where P denotes the set of cores currently available for the application in the data plane, M denotes the size of SPM associated with each processor, and DMA overhead for communicating d KB is given by $f(d) = (0.21 + 0.075 \times d)\mu s$.

Generate a run-time schedule that maps the actors to cores in the data plane subject to the memory constraints and communication overheads with an objective of maximizing the throughput of the application.

4. DYNAMIC SCHEDULING OF STREAM APPLICATIONS

Our approach to dynamic scheduling of stream applications on embedded multi-core architectures consists of two stages (see Figure 2). In the first stage we utilize a compiler to analyze the stream application and generate re-targetable code for the actors along with some other information. During run time a dynamic scheduling framework executes the application on the available cores. The dynamic scheduling

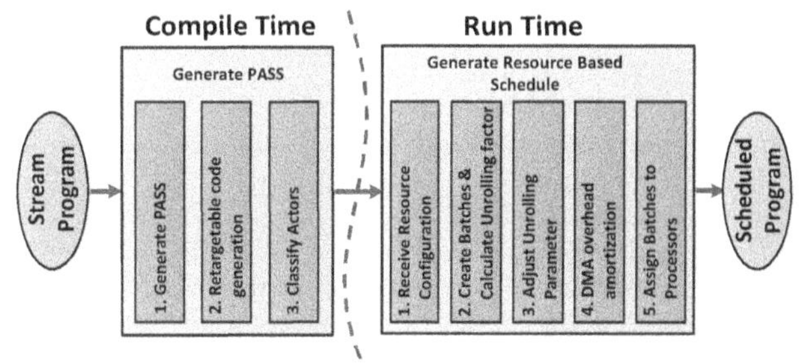

Figure 2: Dynamic Scheduler Framework

framework has the capability to execute the same application on variable number of cores. In the following few sections we discuss the compilation stage, dynamic scheduling algorithm and implementation details. In our approach we have considered StreamIt as the input specification language and IBM Cell BE as the target multi-core architecture.

4.1 Compile time analysis

The key objective of the compilation stage is to statically analyze the application, generate key information for the dynamic scheduling algorithm, generate a periodic sequential schedule for the application, and create re-targetable executables for the actors within the application.

4.1.1 Structure of the application

The compiler analyzes the StreamIt specification to extract the SDF based intermediate representation of the application. The SDF representation captures the graphical structure of the application along with the number and sizes of data tokens produced and consumed on each edge. We make two transformations on the SDF based representation both driven by our focus on dynamic scheduling. We first transform the SDF into a single appearance schedule. Thus, each actor in the transformed schedule has only one firing for one complete execution of the application. Further, we collapse any cycles in to a single actor. Both these optimizations reduce the size of the SDF and complexity of the dynamic scheduling problem. We would like to emphasize that as we are considering SDFs that represent entire applications, cycles are not very common. We call the transformed structure as SDF' and the corresponding graph is denoted by $G'(V', E')$. In the single appearance SDF' each edge $e \in E$ has the same number of tokens that are produced and consumed, and we denote it as $pc(e)$.

4.1.2 Periodic admissible sequential schedule

The compiler conducts the rank test on the application and generates the periodic admissible sequential schedule or PASS for the application if a schedule exists. The PASS is generated by a depth first traversal of the SDF' subject to precedence constraints between parent and child actors. The algorithm requires that a special source actor exist in the application that generates the input data stream. For example in the StreamIt benchmarks the file reader actor acts as the source actor for the application. As the SDF' is a single appearance graph, the generated PASS fires all instances of the same actor in the original SDF as a consecutive sequence. Further, all actors belonging to a cycle are also fired consecutively.

4.1.3 Retargetable code generation

The compiler generates retargetable binaries for all the actors. We are interested in run time scaling up or down of the number of cores available to the application. As we do not know the number of cores available to the application, we initially assume that all the actors are assigned to the same core and executed according to the PASS. In the case that the application does not contain cycles or statefull (described below) actors, replication of the same PASS across the available number of cores is indeed the throughput optimal solution (subject to available memory).

4.1.4 SDF annotation and actor classification

After the binaries have been compiled the static analysis phase generates additional information for the dynamic scheduler. It records the code memory requirements for each actor, workload for one firing of the actor in SDF', total workload for the PASS (W_{pass}), and classification of the actors in SDF' as stateless or statefull. An actor is classified as statefull if the output in each firing is a function of the current and past inputs (stored as state). Alternatively, an actor is stateless if the outputs are purely a function of the current inputs. An actor in SDF' that represents a cycle in SDF is labeled as statefull.

4.2 Dynamic scheduler

The objective of the dynamic scheduler is to generate a highly optimized software pipelined schedule for execution of the streaming application. The dynamic scheduling algorithm utilizes software pipelining and unrolling to maximize the throughput of the application. Software pipelining is achieved by introducing double buffering for inter-core communication. Unrolling is achieved by utilizing a fusion-fission approach. Fusion assigns multiple actors to a single batch. Fission assigns each batch to one or more cores. When a batch is assigned to more than one core it effectively unrolls the SDF'. As the schedule is generated dynamically we are interested in a near linear time algorithm. In the following paragraphs we describe the calculation of optimal/batch workloads, actor to batch assignment, fission/unrolling of a batch, and amortization of DMA overhead. Finally, we discuss the pseudo code for the algorithm.

4.2.1 Calculation of optimal workload per core

The optimal workload for each core for a given application is a function of the number of cores, and maximum workload of a statefull actor, and is given by:

$$W_{opt} = \max\{\frac{W_{pass}}{n}, \max_{\forall u_{stf} \in V'}(W(u_{stf}))\}$$

As multiple instances of a statefull actor in an unrolled SDF' must be executed sequentially, the effective throughput of the statefull cannot be increased by its replication across multiple cores. Alternatively, the effective throughput of a stateless actor can be increased in an unrolled SDF by replicating it on multiple cores. Thus, the optimal workload of the application is also lower bounded by the maximum workload of any statefull actor.

4.2.2 Calculation of workload and memory requirements of a batch

As an actor u is assigned to a batch b, the workload of the batch is summation of its current workload plus the actor workload. Thus,

$$W(b) = W(b) + W(u)$$

The memory requirement of a batch $M(b)$ is summation of the memory required by code for actors assigned to the batch, intra-batch (same as intra-core) communication buffers, and inter-batch (identical to inter-core) communication buffers. Thus,

$$M(b) = M_{code}(b) + M_{intra}(b) + M_{inter}(b)$$

As an actor is assigned to a batch, the code memory requirement of the batch increases by the size of binary executable file for the actor. The increase in buffer memory requirement is dependent upon if the parent or child of the actor have been assigned to any batch or not (currently unassigned). Further, if the parent or child has already been assigned to the same batch as the actor or a different one, the memory requirements are different. Thus, we have the following three cases:

- **Case I :** The parent u of the actor v has not been assigned to any batch. In this case we initially assume that u will be assigned to a different batch, and the inter-batch communication buffer requirement is increased to accommodate for double buffering.

  $$M_{inter}(b) = M_{inter}(b) + 2 \times pc(e) \times s(e), e(u, v) \in E'$$

  Similarly, for a child w of v that has not been assigned to any batch we initially assume double buffering. Thus, the equation is identical except the edge $e(v, w)$ is considered.

- **Case II :** The parent u of the actor v has been assigned to the same batch as v. In this case we remove the double buffers that we had initially assigned for inter-batch communication, and increase the buffer for intra-batch communication. Thus,

  $$M_{inter}(b) = M_{inter}(b) - 2 \times pc(e) \times s(e), e(u, v) \in E'$$

  $$M_{intra}(b) = M_{intra}(b) + pc(e) \times s(e), e(u, v) \in E'$$

  The calculation for a child actor w which has also been assigned to the same batch as v is also similar.

- **Case III :** The parent u of the actor v has been assigned to a different batch b'. In this case we only need to assign space for double buffering in batch b to which v is being assigned. Thus,

  $$M_{inter}(b) = M_{inter}(b) + 2 \times pc(e) \times s(e), e(u, v) \in E'$$

  The buffer space calculation for a child w of actor v is similar.

4.2.3 Actor to batch assignment or fusion

The dynamic scheduling algorithm first assigns statefull actors to batches followed by stateless actors. The strategy for actor to batch assignment is different for each of these two types of actors.

1. *Statefull actors :* We assign statefull actors to a batch in the order that they appear within the PASS. We assign multiple statefull actors to a batch as long as the workload of the batch is less than W_{opt} and memory requirements of the batch are lower than the SPM (M) size. When addition of an actor to a batch results in the violation of either of these two constraints, we

assign the actor to a new batch. We refer to a generic statefull actor batch as b_i^{stf}.

2. *Stateless actors :* The stateless actors are also assigned to batches in the order that they appear within the PASS. However, in the assignment of the stateless actors we only consider the memory constraints. That is we only ensure that the memory requirements of the batch are lower than the SPM size. We ignore the workload of the batch as we can maximize the workload of a stateless actor batch by fission (or unrolling). We refer to a generic stateless actor batch as b_i^{stl}.

It is possible that at this stage after assigning actors to batches the total number of batches are greater than the number of cores. Thus, we cannot do one to one mapping between the batches and cores. The primary reason for mapping statefull and stateless actors to different batches is to be able to improve the throughput of stateless batches by batch replication. If on the other hand the number of batches are already greater than the number of cores, we cannot do replication. In such a case we attempt to generate a new solution where we mix both statefull and stateless actors in batches. The actors are assigned in the order that they appear within the PASS. We again ensure that W_{opt} and SPM memory constraints are not violated. If the solution still has more batches than the number of cores, then we make a final attempt by re-distributing the actors in the smaller workload batches across batches with larger workloads subject to memory constraint. If a valid solution is still not found we declare failure.

4.2.4 Batch replication and core assignment

After the actors have been assigned to batches we improve the throughput of the application by unrolling or fission provided the number of batches are less than the number of cores. During fission we only consider batches that contain stateless actors. Each batch of statefull actors are assigned a unique core. Let P' denote the number of cores that is remaining after the statefull batches have been assigned. We first calculate the optimal fission for each batch of stateless actors b_i:

$$U^*(b_i^{stl}) = \frac{W(b_i^{stl})}{\max_{\forall j}(W(b_j^{stf}))}$$

Notice that $U^*(b_i^{stl})$ is not necessarily an integer. We then estimate the total core requirement after fission as $K = \sum_{\forall i} U^*(b_i^{stl})$. The fission of a stateless batch is then set as:

$$U(b_i^{stl}) = \begin{cases} K > P' & \left\lfloor U^*(b_i^{stl}) \times \frac{P'}{K} \right\rfloor \\ K \leq P' & \lfloor U^*(b_i^{stl}) \rfloor \end{cases}$$

If at the end of batch replication there are some free cores (number of batches less than the number of cores) and the optimal workload of the application is constrained by stateless batch, then we attempt to improve the throughput by generating an alternative solution. In the new solution we mix both statefull and stateless actors together, and assign actors to batches in the order that they appear within the PASS. We compare the new alternative with the previous solution, and select the one with better performance.

4.2.5 DMA overhead amortization

In our actor to batch (and eventually core) mapping we do incorporate double buffers for amortizing DMA overheads.

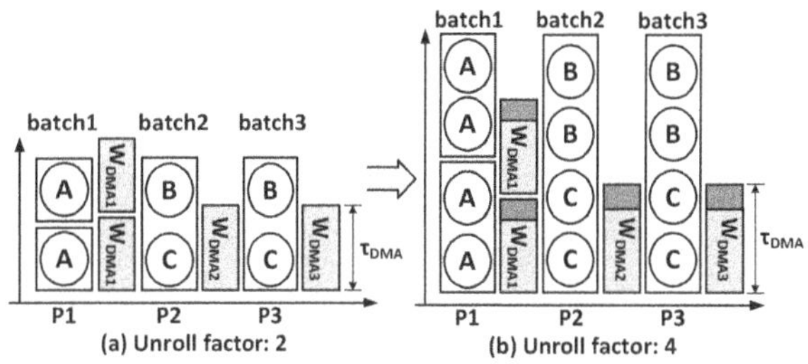

Figure 3: DMA overhead amortization

However, DMA overheads are typically governed by a minimum base cost ($0.21\mu s$ on Cell BE). The base cost is constant below a certain threshold, D_{th} of data transfer (D_{th} is 2KB in Cell BE) and then increases linearly with data size X ($7.5 \times 10^{-2} \times X \mu s$ in Cell BE). Thus, if a DMA operation involves fewer than D_{th} KB of data, its cost can be amortized by block processing. Block processing involves delaying the transfer of data until more data is produced by computation and then initiating bulk transfers. Effectively, block processing involves further unrolling of the application and requires more buffer memory for inter-core communication. Figure 3 shows an example of block processing. The left hand side of Figure 3 depicts the original design produced by the fission stage that has an unrolling factor of 2. However, the DMA transfer size for batch 1 is lower than the threshold, and its overhead is greater than associated computation. We unroll the implementation thereby increasing the unrolling factor to 4 as shown in the right hand side of Figure 3. As the rate of increase of DMA overhead beyond the threshold is quite low, we are able to completely mask the communication overhead by computation. Our algorithm applies block processing only if the DMA overhead for some batch is greater than its associated computation, and if the block processing indeed would result in an improvement.

4.2.6 Algorithm and complexity analysis

The pseudo-code for the dynamic scheduling algorithm is given in Algorithm 1. Line 3 calculates the W_{opt}, Line 4 assigns the statefull actors to batches, and Line 6 assigns stateless filters to batches. Line 8 performs batch replication or fission if the number of batches in current solution is less than number of cores ($F = false$). Line 9 checks for the case if the number of batches is less than the number of cores, and if the optimal workload is constrained by stateless batches. Function $W_{max}()$ returns the maximum workload over a set of batches. Line 10 sets R as true if the condition is satisfied. The *if* block of Line 11 generates a solution by assigning actors in the PASS order to batches. The algorithm enters the block if no valid solution has been generated upto this stage ($F = true$) or R is true. Line 14 attempts to re-distribute the smaller workload batches across the larger workload batches (subject to memory constraint) if the generated solution is not valid. The function *ReAssignBatches()* performs this operation and modifies B'. If the new solution is valid, Line 15 updates F and B accordingly. Line 18 checks if the new solution is better than the previous solution and updates B. Line 20 performs DMA overhead amortization, and finally Line 21 returns the final solution as B (if it is found).

The functions *AssignBatches()* and *ReplicateBatches()* have a complexity of $O(|V|)$. $W_{max}()$ has a complexity of $O(|P|)$.

Input : List of statefull actors L_{stf} in PASS order
: List of stateless actors L_{stl} in PASS order
: List of actors denoting the pass $PASS$
: P, M, G'(V',E')
Output: List of batches B ($|B| = |P|$), or failure

B $\leftarrow \emptyset$;
F $\leftarrow$ false, R $\leftarrow$ false ;
$W_{opt} \leftarrow$ CalcWopt(L_{stf}, L_{stl}, P);
AssignBatches(L_{stf}, B, W_{opt}, M);
if $|B| > |P|$ **then** F $\leftarrow$ true;
if *not F* **then** AssignBatches(L_{stl}, B, ∞, M) ;
if $|B| > |P|$ **then** F $\leftarrow$ true;
if *not F* **then** ReplicateBatches(B);
if $|B| < |P|$ *and* $W_{max}(B_{stf}) < W_{max}(B_{stl})$ **then**
  R $\leftarrow$ true;
if *F or R* **then**
  B' $\leftarrow \emptyset$;
  AssignBatches(PASS, B', W_{opt}, M);
  if $|B'| > |P|$ **then** ReAssignBatches(B');
  if F *and* $|B'| \leq |P|$ **then**
    F $\leftarrow$ false;
    B $\leftarrow$ B';
  if R *and* $|B'| \leq |P|$ *and* $W_{max}(B') < W_{max}(B)$ **then**
    B $\leftarrow$ B';
if *not F* **then** DmaAmortization(B, *f*);
if $F = true$ **then return** *failure* **else return** B;

Algorithm 1: DynamicScheduler()

Input : List of actors A,W_{opt}, M
Input and Output: List of batches B

b $\leftarrow$ newbatch() ;
while $A \neq \emptyset$ **do**
  a $\leftarrow$ A.getactor();
  if *(W(b) + W(a) > W_{opt}) OR*
  (M(b) + M(a,b) > M) **then**
    B.addbatch(b) ;
    b $\leftarrow$ newbatch() ;
  b.addactor(a);
if $b \neq \emptyset$ **then** B.addbatch(b);

Algorithm 2: AssignBatches()

As the function *ReAssignBatches()* sorts the existing batches it has a complexity of $|P|log|P|$. Consequently the overall complexity of the algorithm is given by $O(|V| + |P| + |P|log|P|)$. In other words for a given architecture (P is constant) the complexity of the algorithm is linear in the number of actors in the application ($O(|V|)$.

4.3 Implementation details

In this section we discuss the implementation details for the dynamic scheduler in the context of an embedded multi-core architecture. In the following we have assumed the target architecture as IBM Cell BE. However, the discussion holds true for other multi-core architectures that utilize an SPM. In the following sections we discuss the memory map, software pipeline implementation, and run-time control thread.

4.3.1 SPM layout and allocation

Figure 4 describes the memory layout of an SPM attached to a data plane core. The memory is partitioned into contiguous regions for library functions and global data, code region for our runtime control thread, overlay tables and control blocks, heap, and stack. Given a fixed size SPM, we first preserve the memory for library function and global data. Then, the memory for storing the code of our run time control thread is allocated. Immediately after the static code region, we allocate a fixed size memory for storing overlay tables and control blocks[1]. We maintain two overlay tables, one for storing information of the code source, destination addresses, and size of each actor (_ovly_table). The other table maintains information about whether an actor is present in the on-chip SPM (_ovly_buf_table). The control blocks also have two implementations, namely batch control block (bcb) and actor control block (acb). A batch control block contains information of the entire batch, and an actor control block contains information that is specific to each actor. The remaining memory is designated for heap and stack. The actor code and their data buffers of each SPM are dynamically allocated in heap because they are unknown at compile time. The buffers include space for intra-core communication, inter-core incoming data, and inter-core outgoing data. Section 4.2.2 included the discussion for calculation for data buffer sizes to be allocated.

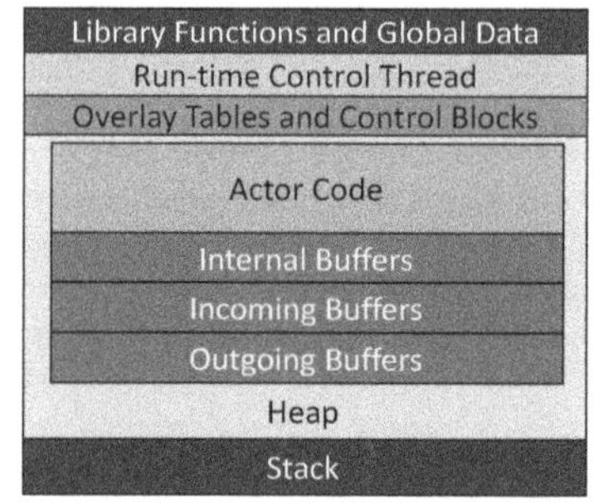

Figure 4: Memory layout for a local SPM.

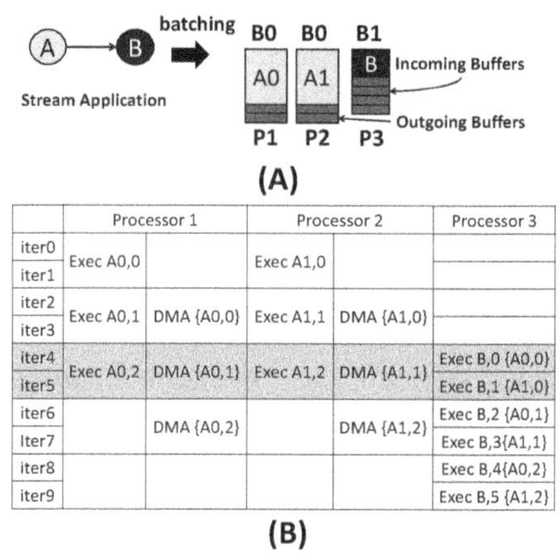

Figure 5: Software pipelined execution.

4.3.2 Software pipelining

As discussed earlier the dynamic scheduler generates a software pipelined schedule for application execution. Figure 5 provides a simple example with 2 actors and 3 processing engines. We will first discuss this example as a case study and then explain the implementation details.

In Figure 5 (A) we have a stream application with one producer A and one consumer B. Assume that the workload of A is twice of B, and B is a statefull actor. After mapping

[1]We assume an upper bound on the memory requirement for the tables.

them to 3 processors we will have actor A mapped to batch B0 then replicated once, and actor B mapped to batch B1. After batch to processing engine mapping, we have the first copy of actor A (A0) mapped to processing engine P1, the second copy of actor A (A1) mapped to processing engine P2, and actor B mapped to processing engine P3. Each copy of A and B has two buffers for every communication edge to implement double buffering. At iteration 0, both A0 and A1 start execution. *Exec A0,0* in Figure 5 (B) denotes the first execution of A0 and $DMA\{A0,0\}$ denotes that the DMA engine transfers the output data of *Exec A0,0* to its destination. Starting from iteration 2, the output data of A0 and A1 are available. We start $DMA\{A0,0\}$ at iteration 2 and in iteration 4 we start the first execution of B that consumes this data, denoted by $Exec\ B,0\{A0,0\}$. We also start $DMA\{A1,0\}$ in iteration 2 that transfers data to the other incoming buffer of B. Consequently, we have parallelized executions of $(A0,1)$, $(A1,1)$, $(DMA\{A0,0\})$, and $(DMA\{A1,0\})$ in this iteration. Then in iterations 4 and iteration 5, we have A0, A1 each being executed once, their data being transferred to B, and Actor B executed twice. This is also the steady state execution of the entire application. We set synchronization barriers across the steady state schedule.

In our implementation, the control block of each batch holds the information of the current execution index and the number of actors mapped to the batch. The control block of each actor contains information of the iteration at which the current actor starts execution and DMA operations, the address location of actor code, pointers for its input and output data buffers in local SPM, and the source and destination of its incoming and outgoing data. All control blocks are initialized in the control plane processor by the dynamic scheduler, and then transferred to each on-chip SPM through DMAs. A main routine that operates on these data and executes a batch is discussed in the following section.

4.3.3 Run-time control thread

Algorithm 3 describes the main routine of our run time control thread that executes on the data plane core (SPE in IBM Cell BE) and implements the previously discussed software pipelined execution. The main body of the control thread is a while loop. Line 2 in the algorithm implements the synchronization barrier, and waits for a message from the control plane core (PPE in IBM Cell BE). The message has four components. The *msg.stop_execution* bit determines whether we terminate the slave thread. If *msg.stop_execution* is true, then the control thread exits immediately and writes a message back to the control plane core, Line 16. Otherwise, it checks *msg.new_schedule_start* bit to see whether the current iteration is a start of a new schedule. If *msg.new_schedule_start* is true, then the control thread frees any heap memory that has been allocated, including previous allocations for actor code and data buffers. Then it reallocates memory for actor code and data buffers of the new schedule. The size of each memory allocation can be extracted from the same mailbox message. It then initializes the control blocks and overlay tables with data that is generated by the dynamic scheduler through DMAs. The *msg.flush_pipeline_start* bit indicates whether we terminate the execution of the current application and flush the entire pipeline. If *msg.flush_pipeline_start* is true, then

```
1  while true do
2      msg = wait_mailbox();
3      if msg.stop_execution==true then
4          break;
5      if msg.new_schedule_start==true then
6          Free previous memory and allocate new memory;
7          DMA control blocks and overlay tables;
8      if msg.flush_pipeline_start==true then
9          DMA control blocks;
10     Initiate DMAs for input data for index + 1;
11     for i = 0; i < bcb.actors; i + + do
12         if bcb.idx ≥ acb[i].start && bcb.idx ≤ acb[i].end
           then
13             Execute actor[i];
14     Check and ensure DMAs complete;
15     write_mailbox(msg);
16 write_mailbox(msg);
```

Algorithm 3: Run-time Control Thread.

benchmark	actors	edges	% statefull
beamformer	56	58	82%
bitonic_sort	40	46	35%
channelvocoder	55	70	65%
dct	8	7	0%
des	53	60	38%
fft	17	16	0%
filterbank	85	99	58%
fm	43	53	65%
mpeg2_subset	23	26	30%
serpent_full	120	128	43%
tde-pp	29	28	3%
vocoder	114	147	72%

Table 1: StreamIt Benchmarks

the control thread updates the actor control blocks. The corresponding end iterations of actor executions and DMA transfers will be updated which flush the software pipeline. Lines 10-14 implement parallel execution of a batch for the current iteration and DMA transfers for the last iteration. The thread first initiates DMA transfers for data that are produced from the previous stage. Then for each actor, if the current batch execution index is no less than its execution start index and no more than its execution end index, it executes the current actor. After execution of every actor in the batch, it ensures that the DMA transfers for data that were produced in the previous are complete. Then it writes a mailbox message back to the control plane processor for starting the next iteration.

5. EXPERIMENTAL RESULTS

We evaluated our technique by compiling and dynamic scheduling of StreamIt benchmark application suite (shown in Table 1). The target architecture was considered to be similar to IBM Cell BE. We compared the performance of our approach with two existing dynamic scheduling techniques proposed by Hormati et al. (Flexstream) [8] and Baker et al.[1]. We also compared the performance of our dynamic scheduler with a static scheduling technique proposed by Che et al. [3]. We characterized the workloads and buffer requirements of the actors by compiling and executing them on IBM Cell BE. In order to evaluate the proposed and existing approaches for architectures with larger number of cores we constructed SystemC models. The run time of actors and the communication overheads in the model

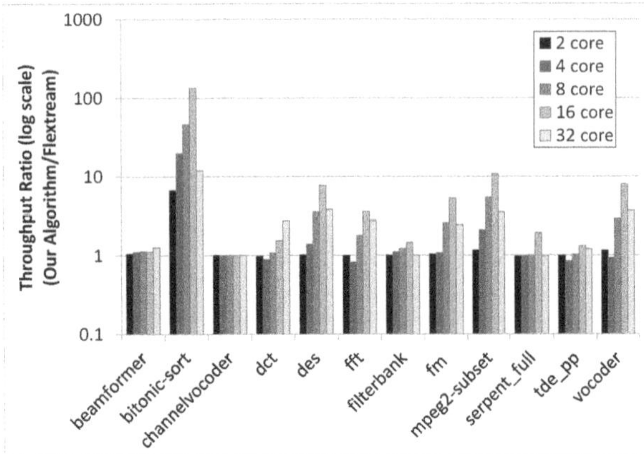

Figure 6: Comparison with Flextream

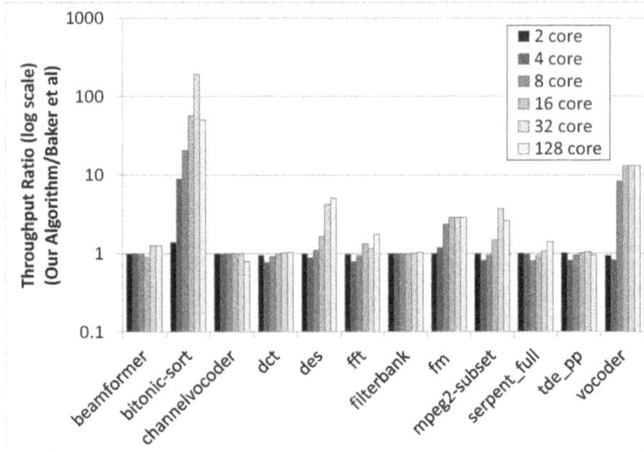

Figure 7: Comparison with Baker et al.

were based on the characterization values obtained from the IBM Cell BE. The run-time of the dynamic scheduling algorithms were obtained by executing them on the PowerPC core of the IBM Cell BE. The run-time of the static analysis stage of the various approaches was obtained on Intel Xeon Quad-core processor at 2.8 GHz.

5.1 Comparisons with existing approaches

Comparison with Flexstream [8].

Flexstream utilizes an integer linear programming (ILP) formulation to obtain a maximal parallel schedule during design time on the available number of cores. It then reduces the degree of parallelism in the implementation dynamically as the number of cores are reduced. In our experiment we set the maximum number of cores as 32. Thus, Flexstream generated an implementation for each application at compile time that required 32 cores. We then evaluated the performance of the Flexstream approach as the number of cores were varied from 2 to 32. Figure 6 plots the performance improvement in throughput achieved by utilizing our approach in comparison to Flexstream for each of the StreamIt benchmarks and for 2-32 cores. A few trends are clearly observable. The designs generated by our approach are overwhelmingly superior to Flexstream in vast majority of the cases. Further, the performance due to our approach improves as the number of cores increase. The rate of increase in performance reduces at 32 cores. This is because the Flexstream implementation at 32 cores is the statically generated design. However, the designs by our approach even at 32 cores is better than Flexstream. The primary reason for the better performance of our approach is the aggressive unrolling that we apply both during fission (or batch replication) and DMA overhead amortization. Our approach generates designs that are on an average 5.55 times faster (standard deviation of 17.91) than Flexstream. Further, our compile time stage on an average executes in $0.03s$ while Flexstream ILP approach requires $49000s$. Finally, our dynamic scheduling stage requires $0.3ms$ on average while Flexstream executes in $0.27ms$.

Comparison with Baker et al. [1].

The static analysis stage of Baker et al. is similar to our technique, and unlike Flexstream they utilize unrolling. We compared the designs generated by our approach against Baker et al. for 2 to 128 cores. Figure 7 plots the performance improvements achieved by our technique in comparison to Baker et al. for each of the benchmark applications. As can be observed from the figure our technique generates superior designs in comparison to Baker et al. In particular for *bitonic-sort, des, fft, fm, mpeg2-subset* and *vocoder* our approach gives large performance improvements. The primary reason for the performance improvement is that we restrict the DMA overheads by assignment of actors to batches and then replicating the batches to perform systematic unrolling which creates symmetric allocations. Baker et al. perform unrolling before assigning actors to batches (which are then one-to-one mapped to cores). Consequently, the distribution of actors across cores is quite arbitrary and results in larger DMA overheads. The average performance improvement due to our approach over Baker et al. is 6.38X with standard deviation of 23.84. Further, our dynamic scheduling algorithm executes in $0.32ms$ on average while Baker et al. requires $0.63ms$ or almost twice as much as our approach. The computational complexity of our dynamic scheduling approach is linear time for a fixed number of cores and therefore we are able to generate solutions in half the time.

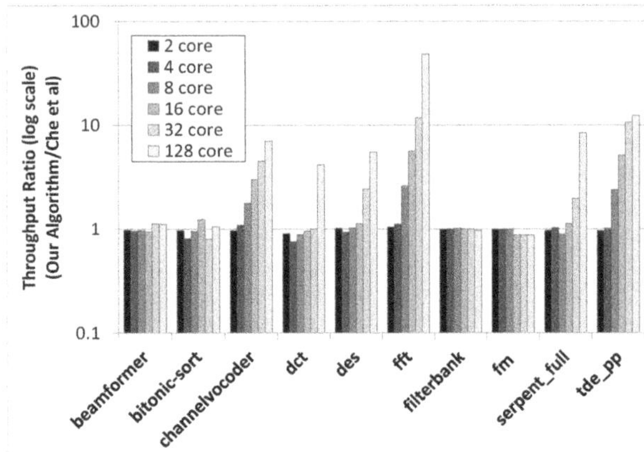

Figure 8: Comparison with compile time approach

Performance comparison with compile time approach.

We also compared the performance obtained by our technique against a compile time approach by Che et al. [3] that generates one solution for an application based on the num-

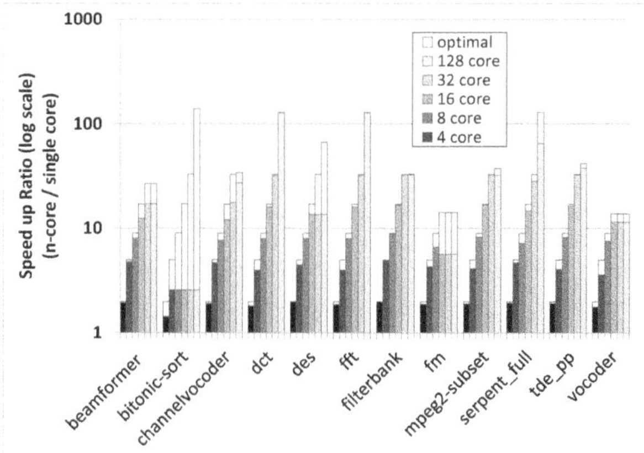

Figure 9: Performance without DMA amortization

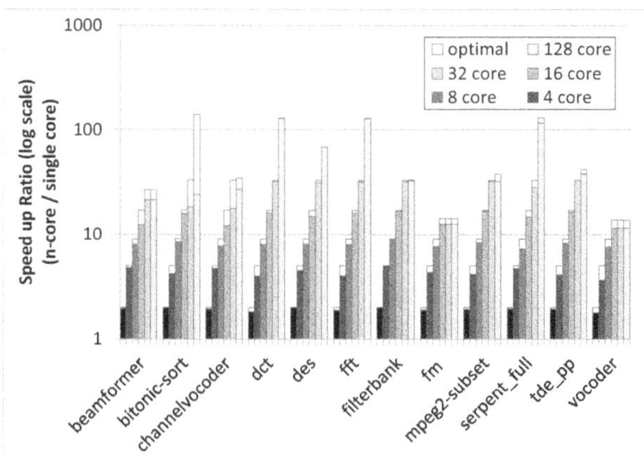

Figure 10: Performance with DMA amortization

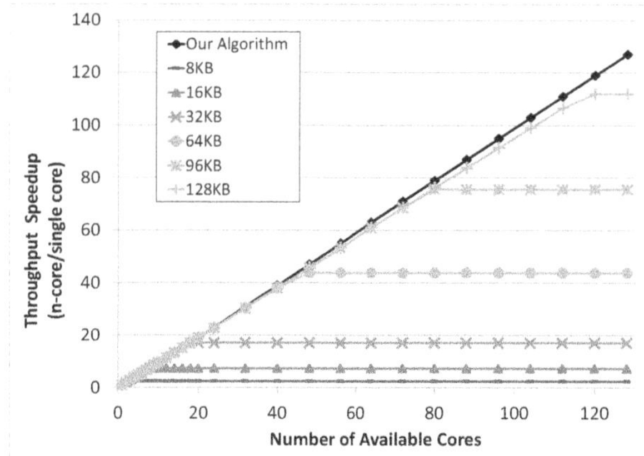

Figure 11: DCT performance scaling

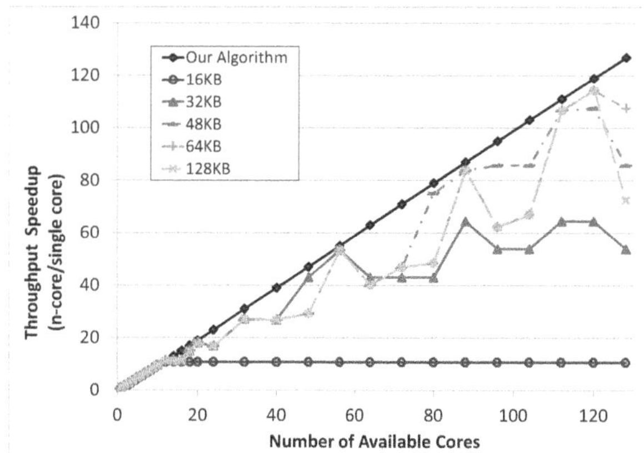

Figure 12: FFT performance scaling

ber of cores specified to the compiler. Unlike, our technique the compile time approach by Che et al. utilizes retiming to address cycles in the application graph. However, in contrast to our approach they do not consider unrolling of the application. We compared the solutions generated by our approach against the static compilation technique for 2 to 128 cores. Figure 8 gives the performance improvement obtained by our dynamic scheduling technique against the static compilation approach. As can be seen from the figure our dynamic scheduling technique out performs the static compilation approach in many cases. The performance improvement is primarily due to the aggressive unrolling utilized by our approach. Further, even though we do not optimize for cyclic dependencies for the StreamIt benchmarks we are still able to out perform the static compilation approach that does optimize cyclic dependencies. The average performance improvement due to our dynamic scheduling approach is 3X (standard deviation 6.48). Further, the average run time of the static compilation approach is $6s$ which is much larger than our dynamic scheduling technique that executes in ms.

5.2 Impact of DMA amortization optimization and comparisons with optimal

We also analyzed the impact of DMA amortization through block processing on the overall performance of the algorithm. Figure 9 depicts the normalized performance obtained by our approach without DMA amortization for 2 to 128 cores. Each performance bar in the figure is normalized to the performance of the same application on a single core. Further, for each bar we also show the maximal theoretical speed-up possible (optimal in the figure). As can be seen from the figure in the absence of DMA amortization the achieved performance is not near the theoretical optimal. This is particularly true for *bitonic-sort, des* and *fm*. The discrete DMA communication overheads limit the achievable performance. Figure 10 depicts the performance achieved with DMA amortization and compares it with theoretical optimal. As is clearly observable from the figure DMA amortization results in considerable speed-up in *bitonic-sort, des* and *fm*, and incremental speed-up in several others. Amortization of communication overhead is a key challenge in multi-core implementations and our technique is effectively able to do so. Further, the designs generated by our approach are quite close to the theoretical optimal solutions.

5.3 Performance scaling with available cores and memory

We also evaluated the performance scaling of the solutions generated by our approach for two applications without any statefull actors as the available memory and cores are scaled up. Further, we compared our designs with those generated by Baker et al. [1]. Figures 11 and 12 plot the performance obtained by our approach and by Baker et al. Each point in the two plots is normalized to the performance achieved by a single core architecture with identical memory. As can be observed from the two plots our approach generates designs that scale up linearly with the number of cores. The primary reason is that in the case of the stateless application our approach exploits the available data-level parallelism to the fullest and replicates the application across each of the cores. However, Baker et al. splits the application across the cores, and the resulting buffer requirements in the presence of memory constraints end up limiting the achievable performance.

6. CONCLUSION

The paper addressed the problem of dynamic scheduling of streaming applications on embedded multi-core architectures. We presented a two stage static-dynamic analysis approach. The static or compile time phase collects useful information about the application and generates re-targetable executables. The dynamic scheduler reads the overall application information generated by the static compilation stage and generates highly optimized parallel implementations on the specified cores. The algorithm complexity of the dynamic scheduler is linear in the number of the cores. We evaluated our approach by comparing its solution quality and run time with two dynamic scheduling and one compile time approach. Our algorithm generates overwhelmingly superior designs in extremely low run times. The block processing based DMA amortization stage was shown to be particularly effective for reducing communication overheads. Further, the solutions generated by our approach was shown to scale up with available cores and memory.

In the proposed approach although we address SPM management through overlay tables we have not addressed problems of code and data overlays. To the best of our knowledge there are no known purely dynamic scheduling approaches that can also address code and data overlay optimizations at run time. Such optimizations have typically been addressed at compile time in the past. Our future work would address incorporating low complexity code and data overlay optimizations that can be integrated with the dynamic scheduler.

7. ACKNOWLEDGEMENT

The research presented in the paper was supported in part by grants from Science Foundation Arizona, Stardust Foundation, National Science Foundation (CCF - 0903513) and Semiconductor Research Corporation.

8. REFERENCES

[1] M. A. Baker and K. S. Chatha. A lightweight run-time scheduler for multitasking multicore stream applications. In *Proceedings of International Conference on Computer Design (ICCD)*, 2010.

[2] F. Blagojevic, D. S. Nikolopoulos, A. Stamatakis, and C. D. Antonopoulos. Dynamic multigrain parallelization on the cell broadband engine. In *Proceedings of the 12th ACM SIGPLAN symposium on Principles and practice of parallel programming*, PPoPP '07, pages 90–100, New York, NY, USA, 2007. ACM.

[3] W. Che and K. Chatha. Compilation of stream programs onto scratchpad memory based embedded multicore processors through retiming. In *Design Automation Conference (DAC), 2011 48th ACM/EDAC/IEEE*, pages 122 -127, june 2011.

[4] W. Che, A. Panda, and K. S. Chatha. Compilation of stream programs for multicore processors that incorporate scratchpad memories. In *Proceedings of the Conference on Design, Automation and Test in Europe*, DATE '10, pages 1118–1123, 3001 Leuven, Belgium, Belgium, 2010. European Design and Automation Association.

[5] M. K. Chen, X. F. Li, R. Lian, J. H. Lin, L. Liu, T. Liu, and R. Ju. Shangri-la: achieving high performance from compiled network applications while enabling ease of programming. *SIGPLAN Not.*, 40:224–236, June 2005.

[6] J. Eker and J. W. Janneck. Cal language report. Technical report, University of California at Berkeley, Tech. Rep. UCB/ERL M03/48.

[7] M. I. Gordon, W. Thies, M. Karczmarek, J. Lin, A. S. Meli, A. A. Lamb, C. Leger, J. Wong, H. Hoffmann, D. Maze, and S. Amarasinghe. A stream compiler for communication-exposed architectures. *SIGARCH Comput. Archit. News*, 30:291–303, October 2002.

[8] A. H. Hormati, Y. Choi, M. Kudlur, R. Rabbah, T. Mudge, and S. Mahlke. Flextream: Adaptive compilation of streaming applications for heterogeneous architectures. In *Proceedings of the 2009 18th International Conference on Parallel Architectures and Compilation Techniques*, PACT '09, pages 214–223, Washington, DC, USA, 2009. IEEE Computer Society.

[9] J. A. Kahle et al. Introduction to the cell multiprocessor. *IBM Journal of Research and Development*, 49:589 -604, 2005.

[10] E. Kilgariff and R. Fernando. The geforce 6 series gpu architecture. In *SIGGRAPH*. ACM, 2005.

[11] K. Knobe and C. D. Offner. Tstreams: A model of parallel computation (preliminary report). Technical report, HP Labs, Technical Report HPL-2004-78.

[12] M. Kudlur and S. Mahlke. Orchestrating the execution of stream programs on multicore platforms. *SIGPLAN Not.*, 43:114–124, June 2008.

[13] S.-w. Liao, Z. Du, G. Wu, and G.-Y. Lueh. Data and computation transformations for brook streaming applications on multiprocessors. In *Proceedings of the International Symposium on Code Generation and Optimization*, CGO '06, pages 196–207, Washington, DC, USA, 2006. IEEE Computer Society.

[14] M. Monteyne and R. Inc. Rapidmind multi-core development platform. Technical report, RapidMind, Tech. Rep.

[15] NVIDIA. *Compute Unified Device Architecture Programming Guide*. NVIDIA: Santa Clara, CA, 2007.

[16] C. Ostler, K. S. Chatha, V. Ramamurthi, and K. Srinivasan. Ilp and heuristic techniques for system-level design on network processor architectures. *ACM Trans. Des. Autom. Electron. Syst.*, 12, September 2007.

[17] J. Pino and E. Lee. Hierarchical static scheduling of dataflow graphs onto multiple processors. In *Acoustics, Speech, and Signal Processing, 1995. ICASSP-95., 1995 International Conference on*, volume 4, pages 2643 -2646 vol.4, may 1995.

[18] J. Stokes. Peakstream unveils multicore and cpu/gpu programming solution. Last accessed April 2012.

[19] J. Stone, D. Gohara, and G. Shi. Opencl: A parallel programming standard for heterogeneous computing systems. *Computing in Science Engineering*, 12(3):66 -73, may-june 2010.

[20] W. Thies, M. Karczmarek, and S. Amarasinghe. Streamit: A language for streaming applications. In R. Horspool, editor, *Compiler Construction*, volume 2304 of *Lecture Notes in Computer Science*, pages 49–84. Springer Berlin / Heidelberg, 2002.

[21] L. Truong. White paper: Low power consumption and a competitive price tag make the six-core tms320c6472 ideal for high performance applications. *Processing Business*, oct. 2009.

[22] S. Wasson. Ageia's physx physics processing unit. *The tech report, PC hardware explored*, Last accessed April 2012.

[23] M. H. Wiggers, M. J. Bekooij, and G. J. Smit. Monotonicity and run-time scheduling. In *EMSOFT '09: Proceedings of the seventh ACM international conference on Embedded software*, pages 177–186, New York, NY, USA, 2009. ACM.

[24] D. Zhang, Q. J. Li, R. Rabbah, and S. Amarasinghe. A lightweight streaming layer for multicore execution. *SIGARCH Comput. Archit. News*, 36(2):18–27, May 2008.

A Distributed Interleaving Scheme for Efficient Access to WideIO DRAM Memory

Ciprian Seiculescu
LSI, EPFL
Lausanne, Switzerland
ciprian.seiculescu@epfl.ch

Luca Benini
DEIS, University of Bologna
Bologna, Italy
luca.benini@unibo.it

Giovanni De Micheli
LSI, EPFL
Lausanne, Switzerland
giovanni.demicheli@epfl.ch

ABSTRACT

Achieving the main memory (DRAM) required bandwidth at acceptable power levels for current and future applications is a major challenge for *System-on-Chip* designers for mobile platforms. *Three dimensional* (3D) integration and 3D stacked DRAM memories promise to provide a significant boost in bandwidth at low power levels by exploiting multiple channels and wide data interfaces. In this paper, we address the problem of efficiently exploiting the multiple channels provided by standard (JEDEC's WIDE-IO) 3D-stacked memories, to extract maximal effective bandwidth and minimize latency for main memory access. We propose a new distributed interleaved access method that leverages the on-chip interconnect to simplify the design and implementation of the DRAM controller, without impacting performance compared to traditional centralized implementations. We perform experiments on realistic workload for a mobile communication and multimedia platform and show that our proposed distributed interleaving memory access method improves the overall throughput while minimally impacting the performance of latency sensitive communication flows.

Categories and Subject Descriptors

B.4.3 [**INPUT/OUTPUT AND DATA COMMUNICATIONS**]: Interconnections (Subsystems)—*topology*

General Terms

Design

Keywords

NoC, WideIO, DRAM controller, interleaving

1. INTRODUCTION

Todays applications that drive the *System-on-Chip* (SoC) design require more and more storage capacity as well as high bandwidth to main memory. To provide the required storage capacity, high-density commodity DRAM is the only cost-effective main memory option, and external DRAM modules are needed. To deliver the required bandwidth when accessing external DRAM is a major challenge and main memory access is the main bottleneck for scaling computing performance, also known in literature as the *Memory Wall* [1]. In mobile SoCs platforms that have strict power consumption constraints, providing the required bandwidth to main memory at manageable power levels is an even more challenging problem. Mobile SoCs rely on parallelization and specialization of the functionality in order to obtain the required performance for the application at low power level. A natural solution for providing increased memory bandwidth with low power would be to parallelize the access to the memory. However, as the main storage is external, the limited number of available off-chip IO ports prevents the design of a parallel memory system.

Three dimensional integration is a promising technology for increasing the number of transistors on-chip [2]. A major advantage of 3D integration is the ability to integrate efficiently heterogeneous manufacturing technologies in a single chip stack, by putting together dies that have been processed separately. 3D-stacked memories that leverage the benefits of heterogeneous integration have been proposed as a solution to overcome the *Memory Wall* [3]. As each layer in a 3D stack is processed separately, high density DRAM memory can be stacked on top of logic to satisfy the large storage needs of applications (at low cost per MB). *Through Silicon Vias* (TSVs) are used to provide vertical connectivity and as 3D integration technology matures the density of TSVs increases. Stacked memories can benefit from the large number of TSVs to provide wide interfaces and multiple channels, such that the large bandwidth requirements can be met at low power levels. Apart from the wider data-paths that allow the memory to operate at lower frequency, while achieving the same bandwidth, power is saved in 3D stacked memories by removing the need to go off-chip through power-hungry IO ports. On the other hand, having access to multiple ports, requires the SoC to be able to efficiently use them to achieve the overall bandwidth requirement.

Given the promise of three-dimensional DRAM stacking, industry is actively pushing standardization of TSV-based interfaces. WideIO 3D-stacked DRAM [4] is an emerging JEDEC standard. WideIO memories use TSVs to provide interfaces to 4 channels each with a 128bit wide data interface. By running at 200MHz with single data rate the WideIO memory can provide a peak bandwidth of 12.8GB/s at lower power levels than current *Low-Power Double Data Rate* (LPDDR) DRAM. According to the JEDEC standard WideIO will provide 50% more bandwidth with 20% less power than an existing dual-channel LPDDR2 off-chip solution. In this work, we focus on WideIO DRAM memory integration in the SoC design and we address the problem of efficiently using the 4 channels to achieve the required application performance.

CODES+ISSS'12, October 7-12, 2012, Tampere, Finland.

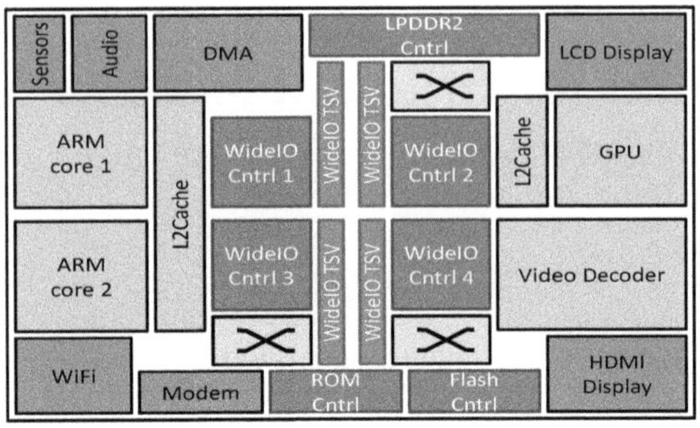

Figure 1: Example of SoC floorplan with WideIO TSV interfaces

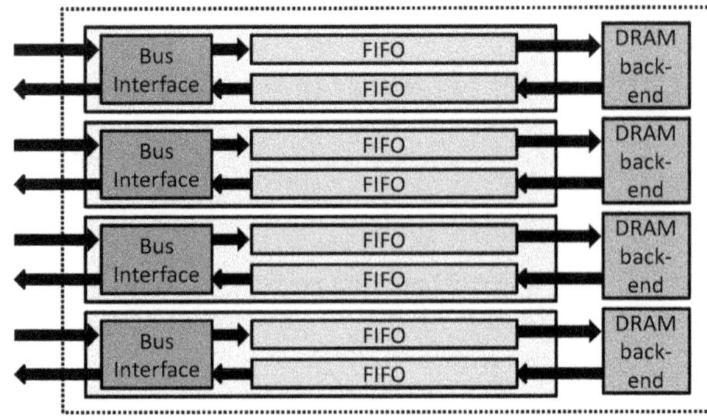

Figure 2: Distributed DRAM controller with 4 separate channels

Networks-on-Chip (NoCs) have been proposed as a scalable interconnect for on-chip communication [5]. NoCs have been already adopted in many high-end mobile SoC products and can be found on most of next-generation SoCs [6]. Therefore in this work, we focus on SoC design that use a Noc for the global interconnect. We analyze two architectures for the memory sub-system that access the 4 channels of the WideIO DRAM: i) a simple to implement architecture that uses 4 DRAM controllers to independently access the four channels that rely on software to balance the traffic between the channels and ii) a complex centralized controller with multiple ports and interleaved address space to balance the traffic among the four channels. Since the TSV size is large, when compared to transistor size, the wide data interfaces that require many TSVs will be far apart on the floorplan. An example of such a heterogeneous SoC floorplan with WideIO connectivity is presented in Figure 1. The position of the TSV interfaces in the example was chosen to accommodate the WideIO interface from [4]. This makes the centralized controller difficult and expensive to implement. Therefore, we also propose a new distributed interleaving method to access the memory controller that leverages the advantages of both of the previously mentioned designs, while avoiding their most serious shortcomings. On one hand it uses a simple memory interface design, as the first method, but provides an interleaved address space such that balancing the traffic to the four channels is transparent to the software. Our proposed approach requires the integrated design of both the NoC and the DRAM controller, as the interleaving support is now distributed within the NoC, which also result in balancing the traffic in the NoC itself.

We perform experiments on a realistic benchmark for a heterogeneous mobile communication and multimedia SoC platform. An important contribution is given by our advanced traffic modeling environment and by modeling the details of the NoC micro-architecture (i.e., packetization, bandwidth inflation). From experiments, we show that our proposed distributed interleaving memory access method improves the overall throughput while minimally impacting the performance of latency sensitive communication flows. For example, our design improves the frame rate of the video decoding and display subsystem by 2 frames/second when compared to simple separated controller with the best memory allocation (42 frames/second with the worst memory allocation) and by 7 frames/second when compared to the complex controller with interleaved address space.

2. RELATED WORK

Several works have presented methods to improve DRAM access efficiency by scheduling and reordering transactions in the DRAM controller [7], [8], [9], [10], [11], [12]. In [8], [10] optimizations for multicore systems are presented, and in [9] a predictable DRAM controller is presented. Memory transaction scheduling is important in increasing the efficiency of DRAM access, but it is orthogonal to the scope of this paper. We use the simulator model from [12] to include these memory access optimizations in our simulation framework.

Many research groups have focused on the technological aspects to manufacture 3D-integrated memory systems [13], [14], [15], [16]. Others have investigated system architectures using 3D-integrated on-chip DRAM [17], [18], [19], [20]. In [3], Weis et al. present a design space exploration of SoCs with 3D-stacked DRAM and in [21] the authors show an overview of 3D-integrated DRAMs and the challenges associated with it. In this work we assume a specific 3D-stacked DRAM architecture, i.e. the WideIO JEDEC standard[4]. A study showing the advantages of using multi-channel memory systems for video encoding SoCs is presented in [22]. The study shows the impact of multiple channels on the system performance and our work is different from that as we are concerned with how to efficiently access multiple channels.

Several researches have looked at the co-design of the NoC with the DRAM controller. In [23] the authors present a way to reorder DRAM transactions while in the network and simplify the DRAM controller. However this work addresses the problem of scheduling and not of accessing multiple channels. To reduce the traffic to DRAM the authors propose in [24] to have a processor base DRAM controller capable to process complex requests and return only the results. A credit based flow control method is used in [25] to prevent the DRAM traffic from waiting into the network and interfering with non DRAM traffic. In [26] the authors propose to give higher priority to transactions waiting in the DRAM queue that have to be sent back to cores in areas of the NoC which are less congested. These works however do not address the problem of accessing multiple channels. Memory centric NoC architectures with real chip implementations are provided in [27] and [28]. However in these systems there are several memories which are on-chip and the communication between cores is done through these memories.

Arteris [29] and Sonics [30] offer memory interleaving support that is integrated with their interconnect solutions. However they do not provide any comparison to traditional solutions. Moreover in the white paper from Sonics [30], experiments are shown only for two channels using existing off-chip DDR3 memories. In this work we target 3D-stacked WideIO with 4 channels and provide an extensive comparison with traditional architectures like centralized controllers and software managed independent channels.

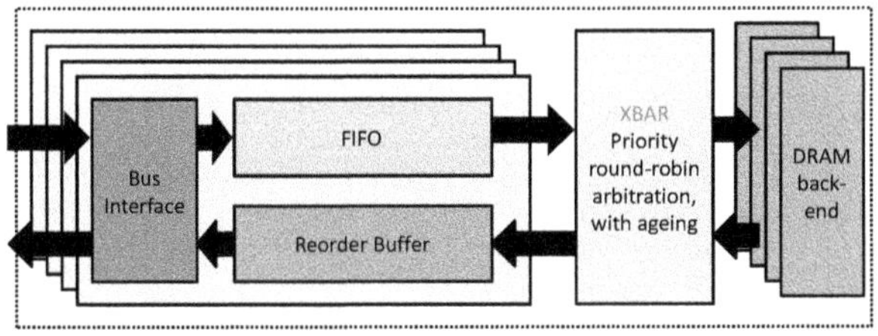

Figure 3: Centralized DRAM controller with interleaving at the controller side

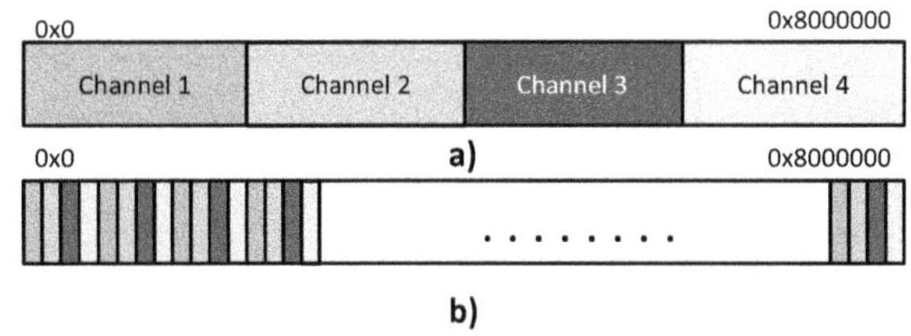

Figure 4: Example of a) partitioned- and b) interleaved address space

3. NOC AND CONTROLLER ARCHITECTURES FOR MULTI-CHANNEL DRAM

WideIO DRAM provides high-peak bandwidth at low power levels by using multiple channels with independent wide data-interfaces operated at low frequency. Efficiently exploiting the 4 channels of the WideIO memories, in order to satisfy the bandwidth demands of the application, is up to the SoC designer. Having multiple channels provides new opportunities for designing the memory controller to efficiently access the memory subsystem. In this section, we introduce three architectures: two traditional ones and we also propose a new architecture that moves part of the DRAM controller complexity into the NoC fabric to provide distributed parallel access to the four channels of a WideIO memory.

In this section we describe the three analyze architecture and discuss their advantages and disadvantages:

- *Distributed controller with separate independent channels.* This is a simple solution where an independent DRAM controller is assigned to each channel.
- *Centralized controller with interleaved address space.* This is a single multi-ported controller that can access all the four channels of the WideIO memory interface. The requests from the four ports are interleaved based on the address to the four channels to balance the traffic.
- *Distributed controller with interleaving in the NI.* This is our proposed method that uses 4 simple DRAM controllers for the 4 channels, but the transactions are split and interleaved based on address within the interconnect at the *Network Interfaces* (NIs) of the NoC.

3.1 Distributed controller

The simplest solution to access the four channels is to have four independent DRAM controllers and to split the address space in four large contiguous blocks. A block diagram of such an architecture is presented in Figure 2. By ensuring at software level that a core does not access more than one channel at the same time, this architecture does not require any changes to existing DRAM controller or NoC architectures. To each channel a DRAM controller is assigned that only needs a bus interface and address generator, with FIFO buffers to drain the requests from the NoC and an out-of-order back-end. Designing the memory subsystem of the SoC in such a distributed fashion, with separate independent DRAM channels, is easy. The main drawback of this simple architecture is that the performance of the memory subsystem is highly dependent on the memory mapping. In the worst case, if the memory regions of all cores are mapped to the same channel (which could happen for certain periods of time in systems where the memory is dynamically managed), then the peak-bandwidth of the WideIO DRAM memory is effectively reduced four times. To tackle this problem, such a system would have to expose hardware details to the software and make sure that at software level, the memory is allocated as to balance the accesses to the 4 channels. However as such an allocation, reliant on the software, would be coarse grained it may not be possible to efficiently balance the accesses to the channels.

To tackle this drawback of separated independent channels a popular technique is to interleave the address space between the channels [31]. By splitting the address space in fine-grained blocks and assigning them interleaved to the channels as shown in Figure 4, we can make sure in hardware that the data is distributed uniformly among the channels. Accessing the memory is now balanced between the channels and it is transparent to the software. The decision to which channel a transaction (or a piece of a transaction) belongs depends on the address of that transaction. Depending on where that decision is taken we look at two solutions: i) centralized in the DRAM controller and ii) distributed at the initiator *Network Interfaces* (NIs) of the NoC.

3.2 Centralized Controller with Interleaving

One way to design an interleaved memory subsystem is to have a centralized DRAM controller with multiple ports toward the NoC and multiple channels to connect to the WideIO DRAM as shown in Figure 3 similar with that from [32] (with different arbitration scheme though as we do not require that level of predictability). The advantage of this solution is that the memory controller and the NoC can be designed separately and regardless of which port you use you have access to the entire memory space. Such a centralized solution would require a crossbar to allow for parallel access between ports and the back-end controllers connected to the channels. In our architecture the bus interfaces, corresponding to each port, take the bus request and generate transactions for the DRAM back-end with the same size as the interleaving blocks. These transactions are stored in the input FIFO of the port. The arbiter takes these transactions from the ports and using the crossbar sends them to the appropriate channel according to the address. A popular schemes for arbitration (which we also assume) is priority with aging to prevent starvation. Ports can have different priorities (in our case we use two) and the transactions in the low priority ports keep an age counter. After a certain age given as parameter their priority becomes the highest and get serviced next. The reordering of the transaction to be memory friendly is done in the back-end and that is beyond the scope of this work. However since transactions from the same port are sent to different back-ends they can be serviced and returned out of order, so the response buffers in the ports have to be able to reorder the transactions.

While this solution fixes the problem of application memory mapping, there are two important drawbacks of this solution. The first drawback relates to the physical implementation of the centralized controller. The WideIO uses TSVs for connectivity, which are considerably larger than other features, and has wide interfaces so re-

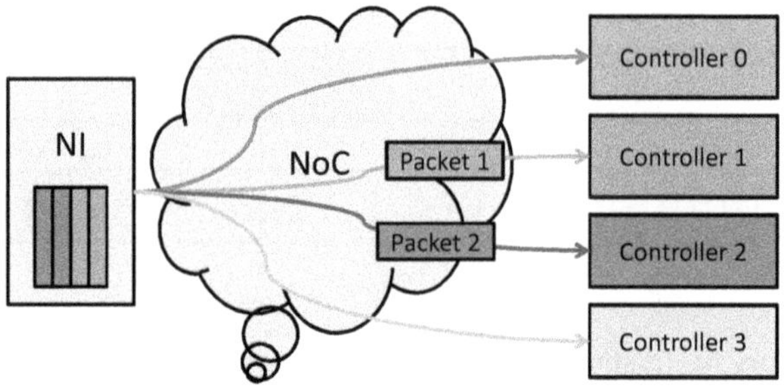

Figure 5: Example of distributed interleaving where the NI sends out a 4 beat burst transaction in 2 packets on different routes

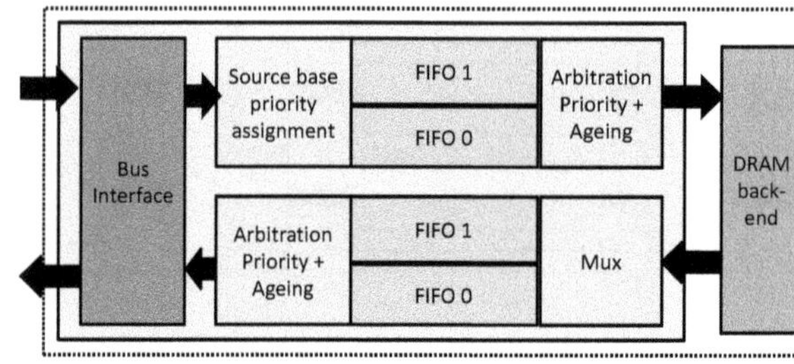

Figure 6: DRAM controller port with priority

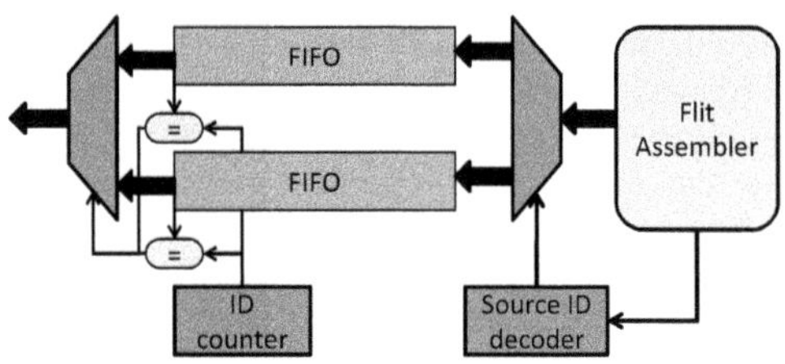

Figure 7: Simple reorder buffer schematic

quiring many such TSVs. According to the JEDEC standard the size of the 4 channels interfaces is around 0.54mm by 5.27mm. So the interfaces are far apart on the floorplan of the resulting chip as shown in Figure 1. Therefore designing the crossbar to connect the ports to the DRAM back-ends may be costly and slow. The second drawback is that the as there are more IP-cores that used the DRAM than ports, it is up to the designer to decide the assignment of the IP-cores to ports. As different IP-cores may be active for different application there could be cases where even a good assignment could still result in over-congesting a port and parts of the NoC. This would result in a degradation of performance.

3.3 Distributed Controller with Interleaving

A compromise between the two solutions discussed before is to distribute the interleaving function from the DRAM controller in the NoC. This solution would require the simpler controllers of the first solution, which could be easily implemented next to the interfaces to the WideIO memory. In this case the source NIs are responsible to implement the interleaving function (performed by the crossbar in the centralized controller). A schematic representation of this architecture which we will call as distributed controller with interleaving in the NIs is presented in Figure 5. The NI needs to have a route to each port of the independent memory controllers. Based on the address the NI chooses the path to the corresponding port. In case of transactions that are larger than the size of the interleaving block, the NI is responsible to split these transactions into multiple packets and to send those packets to the corresponding controllers. In this case the responses or partial responses (as the transaction can receive the responses in multiple packets) have to be reordered and reassembled in the NI. The details describing the NI are presented in Section 4.1. To provide two level of priority as in the centralized controller case, we use two FIFO buffers per port as shown in Figure 6. The assignment of the transactions to the priority queue is done based on the ID of the source.

The disadvantage of this method is that it generates more bandwidth in the NoC, due to the packetization overhead in the case when transactions are split. An important thing to note is that even in the previous case long transactions may need to be split to prevent blocking the interfering traffic for too long from accessing the memory controller as well. In this architecture the NoC and the memory controller need to be designed together. The main advantage of this architecture is that it balances the traffic in both the NoC and at the DRAM controller channels, regardless of the application memory mapping.

3.4 Simple Reorder-buffer Implementation

If the NI has support for interleaving and splitting of packets then it needs to be able to reorder the transactions. However in cases where there are only few routes handled by the NI the reorder buffer can be implemented in a simpler way. By leveraging the property that packets on the same route will arrive in order, then the reorder buffer can be implemented only with FIFOs and few comparators, instead of expensive CAM memories. In Figure 7, we show an example of such a reorder buffer for an NI that uses two routes to interleave the packets.

To track the order, the transactions are assigned an ID (consecutive values of a counter) when they are sent out to the target. The responses from the target will contain the same ID that was assigned to the request. We need as many FIFO buffers as there are routes. As the transaction responses coming from the same path arrive in-order, we can use simple FIFOs to buffer them. Based on the ID of the source (the ID of the target that responds) the transaction are stored to the corresponding FIFO. A counter at the receiver NI also indicates the ID of the transaction that has to be delivered next and it is incremented whenever a transaction is delivered from the FIFO to the bus interface. One comparator per FIFO buffer compares the ID of the transaction that is in the front of the buffer to the ID counter. If the ID of the transaction matches the ID of the counter it indicates that as the next transaction to be transfered.

4. EXPLORATION ENVIRONMENT

Our experimental setup is based on a cycle-accurate NoC simulator. The simulator models accurately the ×pipes NoC library [33] which includes: accurate NI models that account for packetization effects, FLIT size converter models and switch models. On top of that we extended the initiator NI models to add support for multiple outstanding transactions and for reordering responses and for transaction splitting and interleaving. We implemented three types of traffic generators: i) the initiator traffic generator, ii) the target traffic generator and iii) the DRAM target traffic generator. The initiator traffic generator supports multiple outstanding transactions and out-of-order execution and it is described in detail in the next sub-section. The target traffic generator receives the requests from the initiator traffic generators and generates the response traffic. The target traffic generator can also be configured as synchroniza-

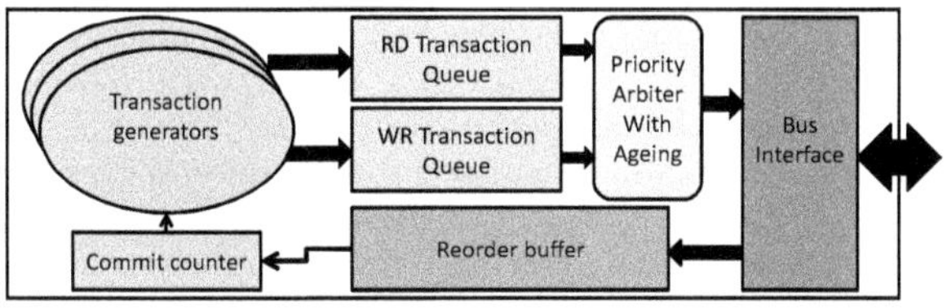

Figure 8: Initiator traffic generator

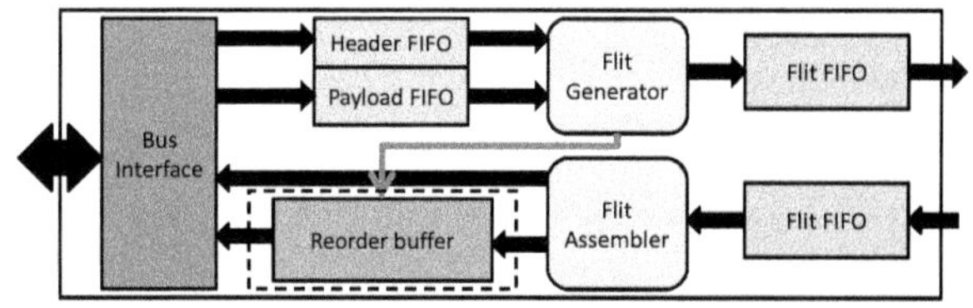

Figure 9: Initiator network interface

tion block. The DRAM target traffic generator uses DRAMSim 2 [12] to accurately emulate the functionality of the back-end of the DRAM controller. The DRAM traffic generator interface the NI to the DRAMSim instances and can be configured with multiple ports as well as channels in order to simulate all the architectures proposed in Section 3. Our benchmarking is oriented to real-life traffic in a state-of-the-art mobile SoC. We model different types of traffic and addressing modes to emulate different IP-cores like: video and graphic accelerators, display drivers, DMAs, peripherals and not just CPUs. Hence our environment is a significant step forward with respect to homogeneous architecture modeling environments with traffic generated only by cache misses.

4.1 Traffic Generators and NIs

The *initiator traffic generator* (ITGen) along with the initiator NI are some of the most important components of the simulator. The ITGen has to be able to emulate the traffic patterns generated by processors, accelerators, custom controllers, communication IP-cores. To be able to emulate all these behaviors, we added described in the simulator the ITGen to have the structure as presented in Figure 8. The basic blocks of the ITGen are the transaction generators, the read and write queues, the arbiter between the read and the write queues, the bus interface and the reorder buffer.

The transaction generators are responsible to generate the high-level read/write transactions (e.g. cache line refill or write-backs in a cache controller). The transaction generator can be programmed to generate different patterns of transactions, with different sizes and different time intervals between them. The types of transactions we use are: i) reads, ii) non posted writes and iii) barriers which are used for synchronization. We only considered non posted writes in this work as we assume that acknowledgments are needed to implement memory consistency protocols since data is shared among some cores. However posted writes can also have be used without impacting the results, especially since no acknowledgment traffic is necessary in that case. The transaction in the pattern are dependent as the transaction generator blocks if it tries to inject a transaction in a full queue. Consequently the following transaction are delayed by the same amount of time that the transaction generator is blocked. A ITGen can have multiple transaction generators which are independent from one another. For example if a transaction generator blocks on a full read queue another transaction generator could still generate write transactions if the write queue is not full. The use of multiple transaction generator can emulate multiple threads in a multi-threaded CPU or multiple independent units in an accelerator. The arbiter selects between the read and the write queue the transaction that has the highest priority, and which will be sent next to the bus interface. The bus interface has to convert the current selected transaction to bus requests (i.e. similar to AXI bus requests), which could comprise of a burst of requests in case of writes. Once a transaction has been processed by the bus interface, it is placed in the reorder buffer to await the response from the target traffic generator. The ITGen can be configured to expect responses in-order or out-of-order. In the first case when a response it received the ITGen checks that the response corresponds to the first transaction in the reorder buffer. In the latter case the response is matched to the corresponding request transaction in the reorder buffer. The serviced transactions in the reorder buffer are committed in-order, and the latency is tracked at commit time.

One important feature of the transaction generators is that they support multiple addressing modes, which can be configured when they are instantiated. The supported addressing modes are: i) *incremental*, ii) *incremental with synchronization*, iii) *block addressing*, iv) *random block addressing* and v) *trace*. *Incremental* addressing as the name suggests generates addresses incrementally with the possibility of wrapping around after a certain number of transactions. This mode can be used to emulate IP-cores that work with arrays or that move large amounts of data (e.g. DMA). In case of the *incremental with synchronization* addressing mode at the end of the accessed address range when it wraps around or moves to another address range it requires to synchronize with other IP-cores. New transactions are not generated until the synchronization completes. This mode can be used for IP-cores like the LCD or HDMI which read a frame with incremental transaction, but require synchronization before moving to another frame. *Block addressing* is designed to emulate the addressing mode of the video decoder. The frame is viewed as an M by N matrix which is further divided in blocks of size m by n ($m < M$ and $n < N$). The blocks are chosen in row order and for each block the addresses are generated in row order as well. This mode also requires synchronization at the end of the frame. In case of *random block addressing*, the next block to be accessed is chosen in a random manner, to emulate the fact that video decoding is data dependent. For *trace* addressing, we read a trace of addresses from file. These traces can be generated beforehand with a functional simulator and can be used to have a realistic behavior of IP-core for which the behavior is harder to emulate.

The initiator NI is described in Figure 9. The initiator NI contains the following blocks: the bus interface, the request queues (as header information and payload data queues), the FLIT generator block, the FLIT assembler block, the FLIT FIFOs and an optional reorder buffer. The bus interface is required to connect the NI to the traffic generators. The FLIT generator and FLIT assembler blocks convert the bus transactions into NoC packets and vice versa. FLIT buffers are used toward the switch as well to improve performance. In the case when the ITGen supports multiple outstanding transaction, but it requires the responses in order, a reorder buffer is necessary. To prevent deadlocks, the FLIT generator block will reserve space in the reorder buffer when generating a packet. If there is not enough space in the reorder buffer, the FLIT generator will block until space becomes available. In case the transaction requires more space than the size of the buffer the FLIT generator will wait until the buffer is completely free before starting to generate the packet. If transaction splitting and interleaving is supported by the NI then the reorder buffer is also necessary as the different pieces of a single transaction sent as different packets have to be reassembled in-order into the response transaction, which will be returned to the ITGen.

The target traffic generator is simpler. It only has the bus interface and a queue in which to store the incoming requests. The bus interface takes the stored requests and generates the appropriate response. The target traffic generator can be configured as a synchronization block as well. In that case it will only generate the responses when it received requests from all the ITGens that need to be synchronized. The DRAM controller simulation is done as described in Section 3. The target NI is similar to the initiator version, but it is simpler as it does not need support for reordering or splitting and interleaving.

4.2 Benchmark and Use-cases

To perform experiments we use a realistic benchmark that describes a mobile multimedia platform capable of running applications on a CPU cluster with 3D acceleration, perform video decoding, support multiple high definition displays and wireless communication. The communication requirements are represented by the graph from Figure 10. The vertices in the graph represent the task/IP-cores. In some case several tasks are performed by the same IP-core (e.g. Display LCD and CPU cluster). The edges in the graph represent a communication flow between two IP-cores. The weights on the edges represent the read/write bandwidth demands in MB/s. As can be seen from the plot this benchmark is DRAM centric with most communication going to the WideIO SDRAM.

The communication graph describes all the possible communication flows in the SoC, however different operating modes may require only a subset of the IP-cores to be active. To emulate this behavior and to see from experiments the trends on bandwidth and latency as more flow become active, we define four use-cases. Three of the use-case activate only a subset of the flows, while the last one will use all. A description of the use-case is provided in Table 1.

Use-case 1 (UC1) uses only the Video decoder IP-core and the HDMI display IP-core to provide basic video playback. Use-case 2 assumes that along with the video playback, applications are also running on the CPU that require 3D graphic acceleration. In use-case 3, two displays are used. In case of the LCD display the resolution is considered to be less than 1080p so downscaling and rotation operations are needed. All the IP-cores that are active in UC3 are high bandwidth. In use-case 4 we consider the influence of the remaining IP-cores most of which are low bandwidth, but may require low latency as is the case of the Modem IP-core.

4.3 Topology

For the experiments we use a 6 switch NoC topology. To prevent message level deadlocks, we use two separate networks so 3 of the switches are used for the request network and 3 for the response network. The request network topology is presented in Figure 11 and the response network is symmetric, the only difference being that the data flows in the opposite direction. In the figure the round nodes represent the IP-core (in the simulator these require an instance of the traffic generator as well as an instance of an NI) and the number below the name represents the size of the data interface for that IP-core. The low bandwidth IP-cores have a 32 bit interface, while the high bandwidth IP-cores use 64 bits. Since the WideIO SDRAM has 4 channels with a data size of 128 bits, to be able to transfer full bandwidth we assume the DRAM controller interface toward the NoC is also 128 bit wide. Similarly some if the IP-core that generate large regular transactions like the display drivers also use 128 bit data interfaces.

As can be seen from the figure the IP-cores that have the same data width are clustered on the same switch. To reduce the power consumption the switches have a FLIT size similar to the data size of the cores connected to it. The only exception is the Video IP-core which is connected directly to the 128 bit switch. When transactions are converted into packets the bandwidth requirements increase due to the extra information that is added in each packet. Since the Video IP-core has high bandwidth demands, a link in the NoC with a 64bit FLIT width could not support the bandwidth resulting after packetization and therefore we connected it directly to the wider switch. Even though the Video IP-core generates significant traffic, it does so in small transaction and therefore we assumed that it has a 64bit data-interface. Also this setup allows us to capture the packetization effects from different data-sizes.

Since the switches have different FLIT sizes, converters need to be used on each link to change the width of the FLITS in each packet. It is important to accurately simulate the size converters as they can also increase the bandwidth when going from narrow to wide. Since we use wormhole switching, once the head of a packet has reserved a channel, that channel remains reserved until the tail of the packet passes through it. Since the narrow network cannot provide sufficient data to generate a FLIT every cycle after the size converter. Since the channels remain reserved until the tail passes, the resulting packet appears to have more FLITs in the wide network. This effect manifests itself as having a higher bandwidth flow. However in case of downstream contention these empty FLITS can be dropped. To have accurate results we model all these effects.

Apart from the IP-cores described in the communication graph of the benchmark, we attached another target IP-core on the narrow 32 bit switch. This core called *Semaphore* is used to synchronize the operation of the Video, LCD and HDMI IP-cores when they change from one frame to another.

5. EXPERIMENTAL RESULTS

In the experiments, using the benchmark described in Section 4.2, we analyze how the bandwidth and latency are affected by the presence of interfering flows at the WideIO DRAM memory. We analyze 5 setups based on the three architectures described in Section 3. The simulations setups with their corresponding names are the following:

- *Separate 1CH*: uses a distributed DRAM controller architecture with separate independent channels. This simulates the worst-case when all the active memory regions addressed by the ITGens are mapped to the same channel;
- *Separate 4CH*: uses the same distributed architecture, but in this case the active memory regions were carefully mapped to different channels. For example for the Video IP-core which generate high bandwidth traffic, the address memory regions have been distributed in all channels.
- *Controller 1 3 Port*: uses a centralized DRAM architecture with interleaving at the controller. As there are more ITGens than ports in this setup several ITGens have been assigned to use the same port (only three of the 4 ports are used).
- *Controller 1 4 Port*: uses the same centralized architecture, but the ITGens have been assigned to all four ports so that there is less contention at the DRAM controller ports.
- *NI I*: uses a distributed DRAM controller architecture, however the address space it is interleaved between the four channels of the WideIO memory. In this case the initiator NIs are responsible to split transactions into packets and to send the packets to the appropriate memory channel according to the address.

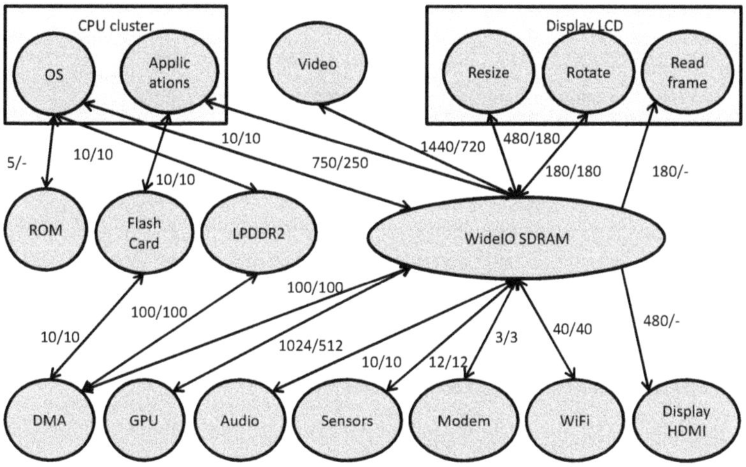

Figure 10: Benchmark communication graph

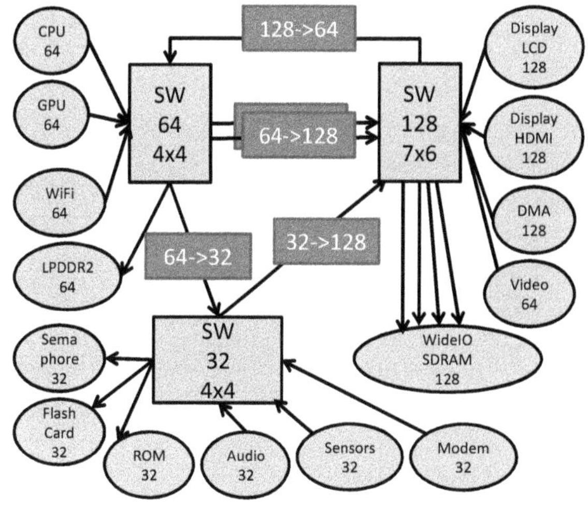

Figure 11: Topology

	CPU	GPU	Video	LCD	HDMI	DMA	Audio	Sensors	WiFi	Modem
UC1			x		x					
UC2	x	x	x		x					
UC3	x	x	x	x	x					
UC4	x	x	x	x	x	x	x	x	x	x

Table 1: Description of the use-cases

The simulation parameters used for the initiator traffic generators are presented in Table 2. For the initiator NIs, we used 2-deep bus transaction buffers and 5-deep FLIT FIFOs. For the setups using the distributed DRAM controller with independent channels and for the centralized DRAM controller, reorder buffers are not needed as there is a single route to reach the memory controller for the ITGens that require responses to be return in-order. In case of the distributed controller with splitting and interleaving at the NI, reorder buffers are not needed for the CPU, GPU and Video IP-cores. That is because the largest transaction is the same size as the interleaving size so no splitting is required. Also these traffic generators accept responses out-of-order. In case of the LCD and HDMI display controllers as well as the DMA, the transactions have to be split and therefore we need a reorder buffer. We used 24-deep reorder buffer (each entry in the reorder buffer is a bus transaction). In case of the Audio, WiFi, Sensor and Modem IP-cores, no splitting is necessary, but the responses have to be delivered in order so, there is a reorder buffer. Since these cores are low bandwidth, we use 16 deep reorder buffers.

5.1 Throughput oriented communication

In our benchmark, we have IP-cores that are throughput sensitive (Video, HDMI, LCD) and some that are latency sensitive (CPU, Modem). In this section, we will have a closer look at two representative throughput sensitive IP-cores, namely he Video accelerator and the HDMI display controller. Both IP-cores require a significant amount of bandwidth and have to synchronize after finishing a frame. The Video controller generates small transactions, while the HDMI display controller transfers data in long 1kB burst transactions. In Figure 12, we show the trend of the average latency for the Video transactions as more interfering bandwidth is introduced with the more complex use-cases (in UC1 only the Video and the HDMI cores are active, while in UC4 all the IP-cores in the benchmark are active). As can be seen from the plot the dis-

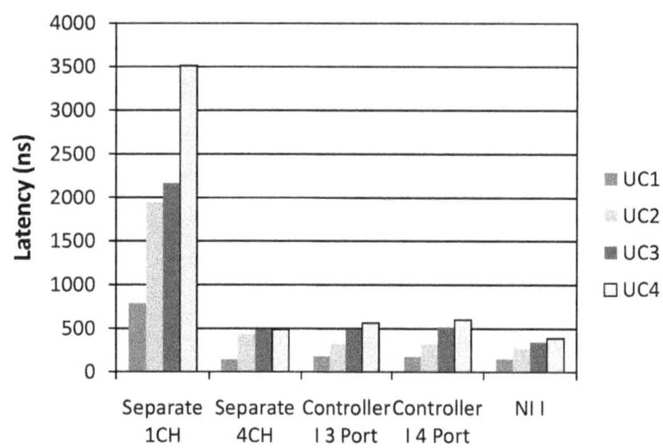

Figure 12: Average latency for the Video IP

tributed interleaving scheme that balances the traffic in the network as well has the lowest latency. Moreover compared to the other schemes, the distributed interleaving is also the least sensitive to the interfering bandwidth, as it has the lowest growth. The figure also shows that the mapping of data in memory has a significant impact on the performance of the distributed controller with independent channels. However with the best memory mapping as well as with the distributed controller with NI interleaving the latency is lower than in the case of the centralized controller. This is because both schemes exploit the parallelism in the NoC as well.

Similarly, in Figure 13, we show the average latency of the HDMI transactions. An important thing to remember is that we measure latency of a transaction from the time it is generated by the ITGen and placed in the read/write buffer of the ITGen until the time it received the response and it is committed by the ITGen (in case

	Out-of-order	Maximum outstanding		Number of	Address	Transaction
		Reads	Writes	transaction generators	mode	sizes
CPU	yes	4	8	6	trace+incremental	64b, 512b
GPU	yes	8	8	1	incremental	512b
Video	yes	30	30	5	block + random block addressing	128b, 256b
LCD	yes	10	10	1	incremental with synchronization	1kB
HDMI	yes	10	10	1	incremental with synchronization	1kB
DMA	yes	10	10	3	incremental	128b, 1kB
WiFi	no	4	4	1	incremental	128b
Sensors	no	2	2	1	incremental	32b
Audio	no	2	2	1	incremental	128b
Modem	no	2	2	1	incremental	256b

Table 2: Simulation parameters for the ITGens

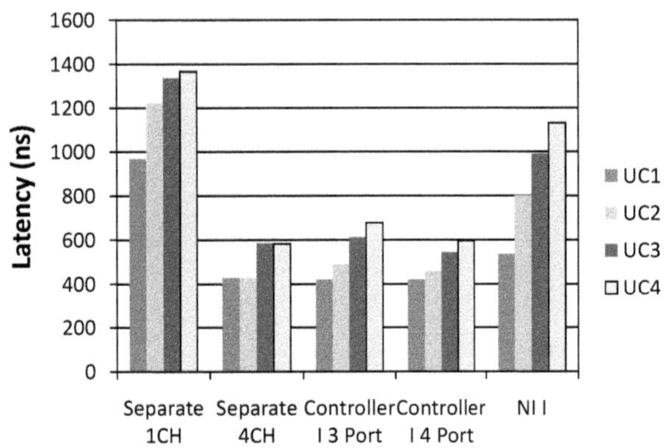

Figure 13: Average latency for the HDMI IP

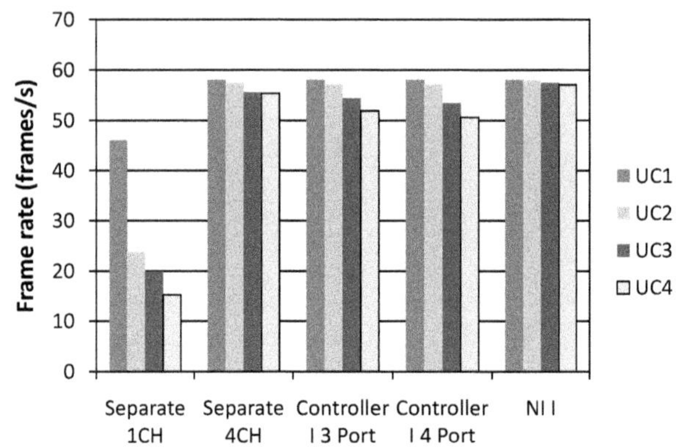

Figure 14: Average frame-rate

of out-of-order ITGens the transactions are committed in-order so any completed transactions cannot be committed until all previous transactions have been completed and committed). In case of the HDMI core, data is transfered in 1kB transactions. Therefore in case of the distributed controller with interleaving in the NI, the transactions have to be split over multiple packets, in order to be sent to the appropriate channel. The different response packets have to be reordered and assembled such that the response from the NI to the ITGen is sent as a single burst of in-order bus transfers. The number of packets of the transactions that can be sent out is limited by the size of the reorder buffer. This results in a higher latency per transaction for the HDMI core as can be seen from the figure. However since a single transactions transfers 1kB of data these transfers are very efficient and the increased latency does not impact the overall performance of the system. If we look at the latency per byte for these 1kB transfers we can see that they are 11 times more efficient than the smaller transfers generated by the Video core (1.1 ns/byte for HDMI and 12.2 ns/byte for the Video in UC4), which explains why the larger latency of the HDMI core does not impact the system performance.

To analyze the overall system performance, in Figure 14, we show the frame rates obtained for the different use-cases in each simulation setup. The distributed DRAM controller with interleaving at the NI obtains the best frame rate and also has the lowest degradation of the frame rate as more interfering communication flows are activated. The frame rate of this setup is better even than that of the distributed controller with separate independent channels even for the best memory allocation scheme, as it balances the traffic from all the cores in the network as well. Surprisingly the centralized controller where only three ports are used has better frame rate than when 4 ports are used. That is because in the case of the three port setup some of the interfering flows that are mapped on the same port interferer among themselves impacting their performances and in this particular case favoring the Video core. This also shows the sensitivity of the centralized controller scheme to the mapping of the communication flows to ports.

5.2 Bandwidth analysis

As the benchmark is representative of real applications, it is DRAM centric with all communication being between the IP-cores and the DRAM controller. Therefore one important metric to assess the performance of the SoC is also the total read/write bandwidth to the DRAM memory. In Figure 15, we show the bandwidth obtained with each simulation setup for all use-cases normalized to the bandwidth required by that use-case. The reported bandwidth refers to the effective data bandwidth measured by the ITgens, the actual bandwidth transfered in the NoC is higher due to packetization and the bandwidth inflation generated by the size converters.

As expected, due to the balancing of traffic through the NoC as well, the distributed DRAM controller with NI interleaving setup achieves the best performance in terms of total average bandwidth as well (6184MB/s out of 6980MB/s demanded by use-case 4). The distributed controller with separate independent channels achieves similar performance for the most demanding use-case when the allocated memory is well distributed in the channels. However, to achieve that performance with independent channels the hardware

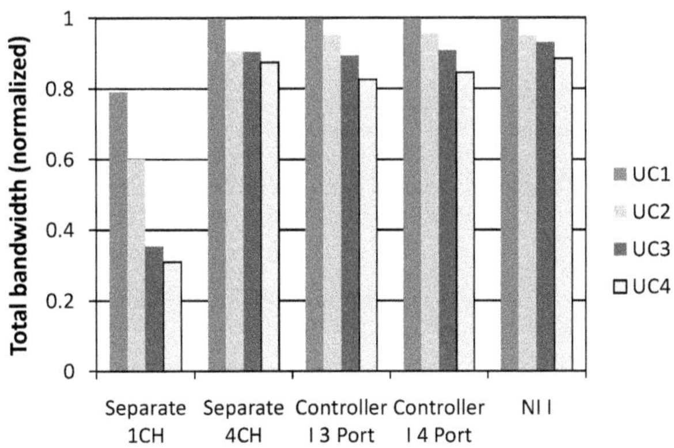

Figure 15: Average total bandwidth

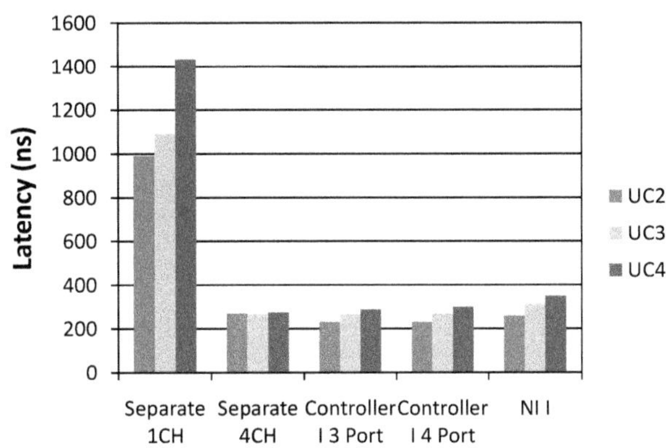

Figure 16: Average latency for the CPU IP

would need to be exposed to the software and the managing operating systems should be smart enough to allocate memory such as to balance the channel usage. In case of the hardware interleaving scheme the memory access is transparent to the software, favoring the NI interleaved scheme which balances traffic in the interconnect as well.

5.3 Latency sensitive communication

So far we have analyzed the bandwidth oriented communication flows. In this section we analyze two of the latency sensitive IP-cores. One of them is the CPU where read are on the critical execution path and therefore the CPU performance is dependent on the latency of reads. On the other hand the CPU generates a significant amount of bandwidth as well. Another latency sensitive core is the Modem which has strict latency requirement imposed by the communication protocol, however the Modem core only requires little bandwidth.

In Figure 16, we present the average latency of the CPU for the three use-cases where the CPU is active. As can be seen from the figure the latency of the CPU is only slightly larger for the distributed controller with interleaving at the NI when compared to the centralized controller (around 17% for UC4). That is because in the NI interleaving scheme the transaction from the CPU are distributed to all ports and they interfere with the traffic of the high-bandwidth cores at all the ports. In the other case the CPU is mapped by itself to one port. One aspect to remember however is that in the case of the distributed controller with separate independent channels the mapping of memory to channels is application dependent and it may not be possible to achieve a good mapping in all cases. As can be seen from the figure for a bad mapping of the memory to channels, the controller with separated channels has very poor performance. Similarly the latency of our solution is slightly larger than that of the centralized controller. Nevertheless, it may be very expensive to physically implement the centralized controller (due to the distance between the channel interfaces), and as such the distributed interleaving method provides a good trade off. Moreover the distributed controller can provide other opportunities for the adaptation of the NoC topology (i.e., connect the different channel controller to different switches).

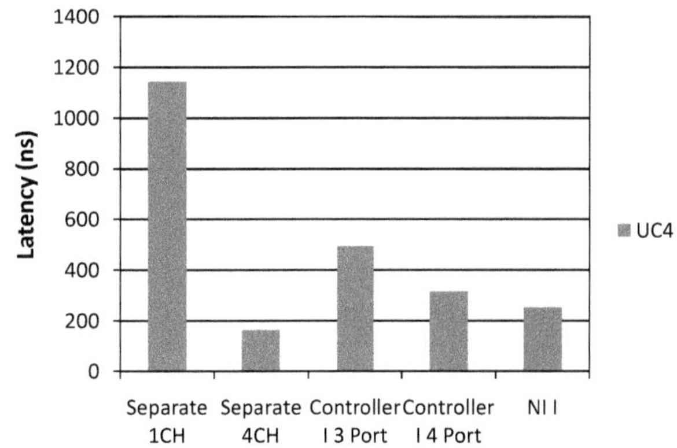

Figure 17: Average latency for the Modem IP

In Figure 17, we show the average latency for the Modem core. This core is latency sensitive, but has low bandwidth requirements. From the setups that perform interleaving the NI interleaved case has the lowest latency. The latency for the controller with separated independent channels, for the best mapping has the lowest latency. That is because in this case the communication of the Modem is to a separated channel where there are no high-bandwidth cores mapped. Interestingly, as the core has low bandwidth its latency is more affected by the port assignment in the case of the centralized controller.

6. CONCLUSIONS

3D-stacked WideIO DRAM memory promises to deliver the required bandwidth to satisfy the demands of current and future application running on mobile SoCs at acceptable power-levels, by providing multiple channels and wide data interfaces. The challenge for SoC designers is to efficiently access the multiple channels provided by the WideIO interface, to achieve the required bandwidth and latency for communication flows.

In this work we analyze three architecture for designing the memory controller that access the WideIO DRAM memory. We propose for one of the architectures a new distributed interleaving method. The new method capitalizes on the advantages of the two analyzed methods, to provide a simple DRAM controller design and to balance the traffic in both the NoC and at the memory channels transparent to the software. From experiments, we show that our proposed distributed interleaving memory access method improves the overall throughput while minimally impacting the performance of latency sensitive communication flows.

Future work will focus on understanding the relationship between network topology and the distributed interleaving scheme, and to analyze how to implement low overhead *Quality-of-Service* support to aggressively reduce latency for critical flows.

7. ACKNOWLEDGMENTS

We would like to acknowledge the contributions of Eric Flamand from STMicroelectronics and Denis Dutoit from CEA LETI, for their help in the construction of a realistic evaluation environment. This work was supported in part by The European Research Council under project AdG-246810-NANOSYS, by the Pro3D project grant agreement number: 248776 and the ARTIST-DESIGN Network of Excellence.

8. REFERENCES

[1] WULF, W. A., AND MCKEE, S. A. Hitting the memory wall: implications of the obvious. *SIGARCH Comput. Archit. News 23*, 1 (Mar. 1995), 20–24.

[2] BORKAR, S. 3d integration for energy efficient system design. In *Proc. 48th ACM/EDAC/IEEE Design Automation Conf. (DAC)* (2011), pp. 214–219.

[3] WEIS, C., WEHN, N., IGOR, L., AND BENINI, L. Design space exploration for 3d-stacked drams. In *Proc. Design, Automation & Test in Europe Conf. & Exhibition (DATE)* (2011), pp. 1–6.

[4] KIM, J.-S., OH, C. S., LEE, H., LEE, D., HWANG, H.-R., HWANG, S., NA, B., MOON, J., KIM, J.-G., PARK, H., RYU, J.-W., PARK, K., KANG, S.-K., KIM, S.-Y., KIM, H., BANG, J.-M., CHO, H., JANG, M., HAN, C., LEE, J.-B., KYUNG, K., CHOI, J.-S., AND JUN, Y.-H. A 1.2v 12.8gb/s 2gb mobile wide-i/o dram with 4x128 i/os using tsv-based stacking. In *Proc. IEEE Int. Solid-State Circuits Conf. Digest of Technical Papers (ISSCC)* (2011), pp. 496–498.

[5] DE MICHELI, G., AND BENINI, L. *Networks on Chips: Technology and Tools; electronic version.* Elsevier, Burlington, MA, 2006.

[6] DE MICHELI, G., SEICULESCU, C., MURALI, S., BENINI, L., ANGIOLINI, F., AND PULLINI, A. Networks on Chips: From research to products. In *Proc. 47th ACM/IEEE Design Automation Conf. (DAC)* (2010), pp. 300–305.

[7] RIXNER, S., DALLY, W. J., KAPASI, U. J., MATTSON, P., AND OWENS, J. D. Memory access scheduling. In *Proc. 27th Int Computer Architecture Symp* (2000), pp. 128–138.

[8] AHN, J. H., EREZ, M., AND DALLY, W. J. The Design Space of Data-Parallel Memory Systems. In *Proc. ACM/IEEE SC 2006 Conf* (2006).

[9] AKESSON, B., GOOSSENS, K., AND RINGHOFER, M. Predator: A predictable SDRAM memory controller. In *Proc. 5th IEEE/ACM/IFIP Int Hardware/Software Codesign and System Synthesis (CODES+ISSS) Conf* (2007), pp. 251–256.

[10] LEE, K.-B., LIN, T.-C., AND JEN, C.-W. An efficient quality-aware memory controller for multimedia platform SoC. *Circuits and Systems for Video Technology, IEEE Trans. on 15*, 5 (2005), 620–633.

[11] RAFIQUE, N., LIM, W.-T., AND THOTTETHODI, M. Effective Management of DRAM Bandwidth in Multicore Processors. In *Proc. 16th Int. Conf. Parallel Architecture and Compilation Techniques PACT 2007* (2007), pp. 245–258.

[12] WANG, D., GANESH, B., TUAYCHAROEN, N., BAYNES, K., JALEEL, A., AND JACOB, B. DRAMsim: a memory system simulator. *SIGARCH Comput. Archit. News 33* (November 2005), 100–107.

[13] DUTOIT, D., AND JERRAYA, A. 3D integration opportunities for memory interconnect in mobile computing architectures. *Future Fab CEA-Leti MINATEC Issue 34* (2010), pp. 38–45.

[14] ANIGUNDI, R., SUN, H., LU, J.-Q., ROSE, K., AND ZHANG, T. Architecture design exploration of three-dimensional (3d) integrated dram. In *Proc. Quality Electronic Design Quality of Electronic Design ISQED 2009* (2009), pp. 86–90.

[15] FACCHINI, M., CARLSON, T., VIGNON, A., PALKOVIC, M., CATTHOOR, F., DEHAENE, W., BENINI, L., AND MARCHAL, P. System-level power/performance evaluation of 3d stacked drams for mobile applications. In *Proc. DATE '09. Design, Automation & Test in Europe Conf. & Exhibition* (2009), pp. 923–928.

[16] WOO, D. H., SEONG, N. H., LEWIS, D. L., AND LEE, H.-H. S. An optimized 3d-stacked memory architecture by exploiting excessive, high-density tsv bandwidth. In *Proc. IEEE 16th Int High Performance Computer Architecture (HPCA) Symp* (2010), pp. 1–12.

[17] LOI, I., AND BENINI, L. An efficient distributed memory interface for many-core platform with 3d stacked dram. In *Proc. Design, Automation & Test in Europe Conf. & Exhibition (DATE)* (2010), pp. 99–104.

[18] LOH, G. H. 3d-stacked memory architectures for multi-core processors. In *Proc. 35th Int. Symp. Computer Architecture ISCA '08* (2008), pp. 453–464.

[19] LOH, G. H. Extending the effectiveness of 3d-stacked dram caches with an adaptive multi-queue policy. In *Proc. MICRO-42 Microarchitecture 42nd Annual IEEE/ACM Int. Symp* (2009), pp. 201–212.

[20] SUN, H., LIU, J., ANIGUNDI, R. S., ZHENG, N., LU, J.-Q., ROSE, K., AND ZHANG, T. 3d dram design and application to 3d multicore systems. *IEEE Design & Test of Computers 26*, 5 (2009), 36–47.

[21] AKESSON, B., HUANG, P.-C., CLERMIDY, F., DUTOIT, D., GOOSSENS, K., CHANG, Y.-H., KUO, T.-W., VIVET, P., AND WINGARD, D. Memory controllers for high-performance and real-time mpsocs requirements, architectures, and future trends. In *Proc. 9th Int Hardware/Software Codesign and System Synthesis (CODES+ISSS) Conf* (2011), pp. 3–12.

[22] AHO, E., NIKARA, J., TUOMINEN, P. A., AND KUUSILINNA, K. A case for multi-channel memories in video recording. In *Proceedings of the Conference on Design, Automation and Test in Europe* (3001 Leuven, Belgium, Belgium, 2009), DATE '09, European Design and Automation Association, pp. 934–939.

[23] JANG, W., AND PAN, D. Z. An SDRAM-Aware Router for Networks-on-Chip. *Computer-Aided Design of Integrated Circuits and Systems, IEEE Transactions on 29*, 10 (2010), 1572–1585.

[24] YOO, J., YOO, S., AND CHOI, K. Multiprocessor system-on-chip designs with active memory processors for higher memory efficiency. In *Proc. 46th ACM/IEEE Design Automation Conf. DAC '09* (2009), pp. 806–811.

[25] WALTER, I., CIDON, I., GINOSAR, R., AND KOLODNY, A. Access Regulation to Hot-Modules in Wormhole NoCs. In *Proc. First Int. Symp. Networks-on-Chip NOCS 2007* (2007), pp. 137–148.

[26] KIM, D., YOO, S., AND LEE, S. A Network Congestion-Aware Memory Controller. In *Proc. Fourth ACM/IEEE Int Networks-on-Chip (NOCS) Symp* (2010), pp. 257–264.

[27] KIM, D., KIM, K., KIM, J.-Y., LEE, S.-J., AND YOO, H.-J. Solutions for Real Chip Implementation Issues of NoC and Their Application to Memory-Centric NoC. In *Proc. First Int. Symp. Networks-on-Chip NOCS 2007* (2007), pp. 30–39.

[28] KIM, D., KIM, K., KIM, J.-Y., LEE, S., AND YOO, H.-J. Implementation of Memory-Centric NoC for 81.6 GOPS object recognition processor. In *Proc. IEEE Asian Solid-State Circuits Conf. ASSCC '07* (2007), pp. 47–50.

[29] ARTERIS. http://www.arteris.com/pr_22_oct_08, 2008.

[30] CASINI, P. SoC Architecture to Multichannel Memory Management Using Sonics IMT. Tech. rep., Sonics, Inc., 2008.

[31] WANG, F., AND HAMDI, M. Scalable router memory architecture based on interleaved dram. In *High Performance Switching and Routing, 2006 Workshop on* (0-0 2006), p. 6 pp.

[32] AKESSON, B., AND GOOSSENS, K. Architectures and modeling of predictable memory controllers for improved system integration. In *Proc. Design, Automation & Test in Europe Conf. & Exhibition (DATE)* (2011), pp. 1–6.

[33] STERGIOU, S., ANGIOLINI, F., CARTA, S., RAFFO, L., BERTOZZI, D., AND MICHELI, G. D. ×pipes Lite: A Synthesis Oriented Design Library For Networks on Chips. In *Proceedings of the conference on Design, Automation and Test in Europe - Volume 2* (Washington, DC, USA, 2005), DATE '05, IEEE Computer Society, pp. 1188–1193.

Minimizing Power Supply Noise Through Harmonic Mappings in Networks-on-Chip

Nizar Dahir [*], Terrence Mak [†], Fei Xia and Alex Yakovlev
School of Electrical and Electronic Engineering
Newcastle University
Newcastle upon Tyne, UK
{nizar.dahir,terrence.mak,fei.xia,alex.yakovlev}@ncl.ac.uk

ABSTRACT

Power supply integrity has become a critical concern with the rapid shrinking of device dimensions and the ever increasing power consumption in nano-scale integration. Particularly, power supply noise is strongly correlated to the spatial distribution of activity densities and this can be attributed to the on-chip communication, which dictates the power dissipation and overall system performance in networks-on-chip. In this paper, we propose a new mapping strategy aiming to create a balanced activity distribution across the whole chip. We formulate the problem of application mapping as a minimization of the activity density by employing a repulsive force-based objective function. Metrics of regional activity density and characteristics of its impact on power supply noise are considered. The proposed method has been rigorously evaluated based on a large set of real-application benchmarks. Significant reduction in power supply noise can be achieved with negligible energy overhead. This new approach would provide a more scalable solution for future large-scale system integration.

Categories and Subject Descriptors

B.7.2 [**Hardware**]: Integrated Circuits—*Design Aids*

General Terms

Performance, Reliability

Keywords

Networks-on-Chip, Power Supply Noise, Application Mapping, Activity Factor, Power Density

[*]Nizar Dahir is also a staff member with the University of Kufa in Najaf-Iraq and they are sponsoring his Ph.D. study at Newcastle University. email: nizar.dahir@uokufa.edu.iq.

[†]Terrence Mak is also with the Department of Computer Science and Engineering, The Chinese University of Hong Kong. email: stmak@cse.cuhk.edu.hk.

CODES+ISSS'12, October 7-12, 2012, Tampere, Finland.

1. INTRODUCTION

Power supply noise (PSN) has adverse effects on digital circuit performance and reliability. It could cause signal deterioration and create soft errors. It has been reported that variations in power supply would have significant impact on operational frequency and system power dissipation [16]. Power supply noise is caused by resistive (IR) drop and inductive (ΔI) droop. The resistive voltage drop occurs mainly due to the resistance of power delivery wires on the chip. While the inductive droop is mainly due to wire inductance in the package and chip wires and is proportional to the rate of change of current di/dt.

Technology scaling exacerbates the problem of power supply noise for many reasons. Firstly, due to the large-scale integration, power density is substantially increasing. Also, wire size in the power network is shrinking, causing resistance to substantially increase, resulting in higher IR drop. Secondly, higher switching frequency increases ΔI droop. Thirdly, lower operating voltage decreases the noise margin. These facts make voltage drop in 65 nm technology be as much as 30% of the supply voltage [2]. Thus, mitigating power supply noise becomes a grand challenge for the sustainability of future large-scale integration development.

In communication centric systems such as Networks-on-Chip (NoCs), the impact of power supply noise is even more prominent. It would deteriorate performance and increase power dissipation significantly. Power supply noise would cause timing inconsistencies due to its impact on timing path delays. Also, it would cause fluctuations of clock frequency. It has been reported that a change of 10% of power supply will cause about 6% of change in frequency and 18% increase in power dissipation due to the increase in leakage power [19].

Power dissipation activity in NoCs is strongly correlated with the network traffic load. This load can be determined in the early design stages, once the application is mapped to the target architecture, offering a unique opportunity to estimate power consumption with good accuracy using high network-level simulators.

In this work, we propose an NoC application mapping method which aims for power supply noise minimization. We use the metric of *activity density* and analyze the impact of core activity density on power supply noise. To minimize activity density, we propose *tile repulsive force* as a mapping objective and argue that using this objective in application mapping for NoCs will result in more scattered and thus higher balanced activity distribution. We also verify, using the NoC power supply noise model, that systems resulting from this mapping have significantly lower power supply noise compared to energy-minimization mappings with low energy penalty. The main contributions of this work are:-

1 Presents a new concept of optimizing power supply noise in application mapping for NoCs.

2 Our work considers NoCs communication workload impact on power delivery network for multi-core NoC-based systems.

3 Introduces the metric of activity density and analyse the impact of its spatial patterns on power delivery. Significant relationships between the spatial distribution of cores and power supply noise are discovered.

4 Proposes tile repulsive force as a mapping objective strategy which, in contrast to other NoC mapping strategies, results in spreading the highly active tiles across the chip and causes significant drop in power supply noise with a relatively low energy overhead compared to energy-aware mapping.

The remainder of this paper is organized as follows: Section 2 presents the related work on power supply noise mitigation and NoCs application mapping. This section will also present the notations, definitions and the main models used in this paper. In Section 3 the methodology used to achieve our power supply noise minimization by application mapping in NoCs is and the metrics of tile repulsive force and activity density are proposed and discussed. Results are presented and discussed in Section 4. Finally, the paper is concluded in Section 5.

2. RELATED WORK AND BACKGROUND

2.1 Related Work

Classical techniques employ on-chip decoupling capacitors to reduce power supply noise. Additional capacitors are inserted into the computational circuits to increase the load and extra current spikes would be filtered. This can be an effective technique at the cost of additional chip area. In [6], methodologies are proposed to optimally determine the physical location for the decoupling capacitors during floor-planning. Alternatively, optimal power-gating technique coupled with dynamic scheduling are also proposed to minimize the voltage drop caused by high-frequency logic switching in the gated blocks [21].

Power supply noise can also be tackled at the system-level. Particularly, workload assignment can have a significant impact on the induced power supply noise in a multi-core system. In [20], a simulated-annealing approach is employed to optimize the assignment of workloads to the cores, such that the resulting power supply noise can be minimized. Although it has been demonstrated that the methodology is efficient in reducing the overall power supply noise, the communication activities between the cores, which would create significant power supply noise, have been ignored.

Networks-on-chip takes up a significant portion of the overall power consumption and produce notable power supply noise around the highly communicating regions. Previously, most of the application mappings focused on minimizing communication delay or energy consumptions. Notable examples include proposing optimization algorithms to minimize energy consumption [11], increasing performance[5], and improving system reliability [1].

The impact of power supply noise and its derived risks to an NoC system has always been ignored. This also been exacerbated as a result of aggressive energy and performance focused optimization. This is because highly communicating cores are usually mapped to regions in a closer proximity and this would lead to some regions in a chip with significantly higher activity density. More power would be drawn into these areas at an expense of voltage drops and power supply noise. This under-balanced communication can be seen as an advantage to energy and performance, but at the expenditure of system reliability.

The concept of activity density in VLSI circuits is first introduced by [15]. The author defines transition density to be the *average switching rate* and develop an algorithm to compute this density based on stochastic models of logic signals. The results show that higher activity density will lead to higher power and ground current densities which would directly affect power supply integrity and introduce thermal hotspots. Also they show that higher activity would have bad impact on circuit reliability in terms of electromigration failures. This can be seen as another problem with higher activity density and motivates balanced activity design in VLSI circuits.

In our previous work, we proposed a computational model that determines the power supply variations across NoC-based chip multi-processors (CMPs) [18]. To determine the voltage variations across the chip at the presence of workload, both energy and traffic models are captured. This follows a characterization of the switching activities for each individual component on the chip. An approximation model, which is based on peak voltage noise estimation for the power delivery network [23], is employed in the overall noise approximation. In this paper, we propose a method to balance both system energy efficiency and reliability by providing a balanced communication activity density across the whole chip.

2.2 Background

We now give definitions and notations used in this paper and present a brief description of the metrics of power supply noise and energy.

2.2.1 Definitions

The NoC architecture is characterized by *Architectural Graph* $ARG = G(T, P)$ which is defined as a directed graph where each vertex, $t_i \in T$, represents an NoC tile and each directed arc $p_{i,j} \in P$, represents the path from tile i to tile j. Each path $p_{i,j}$ consists of a set of links $L(p_{i,j})$. The set $L(p_{i,j})$ is determined by the routing algorithm used to route packets from source to destination.

On the other hand the application communication requirements are described by *Application Graph* $APG = G(S, A)$ which is a directed acyclic graph where each vertex $s_i \in S$ represents a task and each arc $a_{i,j} \in A$ represents the communication from task s_i to task s_j. The quantities associated with $a_{i,j}$ are the bandwidth requirement from s_i to s_j, $b(a_{i,j})$ and data volume $w(a_{i,j})$.

A mapping function (Ω) maps an application characterized by the APG to the target architecture characterized by the ARG.

2.2.2 Mertics for Power Supply Noise

To compute power supply noise, we adopt the definition given in [7]. Consider G to be the set of all power grid nodes. For node $x \in G$ in the power delivery network, power supply noise, during a switching time period T_s, is given as:

$$PSN(x) = \int_0^{T_s} \min(V_{NM} - \Delta V(x,t), 0)dt \quad (1)$$

Where V_{NM} is the noise margin, $\Delta V(x,t)$ is the power supply variation for node x at time t. We determine total power supply noise on the chip as the summation of the power supply noise for all nodes in the power grid, i.e.

$$PSN_{tot} = \sum_{\forall x \in G} PSN(x) \quad (2)$$

Where PSN_{tot} is the total power supply noise on the chip.

2.2.3 Energy Model

To compute the energy cost of a mapping function, we used the bit energy metric, E_{bit}, to compute this cost whenever necessary. The average energy consumed by sending one bit from tile i to tile j ($E_{i,j}^{bit}$) is given by [22]:

$$E_{i,j}^{bit} = (E_S^{bit} + E_B^{bit})n_{hops}(i,j) + E_L^{bit}(n_{hops}(i,j) - 1) \quad (3)$$

Where $n_{hops}(i,j)$ is the number of hops along this path between tiles i and j. E_S^{bit}, E_B^{bit} and E_L^{bit} are the energy dissipated by the crossbar, buffer and link of the router respectively. The total energy cost of a mapping function ($E_{tot}(\Omega)$) is computed as:

$$E_{tot}(\Omega) = \sum_{a_{i,j} \in A} w(a_{i,j}).E_{\Omega(i),\Omega(j)}^{bit} \quad (4)$$

Where $w(a_{i,j})$ is the communication data volume from task s_i task s_j in APG. The number of hops from the source to destination tiles i and j, $n_{hops}(i,j)$ is determined by the routing algorithm. In this work the XY routing algorithm is assumed. XY is a deterministic, deadlock free routing algorithm, which routes the packets from its source along the X direction first and then along the Y direction towards its destination. A summary of all notations used in this paper is shown in Table 1.

3. METHODOLOGY

3.1 Local and Regional Activity Densities

In this work we employ a mapping strategy based on minimizing the activity density. We define the metric of *local activity density* considering an NoC tile k which consists of a set of functional units (floating point unit, SRAM, router etc.). For unit $u \in k$ we define the local activity density (γ_u) in terms of the unit's maximum power consumption (P_u^{max}), switching activity factor (α_u) and area as:

$$\gamma_u = P_u^{max}\left(\frac{\alpha_u}{area_u}\right) \quad (5)$$

Here α_u ranges from 0 to 1 and is the ratio of the unit's average load to its maximum loading capacity.

Now considering an NoC tile k which consists of a set of units, the local activity density, γ_k, can be expressed as:

$$\gamma_k = \frac{\sum_{\forall u \in k} P_u^{max} \alpha_u}{area_k} \quad (6)$$

$G(T,P)$	NoC architectural graph with the set of NoC tiles {T} as verticies and the set of paths {P} among these tiles as arcs.
$G(S,A)$	Application graph with the set of tasks {S} as verticies and the set of communications {A} among these tasks as arches.
$L(p)$	The set of NoC links that constitutes a path p in the architectural graph.
Ω	Mapping function that maps application graph to architectural graph.
PSN_{tot}	Total power supply noise.
V_{NM}	power supply noise margin.
$E_{tot}(\Omega)$	Total energy cost of mapping Ω.
W_r	Channel width of router r.
N_r	Number of channels in router r.
F_r	Frequency of router r.
$B_r(\Omega)$	The bandwidth capacity of router r.
$\hat{B}_r(\Omega)$	The bandwidth load of router r.
α_u	Activity factor of VLSI unit u.
$\gamma_k(D)$	Regional activity density of tile k considering region of diameter D.
Γ_i	Metaphor of charge for tile i which is a function of the tile local activity density $\Gamma_i = e^{k_i \gamma_i}$. k_i is a tuning constant.
$F_{i,j}$	The tile repulsive force between tiles i and j.
F_{tot}	The total repulsive force for all NoC tiles.

Table 1: notations used in this paper

Where $area_k$ is tile area. We now define *regional activity density* of an NoC tile in terms of local activity densities. Consider the activity in a region with a particular size in the vicinity of a tile of interest k. For tile k we define this region as the set of all tiles j that satisfy $\|k,j\| \leq D$, where $\|k,j\|$ is the Manhattan distance between tiles k and j, D is the region radius. Now considering a regular NoC with similar tile size and architecture, the regional activity density of tile k as a function of region radius D, $\gamma_k(D)$. This is expressed as the summation of local activity densities of all tiles that lie within this region i.e.:

$$\gamma_k(D) = \sum_{\forall j \in T, \|k,j\| \leq D} \gamma_j \quad (7)$$

According to this definition the local activity density defined in Eq 6 can also be denoted as $\gamma_k(0)$.

In contrast to other tile units, whose activity is only determined by the task assigned to the tile, the router activity is highly characterized by the communication demand of the application and the placement of the communicating tasks across the NoC system. Considering router r with N_r number of channels with W_r channel width and F_r frequency, the bandwidth capacity of router r, B_r, can be expressed as:

$$B_r = W_r \times N_r \times F_r \quad (8)$$

The actual switching load of the router's logic, $\hat{B}_r$, is the data bandwidth the router is responsible for relaying. This load is determined by the application mapping function (Ω) and the routing algorithm. The router load is the summation of loads of all router channels. For router r with a set of channels (CH_r) the router load is given by:

$$\hat{B}_r = \sum_{ch \in CH_r} \hat{B}(ch) \tag{9}$$

Where $\hat{B}(ch)$ is the communication bandwidth load of channel ch. Now α_r can be readily computed as;

$$\alpha_r = \frac{\hat{B}_r}{B_r} \tag{10}$$

3.2 Power Supply Noise Optimization Objective

Higher switching activity density leads to higher average power and current densities. Moreover, high activity density would also increase peak current demand due to larger simultaneously switching circuitry. This causes both the average and peak IR drops to increase. The inductive, ΔI, droop also increases with activity density due to higher rate of switching which leads to higher fluctuations in the current draw [15, 3, 17]. Thus, minimizing activity density will improve supply integrity and lower power supply noise. These facts are also supported by our analysis of the correlation between power supply noise and both local and regional activity densities presented in Section 4.2. To reduce the regional activity density within a particular region, our objective function must minimize the number of high activity tiles that lie within this region (see Eq. 7). Thus, mappings which result in condensing high activity tiles must have high cost. To define this cost, we introduce the metric of *tile repulsive force* $F_{i,j}$. As an analogy, this force can be considered similar to the repulsive force among like charges which is given by Coulomb's law (see Figure 1(a)). Two tiles i and j repel each other by a force directly proportional to their charge (a function of their local activity) and inversely proportional to the square of the distance between them. We express this force as follows:

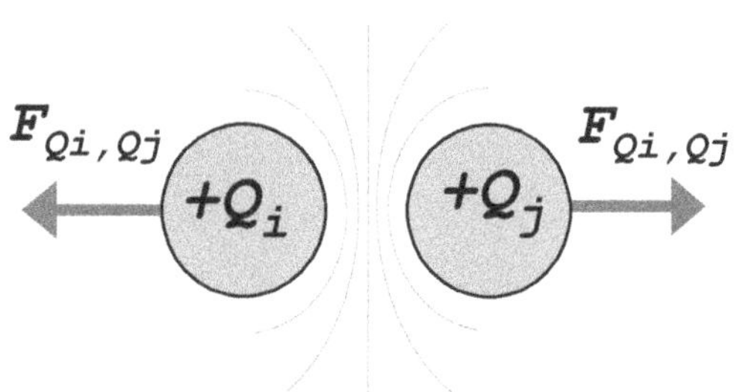

(a) Repulsive force among like charges

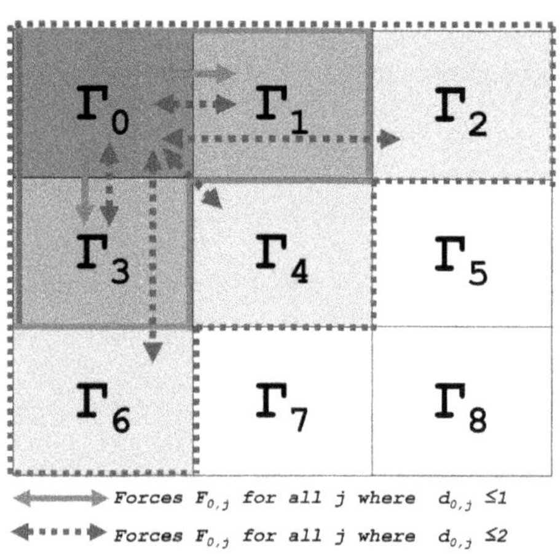

(b) Repulsive force between tile 0 and other tiles for different region sizes. $\Gamma_i = e^{k_i \gamma_i}$ is the tile charge.

Figure 1: Illustration of tile repulsive force

$$F_{i,j} = K \frac{\Gamma_i \Gamma_j}{d_{i,j}^2} \tag{11}$$

Where $\Gamma_i = e^{k_i \gamma(i)}$ and $\Gamma_j = e^{k_j \gamma(j)}$, k_i, k_j and K are constants. The exponential function is used to impose an exponential increase in $F_{i,j}$ when the local activity increases. This is shown to give better results than the linear function. The distance $d_{i,j}$ considered here is the Manhattan distance between the tiles. Since the force defined by Eq. 11 decreases quadratically with distance, and to reduce the computation time required to evaluate this force during mapping optimization, we consider the repulsive force among tiles given that they lie within a region with a predefined radius D (see Figure 1(b)). Thus, we compute the total of this repulsive force as:

$$F_{tot} = \sum_{\forall j \in T} \left(\sum_{\forall i \in T, \|i,j\| \leq D} F_{i,j} \right) \tag{12}$$

A mapping function which results in lower F_{tot} will have more scattered distribution of highly active tiles. This would result in lower regional activity and power supply noise.

3.3 Problem Formulation

Now, we formulate the problem of power supply noise optimization mapping in NoCs as follows:

Given: Application graph, $G(S, A)$ and architectural graph, $G(T, P)$ that satisfy

$$|S| \leq |T| \tag{13}$$

find: A mapping function Ω that maps each task in APG to a tile in ARG

Objective: $\min \sum_{\forall j \in T} \left(\sum_{\forall i \in T, \|i,j\| \leq D} F_{i,j} \right)$

such that:

$$\Omega(s_i) \in T \quad , \quad \forall\ s_i \in S \tag{14}$$

$$\Omega(s_i) \neq \Omega(s_j) \quad , \quad \forall\ s_i \neq s_j \tag{15}$$

$$B(l_k) \geq \hat{B}(l_k) \quad , \quad \forall\ l_k \in L(p_i),\ \forall p_i \in P \tag{16}$$

where $B(l_k)$ is link bandwidth and $\hat{B}(l_k)$ is the link load which is determined by the application mapping function and computed as:

$$\hat{B}(l_k) = \sum_{\forall a_{i,j} \in A} b(a_{i,j}) \times \pi(l_k, p(\Omega(s_i), \Omega(s_j))) \tag{17}$$

Where $\pi(l, p)$ is 1 if l belongs to the set of links constituting path p, $L(p)$, and 0 otherwise.

The first two conditions are for ensuring that each task will be mapped onto only one tile and that no more than one task can be mapped onto one tile, respectively. The third constrain is necessary to guarantee that a link load will not exceed its bandwidth capacity.

3.4 Simulated Annealing-Based Solution

The application mapping problem in NoCs is known to be NP-hard [11]. For an NoC of size $n \times m$ there are $(n \times m)!$ possible mappings. In this work we use simulated annealing-based solution. Simulated annealing can help to avoid being trapped at local minima, as the temperature function would give an opportunity to jump out from the minima throughout searching. It is suitable for NP hard problems where suboptimal solution is required, which is the case in this work. The pseudo code of the this solution is shown in Algorithm 1.

Algorithm 1 Pseudo code of the simulated annealing-based solution

Define: $Temp_f$: final temperature, β: cooling rate.
    $\mathcal{N}(t)$: the set of neighbors of tile t.
Input: APG: application graph $G(S, A)$,
    ARG: architectural graph $G(T, P)$.
Output: Ω is the optimal mapping function.
Initialize: $Temp_c = INI\_TEMP$,
    $\Omega = RAND\_MAPPING$.

1: $\Omega_p \leftarrow \Omega$
2: based on Ω_p, compute $\gamma_t\ \forall t \in T$
3: compute F^p_{tot} using Eq. 12
4: **while** $Temp_c \geq Temp_f$ **do**
5: $\quad t_1 \leftarrow \arg\max_t(\gamma_t),\ \forall t \in T$
6: $\quad$ choose t_2 from $\mathcal{N}(t_1)$ randomly with equal probability
7: $\quad \Omega_p(\Omega^{-1}(t_1)) = \Omega^{-1}(t_2)$
8: $\quad \Omega_p(\Omega^{-1}(t_2)) = \Omega^{-1}(t_1)$
9: $\quad$ **if** bandwidth constrain for Ω_p are satisfied **then**
10: $\quad\quad$ based on Ω_p, compute $\gamma_t\ \forall t \in T$
11: $\quad\quad$ compute F_{tot} using Eq. 12
12: $\quad\quad \Delta F = F_{tot} - F^p_{tot}$
13: $\quad\quad$ **if** $(\Delta F < 0)$ **then**
14: $\quad\quad\quad \Omega \leftarrow \Omega_p$
15: $\quad\quad\quad F^p_{tot} \leftarrow F_{tot}$
16: $\quad\quad$ **else**
17: $\quad\quad\quad$ **if** $e^{-\Delta F/Temp_c} > rand()$ **then**
18: $\quad\quad\quad\quad \Omega \leftarrow \Omega_p$
19: $\quad\quad\quad\quad F^p_{tot} \leftarrow F_{tot}$
20: $\quad\quad\quad$ **end if**
21: $\quad\quad$ **end if**
22: $\quad$ **end if**
23: $\quad Temp_c = \beta Temp_c$
24: **end while**
25: RETURN Ω

The algorithm takes an application graph (APG) and an architectural graph (ARG) as inputs. Also, the final temperature $Temp_f$ and the cooling rate β need to be defined at the beginning of the algorithm. Then, both mapping function and temperature ($Temp_c$) are set to their initial values. In lines 1-3, and based on the initial mapping function (Ω_p), the activity densities of all tiles ($\gamma_t\ \forall t \in T$) and the objective function (F_{tot}) are computed.

The parameters $Temp_c$, $Temp_f$ and β are tuned experimentally. The initial temperature, $Temp_c$ controls the level of relaxation of randomness of exploration at the start of the optimization, which needs to be chosen carefully to enable good exploration of the solution space. The cooling rate β controls the speed of convergence. It need to be chosen to allow slow enough convergence to ensure a good exploration of the solution space but not smaller than necessary since this would make the convergence too slow.

The main optimization loop is at lines 4-24. At lines 6-8 the new mapping (or neighbouring state) is generated by first choosing the tile with the highest activity density, and then randomly choosing another tile from its neighbours. The tasks assigned to these tiles are then exchanged (lines 7 and 8). By always modifying the tile with the highest activity, we ensure that next mapping would have different hotspot which helps in good exploration of solution space and makes convergence faster. The condition at line 9 checks if the new mapping satisfy the bandwidth constrain stated in Eq. 17. If this constrain is not satisfied, the new mapping is ignored and the algorithm goes directly to next iteration. If the bandwidth constrain is met, the new activity densities and the objective function are computed for this new mapping (lines 12 and 13). In lines 14-15 the new mapping is accepted as new state if it has lower value of the objective function (i.e. $\Delta F < 0$)), if not, this mapping can be accepted with a probability of ($e^{-\Delta F/Temp_c}$). Then the current temperature is reduced by the cooling rate and the loop starts again.

4. EXPERIMENTAL RESULTS

4.1 Simulation Setup and Tools

To compute power supply noise in NoCs, we integrate NoC power and area model [12], a traffic simulator [9] and a power delivery network model [23]. This computational model takes application characteristics as input and employs a mapping function to assign tasks to their NoC architecture. This function will determine the traffic distribution which is input to the NoC simulator to compute the communication workload across the chip. This work is not limited to a particular NoC topology of architecture. However, for convenience we will describe it in the context of a regular mesh NoC. We also assume CMPs that run concurrent parallel tasks.

To determine supply voltage variations across the chip in the presence of a workload, two models are needed. The first one characterizes the switching workload of different components on the chip. The second is for power delivery network which delivers power from the power source to these components. We employed a fast power grid model which computes peak voltage noise at the nodes across the power delivery network [23].

For the power delivery network (PDN), we included both off-chip and on-chip power delivery network models. The on-chip PDN consists of a global level mesh structure routed in the top metal layers. In this work we used a lumped model of the power delivery network. The on-chip power network is modelled as RLC mesh with a grid segment length such that we have 5×5 granularity per NoC tile. This granularity was shown to be enough for capturing the power supply voltage variations across the chip [10]. The RLC values for the grid segments were determined using PTM [4]. We employed a SPICE netlist of this PDN. We integrated an NoC cycle accurate simulator [9] and router power model [12] to compute the workload. The floorplan and architecture of Intel's TeraFlop tile is used. Tile's computational units power traces are estimated using the results presented in [20]. Integrating these models enables us to see the temporal and spatial voltage variations as direct function of the activity across the chip. The tool accuracy was also evaluated against SPICE simulation and an average error of only 1.4% was reported [18].

4.2 Activity Density and Power Supply Noise

To illustrate the significance of the problem and the motivation behind our power supply noise-aware mapping in NoCs, we start by analyzing 100 random mappings for both the MMS and the VOPD benchmarks [14]. For each of these mappings we computed the resulting voltage variations. A snapshot of this simulation for the VOPD application is shown in Figure 2. We also compute the resulting total

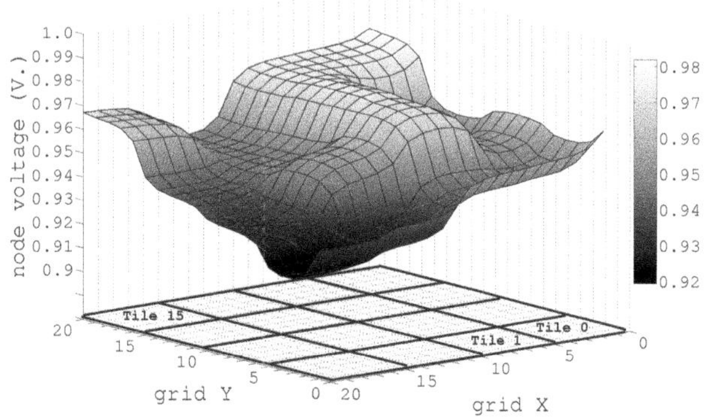

Figure 2: A snapshot of voltage variations during the VOPD benchmark simulation.

power supply noise (see Eq. 1) and the total energy E_{tot} (see Eq. 4) that results from each mapping. The ranges of both PSN and energy for both benchmarks are shown in Figure 3. It can be seen that the range PSN (see Figure 3(b)) is much higher than the range of energy (see Figure 3(a)). This implies that mapping has significant impact on power supply noise. This impact on PSN is significantly higher than the impact impact on energy. This suggests that considering PSN in application mapping for NoCs would have high impact on the power supply noise of the resulting system.

Using the power supply noise results of these random mappings, we also investigated how spatial patterns of regional activity density affects power supply noise. In particular, we investigated the impacts of tile local activity ($\gamma_t(0)$), and regional activity $\gamma_t(D)$ (for two region sizes $D = 1$ and $D = 2$), on power supply noise.

Figure 4 plots the correlation coefficient of total power supply noise with both the tile local and regional activities (for D =1 and D =2) for the VOPD benchmark. The noise margin V_{NM} (see Eq. 1) is varied from 20 mV. to 120 mV. with a step of 10 mV.

It can be noticed that for high V_{NM} (closer to V_{DD}), noise is highly dependent on the local activity $\gamma(0)$. When the noise margin decreases, noise dependence on both local and regional activities decreases. However, the correlation of the regional activity ($\gamma(D)$ for D $>$ 0) with power supply noise does not decrease as rapid as that of local activity ($\gamma(0)$). As a result, at some point, regional activity dominates local activity as a source of noise.

This change in the role of local and regional activity can be explained by the fact that when the noise margin increases, local activity will not be enough to cause voltage to drop below this margin. At this point regional activity starts to play a higher role in noise introduction. Also, we can see that regional activity for $D = 2$ has slightly higher impact on noise than regional activity for $D = 1$. The same trend was found for the MMS benchmark. This implies that the higher the noise margin is, the higher the region size that need to be considered for noise optimization.

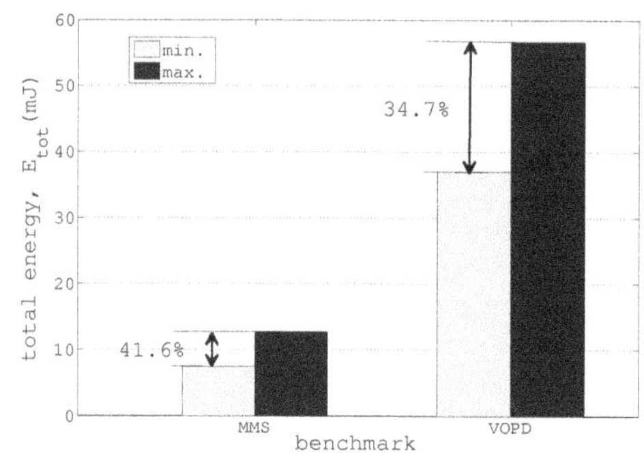

(a) energy range.

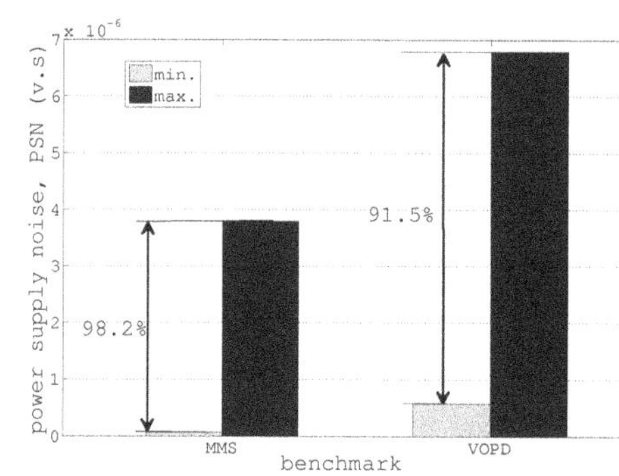

(b) power supply noise range.

Figure 3: Random mappings energy and power supply noise ranges for two benchmarks. Different mappings can have significant difference in power supply noise. This fact is exploited to optimize power supply noise throughout mapping.

Previous works on application mapping for NoCs considered different objectives but, no technique took the activity density of the resulting system into consideration. Even worse, some techniques (energy-aware mapping for instance) usually result in higher activity density in some regions of the chip. This results from placing highly communicating tasks close to each other. Consequently, hotspots results at these regions, which cause the chip to experience unbalanced switching activity, higher power supply noise, and increased temperature. As a result this leads to lower system reliability.

4.3 Application Topology and Activity Density

To better understand the dependence of activity density on application topology, we characterize applications by two parameters: *connectivity* and *bandwidth*. The connectivity of the application tasks is defined as the ratio of the existing connections between tasks to the number of all possible connections. Given an application graph (APG) $G = G(S, A)$,

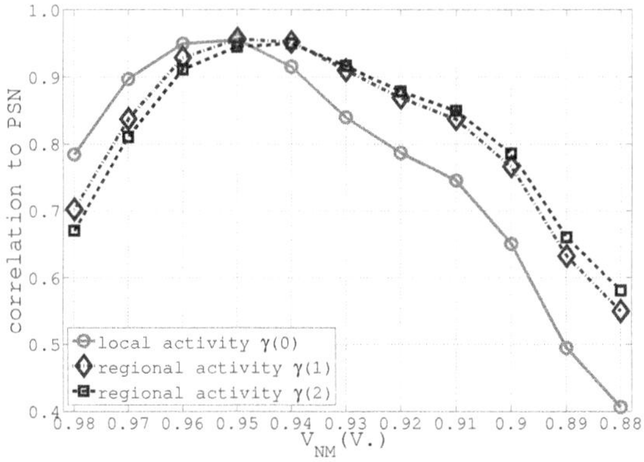

Figure 4: The power supply noise correlation activity density results form 100 random mappings for the VOPD benchmark. Significant correlation between power supply noise and activity density can be seen which is higher for regional activity than local activity.

connectivity is defined as:

$$Connectivity = \frac{|A|}{2\binom{|S|}{2}} \tag{18}$$

While the average bandwidth (BW) is defined as;

$$BW = \frac{\sum_{\forall a \in A} b(a)}{|A|} \tag{19}$$

To analyse how both parameters influence activity density (see Eq. 7), random APG's with a range of connectivity (2% to 10%) and bandwidths (20-100 MB/s.) are generated using TGFF [8] and 64 tasks. For each graph, 1000 random mapping to an 8×8 NoC are generated. The average activity density, over these 1000 random mappings is plotted against both metrics in Figure 5. It can be seen that activity density increases with both bandwidth requirements and connectivity. However, as the connectivity is higher, the activity density increases more sharply with the bandwidth.

To determine the impact of these parameters together and mapping on regional activity density, we characterize the impact of mapping by computing by the standard deviation STD of activity density over the 1000 random mappings. Higher values of STD reflect higher impact of mapping on activity density.

Figure 5(b) plots STD against APG topology parameters (connectivity and average bandwidth). It can be noticed that for applications with lower connectivity the impact of mapping on activity density is higher. This can be explained by the fact that a lower connectivity leaves higher space for the mapping technique to manoeuvre and redistribute the communication activities across the chip. As a result, in applications with highly connected tasks the regional activity does not vary with mapping as much as for applications with low connectivity. It can also be observed that application bandwidth has nearly no impact on STD of regional activity since this trend is nearly similar for different bandwidths.

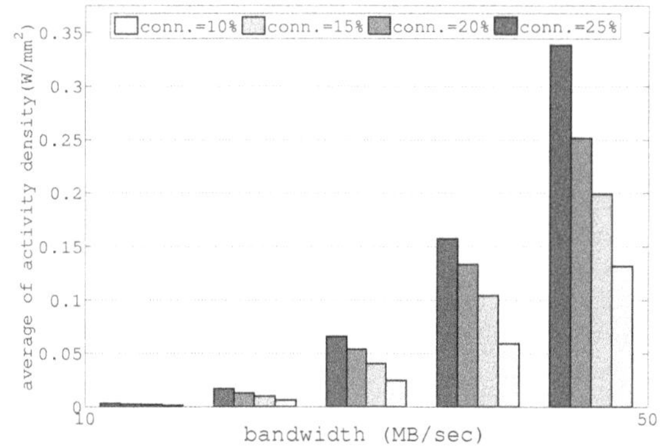

(a) average of activity density

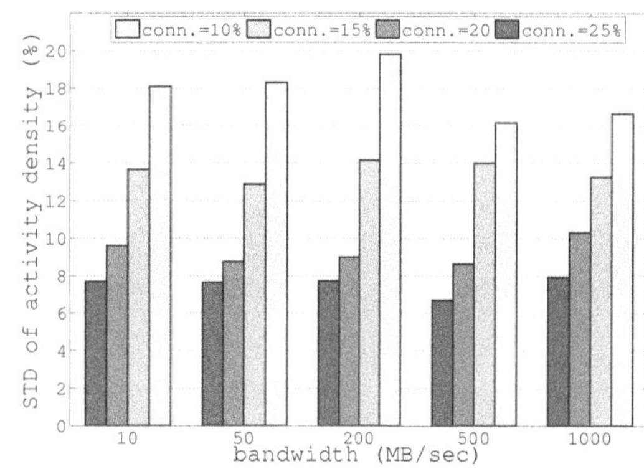

(b) STD of activity density

Figure 5: Average and STD of activity density for application graphs with different bandwidths and connectivities. 1000 random mappings are generated for each graph. Activity density increases with both connectivity and bandwidth. However, mapping has higher impact on activity density for applications with lower connectivity.

4.4 Mapping Results

To evaluate the proposed power supply noise minimization mapping, we used six real benchmarks with different sizes, topologies and bandwidth requirements. These benchmarks include a generic complex MultiMedia system which comprises h263 video encoder and mp3 audio decoder (MMS) [11], Telecommunication benchmark (TELE) and Video Object Plane Decoder (VOPD)[14]. In addition to three benchmarks, AMI49, AMI25 and MPEG4 decoder found in [1]. The details of size and communication bandwidth requirements of these benchmarks are shown in the first four columns of Table 2. Using simulated annealing-based optimization, these benchmarks were first mapped into their target NoC architectures with the objective of minimizing the total repulsive force F_{tot} defined in Eq. 12.

To evaluate each mapping in terms of power supply noise, we used the tool described in subsection 4.1 assuming 65 nm technology with nominal supply voltage V_{DD}=1 V. and 1 GHz clock frequency. We compared our noise-aware mappings with energy-aware mappings in terms of both power supply noise and energy. Since the changes in power supply

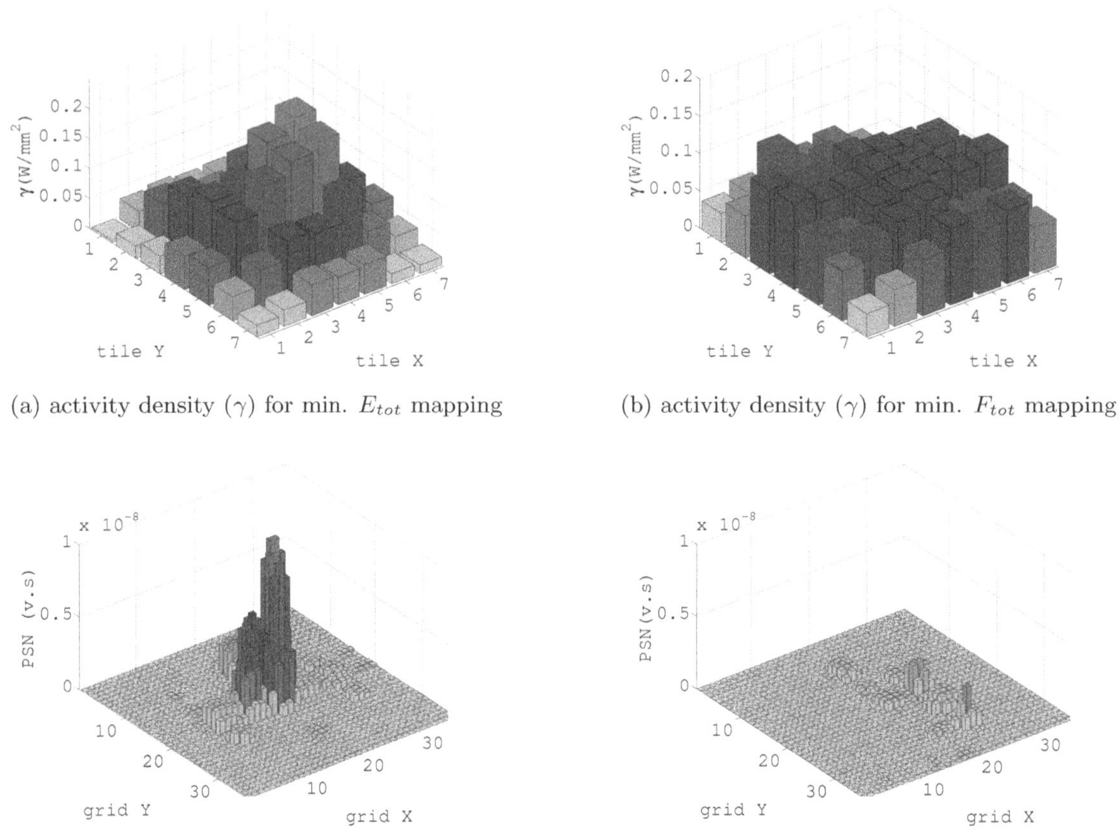

(a) activity density (γ) for min. E_{tot} mapping

(b) activity density (γ) for min. F_{tot} mapping

(c) power supply noise for min. E_{tot} mapping

(d) power supply noise for min. F_{tot} mapping

Figure 6: The spatial distribution of activity density and power supply noise for the AMI49 application. Significant reduction in power supply noise is achieved by harmonic distribution of activity.

time scale are slower compared with clock frequency [13], we used a time window of 100 cycle (0.1 μs) for computing the power supply variations [18]. The simulation runs for 10,000 windows (one million clock cycles) for each mapping. We computed power supply noise using Eq. 1 assuming noise margin, V_{NM} to be 10% of nominal V_{DD} (i.e. 0.1 V.).

An example illustrating the impact of our repulsive force minimization mapping can be seen in Figure 6, which shows the spatial activity density and power supply noise distributions resulting from both energy and repulsive force minimizations for the AMI9 benchmark.

It can be noticed that energy-aware mapping results in condensing highly active tiles resulting in regions with high activity on the chip (see Figure 6(a)). This results in hotspots that experience high power supply noise (see Figure 6(c)). In contrast, our repulsive force minimization mapping results in scattered and more homogenous activity distribution (see Figure 6(b)), which, in turn, reduces the power supply noise significantly (by 76% for this example) as depicted in Figure 6(d).

A summary of the results of both power supply noise and energy, using both mapping strategies for the six benchmarks are shown in Table 2. These results are also depicted graphically in Figure 7. It can be seen that our repulsive force minimization resulted in significant drops in power supply noise (72.5% of noise is removed on average) with low energy penalties (about 4% in average). This implies that considering regional activity in NoC mapping is very useful and can result in systems with lower noise and better power supply integrity.

It can also be noticed that, in general, the difference in energy between energy-aware mapping and repulsive-force based mapping is relatively small (1.1% and 1.5% for the TELE and MPEG4 benchmarks respectively). This can be explained by the fact that F_{tot} defined in Eq. 12 can be reduced by both increasing the distance between highly active tiles and/or lowering the local activities of the tiles. A mapping function which will result in lower total switching activity will also result in lower total energy (see Eq. 4). Thus using F_{tot} as an objective for the mapping function will result in a sub-optimal solution for energy minimization. This fact is also verified experimentally by finding very high correlation between F_{tot} computed using Eq. 12 and E_{tot} computed using Eq. 4 for the mappings mentioned in Section 4.2.

5. CONCLUSIONS

Power supply noise has significant impact on system reliability. Particularly, on-chip communication could easily incur power supply noise without proper isolation. We propose a new mapping strategy which aims at reducing power

no.	benchmark (No. of tasks)	NoC size	min/max BW (MB/s)	E_{tot} optimization		F_{tot} optimization		energy penalty	PSN reduction
				energy(mJ)	PSN($V.s$)	energy(mJ)	PSN($V.s$)		
1	AMI49 (49)	7×7	5.3/85.3	6.44	3.427e-8	6.84	8.215e-9	6.2%	76%
2	AMI25 (25)	5×5	53.3/213.3	3.21	1.046e-8	3.32	2.353e-9	3.3%	78%
3	MMS (25)	5×5	0.025/116.8	5.18	1.416e-8	5.52	5.082e-9	6.1%	65%
4	TELE (16)	4×4	11/71	7.90	4.984e-9	7.98	1.407e-9	1.1%	72%
5	VOPD (16)	4×4	16/500	26.2	6.816e-8	28.3	1.204e-8	7.4%	83%
6	MPEG4 (9)	3×3	8.5/502	26.1	6.846e-8	26.6	2.701e-8	1.5%	61%
							AVERAGE	**4.26%**	**72.5%**

Table 2: Summary of the benchmarks and mappings results

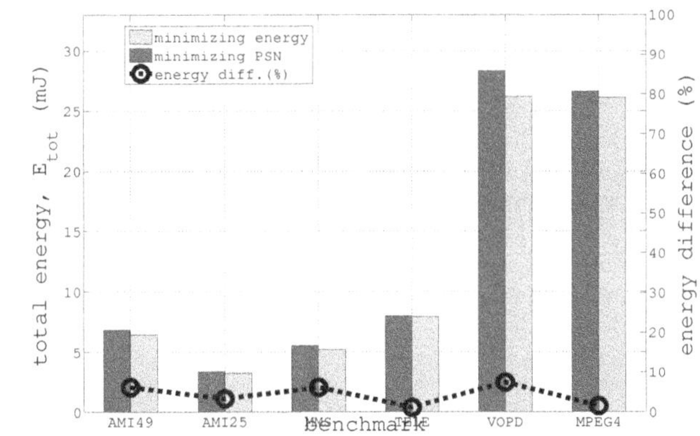

(a) total energy consumption.

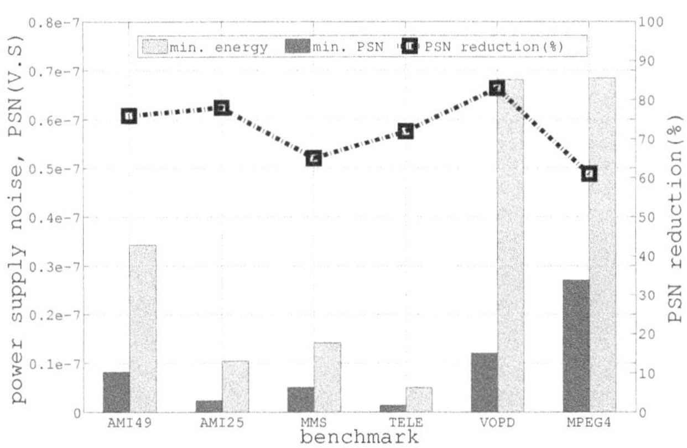

(b) resulting total power supply noise.

Figure 7: Comparison of both power supply noise and energy optimizations. Our noise minimization could achieve significant reduction in power supply noise compared to energy minimization with a low energy penalty.

supply noise in inter-core communication through optimizing activity distribution. We found that different mappings can result in significant variation in terms of power supply noise (up to 98.2%). A new metric based on communication activity density, which has direct impact on power supply noise, has been developed. We integrate this new metric into a new mapping algorithm and employ a repulsive force-based strategy. This new strategy leads to a balanced distribution of activities across the chip and, hence, results in smaller power supply noise. The new mapping strategy can achieve significant power supply noise reduction (up to 83%) with negligible energy penalty (about 4% in average). This work enables better power supply integrity and reliable power delivery for future many-core systems.

6. REFERENCES

[1] C. Ababei, H. S. Kia, O. P. Yadav, and H. Jingcao. Energy and reliability oriented mapping for regular networks-on-chip. In *Networks on Chip (NoCS), 2011 Fifth IEEE/ACM International Symposium on*, pages 121–128, 2011.

[2] A. H. Ajami, K. Banerjee, and M. Pedram. Scaling analysis of on-chip power grid voltage variations in nanometer scale ulsi. *Analog Integrated Circuits and Signal Processing*, 42(3):277–290, 2005.

[3] K. Arabi, R. Saleh, and M. Xiongfei. Power supply noise in socs: Metrics, management, and measurement. *Design Test of Computers, IEEE*, 24(3):236 –244, may-june 2007.

[4] Y. Cao, T. Sato, D. Sylvester, M. Orshansky, and C. Hu. Predictive technology model. *Nanoscale integration and modeling group, Arizona State Univerity, http://ptm.asu.edu/*, 2006.

[5] E. Carvalho and F. Moraes. Congestion-aware task mapping in heterogeneous mpsocs. In *System-on-Chip, 2008. SOC 2008. International Symposium on*, pages 1–4, 2008.

[6] H. H. Chen and D. D. Ling. Power supply noise analysis methodology for deep-submicron vlsi chip design. In *Design Automation Conference, 1997. Proceedings of the 34th*, pages 638–643, 1997.

[7] A. R. Conn, R. A. Haring, and C. Visweswariah. Noise considerations in circuit optimization. pages 220–227. ACM, 1998. Proceedings of the 1998 IEEE/ACM international conference on Computer-aided design.

[8] R. Dick, D. Rhodes, and W. Wolf. Tgff: task graphs for free. In *Hardware/Software Codesign, 1998. (CODES/CASHE '98) Proceedings of the Sixth International Workshop on*, pages 97 –101, mar 1998.

[9] F. Fazzino, M. Palesi, and D. Patti. Noxim: Network-on-chip simulator. *URL: http://sourceforge.net/projects/noxim*, 2008.

[10] M. S. Gupta, J. L. Oatley, R. Joseph, W. Gu-Yeon, and D. M. Brooks. Understanding voltage variations in chip multiprocessors using a distributed power-delivery network. In *Design, Automation and Test in Europe Conference and Exhibition, 2007. DATE '07*, pages 1–6, 2007.

[11] H. Jingcao and R. Marculescu. Energy-aware mapping for tile-based NoC architectures under performance constraints. In *Design Automation Conference, 2003. Proceedings of the ASP-DAC 2003. Asia and South Pacific*, pages 233–239, 2003.

[12] A. B. Kahng, B. Li, L. S. Peh, and K. Samadi. Orion 2.0: A power-area simulator for interconnection networks. *Very Large Scale Integration (VLSI) Systems, IEEE Transactions on*, PP(99):1–5, 2011.

[13] S. Kvatinsky, E. Friedman, A. Kolodny, and L. Scha? andchter. Power grid analysis based on a macro circuit model. In *Electrical and Electronics Engineers in Israel (IEEEI), 2010 IEEE 26th Convention of*, pages 000708 –000712, nov. 2010.

[14] S. Murali and G. De Micheli. Bandwidth-constrained mapping of cores onto noc architectures. In *Design, Automation and Test in Europe Conference and Exhibition, 2004. Proceedings*, volume 2, pages 896–901 Vol.2, 2004.

[15] F. Najm. Transition density: a new measure of activity in digital circuits. *Computer-Aided Design of Integrated Circuits and Systems, IEEE Transactions on*, 12(2):310 –323, feb 1993.

[16] S. R. Nassif. Power grid analysis benchmarks. In *Design Automation Conference, 2008. ASPDAC 2008. Asia and South Pacific*, pages 376–381, 2008.

[17] S. Nithin, G. Shanmugam, and S. Chandrasekar. Dynamic voltage (ir) drop analysis and design closure: Issues and challenges. In *Quality Electronic Design (ISQED), 2010 11th International Symposium on*, pages 611 –617, march 2010.

[18] T. M. Nizar Dahir and A. Yakovlev. Communication centric on-chip power grid models for networks-on-chip. In *VLSI and System-on-Chip (VLSI-SoC), 2011 IEEE/IFIP 19th International Conference on*, pages 180–183, 2011.

[19] M. Saint-Laurent and M. Swaminathan. Impact of power-supply noise on timing in high-frequency microprocessors. *IEEE Transactions on Advanced Packaging*, 27(1):135–144, 2004.

[20] S. Vangal, J. Howard, G. Ruhl, S. Dighe, H. Wilson, J. Tschanz, D. Finan, P. Iyer, A. Singh, and T. Jacob. An 80-tile 1.28 tflops network-on-chip in 65nm cmos. In *Solid-State Circuits Conference, 2007. ISSCC 2007. Digest of Technical Papers. IEEE International*, pages 98–589. IEEE, 2007. Solid-State Circuits Conference, 2007. ISSCC 2007. Digest of Technical Papers. IEEE International.

[21] Y. Wang, J. Xu, Y. Xu, W. Liu, and H. Yang. Power gating aware task scheduling in mpsoc. *Very Large Scale Integration (VLSI) Systems, IEEE Transactions on*, (99):1–12, 2010.

[22] T. Ye, L. Benini, and G. De Micheli. Analysis of power consumption on switch fabrics in network routers. In *Design Automation Conference, 2002. Proceedings. 39th*, pages 524 – 529, 2002.

[23] L. R. Zheng and H. Tenhunen. Fast modeling of core switching noise on distributed lrc power grid in ulsi circuits. In *Electrical Performance of Electronic Packaging, 2000, IEEE Conference on.*, pages 307–310, 2000.

Worst-case Performance Analysis of 2-D Mesh NoCs using Multi-path Minimal Routing

Gaoming Du
Institute of VLSI Design
Hefei University of Technology
Hefei, Anhui Province, China
dugaoming@hfut.edu.cn

Cunqiang Zhang
Institute of VLSI Design
Hefei University of Technology
Hefei, Anhui Province, China

Zhonghai Lu
Dept. of Electronic Systems
KTH Royal Institute of Technology, Sweden
zhonghai@kth.se

Alberto Saggio
Dept. of Electrical Engineering
Sapienza University of Rome
Rome, Italy
saggio@kth.se

Minglun Gao
Institute of VLSI Design
Hefei University of Technology
Hefei, Anhui Province, China
gaominglun@hfut.edu.cn

ABSTRACT

In Network-on-Chip (NoC), multi-path routing is often preferable than single-path routing since it can better balance workload and thus provide better performance. However, performance analysis with multi-path routing is much more difficult due to complicated contention scenarios. Based on network calculus, we study worst-case performance of deterministic multi-path minimal routing on 2-D mesh NoCs. We first present a per-flow delay bound analysis technique for multi-path routing, which extends the analysis for single-path routing but deals with traffic splitting. Then we define a contention matrix to capture network congestion status. Based on the contention matrix, we propose an effective non-uniform traffic splitting strategy to improve worst-case performance. Experiments with synthetic traffic flows and an industrial case show that our analysis can effectively explore the traffic splitting space, and verify the effectiveness of the non-uniform splitting policy.

Categories and Subject Descriptors

B.2.2 [**Performance Analysis and Design Aids**]: Worst-case analysis

General Terms

Performance,Theory

Keywords

Multi-path Routing NoC, Network Calculus, Contention Matrix

1. INTRODUCTION

Quality-of-Service (QoS) [8] as a key issue in NoC design has attracted huge attention from the birth of NoC, since it can raise design confidence by knowing the performance bound that NoCs can provide. But traditionally, performance evaluation is done either with simulation or design reviews. Neither of them is scalable nor can cover corner cases. Furthermore, they have drawbacks such as error prone (for design reviews) and time consuming (for simulations).

Formal approach such as network calculus [4][6] has been proposed to evaluate the performance of NoCs. It can not only derive the performance bounds such as delay, backlog and throughput bounds, but also can make worst-case performance guarantee for application specific NoCs [14]. Previous research has been done on wormhole routing NoC and credit based flow control router [15][16], and profound results have been obtained on the analysis and optimization of delay and backlog bounds. However, existing analysis techniques are only for routing algorithms with one path per flow (a flow is defined as a stream of unicast packets from a source node to a destination node), but NoCs often employ multi-path routing such as oblivious and adaptive routing, to balance workload and to improve network performance. This research gap motivates us to analyze the worst-case performance for multi-path routing.

Unlike those routing algorithms that provide only a single path per flow, multi-path routing allows a flow to use different paths between a pair of source and destination nodes. As a flow may take different paths from source to destination, it can be seen as "being split" into sub-flows. We call this behavior *traffic splitting*. Since it can exploit the network path diversity, multi-path routing can provide better performance in terms of improved load balance, higher network resource utilization and lower network congestion and delay. Previous studies show that multi-path routing in NoCs can reduce network bandwidth requirement around 36.86% and power consumption up to 30.51% [11] on average. However, few of the previous works use a formal approach to study the worst-case performance, while most of them have been done considering average cases with simulations. This is not satisfying for real time applications such as multimedia streaming processing, as the worst-case delay is one of the key parameters that affect the whole system performance and correctness.

On the other hand, multi-path routing is much more complicated than single-path routing, causing other problems.

CODES+ISSS'12, October 7-12, 2012, Tampere, Finland.

The first is traffic over-splitting. In fact, more traffic splitting will bring more traffic contentions, and more contentions may result in longer worst-case delay. Therefore a proper traffic splitting strategy is important to harvest the benefit of multi-path routing. We will study different traffic splitting strategies and propose an effective method to improve the worst-case performance. We will first define a contention matrix to represent the traffic congestion state, and then propose a non-uniform traffic splitting strategy that can improve the worst-case delay.

Another problem with multi-path routing is out-of-order packet delivery, i.e., a packet sent first may arrive at the destination node after a packet sent later. This problem can be addressed by utilizing a packet re-ordering buffer at the network interface [11]. In this work, we focus on applying network calculus to evaluate the worst-case performance in on-chip networks employing multi-path routing, and based on the analysis, propose multi-path routing alternatives and compare their worst-case performance. The results in the paper are independent from the packet reordering policy used after packets are ejected from the network.

The rest of the paper is organized as follows. Section 2 reviews previous work and highlights our contributions. Then we introduce the basic network calculus results for per-flow delay bound analysis with deterministic routing in Section 3. Basic analysis technique for multi-path routing is presented in Section 4. In Section 5, we define the contention matrix and then present the non-uniform traffic splitting strategy. Section 6 presents experiments and results. Finally, we conclude in Section 7.

2. RELATED WORK

Network calculus is a formal tool to evaluate the network performance, which can give worst-case delay and backlog bounds. It was initially proposed by Cruz [4]. Later it has been elaborated in a number of papers and well summarized in two excellent books [3][6]. It has been very successful when applied to various networks, for example, Internet with differentiated and integrated services, Intranet and ATM, recently wireless sensor networks and real-time embedded systems. Real-time calculus [18] combines network calculus with real-time scheduling theory to reason about the worst-case delay and backlog bounds under various scheduling policies (FP, FIFO, TDMA, EDF, etc.) in a compositional way. Only recently, researchers began to use this tool for on chip communication analysis. Lu. *et al.* has derived the closed-form performance bounds in per flow case [15][16] and applied traffic regulation policy for controlling the performance [9]. In [2], based on network calculus, a methodology is presented to analyze and evaluate on-chip interconnects in terms of performance and cost metrics.

Though not many, there are some NoC research works studying multi-path routing. Murali *et al.* [11][10] studied the multi-path routing problem in NoCs and proposed multi-path routing strategy that guarantees both in-order packet delivery and fault tolerance. Jiao *et al.* [5] proposed a multi-path routing scheme to maximize the data throughput for mesh or torus based NoCs. However, they have not considered the worst-case performance and the evaluation tools used are all by simulation, which can hardly get the worst-case results. Stefan *et al.* [17] proposed a multi-path slot allocation method with static resource reservation, especially in TDM NoC, which can guarantee bandwidth and delay by employing circuit switching. We will study the packet switching NoC and focus on the relationship between delay bounds and network congestion using a formal analysis approach.

In this paper, based on network calculus, we study the performance evaluation problem concerning multi-path routing to derive the delay bound per flow on 2-D mesh NoCs. Traffic can be split in every router from source to destination. This means that one flow may be split into two or more sub-flows. These sub-flows may interference with the *tag flow*, i.e. the flow for which we shall derive its delay bound.

Our main contributions can be summarized as follows,

(1) Based on network calculus, we propose a per-flow delay bound analysis technique for multi-path routing, which is suitable for arbitrary sized 2-D mesh NoCs.

(2) Multi-path routing implies traffic splitting. We propose a concept of contention matrix to capture the NoC congestion status. Based on this concept we propose an effective non-uniform traffic splitting strategy to improve worst-case performance.

(3) With experimental results of synthetic traffic and an industrial case, we validate our analysis and show the effectiveness of the traffic splitting techniques.

3. NETWORK CALCULUS BASICS

3.1 Basic Results of Network Calculus

In network calculus [6], a flow $f(t)$ is bounded using an *arrival curve* $\alpha(t)$ to constrain the amount of injected traffic within any time interval. A network element is modeled with a *service curve* $\beta(t)$, which provides a lower bound on the available service capability. With the upper bounded arrival curve and the lower bounded service curve, delay and backlog bounds can be reasoned about.

In order to derive closed-form formulas, special forms of arrival and service curves are commonly assumed. A special case of arrival curve is the *linear* arrival curve $\alpha(t)$, which has the form $\alpha(t) = rt+b$, where r bounds the burstiness and b the average (sustainable) rate. A special service curve $\beta(t)$ can be modeled as a latency-rate function $\beta_{R,T} = R(t-T)^+$, where R is the minimum service rate and T the maximum processing latency of the network element. Here x^+ equals 0 if $x \leq 0$, else x.

When a linear arrival flow f is served by a node guaranteeing a latency-rate server $\beta_{R,T}$ [7], the maximum delay for the flow is bounded by Eq. (1) and the buffer required for the flow is bounded by Eq. (2).

$$\bar{D} = \frac{b}{R} + T \tag{1}$$

$$\bar{B} = b + rT \tag{2}$$

3.2 Delay Bound Analysis: Uni-path Routing

The above equations are for single node analysis. Since a flow often traverses through a series of routers (servers), we need to calculate the *equivalent service curve* (ESC) and then we can use Equation 1 and Equation 2 to calculate the end-to-end delay bound and backlog bound, respectively. As proven in [7], the delay bound using ESC is LUDB (least upper delay bound).

The main challenge for per-flow ESC derivation is how to handle the contention problem. Firstly, different sharing scenarios have different analysis techniques. Following [14], we have classified this into three categories: link sharing, control sharing and buffer sharing. Secondly, different contention flows have different contention relationship, that is, nested, parallel and cross contentions [15]. Algorithms have been developed to automate the analysis for single-path flow with deterministic routing. The basic analysis model considers that a *tag flow* traverses through a tandem of routers, with several *interference flows* in different contention modes. The ESC of the tag flow can be derived. As validated in [15], the delay bound derived with this technique is very tight. All the works above laid a solid basis for per-flow end-to-end delay bound analysis of multi-path routing.

3.3 Basic Assumptions and Notations

We assume that all flows injected into the NoC have a linear arrival curve $\alpha(t) = rt + b$. We also assume that, with one virtual channel per inport and a FCFS (First Come First Serve) policy, a router i uses the latency-rate model with a service curve $\beta_{R_i,T_i} = R_i(t - T_i)^+$ defined above.

We follow the notation conventions for min-plus algebra in book [6]. $\otimes$ represents min-plus convolution of two functions $f, g \in F$, the set of wide-sense increasing functions defined on $[0, \infty)$, $(f \otimes g)(t) = \inf_{0 \le s \le t} \{f(t - s) + g(s)\}$; $\oslash$ represents the min-plus de-convolution of $f, g \in F$ and is defined as:$(f \oslash g)(t) = \sup_{s \ge 0}\{f(t+s) - g(s)\}$. The affine curve $\gamma_{b,r}(t) = rt + b$ for $t > 0$, and 0 otherwise; The burst delay function $\delta_T(t) = +\infty$ for $t > T$, and 0 otherwise. For our traffic splitting analysis, we define more notations in Table 1.

Symbol	Explanation
P_x	Traffic splitting proportion in X axis
$f_{\langle m,n \rangle}$	The flow from source node m to destination n
$f_{(m,n)}$	Flow that passes through node m and n
$f_{[m,n]}$	Flow injected into node m and output from n
P_f	Traffic splitting proportion of flow f
$\otimes$	Min-plus convolution
$\oslash$	Min-plus de-convolution
$\{f_1, f_2\}$	Congregate flow of f_1, f_2
α^f_m	Arrival curve for flow f at node m
$\epsilon(.,.)$	Function to compute the ESC
$\beta^{f,eq}_m$	ESC for flow f at node m
$\wedge$	The minimum operation. $f \wedge g = min\{f, g\}$
&	Logic AND operation
f_{kl}	The l-th sub-flow of the k-th main flow
$C^{kl}_{m,n}$	Contention matrix element for sub-flow f_{kl} of tag flow$f_{\langle m,n \rangle}$

Table 1: Notations and symbols used in this paper

We assume that the NoC topology is two dimensions with arbitrary network size for simplicity. However, the proposed analysis method can easily be extended to other topologies because we define the contention matrix using a generic adjacent matrix approach, which is a key to our performance analysis technique. The base routing algorithm is dimension-order routing. For every router, there is a traffic splitter, which may split the traffic to the next node at different direction with different proportion. As shown in Figure 1, the proportion in X direction is denoted as P_x, so it is $1 - P_x$ in Y direction. When P_x equals 0 or 1, it becomes Y first or X first single-path routing. Otherwise, it is multi-path routing with constant traffic splitting proportion. So the basic theory used is deterministic network calculus. In this study, we obtain this proportion by calculating the network congestion status in an off-line processing manner, which requires a priori knowledge of specific application. The traffic splitting proportion at each router is configurable so that we can apply uniform or non-uniform traffic splitting.

4. PERFORMANCE ANALYSIS FOR MULTI-PATH ROUTING

4.1 The Problem Illustration and Analysis

4.1.1 *An illustrative example*

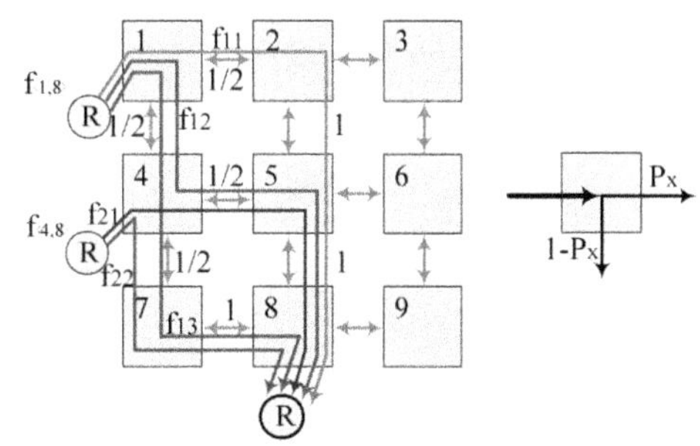

Figure 1: An example of multi-path routing with traffic splitting

From a performance analysis point of view, there exists a considerable difference between multi-path and single-path routing. Firstly, the number of contention flows increases exponentially as a main flow is split into multiple sub-flows. As shown in Figure 1, a NoC with size of 3×3 is presented. Two main flows $f_{\langle 1,8 \rangle}$ and $f_{\langle 4,8 \rangle}$ are transferring in NoC. By traffic splitting, $f_{\langle 1,8 \rangle}$ is split into three sub-flows f_{11}, f_{12} and f_{13}, and flow $f_{\langle 4,8 \rangle}$ is split into f_{21} and f_{22}. Let f_{11} be the tag flow, so the contention flows are f_{12}, f_{13}, f_{21} and f_{22}. Considering the single path case, there is only one tag flow and one contention flow. But in multi-path routing, the number of contention flows has increased from one to four. This is only a very simple example. Consider a slightly large 2-D NoC with 6×5, a flow traversing from node (1,1) to node (6,5) may have 126 sub-flows with full traffic splitting (traffic flow is split at every node it passes by in a minimal path region). This highlights the fact that, with the increased sub-flows brought by traffic splitting, the complexity will increase dramatically.

Secondly, the traffic splitting strategy has great impact on the analytical results. On one side, traffic splitting means distributing the traffic to other links, so it may achieve better usage of the network resource and may have better load balance. But on the other side, in *full traffic splitting* case, the performance results may be worse due to increasing the number of flows in exponent as well as the contention status.

This section will focus on the first problem and propose the delay bound analysis technique for multi-path routing. The other issue will be addressed in the next section.

4.1.2 *General traffic splitting*

We use a 2-D mesh architecture with minimal path routing as an example to clarify the general traffic splitting scheme in multi-path routing, though it can also be applied to other topology easily.

As shown in Figure 1, a flow can be split in two axis, X and Y. Let P_x be the proportion of splitting on the X axis, then the proportion on the Y axis is $1-P_x$. In general traffic splitting, every node can split traffic in this way. What really matters is how to determine P_x or P_y. An example using even traffic splitting is given in Figure 1. We can see that for every node that delivers flow $f_{\langle 1,8\rangle}$, the traffic is split into half on the X axis and half on the Y axis, except those nodes where there is only one possible path to reach the destination.

4.2 Delay Bound Analysis for Traffic Splitting

4.2.1 The analysis steps

Based on the above traffic splitting, we can calculate the parameters of the split sub-flows, perform contention analysis and derive ESCs and delay bounds. The general procedure is given in the following.

- *Step 1*: Sub-flow identification
  Many sub-flows are generated due to traffic splitting, thus, we have to identify all the possible paths. This is the base step for contention state analysis.
- *Step 2*: Proportion calculation
  We calculate not only node dispatch proportion for every node P_n, but also flow proportion for every sub-flow $P_{(f)}$. $P_{(f)}$ is obtained by multiplying all the P_n that the sub-flow experiences.
- *Step 3*: Sub-flow parameters calculation
  Suppose flow $f_{\langle 1,8\rangle}$ has an original traffic arrival curve like (r, b), We calculate the traffic characteristics of sub-flows by multiplying the flow proportion with the original traffic parameters.
- *Step 4*: ESC for each sub-flow
  Through the above steps, we successfully divide the multi-path routing problem into the single-path problem, and some previous results for single-path routing can be reused.
- *Step 5*: Delay bounds calculation for sub-flow
  Finally we can derive the delay bound per sub-flow based on Equation 1.
- *Step 6*: Delay bounds for tag flow
  Through the above six steps, we can obtain the delay bound of one sub-flow. Recursively executing these procedures, all performance bounds of every sub-flow can be obtained. By comparing the results for all sub-flows, the maximum one is determined as the worst-case delay bound.

4.2.2 An analysis example

We show an example using the above method in Figure 1.

Step 1: Sub-flow identification. Two main flows $f_{\langle 1,8\rangle}$ and $f_{\langle 4,8\rangle}$ are in 2-D NoC. Let $f_{\langle 1,8\rangle}$ has a linear flow model (r_1, b_1) and $f_{\langle 4,8\rangle}$ has (r_2, b_2). Through traffic splitting, $f_{\langle 1,8\rangle}$ is split into three sub-flows f_{11}, f_{12} and f_{13}, and $f_{\langle 4,8\rangle}$ is split into f_{21} and f_{22}. Let f_{11} be the tag flow. Our goal is to calculate the end-to-end delay bound for flow f_{11} using the procedure proposed above.

Step 2: Proportion calculation. The traffic splitting proportion map is also shown in Figure 1. and the flow ratio of f_{11} is: $P_{(f_{11})} = \frac{1}{2} \times 1 \times 1 \times 1 = \frac{1}{2}$, $P_{(f_{12})} = \frac{1}{4}$, $P_{(f_{13})} = \frac{1}{4}$, $P_{(f_{21})} = \frac{1}{2}$, $P_{(f_{22})} = \frac{1}{2}$.

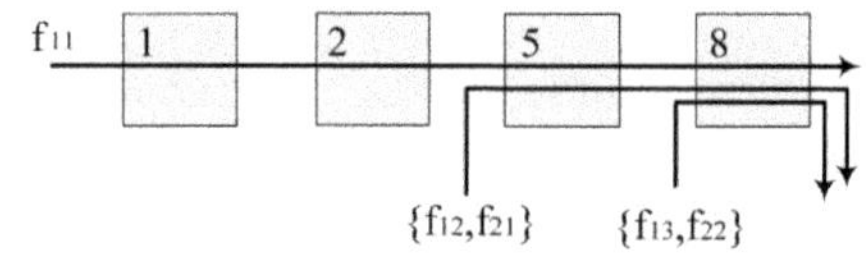

Figure 2: A flow example for ESC derivation

Step 3: Sub-flow parameters calculation. For sub-flow f_{11}, its related parameters are $(P_{(f_{11})} \times r_1, P_{(f_{11})} \times b_1) = (\frac{r_1}{2}, \frac{b_1}{2})$. In the same way, we have $(\frac{r_1}{4}, \frac{b_1}{4})$ for f_{12}, $(\frac{r_1}{4}, \frac{b_1}{4})$ for f_{13}, $(\frac{r_2}{2}, \frac{b_2}{2})$ for f_{21}, and $(\frac{r_2}{2}, \frac{b_2}{2})$ for f_{22}.

Step 4: ESC derivation for each sub-flow.

Step 4.1: Contention flows identification. As shown in Figure 2, for tag flow f_{11}, there are two contention flows: congregate flow $\{f_{12}, f_{21}\}$ at node 5 and congregate flow $\{f_{13}, f_{22}\}$ at node 8. They are in nested contention.

Step 4.2: Arrival curve of contention flows. The arrival curve $(\alpha_5^{\{f_{12},f_{21}\}})$ and $(\alpha_8^{\{f_{13},f_{22}\}})$ for $\{f_{12}, f_{21}\}$ and $\{f_{13}, f_{22}\}$ should be calculated first. So we need to trace through the congregate flows. For congregate flow $\{f_{12}, f_{21}\}$, its sub-flow f_{12} and f_{21} gather at node 4 and contend with f_{11} at node 5. Since f_{12} is the result of splitting from $f_{\langle 1,8\rangle}$, with a flow proportion of $\frac{1}{4}$, the arrival curve $\alpha_4^{f_{12}}$ for f_{12} at node 4 is:

$$\begin{aligned}
\alpha_4^{f_{12}} &= \alpha_1^{f_{12}} \oslash \beta_1^{f_{12},eq} \\
&= \alpha_1^{f_{12}} \oslash \epsilon(\beta_1, \alpha_1^{f_{13}}) \\
&= \gamma_{\frac{1}{4}b_1, \frac{1}{4}r_1} \oslash \epsilon(\beta_1, \gamma_{\frac{1}{4}b_1, \frac{1}{4}r_1}) \\
&= \gamma_{\frac{1}{4}b_1, \frac{1}{4}r_1} \oslash (\gamma_{0, R_1 - \frac{1}{4}r_1} \otimes \delta_{T_1 + \frac{b_1}{4R_1}}) \\
&= \gamma_{\frac{1}{4}b_1 + \frac{1}{4}r_1(T_1 + \frac{b_1}{4R_1}), \frac{1}{4}r_1}
\end{aligned} \tag{3}$$

Due to traffic splitting, path proportion of f_{21} is $\frac{1}{2}$, the arrival curve of f_{21} at node 4 is $\alpha_4^{f_{21}} = \gamma_{\frac{1}{2}b_2, \frac{1}{2}r_2}$. So the arrival curve of congregate flow $\{f_{12}, f_{21}\}$ at node 4 is:

$$\alpha_4^{\{f_{12},f_{21}\}} = \gamma_{\frac{1}{4}b_1 + \frac{1}{4}r_1\left(T_1 + \frac{b_1}{4R_1}\right) + \frac{1}{2}b_2, \frac{1}{4}r_1 + \frac{1}{2}r_2}$$

So the Arrival curve for $\{f_{12}, f_{21}\}$ at node 5 is:

$$\begin{aligned}
\alpha_5^{\{f_{12},f_{21}\}} &= \alpha_4^{\{f_{12},f_{21}\}} \oslash \beta_4^{\{f_{12},f_{21}\},eq} \\
&= \gamma_{\frac{1}{4}b_1 + \frac{1}{4}r_1\left(T_1 + \frac{b_1}{4R_1}\right) + \frac{1}{2}b_2 + \left(\frac{1}{4}r_1 + \frac{1}{2}r_2\right)T_4, \frac{1}{4}r_1 + \frac{1}{2}r_2}
\end{aligned} \tag{4}$$

The congregate flow f_{13}, f_{22} gather at node 4. They have almost the same situations as the previous one. For short, we directly give the results of the arrival curve for $\{f_{13}, f_{22}\}$ at node 4.

$$\alpha_8^{\{f_{13},f_{22}\}} = \gamma_{\frac{1}{4}b_1 + \frac{1}{4}r_1\left(T_1 + \frac{b_1}{4R_1}\right) + \frac{1}{2}b_2 + \left(\frac{1}{4}r_1 + \frac{1}{2}r_2\right)(T_4 + T_7), \frac{1}{4}r_1 + \frac{1}{2}r_2} \tag{5}$$

Step 4.3: ESC of tag flow derivation. The ESC for f_{11} of $f_{\langle 1,8\rangle}$ can be derived as follows,

$$\beta_{(1,8)}^{f_{11},eq} = \beta_1^{f_{11},eq} \otimes \beta_2^{f_{11},eq} \otimes \beta_{(5,8)}^{f_{11},eq} \tag{6}$$

where $\beta_1^{f_{11},eq} = \beta_1$, $\beta_2^{f_{11},eq} = \beta_2$. And $\beta_{(5,8)}^{f_{11},eq}$ can be calculated in the following way,

$$
\begin{aligned}
\beta_{(5,8)}^{f_{11},eq} &= \epsilon(\beta_{(5,8)}^{\{f_{11},f_{12},f_{21}\},eq}, \alpha_5^{\{f_{12},f_{21}\}}) \\
&= \epsilon(\beta_5 \otimes \beta_8^{\{f_{11},f_{12},f_{21}\},eq}, \alpha_5^{\{f_{12},f_{21}\}}) \\
&= \epsilon(\beta_5 \otimes (\epsilon(\beta_8, \alpha_8^{\{f_{13},f_{22}\}})), \alpha_5^{\{f_{12},f_{21}\}})
\end{aligned} \tag{7}
$$

After several intermediate steps, finally,

$$
\begin{aligned}
R_{(1,8)}^{f_{11},eq} &= R_1 \wedge R_2 \wedge \\
&\left(\left(R_8 - \left(\frac{1}{4}r_1 + \frac{1}{2}r_2\right)\right) \wedge R_5 - \left(\frac{1}{4}r_1 + \frac{1}{2}r_2\right)\right) \\
T_{(1,8)}^{f_{11},eq} &= T_1 + T_2 + T_5 + T_8 + \\
&\frac{\frac{1}{4}b_1 + \frac{1}{4}r_1\left(T_1 + \frac{b_1}{4R_1}\right) + \frac{1}{2}b_2 + \left(\frac{1}{4}r_1 + \frac{1}{2}r_2\right)(T_4 + T_7)}{R_8} \\
&+ \frac{\frac{1}{4}b_1 + \frac{1}{4}r_1\left(T_1 + \frac{b_1}{4R_1}\right) + \frac{1}{2}b_2 + \left(\frac{1}{4}r_1 + \frac{1}{2}r_2\right)T_4}{\left(R_8 - \left(\frac{1}{4}r_1 + \frac{1}{2}r_2\right)\right) \wedge R_5}
\end{aligned} \tag{8}
$$

Step 5: Delay bound calculation for sub-flow. Then based on Equation 1, we get the delay bound of f_{11} as follows,

$$
\begin{aligned}
D_{11} = &\frac{\frac{1}{2}b_1}{R_1 \wedge R_2 \wedge \left(\left(R_8 - \left(\frac{1}{4}r_1 + \frac{1}{2}r_2\right)\right) \wedge R_5 - \left(\frac{1}{4}r_1 + \frac{1}{2}r_2\right)\right)} \\
&+ T_1 + T_2 + T_5 + T_8 \\
&+ \frac{\frac{1}{4}b_1 + \frac{1}{4}r_1\left(T_1 + \frac{b_1}{4R_1}\right) + \frac{1}{2}b_2 + \left(\frac{1}{4}r_1 + \frac{1}{2}r_2\right)(T_4 + T_7)}{R_8} \\
&+ \frac{\frac{1}{4}b_1 + \frac{1}{4}r_1\left(T_1 + \frac{b_1}{4R_1}\right) + \frac{1}{2}b_2 + \left(\frac{1}{4}r_1 + \frac{1}{2}r_2\right)T_4}{\left(R_8 - \left(\frac{1}{4}r_1 + \frac{1}{2}r_2\right)\right) \wedge R_5}
\end{aligned} \tag{9}
$$

Step 6: Delay bound calculation for tag flow. Recursively executing the above five steps, we can get the delay bounds D_{12} and D_{13} for sub-flow f_{12} and f_{13}. By comparing D_{11}, D_{12} and D_{13}, we choose the biggest one as the delay bound $\bar{D}$ for tag flow $f_{\langle 1,8 \rangle}$.

4.3 The Analysis Algorithm

We summarize the delay bound derivation procedure in Algorithm 1. Line 1 to line 3 correspond to steps 1-3 above. We calculate the ESC from line 4 to 19. The maximum delay for every split tag flow can be obtained at line 20.

The key steps lie in the ESC derivation. It contains three sub-steps. Firstly, we identify each contention flow $f_{[a,b]}$ and classify using function $ClassifyConFlow(FlowSet)$, whether it is only a single flow or a congregate flow or not. Secondly, we calculate the arrival curve of $f_{[a,b]}$. Note that in this situation, $f_{[a,b]}$ may become a new tag flow to calculate its ESC. Thirdly, we calculate the ESC of one of the original tag flows. Here we adopt the contention flow classification method in [15], that is, cross contention, nested contention and parallel contention. For cross contention, we first cut the contention flow at the first point, and then calculate the arrival curve of the new cut flow at the cutting point. Finally, we complete the cross contention case by merging the cut flows into the existing contention flow. For the other two cases, we can obtain the related ESC using function $ESCNoCrossCon(f_{[a,b]}, ACSet)$. After we have obtained the ESC for a given split tag flow, we can derive the delay bound using Eq. (1). By recursively repeating the procedure and calculating all the delays of all the split tag flows, we can get the maximum value as the worst-case delay bound $\bar{D}$ using traffic splitting.

Algorithm 1 Delay Bound Calculation Algorithm

Require: NoC with router service $\beta_{R_j,T_j} = R_j(t - T_j)^+, 1 \leq j \leq X * Y$, tag flow and contention flows $f\langle m_i, n_i \rangle$ with (r_i, b_i), $1 \leq i \leq FlowNum$
Ensure: determine Delay bound $D(f_{tag}\langle m_t, n_t \rangle)$
1: Identify every sub-flow with full traffic splitting;
2: Calculate the path proportion of every sub-flow $P(f_{kl})$;
3: Calculate the split parameters $Para(f_{kl}) = (P(f_{kl}) \times r_k, P(f_{kl}) \times b_k)$
4: **for all** sub-flows $f_{kl} \in \{SplitTagFlowSet\}$ **do**
5: $ESC(f_{kl})$ // Calculate the equivalent service curve
6: {
7: NodeSet() // List all the nodes across by f_{kl}
8: $CClassSet = ClassifyConFlow(f_i)$ // Classify contention flows through NodeSet
9: **for all** $f_{[a,b]} \in CClassSet$ **do**
10: $ACSet = AC(f_{[a,b]})$ //Arrival curve of contention flows
11: **if** CrossContention **then**
12: Cut all cross-contention flows // For Cross contention
13: $ACSet = AC\_CrossCon(f_{[a,b]}, ACSet)$ // Calculate arrive curves of cutting flows at cutting points
14: Merge flows with the same class
15: **else**
16: $ESC = ESCNoCrossCon(f_{[a,b]}, ACSet)$ // Parallel contention and nested contention
17: **end if**
18: **end for**
19: }
20: $\bar{D} = max(Delay(f_{kl}, ESC, Para(f_{kl})))$
21: **end for**

4.4 Complexity Analysis

We assume that the maximum number of nodes that sub-flow f_{kl} goes through is j. In order to calculate the equivalence service curve for f_{kl}, we have to cut the flows into a form $f_{\langle a,b \rangle}$, where a is the source router node and b the destination. Then the maximum number of such kinds of flows is $j * (j+1)/2$. So the maximum executing time will be $j * (j+1)/2$ for line 9 in Algorithm 1. Let the maximum number of nodes for all the traffic flows be n (including tag flow and contention flows), then the time complexity of computing ESC for each sub-flow is $O((\frac{j*(j+1)}{2})^n)$. Let m be the sub-flow number for tag flow after traffic splitting, then the complexity for the delay bound calculation is $O(m(\frac{j*(j+1)}{2})^n)$.

5. NON-UNIFORM TRAFFIC SPLITTING

Constraining traffic splitting can not only avoid over-splitting but also reduce the algorithm complexity. We use a non-uniform approach, exploiting the network congestion information through a *contention matrix*. In the following, we first introduce the contention matrix, and then present two non-uniform traffic splitting strategies.

5.1 Contention matrix

5.1.1 *Definitions*

We define the contention matrix to capture the contention state of a given application on NoC with a base deterministic routing. Before that, we give related definitions first.

Definition 1: Given a 2-D NoC that can be represented in a weighted directed graph $G = (V, E)$, whose adjacent matrix is $A = (a_{ij})_{\nu \times \nu}$, we call A is G' adjacent matrix if:

$$a_{ij} = \begin{cases} p_{ij}, & \text{if } (v_i, v_j) \in E, \text{ where } p_{ij} \text{ is the traffic splitting} \\ & \text{proportion from node } i \text{ to node } j \\ 0, & \text{else} \end{cases} \tag{10}$$

Definition 2: Logic AND of the adjacent matrix.

Let $\mathbf{A} = \begin{bmatrix} a_{11} & a_{12} \\ a_{21} & a_{22} \end{bmatrix}, \mathbf{B} = \begin{bmatrix} b_{11} & b_{12} \\ b_{21} & b_{22} \end{bmatrix}$, of which $a_{ij} \in \{R^+, 0\}$, $b_{ij} \in \{0, 1\}$. Define:

$$\mathbf{A}\&\mathbf{B} = \begin{bmatrix} a_{11}\&b_{11} & a_{12}\&b_{12} \\ a_{21}\&b_{21} & a_{22}\&b_{22} \end{bmatrix} \tag{11}$$

of which & is the logic AND defined as follows,

$$a\&b = \begin{cases} a & b = 1; \\ 0 & b = 0. \end{cases}$$

Definition 3: Contention matrix.

Assume a $m \times n$ 2-D NoC, there exists multiple traffic flows $f_{s_1,d_1}, f_{s_2,d_2} \cdots f_{s_k,d_k}$, where $f_{s_i,d_i} (1 \le i \le k)$ represents the flow from source node s_i to destination node d_i, and each flow has an adjacent matrix $A_{s_1,d_1}, A_{s_2,d_2} \cdots A_{s_k,d_k}$. The contention matrix for flow f_{s_i,d_i} can be derived as follows,

$$C_{s_i,d_i} = (A_{s_1,d_1} + A_{s_2,d_2} + \cdots + A_{s_k,d_k}) \\ \& A_{s_i,d_i} - A_{s_i,d_i}$$

For simplicity,

$$C_{s_i,d_i} = (A_{s_1,d_1} + A_{s_2,d_2} + \cdots + A_{s_k,d_k}) \\ \& A_{s_i,d_i}, i \neq k. \tag{12}$$

Note that our definition of contention matrix denotes the link contention between routing nodes. Ogras and Marculescu also proposed a contention matrix [12], whose element is defined as the forwarding probability. This is different from ours. Firstly, the element in our contention matrix is defined as the traffic splitting proportion for deterministic multi-path or single-path routing. If all the elements are valued either 0 or 1, it is single-path routing. Otherwise it is multi-path routing with traffic splitting. Secondly, our contention matrix is defined from the adjacent matrix of a graph, it can denote the contention state directly for all links. But their definition is based on the local links for one router. Finally, we define the contention matrix derivation method for any tag flow. This makes it easy to distinguish the tag flow from contention flows.

5.1.2 *Contention speculation*

Again, take Figure 1 as an example. Assuming the XY routing, the contention matrix $C^{12}_{1,8}$ for sub-flow f_{12} can be written as follows,

$$\begin{bmatrix} 0 & 0 & 0 & 0.5 & 0 & 0 & 0 & 0 & 0 \\ 0 & 0 & 0 & 0 & 0 & 0 & 0 & 0 & 0 \\ 0 & 0 & 0 & 0 & 0 & 0 & 0 & 0 & 0 \\ 0 & 0 & 0 & 0 & 0.5 & 0 & 0 & 0 & 0 \\ 0 & 0 & 0 & 0 & 0 & 0 & 0 & 2 & 0 \\ 0 & 0 & 0 & 0 & 0 & 0 & 0 & 0 & 0 \\ 0 & 0 & 0 & 0 & 0 & 0 & 0 & 0 & 0 \\ 0 & 0 & 0 & 0 & 0 & 0 & 0 & 0 & 0 \\ 0 & 0 & 0 & 0 & 0 & 0 & 0 & 0 & 0 \end{bmatrix}$$

As described above, the contention matrix can represent link and flow contention state. Seen from Figure 1, for sub-flow f_{12}, there are three links: $1 \to 4$, $4 \to 5$ and $5 \to 8$. For link $1 \to 4$, it has contention from sub-flow f_{13} with traffic splitting proportion 0.5. Sub-flow f_{21} has contention at link $4 \to 5$ with 0.5. Sub-flow f_{11} and f_{21} have link contention at $5 \to 8$. This is exactly reflected in the contention matrix, with $C^{12}_{1,8}[1,4] = 0.5$, $C^{12}_{1,8}[4,5] = 0.5$ and $C^{12}_{1,8}[5,8] = 2$.

The contention state for all the sub-flows after traffic splitting can also be represented. Again with Figure 1, let $f_{\langle 1,8 \rangle}$ be the tag flow, so there is contention flow $f_{\langle 4,8 \rangle}$. After traffic splitting, the contention matrix for $f_{\langle 1,8 \rangle}$ is as follows,

$$\begin{bmatrix} 0 & 0 & 0 & 0 & 0 & 0 & 0 & 0 & 0 \\ 0 & 0 & 0 & 0 & 0 & 0 & 0 & 0 & 0 \\ 0 & 0 & 0 & 0 & 0 & 0 & 0 & 0 & 0 \\ 0 & 0 & 0 & 0 & 0.5 & 0 & 0.5 & 0 & 0 \\ 0 & 0 & 0 & 0 & 0 & 0 & 0 & 1 & 0 \\ 0 & 0 & 0 & 0 & 0 & 0 & 0 & 0 & 0 \\ 0 & 0 & 0 & 0 & 0 & 0 & 0 & 1 & 0 \\ 0 & 0 & 0 & 0 & 0 & 0 & 0 & 0 & 0 \\ 0 & 0 & 0 & 0 & 0 & 0 & 0 & 0 & 0 \end{bmatrix}$$

This contention matrix also exactly reflects the contention state by the contention flow $f_{4,8}$, which has contention at link $4 \to 5$, $4 \to 7$, $5 \to 8$ and $7 \to 8$, with proportion of 0.5, 0.5, 1 and 1, respectively.

With such representation of traffic contention, we can identify the most congestion part by analyzing from the task graph directly, and derive the exact congestion state through quantity computing. Furthermore, based on the contention matrix, we can extract the congestion information for non-uniform traffic splitting strategy exploration to improve worst-case performance.

In our approach, we create one contention matrix for each tag flow. In general, a contention matrix may have the size of square of the network size, because we define it by using the adjacent matrix. Also, a contention matrix is a sparse matrix, since the nodes in a 2-D NoC have mostly 4 connections with the adjacent nodes. Those elements that have no connection will be zero. As the network size grows, this will require a lot of memory space. In our implementation, we create a tree data structure for every sub tag flow. When searching the node tandem of a flow, we use the tree structure rather than the contention matrix. This helps to improve the processing speed and reduce the storage space.

5.2 Non-uniform traffic splitting

5.2.1 *Splitting options*

As described early, full traffic splitting may generate too much contention, which may worsen the worst-case delay. In order to overcome this drawback, we propose two non-uniform traffic splitting strategies: *node based* and *flow based*. In *node based traffic splitting*, the proportion of traffic splitting of each direction at every node can be different and flexibly determined by exploiting the contention matrix. In *flow based traffic splitting*, we propose partial traffic splitting strategy by selecting some of the sub-flows as target split flow and restrict other flows from splitting.

5.2.2 Node-based non-uniform splitting

For node based non-uniform traffic splitting, the splitting proportion is set according to the contention matrix. In fact, the matrix has been obtained from the adjacent matrix of the target NoC and every value in the matrix can reflect the possible network congestion. So, to decide the proportion that should be given to the X or Y direction, we can refer to this kind of network congestion state. For example, if the next node has m contention flows in the X direction, and n flows in the Y direction, we can decide the proportion as: $P_x : P_y = n : m$, in which $P_x + P_y = 1$.

Algorithm 2 Non-uniform traffic splitting

Require: contention matrix $ConMatrix$
Ensure: determine $Adapting(ConMatrix)$

```
ConXPro ← ConProX(ConMatrix)
ConYPro ← ConProY(ConMatrix)// Calculate the contention proportion in X and Y direction
if (ConXPro = 0)&(ConYPro = 0) then
    TagXPro ← 0.5
    TagYPro ← 0.5
else if (ConXPro = 0)&(ConYPro ≠ 0) then
    TagXPro ← 1
    TagYPro ← 0
else if (ConXPro ≠ 0)&(ConYPro = 0) then
    TagXPro ← 0
    TagYPro ← 1
else
    TagXPro ← ConYPro / (ConXPro+ConYPro)
    TagYPro ← ConXPro / (ConXPro+ConYPro)
end if
```

The algorithm is shown in Algorithm 2. We first get congestion information from the contention matrix by calculating the congestion proportion of two directions ConXPro and ConYPro. When both of them equal zero, it means that there exits no traffic conflict, thus we assign even proportion to the next two directions. Or when one and only one of them is zero, we assign the full proportion to this direction to avoid congestion as much as possible. When none of them is zero, which means both links have contention, we just invert the congestion proportion to be the traffic splitting proportion. Since the traffic splitting proportion is inverted to be the congestion proportion, it is more likely to split more traffic to the less congestion one, and thus to achieve better worst-case performance.

5.2.3 Flow-based non-uniform splitting

The node based traffic splitting may have some drawbacks. First, it may fall into local optimum since all the traffic split decisions are made on the current next-node information. Second, the earlier traffic splitting nodes may have more powerful impact on the performance of the whole flow. So we propose a flow based traffic splitting that considers the whole flow impact from the contention matrix in a global

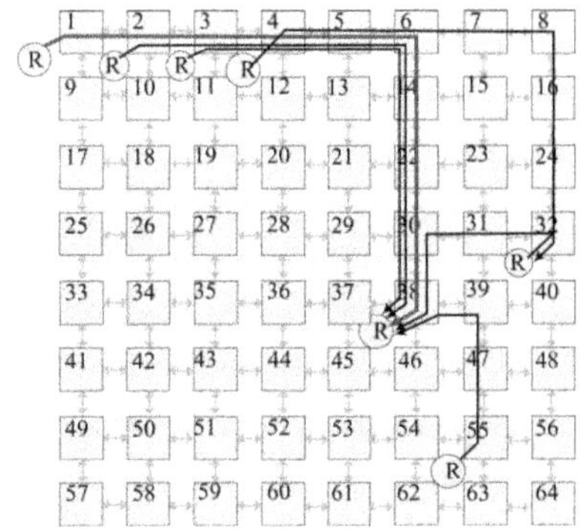

Figure 3: Synthetic communication platform

view to overcome these drawbacks. The basic principle is as follows. First we fully explore the traffic splitting space and give an initial evaluation for every sub-flow. We choose one or more sub-flows with less congestion as the target traffic splitting flows. Then we re-split the traffic using the chosen flows, and only these flows are allowed to transfer packets for the main flow. Thus it may enhance the utilization of the spare routers and achieve higher load balance as well as decreasing the worst-case delay.

This can be easily implemented by setting 0 or 1 to the traffic splitting proportion at different directions of each router. When the proportion is 0, it means that no traffic traverses through this direction. Otherwise, proportion 1 means that the traffic traverses fully through this direction. Thus by switching the traffic splitting proportion to 0 or 1, we can control the main flow be split through the chosen flows.

6. EXPERIMENTS AND RESULTS

The experimental purpose is to verify the effectiveness of the proposed per-flow delay bound analysis technique for multi-path routing, the non-uniform traffic splitting strategy. We experimented with both synthetic communication patterns and an industrial application. Moreover, to verify the correctness of the proposed analysis we conducted simulations using SoCLib [1].

6.1 Analysis with Synthetic Traffic

6.1.1 Setup

To investigate the multi-path traffic splitting effects, we conduct experiments on a 2-D 8×8 mesh NoC. Since our algorithm is parameterized, the network can be of arbitrary size. Although we use the 2-D mesh as the experimental platform, our approach is topology independent, because any network topology can be represented as adjacent matrix and we can speculate the network congestion state.

We set up the following experimental platform shown in Figure 3. There are 6 flows altogether, and we set flow $f_{\langle 1,38 \rangle}$ as tag flow, so the others are all contention flows. All input flows have arrival curve of $\alpha(t) = 0.2t + 2$, which means that two packets are generated in every ten cycles with the burstiness of two packets. All the router nodes use a FCFS policy and have the service capability of $\beta(t) = \delta \otimes \gamma_{0,1}(t) = 1 \cdot (t-2)^+$, and this means that every router can forward one packet per cycle with a delay of two cycles. The router uses first-come-first-served arbitration scheme.

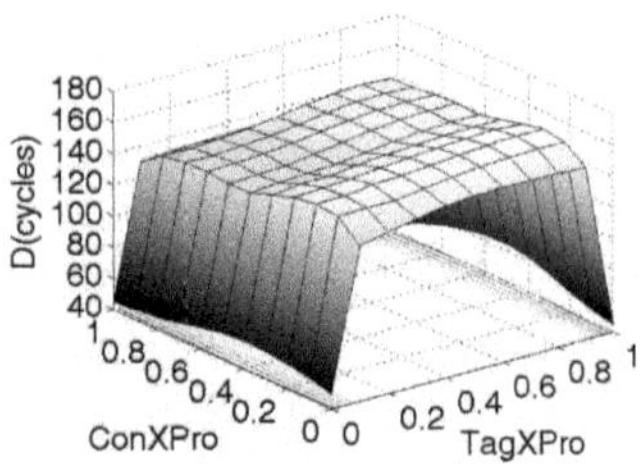

Figure 4: Delay bounds for uniform traffic splitting

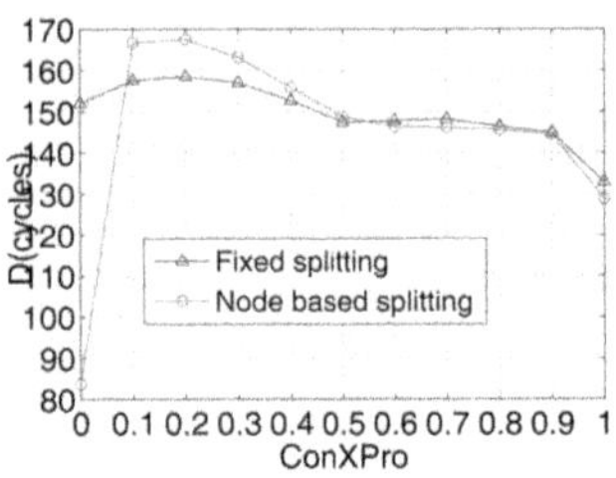

Figure 5: Delay bound comparison between uniform splitting and node based non-uniform traffic splitting

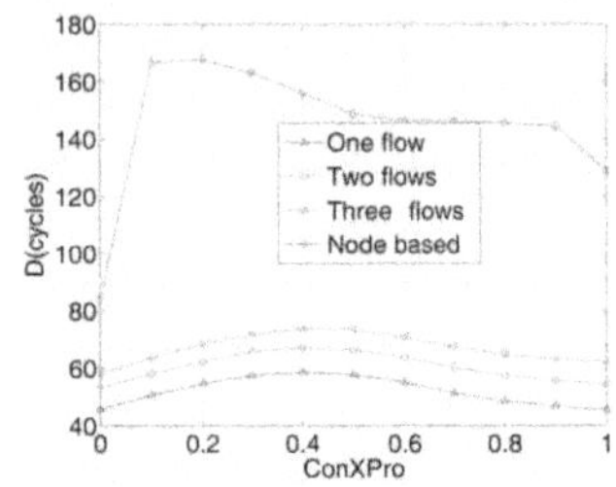

Figure 6: Delay bound comparison between node based and flow based non-uniform traffic splitting

6.1.2 Splitting effect

In order to verify the multi-flow effects, we first set traffic splitting proportion of both tag flow and contention flows to a fixed value to get the related delay bounds, and then vary the proportion in the X axis from 0 to 1. The results are shown in Figure 4. In this figure, TagXPro means the traffic splitting proportion of the tag flow on the X axis, and ConXPro represents that of contention flows. The result is obtained using full traffic splitting. When TagXPro or ConXPro is 0, it is actually the YX routing without traffic splitting. But when $0 \leq TagXPro \leq 1$, the delay bounds are increased. This is because the number of splitting sub-flows is greatly increased when the tag flow or contention flows are split. Take the tag flow for example, there are 126 sub-flows using full traffic splitting. These sub-flows worsen the contention status, resulting in the increased delay bounds.

6.1.3 Exploration of splitting strategy

In order to avoid this kind of side effects, we improve the traffic splitting strategy using non-uniform traffic splitting, which has two variants, node based and flow based. As described before, the node based non-uniform traffic splitting can adjust the flow amount according to the speculated network congestion state. From Figure 5 we can see that the delay has been decreased when $0.5 < ConXPro \leq 1$ or $ConXPro = 0$. The maximum improvement is 44.9% when ConXPro is zero.

But when $0 < ConXPro \leq 0.5$, the delay bound of the node based non-uniform traffic splitting gets worse. This is because more flows are injected into the congesting nodes. This also reflects the drawback of the node based non-uniform traffic splitting. Although the traffic can be split according to the congestion state of the next two nodes, the decision is made based on the current node and is easy to fall into local optimum, which may not be globally optimal.

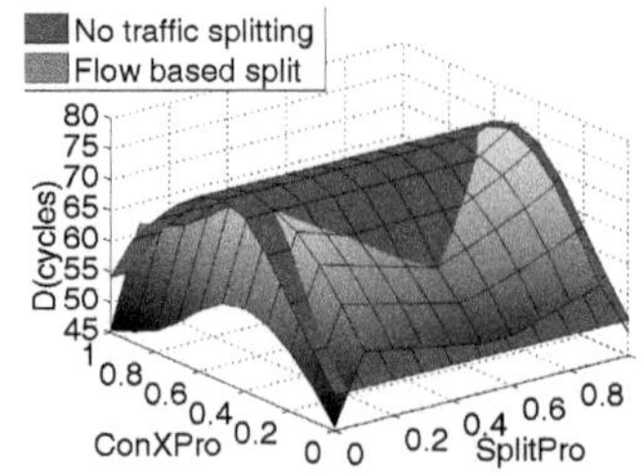

Figure 7: Delay bound comparison between non-traffic-splitting and flow based non-uniform traffic splitting

We also tried the flow based non-uniform traffic splitting. We first fully explored the traffic splitting space, and then computed the globally optimal flows, and chose several flows as the tag flows for traffic splitting. We first chose three flows (flow numbers are 70, 125 and 126), and prohibited all other flows from splitting. These three flows have even splitting traffic proportion. Then we did experiments with three to one flow cases. The experimental results are compared with the node based traffic splitting in Figure 6. We can see that the delay bounds are greatly decreased with a maximum improvement of 61.8%, 65.1% and 69.3% for three-flow case, two-flow case and one-flow case, respectively.

Finally, we compared the delay bounds of no-splitting with the flow based non-uniform traffic splitting. The results are shown in Figure 7. The gray part is the single flow without traffic splitting, still with the contention flow splitting proportion varying from 0 to 1. In order to have a clear picture of the comparison results, we drew a curved surface on the top but, actually, the tag flow has no traffic splitting. The colored part is the delay bound with the flow based non-uniform traffic splitting using two flows. The results show that when the traffic is not so well balanced (TagXPro near 0 or 1), the delay bound is worse than the no traffic splitting cases. But as the tag flows are in a better balanced condition (TagXPro is near 0.5), the flow based non-uniform splitting has better delay than the no traffic splitting case. When the contention flow also has well balanced traffic splitting, the maximum improvement can reach up to 28.5%.

6.2 Simulation with Synthetic Traffic

6.2.1 Setup

We use SoCLib [1] to realize a cycle-accurate simulation platform for the 2-D 8x8 mesh NoC in Figure 3. The network performs wormhole switching with buffered flow control. Each router guarantees the service curve of $\beta(t) = 1 \cdot (t-2)^+$ and uses the packet-by-packet round-robin scheme for link scheduling. We assume no link wire delay.

The simulation experiments are carried out using synthetic traffic used in the analytical calculation of the bounds. Moreover, every value is obtained through a simulation process of almost 10^8 cycles to guarantee an appropriate exploration of the network with all the possible splitting ratios.

6.2.2 Simulation results

In Figure 8 we present detailed simulation results for one basic network configuration without traffic splitting in which both TagXPro and ConXPro equal to 0. The figure plots the packet delay for a sequence of 10^3 packets that includes the worst case delay. The delay bound is represented as a

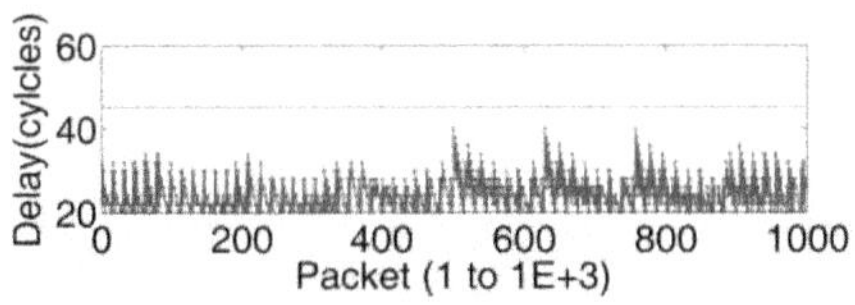

Figure 8: Comparison between the basic analysis results and simulation records

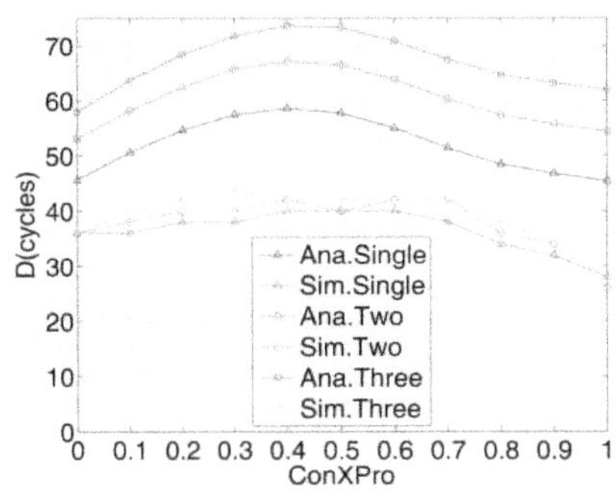

Figure 9: Analysis results and simulation results for flow based non-uniform traffic splitting

red straight line. We can see that the simulated delays are totally constrained by the calculated delay bound proving the correctness of the analysis.

Furthermore, we performed simulation analysis on the flow-based traffic splitting approach which showed the greatest performances in the analytical experiment. As illustrated in Figure 9 the behavior of the single, two and three flows cases is similar to the one obtained with the analytical bounds. The single-flow case still shows the best performance, while the two-flow case curve is constrained by the other two cases. Moreover, this figure can be analyzed from other three aspects: (1) All the simulation values are constrained by the bounds and thus correct. (2) The time difference for obtaining the results between the analytical bounds and the simulation values is huge. One single simulation with the traffic splitting strategy requires more than 4 hours to explore adequately the traffic patterns in the network, while the 33 analytical values for flow based non-uniform traffic splitting are obtained in less than 45 seconds. (3) The gap between delay bounds and simulation values exhibits a certain variation with the increment of the splitting proportion value. We think that this is mainly due to the difficulty of finding through simulations the real worst case configuration of the network when the flows have a certain proportion of splitting in every node. In fact, with traffic splitting strategy we can feed hundreds of possible different sub-flows but simulating all the situations would be impossible due to timing constraints and is hard to detect the worst case. As stressed in [13], this underlines the importance of our research into analytical methods for evaluating NoC performance and QoS.

6.3 Industry case analysis

6.3.1 The application

We use the Ericsson Radio System application [8] as an example to verify the effectiveness of the proposed non-uniform traffic splitting method, as shown in Figure 10. Node 5, 6, 7, 10, 14 and 15 are ASICs, node 1, 2, 3, 8, 11 and 16 are

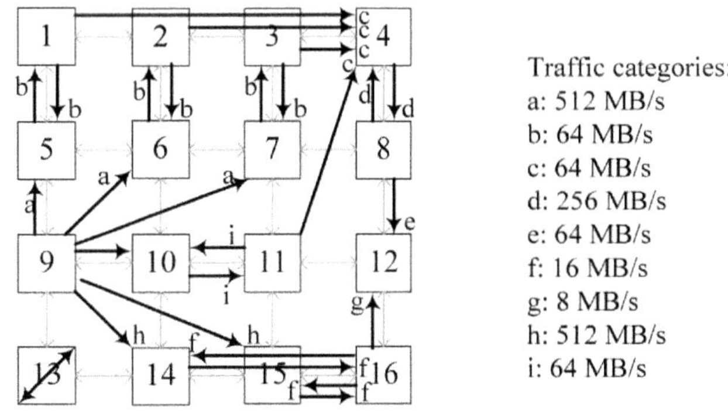

Figure 10: Ericsson radio system example

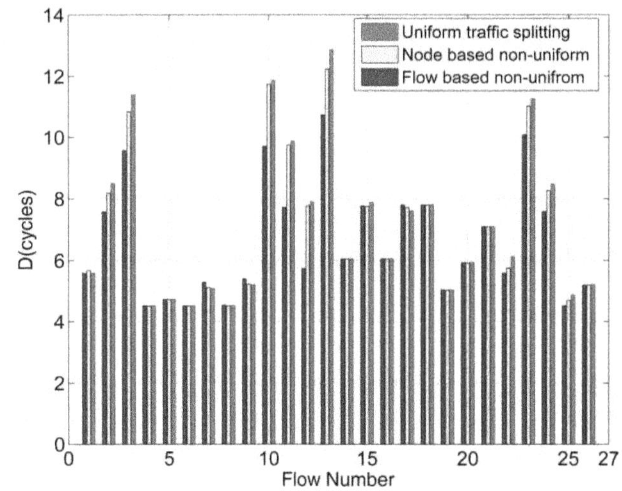

Figure 11: Delay bound comparison between uniform, node based non-uniform and flow based non-uniform traffic splitting

DSP, node 4, 9, 12 are FPGA, and node 13 is a device processor that initiates the data transmission and control the normal operations. There are 26 dedicated flows altogether, and they can be classified into 9 categories in terms of bandwidth requirements represented as $\{a, b, c, d, e, f, g, h, i\}$. We characterize flows according to their bandwidth requirement and set their burstiness to be 128 bits.

We treat each of the 26 flows as a tag flow one by one. For some of the flows ($f_{\langle 9,6\rangle}, f_{\langle 9,7\rangle}, f_{\langle 9,15\rangle}, f_{\langle 9,14\rangle}, f_{\langle 11,4\rangle}$), the delay bounds become worse as the traffic splitting proportion is not 0 or 1. The reason is just the same as with the synthetic communication pattern described above, because the contention state is getting worse as the split sub-flows are greatly increased. But there are still some flows that have no change or minor change in delay bound. For example, flow $f_{\langle 5,1\rangle}, f_{\langle 6,2\rangle}, f_{\langle 4,8\rangle}, f_{\langle 8,12\rangle}$ and $f_{\langle 16,12\rangle}$. This is because these flows are routed through a single link. Their traffic is not split and there is no influence from other flows.

6.3.2 Performance with traffic splitting

We performed both the node based and flow based non-uniform traffic splitting on the application. The results are shown in Figure 11. The red bars represent the delay bounds of all the 26 flows with the full uniform traffic splitting. The yellow bars are with the node based non-uniform traffic splitting and the blue bars are with the flow based method. The node based non-uniform splitting method has a maximum improvement of 6.0% in delay bound against the uniform traffic splitting. The flow based non-uniform traffic splitting achieves more improvement with an average improvement of 6.2% and a maximum of 27.3%.

7. CONCLUSION

Based on network calculus, we have analyzed the per-flow worst-case delay bound with multi-path minimal routing on 2-D mesh NoCs. We first present a per-flow delay bound analysis technique for multi-path routing, which extends the analysis method for deterministic routing but deals with complicated traffic splitting. Then we define a contention matrix to capture network contention status. Based on the contention matrix, we propose effective non-uniform traffic splitting to improve the worst-case network performance with two different strategies, node based and flow based non-uniform traffic splitting. Experiments with synthetic traffic flows and an industrial case verify the effectiveness of the non-uniform traffic splitting techniques and the selection algorithm. Experimental results show that with synthetic communication traffic, it has a maximum of 44.9% improvement with the node based non-uniform traffic splitting against full uniform splitting, and a maximum of 69.3% improvement for the flow based non-uniform traffic splitting. The industrial example shows that the flow based method achieves a maximum improvement of 27.3% against the uniform traffic splitting. Finally, through comparing analysis results against simulation results, we validate the correctness of our analysis and the performance optimizing behavior of flow based non-uniform traffic splitting.

In future work, we will extend our research to three dimensional NoCs using multi-path minimal routing. We will analyze the worst case performance with special focus on the Through Silicon Vias (TSV) based asymmetric communication links.

8. ACKNOWLEDGMENTS

The project is sponsored in part by Intel Corporation through a research gift, National Nature Science Foundation of China (Grant No. 61106020, 61006024 and 61106038) and Doctoral Fund of Ministry of Education of China (Grant No. 20100111120009).

9. REFERENCES

[1] Soclib simulation environment. On-line, available at http://soclib.lip6.fr/.

[2] M. Bakhouya, S. Suboh, J. Gaber, T. A. El-Ghazawi, and S. Niar. Performance evaluation and design tradeoffs of on-chip interconnect architectures. *Simulation Modelling Practice and Theory*, 19(6):1496–1505, 2011.

[3] C.-S. Chang. *Performance Guarantees in Communication Networks*. Springer-Verlag, 2000.

[4] R. L. Cruz. A calculus for network delay, part I: Network elements in isolation. *IEEE Transactions on Information Theory*, 37(1):114–131, January 1991.

[5] Y. Jiao, Y. Yang, M. He, M. Yang, and Y. Jiang. Multi-path routing for mesh/torus-based NoCs. In *Fourth International Conference on Information Technology.*, pages 734–742, Apr. 2007.

[6] J.-Y. Le Boudec and P. Thiran. *Network Calculus: A Theory of Deterministic Queuing Systems for the Internet.* Number 2050 in LNCS, Springer-Verlag, 2004.

[7] L. Lenzini, L. Martorini, E. Mingozzi, and G. Stea. Tight end-to-end per-flow delay bounds in fifo multiplexing sink-tree networks. *Perform. Eval.*, 63(9-10):956–987, 2006.

[8] Z. Lu and A. Jantsch. TDM virtual-circuit configuration for network-on-chip. *IEEE Transactions on Very Large Scale Integration (VLSI) Systems*, 16(8):1021–1034, Aug. 2008.

[9] Z. Lu, M. Millberg, A. Jantsch, A. Bruce, P. van der Wolf, and T. Henriksson. Flow regulation for on-chip communication. In *Design, Automation & Test in Europe Conference & Exhibition.*, pages 578–581. IEEE, Apr. 2009.

[10] S. Murali, D. Atienza, L. Benini, and G. De Micheli. A multi-path routing strategy with guaranteed in-order packet delivery and fault-tolerance for networks on chip. In *43rd ACM/IEEE Design Automation Conference*, pages 845–848. IEEE, 2006.

[11] S. Murali, D. Atienza, L. Benini, and G. De Micheli. A method for routing packets across multiple paths in NoCs with in-order delivery and fault-tolerance gaurantees. *VLSI Design*, 2007:1–11, 2007.

[12] U. Y. Ogras and R. Marculescu. Analytical router modeling for networks-on-chip performance analysis. In *Proceedings of the conference on Design, Automation and Test in Europe*, 2007.

[13] J. Owens, W. Dally, R. Ho, D. Jayasimha, S. Keckler, and L.-S. Peh. Research challenges for on-chip interconnection networks. *Micro, IEEE*, 27(5):96 –108, sept.-oct. 2007.

[14] Y. Qian, Z. Lu, and W. Dou. Analysis of worst-case delay bounds for best-effort communication in wormhole networks on chip. In *Proceedings of the 3rd ACM/IEEE International Symposium on Networks-on-Chip*, pages 44–53, San Diego, CA, May 2009.

[15] Y. Qian, Z. Lu, and W. Dou. Analysis of worst-case delay bounds for on-chip packet-switching networks. *IEEE Transactions on Computer-Aided Design of Integrated Circuits and Systems (TCAD)*, 29(5):802 – 815, May 2010.

[16] Y. Qian, Z. Lu, W. Dou, and Q. Dou. Analyzing credit-based router-to-router flow control for on-chip networks. *IEICE Transactions on Electronics, Special Section on "Hardware and Software Technologies on Advanced Microprocessors"*, E92-C(10):1276–1283, Oct. 2009.

[17] R. Stefan and K. Goossens. A TDM slot allocation flow based on multipath routing in NoCs. *Microprocessors and Microsystems*, 35(2):130–138, 2011.

[18] E. Wandeler, L. Thiele, M. Verhoef, and P. Lieverse. System architecture evaluation using modular performance analysis - a case study. *Software Tools for Technology Transfer (STTT)*, 8(6):649–667, October 2006.

HyCoS: Hybrid Compiled Simulation of Embedded Software with Target Dependent Code

Zhonglei Wang, Jörg Henkel
Karlsruhe Institute of Technology, Chair for Embedded Sytems
Haid-Und-Neu-Str. 7, 76131 Karlsruhe, Germany
{zhonglei.wang, henkel}@kit.edu

ABSTRACT

Source-Level Simulation (SLS) has become a de-facto standard technique for fast simulation of embedded software. The basic idea of SLS is to generate software simulation models by annotating low-level timing information into application source code. The obtained source-level simulation models provide a good alternative to traditional Instruction Set Simulators (ISS) for system-level design space exploration of complex embedded systems.

However, the generation of source-level simulation models requires the source code to be available, and therefore, it is not applicable to software that contains target dependent code (e.g. inline assembler and pre-compiled library functions). Since target dependent code is often used in embedded software development, this problem strongly limits the applicability of SLS. To overcome this limitation, we propose for the first time a novel hybrid compiled simulation approach called *HyCoS* that takes advantage of SLS and provides support for target dependent code by incorporating an instruction-level compiled simulation technique. A major challenge to be addressed in the hybrid simulation is the implementation of synchronization and communication between code simulated at different abstraction levels, in order to achieve functional correctness. In addition, it is also crucial to improve estimation accuracy. In this paper we present novel methods for these goals. Experimental results show that, compared to an ISS, HyCoS achieves an average simulation speed of 464 MIPS on a normal desktop computer, 128.0x faster than a standard ISS while achieving comparable accuracy. Even in comparison to fast instruction-level compiled simulation, it also achieves a speedup of up to 4.2x. We also use a multimedia application to demonstrate the efficiency of our approach that is especially beneficial in complex multiprocessor simulation.

Categories and Subject Descriptors

I.6.5 [**Computing Methodologies**]: Simulation and Modeling—*Model Development*

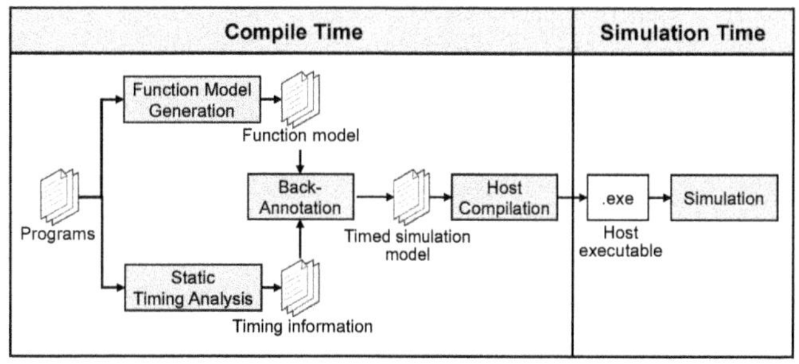

Figure 1: Standard Compiled Simulation

General Terms

Design, Performance

Keywords

Hybrid compiled simulation, source-level simulation, system level design, embedded systems

1. INTRODUCTION

Today's embedded applications often involve a large set of software tasks running on parallel hardware platforms such as Multiprocessor System-on-Chips (MPSoC). The large complexity of embedded systems places great demand for novel simulation techniques to support fast and accurate design space exploration. The traditional Instruction Set Simulator (ISS) based simulation methods, despite some advances, are too slow for comprehensive system-level exploration in an early design phase.

Over the past decade, *compiled simulation* techniques, which achieve significant speedups compared to ISSs, have been increasingly used for software simulation and provide an alternative to ISSs. The idea of compiled simulation is to move some time-consuming operations (e.g. instruction decoding and timing analysis) from simulation time to compile time. A one-time effort required at compile time can avoid repetition of these operations at runtime.

A general approach of compiled simulation is illustrated in Figure 1. As shown, the whole approach consists of two phases: a compile-time phase for generation of simulation models and a simulation-time phase. To generate a compiled simulation model, three issues need to be addressed: function model generation for each program, timing analysis, and back-annotation of the obtained timing information into the function model. According to the representation level of the program where the function model is generated, compiled simulation can be categorized into source-level simulation, intermediate representation (IR) level simulation and instruction-level (or binary-level) simulation [24]. To obtain accurate timing information, the timing analysis should be performed on binary code, by means of a performance model that takes all important timing effects of the target processor into account, such as pipeline effects, cache effects and branch prediction effects. Finally, the obtained timing information is annotated into the function model by relating the binary code and the basic entities of the function model.

Among these compiled simulation techniques, Source-Level Simulation (SLS), due to its very high simulation performance, has gained increasing attention in recent years. It uses source code directly as function model and accurate timing information obtained at compile time is annotated into the source code. In addition to high simulation performance, another advantage of SLS is that the performance statistics can be related to source-level entities and can directly guide the programmer to optimize the algorithms at source level.

However, to make SLS capable of replacing ISSs for software simulation of practical applications, two major challenges need to be overcome. First of all, it is difficult to accurately model low-level timing effects, such as pipeline effects, cache effects and branch predictor effects, in source code. Approximation made for some important timing effects will cause simulation errors. Second, the back-annotation of timing information relies on the mapping between source code and binary code. Since the compiler will heavily alter the code structure during the optimizing compilation, it will make it problematic to find the source-level counterparts of some binary code. This will lead to wrong back-annotation of the timing information of these binary code and may introduce large inaccuracies. In recent years, a large body of previous work deals with the two challenges to improve the simulation accuracy of SLS (see Section 2). With these advances, SLS can achieve simulation accuracy close to ISSs, as shown in the experimental results in many publications [10, 20, 21, 23, 24]. **Nevertheless, SLS still has a large problem that it is not applicable to programs containing target dependent code, such as inline assembler, standard library functions and pre-compiled third party code, which are often used in embedded application development.** This strongly limits the applicability of SLS.

To overcome this limitation of SLS, in this paper, we propose **for the first time** a hybrid compiled simulation approach, called HyCoS, which provides support for target dependent code by employing Instruction-Level compiled Simulation (ILS). We developed a SLS approach that allows for very fast AND very accurate simulation of the available source code. HyCoS employs this SLS approach as the main simulation engine and control is switched to ILS only when target dependent code is encountered. Like source-level models, the simulation models generated by HyCoS can also be easily integrated into a SystemC-based simulation environment for simulation of multiprocessor systems.

Summarizing: The **contribution** of this paper is the HyCoS approach that combines the advantages of SLS (high simulation performance, low modeling complexity and support for source-level optimization) and ILS (support for target dependent code) for the first time and allows for fast and accurate simulation of arbitrary programs on a wide range of embedded processors. Novel methods employed in HyCoS for achieving functional correctness and high simulation accuracy are summarized as follows:

- We present an efficient ILS approach for generating well-organized instruction-level simulation code that can be easily combined with source-level simulation code (see Section 4.1).
- To achieve functional correctness of the hybrid simulation, we propose novel methods to implement correct synchronization and communication between the source-level part and the instruction-level part of a simulation model (see Section 4.2 and 4.3).
- We propose a new data cache simulation method to improve simulation accuracy (see Section 4.4).

The rest of this paper is organized as follows: After reviewing related work in Section 2, the concept of source-level simulation is introduced in Section 3. Section 4 presents the details of HyCoS. Experimental results are presented in Section 5. Finally, the paper is concluded in Section 6.

2. RELATED WORK

The conventional way of software simulation is using ISSs. For multiprocessor simulations, a widely used method is to integrate multiple ISSs into a SystemC-based simulation environment [3]. Many simulators are built in this way, including commercial simulators such as Synopsys CoMET [2] and Imperas OVP [1], as well as academic simulation platforms such as MPARM [5] and the M5 simulator [4]. However, such multiprocessor simulations use multiple ISSs running in parallel, and therefore, they are too slow for iterative system-level exploration in early design phases. In addition, complex timing synchronization between ISSs and the SystemC simulation kernel must be handled, as discussed in [9]. Trace-driven simulation [17, 26] is another choice. However, it rules out functional simulation and a set of traces can simulate the workload of only one execution path of a program.

A large body of previous work deals with improving the simulation performance of ISSs by means of hybrid simulation that combines ISSs with compiled simulation [6, 19] or native execution [12, 15]. These approaches are inherently ISS-centric and therefore cannot avoid the disadvantages of ISSs. Hence, the speedup that can be achieved is very limited. The former approaches [6, 19] increase the simulation speed to around 10 MIPS, only 4x faster than the ISSs. The native execution employed in the latter approaches is either fully functional [15] or provides just very approximate timing estimates [12], so that the gain of simulation performance comes at the large expense of accuracy. If a high simulation accuracy is required as in [15] (error within 5%), little code can be simulated by means of native execution and the speedup was only 70% compared to an ISS. In [12], higher simulation speeds are reported (88 MIPS on average), but the simulation error was up to 17.6%. In contrast, our HyCoS can achieve both high simulation speed (464 MIPS on average) and high accuracy (everage error of 1.5%).

Compiled simulation techniques can achieve significant speedups compared to ISSs. Early work focuses on Instruction-Level Simulation (ILS) [14, 27]. However, with the growing complexity of embedded systems, ILS still cannot achieve the desired simulation speed. In recent years, Source-Level Simulation (SLS) has gained great popularity due to its very high simulation speed combined with low modeling complexity [10, 11, 13, 16, 18, 20, 21, 22, 23, 24, 25]. A large body of previous work addresses the two aforementioned challenges to improve the SLS technique. Early work obtains a latency value for each basic block of binary code by means of measurement using an ISS [13]. Such latency values cannot capture the dynamic timing effects such as cache effects and branch predictor effects. It also cancels the advantage of SLS to rely on an ISS. A more efficient approach is to combine static timing analysis for the pipeline effects and dynamic simulation for the cache and branch predictor effects, as proposed in [20, 24]. However, accurate data cache simulation is still problematic at source level, because, unlike instruction cache simulation and branch predictor simulation, where instruction addresses necessary for simulation can be obtained and annotated at compile time, data addresses required for data cache simulation cannot be statically resolved during source code instrumentation. Previous work either considers only memory accesses made by global variables [16] or uses host data addresses [8, 11, 18, 24]. All these methods are not suitable for our hybrid simulation (see Section 4.4 for more discussion). To solve this problem, we propose a method for obtaining target data addresses at source level, as presented in Section 4.4.

To cope with mapping problems caused by compiler optimizations, one solution is to transform source code to Intermediate Representation (IR) code that has an optimized structure close to the binary code structure [11, 24]. Then, timing information is annotated to the IR-level code to generate simulation models. Since IR-level code is hardly readable, this method rules out source-level optimizations. Some recent approaches [21, 23, 25] aim to overcome the mapping problems while still using the original source code as the function model. In [21, 25] only solutions for mapping problems caused by some specific optimizations are proposed, such as code motion [25], loop unrolling and function inlining [21]. In [23] Wang et al. propose a more general solution, which addresses the mapping problems by translating source code to so-called *partly optimized source code.*

Despite these advances, SLS still has a large limitation that it is not applicable to programs containing target dependent code. There is no previous work that addresses this problem yet.

3. SOURCE-LEVEL SIMULATION

We will first explain the basic concepts of SLS and then introduce our HyCoS approach by demonstrating how they apply to the fragment of code as illustrated in Figure 2. In a typical software development process, a program will be represented as source code (Figure 2(a)), intermediate representation (IR) and binary code (Figure 2(b)), for programming, optimizing compilation and final execution on the target processor, respectively. The structure of both source code and binary code can be described as a Control Flow Graph (CFG) as shown in Figure 2(c) and (d), respectively. Each node in a CFG represents a basic block that is a maximal sequence of source code statements or target instructions without any jumps or jump targets in between. Since the binary code is the code which will be finally executed on the target processor, accurate timing information can be obtained only from binary code. For a program with n binary-level basic blocks, the execution time can be expressed by:

$$T = \sum_{i=1}^{n} t_i \times c_i \quad (1)$$

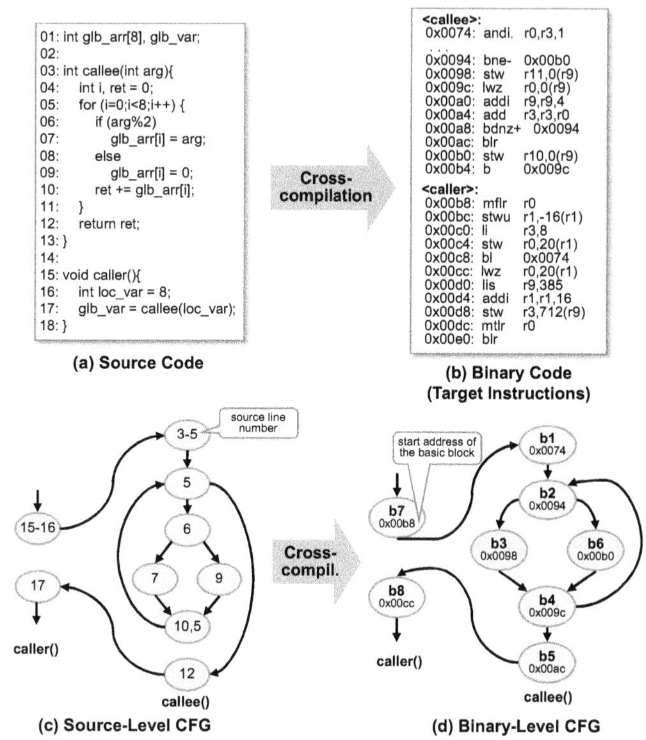

Figure 2: Example Program

where t_i and c_i are execution time and execution count of $i-$th basic block, respectively.

The idea of source-level simulation is to directly use application source code as function model. Since native execution of source code by itself cannot provide estimates of the execution time, annotation of timing information is needed. Therefore, the automatic generation of source-level simulation models consists of three steps: timing analysis, mapping and timing annotation. Timing analysis is aimed to estimate the execution time of each basic block. Accurate timing analysis will obtain t_{est_i} close to t_i ($t_{est_i} \approx t_i$) for $i-$th basic block. Some timing effects such as the pipeline effects can be statically analyzed to avoid repetitive dynamic simulation, while some other timing effects such as the cache and branch prediction effects are highly context-related and therefore must be dynamically simulated. We obtain:

$$t_{est_i} = t_{static_i} + t_{dynamic_i} \quad (2)$$

where t_{static_i} is a constant delay value that accounts for the pipeline effects and $t_{dynamic_i}$ varies at simulation runtime with respect to input data and processor states.

The back-annotation of timing information relies on the mapping between binary code and source code. The mapping can formally be expressed by a function $m : \mathbf{B} \mapsto \mathbf{L}$, where the set $\mathbf{B}$ ($\mathbf{B} = \{b_1, b_2, \cdots, b_n\}$) contains all n basic blocks of a program and $\mathbf{L}$ is a set of source lines. We obtain the mapping information $\mathbf{M}$:

$$\mathbf{M} = \{(b_i, \ell_i) \mid b_i \in \mathbf{B},\ \ell_i \in \mathbf{L},\ \ell_i = m(b_i),\ 1 \le i \le n\} \quad (3)$$

Each tuple (b_i, ℓ_i) indicates that b_i is mapped to the source line ℓ_i. In other words, the timing information of b_i should be annotated before or after ℓ_i. Multiple different basic blocks may be mapped to the same source line. This means

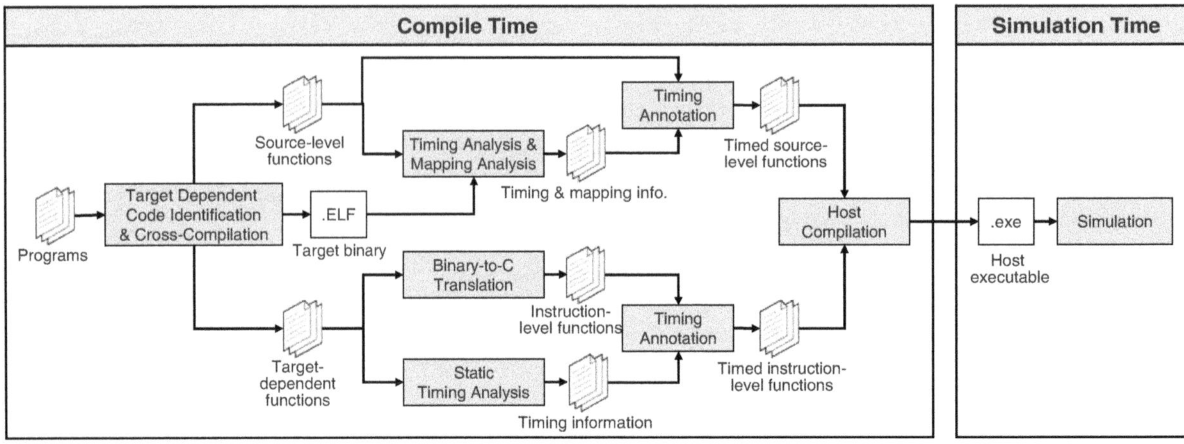

Figure 3: The HyCoS Approach

```
int callee(int arg){
    int i, ret = 0;
    bb_1();
    for (i=0;i<8;i++) {
        bb_2();
        if (arg%2){
            bb_3();
            glb_arr[i] = arg;
        } else {
            bb_6();
            glb_arr[i] = 0;
        }
        bb_4();
        ret += glb_arr[i];
    }
    bb_5();
    return ret;
}
```

```
...
void bb_2(){
    ICACHE(0x0094, 0x0094);
    cycles += 1;
    pred_taken = BP(0x0094);
}
void bb_3(){ //branch is not taken
    if(pred_taken) //predicted as taken
        cycels += BP_MISS_PENALTY;
    ICACHE(0x0098, 0x0098);
}
...
void bb_6(){ //branch is taken
    if(!pred_taken) //predicted as not taken
        cycels += BP_MISS_PENALTY;
    ICACHE(0x00b0, 0x00b4);
    cycles += 1;
}
```

Figure 4: Instrumented Source Code of *callee()*

that it is possible that $\ell_i = \ell_j$ $(i \neq j)$. Accurate mapping should have the following properties:

1. $\forall b_i, b_j \in \mathbf{B}\ (i \neq j) : \ b_i \to b_j \iff \ell_i \to \ell_j$
2. $\forall b_i \in \mathbf{B} : \ \eta(b_i) = \eta(\ell_i)$

where $\eta(\cdot)$ returns the execution count of a basic block or a source line and "$\to$" denotes the execution oder. $b_i \to b_j$ means that b_j is executed after b_i. The first property means that the execution order of binary-level basic blocks should be retained during the source-level simulation, while the second one indicates that a basic block should be simulated the same number of times as its execution count at binary level.

However, compiler optimizations might alter the program structure and hence make it difficult to establish accurate mapping. Solutions to this problem have been proposed in previous work [21, 23, 24, 25]. We adopt the method from [23] for generating accurate mapping information for compiler-optimized programs.

Since $c_i = \eta(b_i)$ and $c_{est_i} = \eta(\ell_i)$, we obtain $c_{est_i} = c_i$. Given $t_{est_i} \approx t_i$, we obtain the estimated execution time of a program:

$$T_{est} = \sum_{i=1}^{n} t_{est_i} \times c_{est_i} = \sum_{i=1}^{n} t_{est_i} \times c_i \approx T \qquad (4)$$

Hence, by native execution of instrumented source code we can obtain accurate estimates of software execution time.

Let's assume that the source code of *callee()* in the example program is available. Its instrumented source code is shown in Figure 4. For example, *bb_2()* contains the timing information of b_2. The delay value that accounts for the pipeline effects is accumulated by the variable *cycles* and the other code is for dynamic simulation of the cache and branch prediction effects. At simulation time, the function calls **ICACHE**(...) and **BP**(...) will send instruction addresses for instruction cache simulation and branch prediction simulation, respectively. Data cache simulation is more complex and will be discussed in Section 4.4.

4. THE HYCOS APPROACH

Figure 3 presents the HyCoS workflow. Similar to the typical compiled simulation approaches (cf. Figure 1), it also consists of a compile-time phase for generating simulation models and a simulation-time phase. Given a program, it is first analyzed to identify target dependent code. The identification is restricted to function call boundaries. If a function contains some target dependent code (e.g. inline assembler), the whole function is treated as target dependent. Then, target-independent functions are simulated at source level, while target-dependent functions are simulated at instruction level. The instruction level simulation of target-dependent functions is described in Section 4.1.

As source-level functions and instruction-level functions represent data at different abstraction levels, this gives rise to the issues of functional correctness and timing accuracy in the hybrid simulation. Functional correctness requires correct data transfer between source-level and instruction-level functions. Data transfer will occur during function calls in the form of function parameters and return values. A conversion is needed when function parameters and return values are passed from C variables of a source-level function to registers in an instruction-level function or vice versa. Data may also be transferred indirectly between source-level functions and instruction-level functions by accessing global variables. Natively executed source-level functions reference data in the host memory, while data used in instruction-level functions are allocated in the target memory model. Therefore, a synchronization mechanism is needed to keep the data consistency of global variables in both memory spaces. Hybrid function calls and global variable synchronization are discussed in Section 4.2 and 4.3, respectively.

The instrumented source-level functions and instruction-level functions along with the involved service routines build the function model as shown in Figure 5(a). The function model is then annotated with some additional code for in-

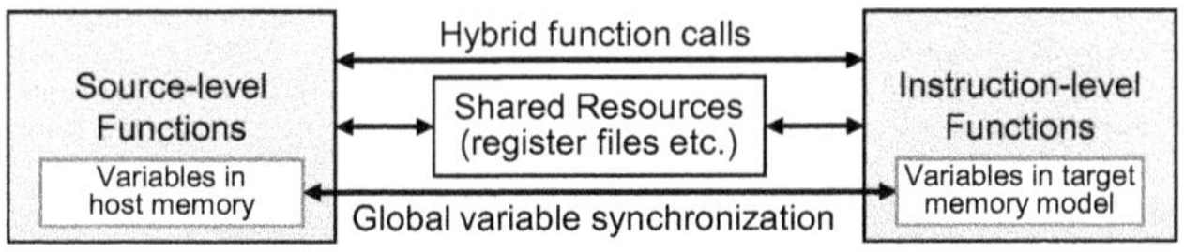

(a) Function Model

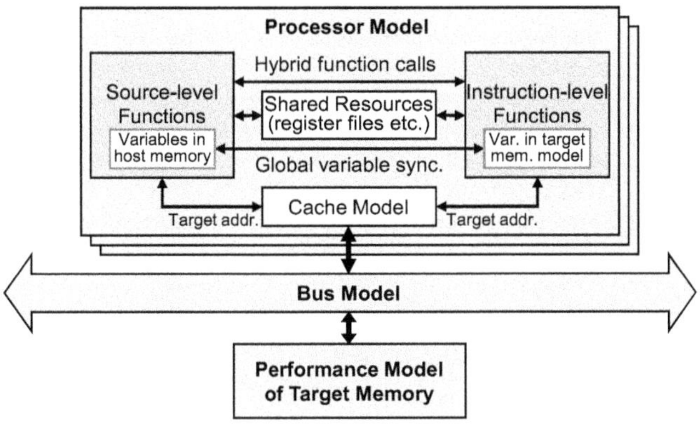

(b) Architectural Model for Multiprocessor Simulation

Figure 5: Hybrid Simulation Model

teraction with the models of the processor's units such as cache and branch predictor. The way of modeling instruction cache and branch predictor at both source level and instruction level has been well studied in previous work [20, 24] and has been discussed in Section 3. However, accurate data cache modeling is difficult because data addresses are specified by register operations in target instructions and cannot be statically resolved during source code instrumentation. We address this problem in Section 4.4.

The function model along with the performance model builds a processor model. Multiple processor models may be integrated into a SystemC-based simulation environment for simulation of multiprocessor systems. A simplified view of a multiprocessor simulator is illustrated in Figure 5(b). As shown, the memory model is separated into a functional part storing the real data that is directly accessed by the instruction-level functions and the service routines for global variable synchronization, and a performance part, which captures memory access delays and is accessed through the cache and communication models. Due to the *decoupling of function model and performance model*, the change of the performance model will not affect the functional correctness of the simulation. This increases the modularity and reliability of the simulation model.

4.1 Instruction-Level Simulation of Target Dependent Functions

The idea of Instruction-Level Simulation (ILS) is to translate the target binary, which cannot be natively executed, to a functionally equivalent program in a high level programming language such as C or C++. In our approach, the binary code of each target-dependent function is translated to a so-called *instruction-level function* that simulates the target-dependent function at instruction level. Each instruction-level function contains *control flow simulation code* that realizes the control transfer between basic blocks within the function.

Let's assume that *callee()* is target dependent in the example program. Its instruction-level function looks as follows:

```
1: void callee_sim(){
2:   PC = 0x0074; // entry address of the function
3:   while(running){
4:    switch(PC){
5:      case 0x0074: bb_1(); break;
6:      case 0x0094: bb_2(); break;
7:      ...
8:      case 0x00ac: bb_5(); return; //b5 contains a return jump
9:      case 0x00b0: bb_6(); break;
10:     default: running = false; break;
11:   }
12:  }
13:}
```

As shown above, the name of the instruction-level function is a combination of the name of the target-dependent function and a suffix "*_sim*" (line 1). The control flow simulation code consists of a *switch* construct in a *while* loop. Each *case* of the *switch* construct corresponds to a basic block. The simulation code of the $i-th$ basic block is contained in a function *bb_i()*. The initial value of the PC is set to the entry address of the target-dependent function (line 2). After the simulation of a basic block, the PC value is updated and the control is transferred to the *case* branch corresponding to the next basic block. The control transfer continues in this way until reaching a basic block that ends with a return jump (e.g. b_5 in the example).

As aforementioned, each basic block is simulated by a function that realizes the data flow within the basic block. For example, the simulation code of b_5 in the example program is contained in *bb_5()*:

```
1: void bb_5(){
2:   cycles += 3;
3:   ICACHE(0x009c, 0x00a8);
4:   GPR(0) = MEM_READ(GPR(9) + 0, 4); // 0x009c: lwz r0,0(r9)
5:   GPR(9) = GPR(9) + 4;              // 0x00a0: addi r9,r9,4
6:   GPR(3) = GPR(3) + GPR(0);         // 0x00a4: add r3,r3,r0
7:   CTR = CTR - 1;                    // 0x00a8: bdnz+ 0x0094
8:   if(CTR != 0) PC = 0x0094;
9:   else PC = 0x00ac;
10:  pred_taken = BP(0x00a8);
11:}
```

In the above code, each target instruction (shown at the right-hand side as comments) is translated to functionally equivalent statements in C. For performance simulation, the same timing analysis is utilized as in the SLS approach: t_{static} is accumulated by *cycles* (line 2) and $t_{dynamic}$ is simulated by some annotated code (line 3 and line 10). As both function model and timing information are obtained from instruction level, the annotation of the timing information into the function model is straightforward.

Compared to an ISS, ILS performs the time-consuming instruction fetching and decoding *prior* to simulation, and hence, it can achieve speedups of two orders of magnitude. The simulation code needs to reference data in a target memory model that maps the target address space to the host memory. The accesses to the target memory model through functions **MEM_READ**(...) and **MEM_WRITE**(...) are time-consuming and are the main cause of slowdown compared to native execution.

4.2 Hybrid Function Calls

A source-level function may call an instruction-level function, or vice versa. Such function calls are called *hybrid function calls*. A function call from a source-level function to an instruction-level function is called *forward hybrid function call*. An inverse function call is called *backward hybrid function call*.

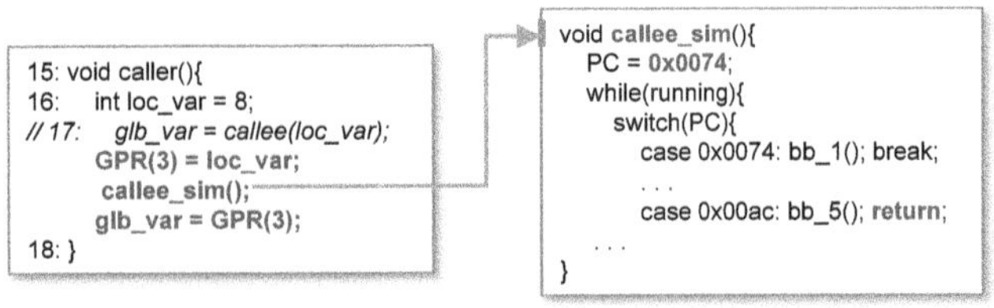

(a) Source-Level Function **(b) Instruction-Level Function**

Figure 6: Forward Hybrid Function Call

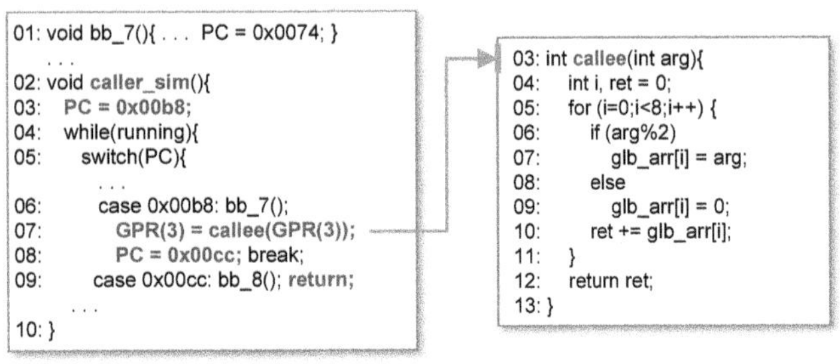

(a) Instruction-Level Function **(b) Source-Level Function**

Figure 7: Backward Hybrid Function Call

As discussed, hybrid function calls require parameter passing from C variables to registers or vice versa. The parameter passing needs to follow the calling conventions of the target processor. For example, according to the typical calling conventions of PowerPC processors, parameters of a function call are placed into General Purpose Registers (GPR) 3 through 10 and Floating-Point Registers (FPR) 1 through 13 from left to right and results are returned into GPR 3 or FPR 1. All parameters that cannot fit into the designated registers are moved to the stack. Following these calling conventions, we just need to annotate some additional code into the calling function for parameter passing of hybrid function calls, as shown in Figure 6 and Figure 7, where *callee()* and *caller()*, respectively, are assumed to be target dependent. In Figure 6(a), the value of the only parameter *loc_var* is passed to *GPR(3)*. Then, the instruction-level function *callee_sim()* (without parameter) is called and control is transferred to the instruction-level function. The return value of the instruction-level function is stored in *GPR(3)* and passed to *glb_var*. In Figure 7(a), *GPR(3)* is used as the function argument and the return value of the source-level function is passed to *GPR(3)* (line 7). Different annotation rules should be made for processors with different calling conventions.

In Figure 7(a), after the simulation of b_7 the PC is set to *0x0074* (line 1), which is the entry address of *callee()* at instruction level. However, since *callee()* is simulated at source level, the PC will not be updated to its return address, which is *0x00cc*. Therefore, after an instruction-level function has called a source-level function, the PC must be explicitly set to the return address of the called function (line 8 in Figure 7(a)). Otherwise, the next control transfer in the instruction-level function will be wrong.

4.3 Global Variable Synchronization

To achieve consistency of the target memory model and the host memory, a straightforward idea could be to modify source code to redirect global data references from the host memory to the target memory model. For example, a statement "$glb1 = glb2 + glb3$;" should be translated to:

```
temp2 = read(A_glb2);
temp3 = read(A_glb3);
temp1 = temp2 + temp3;
write(A_glb1, temp1);
```

where *A_glb1*, *A_glb2* and *A_glb3* are the addresses of the respective global variables in the target memory and *read(...)* and *write(...)* are service routines for reading/writing data from/to the target memory model. There are three major disadvantages of such an approach: (1) Complex pointer analysis is needed to identify the variables that need to be translated. (2) The abundant features of the C language allow a program to contain many complex statements, which make the translation of source code complex and error-prone. (3) Each use of a global variable needs to access the target memory model, which will decrease the simulation performance.

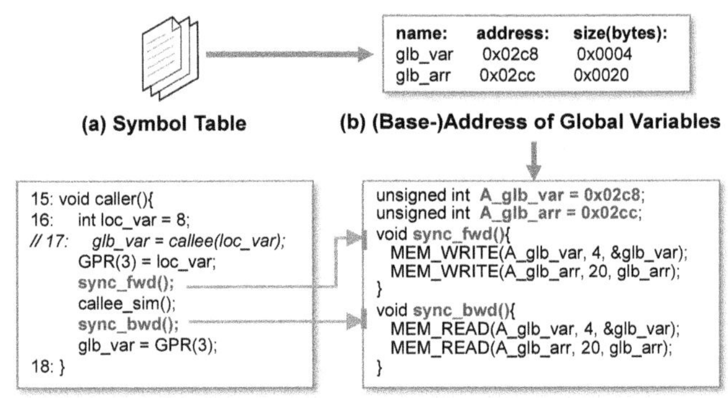

(d) Instrumented Source Code **(c) Synchronization Functions**

Figure 8: Global Variable Synchronization

In HyCoS, we propose a better solution: We do not make any modification to original source code statements. Instead, we insert additional code into source code that copies global data from the host memory to the target memory model (called *forward synchronization*) or from the target memory model to the host memory (called *backward synchronization*). Such synchronizations are needed only at hybrid function call boundaries. As shown in Figure 8(d), before a forward hybrid function call, *sync_fwd()* is invoked to perform the forward synchronization, and when the hybrid function call returns, the backward synchronization is performed by *sync_bwd()*. An inverse process is carried out in the case of a backward hybrid function call. The implementation of *sync_fwd()* and *sync_bwd()* is shown in Figure 8(c). The target data addresses of global variables can be obtained from the symbol table (Figure 8(a) and (b)). As shown in this example, the original source code is not touched at all (except for line 17, which is tuned for the hybrid function call) and the additionally added code will not affect the functionality of the original source code.

Our above implementation synchronizes all global variables at a synchronization point. A further improvement can be made based on the observation that, if a global variable is not changed before a hybrid function call, it is not necessary to save and then to restore it. The improvement can be achieved by performing dynamic data analysis to identify global variables, which have been changed since the last synchronization point, and then synchronizing only these updated global variables. The pseudo code is shown in Algorithm 1. As both source-level and instruction-level functions use target data addresses for data cache simulation (cf. Section 4.4), it checks for each cache write access if the address is within the address range of a global variable (line 7-10). If so, the dirty bit of this variable is set to *true* to indicate that this variable has been updated (line 11). The tuple of this variable is moved to the top of the list in order to improve the searching performance (line 12), because the most recently accessed variable is most likely to be accessed again. Then, during synchronization, the dirty bit of each global variable is checked. If the dirty bit of a variable has been set to *true*, this variable will be synchronized (line 20 - 25) and after the synchronization the dirty bit is cleared (line 26). Otherwise, if the dirty bit of a variable evaluates to *false*, the synchronization of this variable is skipped to improve the simulation performance.

Algorithm 1 Global Variable Synchronization

1: **(a) Recording updated global variables**
2: **Input:** $\mathbf{G} = \{(ptr_i, addr_i, size_i, dirty_i) \mid 1 \le i \le n\}$: a list to store the following information of all n global variables:
3: $-ptr$: pointer pointing to the host memory location
4: $-addr$: target data address
5: $-size$: data size of the global variable
6: $-dirty$: used to identify if the global variable has been changed
7: **for each** cache write access at $address$ **do**
8:   **if** $address$ is in the global variable section **then**
9:     **for each** $(ptr, addr, size, dirty) \in \mathbf{G}$ **do**
10:       **if** $addr \le address \le addr + size$ **then**
11:         $dirty \leftarrow true$
12:         move $(ptr, addr, size, dirty)$ to the top of $\mathbf{G}$
13:       **end if**
14:     **end for**
15:   **end if**
16: **end for**
17:
18: **(b) Global variable synchronization**
19: **for each** $(ptr, addr, size, dirty) \in \mathbf{G}$ **do**
20:   **if** $dirty == true$ **then**
21:     **if** Forward synchronization **then**
22:       MEM_WRITE$(addr, size, ptr)$
23:     **else**
24:       MEM_READ$(addr, size, ptr)$
25:     **end if**
26:     $dirty \leftarrow false$
27:   **end if**
28: **end for**

4.4 Data Cache Simulation

Accurate cache simulation is of paramount importance in multiprocessor systems design because the memory subsystem accounts for a large portion of system performance. We believe therefore that it is mandatory to include cache simulation techniques into HyCoS. Otherwise, the advantages of HyCoS would be overshadowed by cache effects.

Memory accesses can be caused by references to global variables and local variables or due to building up and cleaning up the call stack in a function's prologue and epilogue. Except for global variables, target data addresses of other memory accesses cannot be statically resolved during source code instrumentation. Previous work considers only memory accesses made by global variables [16] or uses host data addresses for data cache simulation [8, 11, 18, 24], based on the assumption that the same data allocated in the host memory and in the target memory has very similar locality of reference. Using the latter method in the hybrid simulation, source-level functions access the cache with host data addresses while instruction-level functions reference data in the target memory model. This mixture of memory spaces will lead to cache simulation errors. In addition, memory accesses made in a function's prologue and epilogue are not visible in the source code and therefore cannot be taken into account in the previous approaches.

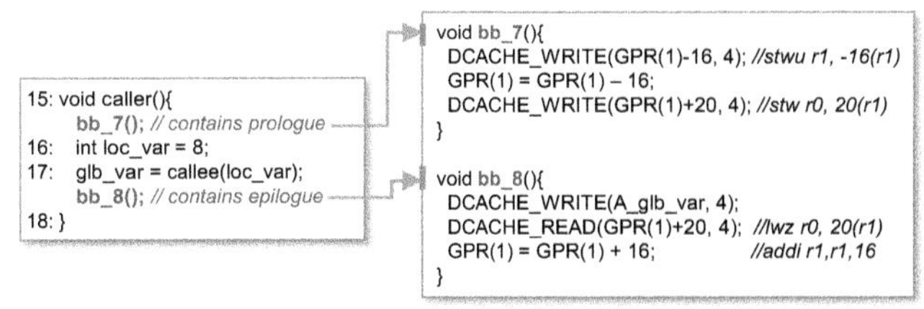

Figure 9: Source Code Instrumentation for Data Cache Simulation

HyCoS is aimed at accurate simulation of any kind of memory access. Our solution is based on the observation that the memory locations of local variables change due to dynamic allocation of the stack frame every time a function is called, whereas the local variables (those that do not fit into registers) are usually assumed to reside at a fixed offset from the stack pointer. The offset of a local variable to the stack pointer can be obtained by decoding load/store instructions. Therefore, if the content of the stack pointer can be maintained in the source-level simulation, the target data addresses of the local variables can be obtained. Figure 9 illustrates the code annotated for simulating operations on the stack pointer. In PowerPC processors, GPR 1 is dedicated as the stack pointer. In *bb_7()*, which contains the prologue of *caller()*, the *stwu* instruction (store word with update) stores the old stack pointer and grows the stack to build a new stack frame. The address of the *stw* instruction is obtained by adding the offset *20* to GPR 1. In *bb_8()*, *A_glb_var* stores the address of the global variable *glb_var*, which is obtained from the symbol table. The address of the *lwz* instruction is obtained by adding the offset *20* to GPR 1. Finally, the *addi* instruction shrinks the stack and the stack frame is deleted. As shown, all data addresses are passed to **DCACHE_READ**(...) and **DCACHE_WRITE**(...) for data cache simulation. Although we demonstrate our method with PowerPC processors, similar rules can be established for other widely used RISC processors.

For memory accesses to an array with a variable index, the above-introduced method is only able to obtain the base address of an array variable and therefore we need to calculate the dynamic offset to the base address by:

$$Offset_{target} = (Addr_{host} - BaseAddr_{host}) * \frac{size_{target}}{size_{host}} \quad (5)$$

where $(Addr_{host} - BaseAddr_{host})$ calculates the offset of the host address, which is then translated to the offset of the target address considering the difference of the size of the data type in the target processor ($size_{target}$) and the host machine ($size_{host}$). The following example illustrates this scheme, assuming $size_{target} = size_{host}$:

```
for (i = 0; i < 10; i++) {
  x[i] = x[i] + y[i];
  DCACHE_READ(A_x+(unsigned int)&(x[i])-(unsigned int)x, 4);
  DCACHE_READ(A_y+(unsigned int)&(y[i])-(unsigned int)y, 4);
  DCACHE_WRITE(A_x+(unsigned int)&(x[i])-(unsigned int)x, 4);
}
```

Figure 10 shows the final instrumented source code of *caller()*, assuming that *callee()* is target dependent. The code at line a2, a4 and a6 are annotated for parameter passing of the forward hybrid function call, while the code at line a3 and a5 synchronizes global variables between the host memory and the target memory model. The whole code is annotated to achieve functional correctness of the hybrid simulation, while the code in *bb_7()* and *bb_8()* is inserted for accurate performance estimation.

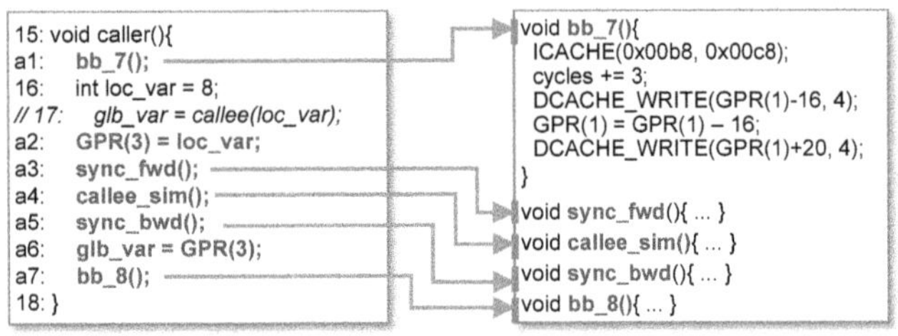

Figure 10: Final Instrumented Source Code

5. EXPERIMENTAL RESULTS

In the experiments, we first evaluate our HyCoS approach in terms of simulation accuracy and performance by means of a set of benchmark programs. Then, we use a case study of an entire video application to demonstrate how the proposed approach facilitates multiprocessor simulation.

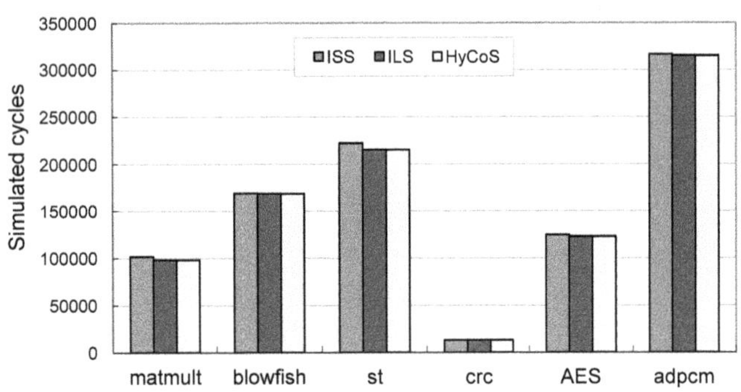

Figure 11: Comparison of Simulation Accuracy

5.1 Single Processor Simulation

Six embedded applications were selected to evaluate HyCoS for single processor simulation. PowerPC 603e (4KB instruction cache and 4KB data cache) was selected as the target processor. A standard interpretive ISS was implemented and used as a reference to evaluate the simulation accuracy of HyCoS. We also compared HyCoS to pure Instruction-Level Simulation (ILS).

The performance estimates are illustrated in Figure 11. HyCoS achieves performance estimates comparable to the ISS, with the error rate ranging from -0.2% to -3.3% (-1.5% on average). The error is mainly caused by the approximation made in the static timing analysis of pipeline effects. Since the same timing information was used in ILS, the estimates obtained by ILS and HyCoS were the same.

Figure 12 illustrates a comparison of methods for source-level data cache simulation in terms of estimation accuracy of cache misses, which is expressed by *normalized cache miss count*: a ratio of estimated cache misses to the actual cache misses. *Method 1* proposed in [8, 11, 18, 24] uses host addresses for cache simulation. Using this method, the same data might be referenced with both target address and host address. Therefore, successive accesses to the same data might lead to cache misses, resulting in a positive estimation error. Such a positive error can be observed in the simulation of *matmult*. Since not all memory accesses are visible at source level, such as memory accesses made by building up and cleaning up the call stack in a function's prologue and epilogue, this results in a negative error in the simulation of some other applications. *Method 2* used in [16] considers only global variables, the target addresses of which can be obtained from the symbol table at compile time. Using this method, the cache simulation accuracy depends on the portion of memory accesses made by global variables. This method incurs large errors for *blowfish* and *adpcm*, where memory accesses made by non-global variables also account for a large portion. As shown in the figure, our cache simulation method employed in HyCoS can accurately estimate all cache misses for all applications.

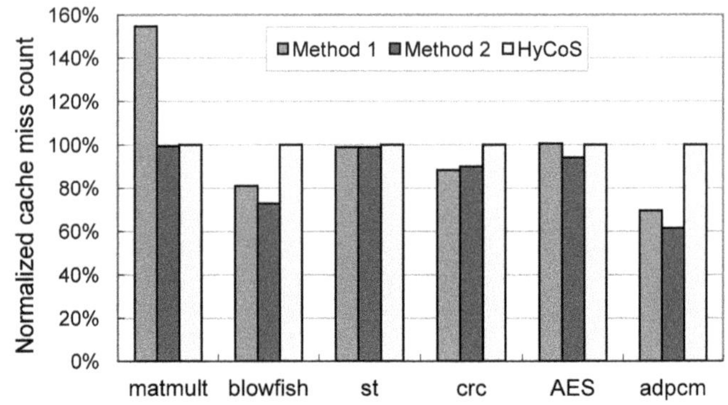

Figure 12: Comparison of Data Cache Simulation Methods: HyCoS vs. *Method 1* proposed in [8, 11, 18, 24] and *Method 2* used in [16]

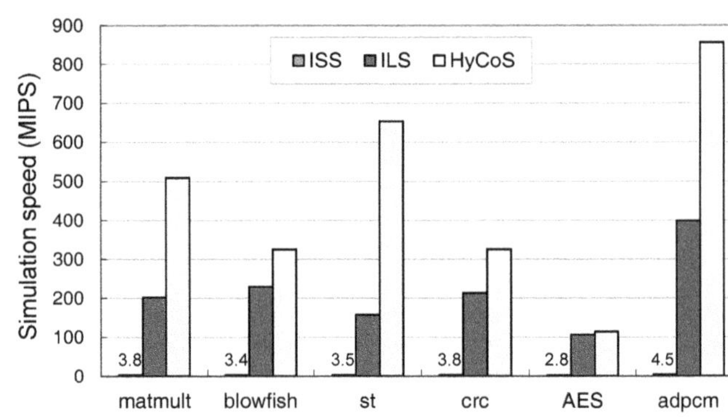

Figure 13: Comparison of Simulation Performance

Figure 13 illustrates a comparison of the simulation performance. The simulation performance was measured on a PC equipped with a 3.2GHz Intel CPU and 2GB RAM. The simulation speed of HyCoS ranges from 114 Million simulated Instructions Per Second (MIPS) to 856 MIPS (463.7 MIPS on average). HyCoS achieved 128.0x and 2.1x speedups, respectively, compared to the employed ISS (3.6 MIPS on average) and ILS (217.5 MIPS). The speedup depends on the portion of target dependent code simulated with ILS. In the selected applications, in addition to library functions, we

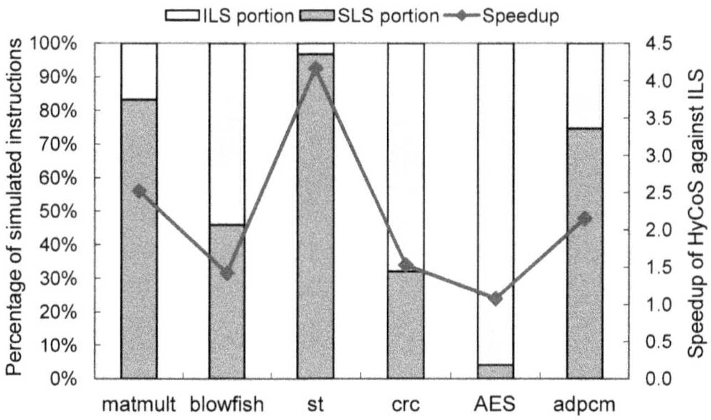

Figure 14: Speedup with Respect to Percentage of Target Dependent Code

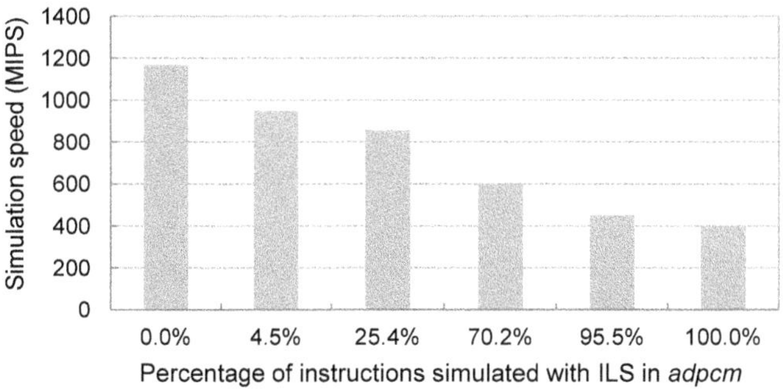

Figure 15: Simulation Speeds with Respect to Percentage of Target Dependent Code for *adpcm*

also purposely assumed some more functions to be target dependent to study the relation of the simulation performance with the amount of target dependent code. This relation is depicted in Figure 14. For *st*, where the instructions simulated with ILS account for only 3.3%, HyCoS achieves a speedup of 4.2x compared to ILS. Whereas, when the instructions simulated with ILS are dominant, the speedup will be trival. For exmaple, for *AES* the speedup is only 1.1x.

This relation of the simulation speed and the portion of instructions simulated with ILS can also be observed in Figure 15, where different numbers of functions in *adpcm* are assumed to be target dependent. With the portion of instructions simulated with ILS changes from 0% (pure SLS) to 100% (pure ILS), the simulation speed slows down from 1167 MIPS to 398 MIPS.

5.2 Multi-Processor Simulation

The proposed HyCoS approach was also applied in an MPSoC system design for a video Downscaler to demonstrate its efficiency in multiprocessor simulation. The Downscaler converts the original CIF video frames (352x288) to the frames with a lower resolution (132x128). The configuration of the system and the task graph of the application are shown in Figure 16. A simple shared-memory architecture was evaluated. All processor cores run at 500MHz. The L1 cache and L2 cache are 8KB and 128KB, respectively.

We built two simulators for the same system. One uses ISSs for software simulation, while the other uses hybrid compiled simulation models generated by the HyCoS approach. The simulation models of the other system components are equal in both simulators. Since modeling communication and synchronization of MPSoC is out of the scope of this paper, only a high-level communication model in TLM [7] was used. To be connected with the communication model, the HyCoS models are annotated with standard TLM interfaces and are regarded as software TLMs.

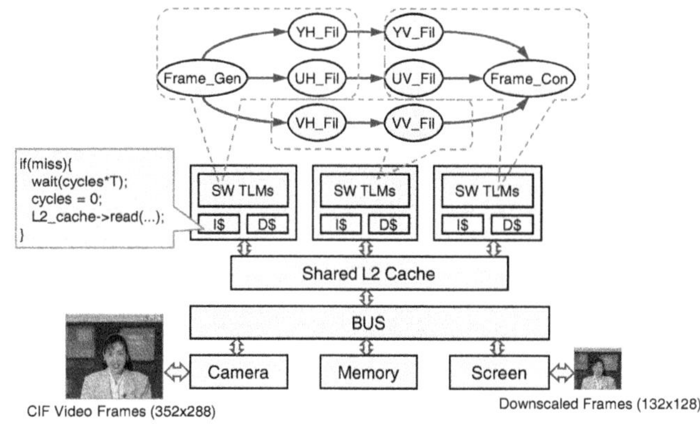

Figure 16: Case Study of a Video Downscaler

Table 1: Simulation Results of Processing 10 Frames

Comparison of Simulated Time			
System Configuration	1 core	2 cores	4 cores
ISS-based Simulator	1233ms	701ms	446ms
HyCoS-based Simulator	1226ms	698ms	442ms
Error	-0.6%	-0.4%	-0.9%
Comparison of Simulation Runtime			
System Configuration	1 core	2 cores	4 cores
ISS-based Simulator	2.5h	2.9h	3.8h
HyCoS-based Simulator	2.3min	2.3min	2.5min
Speedup	66.9x	75.4x	89.5x

The experimental results of processing 10 video frames[1] are shown in Table 1. Three system configurations were simulated. Using HyCoS software models, the estimation error of the overall simulated time remains below 1% in all examined configurations. This justifies the accuracy of the software simulation models generated by HyCoS. The simulation performance of the ISS-based simulator is related to the number of cores. With an increasing number of cores, the overhead for synchronization beteen the ISSs and the SystemC kernel increases. The HyCoS-based simulator has all components in SystemC and has lower synchronization overhead. It achieves an average speedup of 77.3x compared to the ISS-based simulator.

6. CONCLUSIONS

This paper presented a novel hybrid compiled simulation approach, called HyCoS, for fast and accurate performance simulation of embedded software. HyCoS takes advantage of both source-level simulation (high speed, better support for source-level optimization) and instruction-level compiled simulation (applicability to target-dependent code). For functional correctness of the hybrid simulation, the methods for realizing hybrid function calls and global variable syn-

[1]Ten frames are sufficient since more frames will not lead to new scenarios regarding the simulation performance of HyCoS.

chronization were proposed. In addition, a novel method was presented to improve the data cache simulation accuracy. Compared to instruction set simulators and pure instruction-level compiled simulation, HyCoS allows for much faster simulation without compromising accuracy. Our experiment presented that HyCoS achieved an average speedup of 128x compared to an ISS and 2.1x compared to the pure ILS. In the experiment, we purposely assumed that some applications have a large portion of instructions simulated with ILS in order to study the overhead of ILS. In practice, HyCoS might achieve more speedup.

7. REFERENCES

[1] Imperas. http://www.imperas.com/.

[2] Synopsys. http://www.synopsys.com/.

[3] SystemC. http://www.systemc.org/.

[4] The M5 Simulator. http://www.m5sim.org/.

[5] L. Benini, D. Bertozzi, A. Bogliolo, F. Menichelli, and M. Olivieri. MPARM: Exploring the Multi-Processor SoC Design Space with SystemC. *Springer Journal of VLSI Signal Processing*, 41(2):169–182, 2005.

[6] G. Braun, A. Nohl, A. Hoffmann, O. Schliebusch, R. Leupers, and H. Meyr. A universal technique for fast and flexible instruction-set architecture simulation. *IEEE Transaction on Computer-Aided Design of Integrated Circuits and Systems*, 2004.

[7] L. Cai and D. Gajski. Transaction level modeling: an overview. In *Proceedings of the IEEE/ACM/IFIP international conference on Hardware/software codesign and system synthesis (CODES+ISSS '03)*, pages 19–24, 2003.

[8] E. Cheung, H. Hsieh, and F. Balarin. Memory subsystem simulation in software tlm/t models. In *Proceedings of the 2009 Asia and South Pacific Design Automation Conference*, ASP-DAC '09, pages 811–816, 2009.

[9] F. Fummi, G. Perbellini, M. Loghi, and M. Poncino. ISS-centric modular HW/SW co-simulation. In *Proceedings of the 16th ACM Great Lakes symposium on VLSI (GLSVLSI '06)*, pages 31–36, 2006.

[10] Y. Hwang, S. Abdi, and D. Gajski. Cycle-approximate retargetable performance estimation at the transaction level. In *Proceedings of the conference on Design, automation and test in Europe (DATE'08)*, pages 3–8, 2008.

[11] T. Kempf, K. Karuri, S. Wallentowitz, G. Ascheid, R. Leupers, and H. Meyr. A SW performance estimation framework for early system-level-design using fine-grained instrumentation. In *Proceedings of DATE*, pages 468–473, 2006.

[12] S. Kraemer, L. Gao, J. Weinstock, R. Leupers, G. Ascheid, and H. Meyr. Hysim: a fast simulation framework for embedded software development. In *Proceedings of the 5th IEEE/ACM international conference on Hardware/software codesign and system synthesis (CODES-ISSS'07)*, pages 75–80, 2007.

[13] T. Meyerowitz, M. Sauermann, D. Langen, and A. Sangiovanni-Vincentelli. Source-level timing annotation and simulation for a heterogeneous multiprocessor. In *Proceedings of the conference on Design, automation and test in Europe (DATE'08)*, 2008.

[14] C. Mills, S. C. Ahalt, and J. Fowler. Compiled instruction set simulation. *Software-Practice Experience*, 21(8):877–889, 1991.

[15] A. Muttreja, A. Raghunathan, S. Ravi, and N. K. Jha. Hybrid simulation for embedded software energy estimation. In *roceedings of Design Automation Conference (DAC'05)*, pages 23–26, 2005.

[16] A. Pedram, D. Craven, and A. Gerstlauer. Modeling cache effects at the transaction level. In *Analysis, Architectures and Modelling of Embedded Systems*, volume 310, pages 89–101. Springer Boston, 2009.

[17] A. D. Pimentel, M. Thompson, S. Polstra, and C. Erbas. Calibration of abstract performance models for system-level design space exploration. *Journal of Signal Processing Systems*, 50(2):99–114, 2008.

[18] H. Posadas, L. Díaz, and E. Villar. Fast data-cache modeling for native co-simulation. In *Proceedings of the 16th Asia and South Pacific Design Automation Conference*, ASPDAC '11, pages 425–430, 2011.

[19] M. Reshadi, P. Mishra, and N. Dutt. Instruction set compiled simulation: a technique for fast and flexible instruction set simulation. In *Proceedings of Design Automation Conference (DAC'03)*, pages 758–763, 2003.

[20] J. Schnerr, O. Bringmann, A. Viehl, and W. Rosenstiel. High-performance timing simulation of embedded software. In *Proceedings of the Design Automation Conference*, Anaheim, USA, June 2008.

[21] S. Stattelmann, O. Bringmann, and W. Rosenstiel. Fast and Accurate Source-Level Simulation of Software Timing Considering Complex Code Optimizations . In *Proceedings of the 48th Annual Design Automation Conference (DAC'11)*, San Diego, California, 2011.

[22] S. Stattelmann, G. Gebhard, C. Cullmann, O. Bringmann, and W. Rosenstiel. Hybrid source-level simulation of data caches using abstract cache models. In *Proceedings of the conference on Design, automation and test in Europe (DATE'12)*, 2012.

[23] Z. Wang and J. Henkel. Accurate source-level simulation of embedded software with respect to compiler optimizations. In *Proceedings of the conference on Design, automation and test in Europe (DATE'12)*, 2012.

[24] Z. Wang and A. Herkersdorf. An Efficient Approach for System-Level Timing Simulation of Compiler-Optimized Embedded Software. In *Proceedings of the 46th Annual Design Automation Conference (DAC'09)*, pages 220–225, San Francisco, California, July 2009.

[25] Z. Wang, K. Lu, and A. Herkersdorf. An approach to improve accuracy of source-level TLMs of embedded software. In *Proceedings of the Conference on Design, automation and test in Europe (DATE'11)*, pages 1–6, 2011.

[26] T. Wild, A. Herkersdorf, and G.-Y. Lee. TAPES–Trace-based architecture performance evaluation with SystemC. *Journal of Design Automation for Embedded Systems*, 10(2-3):157–179, 2005.

[27] V. Zivojnovic and H. Meyr. Compiled HW/SW co-simulation. In *Proceedings of the Design Automation Conference (DAC)*, 1996.

Fast Simulation of Systems Embedding VLIW Processors

Luc Michel
Tima Laboratory
CNRS/Grenoble INP/UJF
luc.michel@imag.fr

Nicolas Fournel
Tima Laboratory
CNRS/Grenoble INP/UJF
nicolas.fournel@imag.fr

Frédéric Pétrot
Tima Laboratory
CNRS/Grenoble INP/UJF
frederic.petrot@imag.fr

ABSTRACT

Virtual prototyping of MPSoCs requires fast processor simulation models. Dynamic binary translation is an efficient technology for instruction set simulation, but as it is basically used for effortless code migration, it targets mostly general purpose processors. As many heterogeneous MPSoCs include VLIW processors, we propose and detail in this paper a strategy to perform dynamic binary translation of VLIW codes on scalar architectures for simulation purposes. Our simulation experiments show that it is a few orders of magnitude faster than direct instruction interpretation, although the translator includes no optimization.

Categories and Subject Descriptors

C.0 [**General**]: Modeling of computer architecture; B.4.4 [**Performance Analysis and Design Aids**]: Simulation; D.3.4 [**Processors**]: Interpreters

General Terms

Performance, Design

Keywords

VLIW, Simulation, Binary Translation

1. INTRODUCTION

Many current integrated systems are composed of a general purpose processor assisted by one or a few (usually very long instruction word - VLIW - based) digital signal processors (possibly deeply embedded into devices) on which generally regular but computation intensive functions are offloaded. Since depending on the final product target many designs alternatives are possible, efficient simulation of the complete hardware/software system is needed. Studies have shown that the time spent in Instruction Set Simulators (ISS) is a significant part of the whole MPSoC (Multi-Processor System on Chip) simulation time [1], and this part raises with the internal complexity of the processors. As the trend is to embed more and more processors, fast instruction set simulation is of utmost importance.

Instruction interpretation technologies are numerous, as detailed in, *e.g.*, [2], and dynamic binary translation (DBT) is now a solution making its way into MPSoC simulation [3, 4, 5, 6] that is fast while allowing accurate performance evaluation [4]. DBT is a mature technology, and it is used for scalar to scalar and scalar to VLIW codes translations, at first democratized by companies building processors to allow the use of legacy codes on newer [7], sometimes disruptive [8], processor architectures. MPSoC simulation opens a new ground for this technology: translation of VLIW code on a scalar architecture. Indeed, and as far as we know, such a translation has never been reported, due to the fact that this VLIW to scalar translation is of interest only in simulation, since there is no captive VLIW legacy code base.

The focus of this work is thus to define a strategy for the translation of VLIW codes on scalar processors and demonstrate its efficiency for building ISS.

The paper is organized as follows. Section 2 presents the field of work and the related researches. Section 3 defines the problem in a comprehensive way, and section 4 details the solution that we propose to solve it. Section 5 presents and analyzes experimental data, before summarizing our contribution in Section 6.

2. RELATED WORK

Binary translation is aiming at transforming instructions of one ISA to another[7]. This process can be executed at two different instants: offline, for the static binary translation (SBT)[9, 10], or at run-time, for the dynamic binary translation (DBT)[11, 12].

The main and original goal of binary translation has been migration and compatibility. Indeed, numerous works propose solutions based on binary translation (static or dynamic) aiming at exploiting new features of more recent versions of an architecture, for example UQBT with the SPARC ISA[9] or Transmeta with their so called "code-morphing"[13] hardware technology targeting the x86 ISA. Others propose solutions easing migration from some architecture to another [10, 14, 15].

More applications of this technique have emerged in the recent years, for example Just-in-time compilation (JIT) for Java, native binary acceleration[16] or virtualization and system simulation [12]. Even more recently, interpretive languages have benefited from these techniques, in web pages (the Tamarin JIT for Javascript) or for scripting (Python, Ruby, ...). The technique was popularized in the early 80's by the implementation of SmallTalk[17].

In the DBT field, efforts have been made to build machine adaptable binary translator. In that way, the translator can be adapted to numerous architectures with a reduced effort [11, 12, 18]. These translators are all based on an Intermediate Representation (IR) so that the complete process of binary translation can be described in a two-phases manner, as proposed on Figure 1. The IR is machine independent to guaranty the re-targetability of the translator. This representation can be viewed as a generic machine instruction set, it is even called micro-operations in QEMU [12] or I-RTL in Walkabout [11].

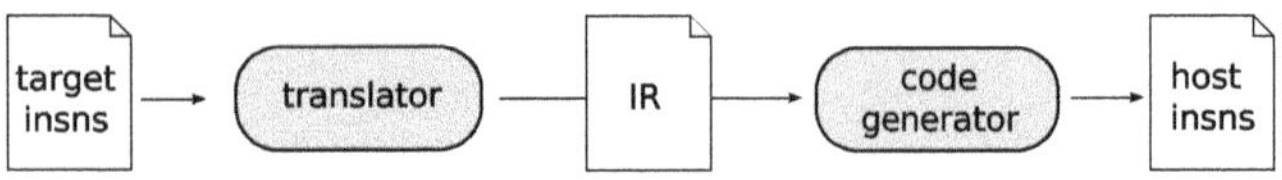

Figure 1: Machine adaptable DBT process

The first phase is in charge of translating the target instruction into the machine independent IR. In most cases, this phase is called translator. The second phase is then in charge of encoding the IR into host instructions. It is called either code generation by some authors, by analogy with the compilation notion, or encoder.

Among all the works presented until now, many have addressed the issue of translating binaries from a scalar target architecture to another scalar architecture. This case is the most straightforward one, since by falling back in an elementary IR, one can always find a valid translation for instructions regardless of their complexity [12].

A few works have focused on the efficient execution of SIMD instructions. Among them we can cite an effort from FX!32 [10] to translate MMX SIMD instructions to the Alpha instruction set, the work of [19] which focuses the SIMD instructions (MMX/SSE) on an IA64, and [20] that proposes a general approach that is demonstrated on ARM Neon extensions.

Other works have proposed translations from scalar architectures to parallel architectures, more precisely to VLIW architectures such as DAISY [14] or the Itanium or IA64 [8, 15]. These solutions are more complex than the previous ones since on top of finding a matching between instructions, these solutions have to extract the instruction level parallelism (ILP) to take advantage of the host architecture for better performances.

The use of Dynamic Binary Translation as an instruction set simulation tool for system level simulation has been introduced only recently[4, 3]. As the translation of VLIW code into sequential code does not have a practical interest outside of this topic (unless for the support of legacy code, but VLIW processor are indeed quite specialized and they do not have a large code base), and to the best of our knowledge, the DBT of VLIW code into scalar code has not been detailed in the literature as of today.

3. PROBLEM DEFINITION

3.1 Dynamic Binary Translation Technique

Figure 1 gives a conceptual overview of the Dynamic Binary Translation (DBT) process, whereas Figure 2 (borrowed from [2]) gives the overall details of the process. As stated before, this translation is made in a two-phase manner with a translation phase (from target instruction to IR) and a code generation (from IR to host instructions). This is mainly for easy retargetability purposes.

As shown on Figure 2 these two phases are not called sequentially on each instructions. Indeed, the translation phase is first accomplished on a complete sequence of instructions. This group of instructions are sequentially executed instructions, which means that the translation of a target branch instruction triggers the end of the group. These groups are called Translation Blocks (TB) and are very close to the compilation notion of Basic Block. The main difference with Basic Blocks is that Translation Blocks also end on other conditions like memory page frontiers. Once a TB is translated into IR operations, the code generator produces at once the corresponding host instructions, called Translated Basic Block (TBB). The TBB is then wrapped with a prologue and an epilogue to match a function template. Finally, the TBB is executed using a function call. At the end of the execution of the TBB, the control returns to the DBT engine to execute the next TBB. For performance reasons, the TBB are cached for later reuse in order to amortize the translation and code generation costs. The DBT engine will then first lookup in the cache to find an existing translation and execute it in case of hit or call the translator in case of miss. As can be realized from this process, the TBs are translated and generated independently of their context of use. Indeed, all possible predecessors of a specific TB are not known at translation time, more precisely only one is known: the one from which the TB was encountered the first time.

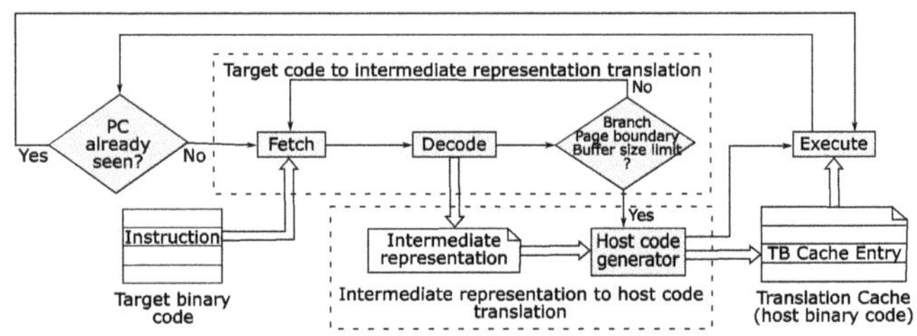

Figure 2: Overview of the DBT process

Figure 3 gives an example of the translation results of an ARM instruction on an x86 host made by the QEMU DBT engine. The example also depicts, in the middle, the IR operations used for this translation, QEMU micro-operations.

```
and r2,r1, r5     mov_i32 tmp0, r5               mov 0x05(%ebp), %esi
                  mov_i32 tmp1, r1               mov 0x04(%ebp), %ebx
                  and_i32 tmp0, tmp0, tmp1       and  %esi, %ebx
                  mov_i32 r2, tmp0               mov %ebx, 0x08(%ebp)
```

Figure 3: DBT example: ARM to x86

As can be realized from this example, the translation of a simple logic instruction results in a sequence of many instructions of the host architecture. Lines 1, 2 and 4 of the x86 generated code also underline the fact that the registers of the target are placed in memory for the simulation. The sequence of extra generated instructions aims at moving values of target registers in memory to host registers and vice-versa. This resembles the *to* and *from* memory moves an unoptimized compiler would produce, where the target registers would be the variables of the source code.

For the sake of readability, in the rest of this article we will simplify the IR by aggregating the memory to host register and the arithmetic and logic IR operations. The previous example IR code will be written as a single IR operation: `and_i32 r2, r1, r5` (whose meaning is $r_2 \leftarrow r_1 \wedge r_5$).

3.2 VLIW Architectures specificities

The VLIW idea can be summarized as making a processor simpler yet powerful by having the compiler provide the Instruction Level Parallelism (ILP) explicitly in the instruction word. The VLIW approach can be implemented in general purpose processing, *e.g.* tilera, transmeta crusoé or IA64, but is most often used for digital signal processing, *e.g.* NXP TriMedia, AD SHARC, STM ST200, Atmel mAgic-VLIW and TI C6x, where applications are data dominated. Many *ad-hoc* processing engines in embedded and integrated systems are also VLIW based, as they provide a high computing vs power efficiency. All match the main concept of VLIW but each offers different architectural implementation choices. The implementation choices are mainly trade-offs regarding simplicity of the design against compiler complexity, the major one being bypasses and stalls against register update latencies (called delay slots in the sequel).

Our goal here is not to give a complete overview of these architectures, but to provide clues about which architectural specificities of VLIW could be issues in the DBT process. For that purpose we illustrate this article using the TI C6x DSP architecture, which contains all of the architectural features making DBT on a scalar architecture difficult. The Listing 1 is a small piece of C6x code that will we use throughout the paper.

Listing 1: VLIW code Example: TI C6x

```
   ;  Instruction               ; Cycle ; L ;
2     add    .L1 a2, a1, a2   ; 1     ; 1 ; a2 <- a2 + a1
   || sub    .D1 a1, a4, a6   ; 1     ; 1 ; a6 <- a1 - a4
4  || mpy32  .M1 a2, a1, a3   ; 1     ; 3 ; a3 <- a2 * a1
      b      .S1 0xbeef       ; 2     ; 5 ;
6                                         ;
      sub    .D1 a6, a3, a3   ; 3     ; 1 ; a3 <- a6 - a3
8     add    .L1 a2, a3, a4   ; 4     ; 1 ; a4 <- a2 + a3
      mpy32  .M1 a2, a3, a5   ; 5     ; 3 ; a5 <- a2 * a3
10    nop     2               ; 6,7   ; X ;
      add    .L1 a2, a3, a5   ; XXX   ; X ; a5 <- a2 + a3
```

First of all, ILP expressed in the instruction word, is illustrated in the example by lines 2, 3, 4. The '||' means that the following instruction will be executed in the same cycle as the previous one in the code. A group of parallel instruction is an Execution Packet. The main characteristic of the execution packet is that multiple instructions can use the same register(s) as input, but more interesting, in the same execution packet, one instruction can write its result in a register whereas other instructions use it as operand. Obviously, the operand will have the value at the beginning of the cycle and not the result value. For example, the register `a2` is an operand register at line 2 and 4, but also a destination register at line 2.

The next characteristic concerns the delay slot of arithmetic and logic instructions. Indeed, some of the instructions available in these processors are too complex to be completed in one cycle. Instead of stalling the pipeline until the availability of the result in the destination register, the compiler has the responsibility to ensure that instructions using the result of this instruction will not be scheduled before the end of the delay. It also means that all instructions executed in between can read this register to get its old value, and it is even possible to write it, the actions occurring after the corresponding latency (result undefined in case of a tie). For example, register `a3` value resulting of the `mpy32` instruction will only be available at cycle 5 for the second `mpy32` since `mpy32` has a three cycle delay. Moreover, the `a3` value of lines 7 is the old value and its new value, used in the `add` line 8 is overwritten by the result of the first `mpy32`.

The last specificity is related to branches. Branch instructions have also delay slots, which means that instructions following the branch will be executed before branching actually occurs. For example, in the C6x the delay of a branch is 5 cycles. This means that the branch will effectively occur after the second cycle of `nop` in the example of Listing 1. The instructions between the branch and the effective branch are executed as if they were placed before the branch and the branch was immediate.

3.3 A Naïve DBT of VLIW code

The Algorithm 1 presents a simple version of the classical scalar DBT algorithm that translates the target code until the end of the translation block. The Listing 2 presents the resulting translation of the VLIW code depicted in Listing 1 after applying this algorithm.

Algorithm 1 Naive VLIW DBT algorithm

```
while ¬end_of_tb() do
    insn ← get_next_insn()
    translate(insn)
end while
```

Listing 2: Naive DBT of VLIW code

```
; IR operation             ;    original instruction ; Cyc
add_i32   a2, a2, a1       ;    add    .L1 a2, a1, a2 ; 1
sub_i32   a6, a1, a4       ; || sub    .D1 a1, a4, a6 ; 1
mul_i32   a3, a2, a1       ; || mpy32  .M1 a2, a1, a3 ; 1
mov_i32   pce1, $0xbeef    ;    b      .S1 0xbeef     ; 2
exit_tb   0x0              ;                          ;
sub_i32   a3, a6, a3       ;    sub    .D1 a6, a3, a3 ; 3
add_i32   a4, a2, a3       ;    add    .L1 a2, a3, a4 ; 4
mul_i32   a5, a2, a3       ;    mpy32  .M1 a2, a3, a5 ; 5
# nop 2                    ;    nop     2             ; 6,7
add_i32   a5, a2, a3       ;    add    .L1 a2, a3, a5 ; XXX
```

Because of the VLIW architectural specificities, the naïve scalar DBT produces code that has an incorrect behavior.

First, the parallel execution and more precisely the parallel read of source registers is broken. As the translation has to sequentialize the instructions of an execution packet, the Write-after-Read (WAR) dependency due to the parallel read of operands which occurs before the result write back in destination registers is not respected. For example, the execution of the first `add` will be finished when the `mul` will be executed. The result of the first `add` will have overwritten the value of the correct operand for the `mul`.

Second, delay slots of arithmetic operations are also not respected, because all IR operations are instantaneous from a simulation point of view. Then results of arithmetic and logic instructions with delay slots will be written back to their destination register before the next cycle is evaluated. For example the result of the `mul` will be available for the following `sub`.

Finally, the translation for instructions following the branch is represented in the Listing 2, but in the standard process, the translator will never translate them since it will end the TB at the branch instruction. The delay slot instructions should be part of this TB, but they are not in the current process. The branch delay slot are thus not respected.

To conclude, the current scalar DBT is not able to translate VLIW code for execution on scalar machines. To solve this issue, it is mandatory to modify the translation process to handle as efficiently as possible the delayed register updates.

4. DBT FOR VLIW

4.1 VLIW DBT Extension principles

First, the DBT has to handle the fact that multiple instructions are executed in parallel which may have destination registers being source registers of others. The simple approach that consists of reordering the instructions in the execute packet so that the instructions writing a register are placed after the one reading it is the most efficient, but does not always have a solution (*e.g.* circular dependencies).

A heavier but systematic approach consists of introducing copies of the original registers for instructions using an overwritten register, so we opt for this solution. A simple way to apply it to solve the WAR dependency due to parallel execution is to rename the target registers using a single assignment scheme. This strategy is similar to the Static Single Assignment (SSA [21]) form used in compilation if we consider target registers as variables.

This renaming is quite simple. Each register, for example `a0`, is present under multiple names build incrementally, *i.e.* `a0_0`, `a0_1`, and so on. We create one new version of the register each time it is assigned as a destination of an instruction and use it in the subsequent execute packets.

Applied to the intra-instruction WAR dependency, we will have at most two living versions of the register in each execute packet, one corresponding to the old value and one corresponding to the updated value.

The Algorithm 2 gives the DBT algorithm adapted for this single assignments in which we create replicates *r* on each output operand *op* assignments in an Execution Packet (*ep*). At the end of each Execution Packet we finally alias the target registers to their newer replicates and remove old ones.

Algorithm 2 Single Assignment registers applied on naïve DBT

```
while ¬end_of_tb() do
    ep ← get_next_execute_packet()
    for insn ∈ ep do
        op ← get_op_out(insn)
        r ← new_replicate(op)
        translate(insn, r)
    end for
    do_end_of_cycle_updates()
end while
```

The application of this algorithm on original VLIW code of Listing 1 produces the IR operations sequence presented in Listing 3.

Listing 3: Single Assignment registers example

```
; IR operation                 ;    original instruction ; Cyc
add_i32  a2_1, a2_0, a1_0 ;    add   .L1 a2, a1, a2 ; 1
sub_i32  a6_1, a1_0, a4_0 ; || sub   .D1 a1, a4, a6 ; 1
mul_i32  a3_1, a2_0, a1_0 ; || mpy32 .M1 a2, a1, a3 ; 1
mov_i32  pce1_1, $0xbeef  ;    b     .S1 0xbeef     ; 2
exit_tb  0x0              ;                         ;
sub_i32  a3_2, a6_1, a3_1 ;    sub   .D1 a6, a3, a3 ; 3
add_i32  a4_1, a2_1, a3_2 ;    add   .L1 a2, a3, a4 ; 4
mul_i32  a5_1, a2_1, a3_2 ;    mpy32 .M1 a2, a3, a5 ; 5
# nop 2                   ;    nop    2             ; 6,7
add_i32  a5_2, a2_1, a3_2 ;    add   .L1 a2, a3, a5 ; XXX
```

This solution clearly solves the WAR problem, since the operand register of the `mul` is the old version of register `a2` and not the newer one that is the outcome of the `add` instruction. Unfortunately this simple register renaming strategy does not solve the issue of arithmetic operations delay slots.

Indeed, `a3_1` will be used for the `sub` instruction whereas this value is not the correct one since it is not available yet in the architecture. To solve this, the old version must be used instead of the new one for all cycles within the producing instruction delay slots. This results in keeping possibly alive more than two versions of the same register at the same moment, which is clearly not the case in conventional SSA.

The translation algorithm is adapted to handle these arithmetic and logic instructions delay slots and presented in Algorithm 3. The creation of replicates takes into account the result availability delay. At the end of each Execution Packet we update the delays of replicates and alias the target registers to new replicates only if delay falls to zero. The translation result of the previous example is given in Listing 4.

Algorithm 3 Delay slot handling

```
while ¬end_of_tb() do
    ep ← get_next_execute_packet()
    for insn ∈ ep do
        d ← get_delay(insn)
        op ← get_op_out(insn)
        r ← new_replicate(op, d)
        translate(insn, r)
    end for
    do_end_of_cycle_updates()
end while
```

The number of living versions of the registers increases, but fortunately, this number is still bounded to a reasonable amount, which is the maximum instruction latency plus 1. Indeed, the worst case is a sequence of largest latency instructions writing to the same register. In that case, one living version must exist for each instruction executed between the execution of the first occurrence and the availability of its result, plus one version for the previous value.

Listing 4: Arithmetic delay slots handling

```
; IR operation                 ;    original instruction ; Cyc
add_i32  a2_1, a2_0, a1_0 ;    add   .L1 a2, a1, a2 ; 1
sub_i32  a6_1, a1_0, a4_0 ; || sub   .D1 a1, a4, a6 ; 1
mul_i32  a3_1, a2_0, a1_0 ; || mpy32 .M1 a2, a1, a3 ; 1
mov_i32  pce1_1, $0xbeef  ;    b     .S1 0xbeef     ; 2
exit_tb  0x0              ;                         ;
sub_i32  a3_2, a6_1, a3_0 ;    sub   .D1 a6, a3, a3 ; 3
add_i32  a4_1, a2_1, a3_2 ;    add   .L1 a2, a3, a4 ; 4
mul_i32  a5_1, a2_1, a3_1 ;    mpy32 .M1 a2, a3, a5 ; 5
# nop 2                   ;    nop    2             ; 6,7
add_i32  a5_2, a2_1, a3_1 ;    add   .L1 a2, a3, a5 ; XXX
```

Finally, the branches are handled in two phases. Firstly, the code responsible for the computation of the branch target address is generated when encountering the branch. Secondly, a TB ending instruction is produced after the delayed instructions. Listing 5 gives the corresponding modified sequence of IR operations.

Listing 5: Branch delay slots handling

```
; IR operation                 ;    original instruction ; Cyc
add_i32  a2_1, a2_0, a1_0 ;    add   .L1 a2, a1, a2 ; 1
sub_i32  a6_1, a1_0, a4_0 ; || sub   .D1 a1, a4, a6 ; 1
mul_i32  a3_1, a2_0, a1_0 ; || mpy32 .M1 a2, a1, a3 ; 1
mov_i32  pce1_1, $0xbeef  ;    b     .S1 0xbeef     ; 2
                          ;                         ;
sub_i32  a3_2, a6_1, a3_0 ;    sub   .D1 a6, a3, a3 ; 3
add_i32  a4_1, a2_1, a3_2 ;    add   .L1 a2, a3, a4 ; 4
mul_i32  a5_1, a2_1, a3_1 ;    mpy32 .M1 a2, a3, a5 ; 5
# nop 2                   ;    nop    2             ; 6,7
exit_tb  0x0              ;
add_i32  a5_2, a2_1, a3_1 ;    add   .L1 a2, a3, a5 ; XXX
```

4.1.1 TBB entry and exit states

Using the above described techniques (plus others not described here but similar in spirit, to handle for example predicated instructions), we obtain a sequential intermediate translation using registers replicates accomplishing the exact functional behavior of the source VLIW code. As can be realized by using the renaming strategy, the working version (currently used versions) of the registers is unpredictable. More precisely, as TB are translated independently, we cannot rely on these working versions. Indeed, when a TBB has several different predecessors, we cannot guaranty that the working version will be identical at the exit of all the preceding TBBs, and the translator does not even know if a TBB has more than one predecessor when performing the translation.

The solution for handling this need of TBB independence is to define an unique entry and exit working register set for TBs. This set will be called the canonical state of replicate registers. In that way, once translated, the TB will be reusable from all TBs pointing to it. The canonical state will be composed of the first replicate of each register, in which are mapped the first version of each register at the beginning of TB translation (`an_0` in our case).

The Algorithm 4 is called at the end of each translation block generation to fulfill the canonical state requirements

Algorithm 4 Canonical state return algorithm

> **for** $r \in$ target_registers **do**
> $rep \leftarrow$ get_current_replicate(r)
>   **if** $\neg$is_first_replicate(rep) **then**
>   gen_mov(get_canonical_replicate(r), rep)
>   **end if**
> **end for**

Unfortunately, in some cases, the delay slots crosses the border of a TBB, for example the `a5_1` register which is the result of the last `mul` in the code example. In that case, an external mechanism needs to be set up to handle these delay slots. This mechanisms needs to be external to the translator because of the TBB independence requirements. Indeed, the translator looses the information about delay slots when exiting a TB and thus only an execution time mechanism can manage the delay slots in that case.

This mechanism records the pending delayed registers with their current cycle delay when exiting the current TBB at run-time. The next TBB executed consults the recorded data during its first execution cycles (bounded by the maximum possible latency) to check if there are some registers needing to be updated as they reach their latency. This is done through function calls inserted by the translator.

4.2 Complexity of the modifications

From a pure functional point of view, all modifications needed to implement the VLIW DBT are part of the translator. The code generator does not strictly need to be modified for this support.

The modifications needed are first a change from a simple array of registers in which each cell represents a target register to an array of these registers in which a line represents all the replicates of one target register. This change requires to modify all mechanisms at translation time to allocate the correct replicate each time an assignment to a target register occurs.

The delay slot handling, delaying use of a newer replicate, can be modeled using a queue, in which future versions of registers can be inserted at the corresponding delay. At the end of each cycle all delayed register versions progress of one cycle in the delay queue. All these computations occur at translation-time. Complexity is once again limited.

The handling of the canonical state implies a modification of the translator, but impacts the generated code. Indeed, the easiest way to return to the canonical state at the end of a translation block is to generate instructions that move current working replicates of registers to the ones defined in the canonical state. This solution has a limited complexity as far as we consider only the translation phase but has the unfortunate side-effect of increasing the TBB size, and thus its execution time.

Finally, the handling of delay slots crossing TBB edges is a pure run-time mechanism. This mechanism has to be identical for all TBB to be valid for all sequences of TBB. The amount of generated code for this purpose is not huge, as it consists of generating function calls (usually called *helpers*) to propagate correctly the register updates. Even though the functions themselves are quite straightforward since they only handle registers updates through a runtime delay queue similar to the one described before, the runtime overheads necessary to set-up and perform these calls are quite large compared to a simple sequence of generated host instructions.

5. EXPERIMENTS

We have implemented a translator for the C6x processor family using the previously presented concepts within the QEMU DBT environment. Firstly, we have performed unitary tests (not reported here) to ensure correctness of the translation. Secondly, we have analysed the generated code to quantify the contribution of each stage of the translation to it. Finally, we have run a few kernels for performance measurements that we compared with execution speeds obtained using the simulator, based on instruction interpretation, included in Texas Instruments Code Composer Studio (CCS).

- The `fibo` program computes the Fibonacci number of a given index using the naïve recurrence relation $F_i = F_{i-1} + F_{i-2}$ with $F_0 = 0$ and $F_1 = 1, \forall i \in \mathbb{N}$. It involves a lot of branches,
- The `matrix` program multiplies two square matrices of size $j \times j$. It performs a lot of memory accesses and operations, and branches occur only at loop boundaries,
- The `idct` program computes the inverse discrete cosine transform of k jpeg macro-blocks of 64 16 bit unsigned integers using Loeffler algorithm. It does a huge amount of arithmetical and logical operations on fixed point integers, but not many loop iterations.

Note that the parameters i, j, k are given as constants in the program so as to benefit from the compiler static optimizations, if any.

The first Figure (Fig. 4) represents the *origin* of the host instructions generated in the TBB in average for varying values of each program parameter. In order to evaluate actual general purpose code, we also translated an application containing calls to the standard C library functions.

The *Target instructions* gives the average target instructions within a translation block for the given test. It ranges from an average of 7 for the stdlib code to up to almost 40 for the matrix one. The *Micro-ops for pure target instructions simulation* represents the number of bare instructions, similar to what is necessary for a scalar to scalar translation, and features a factor of 4 to 5 (`idct` has the biggest factor) compared to the target instructions over all programs. The other origins are due to the VLIW nature of the target code, as explained in Section 4. The *Micro-ops to handle canonical state return* reports the number of prologue and epilogue instructions necessary to make each TBB independent of its calling context. It varies between 20 and 40 instructions, and represents a larger percentage overhead for the smaller translated blocks (`fibo` and `stdlib`). The *Micro-ops to handle cross-border delays* represents the overhead in term of micro-operations due to the calls to the runtime mecanism that handle cross-border delays. It represents overall very few instructions, always less than 10 even for the largest basic blocks. Overall, for these simple programs, the instruction mix is very consistent for the whole range of the parameter.

The following set of curves (Figs. 5, 6 and 7) gives the simulation run times using the exact same binary code produced by the TI compiler on both platforms. The `fibo` and `matrix` tests have an

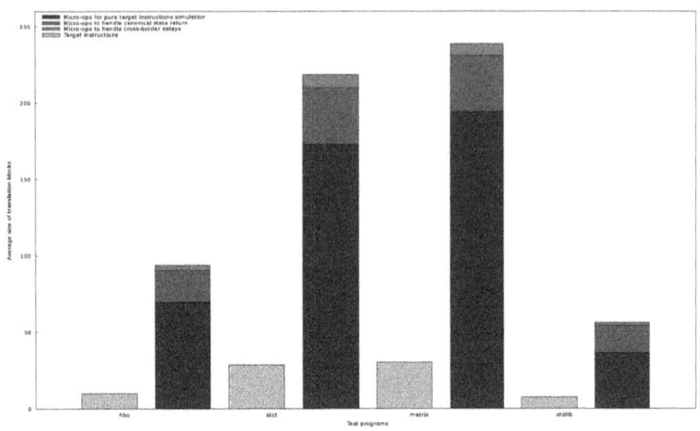

Figure 4: Host instruction origin for the `fibo`, `idct`, `matrix`, `stdlib` test

exponential algorithmic complexity with respect to their parameter, whereas the `idct` has a linear one. Note that for these measures, we didn't take into account the overhead due to the simulators initializations. For the CCS simulator, the entire java environment is loaded, and the program is ready to run when the time measurement begins. For QEMU, the measure is started when QEMU initiates the translation of the very first translation block.

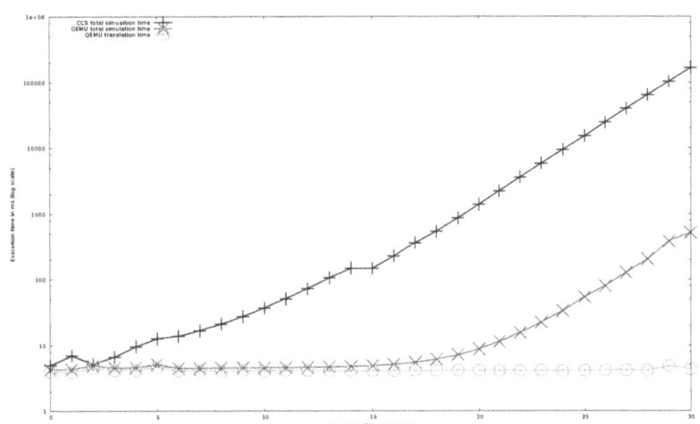

Figure 5: Execution time of the `fibo` program

These tests clearly show the performance advantages of the DBT, compared to the direct interpretation. When the simulated program is very small in term of computation workload, (when the parameter is near 0), we can see that the performances are equivalent. On the `idct` test, the CCS simulator is even better when computing one block. But when the parameter increases, the dynamic binary translator gains a dramatical advantage, thanks to the reuse of the translated code.

For the `fibo` test, there is about a factor 320 for the lasts indexes between QEMU and CCS. For the `matrix` test, the factor is about 175 for the bigger matrices. Finally, for the bigger number of blocks to compute in the `idct` test, QEMU is arount 18 to 25 times faster than the CCS simulator. It shows that, even with all the corner cases workarounds described in Section 4 that make the generated code more complex, the DBT approach is still efficient enough to be considered as a viable solution.

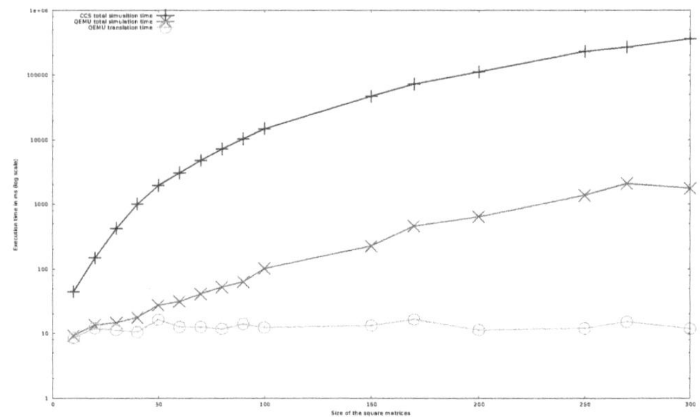

Figure 6: Execution time of the `matrix` program

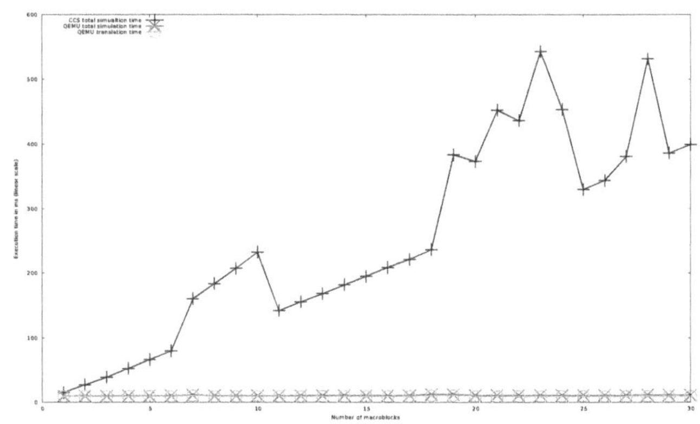

Figure 7: Execution time of the `idct` program

6. SUMMARY AND PERSPECTIVES

In this paper we have presented a solution for the Dynamic Binary Translation (DBT) of VLIW codes onto scalar machines. The approach requires deep modifications in the translator due to the registers update latencies. It has been dealt with through a mix of techniques acting both at translation and execution time. Even though these overheads are not negligible, our experiments have shown gains from 20× to 300×. Nevertheless, the translation is still basic, in the sense that our goal was to demonstrate the feasibility of VLIW code translation on scalar architecture and we did not perform any optimization on it. As a matter of fact, QEMU is known to perform very fast translation, but to produce straightforward host code. Due to the nature of the translated code, it is quite likely that optimizing often executed translated blocks (called hotspots) will result in large gains. Indeed, very naïve local optimization easily gains 20% speed according to [22], and [23], optimizing along the most often used paths, claims a gain of above 60%. A future work is thus to enhance the quality of the translated code while keeping the translation overhead under control, by using the above solutions and by trying to optimize the VLIW specific parts of the translator.

References

[1] A. Nohl, G. Braun, O. Schliebusch, R. Leupers, H. Meyr, and A. Hoffmann. A universal technique for fast and flexible instruction-set architecture simulation. In *39th Design*

Automation Conference, pages 22–27, 2002.

[2] F. Pétrot, N. Fournel, P. Gerin, M. Gligor, M. Hamayun, and H. Shen. On MPSoC software execution at transaction-level. *Design & Test of Computers, IEEE*, 28(3):32–43, 2011.

[3] M. Montón, J. Carrabina, and M. Burton. Mixed simulation kernels for high performance virtual platforms. In *Forum on Specification & Design Languages*, pages 1–6, September 2009.

[4] M. Gligor, N. Fournel, and F. Pétrot. Using binary translation in event driven simulation for fast and flexible MPSoC simulation. In *CODES+ISSS*, pages 71–80, October 2009.

[5] W. Mueller, M. F. da S. Oliveira, H. Zabel, and M. Becker. Verification of real-time properties for hardware- dependent software. In *High Level Design, Verification and Test Workshop*, Anaheim, CA, June 2010.

[6] R. Leupers, L. Eeckhout, G. Martin, F. Schirrmeister, N. Topham, and X. Chen. Virtual manycore platforms: Moving towards 100+ processor cores. In *Proceedings of the Design, Automation and Test in Europe Conference*, pages 715–720, Grenoble, France, March 2011. IEEE.

[7] C. Cifuentes and V. Malhotra. Binary translation: Static, dynamic, retargetable? In *IEEE International Conference on Software Maintenance*, page 340, Los Alamitos, CA, USA, 1996. IEEE Computer Society.

[8] L. Baraz, T. Devor, O. Etzion, S. Goldenberg, A. Skaletsky, Y. Wang, and Y. Zemach. IA-32 Execution Layer: a two-phase dynamic translator designed to support IA-32 applications on itanium-based systems. In *Proceedings of the 36th annual IEEE/ACM International Symposium on Microarchitecture*, pages 191–202, 2003.

[9] C. Cifuentes and M. Van Emmerik. UQBT: Adaptable Binary Translation at Low Cost. *Computer*, 33(3):60–66, 2000.

[10] P. J. Drongowski, D. Hunter, M. Fayyazi, D. Kaeli, and J. Casmira. Studying the Performance of the FX!32 Binary Translation System. In *the First Workshop on Binary Translation*, 1999.

[11] D. Ung and C. Cifuentes. Machine-adaptable dynamic binary translation. In *DYNAMO '00*, pages 41–51, 2000.

[12] F. Bellard. QEMU, a fast and portable dynamic translator. In *the USENIX Annual Technical Conference*, pages 41–46, 2005.

[13] J. C. Dehnert, B. K. Grant, J. P. Banning, R. Johnson, T. Kistler, A. Klaiber, and J. Mattson. The transmeta code morphing software: using speculation, recovery, and adaptive retranslation to address real-life challenges. In *Proceedings of the international symposium on Code generation and optimization: feedback-directed and runtime optimization*, pages 15–24, 2003.

[14] K. Ebcioğlu and E. R. Altman. DAISY: Dynamic Compilation for 100% Architectural Compatibility. In *ISCA 24*, pages 26 – 37, 1997.

[15] C. Zheng and C. Thompson. PA-RISC to IA-64: Transparent execution, no recompilation. *Computer*, 33(3):47–52, 2000.

[16] V. Bala, E. Duesterwald, and S. Banerjia. Dynamo: a transparent dynamic optimization system. In *ACM conference on Programming language design and implementation*, pages 1–12, 2000.

[17] L. Peter Deutsch and Allan M. Schiffman. Efficient implementation of the smalltalk-80 system. In *Proc. of the 11th ACM SIGACT-SIGPLAN Symp. on Principles of programming languages*, pages 297–302, 1984.

[18] B. Yuncheng, L. Alei, and G. Haibing. Design and implementation of crossbit: Dynamic binary translation infrastructure. *Computer Engineering*, 33(23):100 – 134, 2007.

[19] J. Li, Q. Zhang, S. Xu, and B. Huang. Optimizing dynamic binary translation for SIMD instructions. In *Code Generation and Optimization*, March 2006.

[20] L. Michel, N. Fournel, and F. Pétrot. Speeding-up SIMD instructions dynamic binary translation in embedded processor simulation. In *Proceedings of the Design, Automation & Test in Europe Conference*, pages 277–280. IEEE, 2011.

[21] R. Cytron, J. Ferrante, B. K. Rosen, M. N. Wegman, and F. K. Zadeck. Efficiently computing static single assignment form and the control dependence graph. *ACM Transactions on Programming Languages and Sytems*, 13:451–490, 1991.

[22] Y. Hu, H. Jin, Z. Yu, and H. Zheng. An optimization approach for qemu. In *1st International Conference on Information Science and Engineering*, pages 129 –132, dec. 2009.

[23] D. Jones and N. Topham. High speed CPU simulation using LTU dynamic binary translation. In *High Performance Embedded Architectures and Compilers*, volume 5409 of *LNCS*, pages 50–64. 2009.

DIMSim: A Rapid Two-level Cache Simulation Approach for Deadline-based MPSoCs

Mohammad Shihabul Haque
Dept. of Elect. and Comp. Eng.
National University of Singapore
elemsh@nus.edu.sg

Roshan Ragel
and S. Radhakrishnan
Dept. of Computer Eng.
University of Peradeniya
ragelrg@gmail.com

Angelo Ambrose
and Sri Parameswaran
School of CSE
University of New South Wales
ajangelo@cse.unsw.edu.au

ABSTRACT

It is of critical importance to satisfy deadline requirements for an embedded application to avoid undesired outcomes. Multiprocessor System-on-Chips (MPSoCs) play a vital role in contemporary embedded devices to satisfy timing deadlines. Such MPSoCs include two-level cache hierarchies which have to be dimensioned carefully to support timing deadlines of the application(s) while consuming minimum area and therefore minimum power. Given the deadline of an application, it is possible to systematically derive the maximum time that could be spent on memory accesses which can then be used to dimension the suitable cache sizes. As the dimensioning has to be done rapidly to satisfy the time to market requirement, we choose a well acclaimed rapid cache simulation strategy, the single-pass trace driven simulation, for estimating the cache dimensions. Therefore, for the first time, we address the two main challenges, coherency and scalability, in adapting a single-pass simulator to a MPSoC with two-level cache hierarchy. The challenges are addressed through a modular bottom-up simulation technique where L1 and L2 simulations are handled in independent communicating modules. In this paper, we present how the dimensioning is performed for a two-level inclusive data cache hierarchy in an MPSoC. With the rapid simulation proposed, the estimations are suggested within an hour (worst case on considered application benchmarks). We experimented our approach with task based MPSoC implementations of JPEG and H264 benchmarks and achieved timing deviations of 16.1% and 7.2% respectively on average against the requested data access times. The deviation numbers are always positive meaning our simulator guarantees to satisfy the requested data access time. In addition, we generated a set of synthetic memory traces and used them to extensively analyse our simulator. For the synthetic traces, our simulator provides cache sizes to always guarantee the requested data access time, deviating below 14.5% on average.

CODES+ISSS'12, October 7-12, 2012, Tampere, Finland.

Categories and Subject Descriptors

B.8.2 [**PERFORMANCE AND RELIABILITY**]: Performance Analysis and Design Aids

General Terms

Algorithm, Performance, Design

Keywords

Cache Hierarchy, Design Space Exploration, MPSoC, Trace-driven, Simulation

1. INTRODUCTION

Estimating performance in embedded systems, particularly in the face of many choices is difficult. Two separate aspects make it challenging. The first is that there are many differing hardware components which can be varied (for example, the processor, the co-processors, cache sizes and even instructions); and, the second is that the benchmarks which are executed on the system at design time might not be completely representative of the actual load that the system might endure during its lifetime (for example, in a multimedia system the processing load can vary significantly with the images encountered).

Designers tackle the first aspect by fixing as many components as possible; and the second is addressed by allowing a margin for worst case situations, unforeseen operating systems interventions and interrupts.

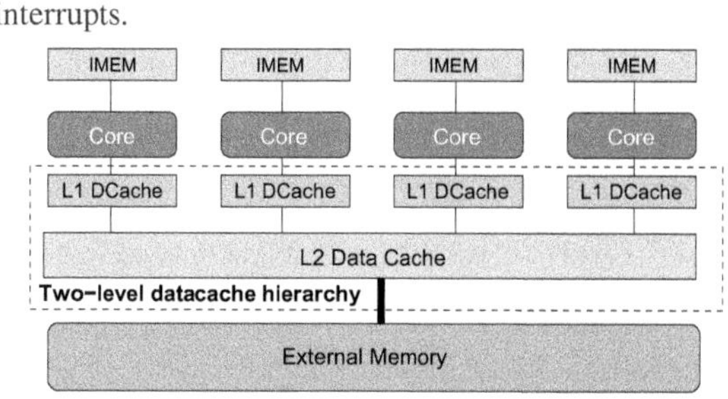

Figure 1: Two-level Cache Hierarchy in MPSoC Architecture

In this paper we examine a method of sizing L1 and inclusive L2 data caches for a multiprocessor embedded system. All other components are fixed (i.e. processor, instruction set, coprocessors, etc.). We first size L2 to meet the requirements needed by the system with the given trace (i.e. we assume that L1 cache does not exist). Then we size L1 caches to allow for the margin desired. In a ten processor system, it is possible that we could have 180^{11} configurations[1], and searching for an optimal scheme, or simulating through all of them is not possible. A trace for 100 micro seconds in a 10 processor system will yield 1 billion memory accesses at 1GHz. Thus an optimal method would be difficult, and thus we provide a fast heuristic to meet our provided miss rates and margins.

Cache simulation techniques can assist the designer in estimating the suitable cache configurations long before the system is implemented. Application trace driven simulation [16] is a well known approach to achieve such an estimation in a very short time. A single-pass simulator [25], which is robust, fast and resource generous, is a type of trace driven simulator. It traverses the memory access trace of an application one entry at a time and calculates the number of cache misses for different cache configurations. As the memory access time and therefore the execution time[2] of an application is influenced by the number of cache misses, this number is used in single-pass simulators to decide a suitable cache configuration to satisfy the application deadline and area budget.

Two-level inclusive[3] data cache hierarchies are widely utilised in MPSoCs [5, 18, 23] for sharing data among processors. Figure 1 depicts a commonly used two-level MPSoC architecture in contemporary chips [15], which is our target architecture. In our architecture, the processor cores include private L1 and shared L2 *inclusive data caches*, together with private instruction memories (note that similar to [7], our system has instruction memories local to each processor).

Utilising a single-pass simulator to simulate a cache hierarchy as in Figure 1 is challenging, nevertheless beneficial in quickly finding the right cache configurations required for a *set of communicating multiprocessor applications or tasks*. The two main challenges are:

1. *Maintaining coherency across processors, where multiple processors can access (read and write) a shared data memory space through a two-level inclusive cache hierarchy.* Current single-pass simulators do not consider such data sharing and therefore the data structure and the simulation strategy have to be adapted and extended to support coherency. Conflict scenarios are already covered for uniprocessors in two-level single-pass simulations [31] and can be directly applied in two-level cache hierarchies for MPSoCs;
2. *Maintaining scalability for both simulation time and storage space of the simulator with the increasing number of L1 private caches (or cores) in the system.* For a given cache hierarchy, such as the one shown in Figure 1, the cache simulator must select the suitable configuration for each and every cache memory used in the hierarchy. Single-pass simulators read the application trace only once and simulate all the cache configurations together. Therefore, a large combination of cache configurations have to be simulated together at once and this number will exponentially increase with the number of private L1 caches. Such a simulation would result in exponential growths in both the time needed and the memory storage required.

In this paper, for the first time, we address the challenges discussed above in selecting the cache configurations in a two-level *inclusive data cache hierarchy* to satisfy application deadlines in MPSoCs. The technique we propose takes a bottom-up approach (from L2 to L1), named "DIMSim" (Dual Independent Modular Simulation), that performs independent simulations on each level of the cache hierarchy. Given that the L2 simulation can be handled by the current single-pass simulators, our approach *reduces the complexity of DIMSim by first simulating the shared L2 cache* and then performing the private L1 cache simulations while addressing coherency. As detailed in Section 3, DIMSim uses its L2 module to satisfy the requested data access time constraint and L1 module to satisfy the requested headroom time (an overhead incurred by the system). It is worth noting that the modular approach we have devised is scalable for both simulation time and storage space with the increasing number of L1 private caches (i.e. the number of cores).

DIMSim considers the most widely used First-In-First-Out (FIFO) replacement policy (e.g., Intel XScale [1], ARM9 [3], ARM11 [2] and Tensilica Xtensa LX2 processors [29]) in our architecture. To the best of our knowledge,caches for embedded systems are designed using area and power constraints and the applications are mapped in a post-production stage. We take a different (and we believe a better) route to this approach by providing a notion of application performance during the design phase in an attempt to further optimise the total cache size.

Problem Statement: Provided the application trace of (cacheless) memory accesses of an MPSoC with shared data, find the cache configurations (set size, associativity and cache line size), for each private L1s and shared L2, to satisfy an allowable number of cache misses.

Layout: The rest of the paper is organised as follows: Section 2 describes the related work, while Section 3 details the DIMSim simulation approach. The experiments and the results are presented in Section 4 and Section 5 respectively. We finally conclude with Section 6.

2. RELATED WORK

Due to power and performance critical nature of modern computer systems, the necessity to find the optimal (or near optimal) cache configuration has become an important issue in computer system design. State-of-the-art cache design space exploration techniques can be broadly categorised into: 1) System Simulations [30], 2) Instruction Set Simulations (in SystemC) [21] and 3) Trace driven simulations [25]. Available system simulation tools such as [30] are difficult to customise and hard to program with respect to cache configurations. These tools incur significant simulation time (even several days) just to simulate a single cache configuration for a specific application in MPSoC. The instruction set simulators [21] are faster to simulate a specific cache configuration, but still simulates one cache configuration at a time and therefore consumes significant amount of time. Trace driven cache simulations [25], however, do not require architecture related information, and are the fastest amongst all, providing cache dimensions well before the design phase. Furthermore, trace driven simulators are capable of simulating multiple cache configurations at a time. Memory footprint of the application in the form of traces is the only input necessary.

Due to higher abstraction with respect to the actual architecture, various types of speedup mechanisms can be applied to trace driven simulation methods. Four of the popular speedup mechanisms applied to trace driven simulations are: 1) Compressed trace simulation, 2) Parallel simulation, 3) Sample-based simulation and 4) Single-pass simulation. *Compressed trace simulation* [20, 22, 26, 27] prunes redundant information to compress the application's

[1]assuming 180 different possible configurations for each cache

[2]when the execution time deadline of an application is given, it is possible to systematically derive the required/*requested memory access time*

[3]shared cache contains the superset of private caches as opposed to exclusive cache where the content will only be present in either level of the cache hierarchy

memory access trace, resulting in a reduced simulation time. *Parallel simulation techniques* perform the simulation of a group of cache configurations in parallel on multiple processors [4, 10, 13]. *Sample based simulation* [6, 17, 19, 28] combines simulation and sampling such as getting the memory trace for a fixed number of cycles to reduce simulation time overhead. In *single-pass simulation*, the application trace is read only once and various cache configurations are simulated together. Unlike parallel simulation, single-pass simulation utilises one processing unit as optimally as possible and can be combined with parallel or compressed trace simulation methods for further speedup [25]. Single-pass simulation approaches usually exploit cache inclusion properties [11, 12] and custom-tailored data structures (such as binomial tree [16, 24]) to reduce processing time without the help of additional hardware.

To find the most appropriate cache configurations for an MPSoC system like the one in Figure 1, most suitable configurations must be found for all the private and shared cache memories. However, to simulate the behaviour of one processor's private/shared cache memory, other private and shared cache memories in the system must also be simulated to maintain coherency. Therefore, when single-pass simulation methods are utilised in finding the appropriate caches in MPSoCs, a large combination of cache configurations has to be simulated by reading the application trace once. As a result, space and time consumption becomes a critical concern. To the best of our knowledge, no single-pass method has ever been adapted to simulate cache hierarchy of an MPSoC and therefore none of them ever had to address coherency issues. In this paper, we focus on designing a fast and space efficient cache simulation technique for *two-level inclusive data cache hierarchies* in MPSoCs.

Therefore, the **contributions** of DIMSim are as follows:

- We propose the first ever cache simulator (DIMSim) for MPSoCs that adapts the *single-pass strategy*. DIMSim will not only simulate a two-level data cache hierarchy (private L1s and shared L2) rapidly, but also work with deadline constraints. Therefore, DIMSim addresses the two main challenges in simulating a data cache hierarchy for deadline constrained MPSoCs: (1) coherency; and (2) scalability.
- The scalability is addressed (1) by breaking the simulator into two *independent* communicating modules (L1 and L2 simulators) and (2) by enabling the private cache simulations to be performed in parallel for each processor (more detail in Section 3).
- The coherency issue is addressed through a novel bottom up (L2 first and then L1s) simulation with *communicating* modules. As detailed later in the paper, the information passed through the interaction was used effectively to handle coherency.

3. METHODOLOGY

Given that DIMSim is expected to take the application deadline (also known as *requested execution time*, RET) as the input and to decide of the suitable cache configurations, we could formulate Equation 1 to represent RET. In Equation 1, RET refers to the requested execution time and AET refers to the actual execution time. $TTDM$ is to the total time spent on data memory access and $TTNM$ is the total time spent on non data memory operations. $TTOH$ refers to the total time spent on overheads such as the time spent for handling the scheduling and operating system overheads which are system specific and are not covered by the application trace. Our timing model as in Equation 1 is formulated such that introducing a cache hierarchy or changing cache sizes would only effect $TTDM$ and not $TTNM$ or $TTOH$.

$$RET \geq AET = TTDM + TTNM + TTOH \qquad (1)$$

The *RET* is provided by the user, considering the application(s) throughput and latency constraints (e.g., JPEG encoder application has to encode an image within 20ms for the K7 Pentax Camera). The user will also provide a requested headroom time, $RHRT$. DIMSim addresses to satisfy both $TTDM$ (via its L2 estimation) and $TTOH$ (via its L1 estimation).

Figure 2 depicts the DIMSim flow. Pre-processing of the trace to create the shared memory trace and add tags (explained later) takes place before the simulation. The DIMSim simulation itself is broken down into three stages: (1) L2 simulation; (2) Secondary trace generation; and (3) L1 simulation. Pre-processing is performed to prepare the trace for the simulator. While the MPSoC embedded system (without caches) is executing an application as communicating tasks or multiple applications, memory accesses are observed and captured at the memory controller hence the order of access is correct. The data accesses from the trace are then extracted and annotated (read/write, memory-address, processor-ID) as depicted.

DIMSim approach consists of the following three stages:

STAGE-1: Finding the suitable shared L2 data cache configuration that satisfies the requested data access time

As depicted in Figure 2, in STAGE-1, DIMSim takes the whole data access trace of the application and the requested data access time $RDAT$ ($= RET - TTNM$) and estimates the shared L2 data cache configuration. In STAGE-1, DIMSim assumes that the system has only a shared memory and there exist no L1 caches. As the total time spent on data memory (when only L2 cache is present ($TTDM_{L2}$)) of an application will increase with the number of cache misses, the acceptable number of cache misses in L2, called "ML", that satisfies the $RDAT$ is calculated using Equation 2. As shown in the equation, when a data is requested by the processor, the L2 is checked first and if not found, the memory is checked. Hence, every miss in L2 will incur T_M[4] seconds. On the other hand, the data which is found in L2 is served by the L2 in T_{L2} [5] seconds.

Considering that the total number of accesses is A by all the processors, the total hit time is $(A - ML) * T_{L2}$ seconds.

$$RDAT \geq TTDM_{L2} = ML * (T_M + T_{L2}) + (A - ML) * T_{L2} \qquad (2)$$

By reading the trace file once, DIMSim simulates all available cache configurations for L2. The result of this simulation would be a set of cache configurations that satisfies the ML. Among them, the smallest one in size is chosen as the suitable L2 shared cache to minimise the area and therefore to minimise the power consumption. The L2 simulation is implemented similar to CIPARSim [11], where pruning is applied to avoid simulating cache configurations which cannot support ML.

STAGE-2: Secondary trace generation to be used by the L1 simulator

When an L2 cache is shared among all the processor cores, co-

[4] T_M includes (the worst case) time to send a request from the L2 cache to memory, search time in memory, and time to send data from the memory to the L2 cache

[5] T_{L2} includes (the worst case) time to send a request from the processor to L2 cache, time to handle the coherency protocol, search time in L2, and the time to send data from L2 cache to processor

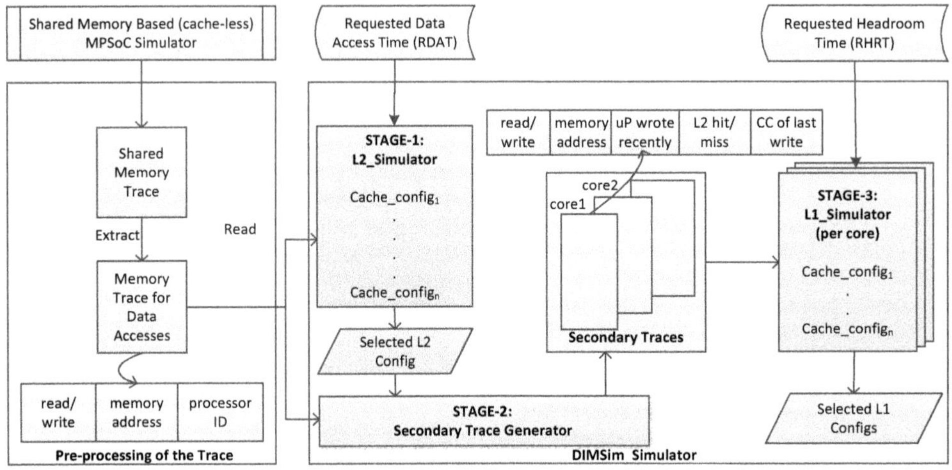

Figure 2: DIMSim Simulation Flow

herency is the first challenge that the simulator must handle in finding the suitable private L1 caches. We propose, both independent and communicating, L1 and L2 simulators, passing information from L2 simulator to L1 simulator. The interaction between the simulators is enabled through a secondary trace file that is derived by instrumenting our original trace depending on the selected L2 cache in STAGE-1.

As depicted in Figure 2, for each memory block address, a secondary trace file records: 1) operation code of the data access (e.g., data read or write), 2) the requested memory address, 3) the name of the processing core that wrote in that particular memory block most recently, 4) whether the block was a hit or miss in the selected L2 cache, and 5) clock cycle when the memory block was last written in the shared L2 cache. All the extra information (compared to the original trace) recorded in the memory block address help in implementing cache coherency protocols for MPSoCs. The next stage describes the process of coherency protocol implementation.

STAGE-3: Finding suitable L1 cache configurations for the selected shared L2 cache

As shown in Figure 2, once the secondary trace file is generated, it is divided into smaller trace files by grouping the accesses from each processing core into a separate file. To find the suitable private L1 cache for a particular processor core, its respective smaller trace file is utilised. Dividing the secondary trace file into smaller trace files allows our simulation process to be parallelised and therefore the L1 simulation can be made faster if desired.

DIMSim makes use of the fact that adding L1 caches will speed up the system to satisfy the second timing requirement, $RHRT$, provided as another input (apart from the requested execution time). The $RHRT$ requirement is distributed among cores proportional to the number of data memory accesses by each core. The suitable L1 cache configurations are selected to satisfy the $RHRT$ requirement of each core. It is worth noting that DIMSim ignores the fact that the individual cores can access their private L1 caches simultaneously as the input trace does not have this information. Therefore, DIMSim might potentially satisfy the $RHRT$ requirement with a larger margin.

By reading the corresponding smaller secondary trace file once, DIMSim simulates all available cache configurations to find the suitable private L1 per core. For every cache configuration simulated per core, the total number of memory access requests that cannot be served by the particular cache configuration (L1 misses) is recorded at runtime. The DIMSim L1 simulation component reads each smaller trace per core and scans through every entry which is fed into Algorithm 1 as explained later in this section.

To calculate the total number of cache misses incorporating coherency, DIMSim records the last content update time in each cache line in the simulated cache configurations. Any memory address which is indicated as a L2 miss in the secondary trace file will also cause a miss in the private cache memory during simulation due to the inclusive property. When a requested memory address content is found in shared cache (L2) as well as in the private cache memory (L1), the last update time written in the private cache line, which is holding the content, and the L2 update time written on the secondary trace file is compared. If it matches, cache hit is declared; otherwise, cache miss is recorded. Cache miss is also recorded if the requested memory address content is missing in the private cache configuration. On a cache miss, the requested content is placed in a cache line in the simulated cache configuration along with its last update time in the shared L2 cache memory. In this way, DIMSim approach implements coherency protocol without additional storage and time consumption.

Algorithm 1 reads every entry in the smaller trace and tries to evaluate whether it is a hit or a miss in each and every simulated cache configurations. The algorithm receives the address entry (i.e., Requested Address RA) from the secondary trace file (for every private L1 there will be one secondary trace file). Every entry in the secondary trace file is tagged with L2 hit or miss information as shown in Figure 2. Due to the inclusive property of the L1 and L2 caches, a miss in L2 will cause a miss in L1 as well. As shown in Algorithm 1, Function HandleCacheMiss is called when the RA is not available in the L2 cache (the L2 hit for that address in the secondary trace file indicates that the entry is available, likewise an L2 miss for that entry indicates that the address is unavailable). If the RA is available in L2 (else statement in Line 3), search in the L1 data structure (i.e., Central Look-up Table (CLT)) whether the RA is available. The Function HandleCacheMiss is called if RA is unavailable in CLT, which indicates a miss in that particular L1. A hit in L1 (i.e., RA is available in CLT; else statement starting at Line 7) requires recording information in the simulation tree. Starting from the root of the simulation tree all the levels in the tree (the simulation tree is explained in detail in Section 3.1) are traversed, until we reach the level with the largest set size. It is worth noting that misses can arise due to a data read or write. For each level (i.e., set size), iterate over all the associativities, starting from the small-

Algorithm 1: AddressEvaluation(RequestedAddress(RA))

```
if (RA was not available in L2 cache) then
    HandleCacheMiss(RA);
else
    Search RA in the look-up Table (CLT);
    if (RA is not available in CLT) then
        HandleCacheMiss(RA);
    else
        select the root tree level L = 0 (for cache set size S = 2^L);
        For both data read and write:
        while 2^L is not larger than the largest set size do
            A = the smallest associativity;
            while A is not larger than the largest associativity do
                if (RA is available in the selected cache configuration in
                the tree) then
                    if (RA writing time does not match with L2 writing
                    time) then
                        Record a cache miss in the cache configuration
                        and update the simulation tree;
                        Attach the writing time with RA in the tree;
                        Update the records of CLT to indicate tag
                        insertion;
                    else
                        Record a cache hit for the cache configuration;
                else
                    Record a cache miss in the cache configuration and
                    update the simulation tree;
                    Attach the most recent writing time with RA in the
                    tree;
                    Update the records of CLT to indicate tag insertion;
                A = Next larger associativity;
            L = L + 1; (continue to the next level)
```

est (this iteration is considered as analysing a cache configuration). If RA is found in the selected cache configuration in the tree, check whether the writing time matches with the L2's writing time. A match suggests an L1 data cache hit, hence will be updated as hit for that configuration in the simulation tree. A mismatch in timings denotes an L1 cache miss. Hence the cache configuration in the simulation tree is updated, including the writing time and a record in CLT to indicate tag insertion. If the cache configuration does not include the RA, record a cache miss in the configuration and update the simulation tree, while attaching the most recent writing time for the RA and an update in CLT to indicate tag insertion. The inner loop is iterated for each associativity and the outer for set size.

Function HandleCacheMiss(RA)

```
Record a cache miss in all the L1 cache configurations
Update the simulation tree and attach the most recent writing time with each
RA tag in the tree;
Update CLT for RA;
```

The Function HandleCacheMiss is called when the RA is either not in L2 cache (i.e., checked using the secondary trace file) or not in L1 (i.e., checked in CLT). All the cache configurations will be recorded as cache miss for the RA. The simulation tree and CLT are updated with the most recent writing time of the RA and RA entry respectively.

3.1 DIMSim Data Structure

The data structures used in DIMSim are influenced by CIPARSim [11], and the single cache configuration simulator DineroIV [8]. DIMSim utilises a central look-up table (CLT), as shown in Figure 3. Simulated cache configurations are represented using a binary simulation tree which is used to update the look-up table. In DIMSim, the binary simulation tree that is utilised in [11] is modified to accommodate the last writing time of each memory address tag, to handle coherency.

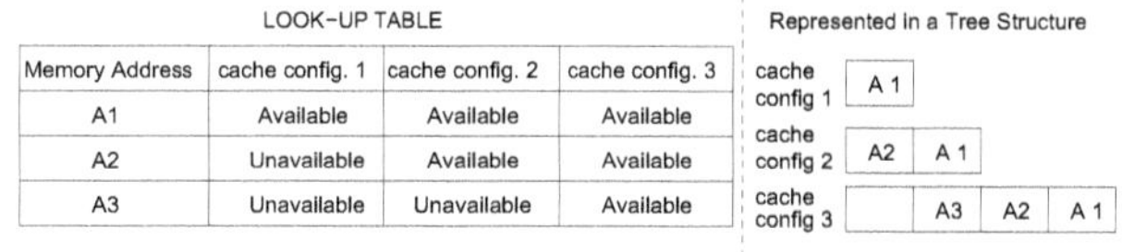

Figure 3: Central Look-up Table in DIMSim

For each cache line size, both the L2 and L1 simulation components in DIMSim utilises a simulation tree to represent cache memories and a Central Look-up Table (CLT), such as the one presented in Figure 4 and Figure 3 respectively, to determine cache hit/misses quickly. Each entry in the CLT records the availability of a memory block content in simulated cache configurations. For example, the memory block address A2 is available in cache configurations 2 and 3, but is unavailable in configuration 1. As the look-up table entries are sorted by memory block addresses, binary search is applied to quickly figure out the availability of a particular memory block in different cache configurations. All the cache configurations are included in the look-up table. In a simulation tree, each level represents a cache configuration. Each tree node represents a cache set in the cache configuration.

Figure 4 illustrates a simulation tree[6] representing three cache configurations with set size two, four and eight. The tree starts with a FIFO cache configuration containing two cache sets. The top left node, named '0', represents the cache set with index 0 in the cache with set size 2. Similarly, the second node '1' refers to cache set 1. At the second level of the two trees, there are a total of four nodes stamped '00', '10', '01' and '11'. Thus the second level represents a FIFO cache with set size of four, and the numbering within the nodes represent the respective cache sets as shown in Figure 4. Similarly, the third level (illustrated as the bottom level in Figure 4), will represent a FIFO cache with eight sets. More caches with bigger set sizes can be represented by expanding the tree further, which is not presented in this paper. It is assumed that the traditional mapping from memory address to cache sets is performed by taking the lower bits of the memory address to determine the set. Thus, the elements that map to any node of a tree will be mapped to its child nodes in the next level and only its child nodes.

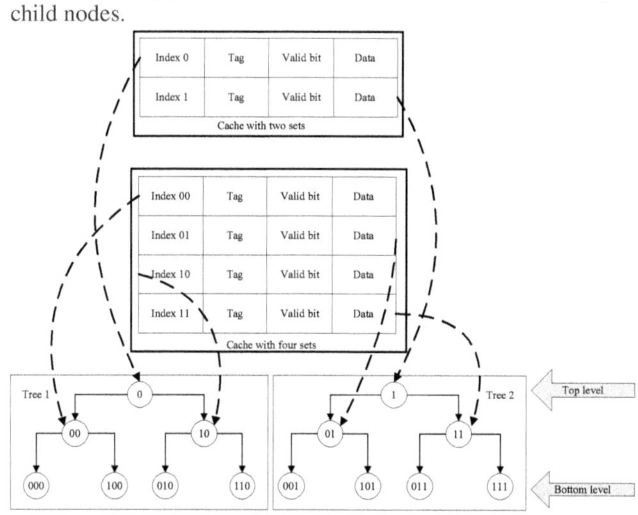

Figure 4: The Simulation Tree

[6]the simulation tree is developed based on CIPARSim [11]

Lists with varying number of nodes are attached with each tree node to represent different associativities. Each node inside a list represents a cache line and will have a pointer to the memory block address inside a look-up table set to indicate which memory block resides there. Each node in a simulation tree also stores the most recently inserted (MRI) memory block address of associativity two when the smallest associativity is two. The contents inside the associativity lists are replaced as in the FIFO caches. A bit called "Track_Flag" is also stored with each tree node when caches with associativity two are simulated. Whenever a new memory block is inserted into the list for associativity two, the Track_Flag is set to false (or 0). When an existing memory block of the associativity two in the selected tree node is re-accessed, the Track_Flag is set to true. A cache hit in the FIFO associativity two with Track_Flag set to true indicates that the memory block content is available in all the larger FIFO cache configurations in the same simulation tree. If the smallest associativity is larger than two, a bit "Intersection_Flag" per larger associativity is associated with each cache line in the smallest associativity list of a simulation tree node. Whenever a new memory block tag is inserted in a cache line in the smallest associativity list of a tree node, the Intersection_Flag is set to true if the same memory block tag is at least $((2 \times A_X) - 3)$ (where A_X is the smallest associativity) elements away from the replacement pointers in the other larger associativity lists in the same tree node. When a memory block content in the smallest associativity in a tree node is re-accessed, simulation can be avoided in the larger associativities if the Intersection_Flag is found true. To simulate direct mapped caches, Most Recently Accessed (MRA) tag must be saved for each simulation tree node.

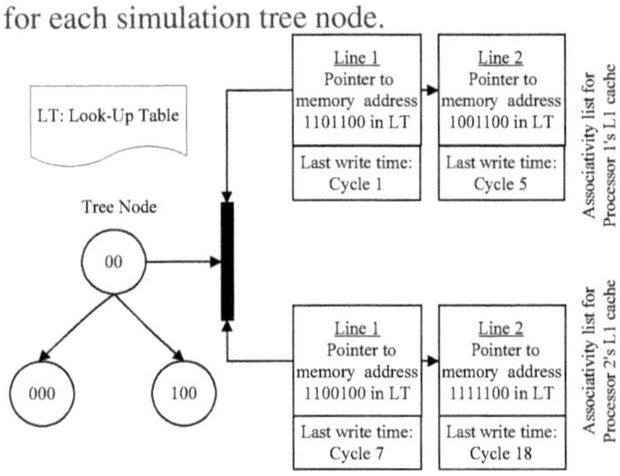

Figure 5: Associativity Lists

In Figure 5, an example tree node '00' from Figure 4 is presented with two FIFO associativity lists illustrated (namely associativity=2 and associativity=4) (this example is from [11]). Node '00' is from the second level in the tree of Figure 4. The second level of the tree of Figure 4 represents a FIFO cache with set size 4. The first cache line of the list for associativity 2 has a pointer to the memory block address "1101100" in the look-up table of DIMSim. Using these pointers, DIMSim can update the look-up table's bit arrays when the address "1101100" will be evicted from the associativity 2's list in tree node '00' due to a miss for that node. In the L1 simulator component of DIMSim, each cache line also stores the last writing time of the containing memory address tag to handle coherency.

4. EXPERIMENTS

We created synthetic data memory access traces to represent intercommunicating applications, mapped on different processors (a four core MPSoC), to perform an extensive analysis in our simulator to cover a significant portion of the design space. The synthetic traces are generated to ensure a better coverage of the data sharing among cores, thus representing coherency and conflict scenarios extensively. As explained in methodology, the memory traces are generated assuming a cache-less system and then the target is to estimate the cache sizes (we assumed a four-core system with private L1s and a shared L2) for different sharing scenarios. The traces are categorised based on the following features:

1. The number of processors that uses the shared memory: we assumed that a selected number of processors out of all four use shared data. Therefore, the rest of the processors use private data. When core1 and core2 sharing data and core3 and core4 accesses private data, we named this scenario **case 1**. When core1, core2 and core3 share data and core4 uses private data, we named this scenario **case 2**. When all four cores share data, we named this scenario **case 3**.

2. Data usage: the percentage of shared data accesses out of the total data memory accesses in the trace. We have used the following percentages in our experiments: 25%, 50%, 75% and 100%. The unshared data will be considered for (and will influence) conflict misses.

To further analyse our simulator on real applications, we implemented a six core (more number of cores compared to the synthetic experiments to verify scalability and performance) cache-less multiprocessor implementation using the Tensilica tool set [29] and executed JPEG encoder and H264 encoder (only the motion estimation kernel) to generate traces for different image and video benchmarks. Both the applications are partitioned into multiple communicating/sharing tasks which are mapped on separate processors. We chose JPEG and H264 since they represent real time applications which are widely used in embedded systems and have distributed sharing of data across all the cores.

For our simulation experiments, we executed the DIMSim simulator on a machine with a dual core Opteron64 2GHz processor, 8GB of main memory and 1MBytes L2 cache pre-distributed among the processing cores.

Cache Set Size=2^i	$0 <= i <= 14$
Line Size=i Bytes	$i \in 4, 16, 64$
Associativity=2^i	$1 <= i <= 4$

Table 1: Cache Configuration Parameters

In our experiment, each private L1 or shared L2 cache has 180 possible FIFO configurations as shown in Table 1. We used *TL* = 5 ns and *TM* = 15 ns (based on Xtensa processor [29]), assuming that all the applications are mapped on a 1GHz processor with one clock cycle L1 cache latency.

5. RESULTS

We evaluated our DIMSim simulator using two different metrics: 1) simulation time, which denotes the time consumed by the DIMSim simulator to produce a solution; and 2) deviation, which indicates the difference between the *requested data access time* ($RDAT$) and the time supported by the selected (i.e., suitable) L2 cache configuration ($TTDM_{L2}$). Since our focus is on data caches, we use $RDAT$ instead of the *requested execution time* (RET).

However, our method can be easily extended for RET using the equations provided in Equation 1. DIMSim is experimented for different block sizes (only 4, 16 and 64 are shown due to lack of space). It is worth nothing that the block sizes are fixed across L1 and L2 cache configurations for a particular experiment. We have selected so to avoid violating the two-level inclusion property as discussed in [14].

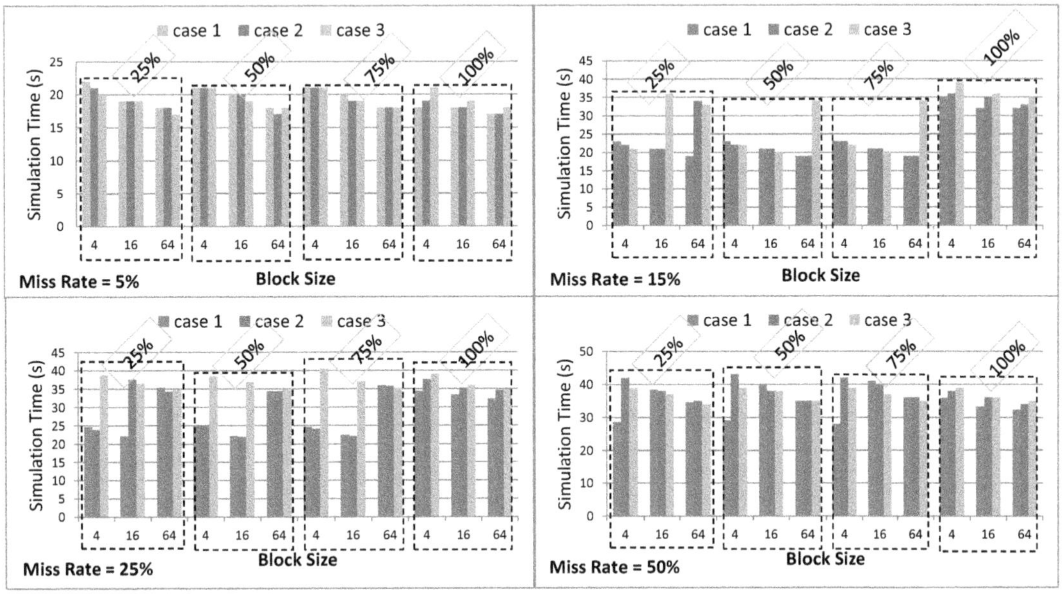

Figure 6: Simulation Time in DIMSim for Synthetic Applications

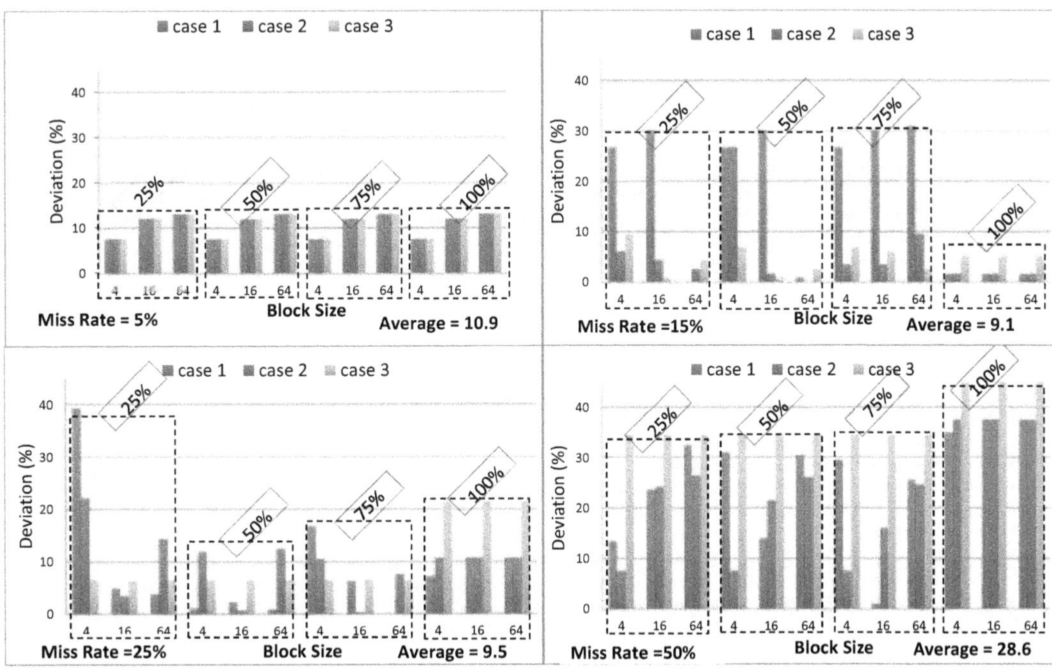

Figure 7: Deviation in Synthetic Applications

As detailed in Section 3, $TTOH$ in Equation 1 is accommodated into DIMSim by selecting the suitable L1 cache sizes. DIMSim allows its user to specify the $TTOH$ demand from the system as a parameter ($RHRT$) and uses the speedup gained by introducing suitable L1 caches to satisfy the demand. We have selected the smallest possible L1 caches and computed the maximum allowable headroom time in our experiments and the results are reported here (in addition to the simulation time and the deviation).

For all our experiments, we used a set of $RDAT$ values to see DIMSim's behaviour across different requested data access times. We use Equation 2 to calculate the number of misses in L2 (ML) when an $RDAT$ is known and the set of $RDAT$ is selected such that the miss rates[7] are 5%, 15%, 25% and 50% for synthetic traces and 5%, 10%, 15%, 20%, 25% and 50% for traces from JPEG and H264 benchmark applications. These miss rates are chosen (more analyzed but not reported due to lack of space) to cover a wide range of miss scenarios.

Figure 6 depicts the simulation time of DIMSim with the synthetic trace files. The simulation time (in seconds), on average, increases when the miss rate increases since more cache configu-

[7]The miss rate, in percentage, is computed as the number of misses in L2 (ML) divided by the total memory accesses (A).

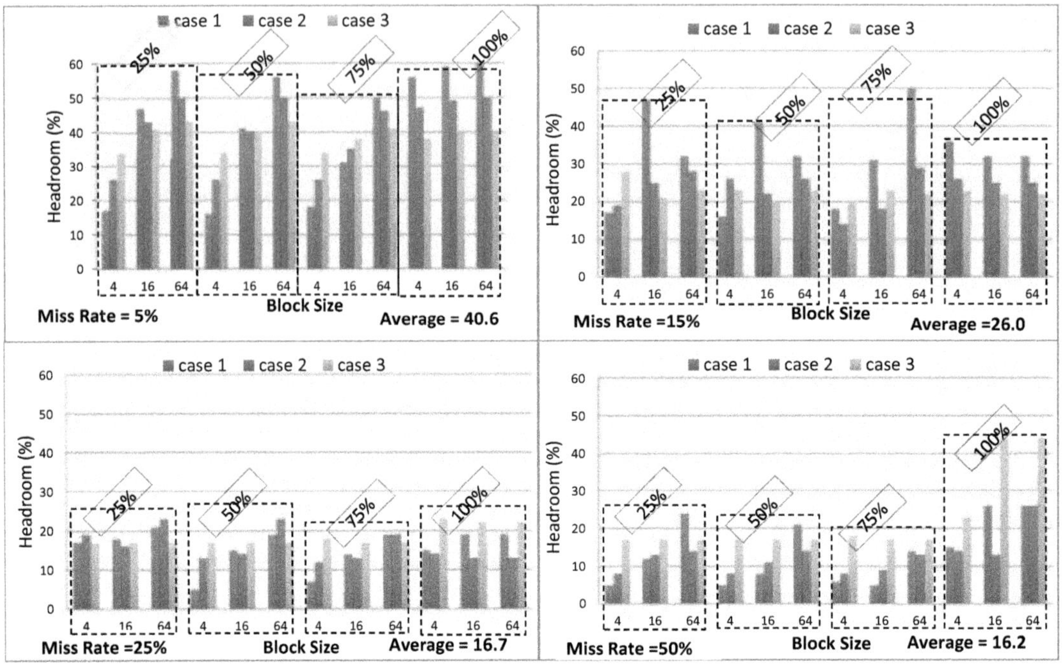

Figure 8: Maximum Allowable Headroom in Synthetic Applications

Apps.	Blk. Size (B)	Miss Rate (Directly related to $TTDM$)																	
		5%	10%	15%	20%	25%	50%	5%	10%	15%	20%	25%	50%	5%	10%	15%	20%	25%	50%
		Simulation time (Sec)						Headroom (%)						Deviation (%)					
JPEG																			
graph.	4	1752	1800	1779	1778	3251	3351	23	19	19	19	12	9	6	4	14	22	7	20
	16	2944	3015	2911	3017	3090	3183	29	29	29	19	19	10	6	17	26	6	14	14
	64	2852	3017	2806	2854	2898	2816	37	37	37	22	22	25	11	21	29	2	11	38
lowg	4	220	243	227	235	451	455	22	20	20	20	13	10	0	4	14	22	7	20
	16	392	406	398	405	416	424	32	32	23	23	23	12	6	17	5	14	21	18
	64	375	376	351	386	399	416	41	41	41	25	25	9	11	21	29	9	16	3
lena	4	1735	1815	1780	1790	3217	3371	23	19	19	19	12	9	6	4	14	22	7	20
	16	2936	3023	2909	2995	3064	3171	29	29	29	19	19	10	6	17	26	6	14	14
	64	2821	3027	2817	2857	2888	2886	37	37	37	22	22	25	10	21	29	2	11	38
criss	4	1758	1855	1782	1781	3259	3331	23	19	19	19	12	9	6	4	14	22	7	20
	16	3015	3153	2912	3013	3055	3113	29	29	29	19	19	10	6	17	26	6	14	14
	64	2838	3011	2828	3002	2943	2892	37	37	37	22	22	25	10	21	29	2	11	38
photo1	4	1722	1763	1797	1830	3289	3318	23	19	19	19	12	9	6	4	14	22	7	20
	16	2985	3004	2998	3120	3086	3169	29	29	29	19	19	10	6	17	26	6	14	14
	64	2797	2835	2826	2880	2902	2842	37	37	37	22	22	25	10	21	29	2	11	38
photo2	4	1751	1788	1822	1824	3303	3316	22	19	19	19	12	9	6	4	14	22	7	20
	16	2967	2944	3038	3067	3073	3140	29	29	29	19	19	10	6	17	26	7	15	14
	64	2799	2798	2804	2889	2901	2864	37	37	37	22	22	25	10	21	29	3	11	38
H264																			
bluesky	4	252	1384	1435	1525	1534	1561	NS	7	6	6	5	5	NS	1	1	6	1	28
	16	1204	1217	1331	1339	2361	2284	17	16	14	13	12	6	1	3	4	5	8	3
	64	1102	1140	1219	2186	2200	2153	20	20	20	14	14	8	0	12	21	3	11	13
river	4	290	1440	1516	1472	1614	1593	NS	7	6	6	5	5	NS	1	1	6	1	28
	16	1228	1269	1295	1215	2347	2365	17	16	14	13	12	6	1	3	4	5	8	3
	64	1156	1140	1203	2043	2278	2261	20	20	20	14	14	8	0	12	21	3	11	13
station	4	277	1432	1488	1422	1549	1550	NS	7	6	6	5	5	NS	1	1	6	1	28
	16	1220	1160	1253	1230	2345	2282	17	16	14	13	12	6	1	3	4	5	8	3
	64	1142	1488	1134	2219	2159	2200	20	20	20	14	14	8	0	12	21	3	11	13
pedest.	4	303	1470	1492	1436	1604	1605	NS	7	6	6	5	5	NS	1	1	6	1	28
	16	1262	1323	1312	1234	2364	2306	17	16	14	13	12	6	1	3	4	5	8	3
	64	1151	1207	1134	2008	2198	2232	20	20	20	14	14	8	0	12	21	3	11	13
rushhr	4	281	1457	1507	1419	1567	1574	NS	7	6	6	5	5	NS	1	1	6	1	28
	16	1250	1267	1256	1236	2353	2396	17	16	14	13	12	6	1	3	4	5	8	3
	64	1160	1167	1155	2222	2210	2243	20	20	20	14	14	8	0	12	21	3	11	13
tractor	4	279	1431	1475	1449	1544	1582	NS	7	6	6	5	5	NS	1	1	6	1	28
	16	1231	1262	1285	1249	2388	2427	17	16	14	13	12	6	1	3	4	5	8	3
	64	1157	1151	1137	2115	2155	2173	20	20	20	14	14	8	0	12	21	3	11	13

Table 2: DIMSim Performance Analysis for JPEG and H264 Benchmarks

rations are simulated for a higher miss rate. In other words, when the given miss rate is smaller, only a few large cache configurations can satisfy its respective ML, while other cache configurations are pruned away. This pruning point in the simulation is reached at a much earlier time for smaller miss rate hence the significant variations in the simulation time. The maximal simulation time of 42 seconds is observed at two places: (i) when 50% miss rate is imposed, at 25% sharing, in case 2 and block size of 4, and (ii) when

50% miss rate is imposed, at 50% sharing, in case 2 and block size of 4. The minimal simulation time of 17 seconds is observed at several places. Compared to the crude exhaustive approach [9] (i.e., simulating every single cache configuration at a time), a seven orders of magnitude in average speedup is estimated in synthetic applications across all the scenarios. The four core system with each core having a private L1 cache and a shared L2 cache will have around 2.3 billion possible cache configurations when each cache has 180 possible configurations.

$$Deviation = \frac{(RDAT - TTDM_{L2}) * 100}{RDAT} \quad (3)$$

Figure 7 depicts the deviation between the requested data access time ($RDAT$) and the total time spent on data memory accesses with only L2 ($TTDM_{L2}$). $Deviation$ is calculated, as per Equation 3, for each application trace on the suggested L2 cache from DIMSim using Equation 2. DIMSim suggested cache hierarchy's $TTDM_{L2}$ is *always smaller than* $RDAT$, hence $Deviation$ will be always positive. This is an indication that DIMSim suggested cache hierarchy never fails to satisfy the timing constraint of the target deadline constrained application on a given hardware platform. The deviation increases with the miss rate for an application until the number of misses result in a different cache configuration being chosen. Since the cache sizes are exponential, deviation incurs significant increase when miss rate increases, until the next (i.e., smaller cache to support more misses) cache configuration is chosen. A sharp decrease in deviation is observed with the next cache configuration. For example, the first bar in each miss rate plot (case 1, block size 4 and 25% sharing) indicates that the deviation increases from 8%, 27%, 38% for 5%, 15% and 25% miss rates respectively, and then drops to 14% for 50% miss rate. The chosen cache size was the same for 5%, 15% and 25% miss rates and then dropped to the next smaller cache for 50% miss rate, because of larger number of misses requested. The deviation fluctuates between 4% and 60% (only in 6% of the bars are over 50% in deviation). As mentioned above, when the miss rate is smaller, only a few large L2 caches will be simulated. An average deviation of 25% is recorded in synthetic applications across all the scenarios (best case 5% and worst case 60%). Variation in deviation is quite unpredictable since it is based on the number of misses and respective supporting cache configuration. Since the cache configuration sizes exponentially increase, a step to the next level cache will significantly reduce $TTDM_{L2}$.

$$Headroom = \frac{(TTDM_{L2} - TTDM) * 100}{TTDM_{L2}} \quad (4)$$

Figure 8 shows the maximum allowable headroom (for the smallest L1) observed in synthetic applications for different miss rates. The Headroom is calculated, as per Equation 4, for each application trace. In Equation 4, $TTDM_{L2}$ is the total data memory access time when only L2 is present in the system. On average, the maximum headroom decreases with the miss rate. A maximum of 60% headroom is observed at 5% miss rate for 100% sharing and case 1, at block size 64. There was a minimum of 5% headroom occurred in several places at case 1. The headroom allows the designer to realize and choose the right cache configurations based on the extra overhead in the design.

The code of JPEG and H264 are partitioned into six different communicating tasks which share information via the shared memory. Table 2 depicts the Simulation time (in seconds), Deviation (in percentage) and Headroom (in percentage), for several JPEG and H264 benchmarks. The first column details the benchmark names for applications JPEG and H264, while the second column indicates the block sizes in bytes and the remaining columns depict the simulation time, deviation and the headroom for different requested miss rates.

The shortest simulation time for JPEG is 220sec and observed for the *lowg* benchmark with block size 4 bytes and 5% miss rate. A time of 3371 sec was the maximum simulation time noted at the *lena* benchmark with block size 4 bytes and 50% miss rate. The average simulation speedup across all the benchmarks of JPEG is 11.0 in $\log_{10}$ scale compared to the estimated (and crude) exhaustive simulation time. The six core system with each core having a private L1 cache and a shared L2 cache will have around 8.4 trillion possible cache configurations when each cache has 180 possible configurations. The maximum headroom was 41% at *lowg* benchmark. On the other hand, the minimum was 9% and observed in several benchmarks for 50% miss rate. On average, the headroom is 18.5%. For H264, the maximum simulation time is 2427 seconds and the minimum is 252 seconds, occurred at (50% missrate, *tractor*, B16) and (5% miss rate, *bluesky*, B4) respectively. The maximum, minimum and average speedups, in simulation time, for H264 benchmarks are 11.2, 10.9 and 11.0 respectively in $\log_{10}$, compared to the crude exhaustive simulation. The minimum for the allowable headroom is 5% and the maximum is 20%. A minimum of 0% deviation is observed at bluesky for block size 64, indicating the exact match of the cache configuration (i.e., $TTDM_{L2}$) with the requested time (i.e., $RDAT$). A maximum deviation of 28% has resulted at several places for H264 benchmarks.

Simulation times of JPEG are relatively larger than H264 due to the fact that the number of memory accesses in JPEG are higher than H264 (i.e., higher number of entries in the trace). It is worth to note that we only partitioned and experimented the motion estimation kernel of the H264, hence the less number of data accesses compared to the full-on JPEG encoder. In several cases, such as at bluesky and riverbed for 4 bytes block size and 5% miss rate, DIMSim is unable (*NS = No Solution*) to provide any cache hierarchy for the requested miss rate. In these cases, DIMSim could not find an L2 configuration which satisfies the requested miss rate (or $RDAT$) from the provided list of L2s shown in Table 1. As a result, the simulation time is significantly low as no L1s are simulated. Even though the images tested for JPEG are of different sizes, each benchmark's simulation time and deviation per block size are quite similar to the other benchmarks. A similar variation is observed for H264. The underlying cause for such a behaviour is similar number of memory accesses and memory access patterns within the selected benchmarks of each application. At the end of the simulation, the smallest L2 and the smallest L1s are chosen as the suitable cache hierarchy from the provided set of solutions (as mentioned in Section 3).

Table 3 presents the suggested set associative cache configurations by DIMSim for all the block sizes and miss rates. The numbers, in the form of a tuple (set size, associativity), are divided for private L1s and shared L2. The L1s are tabulated in the sequence of cores. For example, for cache miss rate of 25% and block size of 64 bytes, the first two processors should have 2-way fully associative (i.e, $2\times(1,2)$) L1 caches, the next three processors should have 2-way set associative caches with 2 sets (i.e, $3\times(2,2)$) and the last processor can deploy a 2-way fully associative cache. The proposed shared L2 cache for this scenario is a 4-way fully associative cache.

6. CONCLUSION

We proposed a bottom-up cache simulation approach to provide estimations that satisfy the deadline constraints for a system containing two-level inclusive data cache hierarchies in deadline-based MPSoCs. For the first time, a trace based single-pass simulator is

	blk. size	Miss Rate					
		5%	10%	15%	20%	25%	50%
JPEG							
L1	4	6×(2,2)	6×(2,2)	6×(2,2)	6×(2,2)	6×(2,2)	2×(1,2),3×(2,2),(1,2)
	16	6×(2,2)	(1,2),(64,2),4×(2,2)	(1,2),(64,2),4×(2,2)	2×(1,2),4×(2,2)	2×(1,2),4×(2,2)	2×(1,2),3×(2,2),(1,2)
	64	(1,2),(16,8),4×(2,2)	2×(1,2),4×(2,2)	2×(1,2),2×(2,2),2×(1,2)	2×(1,2),4×(2,2)	2×(1,2),3×(2,2),(1,2)	(1,2),5×(2,2)
L2	4	(8,8)	(2,16)	(2,16)	(2,16)	(1,16)	(1,8)
	16	(1,16)	(1,16)	(1,8)	(1,8)	(1,8)	(1,4)
	64	(1,8)	(1,8)	(1,8)	(1,4)	(1,4)	(1,2)
H264							
L1	4	NS	6×(1,2)	6×(1,2)	6×(1,2)	6×(1,2)	6×(1,2)
	16	6×(1,2)	6×(1,2)	6×(1,2)	6×(1,2)	6×(1,2)	6×(1,2)
	64	6×(1,2)	6×(1,2)	6×(1,2)	6×(1,2)	6×(1,2)	6×(1,2)
L2	4	No Sol.	1024×16	64×8	16×16	4×16	2×16
	16	16×16	16×8	4×16	2×16	1×16	1×4
	64	4×16	4×16	4×16	1×8	1×8	1×4

Table 3: Suitable Cache Configurations

adapted for simulating a two-level cache hierarchy of an MPSoC. Our simulator addressed the two main challenges on simulating a two-level cache hierarchy in an MPSoC, namely coherency (that occurred due to shared data cache) and scalability (that occurred due to the large number of cache combinations to be simulated) for simulation time and storage space. Our simulator, in the worst case, took less than an hour to simulate an application (from the set of benchmarks considered) to estimate the L2 shared cache and L1 private caches for a two-level cache hierarchy. The cache configurations selected by our simulator deviates from the requested data access time by 16.1%, 7.2% and 14.5% in JPEG, H264 and synthetic applications respectively. The deviations are always positive meaning the deadline requirements are always satisfied. Therefore, our simulator is both fast and reasonably accurate in producing results, satisfying the deadline constraints.

7. ACKNOWLEDGEMENT

The authors would like to thank Hong Chinh Doan and Su Myat Min Shwe from the University of New South Wales, Australia, for providing valuable suggestions in obtaining the JPEG and H264 shared memory traces.

8. REFERENCES

[1] Intel xscale microprocessor data book. www.intel.com.

[2] Arm11 processor datasheet. In *www.datasheetarchive.com/ARM11-datasheet.html*, ARM Limited.

[3] Arm9 processor datasheet. In *www.datasheetarchive.com/ARM9-datasheet.html*, ARM Limited.

[4] L. Barriga and R. Ayani. Parallel cache simulation on multiprocessor workstattions. In *Proc. Int. Conf. Parallel Processing ICPP 1993*, volume 1, pages 171–174, 1993.

[5] J. Casazza. Intel core i7-800 processor serioes and intel core i5-700 processor series based on intel microarchitecture (nehalem). *Intel White Paper, Intel Corporation, USA*, 2009.

[6] T. Conte, M. Hirsch, and W.-M. Hwu. Combining trace sampling with single pass methods for efficient cache simulation. *Computers, IEEE Transactions on*, 47(6):714 –720, jun 1998.

[7] H. C. Doan, H. Javaid, and S. Parameswaran. Multi-asip based parallel and scalable implementation of motion estimation kernel for high definition videos. In *ESTImedia*, pages 56–65. IEEE, 2011.

[8] J. Edler and M. D. Hill. Dinero iv trace-driven uniprocessor cache simulator. http://www.cs.wisc.edu/ markhill/DineroIV/, 2004.

[9] T. Givargis and F. Vahid. Platune: a tuning framework for system-on-a-chip platforms. *TCAD*, 2002.

[10] W. Han, G. Xiaopeng, and W. Zhiqiang. Cache simulator based on gpu acceleration. In *Simutools*, pages 1–6, ICST, Brussels, Belgium, Belgium, 2009.

[11] M. Haque, J. Peddersen, and S. Parameswaran. Ciparsim: Cache intersection property assisted rapid single-pass fifo cache simulation technique. In *Computer-Aided Design (ICCAD), 2011 IEEE/ACM International Conference on*, pages 126 –133, nov. 2011.

[12] M. S. Haque, A. Janapsatya, and S. Parameswaran. Susesim: a fast simulation strategy to find optimal l1 cache configuration for embedded systems. In *Proceedings of the 7th IEEE/ACM international conference on Hardware/software codesign and system synthesis*, CODES+ISSS '09, pages 295–304, New York, NY, USA, 2009. ACM.

[13] P. Heidelberger and H. S. Stone. Parallel trace-driven cache simulation by time partitioning. In *WSC*, 1990.

[14] J. Hennessy and D. Patterson. *Computer Architecture: A Quantitative Approach*, pages 397–398. The Morgan Kaufmann Series in Computer Architecture and Design Series. Elsevier Science & Technology, 2011.

[15] L. Hsu, R. Iyer, S. Makineni, S. Reinhardt, and D. Newell. Exploring the cache design space for large scale CMPs. *SIGARCH Comput. Archit. News*, 33:24–33, November 2005.

[16] A. Janapsatya, A. Ignjatovic, and S. Parameswaran. Finding optimal l1 cache configuration for embedded systems. In *Design Automation, 2006. Asia and South Pacific Conference on*, page 6 pp., jan. 2006.

[17] R. Kessler, M. Hill, and D. Wood. A comparison of trace-sampling techniques for multi-megabyte caches. *Computers, IEEE Transactions on*, 43(6):664 –675, jun 1994.

[18] P. Kongetira, K. Aingaran, and K. Olukotun. Niagara: a 32-way multithreaded Sparc processor. *Micro, IEEE*, 25(2):21–29, march-april 2005.

[19] S. Laha, J. Patel, and R. Iyer. Accurate low-cost methods for performance evaluation of cache memory systems. *Computers, IEEE Transactions on*, 37(11):1325 –1336, nov 1988.

[20] X. Li, H. S. Negi, T. Mitra, and A. Roychoudhury. Design space exploration of caches using compressed traces. In *ICS '04*.

[21] M. Loghi, M. Poncino, and L. Benini. Cache coherence tradeoffs in shared-memory MPSoCs. *ACM Trans. Embed. Comput. Syst.*, 2006.

[22] A. Milenković and M. Milenković. An efficient single-pass trace compression technique utilizing instruction streams. *ACM Trans. Model. Comput. Simul.*, 17(1):2, 2007.

[23] B. Sinharoy, R. N. Kalla, J. M. Tendler, R. J. Eickemeyer, and J. B. Joyner. POWER5 system microarchitecture. *IBM Journal of Research and Development*, 49(4.5):505–521, july 2005.

[24] R. A. Sugumar and S. G. Abraham. Set-associative cache simulation using generalized binomial trees. *ACM Trans. Comput. Syst.*, 13(1):32–56, 1995.

[25] N. Tojo, N. Togawa, M. Yanagisawa, and T. Ohtsuki. Exact and fast l1 cache simulation for embedded systems. In *ASP-DAC*, 2009.

[26] W.-H. Wang and J.-L. Baer. Efficient trace-driven simulation method for cache performance analysis. In *SIGMETRICS*, 1990.

[27] Z. Wu and W. Wolf. Iterative cache simulation of embedded cpus with trace stripping. In *CODES*, pages 95–99, New York, NY, USA, 1999. ACM.

[28] R. Wunderlich, T. Wenisch, B. Falsafi, and J. Hoe. Smarts: Accelerating microarchitecture simulation via rigorous statistical sampling. In *Computer Architecture, 2003. Proceedings. 30th Annual International Symposium on*, pages 84 – 95, june 2003.

[29] Xtensa. Xtensa lx2 product brief. www.tensilica.com.

[30] XTMP. The xtensa modeling protocol and xtensa systemc modeling for fast system modeling and simulation. www.tensilica.com.

[31] W. Zang and A. Gordon-Ross. T-spacs: a two-level single-pass cache simulation methodology. In *ASPDAC*, 2011.

A Traffic-aware Adaptive Routing Algorithm on a Highly Reconfigurable Network-on-Chip Architecture

Zhiliang Qian
HKUST, Clear Water Bay
Kowloon, Hong Kong, China
qianzl@ust.hk

Paul Bogdan
Carnegie Mellon University
Pittsburgh, PA, USA, 15213
pbogdan@cmu.edu

Guopeng Wei
Carnegie Mellon University
Pittsburgh, PA, USA, 15213
danielwei@cmu.edu

Chi-Ying Tsui
HKUST, Clear Water Bay
Kowloon, Hong Kong, China
eetsui@ust.hk

Radu Marculescu
Carnegie Mellon University
Pittsburgh, PA, USA, 15213
radum@cmu.edu

ABSTRACT

In this paper, we propose a flexible NoC architecture and a dynamic distributed routing algorithm which can enhance the NoC communication performance with minimal energy overhead. In particular, our proposed NoC architecture exploits the following two features: i) self-reconfigurable bidirectional channels to increase the effective bandwidth and ii) express virtual paths, as well as localized hub routers, to bypass some intermediate nodes at run time in the network. A deadlock-free and traffic-aware dynamic routing algorithm is further developed for the proposed architecture, which can take advantage of the increased flexibility in the proposed architecture. Both the channels self-reconfiguration and routing decisions are made in a distributed fashion, based on a function of the localized traffic conditions, in order to maximize the performance and minimize the energy costs at the macroscopic level. Our simulation results show that the proposed approach can reduce the network latency by 30% -80% in most cases compared to a conventional unidirectional mesh topology, while incurring less than 15% power overhead.

Categories and Subject Descriptors

C.1.2 [**Computer Systems Organization**]: Multiple Data Stream Architectures—*Interconnection architectures*

Keywords

Network-on-Chip, adaptive routing, bidirectional link, fitness based routing, traffic characteristics, congestion control

1. INTRODUCTION

With technology scaling down, finding a scalable solution and an efficient way to manage the communication between different components become more and more important. Towards this end, the Network-on-Chip (NoC) architecture has been recently proposed as a promising solution to solve the complex on-chip communication problem [8].

The NoC architecture and the corresponding routing strategy play an important role in optimizing the system performance in terms of throughput and latency. Indeed, enhancing the NoC architecture with additional flexibility is appealing since it can offer more opportunities to minimize the impact of traffic congestion by bypassing the intermediate router pipeline stages for some packets at run time [10]. At the same time, a routing strategy, which fully utilizes the characteristics of both the underlying communication infrastructure and the NoC traffic, is equally important since the routing decision made at the run time is critical in optimizing the NoC performance and resources utilization [2,3].

For NoC architecture, the bandwidth, the average distance between the nodes and the traffic characteristics have a significant impact on the overall network performance. Most of the existing NoC architectures have employed a two-dimensional mesh topology with two unidirectional links connecting the neighboring tiles. Although the mesh topology is well suited for silicon implementation [6], the channel bandwidth is not optimally used [5] and it may suffer from long packet latencies due to the lack of short paths between remotely located nodes [13].

For routing strategy design, several adaptive routing algorithms have been proposed for conventional unidirectional mesh NoCs [2,6,12,15]. However, dynamic routing has been far less explored for performance improvement.

In this work, we propose a reconfigurable NoC architecture which combines the advantages of providing higher effective bandwidth between the neighboring nodes and shorter paths between remotely located nodes. Our proposed NoC architecture exploits the following two capabilities, namely: i) self reconfigurable bidirectional channels (BiNoC) [1,5,11] and ii) static express virtual channels (EVCs) [10] with regional hub routers, to dynamically create short-cut paths for transmitting packets. In order to exploit the added flexibility provided by the proposed architecture, we also propose a new fitness-based adaptive routing algorithm for optimizing the network performance.

Experimental results obtained for synthetic traffic and real benchmarks show that our approach can improve the latency by as much as 80% , while involving less than 15% overhead in power dissipation.

The remaining of this paper is organized as follows: In section 2, we review related work on NoC architecture and adaptive routing algorithm design. In section 3, we describe the newly proposed NoC architecture. Section 4 presents the adaptive routing algorithm for the proposed NoC. The practical considerations and simulation results are discussed in section 5. Finally, section 6 concludes this work.

2. RELATED WORK

In NoC architecture design, many efforts are focused on increasing the total bandwidth and reducing the average node distance by proposing new topologies [7, 17]. In [17], a Diagonally-linked Mesh topology is proposed which employs physical diagonal express links between routers to reduce the distances between nodes. In [7], a new topology called Multidrop Express Channels (MECS) is proposed; this uses a one-to-many communication model to enable a high degree of connectivity. Compared to the mesh based NoC, these new topologies can improve the network bandwidth and connectivity at the cost of adding more physical resources such as the link wires and increased router complexity.

To improve the trade-off between the design complexity and the performance, there are also approaches exploiting the mesh topology due to its modularity and scalability. In [10], the NoC architecture with static and dynamic express channels (EVC) is proposed. Instead of adding physical links, a flow control mechanism allows packets to virtually bypass intermediate routers along their path. Static EVC approach uses the express paths of uniform lengths and distinguishes the nodes as either EVC source (sink) nodes or bypass nodes according to whether the EVC originates (terminates) at those nodes. Dynamic EVCs make every node in the network a source (sink) and allow EVCs of various lengths to originate from a node [10].

Besides the idea of bypassing intermediate routers, another important direction in optimizing the mesh NoC architecture is to enable the network to increase the effective bandwidth at run time. Indeed, very often, there is much traffic in one direction, while the channel for the opposite direction is idle. NoCs with run-time reconfigurable bi-directional channels have been recently proposed to fully utilize the bandwidth according to the run-time traffic conditions (BiNoC) [1, 5, 11, 14]. However, adaptive routing is less exploited in these works for simplicity reasons.

Previous adaptive routing algorithms are mainly designed for unidirectional NoCs. In [2], a neighbors-on-path (NoP) selection strategy is proposed to make each node routing selection based on the condition of the nodes adjacent to the neighbors. In [6], a regional contention awareness scheme (RCA) was first proposed to utilize both the local and non-local information to improve the load balancing in NoCs. In [12], the RCA scheme was improved by using the adaptive routing scheme DBAR to leverage the local and non-local network information. In [15], a destination-based adaptive routing algorithm (DAR) is proposed where every node estimates the delay to every other node in the network. However, for a more flexible NoC platform such as the ones employing bi-directional links and EVC channels, these schemes need to be modified with a congestion fitness function to reflect the run time traffic status.

Starting from these overarching ideas, in this work, we aim at improving the NoC performance with respect to both architecture design and routing algorithm development. Towards this end, we propose a flexible NoC architecture which combines the advantages of higher effective bandwidth and router bypass capability and develop an adaptive routing algorithm to optimize the network run-time performance.

3. NEW NOC ARCHITECTURE

In this section, we first present the motivation for adding regional hub routers into the NoC and then elaborate on the new reconfigurable NoC architecture.

3.1 Motivation for adding hub routers

Because of the complexity of the dynamic EVC approach [10], in this work, we adopt a 3-hop static EVC network; this provides a better trade off between performance and design complexity. We also define a region as a 4×4 mesh whose boundary is made up of the EVC source/sink nodes. A regional hub router is added into each region based on the following key observations:

1) The regional traffic represents a significant portion of the total traffic distribution. Here, we define the regional traffic as the communication flow whose source and destination reside within the same region. This is especially true for application-specific NoCs where highly communicating nodes are usually mapped close to each other. For regional traffic, it has been shown that more than 90% of nodes communicate with other nodes residing within a region of three hops away [11].

2) While the static EVCs provide express paths crossing over NoC regions, they typically lack sufficient paths needed to handle the traffic within the NoC regions. If both the source and destination nodes are bypass nodes in a static EVC, then the packets cannot use the EVCs to bypass the intermediate nodes.

3) The static EVCs enable packets to bypass the intermediate nodes following a fixed express path. Also, the EVCs are restricted to a single dimension and cannot turn directly. Consequently, it will be beneficial if we can dynamically build shortcut paths for regional traffic rather than being limited by the single dimension requirement.

Therefore, in this work, we propose to add a light weight hub router to minimize the burden of the regional traffic in NoCs. More precisely, we additionally allocate a dedicated (i.e., static) express path for each node to route to the hub router and utilize the hub router to connect the nodes within the same region; this way, when the hub router is used, the intermediate pipeline stages of the normal routers can be bypassed altogether.

3.2 Overview of proposed NoC architecture

Figure 1-a shows the proposed flexible NoC architecture for 8×8 meshes. In this example, the static EVC hop length is equal to 3. Each region is a small 4×4 mesh. Other static EVC hop length and region size can be used for different sizes of the meshes. The solid line in Figure 1-a represents the physical channels between the tiles which are made up of two bi-directional links. Both bidirectional links can be reconfigured as sending or receiving. For each router, we define one link as a high priority link (master link) and the other as a low priority link (slave link) as in [11]. By default, the master link is the sending link and the slave link is the receiving link when there is traffic in both directions.

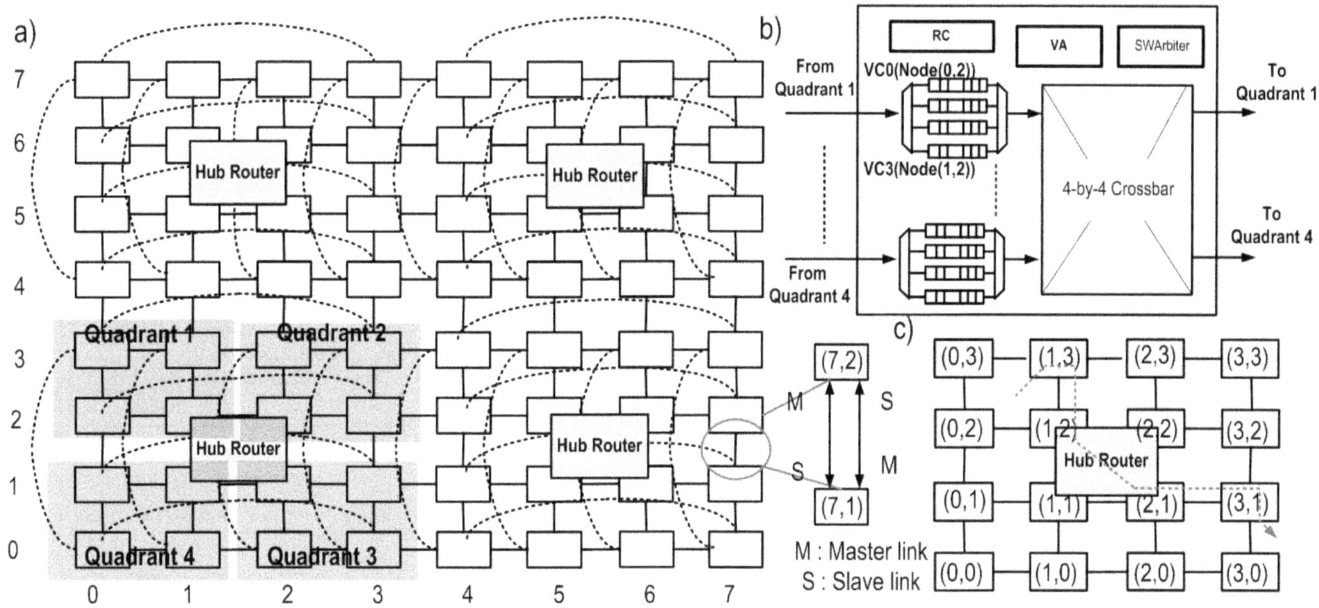

Figure 1: a) Proposed NoC architecture for an 8×8 mesh with bi-directional links, EVCs and hub routers b) The hub router architecture with each VC corresponding to a node in the region c) An example of routing from (1,3) to (3,1) using hub routers

As shown in Figure 1-a, the master link of one router corresponds to the slave link of its neighbor. The dash line in Figure 1-a represents the 3-hop EVCs.

We further divide each 4×4 region into four quadrants (see Figure 1-a). In order to reduce the additional complexity added to the NoC backbone, the regional hub router is a simple and generic four ports router with four virtual channels at each input port as shown in Figure 1-b. Every input port corresponds to a quadrant in the region and each node in the quadrant is assigned a virtual channel at the input port of the hub router. For example, VC0 of the first input port (i.e. the quadrant 1 port) of the hub router is assigned to node (0,2) in Figure 1-a.

At run time, the hub router plays the role of setting a connection between the source and destination pairs within different quadrants of the same region. For example, in Figure 1-c, if node (1,3) in quadrant one needs to communicate with node (3,1) in the quadrant three, it cannot use the static EVCs. Instead, it can communicate via the hub router. The packet will first follow the dedicated express hub path bypassing router (1,2) pipeline stages to reach the input port corresponding to quadrant one of the hub router. After the hub router grants its connection from quadrant one input port to the quadrant three output port in the switch allocation stage, the packet will traverse the crossbar in the hub router and bypass router (2,1) pipeline stages to arrive at the destination node (3,1) directly. Compared with using normal paths to send packets from (1,3) to (3,1), which requires five router pipeline stages, only one router pipeline in the hub router is needed.

In the proposed architecture, we utilize the virtual channel allocator and switch allocator in the hub router to arbitrate the contentions. For instance, if both nodes (1,3) and (1,0) want to send packets to (3,1) using the hub router, after arriving at the hub router, these two packets will request the same virtual channel which corresponds to node (3,1) in the quadrant three output port. The virtual channel allocator will grant one of the requests first, while the other packet needs to wait in the input channel buffer until the virtual channel becomes available again. Similarly, when there are multiple requests from different input quadrant ports to the same output quadrant, for instance, if both the packets from node (1,3) to (3,1) and node (1,1) to (3,0) want to use the quadrant four output port in the hub router, the switch allocator will only serve one request each time.

3.3 Router implementation

In this section, we present the router design that supports the BiNoC with EVC and region hub. First, we will discuss the additional hardware required to support the BiNoC approach. Then the micro-architecture that supports static EVCs will be presented. Finally, we present the modifications required to support the region-hub routing.

Figure 2-a shows the router design for BiNoC with the extra logic required (see the shaded area) to support the bi-directional switching. In BiNoC each input and output port need to be modified to inout ports controlled by the corresponding finite state machines (FSMs) [11]. Also, the arbiter and the crossbar are modified to handle the requests received from the master and slave ports. At run time, the FSM associated to every inout port configures the port mode (i.e., input or output) according to the requests existing in current router and the backpressure feedback from the neighboring routers as discussed in [11].

Figure 2-b shows the router micro-architecture that supports static EVCs for BiNoC. In this work, we build the EVC path using the output ports corresponding to the master links, because the master link has a higher priority in transmitting flits according to the channel direction controlled by the FSM. Compared to the BiNoC router in Figure 2-a, the extra logic need to support the EVC architecture is shaded in Figure 2-b and Figure 2-c. In static EVCs, there are two types of nodes, namely the bypass nodes and the EVC source/sink nodes. In the bypass nodes (as shown in Figure 2-b), an EVC latch is added to hold the packets using the EVC. Once a packet arrives at the EVC latch, it will by-

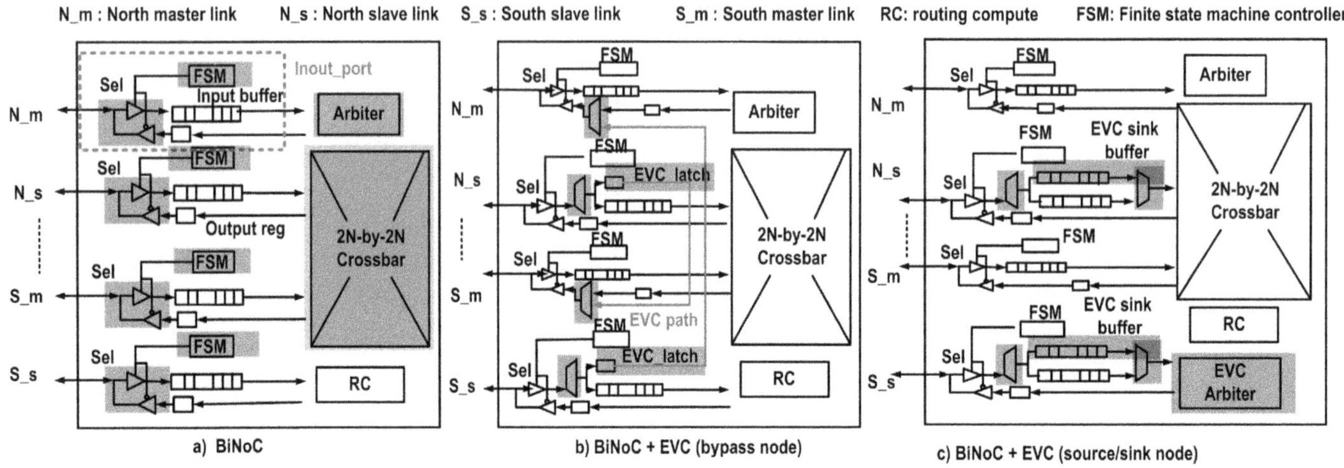

Figure 2: Router architecture of a) BiNoC; b) BiNoC + EVC bypass node; c) BiNoC+EVC source/sink node

pass all the intermediate pipeline stages of the current router (e.g., switch allocation, crossbar traversal) and is directly sent to the output port in the same dimension. In Figure 2-b, the EVC paths along the north/south direction that a packet will take to bypass the router pipeline is highlighted. The architecture of the EVC source/sink routers is shown in Figure 2-c. Here, we add an EVC sink buffer at the slave link port to hold the packets from the upstream nodes. In addition, an EVC arbiter is added to handle the arbitration requests from all the input channels (both the normal input and EVC sink buffers). Once a packet successfully wins the allocation, an EVC flag in the flit is asserted. Based on this flag, the downstream router decides whether to put the flits into the EVC latch or into the normal input buffer.

In the proposed regional hub routing, for every node, there is one static express path assigned to connect to the hub router. Figure 3 shows the paths assigned to the four nodes in the quadrant one of Figure 1. We add hub latches to multiplex with the normal buffers at the input port and hub registers to multiplex with the output registers at the output port (shown in Figure 3). The hub latch and register pair forms an express path for a dedicated node to bypass the pipeline stage within the router.

Figure 4-a shows the router design for node (1,2) in Figure 3 which connects to the hub router using an additional port. The extra logic needed compared to Figure 2-c is shaded. As shown in Figure 4-a, the EVC paths are highlighted in red lines while the express paths formed by hub latch/register pairs are highlighted in blue lines.

At run time, there may be contentions between the hub latches or between the EVC and hub latches. For example, for router (1,3) in Figure 4-b, the hub latch in the local port and the hub latch in the west port may contend with the EVC latch in the north port to use the south output link. In order to resolve such contentions, the express path arbiter in Figure 4-b is needed in every router to handle the hub and EVC latch requests to make sure that, at any one time, only one packet can bypass the pipeline stages and use the physical channel. In this work, we allocate a higher priority to the EVC paths, because the hub paths only serve the regional traffic, while the EVC paths usually work for the traffic meant for longer distances. For example, the express path arbiter will first grant the north EVC latch to use the south output link. The packets from the west and local hub

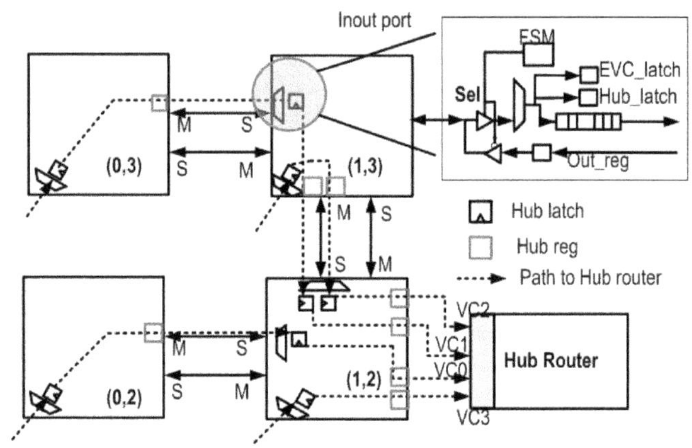

Figure 3: The express paths to the hub router

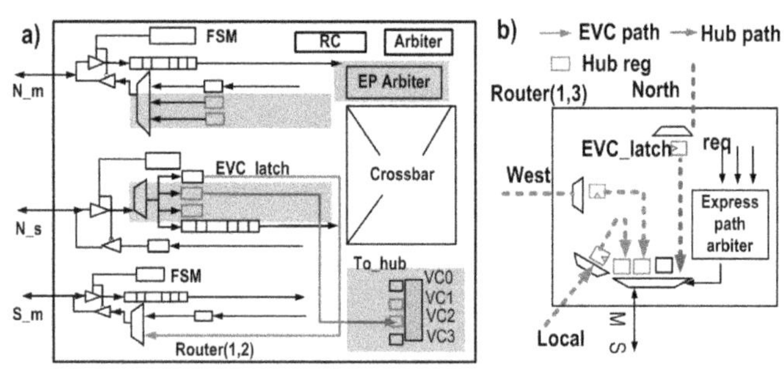

Figure 4: a)Router architecture of node (1,2) b) Contention between EVC and Hub paths

latches, as well as the input buffers will wait in the output port. Then, the express path arbiter will grant the requests from hub latches to use the output link with a higher priority than the normal paths. In order to avoid the starvation of flits in normal buffers and registers, the arbiter will grant the requests from normal paths after serving the EVC and hub latches for n consecutive cycles as in [10]. In this work, n is set to be 30 according to our simulation results.

4. ROUTING ALGORITHM DESIGN

In this section, we present the details of our adaptive routing algorithm for the proposed flexible NoC. We first describe the scheme to choose among the static EVCs, express hub paths and BiNoC for sending a packet. Next, we present the adaptive routing algorithm when using the bi-directional channels to route packets. We develop a fitness function as a metric to evaluate the neighboring node availability based on the channels occupancy. The fitness function not only captures the buffer status but also takes the traffic dynamics, as well as the characteristics of the bi-directional channel into account. Then, a K-step speculative routing selection strategy is proposed to evaluate each candidate direction, which dynamically selects the nodes with the best fitness values that reside on a path towards the destination.

4.1 Choosing the express hub and EVC paths

In the proposed NoC architecture, we can use EVCs, hub routers, as well as the bi-directional channels to send packets around. The network interface (NI) in the source tile determines whether to use the express hub paths for the packet first. More specifically, the NI first compares the source and destination address of the packet. If the source and destination nodes are located in different quadrants of the same region, and if the destination node cannot be reached by EVCs from the source directly, then the NI will check the availability of the hub latch in the local port of the neighboring router. If the hub latch is free, the packet will be sent to it and follow the express hub path to route towards the destination. Otherwise, the packet will be sent to the normal buffer in the local port of the neighboring router.

In the EVC source/sink nodes, for each input channel, the routing computation module decides whether to use the EVCs based on the EVC latch availability and the average waiting time of the sink buffer in the EVC sink node. If the waiting time is larger than a threshold T (which means that there exists heavy congestion at the EVC sink node), the EVC will not be chosen for routing.

At last, for the packets which cannot use EVCs or the express hub paths, the adaptive routing algorithm proposed for bi-directional NoC is used to find an output direction based on the run time traffic status.

4.2 Adaptive routing for BiNoC

4.2.1 Channel and direction fitness

In NoCs utilizing bidirectional channels, for each direction, there are two input/output channels corresponding to the master and slave links, respectively. We define two metrics, namely channel fitness and direction fitness, to reflect the suitability of an input channel to receive packets.

In the channel fitness function, in order to predict the dynamics of the network traffic which may exhibit a non-Markovian behavior [3], we include the channel average waiting time to reflect the channels "memory". The fitness value of an input channel is represented as:

$$fitness_{in} = \alpha \times m_{in} \times w_{in}^{-1}$$

where α is a scaling parameter, m_{in} is the average number of free slots in the channel and w_{in} is the average waiting time that a packet spends in the channel. In this work, according to the simulation results with different α values ranging from 0.5 to 1.5, we observe α equals to 0.8 offers the highest performance.

During the routing stage, since we have not yet determined whether the master or the slave output port will be used, we need to evaluate the input channels at both ports of the downstream router to get a more appropriate metric for choosing the output direction. The direction fitness function is used to indicate the overall availability of one direction in the downstream router. One issue when designing the direction fitness function is to consider the characteristics of the bi-directional channels since the effective bandwidth between two neighboring routers varies with the actual traffic over time. One simple way is to add together the two channels fitness values regardless of them being of master or slave type. However, because the master port has a higher priority in sending and its input channel can only receive flits when there is no sending request at the same port. Then, if we only consider the channel fitness without regarding to the probability of receiving flits using this channel or the actual channel utilization, it may not lead to an optimal selection.

Table 1: Notations in the routing for proposed NoC

Parameter	Description
N	Number of nodes in the mesh network
P	The set of directions $P = N, E, S, W, L$
$f[i][j][k]$	Fitness of the input channel where $i \in P$, $j \in J$, $k \in N$
$P_{block}[i][j]$	Blocking probability of the input channel in master inout port in direction i of node k
$F[i][k]$	Fitness value of direction i of node k
$S_l[i][k]$	Total score from current node l to node k through direction i
$CH[i][k]$	Set of (node, direction) pairs chosen by K-step speculative algorithm from current node to the destination node k along direction i

Algorithm 1 Channel direction fitness calculation

Input: Average waiting time: $w[i][j][k]$; Average available slots $m[i][j][k]$; master inout port input channel block probability $P_{block}[i][j]$; scaling parameter α
Output: Channel fitness: $f[i][j][k]$ and the direction fitness $F[i][k]$

```
for all node k ∈ N do
  for all i ∈ P do
    F[i][k] = 0
    for all j ∈ P do
      f[i][j][k] = α × m[i][j][k] × w[i][j][k]^-1
      if j == 0 then
        F[i][k]+ = (1 − P_block[i][j]) × f[i][j][k]
      else
        F[i][k]+ = f[i][j][k]
      end if
    end for
  end for
end for
```

In order to deal with this issue, we calculate the fitness of a particular direction by distinguishing the input channels at the master and slave ports. For the input channel in the slave port, because the channel can always be used whenever there is a request from a neighbor, its fitness directly contributes to the fitness function calculation. For the input channels at the master inout port, we calculate the average block probability P_{block} due to the write conflict during a time window. This is the probability when the FSM controller configures the port into the output mode and lets the output register use the link for sending packets instead of receiving the packets from the neighboring nodes. The fitness of direction i under consideration is then:

$$F_i = fitness_{slave\_in} + (1 - P_{block}) \times fitness_{master\_in}$$

In Algorithm 1, we present the idea of calculating the fitness function periodically for any given direction. The notations used for the algorithm are listed in Table I. Two counters are needed in each input channel to calculate the average waiting time of packets and the number of available buffer slots during any time window. According to these two metrics, the input channel fitness at the master and slave inout ports can be calculated. An extra counter at the master port FSM is used to record the average blocking probability P_{block}. The fitness of the direction under evaluation is then the weighted sum of the two input channels fitness values.

4.2.2 *Fitness based adaptive routing algorithm*

In order to avoid deadlocks at run time, the odd-even turn rules [4] are used in the minimal path based routing computation. Under this assumption, for any packet in the current router, there are at most two feasible output directions.

As discussed in [2,6,15], if the adaptive routing algorithm only considers the local congestion metric, it will be too slow to re-act to congestion in the more distant parts of the network as it relies on network backpressure to propagate the congestion state. In this work, we propose a scheme that combines the local and remote channel fitness status in order to make a better routing decision (see Algorithm 2).

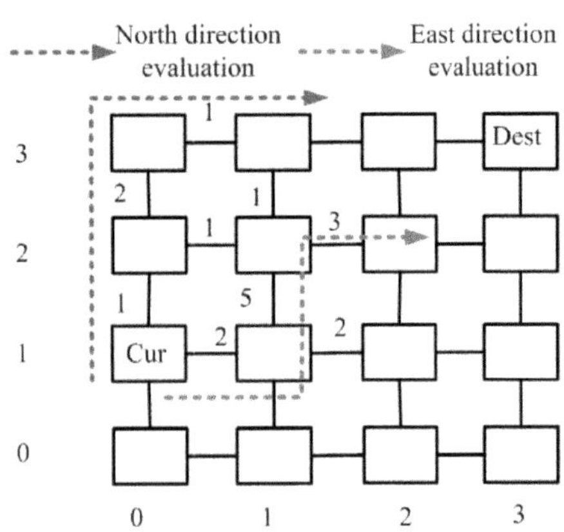

Figure 5: K-step (K=3) speculative routing

Different from previous approaches in [2,6,12], which utilize fixed local and non-local neighbors to evaluate each candidate direction in the router, our proposed adaptive routing algorithm uses a K-step speculative routing to dynamically select a set of nodes on the routing path which have the best fitness value towards the destination currently. Based on the fitness value of these nodes, the routing algorithm decides the optimal output port for the current router.

Figure 5 shows a routing scenario for the proposed K-step speculative routing with $K = 3$. The values on the link indicate the direction fitness level measured at each router. When evaluating the east output direction for the current node, node (1,1) is chosen first. Then, the router compares the two candidate directions from node (1,1) to the destination. Since the north output direction at node (1,1) has a larger direction fitness value (5) than the east output direction. The north neighboring node (1,2) is chosen second. Similarly, for node (1,2), its east neighboring node (2,2) will be selected. Therefore, nodes (1,1), (1,2) and (2,2) form a 3-step speculative path towards the destination using the east output direction of the current router. Similarly, nodes (0,2), (0,3) and (1,3) form a speculative path from the north output direction towards the destination.

Algorithm 2 K-step speculative selection algorithm

Input: Current node **cur**: Destination node **dst**; Set of candidate output directions P_c
Output: Output direction $P_o \in P_c$
Function:$Candidate\_dir(a, b)$:A set of candidate directions for node a to b

```
for all direction i ∈ P_c do
  S_cur[i][dst] = 0;
  CH[i][dst] ← (cur, i);
  check_length = 0;
  while check_length < K&&!CH[i][dst].IsEmpty() do
    (check_node, check_dir) = CH[i][dst].Pop();
    next_node = check_node.get_neighbor(check_dir);
    if next_node! = dst then
      S_cur[i][dst]+ = F[reverse(check_dir)][next_node];
      C_set = Candidate_dir(next_node, dst);
      if F[C_set[1]][next_node] > F[C_set[0]][next_node] then
        CH[i][dst] ← (next_node, C_set[1]);
      else
        CH[i][dst] ← (next_node, C_set[0]);
      end if
    end if
    check_length + +;
  end while
end for
P_0 = Select_highest_score_dir(S_cur, P_c);
```

By adding together the direction fitness values of each path, the scores of using the north and the east output port can be calculated. The router then chooses the direction with the best score for the current router. If the direction fitness value changes at run time, the nodes selected for evaluating each candidate port will also change accordingly to capture the network dynamics.

Algorithm 2 presents the details of the proposed K-step speculative routing algorithm. At run time, each router periodically collects the channel and direction fitness values of the neighbors located in a region less than K-hops away. Then, for each output candidate, we perform a K-step look ahead routing towards the destinations and select a set of K consecutive nodes and directions to form a speculative routing path towards the destinations using current candidate direction. By comparing the total fitness values along the paths between the two candidate directions, the direction with the best path fitness value is chosen as the output port for the current router.

In this work, we adopt a light weight traffic status propagation network similar to [15] which is used to propagate the direction fitness information to the nodes within K-hops distance in the network. More specifically, every T cycles, the direction fitness value updated by the current router is propagated K hops away throughout the network in a hop-by-hop manner. After collecting all the direction fitness values

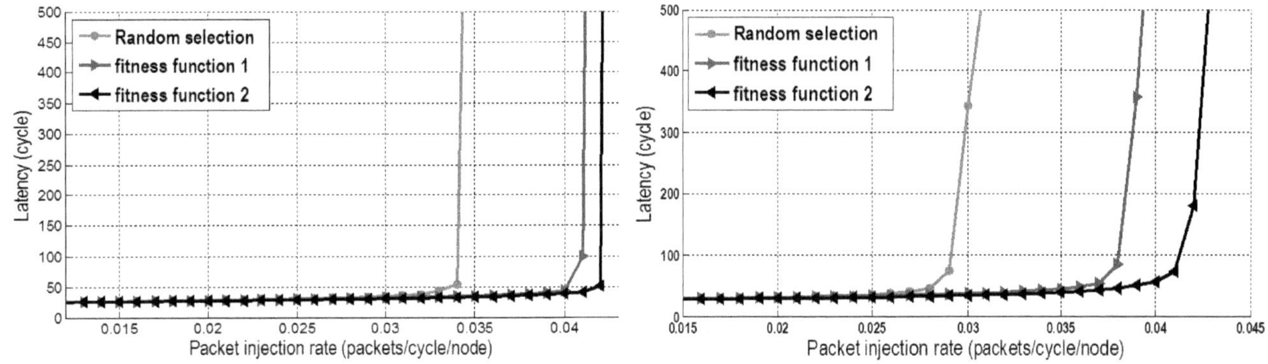

Figure 6: Comparison of the fitness functions for 8×8 meshes using bi-directional channels

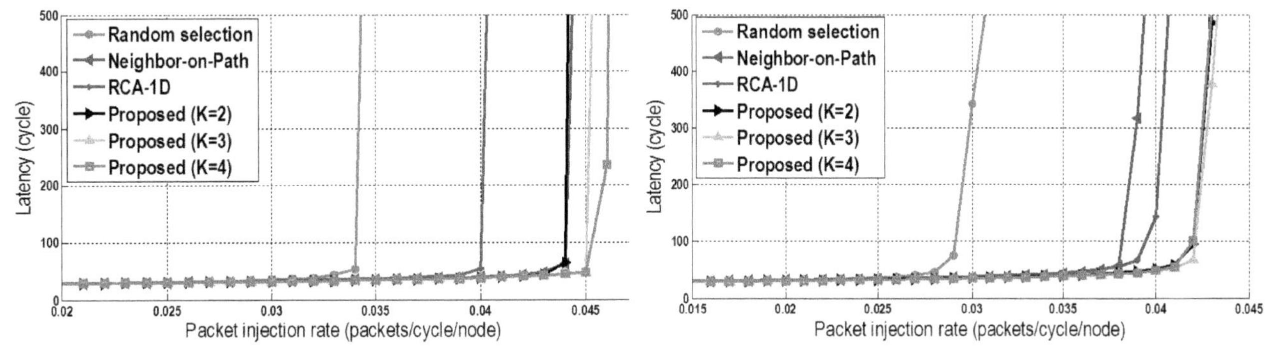

Figure 7: Comparison of different adaptive routing schemes for 8×8 meshes

from the neighboring routers within K-hops distance, these values are stored in the router and used for the proposed K-step speculative routing algorithm. For the case $K \leq 2$, we can further reduce the network complexity by using a specific control channel between the neighboring nodes as in [2] instead of a status propagation network to exchange the traffic information. The signal sent through the control channel contains the fitness of the direction $F[i][k]$ associated to the current router and its 1-hop neighbors. According to the simulation results shown in section 5, there is not too much performance improvement for $K \geq 2$ compared to $K = 2$. Hence we propose to set $K = 2$ (i.e. look only two hops ahead) to achieve the best trade-off between the performance and additional complexity.

5. SIMULATION RESULTS

5.1 Simulation setup

We evaluate the proposed NoC architecture, as well as the adaptive routing algorithm, using a cycle accurate NoC simulator implemented in C++. Simulations were done for different mesh network sizes: 4×4 and 8×8. To investigate the benefits of our NoC architecture and the performance improvements of our adaptive traffic aware routing algorithm, we compare our approach with the following NoC architectures: 1) classical unidirectional NoC; 2) bi-directional NoC [11]; 3) bi-directional NoC with static EVCs [10].

Throughout the experiments, we assume that each input channel has a buffer depth of 6 flits for the NoC using bi-directional channels and a buffer depth of 12 flits for the uni-directional NoC. Both synthetic traffic (i.e., uniform, transpose) and real benchmark traces were used in the simulations. For uniform traffic, each node sends packets to other nodes in the network with an equal probability. For transpose traffic, each node at the (i, j) mesh location sends packets to the node at the (j, i) location on the mesh.

For the real benchmark workloads, we consider several 16-node multithreaded commercial and scientific workloads from DBmbench [16] and SPECweb99 [18]. This type of traffic includes the memory request/response coherence traffic between PEs and caches.

5.2 Comparison of adaptive routing for BiNoC

We compare our proposed adaptive routing algorithm with some widely adopted routing algorithms to evaluate the performance under bi-directional channels. More precisely, we compare the benefits of using a fitness function and a K-step speculative selection algorithm to capture the network traffic status. First, we compare different fitness functions used to evaluate the router channels. In this comparison, we only gather the traffic status from the immediate neighbors and use different fitness functions to evaluate the channels status. The baseline for this comparison is the random selection strategy of the Odd-even routing algorithm [4]. Two direction fitness functions are used in the simulation:

1) Fitness function 1 is the direct sum of the input channel fitness without distinguishing the master and slave channels

2) Fitness function 2 uses the link blocking probability to weight the channels in the combination of the master and slave channels fitness values.

Figure 6 shows the comparison results obtained for an 8×8 mesh under random and transpose traffic patterns. As shown in this figure, using a fitness function to represent the channel traffic status significantly improves the network critical load (by more than 22.5%). Furthermore, if we consider the characteristic of the bidirectional links by distin-

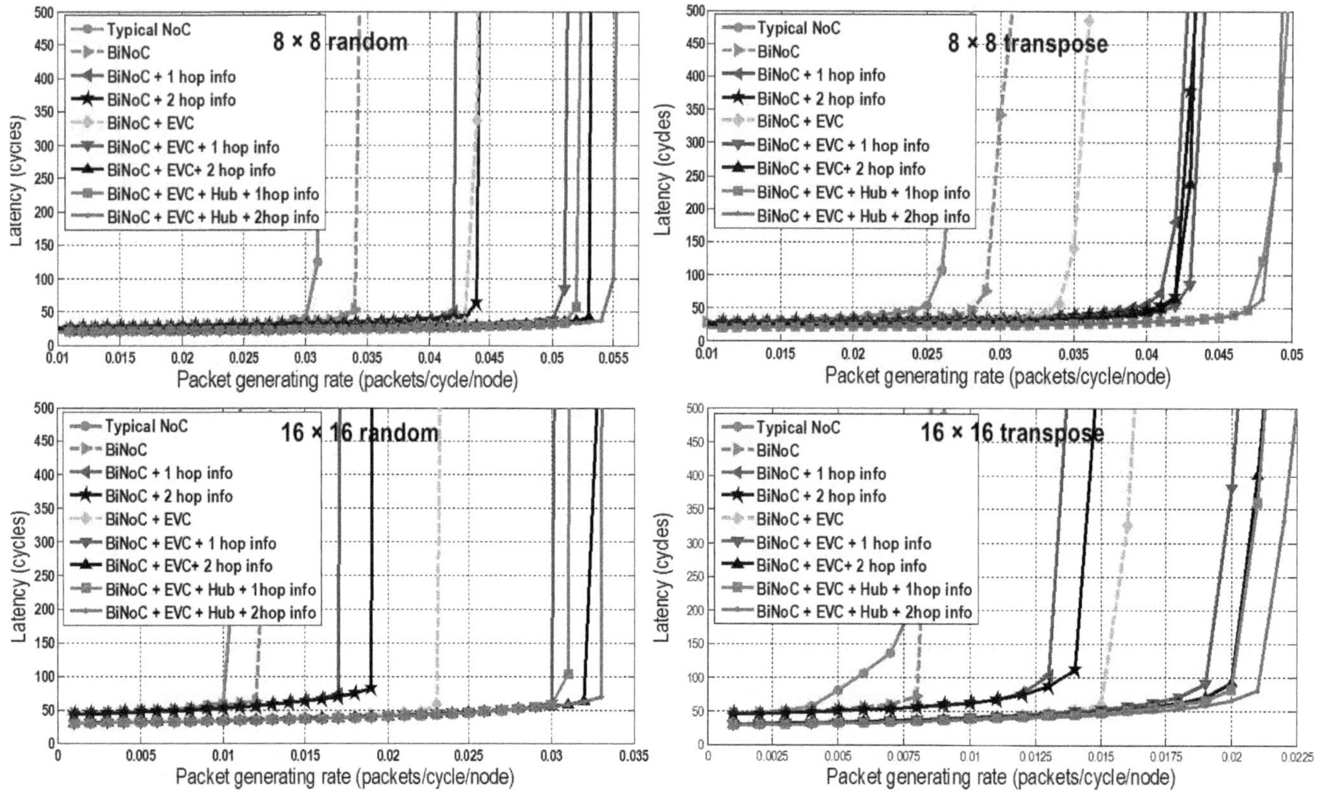

Figure 8: Comparison of different NoC architectures under various mesh size and traffic patterns.

guishing the master and slave channels, an extra 5% - 8% performance gain can be achieved.

Next, using the proposed fitness function for the bidirectional NoC, we make a comparison of different adaptive routing schemes which consider both the immediate neighbors and non-local nodes to evaluate the directions in the routing selection phase. We evaluate our proposed K-step speculative selection scheme with different K values (K=2, 3, 4). At the same time we compare our scheme with two widely adopted schemes, namely neighbor-on-path [2] and regional-contention-awareness (RCA-1D) [6] under random, and transpose traffic patterns on an 8×8 mesh. In order to minimize the intra-region interference in RCA-1D [12, 15], we modify the RCA-1D scheme to integrate the destination into the selection function as in the DBAR approach [12].

As shown from Figure 7, the proposed K-step speculative scheme achieves the best performance results by selectively choosing the intermediate nodes towards destination at run time. Also, it can be seen that there is no significant improvement in the performance for a K value larger than 2. Since the complexity of the fitness value propagation increases dramatically when $K \geq 2$, we use $K = 2$ throughout the remaining simulations.

5.3 Effect of adding EVC and hub routers

In this section, we evaluate the performance improvement resulted by adding EVC and regional hub routers into the BiNoC. Both random selection and K-step speculative selection strategies are used in these simulations. The following architectures were evaluated and compared: the typical NoC with unidirectional channels, the BiNoC proposed in [11], the BiNoC + EVC which combines the features of Bi-directional switching in [11] and express virtual channels in [10], and the proposed NoC with regional hubs.

Figure 8 summarizes the simulation results. We compare the average latency performance under various traffic injection rate for 4×4 and 8×8 meshes. Several observations can be made based on these results:

1) BiNoC outperforms the typical NoC design. Adding EVC into the network can further improve the network criticality by 9.8%-80% for different traffic patterns and mesh sizes. Furthermore, if the regional hub router is added, the throughput can be further improved by 9.3%-15%.

2) For all the NoC architectures using the adaptive routing algorithm, the fitness function employed to evaluate the traffic status can significantly improve the network performance. As shown in Figure 8, using the 1 hop away neighboring info can improve the network criticality by 13% - 30%, while using 2 hop neighbor info can further improve the performance by 3% - 11% in most cases.

5.4 Results using real world workloads

In this section, we show the latency comparison for various real world benchmarks with an 8×8 mesh size. We report seven experiments. The first five experiments collect the traces from the same applications, i.e. Apache, Oracle, Db2V, sparse and Ocean which were mapped onto an 8×8 mesh. The last two experiments named Mixed-1 and Mixed-2 combine the traces from different applications and map them to the same NoC platform. The simulation time of each benchmark is set to 5,000,000 clock circles with a 2,000 cycles warmup period.

As shown in Figure 9, compared with the baseline BiNoC design with random selection strategy, which is normalized

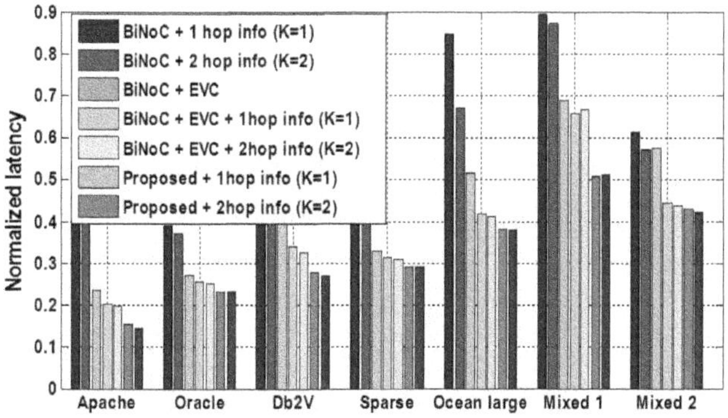

Figure 9: Latency comparison for benchmarks

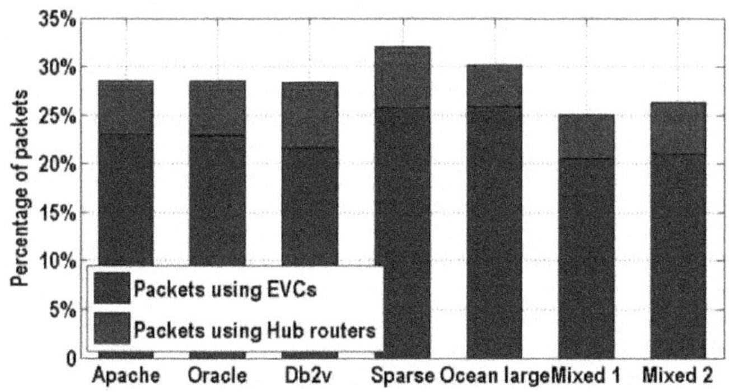

Figure 10: Percentage of packets using EVCs and hub routers

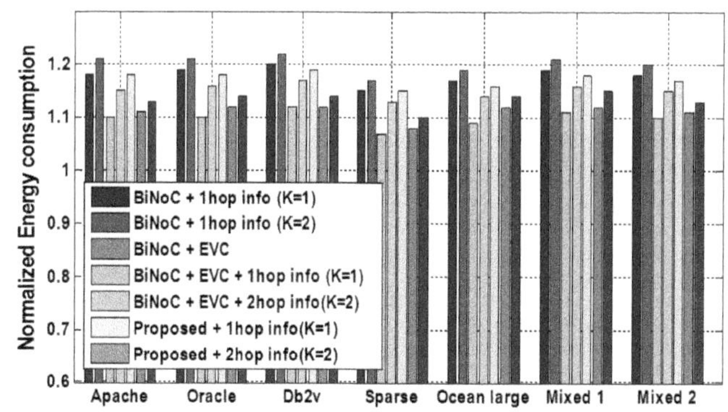

Figure 11: Energy comparison for benchmarks

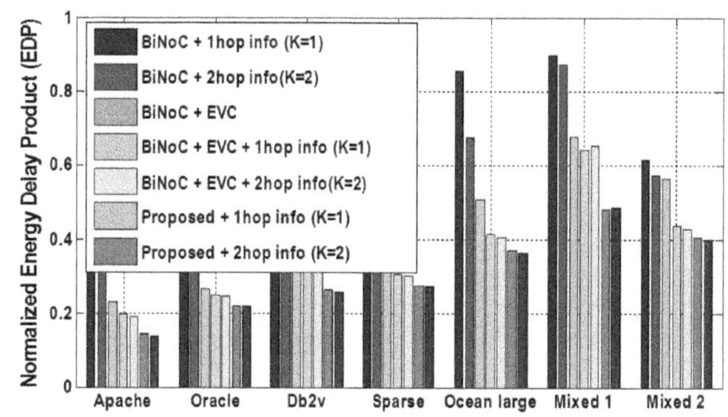

Figure 12: EDP comparison for benchmarks

to 1, by adopting a fitness function to evaluate the channels status can reduce the average latency by 15%-60%. For example, after applying the fitness functions, the latency of the sparse benchmark is reduced to 42% compared with BiNoC routing. The static EVC approach further improves the performance by 6%-28% compared with its BiNoC counterparts for both random selection or fitness function based selection strategies. As in the sparse application, the EVC+BiNoC+2 hop info routing improves the latency by 25.2% over the BiNoC + 2 hop info routing. If a central hub router is added into each region in our proposed NoC architecture, the performance can be further improved by 5%-10%. As shown in Figure 9, for the sparse application, the proposed NoC architecture with $K = 2$ speculative routing improves the latency by 6.5%.

Figure 10 shows the percentage of packets that utilize the EVCs and hub routers when running different benchmarks. As shown, on average, 5.5% of packets utilize the express hub paths to send packets to the destination directly, while 22.9% packets utilize EVCs at least once at run time.

Next, we evaluate the energy overhead of different NoC architectures while running these applications. For this purpose, we have modified the Orion power model [9] to consider the extra energy consumption over the unidirectional NoC. For the BiNoC, the additional energy consumption is mainly due to the larger crossbar size ($2N \times 2N$), and the channel direction control logic [11]. We modified the energy consumption of the crossbar in the Orion power model and added the energy overhead for the link direction switching according to [11]. For BiNoC + EVC architecture, the additional energy consumption for the EVC latch and the EVC arbiter is discussed in [10] and we add this to the Orion model. For the energy consumption of the proposed architecture, the hub latches in the normal router are modeled similarly to the EVC, while the energy consumption of the hub router is modeled as a four-port, four-VC normal router as in the Orion power model. For the calculation of the fitness values for each channel, we need additional adders and multipliers to calculate the fitness values every 100 cycles. This energy overhead is modeled in a similar way as in [2]. In Figure 11, the energy consumption of the unidirectional NoC architecture is normalized to one. The BiNoC approach has about 10%-20% energy overhead due to a large crossbar size and the link direction switching overhead [11]. The EVC and regional hub approach can effectively reduce the energy by allowing some packets use the express paths and bypassing the router pipeline stages. In Figure 11, the energy overhead for the proposed NoC architecture with 2-step selection strategy is 13% on average.

In Figure 12, we show the energy-delay product (EDP) metric for different architectures discussed in this paper. The baseline EDP metric is chosen to be the BiNoC architecture in [11]. As shown in Figure 12, the proposed architecture with regional hub routers, with the fitness based routing approach, consistently improves the system performance. In fact, as much as 80% reduction in EDP can be achieved when combining all these approaches.

5.5 Implementation overhead evaluation

We have modified the Orion 2.0 area model [9] to evaluate the area overhead. In this evaluation, we target a 1.0GHz operating frequency under the 65nm technology. When evaluating the BiNoC, the bi-directional link direction control logic is considered as in [11]. As shown in Figure 13, the area numbers of source/sink nodes and bypass nodes in the BiNoC+EVC architecture, as well as the nor-

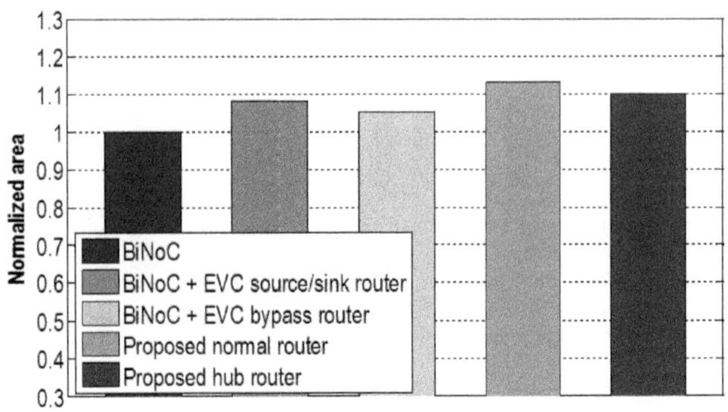

Figure 13: Area overhead comparison

mal router and hub router in the proposed architecture are compared against the baseline BiNoC design which is normalized to one. Router (1,2) in Figure 3 is chosen when evaluating the normal routers in the proposed architecture, since this router is the most complicated one with an extra port connected to the hub router. In Figure 13, compared to BiNoC baseline router, the normal router of the proposed architecture has an overhead of about 13%. Together with the additional hub router in each 4×4 region, the proposed NoC architecture has an area overhead of 19%.

A normal router in the proposed architecture was also implemented in Verilog and synthesized using Nangate 45nm library [19]. Compared to the BiNoC router with $0.10mm^2$ area and $632MHz$ frequency, the proposed router has an area of $0.11mm^2$ and a maximum frequency of $589MHz$. Further optimization on the hardware implementation of the proposed NoC architecture will be discussed in future work.

6. CONCLUSIONS

In this work, we have proposed a flexible NoC architecture which utilizes bidirectional channels, EVC channels and regional hub routers to improve the NoC performance. We have also proposed a traffic-aware, adaptive routing algorithm that considers the characteristic of the bidirectional links. Simulation results on synthetic traffic, as well as real world benchmarks, show that the proposed NoC architecture, together with the routing algorithm, can significantly reduce the latency by as much as 80% with a small energy and area overhead.

7. ACKNOWLEDGMENTS

The authors P.B.,G.W.,and R.M. greatly acknowledge the support from NSF under the CCF-0916752 grant and from GRC under the 2011-HJ-2168 and 2012-HJ-2232 grants. The author Z.Q acknowledges the generous support of a RGC-HK Fulbright Scholarship and HKUST oversea research scholarship. The authors would like to thank the anonymous reviewers for their valuable comments to improve the quality of this paper.

8. REFERENCES

[1] M.A. Al Faruque, T. Ebi, J. Henkel, "Configurable links for runtime adaptive on-chip communication," *Design, Automation & Test in Europe Conf. & Exhibition* (DATE), pp. 256-261, 2009.

[2] G. Ascia, V. Catania, M. Palesi, D. Patti, "Neighbors-on-Path: A New Selection Strategy for On-Chip Networks," *Embedded Systems for Real Time Multimedia* (ESTMedia), pp. 79-84, 2006.

[3] P. Bogdan, R. Marculescu, "Non-Stationary Traffic Analysis and Its Implications on Multicore Platform Design," *IEEE Trans. on Computer-Aided Design of Integrated Circuits and Systems*, vol.30, no.4, 2011.

[4] G.-M. Chiu "The odd-even turn model for adaptive routing" *IEEE Trans. on Parallel and Distributed Systems*, vol.11, no.7, pp.729-738, 2000.

[5] M.H. Cho, M. Lis, K.S. Shim, M. Kinsy, T. Wen, S. Devadas, "Oblivious Routing in On-Chip Bandwidth-Adaptive Networks," *Parallel Architectures and Compilation Techniques* (PACT), 2009.

[6] P. Gratz, B. Grot, S.W. Keckler, "Regional congestion awareness for load balance in networks-on-chip," *14th Intl. Symp. on High Performance Computer Architecture* (HPCA), pp.203-214, 2008.

[7] B. Grot, J. Hestness, S.W. Keckler, O. Mutlu, "Express Cube Topologies for on-Chip Interconnects," *15th Intl. Symp. on High Performance Computer Architecture* (HPCA), pp.163-174, 2009.

[8] A. Hemani et al., "Network on chip: an architecture for billion transistor era," *IEEE NorChip Conf.*, 2000.

[9] A.B. Kahng, B. Li, L.-S. Peh, K. Samadi, "Orion 2.0: A power-area simulator for interconnection networks" *IEEE Trans. on Very Large Scale Integration Systems*, vol.20, no.1, pp. 191-196, 2012.

[10] A. Kumar, L.-S. Peh, P. Kundu, N.K. Jha, "Toward Ideal On-Chip Communication Using Express Virtual Channels" *IEEE Micro*, vol. 28, no. 1, pp. 80-90, 2008.

[11] Y.-C. Lan et al., "A Bidirectional NoC (BiNoC) Architecture With Dynamic Self-Reconfigurable Channel," *IEEE Trans. on Computer-Aided Design of Integrated Circuits and Systems*, vol.30, no.3, 2011.

[12] S. Ma, N.E. Jerger, Z. Wang, "DBAR: an efficient routing algorithm to support multiple concurrent applications in networks-on-chip," *38th Intl. Symp. on Computer Architecture* (ISCA), 2011.

[13] U.Y. Ogras, R. Marculescu, "It's a small world after all: NoC performance optimization via long-range link insertion," *IEEE Trans. on Very Large Scale Integration Systems*, vol.14, no.7, pp. 693-706, 2006.

[14] Z.-L. Qian, Y.F. Teh, C.-Y. Tsui, "A flit-level speedup scheme for network-on-chips using self-reconfigurable bi-directional channels," *Design, Automation & Test in Europe Conf. & Exhibition* (DATE), 2012.

[15] R.S. Ramanujam, B. Lin, "Destination-based adaptive routing on 2D mesh networks," *Architectures for Networking and Comm. Systems* (ANCS), 2010.

[16] M.-L. Shao, A. Ailamaki, B. Falsafi, "Dbmbench: fast and accurate database workload representation on modern microarchitecture" *Centre for Advanced Studies on Collaborative Research* (CASCON), 2005.

[17] C.-F. Wang, W.-H. Hu, N. Bagherzadeh, "Congestion-aware Network-on-Chip router architecture," *Computer Architecture and Digital Systems (CADS)*, 2010.

[18] Spec benchmarks. `www.spec.org/web99`.

[19] Nangate 45nm library. `www.nangate.com`.

The Roce-Bush Router: A Case for Routing-centric Dimensional Decomposition for Low-latency 3D NoC Routers

Miguel Salas
Intel Corporation
Fort Collins, CO, USA
miguel.o.salas@intel.com

Sudeep Pasricha
Electrical and Computer Engineering Dept.
Colorado State University, Fort Collins, CO, USA
sudeep@colostate.edu

Abstract

As 3D System-On-Chips (SoCs) come ever closer to becoming the standard for high performance ICs, 3D Networks on Chips (NoCs) have emerged as a key component in meeting performance constraints and ensuring power-efficiency. Among the proposed 3D router architectures, dimensionally-decomposed routers are widely accepted as an efficient solution to deal with the increased port count and the accompanying exponential power and area increases. All decompositions proposed thus far have however been dimensionally static, that is, they have set in stone a particular bias among the three dimensions. This paper presents a novel router with a routing-centric decomposition and virtual channel buffer sharing called the *Roce-Bush* router. To our knowledge, this is the first work that integrates routing-awareness in the context of dimensional decomposition and buffer resource allocation for NoC routers. Experimental results involving RTL level implementations of our router and synthesis at 45nm show that compared to a dimensional-agnostic decomposed router, the Roce-Bush router can achieve up to 14% better performance and 5% lower power.

Categories and Subject Descriptors
B.5 **[Register-Transfer-level implementation]** - Data-path design
C.1.2 **[Multiple Data Stream Architectures]** - Interconnection architectures

Keywords: Network-on-chips, NoCs, System-on-chips, 3D ICs, router architecture

I. INTRODUCTION

As silicon chips continue to scale into the deep submicron era, the performance bottleneck of Chip Multiprocessors (CMPs) has shifted to their interconnection network. The ever-increasing latency and throughput requirements on CMPs that must stay within a stringent power envelope are slowly making bus-based interconnects impractical due to their limited throughput, power inefficiencies, and poor scaling. More importantly, the number of cores is increasing rapidly, as can be easily seen in the current state-of-the-art CMPs, with some commercial offerings integrating around 100 cores [23].

CODES+ISSS'12, October 7–12, 2012, Tampere, Finland.

Network-on-Chips (NoCs) are quickly becoming the de-facto standard for communication in CMPs with such a large number of cores [1]. However, *one of the main challenges* with NoCs is long packet latencies that can become a major performance bottleneck. To this end, a NoC router is required to not only be extremely power and area efficient, but must also allow for a large throughput and low latency. Figure 1 shows a typical NoC router [2] that supports virtual channels, which is a common way to dramatically lower transfer latencies. It has five key components: Port Buffers, Route-Computation (RC), Virtual-channel Allocator (VA), Switch-Allocator (SA), and a Crossbar Switch. The specific router architecture chosen in a NoC plays a vital role in its performance, and thus much research has focused on designing a highly efficient router across the latency-throughput-area-power spectrum [4]-[11].

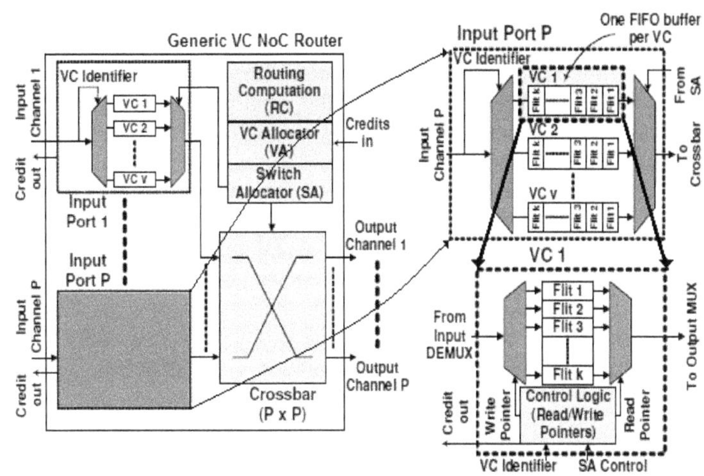

Figure 1. A Generic Virtual Channel (VC) Router [2]

The use of multiple layers of silicon within a die, coined a 3D IC, has very recently emerged as one solution to mitigate the high latencies due to long interconnects as illustrated in Figure 2 [3]. By using order of magnitude shorter vertical Through Silicon Vias (TSVs) to replace long global interconnects, the inter-core communication latency can be dramatically reduced. Since each layer is simply a 2D IC, most circuit design concepts still apply. Thus, it is no surprise that first-pass 3D NoCs proposed in literature [24] are simply made up of 2D routers with two extra ports – the up and down ports for inter-die communication (Z-direction). However, such extension to NoC routers that have an $n \times n$ structure (n is the number of ports) can significantly increase fanout, area, and complexity, *resulting in very inefficient 3D routers.*

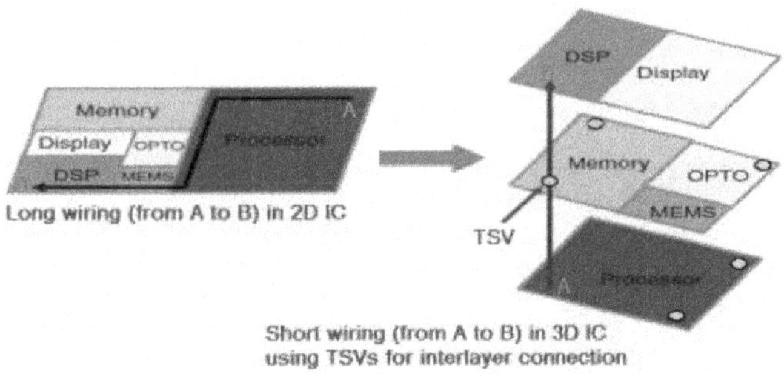

Figure 2. Motivation for migrating from 2D to 3D ICs [3]

In this paper, we propose a novel 3D dimensionally decomposed router (the *Roce-Bush* Router) that is optimized for low-latency and when compared to the state-of-the-art decomposed routers, can achieve significantly better performance with lower power dissipation. Our Routing-Centric Buffer-Sharing (*Roce-Bush*) router supports decompositions that exploit the patterns of a given routing scheme. Furthermore, it allocates shared buffer resources to exploit these patterns to further enhance communication performance. Finally, it also decomposes the arbitration modules within a router. Using all of these enhancements results in a novel 3D router that is power and area efficient while also meeting low-latency design requirements and supporting virtual channels.

II. RELATED WORK

A. 3D Decomposed Routers

Coming up with efficient routers for 3D NoCs has been a topic of avid research. One of the most popular solutions that have recently emerged is a *dimensionally-decomposed* router, that is, a router that is decoupled among certain directions in the XYZ Cartesian plane. A typical decomposed router avoids a 7×7 crossbar and other router components that have $n \times n$ complexities, depending on the actual router implementation, where n is the number of router ports (radix). A decomposed router breaks up these components into a set of smaller components, thereby avoiding the prohibitive area and power increase of a large crossbar and other $n \times n$ components.

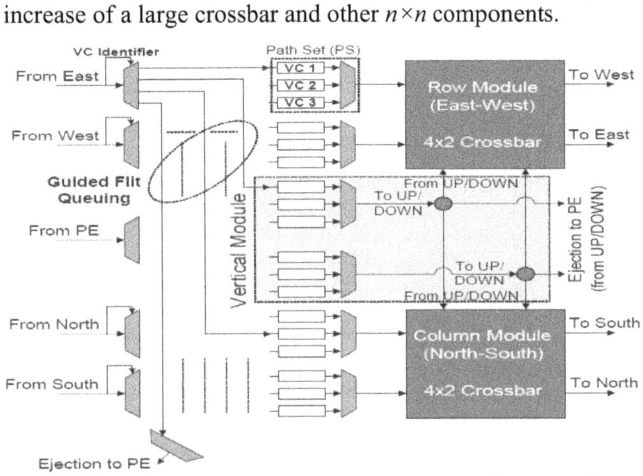

Figure 3. A Fully dimensionally decomposed router [4]

One well known solution in dimensionally decomposed 3D NoC routers is shown in Figure 3 [4]. This router is fully decomposed among each of the 3 dimensions: there is a module for X-routing, one for Y-routing, and one for Z-routing. Implied across each direction are 2 stages of arbitration and a crossbar. For example, for a flit to go to west or east (X-module), it must first go through two 3×2 crossbar stages to select 2 out of the 5 inputs (east, west, north, south, core). Then, it must couple the two winners with the Z-direction via a 4×2 crossbar. The same applies to the Y and Z directions, resulting in a design that sacrifices latency and throughput (due to arbitration as will be discussed in section IV) in favor of a smaller and more power-efficient design.

While the router decomposed in all directions is simple and efficient, it is not practical for latency and throughput-sensitive designs. A more recent and popular decomposed 3D NoC router is shown in Figure 4 [5], [6]. This decomposed router keeps the latency and throughput characteristics of a 2D design and decouples one of the directions, ending up with two 4×4 routers that still finish within 1 full clock cycle, thereby making it fall under the single cycle router category. Thus, the router functions as a single synchronous router with some latency increase due to the two stages of arbitration and logic. The final result is a router with a decomposition that partitions in *core-Zdir* and *Xdir-Ydir* paths, and hence results in a compromise between the area-power efficient decomposition-across-all-directions and a low-latency but implementation inefficient "composed" design. However, this particular implementation has an inherent bias towards the packets traveling in the *Z* direction, which see lower latency as they bypass the *X-Y* arbitration, and just see a net latency provided by its 4×4 crossbar (up, down, core and "other"). It can be argued that this is because all other things equal, the *Z* direction might see the overhead of TSV propagation and thus it might make sense to bias the router towards Z-direction in hopes of cancelling the TSV delay effect. That brings up another question: *What if we chose the X-direction as the preferred direction? Or what if we chose Y?* Our *Roce-Bush* router attempts to answer these specific questions, proving that indeed, there is a notable performance improvement if we decompose the NoC router in the appropriate direction. To this end, we implemented the dimensionally static 3D router from Figure 4 as a comparison point against our *Roce-Bush* router.

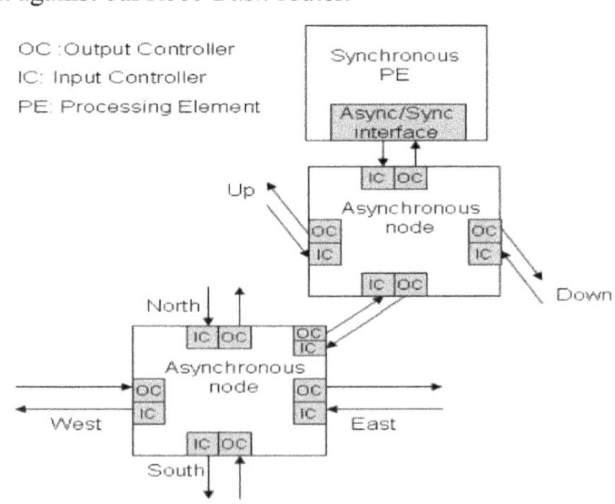

Figure 4. Z-biased 2-level decomposed 3D NoC router [5]

Note that the previous two 3D decomposed routers are not an exhaustive list by any means. Other notable decomposed routers have also been proposed. For example, the MIRA router [7] proposes having a 3D router span among multiple layers, thereby reducing latencies for packets travelling across each layer (Z-direction travel). Nevertheless, routers such as MIRA understate the difficulty in physical design and validation complexity by not being able to keep a given design on a layer. For example, a physical designer of the router might require special synthesis tools to incorporate across-layer information, where small inaccuracies can lead to very low yields. Furthermore, silicon validation across layers would require a very complex interlayer validation scheme [8].

B. Other high performance 3D routers

Decomposed routers are by no means the only proposed high performance NoC routers. Figure 5 shows a speculative router, which is one of the most popular low-latency router designs [9]. The speculative router tries to request crossbar access without knowing whether a packet has reserved a virtual channel or not. Speculative routers have demonstrated good performance in 2D routers. Nevertheless, it has been pointed out that their clock period and power dissipation costs are extremely high, not only due to the abort-logic overhead, but also due the wasted dynamic power every time the speculation does not work [9]. To compare the *Roce-Bush* router performance against other state-of-the-art 3D routers, we also implemented a 3D speculative NoC router.

Finally, large amounts of research on 3D NoC routers have focused on application-specific routers, e.g., [10], [11]. However, the *Roce-Bush* router attempts to improve on generic 3D router architectures for NoCs, and thus avoids an application specific implementation.

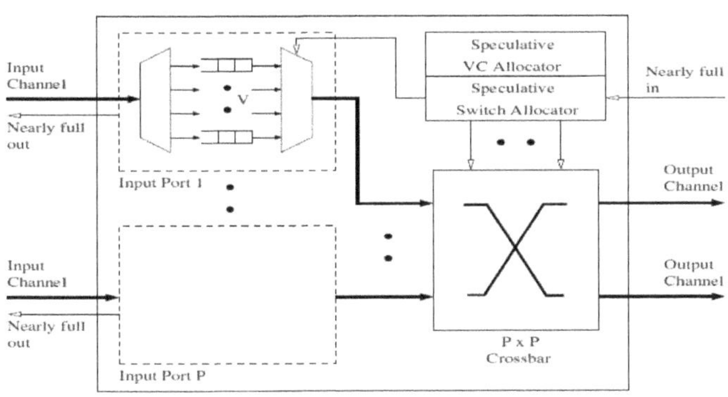

Figure 5. Speculative NoC router design [9]

III. BACKGROUND: 3D NOC ROUTER DECOMPOSITION

In most literature on router decomposition, typically the only part of a NoC router that is considered for decomposition is the crossbar, as it is a fully composed $n\times n$ structure whose complexity grows significantly with increasing n. Some of the proposed decomposed crossbars have been shown to have a large impact on performance [22]. However, decomposing only the crossbar neglects the fact that low latency routers make use of very efficient and more complex arbitration modules for the switch and virtual channel allocation. One of the most popular of these arbitrations is explored in [12], [13], where switch arbitration is done through matrix arbiters and virtual channel arbitration through a tree arbiter made up of parallel matrix arbiters. Switch arbiters are simple $n\times n$ arbiters that through fair arbitration can achieve low latencies. What follows in this section describes the decomposition in each of the typically *composed* router components, for an $n\times n$ complexity.

A. Decomposed Crossbar

A simple extension of the 5×5 crossbar found in typical 2D NoC routers would yield a very large 7×7 crossbar in 3D. Figure 6 shows three efficient ways to decompose a 7×7 crossbar. Figure 6(a) shows a decomposition that, while balancing the 7 loads evenly into two 4×4 crossbars, does not lend itself to any dimensional decomposition. Figure 6(b) shows the type of crossbar that allows for dimensional decomposition. This results in a two-stage 3×3 and 5×5 set of crossbars. Another type of decomposition is explored in figure 6(c), with two-stage 3×3 and 4×4 crossbars in *parallel*, and a 2:1 mux to decide between the two. Note that while Figure 6(c) shows the most power and area efficient design among them all, resulting in the smallest number of gates, Figure 6(b) also has an advantage: because the critical path of an ultra-low latency router is always its control logic, there is a slight latency improvement by using this implementation over the parallel decomposed crossbar. Whichever decomposition is ultimately used in a dimensionally decomposed router depends on whether area, leakage power or latency is the more important design constraint.

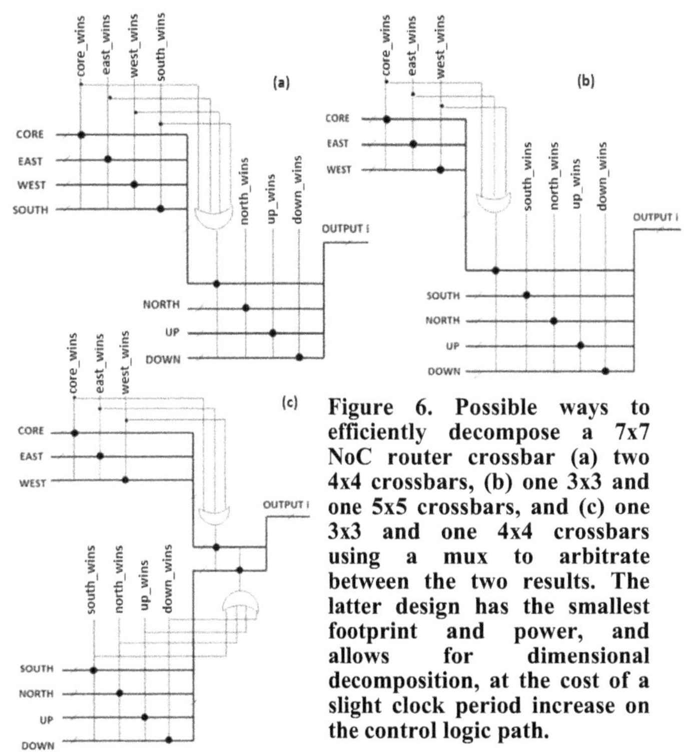

Figure 6. Possible ways to efficiently decompose a 7x7 NoC router crossbar (a) two 4x4 crossbars, (b) one 3x3 and one 5x5 crossbars, and (c) one 3x3 and one 4x4 crossbars using a mux to arbitrate between the two results. The latter design has the smallest footprint and power, and allows for dimensional decomposition, at the cost of a slight clock period increase on the control logic path.

B. Decomposed Switch Arbitration

What is rarely discussed in literature on router decomposition is decomposition of non-crossbar router elements, primarily because the baseline-router for decomposition so far has been extremely simple. Some of the studied routers are simply made out of a naive switch allocator, a crossbar, and a routing module. However, for ultra-low latency, a better complexity-performance compromise is achieved by the matrix arbiters, shown in Figure 7(a). A matrix arbiter keeps track of the requests by setting the corresponding bit in a matrix to 1 and setting the entire row of the requester back to 0 whenever a particular requester wins the current arbitration [13].

However, the matrix arbiter is of $n \times n$ complexity as can be seen in Figure 7(b), resulting in a rather large 49-element matrix for n=7, with fairly complex corresponding control logic. To overcome this challenge, one must decompose the switch arbitration as well. Decomposing the arbiter in a dimensionally-exploitable manner is shown in Figure 7(c), which accomplishes power and area savings from the control logic reduction. The remaining challenge involves deciding how to arbitrate in the case that there is a request from the *preferred* directions (X direction in the figure 7(c)) and the *non-preferred* directions (Y and Z directions in Figure 7(c)) to keep the savings. We define the *preferred* dimension in the decomposition scheme as the dimension that lives next to the core, contending only within the dimension and the core. The other two dimensions are thus called *non-preferred.* This challenge is addressed in section IV.

C. *Decomposed Virtual Channel Allocation*

Finally, in low-latency routers, FIFO-based virtual channels are a common practice to avoid performance bottlenecks such as head-of-the-line blocks (HOL blocking), and to avoid deadlocks [14]. An efficient implementation is presented in Figure 8(a) [13]. It consists of a tree of $n \times (n \times V+1)$ parallel matrix arbiters, where V is the number of virtual channels. The tree functions as follows: each output port contains n arbiters deciding which VC of the given input port wins the arbitration, calculated in parallel to another arbiter that determines which input port gets to win the requested output port. This results in a scheme that contains $n \times V+1$ matrix arbiters per output port. As VC allocation is critical for low-latency routers, this level of VC complexity is often excused with the performance gain.

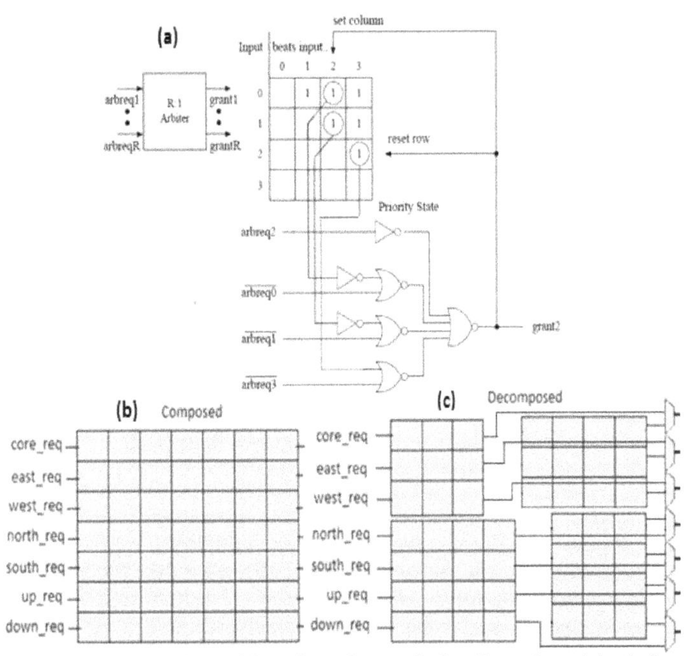

Figure 7. Matrix arbitration for switch allocation (a) 4x4 matrix of arbiters for switch allocation (b) composed 7x7 switch allocation for 3D routers; each block is 1 element of the matrix corresponding to the requestor (row) and requested (column) (c) decomposed switch allocation that decomposes each of the directions and adds a mux per output port for the last stage arbitration.

However, extending this implementation to 3D results in a non-trivial complexity hike. For example, a scheme with 2 VCs, which is the minimum complexity and size required to take advantage of minimal HOL blocking and deadlock freedom provided by VCs, results in a scheme with 15×7 matrix arbiters. Figures 8(b) and 8(c) elaborate on the actual implementation differences. The darker lines indicate the separation among each input port, in this case 2 column-wide to represent 2 Virtual Channels per input port. It can be seen that in the decomposed scheme, we again end up with the dilemma of how to arbitrate among the preferred and non-preferred directions. Furthermore, as in the case of the switch arbitration, all the n-dependant logic of the tree (such as the matrix-arbiter control logic) has exponentially decreased complexity through the use of a 3×3-4×4 decomposed schemes over a 7×7 composed scheme.

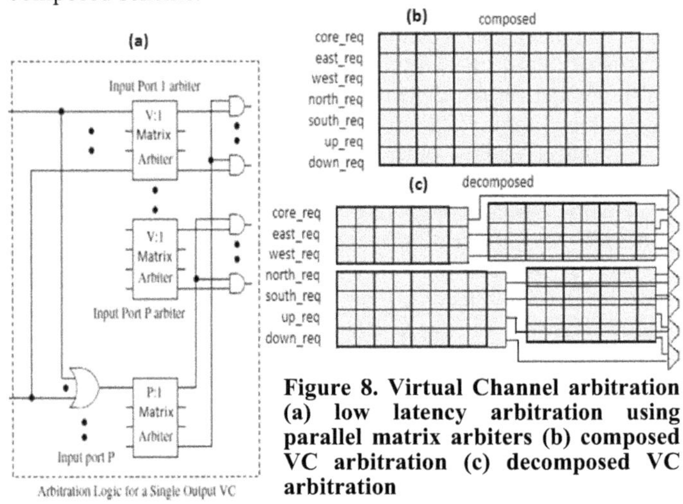

Figure 8. Virtual Channel arbitration (a) low latency arbitration using parallel matrix arbiters (b) composed VC arbitration (c) decomposed VC arbitration

IV. THE ROCE-BUSH 3D NOC ROUTER

In this section, we describe the key components of our Roce-Bush 3D NoC router: routing-centricity, physical optimizations, decomposed arbitraton, and directionality-aware buffering.

A. *Routing centricity*

Although there is literature on routing centric NoC design such as the recent multimedia application-specific design presented in [11], the *Roce-Bush* router is the first work to focus on routing centricity towards decomposed routers. We conjecture that biasing the decomposition in the Roce-Bush router based on the routing scheme chosen can lead to better performance. The motivation for routing centricity is that since dimensionally-decomposed routers rely on some static assumptions (such as TSV effects on 3D SoCs) for choosing a certain dimensional decomposition over another, a systematic routing scheme may present a strong case for providing a better and different dimensional bias. The routing schemes considered for routing-centric decomposition in our router are:

1) *Dimension-ordered Routing*

One of the most popular routing schemes for 3D NoCs is dimension-ordered routing (e.g., XYZ) because of its simple routing logic implementation. However, dimension-ordered routing presents a very systematic way of routing flits through the network: first route in dimension A, then in dimension B, and finally in dimension C. Qualifying a router in terms of how it performs across each direction on a fully symmetrical network often shows differences that can be classified as statistical noise if all the ports and router logic are symmetrical with respect to the *X, Y* and *Z* directions. However, by adding a dimensional-bias, which is the heart of the decomposed routers presented thus far, the original assumption is eliminated altogether. This opens up the question of *which direction to decompose on and how to dimensionally bias that decomposition in the most efficient manner.*

2) Partially adaptive Routing

While simple dimension-order routing remains a popular choice, it certainly is not the de-facto standard for routing. Several enhanced routing schemes for mesh networks have been proposed [15]-[18]. Among them, partially adaptive turn-model based routing schemes such as the west-first routing algorithm, *can exploit dimensional decomposition.* This is because there is a pattern to the routing scheme. For the west-first algorithm, first proposed in [15], flits are routed in the west direction first, and only then is routing in other directions allowed (Figure 9(a)). Such behavior puts a higher load on *X*-direction travel, making it an inherently dimensional biased routing and thus leads itself to routing-aware decomposition. Exploiting these routing scheme patterns, however, is limited by the actual pattern inherent in the chosen routing scheme. For example, in a 3D toggling scheme between XYZ and its other 5 permutations in Figure 9(b), there is no pattern to exploit, and hence, this kind of dimensional bias based decomposition is not beneficial.

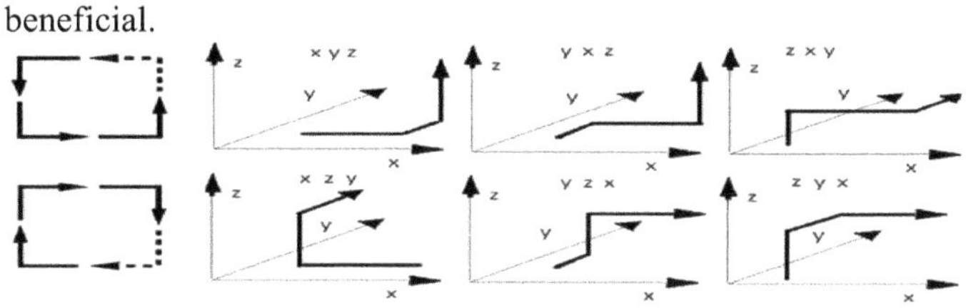

Figure 9. Non dimension-ordered routing schemes (a) 2D West-first turn-based routing, (b) 3D dimension-based toggle routing

B. Physical Optimizations

One of the advantages of directionality-based routing-centric decomposition is that it lends itself to optimizations in certain directions. For example, in an XYZ-routing router, all decomposed logic related to Y going to X, Z to X, or Z to Y can be removed altogether. This results in dimensionally decomposed routers whose parts are dramatically more efficient than their composed counterparts. Compare Figure 7(c) with Figure 10. The latter shows the concept as it is applied to the decomposed switch arbitration logic on a router using XYZ routing.

In Figure 10, since the first stage of arbitration contains the intra-arbitration among the decomposed parts, the diagonal logic is superfluous and thus removed, as it represents requests for a port going to itself. Moreover, the directional optimizations mean that for an XYZ scheme, an X-port must only consider requests from the other X direction and from the core. Similarly, the Y-direction need only consider requests from X, the other Y direction, and the core. These observations can allow us to remove additional logic that is not needed, further reducing router footprint.

The same logic pruning optimization applies to the crossbar and virtual channel allocation decompositions. This optimization makes our proposed dimensional decomposition very appealing. Note that the redundant logic in the decomposition, however, will not be auto-optimized away by commercial synthesis tools, because at a router-level, synthesis is unaware that this logic will remain unused. This implies that all these optimizations must be hard-coded in the RTL code. Finally, note that on schemes that must support routing across all directions, this physical optimization reduces to only pruning of the self-sending directions.

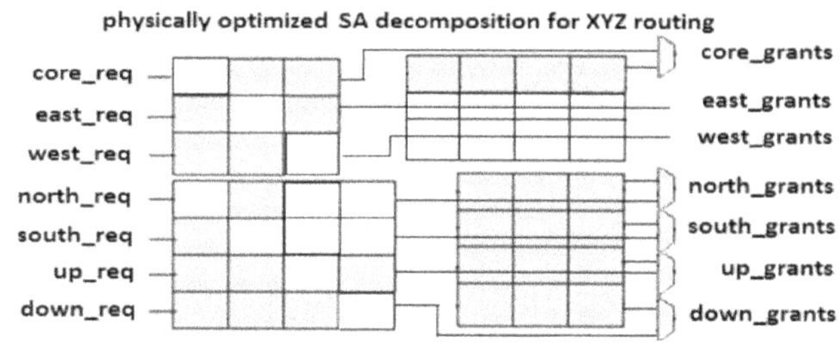

Figure 10. Decomposed SA arbitration with physical optimizations for XYZ routing. Compared to figure 7(c), the logic that will remain unused with XYZ routing has been removed, as shown by the white squares.

C. Efficient Decomposed Arbitration

While asynchronously decomposed crossbars, whose data passes through both stages within the same clock cycle do not change the cycle count (although they affect the clock period), decomposed arbitration does. One of the unanswered questions in decomposed arbitrations is how to efficiently reconcile the arbitration results of the two-stage arbitration scheme. The two inputs to arbitrate are the winner of the *preferred* direction and the winner of the *non-preferred* directions. This arbitration is represented by 2:1 muxes in Figures 7(c), 8(c) and 10. While matrix arbiters provide an efficient way to deal with fair arbitration of multiple inputs, given the amount of inputs to arbitrate, it may be overkill for this problem. Below are four novel simpler schemes that we propose to explore:

- ***Preferred-Takes-All:*** In this default scheme, the preferred direction always wins the arbitration.
- ***Preferred-biased***: Here, the preferred direction wins 66% of the contention times. This scheme tries to provide some relief to the non-preferred contender, to prevent complete starvation.
- ***Preference-Fair**:* In this scheme, when there is contention, half of the time the preferred direction wins, and the other half, the non-preferred directions win. This scheme tries to be fully fair among the preferred and non-preferred contenders. Note that as the first stage of the preferred direction only has 3 requestors (core and dimension A), and the first stage of the non-preferred direction has 4 requestors (dimensions B and C), this scheme still favors the preferred direction, but in a more fair manner. The net effect is that arbitration is slightly biased towards the preferred direction.
- ***Non-Preferred-biased**:* Here, the preferred direction only wins 33% of the contention times. The purpose of this scheme is to have a bias towards the non-preferred directions, to provide a contrast to the other approaches with preferred-direction biasing.

D. Directionality aware buffering

While buffer resources in NoC routers increase throughput and overall performance, they are a very limited resource due to their large power consumption. In a recent NoC power analysis study [19], almost 25% of power dissipated in a router is spent on the FIFO buffers. Hence sharing buffer resources among and within input ports has been proposed as a way to make power-efficient use of them. Among the many sharing permutations, sharing across two of the four directions in a 2D router was recently proposed after a study evaluated each of the permutations [20].

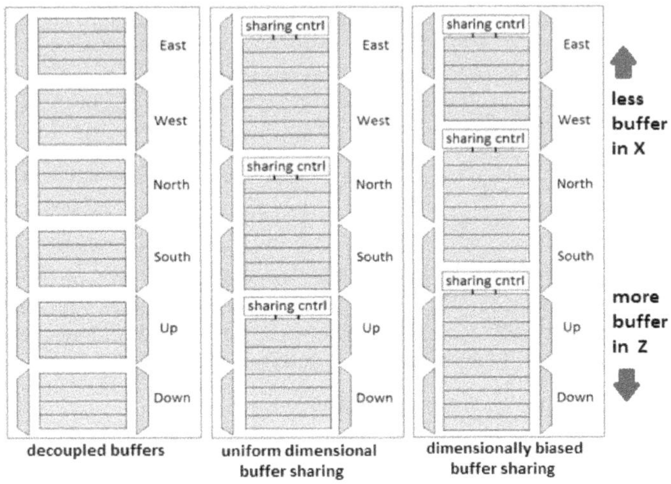

(a) (b) (c)

Figure 11. Buffer resource allocation in VC routers. (a) baseline resource allocation in VC routers is uniform and isolated (b) uniform dimensional buffer sharing (c) dimensionally-biased dimensional buffer sharing.

The *Roce-Bush* router attempts to share buffer resources while exploiting the dimensional bias of decomposed routers. We conjecture that if we can have two ports along a dimension sharing their buffer resources, and allocate these buffers unevenly among each of the directions, we can achieve better performance than a nominal decomposed router that uses a dimensionally-uniform buffer distribution. Figure 11 compares different possible FIFO buffering configurations. Figure 11(a) is the typical scheme where no buffer sharing occurs among ports. Figure 11(b) shows buffer sharing across two input ports along the same dimension. Figure 11(c) shows the same buffer sharing with uneven buffer allocation among each of the dimensional buffer pools. The motivation for dimensionally biasing buffer resources comes from the fact that in a dimensionally decomposed router, there is some inherent bias in the decomposed arbitration. Coupled with the bias on the buffer sharing, a fine-tuned router architecture that outperforms dimensionally oblivious schemes can be developed.

E. Putting it all together: The Roce-Bush 3D NoC router

Combining dimensional biasing, efficient decomposed arbitration and efficient buffer resource utilization leads us to the Roce-Bush router architecture, whose architecture is shown in Figure 12 (for an XYZ routing scheme). Note the optimal location of the decomposed crossbars, facing one another. The shared buffer pool in each direction can be lined up with the ports for an efficient physical implementation.

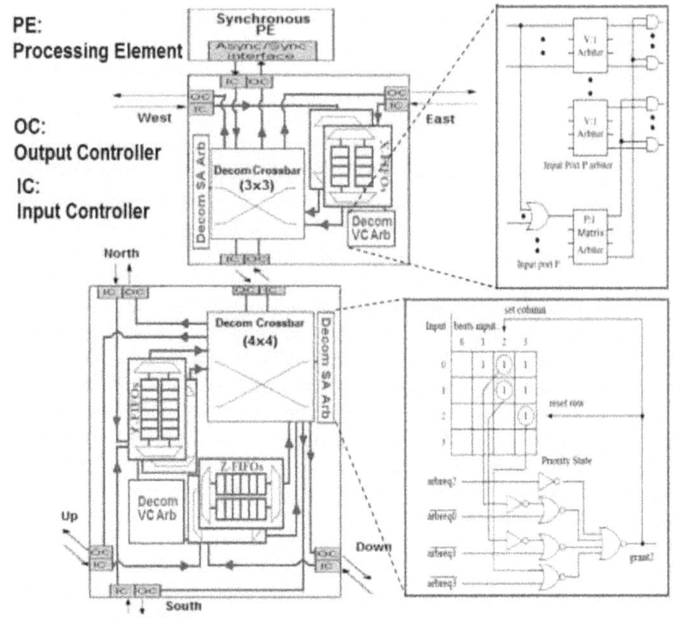

Figure 12. Proposed Roce-Bush router architecture (shown here with an implementation biased towards an XYZ routing scheme).

V. EXPERIMENTAL RESULTS

We implemented our Roce-Bush 3D NoC router at the RTL level using System Verilog, with simulation analysis using VCS and performed logic synthesis using Synopsys Design Compiler. The baseline code used was derived from the 2D NoC Netmaker library [20]. The following results are based on a 2 GHz single-cycle router synthesized using the standard 45nm Synopsys library. Unless otherwise noted, a router is a 7-port 3D router with 2 virtual channels of 4-flit buffers each, and a fixed packet length of 8 flits, running under a *Uniform Random* traffic pattern with a flit injection rate of 0.3 flits per router per cycle. Other simulated traffic patterns include *Neighbor*, *Hotspot-25* [25], *Bit-complement,* and *Tornado*. Each simulation result is based on a symmetrical 3 layer 4×4×4 (64 core) 3D network with 100,000 injected packets. Finally, the datapath/flit width across the routers is 64 bits. The results below measure latency in terms of the average cycle count taken by an 8-flit packet travelling across the NoC, as well as the worst-case cycle count for the slowest packet in the NoC. We measure the worst-case latencies on top of the average latencies because it gives a rough idea of the stability of the chosen design, an important aspect in embedded designs. For example, two designs might yield similar average latencies, but one of them might produce a much larger worst-case latency, which is undesirable for embedded designs.

Figure 13 shows the router performance (average and maximum flit latency) assuming XYZ, YXZ, and ZXY routing respectively, and after dimensionally decomposing a 3D NoC router across the three different dimensions, for five synthetic traffic patterns. *The results reveal a large performance advantage in decomposing the router in the first direction of the dimension-order routing.* This backs our conjecture that router decompositions biased based on the routing scheme can lead to improved performance. By decomposing in the first direction of the chosen dimension-order routing, our router helps reduce congestion. All other things equal, in a fully symmetrical network with an *ABC* dimension-ordered routing, our analysis has shown that by choosing to minimize congestion on the first-dimension *A*, we allow more packets into the network, increasing the probability of higher throughput, and diminishing the probability of wasted cycles on the following dimensions, as the packet travels through the *B* and *C* downstream. If instead, we choose to route on *B*, then we ease some congestion on *B*, but without increasing the amount of packets coming into the network because *A* remains congested. To generalize from our results, *a dimensionally-decomposed router will have the highest performance if its dimensional bias aligns with the first direction of the dimensional routing scheme*, i.e., by giving preference to direction *A* in *ABC* routing.

Note that the larger the latency, whether average or maximum, the larger the spread among the decompositions. This makes intuitive sense, since for best-case traffic patterns such as *neighbor* and *tornado* for the XYZ or ZXY routing schemes, where there is very little congestion in the network (and thus latencies are low), routing-centricity during router decomposition, which aims to reduce congestion, does not have a major performance impact. However, as can be seen for the YXZ routing scheme, an inappropriate choice of decomposition direction bias (e.g., Z) can actually create congestion and drive down performance. In general, choosing a proper decomposition in the appropriate direction gives a larger performance gain when the congestion and latency increases, as can be seen for a majority of the traffic scenarios.

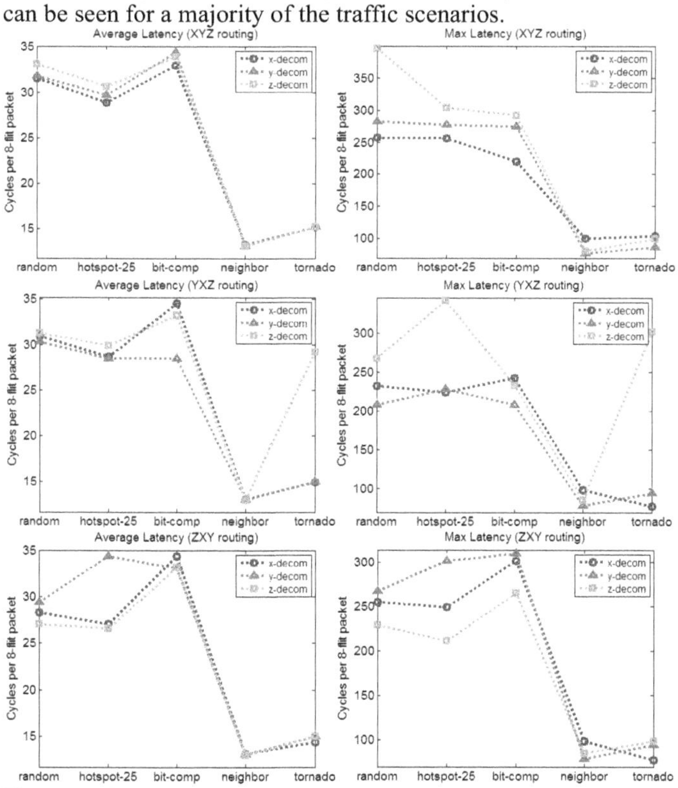

Figure 13. Performance comparison of three different decomposition configurations of the Roce-bush router for five synthetic traffic patterns under XYZ, YXZ and ZXY routing.

Figure 14 shows the performance of different arbitration techniques. In the figure, *pref-bias*, *fair*, *nonPref-bias*, and *Always-Pref* corresponds to the arbitration types "Preferred-bias", "Preference-fair", "Non-Preferred bias", and "Preferred-takes-all", respectively, described in section IV. The figure shows that using the simple preferred-takes-all scheme consistently results in the worst performance, by a significant margin. This is because by choosing a preferred takes all arbitration, we are starving the traffic in the non-preferred dimensions, which can lead to increased congestion along those dimensions due to a lack of load balancing. This is akin to having green lights only on east-west street lights in your drive home: even if your drive consists of mostly east or west roads, at some point you are likely to need to head south or north, and you will be stuck waiting, along with everyone else who was already waiting while you were going east or west.

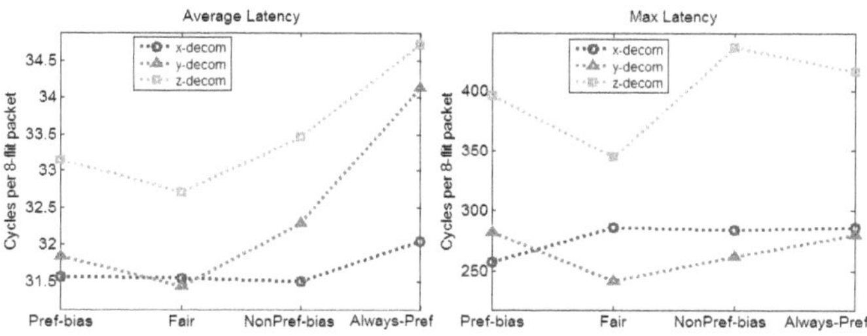

Figure 14. Performance comparison for different decomposed arbitration schemes in Roce-Bush, with XYZ routing. The implemented arbitration schemes (x-axis) correspond to preference-bias, preference-fair, non-preference-bias and preferred-takes-all.

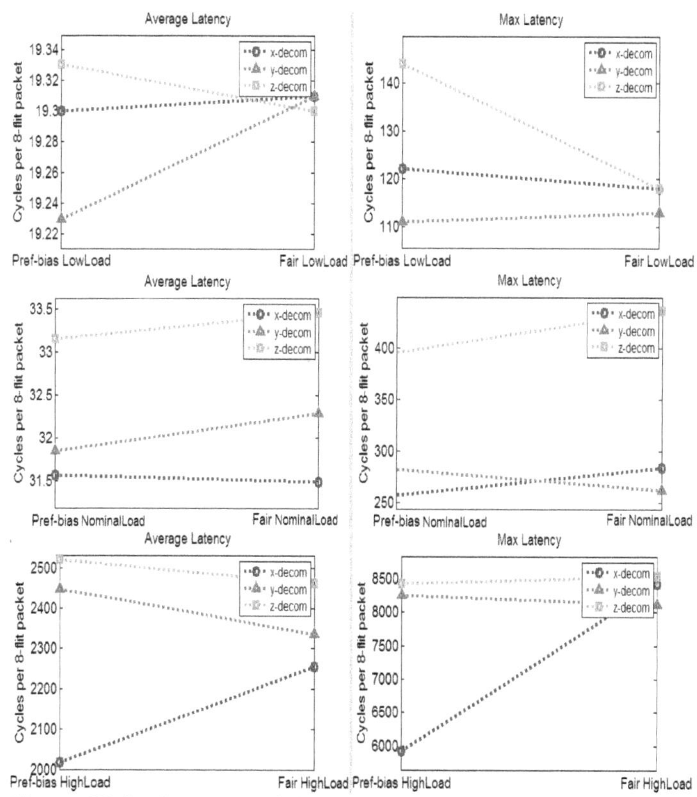

Figure 15. Performance of the three Roce-Bush decomposition configurations under different network loads (injection rates) for uniform random traffic and XYZ routing: Low load of 0.15 flits arriving at a router per cycle, Nominal load of 0.3 flits/cycle/router, and High load of 0.5 flits/cycle/router

On the other hand, a load-balancing arbitration, just as our regular street traffic lights, does a better job balancing the load and thus results in lower latencies. However, *this load balancing should not be direction agnostic. Our results show that a scheme that is slightly biased towards the preferred direction performs best.* This is equivalent to the waiting time on a main street vs. a side street, where an optimal traffic light will give slightly more green time to the main street traffic, though it will not fully starve the side street traffic. Thus, we conclude that *by dimensionally biasing the arbitration towards the dimension we choose to prioritize (based on the directional bias of the chosen routing scheme), we get better performance.* Also, note that we consider the cases favoring the Y-decomposition over X to be within statistical noise due to the proximity of their results.

Figure 15 shows the latencies of each of the decompositions for the XYZ routing scheme under three different network loads for Uniform Random traffic: 0.15 flits/router/cycle (light loading), 0.3 flits/router/cycle (nominal loading), and 0.5 flits/route/cycle (heavy loading), under two different arbitration schemes (*Pref-bias* and *Fair*). In the chosen case of XYZ routing, the Roce-Bush router decomposes with X-direction bias. From the figure, we can see that the *Roce-Bush* router can attain an up to 25% increase in performance under high loads for the XYZ routing scheme. Note that as the load of the network increase, congestion goes up, and as discussed previously, this is where the decomposition used matters most, hence resulting in a much better performance for a *Roce-Bush* router over a statically decomposed router. Finally, although not shown for brevity, similar performance improvements were obtained in experiments with the Roce-Bush router when a YXZ or YZX routing scheme was chosen and a Y-direction bias was employed, and when a ZYX or ZXY routing scheme was chosen and a Z-direction bias was employed.

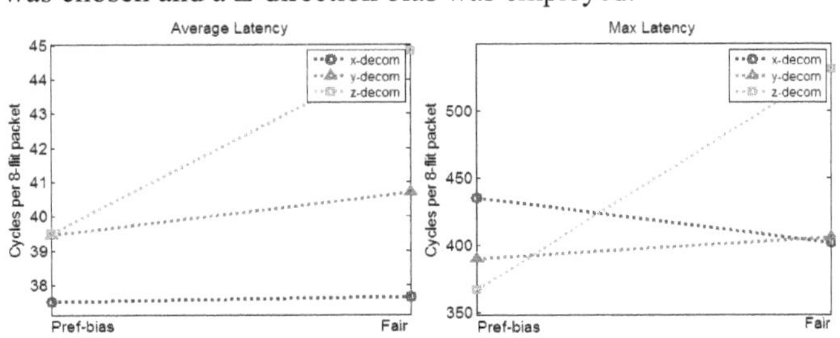

Figure 16. Performance comparison of different decomposition configurations in Roce-Bush for 3D west-first routing scheme.

The Roce-Bush router provides routing-centric performance optimization that can extend beyond simple dimension-ordered routing schemes. Figure 16 shows a comparison of different dimensional decompositions in Roce-Bush for a turn model-based 3D west-first routing algorithm, where the XY plane (typical 2D plane implementation) forbids north-west and south-west turns, the YZ plane forbids up-south and down-south turns, and finally, the ZX plane forbids up-west, and down-west turns. This routing scheme always puts more pressure on the X direction (as implied by its name all flits must go west-first) hence a Roce-Bush optimization with an X-direction decomposition bias yields roughly a 20% increase in performance (average latency) as compared to the static Z-decomposed router on an average loaded network. Note that the Y-preferred design has a slightly lower latency than the Z-preferred design, because the 3D west-first routing first goes west, then it alternates among the Y directions, and then among Z, thus making it more efficient to bias along the Y over the Z.

Figure 17 shows the results of biasing the amount of buffer resources in each of the directions, in a Roce-Bush implementation with an XYZ routing scheme and Uniform Random (nominal injection rate) traffic. Notice that in XYZ routing, regardless of each of the direction of the decomposition chosen or the arbitration scheme, the latency is minimized by adding more buffer resources to either the Y or Z dimensions. This makes sense because these two dimensions are further along the packet's travel where there is a higher chance of seeing HOL blocking.

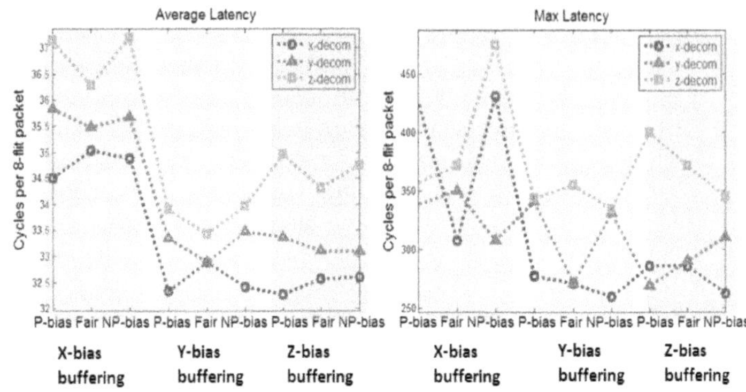

Figure 17. Performance comparison with buffer biasing for each of the dimensional decompositions in Roce-Bush for XYZ routing

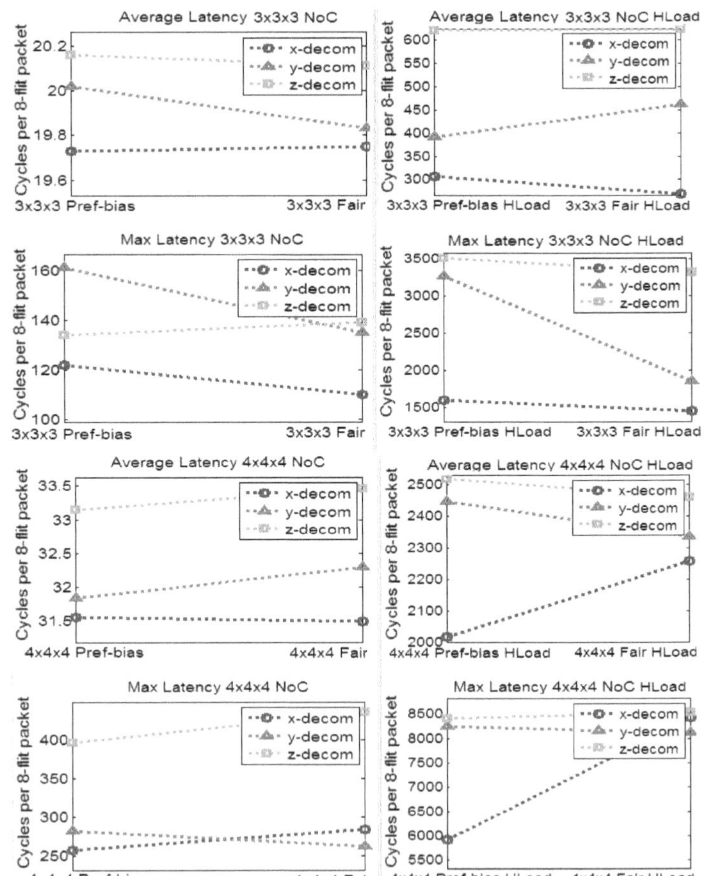

Figure 18. Performance comparison between different dimensional decompositions in Roce-Bush under different network sizes using a random traffic pattern.

Figure 18 shows the promising future of this optimization as we increase the number of cores in the die. On a nominal load, the results show that a 4x4x4 (64-core) network has *3 times the performance increase with respect to different directional decompositions* of a 3x3x3 (27-core) network, where in the 27 core network there is a 0.5 cycle improvement per packet, while in the 64 core network, there is roughly 1.5 cycles improvement. Note that both networks show much higher performance gain using the Roce-Bush router under high-load conditions as expected.

Finally, Figure 19 provides a comprehensive comparison of the *Roce-Bush* router against various state-of-the-art 3D NoC routers for different traffic patterns, for the XYZ routing scheme and a 4x4x4 3D NoC, using Prime Power to extract power estimates. The routers compared are: 3D Composed VC router based on the VC router of [12], a 3D speculative router of [13], a 3D static Z-decomposed hierarchical router [4], and the proposed Roce-Bush router. The *speculative router* extension to 3D results in the highest power dissipation and does not result in a decrease in latency when compared to a state-of-the-art router that uses a minimal amount of virtual channels. A single cycle *composed router* with virtual channels uses the second largest power, but achieves very low cycles to completion. By decomposing the router on the Z-direction, the *static Z-decomposed hierarchical router* takes a performance penalty but has lower power dissipation. However, using a strategic decomposition and buffer allocation using our *Roce-Bush router*, we beat the cycle count of the composed router while also using lower power than all other routers. Our results show power savings of 25% against the speculative router, 12.5% against the composed router and 5% over the statically z-decomposed router, as well as a latency reduction of 39% against the speculative router, 3% against a composed router, and 14% against a statically Z-decomposed hierarchical router.

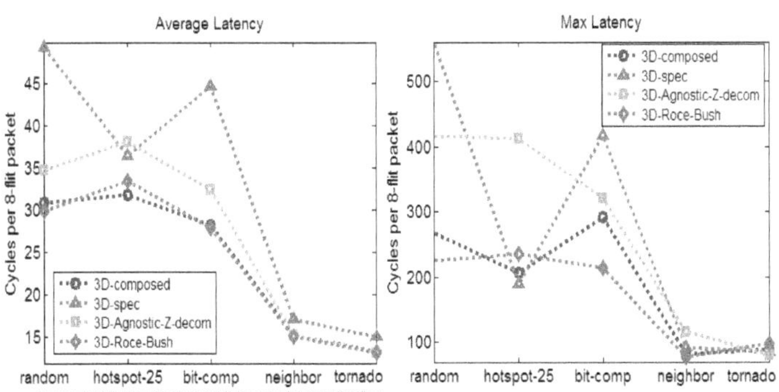

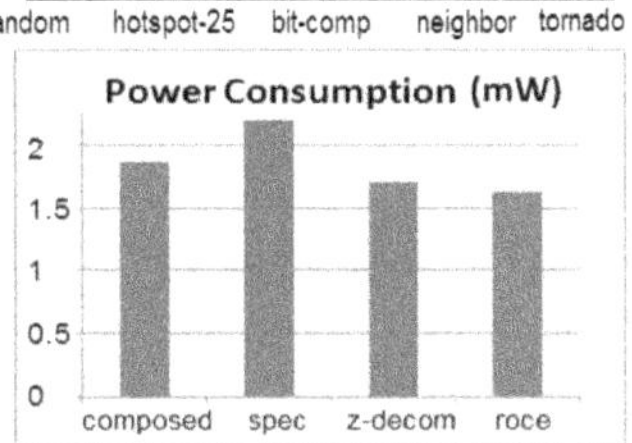

Figure 19. Power and performance comparison between 3D Roce-Bush and different state of the art 3D NoC router architectures across five different traffic patterns.

In summary, based on our experimental results, we have shown that our novel routing-centric decomposed *Roce-Bush* 3D NoC router can achieve significant performance gains while still staying below the power envelope of other state-of-the-art 3D NoC routers.

VI. CONCLUSION

This paper presented a novel dimensionally decomposed 3D router for NoCs, with the ability to exploit inherent dimension biases in routing schemes used with 3D CMPs. The Roce-Bush router highlights the important concept of routing-centric dimensionality awareness in 3D NoC router design by exploiting it in terms of resource decomposition and buffer allocation. While in 2D NoC routers, dimensional decomposition was excused due to the decomposition overhead, in 3D routers, it becomes a necessity. However, as shown in our experimental results, statically decomposed routers that are agnostic to the chosen routing scheme may not achieve desired results. As we migrate from conventional 2D ICs to multilayer CMPs, exploiting the decoupling of dimensional patterns in routers based on routing-centricity will become a handy technique for designers to efficiently tailor to fit more stringent performance needs. Our experimental comparisons for RTL level implementations of Roce-Bush with various state-of-the-art 3D NoC routers confirm this observation.

VII. REFERENCES

[1] L. Benini et al., "Networks on Chip: A New SoC Paradigm," Proc. Computer, 49(1):70-71, Jan 2002.

[2] C. Nicopoulos et al., "Network-on-Chip Architectures: A Holistic Design Exploration", ISBN-9048130301, 2009.

[3] J. Lau, "Advanced MEMS Packaging", ISBN-10: 0071626239, chapter 2, pp 50, 2009.

[4] J. Kim, "A Novel Dimensionally-Decomposed Router for On-Chip Communication in 3D Architectures", Proceedings of the 34th annual international symposium on Computer architecture (ISCA), 2007.

[5] W. Lafi, "An efficient hierarchical router for large 3D NoCs", 21st IEEE International Symposium on Rapid System Prototyping (RSP), 2010.

[6] F. Darve, "Physical Implementation of an Asynchronous 3D-NoC Router using Serial Vertical Links", Proc. IEEE ISVLSI, 2011.

[7] D. Park, "MIRA: A Multi-layered On-Chip Interconnect Router Architecture", Proc. ISCA, 2008.

[8] E. Marinissen, "Testing 3D chips containing through-silicon vias", International Test Conference, 2009.

[9] A. Banerjee, "A Power and Energy Exploration of Network-on-Chip Architectures", Proceedings of the First International Symposium on Networks-on-Chip (NOCS), 2007.

[10] A. G. Wassal, "Novel 3D memory-centric NoC architecture for transaction-based SoC applications", Saudi International Electronics, Communications and Photonics Conference (SIECPC), 2011.

[11] N. Choudhary, "Routing Centric NoC Design for High Performance Multimedia Application", International Journal of Soft Computing and Engineering (IJSCE), ISSN: 2231-2307, Volume-1, Issue-5, 2011.

[12] R. Mullins, "Low-Latency Virtual-Channel Routers for On-Chip Networks", Proc. ISCA, 2004.

[13] R. Mullins, "The Design and Implementation of a Low-Latency On-Chip Network", Asia and South Pacific Conference on Design Automation, 2006.

[14] W. J. Dally and B. P. Towles, "Principles and Practices of Interconnection Networks", ISBN 0-12-200751-4, 2004.

[15] C. Glass, "The Turn Model for Adaptive Routing", The 19th Annual International Symposium on Computer Architecture, 1992.

[16] H. Zhu, "Performance Evaluation of Adaptive Routing Algorithms for achieving Fault Tolerance in NoC Fabrics", IEEE International Conf. on Application -specific Systems, Architectures and Processors, 2007.

[17] R. Manevich, "A Cost Effective Centralized Adaptive Routing for Networks-on-Chip", 14th Euromicro Conference on Digital System Design (DSD), 2011.
[18] K. Shim, "Static virtual channel allocation in oblivious routing", 3rd ACM/IEEE International Symposium on Networks-on-Chip (NoCs), 2009.
[19] A. B. Kahng, "ORION 2.0: a fast and accurate NoC power and area model for early-stage design space exploration", Conference on Design, Automation and Test in Europe (DATE), 2009.
[20] K. Latif, "PVS-NoC: Partial Virtual Channel Sharing NoC Architecture", 19th Euromicro International Conference on Parallel, Distributed and Network-Based Processing (PDP), 2011
[21] R. Mullins, "Netmaker – 2D NoC simulation and synthesis library", http://www-dyn.cl.cam.ac.uk/~rdm34/wiki/index.php, 2009.
[22] S. Y. Nam, "Decomposed crossbar switches with multiple input and output buffers", Global Telecommunications Conference, 2001
[23] Tilera Corp., "Tilera TILE-Gx 3000", http://www.tilera.com/, 2011.
[24] F. Darve et al., "3D Embedded multi-core: Some perspectives", Proc. DATE, 2011.
[25] A. Rahmani et al., "Negative Exponential Distribution Traffic Pattern for Power/Performance Analysis of Network on Chips", International conference on VLSI design, pp 157-162, Jan 2009.

Non-Intrusive Trace & Debug NoC Architecture with Accurate Timestamping for GALS SoCs

Vladimir Todorov
Intel Mobile Communications GmbH
Munich, Germany
vladimir.todorov@intel.com

Alberto Ghiribaldi
University of Ferrara
Ferrara, Italy
alberto.ghiribaldi@unife.it

Helmut Reinig
Intel Mobile Communications GmbH
Munich, Germany
helmut.reinig@intel.com

Davide Bertozzi
University of Ferrara
Ferrara, Italy
davide.bertozzi@unife.it

Ulf Schlichtmann
Technische Universitaet Muenchen
Munich, Germany
ulf.schlichtmann@tum.com

ABSTRACT

This work proposes a flexible and modular solution for non-intrusive tracing and debugging of software on embedded SoC platforms. It utilizes a separate, dedicated Network-on-Chip (NoC) interconnect with a hierarchical unidirectional ring topology to connect a multitude of monitoring devices. The devices are controlled via a debugger attached to the NoC. They use the network to receive control information and send back observations, which the debugger uses to construct a trace. The system utilizes a very accurate and efficient differential timestamping approach. It allows working with multi-synchronous SoCs, identifying concurrencies and other temporal properties in the SoC and coping with partial power downs and clock gatings. The proposed solution requires a low amount of hardware resources and at the same time provides unmatched capabilities.

Categories and Subject Descriptors

B.4.3 [**Input/Output and Data Communications**]: Interconnections (Subsystems); D.2.5 [**Software Engineering**]: Testing and Debugging

Keywords

Trace, Debug, NoC, Non-intrusive, Timestamping

1. INTRODUCTION

On-chip debug and trace solutions are essential to the modern development flow of complex system-on-chip (SoC) integrated circuits, where software has to be developed and optimized for a certain hardware platform. A suboptimal or erroneous software routine can significantly decrease the overall performance of the SoC. Such a decrease in performance can be caused by logical and functional errors. Detecting and observing such errors is a challenging task, e.g. when race conditions are present. Furthermore, there might be other deeper dependencies between a software program flow and the rest of the activity occurring within the SoC. Such complex hardware-software interactions might be hard to predict and find. Therefore, it is advantageous to have a way of observing how a software program interacts with specific hardware components and how the information flow caused by it spreads through the SoC. Hence, it is important that the actual hardware platform becomes observable [1]. Such a transparency is key to better understanding the hardware-software interaction. Information like delay, contents, and effects of different processing blocks on a particular transaction occurring in the SoC can help optimize and debug the SoC and lead to shorter and more precise development cycles.

The observation of a particular SoC must be non-intrusive to its normal operation. This ensures that the produced information is the same as if no tracing has been performed. Otherwise, the observed behavior might differ from the real one and may render the whole observation trace useless. Another requirement is that an observation carries also temporal information, indicating when the observation was generated. Such information is essential for ordering the observations into a complete trace, detecting parallel processes and estimating delays. Unfortunately, a lot of modern SoCs are multi-synchronous and comply to the globally asynchronous, locally synchronous (GALS) paradigm. Thus, it is important that observations from different parts of the system can easily be combined into one single trace with high temporal accuracy. Moreover, SoCs designed for mobile communications and handheld devices rely heavily on power management strategies involving clock and power gating to preserve energy. Therefore, trace consistency has to be maintained in the presence of such conditions. Finally, in the resource-constrained SoC environment the trace and debug architecture should marginally increase the hardware overhead.

This work proposes a novel solution to the afore mentioned problem. The discussed approach utilizes a dedicated trace and debug network-on-chip (TDNoC) architecture for transporting observations between the monitoring devices, producing them, and the debugger, which can be either on-chip or off-chip (connected to a dedicated port). The observations are by definition non-intrusive to the normal operation of the SoC because they are transported on a dedicated in-

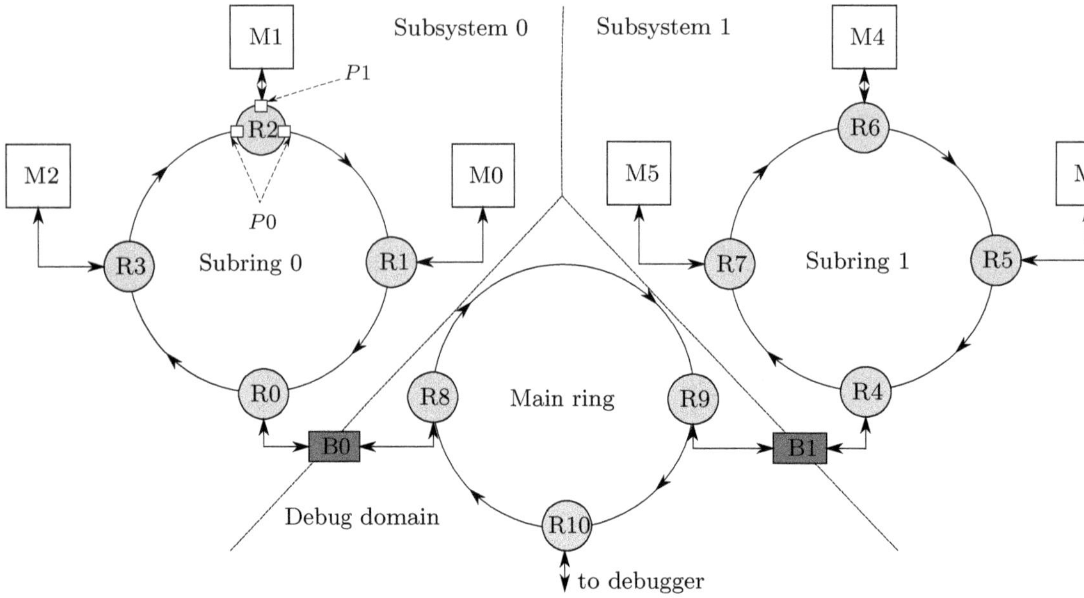

Figure 1: Hierarchical ring topology

terconnect. The topology used to implement the TDNoC is a hierarchical ring, which eases its application in GALS SoCs and has a reduced hardware overhead. This work presents a novel timestamping strategy, which is differential in nature, and is able to give accurate time to observations independent of their subsystem of origin. The timestamping technique ensures trace consistency even after multiple partial power ups and power downs and clock gatings of the individual subsystems. The final trace is assembled by software at the debugger side from all the received observations. For completeness, the work also proposes a dummy abstract model of the monitoring devices, referred to as monitors. Based on the monitors attached to the architecture, the TDNoC can be used also for pure post-silicon hardware trace and debug.

The rest of the paper is structured as follows: Section 2 briefly discusses the related work on the problem. Section 3 presents the architecture and all the components of the TDNoC. Section 4 introduces the novel timestamping approach. Sections 5 and 6 present, respectively, results and conclusions.

2. RELATED WORK

Several approaches exist that propose solutions to the problem of tracing a SoC. For example, [2] and [3] concentrate on AHB tracers, aimed at producing observations from an AHB bus. However, the authors concentrate only on one type of interconnect. The methods lack the notion of time and [2] is also intrusive to the normal system operation. Other works, like [4] and [5] make use of scan-chains and concentrate on directly debugging code executed within the processor. Yet, their work primarily concentrates on inserting breakpoints and is targeted to operate only within the scope of the processor, rather than the system as a whole. The works in [6] and [7] concentrate on transaction level debug, where the communication, rather than the state of the processor is observed. In [6] the regular NoC interconnect of the SoC is reused for passing the observations to their final destination. The work in [7] relies on scan-chains, which can severely limit the bandwidth for observations. The work also does not support accounting of time. The authors in [8] propose a clustering method for generating concurrent trace. However, the observations are intrusive to the system and do not come with timestamps. In [9] the authors propose an intrusive hardware debug method for NoCs with multiple clocks, which uses timestamping. The approach, however, does not consider partial power downs and clock gating. In [1] an intrusive approach for observing and debugging SoCs with multiple clocks is presented. The work in [10] presents a dedicated dual network for control signaling, but its purpose is hardware testing and it is not suitable for trace and debug.

In contrast, the proposed approach provides non-intrusive tracing, highly accurate timestamping and support for GALS SoCs with partial power down and clock gating at the cost of low hardware overhead.

3. PROPOSED ARCHITECTURE

The topology of the TDNoC architecture utilizes a hierarchical ring structure, where there is a single main ring, which is connected to multiple subrings. Each ring encompasses at most one subsystem of the SoC, where a subsystem is defined as all the modules that reside in the same voltage and frequency domain. The rings are constructed by interconnected routers having two input buffered bidirectional ports. Fig. 1 illustrates such a structure for an example SoC with two subsystems. Each subring in the figure has 4 routers ($R0$-$R3$ for subring 0 and $R4$-$R7$ for subring 1). The first port ($P0$) of the routers is used for the rings, where port's output is connected to the input of $P0$ of the next router in the chain. The monitors used to produce observations (e.g. $M0$-$M5$) are connected to the second ports ($P1$) of routers on the subrings. In the figure the ports are shown only for router $R2$. The main ring resides in a separate domain and is connected to the subrings via bridges, which provide crossing between the domains. In Fig. 1 the routers $R8$ and $R9$ on the main ring connect it to the subrings via the bridges

$B0$ and $B1$. The debugger is connected to a router on the main ring (e.g. $R10$). To reduce wiring overhead, all the rings are implemented using unidirectional links. The only bidirectional connections exist between the main ring and the subrings, between the monitors and their corresponding routers and between the debugger and the corresponding router on the main ring. This implementation introduces greater latency upon the traffic on the rings, but, as it will be shown in Sections 4 and 5, the traffic taking place on the TDNoC is highly latency tolerant.

The routing of the packets in the architecture is straight forward. There are two directions of information flow. Packets can either propagate from a monitor to the debugger (*downstream*) or from the debugger to the monitors (*upstream*). The amount of traffic going upstream (configuration packets) is expected to be low compared to the amount of packets traveling downstream (trace packets). The routers inspects the packet headers and decide whether to forward a particular packet on the current port or switch in to the other.

The monitors trace the activity on the buses to which they are attached. The observations are encapsulated in the form of packets, which are injected into the subrings. These packets then circulate around the interconnect until they reach the debugger (in this example attached to $R10$), where they get absorbed and included in the overall trace of the system.

The structure of the monitor module is not discussed in depth because it can differ based on requirements, applications and on the basis of the observed communication protocol. However, all different monitors share a set of common features. The purpose of a monitor is to observe in a non-intrusive way the activity on a transmission channel, such as the input and ports of a core or a memory, to encapsulate it in the form of NoC packets, and to forward the packets on the rings. All monitors use the same timestamping mechanism, presented in Section 4. A monitor is programmable and can be switched on and off. Upon its activation or deactivation a special packet is emitted, as discussed below. As the monitor is able to receive as well as to transmit packets, it can be constructed in such way as to interact with the module, which it is observing. This, for example, may allow the programming of breakpoints and, hence, allows the discussed solution to be used as a trace as well as a debug architecture.

Because of the TDNoC's hierarchical ring structure, a special arbitration scheme has been designed to provide fairness between the packets produced by different monitors. For example, back in Fig. 1 if all monitors $M0$-$M2$ are producing observations, then the combined traffic of $M2$ and $M1$ will arrive at the ring port of $R1$. However, the traffic of $M0$ will be present on the other port. Under the assumption of round robin arbitration, $M0$ will be served more often than either $M1$ or $M2$. Thus, their traffic will have a higher latency. In the general case, let π_K be a packet, which has to traverse $K+1$ hops (routers) before reaching the router bridging the subring to the main ring. Assuming that there is always a competition on the subring, the probability of winning all of the $K+1$ arbitrations is given by Eq. 1.

$$P_{pass}(\pi_K) = \left(\frac{1}{2}\right)^{K+1} = 2^{-K-1} \qquad (1)$$

As it can be seen, the probability varies with K and for

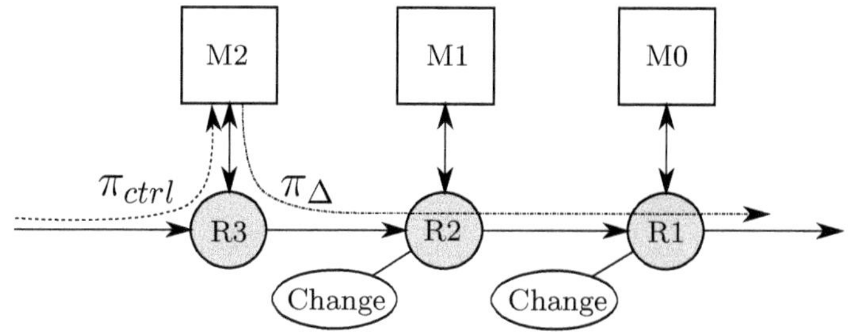

Figure 2: Transmission of a weight change packet

$K >> 0$ it tends to 0. Thus, it is unfair for packets that have to traverse more hops. To resolve this issue a better, weighted arbitration scheme is used. Instead of having equal weights $w_{P0} = w_{P1}$ for the two ports, they are scaled in correspondence to the location of the router. For the router attached to the Kth monitor in a ring of N monitors, the weights are as defined by Eq. 2 – 3.

$$w_{K,P0} = \begin{cases} N-K-1 & \text{if } K \neq N-1 \\ 1 & \text{otherwise} \end{cases} \qquad (2)$$

$$w_{K,P1} = 1 \qquad (3)$$

The new weights allow for a new pass probability expression $P_{pass}^{fair}(\pi_K)$ to be computed (Eq. 4). It is independent of the relative position of the monitor and ensures fairness to all monitors within a subring.

$$P_{pass}^{fair}(\pi_K) = \frac{1}{N-K}\prod_{i=0}^{K-1}\frac{N-i-1}{N-i} = \frac{1}{N} \qquad (4)$$

The fairness, however, can be lost because of monitor programming. If within a subring not all monitors are working, the weighting scheme may become unfair again. Thus, adjustable weights $w_{K,P0}$ are introduced (Eq. 5). None of the weights can be decreased below 1. The adjusting factor Δ signifies the change in the number of working monitors N. Hence, a ring can be seen as having a variable size, with $N_{new} = N_{old} + \Delta$.

$$w_{K,P0} = \begin{cases} N+\Delta-K-1 & \text{if } K \neq N-1 \\ 1 & \text{otherwise} \end{cases} \qquad (5)$$

Whenever a monitor M is activated or deactivated, it emits a special packet π_Δ. When the routers, connected to the monitors, receive it on their ring port ($P0$), they adapt the weights according to the $\Delta \in \{-1, 1\}$ carried by the packet (Fig. 2). Fig. 3(a) illustrates the weights when all monitors are active for a particular subring. Fig. 3(b) shows how the weights are adjusted when $M2$ is not working. The router attached to the last active (K^{th}) monitor has weights equal to the ones of the successive downstream router, attached to the $(K-1)^{\text{th}}$ monitor. This is based on the assumption that the amount of control traffic (upstream) is much less than the one produced by the monitors. If $w_{K-1,P0} > w_{K,P0}$, then the Kth monitor will get advantage over the $(K-1)^{\text{th}}$ one. Therefore, keeping $w_{K-1,P0} = w_{K,P0} = 1$ would be more fair.

4. TIMESTAMPING

Knowledge of the generation time of the observations is important for constructing, inspecting and analyzing the trace

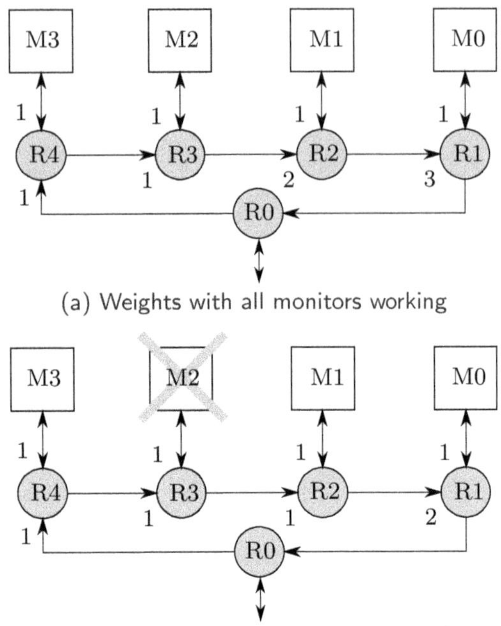

(a) Weights with all monitors working

(b) Weights with monitor $M2$ stopped

Figure 3: Dynamic weight adjustment

of a system. Therefore, each observation has to carry timing information. This can be achieved by inserting timestamps in the packets. The timestamps can be produced in different ways. For example, dedicated counters counting the clock cycles from the starts of the different subsystems can be used. However, such an implementation implies a finite measure of time as the counters will eventually overflow, high bitwidth counters and, eventually, large timestamps, which consume bandwidth on the NoC. Furthermore, this approach fails under the assumption of partial system power downs and clock gating.

In order to overcome the previous limitations, and at the same time to reduce the hardware utilized for this purpose, a differential timestamping approach has been developed. The packets carry small differential timestamps instead of large absolute ones. These timestamps are constructed using $\mathcal{N}$-bit counters. Each counter is further virtually subdivided into two portions of $\mathcal{M}$ higher and $\mathcal{K}$ lower bits. Thus, the higher $\mathcal{M}$ bits can be seen as a count on how many times the $\mathcal{K}$-bit portion has overflowed. Fig. 4 illustrates the partitioning for $\mathcal{N} = 10$, $\mathcal{M} = 2$, $\mathcal{K} = 8$. Each ring S, including the main ring, has its own counter C_S of size $\mathcal{N}_S$, or a number of unique and equivalent counters. All the timestamp counters in the system count from the reset onwards the clock cycles within their respective subrings. The counters need not have the same size or partitioning among different subrings.

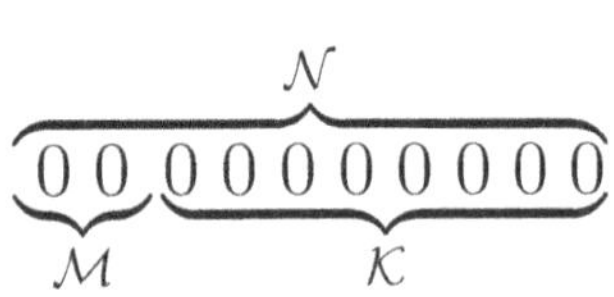

Figure 4: Example 10-bit timestamp counter

When a monitor makes an observation it takes the counter value and includes it as a timestamp in the packet. The routers that bridge the subrings to the main ring (e.g. $R0$ and $R4$ in Fig. 1) and the router interfaced with the debugger (e.g. $R10$) periodically generate special timing packets. Such a packet is generated and emitted by the router every time the $\mathcal{K}$-bit portion of its counter overflows. It is referred to as end of period packet (π_{eop}). Thus, $\pi_{eop,S}$ designates an end of a period of $2^{\mathcal{K}_S}$ clock cycles in subsystem S.

The debugger keeps track of the absolute number of periods E_S for each ring S by counting the number of received $\pi_{eop,S}$. Thus, each time it receives a $\pi_{eop,S}$ it increases E_S by 1. When a normal trace packet π_S, originating from subring S, is received, it is ordered in the trace by the use of its differential timestamp $\delta(\pi_S)$ and E_S. The higher $\mathcal{M}_S$ bits of $\delta(\pi_S)$ serve as an indicator to one of the last $2^{\mathcal{M}_S}$ periods, to which an observation packet π_S relates. A relative period $\hat{E}_S \in [0, 2^{\mathcal{M}_S})$, indicating the relative period number of the last period of E_S of S can be computed as $\hat{E}_S = E_S \; mod \; 2^{\mathcal{M}_S}$. The relative period, to which a packet π_S refers to can be computed as $\lfloor \delta(\pi_S)/2^{\mathcal{K}_S} \rfloor$. The estimate of the absolute time $\hat{t}(\pi_S)$ can now be computed by using Eq. 6 if $\hat{E}_S < \lfloor \delta(\pi_S)/2^{\mathcal{K}_S} \rfloor$, else by using Eq. 7. $T_{clk,S}$ is the clock period of subsystem S, which is known to the debugger. The first equation covers the case when C_S has overflowed between the generation of π_S and $\pi_{eop,S}$ and the second packet has arrived first.

$$\hat{t}_0(\pi_S) = T_{clk,S} \left(\left(E_S - (2^{\mathcal{M}_S} + \hat{E}_S - \left\lfloor \frac{\delta(\pi_S)}{2^{\mathcal{K}_S}} \right\rfloor \right) 2^{\mathcal{K}_S} + \right.$$
$$\left. + (\delta(\pi_S) \; mod \; 2^{\mathcal{K}_S}) \right) \quad (6)$$

$$\hat{t}_1(\pi_S) = T_{clk,S} \left(\left(E_S - (\hat{E}_S - \left\lfloor \frac{\delta(\pi_S)}{2^{\mathcal{K}_S}} \right\rfloor \right) 2^{\mathcal{K}_S} + \right.$$
$$\left. + (\delta(\pi_S) \; mod \; 2^{\mathcal{K}_S}) \right) \quad (7)$$

This approach allows a packet π_S to experience a maximum delay in the range between $(2^{\mathcal{M}_S} - 1) \times 2^{\mathcal{K}_S}$ and $2^{\mathcal{N}_S} - 1$ clock cycles within its ring before being falsely ordered in the trace. Thus, it makes the NoC observations traffic highly tolerant to latencies. As the trace generation is a computationally complex task, it is assumed that the debugger carries it out in software.

Finally, to comply with the partial power down and clock gating, another type of packet, a wake up packet $\pi_{up,S}$, is introduced. The $\pi_{up,S}$ originates from the routers on the main ring, which connect it to the subrings (in Fig. 1 these are $R8$ and $R9$). A packet is created and sent to the debugger, whenever a router on the main ring senses the wake up of the attached subring S. It samples the value of the counter associated with the main ring (C_{main}) and uses it as a timestamp to $\pi_{up,S}$. For simplicity, the time needed for synchronization is not included in the discussion, and it can be additionally added as a constant factor. By using either Eg. 6 or Eq. 7, an offset time $t_{off,S} = \hat{t}(\pi_{up,S})$ is computed. It indicates the time, at which the subsystem S has woken up according to the time of the main ring. This leads to $\tilde{t}(\pi_S) = t_{off,S} + \hat{t}(\pi_S)$ for the approximate absolute time estimate of the packets coming from S after the wake up. Assuming that a subsystem S can wake at any point in time and no synchronization penalty, i.e. the router detects the wake up immediately, the introduced timing error is in $[0; T_{main})$, where T_{main} is the clock period on the main

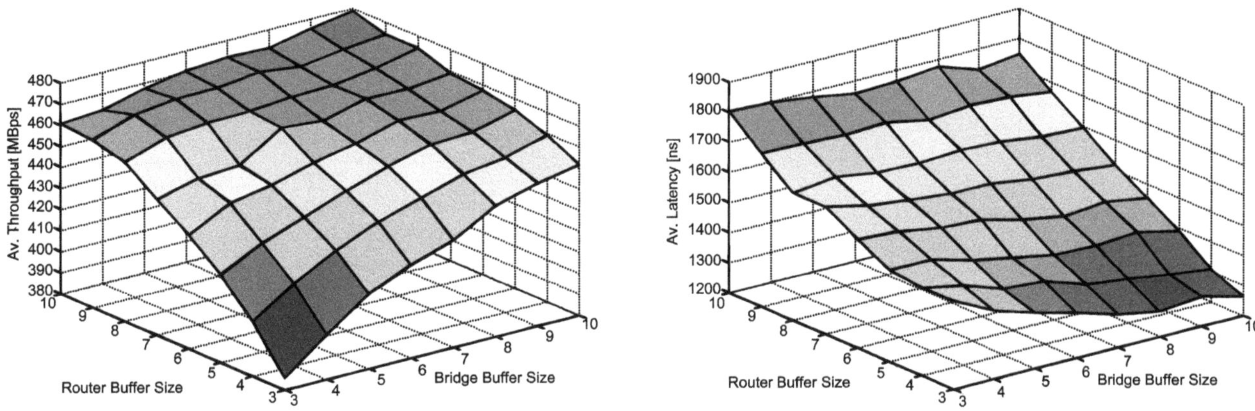

(a) (b)

Figure 5: Throughput and latency vs. buffer size

ring. It is assumed that the clock on the main ring has the highest frequency because it serves as the backbone of the whole TDNoC architecture. Additionally, the main ring is never powered down during trace and debug. The small error range makes the timestamping approach very robust. Compliance with clock gating is achieved in a similar way, by using the clock-gating signal of the subsystem as a reset to the associated subring and its counter.

Algorithm 1 shows how the debugger processes packets and inserts observations in the trace τ.

Algorithm 1 Packet processing algorithm

PROCEDURE: **ProcessPacket**(π)
BEGIN
$S \leftarrow Ring(\pi)$ {Get π's ring of origin}
$\hat{E}_S \leftarrow E_S \ mod \ 2^{\mathcal{M}_S}$ {Compute E_S's relative period number}
if $isEop(\pi)$ **then** {Check if π designates end of period}
  $E_S \leftarrow E_S + 1$ {Increase the period counter of S}
else if $isUp(\pi)$ **then** {Check if π reports a wake-up}
  $X \leftarrow SubringId(\pi)$ {Get the id of the woken up subring}
  if $\hat{E}_S < \lfloor \delta(\pi)/2^{\mathcal{K}_S} \rfloor$ **then** {Check if C_S overflowed}
    $t_{off,X} \leftarrow \hat{t}_0(\pi)$ {Compute offset time}
  else
    $t_{off,X} \leftarrow \hat{t}_1(\pi)$ {Compute offset time}
  end if
else {π contains an observation}
  if $\hat{E}_S < \lfloor \delta(\pi)/2^{\mathcal{K}_S} \rfloor$ **then** {Check if C_S overflowed}
    $\tilde{t} \leftarrow t_{off,S} + \hat{t}_0(\pi)$ {Compute time estimate}
  else
    $\tilde{t} \leftarrow t_{off,S} + \hat{t}_1(\pi)$ {Compute time estimate}
  end if
  $\tau.insert(\tilde{t}, \pi)$ {Insert the observation in τ at time $\tilde{t}$}
end if
END

5. RESULTS

A SystemC transaction level model of the proposed solution has been implemented. The system used for the simulations consists of 2 subsystems (2 subrings) each having 5 monitors. The following clocks were used: $T_{main} = 3$ ns, $T_{clk,0} = 7$ ns and $T_{clk,1} = 9$ ns. The flit size of the packets is 16 bit. All timestamp counters are the same, with $\mathcal{N} = 10$, $\mathcal{K} = 8$ and $\mathcal{M} = 2$. The monitors inject random observations of lengths between 4 and 40 flits.

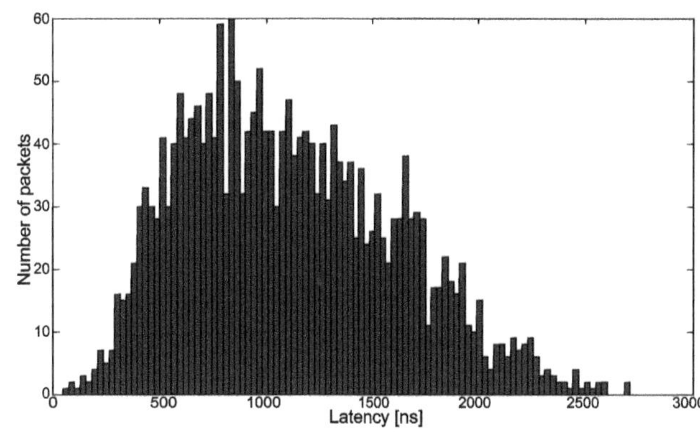

Figure 6: Packet latency histogram

The rate of observations that can be generated depends on the throughput of the TDNoC. Low throughput may cause congestion, which would prevent the monitors from injecting some observations. This effect can be reduced by having a large buffer storage. However, due to the low hardware overhead requirement, large buffers are unwanted.

To explore this tradeoff, the depths of the buffers in the routers and in the bridges are swept between the size of 3 and 10 flits. For each case a simulation has been performed. Fig. 5(a) shows how the throughput changes in accordance to the buffer resources for an average injection rate of 498 MBps. It can be seen that increasing the buffers of all routers has almost the same effect on the throughput (460 MBps) as increasing the buffers only in the bridges (450 MBps). Combining both does not produce a significant benefit (480 MBps). The overhead of the router buffers, however, is much higher because there are a total of 24 buffers affecting the throughput in the routers vs. only 2 in the bridges (only downstream considered).

Next, Fig. 5(b) illustrates how the packet latency scales with buffer size. It can be seen that the latency grows with growth of buffer space in the routers and decreases with increase in buffer space in the bridges. The growth effect is caused by the increased number of packets in transit on the subrings (slow interconnect). The buffers on the bridges

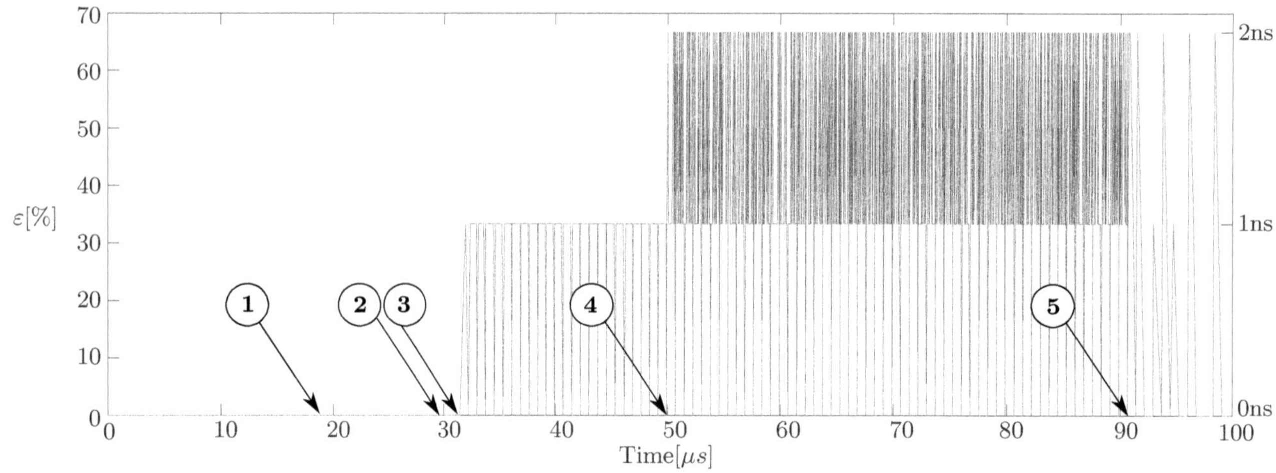

Figure 7: Error of the time estimate $\tilde{t}$ relative to T_{main} in the presence of partial power downs

reduce the latency because they act as a storage space right in front of the fast interconnect (the main ring). This allows flits to be stored slowly and then read rapidly in a bursty fashion. The result also concludes that increasing the bridge buffer space is better compared to increasing the one of the routers.

Fig. 6 shows a packet latency histogram for a simulation run, having bridge and router buffer depths of, respectively, 10 and 3 flits. As it can be seen, the packets exhibit a relatively high latency, which in this particular case goes up to $2.7\mu s$. However, even such a high latency does not introduce errors in the resulting trace and is tolerable.

Fig. 7 shows the error ε of the time estimate $\tilde{t}$ in the presence of partial shutdowns. The figure shows the plot of $\varepsilon = (\tilde{t} - t_{sim})/T_{main}$ in percent for the whole trace, where t_{sim} is the actual simulation time at which an observation is created. Point ① indicates the time when subsystem 0 was powered down. Point ② shows the time when subsystem 1 was powered down. Point ③ indicates the power up of subsystem 0. The absolute error introduced by its traffic is $\varepsilon_0 = 33\% \times T_{main} = 1\ ns$. At ④ subsystem 1 is powered up. The error absolute introduced by its traffic is $\varepsilon_1 = 66\% \times T_{main} = 2\ ns$. The maximum error is then $\varepsilon_{max} = \max(\varepsilon_0, \varepsilon_1) = 2\ ns < T_{main}$. For practical applications this is a very small and negligible error. Therefore, this work is the first to present a highly accurate timestamping approach for GALS SoCs with support for partial power downs. As the error is proportional to T_{main}, it can be further decreased by increasing the clock frequency on the main ring. At ⑤ the debugger starts shutting down the monitors and the traffic starts to decrease. The error periodically drops to 0 because it is also calculated for packets originating from the main ring, which is never powered down.

To demonstrate the small overhead of the TDNoC, RTL models of the routers and the bridge were created and synthesis was performed. The results show that the area consumed for a subring with 6 routers (5 monitors) and a bridge is only 1002 FlipFlops and 2190 gates (3-flit buffers for the routers and 10-flit for the bridge). The maximum clock frequency achieved in 40 nm technology is 800 MHz, where the limiting factor is the bridge, which in its current implementation imposes a timing constraint of half a clock period.

6. CONCLUSION

This paper presented a novel NoC architecture for tracing and debugging GALS SoCs. The proposed solution provides capability for non-intrusive tracing, which is essential to observing and debugging the true interaction between software and hardware. The TDNoC employs a novel, versatile and robust timestamping approach, which works across multiple domains and recovers with minimal error after partial system power downs and clock gatings. Finally, as shown, the solution requires a low amount of hardware resources and at the same time provides unmatched capabilities.

Future work will concentrate on extending the TDNoC to SoCs based on dynamic voltage and frequency scaling.

7. REFERENCES

[1] Bart Vermeulen and Kees Goossens. Interactive Debug of SoCs with Multiple Clocks. In *IEEE Design & Test of Computers*, 2011.

[2] Fu-Ching Yang, Yi-Ting Lin, Chung-Fu Kao, and Ing-Jer Huang. An On-Chip AHB Bus Tracer With Real-Time Compression and Dynamic Multiresolution Supports for SoC. In *IEEE Transactions on VLSI Systems*, 2011.

[3] Chung-Fu Kao, Ing-Jer Huang, and Chi-Hung Lin. An Embedded Multi-resolution AMBA Trace Analyzer for Microprocessor-based SoC Integration. In *DAC*, 2007.

[4] Jianmin Zhang, Ming Yan, and Sikun Li. Debug Support for Scalable System-on-Chip. In *Seventh International Workshop on Microprocessor Test and Verification (MTV'06)*, 2006.

[5] Kuen-Jong Lee, Si-Yuan Liang, and Alan Su. A Low-Cost SOC Debug Platform Based on On-Chip Test Architectures. In *IEEE International SOC Conference*, 2009.

[6] Cheng Kwang-Ting and A.S. Krishnakumar. A Design-for-Debug (DfD) for NoC-based SoC Debugging via NoC. In *17th Asian Test Symposium*, 2008.

[7] Kees Goossens, Bart Vermeulen, Remco van Steeden, and Martijn Bennebroek. Transaction-Based Communication-Centric Debug. In *Proceedings of the First International Symposium on Networks-on-Chip*, 2007.

[8] Jianliang Gao, Jianxin Wang, Yinhe Han, Lei Zhang, and Xiaowei Li. A Clustering-Based Scheme for Concurrent Trace in Debugging NoC-Based Multicore Systems. In *DATE*, March 2012.

[9] Shan Tang and Qiang Xu. A Multi-Core Debug Platform for NoC-Based Systems. In *DATE*, 2007.

[10] Alberto Ghiribaldi, Daniele Ludovici, Michele Favalli, and Davide Bertozzi. System-level infrastructure for boot-time testing and configuration of networks-on-chip with programmable routing logic. In *VLSI and System-on-Chip*, 2011.

Dynamic Property Mining for Embedded Software

Marco Bonato†, Giuseppe Di Guglielmo†, Masahiro Fujita◇,
Franco Fummi†, Graziano Pravadelli†

† University of Verona
Department of Computer Science
Strada Le Grazie 15, Verona, Italy
{name.surname}@univr.it

◇VLSI Design and Education Center
The University of Tokyo, Japan
CREST, Japan Science and Technology Agency
fujita@cad.t.u-tokyo.ac.jp

ABSTRACT

The importance of specification definition in the embedded-software design flow has been proven over the years. The entire design process relies on the specification quality, which inevitably depends on designer knowledge and skills. Automatic property mining is part of the efforts proposed to make this activity easier for the designers. Nonetheless, the existing approaches are limited to the detection of either arithmetic invariants of programs or temporal properties for Boolean designs, e.g., bit-level hardware descriptions. In this work, we present a dynamic mining approach able to infer linear temporal logic (LTL) properties for embedded software. The mined properties are in the form of temporal relationships between arithmetic expressions. The approach considers the execution traces only, thus it is completely independent from the code implementation. Experimental results demonstrate the effectiveness of the approach.

Categories and Subject Descriptors

D.2.1 [**Software Engineering**]: Requirements/Specifications; D.2.4 [**Software Engineering**]: Software/Program Verification—*validation*

Keywords

Temporal Property, Dynamic Mining, Embedded Software

1. INTRODUCTION

Design of embedded software depends significantly on the quality of specifications. *Specification definition* is the first step of the design process, but often it does not receive enough attention by designers: clear and complete specifications can lead to great benefits, as well as incomplete specifications lead to undetected errors and unexpected design behaviors.

Specifications can be given by a set of *properties* that formally describe the design behavior. These properties may concern temporal behaviors, constraints on inputs and outputs, arithmetic relationships between design variables, etc.

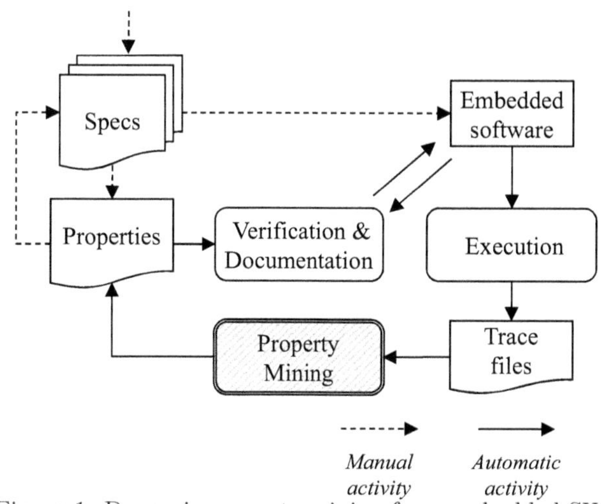

Figure 1: Dynamic property mining from embedded SW.

Properties are widely used in functional verification to formally check the correctness of the design implementation. In particular, static verification, e.g., model checking [6], provides high confidence in design correctness; while, dynamic verification, e.g., Assertion-based Verification (ABV) [16], scales exceptionally well with design size. In both the cases, verification results are good as the used properties. Moreover, properties overcome the ambiguity of natural languages and give to the engineers precise and well-defined specifications for documentation purposes.

The difficulty of achieving good specifications and, therefore, good properties, is due to the complex nature of specifications themselves and to the high expertise required. Property definition is a tedious and error-prone task, which requires knowledge of temporal logics, e.g., Linear Temporal and Computational Tree Logics (LTL and CTL) [21] or specification languages, e.g., Property Specification Language (PSL) [11], in order to define the desired design functionality. Moreover, another issue concerns the maintenance of specifications. During the design process, specifications may result not well-defined or incomplete. There are many possible causes: specifications may not be defined at all or they become obsolete due to design modifications.

In order to make easier the definition and refinement of specifications, automatic *property mining* has been proposed, whose goal is to extract significant properties from the actual implemented design [2]. Property mining approaches can be classified as *static* or *dynamic*. Static property mining infer properties by exploring design models or implementations;

while, dynamic property mining is designed to infer properties from design execution traces.

This paper focuses on this second approach and it particularly targets property mining for embedded SW (Figure 1). Properties extracted from execution traces are generally not intended as an alternative to specification definition. In fact, the purpose of dynamic property mining is to improve the verification process by providing verification engineers with a way for evaluating and extending the initial manually-defined set of properties. In particular, mined properties can be compared to the original manually-defined ones to understand if they match. If they do, the original intent of designer has been respected in the implementation. If they do not, mined properties highlight the incompleteness of the original specifications, which may lead to discover design errors and unexpected behaviors. On the other hand, not all the designs may be provided with initial specifications. In these situations, property mining can be exploited as a "black-box approach" to investigate the design behavior by monitoring its inputs and outputs.

As summarized in Section 2, some approaches have been proposed to mine particular classes of properties, i.e., either arithmetic invariants for software, or Boolean temporal properties for bit-level hardware descriptions. An arithmetic invariant is a mathematical expression that holds at a certain point of a program over all program executions. For example, in C language, they are expressed as *assert()* statements and they are used for run-time verification. Some examples are: $a + b = c$, *x is in the range [0..10]*, and *p != NULL*. Whereas, Boolean temporal properties express formal correctness of a program in terms of ordering and relationships of events during executions. An example of temporal property is the strict relationship between a request and the corresponding acknowledgement, that in LTL can be expressed as $G\ (req \rightarrow F\ ack)$.

However, none of the existent approaches is able to automatically extract properties from embedded SW, since they are unable to extract properties in the form of temporal relationships between arithmetic invariants involving more complex data types than Booleans, like, for example, *G (((Heating=="ON") && (door=="CLOSE")) U ((temp − tolerance) > threshold))*. This work fills in the gap by proposing a methodology, supported by a tool, to mine temporal properties from execution traces of embedded SW. In particular, main contributions of this work are:

- Identification of a timing reference for embedded SW execution which enables us to precisely reason in terms of temporal events.
- Definition of a new dynamic mining approach suitable for embedded SW which relies on the previous timing reference. In particular, the approach is able to infer linear temporal logic properties in the form of temporal relationships between arithmetic expressions.
- Implementation of the proposed approach in a scalable and modular framework.

The remaining part of the paper is organized as follows. Section 2 summarizes existing methodologies for property mining and it compares them with our approach. Section 3 presents the adopted timing reference for embedded SW execution, upon which the extraction of temporal pattern relies. Section 4 describes the methodology proposed to mine temporal properties from embedded SW. Section 5 deals with experimental results. Finally, conclusions are drawn in Section 6.

2. RELATED WORKS

Both static and dynamic approaches have been proposed for property mining. Static property mining is effective and accurate, but it does not scale sufficiently well with program size [1, 13]. On the contrary, dynamic property mining guarantees a better scalability, but the quality of mined properties depends on the observed executions and then on the test suite used to stimulate the design [8].

Dynamic property mining approaches and tools are classified in two main categories: invariants miners [14, 15, 5, 18, 19] and temporal property miners [3, 24, 12, 31, 30, 32, 23].

Among the others, Daikon [14] has proven to be the more effective tool to infer *likely invariants*, i.e., properties that are true in specific *program points* over all the observed executions. The tool permits to specify monitored variables and program points: default program points are all the functions contained in the program. The selected variables will be monitored at entry and exit of each program point. The generated trace files are processed by an inference engine that incrementally detects invariants specified in a grammar configuration file [26]. Daikon has been widely used for documentation, debugging, testing and maintainability [15]. Thus, thanks to its configurability, we have adopted it as a part of our framework (Section 4.1).

Other tools exist for mining invariants, but limited to a specific application field or pre-processed language. In particular, Agitator [5] is a commercial award-winning extension of Daikon that performs likely invariant detection to guide software test generation. DIDUCE [18] is a tool that aids programmers in identifying root causes of Java program errors. It dynamically formulates hypotheses of invariants obeyed by the program. In particular, it hypothesizes the strictest invariants at the beginning, and gradually relaxes the hypothesis as violations are detected to allow for new behaviors. The violations reported help users to catch software bugs as soon as they occur. IODINE [19] infers likely invariants from hardware design descriptions. Inferred invariants refer to state machine protocols, request-acknowledge pairs, and mutual exclusion between signals. Many other tools [20, 27] use dynamic assertion mining transparently to the user and limited to bug detection, e.g., uninitialized-memory reads, memory leaks, array-bound overruns, race conditions, etc.

Most of the existing mining tools for temporal properties infer properties in the form of state machines. Some of them, learn a single complex specification state machine at once, and then extract simpler properties from it. For instance, in [3] a state machine is inferred that captures both temporal and data dependencies. These state machines can be both examined by a programmer to refine the specification and identify errors, and utilized by automatic verification tools to find bugs. A similar approach was proposed in [24] that infers a model representing interactions between software components. The tool automatically generates Extended Finite State Machines (EFSMs) from interaction traces. EFSMs model both data and control aspects that are useful for analyzing and verifying system execution. In particular, the approach generates EFSMs by combining classic algorithms for generating FSMs and Daikon. Daikon describes important properties of the monitored variables, and FSM inference engines capture and generalize component interaction patterns. Some drawbacks exist in both these approaches. First, mining a single state machine from execution traces is a NP-hard problem [17]. Moreover, the problem of extracting formula-based program properties from complex state machines still remains.

To achieve better scalability, an alternative is to first learn multiple small specifications and, in case, post-process them to form more complex specifications. The study in [12] first introduces the idea of mining simple patterns through monitoring checkers. Checkers tailor rule templates to the system behavior, e.g., finding all functions that fit the rule template <*a*> *must be paired with* < *b*>, etc. Several works have followed this first effort.

In [10], the authors defined a set of temporal-property patterns based on case study of hundreds of real property specification. The purpose was to help designers unfamiliar with formal specifications and static verification approaches, e.g., model checking. But the set of defined patterns can be re-used also as a reference in the context of dynamic property mining techniques.

Perracotta [31, 30, 32] is a mining tool developed to detect likely binary patterns from an execution trace. The intuition behind these works is that frequently occurring behaviors that match temporal patterns are likely to be true. Its philosophy is very similar to Daikon's, but the focus of its analysis is on design control flow instead of data flow analysis performed by Daikon. The main idea to achieve scalability to large traces is to mine binary specification first, in form of automata, and then post-process them with inference rules to form more complex state machines. The kind of pattern mined by Perracotta is (P $\mathbf{G}$ S), where P and S are placeholders for generic events and $\mathbf{G}$ a placeholder for a generic binary pattern.

Finally, a further effort [23] makes temporal pattern mining suitable to digital circuits by modifying the used timing reference and adapting concepts to hardware environment. The basic algorithm to mine patterns from trace files is the same proposed by Perracotta, but its purpose is slightly different: this approach tries to mine all the satisfied patterns from the trace file, while Perracotta tries to mine only the strictest pattern satisfied. Both approaches use a set of patterns already codified as state machines.

2.1 Comparison between our approach and previous works

Among all the previous studies, the most relevant ones are graphically summarized in Figure 2 to show their relationship with the work proposed in this paper.

The left side shows milestones in likely invariant mining and the right side shows milestones in temporal property mining. None of the previous approaches is fully suitable for embedded SW for two main reasons: (i) lack of a timing reference suitable for embedded SW, and (ii) incapability of combining arithmetic invariants and temporal operators to form temporal properties on more complex data types than Booleans.

The first issue depends on the fact that existing approaches refer to timing references that may be not suitable mining temporal properties on embedded SW. Perracotta [32] uses the same timing concept proposed by Daikon [15], i.e., variables are monitored at entry and exit points of functions. Thus, in the Perracotta approach, the timing granularity depends on the code structure. The work in [23] is closer to a general timing reference, with the introduction of concepts like clock and delta cycles, but these concepts are strictly related to a hardware context and not suitable for embedded SW. Indeed, the simulation of hardware descriptions exploits either a cycle-based or an event-driven scheduling strategy which make extremely clear how synchronization

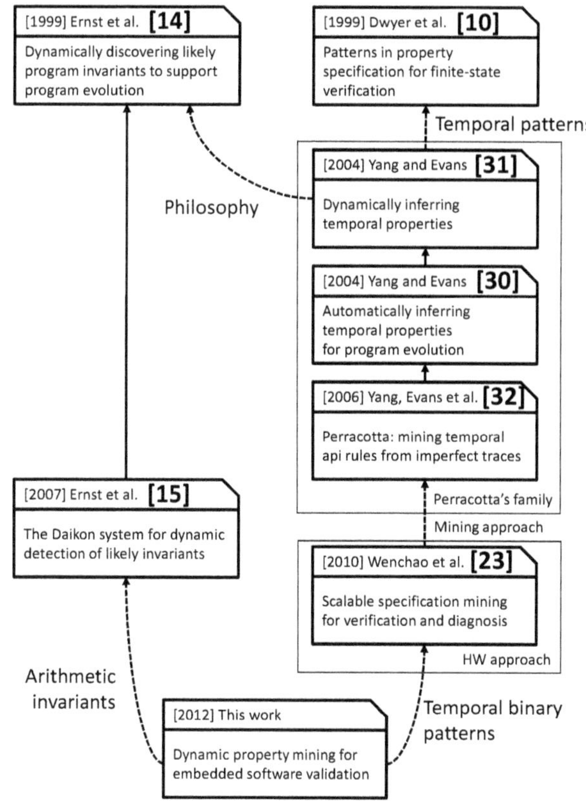

Figure 2: Overview of the main specification mining contributions and the connections between them.

between modules happens, and exactly fixes the time when computation reaches a stable condition. Such timing reference provides designers with the exact time when properties must be evaluated to verify the behavior of the design. In general, the execution of embedded SW lacks such a timing reference, thus the developers are not aware of the right time when embedded SW computation reaches a stable condition.

The second issue is due to the capability of existing approaches of mining only a specific kind of properties: i.e., either arithmetic invariants [15] or Boolean temporal properties [23], not both of them. The temporal properties are Boolean in the sense that they identify temporal relationships between variables defined on the Boolean domain, e.g., events. For example, the property pattern $G(e_1 \rightarrow XFe_2)$, considered in [23], may tailor to an acknowledge-request-and-grant behavior: *Every time the request signal* e_1 *will rise, eventually the acknowledge signal* e_2 *will rise.* The events e_1 and e_2 are Boolean signals. Similarly, the *response pattern* considered in [32] describes cause-effect relationships between two abstract events p and s: p's occurrence must be followed by the occurrence of s (where p and s are, for example, function calls).

The present work (bottom box in Figure 2) addresses both these issues.

- It adopts a timing reference borrowed from the *synchronous reactive paradigm*. This paradigm is adopted by well-known model driven design-based tools for embedded SW [22, 29, 28]. Moreover, this timing reference permits to consider the execution traces only, making the approach independent from the code structure.

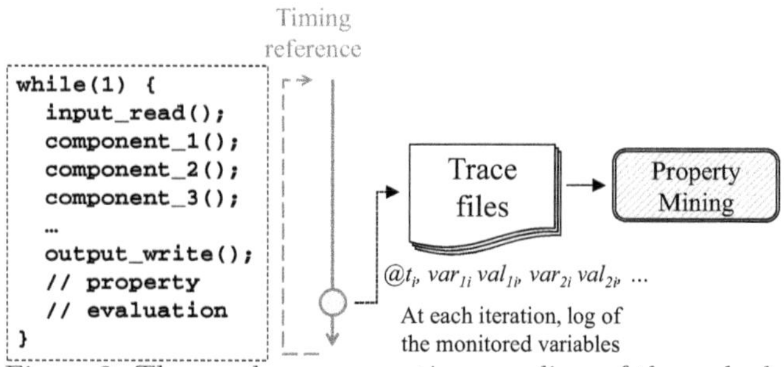

Figure 3: The synchronous reactive paradigm of the embedded SW provides a timing reference for temporal property evaluation.

- It mines properties that are in the form of temporal relationships between arithmetic expressions, e.g., $G((x \geq 0) \rightarrow XF(y < 0))$. First, it infers arithmetic invariants of the monitored variables and, then, it mines binary properties to capture temporal interplay between data values.
- It is designed to maintain the scalability achieved by Perracotta [32] using binary temporal patterns.

3. TIMING REFERENCE FOR PROPERTY MINING

Control applications running on embedded systems consist of periodic tasks that acquire data from environment through sensors, elaborate them, and consequently drive the monitored system.

The most adopted solution for modelling such a kind of control applications is the simple looping approach shown in Figure 3. It implements the synchronous reactive paradigm adopted by well-known model driven design-based tools for embedded SW, such as IAR VisualState [22], MathWorks Simulink [29] and SCADE Suite of Esterel Technologies [28].

In a synchronous reactive environment, components are designed as part of a single application: the synchronous model latches its inputs at the start of a computation step, computes the system next state and related outputs as a single atomic step, and communicates between components using dataflow signals. Signals consist of data values that are aligned with global clock ticks. Such a paradigm represents the state-of-the-practice for safety critical avionics and automotive applications [4].

The synchronous nature of the loop in Figure 3 provides a native timing reference for evaluating properties associated with embedded SW [9]. Properties are evaluated only at the end of the loop, when each component has completed its execution, the stable state is reached, and outputs are written. In particular, at each iteration of the main loop of the embedded application, values of the monitored variables are traced. Monitored variables can be inputs and outputs of the application or internal variables associated with any component. The mined properties will be instantiated over these variables. Each line of the trace file is in the format $< @t_i \; var_1 \; val_{1i} \; var_2 \; val_{2i} \; \ldots >$, where t_i is the execution time and val_{ji} is the value associated with the variable var_j at the specific time t_i. Such trace files will be passed as input of the property mining procedure described in the following sections. Thus, the property mining is independent from the application implementation and it refers to the timing reference provided by the synchronous reactive paradigm.

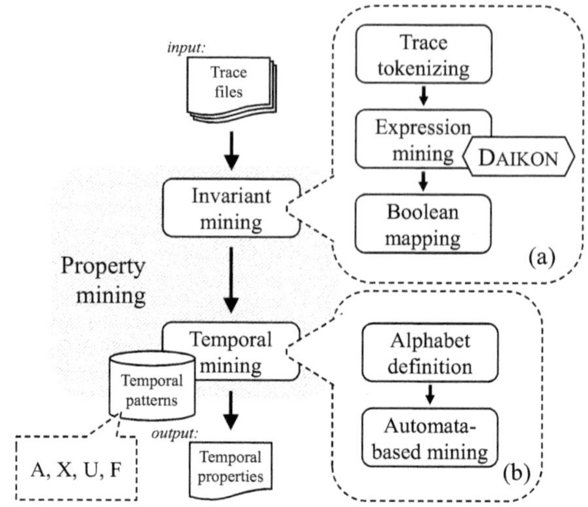

Figure 4: The workflow of the proposed temporal property mining approach from embedded SW.

4. PROPERTY MINING

Most of embedded applications include non-Boolean variables (e.g., double, integer, etc.) that require an alternative approach for property mining, with respect to the state of the art, to capture the complex interplay between data values and temporal relationships.

The methodology workflow proposed in this paper is represented in Figure 4. The input of the analysis are execution traces defined according to the synchronous reactive paradigm reported in Section 3. First, invariants are opportunely mined from such traces, then temporal relationships are inferred between these invariants. The result of the analysis is a set of temporal properties expressed in linear temporal logic. The two main phases of the methodology, i.e., *Invariant mining* and *Temporal mining*, are respectively described in Section 4.1 and Section 4.2.

4.1 Invariant mining

This phase aims at generating expressions defined on variables that hold over time intervals. Figure 4(a) depicts the main steps: first the execution traces are split in sub-traces; then, invariants are inferred for each sub-trace; finally, the original traces are re-defined in terms of occurrences of invariants. These steps are detailed in the remaining of the section.

4.1.1 Trace tokenizing

Invariants are Boolean conditions that hold on the whole execution trace describing steady dependencies between variables, as shown in Fig. 5(a). On the contrary, temporal properties generally define temporal relationships between Boolean conditions that are not necessary true along the whole trace. Saying "the invariants hold on the *whole* execution trace" is equal to assert the absence of a behavior that diversifies in the time. This would lead to the incapability of mining significant temporal properties. Thus, the extraction of invariants from the whole execution trace, e.g., $INV_0 = \{inv_1, inv_2, \cdots, inv_m\}$ in Fig. 5(a), is not the right starting point for temporal mining.

Ideally, to extract temporal behaviors, it is necessary to infer information that is available during the SW execution but lost when considering the whole trace. This result can be achieved by splitting the trace in sub-traces and indepen-

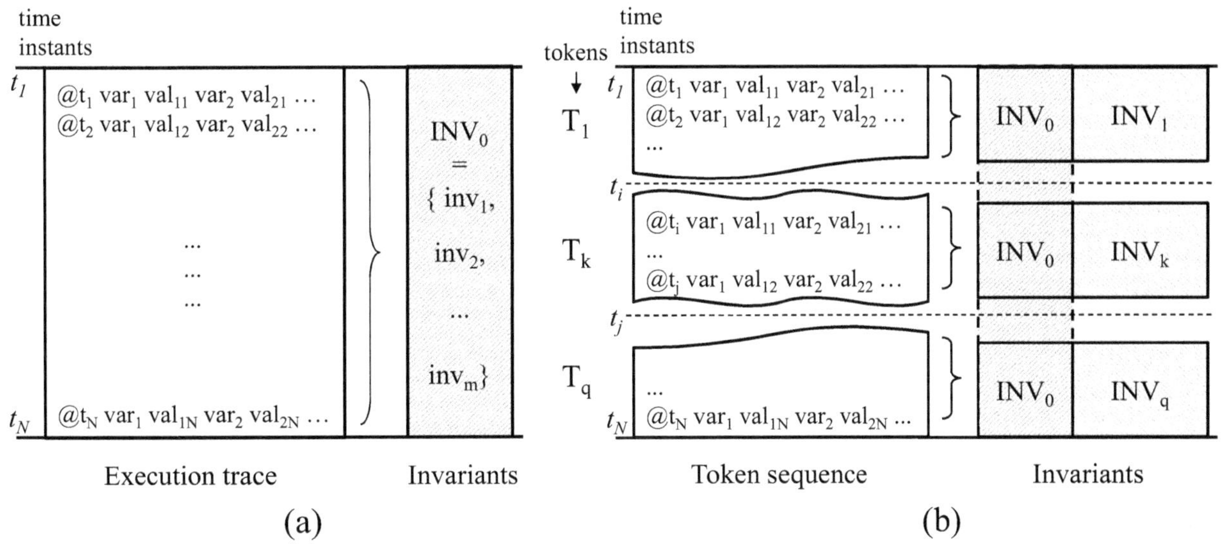

Figure 5: (a) Daikon infers invariants that hold on the whole execution trace. (b) The Daikon's inference engine is applied to sub-traces, i.e., tokens, for generating invariants holding on specific time intervals. The mining procedure infers temporal relationships between these invariants.

dently analyzing them. The process of splitting execution traces is named *trace tokenizing*, where each sub-trace is a *token* of a more complex behavior; the *tokenizing length* is the length of the split sub-traces.

Definition 1. Given an execution trace T and a tokenizing length l, a *token sequence* is an ordered sequence of tokens generated by the trace tokenizing procedure such that $T =< T_1^l, T_2^l, \ldots, T_q^l >$.

The set of invariants inferred from a token concerns a precise time interval, as shown in Figure 5(b) and identifies a local view of the application behavior. For example, the token T_k is defined on the time interval $[t_i, t_j]$. The overall behavior of the application can be described by the sequence of local behaviors and their temporal relationships.

Note that, for each token T_k with $k \in [1, q]$, both the original and the token-dependent sets of invariants hold, i.e., $INV_0 \cup INV_k$. The intuition is that the increasing number of contradictions reduce the number of invariants holding on the whole trace. As a rule of thumb: *Longer is the trace, smaller is the set of associated invariants.* That is INV_k holds on the token T_k, but it does not hold on the whole trace.

Finally, the total number of tokens that can be derived from a N-length execution trace is $\sum_{i=2}^{N} \lceil \frac{N}{i} \rceil$. This includes all the tokens from length 2 to the trace length. Note that when the length N of the execution trace is not a multiple of the chosen tokenizing length l, the length of the last token is N mod l. This does not affect the proposed approach. The complexity of the Algorithm 1 for trace tokenizing is $O(N^2)$. It takes as input the execution trace and it returns the set of all possible token sequences.

4.1.2 Arithmetic expression mining

In this phase, invariants are inferred for each token previously generated. These invariants provide a local view of the design behavior associated with a specific time interval.

Definition 2. Given an execution trace T and a tokenizing length l, the invariant mining procedure associates a *set of invariants* INV_k^l to each token T_k^l of the trace T.

Algorithm 1 Trace tokenizing

```
function TOKENIZER(trace) return token_set
    for length ← 2 to N do
        new token_sequence
        for k ← 0 to N/length do
            new token
            for i ← 0 to length do
                token[i] ← trace[i * k]
            end for
            token_sequence.push(token)
        end for
        token_set.add(token_sequence)
    end for
end function
```

We have adopted Daikon [15] for the purpose. Daikon works on a set of $< variable, value >$ pairs, and automatically generates relations, i.e., invariants, that are satisfied by all input pairs. The generated relations are filtered by probability thresholds to exclude incidental relations. Moreover, the tool allows the user to infer 75 different invariants. Checking a large number of invariants makes it more likely to infer significant behaviors, but it also increases the runtime of the invariant detector. For our purposes, we have configured the tool to mine *arithmetic invariants* only, e.g., boundaries on variable values (e.g., $a \leq 5$), ranges of values (e.g., $3 \leq a \leq 8$), arithmetic relations between variables (e.g., $a \geq b$), etc.

Daikon timing reference and input are different from the ones expected by the proposed approach. Thus a front-end adaption was necessary. In particular, Daikon analysis starts instrumenting the source code of the application in order to monitor values of variables during execution; while, the input of this phase is the simulation result in form of execution traces. This permits to keep the whole approach language-independent and unaware of the application implementation. Moreover, Daikon checks for invariants at entry and exit points of function, resulting in invariants that corresponds to pre- and post-conditions; while, the adopted

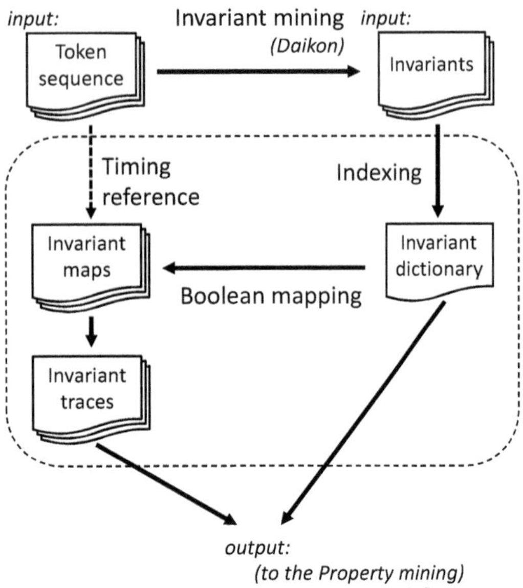

Figure 6: Boolean-mapping workflow.

timing reference is borrowed from the synchronous reactive paradigm and it is independent from the code structure.

In order to exploit the Daikon inference engine, a Daikon-fashion input is generated starting from the embedded SW sub-traces (i.e., tokens) defined in Section 4.1.1. In particular the *Expression mining* module of Fig. 4 mimics the execution of a method `watchpoint()` of the Java class `Watchpoint`. A program point is associated with the method `watchpoint()`, whose implementation code is empty. The method considers all the monitored variables as its input parameters. The values of the monitored variables are read from each token and passed to method `watchpoint()`. The so defined application is passed to the Daikon front-end for Java applications, i.e., *dfej*, that processes and instruments transparently the code.

Finally, the Daikon output invariants are filtered. For example, since the detected invariants are the same for the entry and exit points of method `watchpoint()`, i.e., pre- and post-condition of an empty function, just an half of them are considered. Each token and the associated invariants are stored for the successive processing steps.

4.1.3 Boolean mapping

The purpose of the Boolean mapping is to redefine the execution traces of embedded applications in terms of occurring (and non-occurring invariants), i.e., *invariant traces*.

The Boolean mapping workflow is depicted in Figure 6. The module inputs are a token sequence (Section 4.1.1) and for each token the correspondent set of invariants (Section 4.1). The module outputs are a set of invariant traces, which are built exploiting the timing information of the sub-traces, and an *invariant dictionary*, where all the mined invariants are indexed. A description of each step of this workflow is hereby provided.

Invariant dictionary definition.

At this point of the analysis, a set of arithmetic invariants has already been inferred for each sub-trace. The relationships between the inferred sets of invariants are *a-priori* unknown, e.g., an invariant set can be completely included into another one, or they can be disjoint, etc. Therefore, the main advantage of defining an invariant dictionary is to uniquely identify invariants inferred on different tokens, i.e., the same invariant can occur multiple times on different time intervals.

A dictionary definition procedure has been defined that takes as input the token sequences and incrementally extends the dictionary. An element of the invariant dictionary is a couple $(inv, \#i)$, where inv is an invariant and $\#i$ is the associated index.

Invariant map definition.

The relationship between an invariant and the token of origin permits to associate the presence of an invariant to a specific time interval. Similarly, the knowledge of *all* the invariants concerning an execution trace permits to associate the *absence* of an invariant in a specific time interval. This is the key of the *Boolean mapping*.

In this phase, an *invariant map* is associated with each token. An invariant map is defined on the same time interval of the token and contains information about the invariant presence and absence.

Definition 3. An invariant map IM_k^l associated with a token T_k^l is a pair $(@t, O)$, where $@t$ is the first timestamp of the token and O is a list of *invariant occurrences*. An invariant occurrence $o \in O$ is a pair $(\#i, v)$ composed by an invariant index $\#i$ and a Boolean value v defined as follows:

- v is 1, if the invariant, whose index is $\#i$, holds on the token;
- v is 0, otherwise.

For example, let us consider the token

$$T_1^2 = < \ (@t_1, \{(var_1, val_1 1), (var_2, val_2 1), \ldots\}), \\ (@t_2, \{(var_1, val_1 2), (var_2, val_2 2), \ldots\}) >$$

and the set of invariants associated to T_1^2

$$INV_1 = \{\#1, \#4, \#5\}$$

where $\#1, \#4, \#5$ are elements of the invariant dictionary, i.e., indexes of invariants. Let us assume that the invariant dictionary contains invariants marked with indexes from $\#1$ to $\#d$. Thus, the invariant map associated with the sub-trace T_1^2 is $IM_1^2 = (@t_1, \{(\#1, 1), (\#2, 0), (\#3, 0), (\#4, 1), (\#5, 1), \ldots, (\#d, 0)\})$.

Invariant trace definition.

As an invariant map can be associated with each token, an *invariant trace* can be associated with a token sequence. In particular, invariant maps can be ordered, with respect to their timestamps, to form invariant traces.

Definition 4. Given an execution trace T and a tokenizing length l, an *invariant trace* IT^l is defined as a sequence of length q of invariant maps such that $IT^l =< IM_1^l, IM_2^l, \ldots, IM_q^l >$, where IM_k^l is the invariant map associated with the token T_k^l for $k \in [1, q]$.

An invariant trace resembles the original execution trace, but it contains information about invariant occurrences instead of values of variables.

4.2 Temporal mining

This section defines the mining approach for temporal properties starting from the invariants traces defined in Section 4. The resulting properties will be in the form of temporal relationships between arithmetic expressions that are the Daikon-inferred invariants.

Algorithm 2 Alphabet definition

```
1: function CREATE_ALPHABET(invariant_trace) return alphabet
2:     alphabet ← ∅
3:     for all imap ∈ invariant_trace do
4:         index ← SEARCH(imap, alphabet);
5:         if index = NULL then
6:             index ← NEW_ENTRY(imap.occurrences)
7:         end if
8:         imap.alphabet_index ← index
9:     end for
10: end function
```

Figure 4(b) depicts the workflow for mining temporal properties. The approach checks if invariant traces satisfy a given set of binary temporal patterns defined as accepting automata. If they do, the correspondent temporal properties are generated as output.

The rest of the section provides the description of the remaining two phases, i.e., the alphabet definition (Section 4.2.1) and the automata-based mining (Section 4.2.2).

4.2.1 Alphabet definition

This section provides the definition of the *alphabet* necessary to understand the temporal mining procedure.

Definition 5. An *alphabet* Σ is defined as the set of distinct invariant maps, i.e., *alphabet entries.* With *distinct* invariant maps are intended invariant maps that differ at least for one of their invariant occurrences. On the contrary, two invariant maps containing the same invariant occurrences, but different timestamps, must be considered as the same alphabet entry.

During alphabet definition, each alphabet entry is indexed uniquely, as detailed in Algorithm 2. Given an invariant trace, each invariant map is associated to an alphabet entry. Thus, each invariant map is compared with existing alphabet entries in order to check if it is already known or not. If the invariant map is known, the index of the corresponding alphabet entry is assigned to it; otherwise, a new alphabet entry is created and its index is assigned to the invariant map. As an example, let us consider the invariant trace:

$IT = <$ (@0, {(#1, 1), (#2, 1), (#3, 0)}),
(@1, {(#1, 0), (#2, 1), (#3, 0)}),
(@2, {(#1, 0), (#2, 1), (#3, 0)}),
(@2, {(#1, 1), (#2, 1), (#3, 0)}),
(@3, {(#1, 1), (#2, 1), (#3, 0)}) $>$

The corresponding alphabet is:

$\Sigma = \{$ (##1, {(#1, 1), (#2, 1), (#3, 0)}),
(##2, {(#1, 0), (#2, 1), (#3, 0)}) $\}$

where ##1 and ##2 are unique indexes associated with the alphabet entry (lines 4-7 in Algorithm 2). Moreover, during the alphabet definition (line 8 in Algorithm 2), the original invariant trace is indexed. In the case of the previous example, the resulting trace is

$IT' = <$ (@0, {(#1, 1), (#2, 1), (#3, 0)}, ##1),
(@1, {(#1, 0), (#2, 1), (#3, 0)}, ##2),
(@2, {(#1, 0), (#2, 1), (#3, 0)}, ##2),
(@2, {(#1, 1), (#2, 1), (#3, 0)}, ##1),
(@3, {(#1, 1), (#2, 1), (#3, 0)}, ##1) $>$

Definition 6. Given an invariant trace T, the *indexed invariant trace* T' is obtained from T by labeling each invariant map with its alphabet entry index.

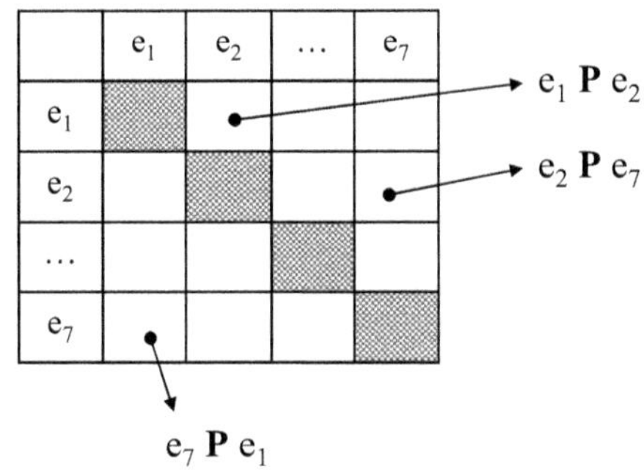

Figure 7: An example of pattern table for a generic temporal pattern **P**: the notation (a **P** b) means that entry a and entry b are in a **P**-relation.

Algorithm 3 Automata-based mining procedure

```
function MINE_PATTERN_P(invariant_trace)
    alphabet ← CREATE_ALPHABET(invariant_trace)
    T ← allocate pattern table(alphabet)
    for all e_a ∈ alphabet do
        for all e_b ∈ alphabet do
            if e_a ≠ e_b then
                T[e_a][e_b] ← MINE_P(e_a, e_b, invariant_trace);
            end if
        end for
    end for
end function
```

4.2.2 Automata-based mining

The temporal property mining uses temporal patterns in form of accepting automata and it analyzes the invariant indexed traces defined in Section 4.2.1. The procedure iteratively selects pairs of alphabet entries and verifies if they satisfy the defined patterns. The adoption of *binary temporal patterns*, instead of more complex ones, provides a scalable methodology [23, 32].

For each binary pattern to be mined, a *pattern table* of dimension K^2 is allocated, where K is the alphabet size. Figure 7 shows a pattern table for an alphabet of size 7. Each cell of the pattern table identifies a pair of alphabet entries by their indexes. The content of the cell stores the current state of the pattern automata. It decides if the occurrences of the invariant maps in the invariant trace satisfy the pattern or not. This content is updated by reading invariant trace and performing the related transitions on the automata. When the whole invariant trace has been processed, the stored state indicates if the corresponding couple of alphabet entries satisfy the pattern. The procedure for a generic pattern P is described in Algorithm 3.

Binary temporal patterns.

We have chosen four binary patterns for temporal specifications mining, i.e., *Alternating*, *Until*, *Next*, and *Eventually*. In particular,

- Alternating pattern (**A**) is defined by the regular expression $(e_a e_b)^*$; it indicates that, for every occurrence of e_a, an e_b must occur, every time e_a occurs in the trace;
- Until pattern (**U**) is defined by the LTL expression $G(e_a \rightarrow X(e_a U e_b))$; it indicates that, after e_a occurs,

Universality		
U	P causes S to happen at the same time	`always (P -> S)`
Responsiveness		
X	P causes S to happen immediately after	`always (P -> next S)`
F	P causes S to happen eventually	`always (P -> eventually! S)`
Precedence		
A	P precedes S repeatedly	`(P before! S) & always (P -> next (S before P))`
Absence		
U	it never happens that P causes S to happen at the same time	`never (P -> S)`

Table 1: Templates of frequently used properties for representing design specification. The adopted set of binary patterns permit to infer them from the execution traces.

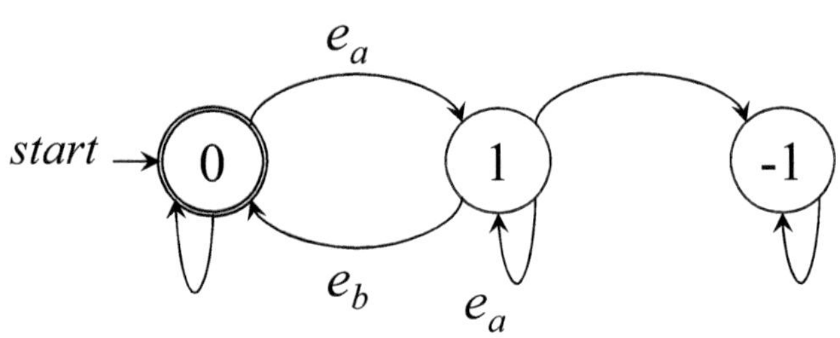

Figure 8: UNTIL pattern automata: 0 is accepting state, 1 is non-accepting state, and -1 is error state.

it must hold until e_b occurs, every time e_a occurs in the trace;

- Next Pattern (**X**) is defined by the LTL expression $G(e_a \to Xe_b)$; it indicates that, after e_a occurs, it must be immediately followed by e_b, every time e_a occurs in the trace;
- Eventually Pattern (**F**) is defined by LTL expression $G(e_a \to XF(e_b))$; indicates that, after e_a occurs, anything could happen if sooner or later e_b occurs.

These patterns are derived from the *practice patterns* introduced in [10] that describe *frequently* used properties for representing design specifications. Thus, they most likely permit to infer interesting behaviors from the execution traces. In Table 1, some of the practice patterns are organized per classes. For each practice pattern, its description in natural language and the corresponding PSL formula are reported. Finally, each of them are marked with one of the patterns adopted in this work, i.e., **A**, **U**, **X**, and **F**.

Accepting automata.

Each of these pattern can be represented with an accepting automata. In Figure 8, the accepting automata for the *Until* pattern is reported. It is implemented in Algorithm 4.

After the automata-based mining finishes to process the indexed invariant trace, values stored in pattern table allow to detect the satisfied temporal properties.

Each cell of a pattern table refers to a pair of alphabet entries. If the value stored in a cell corresponds to the accepting state of pattern automata, all occurrences of that pair of elements satisfy the pattern.

For example, let us consider the UNTIL-pattern table computed on a certain trace of length 4:

Algorithm 4 Mine UNTIL pattern

```
function MINE_UNTIL(e_a, e_b, invariant_trace)
    state ← 0
    for all e ∈ invariant_trace do
        if state = 0 then
            if e = e_a then
                state ← 1
            end if
        else if state = 1 then
            if e = e_b then
                state ← 0
            else if e = e_a then
                state ← 1
            else
                state ← −1
            end if
        end if
    end for
end function
```

	e_1	e_2	e_3	e_4
e_1	⊘	0	2	1
e_2	−1	⊘	0	2
e_3	1	1	⊘	0
e_4	2	0	−1	⊘

This means that the following properties can be mined from the indexed invariant trace, i.e., the following pairs of alphabet entries satisfy the UNTIL pattern: e_1 **U**e_2; e_2 **U**e_3; e_3 **U**e_4; e_4 **U**e_2. Note that, in the UNTIL-pattern automata shown in Figure 8, accepting state is 0, non-accepting state is 1, and error state is -1.

5. EXPERIMENTAL RESULTS

We have implemented the proposed approach in a tool, i.e. ODEN (*Oden* is a Japanese winter dish consisting of several ingredients including *Daikon* radish). The experiments are intended to prove ODEN scalability and effectiveness. We considered 6 benchmarks in our experiments. All of them are applications written in C language.

- two simple designs: (i) a combinational-logic design, i.e. *Sum*, that provides the sum of two randomly generated integer values, and (ii) a counter FSM, i.e. *Fair*, that accepts a Boolean input and prints the FSM-current state as output. The output generated by the automata is described by the regular expression $((010)^* + (0123)^*)^*$. The design ouput is normally described by the regular expression $(0123)^*$, but it changes to $(010)^*$ if the value of the input is *true* when the FSM state is 1.
- two well known behavioral designs from the ITC'99 benchmark suite [7] (adapted to C): (i) *b03* models a resource arbiter dealing with four different requesting devices, and (ii) *b06* models an interrupt handler;
- two industrial designs: (i) *Bus arbiter* models a bus arbiter inspired by AMBA AHB specifications [25] and (ii) *Breadmaker* is an industrial control application composed of periodic tasks that monitor the environment and periodically acquire sensory data.

The experiments have been run on a Intel Pentium Dual 2.2GHz processor equipped with 2.0GB of RAM and running Linux OS.

Quantitative evaluation.

The results are summarized in Table 2. Column I/O indicates the number of observed variables (the temporal properties will be defined on them). Column A.I. indicates the number of mined arithmetic invariants; column T.P. indicates the number of temporal properties mined as temporal relationships between arithmetic invariants. Columns A, X, U, and F report the number of mined properties for each pattern. The execution time is reported in seconds. Column TOT. is the total execution time; column TOK. is the execution time of trace tokenizing; column DAIKON is the Daikon execution time; column B.MAP. is the execution time of Boolean mapping; finally, column T.MIN. is the execution time of temporal properties mining. Note that all these data are intended as the sum of the results obtained from all the considered execution traces. For the academic designs, i.e., *Sum*, *Fair*, *b03*, and *b06*, we used stimuli that guarantee high structural coverage. For the industrial designs, i.e., *Bus arbiter* and *Breadmaker*, we used the factory testbenches.

Arithmetic invariants: the number of arithmetic invariants mined depends on the nature of the design considered, e.g., the number and the type of the design monitored variables and their relationships. This result is provided by the adopted invariant miner, i.e., Daikon. Daikon has been configured to mine exclusively arithmetic invariants.

Temporal properties: we can observe that *Sum* program is not characterized by any temporal property, since it does not have an internal status and receives random values as inputs. Vice versa, some invariants are mined: the most significant one is `a + b - c = 0` that is the specification of *Sum*, where `a` and `b` are the input variables and `c` is the output variable. The high number of mined temporal properties of type *Next* (X) for the *Bus arbiter* and *Breadmaker* are motivated by their nature of controllers; similarly, for the *Alternating* (A) properties in the case of *ITC'99 b03* and *Bus arbiter*.

Execution time: we can observe that the approach scale well with the design size, i.e., number of monitored variables. Moreover, most of the execution time is spent in the invariant mining phase, i.e., the third-party tool Daikon. Further optimizations in the configuration of Daikon, may provide us with better results. The trace tokenizing and Boolean mapping phases requires at most a couple of seconds for each of the design. The temporal property mining based on accepting automata is the most time expensive phase, but in any case it takes only 1 minute and 19 seconds for mining 616 temporal properties for the industrial design *Breadmaker* (total time 44 minutes).

Qualitative evaluation.

The temporal properties mined by ODEN are defined as temporal relationships between arithmetic invariants. Since more arithmetic invariants could occur in the same time interval, the mined temporal properties are characterized by conjunctions of these invariants, in the form

$$inv_i \wedge \cdots \wedge inv_j \wedge \mathbf{P} inv_k \wedge \cdots \wedge inv_h$$

where $\mathbf{P}$ is a generic-temporal pattern and $inv_i, inv_j, inv_k, inv_h$ are arithmetic invariants.

We report some example of the mined temporal properties, where conjunctions are indicated as [&] and the patterns as [A], [X], [U], [F]. These formula can be rewritten in property specification language as defined in Section 4.2.2.

- *Fair*: `(( (output1 one of {0, 1}) [&] (input1 == true) ) [X] ( (input1 == false) [&] (output1 one of {0, 3}) ))`

  This property synthesizes the *Fair* behavior: it describes two contiguous time intervals where the behavior of the system is determined by the value of input variable *input*1. In the first time interval, *input*1 is equal to *true* and the FSM is stuck in a loop between states 0 and 1 (i.e., $(010)^*$). In the second time interval, *input*1 is *false* and the FSM returns to its normal behavior (i.e., $(0123)^*$).

- *ITC'99 b03*: `((req2 == false) [&] (req1 == true) [&] (grant one of {0,8}) ) [X] ((req2 == false) [&] (req3 == true) [&] (req4 == true) [&] (grant one of {1,4}))`

  It is always true that if any request is raised, e.g. $(req1 == true)$, *grant* signal will take the correspondent value within four cycles $(grant == 1$ correspond to $req1)$. This property is exactly part of the specifications of resource arbiter.

- *Bus arbiter*: For lack of space, we report a natural-language transcription of the mined temporal property. Note that the mined properties are instances of the four patterns described in Section 4.2.2. Thus, the transcription in natural language is quite straightforward. *It is always true that when a CPU (i.e, CPU_3) is performing a locked-reading operation, it owns the bus until the operation is completed. Preemption is not performed even if CPU priority is lower than priorities of other CPUs requesting the bus.* The expressiveness of the property proves the effectiveness of the mining approach for temporal properties.

- *Breadmaker*: We report a natural-language transcription of the mined temporal property. Note that the proposed approach is intended to mine properties on the design interface variables. In particular, for the industrial designs a high number of variables are monitored. This contributes to generate properties that are relatively simple to read, but long to be represented. *By using the Alternating pattern, a counter-clockwise-mixing phase is identified for each clockwise-mixing phase inferred during Breadmaker execution. Moreover, both fast and slow mixing involves four sub-phases: (a) stop, (b) clockwise direction, (c) stop, (d) counter-clockwise direction.* The property is significant in terms of the design specifications. Indeed, *Breadmaker* controller is characterized by four phases: (i) mixing for 30s, (ii) kneading for 60s, (iii), proving for 30s, and (iv) baking for 60s. The mined temporal property stresses a specific behavior that occurs during mixing phase: the alternation between clockwise and counter-clockwise directions.

6. CONCLUDING REMARKS

We have provided a new specification mining approach, able to dynamically infer temporal properties from execution traces of embedded SW. In particular, the approach is able to infer linear temporal logic properties in the form of temporal relationships between arithmetic expressions. The

Design	I/O	Number of		Type of temp.prop.				Exec. time (sec.)				
		A.I.	T.P.	A	X	U	F	Tot.	Tok.	Daikon	B.Map.	T.Min.
Sum	3	5	0	0	0	0	0	167	0.279	165	0.275	1
Fair	2	11	44	5	31	0	8	296	0.270	291	0.359	4
ITC'99 b03	5	10	84	29	38	0	17	514	0.211	509	0.461	4
ITC'99 b06	6	12	34	1	27	1	5	431	0.203	426	1.022	4
Bus arbiter	22	109	397	44	329	11	13	1312	0.575	1276	2.289	33
Breadmaker	67	679	616	2	586	4	24	2696	2.030	2552	3.422	139

Table 2: Experimental results.

experimental results confirm the scalability and effectiveness of the proposed approach.

As future works we aim at extending the set of supported temporal patterns for mining a wider set of design behaviors. Moreover, dealing with conjunctions of invariants and high number of monitored variables makes the temporal properties hard to understand. We will try to simplify the set of invariants, even syntactically, in order to provide more readable properties.

7. REFERENCES

[1] R. Alur, P. Černý, P. Madhusudan, and W. Nam. Synthesis of interface specifications for java classes. In *ACM SIGPLAN Notices*, volume 40, pages 98–109. ACM, 2005.

[2] G. Ammons, R. Bodík, and J. Larus. Mining specifications. In *ACM Sigplan Notices*, volume 37, pages 4–16. ACM, 2002.

[3] G. Ammons, R. Bodík, and J. R. Larus. Mining specifications. In *Proceedings of the ACM SIGPLAN-SIGACT Symposium on Principles of Programming Languages*, pages 4–16. ACM, 2002.

[4] M. Baleani, A. Ferrari, L. Mangeruca, and A. Sangiovanni-Vincentelli. Efficient Embedded Software Design with Synchronous Models. In *Proceedings of ACM International Conference on Embedded Software*, pages 187–190, 2005.

[5] M. Boshernitsan, R. Doong, and A. Savoia. From daikon to agitator: lessons and challenges in building a commercial tool for developer testing. In *Proceedings of the 2006 international symposium on Software testing and analysis*, pages 169–180. ACM, 2006.

[6] J. Burch, E. Clarke, K. McMillan, D. Dill, and L. Hwang. Symbolic model checking: 1020 states and beyond. *Information and computation*, 98(2):142–170, 1992.

[7] F. Corno, M. Reorda, and G. Squillero. RT-level ITC'99 benchmarks and first ATPG results. *Design & Test of Computers, IEEE*, 17(3):44–53, 2000.

[8] V. Dallmeier, N. Knopp, C. Mallon, G. Fraser, S. Hack, and A. Zeller. Automatically Generating Test Cases for Specification Mining. *Software Engineering, IEEE Transactions on*, (99):1–1, 2011.

[9] G. Di Guglielmo, L. Di Guglielmo, F. Fummi, and G. Pravadelli. Enabling Dynamic Assertion-based Verification of Embedded Software through Model-driven Design. In *Prof. of ACM/IEEE DATE*, pages 212–217, 2012.

[10] M. Dwyer, G. Avrunin, and J. Corbett. Patterns in property specifications for finite-state verification. In *Proceedings of the International Conference on Software Engineering*, ICSE, pages 411 -420, 1999.

[11] C. Eisner. A practical introduction to psl (series on integrated circuits & systems). *Recherche*, 67:02, 2006.

[12] D. Engler, D. Y. Chen, S. Hallem, A. Chou, and B. Chelf. Bugs as deviant behavior: a general approach to inferring errors in systems code. In *Proceedings of the 18th ACM Symposium on Operating Systems Principles*, pages 57–72. ACM, 2001.

[13] M. Ernst. Static and dynamic analysis: Synergy and duality. In *ICSE Workshop on Dynamic Analysis*, pages 24–27, 2003.

[14] M. Ernst, J. Cockrell, W. Griswold, and D. Notkin. Dynamically discovering likely program invariants to support program evolution. In *Proceedings of the International Conference on Software Engineering*, pages 213–224. ACM, 1999.

[15] M. D. Ernst, J. H. Perkins, P. J. Guo, S. McCamant, C. Pacheco, M. S. Tschantz, and C. Xiao. The Daikon system for dynamic detection of likely invariants. *Science of Computer Programming*, 69(1-3):35–45, 2007. Special issue on Experimental Software and Toolkits.

[16] H. Foster, A. Krolnik, and D. Lacey. *Assertion-based design*. Springer, 2004.

[17] E. Gold. Complexity of automaton identification from given data. *Information and control*, 37(3):302–320, 1978.

[18] S. Hangal and M. Lam. Tracking down software bugs using automatic anomaly detection. In *Proceedings of the International Conference on Software Engineering*, pages 291–301. ACM, 2002.

[19] S. Hangal, S. Narayanan, N. Chandra, and S. Chakravorty. Iodine: a tool to automatically infer dynamic invariants for hardware designs. In *Proceedings of the Design Automation Conference*, pages 775–778. IEEE, 2005.

[20] R. Hastings and B. Joyce. Purify: Fast detection of memory leaks and access errors. In *Proceedinbgs of the Winter USENIX Conference*, 1991.

[21] M. Huth and M. Ryan. *Logic in Computer Science: Modelling and reasoning about systems*. Cambridge University Press, 2004.

[22] IAR Systems. IAR visualSTATE, 2012.

[23] W. Li, A. Forin, and S. Seshia. Scalable specification mining for verification and diagnosis. In *Proceedings of the ACM/IEEE Design Automation Conference*, pages 755 –760, 2010.

[24] D. Lorenzoli, L. Mariani, and M. Pezze. Automatic generation of software behavioral models. In *Proceedings of the ACM/IEEE International Conference on Software Engineering*, ICSE, pages 501 –510, 2008.

[25] A. Ltd. AMBA Open Specifications.

[26] J. Perkins and M. Ernst. Efficient incremental algorithms for dynamic detection of likely invariants. In *ACM SIGSOFT Software Engineering Notes*, volume 29, pages 23–32. ACM, 2004.

[27] S. Savage, M. Burrows, G. Nelson, P. Sobalvarro, and T. Anderson. Eraser: A dynamic data race detector for multithreaded programs. *ACM Transactions on Computer Systems (TOCS)*, 15(4):391–411, 1997.

[28] E. Technologies. Scade suite, 2012.

[29] The MathWorks, Inc. Simulink, 2012.

[30] J. Yang and D. Evans. Automatically inferring temporal properties for program evolution. In *Proceedings of the International Symposium on Software Reliability Engineering*, ISSRE, pages 340–351, 2004.

[31] J. Yang and D. Evans. Dynamically inferring temporal properties. In *Proceedings of the ACM SIGPLAN-SIGSOFT Workshop on Program Analysis for Software Tools and Engineering*, PASTE, pages 23–28, 2004.

[32] J. Yang, D. Evans, D. Bhardwaj, T. Bhat, and M. Das. Perracotta: mining temporal API rules from imperfect traces. In *Proceedings of the International Conference on Software Engineering*, pages 282–291. ACM, 2006.

Efficient Self-Learning Techniques for SAT-Based Test Generation

Ang Li and Mingsong Chen
Shanghai Key Lab of Trustworthy Computing
East China Normal University, Shanghai, China
{ali,mschen}@sei.ecnu.edu.cn

ABSTRACT

SAT-based approaches are promising for automated generation of directed tests. However, due to the state space explosion problem, these methods do not scale well for complex designs. Although various heuristics are proposed to address test generation complexity, most of them require expert knowledge regarding the detailed structure and behavior information of designs explicitly, which limits their usage. This paper proposes promising techniques to derive profitable learnings from the SAT instance itself. The obtained self-learnings can efficiently reduce the chance of long distance backtracks and improve satisfying assignment convergence rate during the SAT search. Experimental results demonstrate that our method can reduce the test generation time by several orders of magnitude.

Categories and Subject Descriptors

B.7.3 [**Integrated Circuits**]: Reliability and Testing—*Test generation*; D.2.4 [**Software Engineering**]: Software/Program Verification—*Validation*

General Terms

Verification, Algorithms, Experimentation

Keywords

Functional Validation, Test Generation, SAT

1. INTRODUCTION

Under the pressure of increasing complexity and decreasing time-to-market, functional validation is becoming a major bottleneck in System-on-Chip (SoC) design. To achieve a coverage goal, current complex designs need to run trillions of random or constrained-random tests. Therefore up to 70% of the design development efforts are wasted in the validation process. As an alternative, directed testing methods have been widely investigated, since they use fewer tests and less simulation time to achieve the required functional coverage. However, most directed test generation approaches [12] need human intervention which is laborious and error-prone. Therefore it is desired that the process of directed test generation can be fully automated.

As a promising method, model checking [7, 22] can be used for automated generation of directed tests. It translates the investigated design into a formal model and the testing target into a property in the form of temporal logic. Then a corresponding model checker searches the state space of the design for a counterexample of the specified property. Such a counterexample is an assignment of variables, which can be used as a directed test to trigger the testing target. However, large designs generally involve complex interactions among multiple components. Model checking of such designs often terminates abnormally due to the out of computation or memory resource. To address the checking complexity, Boolean Satisfiability (SAT) based Bounded Model Checking (BMC) [2] is proposed to restrict the search range to find a shortest path which can falsify the specified property. Assume that the design is M and the property is p. SAT-based BMC unrolls the design and the property k timesteps using the following Boolean formula:

$$BMC(M,p,k) = I(s_0) \wedge \bigwedge_{i=0}^{k-1} T(s_i,s_{i+1}) \wedge \bigvee_{i=0}^{k} \neg p(s_i) \qquad (1)$$

It consists of three parts: i) $I(s_0)$ represents the initial state, ii) $T(s_i,s_{i+1})$ denotes the transition from state s_i to state s_{i+1}, and iii) $p(s_i)$ tests whether p holds on state s_i. Then this formula will be transformed to Conjunctive Norm Form (CNF) and checked by a SAT solver. If M has a false state against p within bound k, the Boolean formula will be evaluated to be *satisfiable*. The derived satisfying assignment for this formula can be used as a directed test against p.

Since the test generation is to find a satisfying assignment for the checking SAT instance, the performance of SAT searching plays an important role in determining the test generation time. To enable quick SAT search, various heuristics based on CNF structures (e.g., literal count [13] and variable dependencies [17]) have been investigated. However, most of them focused on general purpose SAT problems. When the test generation becomes the target, the potential improvement of SAT search can be further exploited. Learning-based approaches [3, 6] are promising candidates to quickly achieve satisfying assignments for SAT instances. It can be used to increase satisfying assignment convergence rate as well as to avoid long-distance backtracks during the SAT search. Therefore it is promising for SAT-based test generation. However, the majority of learning-based approaches are based on the assumption that designs should be well formed to facilitate the exploration of the structure and behavior information, which strongly limits the applicability of these methods. Unlike most approaches that learn from external sources, this paper presents our self-learning techniques which can exploit the profitable learnings from the SAT instance itself to accelerate test generation. It makes two major contributions: i) it investigates the structure of both BMC formulas and CNF clauses as learning objects to derive profitable self-learnings; and ii) it proposes three promising partitioning approaches to derive self-learnings from the SAT instances with low overhead.

The rest of the paper is organized as follows. Section 2 introduces related work on efficient approaches for SAT-based model checking and directed test generation. Section 3 presents the details of our self-learning techniques. Section 4 provides the experimental results. Finally, Section 5 concludes the paper.

2. RELATED WORK

Model checking is being gradually employed for automated generation of directed tests. Unlike traditional Binary Decision Diagram (BDD) based unbounded model checking [7] which easily suffers from the state space explosion problem, SAT-based BMC [2] restricts the search within short possible bounds. The limited search space can reduce BMC validation efforts drastically. Therefore SAT-based BMC succeeds in validating many real industry scale designs [1].

SAT solver acts like the engine of the SAT-based BMC. To improve its performance, various learning-based approaches are developed. Since conflict clauses [14] can avoid repetitive conflicts, they can be used as a kind of learning. For example, when verifying a safety property without knowing the minimum bound in advance, incremental SAT solvers [18] try to check a series of SAT instances with increasing bounds. During the checking, the conflict clauses derived from small-bound SAT instances can be forwarded to large-bound SAT instances as assignment constraints. Such constraints can prune the search space. Hence the overall validation effort can be saved. To exploit more such constraints, Strichman [18] investigated the transition symmetry indicated in Equation (1). He found that conflict clauses derived only from transition relations can be replicated to further reduce the checking time. As an alternative, decision ordering [13] (e.g., VSIDS [14]) plays an important role in determining SAT searching performance, since it can be used to avoid long-distance backtracks when encountering a conflict [17]. To enable quick checking, Zhang et al. [21] proposed an approach which combines clever orchestration of decision ordering and learned information in an incremental framework for BMC. By analyzing the correlation among different SAT instances of a property, Wang et al. [20] used the unsatisfiable core of previously checked SAT instances to derive the decision ordering for unchecked SAT instances. Although all the above approaches can reduce the checking complexity, most of them focus on model checking rather than test generation.

Learning techniques have also been investigated in SAT-based verification and test generation. In [3], Chandrasekar and Hsiao presented an approach to generate tests for path-delay fault models. By dynamically excluding untestable paths, both static and dynamic learning can improve the test generation time. In [10], Lu et al. utilized the circuit topological information and signal correlations to enforce a decision ordering, which enables efficient solving of circuit-based SAT problems. When checking a large set of false properties, Chen and Mishra [4] proposed an approach that can identify the similarity between properties and cluster them together. By sharing the learnings derived from checked properties, the test generation time for the unchecked properties can be drastically reduced. However, the first property checking becomes a major bottleneck due to the lack of learning. To address this issue, they proposed a property decomposition method [6]. By achieving learnings from the spatially and temporally decomposed sub-properties, the test generation time of the original complex property can be reduced. However, the requirement of clear understanding of the structure and behavior information of both properties and designs limits the applicability of these approaches.

This paper is inspired by the intra-property learning approach presented in [5]. The basic idea of [5] is to halve the checking SAT instance and solve one half first. By sharing the learning from the checked half, the test generation time of the original complex property can be reduced. However, this method does not fully investigate other potential learning objects as well as partition heuristics to further reduce the test generation time. To the best of our knowledge, most existing approaches exploit the learnings from a set of correlated properties or sub-properties to reduce test generation time. This paper presents a promising method which can obtain profitable self-learnings from various sources to improve the test generation time.

3. OUR APPROACH

Since our goal is to efficiently generate direct tests using BMC, our approach only focuses on safety properties. Although the bound determination is generally hard in BMC, for directed test generation, the bound can be estimated based on the structure of designs [4]. As shown in Equation (1), BMC encodes a property checking problem into a SAT instance. One satisfying assignment of this SAT instance can be used as a test to activate the property. Therefore the efficiency of the search for a satisfying assignment determines the performance of directed test generation.

Ideally, optimal SAT solvers can find a satisfying assignment without making any decision mistakes. However, such kinds of solvers do not exist. Currently, most SAT solvers adopt the Davis-Putnam-Logemann-Loveland (DPLL) procedure [8] which is widely recognized as an efficient approach in practical searching.

```
while (1){
        run_periodic_functions();
        if (decide_next_branch()) {
            while (deduce() == CONFLICT) {
                blevel = analyze_conflicts();
                if(blevel < 0)
                    return UNSAT;
            }
        }
        else return SAT;
}
```

Figure 1: DPLL search procedure

Figure 1 shows the skeleton of the DPLL implementation used in many SAT solvers, such as zChaff [14] and MiniSAT [15]. It contains three key parts which strongly affect the process of finding satisfying assignments.

- The function *decide_next_branch* decides Boolean variable values based on decision ordering, i.e., the priority of literals.
- The function *deduce* propagates the effect of the new variable assignment using the implication deduction.
- The function *analyze_conflict* removes the effect of variable assignment conflicts using proper backtracks. It marks the reason of a conflict and creates a constraint (i.e., conflict clauses) to avoid the same conflict in future processing.

In most DPLL-based approaches, the decision of next branch is mainly based on the CNF statistics, which cannot properly give a satisfying variable assignment prediction in many situations. Therefore, SAT search performance can be easily deteriorated because of bad decisions, especially in the following two scenarios: i) when a large number of implications are involved between an early incorrect decision and a late conflict, a costly *long distance backtrack* is needed to resolve the conflict, and ii) the *satisfying assignment convergence* will be disturbed due to frequent bad decisions. If all these two scenarios can be avoided during the DPLL search, the test generation time can be drastically improved.

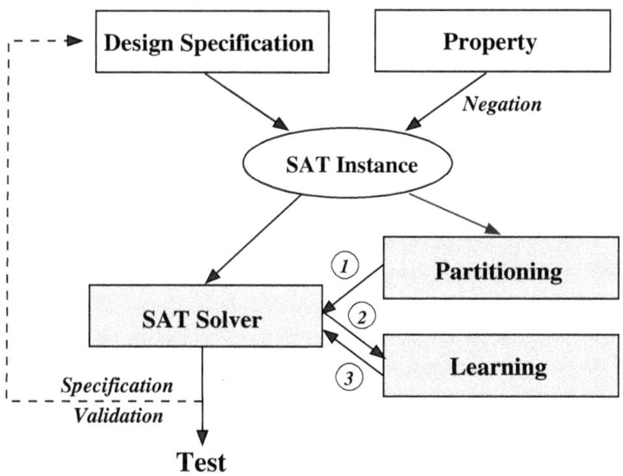

Figure 2: The workflow of our method

This paper presents an approach which adopts self-learning techniques to efficiently address the above two issues. Figure 2 shows the workflow of our method. Firstly, the design specification and a checking property are encoded into a SAT instance. Then the SAT instance is divided into small pieces (indicated by ①) using our partitioning heuristics. By the local search on these small pieces of CNF clauses, proper self-learnings (indicated by ②) can be achieved with much lower cost compared to the original SAT instance checking. However, such accumulated learnings (indicated by ③) are profitable, since it can effectively reduce the chance of both long-distance backtracks and bad decision ordering predictions when processing the unchecked parts. Therefore the overall test generation time can be drastically reduced.

3.1 Self-Learning Objects

Due to lack of external learning sources, our approach tries to exploit learnings from the checking SAT instances to enable quick test generation. It is required that self-learnings are of high quality that can efficiently reduce the chance of long-distance backtracks and bad variable assignment decision as much as possible. Since conflict clauses can be used as guards to avoid specific variable assignment, it is a promising candidate of self-learning. As well, decision ordering heuristics can be utilized as another self-learning to guide the prediction of satisfying variable assignment. However, due to the indistinct study objects, the quality and the effectiveness of self-learnings in traditional SAT search are not well studied. In the context of test generation, the capabilities of both self-learnings are limited. If the learning object is set to avoid long-distance backtracks and accelerate satisfying assignment convergence, the potential of both self-learnings can be further exploited. The following sub-sections present what are good objects for high quality self-learning derivation.

3.1.1 Learn from the Structure of BMC Formulas

The structure information of BMC formulas is a good source to achieve self-learnings. Assume that *prop* is a safety property for design M and it fails at the n_{th} clock cycle. According to the formula shown in Equation (1), the SAT instance for *prop* can be decomposed into three parts, $I = I(s_0)$, $T = \bigwedge_{i=0}^{n-1} T(s_i,s_{i+1})$ and $P = \bigvee_{i=0}^{n} \neg prop(s_i)$. It is important to note that T only constructs the links between states from s_0 to s_n without any explicit variable assignment constraints. When a bad decision is made for a variable, its effect can be propagated along one transition path easily by deduction. If a large number variables are involved in the deduction through the media T, the corresponding backtracking will be costly, since the rollback will cancel all assignments for these variables.

Figure 3 shows two examples which can easily cause conflicts during the SAT search for *prop*. As shown in Figure 3a), a transition variable V in clock cycle k ($0 < k \leq n$) is determined first. Through the deduction on other transition variables of T, its effect will be propagated to either the part of I or the part of P. Since both I and P indicate strong constraints for state variable assignments, when the deduction arrives, it often causes an assignment conflict, i.e., $\neg V$. If the clock cycle k is far away from the the part of I or P, a long-distance backtrack to resolve the conflict is inevitable. As an extreme case shown in Figure 3b), a variable V which belongs to the n_{th} clock cycle is decided in an early stage. Due to lack of disturbance from the constraints imposed by transitions, the effect of the assignment can be propagated easily to the other end, i.e., I. Before encountering a conflict $\neg V$, there may be thousands of implications and new decisions made during this deduction process. Consequently resolving such a conflict is very costly.

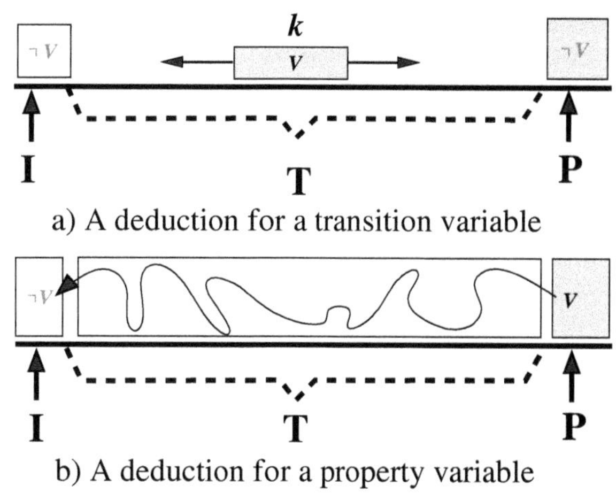

Figure 3: Two cases of variable deduction

From the above examples, we can find that there are two major reasons that lead to long-distance backtracks: i) the constraint imposed by the transition part T is weak; and ii) a bad decision is made too early but detected too late. To enforce constraints on the transition part T, one applicable way is to instrument some local guards along the transition path, which can block the potential long-distance backtracks in an early stage. To improve the accuracy of Boolean variable assignment decisions in the mean time, proper heuristics should be applied. By our observation, conflict clause and decision ordering are two promising self-learning candidates to address the above two problems.

Conventional DPLL-based learnings cannot be directly applied to solve the long-distance backtracks. Since the learning object in conventional SAT searching is the whole SAT instance, the derived conflict clauses act like global improvisatory guards to avoid the second occurrence of the same conflicts. However, it cannot prevent long-distance backtracks in a proactive manner. In addition, traditional VSIDS-based decision ordering is derived according to the statistics of CNF clauses without considering BMC structure information, which results in inaccuracy in decision ordering prediction.

Unlike conventional methods, we set the learning object to a small part of the checking SAT instance. In our method, the SAT instance is divided into several smaller parts as described in Section 3.2. By checking each of them against the constraints of both I and P, some "local" self-learnings can be achieved and applied on the original SAT instance. The collected conflict clauses can be used as local guards of transitions at different clock cycle. It can effectively break down the route of long-distance backtracks. As well, since the small SAT piece indicates the partial behavior of the original SAT instance, its satisfying result can be useful to guide the decision ordering prediction on the original SAT instance. These ideas may have the effect of improving the convergence rate of the SAT search.

3.1.2 Learn from the Structure of CNF Clauses

SAT search heuristics based on CNF structure have been widely investigated. However, most of them focus on deriving decision ordering based on literal and clause statistics as well as variable dependence. Few of them utilize the CNF structure to guide the conflict clause generation to enable efficient search space pruning. Alternatively, this paper takes the clause size into account to derive high-quality conflict clauses. Since smaller conflict clauses can prune more search space, the size of a conflict clause determines its quality. If the derived conflict clauses are of small size, the test generation time can be improved.

For test generation, a SAT instance may consist of a large set of CNF clauses. If all the CNF clauses are of small size, generally the SAT search will be terminated in a reasonable time. This is because, during the SAT search of small-size clauses, the impact of a variable decision can be instantly propagated so that variable assignment conflicts can be detected quickly. That means, due to the strict constraints imposed by small clauses, only a few new decision levels are involved between the level of decisions and the level of the corresponding conflict. Therefore, the long-distance backtracks can be effectively avoided. In addition, since the number of backtracked levels determines the conflict clause size, the derived conflict clauses are more likely to be of small size. Consequently, the SAT search space can be efficiently pruned due to the high quality of the derive learnings.

However, most practical SAT searches encounter a mixture of CNF clauses with both large and small size. The existence and introduction of large clauses can strongly affect the SAT search performance. The following is an example using a SAT instance segment:

$$\ldots(y \vee x_1 \vee x_2 \ldots \vee x_k) \wedge (\neg y \vee x_1 \vee x_2 \ldots \vee x_k \vee z_1 \vee z_2 \ldots \vee z_j)\ldots$$

When adopting the decision sequence $\neg z_1, \neg z_2, \ldots, \neg z_j, \neg x_1, \neg x_2, \ldots, \neg x_k$, a conflict of y's assignment happens. To resolve such conflict, a cancel of $k+j$ decision levels may be needed, which involves a large set of determined Boolean variables in these levels. Moreover, to avoid such scenario again, a conflict clause $(x_1 \vee x_2 \ldots \vee x_k \vee z_1 \vee z_2 \ldots \vee z_j)$ will be generated. Since SAT solvers are not sensitive to large conflict clauses, the influence of such a conflict clause is negligible in most scenarios.

Few of existing SAT solvers try to reduce the chance of large conflict clause generation in a proactive manner. Most of them drop large conflict clauses on-the-fly during the SAT search, which is a waste of validation effort. However, learning directly from the original SAT instance cannot affect the size of conflict clauses. So we adopt the similar strategy as the heuristic proposed in Section 3.1.1. The basic assumption is that a set of small CNF clauses has a high chance to derive small-size conflict clauses. The small CNF clauses of a large SAT instance can be grouped and check together first. The achieved small-size conflict clauses put stricter restrictions during the SAT search, which can efficiently avoid long-distance backtracks. In addition, the satisfying assignment for the small clause group is also a promising source for deriving decision ordering for the original SAT instance.

3.2 Learning Oriented Partitioning Heuristics

Deriving self-learnings directly from a SAT instance is costly. In our approach, a SAT instance is partitioned into small parts and self-learnings can be achieved from them with low overhead. By combining the local learnings together, we can economically form a "global" learning to accelerate the original SAT searching.

3.2.1 Segmental Partitioning

When handling a large SAT instance as a whole, the effect of a bad decision may propagate to a large range. The interleaving of a large quantity of implications and decisions will postpone the conflict detection. Although conflict clauses can prune the search space, it cannot actively reduce the occurrences of long-distance backtracks. To reduce the chance of long-distance backtracks, we developed the segmental partitioning approach which utilizes self-learnings to prevent long-distance backtracks. By dividing the original SAT instance into several segments with equal size and checking each of them separately, we can achieve both local conflict clause and partial decision ordering based learnings in a short time due to the small size of the learning objects.

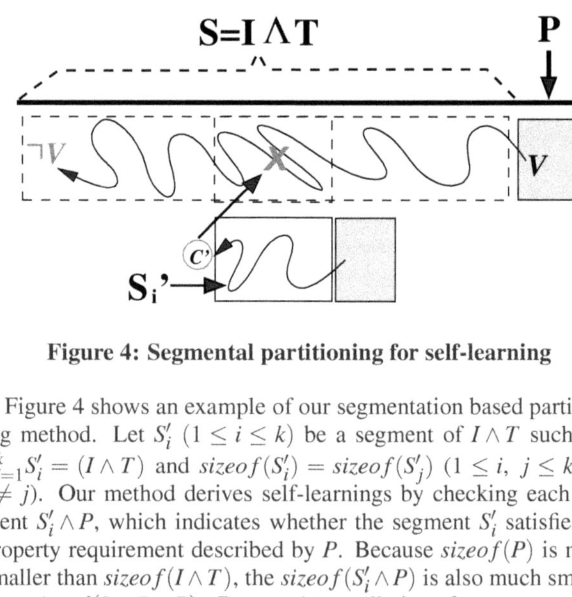

Figure 4: Segmental partitioning for self-learning

Figure 4 shows an example of our segmentation based partitioning method. Let S'_i $(1 \leq i \leq k)$ be a segment of $I \wedge T$ such that $\Sigma_{i=1}^{k} S'_i = (I \wedge T)$ and $sizeof(S'_i) = sizeof(S'_j)$ $(1 \leq i,\ j \leq k$ and $i \neq j)$. Our method derives self-learnings by checking each segment $S'_i \wedge P$, which indicates whether the segment S'_i satisfies the property requirement described by P. Because $sizeof(P)$ is much smaller than $sizeof(I \wedge T)$, the $sizeof(S'_i \wedge P)$ is also much smaller than $sizeof(I \wedge T \wedge P)$. Due to the small size of a segment, self-learnings in the form of conflict clauses and decision orderings can be derived in a short time. In addition, such learnings are very beneficial. By enhancing the variable assignment restrictions on segment S'_i, the derived conflict clauses can be used as local guards to block implications which traverse through this segment. Therefore many long-distance backtracks in the original SAT instance can be efficiently blocked. For example, in Figure 4, the conflict clause C' derived from $S_i' \wedge P$ can be used as a local guard to block a long-distance backtrack which happens in the original SAT instance checking. Furthermore, since $S_i' \wedge P$ is a part of $I \wedge T \wedge P$, the derived satisfying assignment for $S_i' \wedge P$ may have a large overlap with the partial satisfying assignment for $I \wedge T \wedge P$. Thus, the variable assignment for $S_i' \wedge P$ can be used as a learning to tune the decision ordering of the original SAT instance.

3.2.2 Incremental Partitioning

Segmental partition focuses on preventing long-distance backtracks by establishing local guards during the searching. However, the self-learnings derived using this method only have a local view, especially for the decision ordering based learnings.

When composing the satisfying assignments of all segments, conflicts arise due to the lack of global view. In addition, the conflict clauses derived from the local segments may neglect the long-distance backtracks which only happen in the global search. Therefore it is necessary to find a solution which takes both local and global views into account.

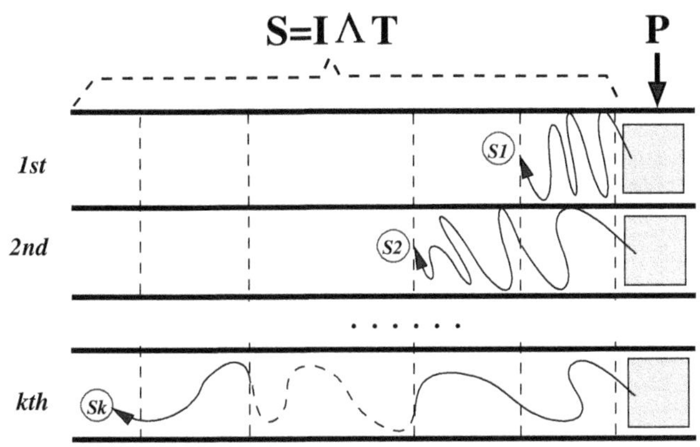

Figure 5: Incremental partitioning for self-learning

Figure 5 presents our incremental approach which can approximate the search range gradually to the original SAT instance. Assume that $I \wedge T$ is divided into k parts (i.e., s_1, s_2, ..., s_k) with same size. The incremental approach does k iterations to achieve a satisfying assignment for the SAT instance. The first iteration checks $s_1 \wedge P$, which is similar to the segmentation method. However, the second iteration checks $s_1 \wedge s_2 \wedge P$, which doubles the size of the non-property part. In our incremental method, the learnings derived from the first iteration are forwarded to help the second iteration checking. Thus the SAT checking time in the second iteration can be drastically reduced. The following iterations deal with the remaining parts with increasing size in the same way until the $(k-1)_{th}$ iteration. Finally, the k_{th} iteration checks the original SAT based on learnings from all previous $k-1$ iterations. Since the larger SAT instance checking is based on the smaller SAT instance checking, the overhead for incremental process is small. However, the accumulated self-learnings in all iterations can drastically improve the overall SAT checking time.

3.2.3 Clause Size Aware Partitioning

As described in Section 3.1.2, the clause size determines the quality of the conflict clauses based self-learning. To guarantee the high quality of the derived self-learning, we develop the clause size aware partitioning strategy which can make the size of derived conflict clauses as small as possible. The implementation of clause size aware partitioning is similar to the incremental partitioning. The only difference is that the SAT instance is partitioned based on the size of clauses rather than the temporal order of transitions.

Figure 6 shows our clause size aware partitioning approach. Let k be the step size chosen to partition $I+T$. $(I+T)_{1..k}$ indicates the set of clauses in $I+T$ which have a size between 1 and k. In an incremental order, $P+(I+T)_{1..k}$ is checked first. Based on the profitable learning from the checked part, checking $P+(I+T)_{1..2k}$ becomes easier. Assume that the iteration has n steps. In the $(n-1)_{th}$ step, $P+(I+T)_{1..(n-1)k}$ will be checked. And all the learnings collected during the $(n-1)$ iterations will be forwarded to help the checking of $I+T+P$. Since the derived small conflict clauses are with strict constraints on variable assignments, it can effectively prevent the long-distance backtracks. Therefore the overall SAT performance can be improved.

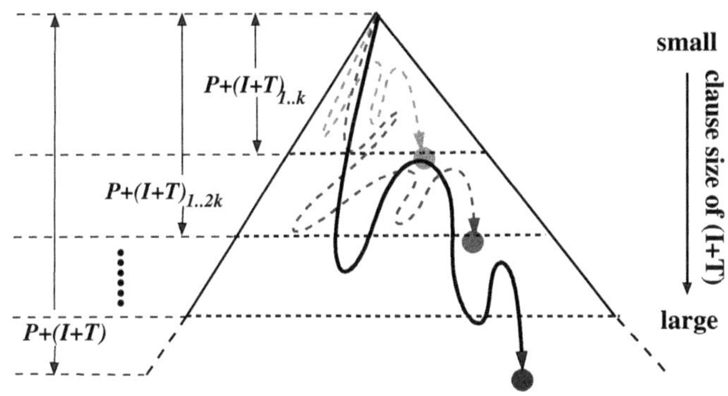

Figure 6: Clause size aware partitioning for self-learning

3.3 Self-Learning Based Test Generation

Test generation using SAT-based BMC focuses on how to efficiently achieve satisfying assignments quickly. Our test generation approach tries to exploit self-learnings to boost the SAT solving using both conflict clauses and decision orderings.

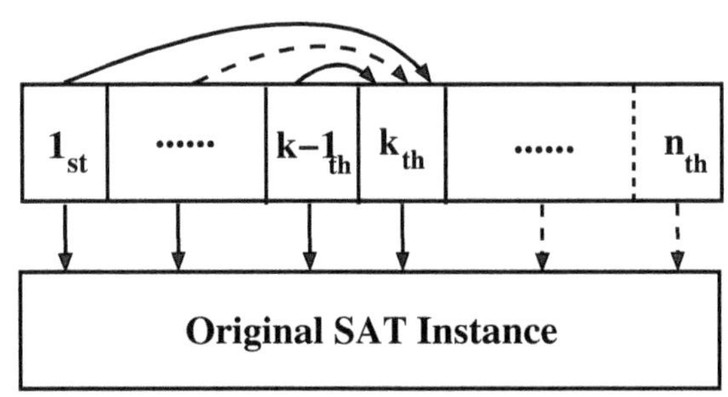

Figure 7: Conflict clause forwarding pattern

In our test generation framework, we collect all the conflict clauses during the checking iterations for partitions. Figure 7 shows our conflict clause forwarding pattern. When handling test generation with n partitions, our method uses an array *lBucket*$[n]$ of n learning buckets to store conflict clause base learnings. It is important to note that the k_{th} $(1 < k \leq n)$ partition checking is guided by the learning stored in *lBucket*$[1..k-1]$, i.e., the learning derived from previous $k-1$ partitions. Therefore the checking time of the k_{th} partition can be drastically reduced. Finally all the learnings collected from each partition checking are applied on the original SAT instance checking. Compared to the original SAT instance checking, the time of self-learning derivation process can be negligible. However, the achieved self-learnings are profitable, which can drastically reduce the complexity of the original SAT instance checking.

Decision ordering is another kind of self-learning to accelerate test generation in our approach. Since each partition is a subset of the original SAT instance, it indicates partial behavior of the original SAT instance. Therefore, the intermediate satisfying results for the partitions may have a large overlap with the original SAT instance on satisfying variable assignments. In our approach, under the help of intermediate satisfying results, the decision ordering of the unchecked partitions is affected and gradually tuned by the results of checked partitions. If all the collected information can be used to derive decision ordering for the original SAT instance, the test generation time can be drastically reduced.

Let $vStat[sz][2]$ (sz is the number of variables in the original SAT instance) be a 2-dimensional array which stores the accumulative results for the checked partitions. Initially the value of all the elements of $vStat[sz][2]$ are 1. After checking one partition, the value of $vStat$ will be updated. Assume that the k_{th} partition is the latest checked part. If the variable v_i is involved in the evaluation and its value is 1, then $vStat[i][1]$ will be increased by 1. If the variable v_i is involved in the evaluation and its value is 0, then $vStat[i][2]$ will be increased by 1. Otherwise, $vStat[i][\,]$ will remain unchanged.

In this paper, we investigate two different SAT solvers - zChaff [16] and MiniSAT [15], which adopt different decision ordering heuristics. zChaff supports the VSIDS heuristic, which calculates the score (i.e., priority) for each literal l dynamically. Initially, the *score(l)* equals to the literal count in the SAT instance. Then during the SAT search, after a certain number of backtracks, *score(l)* will be updated in the period function using the following formula

$$score(l) = score(l)/2 + new\_conflict\_count(l) \qquad (2)$$

where *new_conflict_count(l)* is the number of newly added conflict clauses which contain literal l since last update. Based on the VSIDS framework, our method incorporates the learning information from $vStat[sz][2]$. Instead of replacing the Equation (2), at the initialization of SAT searching and periodic score decaying, our method first calculates the literal score using the Equation (2) followed by the Equation (3):

$$score(l_i) = \begin{cases} max(v_i) + step & (vStat[i][1] > vStat[i][2] \& l_i = v_i) \\ & or (vStat[i][1] < vStat[i][2] \& l_i = v_i') \\ score(l_i) & otherwise \end{cases} \qquad (3)$$

where $max(v_i) = MAX(score(v_i), score(v_i'))$ and the value of $step$ is determined by the type of partitioning. For segmental partitioning, $step$ is set to be 1 since all the partitions have the similar size. When adopting incremental or clause size aware partitioning heuristics, the result of later checked partition will be more approximate to a satisfying assignment of the original SAT instance. In this case, $step$ is set to be k when handling the k_{th} partition, since it can reflect the importance of later checked partitions.

Similar to zChaff, MiniSAT employs a variant of the VSIDS heuristic. However, MiniSAT does not support explicit ordering for literals. It only keeps activity scores for variables and clauses, which cannot be used to predict the variable polarities (i.e., Boolean values of variables). Based on the statistics collected in $vStat$, if a variable has not been determined yet, its polarity can be predicted at the beginning and the restart of the search using the following formula:

$$polarity(v_i) = \begin{cases} true & (vStat[i][1] > vStat[i][2]) \\ false & (vStat[i][1] < vStat[i][2]) \\ skip & (vStat[i][1] = vStat[i][2]) \end{cases} \qquad (4)$$

Algorithm 1 describes our self-learnings based test generation approach. The algorithm has three inputs: i) a formal model of the design; ii) a specified property and its minimum satisfiable bound; and iii) the partition strategy and the number of partitions. The first step initializes the learning buckets $lBucket[n]$ with no learnings and resets the elements of $vStat[sz][2]$ with all 1s. Step 2 encodes the property falsification into a SAT instance in CNF format, and step 3 divides the CNF clauses into n partitions using the specified partitioning strategy. Then the following iterations try to collect both conflict clause and decision ordering based learnings. In the i_{th} iteration, step 4 checks the i_{th} partition based on the accumulative learnings derived from all previous $i-1$ iterations. Step 5 collects the conflict clause based self-learning derived in i_{th} iteration and save it in $lBucket[i]$. Step 6 updates the decision ordering based learning using $vStat[sz][2]$. Step 7 checks the original SAT instance using both the learnings from $lBucket[1..n]$ and $vStat[sz][2]$. Finally, the algorithm reports a test t_P to falsify the property P.

Algorithm 1: *Test Generation using Self-Learnings*
Inputs: i) Formal model of the design, D
    ii) Property P with a satisfiable bound $bound_P$
    iii) Partitioning type $type$ and the number of partitions n
Outputs: A test t_P to falsify P
Begin
  1. Initialize $lBucket[1..n]$ and $vStat[1..sz][\,]$;
  2. $CNF = BMC(D, P, bound_P)$;
  3. $\{p_1, p_2, \ldots, p_n\}$ = Partition(CNF, $type$, n);
  for i is from 1 to n do
    4. $(assign_i, conf_i)$ = SAT(p_i, $lBucket[1..i-1]$, $vStat$);
    5. $lBucket[i] = conf_i$;
    6. **for** j is from 1 to sz do
      if $(assign_i[j] == 0)$
        $vStat[j][2]++$;
      else if $(assign_i[j] == 1)$
        $vStat[j][1]++$;
    endfor
  endfor
  7. $(t_P,)$ = SAT(CNF, $lBucket[1..n]$, $vStat$);
  return t_P
End

4. EXPERIMENTS

By applying our proposed self-learning techniques, this section presents the results of the benchmarks from two different sources: i) a set of SAT instances derived from a VLIW MIPS processor [6] and a stock exchange system OSES [23]; and ii) a set of SAT instances from 10 buggy variants of 12-pipelined processors named *PIPE-SAT-1.1* [19]. All such SAT instances are pre-determined to be satisfiable. The first benchmark set is generated by the BMC tool NuSMV [11]. Although the second benchmark is not generated by any BMC tools, our approach can also be applied to derive corresponding tests quickly. To evaluate the applicability of our approach on unsatisfiable SAT instances, we also conducted the experiment on a set of bigger variants of the pipe_ooo benchmarks named *PIPE-OOO-UNSAT-1.1* provided in [19]. We modified both the SAT solvers MiniSAT-2.2 [15] and zChaff [16] to incorporate our proposed partitioning and learning techniques. In these experiments, all the partitioning heuristics divide SAT instances into 4 partitions. Based on the experimental results of [9], for self-learnings, we only forward conflict clauses whose size is smaller than 9. The experimental results are obtained on a Linux PC with 3.3GHz AMD FX-6100 processors and 4 GB RAM.

Table 1: Test Generation Results for DLX Processor and OSES

SAT Instance	MiniSAT[15] /zChaff[16]	Segmental Partitioning ([15]/[16])			Incremental Partitioning ([15]/[16])			C. S. A. Partitioning ([15]/[16])			Max Speedup
		cls	var	cls+var	cls	var	cls+var	cls	var	cls+var	
DLX-1	1.9/104.5	3.6/72.8	4.3/22.2	**3.3**/23.0	4.6/133.4	4.9/28.6	3.7/24.6	3.5/23.1	4.3/6.7	3.4/**6.2**	0.6/16.9
DLX-2	1.5/58.0	3.5/58.5	3.3/20.8	**3.1**/19.0	4.3/90.0	4.5/19.1	3.8/13.9	3.8/35.3	4.1/9.5	3.2/**5.7**	0.5/10.2
DLX-3	0.8/32.4	1.7/26.3	2.1/12.7	**1.6**/15.2	2.1/189.2	2.0/8.7	2.0/11.8	1.9/16.9	2.1/5.0	1.8/**3.2**	0.5/10.1
DLX-4	0.2/2.1	0.5/2.4	0.6/0.8	0.5/**0.5**	0.7/1.5	0.6/0.7	**0.5**/0.6	0.5/1.4	0.5/0.8	0.5/0.7	0.4/4.2
DLX-5	0.6/7.9	1.3/6.1	1.3/4.2	1.3/3.8	1.4/9.6	1.5/4.9	1.2/2.8	1.1/6.6	1.3/2.9	**1.0/2.7**	0.6/2.9
DLX-6	1.1/101.3	2.6/105.0	3.0/35.5	2.7/31.0	3.2/106.1	2.8/27.2	2.9/25.6	2.6/71.7	2.6/3.7	**2.3/2.9**	0.5/34.9
OSES-1	0.6/5.5	**0.3**/0.6	0.4/18.5	0.4/4.2	0.3/6.3	0.4/1.7	0.3/0.8	0.4/1.0	0.4/**0.5**	0.4/0.7	2.0/11.0
OSES-2	0.6/209.3	**0.5**/80.2	2.1/200.1	0.9/290.6	2.2/131.1	1.6/177.6	1.1/249.0	1.1/246.6	2.3/73.1	1.0/**24.8**	1.2/8.4
OSES-3	4.7/121.7	1.7/89.8	9.5/181.5	1.0/238.9	**0.9**/89.5	2.0/140.8	9.2/269.5	1.9/74.5	1.3/**6.7**	5.4/35.3	5.2/18.2
OSES-4	0.9/28.8	3.5/47.3	7.9/91.4	4.0/99.6	4.0/39.0	3.4/45.2	**1.0**/8.7	5.1/36.4	18.6/**0.8**	5.0/0.9	0.9/32.0
OSES-5	0.1/21.8	**0.2**/20.2	0.3/8.8	0.3/5.2	0.6/12.0	0.3/3.5	0.4/2.7	0.4/21.1	0.3/**0.6**	0.3/0.7	0.5/36.3
OSES-6	0.9/53.8	**0.3**/74.4	0.4/76.5	0.4/67.4	0.7/122.8	0.5/15.2	0.7/78.8	1.2/136.4	1.4/**1.7**	1.5/2.3	3.0/31.6

4.1 Checking BMC-Based SAT Instances

In this case study, we derive tests to validate two designs. The first one is a VLIW MIPS processor with five-stage pipelines. The main testing target is to investigate all the interactions between pipeline paths (i.e., ALU, DIV, FADD and MUL). The second design is an on-line stock exchange system (OSES), which mainly deals with various transactions of customers' orders (market orders and limit orders).

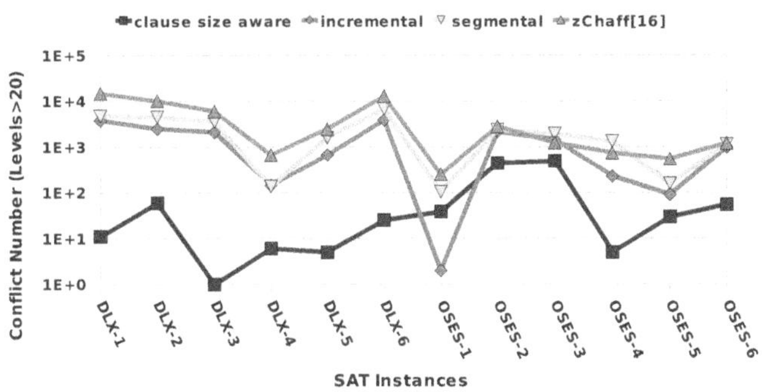

(a) The statistics of canceled levels

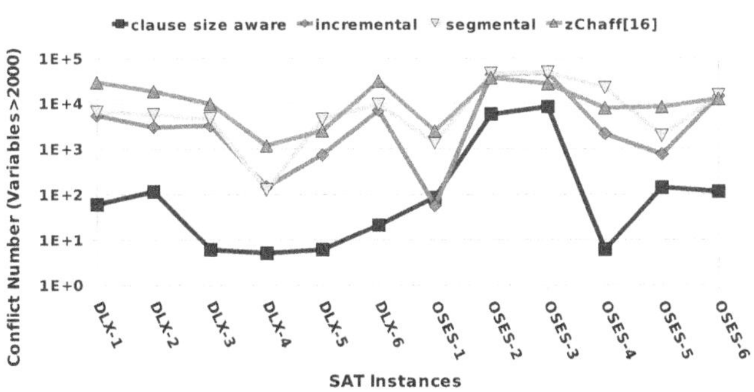

(b) The statistics of canceled variable assignments

Figure 8: Backtrack analysis for Table 1

Table 1 shows the test generation details of both designs using various self-learning heuristics. Due to the limit of the space, we only choose 6 typical tests for each design. All the other remaining tests show the similar results. In Table 1, the first column shows the index of SAT instances. For columns 2-11, we use the notation *MiniSAT/zChaff* to denote the test generation time (in seconds) using MiniSAT [15] and zChaff [16] respectively. The column 2 presents the test generation result without any improvement. Columns 3-5 present the result of segmental partitioning using different kinds of self-learnings. Column 3 shows the result only using conflict clauses based learning. Column 4 utilizes decision ordering as its single self-learning. Column 5 combines both learnings to further improve the checking performance. Similarly, columns 6-8 and columns 9-11 indicate the test generation time using incremental and clause size aware partitioning strategies individually with different self-learnings. For each SAT instance, we mark the best test generation time in bold font. It is important to note that all the results in columns 3-11 include the overhead of learning derivation. The final column presents the speedup of our methods over unmodified MiniSAT and zChaff solvers respectively using the following formula:

$$max\_speedup = \frac{column2}{MIN(column3,\ column4,\ \ldots,\ column11)} \quad (5)$$

In this benchmark, it can be found that the self-learnings do not take the effect in MiniSAT searching in most cases, since the test generation time using MiniSAT without learnings is already small enough (i.e., smaller than 1 second). The introduction of extra learnings may degrade the search performance. However, the self-learnings are still effective for MiniSAT in the complex scenarios. For example, in the case of OSES-3, we can achieve 5.2 times improvement with self-learnings. Unlike MiniSAT, zChaff needs more time to derive tests in this benchmark. It is important to note that in this case our self-learning techniques can reduce the test generation time drastically. Especially the clause size aware partitioning method is best suited to this benchmark. When employing clause size aware partitioning heuristic, 5 out of 12 SAT instances can achieve the minimum test generation time by using decision ordering based self-learning only, and 6 out of 12 SAT instance can achieve the minimum test generation time because of the synergy of different kinds of learnings. By using our self-learning approaches in zChaff, a 3-37 times improvement can be achieved.

In the experiment, we assume that a long-distance backtrack involves a rollback with more than 20 decision levels or a cancel of more than 2000 variable assignments. Since zChaff needs more test generation time in this benchmark, the effect of our self-learnings can be observed more easily. Figure 8 analyzes the long-distance backtrack details for Table 1 using zChaff with different partitioning heuristics. For each partitioning method, we only investigated the composite learning using both conflict clauses and decision orderings. For each SAT instance, Figure 8a) counts the conflicts which require backtracks with more than 20 decision levels, and Figure 8b) indicates the number of conflicts which involve cancels of more than 2000 variable assignments. The result shows that,

Table 2: Test Generation Results for PIPE Processors

SAT Instance	MiniSAT[15] /zChaff[16]	Segmental Partitioning ([15]/[16])			Incremental Partitioning ([15]/[16])			C. S. A. Partitioning ([15]/[16])			Max Speedup
		cls	var	cls+var	cls	var	cls+var	cls	var	cls+var	
PIPE1	12/854	28/488	234/761	190/572	8/507	**1**/242	**1**/924	26/844	2/**7**	2/8	12.0/122.0
PIPE2	1/1090	**1**/2085	**1**/421	**1/1**	11/943	**1**/174	**1**/217	**1**/1124	**1**/11	**1**/11	1.0/1090.0
PIPE3	15/524	8/879	169/1185	144/1495	8/692	**1**/521	1/**142**	16/707	4/276	4/276	15.0/3.7
PIPE4	6/670	36/77	1055/162	**1**/12	5/311	NA/**4**	118/4	18/684	2/237	2/236	6.0/167.5
PIPE5	5/395	2/1345	3/2544	2/2613	9/90	2/595	10/1240	16/401	**2/55**	4/**55**	2.5/7.2
PIPE6	1/1	**1**/98	4/106	11/55	1/2	2/122	4/142	**1/1**	**1/1**	**1/1**	1.0/1.0
PIPE7	13/1117	284/505	322/2069	112/1184	450/681	6/1188	**4**/162	13/1059	4/**38**	4/39	3.3/29.4
PIPE8	2/73	**6/1**	44/69	91/61	7/110	NA/75	NA/76	9/73	**6**/30	11/30	0.3/73
PIPE9	30/3897	32/2522	2/404	2/**395**	43/421	3/1295	**1**/964	6/3874	1/1022	1/1020	30.0/9.9
PIPE10	174/907	112/647	672/973	4/497	111/446	**2**/139	**2/118**	17/661	4/148	4/147	87.0/7.7

Table 3: SAT Solving Results for UNSAT Instances of PIPE Processors

SAT Instance	MiniSAT[15] /zChaff[16]	Segmental Partitioning ([15]/[16])			Incremental Partitioning ([15]/[16])			C. S. A. Partitioning ([15]/[16])			Max Speedup
		cls	var	cls+var	cls	var	cls+var	cls	var	cls+var	
pipe2-ooo	0.3/0.06	0.1/**0.05**	**0.04**/0.08	0.05/0.09	0.1/0.06	0.1/0.10	0.1/0.10	0.3/0.08	0.1/0.19	0.1/0.13	7.5/1.2
pipe3-ooo	10.7/0.8	12.5/0.9	6.7/0.9	5.9/1.1	11.6/1.1	12.5/1.0	8.0/0.9	8.4/**0.8**	**0.8**/1.5	1.2/1.1	13.4/1.0
pipe4-ooo	94/6	142/4	118/3	111/4	114/**3**	77/4	197/4	50/6	13/5	**10**/5	9.4/2.0
pipe5-ooo	280/18	356/15	64/15	**47**/14	498/14	NA/12	1065/**11**	476/13	51/18	62/21	6.0/1.6
pipe6-ooo	731/69	NA/65	NA/64	NA/61	279/67	NA/50	NA/**48**	645/66	74/78	**70**/70	10.4/1.4
pipe7-ooo	1016/266	**702**/278	NA/285	NA/294	NA/303	NA/**199**	NA/208	NA/285	NA/304	NA/295	1.4/1.3
pipe8-ooo	NA/1107	NA/1330	NA/1083	NA/1104	NA/1387	NA/772	NA/**684**	NA/1326	NA/1354	NA/1334	1.4/1.6
pipe9-ooo	NA/1697	NA/1716	NA/1565	NA/1656	NA/1688	NA/**940**	NA/989	NA/1497	NA/2005	NA/1913	NA/1.8

compared to the method using zChaff, our self-learning techniques are effective to reduce the number of long-distance backtracks. Especially, the clause size aware partitioning approach achieves the best performance in most cases, which is consistent with the result presented in Table 1.

4.2 Checking Non-BMC-Based SAT Instances

Our approach can not only accelerate the test generation for SAT instances generated by BMC tools, but also it can be applied on SAT instances derived by other tools. Table 2 shows the test generation results for buggy variants of PIPE processors which are generated by a non-BMC tool [19]. The table structure is the same as the Table 1. The notation *NA* (i.e., INDETERMINATE) in the cells of the table indicates that the search run out of the specified memory when using the MiniSAT. In this case study, we can achieve an up to 87 times improvement using MiniSAT with our self-learning techniques. By using zChaff, we can achieve an up to 1090 times improvement, which is consistent with the results presented in Table 1. It can be observed that, although it cannot always achieve the best results, the clause size aware partition with composite learnings (i.e., column 11) outperforms other methods in most cases.

4.3 Discussion

From Section 4.1 and Section 4.2, we can find that MiniSAT needs less time than zChaff in test generation for both BMC-based and non-BMC-based methods. Since zChaff needs longer time for directed test generation, it implicitly needs to handle more long-distance backtracks during the SAT search. Therefore, we can clearly observe the effects (up to 1090 times improvement) of self-learning methods. As a state-of-art SAT solver, MiniSAT-2.2 can efficiently solve the simple SAT instances with less long-distance backtracks. But it does not mean that our self-learnings are not beneficial during the MiniSAT searching. In Table 2, we can find that the more complex the test generation problem is for MiniSAT, the more speedup can be achieved using our self-learning methods. For example, the test generation for PIPE10 costs 174 seconds without learnings, however by using the composite learnings as well as the incremental partitioning, the modified MiniSAT only needs 2 seconds to achieve the directed tests.

As shown in Section 4.1 and Section 4.2, the clause size aware partitioning coupled with the composite learning can achieve the best test generation time generally. However, no matter what SAT solvers are used for test generation, it is true that no single heuristic can guarantee the best performance for all cases. Resorting to the multi-processing capability is a feasible way to address this problem. Since most present computers have multiple cores, we can check a SAT instance with different partitioning approaches on different cores using the similar parallel strategy proposed in [9]. It means that if one of the cores finishes first, all the remaining SAT searches on the other cores can be terminated safely. In this way, we can always achieve the best test generation performance.

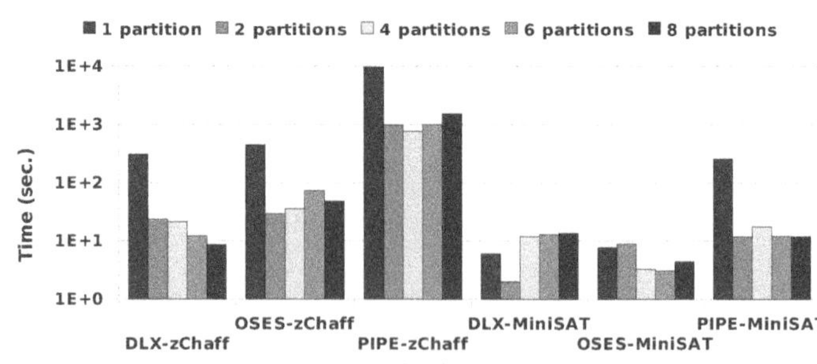

Figure 9: The analysis of the number of partitions

In our approach, the number of partitions plays an important role in determining the test generation time. We re-conducted all the benchmarks using both MiniSAT and zChaff with different number of partitions. Figure 9 shows the comparison results. The height of each bar in the figure indicates the overall minimum test generation time (i.e., the best one in all the 9 possible options as shown in columns 3-11 in Table 1 and Table 2) for all the SAT instances in the same benchmark. For example, the blue bar in the cluster *DLX-zChaff* indicates the overall minimum test generation time for all the 6 DLX SAT instances using zChaff. It can be found that MiniSAT generally needs less time than zChaff to derive tests. For MiniSAT, the approaches using 2 partitions or 4 partitions are good enough for test generation. And for zChaff, we can find that all the cases using 2, 4, 6, 8 partitions can achieve a drastic improvement for the three benchmarks. Especially, the methods using 4 partitions show a better performance for these three benchmarks.

Since our approach can effectively reduce long-distance backtracks, our self-learning can also be applied in the checking of UNSAT instances. We applied our self-learning and partition approaches on the *pipe_ooo* benchmarks generated by [19]. Here we only selected 8 out of 14 cases since the unselected ones cannot be solved by both MiniSAT and zChaff in one hour. Table 3 shows the checking result. Interestingly, we can find that zChaff outperforms MiniSAT in this benchmark, and our self-learning techniques can achieve an up to 13.4 times improvement.

5. CONCLUSIONS

Directed testing is promising for function validation, since coverage requirements can be achieved using fewer tests and less simulation effort. However, most automatic directed test generation methods, especially SAT-based approaches, are impeded by the state space explosion problem as well as the requirement of expert knowledge. This paper presented an efficient approach which utilizes our self-learning techniques to accelerate test generation. By exploiting high quality self-learnings to avoid long-distance backtracks and improve satisfying assignment convergence rate, the test generation time using SAT-based methods can be drastically reduced. Since our approach does not need the structure and behavior information of designs, it can be fully automated. The experimental results using various benchmarks demonstrated the effectiveness (by several orders of magnitude) of our approach.

6. ACKNOWLEDGEMENTS

This work was partially supported by the grants from Doctoral Fund of Ministry of Education of China 20110076120025, State High-Tech Development Plan of China 2011AA010101 and Natural Science Foundation of China 61021004, 90818024.

7. REFERENCES

[1] N. Amla, X. Du, A. Kuehlmann, R. P. Kurshan, and K. L. McMillan. An analysis of SAT-based model checking techniques in an industrial environment. In *Proceedings of Correct Hardware Design and Verification Methods (CHARME)*, pages 254–268, 2005.

[2] A. Biere, A. Cimatti, and E. M. Clarke. Bounded model checking. *Advances in Computers*, 58(3):118–149, 2003.

[3] K. Chandrasekar and M. S. Hsiao. Integration of learning techniques into incremental satisfiability for efficient path-delay fault test generation. In *Proceedings of Design, Automation and Test in Europe (DATE)*, pages 1002–1007, 2005.

[4] M. Chen and P. Mishra. Functional test generation using efficient property clustering and learning techniques. *IEEE Transactions on Computer-Aided Design of Integrated Circuits and Systems (TCAD)*, 29(3):396–404, 2010.

[5] M. Chen and P. Mishra. Property learning techniques for efficient generation of directed tests. *IEEE Transactions on Computers*, 60(6):852–864, 2011.

[6] M. Chen and P. Mishra. Decision ordering based property decomposition for functional test generation. In *Proceedings of Design, Automation and Test in Europe (DATE)*, pages 167–172, 2011.

[7] E. Clarke, O. Grumberg, and D. Peled. *Model Checking*. MIT Press, Cambridge, MA, 1999.

[8] M. Davis, G. Logemann, and D. W. Loveland. A machine program for theorem proving. *Communication of the ACM*, 5:394–397, 1962.

[9] Y. Hamadi, S. Jabbour and L. Sais. ManySAT: a parallel SAT solver. *Journal on Satisfiability, Boolean Modeling and Computation (JSAT)*, 6(4):245–262, 2009.

[10] F. Lu, Li-C. Wang, K. Cheng, and R. Huang. A circuit SAT solver with signal correlation guided learning. In *Proceedings of Design, Automation and Test in Europe (DATE)*, pages 10892–10897, 2003.

[11] NuSMV. Available from: http://nusmv.irst.itc.it/.

[12] S. Fine and A. Ziv. Coverage directed test generation for functional verification using bayesian networks. In *Proceedings of Design Automation Conference (DAC)*, pages 286–291, 2003.

[13] J. P. Marques-Silva and K. A. Sakallah. The impact of branching heuristics in propositional satisfiability. In *Proceedings of the 9th Portuguese Conference on Artificial Intelligence*, pages 62–74, 1999.

[14] M. W. Moskewicz, C. F. Madigan, Y. Zhao, L. Zhang, and S. Malik. Chaff: Engineering an efficient SAT solver. In *Proceeding of Design Automation Conference (DAC)*, pages 530–535, 2001.

[15] MiniSAT-2.2.0. Available from: http://minisat.se/.

[16] zChaff. Available from: http://www.princeton.edu/~chaff/zchaff.html.

[17] O. Strichman. Tuning SAT checkers for bounded model checking. In *Proceedings of Computer Aided Verification (CAV)*, pages 480–494, 2000.

[18] O. Strichman. Pruning techniques for the SAT-based bounded model checking problem. In *Proceedings of Correct Hardware Design and Verification Methods (CHARME)*, pages 58–70, 2001.

[19] M. N. Velev. Automatic abstraction of equations in a logic of equality. In *Proceedings of Automated Reasoning with Analytic Tableaux and Related Methods (TABLEAUX)*, pages 196–213, 2003.

[20] C. Wang, H. Jin, G. D. Hachtel, and F. Somenzi. Refining the SAT decision ordering for bounded model checking. In *Proceedings of Design Automation Conference (DAC)*, pages 535–538, 2004.

[21] L. Zhang, M. R. Prasad, and M. S. Hsiao. Incremental deductive & inductive reasoning for SAT-based bounded model checking. In *Proceedings of International Conference on Computer-Aided Design (ICCAD)*, pages 502–509, 2004.

[22] M. Chen, X. Qin, H. Koo and P. Mishra. *System-Level Validation: High-Level Modeling and Directed Test Generation Techniques*. Springer, 2012.

[23] M. Chen, X. Qiu, W. Xu, L. Wang, J. Zhao and X. Li. UML activity diagram-based automatic test case generation for Java programs. *The Computer Journal* , 52(5):545–556, 2009.

Using Static Analysis for Coverage Extraction from Emulation/Prototyping Platforms

Viraj Athavale*
Coordinated Sci. Lab.
University of Illinois at Urbana-Champaign
Urbana, IL 61801
athaval1@illinois.edu

Sam Hertz
Coordinated Sci. Lab.
University of Illinois at Urbana-Champaign
Urbana, IL 61801
slhertz2@illinois.edu

Darshan Jetly
Qualcomm Inc.
San Diego, CA 92121
djetly@qualcomm.com

Vijay Ganesan
Qualcomm Inc.
San Diego, CA 92121
vganesan@qualcomm.com

Jim Krysl
Qualcomm Inc.
San Diego, CA 92121
jkrysl@qualcomm.com

Shobha Vasudevan
Coordinated Sci. Lab.
University of Illinois at Urbana-Champaign
Urbana, IL 61801
shobhav@illinois.edu

ABSTRACT

Full-system emulation and prototyping is now being used widely in the industry for System-on-Chip (SoC) verification. Emulation/prototyping platforms run tests in a fraction of time compared to the traditional simulation based verification. However, unlike simulation, they do not provide visibility into the hardware design source code. As a result, they fail to provide any information about code coverage achieved, which is an important metric to measure the completeness of the verification process.

In this paper, we present a novel technique to extract code coverage from emulation/prototyping platforms. Through analysis of the source code for the hardware design, we relate the evaluation of branch conditions to other statements in the code. Evaluation of the branch conditions is recorded using additional logic during emulation, and mapped back to the code to obtain coverage information. We apply our technique to an industrial system, and show that it can efficiently provide code coverage statistics that are faithful to the coverage obtained from simulation. We also perform experiments on the publicly available OpenRISC processor and demonstrate similar results.

Categories and Subject Descriptors

B.5.2 [**Register-Transfer-Level Implementation**]: Design Aids—*Simulation, Verification*

General Terms

Algorithms, Performance, Verification

*The author is currently at Oracle Corp., Santa Clara, CA 95054 (viraj.athavale@oracle.com)

Keywords

Emulation, FPGA, Code Coverage, Static Analysis

1. INTRODUCTION

Today, verification consumes a considerable amount of resources in the System-on-Chip (SoC) development life cycle [1]. With increasingly complex SoCs and shorter times-to-market, over 70% of the engineering resources and time are spent on various forms of verification alone. Full-system simulation based verification with real-world workloads running on the underlying hardware designs has become extremely time consuming. Emulation/prototyping, such as that based on Field Programmable Gate Array (FPGAs) platforms, has emerged as a prominent technique to accelerate verification in recent years [2–5]. The primary motivation for using these alternative platforms is speed: runtime of a test during emulation is orders of magnitude lower compared to simulation [2]. For example, we found that for an industrial design, running a test in emulation was up to 360x faster than in simulation. The difference in runtimes becomes even more pronounced with increasing design complexity. As a result, some complex tests are run on emulators alone, due to extremely long simulation runtimes.

In the early (pre-silicon) stage of SoC development, hardware designs are described at the register-transfer level (RTL). The RTL design abstraction models hardware in terms of the flow of data between registers, and the logical operations performed on the data. Hardware Description Languages (HDLs) such as Verilog and VHDL that are employed for this purpose express the hardware behavior in a C-like design source code.

Traditional simulation based hardware verification involves applying a set of input vectors or *tests*[1] to the hardware designs described in HDLs. Various testbench checkers are employed during and at the end of each test to verify that the design functions according to the specification. Each test exercises a different execution of the design, and a design is correct if it behaves as required for all possible tests. Since checking all possible executions of a design is infeasible, a subset of tests is heuristically chosen for verification. If the tests fail to exercise some parts of the design, these parts re-

[1]Here we use *tests* to refer to input vectors applied to a design for the purpose of verification.

main untested, thus leading to low confidence in the verification process.

Since exhaustive testing is infeasible, the extent of coverage of a test is critical in evaluating the goodness of the test, as well as the verification progress. Various coverage metrics help in quantifying the exhaustiveness of verification. These metrics include code coverage, toggle coverage, functional coverage etc [6, 7]. *Code coverage* metrics measure the amount of RTL code executed while running a test. Among different types of code coverage, *statement coverage* denotes the fraction of statements executed. Nowadays code coverage is a key signoff criterion for tapeout in the hardware industry.

Simulation based verification, being a "white box" verification approach, has complete visibility into the design source code. Measuring code coverage during simulation is therefore relatively straightforward. On the other hand, during emulation/prototyping, the design is mapped to the underlying platform providing little or no visibility into the source code. Therefore, coverage measurement of a test when it is being emulated in a "black box" emulation environment remains a daunting challenge. To the best of our knowledge, no widely used method exists to achieve this.

In this work, we solve the important real-world problem of code coverage extraction from emulation/prototyping platforms. We mainly focus on the statement coverage metric. Our novel technique enables extraction of code coverage during full-system SoC emulation with minimal area overheads. Coverage of an emulation test extracted using our technique is shown to be faithful to that measured by running that test in the simulation environment. Furthermore, these results are demonstrated on an industrial design emulated on an FPGA platform.

Code coverage statistics are reported by most simulators either by adding code instrumentation (instrumentation based coverage analysis) or by analyzing the value change dumps produced during simulation (dumpfile based coverage analysis) [7]. In contrast, our technique is based on control and data flow analysis of the design source code treated as an "HDL program" [8,9]. Through such program analysis, we relate the evaluation of the branch conditions in the code to the execution of statements in the code. We add logic to record if the branch condition evaluates to true during emulation. If a condition evaluates to true during emulation, we conclude that the corresponding statements are executed. The recorded information is then used to derive statement coverage statistics. Thus, we use program analysis techniques on the design source code to make inferences about emulation behavior.

In order to analyze the design source code, we represent it as a control flow graph (CFG) augmented with limited data flow information. For each branch condition, we identify the set of statements such that the branch condition evaluating to true can help infer that these statements are executed. This set consists of the statements that must be executed *for* the condition to be true (*backward cone*) and the statements executed *due to* the condition evaluating to true (*forward cone*). This static analysis is performed in a way that the coverage from our technique closely approximates the statement coverage reported by a simulator. The static analysis is best suited for behavioral RTL code, where control flow is expressed in the form of `if` and `case` statements.

Extra logic is added to record evaluation of the branch conditions. During emulation, we use the added logic to identify the conditions that evaluate to true at least once during running of a test. This information is cross referenced with the source code to determine the statement coverage of the test.

The total area cost of the added logic is roughly proportional to the number of branch conditions whose evaluation is recorded. In order to keep the area overheads under control, we optimize the set of conditions according to user specified constraints, using a set-cover based approach. These "knobs" allow the user to make the best use of the resources available on the emulation platform.

We demonstrate our technique through experiments on (i) an industrial design and (ii) the OpenRISC processor [10], emulated on Xilinx FPGA platforms [11]. The runtime to generate coverage recording logic was within 30 seconds for both the designs with a few thousand lines of source code each, which shows that the technique is scalable and efficient. For the industrial design, the statement coverage reported using our technique is compared to that from an RTL simulator. We find that with around 10% FPGA usage overhead, the error in reported coverage by our technique is within 2% on average. Moreover, using optimization, the overhead can be reduced at the cost of slightly higher error.

Our contributions in this paper are as follows.

- We present a low overhead solution to the problem of code coverage extraction from full-system emulation/prototyping for SoC verification. Our results are faithful to the coverage obtained from standard simulation tools.
- We introduce an approach that employs program analysis techniques on the design source code to make inferences about emulation behavior.
- We provide a set-cover based optimization framework to reduce area overheads of the coverage extraction logic.

2. RELATED WORK

Some commercial approaches [12–14] have been proposed for code coverage extraction during emulation. However, these approaches do not use static analysis for this purpose, and add logic to explicitly record the execution of *each* statement. Through the CFG based coverage analysis, our technique relates the evaluation of the branch conditions to statements in the code, so that only branch condition evaluation needs to be recorded during emulation for coverage analysis. The optimization step further reduces this set of branch conditions whose evaluation is recorded. As a result, our technique is able to give statement coverage statistics with minimum overheads during emulation[2]. MBAC [15] generates hardware checkers that can check manually specified pre-silicon assertions during emulation. However, the checkers provide no information about code coverage.

Code coverage metrics in pre-silicon verification are largely derived from software testing [16], where the use of static analysis for efficient coverage instrumentation has also been studied to some extent [17, 18]. A recent work [19] uses these static analysis techniques derived directly from software to measure code coverage during post-silicon validation. We, on the other hand, adapt the static analysis to RTL semantics. For instance, the backward cone computation (Sec. 5.2.1), a part of our coverage analysis, involves a data flow analysis across the concurrent processes. Moreover, According to the conclusions in [19], the area overheads, even after optimizations, are found to be unacceptably high in practice. In our case, the overheads are acceptable, as area constraints in emulation/prototyping are typically not as stringent as in post-silicon validation.

[2] An experimental comparison to the VN-Cover Emulator tool [13] was not possible due to the unavailability of the tool.

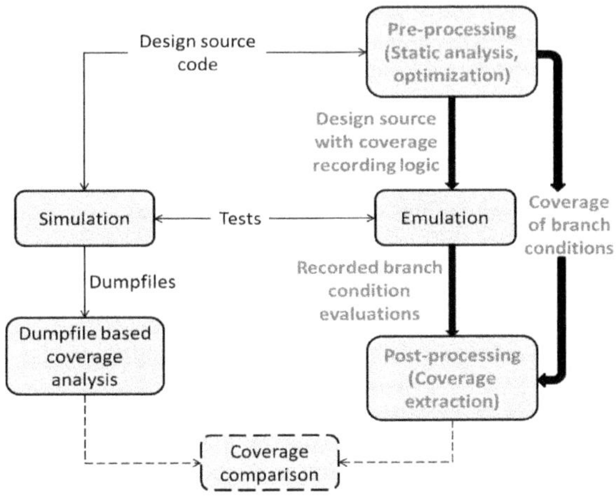

Figure 1: Overall flow of our technique (shown on the right), compared to the dumpfile based coverage flow of standard simulators (shown on the left). Components of our technique are shown in red. The coverage comparison block at the bottom of the figure is for validation purposes, and not a part of our technique.

3. METHODOLOGY OVERVIEW

Fig. 1 illustrates the overall flow of our technique, and compares it to the dumpfile based coverage analysis performed by standard simulators.

In our technique (shown on the right), a given design source code is first passed through the pre-processing step. In this step, static analysis is used to identify branch conditions, and to relate them to execution of statements. The set of branch conditions is then optimized according to user-specified coverage and size constraints. Finally, logic to record evaluation of the optimized set of branch conditions is added to the design. The design is then synthesized on the target emulation platform and a test is applied to it. In the post-processing step, code coverage statistics are derived from the information recorded during emulation, with the help of the coverage information for each branch condition as obtained from the pre-processing step.

For validating the coverage obtained by our technique, we compare it to the coverage reported by the simulator for the same test.

4. ILLUSTRATIVE EXAMPLE

We now present a simple example to motivate our static analysis based technique for coverage extraction from emulation. The Verilog RTL code for the example is shown in Figure 2.

```
1. assign z_o = z;
2. always @ (posedge clk)
3.    if (rst) begin
4.       state <= 0;
5.       z <= 0;
6.    end else
7.       case (state)
8.          0: state <= 1;
9.          1: z <= 1;
10.      endcase
```

Figure 2: Example Verilog code snippet. `clk`, `rst` are inputs, `state`, `z` are internal variables and `z_o` is an output.

Now suppose that this code is synthesized onto an emulation platform and a test is applied to it. Our aim is to find the statement coverage of the test i.e. determine the statements that are executed at least once during the emulation run.

A naïve approach to determine the statement coverage is to add logic to record if each statement is executed [12, 14]. Clearly, the approach is infeasible due to the prohibitive area overheads. The overheads can be greatly reduced by only recording the execution of certain key statements in the code, such that the execution of these statements can be used to infer the execution of other statements.

For example, let us assume that we record if the branch condition (`state = 1`) evaluated to true. Suppose we find that that the branch condition indeed evaluated to true at least once during emulation. From this single piece of information, we can infer the following:

(1) For `state` to have the value `1`, the assignment on line 8 must have been executed. Since this assignment is in turn conditioned on `state = 0`, the assignment on line 4 which assigns the initial value of `0` to `state` must have also been executed.

(2) The statement on line 9 must have been executed, since it is conditioned directly on the `state = 1` branch.

(3) Being a continuous assignment, the statement on line 1 must have been executed.

(4) The statement on line 5 must have been executed, since it is in the same basic block as line 4 and from (1), that line must have been executed.

Note that in this case, recording the evaluation of one branch condition can give us information about coverage of all the statements in the code. This hints at the effectiveness of branch conditions as key recording points for code coverage extraction.

The analysis presented above relates the evaluation of a branch condition to the execution of a set of statements. This information can be obtained from control and data flow based static analysis [20] of the Verilog RTL code. For instance, given that `state = 1`, we need to find the statement which assigns the value `1` to `state` (data flow). Also, we need to find the statements conditioned on `state = 1` (control flow). We employ a CFG framework augmented with limited data flow information (called *extended CFG* in this work) to facilitate this analysis.

5. METHODOLOGY

Fig. 3 illustrates the main steps in our technique. In this section, we describe each of these steps in detail.

5.1 Verilog Code as a Control Flow Graph

This section describes our extended CFG framework used to identify the branch conditions in the RTL source code for a design and perform the required static analysis tasks on the code. The framework is similar to the Process Dependence Graph described in [8].

Each statement in the code corresponds to a node in the extended CFG. An *assignment node* represents an assignment statement (a blocking or a non-blocking assignment in Verilog). A *decision node* represents conditional statements i.e. `if` and `case` statements. Edges in the CFG represent the control flow between statements. A *basic block* [21] denotes a sequence of assignment statements in the code that does not pass through any branches.

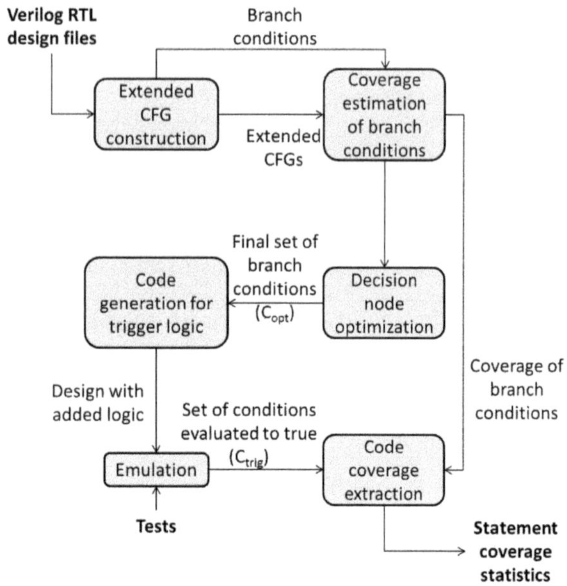

Figure 3: Block diagram describing in detail the various steps in our technique.

We augment the CFG with variable dependency information that partially captures the data flow in the code, thus forming the *extended CFG*. It contains a list of variables used in the code. The variables are classified into *inputs, outputs* and *internal variables*. The data flow information for a variable v is recorded in the form of *decisions* (nodes which use v in a conditional statement) and *assignments* (nodes corresponding to assignments to v). This is similar to the define-use information in the context of software programs commonly used by compilers [22].

Extended CFG for a design module consists of the union of extended CFGs for each of the concurrently running processes in the module. The set of extended CFGs for all modules captures the complete static behavior of the design.

We illustrate the terms introduced above with the help of the example code in Fig. 2. The extended CFG for the module (Fig. 4) consists of the extended CFGs for the continuous assignment and the `always` process.

We traverse the extended CFGs and identify branch conditions for each module. For instance, following three branch conditions are identified from the example code in Fig. 2:

c_1: `(rst == 1)`
c_2: `(rst == 0) && (state == 0)`
c_3: `(rst == 0) && (state == 1)`

Note that c_2 and c_3, which correspond to two different evaluations of the same `case` statement, are considered separately for further coverage analysis and addition of evaluation logic. This is required since during emulation, it is possible that both c_2 and c_3 evaluated to true at least once, or neither of them evaluated to true even once because `rst` was never deasserted. At the same time, we do not consider the condition c_4: `(rst == 0)` for further analysis, since either of c_2 or c_3 evaluating to true implies that c_4 also evaluated to true. Therefore, to obtain a conservative estimate of coverage, it is not required to record the evaluation of c_4. This reduces the number of branch conditions considered for subsequent steps in our technique.

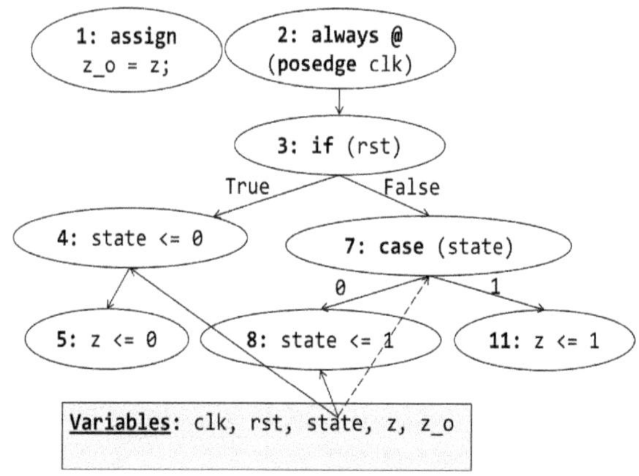

Figure 4: Extended CFG for the example design from Fig. 2 augmented with data flow information in the form of *assignments* (solid line) and *decisions* (dashed line) for variables. For clarity, this information is shown only for the internal variable `state`.

5.2 Estimating Coverage of Branch Conditions

Statements whose execution can be inferred given that a branch condition evaluates to true, are said to be *covered* by the branch condition. This if formalized as follows.

Definition 1. A statement s is *covered* by a branch condition c if it belongs to one of the following categories.

(1) s must be executed in order for c to evaluate to true.

(2) s is executed due to c evaluating to true.

(3) s is always executed irrespective of the evaluation of c.

(4) s belongs to the same basic block as a statement s' from (1) or (2) and consequently execution of s' ensures the execution of s.

Statement coverage of a branch condition is defined in a way that it closely approximates the statement coverage of a test that causes the condition to evaluate to true. Our coverage analysis ensures that the coverage reported by our technique is an under-approximation or a conservative estimate of the test coverage reported by a simulator. In other words, if a statement is reported as covered by our technique, it must be reported as covered by the simulator as well, while the converse may or may not be true.

Together, these categories identify statements in the code such that if a test causes c to evaluate to true, it is guaranteed to execute each of these statements. We call the set of statements in categories (1) and (2) as *backward cone* and *forward cone* of c respectively. We use the term *ancillary cone* to denote the statements belonging to categories (3) and (4).

The four categories in Definition 1 correspond to each of the four sets of statements inferred as covered in the motivating example (Sec.4), respectively. The motivating example essentially finds the statements covered by c_3: `(rst == 0) && (state == 1)` according to Definition 1.

It should be noted that, every statement is either unconditionally executed, or is in the forward cone of some branch condition. However, we compute the backward and ancillary cones of every condition to compact the set of conditions whose evaluations are to be recorded, thus reducing the overheads of coverage extraction. For instance, in the motivating example (Sec.4), we can use backward cone analysis of the c_3 to infer that the assignment `state`

<= 0 on line 4 must have been executed. Although this assignment is in the forward cone of c_1, it is not necessary to record c_1 given that c_3 is recorded.

Let c be a branch condition in the source code. Let B_c, F_c and A_c be the sets of lines in backward, forward and ancillary cones of c. Let S_c be the set of lines covered by c. Then $S_c = B_c \cup F_c \cup A_c$. We now describe our algorithms to compute each of B_c, F_c and A_c. We express c as a proposition or conjunctions of propositions. Here a proposition is of the form $(v == val)$ where v is a variable in the source code.

5.2.1 Backward Cone

We look at each proposition p in c individually to compute B_c (Procedure 1). We find the statements that must be executed for p to evaluate to true. Since c is a conjunction of such propositions, each of these propositions must evaluate to true for c to be true. As a result, the union of backward cones of propositions gives the backward cone of c. Backward cone computation is mainly data flow based and highlights the utility of the variable dependency information present in the extended CFG.

For every proposition p : (`v == ` val), we first find statements which assign the value val to variable `v`. Apart from direct assignments, `v = ` val, we also look for indirect assignments, that is assignments of the form `v = v'` such that `v'` in turn is assigned val directly or indirectly. It is possible that `v` can be assigned val in multiple statements of a process. Since our goal is to find the statements that must be executed for c to evaluate to true, we stop the backward traversal in such cases. When there is exactly one matching assignment n, it is included in B_c. If n is an indirect assignment of the form `v = v'`, a backward cone computation is performed for a new proposition p' : (`v' == ` val) recursively. In case of complex assignments to v (e.g. `v <= a + b`), no further analysis is performed on v.

Finally, all conditional statements on which n depends are also included in B_c. Backward cone computation is then recursively performed on each of these conditions.

Procedure 1 Backward cone computation procedure

$getBackwardCone(c)$
Input: Extended CFG G, branch condition c
Output: Set of statements B_c in backward cone of c

```
B_c ← φ
for Each proposition p : (v == val) ∈ c do
    n ← matchingAssignment(p)
    B_c ← B_c ∪ {n}
    if n is of the form v = v' then
        B_c ← B_c ∪ getBackwardCone(p' : (v' == val))
    end if
    for Each branch condition c' on which n depends do
        B_c ← B_c ∪ getBackwardCone(c')
    end for
end for
```

Note that c needs to be represented as a conjunction of propositions prior to applying the algorithm described above. In cases where this is not possible due to a c having a complex conditional expression, B_c is pessimistically set to ϕ.

5.2.2 Forward Cone

To compute F_c, we use the information provided by c in the form of propositions. Since we assume that c is true, we have available a list of values (L) for some of the variables.

For each process in the code, we traverse the extended CFG starting from the top level node. When a decision node is encountered, we attempt to evaluate the corresponding condition using the values in L. If it can be evaluated, we traverse along the respective edge. If the expression cannot be evaluated, we stop the traversal. The statements corresponding to the nodes encountered during this traversal are included in F_c.

When the conditional expression for c cannot be represented as a conjunction of propositions, we simply start at the decision node corresponding to c and traverse downwards until another decision node is encountered. The statements corresponding to the visited nodes are included in F_c.

5.2.3 Ancillary Cone

Extracting ancillary cone A_c consists of the following two steps, one for each of the categories (3) and (4) from Definition 1.

(1) Firstly, all continuous assignments are included in A_c. Then, starting at the top level node of each process, we traverse the CFG until a decision node is encountered. Statements corresponding to all visited nodes are included in A_c.

(2) For each assignment in $B_c \cup F_c$, we include the other assignments in the same basic block as the original assignment, in A_c.

We demonstrate our algorithm to find the coverage of c: `(rst == 0) && (state == 1)` for the example design from Figure 2. Note that in this case, c is represented as a conjunction of propositions.

Backward cone (B_c) computation: The condition c consists of two propositions, namely p_1: `(rst == 0)` and p_2: `(state == 1)`. Since p_1 involves the input variable `rst` which is always assigned externally, it is not considered for further analysis. For p_2, we look for statements that assign the value 1 to `state` and find that there is a unique one on line 8. This statement is included in B_c. Since it depends on the branch condition c': `(rst == 0) && (state == 0)`, $getBackwardCone(c')$ is called which includes the initial assignment on line 4 in B_c.

Forward cone (F_c) computation: Starting at the top level node of the `always` process, we traverse downwards. The condition on line 3 can be evaluated using the proposition `(rst == 0)` and we take the `False` branch. Similarly, the statement on line 9 is also included in F_c.

Ancillary cone (A_c) computation: In step (1), we include the continuous assignment on line 1 in A_c. In step (2), the assignment on line 5 is included in A_c, since it belongs to the same basic block as line 4 that is already included in B_c.

Fig. 5 shows the CFG nodes included in backward, forward and ancillary cones after this analysis.

5.3 Optimization

It is possible to have multiple branch conditions covering the same statement. We require at least one branch condition covering each statement. Moreover, synthesizing the recording logic for branch conditions incurs area costs. Therefore we perform optimization to obtain a subset of the branch conditions that satisfy certain user defined constraints. Specifically, we find a subset of branch conditions with maximum total coverage that satisfies the following constraints:

1. Total number of branch conditions $\leq max\_cond$.

2. Fraction of total lines covered in the source code for each module $\geq min\_cover$.

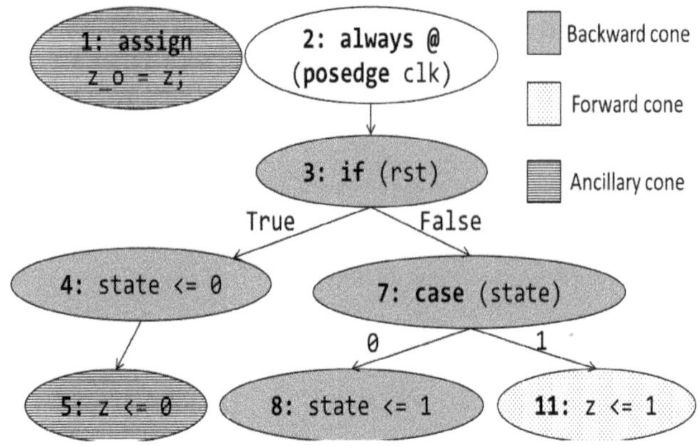

Figure 5: Extended CFG from Fig. 4 with nodes included in backward, forward and ancillary cone for c_3: `(rst == 0) && (state == 1)` shown.

Here max_cond and min_cover are user-specified.

This problem is identified as a variant of *Maximum coverage problem* and is formulated as an Integer Linear Program (ILP) [23]. This ILP is solved to get the final set of branch conditions, denoted by C_{opt}.

Note that when $min\_cover < 1$ is used, there could be statements in the code not covered by any branch condition in C_{opt}. As a result, the coverage information for such statements extracted from emulation may not be accurate. However, fewer branch conditions may be required to be evaluated in this case, which reduces the area cost. This trade-off between accuracy of coverage results and area cost is demonstrated by the case study in Sec. 6. Note also that, even when there are no branch conditions covering some statements, the coverage extracted using our technique is a conservative estimate of the actual statement coverage.

5.4 Synthesis of Branch Condition Evaluation Logic

We add a variable `cov_c` to record the evaluation of each branch condition `c` $\in C_{opt}$. The code added is shown in Fig. 6. When reset is asserted, `cov_c` is initialized to 0. When `c` evaluates to true during running of a test, `cov_c` is set to 1. Thus at the end of the test, the value of `cov_c` denotes if c evaluated to true *at least once* during the emulation run. The value must be captured before subsequent resets since a reset clears `cov_c`.

```
always @ (posedge clk)
  if (rst)
    cov_c <= 0;
  else if (c)
    cov_c <= 1;
```

Figure 6: Code to record if `c` ever evaluated true during emulation.

5.5 Coverage Extraction from Emulation

The target design is synthesized with the additional logic for branch conditions and downloaded to an emulation platform. The additional logic consists of a flip-flop for `cov_c` along with some combinational logic for the condition itself. An emulation test is run, and at the end of the test, the values of `cov_c` flip-flops are extracted.

The subset $C_{true} = \{c \in C_{opt} | \texttt{cov\_c}= 1\}$ gives the set of branch conditions that evaluated to true at least once during the test. The set of statements covered by c, i.e. S_c, is available from the coverage estimation step. Therefore, we can find the set $S_{cov} = \bigcup_{c \in C_{true}} S_c$ of statements that were definitely executed during the test. Let S_{sim} be the set of statements reported as covered by a simulator for the same test. Note that S_{cov} may not include all the lines in S_{sim}, but is guaranteed to be a conservative estimate of S_{sim}, or in other words, $S_{cov} \subseteq S_{sim}$.

6. EXPERIMENTAL RESULTS

We evaluated our methodology using an industrial SoC and the publicly available OpenRISC processor [10]. The subblock of the industrial SoC we considered consists of a signal processing module that generates timing recovery strobes for a receiver front end. The sub-blocks include state machines, counters and math computations. The OpenRISC is an open source RISC processor with a five-stage integer pipeline, virtual memory support (MMU) and basic DSP capabilities.

Experiments were carried out on an Intel Xeon Quad Core @ 3.16 GHz with 32 GB RAM running Red Hat Linux v2.6. The entire tool flow to generate the evaluation logic for final branch conditions completed within 30 seconds. We used the MATLAB solver `bintprog()` for optimization. Xilinx FPGA platform was used to emulate the original design as well as the modified design with the additional evaluation logic for branch conditions (Sec. 5.4). The values of `cov_c` flip-flops were extracted using the Xilinx ChipScope tool. For comparison of statement coverage statistics, we used the ModelSim RTL simulator.

6.1 Branch Conditions and Optimization

Table 1 shows the code sizes (number of lines of code), number of statements and the number of branch conditions after optimization, for the modules under consideration from the two designs. Blank lines and comments are not included while calculating code sizes. The number of statements is less that the code size because lines containing declarations, module instantiations, etc. are excluded. We only consider the modules that contain sequential code, since they contain a clock and a reset signal required by the added evaluation logic for branch conditions. Also, top-level modules containing only module instantiations are not analyzed, since they contain no statements for coverage.

We ran branch condition optimization with two configurations. Let C_{opt_1} and C_{opt_2} denote the final set of branch conditions after performing optimization according to the two configurations, respectively. In optimization configuration (1), $min\_cover = 1$ was used, which ensures that all statements are covered by C_{opt_1}. The total number of branch conditions in this case was 411 for the industrial design and 310 for the OpenRISC design. This was done in order to prune out redundant branch conditions while keeping the coverage target to 100%. In optimization configuration (2), we bounded the total number of branch conditions by a number smaller than 411 and 310 ($max\_cond = 256$). For the industrial design, an additional constraint: $min\_cover = 0.9$ was used in configuration (2). It should be noted that, as explained in Sec. 5.3, the optimization is performed on the complete design, even though the C_{opt_1} and C_{opt_2} are reported for each module in Table 1.

Table 1 shows that the number of branch conditions is much smaller than the number of statements in the code (on average, $2.6x$ and $4.3x$ smaller in C_{opt_1} for the industrial design and the OpenRISC design, respectively). This observation highlights the benefit

Table 1: Number of lines of code, number of statements and the number of branch conditions after optimization, for the two optimization configurations, for each module. Modules M_1 through M_6 are from the industrial design while the remaining modules are from OpenRISC.

Module	Code size	Statements	$\lvert C_{opt_1}\rvert$	$\lvert C_{opt_2}\rvert$
M_1	1855	927	177	85
M_2	271	3	2	2
M_3	254	85	39	38
M_4	195	50	15	10
M_5	588	210	95	80
M_6	907	255	59	26
`ctrl`	802	406	63	59
`except`	487	189	34	27
`fpu`	234	75	13	11
`freeze`	75	31	9	9
`genpc`	162	55	15	14
`if`	88	52	4	4
`lsu`	126	54	25	4
`operand-muxes`	82	35	13	10
`rf`	154	21	3	3
`sprs`	301	125	36	36
`wbmux`	71	19	8	6
`dc_fsm`	330	134	16	15
`dmmu_top`	118	20	3	2
`du`	1241	119	28	24
`ic_fsm`	136	70	17	11
`immu_top`	165	53	6	6
`pic`	84	23	6	5
`pm`	86	39	3	3
`tt`	75	27	8	7

of only recording the evaluation of a subset of branch conditions, and using static analysis to relate it to execution of statements for coverage extraction.

Configuration (2) shows further reduction in the number of branch conditions in nearly all modules from the industrial design. The reduction is more significant in M_1 and M_6. This is because they contain branch conditions that add very little extra coverage, and hence the per-module $min\_cover = 0.9$ constraint can be met even after removing those. The reduction is less significant in the case of OpenRISC mainly because $\lvert C_{opt_1}\rvert$ itself is relatively less (310) for OpenRISC compared to the industrial design (411).

6.2 FPGA Overheads

Table 2 summarizes the FPGA usage overheads of the evaluation logic for C_{opt_1} and C_{opt_2}. The usage is expressed in terms of the flip-flop (FD_LD) and lookup table (LUT) counts. Changes in the usage of remaining FPGA primitives were insignificant. The FD_LD overhead mainly corresponds to the `cov_c` flip-flops to store evaluation information. The overhead in LUT counts is due to additional combinational logic to evaluate the condition.

We find that the overheads are within 11% in all cases. Moreover the overheads for C_{opt_2} are up to 42% lower than C_{opt_1} which shows how optimization can help lower overheads. As expected, the FD_LD overhead for a given design is found to be roughly proportional to the number of branch conditions whose evaluation is being recorded.

Table 2: Percentage FPGA usage overheads of the evaluation logic for the set of branch conditions optimized for the two optimization configurations.

Design	C_{opt_1}		C_{opt_2}	
	FD_LD	LUT	FD_LD	LUT
Industrial design	9.21%	3.28%	5.36%	2.71%
OpenRISC	10.41%	3.53%	7.55%	2.67%

6.3 Coverage Comparison with Simulator

For the industrial design, we ran a system-level test (Test 1) on the modified designs corresponding to the optimization configurations (1) and (2), and our technique was used to extract statement coverage statistics of the test. The same test on the original design was run in a simulator and statement coverage information was obtained from the simulator. For modified design for configuration (2), the process was repeated for a much longer system-level test (Test 2).

Comparison between the statement coverage reported from emulation and by the simulator revealed that in all cases, coverage obtained from emulation is indeed a conservative estimate of the actual coverage from simulation. We report the number of statements that were covered according to the simulator, but reported as *not covered* by our technique, as a percentage of the total number of statements.

Table 3: Percentage error in statement coverage extracted from emulation using C_{opt_1} and C_{opt_2} for Test 1, and C_{opt_2} for Test 2. The error represents the number of covered statements *not* reported as covered using our method, as a percentage of total number of statements.

	Simulation runtime	Emulation runtime	Module	Error for C_{opt_1}	Error for C_{opt_2}
Test 1	3 hours	30 seconds	M_1	0.22%	0.86%
			M_2	0%	0%
			M_3	4.71%	5.88%
			M_4	4%	4%
			M_5	2.86%	2.86%
			M_6	0.78%	7.06%
Test 2	20 hours	5 minutes	Average	-	3.80%

We report detailed results for Test 1 in Table 3. When branch conditions from C_{opt_1} were used, the average error was only 1.8%. A more detailed analysis showed that the discrepancy between coverages can be mainly attributed to some `default` cases of combinational `case` statements. The `cov_c` flip-flops require a reset in order to start recording branch condition evaluations. Therefore for the default cases that were hit before reset was asserted, the corresponding flip-flops failed to record the evaluation correctly.

As expected, the error in reported coverage was found to be slightly higher when a lower number of branch conditions were used. Table 1 shows that $\lvert C_{opt_2}\rvert$ is significantly lower compared to $\lvert C_{opt_1}\rvert$ for modules M_1 and M_6. Table 3 shows that this resulted in around 3 and 9 times increase in error in reported coverage. However, for other modules, the increase in error was less significant. Therefore the average error increased only to 3.8% from 1.8%.

We observed similar coverage statistics for Test 2. In Table 3, we only report the average error in coverage across all modules in this case.

Note that running a test in emulation is about 300x faster than simulation. In particular, Test 2 has a prohibitively large runtime of 20 hours during simulation. However, we are able to obtain coverage statistics within 4% error from emulation for this test as well, thus illustrating the key benefit of our technique.

7. CONCLUSION

We present a novel technique which applies static analysis to code coverage extraction from emulation/prototyping platforms, with minimal overheads. We adapt the static analysis techniques to use the inherent concurrent nature of RTL code. We focus on statement coverage in this paper. However, since our technique relies on recording branch condition evaluations, it can be readily extended to the computation of branch coverage.

Through experiments, we show that our technique is efficient and scales well to industrial-level designs. We also show how the optimization step helps make the best use of available FPGA resources for coverage. Although FPGAs are used as the emulation platforms in our experiments, we are confident that the technique described can be readily extended to other platforms. This is due to the fact that we represent the coverage recording logic as synthesizable Verilog HDL code, which can be converted to hardware by standard logic synthesis tools.

In future, we plan on using FPGA RAMs to record the branch condition evaluations, instead of, or in addition to the FFs. This could potentially reduce or completely eliminate the FD_LD overheads. Another possible reduction of overheads under consideration is to use the coverage obtained from simulation, and focus only on the uncovered parts during emulation. Moreover, we plan to resolve the issue of errors in coverage due to the reset condition (Sec. 6.3) by adding a special reset signal for the coverage evaluation logic.

8. REFERENCES

[1] Adrian Evans et al. Functional verification of large ASICs. In *Proc. DAC '98*, pages 650–655.

[2] James Gateley et al. UltraSPARC-I emulation. In *Proc. DAC '95*, pages 13–18, 1995.

[3] Gopi Ganapathy et al. Hardware emulation for functional verification of K5. In *Proc. DAC '96*, pages 315–318.

[4] M. Gschwind, V. Salapura, and D. Maurer. FPGA prototyping of a RISC processor core for embedded applications. *IEEE Trans. Very Large Scale Integr. Syst.*, pages 241–250, April 2001.

[5] Joydeep Ray and James C. Hoe. High-level modeling and FPGA prototyping of microprocessors. In *Proc. FPGA'03*, pages 100–107.

[6] Serdar Tasiran and Kurt Keutzer. Coverage metrics for functional validation of hardware designs. *IEEE Design and Test of Computers*, pages 36–45, 2001.

[7] Jing yang Jou and Chien nan Jimmy Liu. Coverage analysis techniques for HDL design validation. In *Proc. APCHDL '99*, pages 48–55.

[8] Edmund M. Clarke et al. Program slicing for VHDL. *Int. J. Softw. Tools Technol. Transf.*, 4(1):125–137, 2002.

[9] Shobha Vasudevan, E. Allen Emerson, and Jacob A. Abraham. Improved verification of hardware designs through antecedent conditioned slicing. *Int. J. Softw. Tools Technol. Transf.*, pages 89–101, February 2007.

[10] Openrisc 1200. http://opencores.org/openrisc,or1200.

[11] Xilinx FPGAs. http://www.xilinx.com/products/silicon-devices/fpga/index.htm.

[12] Steven T. Hurlock, Stephen Kun, Robert A. Johnson, Jeremy S. Nichols, and Arthur J. Nilson. Code coverage testing in hardware emulation. *U.S. Patent 7502728*, March 2009.

[13] VN-Cover emulator product overview. http://www.transeda.-com/site/images/stories/vn-cover-emulator.pdf, 2005.

[14] Nils Endric Schubert, John Mark Beardslee, Gernot Heinrich Koch, and Ewald John Detjens. Hardware-based HDL code coverage and design analysis. *U.S. Patent 7222315*, May 2007.

[15] Marc Boule and Zeljko Zilic. Incorporating efficient assertion checkers into hardware emulation. In *Proc. ICCD '05*, pages 221–228.

[16] Hong Zhu, Patrick A. V. Hall, and John H. R. May. Software unit test coverage and adequacy. *ACM Comput. Surv.*, pages 366–427, December 1997.

[17] Hiralal Agrawal. Dominators, super blocks, and program coverage. In *Proc. POPL '94*, pages 25–34.

[18] Mustafa M. Tikir and Jeffrey K. Hollingsworth. Efficient instrumentation for code coverage testing. In *Proc. ISSTA '02*, pages 86–96.

[19] Mehdi Karimibiuki, Kyle Balston, Alan J. Hu, and Andre Ivanov. Post-silicon code coverage evaluation with reduced area overhead for functional verification of soc. In *Proc. HLDVT '11*.

[20] Flemming Nielson, Hanne R. Nielson, and Chris Hankin. *Principles of Program Analysis*. Springer, 2010.

[21] S-T. Cheng and Robert K. Brayton. Compiling verilog into automata. Technical Report UCB/ERL M94/37, EECS Department, University of California, Berkeley, 1994.

[22] Alfred V. Aho, Ravi Sethi, and Jeffrey D. Ullman. *Compilers: principles, techniques, and tools.* Addison-Wesley, 1986.

[23] Vijay V. Vazirani. *Approximation Algorithms*. Springer, March 2004.

Synthesis of Custom Networks of Heterogeneous Processing Elements for Complex Physical System Emulation

Chen Huang[1], Bailey Miller[1], Frank Vahid[1, 3], Tony Givargis[2]
[1] Department of Computer Science and Engineering – University of California, Riverside
{chuang, bmiller, vahid}@cs.ucr.edu
[2] Center for Embedded Computer Systems – University of California, Irvine; givargis@uci.edu
[3] Also with the Center for Embedded Computer Systems – University of California, Irvine

ABSTRACT

Physical system models that consist of thousands of ordinary differential equations can be synthesized to field-programmable gate arrays (FPGAs) for highly-parallelized, real-time physical system emulation. Previous work introduced synthesis of custom networks of homogeneous processing elements, consisting of processing elements that are either all general differential equation solvers or are all custom solvers tailored to solve specific equations. However, a complex physical system model may contain different types of equations such that using only general solvers or only custom solvers does not provide all of the possible speedup. We introduce methods to synthesize a custom network of *heterogeneous* processing elements for emulating physical systems, where each element is either a general or custom differential equation solver. We show average speedups of 45x over a 3 GHz single-core desktop processor, and of 11x and 20x over a 3 GHz four-core desktop and a 763 MHz NVIDIA graphical processing unit, respectively. Compared to a commercial high-level synthesis tool including regularity extraction, the networks of heterogeneous processing elements were on average 10.8x faster. Compared to homogeneous networks of general and single-type custom processing elements, heterogeneous networks were on average 7x and 6x faster, respectively.

Categories and Subject Descriptors

B.5.2 [**Design Aids**]: Automatic synthesis;

C.3 [**SPECIAL-PURPOSE AND APPLICATION-BASED SYSTEMS**]: Real-time and embedded systems

General Terms

Design, Performance, Experimentation

Keywords

Real-time emulation, field-programmable gate array (FPGA), ordinary differential equation (ODE) solving, physical models, cyber-physical systems, differential equation synthesis, high-level synthesis, system-level synthesis, processing elements.

1. INTRODUCTION

Fast accurate digital emulation of physical systems is useful in various cyber-physical systems [11]. For instance, a complicated patient simulator that emulates a human's circulatory, respiratory, and nervous system can be used for training clinicians [15]. Compared to mechanical systems used for emulation purposes, the parameters of a digital model can be easily modified. For instance, a digital lung model's parameters can be changed for capturing varied lung pathologies, which is more flexible than typical lung emulation approaches using mechanical balloons.

Most physical systems can be modeled with ordinary differential equations (ODEs). A heterogeneous physical system may contain thousands of ODEs. Because ODEs for real physical systems typically cannot be solved exactly, simulations/emulations typically step forward using small time steps and estimate the next values of all variables using the current variable values and the slope of the variables' function at that time (the slope coming from the derivative terms). Such iterative solvers typically solve 1000 times per second or faster to achieve sufficient accuracy, thus real-time emulation of a physical system can be computationally intensive. A modern multi-core desktop computer may not satisfy the real-time constraint, because of the mostly-sequential computation of a CPU (centralized processing unit). GPU (graphical processing unit) platforms perform better than CPUs in emulating a physical system because of more parallel computation resources. However, we have found that the memory architecture of a GPU may not match the communication pattern of a physical system model, thus greatly limiting the performance of a GPU.

We previously [7][8] proposed a network of *homogeneous* processing-elements on FPGAs approach for even faster emulation of a physical system. A set of lightweight custom processors each solve a subset of ODEs in the physical system. The structure of the network and interconnections of the PEs is based on ODE interdependencies. Models with widely-varying structures can be efficiently implemented on FPGAs due to FPGA configurability. Initially, we used a custom network of *general* PEs [7], with each general PE able to solve any ODEs, yielding 10x-20x speedups over a single-core Intel I7 desktop processor running at 3.07 GHz. Later, we introduced a custom network of *custom* PEs [8], where a single custom PE was first created to best

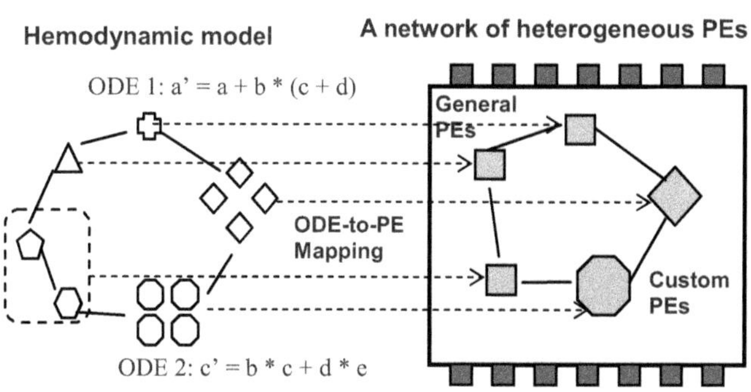

Fig. 1. Synthesizing a hemodynamic model into a network of heterogeneous PEs on an FPGA. Each shape type in the model represents a different type of ODE. Two simplified ODEs are shown for illustration purpose

match the needs of the model's ODEs and then a network of those custom PEs was used to achieve 5x-10x speedups over the network of general PEs.

In this paper, we propose to create a custom network of *heterogeneous* PEs consisting of general PEs and multiple custom PEs together, as shown in Fig. 1. The proposed method greatly expands the exploration problem associated with mapping model equations to the correct type of PE, but can yield substantial speedups of model emulation. A simplified hemodynamic model [25] for modeling a human circulatory system is shown in the figure, containing six *ODE types* for modeling different sub-systems; each type is represented as a different shape in the figure. Each ODE type is unique, and requires a particular ordered set of operations that differ from the operations of other ODE types (e.g., ODE 1 and ODE 2 in the figure are different types). There can be different numbers of ODEs per type. For example, the left four sub-systems in Fig. 1 consist of unique ODE types with a single ODE per type, while the two sub-systems on the right have four ODEs per type. We can build a custom network of 5 PEs that contains two custom PEs for the types with four ODEs, and three general PEs for the left four ODEs (one of the PEs solves 2 ODEs). Note the custom network of PEs has a similar circular connection structure as the circulation model as the communication between model sub-systems remains unchanged.

Heterogeneous PEs substantially changes the synthesis problem due to introducing an enormous design space, involving not just the number of PEs and mapping of ODEs to PEs, but also instantiation of different types of PEs, numbers of each types, and mappings of ODEs to different types. We propose an allocation and binding heuristic for this problem and build an HDL (hardware description language) code generation tool to generate synthesizable VHDL code from the obtained solution.

This paper is organized as follows. Sections 2 reviews related works. Section 3 reviews a processing element network approach. Section 4 introduces an allocation and binding heuristic for a network of heterogeneous PEs and HDL code generation. Section 5 summarizes experimental results, and Section 6 concludes.

2. RELATED WORK

Simulation of physical system models has been studied extensively in the past decades. Tools have been developed to facilitate physical system simulation, such as Matlab [13], JSim [9], LabView [18], etc. These tools usually aim at producing accurate results rather than real-time emulation, commonly executing models much slower than real time.

Researchers have sought methods to speed up simulation by using multi-core processors and GPUs (Graphic Processing Units). For example, a 768-core SGI super-computer executed a 2-billion equation heart model, simulating 0.4 ms in 2 hours [14]. A Flaim heart model was executed on an Nvidia [19] GTX 295 GPU, running 30x faster than OpenMP running on an Intel I7 quad-core processor at 2.93 GHz, but still much slower than real-time, with execution of one heartbeat (300 ms) requiring 7.7 minutes. Amorim [1] used an Nvidia GTX 285 GPU to solve cardiac membrane dynamics, claiming 22-86x speedups over an Intel I7 quad-core processor at 2.8 GHz, though still running >100x slower than real-time.

FPGAs have been used for emulating physical systems. Yoshimi [29] obtained 100x speedups using an FPGA for fine-grained biological emulation compared to a single-core processor. Salwinski and Eisenberg [22] used an FPGA to speedup fine-grained intra-cellular simulation, showing that an FPGA could hold 500 reactions related to gene expression. However, these implementations are mostly manually designed and optimized, which requires significant design time. High-level synthesis (HLS) tools are another way to implement physical system solvers on an FPGA. Various tools have evolved that perform synthesis from C code, such as Stream-C [6], AutoESL [3], ROCCC [26], SynphonyC [23], etc. We compare our approach to a commercial HLS tool. Due to the regularity of most physical systems, we incorporate the idea of regularity extraction [21] in the design for a more fair comparison.

We previously [7][8] proposed a homogeneous processing element network approach for physical system emulation, and built a compiler to convert a model specification to synthesizable VHDL code. The previous custom PE networks contained homogenous processing elements, either general PEs, or custom PEs, but not both. The work in this paper allows different PE types in the network, greatly expanding the solution space and thus requiring additional exploration heuristics, but yielding substantial speedups.

3. PHYSICAL SYSTEM EMULATION WITH A CUSTOM NETWORK OF PROCESSING ELEMENTS

3.1 Modeling physical systems using ODEs

Fig. 2 shows the structure of a four generation Weibel lung model with basic gas exchange at the leaf branches. The Weibel lung has a binary tree structure. The first generation represents the airway (or trachea) between the mouth and lung. The 2nd and 3rd generations represent two bronchi and smaller bronchioles, and the fourth generation represents alveoli that handle gas transfer between lung and capillary cells.

The Weibel lung can be captured as RLC circuits [7], where each branch contains two state variables (flow and volume). The ODEs of each branch can be written in a general format (for simplicity, we use C_i to represent constant parameters):

$$V_i' = F_{parent} \cdot C_1 + V_i \cdot C_2 + F_i \quad (1)$$

$$F_i' = V_i \cdot C_3 - F_i \cdot C_4 - V_{R\_child} . C_5 - V_{L\_child} \cdot C_6 \quad (2)$$

Equation (1) and Equation (2) show that the derivative of *Vi* and *Fi* are linear functions of the volume and flow of branch *i* and neighboring branches. The ODE that governs the model gas exchange is:

$$Po2_i' = C_1 \cdot (Pco2_i - Po2_i) + C_2 \cdot (V_i \cdot C_3 - Po2_i) \quad (3)$$

The derivative of O_2's pressure is a linear function of the pressure

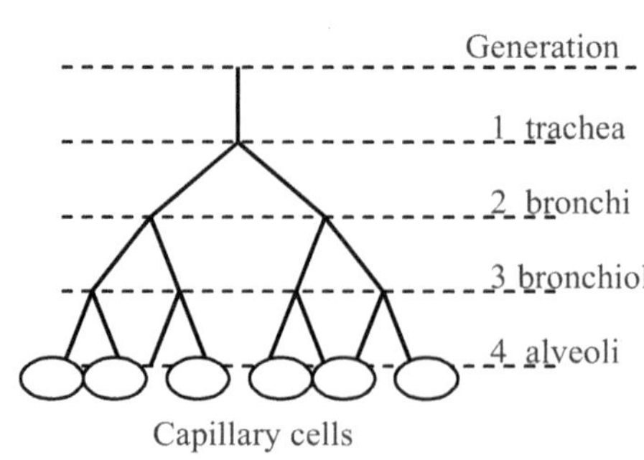

Fig. 2. A four generation Weibel lung with gas exchange model

of CO_2, volume of the alveoli, and the pressure of current O_2. The Weibel lung with gas exchange model contains three types of ODEs, because equations (1) (2) (3) each have a uniquely ordered set of operations.

To calculate the value of a state variable at a given time, the ODEs can be solved using iterative solvers such as Euler [2] or Runge-Kutta [4]. Starting from time 0, iterative solvers move forward in time by a given *time step* such as 1 ms. At each time step, two major tasks are performed by the Euler method:

Evaluate: Calculate each state variable's derivative value, e.g., $V_i' = F_{parent} \cdot C_1 + V_i \cdot C_2 + F_i$

Update: Estimate the value of each state variable for the next time step using the current values and the derivatives calculated above, e.g., $Vi = Vi + d(Vi) / dt * h$, where h is the time step.

3.2 Physical system ODE properties

The ODEs of a physical system often exhibit spatial locality similar to the system's physical counterparts. For instance, the volume of each branch in the Weibel lung is determined only by itself and the neighboring branches.

An *ODE data-dependency graph* [8] captures data-dependencies among the state variables. Each node represents one state variable (or a set of variables), while each edge represents the data dependency between two nodes. For instance, Fig. 3 shows the ODE data-dependency graph of the four-generation Weibel lung. Each node represents a branch which contains two state variables (volume and flow). Note the ODE data-dependency graph has a similar binary tree structure as the Weibel lung model. Since a state variable in a physical system only depends on the variable's neighboring variables, the ODE data dependency graph of a physical system is often very sparse. The number of edges increases linearly with the number of nodes.

3.3 Custom network of processing elements

To increase the speed of physical system emulation, we previously [7][8] proposed an approach to map the ODEs of a physical system to a homogeneous network of processing elements. For example, Fig. 3 maps the ODEs of the four-generation Weibel lung to a custom network of 5 PEs. The state variables in each of the dotted rectangles are mapped to one PE. The custom network of PEs uses a point-to-point communication scheme between PEs. The structure of a PE network is determined by the ODE-to-PE mapping and the ODE data-dependency graph, as in Fig. 3. The state variables and their relevant parameters persist in each PE's local memory. Such distributed data storage eliminates the bottleneck of a centralized memory.

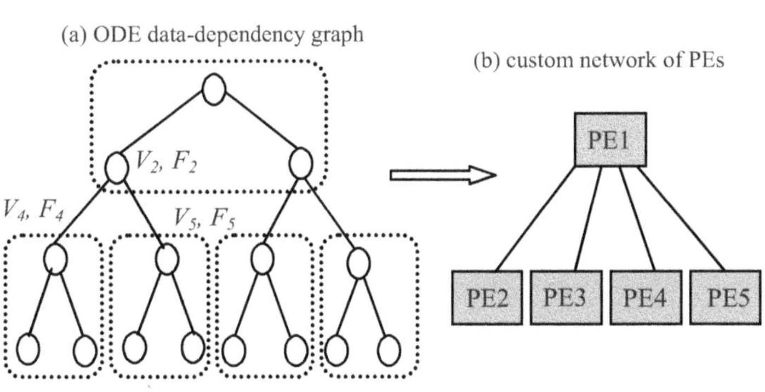

Fig. 3. Mapping a four generation Weibel lung model to a custom network of 5 PEs.

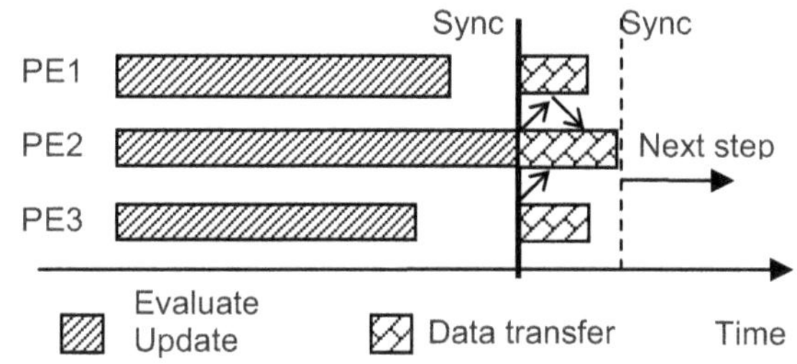

Fig. 4. ODE solving process in a network of 3 PEs

At each time step, a PE performs the "evaluate" and "update" tasks for the state variables mapped to the PE, which are known as the PE's *resident variables*. In order to evaluate each resident variable, the PE may need the state variables that reside in other PEs. For instance, PE1 needs the latest value of *V4* and *V5* in order to calculate *F2'* according to Equation (2). We call such state variables *dependent variables*. At the end of every time step, each PE outputs the latest values of the PE's resident variables, and stores local copies of the PE's dependent variables from other PEs. We call this additional task *data transfer*.

The ODE solving process of a network of PEs is illustrated in Fig. 4. The system has three PEs. The "evaluate" and "update" tasks can be done independently in each PE. All PEs are synchronized at the point when the slowest PE has finished updating the PE's resident variables (PE2 in this example), to ensure that every state variable is updated. Then communications between PEs are performed according to a static schedule built from the ODE data dependency graph. When all the data-transfer tasks have finished, all PEs are synchronized again for the next time step.

3.4 Processing element architecture

Two types of processing elements were proposed in the previous works that trade off performance and flexibility. A general PE [7] can solve any type of ODE. The architecture of the general PE is illustrated in Fig. 5. An instruction is directly mapped to a control word that controls an input mux, a data-ram and a general purpose arithmetic logic unit (ALU). The PE contains a few input ports and one output port for communication purposes. The data ram stores state variables and parameters mapped to the PE. The ALU calculates the equations by the "compute" and "store" operations. The general PE can handle different types of ODEs by parsing the equations into basic compute operations like ADD, MUL, etc.; thus the general PE is flexible.

Since a physical system often exhibits homogenous properties (only contains a few types of ODEs and each type appears many

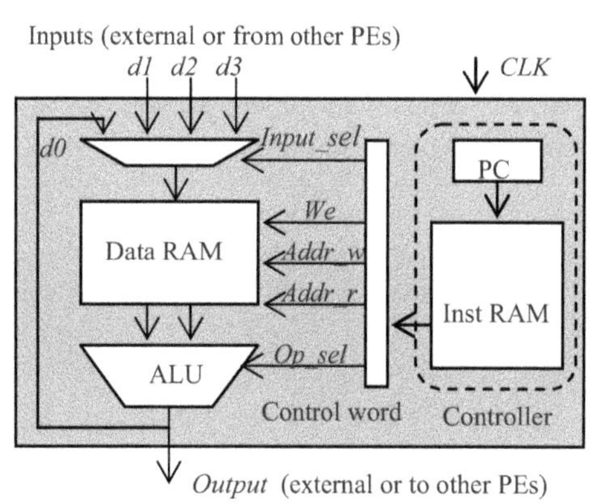

Fig. 5. General PE architecture.

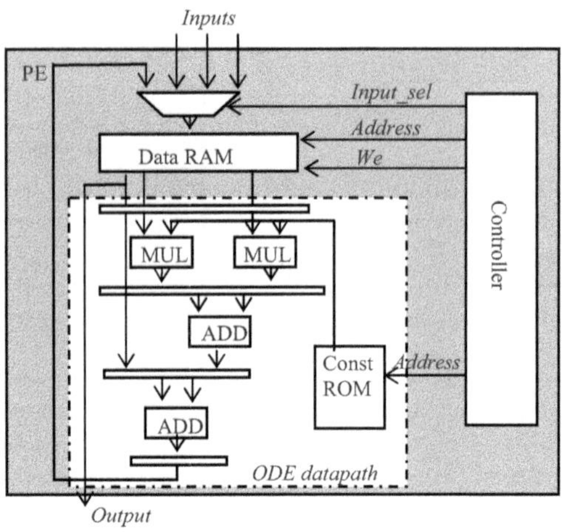

Fig. 6. Custom PE architecture.

times), a custom PE that captures the unique structure of a certain ODE type can provide significant speedup (>10x) over a general PE [8]. A custom PE for equation (1) is illustrated in Fig. 6. Note that the custom PE has a similar architecture compared to the general PE, except the ALU components is replaced with a *custom ODE datapath*. The custom ODE datapath is customized for one type of ODE. With the fully-pipelined design, the maximal throughput of the custom PE is one ODE per cycle. However, the custom PE is not flexible and can only solve a certain type of ODE. The custom PE also consumes more FPGA resources (1.5-3x) compared to the general PE due the ODE datapath and wider data ram.

Both the general and custom PE use fixed point computation, because a floating point core in an FPGA is inefficient in size and latency. Floating point physicals models are manually converted into fixed point using the method described by Kum [10]. The fixed-point results are nearly identical compared to a double precision floating point implementation (the relative error is usually within 0.5%) [7]. Automated conversion from floating point numbers to fixed point numbers is desired in the future.

4. NETWORK OF HETEROGENEOUS PES

The custom network of custom PEs is 5-10x faster than the custom network of general PEs and consumes fewer FPGA resources (due to fewer number of PE instances). However, the models examined in previous work were all homogenous models that contained only 1 or 2 types of ODEs.

A heterogeneous physical system model contains many types of ODEs, such as the hemodynamic model in Fig. 1, where each ODE type can have different numbers of ODEs. Using custom PEs where possible can yield performance improvements, however if the number of ODEs of a certain type is small, than using general PEs to solve those ODEs is likely more efficient in terms of size because multiple ODE types can use the same general PE. Thus, a custom network of *heterogeneous* processing elements, both general and custom, can provide improvements in performance and area due to more fine-grained control over the network implementation.

4.1 Different PE types

A custom network of heterogeneous PEs may contain different types of processing elements. A general PE can solve any type of ODE, but performance is slow. A custom PE can only solve one type of ODE, but performance is 10x faster than a general PE. However, in a real physical system, two or more types of ODEs might be tightly coupled. For instance, the Weibel lung model described in Section 3.1 contains two types of ODEs, for volume and for flow, for each branch, and the volume and flow have data dependencies with each other as shown in Equations (1) and (2). If the system only has custom PEs for flow and volume respectively, there will be excessive communication overhead. We thus extend the custom PE to support multiple ODE types, called *multi-type custom PEs*.

The idea is to put multiple ODE datapaths of different ODE types into one custom PE. To fully utilize those components, these ODE datapaths can execute in parallel, thus the theoretical throughput of a multi-type custom PE can be >= 2 ODEs / cycle. The idea is similar to VLIW (very long instruction word) architectures. The multi-type custom PE is larger than the single type custom PE, because of extra ODE datapaths and wider data ram. With the multi-type custom PE, different types of ODEs that are tightly coupled may be mapped to one custom PE to reduce communication overhead.

4.2 Problem definition

Given the ODEs of a physical system and different PE options, the question is how to select the number of each PE type and how to map the ODEs to the PEs in order to build a custom network of PEs that efficiently emulates the physical system. We formally define an allocation and binding problem as follows. Given are:

- A set of ODEs in the physical system: $O = \{o1, o2, ..., on\}$.
- A set of ODE types of the physical system: $T = \{t1, t2,.., tn\}$.
- A mapping function from O to T: *ode2Type*, e.g., *ode2Type(oi)* returns the ODE type of *oi*.
- An ODE data-dependency graph of the physical system: G, where $G(i, j) = 1$ stands for *oj* depends on *oi*.
- A set of all possible PE types, $PT = \{pt1, pt2, ..., ptn\}$, which includes general PE, single type custom PEs, and all possible multi-type custom PEs.
- A Boolean function determines if an ODE to PE mapping is valid: *Valid(pt, t)*. E.g., *Valid(pti, tj) = true* means *tj* (ODE type *j*) can be mapped to *pti* (PE type *i*).
- A FPGA resource consumption function for each PE type: *RES*, e.g., *RES(pti)* returns the FPGA resource consumption for PE type *i*. (Current we developed a function to estimate the resource consumption of a custom PE based on the ODE types the PE can solve. More accurate result can be obtained by actually synthesis each PE type)
- The total available FPGA resource: *T_RES*.
- A computation cost function: *CompCost(pti, set<ODE>)*, which returns the number of cycles to evaluate and update a set of ODEs with PE type *i*. (For a general PE, the computation cost is obtained by parsing the ODEs into basic computation operations. For a custom PE, the computation cost is depends on the number of ODEs of each type)
- A communication cost function: *CommCost*, the total communication cycles of the network of PEs. The communication cost depends on G and the mapping function *pe2Ode* defined below.

The solution is:

- A set of allocated PEs: $PE = \{pe1, pe2, ..., pe3\}$.

- A mapping function from PE to PT: *pe2Type*, e.g., pe2Type(pei) returns for the PE type of pei.
- The ODEs mapped to each PE: *pe2Ode*, where pe2Ode(pei) return a set of ODEs mapped to pei .

Constraints are:

- FPGA resource constraint: $\sum_i (RES(pe2Type(pei))) <= T\_RES$
- ODE Binding constraint: $\forall oi \in pe2Ode(pei)$
- $valid(pe2Type(pei), ode2Type(oi)) = true$
- Each ODE has been mapped to one PE.

The objective is (minimize cycles per step):

Min {max (CompCost(pe2Type(pei), pe2Ode(pei))) + CommCost}

In other words, the objective is to allocate a valid set of PEs (satisfy the FPGA resource constraint), and to find a valid mapping from ODEs to PEs (satisfy the ODE binding constraint) such that the throughput of the system is maximized.

The throughput of the network of PEs is equal to the number of ODEs divided by the time to emulate one step. Since the number of ODEs is a constant, maximizing the throughput is equivalent to minimizing the time to emulate one step. Assuming the clock frequency is a constant, the time per step is determined by the cycles per step. According to the ODE solving process illustrated in Fig. 4, the total cycles per step is equal to the maximal computation cost of the PEs plus the communication cost, or the objective function.

4.3 Allocation and binding heuristic

4.3.1 Choosing PE types

Since a multi-type custom PE can be built for any subset of the ODE types of a physical system, the number of all possible custom PE types increases exponentially with the number of ODE types. To consider all possible custom PEs might be too expensive in terms of algorithm runtime. However, not all ODE types need a custom PE. For instance, if an ODE type contains only a few ODEs (e.g., <5 ODEs), using a general PE is more size efficient. We thus define a *custom PE threshold*, such that we only build a custom PE for the ODE types with more ODEs than the custom PE threshold.

The multi-type custom PE is only needed when two or more ODEs are tightly coupled, which is reflected by the number of connections between 2 ODE types in the ODE dependency graph. Our solution is to keep merging the ODE types that pass the custom PE threshold, using a *custom PE merge criteria.*

The criteria is that two sets of ODE types can be merged only if the number of connections between the two sets is greater than (or equal to) the number of ODEs of any type in the two sets. Fig. 7

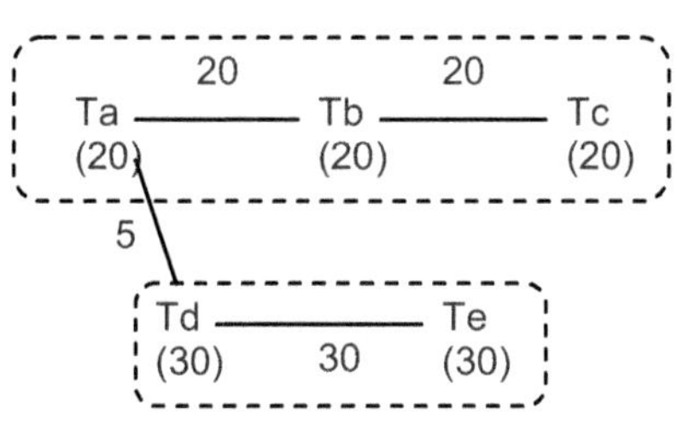

Fig. 7. Merging tightly coupled ODE types

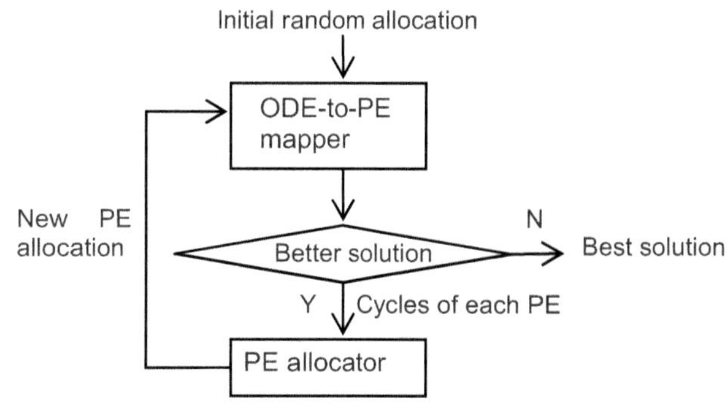

Fig. 8. Overall structure of the allocation and binding heuristic for the network of heterogeneous PEs

shows an example of merging 5 ODE types (*Ta, Tb, ... Te*), the number below each ODE type is the number of ODEs of that type. The line between two types shows the number of connections between two ODE types. After the merge process, two multi-type custom PE can be built ({*Ta, Tb, Tc*}, {*Td, Te*}). Note {*Ta, Tb, Tc*} can not merge with {*Td, Te*} because the number of connections between these two sets (5) do not satisfy the merge criteria. With the custom PE threshold and the merge criteria, the custom PE types are chosen based on the ODE data-dependency graph of the target physical system.

4.3.2 Allocation and binding heuristic overview

Once the PE types have been chosen, we allocate a number of each PE type, and map the ODEs to each PE. The overall structure of the allocation and binding heuristic is illustrated in Fig. 8. The allocation and binding heuristic includes two major components: an ODE-to-PE mapper and a PE allocator. The ODE-to-PE mapper tries to find the best ODE-to-PE mapping for the current PE allocation based on the objective function defined in Section 4.2. The PE allocator adjusts the PE allocation based on the feedback from the ODE-to-PE mapper.

The heuristic first generates a random PE allocation, which includes at least one instance for each PE type. Then the ODE-to-PE mapper will try to find the best mapping based on current PE allocation, and return the number of computation cycles for each PE to the PE allocator. The PE allocator will adjust the number of each PE type based on the mapper's feedback, and generate a new PE allocation. This iterative improvement process will terminate when the mapper cannot find a better solution.

4.3.3 ODE-to-PE mapper

The ODE-to-PE mapping algorithm is based on the mapping algorithm for the network of general PEs [7], with the objective as the cost function. The basic idea of the mapping algorithm is to move one ODE from one PE to another PE, which is called a *neighbor mapping*. To speedup the mapping algorithm, two types of *neighbor functions* are developed to generate neighbor mapping that has higher changes of improving the solution.

The "performance neighbor function" tries to balance the load (or total number of cycles) among PEs by moving ODEs from a heavily loaded PE to a light loaded PE. The "size neighbor function" tries to utilize the spatial locality of the ODEs, and group ODEs nearby to one PE. Thus the total number of connections and communications among the PEs would be reduced.

To adapt the original mapping algorithm to networks of heterogeneous PEs, we added constraints when generating the neighbor mappings such that the neighbor mapping still satisfies the ODE binding constraint (custom PEs can only solve a sub-set of ODE types) defined in Section 4.2. The ODE-to-PE mapper will output the number of cycles for each PE for the best mapping has been found.

4.3.4 PE allocator

The PE allocator adjusts the number of PEs for each PE type based on the feedback from the ODE-to-PE mapper. The PE adjustment algorithm is shown as follows:

Step 1: Choose top K% PEs with most loads (#cycles).

Step 2: Allocate a new PE (same PE type) for each PE chosen in step 1, move half of the ODEs mapped to the original PE to the new PE.

Step 3: Remove the PE with least loads (#cycles), and randomly redistribute the ODEs mapped to the removed PE to other PEs (satisfying the ODE binding constraint).

Step 4: Repeat step 3 until the resource constraint is satisfied.

The basic idea is to look at the number of cycles for each PE, and duplicate the most heavily loaded PEs. The allocator allocates new PEs for top 10% loaded PEs in this work. We notice two possibilities why a PE is heavily loaded. The first possibility is that this PE type doesn't have enough instances because some ODEs can only be mapped to this PE type. The second possibility is that this PE type is very efficient in solving the ODEs, thus many ODEs are mapped to it. Either possibility means that more instances of this PE type are required. However, adding new PEs may violate the FPGA resource constraint, thus we remove the least loaded PEs until the resource constraint is satisfied.

Since the PE adjustment algorithm depends on the ODE-to-PE mapping results, the quality of the mapping algorithm is critical for the entire allocation and binding heuristic. We let the ODE-to-PE mapper run long enough (200K-500K iterations) in order to produce a good solution. The overall time complexity of our approach is: *O(#allocator iterations * #mapper iterations * C)*, where *C* is the cost of generating a new mapping and re-computing the cost. C is mainly determined by the average number of edges of an ODE (not by the total number of ODEs), because the neighbor function and the incremental cost function only modifies one ODE and the neighbors.

4.4 HDL code generation

Once the processing elements have been allocated, and the ODEs are mapped to the PEs, the next task is to generate HDL code for the entire network. The code generation includes two steps:

1. Generate PE components for each PE type.
2. Generate and inject instructions for each PE instance, and connect them at top level.

4.4.1 PE components generation

Since the general PEs only differ in the data-ram size, instruction ram size, and input ports number [7], we developed a script to generate PE components with all possible combinations of the three parameters.

A custom PE contains unique ODE datapaths designed for the ODE types that the PE can solve. Thus we cannot pre-generate all possible custom PE components. Instead, we developed an automatic ODE datapath generator to facilitate custom PE generation. The ODE datapath generator reads an ODE string, and outputs a fully pipelined ODE datapath component for calculating this ODE. The datapath generator parses the input ODE into an expression tree, and uses an ASAP (as-soon-as-possible) scheduling algorithm [20] to schedule the operations. The generator adds pipeline registers for each stage. An ODE datapath usually contains 5-15 stages (or delays), depending on the ODE. The datapath generation task can be done with a high-level synthesis tool.

We also developed a custom data-ram generator to generate data-ram components with different number of ports and depth, because different ODE datapath may require different custom data ram. With the ODE datapath generator and the custom data-ram generator, a custom PE component of any type can be generated on the fly.

4.4.2 PE instruction generation and top level network generation

The PE instructions can be divided into two parts: (1) "evaluate and update" instructions, and (2) "data transfer" instructions, as shown in Fig. 4. The "evaluation and update" instructions are scheduled independently on each PE instance based on the ODEs mapped to the PE, while the "data transfer" instructions are scheduled globally.

The general PE handles the "evaluate and update" instructions by parsing the ODEs into basic instructions for the general purpose ALU component. The general instructions are then converted into the control word by a general instruction assembler [7]. The custom PE schedules the "evaluate and update" instructions by an instruction scheduler, and converts the instructions into control words by a custom instruction assembler [8].

The general PE and the custom PE have the same input/output interface. At each clock cycle, one PE can output a variable and store a variable concurrently. Thus the "data transfer" instructions are handled globally with a communication scheduler. The inputs to the communication scheduler are the ODE data-dependency graph (*G*) and the each PE's ODE set (*pe2Ode*). The scheduler tries to schedule as many "data transfer" instructions as possible if those instructions do not conflict with each other (each PE can only output one variable and store one variable at one cycle). The "data transfer" instructions are appended to the back of the "evaluate and update" instructions for each PE. The complete instructions are then injected into each PE from the generic interface for the instruction ram.

The structure of the top level network is determined by the ODE data-dependency graph and the ODE-to-PE mapping. The code generation tool will finally connect all PE instances according to the network structure, and output synthesizable VHDL files.

5. EXPERIMENTAL RESULTS

This section describes experimental results using five physical system models as benchmarks. The section compares our network of heterogeneous PEs with a high-level-synthesis approach including regularity extraction, networks of general/custom PEs, a GPU implementation, and a modern desktop processor.

Performance numbers are in milliseconds (ms) and represent the time for an implementation to execute one second of simulated time. Throughout this section, we execute the physical system using an Euler solver with a 0.01 ms step.

All FPGA based approaches targeted a Xilinx XC6VLX240T-2 FPGA, having 150,720 LUTs (lookup tables), 768 DSP units (built-in hardcore multipliers), and 416 BRAMs (built-in 32Kb hardcore block RAMs). We used the Xilinx ISE 12.3 tool [28] for synthesis. Note that this work is not limited to a particular FPGA or synthesis tool.

5.1 Physical system models

The five physical system models are all physiology models, and each contains more than one type of ODE. The five models have different connection structures such as binary trees, 2-dimensional meshes, rings, etc.

1. *Weibel lung*: 11 generation Weibel lung model that contains 4094 ODEs and calculates internal lung states. The Weibel lung has two types of ODEs (flow and volume) as discussed in Section 3.1. The Weibel lung has a binary tree structure.
2. *Neuron network*: a neuron network model [24] contains a number of neuron cells for modeling a neuron system in the brain. The neuron network contains three types of ODEs for membrane potentials, channel gating and synaptics. We use a 40 x 40 2-dimensional neuron network, which contain 1600 neurons or 4800 ODEs. The neurons are connected in a 2-dimensional mesh network.
3. *Weibel lung with gas exchange*: 11 generation Weibel lung model with 500 capillary cells connected to leaf branches. The model contains 3 types of ODEs as discussed in Section 3.1, and contains 4594 ODEs and has a binary tree structure.
4. *Hemodynamic*: the hemodynamic model [25] is a system circulation model which contains pulmonary tissues, systemic tissues and left/right ventricles. The model contains 36 types of ODEs for modeling different types of organs/cells. Within the 36 types of ODEs, 12 ODE types each with more than 100 ODEs. The remaining 24 ODE types each with only 1 ODE. The hemodynamic model contains 4800 ODEs, and has a circular connection structure.
5. *Weibel lung with hemodynamic model*: We combine the Weibel lung model with the hemodynamic model, because the pressure of the lung is an input to the hemodynamic model. We use a 10 generation Weibel lung with the hemodynamic model. The entire model contains 4266 ODEs, and 38 types of ODEs. The model has a hybrid connection structure with a binary tree connected with a ring.

5.2 Heterogenous networks vs. HLS and homogeneous networks

We implemented the ODE solver for each model using a commercial high-level synthesis tool[1]. Since physical systems exhibit many commonly recurring patterns we incorporate the idea of regularity extraction [21] into the design. Each ODE type represents a sub-pattern in the system, thus we generate a fully pipelined ODE data-path to compute each ODE type with the HLS tool.

We first attempted to input the entire PE network design into the HLS tool, however the tool used a centralized block ram to store all the data and the created design was not efficient. To eliminate the memory bottleneck of the system, we manually optimized the communication structure of the HLS approach (Fig. 9) to provide a better comparison to our custom network approach. The state

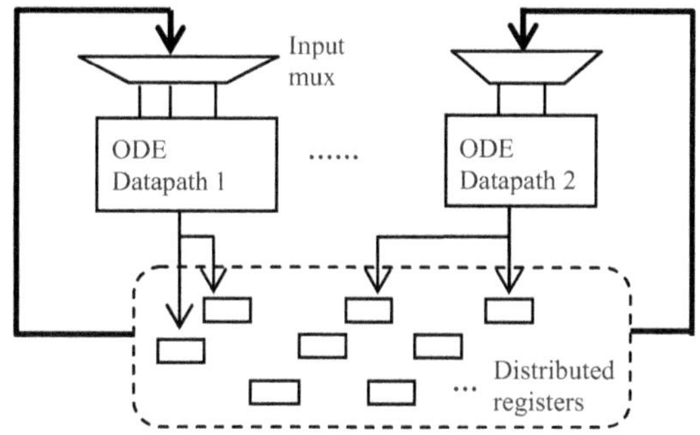

Fig. 9. The overall architecture of the ODE solver using an HLS tool with regularity extraction.

variables of a physical system are placed into distributed registers throughout the design. Each ODE datapath is mapped with a subset of ODEs of the physical system, thus each ODE datapath is responsible of updating multiple registers as shown in the figure. To utilize the spatial locality of the ODEs, one input mux is shared by all ports of the ODE datapath (shown in the figure) using a time multiplexing scheme. Using time multiplexing decreases the performance, however using the shared input mux significantly reduces the number of wires and results in synthesizable designs (one mux per port cannot be fully synthesized due to a large number of wires). We use the same allocate and binding heuristic in Section 4.3 to allocate the ODE datapath, and balance the number of ODEs in each ODE datapath. Since each ODE datapath is mapped with multiple ODEs (usually >50 ODEs), the shared input mux is often very large (64-256 inputs).

The networks of heterogeneous PEs are generated by the PE allocation and binding heuristic, and the code generation tool discussed in Section 4. The total algorithm runtime to generate the VHDL code for each model is about 5-10 minutes. For comparison purpose, we implemented the 5 models using networks of general PEs. We also included the results for networks of single-type custom PEs. All FPGA results are fully synthesized and implemented on the target FPGA.

The summary of the results is shown in Table I. We recorded the resource utilization of each approach. For easy comparison purposes via a single number, we define an *equivalent LUTs* term as is commonly done for FPGA designs [16]. By implementing of equivalent DSP and BRAM components using LUTs, we assign a DSP unit a value of 250 LUTs and a BRAM of 360 LUTs. The bottleneck of each design is highlighted with underlines.

5.2.1 Bottleneck of each approach

We tried to implement the fastest circuit for each design. We notice that performance each design may be constrained by one of the FPGA resource (LUTs, DSPs, BRAMs), or by the clock frequency.

For instance, the HLS designs are constrained by the available LUTs (the FPGA has 150,720 LUTs), because each ODE datapath requires a large input mux as shown in Fig. 9, requiring many LUTs. The networks of general PEs are mainly constrained by BRAMs (the FPGA has 406 BRAMs), because each general PE requires a BRAM instance. The networks of single-type custom PEs are mainly constrained by the clock frequency (or the number of wires in the system). Putting more single-type custom PEs into the network will result in long routing time and lower clock frequency (the reason will be discussed in Section 5.2.3).

[1] The tool name is not included due to the licensing agreement. The tool is commercially available and used by dozens of companies and universities, including the U.S. Dept. of Defense. Reproduction of our experiments using other HLS tools is highly encouraged; we will provide our models for such purposes upon request.

Table I. Synthesis results of custom networks of heterogeneous PEs, HLS, and general/single-type custom PEs. *PEs:* the number of PE or ODE datapath in the design. *Cycles:* total clock cycles to compute one time step. *Freq:* Maximum clock frequency after place and route. *Syn. time:* total synthesis time (including place and route) of a design. The underlined entries show the FPGA resource bottleneck of a design, i.e., the issue that prevents further improvement via more PEs.

HLS	LUTs	BRAMs	DSPs	Equiv. LUTs	PEs.	Cycle	Freq (Mhz)	Perf. (ms)	Syn. Time (min)
Weibel	101,031	131	245	*209,441*	67	296	112	*264*	752
Neuron	139,118	156	190	*242,778*	80	370	102	*363*	664
Weibel_gas	106,008	144	225	*214,098*	72	332	110	*301*	746
Hemodynamics	82,007	145	246	*195,707*	69	420	131	*321*	356
Weibel_hemo	79,735	143	230	*188,715*	75	340	115	*295*	520
General PEs									
Weibel	89,761	396	396	*331,321*	396	184	130	*142*	230
Neuron	74,632	294	294	*253,972*	294	290	150	*193*	147
Weibel_gas	78,178	281	281	*249,588*	281	302	105	*288*	123
Hemodynamics	75,311	281	281	*246,721*	281	364	190	*192*	107
Weibel_hemo	74,956	281	281	*246,366*	281	326	165	*198*	106
Custom PEs									
Weibel	48,579	56	205	*119,989*	56	221	129	*171*	72
Neuron	49,762	71	129	*107,572*	53	397	123	*323*	114
Weibel_gas	50,491	62	202	*123,311*	61	253	123	*206*	78
Hemodynamics	50,743	111	386	*187,203*	111	185	143	*129*	90
Weibel_hemo	72,828	154	553	*266,518*	175	84	167	*50*	146
Heterogeneous PEs									
Weibel	65,036	160	560	*262,636*	80	52	219	***24***	174
Neuron	63,458	133	462	*226,838*	67	69	204	***34***	185
Weibel_gas	58,800	141	494	*233,060*	86	72	222	***32***	122
Hemodynamics	48,652	118	444	*202,132*	142	56	250	***22***	69
Weibel_hemo	58,795	141	494	*233,055*	86	71	213	***33***	130

Thus adding PEs, while achieving more parallelism, yields overall performance decrease due to the slower clock frequency.

The networks of heterogeneous PEs are mainly constrained by DSPs (the FPGA has 768), because the custom ODE datapath (especially multi-type custom PEs) requires more DSPs than a general PE. Since the custom ODE datapaths are fully pipelined, these DSPs are highly utilized in the design. Thus the networks of heterogeneous PEs have the best performance. Note that the FPGA resource utilization of each design may not be close to the upper-bound of the total FPGA resource, because we also consider the clock frequency. Increasing the size of each design will decrease the clock frequency, thus the overall performance will decrease.

5.2.2 Comparison with high level synthesis

Compared to the HLS approach, the network of heterogeneous PEs uses around 40% fewer LUTs, a comparable number of BRAMs, and 2x more DSPs. In terms of equivalent LUTs, the network of heterogeneous PEs uses on average 10% more FPGA resources than the HLS approach.

The performance of the network of heterogeneous PEs approach is on average 10.8x (9x-14x) faster than the HLS approach because the network of heterogeneous PEs makes better usage of memories and computational components like DSPs. Since a large input mux consumes many LUTs in the HLS design, the HLS approach can only place a limited number of ODE datapaths, which limits the performance of the HLS approach. The time multiplexing of the shared input mux further decreases the performance of the HLS approach. Our approach using encapsulated processing elements better utilizes the spatial locality of a physical system. The network of heterogeneous PEs also obtained higher clock frequencies and shorter synthesis times due to fewer wires in the design.

5.2.3 Comparison with networks of general/single-type custom PEs

The network of general PEs consumes on average 15% more equivalent LUTs compared to networks of heterogeneous PEs due to having more PE instances. The performance of the network of heterogeneous PEs is on average 7x (6x~8.8x) faster than the network of general PEs, because the former contains custom PEs that solve certain types of ODEs faster than the general PEs. The networks of heterogeneous PEs also obtained 50% faster clock frequency, due to containing fewer PE instances and fewer wires in the network.

The networks of single-type custom PEs consumed on average 30% fewer equivalent LUTs than the networks of heterogeneous PEs because the former contained fewer PE instances. The reason is that all five models contain tightly coupled ODEs of different types, and the tightly coupled ODEs are split into different single-type custom PEs as discussed in Section 4.1. Thus the network requires more connections and communications. The wire congestion problem limits the clock frequency and the number of single-type custom PEs in the network.

The networks of heterogeneous PEs contain multi-type custom PEs, which reduce the number of connections and communication in the network. The network of heterogeneous PEs may also contain general PEs in case the number of ODEs of a type is too small. For instance, the hemodynamic model has 24 ODE types with only one ODE. Assigning the 24 individual ODEs to a few general PEs instead of creating a custom PE for each type is reasonable. With the multi-type custom PEs and general PE options, the network of heterogeneous PEs is on average 6x (1.5x-9.4x) faster than the network of single-type custom PEs. Note the performance of single-type custom PE networks depends heavily on the model; certain models may have faster performance when implemented as general PE networks (e.g., Nueron).

5.3 Heterogeneous network vs. CPU and GPU

We compared the custom network of heterogeneous PEs with a modern desktop processor and a GPU. The configurations of the processor and the GPU are listed as follows:

1. PC: C code on a 3.06 GHz Intel I7-950 quad-core processor with 16G DDR3 RAM, compiled with Microsoft VS2010 with –O3 flag
2. GPU: CUDA C code on a 763 MHz NVIDIA GTX460 Fermi GPU with 336 CUDA cores, compiled using nvcc with –O3 flag.

A fixed-point implementation was used for all test cases for a fair comparison. The C code on the desktop was manually optimized. The time to optimize each model is around 1-3 hours, which is comparable to the synthesis time of the network of heterogeneous PEs. We first obtained the single threaded performance (PC(1)) for the PC, and calculated an optimistic performance bound for multi-cores (PC(4)) by dividing the single threaded result by the number of cores.

We implemented a GPU kernel function for calculating the ODEs for each model. The kernel function may contain multiple branches for different ODE types as illustrated in Fig. 11(a). Another approach is to implement different GPU functions for each ODE type, shown in Fig. 11(b). However, the second approach executes each function sequentially, which is slower than the first approach. We use the first approach that better utilizes the resource on the GPU.

The ODE kernel function is executed on multiple GPU blocks, and each block contains multiple threads. We tuned the number of blocks and the number of threads to obtain the best performance. We also considered the coalesced access pattern when reading the global memory on the GPU. Since global memory access is more expensive than accessing the shared memory within each GPU block. We utilized the spatial locality of each model by mapping related ODEs to one GPU block. Thus nearby state variables are loaded to shared memory to reduce global memory accesses. The total GPU implementation time for each model is around 2-4 hours, which is comparable to the synthesis time of the custom network of heterogeneous PEs. To ensure that our GPU implementations are of high quality, we asked an experienced GPU programmer to optimize our CUDA code. Runtime was reduced an additional 5-15%, mainly by utilizing coalesced global memory accesses.

The performance of each approach is illustrated in Fig. 10. The single threaded PC failed the real-time constraint for four models, while the optimal multi-threaded version runs each model 2-4x faster than real-time. The average speed of the network of heterogeneous PEs is 45.3X (36x-60x) faster than PC(1), and 11.3x (9x-15x) faster than PC(4). Note the performance is the pure execution time of each model. Further monitoring and debugging logic will cause extra overhead. The network of heterogeneous PEs gives more slack than the C implementation

```
For each step
 ODE_kernel() {
   branch1: type1
   branch2: type2
   branch3: type3
  ... }
```

(a)

```
For each step
 ODE_kernel1() {type1}
 ODE_kernel2() {type2}
 ODE_kernel3() {type3}
 ...
```

(b)

Fig. 11. GPU kernel function implementation options

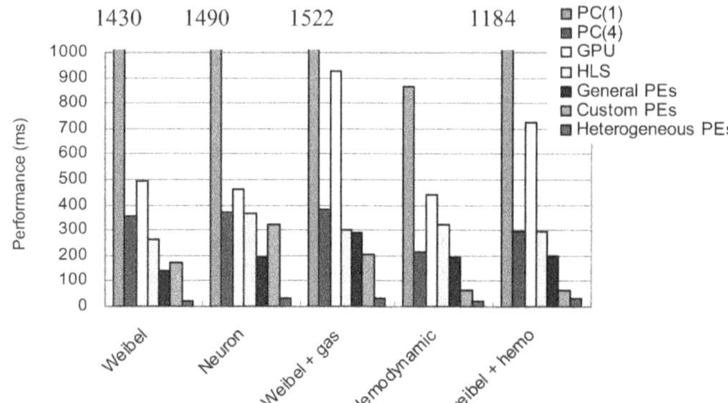

Fig. 10. The performance for each approach. 1000 ms is the real-time constraint and some PC(1) numbers extend off the chart top.

on the PC, which provides opportunity for real-time tracing of model state variables. The network of heterogeneous PEs is also more preferable in case fast-forward emulation is needed.

The GPU performs comparably to the multi-threaded PC approach when the number of ODE types is small (e.g., Weibel lung and Neuron models). The model with larger number of ODE types requires more branches in the kernel function, which decreases the performance. The network of heterogeneous PEs is on average 20.7X (13.7X~29X) faster than the GPU implementation. The major advantage of our approach is the custom communication network. For the target GPU, the only method to synchronize the GPU blocks is through a new function invocation, according to the CUDA programming guide [5]. Thus the frequent function invocation (10^5 times per second) greatly impacts the GPU's performance. According to profiling of the GPU-accelerated program, the pure function invocation overhead consumes 30% - 60% of the total execution time.

We included some approximate cost comparison for different approaches, in particular to acknowledge that FPGA platforms are costlier than PCs and GPUs. We consider the minimal required components for each platform in order to performance the emulation. The approximate cost of each platform is as follows:

1. CPU (I7-950 + Intel X58 board): $ 480
2. GPU (NV GTX460 + I3-540 processor + H55 board) $ 380
3. FPGA (Xilinx Virtex6 240T-2 board): $1800

We consider a *normalized speedup* term, namely: (speedup over real-time) / cost. The normalized speedup of each approach is shown in Fig. 12. The network of heterogeneous PEs obtained the best normalized speedup (3x over the I7-950 CPU and 4.4x over the GTX460 GPU), because of much higher emulation speed. The FPGA based solution has other advantages, such as smaller device

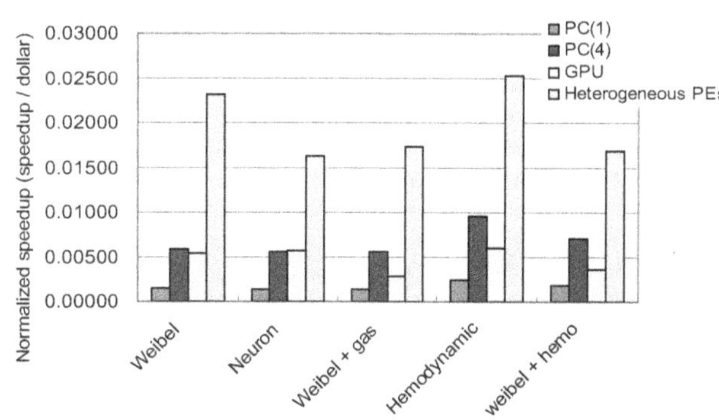

Fig. 12. The normalized speedup for each approach

size and the flexibility to build custom interfaces to the physical world [17].

6. CONCLUSION

We introduced a custom network of heterogeneous (both general and custom) processing-elements for real-time emulation of complex physical systems. We developed an automated tool to generate a custom PE network for a given set of ODEs. We developed an automatic allocation and binding heuristic for allocating different types of PEs, and mapping the ODEs of the target physical system to the PEs. We created a tool to generate synthesizable VHDL code from the allocation and binding results.

Comparing to a commercial high-level synthesis tool with regularity extraction, the custom networks of heterogeneous PEs were on average 10.8x faster and of comparable size. Compared to the custom networks of general and single-type custom PEs, the networks of heterogeneous PEs were on average 7x and 6x faster. The network of heterogeneous PEs was also on average 45x faster than a single threaded 3GHz I7-950 processor, and 20x faster than a 763 MHz NVIDIA GTX460 GPU given comparable implementation time. The speedups are due to the custom communication structure and also due to the custom datapath for each type of ODE.

7. ACKNOWLEDGMENTS

This work was supported in part by the National Science Foundation (CNS1016792, CPS1136146), the Semiconductor Research Corporation (GRC 2143.001), and a U.S. Department of Education GAANN fellowship.

8. REFERENCES

[1] Amorim, R.M., Rocha, B.M., Campos, F.O., dos Santos, R.W. 2010. Automatic code generation for solvers of cardiac cellular membrane dynamics in GPUs, EMBC.

[2] Atkinson, K. 1993. Elementary. Numerical Analysis, 2nd Edition, John Wiley & Sons, Inc. New York, New York.

[3] AutoESL 2012. http://www.xilinx.com/tools/autoesl.htm

[4] Butcher, J.C. 2003. Numerical methods for ordinary differential equations, ISBN 0471967580.

[5] CUDA programming guide 2011. http://developer.download.nvidia.com/compute/cuda/4_0-/toolkit/docs/CUDA_C_Programming_Guide.pdf

[6] Gokhale, M. B., Stone, J.M., Arnold, J., and Lalinowski, M. 2000. Stream-oriented FPGA computing in the Streams-C high level language. FCCM.

[7] Huang, C., Vahid, F., Givargis, T., 2011. Automatic synthesis of physical system differential equation models to a processing element network on FPGAs. Under submission.

[8] Huang, C., Miller, B., Vahid, F., Givargis, T., 2012. Synthesis of networks of custom processing-elements for real-time physical system emulation. Under submission.

[9] JSIM. 2012. http://nsr.bioeng.washington.edu/jsim/

[10] Kum, K., Kang, J., Sung, W. 2000. AUTOSCALER for C: an optimizing floating-point to integer C program converter for fixed-point digital signal processors. IEEE Transactions on Analog and Digital Signal Processing, vol. 47, no. 9, pp. 840-848, September 2000.

[11] Lee, E. A. 2008 Cyber Physical Systems: Design Challenges. Technical Report UCB/EECS-2008-8, University of California, EECS Department, 2008.

[12] Lionetti, F. 2010. http://cseweb.ucsd.edu/groups/ - hpcl/scg/papers/2010/Europ10-src-src-GPU.pdf

[13] Mathworks 2012. Matlab and Simulink. http://www.mathworks.com/.

[14] MedGadget,2008. Supercomputer Creates Most Advanced Heart Model, Internet Journal of Emerging Medical Technologies.

[15] METIman. 2012 available online: http://www.meti.com/products_ps_metiman.htm

[16] Meyer, J., Kocan, F. 2007. Sharing of SRAM Tables Among NPN-Equivalent LUTs in SRAM-Based FPGAs, Very Large Scale Integration (VLSI) Systems, IEEE Transactions on, vol.15, no.2, pp.182-195, Feb. 2007 doi: 10.1109/TVLSI.2007.893581

[17] Miller, B., Givargis, T., Vahid, F. 2011. Application-Specific Codesign Platform Generation for Digital Mockups in Cyber-Physical Systems IEEE Electronic System Level Synthesis Conf. (ESLsyn)

[18] National Instruments. 2011. LabView FPGA Module. http://www.ni.com/fpga/

[19] Nvidia Corporation. 2011. http://www.nvidia.com/object/gpu.html.

[20] Paulin, P.G., Knight, J.P., and Girczyc, E.F. 1986. HAL: a multi-paradigm approach to automatic data path synthesis. In Proceedings of the 23rd ACM/IEEE Design Automation Conference (DAC '86).

[21] Rao, D.S., Kurdahi, F.J. 1993. On clustering for maximal regularity extraction, Computer-Aided Design of Integrated Circuits and Systems, IEEE Transactions on, vol.12, no.8, pp.1198-1208, Aug 1993

[22] Salwinski, L., and Eisenberg, D. 2004. In silico simulation of biological network dynamics. Nature. Nature Publishing Group. pp 1017-1019.

[23] SynphonyC. 2011. http://www.synopsys.com/Systems/BlockDesign/HLS/Pages/SynphonyC-Compiler.aspx

[24] Terman, D., Ahn, S., Wang, X., Just, W. 2008. Reducing neuronal networks to discrete dynamics, Physica D: Nonlinear Phenomena, Volume 237, Issue 3, March 2008.

[25] Van Meurs, WL. 2011. Modeling and Simulation in Biomedical Engineering: Applications in Cardiorespiratory Physiology. McGraw-Hill Professional

[26] Villarreal, J., Park, A., Najjar, W., and Halstead, R. 2010 Designing modular hardware accelerators in C with ROCCC 2.0, FCCM, 2010.

[27] Weibel, E.R, Morphometry of the Human Lung. Berlin, Germany: Springer-Verlag, 1963

[28] Xilinx ISE. 2011. http://www.xilinx.com/

[29] Yoshimi, M., Osana, Y., Fukushima, T., and Amano, H. 2004. Stochastic Simulation for Biochemical Reactions on FPGA. FPL. pp 105-114.

Knowledge-Based Design Space Exploration of Wireless Sensor Networks

Paolo Roberto Grassi[1], Ivan Beretta[2], Vincenzo Rana[1,2], David Atienza[2] and Donatella Sciuto[1]

[1] Politecnico di Milano, DEI, Italy, {grassi, rana, sciuto}@elet.polimi.it
[2] École Polytechnique Fédérale de Lausanne, ESL, Switzerland, {ivan.beretta, david.atienza}@epfl.ch

ABSTRACT

The complexity of Wireless Sensor Networks (WSNs) has been constantly increasing over the last decade, and the necessity of efficient CAD tools has been growing accordingly. In fact, the size of the design space of a WSN has become large, and an exploration conducted by using semi-random algorithms (such as the popular genetic or simulated annealing algorithms) requires an unacceptable amount of time to converge due to the high number of parameters involved. To address this issue, in this paper we introduce a knowledge-based design space exploration algorithm for the WSN domain, which is based on a discrete-space Markov decision process (MDP). In order to enhance the performance of the proposed algorithm and to increase its scalability, we tailor the classical MDP approach to the specific aspects that characterize the WSN domain. We exploit domain-specific knowledge to choose the best node-level configuration in WSNs using slotted star topology in order to reduce the exploration time. The proposed approach has been tested on IEEE 802.15.4 star networks with various configurations of the number of nodes and their packet rates. Experimental results show that the proposed algorithm reduces the number of simulations required to converge, with respect to state-of-the-art algorithms (e.g., NSGA-II, PMA and MOSA), from 60 to 87%.

Categories and Subject Descriptors

C.4 [**Computer Systems Organization**]: Performance of Systems—*Design studies, modeling techniques*; C.3 [**Computer Systems Organization**]: Special-Purpose and Application-Based Systems—*Real-time and embedded systems*

General Terms

Design, Algorithms

Keywords

Design Space Exploration, Markov Decision Process, Wireless Sensor Networks

1. INTRODUCTION

The increasing complexity of Wireless Sensor Networks (WSNs) is leading towards the deployment of very sophisticated and ubiquitous networked systems. A WSN is composed by several nodes that communicate through a wireless channel: these nodes are typically battery-powered, and equipped with low-performance processors and small memories in order to reduce the power requirements. A common WSN node comprises five main components [19]: a processing element (microcontroller, processor, etc.), memory elements (RAM, SD, Flash, etc.), multiple communication layers (physical radio, MAC, Routing), a power supply and a sensing unit (including sensor, transducer, ADC). During the design phase, the contribution of all these components must be combined to identify the configuration that best fits the design objectives. The combination of different layers and the large number of configurable hardware and software parameters often generates an extremely large design space, which requires a powerful CAD algorithm to carry out the exploration.

A critical aspect of the Design Space Exploration (DSE) is the evaluation of a WSN configuration. Among the possible evaluation techniques, network models provide a deep understanding of the network dynamics that can be exploited during the DSE, but their definition is generally difficult and requires a deep knowledge of the working domain [4]. As a consequence, evaluation is typically performed using extensive network simulations [7], which are more accurate and reusable. However, a WSN simulation may take from several minutes to hours (depending on the network size) to be completed, and it should be repeated tens of times (generally more than 30) to mitigate the effects of randomness and ensure reliable statistical results.

In this paper, we propose a knowledge-based DSE algorithm that effectively tackles the design complexity of WSNs, by combining the domain knowledge of the analytical models with the generality and the flexibility of network simulators. Unlike semi-random algorithms, which require an evaluation at each step, the proposed approach performs several moves by relying on a set of domain-specific rules, thus greatly reducing the number of simulations. For this purpose, we adapt the *Markov decision process* (MDP) algorithm [5] to the WSN domain, and we solve its inherited scalability issues to face the large design spaces of WSNs. We also introduce a general domain knowledge for the most popular WSN MAC layer, i.e., the IEEE 802.15.4 [3], which can be reused on any WSN based on this protocol. Validation results prove that the proposed approach effectively reduces the number of simulations with respect to state-of-the-art semi-random algorithms from 60 to 87% on multiple real-world scenarios.

2. PROBLEM DEFINITION

In this section, we provide a characterization of the design space (denoted as S) of WSNs, in order to show the complexity of this kind of systems. The parameter space of a WSN is divided into two parts: a set of *node parameters* (P_n), which can assume different values on each nodes, and a set of *network parameters* (P_r), which assume one value throughout the whole network (or at least a part of it). For example, the memory size or the type of processor are specific of each node, hence they belong to P_n, whereas the network protocol must be the same among the nodes, therefore it belongs to P_r. Each parameter $p \in (P_n \cup P_r)$ is assigned to a discrete set of values in an interval $[p_{min}, p_{max}]$, whose cardinality is denoted as $|p|$.

Node parameters heavily affect the design space size $|S|$, since each parameters can assume an independent value on each node. Thus, when network size (expressed in terms of the number of nodes, N) increases, then $|S|$ increases exponentially. More formally, we can express the size of the design space of a WSN:

$$|S| = \left(\prod_{p \in P_r} |p| \right) \cdot \left(\prod_{q \in P_n} |q| \right)^N . \quad (1)$$

To understand the order of magnitude of $|S|$, let us show a relatively small example for structural or environmental monitoring. Let us assume that 8 nodes are placed on a $2\times2\times2$ tridimensional grid in the monitored area, and that the communication is regulated by the IEEE 802.15.4 MAC protocol [3]. Even without considering any hardware parameter, the configuration of the MAC protocol itself contains a wide set of possible parameters in P_r (e.g., the *frame* and the *beacon orders* [3]) and in P_n (e.g., the choice of using the contention active communication, or the number of requested *guaranteed time slots* [3]). Overall, the design space contains approximately 290 *billions* of solutions.

Thus, an extensive DSE would take an unacceptable amount of time when network simulation is the only viable way to evaluate a solution. As a consequence, a technique that is able to reduce the number of simulations is required.

3. STATE OF THE ART

Design space exploration is a well established research topic in many different fields, such as embedded architectures or system-level design. However, automatic DSE is still immature in WSN design, where the complexity of the network and the peculiarity of each application domain often push the developers towards manual and *ad hoc* optimizations (e.g., the work in [10] for wildlife monitoring).

The main obstacle towards the complete automation of the DSE of WSNs is a rapid and accurate evaluation of a solution. Currently, the two evaluation techniques [1] are models and simulations. Analytical models describe the WSN dynamics by means of a set of equations that provide a *white-box* view of the system, thus extensive analysis are possible. When a model-based evaluation is employed, the DSE is considerably faster compared to simulation-based approaches, but the accuracy of the model is typically guaranteed only for specific domains or for specific aspects of the WSN. In fact, only models that have been proposed for single classes of WSNs (e.g., [21] for body area networks) or for specific protocols (e.g. [11],[6] and [18] for three different operations of the IEEE 802.15.4 MAC layer) show an accuracy that is comparable to a simulation. In [14] an MDP is used to detect optimal sensor node operation in order to meet the application requirements. In this case, the solution is identified analytically solving the MDP via custom reward functions. However, it requires an accurate model to both guide and evaluate the solutions, which is a very important limitation. On the other hand, simulations better profile all the aspects related to communication, energy and resource usage of distributed applications. However, a robust simulation takes several from minutes to hours, thus making it impractical for extensive DSEs.

Table 1: Speed and accuracy of existing DSE techniques

	Low Accuracy	**High Accuracy**
Slow		Simulation-based ([7][16][13])
Fast	Model-based ([8][15])	MDP

In this context, the evaluation technique heavily affects the choice of the optimization algorithms. When an analytical description of the WSN (or, at least, of a specific part of it) is available, the optimization can be performed using *ad hoc* heuristic algorithms (e.g., in [8] to solve the network connectivity problem) or efficient techniques such as convex optimization (e.g., [15] for energy/delay optimization). The simulation-based estimation, on the other hand, has a black-box nature that does not allow any analytical consideration during the execution of the algorithm. This limitation leads to the employment of semi-random approaches such as genetic algorithms (e.g., [7] for placement and role assignment), multi-objective evolutionary algorithms (e.g., [16] for gossip-based WSNs), simulated annealing and Bayesian networks (e.g., [13] for a cross-layer optimization of cognitive wireless networks). However, given the high execution time required by a simulation, the class of semi-random algorithms does not scale well on large design spaces that are typical of real-world WSNs.

According to these considerations, model-based and simulation-based exploration are currently the two alternative approaches for the DSE of WSNs, and each one offers a speed/accuracy tradeoff that is summarized in Table 1. In this work, we aim at combining the high accuracy and reliability of a solution that is evaluated by a simulator, and the high speed that can be achieved when we include model information, calibrated with the simulator, in the DSE. In particular, the rationale is to move within the design space by exploiting the model information until they are accurate, and then use the simulation whenever it is strictly necessary.

4. MARKOV DECISION PROCESS

In this work we propose a knowledge-based design space exploration algorithm for the WSN domain, which is based on a discrete-space Markov decision process (MDP). In particular, we tailor the the classical MDP approach, which has been successfully applied in other domains such as multiprocessor systems design [5], to the WSN domain in order to enhance its performance and to increase its scalability. The proposed algorithm combines the available domain knowledge – which may come from an analytical model or by an analysis of the specific application – with a simulation-based network evaluation, in order to obtain an accurate and yet efficient DSE for WSNs.

In our approach, the DSE is considered as a path from the initial configuration P to a final configuration $\widehat{P}$. The path is identified by applying sequential transformations on the parameters, and the quality of these transformations is evaluated thanks to both models and simulations. The configuration P is composed by a set of parameters such as $P = \{p_1, ...p_k...p_n\}$ and an action $a \in A$ specifies how a configuration should be modified (i.e. *"double the CPU frequency"*). Actions transforms the configurations as follows:

DEFINITION 1. *Given a configuration of parameters $P = \{p_1, ...p_k...p_n\}$ and an action $a \in A$, a transformation $\tau(p_k, a)$ produces a new configuration $P' = \{p_1, ...p'_k...p_n\}$ where $p_k \neq p'_k$*

Once a transformation $\tau(p, a)$ has been performed, its effect on the metrics is evaluated using *movement vectors*:

DEFINITION 2. *A movement vector is a vector of intervals in the metrics space corresponding to a transformation vector in the parameter space defined as:*

$$\Phi = \langle f_1(\tau(p_k, a)), f_2(\tau(p_k, a)), ...f_i(\tau(p_k, a)), \rangle$$

where $i = |M|$, and $\overrightarrow{f} = f_1, f_2, ..., f_i$ are functions that determine the effect of the transformation τ on each metric $m_j \in M$.

Movement vectors are used to estimate the metrics of a configuration P' generated from an action a applied to a configuration P. For each metric $m_i \in M$, an interval in the metrics space $[m_i^L, m_i^H]$ specifies the range where the actual (real) value of the metric is included. $\overrightarrow{f}$ functions and movement vectors Φ are problem-specific (based on a model), thus problem-specific models are required.

For instance, the effect of the action *"double the operational frequency of a processor"* could in the worst case increase of up to two times of the energy consumption (m^H) or, in the best case, leave it unaltered (m^L). Thus, the movement vector associated with this action is $[E, 2E]$, where E indicates the current energy consumption. It indicates that, whereas the action *"double the operational frequency of a processor"* is applied on a configuration P, the energy consumption of the resulting configuration P' belongs to the interval $[E, 2E]$. In Section 5, we provide a set of movement vectors for networks based on the IEEE 802.15.4 protocol.

To tackle exploration accuracy, the metrics space is partitioned according to a parameter $\overrightarrow{\lambda}$ defined for the exploration. $\overrightarrow{\lambda}$ is a vector of scalars that specifies the maximum width of a partition for each metric. Partitioning is used to divide large areas into smaller areas such as the maximum error is defined by λ, given by the difference between the present value of the metrics (to be determined through simulation) and the centroid of the partition that best approximates it. An example of an action on a parameter is illustrated in Figure 1 where action a, applied to P, generates $P' = \tau(P, a)$. The metrics $M(P')$ are evaluated from

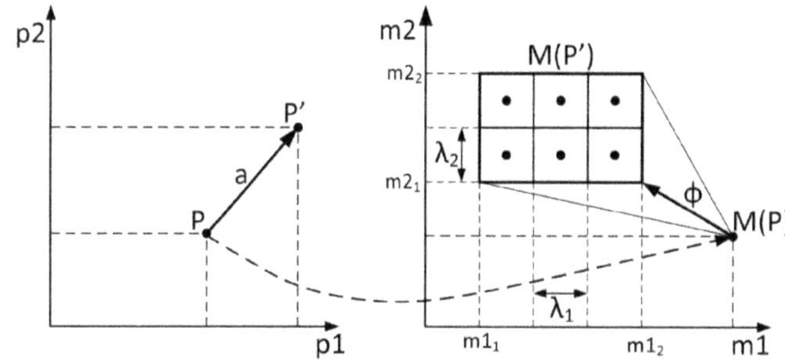

Figure 1: An example of actions on P. The metrics space is partitioned in 6 areas and centroids are illustrated with black dots

$M(P)$ through domain knowledge Φ and results in an area included into $\langle [m1_1, m1_2], [m2_1, m2_2] \rangle$. The area is partitioned in six partition (whose centroids are depicted with black dots) according to $\overrightarrow{\lambda}$.

The utility function (Ψ) has the utility property [20] and is a function of the metrics M. In a multi-objective exploration, metrics are combined in order to be able to enumerate the solutions. Ψ can be linear ($w_1m_1+w_2m_2+...+w_im_i$) or exponential ($m_1^{w_1}+m_2^{w_2}+...+m_i^{w_i}$). To obtain the pareto curve, the exploration is performed in a multivariate environment, thus $\overrightarrow{W} = \{w_1, w_2, ...w_i\}$ must change during the exploration in order to explore all the directions of the metrics space. In a two-dimensional metrics space, this can be achieved, i.e., using the scalarizing function $m_1^{\alpha} m_2^{(1-\alpha)}$ with α in $[0, 1]$.

The exploration is modeled as a MDP:

DEFINITION 3. *A MDP is a tuple $< S, A, TP, R >$ where:*

- *S is the set of possible states describing a solution of the DSE problem;*
- *A is the set of possible actions that can be applied on the states;*
- *$TP : S \times A \rightarrow \Pi(S)$ is the state transition function as the probability density function for every state-action pair;*
- *$R : S \times A \times S' \rightarrow R$ is the expected reward for each state-action pair.*

The behavior of the MDP is described with the Decision Tree D, a tree-based structure used to evaluate the various configurations. A node $s \in S$ in D represents a state of the system expressed by the tuple $\langle P, M \rangle$, where P is a point in the parameters space and M a point in the metrics space. An edge $e \in E$ is defined as:

$$e = \langle s_i, s_j, a, TP(s_i, a, s_j) \rangle$$

and it represents the transition probability (given by the transition function TP) from state s_i to state s_j when action a is applied.

Each partition identifies a new node in the decision tree, and the reward of the actions (R) is computed as the difference between parent (Ψ_p) and child (Ψ_c) utility functions:

$$R = \Psi_p - \Psi_c \quad (2)$$

For each partition $\langle s, a, s' \rangle$, the probability $TP_i(s_i, a, s_k)$ is computed as the number of times $\langle s, a \rangle$ ends in s' when traversing the decision tree from root to leaf. The decision

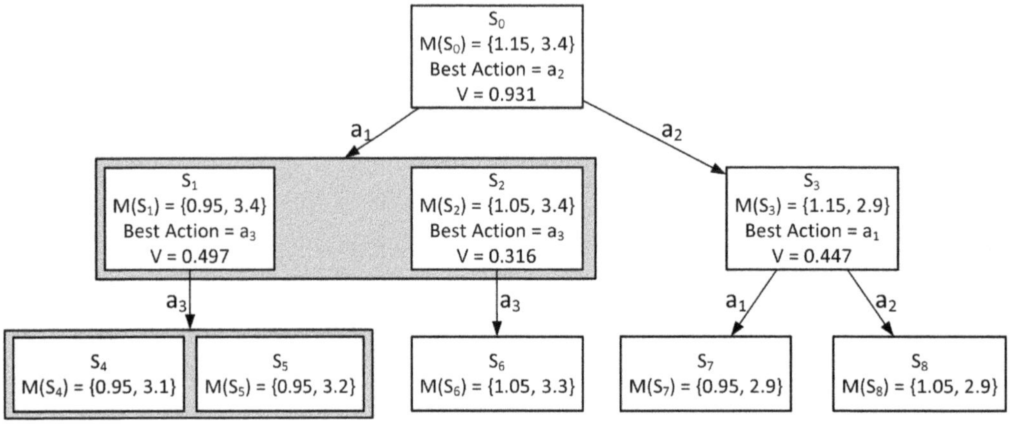

Figure 2: Example of a Decision Tree D. Cumulative return V is computed using the Value Iteration Algorithm (see Algorithm 1)

tree is progressively built by iterating on the newly generated nodes breadth-first, until either is not possible to apply any other action on the leaf nodes or the l-th level is reached. During the creation of D, in order to avoid useless exploration, *opposite* actions are included into a *forbidden list* such as they will not be applied. For example, if the action *Increase CPU frequency* is applied, the action *Decrease CPU frequency* in included into the *forbidden list* since it voids the previous action.

An example of the Decision Tree D is shown in Figure 2. From the initial state s_0, two actions are applied (a_1, a_2) resulting in three states (s_1, s_2, s_3) where s_1 and s_2 are two partitions. Actions a_3 and a_1 are further applied on the second level of the tree. For each state, metrics are associated; this example has two metrics that must be minimized. Rewards estimate the benefits of the actions on Ψ and are used to guide the exploration to better solutions. To determine the reward of the actions, Value Iteration Algorithm (see Algorithm 1) is used on D. For all the states in the tree and for all the available actions, the reward of an action $Q(s,a)$ is computed by adding the reward of choosing that action $(R(s,a,s'))$ with the cumulative return on the destination node $(V(s'))$ scaled by γ. γ is a scalar value $(0 \leq \gamma \leq 1)$ used to control the influence of (expected) cumulative returns. Transition probability $TP(s,a,s')$ is considered in the formula. In this specific example, V is computed by considering $\gamma = 0.6$ and the utility function $m_0^{1-\alpha} + m_1^{\alpha}$ with $\alpha = 0.5$. According to the metrics, the algorithm identifies a_2 as the best action in this situation; in fact, s_7 is optimal with respect to the given metrics. The new state is s_3 and no simulation is required since no uncertainty is detected here.

The overall exploration strategy is illustrated in Algorithm 2. It starts (**first step**) by generating an initial configuration P_0 (line 5) – that can be identified randomly or pseudo-randomly. Once P_0 has been evaluated by simulation and the initial state s_0 has been generated (line 6), the set of states to be examined $(\overline{S})$ is initialized (line 7).

The **second step** of the algorithm solves the MDP. For each state in $\overline{s}$, all possible actions are applied, generating the configurations that differ from s_0 by one parameter (lines 13-26). For all the generated configurations (obtained by applying a in s_i), s_k metrics are partitioned, D and $TP(s_i, a, s_k)$ are updated. The generation of the Decision Tree continues until no new states are available or the maximum depth l has been reached. At this point (line 27) the best value iteration algorithm [20] is applied and the *best_actions* are updated on D.

Algorithm 1: Strategy Evaluation Algorithm

```
initialize V(s) = 0
repeat
    forall the s ∈ S do
        forall the a ∈ A do
            Q(s,a) = Σ_{s'∈S} TP(s,a,s')[R(s,a,s') + γV(s')]
        end
        V(s) = max_a Q(s,a)
    end
until strategy converges;
```

The **third step** applies the *best_action* of s_0 in s_0 to get the set of reachable states (NS). At this point, three situations are possible:

1. **No Uncertainty**: the action can lead to a single state. The action is determined with an accuracy λ and no simulation is necessary;
2. **Uncertainty of the First Kind**: the action leads to a set of states and the algorithm maps the same action to all of them. It means that, whichever state the system will end into, the same next action is chosen. In case the amount of states is below a given threshold K, simulation is not required and parallel exploration will follow, otherwise simulation is required; K controls the amount of solutions to be explored and is used to tackle the scalability of the algorithm. Parallel explorations could evolve differently since they start from different partitions, thus they must be considered separately;
3. **Uncertainty of the Second Kind**: the action leads to a set of states, but the algorithm maps two or more different actions on those states. In this situation, simulation is needed to determine to which state the action really leads to.

Three examples of uncertainties are depicted in Figure 3. In 3(a) an uncertainty of the first kind is detected and $|NS| < K$ thus simulation is not required. In 3(b) an uncertainty of

Algorithm 2: Overall Exploration Strategy

1 Identify the configuration parameters $\overrightarrow{P}$
2 Define the movement vectors Φ
3 *num_runs=0*
4 **repeat**
5 Generate an initial configuration P_0
6 s_{init} = Simulate(P_0)
7 Initialize the set of states to be examined $\overline{S} = s_{init}$
8 **repeat**
9 depth = 0
10 reset D
11 get an element $s_0 \in \overline{S}$, $\overline{S} = \overline{S} - s_0$
12 $\overline{s} = s_0$
13 **repeat**
14 $\overline{s}_{new} = \{\}$
15 **forall the** s_i *in* $\overline{s}$ **do**
16 **forall the** *a applicable in* s_i **do**
17 apply a in s_i creating child nodes s_k
18 partition s_k metrics
19 update D and $TP(s_i, a, s_k)$
20 $\overline{s}_{new} = \overline{s}_{new} + s_k$
21 add a to forbidden action list of s_i
22 **end**
23 **end**
24 $\overline{s} = \overline{s}_{new}$
25 depth++
26 **until** $\overline{s} = \emptyset$ *or depth* $== l$;
27 Value Iteration Algorithm(D)
28 NS = $\tau(s_0, best\_action(s_0))$
29 **if** $|NS| \geq K$ *or* ($\exists s_i, s_j \in$ *NS*: *best_action*(s_i) $\neq$ *best_action*(s_j) *and* $i \neq j$) **then**
30 s_{next} = Simulate(P_{s_0})
31 **if** $s_{next} \notin NS$ **then**
32 Error $\longrightarrow$ Restart From Line 5
33 **end**
34 $NS = s_{next}$
35 **end**
36 **if** *convergency* **then**
37 Simulate(P_{s_0})
38 **else**
39 $\overline{S} = \overline{S} + NS$
40 **end**
41 **until** $\overline{S} = \emptyset$;
42 *num_runs++*
43 **until** *num_runs* $\geq$ *MAXRUNS*;
44 Change Utility Function
45 Repeat All

the first kind is detected but $|NS| \geq K$ thus simulation is required. In 3(c) simulation is required since an uncertainty of the second kind is detected.

In other terms, simulation is performed only if the cardinality of NS (the amount of states reached by the best action) is above a given value K or the action a brings the system to *a set* of states and the Value Iteration Algorithm mapped different actions to each of those states. In case simulation results s_{next} are not contained in NS exploration restarts from line 5, otherwise NS is update with the real value s_{next}. At this point the algorithm checks if convergency has been reached (line 36); in the positive case, a

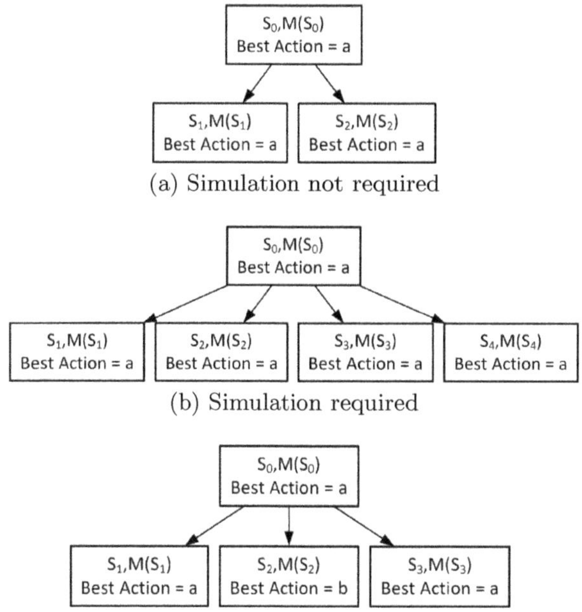

(a) Simulation not required

(b) Simulation required

(c) Simulation required

Figure 3: Uncertainties of First and Second Kind with $K = 3$

simulation is performed (line 37) to get the real values of the metric of s_0 (unless it has been previously simulated), otherwise, $\overline{S}$ is updated and the exploration continues.

Step one, two and three are repeated until a maximum number of runs (*MAXRUNS)* has been performed.

In the **last step**, the weights $\overrightarrow{w}$ of the utility function Ψ are updated (line 44) and the algorithm is entirely repeated. It allows to *change the direction* of the exploration in order to cope multi-objective optimizations. The algorithm stops when no more utility functions would be used.

In conclusion, the algorithm explores all the possible actions for all the reachable states with an event horizon of l to determine an optimal local action considering various sequences of actions. The effectiveness of the approach strictly depends on the quality of the movement vectors; as the accuracy of movement vectors increases, the amount of required simulations decreases. In fact, in the optimal case, movement vectors identify areas with size lower than λ, thus *No Uncertainty* is detected. In this case, assuming that movement vectors are accurate, simulation is required at the beginning (line 6) and end (line 37) only, thus simulations are minimized and exploration speed is maximized. In the worst case, non accurate movement vectors may conduct to *Uncertainties of First* (with $|NS| > K$) or *Second Kind*, thus simulations are required at each step, leading to slower explorations. More generally, to control the accuracy and the speed of the exploration (number of states in the MDP) two mechanisms have been identified:

- **Control the minimum desired accuracy with λ.** It identifies the size of the partitions during the generation of the Decision Tree; increasing λ reduces the number of partitions (states), improving the evaluation speed, but it increases the approximation error;
- **Define a good event horizon l**, which determines the maximum depth of the Decision Tree. It limits the number of steps required to the creation/evaluation

of the MDP. Reducing l improves the speed of MDP evaluation since fewer states are generated into the decision tree D. On the other hand, the higher is l the higher is the lookahead of the algorithm.

5. DOMAIN KNOWLEDGE DEFINITION FOR IEEE 802.15.4 NETWORKS

The proposed approach requires movement vectors to guide the exploration to optimal solutions. In this section, we discuss a domain knowledge definition for the IEEE 802.15.4 MAC layer. The proposed MDP does not require accurate movement vectors to operate [5], thus it is not required that the users give accurate models to use this methodology; moreover, movement vectors are reusable. However, the analysis proposed in this Section has two main goals: first, to show in practice how to build a set of domain-specific rules to exploit the potential of the MDP algorithm. Second, it provides a good characterization of one the most popular MAC protocols in WSNs, hence the proposed rules can be reused.

The IEEE 802.15.4 standard [3] has been introduced to satisfy energy requirements of emergent devices. The protocol is quite common, thus the knowledge domain defined in this Section can be useful for future works. The results presented here are based on the models presented in [12] [21] [11] [6] [9] [18]. IEEE 802.15.4 network is composed by a central node, called coordinator, and a set of nodes, called members. In IEEE 802.15.4, the coordinator is the head of the network and determines the structure of the communication. In the standard, the communication is divided into sequential frames delimited by specific packets called beacons (Figure 4). A frame is divided into an active and an inactive period, and the active part is further divided in two periods named Contention Active Period (CAP) and Contention Free Period (CFP). During the CAP, nodes access the channel by using the CSMA/CA protocol, while, during the CFP, the nodes access the channel using a time division protocol which slots, namely Guarantee Time Slots (GTS), are assigned by the coordinator by means of a policy *First Come First Served* (FCFS) [3].

The metrics of interests are Average Energy Consumption (E), to be minimized, and Percentage of Packets Received (P), to be maximized. The IEEE 802.15.4 is characterized by a certain amount of node and network parameters. For the sake of simplicity, we decide to restrict the analysis to four parameters: **SuperframeOrder**, **BeaconOrder**, **enableCAP** and **requestGTS**. According to the state of the art, these parameters have considerable effects on the metrics of interests, thus their optimization is important to the final design. In all the equations the following constraint

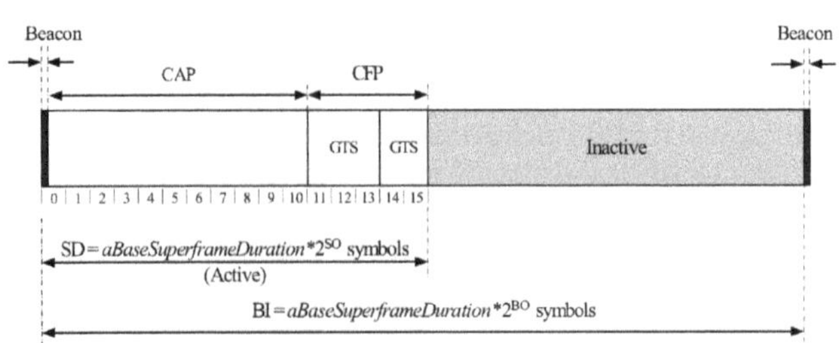

Figure 4: An example of the superframe structure (from [3])

must be satisfied:

$$(0 \leq P \leq 100) \wedge (E \geq 0) \qquad (3)$$

In case the equation is not satisfied, P and E are set to the nearest value which satisfies the equation. I.e., if $P < 0$ then P is set to zero. The next two sections presents in detail the movement vectors. In all the equations, E and P represents the actual value of the metrics while $\widehat{E}$ and $\widehat{P}$ represents their estimated (next) value.

5.1 Beacon Order and Superframe Order

Beacon Order (BO) and Superframe Order (SO) define the main structure of the superframe since they determine the distance between the beacons and the size of the active period. The ratio between SO and BO defines the duty cycle between active and inactive period. The overall effect of increasing BO and decreasing SO is similar, since both actions modify the duty cycle in the same way. Increasing BO or decreasing SO will halve the duty cycle, thus both E and P can be reduced by 2. Resulting movement vectors to actions **increase BO** and **decrease SO** are:

$$\widehat{E} = \left[\frac{E}{2}, E\right] \qquad (4)$$

$$\widehat{P} = \left[\frac{P}{2}, P\right] \qquad (5)$$

On the other hand, actions that **decrease BO** and **increase SO** have an opposite behavior, since duty cycle is doubled:

$$\widehat{E} = [E, 2E] \qquad (6)$$

$$\widehat{P} = [P, 2P] \qquad (7)$$

All these actions can be applied if and only if the constraint:

$$SO \leq BO \qquad (8)$$

is satisfied. This constraint is imposed by the standard [3].

5.2 Guaranteed Time Slots

Each node requires a certain amount of GTS to the coordinator, according to the *requestGTS* parameter. The coordinator assigns the GTS according to the FCFS policy. It implies that if requested GTS are not designed properly, performances of the network dramatically decreases.

The maximum amount of available slots in slotted IEEE 802.15.4 is given by the following formula:

$$M = NSS - \left\lfloor \frac{minCAP}{BSD * 2^{FO}} \right\rfloor \qquad (9)$$

where NSS is the *Number of Superframe Slots*, minCAP is the minimum number of symbols in CAP and BSD is the *Base Slot Duration*.

The average amount of slots per node is equal to:

$$A = \frac{M}{N} \qquad (10)$$

and the overall amount of requested slots is equal to:

$$U = \sum_{i=0}^{N} G(i) \qquad (11)$$

where $G(i)$ represents the value of *requestGTS* of node i. From [18] and experimental results, we notice that, increasing the GTS requests improves P and reduces E. P is improved because contention is reduced and E decreases since nodes wake-up are scheduled more efficiently in CFP with respect to CAP. In particular, when a GTS slot is allocated and few packets are in the buffer, the node sleeps during CAP and wake-ups just at the beginning of the GTS slot. In addition, since IEEE 802.15.4 uses a TDMA protocol during CFP, no additional energy is required to perform *Carrier Sense.*

According to the FCFS policy, if GTS have been already allocated and it is not possible to satisfy the request, the request is rejected and the node is obliged to communicate into the CAP. GTS requests are rejected if the amount of requested GTS slots (Equation 11) overcomes the maximum amount of slots in CFP (Equation 9). Moreover, in order to balance GTS requests, the amount of GTS requests per node n ($G(n)$) should not overcome the average GTS requests (Equation 10). The effect of increasing/decreasing GTS is limited to a single-slot of a single-node, so the value of P and E should be divided by NM to provide more accurate movement vectors.

Action **increase requestGTS** on node n results in:

$$\widehat{E} = \begin{cases} \left[E - \frac{E}{NM}, E\right] & \text{if } U \leq M \wedge G(n) \leq A \\ \left[E, E + \frac{E}{NM}\right] & \text{otherwise} \end{cases} \tag{12}$$

$$\widehat{P} = \begin{cases} \left[P, P + \frac{P}{NM}\right] & \text{if } U \leq M \wedge G(n) \leq A \\ \left[P - \frac{P}{NM}, P\right] & \text{otherwise} \end{cases} \tag{13}$$

On the other hand, action **decrease requestGTS** has the following movement vectors:

$$\widehat{E} = \begin{cases} \left[E, E + \frac{E}{NM}\right] & \text{if } U \leq M \wedge G(n) \leq A \\ \left[E - \frac{E}{NM}, E\right] & \text{otherwise} \end{cases} \tag{14}$$

$$\widehat{P} = \begin{cases} \left[P - \frac{P}{NM}, P\right] & \text{if } U \leq M \wedge G(n) \leq A \\ \left[P, P + \frac{P}{NM}\right] & \text{otherwise} \end{cases} \tag{15}$$

5.3 Enable CAP

Considering the enableCAP parameter, two actions are possible: activate and deactivate CAP. The overall effect of enabling CAP is the increase of energy consumption (due to CAP period) and an increase of packets received. Similarly to GTS, the action has an effect on a single node only, thus both E and P changes are scaled to N. Moreover, the higher is the amount of GTS requests of a node, the lower is the effect of activation/deactivation of CAP, so the metrics are divided by G(n)+1.

Differently from energy, packets received have a known behavior in case $G(n)$ is equal to zero. In fact, when $G(n) = 0$ and CAP is not enabled, the amount of packets sent by a node n is equal to zero, thus activating CAP when $G(n) = 0$ has a increases the number of packets received ($\left[\frac{P}{N}, \frac{100}{N}\right]$); the deactivation of CAP when $G(n) = 0$ has the opposite effect. The movement vectors of the action **activate CAP** are:

$$\widehat{E} = \left[E, E + \frac{E}{N(G(n)+1)}\right] \tag{16}$$

$$\widehat{P} = \begin{cases} \left[P + \frac{P}{N}, P + \frac{100}{N}\right] & \text{if } G(n) = 0 \\ \left[P, P + \frac{P}{N(G(n)+1)}\right] & \text{otherwise} \end{cases} \tag{17}$$

for the action **deactivate CAP**, the movement vectors are:

$$\widehat{E} = \left[E - \frac{E}{N(G(n)+1)}, E\right] \tag{18}$$

$$\widehat{P} = \begin{cases} \left[P - \frac{100}{N}, P - \frac{P}{N}\right] & \text{if } G(n) = 0 \\ \left[P - \frac{P}{N(G(n)+1)}, P\right] & \text{otherwise} \end{cases} \tag{19}$$

5.4 Initial Points Selection

In the classical MDP, the set of initial points is randomly generated but, especially with large design spaces, the probability to obtain bad (or even unfeasible) solutions is high. Therefore, the selection of the initial points can be guided by the model since, considering that the knowledge base has been already created to compute the actions, the same information can be used to extract the initial points.

To define the rules for the selection of the initial points, we conduct several experiments on star networks with 4, 6 and 8 nodes with various packet rates (5, 15, 30, 50, 65, 80 $\left[\frac{pkts}{sec}\right]$) in order to cover a large set of applications. All the experiments where conducted with Castalia simulator [2] (see next Section). From the experimental results, we notice that assigning a *requestGTS* greater than the average (A), reduces the quality of the solution, so we suggest to create the initial population with a starting value of *requestGTS* randomly chosen in the interval $[0, A]$. In addition, a value of Beacon Order lower than 3 or greater than 12 does not usually provide good results, thus we generate the initial solution with BO included into $[3, 12]$. Another aspect concerns the duty cycle ($\frac{SO}{BO}$); good solutions usually have a duty cycle included into $[0.25, 0.85]$ in all the configurations.

Summarizing, to determine the initial points, we propose to generate the set of initial points in such a way:

$$\begin{cases} 0 \leq G(n) \leq A & \forall n \in N \\ 3 \leq BO \leq 12 \\ 0.25 \leq \frac{SO}{BO} \leq 0.85 \end{cases} \tag{20}$$

so that these constraints are all satisfied.

Experimental results in the next Section show that a considerable improvement on search efficiency is obtained if initial points are determined using this technique.

6. EXPERIMENTAL RESULTS

This Section presents two sets of experiments to validate the proposed approach. The solutions were evaluated with Castalia [2], a popular simulator for Wireless Sensor Networks and Body Area Networks, based on the OMNeT++ framework [22]. The design space for all the experiments is presented in Table 2. The design space has been explored in four different scenarios described in Table 3. These scenarios have been chosen in order to cover a large set of applications (i.e. Body Area Networks).

Since the cardinality of the design space is extremely high in all the scenarios, the optimal Pareto curve cannot be extracted with an exhaustive search, thus it has been obtained running all the exploration algorithms for 3000 iterations (solutions) for 20 iterations each. The distance between the

Table 2: **Explored Design Options for the Experimental Results**

Parameter	From	To
Beacon Order	1	14
Frame Order	1	14
Enable Cap	false	true
requestGTS	0	6

Table 3: Experimental Scenarios

	Num of Nodes	Packet Rate (Pkts/Sec)	Size of the Design Space
Scen. 1	4	30, 65, 80	$7.5 * 10^6$
Scen. 2	6	15, 40, 60	$1.4 * 10^9$
Scen. 3	8	5, 15, 30	$2.9 * 10^{11}$
Scen. 4	10	5, 10, 15	$5.6 * 10^{13}$

Pareto sets have been compared using the *Average Distance from Reference Set* (ADRS) [17]. The ADRS is usually measured in terms of percentage and should be minimized.

6.1 Evaluation of the Proposed Algorithm

The first set of experiments aims at evaluating the improvements achieved thanks to the tailoring of the standard MDP technique to the WSN field. In particular, Table 4 presents a comparison between the standard implementation of the MDP algorithm and the one proposed within this work. The experimental results shown in Table 4 demonstrate that the ADRS of the initial points of the proposed algorithm is considerably lower than the ones obtained with [5]. This advantage makes it possible to increase the overall performance of the algorithm, so that the ADRS of the final solutions found by our algorithm is always lower than the ones obtained with [5]. In addition to this, the proposed algorithm is able to converge with a lower number of evaluations, except for Scenarios 3 and 4, where the algorithm presented in [5] often falls in local minima (as shown by the quite high ADRS of the solutions found by the algorithm).

A critical aspect of the standard MDP algorithm is its scalability. In order to analyze this factor, we suggest to handle uncertainties of the first kind with simulations only if the number of states ($|NS|$) is larger than a given threshold K. To evaluate the effect of K on the exploration speed

Table 4: Comparison between original and proposed implementation of the MDP

Scenario 1	[5]	[proposed work]
ADRS[%] init	45.5	21.7
ADRS[%] final	3.9	2.34
Eval. for Convergence	110	70
Scenario 2	[5]	[proposed work]
ADRS[%] init	44.7	21.47
ADRS[%] final	5.73	2.70
Eval. for Convergence	170	120
Scenario 3	[5]	[proposed work]
ADRS[%] init	35.93	24.3
ADRS[%] final	11.35	3.52
Eval. for Convergence	70	80
Scenario 4	[5]	[proposed work]
ADRS[%] init	38.93	27.3
ADRS[%] final	14.18	5.16
Eval. for Convergence	110	70

we perform several experiments with different values of K; Scenario 2 has been chosen as reference example for this analysis. We vary the values of λ such as the average number of generated states for each action is between 3 (higher λ) and 30 (lower λ). Figure 5 illustrates the average number of parallel explorations for different values of K with respect to the average number of states for each step. The bigger is K, the higher is the amount of parallel (independent) explorations. However, the effective exploration time is not directly correlated with the amount of parallel explorations. Figure 6 illustrates the average amount of time (in minutes) required for the exploration with different values of K. Although the number of parallel evaluations increases with both K and the number of generated states, the overall time behaves differently. In fact, for small values of generated states, *K=5* performs better then *K=2* even if the amount of parallel exploration is bigger. However, for high values of generated states (i.e. 30), *K=2* performs better. *K=inf* have no better performances in all the situations; it confirms that a bound on the generated states increase the exploration's speed. Moreover, we notice that exploration efficacy (ADRS and convergence speed) is not affected by *K* since it strictly depends on λ, thus it is suggested to tune K such that the exploration time is minimized.

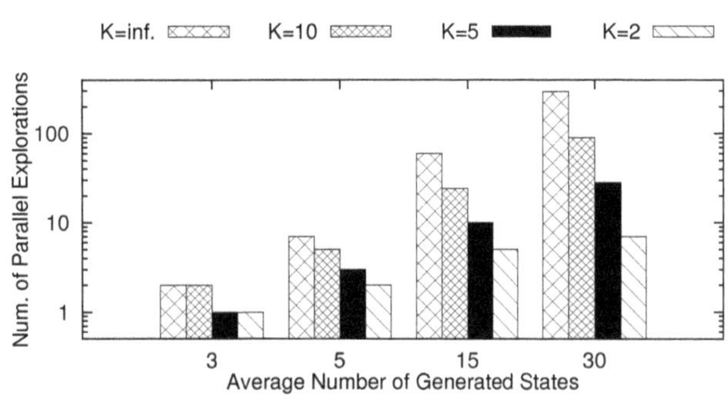

Figure 5: Number of parallel explorations with different values of K (K=inf. refers to the original algorithm). The average number of generated states depends on the chosen λ and movement vectors' accuracy

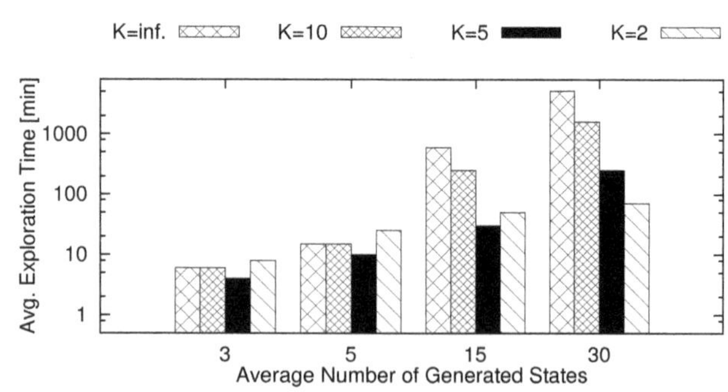

Figure 6: Amount of time (in minutes) required for the exploration with different values of K (K=inf. refers to the original algorithm). The average number of generated states depends on the chosen λ and movement vectors' accuracy

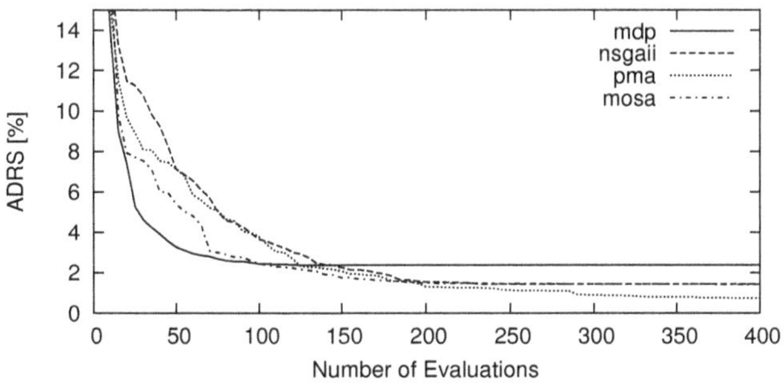

Figure 7: ADRS per Number of Evaluations in Scenario 1

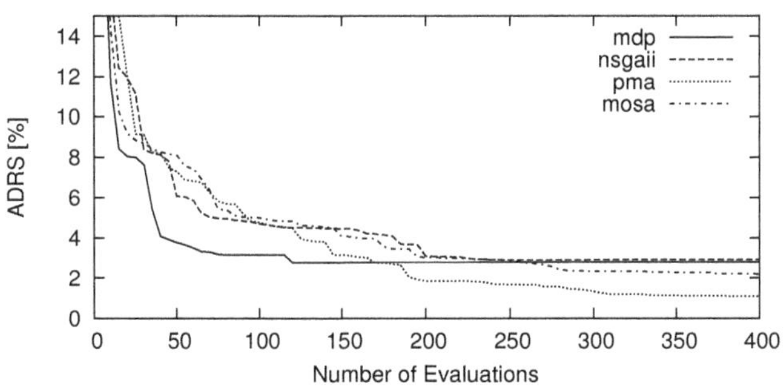

Figure 8: ADRS per Number of Evaluations in Scenario 2

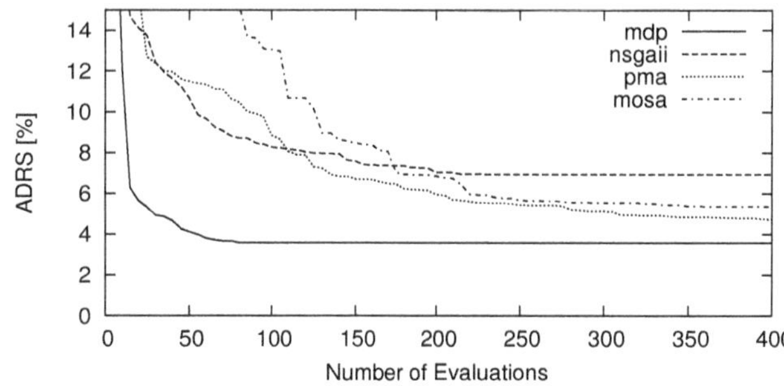

Figure 9: ADRS per Number of Evaluations in Scenario 3

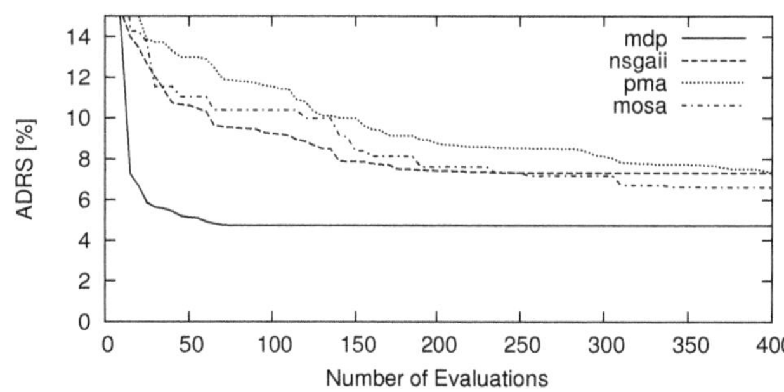

Figure 10: ADRS per Number of Evaluations in Scenario 4

The proposed algorithm is able to reduce/control the exponential growth of the number of parallel executions with respect to the original approach presented in [5] (where the threshold K has not been defined). Then, in addition to improving the quality of the final solution, the proposed approach is also able to reduce the number of explorations to be performed, thus reducing the computational costs and time required by the algorithm itself.

6.2 ADRS and Number of Evaluations

The second set of experiments compares the proposed MDP with three state-of-the-art multiobjective optimization algorithms: controlled non-dominated sorting genetic algorithm (NSGA-II), Pareto memetic algorithm (PMA) and multiple objective simulated annealing (MOSA). The MOMHLib++ [1] library was used as a reference implementation of these algorithms. In order to ensure a fair comparison, all the algorithms exploits the technique described in Section 5.4 to generate the initial points.

Each configuration of all the optimization algorithms has been executed for 20 times in the four scenarios and the average ADRS has been evaluated. We compute the ADRS every 5 evaluations in order to understand its trend with respect to the number of evaluations. The results of these experiments are presented in Figure 7 (Scenario 1), Figure 8 (Scenario 2), Figure 9 (Scenario 3) and Figure 10 (Scenario 4), which show that MDP is able to reach a low ADRS (below 5%) using less than 40 evaluations, while the other algorithms require from 100 to almost 300 evaluations to reach the same objective. This is a reduction of 60-87% in the number of required simulations. The time required to evaluate a single solution varies from 7 (Scenario 1) to 18 minutes (Scenario 4), that implies an exploration time of almost 5 hours for MDP and 12-36 hours for others in Scenario 1, 12 hours for MDP and 30-60 hours for others in Scenario 4. These numbers illustrate the practical efficacy of the proposed approach for real-life WSN designs exploration and optimization.

As design space cardinality increases, the identification of the Pareto curve is more difficult, thus exploration efficiency decreases. It is interesting to notice that the reduction of effectiveness of MDP is considerably lower than the other algorithms (See Table 5). These results encourage the use of such algorithm on large design spaces.

During the Design Space Exploration, optimization algorithms should be run several times in order to guarantee the quality of the identified Pareto curve. Analyzing the standard deviation of the ADRS on the independent runs, we observed that standard deviation on MDP is the lowest. Table 6 summarized the computed standard deviations. A low standard deviation implies that the optimization algorithm requires few repeats to guarantee the quality; it

Table 5: Final ADRS of search Algorithms

	MDP	NSGA-II	PMA	MOSA
Scenario 1	2.34	1.42	0.83	1.43
Scenario 2	2.70	2.88	0.78	2.20
Scenario 3	3.52	6.52	4.76	5.36
Scenario 4	5.16	9.55	8.78	7.32

Table 6: Standard Deviation of ADRS

	MDP	NSGA-II	PMA	MOSA
Scenario 1	0.34	1.20	1.01	1.34
Scenario 2	0.55	2.56	1.94	1.91
Scenario 3	0.64	2.44	2.38	2.81
Scenario 4	0.77	2.59	2.96	2.92

further reduces the overall time required for Design Space Exploration.

7. CONCLUDING REMARKS

This paper has presented a technique to reduce the amount of simulations necessary to obtain the Pareto set of the design space exploration of Wireless Sensor Networks. The proposed technique uses models as soon as they provide an acceptable accuracy and simulates only when it is needed. The knowledge domain about slotted IEEE 802.15.4 has been extracted from the models of the state of the art. Experimental results have shown that proposed algorithm significantly improves the efficiency and scalability with respect to the classical algorithm. To confirm the efficacy of the technique, we also compared the proposed approach with semi-random algorithms such as NSGA-II, PMA and MOSA. Experimental results have shown that MDP reduces the number of simulations required to converge (ADRS lower than 5%) from 60 to 87%. This reduction is more effective as the cardinality of the design space increases, making it an effective approach for the design space exploration of WSNs.

8. REFERENCES

[1] MOMH: multiple objective meta heuristics [online]. available: http://home.gna.org/momh/.

[2] OMNET++ castalia simulator, [Online] http://castalia.npc.nicta.com.au/.

[3] IEEE standard for information technology. 802.15.4 standard specification, 2006.

[4] L. S. Bai, R. P. Dick, P. H. Chou, and P. A. Dinda. Automated construction of fast and accurate system-level models for wireless sensor networks. In *Design, Automation & Test in Europe Conference & Exhibition (DATE), 2011*, pages 1–6. IEEE, Mar. 2011.

[5] G. Beltrame, L. Fossati, and D. Sciuto. Decision-Theoretic design space exploration of multiprocessor platforms. *IEEE Transactions on Computer-Aided Design of Integrated Circuits and Systems*, 29(7):1083–1095, July 2010.

[6] C. Buratti. A mathematical model for performance of IEEE 802.15.4 beacon-enabled mode. In *Proceedings of the International Conference on Wireless Communications and Mobile Computing: Connecting the World Wirelessly*, IWCMC '09, pages 1184–1190, New York, NY, USA, 2009. ACM.

[7] K. P. Ferentinos and T. A. Tsiligiridis. Adaptive design optimization of wireless sensor networks using genetic algorithms. *Computer Networks*, 51(4):1031–1051, Mar. 2007.

[8] O. Goussevskaia, R. Wattenhofer, M. M. Halldorsson, and E. Welzl. Capacity of arbitrary wireless networks. In *IEEE INFOCOM 2009*, pages 1872–1880. IEEE, Apr. 2009.

[9] J. He, Z. Tang, H. Chen, and Q. Zhang. An accurate and scalable analytical model for IEEE 802.15.4 slotted CSMA/CA networks. *IEEE Transactions on Wireless Communications*, 8(1):440–448, Jan. 2009.

[10] Z. He, J. Eggert, W. Cheng, X. Zhao, J. Millspaugh, R. Moll, J. Beringer, and J. Sartwell. Energy-aware portable video communication system design for wildlife activity monitoring. *Circuits and Systems Magazine, IEEE*, 8(2):25 –37, 2008.

[11] M. Kohvakka, M. Kuorilehto, M. Hännikäinen, and T. D. Hämäläinen. Performance analysis of IEEE 802.15.4 and ZigBee for large-scale wireless sensor network applications. In *Performance evaluation of wireless ad hoc, sensor and ubiquitous networks*, pages 48–57, New York, NY, USA, 2006. ACM.

[12] G. Lu, B. Krishnamachari, and C. S. Raghavendra. Performance evaluation of the IEEE 802.15.4 MAC for low-rate low-power wireless networks. In *2004 IEEE International Conference on Performance, Computing, and Communications*, pages 701– 706. IEEE, 2004.

[13] E. Meshkova, J. Riihijarvi, A. Achtzehn, and P. Mahonen. Exploring simulated annealing and graphical models for optimization in cognitive wireless networks. In *IEEE Global Telecommunications Conference, 2009. GLOBECOM 2009*, pages 1–8. IEEE, Dec. 2009.

[14] A. Munir and A. Gordon-Ross. An mdp-based application oriented optimal policy for wireless sensor networks. In *Proceedings of the 7th IEEE/ACM international conference on Hardware/software codesign and system synthesis*, CODES+ISSS '09, pages 183–192, New York, NY, USA, 2009. ACM.

[15] S. Nabar, J. Walling, and R. Poovendran. Minimizing energy consumption in body sensor networks via convex optimization. In *Body Sensor Networks (BSN), Int. Conf. on*, pages 62 –67, June 2010.

[16] M. Nabi, M. Blagojevic, T. Basten, M. Geilen, and T. Hendriks. Configuring multi-objective evolutionary algorithms for design-space exploration of wireless sensor networks. In *Proceedings of the 4th ACM workshop on Performance monitoring and measurement of heterogeneous wireless and wired networks*, PM2HW2N '09, pages 111–119, Tenerife, Canary Islands, Spain, 2009. ACM.

[17] G. Palermo, C. Silvano, and V. Zaccaria. ReSPIR: a response Surface-Based pareto iterative refinement for Application-Specific design space exploration. *Computer-Aided Design of Integrated Circuits and Systems, IEEE Transactions on*, 28(12):1816 –1829, Dec. 2009.

[18] P. Park, C. Fischione, and K. H. Johansson. Performance analysis of GTS allocation in beacon enabled IEEE 802.15.4. In *6th Annual IEEE Communications Society Conference on Sensor, Mesh and Ad Hoc Communications and Networks, 2009. SECON '09*, pages 1–9. IEEE, June 2009.

[19] M. A. Pasha, S. Derrien, and O. Sentieys. System-Level synthesis for wireless sensor node controllers. *ACM Transactions on Design Automation of Electronic Systems*, 17(1):1–24, Jan. 2012.

[20] S. Russel and P. Norvig. *Artificial Intelligence: Modern Approach.* 1st ed. englewood cliffs, NJ: prentice hall edition, 1995.

[21] N. F. Timmons and W. G. Scanlon. Analysis of the performance of IEEE 802.15.4 for medical sensor body area networking. pages 16– 24. IEEE, Oct. 2004.

[22] A. Varga. The OMNET++ discrete event simulation system. In *Proceedings of the European Simulation Multiconference*, pages 319–324. SCS – European Publishing House, 2001.

Spatially- and Temporally-Adaptive Communication Protocols for Zero-Maintenance Sensor Networks Relying on Opportunistic Energy Scavenging

Xuejing He
EECS Department
University of Michigan
1301 Beal Ave
Ann Arbor, MI, 48019
xjhe@umich.edu

Robert P. Dick
EECS Department
University of Michigan
1301 Beal Ave
Ann Arbor, MI, 48019
dickrp@eecs.umich.edu

Russ Joseph
EECS Department
Northwestern University
2145 Sheridan Road
Evanston, IL, 60208
rjoseph@eecs.northwestern.edu

ABSTRACT

Wireless sensor networks allow scientists to gather data from remote, difficult to access, and dangerous locations. However, maintenance of aging networks and removal of obsolete or inactive nodes containing toxic materials is expensive and time consuming. Moreover, node lifespan is generally constrained by the reliability of the batteries used in most deployments, especially in the presence of extreme variation in environmental conditions such as temperature and humidity. We consider the problem of designing wireless sensor networks capable of indefinite deployment periods measured in decades, not months. We describe the architectural and capability implications of eliminating batteries from sensor networks and instead relying on opportunistic energy scavenging. Sensor nodes using ambient energy sources become temporarily active at unpredictable but possibly correlated times. In this paper, we use wind power as an example of such a power source, which we model using temporally and spatially correlated random processes. Such models can be built using historical measurements over a geographical range. We describe a method to use energy models in the design of latency-optimized and cost-constrained battery-less wireless sensor networks, and explain the required changes to network architecture, communication protocol, and node hardware. In the context of environmental monitoring applications, we compare the performance of a network designed and managed using our techniques with that of existing design styles.

Categories and Subject Descriptors

C.2.1 [**Computer-Communication Networks**]: Network Architecture and Design—*Distributed networks*; C.3 [**Computer Systems Organization**]: Special-purpose and application-based systems—*real-time and embedded systems*

Keywords

energy scavenging, routing protocol

This work was supported in part by the NSF under awards CNS-0720820 and CNS-0721978.

1. INTRODUCTION

Long unattended lifespans are important for wireless sensor networks because they are often deployed in locations that are difficult to access. Replacing sensor network node components or retrieving nodes can be prohibitively expensive. Therefore, sensor node lifetime is of central importance. Most sensor nodes last a few months; some last a few years. This implies that component or node replacement is necessary in long-term deployments. Our work provides a novel method of designing wireless sensor networks to operate for decades without periodic repair or replacement of sensor nodes.

Several factors constrain sensor node life time. The battery lifespan constraint is typically encountered first. Rechargeable batteries used in many sensor nodes wear out faster than other components. Even when energy constraints are loose, batteries have lifetimes ranging from 1.5 year to 6 years [1, 2]. Battery lifetime is even worse among sensors deployed in outdoor environments because the batteries suffer from ambient temperature and humidity changes, which can degrade the battery lifespans by 75% [2]. Frequent depletion/recharge cycles can result in 20% decrease in battery lifespans. Consequently, sensor nodes must periodically have their batteries replaced, wasting time and effort. Even for sensor nodes that use batteries with lifespans exceeding that of the application, it is still commonly necessary to eventually collect the nodes because many batteries contain toxic materials such as heavy metals [3]. The elimination of batteries opens the possibility of designing wireless sensor nodes that are suitable for long-term, one time deployment. Battery-less wireless sensor nodes using energy scavenging devices as power supplies can meet this requirement.

Eliminating batteries can potentially make long-term deployment maintenance free. However, existing battery-less sensor network designs still have problems. Previous works do not eliminate the need for lifetime-constraining energy storage devices [4, 5]; such nodes use supercapacitors or battery-supercapacitor hybrid systems for energy storage, which still constrain the sensor node lifespan [6, 7]. In contrast, we consider a wireless sensor node design that completely eliminates the need for lifetime-constraining energy storage devices. The sensor nodes use ambient power sources, such as solar power, wind power, and water flow as their energy source, replacing the battery with long-term, stable energy scavenging devices. As a result, the sensor nodes no longer suffer under batter-imposed lifetime constraints.

Eliminating batteries requires changing the sensor node architecture and modifying the sensor network protocol design to specifically adapt to the changes in sensor node activities caused by using ambient power sources: sensor nodes wake up at imperfectly predictable times. Therefore, existing protocols that rely on pre-scheduled data transmission do not work. Storage and time synchronization constraints in the sensor node architecture design also limit the use of battery-less energy scavenging. We propose a protocol that takes power source availability and remaining memory into consideration.

We consider applications in which the sensing target moves infrequently, as is often the case for long-term environmental monitoring. They fall into one of the two categories: (1) the wireless sensor network only needs to sense when events occur, and these events also provide energy or (2) sensor nodes are deployed in an environment that provides access to time-varying energy sources that are event-independent. These properties are commonly seen in existing distributed sensing applications.

We propose the following modifications to existing wireless sensor network architectures: (1) replace the power supplies of sensor nodes with energy scavenging devices, which may be wind or water turbines, piezoelectric generators, or solar panels, depending on the application and available energy sources; (2) adapt routing decisions based on the spatial and temporal distributions of power availability for nodes; and (3) store intermediate results to non-volatile memory, when appropriate, to compensate for loss of power.

Based on these changes, we describe a new sensor network design that is well suited to energy scavenging. Our major contributions follow.

- We describe a novel routing protocol that works well for sensor networks using battery-less energy scavenging. The routing protocol reacts to imperfectly predictable changes in ambient energy sources. It minimizes the end-to-end latency of packet transmission and achieves 1.3–3$\times$ performance improvement over existing designs for four environmental sensing applications.
- We describe architecture changes to sensor nodes that make them more appropriate for use with intermittent and imperfectly predictable power supplies.
- We categorize commonly used sensor network applications and provide application dependent guidance for designers considering battery-less energy scavenging.

We will discuss the details of our design in later sections and compare it with existing design strategies.

2. RELATED WORK AND MOTIVATION

Large scale, long-term monitoring applications rely on low-maintenance sensor nodes because in-field repairs and replacement are expensive. Energy scavenging nodes offer a compelling solution for reducing maintenance costs; they gather ambient energy from the environment and consequently eliminate the need for battery replacement. However, existing energy scavenging nodes still have practical limitations that either constrain their lifetimes or prevent them from being used to build large-scale network applications. In this section, we point out shortcomings in existing design techniques, summarize our contributions, and argue for new sensor node and network architectures.

2.1 Engery Scavenging with Battery Assistance

Many researchers have proposed using sensor nodes powered by a combination of rechargeable batteries and scavenged energy including power derived from the sun, ambient vibration, wind, water flow, and the motion of animals. Among these, solar-power is most widely used due to its high and stable energy density.

Raghunatha et al. [8] describe a procedure for designing efficient solar-powered sensing systems. Taneja et al. [9] provided network architecture and node design guidelines for micro-solar powered sensor networks. Researchers have also developed routing protocols suitable for solar-powered sensor networks. Voigt et al. [10] proposed and compared two such protocols. Existing work has used solar-powered sensors for environmental monitoring. Main waring et al. [5] developed a wireless sensor network using solar-powered Mica Motes for habitat monitoring on Great Duck Island. They used solar panels that can provide between 60 and 120 Watts in full sunlight. The sensor networks in this paper used rechargeable batteries to store scavenged energy. However, the batteries themselves constrain the sensor node lifetime and hence limit the applicability of these nodes in very long deployments.

2.2 Why Battery-Less Energy Scavenging?

Batteries are the primary energy storage devices in many sensor nodes. However, they typically have short lifespans and frequently limit the lifespan of the whole node. Consequently, researchers have proposed the following methods of eliminating them.

Replace the rapidly degrading rechargeable battery with a supercapacitor. Minami et al. designed Solar Biscuit [4], a battery-less sensor network that only relies on a solar panel and a supercapacitor to power the sensor node. They also developed a routing protocol suited to the long charging time of the supercapacitor. The use of supercapacitors can extend the lifespan of sensor nodes, but only to a point; supercapacitors also degrade. Studies have reported that supercapacitors have 13%–15% capacity degradation and double their internal resistance after one year of power cycle testing [6, 7]. Moreover, the lifetimes of supercapacitors are temperature-dependent. The expected lifetime halves with every 10° Celsius increase of ambient temperature [11, 12]: supercapacitors degrade when deployed outdoor. In addition, supercapacitors are 4–10 $\times$ more expensive than rechargeable batteries with the same energy capacities and densities. Supercapacitors remain unsuitable for our goal of long-term deployment, although this may change in the future if their reliable lifespans are increased.

Reduce the number of charge/discharge cycles in the battery. This can be done by attaching a supercapacitor or energy scavenging device to the battery, and only discharging the battery when the other energy supplies fail. Jiang et al. proposed a multi-stage energy transfer system that uses a solar panel together with a supercapacitor as the first stage and a rechargeable battery as the second stage [13]. They argued that, when ambient power is sufficient to power the sensor node, the system can avoid discharging or charging the battery. This approach can increase the sensor node lifetime to 4 years given a 10% duty cycle. However, it does not eliminate batteries, which must eventually be gathered from the environment. We argue that the sensor node lifetime problem should be solved by removing the battery entirely.

A few researchers have proposed battery-less sensor nodes with the goal of increasing sensor node lifetime. Philipose et al. [14] attached an RFID to a battery-less sensor node, powering the sensor node via the RFID reader. Their work completely removed the energy storage device. Vyas et al. [15] and Patel et al. [16] combine a battery-less, wireless tag and a low power sensor node for use in a passive sensor. However, these works require that energy be directed to each active sensor from an external radio frequency energy source. This prevents use in distributed applications. Ng et al. [17] design a near-body network with battery-less wearable biomedical sensors to monitor patient physiological state. This solution is appropriate for body-range transmission and consists of only a few nodes. Our work focuses on applications requiring larger scale distribution of sensors.

2.3 Node Design and Protocol Support

Existing routing protocols and sensor node architectures are not well suited to energy scavenging sensor networks. We propose an architecture that is based on partial knowledge of the spatial and temporal properties of ambient power sources.

The designers of energy scavenging sensor networks face special difficulties in maintaining functionality and performance. Many environmental power sources, such as solar, wind, and water flow have intermittent availability. This complicates routing protocol and node architecture design. First, the scavenging sensor network is dynamic: its connectivity structure changes dynamically depending on environmental power source status of each node. Routing protocols must adapt to these changes. Second, the wake-up schedule of sensor nodes cannot be controlled by the designer. Algorithms that rely on coordinated activations at pre-determined times to sense, transmit, or receive cannot be used. Third, sensor nodes lose their power sources at imperfectly predictable times, leaving little time for nodes to react by transmitting data or preserving it in non-volatile memory. The designers of energy scavenging wireless sensor networks must consider these domain-specific challenges.

How well would existing sensor node and communication protocol designs fare in a battery-less environment? Prior work has proposed flooding-based routing techniques for energy scavenging sensor networks [4, 8]. These protocols require nodes to wake up at pre-determined times and use redundant transmissions to compensate for the lost messages. They are adequate for small-scale networks. However, they would perform poorly in larger-scale applications such as environmental monitoring. In medium- to large-scale networks, flooding overwhelms the communication channels, resulting in high latencies and data loss rates. Geographic routing is another popular candidate protocol; it is easy to implement and may not require pre-determined schedules for transmissions. However, only using geographic information for routing in energy scavenging sensor network can cause packets to be trapped in inactive nodes (as described in detail in Section 3). The main weakness of existing geographic routing protocols in this application is their failure to account for the fact that nodes frequently become unavailable at imperfectly predictable times and some nodes are available more frequently than others. This limits network scale, and prevents operation when many nodes are frequently inactive. Other candidate protocols require scheduling nodes to transmit at precise times, and therefore cannot be used in battery-less energy scavenging networks.

3. PROBLEM DEFINITION

Our goal is to provide routing protocol and node design techniques suitable for indefinitely deployed sensor networks. We begin by eliminating the use of energy storage devices with highly constrained lifespans. Given temporary losses in node power, we attempt to determine the design techniques yielding the highest end-to-end successful data delivery rate under a (designer-specified and application-specific) constraint on acceptable latency.

We now describe our model of an energy-scavenging sensor network. Ideally, when all nodes have access to sufficient power, they form a connected graph N containing $|N|$ nodes, in which there is a directed edge between two nodes if the first can successfully transmit directly to the second. In this situation, nodes can transmit sensed data to the base station using existing routing protocols. However, the probability of all nodes concurrently having power at any particular time is small. In each time interval, only a subset of sensor nodes have enough scavenged power to operate. The graph of these nodes, N_i, is referred to as the *active subset* for the ith time interval and does not change within the interval. Note that intervals can be defined to end whenever the active subset changes.

We model the network packet transmission latency using active subsets. It is likely that two temporally adjacent active subsets N_i and N_{i+1} have a non-empty intersection due to the temporal correlation of the power source (described in detail in Section 5). As shown in Figure 3, packets from a faraway node S can travel through multiple active subsets N_{i0} through N_{i3} via their intersections to finally arrive at B.

The packet transmission delay is the sum of t_{trans_i} and t_{int_i} for all active subsets along the path. t_{trans_i} is the transmission latency to populate packets within an individual active subset N_i. t_{int_i} is the time interval between active subset N_i and the next active subset N_{i+1}, which is the time when sensor nodes are inactive.

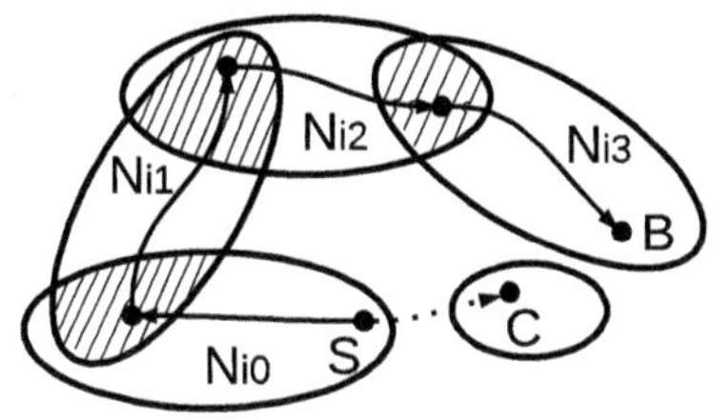

Figure 1: Battery-less energy scavenging sensor network. A node S transmits its packets to base station B through temporally intersecting active subsets.

We define the latency of data transmission in the network to be the time required for all nodes to send their sensed data packets to the base station, i.e., the maximum packet transmission delay. In reality, some packets will be dropped due to channel overuse or collision. Others will be trapped in nodes that wake up infrequently. Thus, we define *packet delivery rate* to be the percentage of packets that reach the base station at a particular time. When we compare protocols in later sections, we will compare transmission latencies associated with particular packet delivery rates.

The limited predictability of ambient power sources reduces designer control of wireless sensor networks. It prevents the designer from using pre-computed routing paths and requires routing protocols that adapt to changes in the ambient power source. Pre-computed routing may falsely send packets to nodes that are not in the temporal intersection of two adjacent active subsets, preventing packets from further transmission. As can be seen in Figure 3, node S may send its packet to another node C, which is geographically closer to the base station B but is in a rarely awake, isolated subset. This can delay packet transmission; the 4-hop path via N_{i0} through N_{i3} is faster. Instead, we consider the temporal and spatial statistics of ambient power sources to dynamically change the routing for every active subset and avoid trapping packets.

We will further describe the design and implementation of our battery-less wireless sensor network routing protocol in the following sections.

4. DESIGN AND IMPLEMENTATION

We have developed a routing protocol for sensor nodes that become active at imperfectly predictable times. Sensor node activation events occur at random times prescribed by the temporally and spatially correlated statistical processes used to characterize ambient energy sources. Therefore, nearby nodes have similar behavior. We describe a protocol informed by these properties, and then discuss four variations of it appropriate for a range of sensing applications.

We will first describe a network architecture suitable for energy scavenging environmental monitoring applications. The sensor nodes are widely deployed, and a group of sensor nodes share a base station. The nodes transmit their sensed data to the base station, potentially indirectly via other nodes. The base station uses a high-capacity power supply that will require replacement every few years at much lower cost than recovering all sensor nodes. In the remainder of this section, we describe how we perform routing given this network structure.

4.1 Sensor Node Architecture

We modify the sensor node architecture to support battery-less energy scavenging and to guarantee that the sensed data contain valid time stamps.

4.1.1 *Energy Scavenging Devices*

We consider two major modifications to a conventional wireless sensor network node: (1) removing the battery and (2) attaching an energy scavenging device, e.g., a solar panel, wind turbine, water turbine, or piezoelectric device [18]. Our design relies on non-volatile memory to save states between active intervals. Most existing sensor nodes contain non-volatile memory. Depending on the power source distributions, it may also be appropriate to use a higher-performance processor and network interface than is typical, in order to quickly finish processing and communication tasks when power is available.

4.1.2 *Time Synchronization*

Sensor nodes must generally associate times with samples. The local timer in a sensor node stops working when power is lost, and it needs to be re-synchronized when power is available. Activation events happen at random times, meaning that sensor nodes cannot determine how long their timers have been inactive when reactivated. A node can synchronize with the base station or its neighbors, which have valid local timers. However, this synchronization still has some delay because a node can be synchronized only when it is in the same active subset with other nodes maintaining correct times. The samples gathered during the synchronization delay will have incorrect time stamps.

We now describe a technique to compensate for time uncertainty in intermittently powered sensor nodes. Nodes are desynchronized by power loss. They attempt to resynchronize with neighboring nodes, but until that time they mark data samples with time ranges that are later used by the base station, together with other sample time stamps, to more accurately estimate when the data were gathered. This approach can achieve time stamp errors of less than 80 minutes for 91% packets in a medium scale (500 nodes) sensor network. The environmental monitoring applications we consider usually gather samples several times a day (as described in Table 1). Therefore, samples with time stamp errors of minutes or even hours are acceptable.

Our proposed process works in the following steps.

1. The local timer of a sensor node contains an invalid value at the beginning of deployment. Every sensor node will first try to synchronize with the base station to obtain the correct time.

2. The sensor node refreshes its local timer value (stored in a non-volatile memory) every fixed time interval (e.g., one minute) and at every time it is synchronized to nodes with correct timers. When a sensor node again has access to power, it restarts its local timer using the stored time stamp in the memory.

3. Every node attaches a node identifier and a unique packet identifier maintained in non-volatile memory to each packet, guaranteeing that for a particular node, packets with smaller packet identifiers are always produced earlier than the ones with larger packet identifiers. Packets also carry time stamp upper bounds (initialized to the latency constraint) and lower bounds (initialized to the value of the local timer). A valid bit is also included, which is set to "true" only when the local timer is known to have low error at the time of packet generation.

4. The base station refines the time stamps of packets, working within a fixed time interval. This time interval should be long enough such that most packets generated at a similar time arrive at the base station before the end of the interval. The generation time of a packet (with identifier p) is estimated by examining the packets with the closest smaller and larger packet identifiers (noted as l and u). If these packets have valid time stamps, the upper and lower bounds for the packet of interest are refined as follows:

$$packet_p.lower = packet_l.upper,$$
$$packet_p.upper = packet_u.lower. \quad (1)$$

4.2 Precomputed Information

Our routing technique bases decisions on temporal power source distributions. Each node knows the probability of having sufficient power for computation and transmission and its distance to the base station. This information can either be precomputed from the power source distribution or gathered after deployment.

The *activity rate* P_{active} of a sensor node is the probability of it having sufficient power to compute and transmit data [18]. If a sensor node is powered by a wind turbine, it will only be activated when the wind speed exceeds a threshold value providing enough power. The probability of a sensor node being awake is $\int_0^{w_{th}} f(x,\lambda,k)$, where w_{th} is the threshold wind speed and $f(x,\lambda,k)$ is the wind speed distribution at that location. The node activity rate can be computed from historical wind speed distribution data.

The distance d from the sensor node to the base station is the number of wireless communication hops, assuming all nodes are active. This distance can be gathered during network deployment.

4.3 Routing Protocols

In order to determine whether existing protocols are sufficient for indefinitely deployed energy scavenging sensor networks, we make comparisons between several existing routing protocols: simple flooding, geographic routing, buffer size dependent routing, and undirected routing. We also evaluate the Ambient Energy Aware routing protocol we designed specifically for this problem.

Flooding is the most commonly described routing protocol for energy scavenging sensor networks [4, 8]. It is easy to implement in sensor nodes with limited computation power and has adequate performance for small-scale networks in which the data generation rate is low. Multiple nodes keep copies of the same packet; thus, even when some of the nodes lack power and become inactive, the redundant copies of the packet are transmitted by other nodes. In larger networks, flooding faces two problems: (i) limited resources and (ii) undirectional transmission. Simple flooding creates redundant packets that can exceed sensor node memory capacities resulting in dropped packets. In addition, flooding protocols suffer greatly from limited channel capacity. The network-wide channel capacity is constrained in battery-less energy scavenging sensor networks by the possibly frequent deactivation of nodes that are (temporarily) without power. Flooding creates duplicate packets and easily overwhelms the network. This is especially problematic when nodes wake up infrequently.

Based on the above observations, we now consider routing protocols appropriate for battery-less energy scavenging sensor networks. These protocols aim to avoid the poor performance caused by limited buffer size, packet collision, and the randomness of node active intervals. These protocols have the following characteristics.

- *Acknowledgment.* We enable acknowledgment by both sender and receiver nodes. Receivers acknowledge packet acceptance. When a sender receives the first acknowledgment, it broadcasts a drop request to its neighbors, allowing all but the node that transmitted the first acknowledgment to drop their copies of the packet. This avoids unnecessarily use of memory and communication resources for duplicate packet copies in multiple nodes, while preserving at least one copy of the packets. The acknowledgment delay described later reduces the probability of acknowledgments collision.

- *Directional transmission.* Packets transmit along the path with the smallest expected latency to reach the base station. When receiving a packet, instead of acknowledging immediately, a receiver use a *ranking function* to delay the acknowledgment. The time delay is set to give priority to nodes with higher probability of successfully reaching the base station. The choice of ranking function is a key design feature. Later in this section, we will discuss the selection of the ranking function in greater detail.

- *Random Back-Off.* Nodes perform random retransmission back-off on packet collisions to avoid future collisions.

Given these starting properties, we consider several candidate routing protocols. Three of the protocols (geographic routing, buffer size dependent routing, and undirected) adapt well-known algorithms to the energy scavenging sensor networks considered in this work.

Geographic routing [19]. Nodes always accept packets from the neighbors that are geographically further away from the base station. This increases the probability of the packet reaching the base station. The ranking function is $delay_i = t_{unit} \cdot d_i$, in which $delay_i$ is the delay of the ith node to acknowledge, t_{unit} is a unit time period, and d_i is the number of hops from the ith node to the base station, assuming all nodes are active. As mentioned earlier in this section, this distance d can easily be gathered during node deployment. One significant drawback of this approach is the likelihood of creating holes in the network: some nodes are geographically closer to the base station, but rarely active. Packets will sometimes be transmitted to these nodes shortly before they become active and then remain trapped for a long time.

Buffer size dependent routing. Nodes accept packets from neighbors with less free space in their message buffers. This avoids buffer overflows, which may result in data loss. The ranking function is $delay_i = t_{unit} \cdot (b_{max} - b_i)$, where b_{max} is the maximum buffer size and b_i is the remaining size in the node receiving buffer. Unfortunately, this protocol does not consider the importance of transmission directions. Nodes that frequently wake up or are closer to the base station receive more packets. As a result, the ranking function will assign these nodes longer delays, forcing packets to be forwarded to nodes from which packets are less likely to reach the base station.

Undirected protocol [19]. Nodes are assigned random priorities using ranking function $delay_i = t_{unit} \cdot random(n_i)$, where $random(n_i)$ returns a random number between 1 and n_i, the number of one-hop neighbors of node i. This protocol has the benefit of simplicity but is usually inefficient because random prioritization results in slow, indirect paths for many packets.

The final protocol is a novel approach which is specifically designed to overcome challenges in battery-less sensor networks:

Ambient Energy Aware protocol. Nodes with the highest probabilities to be (possibly indirectly) connected to the base station have the highest probabilities of accepting packets from their neighbors. This protocol makes use of the statistical data on power source availability and the node activity rate (as described in Section 4.2) to compute the ranking function. Our goal is to combine the best attributes from the four protocols described above, while also using available information on the statistical properties of the ambient power source. The ranking function is $delay_i = t_{unit} \cdot (b_{max} - b_i) \cdot d_i / P_{active,i}$, where b_{max} is the maximum buffer size, b_i and d_i are the remaining buffer size and distance from the base station of node i, and $P_{active,i}$ is the activity rate of node i. The drawback of this protocol is its requirement for additional memory on sensor nodes to store power source statistical properties. Fortunately, this is not a problem in practice because the statistical data can be preprocessed and reduced to a single number: the node activity rate.

The most appropriate protocol depends on application characteristics. Therefore, we will compare the existing and new protocols described above under a variety of operating conditions.

5. EVALUATION

In this section, we provide evaluation results for the protocols discussed in the previous section. We first evaluate the protocols when used in different sensing applications. Then we determine the sensitivity of protocol quality metrics to variations in application characteristics.

5.1 Experiment setup

Our evaluation considers sensor networks that scavenge energy from wind. To model changes in wind conditions, our simulation takes location-dependent time-varying wind traces as input. However, the raw measured wind speed data for large regions and long duration are not publicly available. Therefore, we generate similar wind traces with statistical properties based on recorded wind speed distributions [20]. Wind speed traces are then fed into the discrete-event simulator described later in this section.

Our generated wind speed traces have the following properties. First, the trace for each particular location has particular temporal correlation values. Second, traces at different locations have spatial correlation. We can represent the wind speed traces by a group of correlated Weibull random variables. To generate these random variables, we make use of two sources of information: (1) a regional wind speed atlas [20] and (2) spatial and temporal correlation models.

The World of Wind Atlases houses a publicly available archive of wind data from many regions around the world [20]. For a given region, the atlas logs detailed location-specific information about wind patterns. Specifically, for each location on the map, the atlas records the Weibull parameters (k, λ) that describe variation in wind speed at several altitudes. We select the wind atlas of one island in Denmark as the source of wind data, because its wind atlas is representative of many coastal regions in the world.

We use existing wind speed spatial correlation models [21–23]. The spatial correlation coefficient for wind speed at two different locations is exponentially dependent on the distance between the locations: $c = \exp(-d/d_0)$, where d is the distance between the locations and d_0 is called *correlation distance*. This is the distance at which the correlation between two locations equals $exp(-1)$. We model the temporal correlation coefficient as exponentially dependent on elapsed time based on the observations of Archer and Jacobson [21].

We use a wind trace duration equal to the maximum tolerable latency for data transmission. In environmental monitoring applications, it is common for the base station to processes or transmit data in a daily or weekly pattern [5, 24]. Some packets will carry incorrect time stamps due to the intermittent power loss of the sensor nodes. Their time stamps will be refined after reaching the base station using the method described in Section 4, with the largest error being the packet transmission latency. Thus, packets arriving at the base station later than one week are likely to have indistinguishable time stamps. They are considered to be invalid. We set our latency constraint to be one week.

We developed a discrete event wireless sensor network simulator in which changes in wind speed are events. We generate wind speed traces based on the parameters described above [20,21] and provide them to our simulator. The simulator models the activation and deactivation of sensor nodes when the input wind speeds at the sensor locations change, forming different active subsets. Within each active subset, it simulates the behavior of sensing and data transmission of sensor nodes executing any of the four protocols described in Section 4. The network packet delivery rate, node level channel utilization, and transmission latency are recorded.

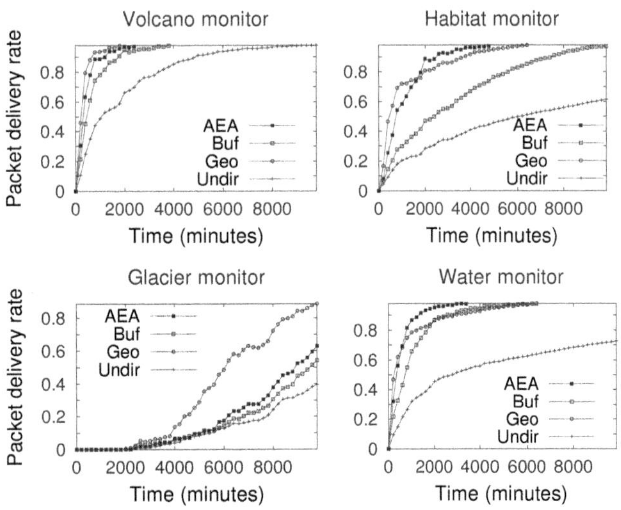

Figure 2: Packet delivery rate comparison for four protocols under different applications.

5.2 Application Based Evaluation

Several sensor network applications are suitable for using energy scavenging techniques. Table 1 lists these applications and their properties [5,24–30]. In the context of these applications, we evaluate four protocols that were discussed in Section 4: Ambient Energy Aware routing (*AEA*), geographic routing (*Geo*), buffer size dependent routing (*Buf*), and undirected routing (*Undir*). Our results show that no single protocol is best for all applications.

We consider four wireless sensor network applications from Table 1 as our examples for energy scavenging sensor network: habitat monitoring (*habitat*) [5], volcano monitoring (*volcano*) [24,25], glacier monitoring (*glacsweb*) [26], and meteorology and hydrology monitoring (*water*) [27]. Each application has a set of parameter values that are used in their setup, as described in Table 1. These four applications have distinct parameters. *habitat*, *volcano* are both small- or medium-scale sensor networks (10–100 nodes evenly distributed in an area with 2 km radius) in which sensor nodes require a moderate amount of ambient power (100–200 mW), and only perform data sensing several times a day. *water* is a large-scale network (600 nodes) with moderate power requirement. *glacier* is a medium-scale sensor network but requires high power supply to sensor nodes. We first evaluate our protocols on these four applications with fixed parameter values listed in Table 1.

Figure 2 shows the time-dependent variation in packet delivery rate throughout the whole network for these four applications. Based on the application constraints described in Section 5.1, we set the maximum tolerable packet transmission latency for all packets to be one week. While some applications (*habitat* and *volcano*) have acceptable delivery rates using simpler routing protocols, others (*water*) require our proposed Ambient Energy Aware Protocol to achieve satisfactory performance (i.e., packet latencies less than a week). For *glacier*, none of the protocols considered achieve the packet delivery rate within the latency constraint.

This difference in performance of different protocols can be briefly explained by reference to the abstract model described in Section 3. First, let us consider the *habitat* and *volcano* applications. They share common properties: small- or medium-scale and medium power requirement. The first property means that there are always sufficient sensor nodes active at the same time. This results in an active subset N_i that covers a large portion of the network. The second property guarantees that the sensor nodes are likely to have enough memory to store the sensed data without dropping packets. As a result, using simpler approaches such as geographic routing is sufficient. Second, we consider *water*, which has a large-scale sensor network and wider distribution of sensor nodes. This results in a large active subset N_i that has the potential to overwhelm the network with traffic. It is therefore favorable to transmit packets through nodes that are more likely to be active, rather than concentrating the traffic close to the base station. For this application Ambient Energy Aware routing works best. Third, *glacier* has a high node power consumption requirement. Only very high wind speed can provide enough power to activate a node. The resulting active subset N_i is a sparse network, making it less likely to cover the whole network for a given latency constraint. As a result, none of the protocols considered have good performance for this application. To improve the situation, one might switch to a more powerful energy scavenging device, e.g., a larger turbine.

5.3 Delivery rate for varying parameters

No single protocol is best for all application scenarios. To assist application developers to select the most appropriate protocol, we now show the application-dependent parameter ranges for which each protocol is best suited.

From the example applications described above, we observe several variable parameters, which are subject to changes due to special requirements of the application or user preference. These parameters include: (1) network scale, which is the total number of nodes in the network; (2) sample size, which is the size of data gathered at every sensing event; (3) required power consumption, which is the maximum power required for a sensor node to perform data processing and transmission; and (4) maximum direct transmission range.

We evaluate how each parameter affects selection of a protocol using a series of parameter studies. The parameter studies are conducted by varying parameters one at a time while keeping others constant. We select a set of constant values for these parameters: medium scale network (300 nodes distributed in a 3 km×3 km region), small sample size (16 B), medium required power consumption (100 mW), and transmission range for commonly used nodes (400 m).

The properties of the sensor network influence the selection of protocols. On the one hand, in large-scale sensor networks, the edge of the network is far from the base station, requiring more hops to send packets to the destination. Since the wind speed at each sensor node location varies randomly over time, the probability of transmitting a packet from a distant node to the base station depends on the node activity rate along the transmission path. It will often be best to route through a longer path with higher activity rate, rather than the shortest path. Ambient Energy Aware routing uses knowledge of ambient power source statistical parameters, giving it an advantage over other routing techniques in large-scale sensor networks. On the other hand, simpler protocols that

Table 1: Applications And Their Parameters

Application	Sensors	Energy source	Project period	Threshold wind speed (m/s)	Required power (mW)	Scale	Node type	Trans-mission range (m)	Sample rate	Sample size	Buffer size
CORIE	conductivity, temperature, depth	solar	1–3 years	9.0	N/A	large	N/A	N/A	several / day	N/A	N/A
Pipe network	MEMS based accelerometer	water flow	1 year	N/A	N/A	large	Gopher	300–32000	150/sec	N/A	256 kB or 16 GB
habitat	temperature, humidity, thermopile	solar or wind	9 months	3.0	68	small	mica2 mote	100	6/day	2 B	512 kB
Volcano	microphone, seismometer	solar or wind	5 years	4.0	100	small	TMote sky	200–400	1–2/day	128 B	4 MB
Glacsweb	pressure, temperature, orientation, external conductivity, strain	solar	1 year	9.0	500	med-ium	mica2 mote	100	6/day	16 B	512 kB
meteorology and hydrol-ogy	water level and temperature	water flow	3 years	4.0	100	large	mica2 mote	100–200	6/day	16 B	512 kB

simply send many redundant messages may be sufficient in small-scale networks.

Figure 3 shows transmission latencies for different network scales. When the packet delivery rate requirement is loose, all protocols have similar performance. However, performance differs under stricter packet delivery rate requirements. Geometric routing works well for small- and medium-scale networks, while buffer size dependent routing works well only for large networks. In contrast, Ambient Energy Aware routing works well for small, medium, and large networks.

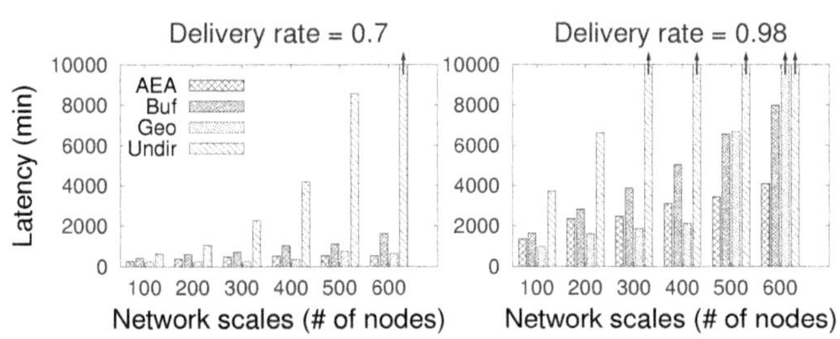

Figure 3: Transmission latency comparison of four protocols when network scale changes. Arrows indicate that latency exceeded application latency constraint.

5.3.1 *Sample size*

Sample size is the amount of data gathered by a node per sample. The sample size affects how long a sensor node spends sensing and transmitting data. If the data gathering and transmission time is too long, the sensor node will not have enough time for data transmission, reducing the packet transmission rate. We now discuss the effect of sample size on the network latency.

Figure 4 shows packet finish time as a function of sample size for the four protocols. The packet delivery rates of all protocols stays almost the same when sample size changes. This is because the sensing time takes up only a small portion of the sensor node active time even for the largest sample size that we consider. We conclude that the sample size for similar applications will not significantly affect the packet transmission latency.

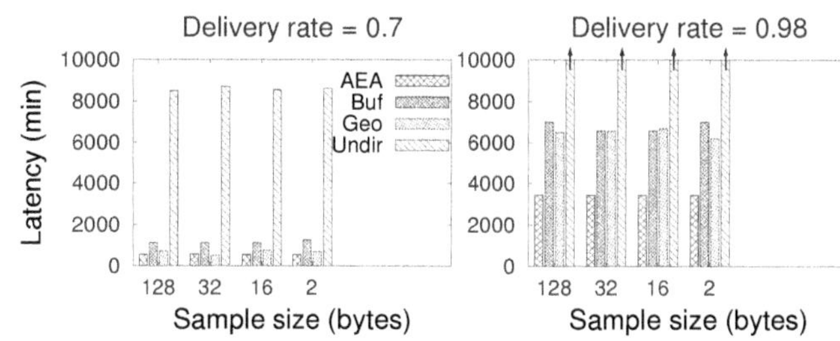

Figure 4: Transmission latency comparison of four protocols when sample size changes. Arrows indicate that latency exceeded application latency constraint.

5.3.2 *Transmission range*

The transmission range of sensor nodes affects routing protocol selection. The larger the transmission range, the more immediate neighbors per sensor node. This is especially important to energy scavenging sensor networks, in which only a subset of neighbors are active at any time.

Figure 5 shows the packet delivery rate as a function of node transmission range for the four routing protocols. The transmission range of a sensor node depends on the radio device used in the sensor node, normally ranging from 100 m to 1 km. When the transmission range is large, simple protocols work as well as Ambient Energy Aware routing. When the transmission range is small, there are so few immediate neighbors per sensor node that selection of neighbors during routing is critical. In this case, Ambient Energy Aware routing protocol outperforms existing alternatives. This result holds for all packet delivery rate requirements.

5.3.3 *Power requirement*

The power required by a sensor node and an ambient power trace determine when the node will be active. Required power depends on the hardware platform and the software workload. In our example application, ambient power is determined by wind speed. We define the minimum wind speed required by an application as *threshold wind speed.*

The impact of threshold wind speed on packet transmission latency in the sensor network is plotted in Figure 6. When the threshold wind speed is low, all protocols have short packet transmission

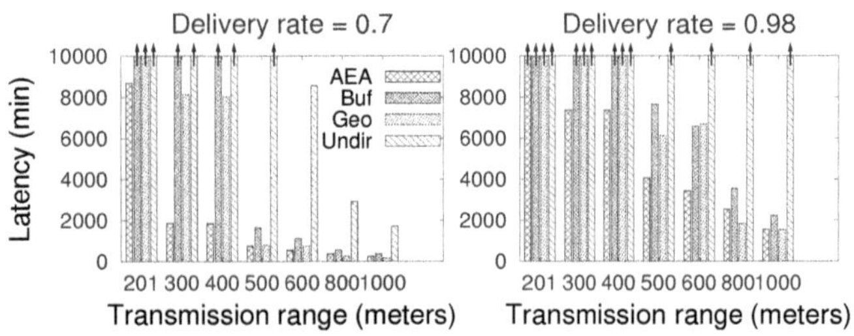

Figure 5: Transmission latency comparison of four protocols when transmission range changes. Arrows indicate that latency exceeded application latency constraint.

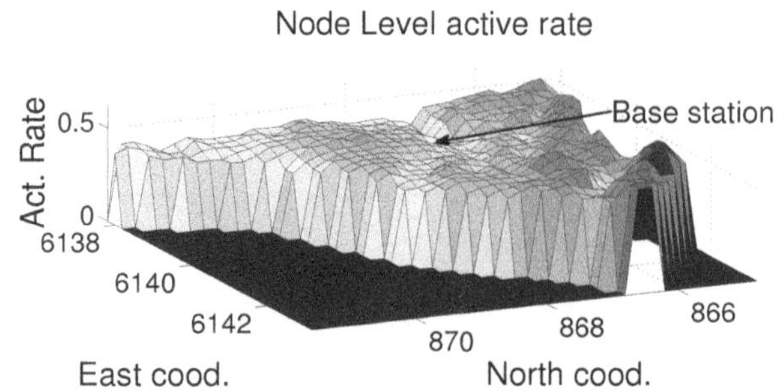

Figure 7: The node-level activity rate given by the statistical data.

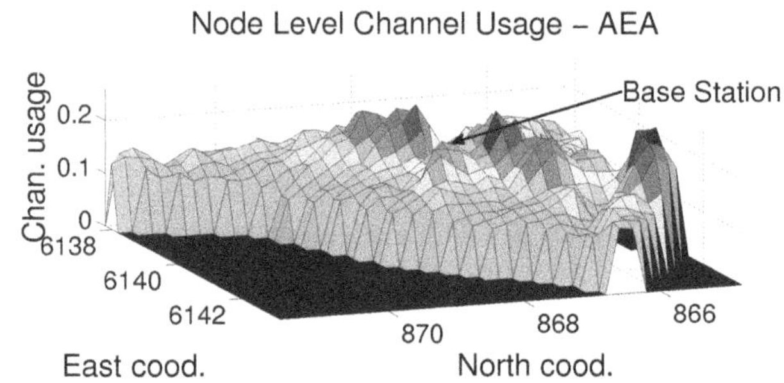

Figure 8: The node channel utilization for Ambient Energy Aware routing.

latencies. For high threshold wind speeds, the Ambient Energy Aware protocol is superior. However, when threshold wind speed is very high, no protocol can finish transmitting enough packets during the active time periods to meet application requirements.

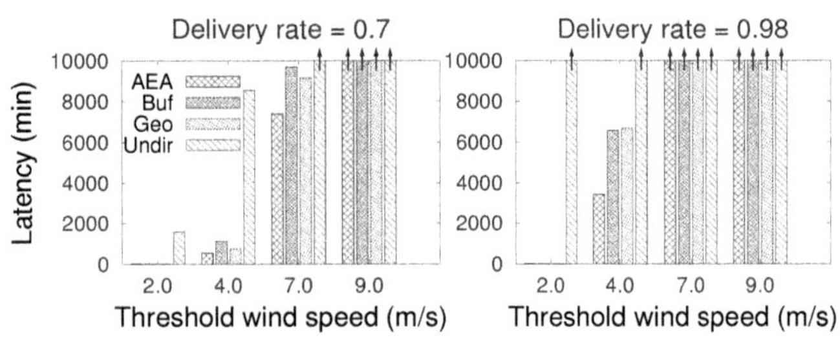

Figure 6: Transmission latency comparison of four protocols when threshold wind speed changes. Arrows indicate that latency exceeded application latency constraint.

6. PROTOCOL SELECTION

This section describes the relationship between protocol performance and both channel utilization and per-node packet delivery rate. It then explains a strategy for selecting an appropriate communication protocol.

6.1 Channel Utilization

Channel utilization is an important additional metric for evaluating our proposed protocols. The channel capacity is limited by the activity rates of nodes in an energy scavenging sensor network. We show the channel utilization for every node in a 500-node sensor network using four protocols. Geographic routing has high channel utilization around the base station, and has very low channel utilization at distant nodes. This increases collision rate near the base station, causing packets to be dropped. Ambient Energy Aware routing has less traffic concentrated at the base station (Figure 8), reducing the packet drop rate. Buffer size dependent routing and undirected routing have higher average channel utilizations compared to the previous two protocols, and their node-level channel utilization distributions follow the node activity rate (Figure 7). This is reasonable because nodes with higher activity rates are available more frequently and therefore may receive more packets. Whether or not this natural bias is helpful depends on the distribution of wind speed. If the wind speed is similar in most sensor locations, the natural bias will lead to spatially balanced channel use. Otherwise, channel traffic will concentrate on active nodes, and is likely to increase packet drop rates around those nodes. In this case, Ambient Energy Aware routing helps by distributing the channel capacity among nodes with higher probability in delivering packets to the base station.

6.2 Per-Node Packet Delivery Rate

We now consider the *fairness* of the protocols under evaluation, i.e., the variation of packet delivery rates of all nodes in the network. We evaluate the fairness by plotting the location-dependent per-node packet delivery rate across the whole network.

Figure 9 shows the per-node packet delivery rate for a medium-scale sensor network. Ambient Energy Aware routing achieves good fairness among nodes, and results in higher average per-node packet delivery rate, while geographic, buffer size dependent, and undirected routing favor nodes that are closer to the base station. This result is consistent with the ranking function used in each protocol. Geographic routing relies on a ranking function that gives higher priority to nodes closer to the base station. Therefore, it is biased toward causing heavy communication on the nodes around the base station. Ambient Energy Aware routing considers the node distance to the base station as well as its activity rate, and therefore has less severe bias on nodes with different distances to the base station, resulting in better fairness.

6.3 Protocol Selection Strategy

Using the results from this section and Section 5, we are able to provide protocol selection strategies for energy scavenging sensor network designers. We first give the conditions under which the four candidate protocols are appropriate. Undirected routing can only work efficiently in small-scale networks, and when ambient power is sufficient to power sensor nodes for most of the time. Buffer size dependent routing works best for small-to-medium size networks and medium transmission ranges. Geographic routing works best for small scale network and large transmission ranges. Ambient Energy Aware routing works well under most conditions,

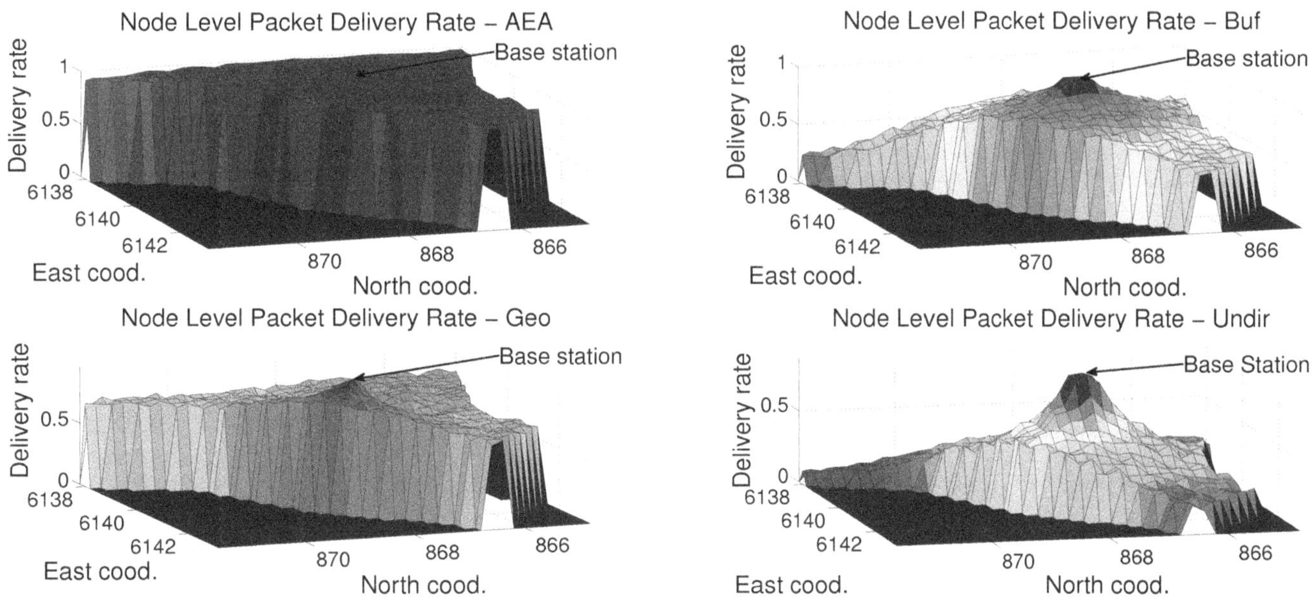

Figure 9: The node level packet delivery rates using four different routing protocols.

and can out-perform others in large-scale networks, even when ambient power is not sufficient to frequently wake up sensor nodes. It adapts better to extreme conditions than other protocols. Based on these working conditions, we provide the designer with several guidelines.

1. Determine required packet delivery rate and latency. The most appropriate protocol depends on these requirements.

2. Select values for sensitive parameters. The values for these parameters should be determined first, since they are very likely to affect the result. These parameters include network scale and sensor node transmission range. The optimal protocol depends strongly on these parameters. On the one hand, Ambient Energy Aware routing outperforms others under "harsh" conditions: when network scale is large or sensor nodes have small transmission range. In addition, it performs well under looser requirements. Designers should choose this protocol when applications require a large number of sensor nodes, or when they are limited by sensor node communication hardware. On the other hand, in a small-scale network using nodes with long transmission ranges, users can instead use simpler protocols.

3. Select values for less sensitive parameters. These parameters either do not greatly affect packet transmission latency, or always result in the same optimal protocol when their values vary. These parameters include sample size and the maximum power consumption of the sensor node. Users are relatively free to select these parameter values; indeed, to improve the overall performance, we recommend selecting the most favorable parameter values for a given budget. For instance, using a larger energy scavenging device can provide more power to the sensor nodes under the same ambient energy conditions; this then allows users to use more powerful sensor nodes that boost the performance.

7. DISCUSSION AND CAVEATS

In this section, we address some of the simplifying assumptions made during our evaluation and discuss the impact that they might have on our reported results. We believe that our experiments capture the most important features of the environment and sensor network well enough to provide a reasonable evaluation of the routing protocols. However, our evaluation framework does not consider some secondary effects including long-term wind speed variation and adjusting node activity rates online. We now address these issues and consider combining Ambient Energy Aware Design with more sophisticated protocols.

7.1 Long-term Wind Speed Variation

There can be long-term variations in wind speed distribution, on time scales ranging from three months to half a year [21] due to seasonal changes and long-term weather patterns. This means that the wind speed distribution will change multiple times during the lifetime of a long-term deployment. In our previous evaluation, we only use one fixed wind speed distribution at one location. This distribution is used in the ranking function. For a real system deployment, long-term wind speed variation should be considered.

The sensor network design can adapt to this variation by prestoring multiple wind distributions. The variation of wind speed distribution in one location is periodic, repeating yearly. This periodic distribution is usually available from the wind atlas of local government websites [20, 31]. Therefore, even for long-term operations, only a limited number of wind speed distributions need to be stored in the nodes. We can then program nodes with multiple wind speed distributions and corresponding times at which the wind speed distribution changes. Sensor nodes will know to switch to a new activity rate by monitoring time stamps.

7.2 Online Adjustment Of Node Activity Rate

Sensor nodes can gather information on their activity rates after deployment. These activity rates are representative of the actual power source condition at the node's location. Therefore, using this value to adjust the pre-stored node activity rates makes them more accurate.

Sensor nodes use timers to gather activity rates. Due to power losses, a node's timer may not record the correct time. It can nonetheless record how long a sensor node has been active. Every time the node has an opportunity to synchronize its timer, it computes its activity rate by dividing the measured node active time by the total elapsed time since the last synchronization event and this value is used to update the pre-stored node activity rate.

7.3 Protocol Extensions

Although we mainly compare Ambient Energy Aware routing to geographic routing, other sophisticated geographic routing protocols, such as Greedy Perimeter Stateless Routing (GPSR) [19], also face similar problems when applied to energy scavenging sensor network. GPSR can prevent data from being stuck at the edges of holes in a sensor network. However, it still cannot avoid sending packets to an infrequently active node in an energy scavenging sensor network.

It would be possible to use the concepts described in Section 4 to design an ambient energy aware variation of GPSR by using a similar ranking function for each node. Such a protocol would avoid low activity rate nodes when searching for paths around holes.

8. CONCLUSION

We have described and evaluated a novel class of design techniques for indefinitely deployed sensor networks. To enable this increased lifespan, we proposed eliminating batteries from sensor nodes and introducing a new routing protocol that account for the resulting restrictions in node activity. This protocol can achieve high delivery rate, even when sensor nodes randomly lose their power sources. It uses stochastic models for ambient power sources and takes advantage of spatial and temporal correlation to make routing decisions. We evaluated the newly proposed protocol together with three existing approaches for four commonly used applications. Finally, we provided guidance on selection of routing protocols for specific applications.

9. REFERENCES

[1] D. Linden, *Handbook of Batteries*, 3rd ed. New York: McGraw-Hill, 2002.

[2] D. Berndt., *Maintenance-free batteries : lead-acid, nickel/cadmium, nickel/metal hydride : a handbook of battery technology*, 2nd ed. Somerset, England : Research Studies Press, 1997.

[3] "Health concerns with batteries," http://batteryuniversity.com/learn/article/health_concerns.

[4] M. Minami, T. Morito, and H. Morikawa, "Solar biscuit: a battery-less wireless sensor network system for environmental monitoring applications," in *Proc. 9th Int. Conf. on Networked Sensing Systems*, 2005.

[5] A. Mainwaring, et al., "Wireless sensor networks for habitat monitoring," in *Proc. Int. Wkshp. Wireless Sensor Networks and Applications*, Sept. 2002, pp. 88–97.

[6] E.-H. El Brouji, et al., "Impact of calendar life and cycling ageing on supercapacitor performance," *IEEE Trans. Vehicular Technology*, vol. 58, no. 8, pp. 3917–3929, Oct. 2009.

[7] "Using a small solar cell and a supercapacitor in a wireless sensor," http://www.sensorsmag.com.

[8] V. Raghunathan, et al., "Design considerations for solar energy harvesting wireless embedded systems," in *Proc. Int. Conf. Information Processing in Sensor Networks*, Apr. 2005, pp. 457–462.

[9] J. Taneja, J. Jeong, and D. Culler, "Design, modeling, and capacity planning for micro-solar power sensor networks," in *Proc. Int. Conf. Information Processing in Sensor Networks*, Apr. 2008, pp. 407–418.

[10] T. Voigt, H. Ritter, and J. Schiller, "Utilizing solar power in wireless sensor networks," in *Proc. Int. Conf. Local Computer Networks*, Oct. 2003, pp. 416–422.

[11] "SMART modular technologies," http://www.smartm.com.

[12] J. Schiffer, D. Linzen, and D. U. Sauer, "Heat generation in double layer capacitors," *J. Power Sources*, vol. 160, no. 1, pp. 765–772, 2006.

[13] X. Jiang, J. Polastre, and D. Culler, "Perpetual environmentally powered sensor networks," in *Proc. Int. Conf. Information Processing in Sensor Networks*, Apr. 2005, pp. 463–468.

[14] M. Philipose, et al., "Battery-free wireless identification and sensing," *IEEE Pervasive Computing*, vol. 4, no. 1, pp. 37–45, Jan. 2005.

[15] R. Vyas, et al., "Design and characterization of a novel battery-less, solar powered wireless tag for enhanced-range remote tracking applications," in *Microwave Conference, European*, Oct. 2009, pp. 169–172.

[16] A. Patel, et al., "Power harvesting for low power wireless sensor network," in *Antennas Propagation Conference, 2009. LAPC 2009. Loughborough*, Nov. 2009, pp. 633–636.

[17] J. W. Ng, et al., "Ubiquitous monitoring environment for wearable and implantable sensors (ubimon)," in *Proc. 6th Int. Conf. on Ubiquitous Computing*, Sept. 2004.

[18] R. Morais, et al., "Sun, wind and water flow as energy supply for small stationary data acquisition platforms," *Computers and Electronics in Agriculture*, vol. 64, pp. 120–132, Dec. 2008.

[19] F. Zhao and L. J. Guibas, *Wireless Sensor Networks: An Information Processing Approach*. Morgan Kaufmann, 2004.

[20] "World wind maps – wind atlases of the world," http://www.mywindpowersystem.com.

[21] C. L. Archer and M. Z. Jacobson, "The spatial and temporal distribution of U.S. winds and windpower at 80 m derived from measurements," *American Geophysical Union*, p. C82, Dec. 2002.

[22] S. Chan, et al., "Operations requirements of utilites with wind power generation," *IEEE Trans. Power Apparatus and Systems*, vol. PAS-102, no. 9, pp. 2850–2860, Sept. 1983.

[23] I. Damousis, et al., "A fuzzy model for wind speed prediction and power generation in wind parks using spatial correlation," *IEEE Trans. Energy Conversion*, vol. 19, no. 2, pp. 352–361, June 2004.

[24] G. Werner-Allen, et al., "Deploying a wireless sensor network on an active volcano," *IEEE Internet Computing*, vol. 10, no. 2, pp. 18–25, Mar. 2006.

[25] G. Werner-Allen, et al., "Fidelity and yield in a volcano monitoring sensor network," in *Proc. Int. Symp. Operating Systems Design and Implementation*, Nov. 2006, pp. 381–396.

[26] K. Martinez, R. Ong, and J. Hart, "Glacsweb: a sensor network for hostile environments," in *Proc. Conf. Sensor and Ad Hoc Communications and Networks*, Oct. 2004, pp. 81–87.

[27] J. Lundquist, D. Cayan, and M. Dettinger, "Meteorology and hydrology in Yosemite national park: A sensor network application," in *Proc. Int. Conf. Information Processing in Sensor Networks*, Apr. 2003, pp. 553–553.

[28] S. N. Simic and S. Sastry, "Distributed environmental monitoring using random sensor networks," in *Proc. Int. Conf. Information Processing in Sensor Networks*, Apr. 2003, pp. 582–592.

[29] "Center of costal margin observation and prediction," http://www.ccalmr.ogi.edu/CORIE/.

[30] M. Shinozuka, et al., "Nondestructive monitoring of a pipe network using a MEMS-based wireless network," in *Proc. SPIE*, Mar. 2010, p. 7649.

[31] "Wind energy resource atlas of the United States," http://rredc.nrel.gov/wind/pubs/atlas/atlas_index.html.

Performance Enhancement under Power Constraints using Heterogeneous CMOS-TFET Multicores

Emre Kultursay, Karthik Swaminathan, Vinay Saripalli
Vijaykrishnan Narayanan, Mahmut T. Kandemir, Suman Datta
The Pennsylvania State University
{euk139,kvs120,vijay,kandemir}@cse.psu.edu,vxs924@psu.edu,sdatta@engr.psu.edu

ABSTRACT

Device level heterogeneity promises high energy efficiency over a larger range of voltages than a single device technology alone can provide. In this paper, starting from device models, we first present ground-up modeling of CMOS and TFET cores, and verify this model against existing processors. Using our core models, we construct a 32-core TFET-CMOS heterogeneous multicore. We then show that it is a very challenging task to identify the ideal runtime configuration to use in such a heterogeneous multicore, which includes finding the best number/type of cores to activate and the corresponding voltages/frequencies to select for these cores. In order to effectively utilize this heterogeneous processor, we propose a novel automated runtime scheme. Our scheme is designed to automatically improve the performance of applications running on heterogeneous CMOS-TFET multicores operating under a fixed power budget, without requiring any effort from the application programmer or the user. Our scheme combines heterogeneous thread-to-core mapping, dynamic work partitioning, and dynamic power partitioning to identify energy efficient operating points. With simulations we show that our runtime scheme can enable a CMOS-TFET multicore to serve a diversity of workloads with high energy efficiency and achieve 21% average speedup over the best performing equivalent homogeneous multicore.

Categories and Subject Descriptors

C.0 [**Computer Systems Organization**]: General—*Hardware/software interfaces*; C.1.3 [**Processor Architectures**]: Other architecture Styles—*Heterogeneous (hybrid) systems*

Keywords

Heterogeneous multicores, TFETs, power aware systems, power partitioning

1. INTRODUCTION

Industrial scaling trends [1] show that each step in process technology comes with a larger number of cores that can be fit into a single chip, and yet, the power deliverable to the chip stays relatively constant. The lack of enough power to turn on all the cores simultaneously at their peak frequency manifests itself either as *dark silicon* where only a small number of cores can be turned on, or as *dim silicon* where all the cores are turned on but execute at very low voltages/frequencies [2].

CODES+ISSS'12, October 7-12, 2012, Tampere, Finland.

Depending on the characteristics of the application to be executed on a multicore, the answer to which of the two possible configurations, i.e., dark silicon or dim silicon, performs better, can vary. Scalable applications may prefer using a large number of cores at a low frequency to achieve a higher energy efficiency. Other applications that do not scale beyond some degree of parallelism would rather be restricted to run on a smaller number of cores (sequential applications being at one extreme of this case, running on only one core). In the latter case, the power saved by turning the remaining cores off can be used to increase the clock frequency of the active cores. Clearly, a general purpose processor with a goal to perform well on a diversity of workloads must be optimized for both scenarios.

Heterogeneous multicores employ separate cores for high performance and low power operation modes. As a result, a heterogeneous multicore has the potential to achieve better power and performance characteristics than an equivalent homogeneous multicore over a variety of workloads. In this work, we first pose the question: *How to design an energy efficient heterogeneous multicore?* We first identify that as the number of cores increase, the dim silicon approach results in very low per-core power budgets. When cores are implemented using the CMOS technology, such a low per-core power budget forces the transistors to operate at near or sub-threshold voltages at which CMOS devices show very poor energy efficiency. Hence, CMOS technology is not very suitable for a dim silicon approach.

TFET technology [3][4] is a very promising alternative to sub-threshold CMOS, offering better energy-delay performance in the low voltage regime. Building TFET cores and employing them in a multicore can significantly improve performance when operating at low per-core power budgets. Yet, TFETs are not energy efficient at higher voltages and perform poorly in a dark silicon setting. At such high voltages, CMOS technology is still the most energy efficient choice. Motivated by these observations, we identify a heterogeneous CMOS-TFET multicore as the best solution to serve a diversity of workloads. However, porting applications to this heterogeneous multicore is not a trivial task. Specifically, it involves finding the best performing thread-to-core mapping, work-to-thread distribution, and core power distribution.

In this work, we propose an *automatic runtime scheme* to extract high performance from heterogeneous CMOS-TFET multicores that operate under fixed power budgets. Our scheme can be implemented as a part of the operating system (OS) and uses (i) heterogeneous thread-to-core mapping (i.e., it can utilize both types of cores simultaneously), (ii) dynamic work partitioning (i.e., it distributes work unequally across threads), and (iii) dynamic power partitioning (i.e., it distributes power unequally across cores). This scheme analyzes the efficiency of the application threads running on the target heterogeneous multicore and redistributes the available chip power across cores to improve overall performance. Our specific contributions in this work are:

- We identify device-level heterogeneous CMOS-TFET multicores as a promising approach to effectively serve a diversity of workloads.
- We build a core power model starting from device models. We validate this model by comparing its results with data reported for existing processors. We use this model with the emerging FinFET and TFET technologies and construct a CMOS-TFET heterogeneous multicore power model.
- We evaluate a CMOS-TFET multicore under a fixed power budget and compare it against homogeneous CMOS and homogeneous TFET multicores. We show that with simple, homogeneous (i.e., single core type) thread-to-core mapping and static work partitioning, a heterogeneous multicore can achieve performance comparable to the best performing homogeneous multicore.
- We propose an automatic runtime scheme that performs dynamic power partitioning across different types of cores in the CMOS-TFET heterogeneous processor. This scheme considers the power/performance tradeoffs and quantities of different types of cores, and can improve the performance of a variety of applications running on heterogeneous processors with different configurations. We show that, when used with heterogeneous thread-to-core mapping and dynamic work partitioning, this runtime scheme enables our heterogeneous CMOS-TFET multicore to achieve an average performance improvement of 21% over the best performing homogeneous multicore, without any effort from the programmer or the user.

2. THE CASE FOR A HETEROGENEOUS CMOS-TFET MULTICORE

In this section, we demonstrate the need for heterogeneous architectures to cater to a diversity of applications. We focus our attention on device-level heterogeneity in multicore processors and examine the viability of using Tunnel-FET based cores in processor design.

2.1 Power Constrained Multicores

The ITRS roadmap [5] indicates that the maximum allowable chip power will remain constant over the next several generations even amidst technology scaling. This makes the chip power the most important parameter that constrains the maximum performance that can be extracted from a processor. Improving energy efficiency has become a major goal, which has lead to servers-on-chip with an entire power budget of a few Watts have been built [6] for web applications as well as 'big data' applications like MapReduce and Hadoop. The corresponding per-core power comes out to be less than 1W. power budgets corresponding to less than 1 Watts per-core. Under such restricted power budgets, the

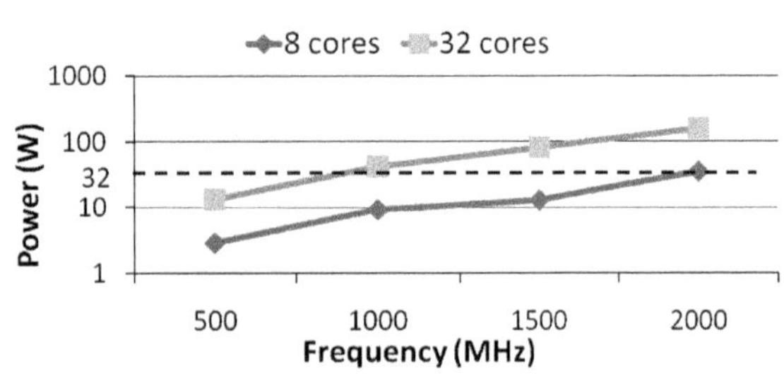

Figure 1: Power consumption of *swim* using 8 and 32 cores at a frequency range of 500 MHz to 2 GHz. The dashed line represents a power budget of 32 W.

number of active cores and their frequencies must be carefully determined to preserve efficiency. Figure 1 shows the power consumption of *swim* from the SPEC-OMP benchmark suite [7] using an 8-core and a 32-core multicore operating over a range of frequencies. It is observed that the power demand for 32 cores to run at 2 GHz, which is around 120W, far exceeds a power budget of 32W (1W per core), which is barely sufficient to turn on 8 cores running at 2 GHz. Thus the only way of reaching 2 GHz frequency with the 32 core processor is by completely shutting down at least 24 cores, i.e, 24 cores must remain *dark*. Conversely, we see that in order to be able to use all the 32 cores, the clock frequency must be limited to less than 1 GHz, i.e, the cores are run in a *dim* manner. This dark/dim behavior is common to many other applications as well (e.g., *apsi* and *wupwise*). These scenarios represent the two extreme operating points, and which one of the two achieves higher performance depends on the properties of the target application.

2.2 Serving a Diversity of Applications

In order to efficiently map applications onto multicore processors under power constraints, two properties of the target applications must be studied: (1) scalability of the application with number of cores, and (2) scalability of the application with frequency.

Figure 2 compares the scalability of two applications, *swim* and *equake*, with the number of cores. It can be observed that while *swim* scales well even when run on 32 cores, the speedup of *equake* is limited when executed on more than 8 cores, in fact degrading when the number of cores is increased from 16 to 32. Hence, *equake* is not able to utilize the cores allocated to it as effectively as *swim*. Analyzing the scalability of two applications with frequency, Figure 3 shows the speedup of two applications, *swim* and *gafort*, when they are executed on a 32-core processor at a range of frequencies. As frequency is increased, the speedup achieved by *gafort* is higher than *swim*. In general, applications with a higher resource utilization in the cores see a higher benefit from increased core clock frequency.

These application characteristics can be used to find better operating points (number of cores, frequencies) that *improve performance under a given power budget*. For instance, given a power budget of 1W/core (32W overall) and considering a baseline configuration with a single CMOS core running at 500 MHz, a well scaling application like *swim* achieves its best performance when running on 32 cores at 1 GHz to give a 52X speedup. On the other hand, *equake*, which scales poorly, achieves its optimal speedup of 15X at 2 GHZ with 8 cores. This indicates that different multithreaded applications can prefer different operating points to maximize their performance under a power budget.

2.3 Exploiting Device-Level Heterogeneity

The best configuration for running a particular application can be significantly different depending on the properties of the target application. In the dark silicon case, cores must be optimized to be efficient at high frequencies, and in the dim silicon case, they must be optimized for low frequency operation. As these two requirements are at the two ends of the power-performance spectrum, they *cannot* be satisfied by a single device technology simultaneously. On the other hand, it is possible to combine two technologies in implementing a multicore, where one technology is used to implement low-frequency/low-power cores and another technology is used to implement high-frequency/high-performance cores. This heterogeneous processor can be a common platform to serve a diversity of applications with

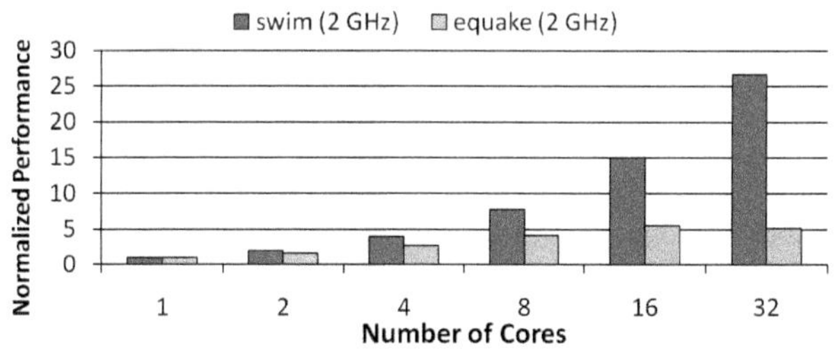

Figure 2: Scaling of the parallel regions of *swim* and *equake* under various core counts for a system running at 2 GHz. Performance values are normalized with respect to the 1 core case.

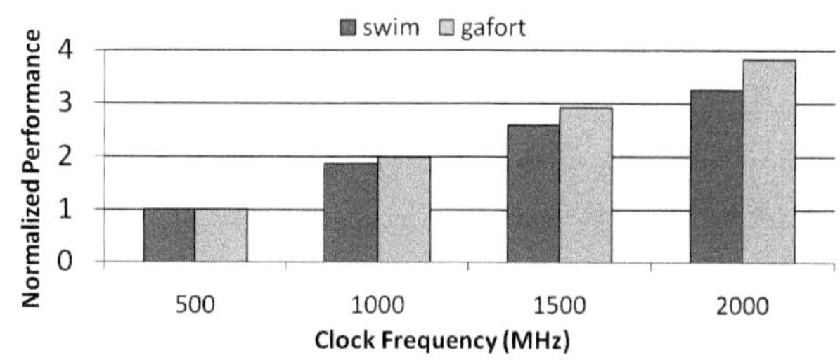

Figure 3: Scaling of applications *swim* and *gafort* with clock frequency for a 32 core system. Performance values are normalized with respect to the 500 MHz case.

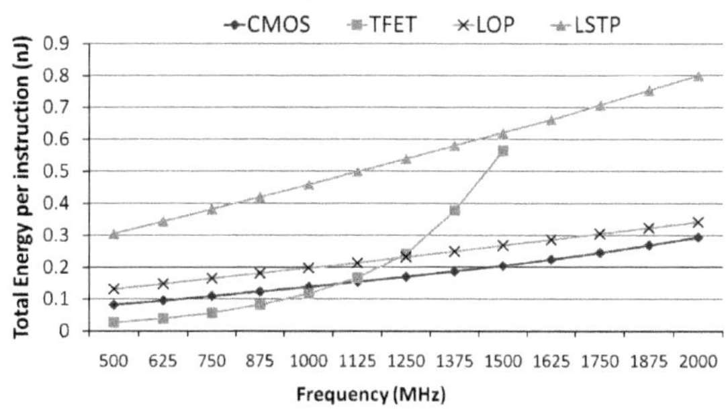

Figure 4: Variation in dynamic energy with frequency for different transistor technologies.

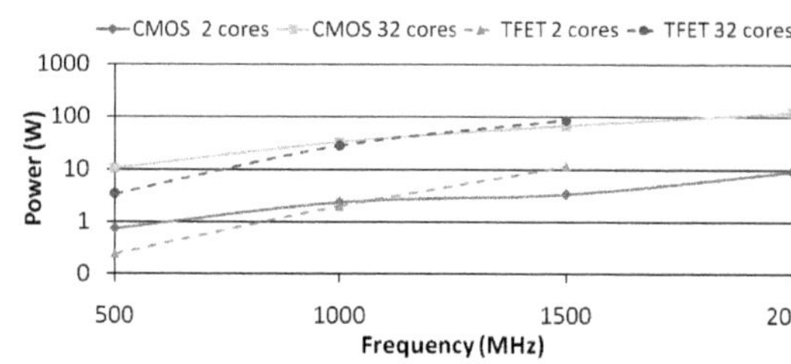

Figure 5: Variation in CMOS and TFET processor power at different frequencies for different number of cores.

high performance. While the standard CMOS technology that can reach high frequencies is a good candidate to be used for implementing high-performance cores, its low supply voltage ($V_{cc} < 300mV$) operation is extremely inefficient because of its limited overdrive voltage. Under a small overdrive voltage, CMOS devices are limited by a 60 mV/decade minimum sub-threshold slope, which provides a very low drive current. Stronger drive currents at low supply voltage can be achieved by reducing the CMOS threshold voltage (V_t). However, reduced threshold voltage results in an unacceptable increase in off-state leakage current. Therefore, the sub-threshold slope of CMOS technology results in poor I_{on}/I_{off} ratio at low voltages, leading to an energy-inefficient low frequency operation.

Variants of standard high-performance (HP) CMOS devices are low standby power (LSTP) and low-power (LOP) devices. Figure 4 shows the variation in core dynamic energy with core frequency for these CMOS-based transistor technologies. LSTP transistors have a higher oxide thickness than HP CMOS transistors which leads to lower I_{on} as well as I_{off} . While this decreases the leakage power, a higher V_{cc} is needed for an LSTP transistor to operate at the same clock frequency as an HP transistor, which in turn results in a higher dynamic energy consumption. Similarly, using LOP transistors which operate at a lower V_{cc} but have a higher threshold voltage also cannot reach better energy efficiencies at any frequency. As a result, using LSTP or LOP transistors is not an effective solution for the design of dynamic energy dominated cores.

Any solution to implement energy-efficient cores must clearly have a better sub-threshold behavior than CMOS technology. Interband Tunnel Field Effect Transistor (TFET) technology is a very promising alternative to sub-threshold CMOS, showing a characteristic sub-60 mV/decade sub-threshold slope. This steep slope brings a good I_{on}/I_{off} ratio at low voltages, which translates into high drive current and low off-state leakage current. Thus, TFET-based cores are clearly more energy efficient than any of the other technologies at low frequencies, as shown in Figure 4.

Figure 5 shows the average power consumption of the *swim* application when running on both CMOS and TFET-based homogeneous multicores with 8 and 32 cores. At the lowest frequency of 500 MHz, 32 TFET cores consume $3X$ less power than 32 CMOS cores. When working under a fixed power budget, this can translate into more number of cores being turned on. Consequently, the massive parallel computational capacity brought in by 32 TFET cores can easily outperform the CMOS configuration when running a scalable application such as *swim*. At low voltages, it is also possible to operate the TFET at higher clock frequencies than CMOS. This enables the TFET cores to achieve superior performances than CMOS cores under power constraints for highly scalable applications.

When executing poorly scaling applications or sequential parts of parallel applications, it is better to restrict the entire power budget to a small number of cores running at a high operating frequency. The high-frequency optimized CMOS cores are very suitable for this operating point. From our profiling simulations we observed that, given a power budget of 32W, we can typically run only 8 CMOS cores at a peak frequency of 2 GHz. As a result, we designed a 32 core heterogeneous CMOS-TFET architecture with 8 CMOS cores and 24 TFET cores. This ensures that, when needed, 8 CMOS cores can be executed at the maximum frequency.

3. MODELING CMOS AND TFET CORES

In this section, we first present our FinFET and TFET device models, and then, describe the method we use to construct an entire processor model from these devices.

3.1 Device Modeling

There have been numerous experimental demonstrations of novel tunneling (TFET) devices. The first such demon-

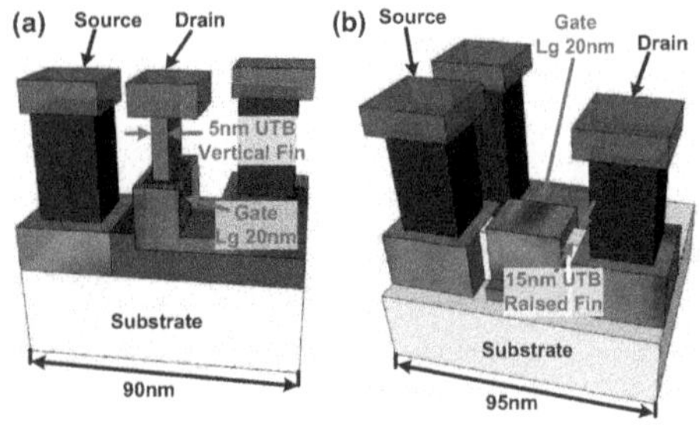

Figure 6: (a) Structure of an UTB 3D TFET, (b) structure of a 3D Si FinFET.

stration was an $In_{0.53}Ga_{0.47}As$ homojunction TFET [8] which illustrated the concept of a vertical interband tunneling transistor. The problem of low I_{on} in homojunction TFETs was overcome by using a $GaAs_{0.1}Sb_{0.9}/InAs$ heterojunction TFET. On account of the P-N heterojunction being staggered, and InAs having a lower bandgap (E_G), this device was observed to have a higher I_{on} than a homojunction TFET. Recently, a vertically-oriented, gate-all-around silicon nanowire was demonstrated, showing 50 mV/decade sub-threshold slope over 3 decades of drain current [9], thus experimentally illustrating a sub-60 mV/decade slope. Further, a process flow for the creation of a side-gated vertical-mesa TFET which can be scaled down to achieve an Ultra-Thin-Body (UTB) double-gated structure has also been demonstrated [3, 10]. Continuous improvements in vertical 3D UTB heterojunction tunneling structures are bringing us closer to the promise of sub-60 mV/decade sub-threshold slope operation.

Figure 6(a) shows the 3D schematic of a vertically-oriented UTB TFET, the fabrication of which has been demonstrated in [10]. Modeling of such a transistor has been performed for different materials using advanced atomistic simulations [11, 12]. This TFET device is compared against bulk-CMOS devices in 20nm CMOS technology in [4]. However, based on recent trends [13, 14], it has become clear that beyond 20nm technology node, instead of bulk-CMOS, CMOS transistors will be implemented using the tri-gate transistor technology (i.e., FinFETs). The 3D schematic of a silicon FinFET is shown in Figure 6(b). The experimental demonstration of such a transistor for the 20nm technology node has been shown in [15]. In this work, we work with these emerging heterogeneous TFET and silicon FinFET transistors.

We performed device level modeling of TFET devices using TCAD Sentaurus [16]. TCAD simulations for TFETs are calibrated with the atomistic simulations [11, 12], the results of which are shown in Figure 7(a) together with the device parameters used. The steep slope in this figure shows that radically different device physics of TFETs allows departure from 60 mV/decade limit imposed by nature on conventional devices such as BJTs and MOSFETs. We verified that our TCAD simulation results agree with the experimental TFET data reported in [3, 10]. Similarly, we performed TCAD simulations for the 20nm Si FinFET. Figure 7(b) shows that our TCAD simulation of this device is in close agreement with the experimental data shown in [15].

Using our device models, we obtained the performance data for a 20nm high performance (low V_t) Si FinFET NMOS and a 20nm heterojunction n-channel TFET, which are shown in Figure 8. This figure shows the I_{on} versus I_{on}/I_{off} for the two types of transistors for different operating points along the I_d-V_g curve, for a given V_{cc} window, and at two supply voltages, namely, $1V$ (high voltage) and $0.3V$ (low voltage). From this figure, we observe that at $1V$, the Si FinFET outperforms the heterojunction TFET both in I_{on} as well as I_{on}/I_{off} ratio. However, when the supply voltage is reduced to $0.3V$, the TFET becomes better in I_{on} and the I_{on}/I_{off} ratio, compared to the high performance Si FinFET at $0.3V$. Even using a low-power FinFET with high V_t exhibits a similar behavior, because TFETs are much more energy efficient at low voltages on account of their sub-60mV sub-threshold slope. While TFET is preferred at low V_{cc} values less than $0.3V$, CMOS is preferred at high V_{cc} values of around 1V. Table 1 summarizes the performance of the two types of transistors at $1V$ and $0.3V$.

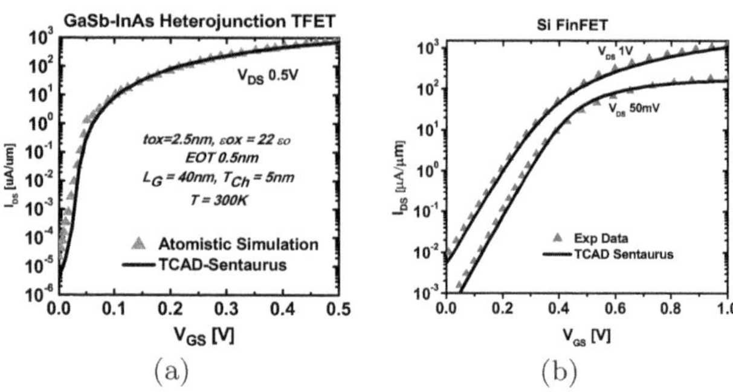

Figure 7: (a) Comparison of TCAD simulation with atomistic simulation for heterojunction TFET [11]. (b) Comparison of TCAD simulation with experimental data for Si FinFET [15].

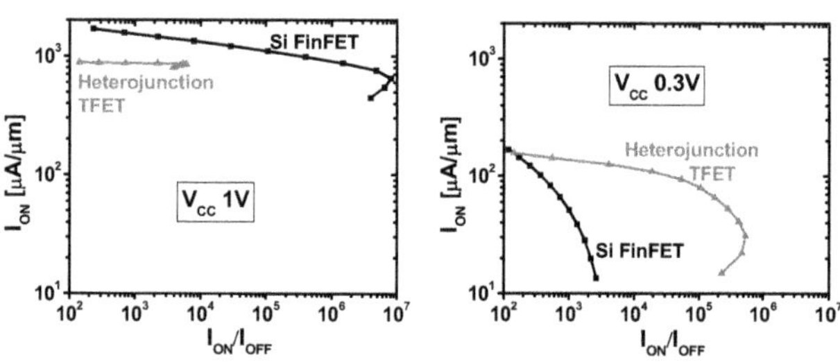

Figure 8: I_{on} vs I_{on}/I_{off} ratio comparison for Si FinFET and HTFET at V_{cc} of 1V and 0.3V.

Table 1: Summary of transistor performance.

Tech	V_{cc}[V]	I_{on}[uA/um]	I_{off}[nA/um]	I_{on}/I_{off}
FinFET	1	1200	5	2×10^5
TFET	1	850	150	6×10^3
FinFET	0.3	5.5	1.25	4.5×10^3
TFET	0.3	115	6	2×10^5

3.2 Transistor-to-System Abstraction

Processor-level power-performance comparison for CMOS and TFET-based processors, including simulations of memory and datapath elements, was done using a device-to-system architecture abstraction in [4]. We use a similar abstraction with two key enhancements in modeling: (1) our TFET models are calibrated with atomistic simulations and experimental data, and (2) our CMOS models use an advanced tri-gate (FinFET) technology rather than an older bulk-CMOS technology.

The maximum operating frequency of a processor is set by its critical path, which we model using a ring-oscillator chain of NAND gates each driving five NAND gates, as shown in Figure 9(a), resulting in a 45 FO4 delay for the ring-oscillator. We observe that, using a 45nm bulk-CMOS model [17], this logic chain is able to accurately model the

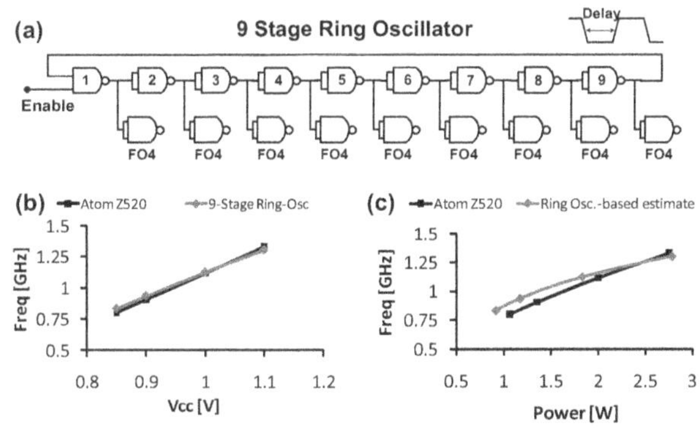

Figure 9: (a) 9-stage ring-oscillator used to model the critical path in the processor, (b) frequency vs V_{cc} behavior for the Atom processor, and (c) frequency vs power behavior for the Atom processor.

V_{cc}-frequency behavior of the Intel Atom processor [18], as shown in Figure 9(b). The switching energy per transistor is estimated from the ring oscillator. Typical switching factors obtained during logic benchmarking range from 12.5% (in logic intensive designs) to 50% (in arithmetic intensive designs), making an average activity factor of 30% a reasonable assumption [19]. Using the Atom processor's transistor count of 47 million and this 30% transistor switching activity factor, we were able to reproduce the power-frequency characteristics of the Atom processor.

In order to model a forward-looking processor, we moved from the 45nm technology node to 20nm technology node in our model. Assuming an average IPC of 1, which can be representative of the 2-issue Intel Atom processor architecture, we obtained the energy per instruction of our target processor using 20nm Si FinFET and 20nm heterojunction TFET technology, considering the energy per instruction to be largely independent of the specific instruction being executed [20]. In our evaluation, we considered both the dynamic and leakage energy of the processor.

As observed in Figure 4, on account of the steep subthreshold slope, TFETs deliver better performance compared to Si FinFETs in low-V_{cc} operation ($\leq 0.5V$). Since the tunneling current saturates for higher Vcc ($> 0.5V$) values, TFET processors are less efficient than FinFET based processors at frequencies in excess of around 1.1 GHz. Due to this behavior, there is an energy-delay crossover point, below which the TFET processor is more energy efficient and above which the Si FinFET processor becomes the energy efficient choice.

3.3 The Manufacturing Barrier: Integrating TFET and FinFET Technologies

TFET technology is at an exploratory stage and it is too premature to analyze it from the yield and cost perspectives. However, from an integration perspective, TFET and FinFET devices can be fabricated on a single chip in a monolithic fashion using a silicon substrate. Such integration has already been demonstrated through experimental fabrication of indium gallium arsenide (InGaAs) based Quantum-Well FETs (QWFETs) on silicon substrate using a metamorphic buffer layer growth scheme [21]. Another important parameter in the adoption of new technologies is their sensitivity to process variations. In [22], it is shown that TFET and FinFET devices are affected similarly from process variations. Their work also presents examples of process variation-aware TFET SRAM cell design.

4. PORTING APPLICATIONS TO HETEROGENEOUS MULTICORES

When executing a multi-threaded application on a CMOS-TFET heterogeneous multicore, there are two important questions that must be answered: (1) how will the threads be mapped to cores, and (2) how will the work be partitioned across threads? The performance of the target application can significantly vary based on these decisions, yet analyzing and evaluating alternative schemes to make the right decision is a time consuming task. In this section, after presenting alternative mapping and work partitioning schemes, we propose an automatic scheme that can, without any programmer effort, achieve high performance, by answering a third question: *How should the available power be partitioned across cores?*

4.1 Thread-to-Core Mapping

We first examine how the threads of a multi-threaded application should be mapped to the cores of a heterogeneous multicore. Considering a CMOS-TFET heterogeneous multicore, two possible methods are homogeneous mapping and heterogeneous mapping. Homogeneous mapping assumes that, while running a parallel region of an application, all threads will use the same type of core. In this case, when a parallel region starts, a binary decision is performed and the parallel region is executed either only on CMOS cores or only TFET on cores. This mapping strategy is used by traditional accelerator-based systems (e.g., a host processor with GPGPUs). However, the decision of what type of core leads to better performance under a fixed power budget must be made manually and is a non-trivial task.

An alternative way of mapping application threads to a heterogeneous processor is to run the application on both types of cores simultaneously. However, cores of different types will be executing at different operating points, which can cause significant performance discrepancy. Therefore, heterogeneous thread-to-core mapping can be expected to perform well only when used together with a heterogeneity-aware work partitioning scheme.

4.2 Work Partitioning

The simplest way of partitioning work across the threads of an application is to distribute the total work equally. This method is typically preferred in homogeneous systems where all application threads will be executed on the same type of core. Running on the same core type results in all threads completing their computations at about the same time, minimizing the time during which cores sit idle at synchronization points. On a loop-level parallelized system, static work partitioning distributes work statically at compile time, by assigning equally sized chunks of loop iterations to all threads.

In a heterogeneous multicore, the performance of threads running on different types of cores can be quite different under a heterogeneous thread-to-core mapping. Under static work partitioning, it can take some threads significantly more time to complete their computations. In this case, threads that complete their work early are forced to wait idle until all the other threads reach the synchronization point, which leads to poor processor utilization, and eventually, poor overall performance. One solution is to use *dynamic work partitioning*, the most widely used form of which is *dynamic loop scheduling* [23]. In this scheme, iterations of a parallelized loop are not distributed equally across threads. Instead, each thread executes a different number of iterations proportional to its dynamic performance. As a result,

```
PartitionPower(interval, pct, CorePower, N_CMOS, N_TFET)  :
IPS_old ← 0
direction ← +1
while ( true )
    SLEEP(interval)
    Power_CMOS ← Σ_{i∈CMOS} CorePower[i]
    Power_TFET ← 1 − Power_CMOS
    IPS_new ← Σ_{i∈[0,31]} instructions[i] * frequency[i]/cycles[i]
    if IPS_new < IPS_old
        direction ← −1 * direction
    end if
    if direction = +1
        ΔPower ← Power_CMOS * pct/100
        Power_CMOS ← Power_CMOS − ΔPower
        Power_TFET ← Power_TFET + ΔPower
    else
        ΔPower ← Power_TFET * pct/100
        Power_CMOS ← Power_CMOS + ΔPower
        Power_TFET ← Power_TFET − ΔPower
    end if
    for i ∈ [0, (N_CMOS + N_TFET − 1)]
        if type[i] = CMOS
            CorePower[i] ← Power_CMOS/N_CMOS
        else
            CorePower[i] ← Power_TFET/N_TFET
        end if
    end for
end while
```

Figure 10: The pseudocode for our dynamic power partitioning algorithm.

all threads complete their allocated work at about the same time, maximizing the utilization of the parallel hardware.

4.3 Power Partitioning

In addition to distributing the workload across threads in the form of loop iterations, the way we partition the available chip power across cores can also significantly impact the performance of the system. As the total power is limited, it must be partitioned across cores such that the processor executes at an energy-efficient operating point. The optimum power distribution depends on the mapping and work partitioning policies adopted by the application. In case of homogeneous mapping and equal work partitioning, dividing power equally across all cores results in almost identical thread performance. However, for other mapping and work partitioning schemes, equal power partitioning may not be the best approach. Instead, adjusting the power distribution across cores can lead to more efficient operating points for the heterogeneous multicore.

Consider the combination of heterogeneous thread-to-core mapping and dynamic work partitioning. While the heterogeneous mapping removes the burden of manually finding the best type of core, dynamic work partitioning eliminates the barrier-wait problems due to load imbalance. Note that when two threads of an application are executed on different types of cores under an equal per-core power budget, we can easily calculate how efficiently they are utilizing this power. For instance, if all cores are running at frequencies below 1 GHz, then clearly TFET cores are operating more efficiently than CMOS cores. Further, determining which type of core uses the available power more efficiently is application-dependent and can even change within an application based on the current phase of execution. Therefore, a runtime scheme that (1) identifies the energy efficiencies of different types of cores and (2) dynamically *repartitions* available power across cores to allocate more power to the efficient core type can potentially improve the overall performance.

To improve performance of our CMOS-TFET heterogeneous multicore under a fixed power budget, we employ a *dynamic power partitioning algorithm* based on a "perturb-and-observe" method. Our algorithm considers the TFET cores and CMOS cores as two power domains and partitions the total chip power across these two domains. Figure 10 gives the pseudocode for this algorithm. At every epoch, a fraction of the power is taken from one power domain (e.g., from TFET) to the other domain (e.g., to CMOS). At the end of the epoch, we observe whether this action resulted in an improvement in the total performance in terms of *instructions per second* (IPS). If the performance improves, then we continue to transfer power in the same direction; otherwise, we reverse the direction of power transfer. Using such a dynamic scheme also enables us to react to behavioral variations occurring within the application. Our dynamic power partitioning algorithm takes the epoch length, percentage of power to transfer at each epoch, total available chip power, and the number of cores in either type as input parameters, and hence, is *portable* across various heterogeneities and power budgets. By employing power partitioning together with a heterogeneous mapping and dynamic loop scheduling, our goal is to reach higher performance automatically, without putting the burden of detailed analysis and testing on the programmer or the user.

4.4 Overview of Evaluated Schemes

Table 2 shows the schemes tested in our evaluation. Starting from a baseline homogeneous processor that is either all-CMOS or all-TFET with equal work partitioning and equal power partitioning (*CMOS-Base* and *TFET-Base*), the first step we take is to switch to a 8-CMOS, 24-TFET heterogeneous processor. For each multi-threaded application, the programmer makes the binary decision of running parallel regions of the application on 8-CMOS or 24-TFET cores. Based on the ability of the programmer in making correct thread-to-core mapping decisions, the performance obtained varies. The schemes with the best and the worst mappings are referred to as *Hetero-Manual-Best* and *Hetero-Manual-Worst*, respectively. To explore the benefits of using all cores in the heterogeneous processor simultaneously (as opposed to using only one type at a time), we also evaluate the *Hetero-Simple* scheme which performs heterogeneous thread-to-core mapping. In the *Hetero-DynWork scheme*, on the other hand, we modify the application to be heterogeneous multicore-aware by adopting dynamic work partitioning. Our goal with this scheme is to evaluate the benefits of dynamic work partitioning on the heterogeneous system. Finally, we introduce our dynamic power partitioning scheme (*Hetero-Auto*) which also includes heterogeneous mapping and dynamic work partitioning.

5. EXPERIMENTAL SETUP

5.1 Simulation Infrastructure

We use the Simics full system simulator for running our simulations [24]. We assume a 32 core system consisting of 8 CMOS cores and 24 TFET cores as our heterogeneous processor model. The performance of this system is compared to our *baseline* system consisting of 32 cores (CMOS or TFET). The architectural parameters of the simulated systems are shown in Table 3.

5.2 Dynamic Work and Power Partitioning Implementation

In order to eliminate the effects of load imbalance, we use dynamic parallel loop scheduling which performs work partitioning at runtime. Dynamic loop scheduling can be done in two ways. In one method, the workload chunk size allotted to each thread is fixed. However, this may not be

Processor	Mapping	Work Partitioning	Power Partitioning	Code
32 CMOS cores	Homogeneous: CMOS	Equal	Equal	CMOS-Base
32 TFET cores	Homogeneous: TFET	Equal	Equal	TFET-Base
8 CMOS and 24 TFET cores	Homogeneous: CMOS *or* TFET	Equal	Equal	Hetero-Manual-Best
	Homogeneous: CMOS *or* TFET	Equal	Equal	Hetero-Manual-Worst
	Heterogeneous: CMOS *and* TFET	Equal	Equal	Hetero-Simple
	Heterogeneous: CMOS *and* TFET	Dynamic	Equal	Hetero-DynWork
	Heterogeneous: CMOS *and* TFET	Dynamic	Dynamic	Hetero-Auto

Table 2: Evaluated multicore configurations. The performance of these schemes are presented in Section 6.

Parameter	Value
No. of Cores (Homogeneous)	32 CMOS *or* 32 TFET
No. of Cores (Heterogeneous)	8 CMOS *and* 24 TFET
L1 D/I-Cache	Private, 32KB each, 4-ways set-assoc., 1-cycle latency
L2 Cache	Shared, 4MB, 16-ways set-assoc. 10-cycles latency (2GHz)
Memory Access Latency	120-cycles (at 2GHz)
DVFS Epoch Size	1ms
Power Partitioning Epoch Size	5ms
Power Transfer Percentage	10%

Table 3: System parameters.

optimal, since a large chunk size can still result in load imbalance across threads and a small chunk size can significantly increase the overhead incurred during the request of a new chunk. A modified version of dynamic scheduling is *guided* scheduling [23], where the chunk size is not fixed, but variable. In guided scheduling, the chunk size starts large but gradually reduces as more loop iterations are completed, which achieves a smaller scheduling overhead. We modified our target benchmarks such that, all OpenMP parallelized loops use guided scheduling.

We implemented power partitioning as a part of our simulator. At every epoch, the total number of instructions executed by all cores in the processor is calculated and the total number of instructions per second (IPS) is obtained. This calculation can be implemented as an OS daemon process on a real system. In this case, an interrupt will be generated at every epoch, causing the daemon to read hardware performance counters and recalculate the total IPS in the last epoch. Comparing the total IPS for the current and previous epochs, it either decides to move power from the TFET domain to the CMOS domain or vice versa. The result of the power partitioner is a vector of per-core power budget values whose entries are stored in per-core power budget registers. Power re-distribution is carried at a period of 5 ms.

Our hardware DVFS implementation reads per-core power budget values from special purpose registers at every epoch. For each core, it determines the ratio of the power of the core to its power budget. It scales the voltage and frequency of the core such that it will match its allocated power budget in the next epoch. Note that in our heterogeneous CMOS-TFET multicore, DVFS is carried out on a per-core basis so as to take the difference in the power and performance characteristics of different types of cores into account. Assuming a 50 mV/ns latency for on-chip per-core voltage regulators as presented by Kim et al. [25] and a PLL locking time of a few microseconds, we set our DVFS epoch length to be 1 ms. By selecting such a large DVFS epoch length, we ensure that the performance overheads due to DVFS are negligible. Note that our baseline systems also employ per-core DVFS, in which case, the energy and area overheads of having per-core voltage domains is common to both our baseline homogeneous and proposed heterogeneous multicores. In our implementation, we assign DVFS levels at frequency intervals of 125 MHz, ranging from 500 MHz to 2 GHz.

5.3 Benchmarks

For the purpose of running our simulations, we use applications with train input sizes from the SPEC OMP 2001 suite [7]. These applications are parallelized using OpenMP [26] pragmas. We ran our simulations from the start until the end of each application, and measured the performance improvement based on the reduction in execution time of the application.

6. EXPERIMENTAL RESULTS

To evaluate the performance of our 32-core heterogeneous processor with 8 CMOS and 24 TFET cores, we consider a 32-core homogeneous CMOS and a 32-core homogeneous TFET processor as baselines. We assume a fixed power budget of 32W (i.e., 1W per core) in all evaluated configurations (we later analyze sensitivity to power budget). In all configurations, sequential regions of the target applications are executed on CMOS cores, except with the homogeneous TFET system where the sequential regions are also executed on TFET cores. During the execution of the applications, if any cores are detected to be idle, then the power budgets of the idle cores are redistributed among the active cores. For instance, only one core can be active during the sequential region of an application, in which case this core is allocated the entire power budget of 32W.

6.1 Hetero-Manual-Best vs. Baseline

We first compare the performance of our heterogeneous multicore against both homogeneous baseline processors, namely, a 32-core CMOS and a 32-core TFET multicore. Figure 11 shows the performance of our baseline and proposed configurations. We also include a *Best-Base* bar in this figure, which represents the maximum of *CMOS-Base* and *TFET-Base* performance, and normalize all bars with respect to *Best-Base*. The *Hetero-Manual-Best* scheme assumes that the application programmer maps parallel regions exclusively to either CMOS or TFET cores of the heterogeneous processor, whichever one achieves higher performance. We observe that, on average, our heterogeneous CMOS-TFET multicore performs within 4% of the *Best-Base* performance. In case of applications like *apsi* and *equake*, we see that *apsi* performs best on 32-TFET cores and *equake* performs best on 32-CMOS cores. In both cases, by using a heterogeneous processor (without any heterogeneity-aware dynamic schemes), we are able to reach the performance of the best homogeneous system, which shows that our heterogeneous multicore is suitable for serving a variety of applications.

6.2 Hetero-Manual-Best vs. Hetero-Manual-Worst

When comparing our heterogeneous multicore against the baseline systems, we assumed that the programmer is capable of making perfect mapping decisions. In other words, the programmer analyzes each application and decides whether it is better to run the parallel regions of the application on the CMOS or TFET part of the heterogeneous processor. Making a bad thread mapping decision (e.g., mapping threads to CMOS cores although TFETs would perform better) can lead to sub-optimal performance. In Figure 12, we compare the two programmer-directed mapping schemes Hetero-Manual-Best and Hetero-Manual-Worst, which represent the best and worst mapping schemes for the target applications. From this figure we observe that bad mapping decisions can degrade the heterogeneous system performance by 32% on average, which easily eliminates any benefit of using the heterogeneous system. Therefore, making correct mapping decisions on heterogeneous systems is key to optimizing performance.

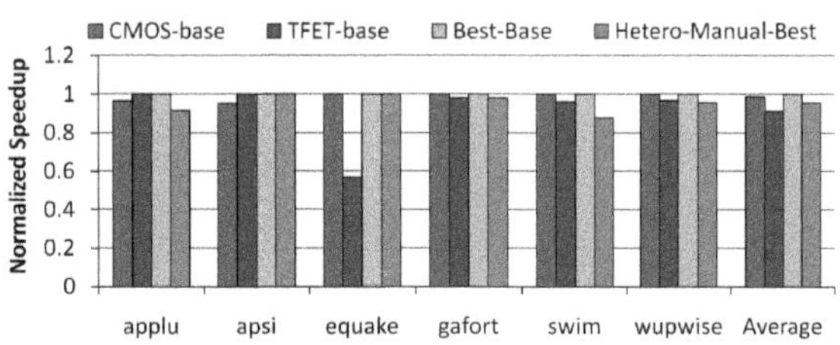

Figure 11: Performance of the baseline homogeneous and the proposed heterogeneous multicores.

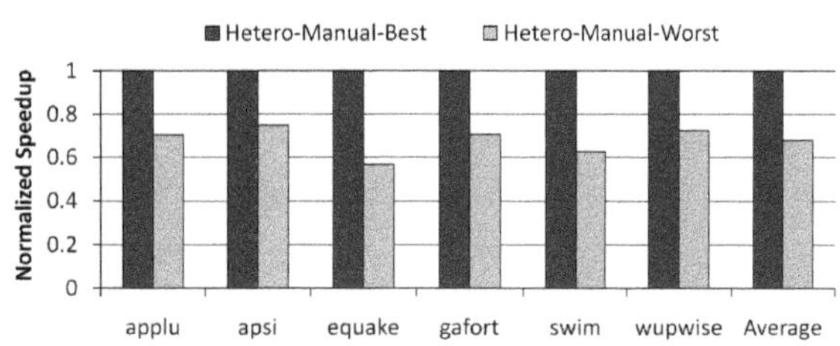

Figure 12: Performance comparison of the best and worst thread mappings on our CMOS-TFET heterogeneous multicore.

6.3 Hetero-Auto vs. Hetero-Manual-Best

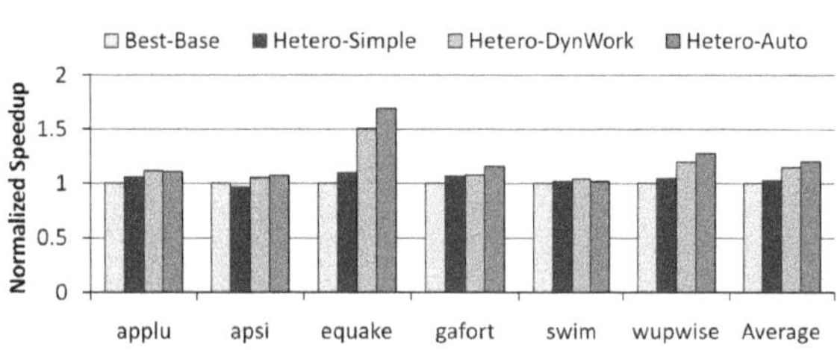

Figure 13: Performance of our CMOS-TFET multicore with and without dynamic work and power partitioning schemes.

We now evaluate our proposed dynamic power partitioning scheme and compare its performance against that of the best programmer-directed mapping. This dynamic scheme is performed *automatically* by a runtime system and requires no effort on the programmer's part. Note that, while the programmer-directed mapping uses only one type of core at any time, our dynamic scheme uses both types of cores simultaneously. Further, applications running under our scheme also use dynamic work partitioning, whereas the manual scheme assumes a static, equal work partitioning.

Figure 13 shows our results with the two schemes, as well as two intermediate schemes. The *Hetero-Simple* scheme uses the heterogeneous CMOS-TFET processor with only heterogeneous mapping, i.e., it employs neither dynamic work partitioning nor dynamic power partitioning. We can see that, heterogeneous mapping alone makes our heterogeneous multi-core perform 4% better than the baseline. Adding dynamic work partitioning on top of heterogeneous mapping (*Hetero-DynWork*) brings an additional 12% performance improvement. Finally, we observe that, on average, our dynamic power partitioning scheme (*Hetero-Auto*) performs 21% better than the best baseline performance.

In conclusion, superior sub-threshold characteristics of TFETs enable them to operate at points that cannot be realized by CMOS devices. Hence, by incorporating TFET devices, heterogeneous multicores can achieve higher performance, and serve a wider variety of applications. It is true that this improvement comes with an additional cost of using TFET technology and integrating CMOS and TFET technologies. However, a recent technology change to tri-gate transistors provided 18-37% improvements at the device-level [13], at a similar cost. Hence, we believe that the 21% system-level improvement presented in this work is very significant.

6.4 Runtime Characteristics

Figure 14 shows the dynamic variation in power consumption of *wupwise* application for the CMOS baseline (middle) and CMOS-TFET heterogeneous multicore (top), as well as the number of active cores (bottom). The total power consumption of both systems follow a similar trend: the entire power budget can be utilized in parallel regions, but sequential regions use only a fraction of available power as only a single core is active. The top figure also shows how our dynamic power partitioning scheme distributes the chip power across CMOS and TFET domains, which results in an improved overall performance.

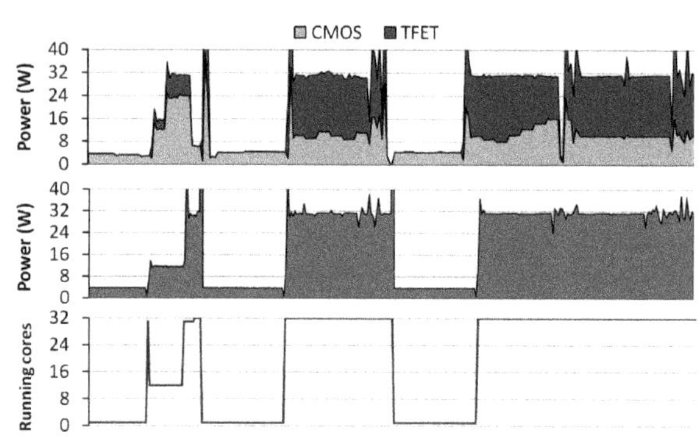

Figure 14: Power consumed by heterogeneous (top) and homogeneous (middle) systems, and number of active cores (bottom) over time (*wupwise*).

6.5 Sensitivity Analysis

As part of our sensitivity analysis, we show the performance of our heterogeneous processor under varying power budgets and ratios of CMOS and TFET cores.

• **Sensitivity to Power Budget:** Our results with the 8-CMOS, 24-TFET multicore with different power budgets for *wupwise* are shown in Figure 15. We observe that, for low power budgets, our heterogeneous multicore achieves a higher speedup. The reason for this behavior is that when power is scarce, cores in the homogeneous CMOS system are forced to operate at very inefficient operating conditions when compared to TFET cores employed in our heterogeneous processor. On the other hand, the homogeneous TFET processor still suffers from the limited maximum frequency of TFETs, which significantly degrades sequential region performance. In contrast, the heterogeneous multicore is able to utilize the available power more efficiently, leading to significant speedup. Since future processor trends point to a decrease in available power per core, we believe that the performance improvement obtained by the heterogeneous CMOS-TFET multicore will increase even further.

• **Sensitivity to CMOS-TFET Core Ratio:** Figure 16 shows the variation in speedup with the number of CMOS cores in our 32 core processor. The two benchmarks demonstrated in this figure, namely, *wupwise* and *apsi*, show different trends as the CMOS core quantity is increased. *wupwise* scales well with number of cores and prefers running at low frequencies on the largest possible number of TFET cores. Yet, a single CMOS core is needed to achieve high performance while executing the sequential regions of the application. Therefore, neither the CMOS-only nor the TFET-only baseline performs satisfactorily and we achieve a performance improvement of up to 37% for the single CMOS core case. On the other hand, the scalability of *apsi* is limited, on account of which it prefers running on a moderate number of CMOS cores. In this case, the best performance improvement of around 10% is observed with the 4 and 8 CMOS core systems. Having more or less number of CMOS cores results in a shift in the operating point of all CMOS cores and leads to a relatively inefficient execution.

We also experimented with different power transfer percentages and found that while amounts higher than 10% lead to oscillations, smaller amounts (large enough to trigger DVFS level changes) still perform satisfactorily.

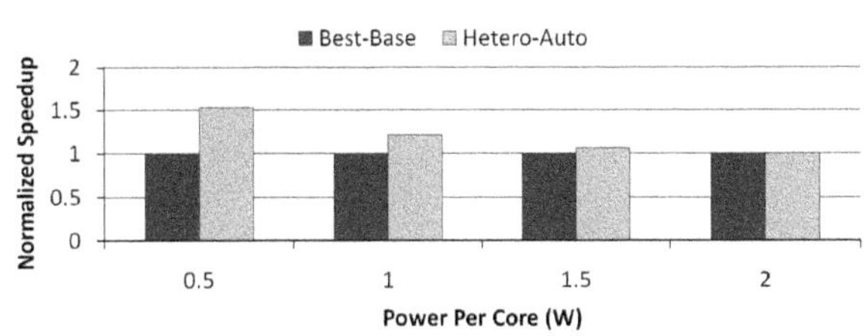

Figure 15: Performance of CMOS-TFET multicore under different power budgets(*wupwise*).

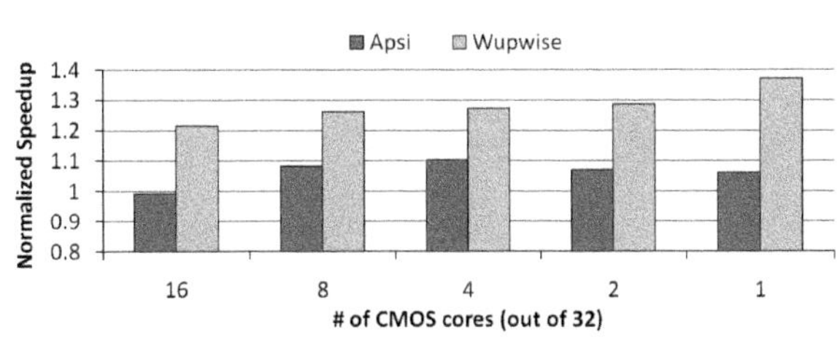

Figure 16: Performance of CMOS-TFET multicore for varying number of CMOS cores.

7. RELATED WORK

The ideas presented in this work can be distinguished from the prior work at two main points: constructing heterogeneous multicores and mapping applications to heterogeneous multicores. There have been various prior works on heterogeneous multicores, most of which consider architectural heterogeneity and process variations in multicore processors. [27] proposes a heterogeneous multicore processor to exploit different points in the power/performance space in an application's execution. [28] shows that heterogeneous multicores can bring significant power reduction for similar performance or significant performance improvement for the same power budget. [29] proposes a dynamically reconfigurable processor that can adapt itself to changing workload behavior dynamically. Showing that critical sections in applications can also be causes for serialization, [30] illustrates use of high performance core for critical section execution and low power worker cores for parallel execution. An analysis of heterogeneous computing using on-chip custom logic, reconfigurable logic, and GPGPU cores is performed in [31]. [32] uses specialized processors with high energy efficiency to fight against the power budget. Various prior works [33, 34, 35] focused on process variations, which is an unintentional source of heterogeneity in multicores. The common goal in these work is to address performance asymmetry across cores by finding the voltage and frequency levels that maximize performance.

There has been only a handful of prior work on device level heterogeneity. In [4], TFET devices are used to design processor cores that have very high efficiency at low frequencies. The authors show large improvements in energy efficiency of embedded processors by running sequential applications on TFET cores at lower frequencies. [36] presents a heterogeneous multicore processor running multithreaded applications under DVFS. They observe that, due to the dynamic behavior of applications and the unequal distribution of work, most of the execution time is spent at low frequencies. Exploiting the fact that TFET devices can provide significant energy savings at those frequencies, they propose a dynamic thread migration scheme across TFET and CMOS cores.

Most of the prior work in multicore heterogeneity is based on architectural heterogeneity and are orthogonal to what is presented in this work, and the works in device level heterogeneity used TFET devices only as a way to improve the energy-delay product of processors by reducing its power consumption, sometimes even sacrificing from performance. In contrast, in this work, our primary target is to achieve the *maximum possible performance while working under a maximum power budget*, which has not been studied in any of these works.

Various efforts have also been made to address the problem of how to map applications to multicore processors. In [37], the behavior of commercial applications running on asymmetric multicores is analyzed. The authors indicate that the application itself needs to be aware of asymmetry, and stress that when running multithreaded OpenMP applications on heterogeneous systems, guided scheduling typically performs better. [38] analyzes multithreaded applications running on a frequency-heterogeneous real multicore system and points out the use of hardware counters in quantifying application progress, which can in turn be used to determine the best number of threads to use at runtime. [39] also indicates the difficulty in mapping applications to cores on a heterogeneous processor and indicate that this is no longer a task that can easily be performed by the programmer. To simplify the process, they propose an automated method that performs runtime adaptive mapping of computations to processing elements. These prior works agree on the fact that simple static work partitioning constructs do not perform well for heterogeneous processors and some form of dynamic load balancing is required to better make use of the performance asymmetry across cores. In an effort to efficiently port applications to heterogeneous processors, these prior work (i) run cores at their respective maximum frequencies without being concerned about power limitations (which required dynamic work partitioning due to performance imbalance) [27, 40], (ii) adjust the frequency/voltage of different types of cores so that static scheduling can still perform satisfactorily [33, 34, 35], or (iii) exploit architectural heterogeneity solely from a perspective that accelerates sequential or critical regions of applications [30, 29, 41]. None of the prior works consider accompanying dynamic work partitioning across application threads with *dynamic power management across cores* as a method to better utilize heterogeneous multicore processors, which is another contribution we make in this work.

8. CONCLUSIONS

ITRS projections for multicore chips indicate continuous decrease in per-core power budget which requires cores to be optimized to consume very low power. However, low power optimized homogeneous multicores cannot satisfy the needs of sequential applications, sequential parts of parallel applications, or applications with limited scalability. In such cases, heterogeneous multicores that use different types of cores for different purposes can perform better. However, it is not a straightforward task to efficiently port an application to a heterogeneous multicore. Extracting high performance from a heterogeneous processor requires both application-specific and processor-specific information and cannot be efficiently performed by the programmer. In this paper, we attacked the problem of how to extract the best performance from a device-level heterogeneous CMOS-TFET multicore. We proposed a runtime system that employs dynamic power partitioning to extract high performance from heterogeneous multicores without requiring any extra effort for application porting. Our power partitioning scheme works in conjunction with heterogeneous thread mapping and dynamic work partitioning, and distributes the available power across cores of the heterogeneous processor in an attempt to achieve better performance. Our results show that, on an average, under a fixed power budget of 1W per core, an 8-CMOS 24-TFET heterogeneous multicore with dynamic power partitioning can achieve 21% performance improvement over the best equivalent homogeneous multicore.

9. ACKNOWLEDGEMENTS

This work was supported in part by NSF awards 1147388, 0903432, 0903432, 1152479, 1017882, 0702617, 0963839, 1213052 and 1017882; and SRC NRI MIND. Karthik Swaminathan is supported by IBM PhD Fellowship.

10. REFERENCES

[1] S. Borkar. Thousand Core Chips: A Technology Perspective. In *DAC*, 2007.

[2] H. Wei et al. Scaling with Design Constraints: Predicting the Future of Big Chips. *IEEE Micro*, 2011.

[3] D.K Mohata et al. Demonstration of MOSFET-Like On-Current Performance in Arsenide/Antimonide Tunnel FETs with Staggered Hetero-junctions for 300mV Logic Applications. In *IEDM*, 2011.

[4] V. Saripalli et al. An Energy-Efficient Heterogeneous CMP based on Hybrid TFET-CMOS cores. In *DAC*, 2011.

[5] International Technology Roadmap for Semiconductors. 2011.

[6] B. Wheeler. Calxeda Spins 4W Server-on-a-Chip. In *Microprocessor Report*, Nov 2011.

[7] V. Aslot et al. SPECOMP: A New Benchmark Suite for Measuring Parallel Computer Performance. In *International Workshop on OpenMP Applications and Tools*, 2001.

[8] S. Mookerjea et al. Experimental Demonstration of 100nm Channel Length In0.53Ga0.47As-based Vertical Inter-band Tunnel Field Effect Transistors (TFETs) for Ultra Low-Power Logic and SRAM Applications. In *IEDM*, 2009.

[9] R. Gandhi et al. Vertical Si-Nanowire n -Type Tunneling FETs With Low Subthreshold Swing ($\leq$ 50mV/decade) at Room Temperature. *IEDM*, 2011.

[10] D.K. Mohata et al. Self-aligned Gate NanoPillar In0.53Ga0.47As Vertical Tunnel Transistor . In *DRC*, 2011.

[11] M. Luisier and G. Klimeck. Performance Comparisons of Tunneling Field-Effect Transistors Made of InSb, Carbon, and GaSb-InAs Broken Gap Heterostructures. In *IEDM*, 2009.

[12] U. E. Avci et al. Comparison of Performance, Switching Energy and Process Variations for the TFET and MOSFET in Logic. In *VLSIT*, 2011.

[13] Intel Corporation. Intel 22nm 3-D Tri-Gate Transistor Technology, May 2011.

[14] M. LaPedus. TSMC to make FinFETs in 450-mm fab, February 2011.

[15] C.C. Wu et al. High Performance 22/20nm FinFET CMOS Devices with Advanced high-K/metal Gate Scheme. In *IEDM*, 2010.

[16] Synopsys. *TCAD Sentaurus Device Manual, Release: C-2009.06*, 2009.

[17] Wei Zhao and Yu Cao. New Generation of Predictive Technology Model for Sub-45nm Design Exploration. In *ISQED*, 2006.

[18] Intel Corporation. Intel Atom Processor Z5xx Series - Datasheet, June 2010.

[19] Xilinx. Xilinx Power Tools Tutorial: Spartan and Virtex 6 FPGAs.

[20] A. Sinha and A.P. Chandrakasan. JouleTrack-a Web based tool for software energy profiling. In *DAC*, 2001.

[21] S. Datta et al. Ultrahigh-Speed 0.5 V Supply Voltage In0.7Ga0.3As Quantum-Well Transistors on Silicon Substrate. *IEEE Electron Device Letters*, 28(8):685 –687, Aug. 2007.

[22] V. Saripalli et al. Variation-tolerant Ultra Low-Power Heterojunction Tunnel FET SRAM Design. *Nanoscale Architectures*, 2011.

[23] C. D. Polychronopoulos and D. J. Kuck. Guided self-scheduling: A practical scheduling scheme for parallel supercomputers. *IEEE Trans. Comput.*, 36(12), December 1987.

[24] P. S. Magnusson et al. Simics: A Full System Simulation Platform. *Computer*, 35, February 2002.

[25] W. Kim et al. System Level Analysis of Fast, Per-Core DVFS using On-Chip Switching Regulators. In *ISCA*, 2008.

[26] OpenMP. OpenMP, url = http://www.openmp.org.

[27] R. Kumar et al. Single-ISA Heterogeneous Multi-Core Architectures: The Potential for Processor Power Reduction. In *MICRO*, 2003.

[28] T. Y. Morad et al. Performance, Power Efficiency and Scalability of Asymmetric Cluster Chip Multiprocessors. *IEEE Comput. Archit. Lett.*, 5, January 2006.

[29] E. Ipek et al. Core Fusion: Accommodating Software Diversity in Chip Multiprocessors. In *ISCA*, 2007.

[30] M. A. Suleman et al. Accelerating Critical Section Execution with Asymmetric Multi-core Architectures. In *ASPLOS*, 2009.

[31] E. S. Chung et al. Single-Chip Heterogeneous Computing: Does the Future Include Custom Logic, FPGAs, and GPGPUs? In *MICRO*, 2010.

[32] Ganesh Venkatesh et al. Conservation Cores: Reducing the Energy of Mature Computations. In *ASPLOS*, 2010.

[33] E. Humenay et al. Impact of Process Variations on Multicore Performance Symmetry. In *DATE*, 2007.

[34] R. Teodorescu and J. Torrellas. Variation-Aware Application Scheduling and Power Management for Chip Multiprocessors. In *ISCA*, 2008.

[35] U. R. Karpuzcu et al. The BubbleWrap many-core: popping cores for sequential acceleration. In *MICRO*, 2009.

[36] K. Swaminathan et al. Improving Energy Efficiency of Multi-Threaded Applications using Heterogeneous CMOS-TFET Multicores. In *ISLPED*, 2011.

[37] S. Balakrishnan et al. The Impact of Performance Asymmetry in Emerging Multicore Architectures. In *ISCA*, 2005.

[38] M. Bhadauria et al. Accomodating Diversity in CMPs with Heterogeneous Frequencies. In *HiPEAC*, 2009.

[39] C-K. Luk et al. Qilin: Exploiting Parallelism on Heterogeneous Multiprocessors with Adaptive Mapping. In *MICRO*, 2009.

[40] R. Kumar et al. Single-ISA Heterogeneous Multi-Core Architectures for Multithreaded Workload Performance. In *ISCA*, 2004.

[41] M. D. Hill and M. R. Marty. Amdahl's Law in the Multicore Era. *Computer*, 41, July 2008.

COOL: Control-based Optimization Of Load-balancing for Thermal Behavior

Thomas Ebi, Hussam Amrouch, Jörg Henkel
Karsruhe Institute of Technology
{thomas.ebi, hussam.amrouch, henkel}@kit.edu

ABSTRACT

The thermal behavior of on-chip systems is crucial in order to maintain a reliable operation throughout its lifetime. Potential thermal hotspots like, for example, register files are particularly responsible for unreliable behavior and have therefore been the focus of related research. Within this paper we demonstrate that a pro-active thermal strategy is necessary in order to avoid thermal hotspots by performing load balancing – in regards to the temperature produced by the computational load – through the means of activity migration. We have found that *extremum-seeking control* is a powerful way to achieve this goal because of its properties that are tailored to the thermal management problem. Our work deploys a thermal camera that captures the infrared emissions from the silicon wafer of an FPGA chip enabling us to accurately analyze and evaluate the impact of our load balancing approach with respect to the chip's thermal behavior. The obtained reduction of peak temperature is $9°C$ and the reduction in thermal spatial variation is from $6°C$ to $1°C$. We additionally apply *extremum-seeking control* to the register file of a superscalar ASIC microarchitecture. Our results using thermal simulation show on average a $13°C$ (up to $21°C$) reduction of peak temperature in the register file while exhibiting a 49% reduction in thermal spatial variation compared to State-of-the-Art while incurring an average performance penalty of 1.4% but without increasing the area footprint of the register file.

Categories and Subject Descriptors

C.0 [**General**]: System architectures; C.3 [**Special-Purpose and Application-Based Systems**]: Real-time and embedded systems

General Terms

Algorithms, Design

Keywords

Dynamic Thermal Management, Multi-core Architectures, MPSoC's, Proactive Algorithm

1. INTRODUCTION AND RELATED WORK

As technology scales to smaller technology nodes, on-chip power densities increase continuously [15]. This increase in power per area, in turn, leads to high temperatures, which cause problems in reliability, performance degradation, and incurs additional cooling costs. Elevated temperatures directly impact electromigration, and thereby reduce the *Mean Time to Failure* (MTTF) of the chip. Additionally, thermal cycling and thermal variation [5] across the chip also affect electromigration etc., and lead to permanent irreversible errors, as they can lead to cracks in on-chip structures and thus also negatively impact chip lifetime. Higher temperatures are also responsible for transient faults caused by timing errors, as an increase of $10°C$ increases interconnect delay by around 5% [15]. Through thermal variations, the delay varies across the chip and the clock tree becomes vulnerable to clock skew [3]. These and other thermal effects make it crucial to employ thermal management in on-chip systems that deal with multiple aspects such as thermal balancing to reduce thermal variation as well as reducing both peak and average temperatures.

There are several fundamental approaches for reducing the power that dissipates into heat per area using *Dynamic Voltage and Frequency Scaling* (DVFS) and *Power Gating*. While effective in reducing peak temperatures, these approaches suffer often from loss of performance and do not consider thermal variation [5]. Another possibility is to improve the power per area gradients through balancing of the computational workload and hence to avoid temperature peaks of local thermal hotspots.

Thermal hotspots often occur in components of small area and high power consumption. An example of such a component is the register file in a superscalar CPU. In spite of the fact that it occupies a relatively small amount of area, it is often responsible for the majority of the generated peak temperatures across the chip over the runtime. This is mainly due to its high utilization (it is accessed more frequently than any other architectural component and its small area – occupying only 6% of the total area of an Alpha processor [22], for example). K. Skadron [21] recognized the register file as the hottest component when running a majority of applications. The experimental simulations in [8] have shown that the temperature of the register file may reach $120°C$ for some applications from the SPEC 2000 benchmarks suite due to its high power density compared to other components. The real temperature measurement of modern processors using an infrared thermal camera [19] also shows that the hotspot is often located in the register file and it has the highest average temperature. The aforementioned reasons make controlling the thermal behavior of the register file inevitable. To minimize the generated temperature from the register file, Patel et al. [20] proposed to divide the physical register file into two equal-sized banks and to migrate switching activity between them by controlling which bank is active. Their scheme can reduce the steady-state temperature at a slight performance penalty.

State-of-the-Art approaches for scheduling activity migration are largely threshold-based [5]. That is, one component is continuously active until a threshold temperature is met, at which time the execution (i.e. switching activity) is migrated to the other component [17]. While existing pro-active approaches act before a threshold is met, they still rely on the given threshold. In other words, all these approaches focus on keeping thermal constraints rather than minimizing temperatures.

The rest of the paper is organized as follows: after presenting our contribution in Section 2 we introduce our thermal model in Section 3. In Section 4 we formalize *extremum-seeking control* as an efficient way of optimizing thermal behavior (i.e. peak temperatures and thermal variations). In Section 5 we analyze our approach using thermal measurements obtained from an infrared camera before applying it to the register file of a superscalar processor in Section 5.1. Finally, we conclude our work in Section 6.

2. CONVENTIONS AND CONTRIBUTIONS

A chip's *Mean Time To Failure* (MTTF) can be expressed as a probability function based on temperature and thermal variation. Focusing, as an example, on electromigration, the MTTF for temperature T is expressed through Black's equation [16]:

$$\mathrm{MTTF} = AJ^{-n}e^{q/(k(T))}$$

where A is a constant, J the current density, n is the technology parameter, q the activation energy, and k is the Boltzmann constant. Additionally, an increase in thermal variation with gradients dT/dx from 0.09 – $0.28°C/\mu m^2$ decreases the time to failure by approximately a factor of 10 in [16]. In order to minimize the aging due to electromigration and increase a chip's expected lifetime, it is thus necessary to minimize both T and dT/dx.

On-chip temperatures are directly affected by the switching *activity* of transistors which cause an increase in dynamic power. Given a system where it is possible to constrain the causes of the switching activity to specific chip areas, e.g. by limiting tasks to a subset of cores or only accessing a subset of registers, we define the changing of these constraints as *activity migration* [9]. In other words, activity migration can be seen as moving switching activity from area A to area B (for instance, R and L in Figure 1). These separate areas are referred to as *components*.

As an example, activity in the register file in Figure 1 is controlled by limiting the write accesses to a subset of the registers (in the example: component R) of the register file through the register renaming unit. Thus, activity migration is performed through the renaming unit by limiting write accesses to a different subset of registers (e.g. component L). There may be some read accesses to the now idle component (R), however as shown in Section 5.1, these are infrequent across all observed benchmarks. Figure 1 shows two different rates of activity migration in a register file with two components: a) using infrequent migration, and b) using frequent migrations. Case b) is able to reduce thermal variations between the two components but, due to mutual heating resulting from the thermal conductivity between the components and insufficient cooling periods, it may lead to higher peak temperatures if the migrations are too frequent.[1] Case a) on the other hand, has a lower peak temperature, but a higher thermal variation. In this paper, we aim to balance the load between components by finding the optimal rate of activity migration which minimizes the temperature T and dT/dx for a given workload.

Our novel contributions:

(1) Unlike previous approaches, the goal of our approach COOL is not keeping thermal constraints, but instead optimizing the spatial temperature distribution, i.e. aiming to minimize peak temperatures and optimizing thermal balancing by finding an optimal scheme of activity migration based on observed temperatures.

(2) Our approach includes both heterogeneous components as well as multiple components (i.e. more than two) running multiple activities.

(3) We verify our approach by means of a State-of-the-Art thermal camera that captures the infrared images emitted from the die of the tested chip to accurately analyze on-chip thermal behavior and the effects of COOL. That means, the results we achieve are *real* improvements and do not underlie estimation errors.

For evaluation, we apply COOL to the register file of a superscalar processor in order to minimize the peak temperature and the thermal variation considering various applications from the SPEC 2006 and SPEC 2000 benchmarks.

3. ACTIVITY AND THERMAL MODELS

In order to formulate the properties of the thermal impact of activity migration, we examine the case where activity is migrated between two homogeneous components. To express the properties mathematically, we first assume an ideal system, i.e. where the overhead of activity migration is considered to be zero, and in the evaluation we apply our approach using both real thermal measurements (obtained from a thermal camera) and thermal simulations and we account for incurred performance penalty. Furthermore, only within this section, it is assumed that the power consumption is constant during execution. The ideal activity on the two components can thus be modeled using the *heaviside* function Θ.

$$\Theta(x) = \begin{cases} 0, & x < 0 \\ 1, & x \geq 0 \end{cases} \tag{1}$$

with the execution on each component modeled as $\Theta_1(\omega, t) := \Theta(\sin \omega t)$ and $\Theta_2(\omega, t) := \Theta(-\sin \omega t)$, respectively, with the angular frequency ω determining the frequency of activity migrations (migration rate). The thermal development over time is then the *step response* for Θ, $\mathcal{R}(\Theta)$ as is shown in Figure 2, and can be expressed as

$$\mathcal{R}(\Theta) \equiv T(t) = S_n + (T(n) - S_n)e^{-t/a(n)}$$

where $T(n)$ is the initial temperature at a change in Θ, S_n is the *steady state* temperature after the change in Θ, and $a(n)$ controls the rate of heating/cooling. If $T_n < S_n$, the component is heating up, and if $T_n > S_n$, it is cooling. This corresponds to the solution of the differential equation of the first law of thermodynamics ($[c \cdot m \cdot \frac{dT}{dt} = P \cdot \Theta + \dot{Q}]$, $c \cdot m$ is the thermal capacity, P is the power consumption, and $\dot{Q}$ is the heat transferred to or from the system) under the assumption that the two components are symmetrical (i.e. both generate the same amount of heat). To calculate

[1] What is deemed as "too frequent" is highly dependent on what the components are. In the case of the register file, this is around more frequent then once every 15K execution cycles, see Figure 11.

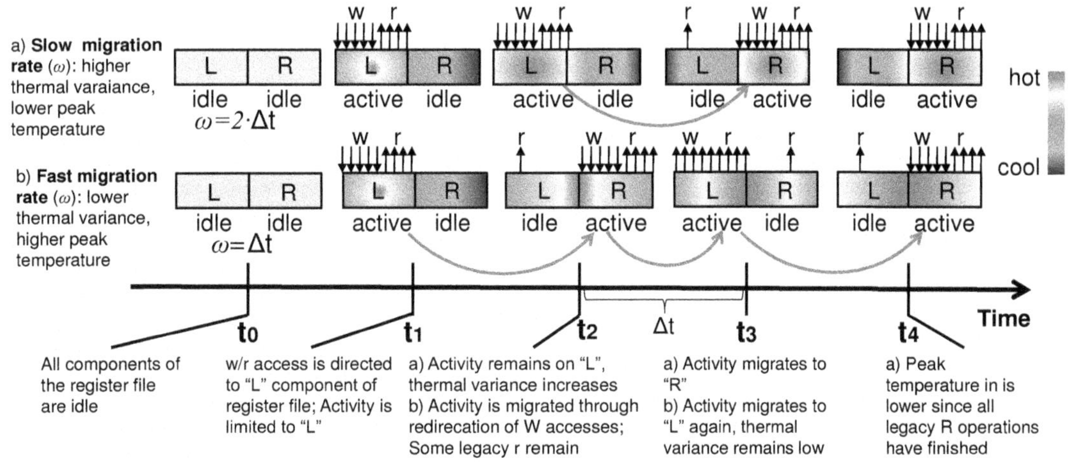

Figure 1: The effects of *activity migration* on a register file (for details see Section 5.1) over time

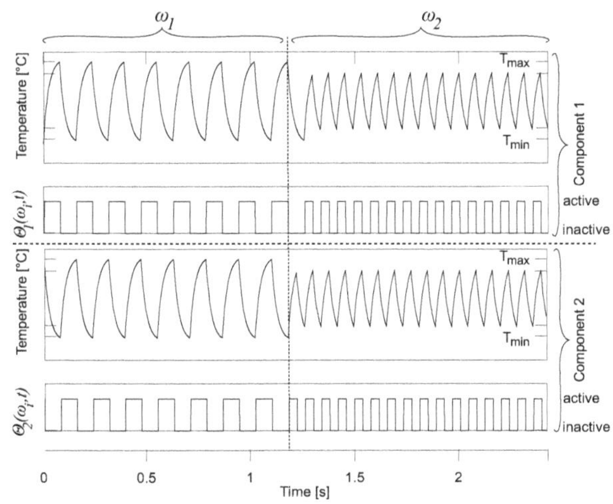

Figure 2: Ideal activity migration and resulting temperature considering homogeneous components

the thermal properties, it is necessary to examine the temperatures of both components T_1 and T_2. For each different value of ω we can use these temperatures to determine the peak and average temperatures as well as the thermal variation between the two components for thermal balancing. As can be seen in Figure 2, these different values of ω will result in different $T_{\max}$ and $T_{\min}$, allowing us to optimize thermal behavior – and thereby chip reliability and lifetime – by finding an optimal ω. To accomplish this, we employ the principles of *extremum-seeking control*.

4. APPLICATION OF EXTREMUM-SEEKING CONTROL

Control theory deals with the control of dynamic systems using a feedback loop to drive a system into a desired state. Akin to the goal of optimizing the temperature/thermal balancing, the model of *extremum-seeking control*, also referred to as *self-optimizing* control, is exploited in order to optimize the output function f of a system as long as this function has an *extremum* value (minimum/maximum) and is at least differentiable two times ($f \in C^2$). Its notable difference to standard control theory is that it does not rely on a predetermined set point, i.e. a predetermined value for the output function to reach, but instead it aims to drive the output function to an extreme value, e.g. to a minimum, and is thus particularly suited for the challenge of minimizing peak temperatures and thermal variations. To fulfill this goal, the controller controls components of an on-chip processor architecture. The output function f of the components is based on the temperature measured during runtime, as shown in the right part of Figure 3. In order to influence this temperature function, the controller changes the activity migration rate between the components. By observing how this change affects the temperature function the controller can adapt the activity migration rate to drive the temperature function to a minimum.

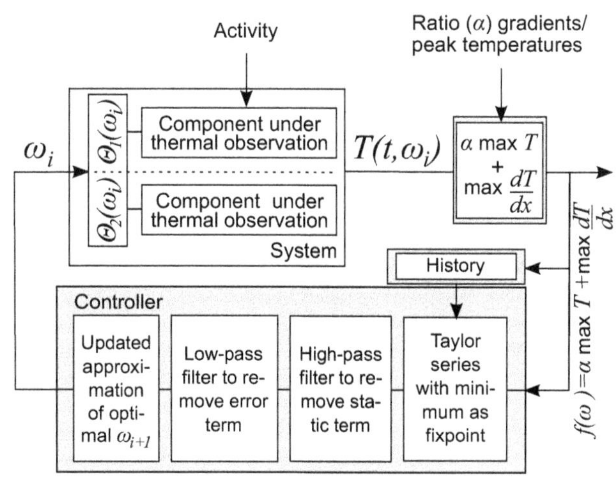

Figure 3: Overview of *extremum-seeking* controller

According to Taylor's theorem, we can approximate f around a neighborhood a as:

$$f(\omega) \approx f(a) + f'(a)(\omega - a) + \frac{f''(a)}{2}(\omega - a)^2 + \epsilon \qquad (2)$$

with an error term ϵ. In order to find the extremum of the output function (e.g. the minimum temperature), we are interested in finding a such that $f'(a) = 0$.

In summary, our *extremum-seeking* control works as follows: assuming the output function of the system $f(\omega)$ can be expressed as Equation 2 with an error ϵ, passing $f(\omega)$ through a high-pass "washout" filter will filter out the constant term $f(a)$. Likewise, the low-pass filter serves the purpose of filtering out the error ϵ which can be seen as high-frequency noise. The result is an approximation for $f''(a)$, which is given in [1]:

$$\dot{\hat{\omega}} \approx -\frac{kbf''(a)}{2}\tilde{\omega} \tag{3}$$

where $\tilde{\omega}$ is the estimation error $(a - \hat{\omega})$, k is the *adaptation gain* of the low-pass filter, b the amplitude of the probing signal used for modulation. This is then employed to determine the changed input ω to the activity migration in order to drive the output function towards $f(a)$.

First we examine the case of optimal *thermal balancing*, in which the goal is to keep the system temperature as steady as possible, i.e. having a minimal thermal gradient between the two components, and avoiding thermal cycling. This is the case when the largest difference between the temperature of the first component, T_1, and the temperature on the second, T_2, is minimal.

$$f(\omega) = \max_{\Delta t} \frac{(T_1(t,w) - T_2(t,\omega))}{dx} \tag{4}$$

Applying *extremum-seeking* control of Equation 3 shows that an optimal thermal balancing occurs when $\omega \to \infty$, or in other words, when activity migration is applied as frequent as possible. However, that is not feasible for practical thermal management, since too frequently applied migrations will negatively impact system performance. As such, when only optimizing for thermal balancing, we need to additionally specify an upper bound for ω. Furthermore, a system optimized only for thermal balancing does not necessarily have the best overall thermal characteristics (i.e. it may still exhibit a high peak temperature whose negative effects on chip reliability and lifetime may outweigh the gain in reliability through minimizing thermal variations). This is a result of the latency of heating and cooling, i.e. there is not sufficient time for cooling if the component is only idle momentarily resulting in a system where the components being controlled are constantly heating up.

It is thus necessary to consider the additional thermal properties, i.e. the average and peak temperatures. We can express the average temperature as:

$$f(\omega) = \frac{1}{2}\left(\frac{\sum_t T_1(t,\omega)}{\Delta t} + \frac{\sum_t T_2(t,\omega)}{\Delta t}\right) \tag{5}$$

Likewise, to optimize peak temperatures we consider

$$f(\omega) = \max_{\Delta t}(T_1(t,\omega), T_2(t,\omega)) \tag{6}$$

In practice, all three of these factors must be considered, and hence, the output function is a weighted combination of Equations 4, 5, and 6 with respective weights. However, in our experiments we found a correlation between average and peak temperatures (see Figure 5), making it sufficient to only optimize for peak temperatures and thermal balancing. This is typically the case when the components occupy a small chip area footprint, due to thermal conductance within the components. If both the area of the components is large and activity is focused on a small part of the components (e.g as may be the case if a component is an entire core, and not only a part of its microarchitecture), however, the average and peak temperatures may no longer be correlated to each other and the average temperature must be taken into consideration and included in the output function. Determining the weight values (α) is device-specific, and as such they must be obtained using an architecture-dependent device exploration. In Figure 3, the weight is given by α which determines the ratio of optimization between the peak temperature and thermal balancing.

Our approach can be implemented using either online or offline optimization depending on how much *a priori* knowledge is available, i.e. if the activity during runtime is known, the optimal migration strategy can be obtained by running our approach offline and applying the devised strategy for runtime activity migration. If this is not possible, e.g. due to non-deterministic activity e.g. resulting from different application inputs or user behavior, the optimization of the migration strategy can be accomplished online using our controller. While the online approach is more flexible, it also requires additional hardware resources to implement our controller.

It is important to differentiate between heterogeneous and homogeneous components. Homogeneous components means that they use the same amount of switching activity (and occupy the same area footprint) for computation and thereby produce equal amounts of heat. In this case migration is applied between the components with each component being active for the same time duration. In the general case, the components are heterogeneous and consume different amounts of power and/or occupy a different amount of area, and, therefore, generate different amounts of heat. In order to optimize the thermal behavior, these heterogeneous components must therefore be active for different amounts of time. The activity can thus be modeled using an extension of Equation 1, using two components as an example:

$$\Theta_1(\omega,\beta,t) := \Theta(\sin\omega t + \beta) \text{ and}$$
$$\Theta_2(\omega,\beta,t) := \Theta(-\sin\omega t - \beta)$$

where $\beta \in [0,1)$. As a result, Θ_1 and Θ_2 are alternating active for the intervals $\frac{\omega}{4\pi}(1+\beta)$ and $\frac{\omega}{4\pi}(1-\beta)$, respectively, and $\beta = 0$ corresponds to the homogeneous case. Without loss of generality, Θ_2 represents the component with increased computation time, i.e. the component that generates less heat. The values for β are optimized offline with the *extremum-seeking* controller using a fixed ω.

4.1 Extension to higher-dimensional problem space

To cover a larger range of architectures, i.e. architectures with more than two components and one activity, the above example must be extended to the multi-dimensional case with n components and m activities. This can be accomplished by using a chain of *extremum-seeking* controllers [7], each responsible for deciding when to migrate activity from one component. An example of such a controller chain is shown in Figure 4 and described in Algorithm 1. The inputs of a component are averaged between *extremum-seeking* controllers it shares with adjacent components, i.e. components located physically next to each other. Thus, in assuming a two-dimensional mesh architecture, each component will have between two and four inputs depending on its location (e.g. if it is somewhere in the middle or at the border).

Here, the migration rate is no longer fixed, but instead each activity $\tau_j, j \in \{1,..,m\}$ has its distinct migration rate ω_{τ_j}. Thus each of the n cores has as its inputs ω of the activity currently running on the component. For instance, Component$_i$, $i \in \{1,..,n\}$ will have the inputs ω_{i,τ_j} if activity τ_j is running. Each component can have up to m inputs

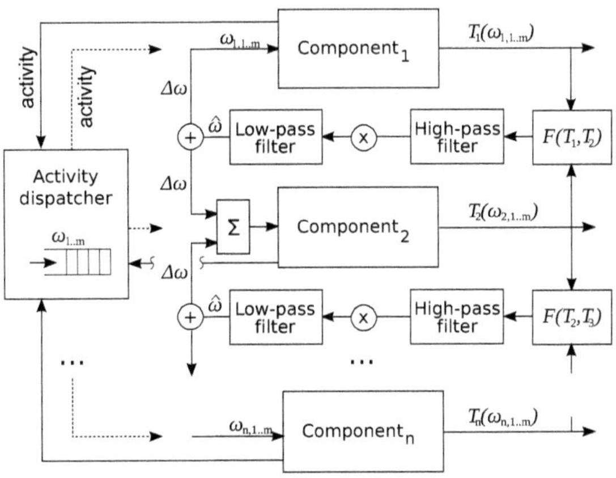

Figure 4: Chaining of multiple *extremum-seeking* controllers

as shown in Figure 4. For each activity migration the activity is migrated from the component it is running on and placed to the queue of the *activity dispatcher* which chooses a new component to migrate the activity to.

There are two parameters which influence the effectiveness of the chained controller.

- The first one is the policy of the activity dispatcher. Where it decides to migrate activity to is dependent on the weight α (see Figure 3). For instance, when optimizing for spatial thermal variation it is most efficient to migrate an activity to the coolest core in the region (where the variation is maximal).
- Second, in the general case where there is more than one activity scheduled on a component, it must be decided how $\sum(\Delta\omega)$ influences the individual ω_τ. For homogeneous activity workloads, we simply reduce the maximum ω_τ. However for heterogeneous workloads, the load also needs to be considered. Thus, assuming that a normalized load parameter L_τ is known (i.e. through performance counters), the ω_τ is reduced where $L_\tau \cdot \omega_\tau$ is maximal.

Due to the properties of *extremum-seeking control*, we are able to manage on-chip temperatures, minimizing both peak temperatures and thermal variations. In the following we analyze the effectiveness of the application of COOL for thermal optimization in different systems. First we analyze the effect of activity migration in FPGA-based systems which enable us to obtain detailed thermal measurements. Subsequently, as one possible application example, we apply our approach to the register file of a superscalar microarchitecture in an ASIC and analyze its effectiveness using thermal simulation.

5. THERMAL ANALYSIS

To analyze our approach using real measurements, we employ a thermal camera that monitors the infrared emissions from a die to illustrate the effectiveness of COOL. Using Xilinx Virtex-II and Virtex-5 FPGAs we are able to examine the effects of various values for ω which determine how often the activity is migrated between two switching regions. The on-chip temperature distributions are observed using a DIAS Pyroview 380L compact infrared thermal camera [25]. The utilized infrared camera is able to measure the emitted temperatures from the FPGA die with an accuracy of ($\pm 1°C$).

Algorithm 1: COOLChain: Chained *extremum-seeking* control at time t

Input: Set of m Activities: $\{\tau_j\}$
Input: set of n components: $\{C_i\}$
Input: Initial allocation at time t: $A_{ij}(t) = \{\tau_j \rightarrow C_i\}$
Input: Corresponding migration rates $\omega_{\tau_j}(t)$
Output: Modified migration rates $\omega_{\tau_j}(t+1)$
Output: Modified allocation: $A_{ij}(t+1)$

begin
  foreach *Controller* $\mathfrak{C}_k$ **do**
    foreach *Input* $C_{i'} \subset \{C_i\}$ **do**
      Get sensor data $T_{i'}(t)$
      foreach *Activity* $\tau_{j'} \in A(i'j)$ **do**
        // Using Equation 3:
        $tildew\omega_{\tau_{j'}} = \mathfrak{C}_k(\omega_{\tau_{j'}}, T_{i'}(t))$
      end
    end
    $l = \text{MAX}_i\ \tilde{\omega}_{\tau_{j'}}$
    $\Delta\omega = \text{VECTOR}_m\ (0..0)$
    $\Delta\omega_l = \tilde{\omega}_{\tau_{j'}}$
  end
  foreach C_i **do**
    foreach *Input from* $\mathfrak{C}_k$ **do**
      $\{\omega_{\tau_j}(t+1)\} = \{\omega_{\tau_j}(t)\} + \Delta\omega$
    end
  end
  foreach *Activity* $\tau \in \{\tau_j\}$ **do**
    if $\omega_\tau = n \cdot t, n \in \mathbb{N}$ **then**
      $A_{ij}(t+1) = A_{ij}(t) \setminus \{\tau\}$
      dispatcherQueue.add(τ)
    end
  end
  foreach *activity* τ *in dispatcherQueue* **do**
    $C_{\tilde{i}} \leftarrow$ getNextComponent(policy)
    $A_{ij}(t+1) = A_{ij}(t) \cup \{\tau \rightarrow C_{\tilde{i}}\}$
  end
end

The implemented designs on the tested FPGAs emulate two computational components by means of switching activity using Toggle-Flip Flops (T-FFs) in rectangular regions on the FPGA, representing the worst-case of switching activity. Each of these components can be in one of two states: *active* or *idle*. A running component consumes 100% switching power (a normalized value regarding to the average switching activity of that component), and, in our implementation, an idle component is clock gated, consuming 0% switching power. Activity migration is performed by swapping the states of the two components, i.e. the active component is clock gated and becomes idle, whereas the clock of the idle component is enabled, making it active. While the FPGA chip is unable to produce temperatures as high as ASIC chips of current technology nodes may reach, the concepts presented can be used at any technology node and are equally applicable to higher temperatures, as is seen in Section 5.1.

Since the input to the controller is discrete, the continuous Laplace is replaced by the discrete z-transform. The *rate of control* is limited by the camera frequency (50Hz), meaning that changing the activity migration rate can at most be done whenever new temperatures are observed. However, it is also necessary to wait for multiple temperature measurements in order to accurately regard the current state and its relation to the extremum $f(a)$, and especially also in order to decrease the effect of measurement noise. Through our thermal measurements, we have determined that for our evaluation platform, a rate of control of once per second is sufficient since the heating of the chip to the peak temperature takes several minutes (between 5 and 10 minutes depending on ambient temperature). However, if a system requires more dynamic thermal management, and has faster on-chip thermal sensors (e.g. reading a thermal sensor takes 54ms in [2]), the rate of control can be in the range of milliseconds (e.g. once every 10-100ms).

The analysis of the effects on the chosen ω on the thermal characteristics of the chip are summarized in Figure 5. We can see that optimizing for peak temperature corresponds to an optimization for average temperature, i.e. here the ω resulting in the lowest peak temperature will also have the lowest average temperature. As such, we limit our optimization to peak temperatures and thermal balancing. Since the maximum thermal variation, which quantifies the degree of thermal balancing, ranges from 0 to $1.6°C$, we choose $\alpha = 1/30$ (see Figure 3) such that the impact of thermal balancing is comparable to that of peak temperatures. The obtained weight can then be used in the *extremum-seeking* controller to optimize activity migration at runtime.

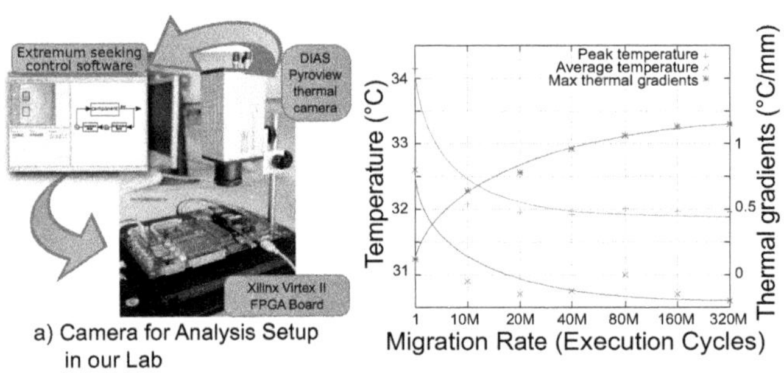

Figure 5: b) Summary of thermal characteristics for various activity migration rates ω

Figure 6 a) shows the application of the controller implementation on our evaluation platform. After the interval of one second, determined by the rate of control, the controller performs a change to the input ω. Initially, the thermal balancing component of the output function is the deciding factor, and thus the input is changed by increasing the frequency of activity migrations in order to achieve a better thermal balancing. At the second controller iteration at $t = 2$s, the peak temperature has risen above the peak temperature of the previous input ω, resulting in the next input decreasing the migration frequency. This process continues until the optimal ω is reached, in the example scenario decreasing the peak temperature by 6.3% ($°C$) compared to only optimizing for thermal balancing. It should be noted, however, that due to the monotonous increase in peak temperature during the initial heating phase, the *extremum-seeking* control drives the output function towards *local* maxima/minima. If this is no longer optimal, once the initial heating phase is complete, the controller will again change the input ω towards the global optimal state. The initial heating phase is shown here in order to illustrate the dynamics of the approach, since in the worst-case scenario (and in particular since the total activity is constant, i.e. not application dependent), ω will become constant. In Figure 6 b), the change in ω over multiple control intervals is shown in terms of activity migrations per second, which illustrates the convergence of the controller towards an optimal ω.

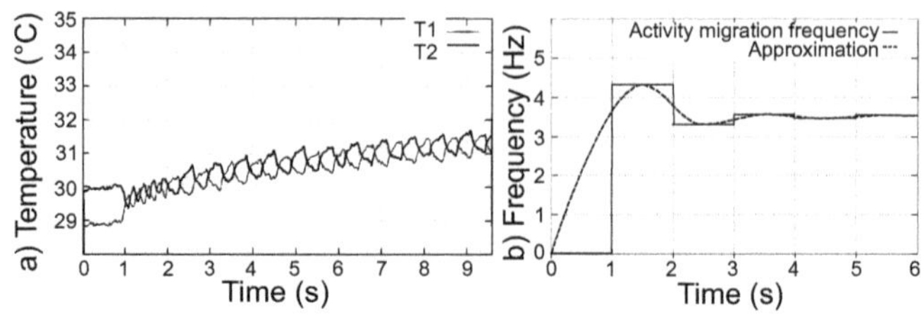

Figure 6: a) Typical runtime control example showing the temperatures T_1 and T_2 of the two components and b) Refinement of ω by *extremum-seeking* controller towards optimal value

For the evaluation with the Virtex-5, we examine the temperatures after several minutes of operation when the thermal state of the system has stabilized to the steady state temperature. At this point, the peak/average temperatures and max thermal variation no longer changes (except for noise temperature variations). Since the temperature has stabilized, optimizing for ω will result in a fixed value. For instance, when using the *extremum-seeking* controller to find optimal values with the 2000 T-FF design, the resulting ω is 96M cycles, with a peak temperature of $58.2°C$ and a thermal gradient of $0.98°C$, a reduction of $9°C$ and $5°C$, respectively. Table 1 shows a summary of the thermal characteristics of several evaluation runs.

To evaluate the multi-dimensional problem with multiple components we have implemented a four component version of the 2000 T-FF Virtex-5 design running two activities, τ_1 and τ_2 on a 2×2 grid. Each activity has its own corresponding ω value, ω_{τ_1} and ω_{τ_2}. The thermal exploration of this setup is shown in Figures 7 and 8. When regarding peak temperatures in Figure 7 we can see two effects which contribute to the peak temperature. The first is that a high migration rate results in higher temperatures, analogous to the two component system. The other is that a correlation between ω_{τ_1} and ω_{τ_2} can result in more mutual heating. Thermal gradients, however are still mostly dependent on ω, with larger values (and thus lower migration rates) resulting in higher gradients. The maximum peak temperature measured is $65.8°C$, and the maximum thermal gradient $1.5°C$. In our approach, the thermal optimization for four components consists of four controllers, each with two inputs and two outputs. When starting from the worst case ($\omega_{\tau_1} = \omega_{\tau_2} = 1$), the COOL first results in an increase in both ω values. The increase of both is slightly different resulting from the different controllers and shifting the peak temperature away from the center in Figure 7 (i.e. where there are higher peak temperatures resulting from correlated values of ω). The resulting values for ω obtained are $\omega_{\tau_1} = 76.8$M cycles, and $\omega_{\tau_2} = 25.6$M cycles with an overall peak temperature of $63.1°C$ and thermal gradient of $0.84°C$. Similar results were achieved over multiple runs, with one ω value being approximately three times the other. This corresponds to the situation where both activities start

FPGA	T-FFs	MHz	ω (cycles)	T_A ($°C$)	T_{max} ($°C$)	T_{avg} ($°C$)	ΔT ($°C$)	ω (cycles)	T_A ($°C$)	T_{max} ($°C$)	T_{avg} ($°C$)	ΔT ($°C$)
Virtex-II	1000	77.5	1	29	34.15	32.6	0.12	10M	29	32.08	30.9	0.64
			20M	29	31.96	30.7	0.78	40M	29	31.36	30.75	0.96
			80M	29	32.14	31.0	1.06	160M	29	32.01	30.7	1.13
Virtex-5	2000	400	8M	32	64.91	57.5	0.64	400M	32	57.9	55.5	2.74
			800M	32	57.64	55.22	3.06	2040M	32	58.4	55.54	3.1
			8K	29.4	57.62	56.43	0.4	400K	29.4	56.1	55.3	0.46
			800K	29.4	55.8	54.93	0.49	2040K	29.4	55.46	54.6	0.46
Virtex-5	4000	400	8K	29.5	68.7	67.28	0.51	400K	29.5	68.16	66.7	0.76
			800K	29.5	68.16	66.31	0.8	2040K	29.5	67.12	65.63	0.71

Table 1: Summary of Thermal Behavior (peak temperature and thermal variation)

diagonally from each other at time t. Then, at time $t + \omega_{\tau_2}$, τ_2 is migrated to the component adjacent to the one with τ_1, and then migrated diagonally again at time $t + 2\omega_{\tau_2}$. This process then repeats after both activities migrate at $t + \omega_{\tau_1}$.

In summary, the analysis presented in this section shows the runtime behavior of our approach measured using an infrared thermal camera. This provides us with a verification of the concepts presented in Section 3, showing that there is an optimal activity migration rate ω and that our controller is able to determine that. We achieve a reduction of peak temperature of $9°C$ and a reduction in thermal variation from $6°C$ to $1°C$ by optimizing ω in the case of two components in a Virtex-5 FPGA. When more components and activities are considered the reductions achieved are lower due to the overall increase in activity, however the controller is still able to reduce temperatures to the minimums seen in Figures 7 and 8.

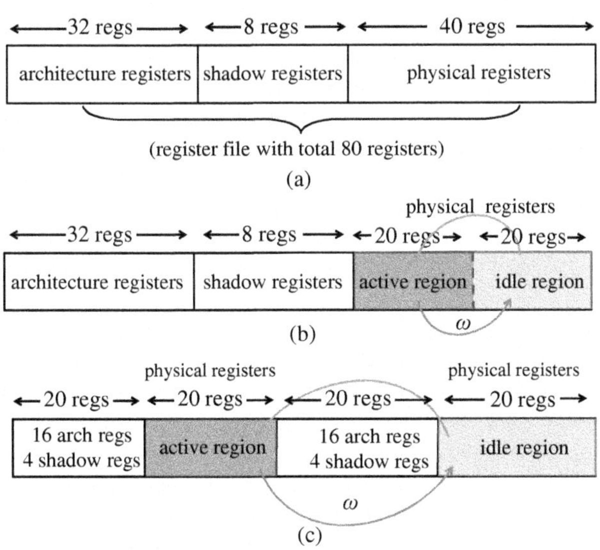

Figure 9: Register file arrangement (a) Base case, (b) activity migration (c) distributed activity migration

5.1 Activity Migration for Register Files

In order to further evaluate our COOL approach, we apply it on the register file component in a superscalar architecture. The key reason behind this decision is that the register file is often the hottest part in the modern microarchitectures as shown in the temperature measured from real processors [19]. This is mainly akin to the fact that the register file occupies a relatively small footprint and is frequently accessed during program execution. Indeed, the *extremum-seeking* control can be effectively used to optimize the thermal behavior of the register file by duplicating the register file unit and balancing the load by activity migration between the two units. However, such a solution would be costly as it comes with a 100% area overhead, which may not be tolerated in many systems (like embedded).

Our main goal in this scope is applying the *extremum-seeking* control to both of the peak temperature and thermal variation in the register file without increasing the register file footprint and with minimum impact on the performance.

Generally, superscalar architectures (such as Alpha 21464 processor [18]) have 32 architecture registers and a lager number of physical registers (e.g. 40 registers), in addition to 8 shadow registers reserved for the operating system. Our various experiments for different applications from the State-of-the-Art benchmark suites (SPEC 2006 and SPEC 2000 [24]) have unveiled the following findings: Due to the imbalanced register file accesses, it is often that major localized heating builds up in one part of the register file component as seen in the thermal map in Figure 10(a). It has been also observed that not all of the register file entries are used at a certain point of time and the average occupancy of the register file is relatively low across different benchmarks from SPEC 2006 and SPEC 2000 suite[2]. According to our own simulations, we found that about half of the physical registers in the register file are not occupied in around 90% of clock cycles. Indeed, this observation is consistent with related work [10, 20, 13]. The aforementioned observations motivate us to use an *extremum-seeking* controller to migrate, now within the register file itself, the activity of a set of registers that are responsible for the thermal hotspots instead of migrating the activity to a duplicated unit.

Practically, only half of the physical registers, instead of all of the physical registers, is seen from the renaming unit (`IntMap`) at a point of time. The resulting impact on the performance degradation is expected to be low and therefore acceptable i.e. around 1,4% as presented later, due to the observation of half of the physical registers are not occupied during the majority of the execution time. Then, the *extremum-seeking* controller is consulted to migrate the activity between the unused half (the cool region) and the occupied half (the hot region) of the physical registers. The optimal migration rate (ω) required for migrating between

[2]In spite of this observation, it is worthy to note that decreasing the register file size too much would have a severe impact on the performance, and thus an extensive exploration of the benchmarks is highly needed.

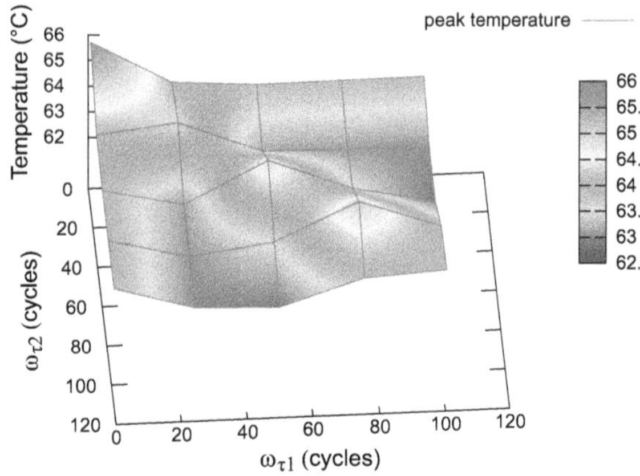

Figure 7: Peak temperatures with 4 cores dependent on ω measured by thermal camera

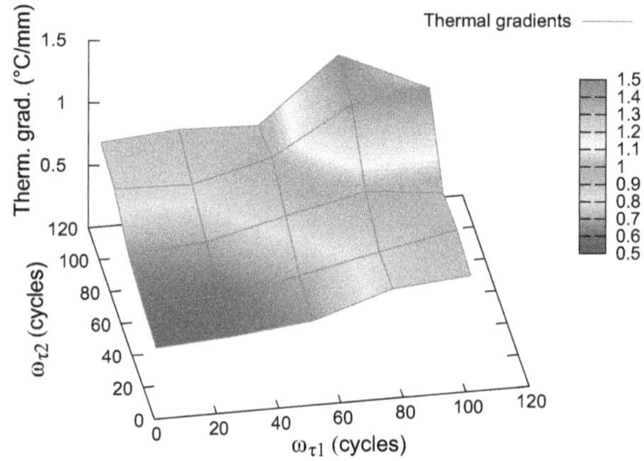

Figure 8: Thermal gradients with 4 cores dependent on ω measured by thermal camera

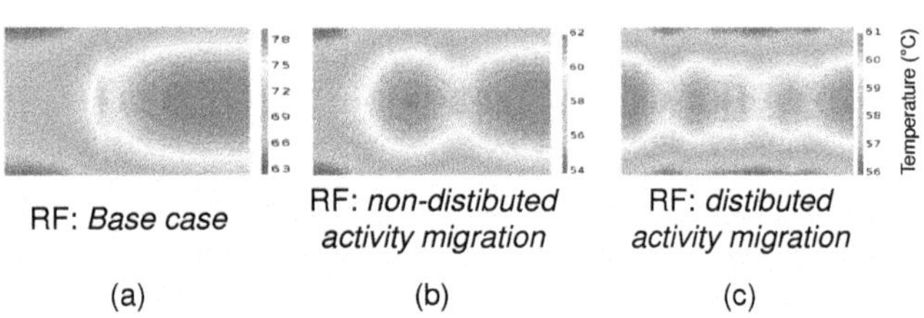

Figure 10: Simulated thermal maps of the register file (RF) with total 80 registers for the gzip benchmark (a) Base case, (b) and (c) after applying the *extremum-seeking* controller

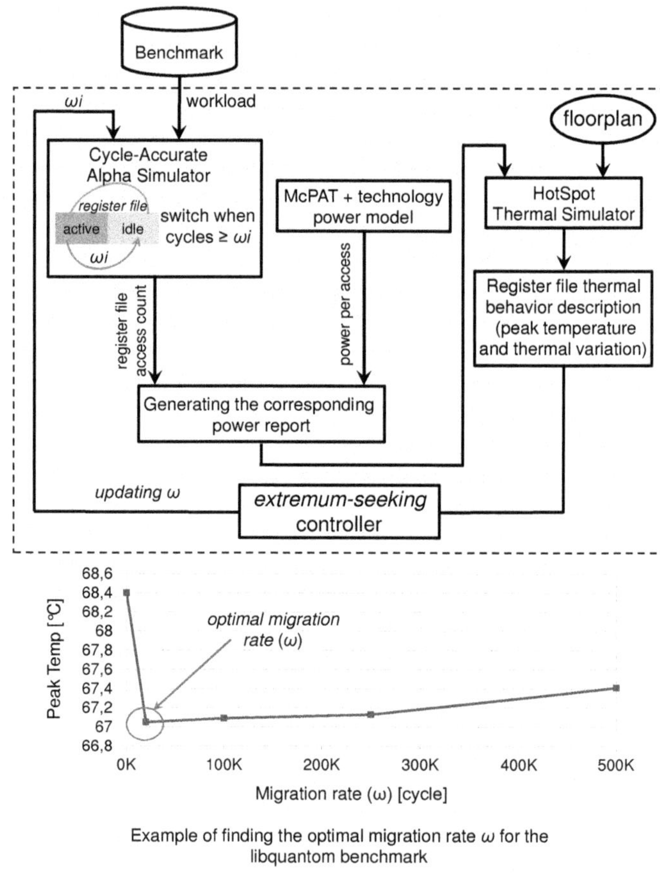

Figure 11: Finding the optimal migration rate (ω)

the active and idle region are computed offline. It is necessary to note that ω is not the same for each benchmark as shown in Figure 17 and it highly depends on the utilization of the register file determined by the application scenario.

Figure 9(a) shows the basic architecture of the register file in the Alpha processors and Figure 9(b) presents how the activity migration between the two regions can be accomplished, the corresponding thermal map of the register file can be seen in Figure 10(b). In order to achieve a better load balancing, we arrange the registers as shown in Figure 9(c). This leads to a better temperature distribution which in turn results in mitigating the thermal variation (as noticed in Figure 10(c)) and it also provides a better cooling down of the hot region.

Towards a fair comparison, we implemented two different approaches which address the same problem of the elevated temperature of the register file. The first approach *"Odd Even"* [12] suggests to evenly redistribute the accesses to the full range of the register file through modifying the renaming unit. The second approach *"Bank Switching"* [20] divides the register file into two equal-sized banks and uses only one bank at a time. Only when a bank is entirely used, the allocation is started for the second bank. These two techniques have been selected here because they have the similar goal (optimizing both peak temperature and thermal variation of the register file with minimum overheads). We derive our instruction set simulations from a widely used simulator for the Alpha architecture called Sim-alpha [6] with McPAT [22] (for the 65nm technology node power consumption models) and HotSpot [11] incorporated to model a high-performance microprocessor operating at 2GHz with eight-issue and 80 registers (based on the Alpha architecture). Our floorplan is for the standard Alpha layout. Figure 11 illustrates the state diagram of the interaction between the parts of our simulation platform when applying our COOL approach to the register file to compute the optimal migration rate of a benchmark (ω). For more accurate results, the thermal simulation was done twice to confirm; the steady-state temperature generated from the first phase was used as the initial temperature for the next phase. The peak temperature and

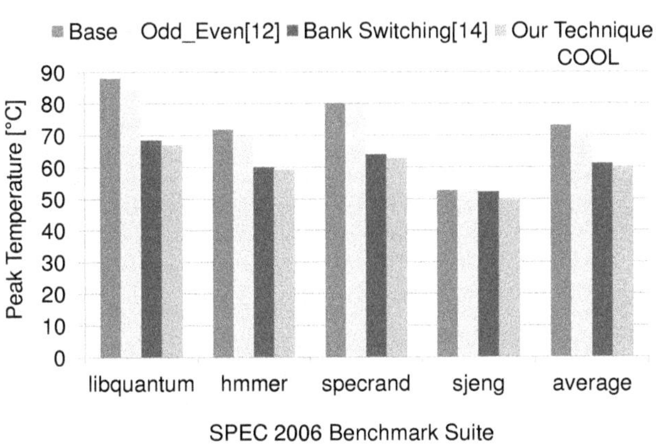

Figure 12: The peak temperature of the register file comparison to the State-of-the-Art for different benchmarks from SPEC 2006 suite

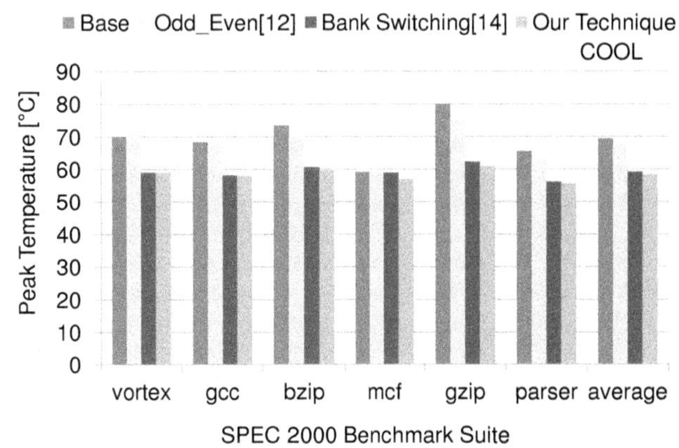

Figure 13: The peak temperature of the register file comparison to the State-of-the-Art for different benchmarks from SPEC 2000 suite

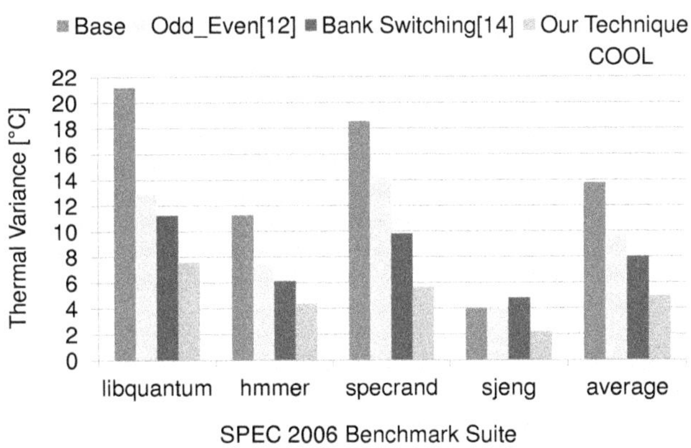

Figure 14: The thermal variation of the register file comparison to the State-of-the-Art for different benchmarks from SPEC 2006

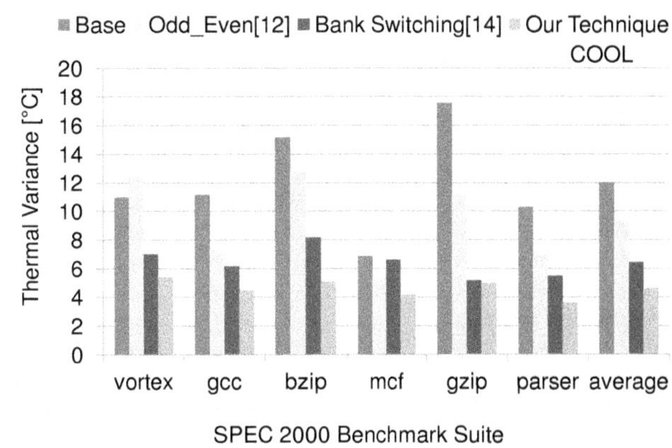

Figure 15: The thermal variation of the register file comparison to the State-of-the-Art for different benchmarks from SPEC 2000

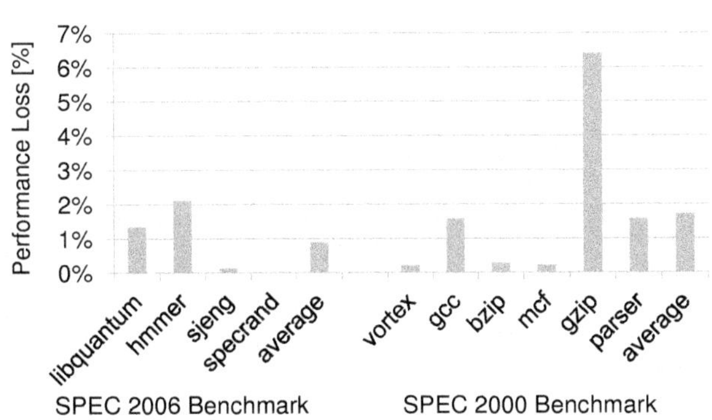

Figure 16: The performance degradation after implementing our approach COOL

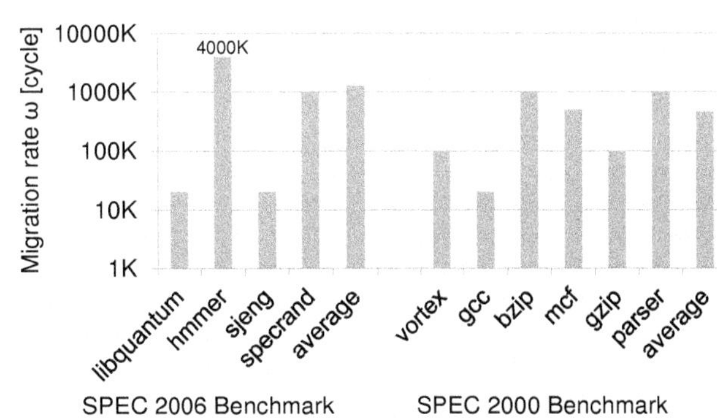

Figure 17: The optimal migration rate (ω) of different benchmarks

the thermal variation of the register file after implementing our technique compared to the *Base* case (the unmodified version of the register file) and the other competitors (*"Odd Even"* [12] and *"Bank Switching"* [20]) are presented in the Figures (12, 13) and Figures (14, 15), respectively.

As seen, the peak temperature reduction after implementing our approach reaches up to $21°C$ and, on average, around $13°C$ and $11°C$ for the SEC 2006 and SPEC 2000 benchmark suite, respectively. On the other hand, the activity migration rate derived from the *extremum-seeking* controller effectively minimizes the thermal variation. Compared to the *Base* version, the thermal variation has been reduced, on average, by 64% and 62% for the SEC 2006 and SPEC 2000 benchmark suite, respectively. It also achieves better results compared to State-of-the-Art techniques. For instance, the thermal variation inside the register file has been decreased, on average, by 38% and 49% in comparison to the *"Odd Even"* and *"Bank Switching"* approaches, respectively.

Finally, Figure 16 illustrates that the performance degradation incurred by our technique, as expected earlier, is slight (1,4% on average considering both SPEC 2000 and 2006 benchmark suites). Indeed, this is consistent with the observation that half of the physical registers are not busy during the majority of the execution time of an application.

It can be summarized that our proposed technique based on applying the *extremum-seeking* controller is capable to effectively reducing both the peak temperature and the thermal variation with negligible impact on the performance and without increasing the footprint of the register file.

Overhead: for controlling the thermal behavior of the register file, we have applied the *extremum-seeking* optimization offline as we are able to estimate the register file utilization by analyzing the application scenario. Thus, the only overhead that comes with our approach is the overhead from the controller implemented in the `IntMap` component of the Alpha processor. Towards investigating the overhead of the employed controller, we designed it in VHDL and synthesized it using the Synopsys Design Compiler with the 65nm TSMC technology library [23]. The required area is 826 μm^2. More precisely, the controller increases the area of `IntMap` by only 1%. From the power perspective, the controller leads to an increase of the dynamic power and leakage of `IntMap` by 4.6% and 0.02% respectively.

6. CONCLUSION

Load balancing through activity migration is a powerful means to optimize the thermal behavior of on-chip systems. COOL utilizes the concept of *extremum-seeking* control and applies it to dynamic thermal management for components of an on-chip microarchitecture. Thermal imaging analysis shows a reduction of peak temperatures by $9°C$ and a reduction of thermal spatial variation from $6°C$ to $1°C$ in an FPGA chip, and shows that the activity migration rates derived from the controller are optimal with respect to minimizing peak temperature and thermal spatial variation. When applying our approach to the register file of a superscalar ASIC microarchitecture, we are able to achieve a reduction of peak temperatures compared to a State-of-the-Art approach in a register file thermal management (with an average peak temperature reduction of $13°C$) while at the same time reducing thermal variation by 49% (which increases the lifetime of a system) at a performance loss of only 1.4%.

7. REFERENCES

[1] K. B. Ariyur and M. Krstic, "Real Time Optimization by Extremum Seeking Control," John Wiley & Sons, Inc., New York, NY, 2003.

[2] A. Bartolini, M. Sadri, J. Furst, A. Coskun, and L. Benini, "Quantifying the Impact of Frequency Scaling on the Energy Efficiency of the Single-Chip Cloud Computer," Design, Automation & Test in Europe (DATE), pp. 181–186, 2012.

[3] A. Chakraborty, K. Duraisami, A. Sathanur, P. Sithambaram, L. Benini, A. Macii, E. Macii, and M. Poncino, "Dynamic Thermal Clock Skew Compensation Using Tunable Delay Buffers," IEEE Transactions on Very Large Scale Integration (VLSI) Systems, vol.16, no.6, pp.639–649, June 2008.

[4] A. K. Coskun, T. S. Rosing, Y. Leblebici, G. De Micheli, "A simulation methodology for reliability analysis in multi-core SoCs," ACM Great Lakes Symposium on VLSI (GVLSI), pp 95–99, 2006.

[5] A. K. Coskun, T. S. Rosing, K.A. Whisnant, K.C. Gross, "Temperature-Aware MPSoC Scheduling for Reducing Hot Spots and Gradients," Proceedings of the 2008 Asia and South Pacific Design Automation Conference (ASPDAC), pp. 49–54, 2008.

[6] R. Desikan, D. Burger, S. Keckler, and T. Austin, "Sim-alpha: A Validated, Execution-Driven Alpha 21264 Simulator," Tech Report.

[7] C. Dixon and E. W. Frew, "Controlling the Mobility of Network Nodes using Decentralized Extremum Seeking," 45th IEEE Conference on Decision and Control, pp. 11–12, 2006.

[8] Y. Han, I. Koren and C. Mritz, "Temperature aware floorplanning," In the second workshop on Temperature-Aware Computer Systems (TACS), 2005.

[9] S. Heo, K. Barr, and K. Asanovic. Reducing power density through activity migration. ISLPED, pages 217–222, 2003.

[10] H. Homayoun et al., "RELOCATE: register file local access pattern redistribution mechanism for power and thermal management in out-of-order embedded processor," In Proceedings of the 5th international conference on High Performance Embedded Architectures and Compilers (HiPEAC'10), 2010.

[11] W. Huang, et al, "An Improved Block-Based Thermal Model in HotSpot-4.0 with Granularity Considerations,"

[12] J. Kim et al, "Register-relocation: a thermal-aware renaming method for reducing temperature of a register file," In SIGAPP Appl. Comput. Rev., vol. 11, nr. 1, pp 41–51, 2010.

[13] G. Memik, M.T. Kandemir, O. Ozturk, "Increasing register file immunity to transient errors," Design, Automation and Test in Europe Proceedings, pp. 586- 591, 2005.

[14] W. Liu Montesinos, and J. Torrellas, "Using register lifetime predictions to protect register files against soft errors," in Dependable Systems and Networks (DSN), pp. 286–296, 2007.

[15] V. Narayanan and Y. Xie, "Reliability concerns in embedded system designs," Computer , vol.39, no.1, pp. 118–120, Jan. 2006.

[16] H.V. Nguyen, et al., "Effect of thermal gradients on the electromigration life-time in power electronics," Reliability Physics Symposium Proceedings, 2004. 42nd Annual. 2004 IEEE International , vol., no., pp. 619- 620, April 2004

[17] M. D. Powell, M. Gomaa, and T. N. Vijaykumar, "Heat-and-Run: Leveraging SMT and CMP to Manage Power Density Through the System", ASPLOS, pp. 260–270, 2004.

[18] R.P. Preston et al., "Design of an 8-wide superscalar RISC microprocessor with simultaneous multithreading," Proceedings of the IEEE International Solid-State Circuits Confrence, vol.1, pp. 334–472, 2002.

[19] F.J. Mesa-Martinez, M. Brown, J. Nayfach-Battilana , and J. Renau, "Measuring power and temperature from real processors," In IEEE International Symposium on Parallel and Distributed Processing (IPDPS), pp. 1–5, 2008.

[20] K. Patel, W. Lee, and M. Pedram, "Active bank switching for temperature control of the register file in a microprocessor," In Proceedings of the 17th ACM Great Lakes symposium on VLSI (GLSVLSI), pp. 231–234, 2007.

[21] K. Skadron et al., "Temperature-aware microarchitecture," Proceedings of the 30th Annual International Symposium on Computer Architecture, pp. 2–13, 2003. In Proceedings of the Workshop on Duplicating, Deconstructing, and Debunking, in conjunction with the 34th International Symposium on Computer Architecture (ISCA), June 2007.

[22] http://www.hpl.hp.com/research/mcpat/

[23] http://www.tsmc.com/english/default.htm

[24] http://www.spec.org/

[25] http://www.dias-infrared.com/pdf/pyroview380lcompact_eng.pdf

Adaptive Online Heuristic Performance Estimation and Power Optimization for Reconfigurable Embedded Systems

Jingqing Mu, Roman Lysecky
Department of Electrical and Computer Engineering
University of Arizona, Tucson, AZ
{jqmu, rlysecky}@ece.arizona.edu

ABSTRACT

For dynamically adaptable systems, accurate online estimation methods can significantly improve the performance and power consumption of using reconfigurable hardware coprocessors implemented within an FPGA. Complex interactions between multiple application tasks, non-deterministic execution behavior in response to varying system inputs, and effects of operating system scheduling introduce significant challenges. We present an adaptive online performance and power estimation framework and heuristic power optimization method that monitors and adapts to dynamically changing application behavior. We further demonstrate the power savings that can be achieved using this approach for dynamic optimization of multitasked applications.

Categories and Subject Descriptors

C.3 **[Computer Systems Organization]** Special-Purpose and Application-Based Systems - *Real-time and Embedded Systems.*

General Terms

Design, Measurement, Performance.

Keywords

Online estimation, performance and power estimation, dynamically reconfigurable embedded systems.

1. INTRODUCTION

Field-programmable gate arrays (FPGAs) are an increasingly attractive design choice due to the programmability, flexibility, parallel computational capabilities, rapid prototyping, and debugging advantages that FPGAs offer over their ASIC counterparts. Dynamically reconfigurable FPGAs offer several benefits ranging from performance improvements to lower hardware costs as the same FPGA device can implement multiple hardware circuits simply by downloading the corresponding hardware configuration into the FPGA. Significant research has demonstrated the benefits of runtime reconfiguration of FPGAs and microprocessor/FPGA devices. Many FPGAs support partial reconfiguration that allows a single region of the FPGA to be reconfigured without affecting the hardware within the remaining regions, thereby allowing multiple hardware circuits to execute simultaneously.

For some reconfigurable systems, a static reconfiguration schedule can be determined at design time – often due to a need to leverage dynamic reconfiguration to serially implement several computations in hardware to compute the result. However, several dynamic reconfiguration approaches dynamically select which hardware kernels to implement within the FPGA based on information collected at runtime. Such systems offer the added benefit of being able to adapt the execution at runtime to either increase performance or reduce power consumption.

Dynamic reconfiguration is utilized within [7] to dynamically select among multiple hardware coprocessors for the same hardware kernel with varying area/speed tradeoffs. With the overall focus on improving performance or reducing power consumption, accurate online performance estimates are needed to guide the selection based on current application needs – as determined by the changing application phase behavior [8]. In [2], dynamic reconfiguration is employed to reconfigure custom instructions implemented within the datapath of a transmutable processor. Due to the non-deterministic behavior of many applications, runtime decisions are made to reconfigure the transmutable processor to best accommodate the custom instructions given the current needs. This approach can achieve average speedups of 3.6X or reduce energy consumption [18]. Alternatively, online self-reconfiguration can be utilized to rapidly reconfigure hardware circuits implemented within an FPGA in response to changes in the input parameters, thereby requiring fewer resources [5]. Dynamic reconfiguration is utilized in conjunction with runtime software to hardware translation by dynamically detecting a software binary's critical kernels and re-implementing those kernels within an on-chip FPGA [15]. Researchers have also extended the MOLEN programming paradigm to support runtime reconfiguration of kernels within multitasked applications through the integration of MOLEN execution/reconfiguration primitive's within the operating system [17].

These reconfiguration approaches focus on dynamically optimizing performance or power consumption using information only available at runtime. In addition, for many applications, partitioning and reconfiguration decisions can be significantly affected by the input data and deployed environment. Thus, for dynamically reconfigurable systems in which the selection of hardware coprocessors is determined at runtime, efficient online estimation methods are needed to evaluate and optimize the dynamic hardware coprocessor selection process on system performance or power consumption.

In this paper, we present an adaptive online performance and power estimation framework that dynamically monitors the accuracy of the performance and power estimation for multitasked applications to provide accurate runtime performance and power estimates. While building upon our previous efforts [16], the presented estimation framework achieves new advances by directly considering multitasked applications, utilizing control dataflow graph (CDFG) analysis to determine upper and lower bounds for hardware and software kernel speedups, and adjusting

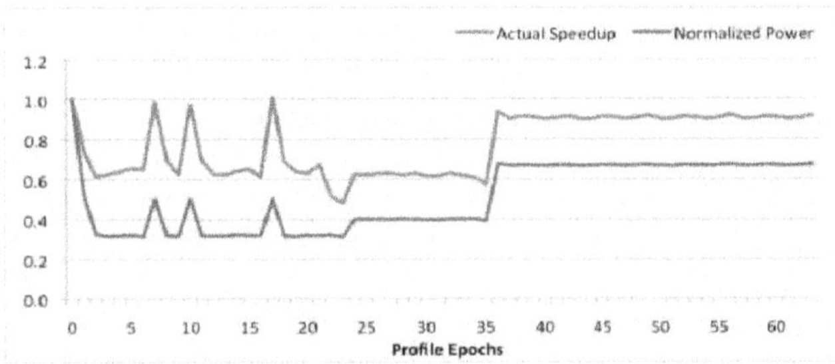

Figure 1: Speedup and normalized power consumption for *brev_g3fax_tblook* without kernel speedup coefficient adaptation.

kernel speedups at runtime by evaluating the accuracy of previous performance estimates. We further present an efficient, heuristic low-power optimization approach for quickly determining kernel selection and voltage/frequency configurations suitable for runtime optimization. Using the adaptive estimation framework and heuristic optimization, we demonstrate the overall system-level power savings that can be achieved for several multitasked benchmark applications.

This paper is organized as follows. In Section 2, we provide an overview of the targeted class of dynamically reconfigurable systems and highlight the required static and dynamic information needed for online performance and power estimation. In Section 3, we present our adaptive online performance and power estimation framework that is periodically utilized to accurately estimate the runtime system performance and power. In Section 4, we present a heuristic online power optimization method to efficiently determine the current hardware kernel selection and voltage/frequency configurations minimizing the runtime power consumed by the system without affecting the system performance. In Section 5, we present several experimental results demonstrating the system-level power reductions that can be achieved using the online estimation and optimization methods compared to the base software only implementation. Finally, in Section 6, we conclude and highlight several future research directions.

2. PREVIOUS WORK

Performance and power estimation methods have been extensively studied, most commonly within design space exploration and hardware/software codesign. However, many of these approaches are not suitable for online execution as they rely on information not available at runtime or utilize simulation to improve accuracy of critical elements. A power state machine approach presented in [3] estimates the power consumption by modeling power states and conditions for transitioning between these states. However, low-level HDL-based simulations are used to determine the overall system power. Fast, accurate system-level power estimation methods targeted at design space exploration have also been developed but rely on simulation methods [22]. To estimate the power consumption of hardware coprocessors, researchers proposed a method to estimate the upper-bound power consumption for different hardware coprocessor implementations without requiring each coprocessor to be synthesized for the target FPGA [1]. While this approach can reduce the time to explore different design alternatives, it is not suitable for runtime system level power estimation as it relies on low-level estimates of switching activity for the FPGA's configurable logic elements.

Several approaches for estimating system-level power consumption using performance counters within microprocessor, caches, memories, or buses have been proposed [4][9][12][11][20][21]. While effective for estimating power for software based systems, these approaches alone are not directly applicable or suitable for estimating power consumption of reconfigurable hardware coprocessors. As the performance and execution of hardware coprocessors is highly dependent on the data being processed, a more detailed profile of the execution behavior is required for the critical computational kernels. On the other hand, performance counters are well suited for estimating power consumption of the specific systems-level components – e.g. cache and memory accesses – and are utilized within the presented approach.

We previously developed a profile assisted online system-level performance and power estimation framework for estimating the speedup and power consumption of dynamically reconfigurable embedded systems consisting of a voltage and frequency scalable processor coupled with a dynamically reconfigurable FPGA focusing on both performance-driven and low-power optimization [15]. In performance-driven optimization, the target system dynamically reconfigured the FPGA to utilize the set of kernels achieving the greatest overall performance. In low-power optimization, the system dynamically reconfigured the FPGA to utilize the set of kernels and voltage and frequency settings achieving the lowest power consumption while providing performance equivalent to software only execution. The resulting performance or power consumption depends on the current dynamic application execution behavior. While the estimation method performed well for determining the correct runtime configuration decisions, the work focused on estimating performance and power consumption for individual application tasks. Although these individual tasks may execute within a multitasked operating system, the impact of kernel selection and voltage/frequency configuration was isolated to a single application task.

When considering all tasks within a multitasked application, predicting the overall performance and power consumption presents additional challenges. For low-power optimization, ensuring that the hardware/software application execution performs equally well compared to the software only implementation – i.e. a speedup greater than one – is required. Considering the complex interactions between multiple task executions, operating system scheduling, and dynamic application execution behavior changes, our previous estimation framework often results in application speedups below one when directly applied to multitasked applications.

Figure 1 presents the performance speedup and normalized power consumption for a multitasked application, *brev_g3fax_tblook*, consisting of three independent tasks *brev*, *g3fax* and *tblook* that correspond to embedded benchmarks from PowerStone [14] and EMMBC [6]. While significant power reductions are possible, the actual system performance drops below that of the software only performance with an average performance speedup of only 0.77X. As performance degradation is not feasible for the intended runtime low-power optimization framework, new online estimation methods are needed to provide an accurate performance estimate within the proposed approach.

3. ADAPTIVE PERFORMANCE AND POWER ESTIMATION

We consider a dynamically reconfigurable system consisting of a voltage-scalable processor and reconfigurable FPGA connected via the system bus. Although voltage-scalable processors often support many voltage and frequency scaling options, we limit the possible selections to a predefined set of voltages and frequencies.

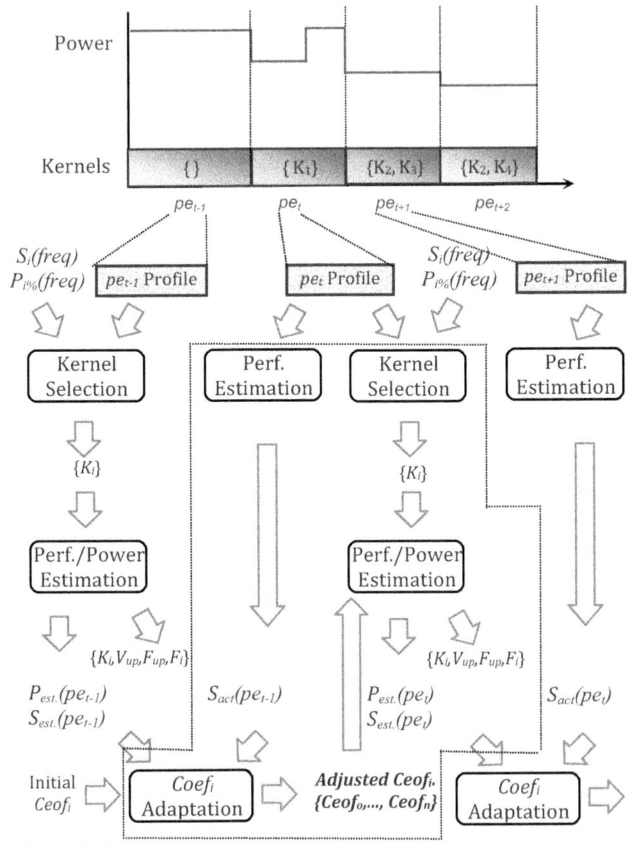

Figure 2: Overview of epoch based profiling, performance and power estimation, and kernel speedup coefficient adaptation.

The FPGA consists of multiple independent reconfigurable regions in which hardware coprocessors can be configured at runtime. The reconfigurable regions incorporate dynamic clock management to support frequency scaling of individual coprocessors implemented within the FPGA. The overall application consists of a complete multitasked software implementation along with hardware coprocessors for specific kernels within the application tasks.

To facilitate online estimation, both static and dynamic information is needed to provide an accurate estimate. As the software and hardware coprocessors are known a priori, design time analysis methods are utilized to characterize the software and hardware coprocessor elements. This statically determined information includes:

- *Software Loop/Kernel and Coprocessor Identification*: Set of software kernels, K_i, for which a hardware coprocessor is available.
- *Software Loop/Kernel Execution Estimate*: Estimate for the average number of instructions required per software kernel iteration. Analysis of the CDFG for each software kernel is utilized to determine the to determine the minimum execution path, $MinExecPath_i$, maximum execution path, $MaxExecPath_i$, and average execution path $AvgExecPath_i$
- *Hardware Coprocessor Performance*: Synthesis results for each hardware coprocessor determining the maximum operating frequency, $F_{i(max)}$, coprocessor execution cycles per iteration $K_{iCycle/Iter}$, and communication cycles per coprocessor execution $K_{iCommCycles}$.
- *Hardware Coprocessor Power*: Estimate or measurement of static power consumption for hardware coprocessors, $P_{i(static)}$ and dynamic power consumption at the maximum operating frequency $P_{i(dynamic)}(F_{i(max)})$.
- *Coprocessor Reconfiguration*: Estimate or measurement of the reconfiguration time $T_{i(reconf)}$, and reconfiguration power, $P_{i(reconf)}$, for individual reconfigurable regions within the FPGA.

The online estimation and optimization framework is executed at the end of each periodic profile epoch, pe_t, in which a non-intrusive dynamic application profiler [19] is employed to determine the current application execution behavior. The profile epoch defines the granularity during which the periodic profiling statistics are collected. Execution statistics available from performance counters within the processors are also utilized. The dynamically determined execution statistics utilized to estimate the system performance and power consumption include:

- *Dynamic Application Profile*: Set of most frequently executed kernels within the current profile epoch with execution statistics for each kernel including average iterations per execution, $AvgIter_i$, and number of executions $Execs_i$.
- *Processor/Cache Statistics*: Information available for processor performance counters including average cycles per instruction, CPI, instruction cache hits, $I\$_{Hits}$, and instruction cache misses, $I\$_{Misses}$, data cache hits $D\$_{Hits}$, data cache misses, $D\$_{Misses}$, data cache write backs, $D\$_{WriteBacks}$, and data cache replacements, $D\$_{Replacements}$.

Figure 2 presents an overview of the proposed online performance and power estimation framework in which at the end of each profile epoch, the previous performance estimate will be re-evaluated given the updated application profile in order to adapt the performance estimation framework. The basis of the performance estimation adaptation is a kernel speedup coefficient utilized to increase the accuracy of the performance estimation for individual application kernels. For each profile epoch, the performance speedup, $S_{est}(pe_t)$, and power consumption, $P_{est}(pe_t)$, estimates are utilized to determine the kernel selection and voltage/frequency configuration for the processor and individual kernels for the following epoch. For instance, at the end of the current profile epoch, pe_t, the adaptive estimation framework first uses the execution statistics and application profile to determine the actual performance speedup, $S_{act}(pe_t)$, for this profile epoch. The estimated and actual performance speedups are then used to adapt the kernel speedup coefficients for kernels utilized within the epoch. The adapted kernel speedup coefficients are utilized during the performance and power estimation for determining the kernel selection and voltage/frequency configuration for the following epoch, pe_{t+1}.

3.1 Performance Estimation

The base estimated speedup, $S_{base\_est.}(pe_t)$, of the hardware/software execution compared to a software execution given the set of kernels implemented with the FPGA is estimated for the following profile epoch pe_{t+1}, assuming reconfiguration of the FPGA is not required. Amdahl's law can be utilized to estimate the speedup for the hardware/software as:

$$S_{base\_est}(pe_{t+1}) = \frac{1}{1 - \sum \%Exec_i + \sum \frac{\%Execs_i}{S_i}},$$

Table 1: Average (AvgExecPath), minimum (MinExecPath), and maximum (MaxExecPath), execution paths determined using CDFG analysis for kernels within *brev_g3fax_tblook* application.

	brev	*g3fax (1)*	*g3fax (2)*	*tblook*
AvgExecPath	39	13	9.5	8
MinExecPath	5	2	5	8
MaxExecPath	72	15	15	8

where the $\%Exec_i$ is the percentage of total software execution time required for kernel K_i implemented within the FPGA and S_i is the kernel speedup obtained by executing kernel K_i in hardware. The percentage of execution time required for a software kernel K_i is initially estimated by analyzing the CDFG for the software kernel. Using the dynamic application profile, and average execution path, $AvgExecPath_i$, the percentage of execution time can be calculated for each software kernel K_i as:

$$\%Exec_i = \frac{AvgExecPath_i * Execs_i * AvgIters_i}{\sum AvgExecPath_i * Execs_i * AvgIters_i}.$$

As earlier demonstrated in Figure 1, this base estimate alone is insufficient in accurately estimating the system performance and power consumption for multitasked applications. For individual application kernels, the application data inputs can affect the execution behavior of individual kernels, which is not accurately reflected by using only the average execution path estimate. Furthermore, while the dynamic application profile has been demonstrated to be 98.5% accurate on average, the profile statistics for individual kernels can exhibit worst case errors of as much as 25% [19]. The resulting performance speedup estimation using this base estimation may lead to overestimation or underestimation of the actual system performance.

For low-power optimization, the overestimation or underestimation can lead to both undesired system behavior and sub-optimal optimization. On the one hand, if the speedup is overestimated, the low-power optimization may reduce the voltage/frequency configuration too low, resulting in an actual speedup below the original software only execution. On the other hand, if the speedup is underestimated, the low-power optimization may miss an opportunity to further reduce power.

To overcome the limitation of the base estimation, for each application kernel, K_i, a kernel speedup coefficient, $Coef_i$, is utilized to dynamically adapt the performance and power estimates. The estimated speedup in the absence of reconfiguration, $S_{no\_reconf}(pe_{t+1})$, for the following epoch is:

$$S_{no\_reconf}(pe_{t+1}) = \frac{1}{1-\sum\%Exec_i + \sum\frac{\%Execs_i}{S_i} * Coef_i}.$$

Given the adaptive performance speedup, the speedup considering reconfiguration overhead can be determined given the set of kernels that need to be configured within the FPGA. If reconfiguration is needed given the selected kernels, the estimated speedup for the following epoch is:

$$S_{est}(pe_{t+1}) = 1 * \%ReconfTime + S_{no\_reconf}(pe_{t+1}) * (1-\%ReconfTime),$$

where %ReconfTime is the percentage of time required for reconfiguration during the following profile, calculated as:

$$\%ReconfTime = \frac{\sum T_{i(reconf)}}{|pe|}, \forall K_i \notin \Gamma_{current},$$

where $|pe|$ is the duration of a profile epoch and $\Gamma_{current}$ is the set of current kernels configured within the FPGA.

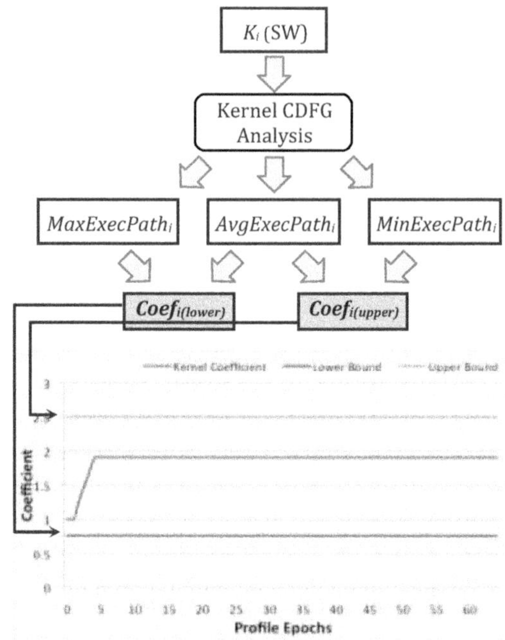

Figure 3: Kernel speedup coefficient lower bound and upper bound calculation method.

Figure 3 provides an overview of the kernel speedup coefficient adaptation. To avoid over adjusting the kernel speedup coefficient, an upper bound, $Coef_{i(upper)}$, and lower bound, $Coef_{i(lower)}$, are determined for each kernel. As all instructions within a kernel may not be executed, the CDFG for each kernel is analyzed to determine the minimum execution path, $MinExecPath_i$, and maximum execution path, $MaxExecPath_i$. For example, Table 1 highlights average, minimum, and maximum, execution paths determined using CDFG analysis for kernels within the *brev_g3fax_tblook* application. Given the average execution path utilized to determine the percentage of execution time of each kernel at runtime and the worst case profiling error of 25%, the kernel speedup coefficient lower and upper bounds can be calculated as:

$$Coef_{i(lower)} = \frac{AvgExecPath_i}{MaxExecPath_i} * 0.75,$$

$$Coef_{i(upper)} = \frac{AvgExecPath_i}{MinExecPath_i} * 1.25.$$

Figure 4 presents the kernel speedup coefficient adaptation algorithm that adjusts the coefficients based on the current kernel selection, $\Gamma_{current}$, speedup estimated before the current profile epoch, $S_{est}(pe_t)$, and the actual speedup estimated after the current profile epoch, $S_{act}(pe_t)$. To ensure that kernel speedup coefficients are not adapted too frequently, the coefficient adaptation algorithm only adapts the coefficients for kernels currently implemented within the FPGA that are considered adaptable, defined by the set A. Initially, all kernel coefficients, $Coef_i$, are adaptable. At the end of an epoch, if the actual speedup is greater than one, all coefficients for kernels within the FPGA will no longer be adaptable. Alternatively, if the actual speedup is less than one and if all coefficients for kernels within the FPGA are currently not adaptable, the coefficients will be added to the adaptable set. The set of adaptable coefficients, A, is utilized within the adaptation algorithm to determine how the coefficients should be adapted for each epoch.

$R = \{\, i : K_i \in \Gamma_{current} \,\}$, $A = \{\, i : \mathrm{Coef}_i \in \mathrm{Adaptable} \,\}$

```
if ( Sact(pet) < 1 ∧ ∃ i ∈ R : i ∈ A ) {
    if (R ⊆ A) {
        ∀ i ∈ R, Coefi = Coefi * Sest(pet) / Sact(pet)
    }
    else {
        CoefAdjustment = ( ∑%Execi : i ∈ R ) /
                         ( ∑%Execi : i ∈ R ∩ A )
        ∀ i ∈ R ∩ A {
            Coefi = Coefi * Sest(pet) / Sact(pet) * CoefAdjustment
        }
    }
    ∀ i ∈ R, adjust Coefi
            until Coefi ≥ Coefi(lower) ∧ Coefi ≤ Coefi(upper)
}
else if (Sact(pet) > 1 ) {
    ∀ i ∈ R {
        A = A − {i}
        if (Sact(pet) > 1.2 )  Coefi = Coefi * 1.1 / Sact(pet)
        adjust Coefi
        until Coefi ≥ Coefi(lower) ∧ Coefi ≤ Coefi(upper)
    }
}
else if (Sact(pet) < 1 ∧ ∀ i : i ∈ {R − A} ) {
    ∀ i ∈ R {
        A = A ∪ {i}
        Coefi = Coefi * Sest(pet) / Sact(pet)
        adjust Coefi
        until Coefi ≥ Coefi(lower) ∧ Coefi ≤ Coefi(upper)
    }
}
```

Figure 4. Kernel Speedup Coefficient Adaptation Algorithm

The coefficient adaptation algorithm adjusts the adaptable coefficient using one of three methods. First, if the actual speedup estimate is less than one and all kernel coefficients are adaptable, the coefficients are directly adjusted using the ratio between the estimated and actual performance. Otherwise, if the actual speedup estimate is less than one and not all kernel coefficients are adaptable, the coefficient adjustment is further adjusted by the ratio of the percentage of execution time for all adaptable kernels implemented in hardware, $\sum \%Exec_i : i$ □ $R \cap A$, to the total percentage of execution time for all kernels, $\sum \%Exec_i : i$ □ R.

Second, if the actual speedup estimate is greater than one, the coefficient adaptation algorithm will adjust the coefficients if the performance estimation underestimated an actual speedup greater than 1.2X. The adaptable coefficients are scaled to achieve an adjusted speedup estimate of 1.1X. In an effort to ensure the resulting system configuration achieves a speedup greater than one, the adaptation algorithm targets achieving a speedup of 1.1X. This effectively accounts for the worst case performance estimation error of approximately 10%, discussed in Section 5.1. In addition, as the performance speedup is greater than one, all coefficients for kernels currently implemented within the FPGA will be removed from the adaptable set. This process reduces the underestimation in order to achieve an actual speedup close to the software only performance during low-power optimization.

By adjusting for speedup underestimation and overestimation, the low-power optimization can more effectively reduce the power consumption while ensuring performance at least equivalent to the software only implementation is achieved. The kernel speedup coefficient adaptation attempts to achieve an accurate estimated speedup near 1.1X, which provides sufficient flexibility to reduce power consumption and ensure performance requirements are met even in the event of rapid changes in execution demands.

Finally, if the actual speedup is less than one but no coefficients are adaptable, all coefficients for kernels implemented within the FPGA are adjusted using the ratio between speedup estimate and the actual speedup. These adjusted coefficients will be added to the adaptable set of coefficients.

For all cases, whenever any coefficient is adjusted, the algorithm will check to ensure that the coefficients remain within the upper and lower coefficient bounds.

3.2 Power Estimation

Utilizing the adaptive performance estimate, processor and cache execution statistics, and statically determined power consumption estimate for individual system components, the overall system-level power consumption without considering the power consumption required during reconfiguration of the FPGA is calculated as:

$$P_{no\_reconf}(pe_{t+1}) = P_{uP} + P_{i\$} + P_{D\$} + P_{FPGA} + P_{Mem}.$$

The total power consumption including reconfiguration overhead of the FPGA is then calculated as:

$$P_{est}(pe_{t+1}) = P_{no\_reconf}(pe_{t+1}) + \sum \frac{P_{i(reconf)} * T_{i(reconf)}}{|pe|}, \forall K_i \notin \Gamma_{current},$$

where |pe| is the duration of a profile epoch and $\Gamma_{current}$ is the set of current kernels configured within the FPGA. We provide a brief summary of the power estimation models for the processor and FPGA components. We refer the interested reader to [16] for complete details of the system-level power model. We further note that the accuracy of the power estimation framework is directly related to the accuracy of the performance estimation method and all power models have been developed to estimate power consumption using the performance estimates.

The power consumption for the XScale processor can be calculated as:

$$P_{uP} = P_{uP(Active)} * uP_{\%Active} + P_{uP(Idle)} * uP_{\%Idle},$$

where $uP_{\%Active}$ is the percentage of time the microprocessor is active and $uP_{\%Idle}$ is the percentage of time the microprocessor is idle given the set of hardware kernels currently be utilized within the FPGA. $uP_{\%Active}$ is estimated as:

$$uP_{\%Active} = S_{est.}(pe_{t+1}) * \left(1 - \sum \%Exec_i + \sum \left(\frac{\%Exec_i}{S_i} * \frac{K_{iCommTime}}{K_{iCommTime} + K_{iTime}} \right) \right).$$

Given the power consumption data provided for each hardware kernel, the total power consumption of the FPGA can be estimated as:

$$P_{FPGA} = \sum P_{i(static)} + \sum \left(P_{i(dynamic)}(F_i) * K_{i\%Active} \right),$$

where $P_{i(static)}$ is the static power consumption for hardware kernel K_i, $P_{i(dynamic)}(F_i)$ is the dynamic power consumption for the hardware kernel excuting at frequency F_i, and $K_{i\%Active}$ is the percentage of time the kernel is actively executing. While the dynamic power consumption is known a priori, the provided power consumption corresponds to the maximum operating frequency for the hardware kernel. As the frequency of hardware

Table 2: Power reduction of partitioning kernels within *brev* and *tblook* at each XScale operating voltages and frequencies, based upon the statically determined $S_i(F_{\mu P})$, $P_i(\%Exec_i,F_{\mu P})$, and $F_{i(min)}(F_{\mu P})$ for each kernel and $\%Exec_i$ estimated from profiling results.

μP		***K₁ (21.8%)***			***K₆ (28.5%)***			
Volt. (V)	**Freq. (MHz)**	**Est. Kernel Speedup** $S_1(F_{\mu P})$	**Est. Power Reduction (per *%Exec_i*)** $P_1(28.5\%, F_{\mu P})$	**Est. Min Kernel Freq.** $F_{1(min)}(F_{\mu P})$	**Est. Kernel Speedup** $S_6(F_{\mu P})$	**Est. Power Reduction (per *%Exec_i*)** $P_6(21.8\%, F_{\mu P})$	**Est. Min Kernel Freq.** $F_{6(min)}(F_{\mu P})$	**Potential Power Reduction (mW)**
0.85	13	1.77	633.01	10	1.67	791.22	145	-
0.90	104	1.77	591.76	10	4.98	784.65	145	-
1.05	208	1.77	523.69	10	5.41	662.46	145	-
1.10	312	1.77	493.59	10	1.87	579.72	50	-
1.35	416	1.77	455.67	10	1.31	492.93	35	-
1.45	520	1.77	412.53	10	1.12	393.54	30	202.09
1.55	624	1.77	365.90	10	1.12	272.57	30	157.45

kernels can be scaled at runtime, the kernel's dynamic power consumption for the dynamically determined frequency F_i is:

$$P_{i(dynamic)}(F_i) = P_{i(dynamic)}(F_{i(\max)}) * \frac{F_i}{F_{i(\max)}}.$$

For low-power optimization, the resulting performance and power estimates are utilized to determine the optimal hardware kernel selection and voltage/frequency configuration for the processor and hardware coprocessors resulting in the lowest overall power consumption with an estimated speedup greater than one. Compared to our previous non-adaptive estimation framework, the adaptive online performance and power estimation framework better achieves this low-power optimization goal, as illustrated in Figure 5 for the *brev_g3fax_tblook* application presented earlier. Utilizing the adaptive speedup estimate, the overall actual application speedup is 1.04X, in contrast to the performance slowdown previously highlighted in Figure 1. As such, the online power optimization process can effectively and accurately minimize power consumption without negatively affecting performance.

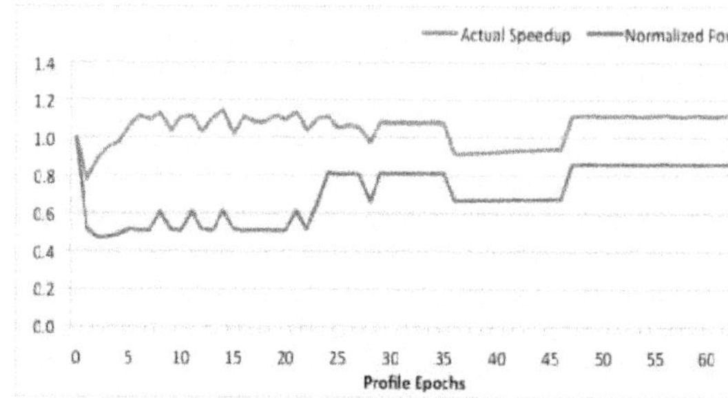

Figure 5: Speedup and normalized power consumption for *brev_g3fax_tblook* with kernel speedup coefficient adaptation.

4. ONLINE HEURISTIC OPTIMIZATION FRAMEWORK

As illustrated in Figure 2, at the end of each profile epoch, the adaptive speedup performance method is first utilized to adapt the performance estimation framework. The adapted performance estimation and current profile information is then utilized within the low-power optimization method to determine the kernel selection and voltage/frequencies for the processor and hardware coprocessors. The low-power optimization utilizes a two-step optimization method in which a heuristic dynamic kernel selection algorithm is first utilized to rapidly select which kernels will be used in the following epoch. Given the kernel selection, the voltage and frequency settings will then be determined for the processor and hardware coprocessors.

The heuristic dynamic kernel selection process utilizes profile information for the percentage of execution time consumed by each software kernel, $\%Exec_i$, and statically determined speedup and power estimates to determine which kernels to implement within the FPGA in order to achieve the largest power reduction while ensuring no performance degradation. Given the significant impact of the processor voltage/frequency setting on the system's performance and power consumption, for each kernel, we statically calculate the estimated kernel speedup as a function of the processor frequency, $S_i(F_{\mu P})$, which is normalized to software execution time running at the maximum frequency, $F_{\mu p(max)}$, and an estimated power reduction, $P_i(\%Exec_i, F_{\mu P})$, as a function of the percentage of execution time for that kernel and processor frequency. Additionally, we determine an estimated minimum hardware kernel frequency, $F_{i(min)}(F_{\mu P})$, that corresponds to the minimum frequency required to achieve a kernel speedup as close to one as possible. Importantly, the estimated power reduction for each kernel is determined using this estimated hardware kernel frequency. This information can be utilized to rapidly estimate which kernels will yield the lowest overall power consumption while still achieving an overall system speedup greater than one.

For example, Table 2 presents the estimated system power reduction considering two kernels, K_1 and K_6, where K_1 is a kernel within the task *brev* and K_6 is a kernel within the task *tblook*. We further consider each of the XScale's operating voltage and frequency settings. Given the dynamic execution profile, the percentage of execution time required for kernels K_1 and K_6 is 21.8% and 28.5%, respectively. The potential system speedup and power reduction can be determined for each processor frequency. For the example application, a potential system power reduction with an estimated speedup greater than one can only be achieved for two processor frequencies, specifically 520 MHz and 624 MHz. For a processor frequency of 520 MHz, the potential power reduction from using only kernel K_1 is 89.9 mW (412.53 * 21.8%) and the potential power reduction from using only kernel K_6 is 112.2 mW (393.54 * 28.5%), resulting is a total potential power reduction of 202.09 mW using both kernels.

Figure 6 presents the heuristic performance and power optimization algorithm. In order to estimate the speedup and power for the profile epoch pe_{t+1}, profile statistics collected at the epoch pe_t are utilized. For all possible subsets of candidate kernel selections, *CK* – i.e. all possible subsets, $P_{<|\Gamma|}(\square K_i)$, of kernels with size less than the number of reconfigurable regions, $|\Gamma|$, within the FPGA – the approach estimates the overall system speedup using a statically determined kernel speedup as a function of the processor frequency, $S_i(F_{\mu P})$. This estimated kernel speedup is represents the lowest feasible hardware frequency that will achieve a speedup given a specific microprocessor frequency. The

1. **determine** all candidate kernel, CK = $\mathcal{P}_{\leq|\Gamma|}(\forall K_i)$
2. $\forall$ KS $\in$ CK {
3. $\quad\forall F_{\mu P}$ {
4. $\quad\quad$ **if** ($S_{KS}(F_{\mu p}) > 1$) **calculate** $P_{est}(pe_{t+1}, KS, F_{\mu p})$
5. $\quad\quad$ **else** $P_{est}(pe_{t+1}, KS, F_{\mu p}) = \infty$
6. $\quad$ }
7. $\quad P_{KS(Min)} =$ **min**($P_{est}(pe_{t+1}, KS, F_{\mu p})\ \forall F_{\mu P}$)
8. }
9. $K' = KS \in CK : \forall j \in CK, P_{KS(Min)} \leq P_{j(Min)}$
10. $\forall K_i \in K'$ {
11. $\quad F_{i(min)} =$ **max** (5, $F_{i(min)}(F_{uP})$-10)
12. }
13. **determine** W,

    $W = \{(V_{\mu P}, F_{\mu P}, \{F_i\}) : (\forall i,\ F_i \geq F_{i(min)} \wedge F_i \leq F_{i(max)} \wedge S_{est}(p_{et+1}, V_{uP}, F_{uP}, \{Fi\}) > 1\}$
14. **find** $w \in W : \forall j \in W, P_{est}(pe_{t+1}, w) \leq P_{est}(pe_{t+1}, j)$
15. $(V'_{\mu P}, F'_{\mu P}, \{F'_i\}) = w$
16. $S_{est}(pe_{t+1}) = S_{est}(pe_{t+1}, V'_{uP}, F'_{uP}, \{F'_i\})$
17. $P_{est}(pe_{t+1}) = P_{est}(pe_{t+1}, V'_{uP}, F'_{uP}, \{F'_i\})$

Figure 6: Heuristic performance and power optimization algorithm.

estimated system speedup for a set of kernels, and microprocessor frequency, $F_{\mu P}$, is estimated as:

$$S_{est}(pe_{t+1}, KS, F_{uP}) = \frac{1}{1 - \sum_{i \in KS} \%Exec_i + \sum_{i \in KS} \frac{\%Exec_i}{S_i(F_{uP}) * \frac{F_{uP(\max)}}{F_{uP}}}} * \frac{F_{uP}}{F_{uP(\max)}}.$$

An estimated speedup of greater than one implies that implementing this set of kernels in hardware can achieve some performance improvement compared to the base software implementation executing at the maximum processor frequency. Therefore, this kernel selection is a candidate for low-power optimization, and the potential system power reduction that can be achieved by partitioning this kernel to hardware given the current processor frequency, $P_{est}(pe_{t+1}, KS, F_{\mu P})$, is calculated. At each microprocessor frequency setting, all possible kernel selections will be evaluated to determine the potential system-level power reduction. The resulting set of kernels, K', to be implemented in hardware for the following epoch pe_{t+1} is determined by finding the kernels that achieve the greatest overall potential system-level power reduction for any microprocessor frequency – i.e. the kernel selection with the lowest overall power consumption.

While this initial kernel selection process can quickly determine which kernels to implement in hardware, this estimation approach is not accurate enough to determine the voltage and frequency settings for the processor and hardware coprocessors. Instead, a heuristic online performance and power estimation is utilized to more precisely estimate the resulting system performance and power consumption to determine the voltage/frequency for the processor and frequency for the selected hardware kernels. In addition to rapidly determining the kernel selection, the statically determined kernel information is utilized to restrict the range of frequencies for each kernel that will be explored to determine the final system configuration. Whereas the full range of possible frequencies is from 5 MHz to the maximum kernel frequency, $F_{i(max)}$, the online optimization process will consider a reduced frequency range of 10 MHz below $F_{i(min)}(F_{\mu P})$ – with an absolute minimum of 5 MHz – to a maximum of $F_{i(max)}$. The online optimization process will explore this reduced design space and determine the voltage/frequency for microprocessor, V'_{uP}, F'_{uP}, and frequency for each hardware coprocessor, $\{F_i'\}$, that achieves the lowest power consumption without performance degradation.

The online heuristic estimation framework is only required in determining the voltage/frequency for the processor and hardware kernels for a single set of selected kernels. As such, the search space and execution time are dramatically decreased compared to an exhaustive search, by the exploration of all possible kernel selection and voltage/frequency settings in one step. As expected, this heuristic approach may lead to increased power consumption compared to the optimal system configuration. But, as we will demonstrate in the following section, the heuristic online optimization method achieves significant power reductions compared to the base software implementation.

5. EXPERIMENTAL RESULTS

We consider a dynamically reconfigurable system consisting of a voltage-scalable 624 MHz XScale PXA270 processor with a 32 KB instruction cache, a 32 KB data cache, a loosely coupled reconfigurable FPGA connected via the system bus, and an off-chip 32 MB memory. Although the XScale processor supports many voltage and frequency scaling options, we limit the possible selections to a predefined set of voltages and frequencies. The FPGA is modeled on a partially reconfigurable Xilinx Virtex-4 FPGA supporting four independently reconfigurable regions. As all hardware kernels require the entire reconfigurable region to be reconfigured, the reconfiguration time for each kernel is 2.6 ms and reconfiguration power for each kernel is 20 mW. A profile epoch of 10 ms was utilized for the current system implementation.

We evaluate the efficiency of our adaptive profile assisted online estimation framework and heuristic power optimization method for the several multitasked embedded benchmark applications. These multitasked applications consist of four or five independent tasks, where the individual tasks are applications from embedded benchmarks, including, *brev*, *g3fax*, *matmul*, *g721* from PowerStone [14], *fir*, *tblook*, and *ttsprk* from EEMBC [6], and *mepg2* from MediaBench [10]. The names for the multitasked applications utilize the names of the individual applications separated by an underscore. We manually created hardware coprocessors for all kernels that achieve any speedup over the software only execution. We synthesized each hardware kernel, which were restricted in size to a single reconfigurable region, to determine both the maximum operating frequency and power consumption using gate-level simulations of the FPGA.

5.1 Performance and Power Estimation Accuracy

To analyze the accuracy of the presented estimation framework and low-power optimization, we simulated our reconfigurable system for each application using the XEEMU simulator [10] coupled within cycle accurate simulation of the hardware kernels. Importantly, we note that XEEMU's performance and power estimates for the XScale processor have been shown to be highly accurate with average and worst case performance errors of 3.0% and 6.4%, respectively, and average and worst case energy errors of 1.6% and 4.5%, respectively.

Figure 7 presents the estimated and actual power consumption for a dynamically adaptable implementation considering low-power optimization using the adaptive online performance and power estimation framework for six multitasked applications, (a) *brev_matmul_fir_g721*, (b) *g3fax_matmul_ ttsprk_mpeg2*, (c) *brev_g3fax_matmul_tblook_mpeg2*, (d) *brev_matmul_tblook_*

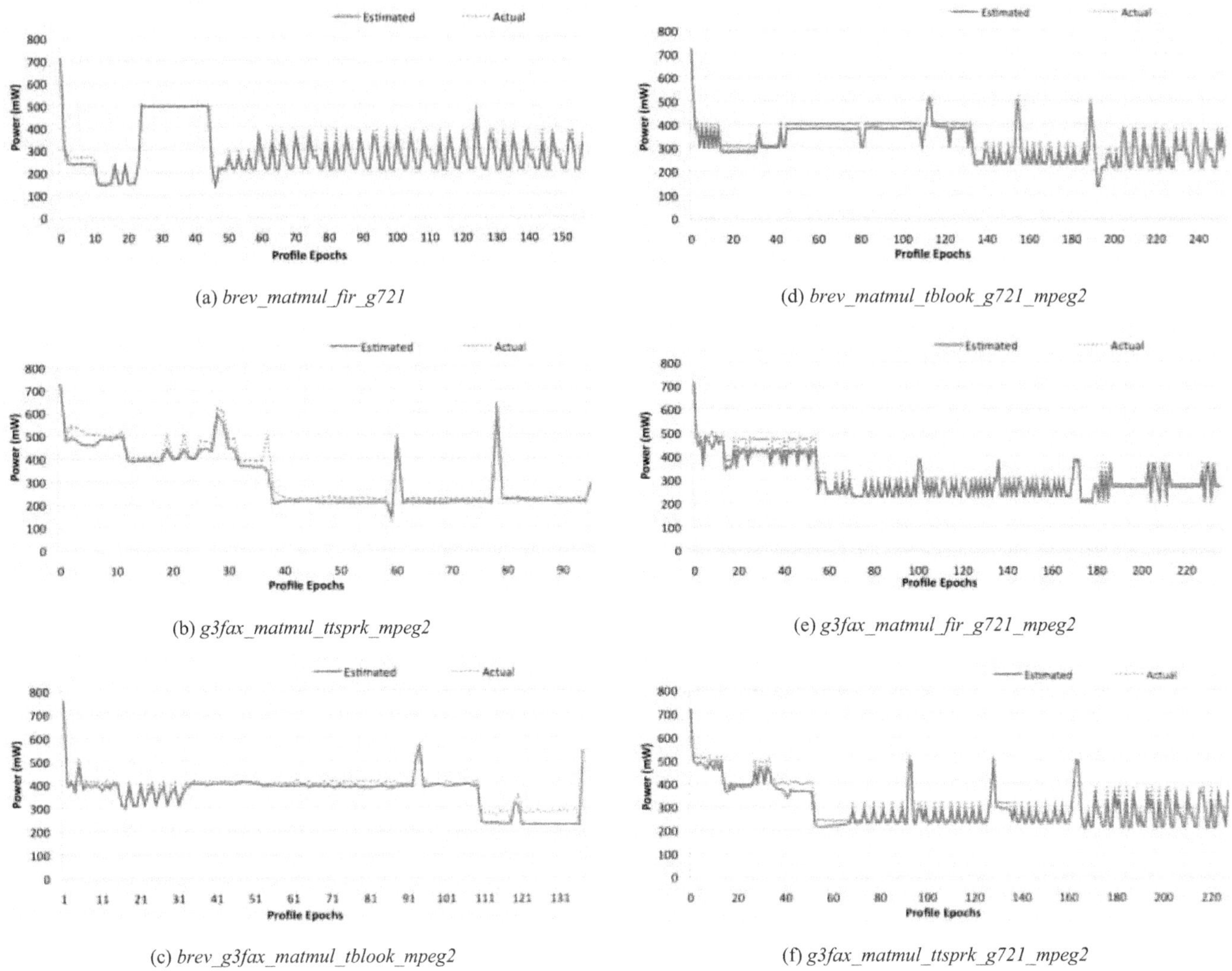

(a) *brev_matmul_fir_g721*

(d) *brev_matmul_tblook_g721_mpeg2*

(b) *g3fax_matmul_ttsprk_mpeg2*

(e) *g3fax_matmul_fir_g721_mpeg2*

(c) *brev_g3fax_matmul_tblook_mpeg2*

(f) *g3fax_matmul_ttsprk_g721_mpeg2*

Figure 7: Estimated and actual power consumption using the adaptive online performance and power estimation framework.

g721_mpeg2, (e) *g3fax_matmul_fir_g721_mpeg2*, and (f) *g3fax_matmul_ttsprk_g721_mpeg2*.

For these multitasked applications, hardware coprocessors are available for 8, 9, 9, 10, 12, and 12 kernels, respectively. The adaptive online power estimation achieves an average accuracy 94.6% with a worst case accuracy of 93.5%. Furthermore, the actual speedup for all applications considered is greater than one, with speedups of 1.00X, 1.04X, 1.02X, 1.01X, 1.06X, and 1.01X, respectively.

For several applications, the system encounters periods during which the power consumption oscillates between a higher and lower power consumption phase. This behavior is due to periods of time during which the interactions of the multiple tasks and operating system scheduling lead to oscillations in the application profile. While the current estimation frame does not use predictive techniques to detect this execution behavior, through development of new phase detection methods, the low-power optimization method could utilize such predictive methods. However, existing phase detection methods may not be adequate, as these behaviors are not just within a single application, but rather due to interactions between application tasks and operating system.

5.2 Heuristic Low-Power Optimization

We measured the total execution time for the both the exhaustive and heuristic optimization methods, including the time required for the adaptive performance and power estimation, using the XScale processor executing at 624 MHz within the reconfigurable embedded system. As discussed earlier, the exhaustive search procedure needed to determine the optimal systems configuration is infeasible, as it requires 0.17 seconds – or 17X the profile epoch duration – when considering a system with four reconfigurable regions and a multitasked application with nine hardware coprocessors. In contrast, the presented heuristic approach only requires 0.08 µs to determine the kernel selection and 341 µs to determine the final voltage/frequency settings – or approximately 3% of the profile epoch duration. Thus, the resulting adaptive estimation and heuristic optimization method is well suited for the applications and profile epoch considered.

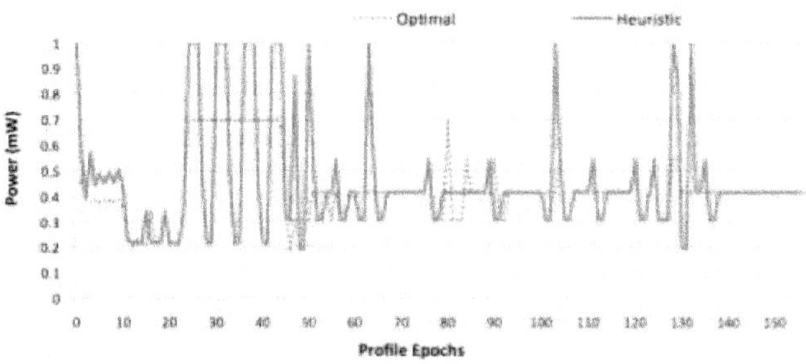

(a) *brev_matmul_fir_g721*

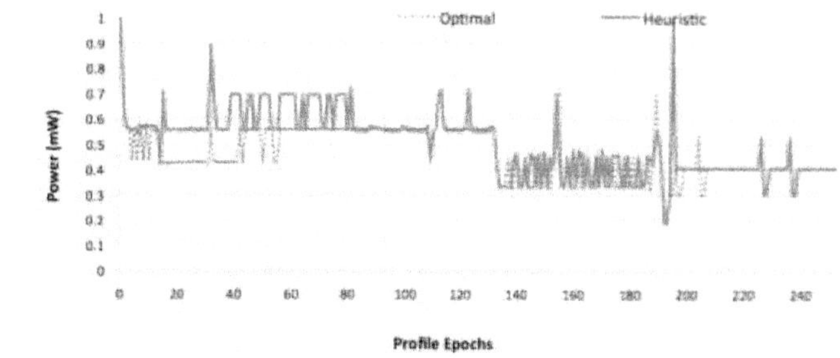

(d) *brev_matmul_tblook_g721_mpeg2*

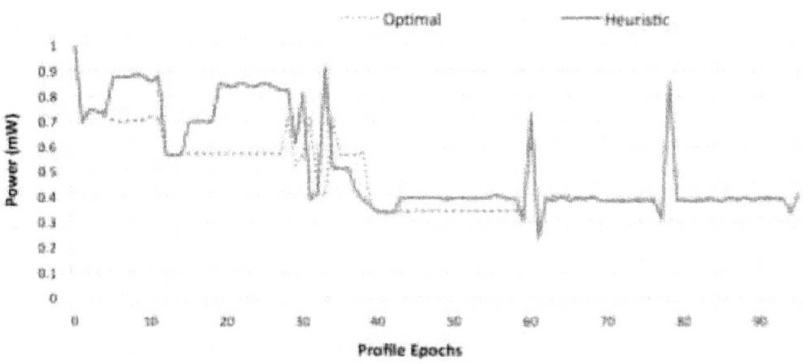

(b) *g3fax_matmul_ttsprk_mpeg2*

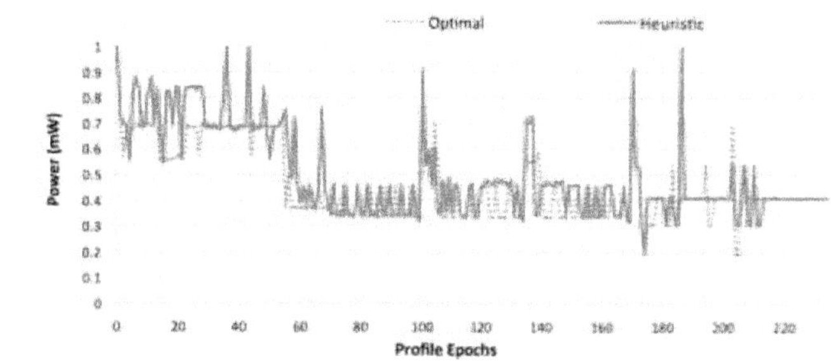

(e) *g3fax_matmul_fir_g721_mpeg2*

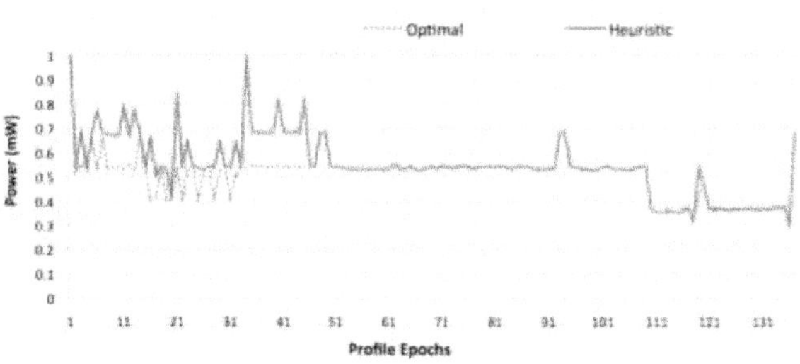

(c) *brev_g3fax_matmul_tblook_mpeg2*

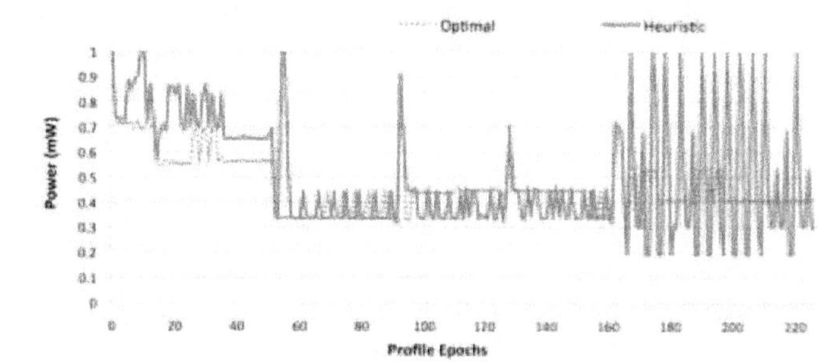

(f) *g3fax_matmul_ttsprk_g721_mpeg2*

Figure 8: Normalized actual power consumption for low-power dynamic optimization using Optimal and Heuristic online power optimization methods.

Figure 8 presents the normalized actual power consumption for low-power dynamic optimization using the presented dynamic estimation and heuristic (Heuristic) online performance and power estimation framework. For these multitasked applications, hardware coprocessors are available for 8, 9, 9, 10, 12, and 12 kernels, respectively. Overall, the adaptive estimation and heuristic optimization method achieves an actual speedup greater the original software implementation for all applications considered.

Additionally, Figure 8 compare the heuristic optimization method with an optimal (Optimal) dynamic configuration determined using an exhaustive exploration of all possible hardware coprocessors and voltage/frequency settings. As the runtime and power overhead of exhaustive evaluation is infeasible, the power consumption reported for the optimal configuration does not include these overheads. This comparison helps illustrate the effectiveness of the heuristic method, the resulting impact of executing the heuristic online, and identify potential opportunities for further improvements.

On average, the heuristic kernel selection approach achieves a 49% power reduction compared to the base software implementation. In the best case for the application *brev_matmul_fir_g721*, this heuristic approach achieves a 54% power reduction compared to the software implementation. Compared to the optimally determined configuration, the heuristic kernel selection approach requires on average 8% greater power consumption, with a worst case and best case power overhead of 11% for *g3fax_matmul_ttsprk_mpeg2* and 5% *brev_g3fax_matmul_tblook_mpeg2*, respectively.

During some profile epochs, the dynamic kernel selection method is unable to determine a set of coprocessors that will yield a speedup of greater than one. For these situations, the base software will be utilized leading to brief period in which the systems will reach its peak power consumption. Fortunately, the percentage of epochs with this peak power consumption is small compared to the total execution duration. In the best case for *brev_g3fax_matmul_tblook_mpeg2*, peak power consumption is only experienced during two profile epochs, accounting for only 1.5% of the total execution time. On average, the percentage of profile epochs that consume the peak power consumption is 4.3%.

6. CONCLUSIONS AND FUTURE WORK

Utilizing the presented online estimation and low-power optimization approach, average reductions in system power consumption on 49% can be achieved for multitasked software applications without performance degradation. The proposed approach is able to effectively leverage dynamic profile to accurately estimate performance and power consumption of dynamically reconfigurable implementations. Using these estimates, efficient heuristic methods are employed to determine a near optimal set of kernels and voltage/frequency assignments that minimize power consumption. Immediate future work includes investigating multitasked and operating system aware program phase detection method that be utilized to learn and predict the application behavior in future profile epochs. Such advances would help to enable better low-power optimization methods that can more effectively and rapidly adapt to changes in execution behavior.

7. ACKNOWLEDGEMENTS

This work was supported in part by the National Science Foundation under Grant CNS-0844565.

8. REFERENCES

[1] Abdelhalim, M. S. Habib. Fast Hardware Upper-Bound Power Estimation for a Novel FPGA-Based HW/SW Partitioning Scheme. IEEE Symposium on VLSI (ISVLSI), 2008.

[2] Bauer, L., M. Shafique, J. Henkel. Run-time Instruction Set Selection in a Transmutable Embedded Processor. In Proceedings of the Design Automation Conference (DAC), 56-61, 2008.

[3] Benini, L., R. Hodgson, P. Siegel. System-Level Power Estimation And Optimization. International Symposium on Low Power Electronics and Design (ISLPED), 1998.

[4] Bircher, W. L., K. John. Complete System Power Estimation: A Trickle-Down Approach Based on Performance Events. International Symposium on Performance Analysis of Systems & Software (ISPASS), 2007.

[5] Bruneel, K., F. Abouelella, D. Stroobandt. Automatically Mapping Applications to a Self-reconfiguring Platform. In Proceedings of the Design, Automation and Test in Europe (DATE), pp. 964-969, 2009.

[6] EEMBC. Embedded Microprocessor Benchmark Consortium. http://www.eembc.org, 2009.

[7] Fu, W., K. Compton. An Execution Environment for Reconfigurable Computing, In Proceedings of the International Symposium on Field-Programmable Gate Arrays (FPGA), pp. 149-158, 2005.

[8] Fu, W., K. Compton. Scheduling Intervals for Reconfigurable Computing. In Proceedings of the International Symposium on Field-Programmable Custom Computing Machines (FCCM), pp. 87-96, 2008.

[9] Gurun, A., C. Krintz. Run-Time Feedback-Based Energy Estimation Model for Embedded Devices. International Conference on Hardware/Software Codesign and System Synthesis (CODES+ISSS), 2006.

[10] Herczeg, Z., Ákos Kiss, D. Schmidt, N. Wehn, T. Gyimóthy. XEEMU: An Improved XScale XScale Power Simulator. Workshop on Power and Timing Modeling, Optimization and Simulation (PATMOS), 2007.

[11] Joseph, R., M. Martonosi. Run-Time Power Estimation in High-Performance Microprocessors. International Symposium on Low Power Electronic Devices (ISLPED), 2001.

[12] Kim, Y., S. Park, Y. Cho, N. Chang. System-level Online Power Estimation using an On-Chip Bus Performance Monitoring Unit. IEEE Transactions on Computer-Aided Design of Integrated Circuits and Systems, 30, 11, pp. 1586-1598, 2011.

[13] Lee, C., M. Potkonjak, W. Mangione-Smith. MediaBench: A Tool for Evaluating and Synthesizing Multimedia and Communications Systems. In Proceedings of the International Symposium on Microarchitecture (MICRO), pp. 330-335, 1997

[14] Malik, A., B. Moyer, D. Cermak. A Low Power Unified Cache Architecture Providing Power and Performance Flexibility. In Proceedings of the International Symposium on Low Power Electronics and Design (ISLPED), pp. 241-243, 2000.

[15] Mu, J., R. Lysecky. Autonomous Hardware/Software Partitioning and Voltage/Frequency Scaling for Low-Power Embedded Systems. ACM Transactions on Design Automation of Electronic Systems (TODAES), 15, 1, pp. 1-20, 2009.

[16] Mu, J., R. Lysecky. Profile Assisted Online System-Level Performance and Power Estimation for Dynamic Reconfigurable Embedded Systems. In Proceedings of the Asia and South Pacific Design Automation Conference (ASP-DAC), pp. 737-742, 2011.

[17] Sabeghi, M., K. Bertels. Interfacing Operating Systems and Polymorphic Computing Platforms based on the MOLEN Programming Paradigm. In Proceedings of the Workshop on the Interaction Between Operating System and Computer Architecture (WIOCSA), pp. 30-35, 2010.

[18] Shafique, M., L. Bauer, J. Henkel. REMiS: Run-time Energy Minimization Scheme in a Reconfigurable Processor with Dynamic Power-Gated Instruction Set. In Proceedings of the International Conference on Computer-Aided Design (ICCAD), pp. 55-62, 2009.

[19] Shankar, K., R. Lysecky. Non-Intrusive Dynamic Application Profiling for Multitasked Applications. In Proceedings of the Design Automation Conference (DAC), pp. 130-135, 2009.

[20] Singh, K., M. Bhadauria, S. A. McKee. Real Time Power Estimation and Thread Scheduling via Performance Counters. ACM SIGARCH Computer Architecture News, 37, 2, pp. 1-10, 2009.

[21] Xiao, Y., R. Bhaumik, Z. Yang, M. Siekkinen, P. Savolainen, A. Ylk-Jaaski. A System-Level Model for Runtime Power Estimation on Mobile Devices. Conference on Green Computing and Communications, 2011.

[22] Varma, A., B. Jacob, E. Debes, I. Kozintsev, P. Klein. Accurate and Fast System-Level Power Modeling: An XScale-Based Case Study. ACM Transactions on Embedded Computing Systems (TECS), Vol. 6, No. 3, Article 25. 2007.

BPR: Fast FPGA Placement and Routing Using Macroblocks

James Coole and Greg Stitt
Department of Electrical and Computer Engineering
University of Florida
Gainesville, FL 32611
{jcoole, gstitt}@ufl.edu

ABSTRACT

Numerous studies have shown the advantages of hardware and software co-design using FPGAs. However, increasingly lengthy place-and-route times represent a barrier to the broader adoption of this technology by significantly reducing designer productivity and turns-per-day, especially compared to more traditional design environments offered by competitive technologies such as GPUs. In this paper, we address this challenge by introducing a new approach to FPGA application design that significantly reduces compile times by exploiting the functional reuse common throughout modern FPGA applications, e.g. as shared code libraries and unchanged modules between compiles. To evaluate this approach, we introduce Block Place and Route (BPR), an FPGA CAD approach that modifies traditional placement and routing to operate at a higher-level of abstraction by pre-computing the internal placement and routing of reused cores. By extending traditional place-and-route algorithms such as simulated-annealing placement and negotiated-congestion routing to abstract away the detailed implementation of reused cores, we show that BPR is capable of orders-of-magnitude speedup in place-and-route over commercial tools with acceptably low overhead for a variety of applications.

Categories and Subject Descriptors

J.6 [**Computer-aided Engineering**]: Computer-aided Design

General Terms

performance, design

Keywords

macroblock, placement and routing, core, reuse, coarse-grain, FPGA, speedup

CODES+ISSS'12, October 7-12, 2012, Tampere, Finland.

1. INTRODUCTION

Existing work has shown the performance and power advantages of hardware/software co-design using FPGAs [1, 2]. However, the complexity of current FPGA design methodologies has been a barrier to mainstream adoption of this promising technology [3]. Chiefly, typical placement and routing (PAR) times of tens of minutes to hours and even days [4] present significant challenges in the development of FPGA systems by lengthening the design-debug cycle and decreasing the turns-per-day of designers, resulting in decreased design quality and increased time to market. FPGAs also increasingly compete for the attention of designers against technologies without such problems, such as DSPs and GPUs, which even if not ideal in terms of performance, have compile times of seconds to minutes. In fact, increasingly popular languages such as OpenCL rely on these fast compile times for runtime compilation, which prevents fully compliant OpenCL usage on FPGAs. Furthermore, ever larger designs making use of rapidly increasing device resources means that PAR times will only continue to grow. Because this trend does not hold for competing technologies such as CPUs and GPUs, without a new approach, today's FPGA productivity gap will only be exacerbated by tomorrow's devices.

In this paper, we present an approach for significantly reducing PAR times based on functional reuse. Many modern FPGA designs often incorporate custom datapaths for efficient computation as part of a larger system on chip (SoC) that includes large cores such as soft processors and interfaces to external board components. Because their design and verification is inherently time consuming, SoC cores are good opportunities for reuse and are often selected by the designer from shared or vendor libraries such as Altera's SOPC builder [5] or OpenCores [6], or are imported from previous designs. Custom datapaths, too, often make use of widely used cores such as floating-point arithmetic operators. Even in cases where truly unique cores must be developed for a single instance in an application, the core is ultimately reused in time, present in numerous compiles over the course of the system's development and testing. Our approach to placement and routing allows this existing reuse to enable large PAR speedups for most designs.

Towards this end, we've developed a new FPGA CAD approach, Block Place and Route (BPR), that modifies traditional FPGA placement and routing to operate at a higher level of abstraction. Unlike traditional FPGA CAD flows, shown in Figure 1(a), which decompose a circuit into numerous fine-grained lookup-tables (LUTs) during every compi-

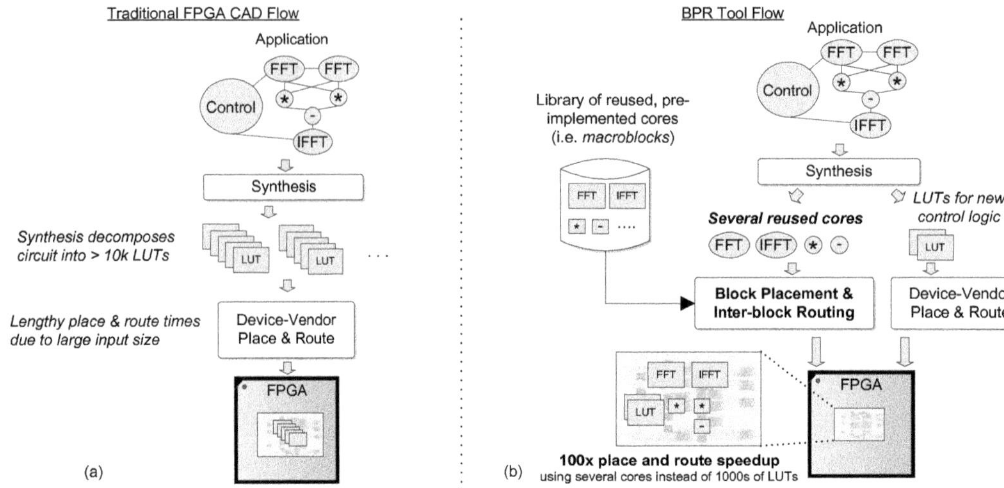

Figure 1: (a) Traditional CAD flows decompose circuits into numerous LUTs, resulting in lengthy place and route. (b) BPR enables fast placement and routing of reused cores with a database of pre-computed core implementations for different FPGA locations. For each reused core, BPR only has to place the black-box footprint (i.e. *macroblock*) of the core, and routes only the connections between macroblocks, providing 100x speedup compared to commercial tools.

lation, BPR pre-computes the internal placement and routing of reused cores for numerous positions in the FPGA. As shown in Figure 1(b), BPR enables reused cores to be compiled a single time into a core database and then reused in different locations on the FPGA in subsequent compiles, with only new logic requiring a full-detail PAR. We extend traditional PAR algorithms such as simulated-annealing placement [7] and negotiated-congestion routing [8] to place only the footprints of these pre-computed cores, called *macroblocks*, and route only the communication between cores. This abstraction achieves large speedups in PAR up to 190x over commercial tools, enabling average 1.1s compile times in line with competing technologies such as GPUs. By extending the best current approaches to traditional placement and routing, BPR achieves these speedups with acceptable overhead in terms of area (up to 49% utilization) and performance (average 34% decrease in clock frequency) relative to full-detail PAR performed by commercial tools for many applications. For situations where such overhead is prohibitive, BPR could speedup debugging iterations and be replaced with a full-detail PAR upon completion. Furthermore, BPR achieves these fast compilation times while using under 25MB for a large Altera EP3C120 Cyclone III, compared to up to 500MB for commercial tools. This small memory footprint potentially enables just-in-time (JIT) compilation of FPGA circuits for languages such as OpenCL.

2. PREVIOUS WORK

One previous method of accelerating PAR uses specialized devices that substitute fine-grain FPGA resources with coarse-grain functionality specific to various domains [9, 10]. This specialization can result in substantially faster synthesis and PAR through large reductions in problem size. Specialized devices can additionally achieve higher performance with reduced area through optimized hardware, but sacrifice the flexibility provided by the fine-grain reconfigurability of FPGAs. These specialized devices also require costly design and manufacture without the economies of scale of more general architectures.

Intermediate fabrics [11] and similar approaches [12, 13] achieve the PAR acceleration of coarse-grain physical architectures on commercial-off-the-shelf (COTS) FPGAs through virtualization, implementing the specialized architecture as an overlay network. Virtualization can retain some of the flexibility of the underlying FPGA by switching between any number of virtual fabric instances, each designed for different application domains. One limitation of intermediate fabrics is the area and clock (alternately, latency) overhead caused by implementing the architecture's routing resources on top of the underlying FPGA. Also, although fabric selection can be deferred to increase flexibility, the fabric instances used must still be designed offline and *a priori*, since the fabric itself must be compiled for the target device, typically requiring hours. This limitation leads inevitably to some additional overhead due to functional mismatches between a design and the available fabrics, and makes intermediate fabrics impractical for SoC-style design, where it isn't possible to incorporate every possible interface or large core *a priori*. BPR similarly uses abstraction to achieve PAR speedup, but has less overhead and does not have these flexibility limitations. BPR can also be complementary to intermediate fabrics, potentially improving the flexibility of intermediate fabrics by allowing fabric instances to be generated rapidly from precompiled functional units and fabric resources.

Other approaches have looked at modifying PAR algorithms to reduce runtimes at the expense of some quality. Lysecky introduced JIT FPGA compilation [14] and dynamic FPGA routing [15] to speedup place and route. However, that work required a specialized FPGA fabric and didn't directly support COTS FPGAs. Mulpuri and Hauck [16] explored routing quality and execution time tradeoffs, enabling up to 3x PAR speedups with 27% clock overhead. Although this speedup is significant for many uses, potential applications such as JIT compilation require larger speedups.

Wires on Demand [17] introduced a fast PAR approach for partial reconfiguration (PR) flows, enabling rapid synthesis of interconnect between pre-PARed modules in a PR system. BPR is conceptually similar, but doesn't focus on statically planned PR regions, and might be used in conjunction with Wires on Demand to quickly synthesize additional modules whose performance or area is not of chief concern.

Previous work has also looked at reducing placement and routing times, or both, through the use of precompiled logic, called *macroblocks* or *hard macros*, by analogy with ASIC floorplanning approaches. Tessier [18] proposed using internal placement data for precompiled cores to speedup placement, using a multiple-step custom floorplanning and placement algorithm, achieving a total 2.6x speedup over commercial PAR times. Our approach also attempts to reuse internal placement data, except that we use modified versions of traditional simulated annealing FPGA placement algorithms. We also attempt to reuse pre-computed internal routing, resulting in substantially larger PAR speedups.

Most recently, Lavin et al. introduced HMFlow [19], a tool that makes use of both placement and routing information for precompiled cores, achieving 10x speedups over commercial PAR, with a 2-4x decrease in clock rate for designs up to 50% of device area. The current version of HMFlow focuses on smaller cores than BPR, using case studies with an average of 16 slices per core. HMFlow also uses a custom greedy-based placement heuristic and a single-pass congestion-avoiding router. BPR focuses on larger cores, including those encountered in SoC design and floating-point computations. Using larger cores can permit greater speedups, but introduces complexities which we discuss in this paper, including leaking routes and core packing/performance tradeoffs. BPR also uses modified versions of traditional and (at least theoretically) higher quality placement and routing algorithms, contributing to comparatively lower overhead in many cases.

Finally, many commercial FPGA toolchains include some support for manual incremental compilation and manual floorplanning, with a goal of avoiding re-synthesizing or re-computing the placement and routing of unchanged modules in a large design [20]. BPR accelerates compilation similarly, but instead pre-computes the PAR for each module in the design at many (typically all) possible locations on the device. This data gives BPR the ability to adjust to even large changes in communication between core instances in a design by essentially re-floorplanning the design, automatically, during BPR's placement phase. Note that BPR's more dynamic approach is more similar to the flexible placement of hard macros in ASIC design flows. One difficulty in adapting this technique for use with FPGAs is accommodating variations in the logic and routing resources across modern FPGAs, which is discussed in more detail in Section 3.2.

3. BPR: MACROBLOCK-BASED PAR

This section describes the Block Placement and Routing (BPR) tool. Section 3.1 presents an overview of the tool flow. Section 3.2 explains how cores are integrated with BPR and converted into relocatable macroblocks. Section 3.3 discusses the BPR placement algorithm. Section 3.4 explains BPR routing.

The current version of BPR is compatible with Altera Cyclone III devices [21], so much of the discussion involves terminology specific to that vendor's devices. However, this practical limitation of our tool is due to the limited public information on commercial FPGA architectures. Note that BPR could be made to work for any island-style FPGA architecture with directional routing, given information about the device's layout and routing connectivity, and with the addition of any PAR data formatters appropriate for the platform. To our knowledge, BPR is the only non-proprietary router that can target Altera devices.

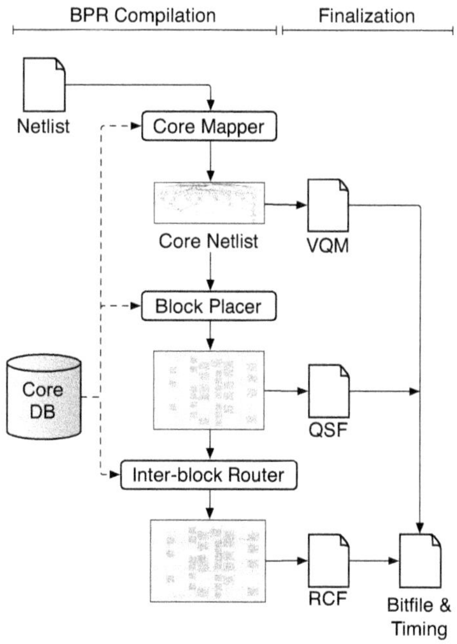

Figure 2: Overview of BPR tool flow. High-level BPR netlists are matched against relocatable core data, including intra-block PAR and port specifications. BPR then places each core as blocks and stitches blocks together through inter-block routing. The output files include an Altera Quartus-specific netlist file (VQM), placement (QSF) and routing (RCF) data for the full design. This design is validated and final bitfiles and timing are produced by Altera's Quartus.

3.1 Overview

From the highest level, BPR performs placement for a complete design using black-box footprints of pre-implemented, coarse-grain cores, referred to as *macroblocks*. Such *block placement* is possible because every macroblock is relocatable to potentially any location on the FPGA, due to a BPR pre-processing step that computes PAR for the internals of the corresponding core at each block location, which we refer to as *intra-block PAR*. After placing each macroblock, BPR performs *inter-block routing* by stitching together the internal placement and routing of each placed macroblock. Speedup in placement and routing is realized by using coarse-grain cores, which reduces the problem size of PAR by ignoring the details of intra-block PAR, and focusing instead on how the system of macroblocks fit together on the device. The BPR tool flow that implements this approach is illustrated in Figure 2 and summarized in the following subsections.

3.1.1 Core Database (DB) and Mapping

BPR must initially be provided with a library of precompiled cores to stitch together to compose larger designs. The contents and construction of this database will be discussed more in Section 3.2, but it contains three main pieces of data needed by BPR: the name and port specification of each core, the rectangular size and origin of all legal placements of each core on the device, and the specific device resources (logic and routing) used by the core for each legal placement.

BPR accepts a simple high-level netlist format that supports core instances and nets capable of connecting arbitrary subranges of instances' ports. BPR performs *core mapping* on these netlists, similar to functional mapping in traditional FPGA tools, by matching instance types to the core types available in the core database, producing a legal *core netlist*. The mapper also takes care of miscellaneous issues such as clock net promotion (BPR currently uses Quartus to route clock signals). Although there are interesting opportunities for optimization of these high-level netlists, such optimizations are outside the scope of this paper. Furthermore, as shown in Figure 1(b), BPR can support a mixture of reused cores (high-level BPR netlists) and non-reused HDL handled in a post-processing step of traditional PAR (e.g. allowing the specification of unique control logic). However, in this paper we solely evaluate reused cores. For Altera target devices, BPR exports a core netlist to Quartus as a two-level hierarchical netlist for the complete design as VQM files specifying the top-level entity and core implementations.

3.1.2 Block Placement and Inter-block Routing

Once a core netlist has been created by the mapper, BPR's block placer attempts to choose between all legal block placements for each core (specified in the core database) in a way that fits all core instances on the device while minimizing the distance and expected routing congestion between connected instances. Note that a legal block placement for one core type will typically overlap many legal placements for other core types (and even other placements of the same type). Our approach to block placement uses a modified version of the VPR [7] simulated-annealing placement algorithm that we have extended to handle these issues. We provide a more detailed discussion of the block placer in Section 3.3. For Altera targets, the placement of each resource is exported as full placement constraints in a QSF file.

Finally, once the blocks for all core instances have been placed on the device, the inter-block router is only responsible for handling the nets connecting blocks because all intra-block routing can be loaded from the core database. First, the router must load from the core database and mark as unavailable all the routing resources utilized internally by each block. The router then loads the resource endpoints of each block's ports. Given these hard constraints, the nets between blocks are routed while minimizing route length. Our inter-block routing approach, discussed in more detail in Section 3.4, is a negotiated-congestion router based on PathFinder [8]. For Altera targets, BPR exports these inter-block routes, along with the internal routes of each block, as full wire-level routing constraints in an RCF file.

3.1.3 Bitfile and Timing

BPR provides the various output files shown in Figure 2 to Quartus for validation and bitfile creation. In the current version of BPR, Quartus is responsible for two other tasks due to limited available information for the Cyclone III device architecture. First, although BPR has information about the connectivity of most routing resources on Cyclone III devices, it does not have information about the device's clock distribution networks. Thus, we currently rely on Quartus to handle clock distribution. Second, for block PAR, the maximum clock frequency f_{max} is determined by two factors: the minimum clock rate of any of the core placements used in the final design and the maximum delay of the inter-block routes. The core database contains block timing data; however, BPR lacks detailed delay information for the Cyclone III's routing resources, currently requiring Quartus to compute the inter-block delays.

3.2 Core DB: Making Blocks Relocatable

As previously discussed, cores supported by BPR must be supplied in a pre-existing core database. BPR is capable of adding arbitrary cores to this database, specified as standard VHDL or Verilog modules. In this section we describe how the core database is populated and the process used to create the relocatable macroblocks used by the placer and router. This process is illustrated in Figure 3. Rather than performing these steps manually, we have created a collection of Python tools that integrate with external programs such as Altera Quartus for intra-block PAR and Synopsys Synplify for core synthesis.

3.2.1 Specification

Cores are added to the database by providing two sets of files to BPR: the standard VHDL or Verilog specification of the core module and an XML-based core specification file, *corespec*, that describes how the core should be handled by the tools. The corespec contains the core's name for use in netlists, a human-readable description for tools and debugging, and identifies the implementing HDL files and top-level entity name. The corespec also identifies and describes the ports that should be exposed in BPR, and allows specifying generics for parameterized modules. Cores may use multiple HDL files in their implementation, but must only contain a single top-level entity.

3.2.2 Synthesis and Resource Determination

The BPR database tools first wrap the core entity by a top-level interface enforcing the corespec. The wrapped entity is then synthesized using standard HDL synthesis tools, currently either Quartus or Synplify. This synthesis pass is required for future steps, but also provides standard optimizations for logic inside the module. Note that because the top-level entity is synthesized in this stage in isolation, optimization between cores is prevented, potentially reducing the quality or fit of the overall circuit. This limitation could be addressed through the use of high-level optimizations, but such approaches are likely to be domain-specific, and are outside the scope of this paper. Finally, the results of synthesis are cleaned up to remove entities inferred by Quartus, such as IO and clock buffers, and stored in the database for future export.

The core is then placed and routed on the device using Quartus, with top-level ports assigned to device pins. This *trial PAR* pass is used to find the device primitive types and counts required by the module, enumerating the device primitives used through back-annotating Quartus'

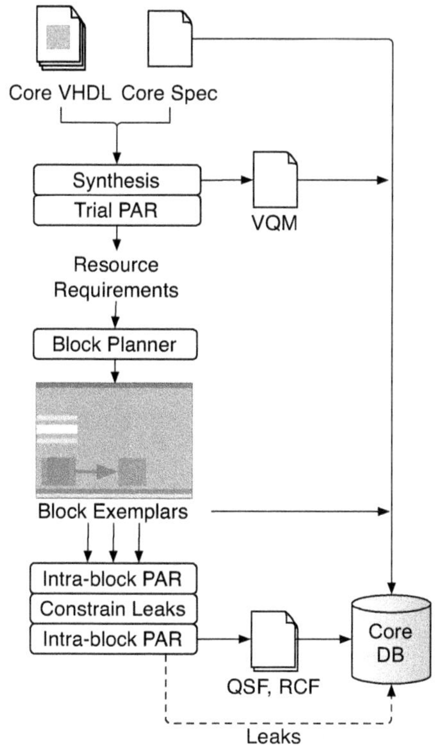

Figure 3: Overview of the BPR core database generation tool flow. New cores are added to the database using their HDL source files and a *corespec* file describing the core's generics and port structure. The tools plan possible placements of cores using black-box footprints (i.e. *blocks*) based on the core's resource requirements and then perform the intra-block PAR using vendor tools, taking care to remove *leaking routes* outside the block area.

placement to QSF. This method works even for cores incorporating protected IP (e.g. some Altera Megafunctions), where the primitives used would otherwise by obscured behind black-box instances in the VQM after synthesis.

3.2.3 Block Planning

Once Quartus or Synplify has optimized the core logic and determined the core's resource requirements, the BPR database tools can begin planning potential placements of blocks on the device. BPR is currently limited to handling cores shaped as rectangular blocks. On Altera devices, we measure block geometry in terms of the coordinates of island structures such as the Logic Array Blocks (LABs) and special resources like M9Ks memory units [21].

The first step of block planning is determining block size. For cores composed of mostly logic (i.e. flip-flops and LUTs), block size is determined by the number of resources required for the core and the packing ratio of the LABs (i.e. the average ratio of flip-flops or LUTs occupied in each LAB). Low packing ratios waste device resources, as the placer can't resolve placement of the fine-grain structures within overlapping blocks. For large cores, very high packing ratios will sometimes fail intra-block PAR using Quartus, typically due to routing pressure within the core. However, even before

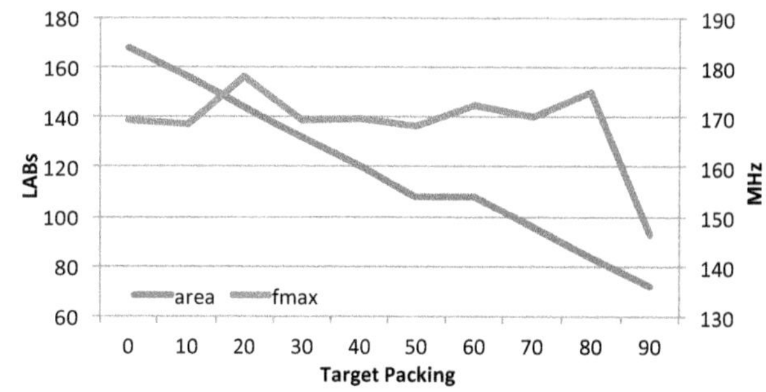

Figure 4: Packing tradeoffs for a floating-point adder core. Depending on the core's internal routing pressure, f_{max} decreases for smaller block sizes (i.e. higher packing ratios).

intra-block PAR fails outright, high packing can reduce the f_{max} Quartus achieves for the block. In practice, choosing an appropriate packing ratio, and thus block size, is currently performed manually, with target ratios of 80-95% providing good area utilization without overly impacting performance. An example of these trends is shown in Figure 4. Note that the actual area used by the core (red line), set through the target packing ratio, changes in steps, depending on the closest rectangular area and other constraints on shape including the device's spacing for any required special resources. As the figure illustrates, for many cores, packing can be increased up to a point without significantly affecting f_{max}, but dropping rapidly after (e.g. 80% packing).

The second step of block planning involves identifying rectangular regions on the device that contain the necessary number and type of resources. To determine legal placements, the block planner uses a sliding-window approach, moving a block-sized footprint across the device one unit at a time while checking whether the resources covered are sufficient, as illustrated in Figure 3.

Once all the legal placements have been identified, the database tools group the placements into sets based on portability. The internal placement and routing of one block is portable to another location only if the logic and routing resources used inside the block exist at the same relative locations (and have the same connectivity) at the other location. The block planner determines portable sets by assigning signatures to each placement that incorporate information about the logic and routing resources within each placement footprint. From each of these sets, one block is chosen as a representative, called a *block exemplar*, which reduces the work in subsequent stages by serving as a stand-in replacement for all the blocks in the set. The block planner ultimately stores a grid of all legal placements in the database, with each placement identifying its exemplar block, for the later use of the BPR placer.

3.2.4 Intra-block PAR and Leaking Routes

Finally, BPR determines the intra-block PAR of each exemplar block by another pass through Quartus. BPR can stitch together the intra-block PAR of blocks without conflict only if all the placed primitives and routes are contained within the block's footprint. For Altera targets, intra-block placements are confined to the rectangular placement footprint by specifying a LogicLock floorplanning constraint

[22] on the top-level module. Unfortunately, current versions of Quartus don't guarantee that intra-block routing will be confined to the LogicLock region, so the output of this second pass often includes internal routes making use of resources outside the block footprint, which we call *leaked routes*.

Though we might wish LogicLock could take care of these issues for us, the inability of LogicLock to make guarantees about routing reflects the limitations of modern FPGA routing architectures. The general-purpose routing of modern FPGA architectures relies heavily on *long wires*, wires spanning multiple islands before terminating in a switch box [23]. For example, the primary general-purpose routing resources on the Cyclone III architecture are the R4 and C4 wires, which span four LABs in row and column channels, respectively. Length-16 and even -24 (C16 and R24) are available on the large devices in the Cyclone III family. These long wires complicate the confinement of intra-block routing. For example, for a 2x2 block footprint, no length-4 wires starting within the block can terminate within the block. Though local wires can usually handle the routes for such small blocks without leaks, in general, the more logic contained within a core and the smaller its block footprint, the more routes will leak. The effects and trends of these leaks are illustrated in Figure 5 for an example core, showing that, due to internal routing pressure and the use of long tracks, an increasing number of a core's internal routes leak from the core's placement footprint (# of LABs) as the size of the footprint is reduced. In the future, as FPGA device sizes continue to increase, we can expect an even greater reliance on long wires to keep interconnect delays low [23], meaning more leaked routes complicating intra-block PAR.

In most cases, there are two factors leading to leaked routes. First, for some nets, a leaking route may provide lower delays than any non-leaking route, helping achieve a high f_{max} for the block. Second, at high routing pressures it may not even be possible to route a net without leaking. Thus, BPR deals with leaked routes in two stages. First, any leaking routes are detected after the first pass through Quartus. The worst leaks are then constrained using additional routing constraints (RCF interval constraints) to the block footprint, and Quartus is re-run with all other routes locked. This process is effective to remove a large number of leaks, at some cost to f_{max} increasing with the number of routes re-routed. However, for large blocks, it is rare that all leaks can be fixed in this way. In this case, we currently add padding to the block's footprint to avoid overuse of the leaked routes' resources.

It should be noted that capturing the intra-block PAR for all the legal placements of a core is typically the most time-consuming step involved in populating BPR's core database. For a large device, most cores will yield hundreds of exemplars after block planning, requiring hundreds of runs through Quartus, which can take considerable time. The time required to add a new core can be substantially reduced in two ways. First, although a core may have many exemplars, each exemplar is not equally valuable in terms of placement flexibility, with some exemplars corresponding to only a single placement option, and others covering tens or hundreds. Thus, we have added an option to our tools to *sift* exemplars, throwing out low-value exemplars until flexibility is impacted to some degree, specified as a percentage. Second, the intra-block PAR of each block placement is independent, and thus is computed in parallel by our tools (using up to one instance of Quartus per machine thread). For some use-cases, for example traditional offline FPGA design, this process could be parallelized over multiple machines making core addition extremely fast.

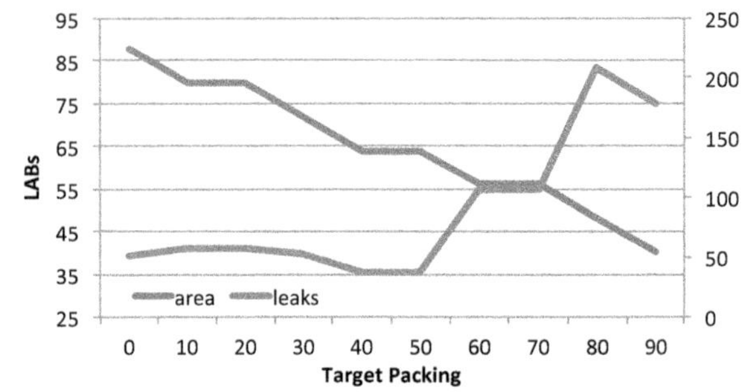

Figure 5: Number of leaked routes for different packing ratios for a floating-point multiplier. The number of routes extending outside the LAB block area (*leaking*) increases with larger packing ratios due to internal routing pressure.

3.3 Block Placement

Given a legal core netlist, BPR's first task is determining where each core instance should be placed on the device. BPR's block placer is responsible for fitting all cores on the device by choosing between legal placement blocks, while considering routability by minimizing the distance between communicating instances and minimizing the expected congestion experienced by those nets.

Because of the similarities with traditional FPGA placement, we based our block placer on the well-known simulated-annealing placement strategy of VPR [7]. However, block placement differs significantly from traditional FPGA placement in two important ways: 1) blocks placed by BPR are not atomic in size and type, conflicting through overlap with multiple other placements, and 2) conflicting with placements of other core types. In this section we discuss how we modified VPR's placement algorithm to handle these complexities and support block placement.

Like VPR, our block placer begins with an initial, poor (randomly generated) placement and evolves an improved solution through many iteratively applied random adjustments, with a tendency to prefer improvements based on an annealing schedule. The solution is perturbed in each iteration by randomly selecting a block instance, placed or unplaced, and moving it to a new randomly selected placement, displacing or evicting any other instances whose placements are newly in conflict.

The primary challenge of adapting this process to place blocks, rather than atomic device resources, is the need for efficient bookkeeping. For example, to determine if a particular block is in conflict with other placed blocks, it is necessary to check if any of the device resources under its footprint are already used by the placement of another instance, which is equivalent to checking if the block footprint intersects the footprint of any other instance. Because this check is performed every iteration, it is also essential that the check be performed efficiently.

In BPR's placer, we require two pieces of information in

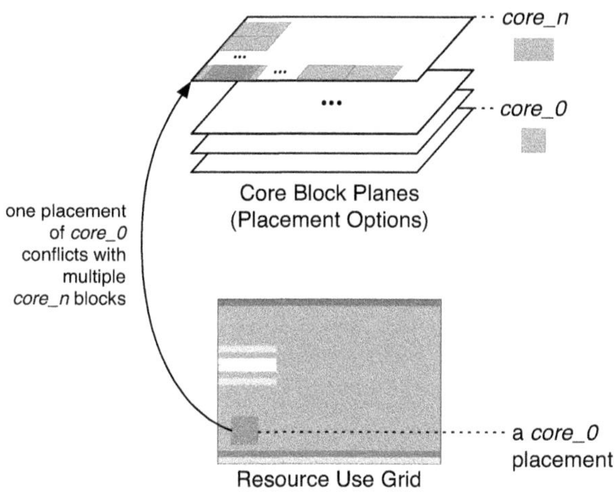

Figure 6: Placer conflicts and bookkeeping. The block placer uses an array of *planes* to keep track of the blocks of each core type available under the current placement. Individual device resources are marked as used or free on a common *use grid.* Note that the placement of a single block, here a block of type *core_0*, typically conflicts with multiple other blocks on each plane.

each iteration: which blocks of each core type are in conflict, and which instances, through which block placements, are making use of each device resource. BPR efficiently determines this information through a data structure resembling Figure 6. We maintain a grid representing the device cell layout (e.g. LAB or M9K) as a common reference for area utilization. Each coordinate in this grid contains two pointers, referencing the instance and block (a *placement*) making use of the cell, or *nil* if the resource is free. Upon choosing a random placement during an iteration, this grid can be used to efficiently find any affected instances for displacement or eviction. We track the availability of placement blocks through an array of *planes*, one for each core type used in the netlist. Each plane holds a grid of legal placements, referenced by origin, as well as *used* and *unused* lists, permitting efficient random access to available placements (e.g. for displacement operations).

One other challenge faced by block placement is that, in terms of block performance, all placements are not created equal. Because the distribution of logic and, to a greater extent, the distribution and connectivity of routing resources varies across the device, there is also variation in the f_{max} achieved for the same core placed at different locations. The amount of variation depends on the core, but can be significant in the worst cases, with deviations of up to 20% for large blocks such as memory interfaces. The BPR placer handles this issue by incorporating the frequency of the minimum-performing block in the current solution as a term in the cost function, preferring the selection of faster blocks in these situations.

3.4 Inter-block Routing

Once the block placer has determined the location of each block instance, and thus the specific intra-block PAR being used, it is the inter-block router's task to stitch the design together by routing the nets connecting each placed block. Inter-block routing is identical to traditional FPGA routing, except that much of the design has already been routed as part of the placer's selection of blocks, and, in this sense, the router has less flexibility to minimize net delays. Due to these similarities, we chose the PathFinder [8] negotiated-congestion router as the basis for the inter-block router in BPR.

The router begins by loading the device's routing resource graph, stored alongside cores in the core database. Because of the large size of modern FPGAs, one of the major challenges in making BPR's router fast was finding an efficient in-memory representation for this graph. Our representation stores the graph as an array of grids, one for each permutation of resources (e.g. R4-C4 or R4-R4), using the device's coordinate system. For each resource pair, the connectivity at each coordinate, equivalent to an individual switch- or connection-box, is stored efficiently as a grid of bitfields for offsets in a neighborhood around the driving resource's (x, y) position. In the database, space is saved by sorting these connectivity patterns and storing each unique pattern, or box topology, exactly once. The router's dynamic cost data is stored similarly. In addition to providing an efficient representation of the device's resource graph, this method of storage has other advantages when performing pathfinding, which will be discussed later.

After loading the device's routing graph, the router loads the routing resource utilization data from the core databse for each block appearing in the final placement. This data represents routes that BPR's router cannot disrupt. To ensure that BPR will not overuse these routing resources, this data is used to break connections in the router's representation of the device's routing resource graph. The endpoint routing resources corresponding to blocks' ports are also loaded at this time and used to annotate the nets.

With the newly modified graph, BPR routes all nets using essentially the same process described in PathFinder [8]. In the details, though, we have made a couple of optimizations to keep run times low. First, instead of using Dijkstra's method to find shortest-paths, we have used a much faster implementation of A* [24], providing speedups of up to 16x on large devices. Second, we reduce the effective size of the routing resource graph when exploring shortest-paths by making the approximation that wire cost is independent of a wire's index within the channel and depends only on the distance the wire covers. Under this assumption, our router simultaneously considers all legal wire indexes at each point in the search, leveraging our bitfield implementation for the storage of resource connectivity to track this information efficiently as an accumulation. The search can progress from a vertex as long as some index is valid in this accumulation. When the search terminates, the exact index used at each step is determined through backtracking, selecting arbitrarily when multiple paths are possible.

4. EXPERIMENTS

In this section we evaluate the performance of BPR compared to the traditional full-detail FPGA placement and routing flow implemented in commercial tools. We evaluate BPR's performance for a number of case study netlists incorporating a variety of cores, implemented in BPR's custom netlist format. For each case study, we compare BPR's execution time against the time required for Altera Quartus to implement the same circuit from an equivalent VHDL design using the same core HDL, treating synthesis and place and route times separately. We also evaluate the performance overhead of BPR's methodology by comparing the area utilization and maximum clock rate f_{max} achieved by each tool.

In our analysis, we compare against Altera Quartus 9.1 SP2 using low placement effort and optimization level settings for faster compilation at the expense of some circuit quality. Execution times were compared on a quad-core 2.66 GHz Intel Xeon W3520 workstation with 12GB RAM, running CentOS 6.1 x86_64. We compare circuit implementations for the Altera Cyclone III family of devices [21].

4.1 Case Studies

We evaluated BPR's performance on 13 case studies, shown in Table 1, covering a variety of applications. *SAD* computes the sum-of-absolute differences for image comparison. *Gaussian* performs a Gaussian blur on an image. *Sobel* performs image edge detection. *FIR* is a finite impulse response filter. Where appropriate, we tested multiple instances of the same netlist at different sizes (e.g. by changing the kernel size for the image processing applications) to demonstrate how BPR's performance scales with problem size. In many cases we also evaluate both single-precision floating point (indicated by *float*) and 16-bit fixed point versions of the same circuit. To determine the effect of device size, we tested BPR with two devices in the Cyclone III device family: the small EP3C5 (EP3C5F256C8) with 5k logic elements, 46 M9K memories, and 23 DSPs; and the large EP3C120 (EP3C120F484C8) with 119k logic elements, 432 M9Ks, and 288 DSPs.

Most of the case studies in Table 1 incorporate large fixed-point or floating-point arithmetic datapaths. The arithmetic operators in these datapaths consist of tens (fixed point) to hundreds (floating point) of LUTs and make use of the Cyclone III architecture's DSP and M9K memory units when applicable, as determined by the vendor tools' synthesis optimizations. The floating-point operators were generated from Altera Megafunctions [20]. Because arithmetic components are prevalent in common applications of FPGAs, and are often instantiated in large quantities within a single netlist, they were added to the database without sifting of low-valued placements to maximize flexibility, with database population requiring up to several hours running on one workstation.

The 2D DSP examples (e.g. *Gaussian 3x3 1080p 16b*) also include sliding window interfaces to external memory, with the various window and image dimensions specified for each instance through corespec parameters wrapping a common parameterized VHDL implementation. Because these memory interfaces are large and appear in limited quantities in most applications, high sifting values were used to speedup database population by discarding all but a small percentage of possible placements, limiting the collective time required for database population to under an hour. Although this sifting limits placement flexibility for instances of these memory interfaces, we have found that good results can still be achieved for designs whose other components (e.g. arithmetic operators) retain high placement flexibility. Note that these decisions were made on an ad-hoc basis, and are likely not optimal. We leave a detailed analysis of sifting tradeoffs for different core types and sizes as future work.

4.2 Results

Table 1 illustrates BPR's place and route speedup, device resource utilization, and performance overhead for each case study. The left-most major column gives a short description of the case study application as well as the Cyclone III device it was compiled for. The second major column compares BPR's execution time to the time required for Quartus' PAR flow (`quartus_fit`) to place and route an equivalent VHDL design. Because the original HDL source for each core is retained in the core database, the BPR tool is capable of generating these equivalent designs itself, ensuring identical core HDL is used for a fair comparison.

For BPR, we measure execution time including the time to initialize BPR's PAR data structures with the mapped netlist, and ending when the final PAR solution is produced in memory. We exclude the time required to export the solution to Quartus in the large human-readable QSF and RCF formats. The PAR time reported for Quartus is the elapsed time reported by `quartus_fit` when run with low effort settings for placement and physical optimizations. Note that Quartus also does not write out QSF and RCF constraints in the normal course of PAR, requiring the use of a second tool (`quartus_cdb`) when back-annotating this data. We exclude the time required to run `quartus_cdb`, which is typically on the order of a few seconds, in the times for Quartus.

The results show an average 93x PAR speedup over all case studies, requiring an average of 1.1s. The speedup numbers are higher on average for the floating-point examples, at 154x, compared to the fixed-point examples, at 76x. This larger speedup is caused by a larger reduction in problem size for the floating-point examples over detailed PAR, with a typical float operator containing 100s of LUTs, compared to 10s for the fixed-point operators, all of which is hidden behind black-box footprints in BPR.

The third major column shows the percentage of device resources required to implement the design as reported by Quartus for each netlist case study, without BPR's PAR constraints. We include this data to give an idea of the size of each design, which impacts the execution times of placement (by complicating fit) and routing (through increased obstacles). Note that although area overhead due to overly generic cores is possible in BPR's methodology, it was not significant for these case studies. *LABs* are an Altera primitive consisting of 16 logic elements, *LEs*, which each consist of a configurable LUT. *DSP* corresponds to multiplier blocks and *M9K* represents on-chip block RAMs.

BPR was able to use up to 49% of the small (C5) Cyclone III when working with fixed-point datapaths. This high utilization is possible because of the placement flexibility of the smaller fixed-point cores, one of which (add16) is purely logic. These smaller cores also achieve high packing ratios due to low internal communication requirements, as discussed in Section 3.2.3, resulting in a higher ceiling for area. Higher utilization was also achieved for the floating-point DSP circuits on the large (C120) device. However, for these larger cores, another factor limits circuit size: competition for the device's scarce resources such as DSPs and M9Ks. The typical floating-point core incorporates one or more of these resources, but has a black-box footprint (due to logic requirements) that covers many more, leading to a large amount of waste. We plan to address this challenge as future work, and discuss this problem in more detail in that section.

Table 1: BPR place and route speedup and overhead of case study circuits.

Applications		Place and Route (PAR) Times					Area				Clock		
Netlist	Device	BPR	BPR Placer	BPR Router	Quartus	Speedup	LABs	LEs	DSP	M9K	BPR	Quartus	Overhead
SAD 3x3 480p 16b	C5	0.629	0.039s	0.59s	0m 11s	**17x**	45%	38%	0%	13%	72 MHz	73 MHz	**1%**
FIR 14-tap 16b	C5	0.076s	0.048s	0.028s	0m 9s	**118x**	56%	34%	61%	0%	222 MHz	225 MHz	**1%**
FIR 20-tap 16b	C5	0.176s	0.12s	0.056s	0m 13s	**74x**	80%	49%	87%	0%	208 MHz	225 MHz	**8%**
Gaussian 3x3 1080p 16b	C120	0.285s	0.239s	0.046s	0m 38s	**133x**	6%	2%	3%	3%	69 MHz	76 MHz	**10%**
Gaussian 5x5 1080p 16b	C120	0.595s	0.478s	0.117s	0m 53s	**89x**	15%	4%	9%	5%	63 MHz	75 MHz	**19%**
Gaussian 7x7 480p 16b	C120	2.059s	1.772s	0.287s	1m 9s	**34x**	31%	8%	11%	4%	62 MHz	64 MHz	**3%**
FIR 48-tap 16b	C120	1.319s	1.168s	0.151s	0m 54s	**41x**	24%	5%	17%	0%	157 MHz	224 MHz	**43%**
FIR 76-tap 16b	C120	2.857s	2.672s	0.185s	1m 33s	**33x**	38%	8%	26%	0%	124 MHz	224 MHz	**81%**
FIR 96-tap 16b	C120	3.69s	3.473s	0.217s	1m 35s	**26x**	48%	10%	33%	0%	95 MHz	224 MHz	**137%**
Sobel 1080p 16b	C120	0.188s	0.156s	0.032s	0m 35s	**186x**	2%	2%	4%	0%	62 MHz	77 MHz	**24%**
SAD 3x3 1080p float	C120	0.768s	0.662s	0.106s	1m 58s	**154x**	23%	17%	0%	11%	51 MHz	72 MHz	**40%**
FIR 9-tap float	C120	0.41s	0.354s	0.056s	1m 18s	**190x**	16%	11%	11%	2%	123 MHz	140 MHz	**14%**
FIR 16-tap float	C120	1.171s	1.051s	0.12s	2m 19s	**119x**	29%	21%	19%	3%	109 MHz	146 MHz	**34%**
Average		1.094s			1m 2s	93x	32%	16%	22%	3%	109 MHz	142 MHz	32%
Geometric Mean		0.637s			0m 46s	72x	23%	10%			97 MHz	124 MHz	14%

The right-most major column compares the maximum frequency f_{max} of BPR's exported designs against designs using Quartus' full-detail place and route. For each case study, we report the clock frequency achieved by BPR's place and route against the frequency achieved by Quartus from the equivalent HDL design without constraints. The frequency for BPR is the value reported by Quartus timing analysis after running BPR's constrained design through `quartus_fit` for finalization, as discussed in Section 3.1. In all cases we report the unrestrained f_{max} number reported by `quartus_sta`.

BPR's speedups were achieved with an average 34% reduction in circuit frequency. This overhead was lowest for the small C5, down to 1%, in part because of the reduced impact of poor quality placements on a small device. The highest overhead numbers were experienced by the large fixed-point FIR filters on the C120, at up to 137%. Part of the large overhead of these large circuits is due to a limitation in BPR's current router where it doesn't have access to very long wires in the Cyclone III architecture (e.g. C16). Note that although the worst-case overhead for these circuits is significant, they are comparable to previous work with typical 2-4x overhead [19]. For many of the 2D DSP examples, e.g. the *Gaussian* kernels, the circuit's performance overhead is determined by the f_{max} of the sliding-window buffer. Here, the overhead is caused by the need to confine the window core to a compact rectangular footprint, as discussed in Section 3.2.3. These examples illustrate that area/frequency tradeoffs are especially important for slower cores which may set a circuit's f_{max} before other, faster components or inter-block routes. We leave a thorough evaluation of these tradeoffs as future work.

5. FUTURE WORK

The performance of BPR's placer is often limited by crowding around special device resources such as DSPs and M9Ks, which are scarce compared to LABs and are arranged densely in columns on the Cyclone III. It is common for a single core (e.g. floating-point arithmetic operators) to incorporate only one or two such resources along with a large amount of logic, which has the effect of requiring large block footprints. Because BPR is limited to placing these cores as rectangular blocks which cannot overlap, a single block will often cover multiple unused DSPs and M9Ks, preventing access to these resources by other blocks. We plan to address this in future versions of BPR by stripping out such scarce resource types when they're used by a core, to be placed and routed separately as small sub-blocks.

The limitations of BPR's current placer are exacerbated by BPR's simplistic core mapper. In the current version of BPR, core mapping does not consider the limited number of resources such as DSPs available on the device. Thus, the core mapper will continue to map core instances to implementations making use of DSPs and other scarce resources even after all such resources on the device have been exhausted, making placement of subsequently mapped blocks impossible. We plan to address this in future versions of BPR by expanding core database population to include secondary core implementations that don't include scarce resources, giving the mapper other options in these situations.

The performance of BPR's router is also limited by the inflexibility of the many intra-block routes imported after placement, which are currently immutable. In addition to reducing the f_{max} achieved by BPR, this inflexibility can potentially make large designs with dense blocks unroutable. We plan to extend future versions of BPR by allowing the router to rip-up imported intra-block routes as necessary in these situations, possibly subject to some tunable effort level to allow for tradeoffs between quality and execution time.

6. CONCLUSIONS

In this paper, we introduced BPR, a new FPGA CAD tool for the fast compilation of FPGA circuits that exploits the functional reuse common in modern FPGA design. BPR modifies traditional FPGA place and route algorithms to abstract the low-level implementation details of reused cores in a design, with the corresponding reduction in problem size enabling large speedups over full-detail commercial FPGA place and route, while also requiring significantly less memory. The main limitation of BPR is performance (f_{max}) overhead and limited scalability due to reductions in placement and routing flexibility caused by limiting the implementation of cores to immutable rectangular footprints. However, we show that over 13 case studies covering a variety of applications, the current version of BPR achieves an average 93x speedup, with a relatively low 34% average reduction in circuit f_{max} compared to full-detail PAR performed by commercial tools, which is acceptable for many applications. Furthermore, these results bring FPGA compilation times much closer to those of competing technologies including GPUs, potentially enabling FPGA support for emerging just-in-time compilation models such as OpenCL.

Future work addressing limitations in the current version of BPR, identified in this paper, may make BPR and similar approaches more competitive with traditional FPGA compilation flows.

7. ACKNOWLEDGMENTS

This work was supported in part by the I/UCRC Program of the National Science Foundation under Grant Nos. EEC-0642422 and IIP-1161022. The authors gratefully acknowledge vendor equipment and/or tools provided by Altera and Synopsys.

8. REFERENCES

[1] A. DeHon, "The Density Advantage of Configurable Computing," *Computer*, vol. 33, pp. 41–49, April 2000.

[2] G. Stitt and F. Vahid, "Energy Advantages of Microprocessor Platforms with On-Chip Configurable Logic," *IEEE Des. Test*, vol. 19, pp. 36-43, November 2002.

[3] E. Girczyc and S. Carlson, "Increasing design quality and engineering productivity through design reuse," in *Proceedings of the 30th international Design Automation Conference*, ser. DAC '93, 1993.

[4] C. Mulpuri and S. Hauck, "Runtime and quality tradeoffs in FPGA placement and routing," in *Proceedings of the 2001 ACM/SIGDA ninth international symposium on Field programmable gate arrays*, ser. FPGA '01, 2001.

[5] *SOPC Builder User Guide*, Altera Corporation, December 2010.

[6] OpenCores. (2012, Mar.) OpenCores. [Online]. Available: http://opencores.org/projects

[7] V. Betz and J. Rose, "VPR: A new packing, placement and routing tool for FPGA research," in *Proceedings of the 7th International Workshop on Field-Programmable Logic and Applications*. London, UK: Springer-Verlag, 1997, pp. 213–222.

[8] L. McMurchie and C. Ebeling, "PathFinder: a negotiation-based performance-driven router for FPGAs," in *Proceedings of the 1995 ACM third international symposium on Field-programmable gate arrays*, ser. FPGA '95, 1995.

[9] J. Becker, T. Pionteck, C. Habermann, and M. Glesner, "Design and Implementation of a Coarse-Grained Dynamically Reconfigurable Hardware Architecture," in *Proceedings of the IEEE Computer Society Workshop on VLSI 2001*, ser. WVLSI '01. Washington, DC, USA: IEEE Computer Society, 2001, pp. 41–.

[10] G. K. Rauwerda, P. M. Heysters, and G. J. M. Smit, "Towards software defined radios using coarse-grained reconfigurable hardware," *IEEE Trans. Very Large Scale Integr. Syst.*, vol. 16, pp. 3–13, January 2008.

[11] J. Coole and G. Stitt, "Intermediate fabrics: virtual architectures for circuit portability and fast placement and routing," in *Proceedings of the eighth IEEE/ACM/IFIP international conference on Hardware/software codesign and system synthesis*, ser. CODES/ISSS '10, 2010.

[12] S. Shukla, N. W. Bergmann, and J. Becker, "QUKU: A Two-Level Reconfigurable Architecture," in *Proceedings of the IEEE Computer Society Annual Symposium on Emerging VLSI Technologies and Architectures*. Washington, DC, USA: IEEE Computer Society, 2006, pp. 109–.

[13] A. Koch, "Structured design implementation: a strategy for implementing regular datapaths on FPGAs," in *Proceedings of the 1996 ACM fourth international symposium on Field-programmable gate arrays*, ser. FPGA '96, 1996.

[14] R. Lysecky, F. Vahid, and S. X. D. Tan, "A Study of the Scalability of On-Chip Routing for Just-in-Time FPGA Compilation," in *FCCM '05: Proceedings of the 13th Annual IEEE Symposium on Field-Programmable Custom Computing Machines*. Washington, DC, USA: IEEE Computer Society, 2005, pp. 57–62.

[15] R. Lysecky, F. Vahid, and S. X.-D. Tan, "Dynamic FPGA routing for just-in-time FPGA compilation," in *DAC '04: Proceedings of the 41st Annual Conference on Design Automation*. New York, NY, USA: ACM, 2004, pp. 954–959.

[16] C. Mulpuri and S. Hauck, "Runtime and quality tradeoffs in FPGA placement and routing," in *FPGA '01: Proceedings of the 2001 ACM/SIGDA Ninth International Symposium on Field Programmable Gate Arrays*. New York, NY, USA: ACM, 2001, pp. 29–36.

[17] P. Athanas, J. Bowen, T. Dunham, C. Patterson, J. Rice, M. Shelburne, J. Suris, M. Bucciero, and J. Graf, "Wires on demand: Run-time communication synthesis for reconfigurable computing," in *FPL '07: International Conference on Field Programmable Logic and Applications*, Aug. 2007, pp. 513–516.

[18] R. Tessier, "Frontier: A Fast Placement System for FPGAs," in *VLSI: Systems on a Chip, IFIP TC10/WG10.5 Tenth International Conference on Very Large Scale Integration (VLSI 99), December 1-4, 1999, Lisbon, Portugal*, ser. IFIP Conference Proceedings, L. M. Silveira, S. Devadas, and R. A. da Luz Reis, Eds., vol. 162. Kluwer, 1999, pp. 125–136.

[19] C. Lavin, M. Padilla, J. Lamprecht, P. Lundrigan, B. Nelson, and B. Hutchings, "HMFlow: Accelerating FPGA Compilation with Hard Macros for Rapid Prototyping," in *Proceedings of the 2011 IEEE 19th Annual International Symposium on Field-Programmable Custom Computing Machines*, ser. FCCM '11. Washington, DC, USA: IEEE Computer Society, 2011, pp. 117–124.

[20] *Quartus II Handbook Version 11.1*, Altera Corporation, November 2011.

[21] *Cyclone III Device Handbook*, Altera Corporation, December 2011.

[22] *Application Note 161: Using the LogicLock Methodology in the Quartus II Design Software*, Altera Corporation, June 2003.

[23] V. Betz and J. Rose, "FPGA routing architecture: segmentation and buffering to optimize speed and density," in *Proceedings of the 1999 ACM/SIGDA seventh international symposium on Field programmable gate arrays*, ser. FPGA '99, 1999.

[24] R. Dechter and J. Pearl, "Generalized best-first search strategies and the optimality of A*," *J. ACM*, vol. 32, no. 3, pp. 505–536, Jul. 1985.

Generating Interlocked Instruction Pipelines from Specifications of Instruction Sets

Ralf Dreesen
University of Paderborn
Fürstenallee 11
33102 Paderborn, Germany
rdreesen@upb.de

ABSTRACT

The development of application specific processors (ASIPs) for systems-on-a-chip (SoCs) became increasingly popular in recent years. To efficiently develop such processors, respective tools are crucial. This paper presents methods to generate pipelined processors from a bare instruction set specification in ViDL . All microarchitectural aspects of the processor are contributed by a generator. Hazard resolution by forwarding, interlocking and branch prediction is automatically derived from instruction semantics, information on the targeted chip technology and an user supplied timing constraint. By variation of the latter, a set of compatible processor implementations is generated with different physical and dynamic characteristics. The processor generator has been evaluated using realistic instruction sets, such as ARM, MIPS, Power, SRC, DNACore and CoreVA. The generated processors have been tested on register-transfer-level and gate-level. In total, 83 processors have been generated and synthesized for a 65 nm STM low power technology, yielding clock frequencies of 260 – 680 MHz for 2 – 7 stage pipelines. Clock frequency and the number of cycles per instruction (CPI) is similar to handcrafted designs.

Categories and Subject Descriptors

B.5.2 [**Register-Transfer-Level Implementation**]: Design Aids—*Automatic synthesis, Optimization*

Keywords

Processor, ASIP, ViDL, Instruction Set, Specification, Generator, Microarchitecture, Pipeline, Forwarding, Bypass, Interlocking, Exploration, DSE

1. INTRODUCTION

The generation methods that are presented in this paper are part of a processor generator. This generator is one component of a system for processor development. The system of the instruction set specification language ViDL [5] and its generators is illustrated in Figure 1. A developer defines an instruction set in ViDL, for instance by formalizing an existing instruction set manual. In contrast to related approaches, the language ViDL strictly abstracts from microarchitectural aspects. It belongs to the class of functional languages, implements domain specific concepts, and obeys fundamental language design guidelines, which greatly improves reliability and reuse [20]. It features a sophisticated type-system to detect undefined behaviour using type-analysis techniques [6].

Great parts of practical instruction sets, such as ARM [1], MIPS [14], and Power [12] have rapidly been specified in two month to one day, by inexperienced and experienced users. The example in Figure 1 shows the definition of a conditionally executed vector-add instruction. The function `ce` encapsules the definition of conditional execution for this instruction set. The functional `SIMD2bin` implements the concept of a binary 2-way SIMD instruction. The actual operation (add) is passed as a parameter. Both functions are defined in ViDL itself and can be extended as desired.

Processors, simulators and development tools are automatically generated from a ViDL specification and only from this specification. No further aspects of the implementations need to be contributed by the developer. In particular, microarchitectural aspects, such as the pipeline structure and its control are not defined. These aspects are entirely derived by the processor generator, on which this paper focuses.

The input of the processor generator is the instruction set specification, a timing constraint (target frequency) and a database containing technology dependent timing estimates of hardware entities. The target frequency defines the desired frequency of the final processor. By invoking the generator with different target frequencies, a set of compatible processors with respective physical and dynamic characteristics is generated. A low target frequency typically leads to a small processor with low instruction latencies, whereas a high target frequency leads to a fast and deeply pipelined implementation with a higher CPI[1].

2. RELATED WORK

The majority of processor related specification languages define processors (on a microarchitectural level) rather than instruction sets. This includes *ASPI Meister* [15], *nML* [17], *Expression* [9], and *Lisa* [13]. Aspects of the microarchitecturea are therefore not derived by the generator, but need to

[1]cycles per instruction

CODES+ISSS'12, October 7–12, 2012, Tampere, Finland.

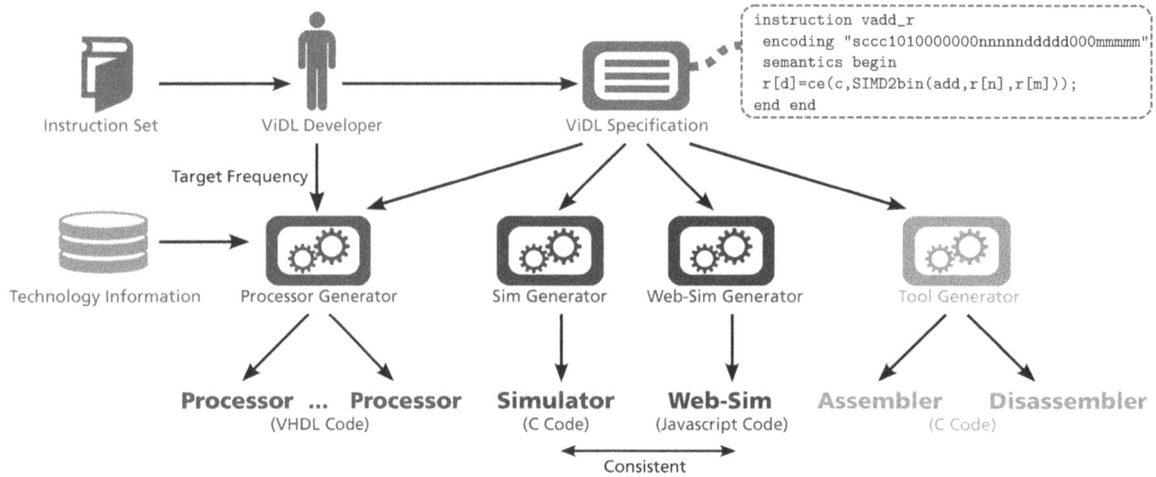

Figure 1: Overview of the entire system to generate generate processors, simulators, and tools from specifications of instruction sets.

be contributed by the developer. This has a major impact on development time, error rate and maintainability. In the following, two of the predominant systems to develop application specific processors are regarded, namely Tensilica and Lisa.

The specification language Lisa defines aspects of the instruction set as well as aspects of the microarchitecture. It is therefore bound to one specific processor implementation. The instruction set is specified on the foundation of the microarchitecture, i.e. the microarchitecture can hardly be changed later. Pipelining has to be specified explicitly in Lisa. The specification includes all pipeline registers and the number and names of pipeline stages. These names are then used to manually assign operations to specific stages. To resolve hazards, a forwarding circuit needs to be defined manually on a microarchitectural level, as it is done in a VHDL specification of a processor. The definition of a typical forwarding circuit in Lisa may be considered complex. Although forwarding is a key technique to resolve data hazards, respective examples have not been published. In contrast, a ViDL developer does not have to consider forwarding, as the forwarding circuit is automatically contributed by the generator.

A Lisa developer also has to define pipeline control manually, as part of instruction semantics. In case of a mispredicted branch, all speculatively executed instructions have to be canceled, by flushing their stages. If a register is read, that is written by a preceding instruction X and the result of X can not be forwarded due to its latency, the read stage and its predecessors have to be stalled, until the result is computed and can be forwarded. The designer is responsible to define correct pipeline control that solves all hazards for all sequences of instructions. This task can be considered complex and error-prone. For instance, development of a simple SRC [11] processor in Lisa by Franz [7] took about 1–2 months. Specification in ViDL, including generation of processors and simulators took 90 minutes. The ViDL specification of SRC is publicly available [4].

As the name suggests, the *Tensilica Instruction Extension* (TIE) language [8, 19, 18, 16] is intended to define instruction set extensions. An existing instruction set can be extended by application specific instructions to accelerate hot-spots of applications. In contrast to related approaches, the basic instruction set (Xtensa core) is fixed and remains unchanged. The specification of complete instruction sets seems not to be intended and respective examples have not been published. Although TIE is very close to an instruction set specification language, there are some exceptions, that break strict abstraction.

For instance, the `schedule` directive in TIE is used to explicitly specify the relation between datapath and pipeline. In particular, the publication stage of an instruction result is specified. Technically, this is the stage in which a result is fed into the bypass. Effectively, the `schedule` directive thereby defines the bypass and the resulting interlocking. In addition, the `schedule` directive is used to assign the stages of read ports and assign intermediate signals to stages. Section 3.4 shows, how these aspects can be derived from instruction semantics.

Finally, a short glance is taken at the Sim-HS tool [2]. It generates synthesizeable Verilog code from a Sim-nML specification, which is an extension of nML, including microarchitectural aspects. The tool maps instruction semantics to a non-pipelined datapath. The approach thereby circumvents generation of hazard resolution in terms of bypasses, interlocking, and branch prediction, at the expense of a limited clock frequency.

3. PROCESSOR GENERATOR

This section describes the generation of a microarchitectural processor implementation. The generation is based on a dataflowgraph (Section 3.1), which represents the semantics of all instructions. The graph is then successively transformed into a pipelined dataflow graph. An overview of a generated pipeline structure is shown in Figure 2. The Figure is just meant to give a basic impression of the structure of one specific processor. The processor in this example consists of a pipeline and a register file. The pipeline has several stages, which are divided by pipeline registers. An instruction is fetched in stage 0, decoded in stage 1, traverses the entire pipeline and is finally retired in stage 5. The execution of instructions in the pipeline is controlled by the

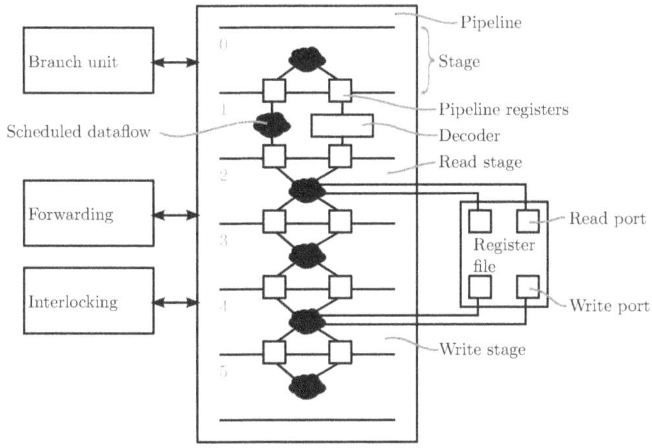

Figure 2: Components of the generated microarchitectural processor implementation.

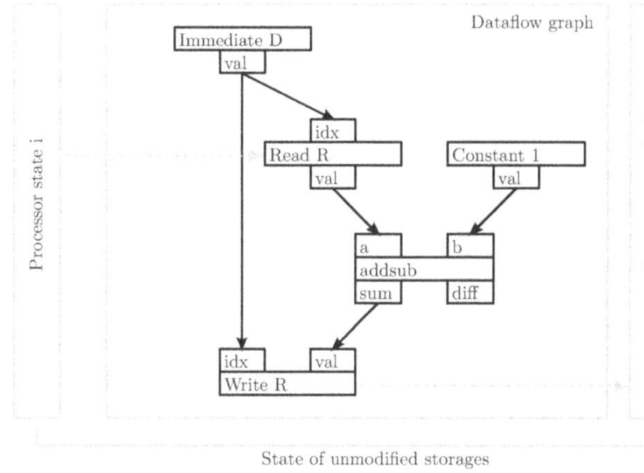

Figure 3: Example of a simple dataflow graph (DFG).

branch unit and interlocking. Parts of the dataflow graph are visualized by black clouds, which are distributed among the entire pipeline.

The figure is referred in the following, to introduce the components of the processor generator. The processor's instruction decoder is produced by a *decoder generator*, which is based on a decision tree. The next phases are highly dependent, i.e. one phase relies on the result of the previous phase. The first phase called *port assignment* generates read and write ports for each register file and each data memory. The example in Figure 2 shows a register file with two read ports and two write ports. Accesses in the DFG are statically mapped to these ports, such that no resource-hazards occur. The method is based on graph coloring and yields a minimal number of ports. Before the pipeline is constructed, some primitives (e.g. multiplier) may be pipelined by the *operation pipelining* phase (Section 3.2). This phase affects the latency[2] of operations and must therefore be executed before any other pipeline related phase. The read stage and the write stage of each storage element are determined in the subsequent *port scheduling* phase (Section 3.4). The resulting stages are connected to the read and write ports that have been derived in the previous phase. In the example (Figure 2), the register file is read in stage 2 and written in stage 4. Depending on the location of read and write ports, the remaining nodes of the DFG are scheduled by the *operation scheduler* (Section 3.5). The dataflow that is assigned to stages is indicated by black clouds in the example. Once all nodes of the DFG are scheduled, *pipeline registers* are inserted (Section 3.6). The insertion of pipeline registers depends on the previous operation scheduling. As shown in the example, pipeline registers are placed on the boundaries between stages, which effectively interrupt dataflow between stages. To eliminate resulting data-hazards, a *forwarding circuit* (Section 3.7) is generated for each register, unless such hazards can be excluded. The generation involves sophisticated analysis of the dataflow. Forwarding is always applied, unless it would introduce further critical paths. The forwarding circuit must be inserted *after* pipeline registers have been inserted. Otherwise, the DFG would become a cyclic graph. If a data-hazard can not be resolved by forwarding, *interlocking* (Section 3.8) is applied. The generation of interlocking is based on analysis information from the previous forwarding phase. The processor generator aims to construct pipeline control such, that the number of pipeline stalls is minimized. The final phase of the transformation constructs a *branch unit* (Section 3.9). The branch unit applies speculative execution and instruction canceling in case of misprediction. The generation involves analysis of dataflow and optimizations to simplify control logic. It depends on results from the forwarding phase.

3.1 Intermediate representation

The frontend of the processor generator translates a textual ViDL specification into a normalized and optimized intermediate representation. The intermediate representation includes the structure of storage elements and the semantics of instructions. The semantics of all instructions are represented by a single dataflow graph (DFG). The DFG consists of operations and their interconnection. It is a directed acyclic graph (DAG), i.e. the dataflow does not include any cycles. Figure 3 shows a very simple example of a DFG. It describes the semantics of an "increment" instruction, which operates on a register `r[d]`. In practice, DFGs are much larger. During processing of the ARM instruction set, the number of nodes ranges from 2.000 to 100.000 nodes.

ViDL provides a set of approximately 50 operations, such as *Immediate*, *Read*, *Constant*, *Write*, and combinatorial logic[3], which are generic with respect to their bitwidth. The set of operations can be extended by the user, although there is typically no need for usual instruction sets.

It is important to note that nodes in the DFG do not carry any state. As a result, the value at out-ports solely depends on the values at in-ports. This enables numerous optimizations and leads to a clear understanding of processor state.

3.2 Operation pipelining

To increase the clock frequency of generated processors, operations may be pipelined by the generator. For instance,

[2]The pipeline depth of an operation, not to be confused with propagation delay.

[3]such as "add", "count-leading-zeros", "rotate-right", "sign-extend", etc.

the multiplier may be pipelined, such that it is distributed among multiple stages. However, pipelining of operations typically increases instruction latencies, chip area and power consumption of the processor. It is therefore only applied if necessary. The decision if an operation is pipelined depends on its estimated delay and the user supplied target frequency, which is introduced in the next section.

Operation pipelining is implemented using a term rewriting system and timing sensitive rewrite rules. For a certain range of the target frequency, a rewrite rule is defined, which exchanges a non-pipelined operation by a pipelined counterpart. For instance, for a range between 300 MHz and 400 MHz, a non-pipelined multiplier may be replaced by a 3-stage multiplier.

3.3 Timing

To generate a pipeline processor, the generator has to consider two kinds of timing, namely the *timing of operations* in the DFG and the targeted timing of the processor. The latter is supplied in terms of a *target frequency* f_{target} by the user. The timing of each operation is defined in the *technology database* (Figure 1). The database defines propagation delays and latencies for all operations. The propagation delay depends on the chip technology that is targeted during synthesis. For this reason, several databases may be defined, one for each technology. The databases itself are processor independent and reused among all instruction sets.

Pipeline related decisions of the generator are guided by the timing of operations and by the user defined target frequency f_{target}. The generator tries to organize the pipeline such, that the critical path does not exceed the timing constraint f_{target}^{-1}. On the other hand, unnecessary pipelining is avoided to save resources. The target frequency is a significant parameter, which has a major impact on the processors frequency (as determined by synthesis), chip area, power consumption and instruction latencies. Using f_{target}, the developer can generate very different processor implementations from the same instruction set specification. The relation between f_{target} and physical characteristics of the processor is evaluated in Section 4. Its impact on instruction latencies is discussed in Section 4.2.

The remaining sections describe methods to construct the instruction pipeline[4]. Most methods consider the target frequency and the timing of operations in some respect.

3.4 Port scheduling

The port scheduling phase determines the read stage and the write-back stage of each storage element, by assigning read ports and write ports to stages. For instance, the read ports of a register X may be assigned to stage 2 of the pipeline and the write ports may be assigned to stage 5, as shown in Figure 4a. In this case, stage 2 is called the read stage and stage 5 is called the write-back stage of X. Note, that distinct stages may be assigned for each storage element, as demonstrated in the example for X and Y.

For port scheduling the generator considers the structure of the DFG, the timing of its nodes and the targeted frequency of the final processor. The resulting port assignment must be valid and should be optimized. The optimization criteria are discussed later.

A valid schedule must satisfy two constraints, namely *causality* and *schedulability*. The causality constraint demands that the write stage of a storage element Y must not precede the read stage of Y. Otherwise, a processor state i may depend on a state $i + 1$, which violates causality. In Figure 4b, causality is violated, as Y is written before it is read. For data dependent read-write accesses (see storage element x) causality always holds. However, if there is no such dependence, causality may be violated. The causality constraint is therefore enforced by the port scheduler.

[4]Simply called pipeline in the following

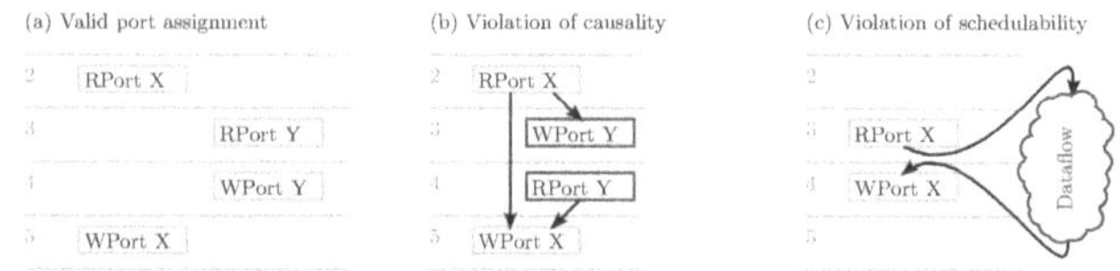

Figure 4: Examples of valid and invalid port schedules.

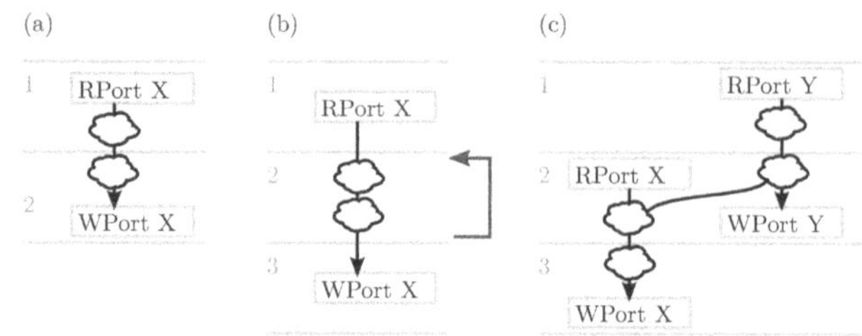

Figure 5: Example of valid port schedules of different quality.

The second constraint regards the schedulability of the entire dataflow graph. The constraint demands that the dataflow graph can be scheduled among pipeline stages, as described in Section 3.5. If data dependent ports are scheduled too tight, as in Figure 4c, the intervening dataflow may not be schedulable without violating timing constraints. The port scheduler therefore considers the target frequency f_{target} and the timing of DFG nodes.

Any port schedule that satisfies the previously mentioned constraints is suited to generate a processor that obeys f_{target}. However, the implementation may be inefficient. In particular, the pipeline of the processor and write latencies may be unnecessarily long. Figure 5 shows two valid port assignments for storage element X. The first assignment (a) requires two pipeline stages, whereas the second (b) uses three stages and requires forwarding (red).

To yield an efficient processor implementation, the port scheduler aims to minimize the write latency and the pipeline length. The write latency is defined as the difference between the write and read stage of a storage element. A low latency reduces data-hazards and simplifies the forwarding circuit. A long latency likely results in many pipeline bypasses. The implemented port scheduler also aims to minimize the pipeline length. Figure 5c outlines a more complex dataflow graph and a port assignment, which minimizes write latencies as well as the pipeline length.

3.4.1 Algorithm

The scheduling of ports can be modeled as a linear integral optimization problem. For each storage element one variable is introduced for the read stage and one for the write stage. For n storage elements this makes $2n$ variables. The scheduling constraints are expressed by inequalities on the variables.

```
foreach x in storages do
  relaxed[x]=false
  rport[x].lastinstage=false
done

do
  scheduleports(wport,rport) /* Section 3.4 */
  stable=true
  foreach x in storages do
    if wport[x].stage-rport[x].stage>1 && !relaxed[x]
      relaxed[x]=true
      rport[x].lastinstage=true
      stable=false
    endif
  done
while (!stable)
```

Figure 6: Pseudocode of bypass-relaxing.

The objective function is given by the distance between read and write stages, which is to be minimized. The solution of this problem corresponds to a valid assignment of stages to each port.

3.4.2 *Bypass-relaxing*

If the distance between read and write stages is larger than one, a forwarding circuit is to be inserted in a later phase (Section 3.7). The bypasses of the forwarding circuit may introduce further critical paths. These critical paths are relaxed at the expense of an additional propagation delay on the datapath. The delay in turn affects the port scheduling and may increase the distance between ports.

The port scheduler therefore iteratively schedules ports and relaxes bypasses, as described by the pseudocode in Figure 6. The number of forwarding circuits thereby rises monotonic. As the number of forwarding circuits is limited by the number of storage elements, the iterative computation is guaranteed to converge. In practice, the generator likely reaches a fixpoint after two iterations. Bypass relaxing has a major effect on the final processor frequency, as shown in Section 4.1.

3.5 Operation scheduling

After ports have been scheduled, the remaining nodes of the DFG are assigned to pipeline stages. The scheduler is similar to the port scheduler. It considers the user supplied target frequency f_{target}, the port schedule, the DFG, and the estimated propagation delay of its nodes.

3.5.1 *Modeling*

The scheduling constraints on DFG nodes can be modeled by a system of equations. The position of a node x is characterized by two values: The *stage* s_x of the node and the *arrival time* a_x within the stage. The arrival time a_x is the estimated signal delay from pipeline registers to x's inputs. The *propagation delay* that is contributed by node x is denoted d_x in the following. It must lie in the range of the *period* p, which is the inverse of the user supplied target frequency.

$$p = f_{\text{target}}^{-1}$$
$$0 \leq d_a \leq p$$

If this property does not hold, the DFG is not schedulable and the generator reports an error. The user then has to reduce the target frequency f_{target}.

The *finish time* at x's outputs is given by the node's arrival time and propagation delay

$$f_x = a_x + d_x.$$

For instance, a node x with a propagation delay of $d_x = 800\,\text{ps}$ (picoseconds) may be scheduled in stage $s_x = 2$ with an arrival time of $a_x = 150\,\text{ps}$, which results in a finish time of $f_x = 950\,\text{ps}$. For read and write nodes, the stage is already fixed by previous port scheduling. These variables can therefore be considered constant.

$$s_x = s_{\text{port}(x)}$$

3.5.2 *Scheduling constraints*

The scheduling constraints are modeled by inequalities on the variables that have previously been introduced. The timing of a node must lie within the user defined period p. Otherwise, the generated processor may not yield the targeted clock frequency.

$$0 \leq a_x \wedge f_x \leq p$$

For two data dependent nodes $x \rightarrow y$, the result of x must be available before it is expected by y. This constraint holds, if x is located in an earlier stage then y. In this case, both nodes are separated by pipeline registers and there is no direct dataflow between both nodes. If instead both nodes are located in the same stage, the finish time of x must be smaller than the arrival time of y.

$$s_x < s_y \vee (s_x = s_y \wedge f_x \leq a_y)$$

Note that this equation implies $s_x \leq s_y$, i.e. the dataflow between x and y must obey the dataflow direction of the pipeline. If s_x would be greater then s_y, data would flow from later stages to earlier stages.

The processor generator solves the system of equations by a two pass algorithm in linear time. For the ARM instruction set, stage numbers are assigned to approximately 2.000 nodes in less then a minute. The arrival and finish times are discarded after scheduling, as they are not needed for any subsequent transformations.

3.6 Pipeline registers

The previous assignment of DFG nodes to stages implies the location of pipeline registers. If two consecutive nodes in the DFG are assigned to different stages, pipeline registers have to be inserted on their connecting edge. For two nodes $x \rightarrow y$ exactly $s_y - s_x$ pipeline registers have to be inserted between x and y.

A pipeline register interrupts the dataflow between nodes. In the dataflow graph, a pipeline register is represented by two associated nodes. A write node in stage s, which receives a value and a read node in stage $s+1$, which yields a value. Figure 7 shows an example for the insertion of two pipeline registers between nodes X and Y. Each pipeline register consists of the pair `PW` and `PR`. These nodes are associated, but not connected in terms of the DFG. After insertion, nodes of different stages are not connected by a path in the DFG. The dataflow graph is thereby divided into at least n connected components, where n is the number of pipeline stages.

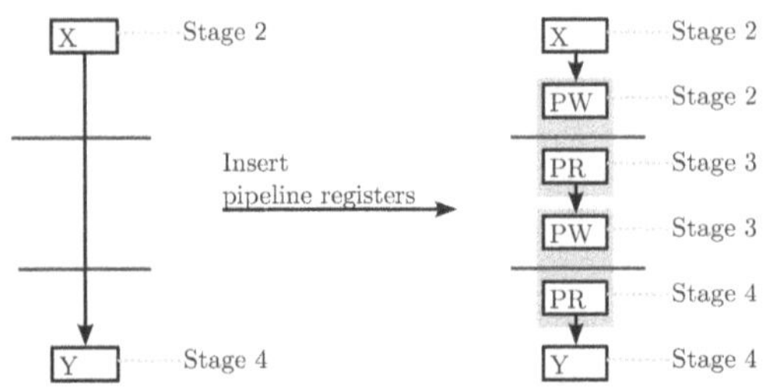

Figure 7: Insertion of pipeline registers.

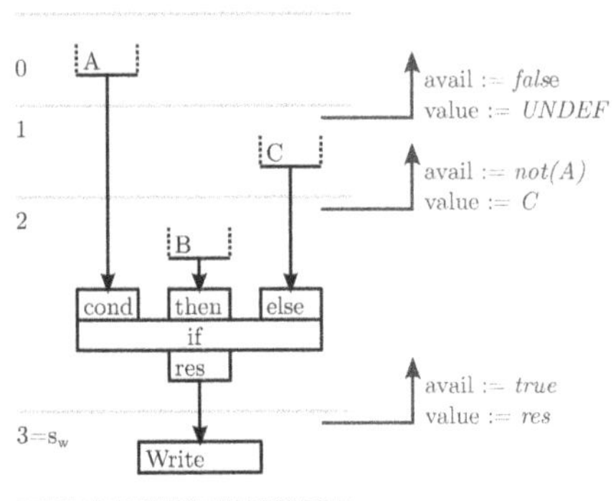

Figure 8: Example of early result forwarding.

3.7 Forwarding circuit

The pipelined DFG that has been constructed so far can be used to generate a pipelined processor implementation. However, the implementation likely includes unresolved data-hazards, which appear as write delays[5]. These hazards must be resolved, to retain execution semantics of instructions. Hazards are primarily resolved by forwarding as described in this section. If forwarding can not be applied, interlocking is used to resolve the hazard (Section 3.8).

To give an impression of the forwarding circuit's construction, a small forwarding example is discussed first. Using this example, the actual construction method is explained.

For a storage element with read stage s_r and write stage s_w, bypasses must be inserted from all stages $s, s_r+1 < s \leq s_w$. Actually, a bypass must be inserted for each stage s, each write port and each read port. The bypasses are then merged by a generated priority multiplexer in stage $s_r + 1$.

What makes forwarding hard, is the fact that the generator has to decide, in which stage a result is fed into the forwarding circuit and under which condition. A result can only be bypassed from a stage s, if it is already available in that stage. Figure 8 shows a highly simplified example of forwarding. The values A, B and C are fed into a condition node (if). Its result is written back in stage $S_w = 3$. The positions of the nodes A, B and C are assumed to be fixed, as shown in the Figure. Due to the position of B, the if-node must be scheduled in stage 2 or later. The final result can therefore only be forwarded from the beginning of stage 3 ("value:=res" in the Figure). The result is always available in this stage, which is expressed by "avail:=true".

In stage 2, the final result is not computed yet. However, if A does not hold, the result is equal to C, which is already available at the beginning of stage 2. The value of the bypass is therefore set to C and the availability to the expression *not(A)*. In stage 1, the result is not known in any case. The availability is therefore set to *false* and the value to *UNDEF*. A bypass from this stage is omitted.

The structure shown in the example is typically produced by the generator's port and hardware sharing transformations. The term A may for instance distinguish between two instructions, which yield the results B and C.

3.7.1 Construction method

The previous example was intended to give a rough impression of the construction task. This section describes the method that is implemented in the generator to systematically construct the forwarding circuit.

In the following, the value that is written-back is regarded as a term t. For the example this is

$$t = \text{if}(A, B, C)$$

The algorithm derives the "*value*" and the "*defined*" expression for each stage s separately. Therefore, the write back node is conceptually moved to stage s. This typically leads to a violation of scheduling constraints.

The violation is resolved by a so called *thin-out* phase. This phase removes all subterms from t that contribute to the violation. For the example and stage $s = 2$, node B is removed, which results in the term

$$t_{\text{thin}} = \text{if}(A, \text{UNDEF}, C)$$

The term t_{thin} thereby becomes partially defined. If A holds, the result of the term is undefined.

A subsequent *is-defined analysis* determines when the term is defined. For the example, the analysis yields the expression

$$t_{\text{def}} = not(A)$$

If this expression holds, the term t_{thin} is defined, otherwise it is not. The expression t_{def} is used to control interlocking, as described in the next section.

In a third *reduction* phase, the term t_{thin} is simplified, yielding a term t_{red}. Basically, all parts of the term that contribute only to an undefined result are removed. This likely enables the simplification of other operations in the term. In the example, the "if" operation is eliminated, as only one alternative yields a defined value. This also eliminates the subterm A, which evaluates the condition. The resulting simplified term is

$$t_{\text{red}} = C$$

This simplified term $t_{\text{simp}} = C$ is finally fed into the forwarding circuit, as shown in stage 2 of Figure 8. Timing constraints of the forwarding circuit are obeyed due to the previous thin-out phase. If t_{def} holds, the forwarded value t_{simp} is equal to the value t that is finally written back to the register. If t_{def} does not hold, the undefined forwarded value is not used due to interlocking. Interlocking is discussed in the next section.

This section gave only a very simple example to demonstrate the construction of forwarding. In practice, the generator processes terms that consist of hundreds of nodes, including nested conditions, arithmetic operations and switch statements. Figure 9 gives an impression of such a term. It has been exported by the processor generator during generation of a 6 stage MIPS processor. The term represents the

[5]by means of delay slots from a programmers perspective.

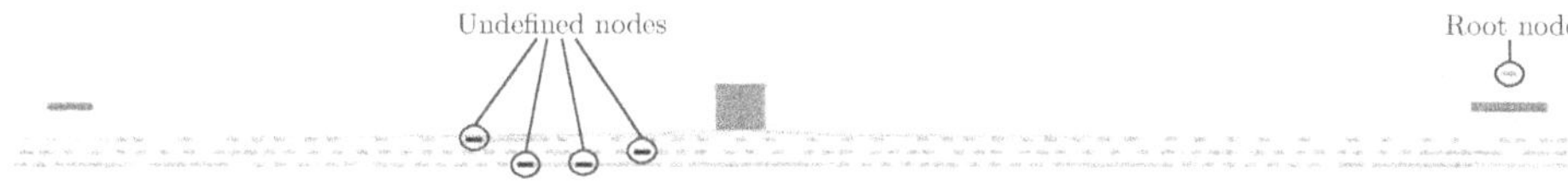

Figure 9: Expression tree of a partially defined result term as used to derive the forwarding of a 6-stage MIPS processor.

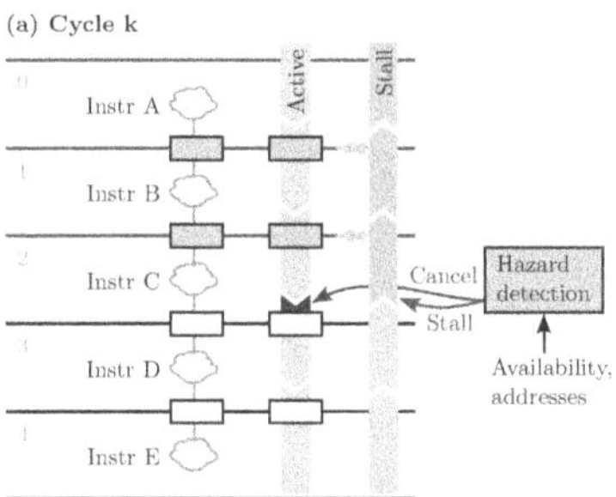

Figure 10: Scheme of constructed interlocking.

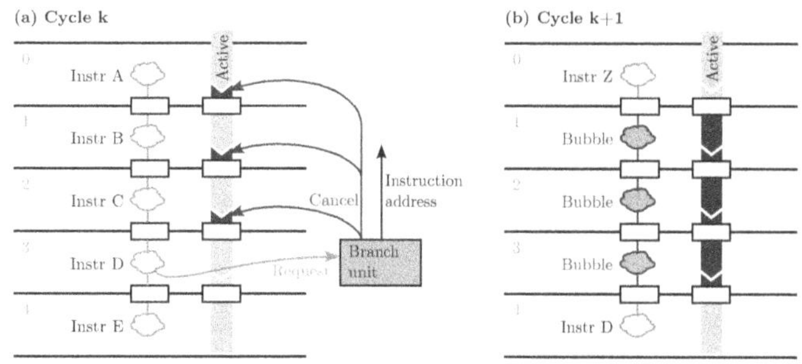

Figure 11: Example of a branch and its processing by the branch unit.

partial result t_{thin} of the GPR registers at the end of the execute stage (EX). The black nodes are undefined, as they would lead to a violation of scheduling constraints. One of these nodes is for instance a read access on data memory, which is scheduled in a later stage (MA).

3.8 Interlocking

The previous section explained how availability information is computed. This information is now used to control the pipeline, as shown in Figure 10a. The availability information from all stages is fed into a hazard detection circuit, along with the addresses of forwarded values. If a forwarded value is accessed, but not yet available, this circuit stalls one part of the pipeline and inserts a bubble. Therefore, the processor generator creates two signal paths called "active" and "stall", which range through all stages. The *stall* path propagates stall information upwards, i.e. from stages i to stages $j, j < i$. Note, that this path is not interrupted by any pipeline registers. In case of a data hazard, the detection circuit triggers a stall. In the example, the stall is triggered in stage 2, which is then propagated to stage 1 and 0. The stall path disables the pipeline registers between stages 0/1 and 1/2 (drawn red in the Figure). Thereby, instructions B and C remain in stages 1 and 2. In addition, the instruction fetch logic (IF) is controlled such, that instruction A remains in stage 0.

To insert a bubble in stage 3, the *active-path* is used. The hazard detection circuit triggers an instruction cancel at the end of stage 2. Note, that this does not affect any instruction, until the next clock cycle. On the next clock edge, the cancelation is passed to stage 3, as shown in Figure 10b. This stage is thereby deactivated in stage $k + 1$, i.e. it is regarded to contain a bubble.

Actually, the explanations given in this section are simplified. The construction method that is implemented in the processor generator considers additional aspects of a pipeline of arbitrary length. For instance, hazard detection also considers write enable signals and has to prioritize availability information according to originating stages. A stall signal need not only disable pipeline registers, but also has to disable registered memories. To optimize the generated processor, the active- and stall-paths are only generated in part. The active-path likely starts in the execute stage. Logic to interconnect hazard detection is omitted in most stages. This depends on the specified instruction set and the generated microarchitecture. Besides, the hazard detection circuit is simplified, by eliminating address comparisons for single registers and static addressing.

3.9 Branch prediction

The processor generator constructs a branch unit based on the specified instruction set and the derived pipeline structure. Its complexity basically depends on the number of branch instructions that have different timings. Currently, the generated branch unit implements a very simple "not-taken" prediction scheme. However, the generation method can be extended to yield other branch predictors.

The branch unit basically has two tasks: To supply the (predicted) *next instruction address* and second, to *cancel* speculatively executed instructions in case of misprediction. For the "not-taken" scheme, the branch unit predicts the next instruction address to be the successor of the current address.

To change the control flow, the branch unit receives branch requests from branch instructions. Branch requests may typically be issued from different pipeline stages, depending on the kind of branch instruction. Figure 11a shows the effects of a branch instruction (Instr D). The branch instruction issues a branch request from stage 3, which is processed by the branch unit. As the prediction scheme is "not-taken", the branch unit cancels instructions A to C, which have been executed speculatively. The cancelation takes effect from cycle $k + 1$ on, as shown in Figure 11b.

A branch request consists of two values, the branch's *target* address and a *taken* flag, which triggers the request. Using such pairs of signals, several stages are connected to the branch unit. Each stage that is connected may trigger a branch. Based on the instruction set and timing of the technology, the generator determines, which stages are to be connected. For instance, an "unconditional relative" branch may be issued from stage 1, a "register" branch from stage 2

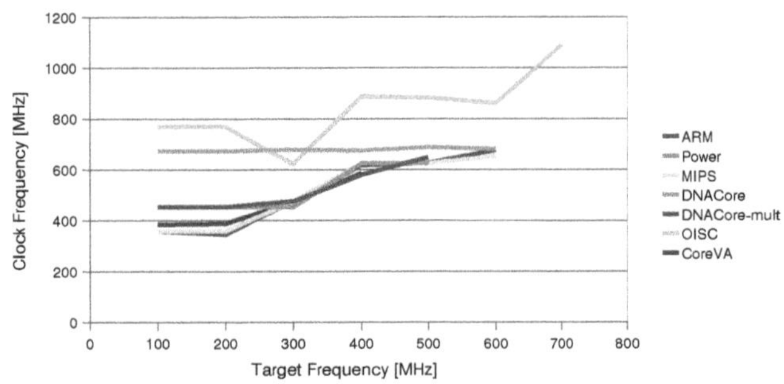

Figure 12: Relation between targeted frequency and achieved clock frequency of synthesized processors.

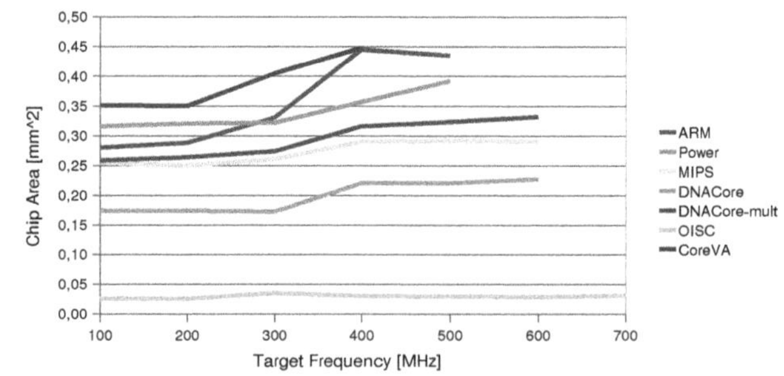

Figure 13: Effect of target frequency on chip area.

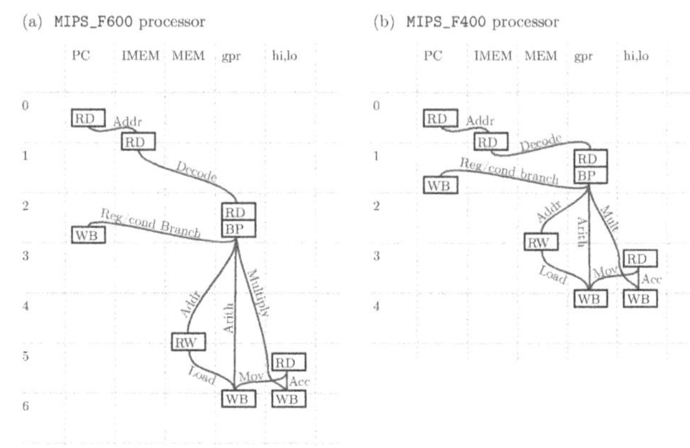

Figure 14: Structure of generated MIPS pipelines for a target frequency of (a) 600 MHz and (b) 400 MHz.

and a "register+offset" branch from stage 3. The generator therefore connects stages 1 to 3 to the branch unit. The branch unit then prioritizes requests with respect to their originating stage. The construction of the *target* and *taken* signal uses methods from forwarding and interlocking construction.

Since the branch unit may cancel instructions, additional constraints must be considered by the generator. In general, a branch request from stage i may cancel instructions in stages 0 through $i - 1$. The instructions in these stages must therefore be cancelable. An instruction is cancelable in a specific stage, if all its effects on the processor state can be eliminated. That is the case, if the instruction has not committed any changes by register write-back. As a result, write-back stages must not precede the latest stage that may trigger a branch. The generator considers this constraint already during port scheduling.

4. EVALUATION

The impact of the target frequency on clock frequency and chip area of the generated processors is presented in the following. Therefore, at least 5 processors have been generated for each instruction set. All processors of one instruction set have automatically been generated from the very same ViDL specification. Only the target frequency parameter has been varied.

As Figure 12 shows, the target frequency that is passed to the processor generator successfully guides generation. With an increasing target frequency, the generator reduces the critical path by deepening the pipeline and by deferring forwarding. This in turn leads to a higher feasible *clock frequency*, of the synthesized processor. The gain between 200 MHz and 500 MHz is mainly caused by successive pipelining of the multiplier. The clock frequency of DNA-Core processors is nearly constant, as its instruction set does not include multiplication instructions.

As you can see in the Figure, the maximal clock frequency of the synthesized processor lies approximately 100 MHz over the user supplied target frequency. This gap is caused by conservative timing estimates in the technology database. Tighter estimates should lead to a more precise relation.

Increasing the target frequency also leads to an increase in chip area, as shown in Figure 13. A major rise in power consumption can be seen between 300 MHz and 400 MHz. This can be attributed to additional resources for pipelining and forwarding.

Generated processors have also been compared to a handcrafted and optimized implementation in terms of VHDL code. The CoreVA instruction set has been used for this comparison, as implementations for the other instruction sets are not publicly available. The CoreVA VHDL code has been written and optimized independently by an experienced circuit engineer in the context of another project. The clock frequencies of generated processors lie in the order of the handcrafted implementation. The 4-stage processor `CoreVA_F100/nRx` (target frequency 100 MHz; no bypass-relaxing) is 18% slower, whereas the generated 7-stage processor `CoreVA_F400` is 37% faster compared to the handcrafted implementation. This speed advantage can be accounted to the longer pipeline and a less agressive hardware sharing. Considering the same pipeline depth, the `CoreVA_F300` processor is faster, but requires approximately 3 times as much power and area. Power consumption and area requirement are comparably high, but are expected to be reduced in future by more aggressive hardware sharing methods.

4.1 Structure of generated pipelines

This section presents a structural analysis of several generated MIPS pipelines. The MIPS instruction set has some nice peculiarities, such as a dedicated register for multiply-accumulate instructions.

The diagram in Figure 14a shows the location of ports and intervening dataflow of a MIPS pipeline that has been generated for a target frequency of 600 MHz. Each row in the figure corresponds to one pipeline stage, which are numbered from 0 through 6. Each column is associated with

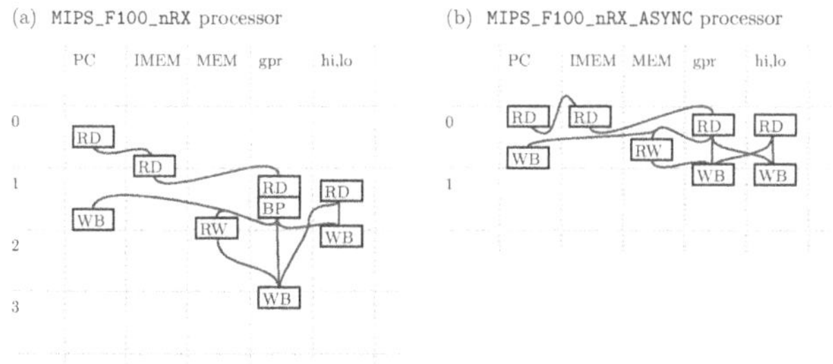

Figure 15: Structure of generated MIPS pipelines of minimal length for (a) synchronous and (b) asynchronous memory.

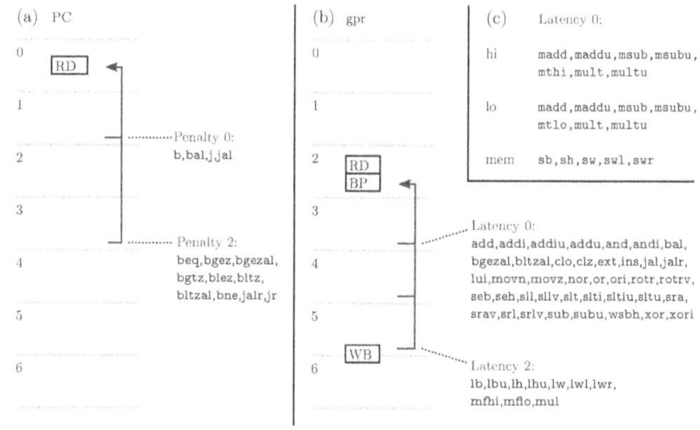

Figure 16: (a) Branch penalties and (b,c) instruction latencies for the generated MIPS_F600 processor.

one storage element. The storages hi and lo use a common column, to simplify visualization. The red lines represent significant dataflow that constraints port scheduling. The general purpose registers (gpr) are for instance read (RD) in stage 2 and written back (WB) in stage 6. The bypasses of the forwarding circuit are joined (BP) in stage 2. For the other storage elements, forwarding is automatically omitted, as the distance between read and write stage is 1. Note, that the program counter (PC) is regarded as register for the task of scheduling.

Multiplications read their source operands from the gpr register file in stage 2. Due to the latency of a pipelined 3-stage multiplier, the result is written back to hi/lo registers in stage 6. Multiply-accumulate instructions also read these registers for accumulation. The "move from high/low" instructions (mfhi/mflo) transfer values to the general purpose register file, which is written in stage 6.

For a target frequency of 400 MHz (Figure 14b), the generator derives the same pipeline structure, that is proposed by Hennessy and Patterson, namely IF,DC/RD,EX,MA,WB [10]. Both architectures apply forwarding only on general purpose registers and have a load latency of one cycle, which is interlocked. Compared to the structure in 14a, the multiplier uses only two stages and ports are scheduled such, that decode and read are combined in one stage. As a result, the pipeline length is reduced by two stages.

For a target frequency of 100 MHz and deactivated bypass relaxing, the 4-stage pipeline in Figure 15a is generated. All instructions in that pipeline have zero latency, i.e. the pipeline is never stalled. The interlocking circuit is therefore omitted by the generator. A major disadvantage of this simple pipeline is a longer critical path, which leads through the non-relaxed bypass. Synthesis shows, that the 4-stage pipeline yields a frequency of only 260 MHz, whereas the relaxed 5-stage pipeline exceeds 350 MHz. The length of 4 stages is minimal for a processor with synchronous (registered) data- and instruction-memory.

Defining the memories to be asynchronous, the generator produces a non-pipelined processor. Technically, this is achieved by setting the memory's latency in the technology database from 1 to 0. This change is a matter of seconds and does not require any modifications in the generator. The resulting pipeline is shown in Figure 15b. It consists of two stages and does neither include interlocking, nor forwarding. In general, a two-stage pipeline is equivalent to a *non-pipelined* implementation.

4.2 Latencies and penalties

Figure 16 shows the latencies and penalties of a MIPS_F600 processor. Although, this processor has a quite long 7-stage pipeline, most instructions have zero-latency, i.e. can be executed consecutively without causing any pipeline stalls. Write accesses to hi, lo and mem always have a latency of zero (Figure 16c), due to the location of read and write stages. Data-hazards on the general purpose register file are mostly resolved by forwarding (blue arrow). Only the load instructions and the "move from hi/lo" instructions (mfhi, mflo) have non-zero latencies. The latency of the latter can be attributed to the pipelined multiplication. Effectively, the latency of multiplication instructions is transferred to mfhi and mflo via the hi/lo registers. As a result, data-dependent multiply-accumulate instructions can be issued in every cycle (e.g. in the context of signal processing applications), without causing any stalls. The latency of load instructions results from the synchronous data memory and address computations. Summing up, most data-hazards are resolved by forwarding. Only few "critical" instructions involve interlocking and have a non-zero latency. The majority of instructions has zero-latency and can tightly be scheduled without causing any stalls during execution.

The penalty for mispredicted branches depends on the semantics of branch instructions. Relative branches that are executed unconditionally have a penalty of zero. Executing such instructions does not involve any speculative execution and instruction-canceling. Misprediction of other branches (register branches and conditional branches) causes a penalty of 2 cycles. These branches rely on results that are computed in stage 3. The instructions in stage 1 and 2 are therefore executed speculatively and may be canceled, which implies a penalty of 2.

Correctness of hazard resolution has been tested by simulating generated processors on register-transfer-level and gate-level in ModelSim. Artificial test programs with extensive hazards have successfully been executed on all generated processors. Waveforms of these simulations are shown in [3].

5. CONCLUSION

This paper has presented methods to generate efficient processors from specifications of instruction sets and only from those specifications. All microarchitectural aspects of processors are automatically derived from instruction semantics, without exception. This principle sets the presented approach apart from related work. A developer can focus on the instruction set, which is rapidly and concisely specified in ViDL. Abstraction from microarchitecture, an irredundant language design, and static type-checking significantly increase reliability, as well as maintainability. Since many tasks of processor development have been shifted to the generator, inexperienced students from computer science and electrical engineering were able to develop Power and CoreVA processors in only 2–3 months.

Very different processors with well balanced physical and dynamic characteristics are generated from the very same instruction set specification, guided by a user supplied target frequency only. Processor implementations range from non-pipeline processors, via stall and penalty free implementations to 7 stage pipelines, which solve hazards by forwarding, interlocking and canceling. Thanks to automated hazard resolution, all generated processors are guaranteed to be consistent to the instruction set specification. There is no way, a ViDL developer can break this consistency, neither by accident, nor by intention. The need to test equivalence of different implementations is thereby eliminated.

The methods for pipeline-construction have proven to be effective for real instruction sets, such as ARM, MIPS, Power, and CoreVA. The clock frequency of generated processors lies in the order of handcrafted VHDL code. Power consumption and area requirements are approximately 3 times higher, but first examinations have revealed a high potential for hardware sharing methods in the generator. The average CPI of generated processors is close to one, i.e. in the order of manually designed processors. A generated processor does therefore actually utilize its high clock frequency, to yield a high throughput of instructions.

6. REFERENCES

[1] ARM Limited. *ARM Architecture Reference Manual*, ARM DDI 0100E edition, 2000.

[2] S. Basu and R. Moona. High level synthesis from Sim-nML processor models. In *VLSI Design, 2003. Proceedings. 16th International Conference on*, pages 255 – 260, Jan. 2003.

[3] R. Dreesen. *Generating Processors from Specifications of Instruction Sets*. PhD thesis, University of Paderborn, Germany, 2011.

[4] R. Dreesen. ViDL specification of the Simple RISC (SRC) instruction set. `http://www.vidl.de`, 2011.

[5] R. Dreesen. ViDL: A versatile ISA description language. In *19th Annual IEEE International Conference and Workshops on the Engineering of Computer Based Systems (ECBS-19)*, Apr. 2012. (accepted for publication).

[6] R. Dreesen, M. Thies, and U. Kastens. Type analysis on bitstring expressions. In *Proceedings of the 9th Workshop on Optimizations for DSP and Embedded Systems (ODES-9)*, Apr. 2011.

[7] J. D. Franz. An evaluation of CoWare Inc.'s processor designer tool suite for the design of embedded processors. Master's thesis, Department of Electrical and Computer Engineering, Baylor University, 2008.

[8] R. Gonzalez. Xtensa: a configurable and extensible processor. *Micro, IEEE*, 20(2):60 –70, mar/apr 2000.

[9] A. Halambi, P. Grun, V. Ganesh, and A. Khare. Expression: A language for architecture exploration through compiler/simulator retargetability. In *In Proceedings of the European Conference on Design, Automation and Test*, pages 485–490, 1999.

[10] J. Hennessy and D. Patterson. *Computer Architecture - A Quantitative Approach*. Morgan Kaufmann, 2006.

[11] V. P. Heuring and H. F. Jordan. *Computer Systems Design and Architecture (2nd Edition)*. Prentice-Hall, Inc., Upper Saddle River, NJ, USA, 2003.

[12] IBM. *Power ISA*, Version 2.04 edition, April 2007.

[13] C. Inc. *LISA Language Reference Manual*, 2008.

[14] M. T. Inc. *MIPS Architecture For Programmers Volume II-A: The MIPS32 Instruction Set*, 2010.

[15] M. Itoh, S. Higaki, J. Sato, A. Shiomi, Y. Takeuchi, A. Kitajima, and M. Imai. PEAS-III: an ASIP design environment. In *Computer Design, 2000. Proceedings. 2000 International Conference on*, pages 430 –436, 2000.

[16] S. Leibson. *Designing SOCs with Configured Cores*. Morgan Kaufmann, 2006.

[17] J. V. Praet, D. Lanneer, W. Geurts, and G. Goossens. nML: A structural processor modeling language for retargetable compilation and ASIP design. In P. Mishra and N. Dutt, editors, *Processor Description Languages*, pages 65–93. Morgan Kaufmann, 2008.

[18] I. Tensilica. *Tensilica Instruction Extension (TIE) Language*, 2006.

[19] A. Wang, E. Killian, D. Maydan, and C. Rowen. Hardware/software instruction set configurability for system-on-chip processors. In *Proceedings of the 38th annual Design Automation Conference*, DAC '01, pages 184–188, New York, NY, USA, 2001. ACM.

[20] D. A. Watt. *Programming Language Design Concepts*. John Wiley & Sons, 2004.

Designing Parameterized Signal Processing IPs for High Level Synthesis in a Model Based Design Environment

Shahzad Ahmad Butt
Electronics and Telecommunication Department
Politecnico di Torino Italy
Corso Duca Degli Abruzzi, 24
Shahzad.Butt@polito.it

Luciano Lavagno
Electronics and Telecommunication Department
Politecnico di Torino
Corso Duca Degli Abruzzi, 24
Luciano.Lavagno@polito.it

ABSTRACT
Model based hardware/software synthesis can lead to fast and efficient embedded system implementations, by enabling quick design space exploration. High level hardware modeling and implementation can be accelerated by using functionally verified parameterized models that are optimized for high level hardware synthesis. Such models can be designed so that they can be easily integrated with a high level modeling environment, such as Simulink, and at the same time provide ample flexibility to perform design space exploration when mapped to hardware.

During signal processing hardware design, the focus is mostly on the architectural representation (data parallelism, pipelining, memory access, etc.) to meet throughput requirement and on data path modeling to analyze the effects of quantization. In this paper we present our experience of modeling an FFT block that can be integrated with the Simulink model based design environment for simulation and verification, and later can be used to perform architectural design space exploration and hardware implementation with optimal data path selection. A key advantage of our model is that the very same bit-accurate C code is used for simulation and for high-level synthesis, because it has been written with both aspects in mind (while for software implementation either our code or the code provided by the Mathworks can be used equally well). To prove the feasibility of our proposed approach we synthesized our FFT for two DSP applications with very different performance and cost requirements, namely a frequency domain audio detector and a GPS acquisition algorithm, and compared it with existing manual implementations

Categories and Subject Descriptors
B.5.2 [Register-Transfer-Level Implementation]: Design Aids – *automatic synthesis, hardware description languages, simulation, verification, optimization*

B5.1 [Register-Transfer-Level Implementation]: Design – *data-path design*

General Terms
Algorithms, Design, Verification.

Keywords
Model-based design, Model-based high level synthesis, Synthesis from Simulink models, Parameterized IPs, Design reuse, Audio detector, GPS acquisition, C/C++ Hardware IP description, FFT.

1. INTRODUCTION
Model-based design environments, such as Simulink, are becoming more widespread as they expand their capabilities of synthesizing efficient hardware and software from abstract models. One of the major concerns of model-based design is to let the algorithm designer work mostly at an abstract level without caring about the low level implementation details. This is because the area, performance and power optimizations that can be achieved at this level outweigh by far anything that can be obtained at the micro-architectural level and below, and also result in improved productivity and faster time to market. The latter gains are achieved mostly by reusing already modeled and verified macro blocks, and by easing the verification task by allowing to use a single golden reference model throughout the design flow. However, implementation efficiency must not be forgotten if one wants to use model-based design in practice.

Commercially available model-based design tools allow automatic generation of software and hardware from a single model. The automatically generated software can be optimized by using knowledge of the target processor architecture and its memory hierarchy. But when it comes to model-based hardware design and implementation (which essentially entails the generation of a cycle accurate RTL model from very abstract block level models that have no of notion clock cycles), manual re-implementation is still often required. *This paper attempts to avoid this expensive step, by using a model-based design paradigm in which the code used to simulate a block in Simulink is optimized for HW synthesis (and good for SW synthesis as well), as opposed to being tuned only for SW synthesis..*

Simulink provides a rich set of modeling components which range from simple blocks like addition and subtraction, to complex macro blocks like frequency domain transforms, digital filters, etc. The computationally complex blocks are normally represented in Simulink as S-functions, whose body is written in C or Matlab. S-functions can be easily integrated in the Simulink environment because they implement the core functionality of the block plus a wrapper around it to satisfy the semantics of the simulation environment. Real Time Workshop (RTW) is a MathWorks tool that translates a Simulink model composed of S-functions and simple blocks to C code, meant for use on micro-controllers and DSPs. The MathWorks also provides a tool, called HDL coder, which can translate Simulink models to RTL for hardware implementation. However, it cannot handle all blocks, and even the latest version, which can perform a limited amount of micro-architectural design exploration (e.g. by changing the latency and pipelining level of a model), does so by *modifying the source model, which partially defies the purpose of model-based design.* Recent work [3][9] has shown that Simulink models can be used for efficient hardware/software synthesis, design space exploration and rapid prototyping when they are used as input for high level hardware synthesis tools. Most of these tools take as input a functional specification written in some variant of C/C++/SystemC. The interface between the Simulink model and high level synthesis was thus obtained in that work by using the automatic C code generation capability provided by RTW.

From our experience we observed that the C code generated by RTW can be used efficiently for hardware synthesis if it involves mostly simple blocks. But when it comes to using complex macro block like Fast Fourier Transform (FFT), Discrete Cosine Transform (DCT), etc. then the software-oriented C code that is generated limits the hardware design space that can be explored. This is because the SW-oriented C code used to model such blocks has a signal flow representation that inherently limits, as we will argue below, the kind of micro-architectures that can be explored. *In this paper we propose the modeling of such complex macro-blocks still using plain C, which is essential for smooth integration with Simulink verification and SW generation, but using a code structure that lends itself to better HW design space exploration as a parameterized high-level Intellectual property (IP) block.* Figure-1 illustrates in detail the integration of FFT IP in Simulink model-based design flow for high level hardware synthesis.

2. RELATED WORK

Simulink models have been used for hardware synthesis and hardware/software co-design in the past. For example, [2] presents a Simulink image processing blockset for hardware/software codesign, using Xilinx System Generator at the backend for hardware generation. In [1] an ESL design tool is presented that can do automatic design space exploration starting from behavioral SystemC models. [1] presents a design flow for mapping a Simulink model to a full Multi-Processor System-on-Chip. The design flow allows processor and task design space exploration at various abstraction levels, but does not provide any support for mapping part of the model to dedicated hardware.

In [3] the authors discuss how to configure RTW for generating C code from Simulink models and also to how to wrap the automatically generated code into a SystemC wrapper that can be used for hardware implementation. They focus on how to tune RTW for generating code that is suited for high level synthesis and on how to obtain different points in the design space without requiring a deep understanding of the automatically generated SystemC code. On the other hand, [4] discusses the design of a register based FFT IP that can be parameterized and used for high level synthesis. The authors focused on representing the design using advanced C++ templates and some specific data type libraries that can be used to describe bit accurate hardware. However, these models cannot be used in Simulink, which cannot use templatized C++ and would have difficulties incorporating external libraries within S functions On the other hand, our parameterized IP blocks are modeled in plain C, to be compatible with Simulink S-function modeling. In [10] authors compare SW

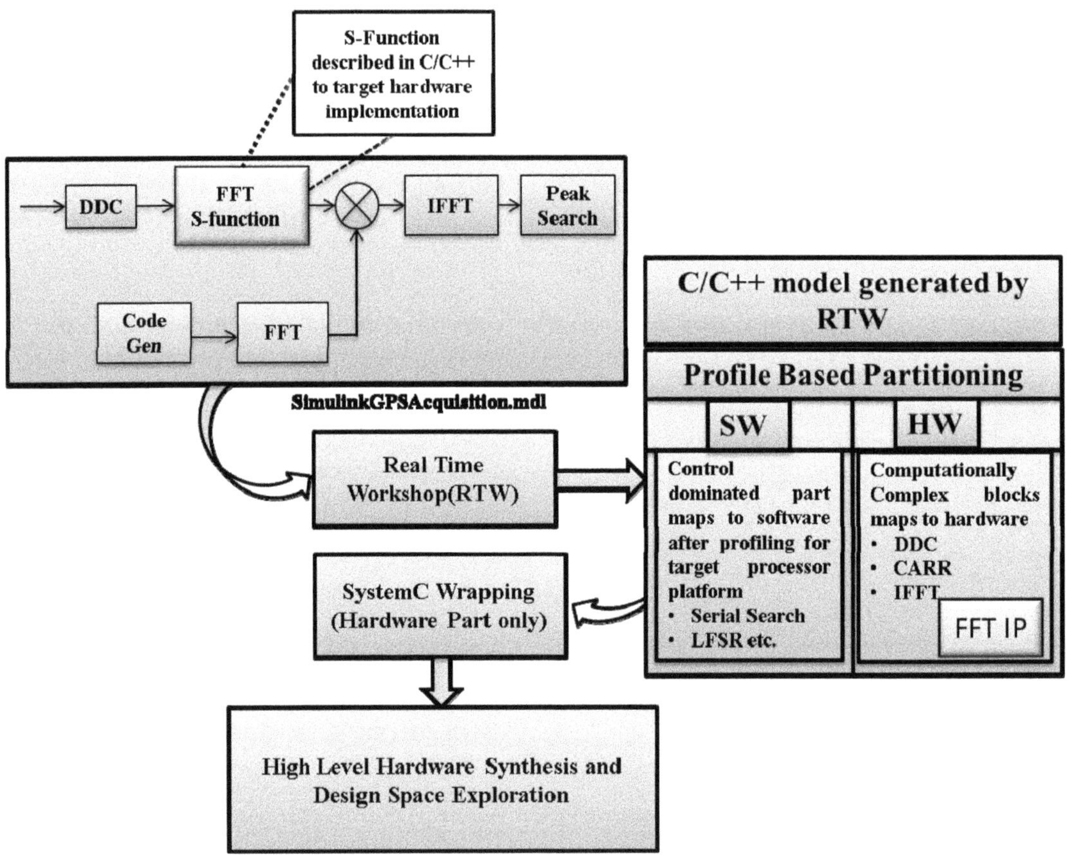

Figure 1. Complete Model-based design flow enhanced by FFT S-function IP.

and a HW implementation of several applications (2-body JPEG and AES), identifying from where hardware actually extracts parallelism and execution speed. We exploit this when creating the IP block. [11] defines a modeling style that allows for efficient HW/SW tradeoffs. We use Simulink as a well-known industrial implementation of a similar modeling style, based on a dataflow paradigm. [12] presents a tool named Compaan that automatically transforms a nested loop program written as Matlab Script or C code into a process network specification. It can extract parallelism from Matlab and C code, but requires code rewriting to fit the Compaan modeling style (affine array indices within nested loops without control) while in our case we exploit designer-provided top-level parallelism among Simulink blocks.

Simulink HDL Coder [5] generates synthesizable RTL code from Simulink models. However, the generated RTL code has a close 1-to-1 correspondence with the Simulink model, hence different micro-architectures in hardware require very different Simulink models, thus defeating the separation between functionality and architecture that is essential for true model-based design. Moreover, most architectural trade-offs like resource sharing, pipelining and exposing more parallelism are tedious to model in Simulink. System Generator for DSP [6] is another model-based hardware design tool that can generate synthesizable RTL for Xilinx FPGAs from Simulink models. It adds to Simulink specialized block sets, i.e. libraries of components that are used for RTL modeling, thus resulting in a flow that is very similar to HDL Coder. Due to strict 1-to-1 mapping between Simulink model and the final RTL representation, it is difficult to represent macro blocks like FFTs as parameterizable IPs that can be mapped to different hardware architecture depending on the application requirements. Altera also offers a tool named DSP Builder [13] that has more or less same capabilities and limitations as Xilinx System Generator.

3. Our IP Modeling strategy

Modeling IP in plain C that still enables HW design space exploration through high level synthesis can be challenging. Even though high level synthesis can vary several micro-architectural parameters such as architectural parallelism, loop pipelining, resource sharing and so on, several of these options are available only when the appropriate modeling style is used in C. For example in DSP applications the datapath width is decided based on the results of several bit-accurate simulations (e.g. using the fixed point optimization capabilities of Simulink). However, representing bit-accurate types in plain C can be tricky. Moreover, DSP applications derive most of their performance from both architectural level and fine-grained parallelism and pipelining.

We developed a modeling strategy based on a representation which can be easily used to explore different micro-architectures. It also accurately models different datapath bit widths and arithmetic overflow/saturation modes in a single C model, which is both compatible with the S-function modeling style and amenable to efficient HW synthesis. This strategy is illustrated in this paper for the sake of explanation with an FFT block, but is applicable to a much more general class of complex Simulink blocks.

3.1 FFT Signal Flow Graph Representations

The Fast Fourier Transform (FFT) is widely used to calculate a Discrete Fourier Transform and its inverse efficiently. The FFT exploits the symmetry of the calculation and the re-use of already performed calculations to reduce the implementation complexity. FFT calculations have many signal flow graph representations which can prove beneficial for targeting different application domains with different performance requirements under different constraints.

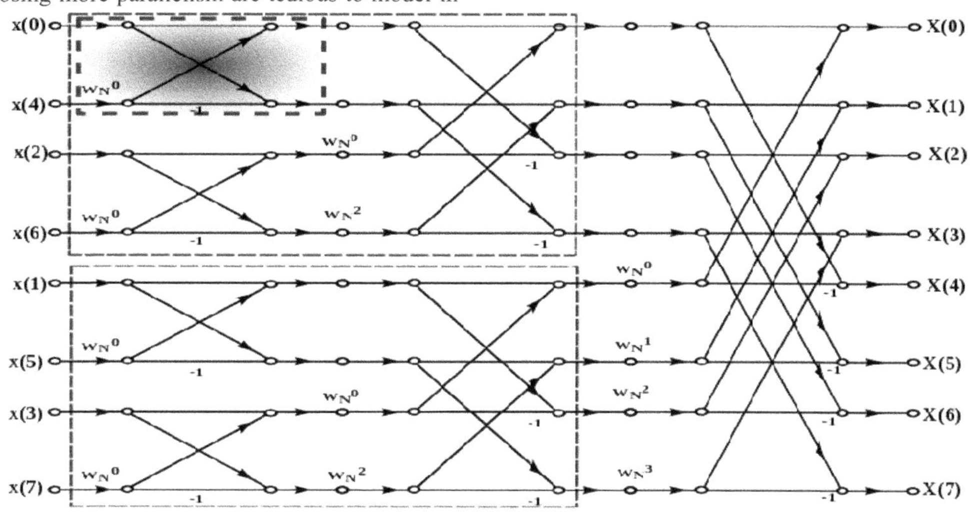

Figure 2. Signal flow graph for radix-2, 8-point in place FFT computations

Figure-2 shows the signal flow graph (SFG) for computing an FFT with 8 samples. The SFG represents the fully unrolled computations and data dependencies (and thus the full available parallelism) implied by the C code structure used by RTW for a software-oriented FFT implementation. In this SFG each node represents a complex operator and each arc represents a complex value. It is called radix-2 FFT since its basic unit, called butterfly and marked by the dotted box at the top left of the figure, consumes two input samples to produce two output samples. Constants marked as W_N^0, W_N^1...W_N3 are complex exponentials which are known as twiddle factors. Inputs x(0),x(1),...x(7) are the complex time domain samples of the signal to be transformed and outputs X(0),X(1),...X(7) are the complex values of the frequency spectrum of the signal. Each butterfly represents the multiplication of twiddle factors with input samples and then one addition and subtraction to calculate outputs.

The signal flow graph in Figure-2 is called in-place FFT because every butterfly can write outputs to the same memory from where it has read the inputs. Such a representation is useful for implementing a resource shared FFT with relatively low throughout requirements targeting low power applications and with limited on chip memory size and bandwidth. But *this kind of signal flow graph is not well suited when throughput requirements are high and either a pipelined implementation or a fully unrolled register based* (rather than memory-based) *implementation is required.* For example, let us assume that in order to increase throughput we unroll the inner loop that performs butterflies in a stage (a column of Figure-2), and that stage inputs are mapped to registers. After performing a butterfly computation, the inputs for the next butterflies mapped to the same multiplier/adder/subtractor resources will come from signal flow graph positions that are different from the first stage, which in hardware will imply high multiplexing cost and hence will not be efficient. Similarly, some tools and memory architectures may not efficiently support pipelining of loops in which computations read and write from the same memory, due to the need to use multi-ported memories. This, on the other hand, would be easy in software, for which the graph in Figure-2 works best.

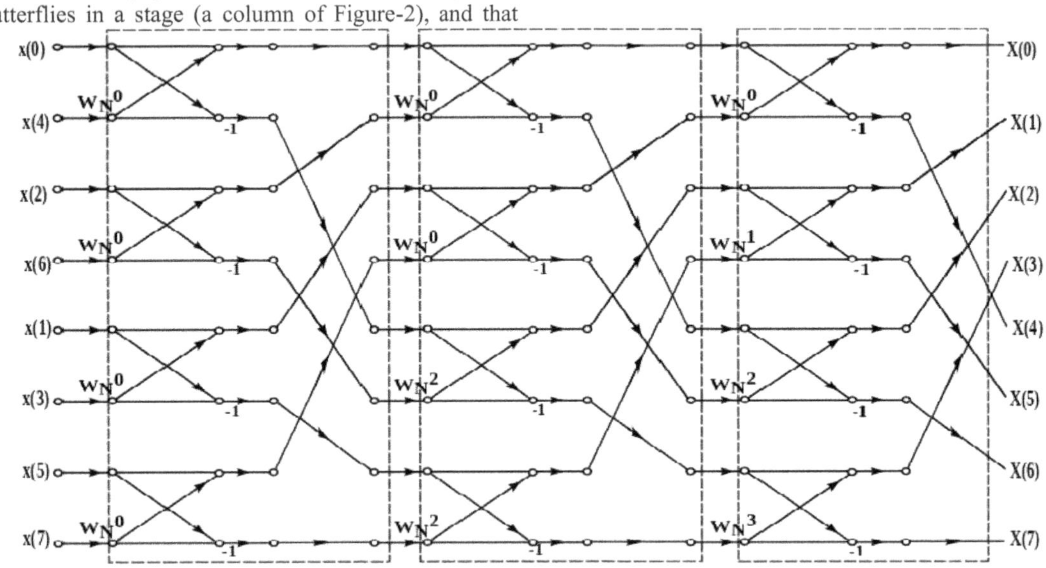

Figure 3. The Signal flow graph for radix-2, 8-point FFT computations

Figure-3 shows another signal flow graph for FFT, which also can be represented in C in the form of nested loops, but is much more flexible than the one in Figure-2 to derive many possible implementations using high level synthesis. In particular, it can be mapped to a register-based unrolled implementation.

The advantage of such an FFT representation with respect to Figure-2 is that the interconnection network between the stages is the same for all the stages, which results in less multiplexing cost when a stage is partially or fully unrolled and subsequent stages are implemented by iteration. Even when a memory-based implementation with more aggressive resource sharing and lower throughput is required, still the signal flow graph in Figure-3 is more flexible because one can always map inputs and outputs of a butterfly to two different memories, while still allowing partial unrolling depending on the memory read/write bandwidth. The signal flow graph in Figure-3 can even be mapped to a single on-chip memory implementation by utilizing the memory merging capability offered by high level synthesis tools, which allows one to map two different memories of different length and width (arrays in C) to a single aggregate memory. In our FFT IP we used the SFG in Figure-3 because it can offer broader design space exploration as compared to Figure-2, which corresponds to the default software implementation from Simulink RTW.

3.2 FFT Butterfly Operations

A more detailed representation of the signal flow graph of a radix-2 butterfly is shown in Figure-4, where values and operators are on real, rather than complex, numbers.

Here X_0^r, X_0^i and X_1^r, X_1^i represent inputs, Y_0^r, Y_0^i and Y_1^r, Y_1^i represent outputs and W_N^r, W_N^i represent twiddle factors. Superscript 'i' and 'r' identify the real and imaginary parts respectively. For hardware implementation this local signal flow graph must be represented as a fixed point datapath with precise

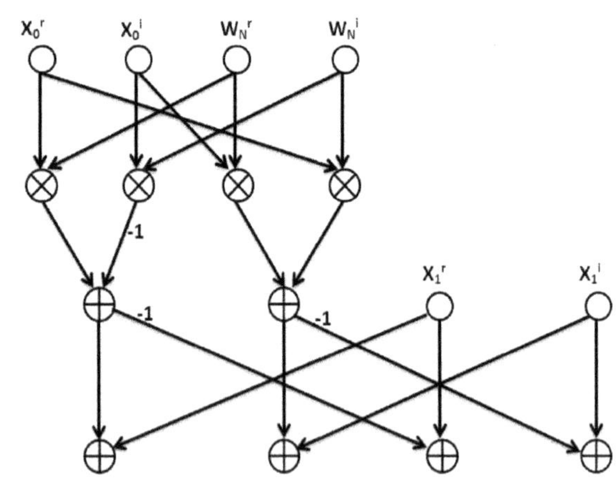

Figure 4. Radix-2 butterfly signal flow graph

bit widths. Based on our design flow requirements, the same representation must be usable for high level synthesis and for simulation in Simulink. In the next section we discuss how we modeled fixed point operators with different arithmetic modes to satisfy all these requirements.

3.3 Modeling Arithmetic Operators for HLS

Fixed point operators take two inputs and produce an output, each with a given bit width, location of the decimal point, and rounding and overflow mode. To correctly perform arithmetic operations some pre and post processing steps such as decimal point alignment, rounding and overflow management are necessary. We divided our C-based implementation of fixed point arithmetic in three steps.

- core operation (including alignment),
- rounding,
- overflow management.

Alignment is included in the core operation because it depends on the operation (e.g. for addition or subtractions inputs need to be aligned, while for multiplication they do not).

Rounding, overflow management and core operation are modeled as generic C functions. For example, the overflow manager function (implementing wrapping and saturation) is called when any addition, multiplication or subtraction operation requires an output to be stored in fewer bits than the full bit width of the core operation result, which can be computed from the input operands. The rounding function on the other hand (implementing truncation, ceil, floor and round) is called when the number of bits for the output fractional part is reduced. Finally, functions that are used to model the core operation take as input the operands with bit width and decimal point information and produce an output with the desired bit width and decimal point. They call rounding and overflow automatically as needed.

All these functions are automatically inlined during hardware synthesis, and since the precision, point position, rounding and overflow selection arguments are constant, the high-level synthesis tool can perform efficient bit width inference for all needed hardware resources.

Note that this method is only applicable if the total bit width for each input or output (including temporary outputs before overflow and rounding management) is less than or equal to the maximum integer size supported by the compiler where Simulink and the high-level synthesis tool are executed.

Normally high level synthesis tools use data types, like sc_fixed or ac_fixed, which use C++ templates to make arithmetic expression representation and automated conversions and casting easier and more natural to handle. However, such sophisticated mechanisms are not available in the plain C which is required by our methodology, since *we do not want to use different models for verification and hardware synthesis, which would require one to re-verify the HW-oriented models to be used by the high-level synthesis tool.* However, we observed that if masking coupled with sign extension is applied at appropriate places in the datapath, then a high level synthesis tool can identify and optimize the data widths of the allocated resources even with our plain C representation of fixed-point data types. Moreover, *we are*

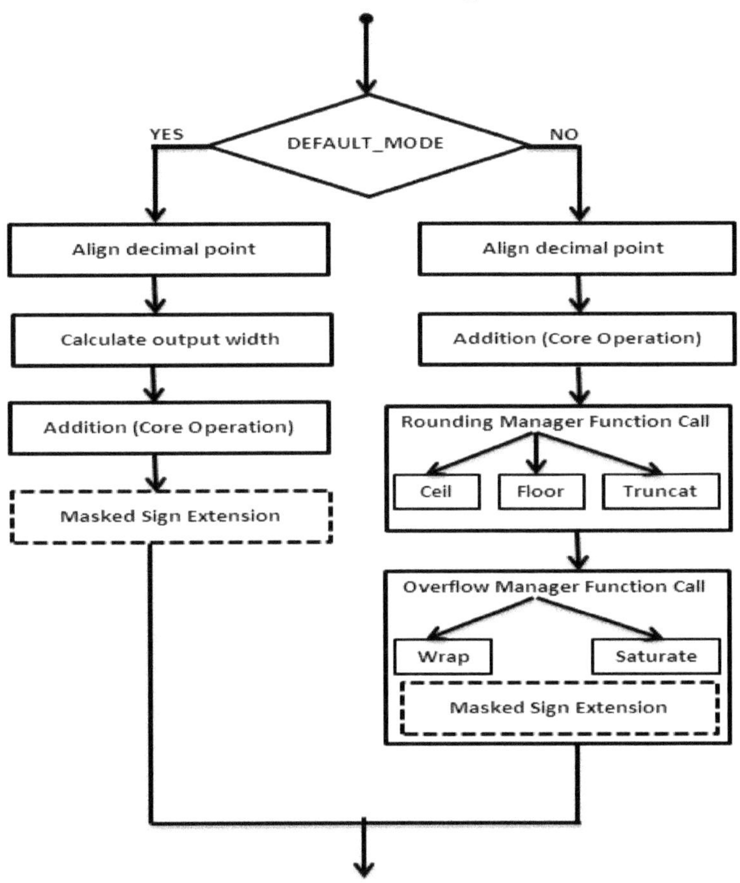

Figure 5. Flow chart for addition operation with masked sign extension

advocating this style only for frequently re-used IP blocks, where hardware implementation flexibility and efficiency are more important than ease of modeling within the blocks. Figure-5 represents the flow chart of a fixed point addition operation.

Note that for an FFT, butterflies in the same stage have the same datapath and produce output with the same fixed point representation. But butterflies in different stages can have different bit widths, which can be handled either by increasing the width by one at each stage, or by appropriate rounding. We used the latter technique, since it lends itself to better resource sharing among stages, and is commonly used in practice. The fixed point parameters passed to the various arithmetic operators can thus be derived from input bit width, output bit width and length of FFT.

3.4 C model of the FFT IP

In this section we discuss how we represented the FFT as a parameterized C IP block that can be used for verification with Simulink and for high level synthesis using a C or SystemC-based tool.

Simulink integration is performed by implementing and using several C functions defined by the S-function APIs that allow the Simulink engine to interact with the block. S-functions can model discrete, continuous and hybrid blocks and be written in a variety of languages, such as C and Matlab (but not C++ or SystemC). Here our focus is on modeling discrete blocks in C. Figure-6 illustrates how the Simulink engine interacts with the blocks, bo6h S-function based are native.

Initialization is carried out at the start of simulation by calling a function provided by each block to initialize state or global variables. Then simulation enters a loop in which it calls two other block functions to calculate outputs and update states. Simulink provides a unified access to inputs, outputs and other

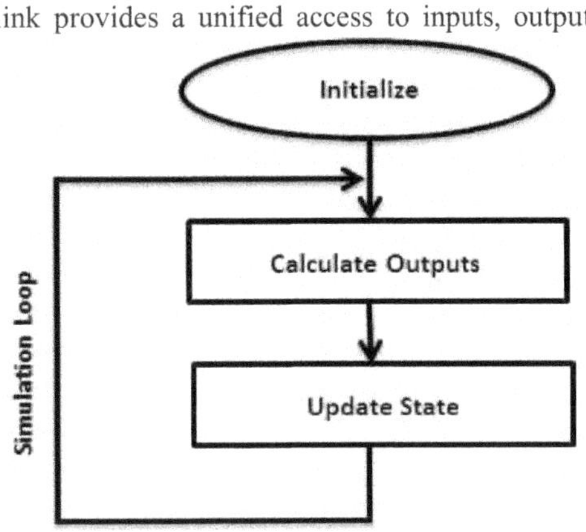

Figure 6. Interaction of Simulink simulation engine with S-function blocks

parameters of an S-function block through a structure called SimStruct. The members of the structure can be accessed for reading and writing through a set of functions provided by Simulink.

Our FFT model is written in plain C, split in different files as shown in Figure-7, in order to make it more understandable and ready for easy encapsulation in an S-function wrapper or SystemC wrapper.

- The "params.h" file defines all the constants to model the fixed point datapath, the parameters of the FFT computation, such as for example the FFT length, radix, as well as bit width and point position for inputs and outputs. It also allows one to switch between fixed point and floating point in order to ease fixed point conversion.
- The "globals.h" file defines all the global variables, such as the buffer memories, which should be defined as public members when encapsulated in SystemC.
- The "const_members.h" file defines all constant data, such as the twiddle table defining all the complex twiddle factors that are required to perform butterflies in different stages. Unfortunately they are different for every FFT length. Then the twiddle table must be pre-computed and saved as a C text

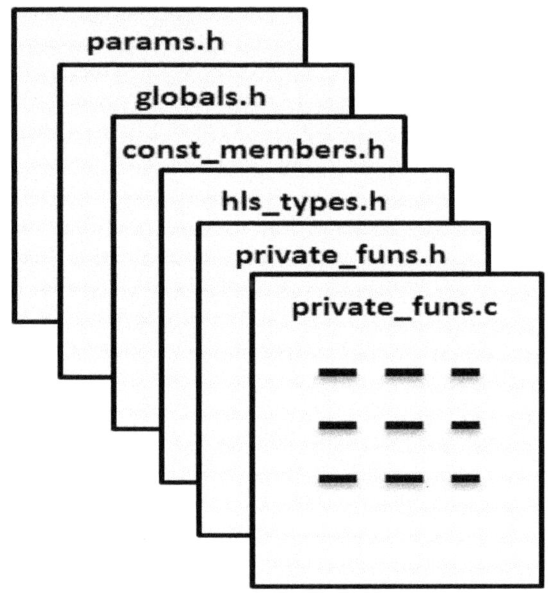

Figure 7. IP C code organization in different files

file used to initialize a constant array for any given parameterization of the IP.

- The "hls_types.h" file conditionally defines basic data types as floating point or integer, as selected in "params.h".
- The "private_funs.c" and "private_funs.h" files define and declare all the other functions required to implement the FFT, including the top level core wrapper function that iterates over butterflies to implement the FFT execution.

3.5 SystemC wrapper for the FFT IP

When I/O signal names and bit widths and the communication protocol are selected for the FFT IP, then a SystemC wrapper can be generated for high level synthesis. This wrapper serves two purposes; it defines the synthesizable RTL interface of the block and it integrates the plain C code in a class structure, where global variables appear as public members and all constants appear as constant public static members. It also defines the SystemC thread behavior by appropriately calling the top-level function defined in "private_funs.c", as shown in Figure-8 I/O interfaces are implemented as two separate cycle accurate functions that inherit the I/O data types from "hls_types.h". For the FFT IP we used a simple streaming I/O protocol with handshake signal to initiate data transfers. Note that generation of this boilerplate code can be easily automated with a script.

```
#include "params.h"
#include "hls_types.h"
#include "private_funs.h"

class FFT: public sc_module {

public:
 #include "globals.h"

 sc_in<bool> clk;
 sc_in< bool > reset;
 sc_in< bool > start;
 sc_in< sc_int <INPUT_WIDTH> > data_in_real;
 sc_in< sc_int <INPUT_WIDTH> > data_in_imag;
 sc_out< sc_int <OUTPUT_WIDTH> > data_out_real;
 sc_out< sc_int <OUTPUT_WIDTH> > data_out_real;

        void core_wrapper_function (------);
        void output_interface(OutDataType BUFF[],
        unsigned int LEN);
        void input_interface(InDataType BUFF[],
        unsigned int LEN);
}
```

Figure 8. SystemC wrapper for IP

3.6 S-function wrapper for the FFT IP

The S-function wrapper can be generated in two ways. First it can be written manually, by following all the rules described by the MathWorks. As an alternative, Simulink provides a graphical environment, called S-function builder, that can be configured to include all the header and source files to generate the S-function wrapper automatically. In this case only a few lines of manually written code are required to describe how the top level function that implements the FFT kernel accesses the input and output (the FFT block has no state to be carried across executions).

4. Use Cases

To demonstrate the effectiveness of our design methodology for IP blocks to be used in a model-based hardware design environment based on high level synthesis, we considered two very different use cases for our FFT example. One is an FFT processor for frequency domain audio detection and the other is an FFT processor for a GPS acquisition front end. Both use cases were synthesized using UMC-90nm technology libraries.

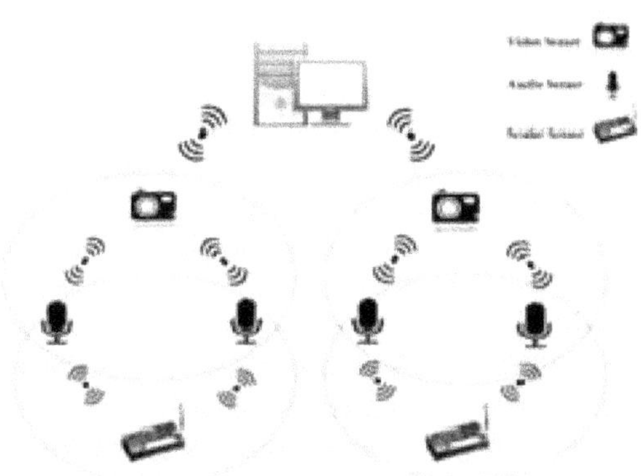

Figure 9. Sound triggered multi-modal wireless surveillance network

4.1 Frequency Domain Audio Detector

In sound-triggered wireless security camera applications, a front end audio detector is employed at the start of the alarm processing chain. Still images and video streams are very expensive to collect and process, hence the video cameras are only turned on when the low-power sound sub-system detects an event of interest, as illustrated in Figure-9.

A frequency domain audio detector is considered in this case, as shown in Figure-10. It consists of two main blocks: "power spectral density estimation" (PSD) and "threshold estimation and signal detection" that we fully modeled in Simulink.

After code generation from Simulink and profiling, the FFT within PSD estimation is identified as the power and performance bottleneck, and thus selected for HW implementation. We then compared the results of high level synthesis when performed on our IP and when performed on the C code automatically generated by RTW.

In this use case, due to the relatively low frequency of the audio input, performance requirements are low, namely one 256-sample FFT with 14 bits of precision every 4 msec. Hence the goal is essentially area and power optimization.

Table-1 compares the implementation results obtained after high level synthesis and RTL level power estimation of our IP block and of the default RTW C code implementation, also encapsulated in SystemC. Our (hardware-oriented) IP consumes 45 percent less area and has essentially the same throughput as the

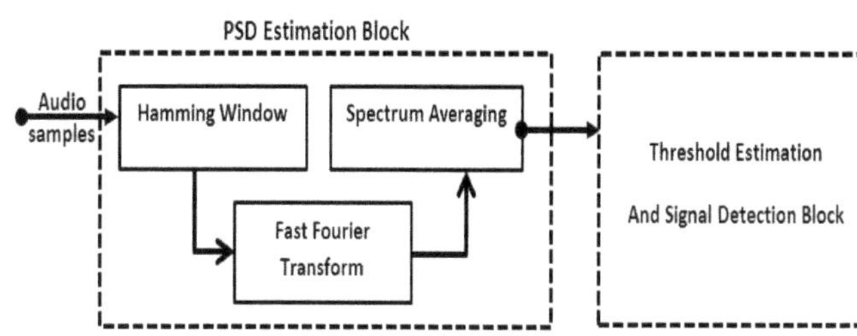

Figure 10. Front audio detection algorithm block diagram

(software-oriented) RTW code. The power consumption is also lower in our case.

One important reason for the area difference is the better bit-width optimizations that are enabled by our bit-accurate representation of the individual butterflies. Both the data path and the memories were trimmed to the exact 14 bit width required by the usage scenario, instead of the default 16 bits used by the RTW implementation (which is limited to C data types).

Table 1. RTW FFT vs. FFT IP for audio detector application

Design	Area(mm^2)	Power(mW)
RTW FFT	0.60	4.14
Our FFT IP	0.42	2.16

4.2 FFT-based GPS Acquisition

A GPS receiver must be able to capture and demodulate signals transmitted by at least four GPS satellites. Every satellite convolves its signal with a code that spreads its power over a relatively large spectrum. When a GPS receiver is turned on, it first task is to identify which satellites are visible at that time and

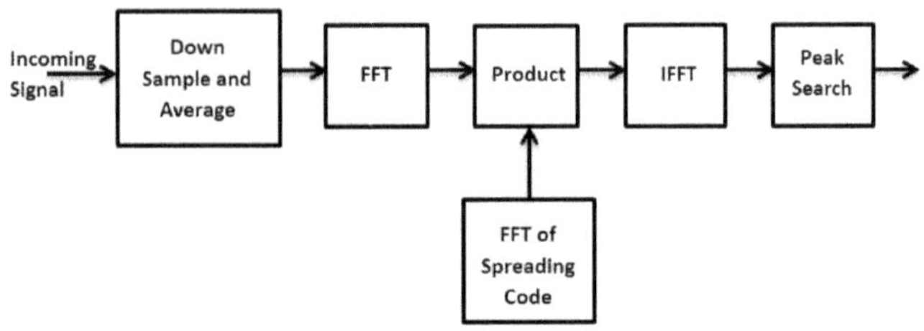

Figure 11. Core GPS acquisition algorithm

place. This means sampling the received signal and figuring out which codes have been used by the visible satellites for spreading and what is the approximate phase of the (known) spreading sequence at that time. Because of the relative movement of satellites with respect to the receiver, there is also a Doppler frequency shift which the receiver is required to estimate.

There are many different techniques for acquisition, including parallel search techniques based on FFT. The FFT-based GPS acquisition algorithm block diagram is shown in Figure-11. The first block in the chain performs two tasks. First it down converts data to baseband, and then it averages data samples to have a lower sampling rate at the output. The next block performs the frequency domain transformation using the FFT algorithm. Then the data is multiplied with the transform of the spreading code. This is followed by an inverse FFT and the peak search in the time domain.

We modeled this algorithm in the Simulink environment, verifying it with both the native Simulink FFT block and the S-function FFT IP developed by us. Then we synthesized both FFTs (our IP and the RTW version) under the very stringent timing constraints required by this usage scenario, namely one 1024-sample FFT with 4 bits of precision every msec.

Note that the throughput is16 times higher than in the frequency domain audio detector case, but the datapath requires only about 1/4 of the bits of the previous case (4 versus 14).

Table-2 compares the results of these two implementations. Our IP is much better in terms of area than the RTW version, with essentially the same throughput. Power consumption is also smaller in our case.

Table 2. RTW FFT vs. FFT IP for GPS acquisition application

Design	Area(mm^2)	Power(mW)
RTW FFT	0.87	6.8
Our FFT IP	0.60	5.7

We also compare our implementation with a manually optimized RTL that was specifically designed for FPGA implementation in [7], while our IP model was not specifically tuned for FPGAs but only for generic HW implementation. The results are reported in Table-3, showing that *our implementation is comparable with a hand optimized RTL*. The SRAM requirements are exactly the same, while we are about 20% worse in terms of area.

Table 3. Hand optimized RTL implementation vs. FFT IP for GPS acquisition application

Design	No of Slices	SRAM(Kbits)
Manual Design	4.2K	18
Our FFT IP	5.2K	18

5. Conclusions and Future Work

In this paper we demonstrated how one can design a parameterized bit-true IP, coded in plain C. This IP can be integrated with Simulink for modeling, simulation and verification and then can be easily used for efficient high level synthesis by wrapping it into SystemC. To prove the effectiveness of our approach we also compared our synthesis results with other implementations that are based on hand optimized RTL or generating C code automatically from Simulink models.

In the future we will expand the capabilities of our FFT IP by exploiting other signal flow graph structures, including for example implementing the FFT stages in pipeline, in order to further improve the throughput for high-performance real time streaming applications.

6. REFERENCES

[1] Kai Huang; Sang-il Han; Popovici, K.; Brisolara, L.; Guerin, X.; Lei Li; Xiaolang Yan; Soo-lk Chae; Carro, L.; Jerraya, A.A.; , "Simulink-Based MPSoC Design Flow: Case Study of Motion-JPEG and H.264," Design Automation Conference, 2007. DAC '07. 44th ACM/IEEE , pp.39-42, 4-8 June 2007

[2] Haubelt, C.; Schlichter, T.; Keinert, J.; Meredith, M.;, "SystemCoDesigner: Automatic design space exploration and rapid prototyping from behavioral models," Design Automation Conference, 2008. DAC 2008. 45th ACM/IEEE, pp.580-585, 8-13 June 2008

[3] Butt, S.A.; Lavagno, L.; , "Model-based rapid prototyping of multirate digital signal processing algorithms," NORCHIP, 2011 , vol., no., pp.1-4, 14-15 Nov. 2011

[4] Takach, A.; "Creating C++ IP for High Performance Hardware Implementations of FFTs," DesignCon 2010

[5] Simulink HDL Coder - Generate HDL code from Simulink models and MATLAB code. http://www.mathworks.comlproducts/slhdlcoder

[6] System Generator for DSP http://www.xilinx.com/tools/sysgen.htm

[7] Molino, Andrea; Girau, Gianmarco; Nicola, Mario; Fantino, Maurizio; Pini, Marco; , "Evaluation of a FFT-Based Acquisition in Real Time Hardware and Software GNSS Receivers," Spread Spectrum Techniques and Applications, 2008. ISSSTA '08. IEEE 10th International Symposium on , vol., no., pp.32-36, 25-28 Aug. 2008

[8] A.; Suardiaz, J.; Cuenca, S.; Grediaga, A.; , "Novel Simulink blockset for image processing codesign," Electrotechnical Conference, 2006. MELECON 2006. IEEE Mediterranean , vol., no., pp.117-120, 16-19 May 2006

[9] Sayyah, P.; Butt, S.A.; Lavagno, L.; , "Simulink-based hardware/software trade-off analysis technique," Applied Electrical Engineering and Computing Technologies (AEECT), 2011 IEEE Jordan Conference on , vol., no., pp.1-7, 6-8 Dec. 2011

[10] Scott, S. and Alessandro, F. September 2008. Where's the Beef? Why FPGAs Are So Fast. Technical Report Microsoft Research Center Redmond.

[11] John, R. W. and Greg, St. 2010. Elastic computing: a framework for transparent, portable, and adaptive multi-core heterogeneous computing. SIGPLAN Not. 45, 4 (April 2010), 115-124. DOI=10.1145/1755951.1755906 http://doi.acm.org/10.1145/1755951.1755906

[12] Bart, K., Edwin, R. and Ed Deprettere. 2000. Compaan: deriving process networks from Matlab for embedded signal processing architectures. In Proceedings of the eighth international workshop on Hardware/software codesign (CODES '00). ACM, New York, NY, USA, 13-17. DOI=10.1145/334012.334015 http://doi.acm.org/10.1145/334012.334015

[13] http://www.altera.com/products/software/products/dsp/dsp-builder.html

Testbenches for Advanced TLM Verification

Wolfgang Mueller
University of Paderborn/C-LAB
33102 Paderborn, Germany
wolfgang@acm.org

Wolfgang Ecker
Infineon Technologies AG
85579 Neubiberg, Germany
wolfgang.ecker@infineon.com

ABSTRACT

As verification activities dominate the systems development process efficient testbenches at an adequate level of abstraction are crucial factors to shorten time-to-market. We give an overview of the current state of ESL testbenches and the corresponding articles of the special session show advances and future directions of IEEE-1600-2011 SystemC in the context of testbenches for Transaction Level Modeling (TLM) [5][6][12][15][16].

Categories and Subject Descriptors

J.6 [**Computer-Aided Engineering**]: Computer-aided Design

Keywords

SystemC, Testbenches, Verification

1. Testbenches for ESL and RTL Verification

Several years ago, the move from Register-Transfer Level (RTL) to Electronic System Level (ESL) design also pushed the development of new verification methodologies and testbench libraries from Cadence, Mentor, and Synopsys: Universal Reuse Methodology (URM) [4], Advanced Verification Methodology (AVM) [11], and Verification Methodology Manual (VMM) [2]. They merged into the Open Verification Methodology (OVM) [14] and finally into the Universal Verification Methodology (UVM) [1]. UVM/OVM basically introduces extensible standard classes for structured implementation of RTL centric testbenches like (test) *environments*, *drivers*, *agents*, *sequences*, *monitors*, and *scoreboards* where transaction modeling (TLM) oriented styles are used for the testbench internal communication and for reference models (scoreboards). Complementary, to the previous methodologies, approaches for test specification [6] and testbench quality measures are developed. The most prominent approaches of latter are based on mutation based testing where also TLM testbench generation is under investigation [15].

Going in hand with the evolution of verification methodologies, several high level verification languages came up like the Property Specification Language (PSL) [8], the e language [7], and SystemVerilog [9] where the latter is a combined design, verification, and property language. All of them support (constrained) random test stimulus generation and a functional coverage metrics. At the same time, SystemC [10] became popular and well accepted as an ESL modeling and fast simulation language for mixed HW/SW virtual prototyping environments. With SystemC, the TLM 2.0 (Transaction Level Modeling) standard became accepted in industrial platform based design flows [5] and became finally combined with the most recent SystemC IEEE Std 1666-2011 [10]. TLM designs typically simulate 100x – 1000x faster than RTL models and thus enable early simulation and validation of the complete system including software. Most recent studies based on the application of GPUs give promising results to even faster simulations [16].

However, SystemC lacks verification features which were partly supported by SystemC libraries like the SystemC Verification Library (SCV) [13]. Additionally, RTL centric verification methodologies and languages can be linked to SystemC models via EDA tool specific transaction level interfaces. However, a SystemC implementation of a very small OVM subset came up [3], which was most recently extended towards functional coverage and constrained random stimulus generation and enhanced/migrated towards most relevant features of UVM for ESL verification [12]. Nevertheless, several points such as time quantum for coverage collection, time simultaneity of transactions, or reference models for TLM remain to be solved.

CODES+ISSS'12, October 7–12, 2012, Tampere, Finland.
ACM 978-1-4503-1426-8/12/09.

REFERENCES

[1] Accellera Organization Inc. Universal Verification Methodology (UVM), May 2012. `www.uvmworld.org`.

[2] J. Bergeron et al. Verification Methodology Manual for SystemVerilog. Springer, 2008.

[3] Cadence Design Systems, Inc. OVM-SC Library Reference Version 2.0.1, February, 2009.

[4] Cadence Design Systems, Inc. Universal Reuse Methodology (URM). `www.cadence.com`.

[5] W. Ecker et al. SystemC as A Completing Pillar in Industrial UVM Based Verification Environments. CODES+ISSS 2012, Tampere, FL, 2012.

[6] G. Di Guglielmo, G. Pravadelli. A Testbench Specification Language for SystemC Verification. CODES+ISSS 2012, Tampere, FL, 2012.

[7] IEEE Computer Society. Standard for the Functional Verification Language e. IEEE Std 1647-2011, 2011.

[8] IEEE Computer Society. IEEE Standard for Property Specification Language (PSL) - IEEE Std 1850-2010, 2010.

[9] IEEE Computer Society. IEEE Standard for SystemVerilog - Unified Hardware Design, Specification, and Verification Language - IEEE Std 1800-2009, 2009.

[10] IEEE Computer Society. Standard SystemC Language Reference Manual. IEEE Std 1666-2011, 2011.

[11] Mentor Graphics. Advanced Verification Methodology (AVM). `www.mentor.com`.

[12] M. F.S. Oliviera et al. The System Verification Methodology for Advanced TLM Verification. CODES+ISSS 2012, Tampere, FL, 2012.

[13] Open SystemC Initiative. SystemC Verification Library v1.0p2, 2006.

[14] OVM Homepage. `www.ovmworld.org`.

[15] M. Sousa, A. Sen. Generation of TLM Testbenches Using Mutation Testing. CODES+ISSS 2012, Tampere, FL, 2012.

[16] S. Vinco et al. SystemC Simulation on GP-GPUs: CUDA vs. OpenGL. CODES+ISSS 2012, Tampere, FL, 2012.

SystemC as Completing Pillar in Industrial OVM Based Verification Environments

Wolfgang Ecker
Infineon Technologies
Am Campeon 1-12
85579 Neubiberg
+49 89 234 45334
Wolfgang.Ecker@Infineon.com

Volkan Esen
Infineon Technologies
Am Campeon 1-12
85579 Neubiberg
+49 89 234 27814
Volkan.Esen@Infineon.com

Michael Velten
Infineon Technologies
Am Campeon 1-12
85579 Neubiberg
+49 89 234 65758
Michael.Velten@Infineon.com

Tudor Timisescu
Infineon Technologies
Am Campeon 1-12
85579 Neubiberg
+49 89 234 20144
Tudor.Timisescu@Infineon.com

ABSTRACT

This paper presents a novel TLM verification approach utilizing TLM+ as a reference model and providing a systematic path to RTL simulation as well. The approach is based on SystemC only but follows the established structure on an OVM testbench. Industrial relevant aspects as use of standards, early verification, and re-use of design items are established in this way.

Categories and Subject Descriptors

J.6 [**Computer-Aided Engineering**]: Computer-aided Design

General Terms

Standardization, Languages, Verification.

Keywords

SystemC, Testbenches, Verification

1. INTRODUCTION

The SystemC based virtual prototypes following the TLM abstraction and using the OSCI TLM 2.0 interface standards gain more and more momentum in today's industrial platform based design flows. They simulate 100x – 1000x faster than RTL models and thus enable early simulation and validation of the complete system including software. However making such a model is no unique process, neither in their time of making nor in their validation.

In a bottom-up approach, RTL models exist before TLM models. The task of verification is to guarantee that the TLM model represents all important features of the RTL model - but in an abstracted way. Simulation uses selected RTL testcases and makes an RTL co- and reference-simulation. The TLM model is connected to the RTL testbench via transactors acting as abstractors. The comparison requires a hand written module to consider the accuracy of the selected TLM modeling style.

In a top-down approach, the TLM model exists before the RTL model. An own testbench has to be built using all features of a state-of-the-art constrained random simulation methodology.

Unfortunately, there is no systematic and standardized way for such kind of testbench. Sometimes classic RTL testsbenches using HVLs [3,4] are linked via TLM interface to SystemC TLM models [5]. Mainly issues as reference model, stimulus generation, or coverage are not addressed. Further on, multi-language simulation has to be established, which relies on EDA vendor specific implementations, requires object to object translation, and often causes overhead to overcome some HVL feature limitations as in object oriented features.

In this paper we present an approach that relies on the classic OVM [1] approach but moves its abstraction one level higher. Further on, the complete framework is implemented in SystemC to avoid object translation and make full use of C++'s OOP features. Therefore, we use the SystemC OVM library from Uni Paderborn [6], a coverage library from Uni Paderborn and Infineon [7], an assertion library from Infineon [8], and the constraint random library CRAVE from University of Bremen [9].

The paper is structured as follows: First, we introduce the idea of moving an OVM framework one abstraction level higher by using TLM+ abstraction techniques [10]. Next, we discuss testcase abstraction as a consequence of the OVM framework abstraction and finally, we present an approach, how the TLM testbench can be reused for RTL verification in a top-down fashion.

2. Abstracting OVM

2.1 Classic OVM structure

In Figure 1, a typical OVM testbench structure for RTL verification is shown. The sequencer is fed with items via constrained randomization. These are abstract transactions. They get translated to signal level activity by the driver, which applies them to the pins of the RTL DUT.

Sequencer, driver, and monitor are combined into a so-called agent. Several agents are used in a testbench to apply stimuli to the RTL DUT and/or take responses hereof.

The monitor does the opposite operation as the driver, converting the activity on the RTL DUTs pins back to abstract transactions. These transactions collected by the monitor are then sent to a scoreboard.

The scoreboard contains a TLM reference model of the RTL DUT and a comparator comparing the responses of the DUT and the TLM reference. Therefore, the scoreboard is fed the exact same inputs and its outputs as the DUT's. It also takes care of collecting coverage to measure the overall progress. This structure allows for the best separation of concerns, vertical and horizontal reuse, and is used by all OVM verification IPs.

CODES/ISSS'12, October 7–12, 2012, Tampere, Finland.

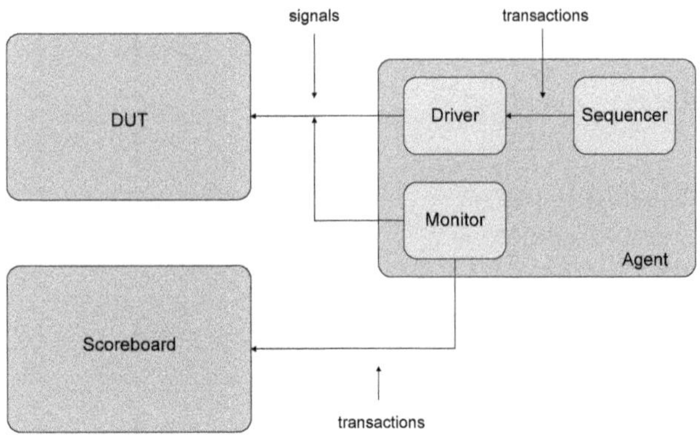

Figure 1 - Classic OVM testbench

2.2 OVM Abstraction

As mentioned before, to be able to build a TLM constrained random testbench, the testbench should operate at a higher level of abstraction than the DUT. This would mean moving from the structure shown in Figure 1 to something as in Figure 2.

In this setup, the sequencer is fed "transactions" at a higher level of abstraction than the DUT, which we call TLM+. What this higher level of abstraction exactly is will be discussed later in this paper. Exemplarily, collections of simple TLM transactions - that are functionally related and that are passed in one call (for example a set of configuration transactions) - might act as TLM+ abstraction.

The transactor has the same role as the driver in the previous picture, in that it translates from abstract stimulus (TLM+) to a format the DUT understands, in our case TLM. The observer does the same as the monitor, converting from TLM to the more abstract TLM+ and sending these to the scoreboard.

The scoreboard in the previous case contained a TLM reference model of the DUT. The challenge here is finding a more abstract description of the TLM model (which in itself is pretty abstract). A purely functionally oriented model that is register agnostic (as opposed to the TLM which is supposed to be register accurate) is an option for the TLM+ abstraction.

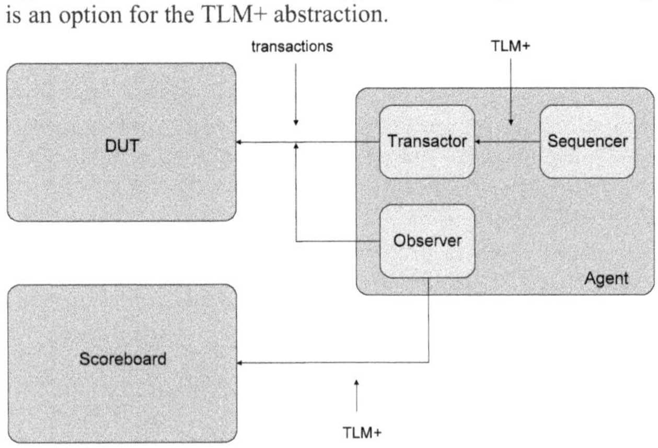

Figure 2 - Abstracted OVM testbench

3. Layered Approach to Stimulus Generation

3.1 TLM to TLM+

In the context of the current RTL verification methodology, the stimulus applied to the DUT is written at a higher level of abstraction than the DUT – instead of thinking at the signal protocol level, verification engineers can be much more productive by thinking in terms of transactions, called sequence items. For example, a write transaction to a certain address would abstract raising the write signal, putting the address on bus, putting the data on the bus and raising the ready signal. It is much easier for a human to think in terms of transactions and then have the driver convert to the signal protocol level. Such sequence item can be grouped together to create complex stimuli. The testbench also contains a reference model of the DUT, which works on the transaction level. This prevents the situation where the reference model ends up re-implementing the DUT.

For TLM verification, the two observations above apply as well. As a higher level of abstraction than TLM, TLM+ as defined in [10] is used. TLM+ achieves this higher level of abstraction in two dimensions:

- Interface abstraction: the underlying operation of the bus is not important anymore, data is no longer sent as a series of bus transactions limited by the bus width, but as a continuous stream; this saves on function calls and context switches, thus speeding up simulation

- Data abstraction: data is no longer processed throughout the chain, instead raw data is sent, along with the parameters with which it would have been processed; this saves on computational complexity, thus speeding up simulation

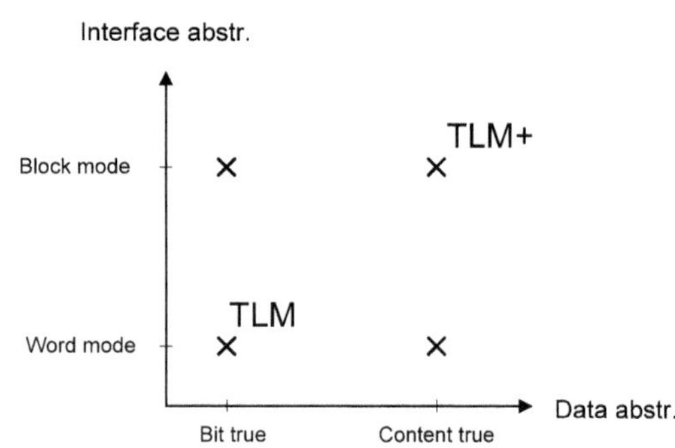

Figure 3 - TLM+ abstraction

The transactor (equivalent to the driver in RTL verification, but the name is different in order to avoid confusion) has the responsibility of converting from TLM+ stimulus to TLM transactions that the DUT can understand.

Let us analyze a simple example to better understand how such a setup would work. As a DUT let us take a simple serial to parallel peripheral, where the protocol of the serial ports is configurable through some control registers in the module. We will be concerned mostly with the parallel bus side.

If the DUT were an RTL model, as a sequence item for the bus side we would have an object that contains the command to be executed (read or write), the address to which the access is to be executed and a data member. The data member for a write item would contain the data to be applied and for a read it would contain the value with which the DUT responded to the request. The driver would take these values and apply them to the appropriate signals according to the protocol.

For a TLM DUT, a simple sequence item has instead of a data member which is of the same size as the bus width, a stream of data we would like to pass to the model (or to read data in, for the case of a read transaction). The transactor would separate this long stream into individual transactions that the DUT would be able to interpret. Such a sequence item is more abstract than the TLM transactions the DUT operates with in just the interface abstraction dimension. We could do better, by applying data abstraction as well.

In the case of data abstraction, we actually have to interpret the data being sent. For our simple case of a serial to parallel peripheral, three simple operations can be performed on the bus: send via serial, receive from serial and configure for a certain serial protocol. Serial send and receive are just writes and reads, respectively to specific register addresses. The benefit in actually defining them as a send and a receive sequence item comes in the reference model; instead of having to examine the address field and the command to see if it was a write to the TX register or a read from the RX register, it would know directly what operation was performed and predict a certain output from the DUT. This will result in less code that focuses more on the functional aspects of the DUT. The third sequence item type, configuration, would go even further: instead of abstracting an access to just one register, it would abstract a sequence of accesses to the configuration registers. It would also contain the desired parameters of the serial protocol in an abstract form, a configuration object with fields for each parameter. The transactor would take this configuration object and encode it into the appropriate data values for each configuration register and create a TLM transaction for each.

Clearly, applying also data abstraction will result in a bigger productivity gain than just applying interface abstraction. The problem with data abstraction is that it requires DUT specific information. In the previous example, send and receive items require knowledge of the offsets for the TX and the RX register. The configuration item, aside from the offsets of the configuration registers, also requires information about the serial protocol and the modes that the DUT supports. The interface abstraction does, however, not require any DUT specific information, just protocol specific information (the way in which a data stream is split into multiple transaction may be different – some protocol may support pipelined accesses, some may support bursts, etc.).

As the effort spent on verification tasks does not directly contribute to the profit a chip will make, it is desired that the amount of code developed be minimized, hence reuse is very important. Mixing in DUT specific information in a piece of VIP will reduce its reuse drastically. As we have seen above, data abstraction does have this drawback, but interface abstraction does not.

The conversion from a data stream to a series of TLM transactions is non-trivial and is something that would be of interest for reuse. Data abstraction does however provide big leaps in productivity and is not to be ignored either. To leverage the advantages of both while mitigating the drawbacks, a layered approach is used.

3.2 Layering for RTL Verification

The foundation of any piece of VIP is the sequence item. For RTL verification, there is usually just one sequence item that can abstract all types of transactions the DUT can handle. Any other sequence item types would just add extra constraints to this item or facilitate error injection.

Sequences are built from sequence items, with the constituent items having some sort of temporal relation. A series of protocol specific sequences can be developed, for example, writing to an address and then reading the value from the same address back one clock cycle later, etc. A DUT specific layer can be built on top, which introduces some DUT specific information, such as writing a '1' to all registers in the design (requires knowledge of what offsets are actually present in the design from the whole address space of the protocol). Such sequences can be then used at the highest level of layering, virtual sequences, which coordinate stimulus between multiple verification components.

In Figure 4, such a layered stimulus hierarchy is presented. Light grey elements are part of the VIP package and can be reused across projects. White elements are project specific and cannot be reused (except for related projects, such as new derivatives, etc.).

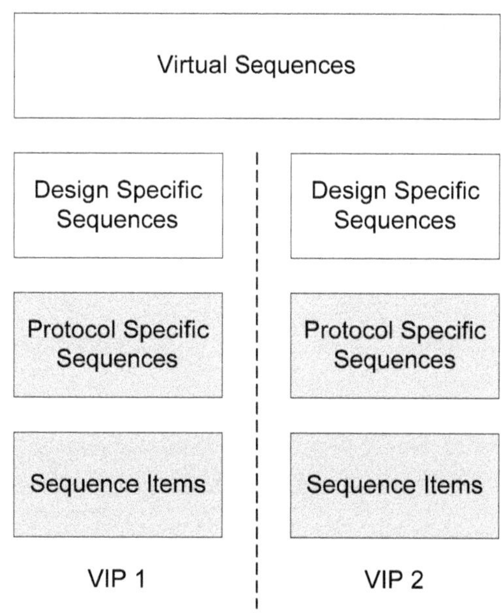

Figure 4 - Layered RTL stimulus

3.3 Layering for TLM Verification

We can have a nicely layered approach for TLM verification as well, in order to be able to achieve as much reuse as possible. The picture looks slightly different in this case (ignoring virtual sequences).

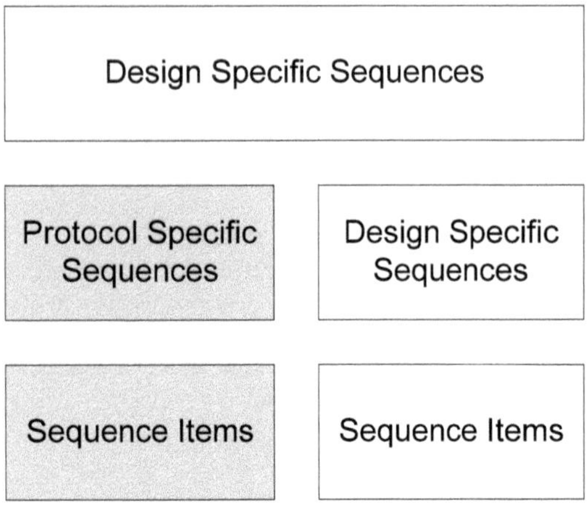

Figure 5 - Layered TLM stimulus

In Figure 5 sequence items in light gray only have interface abstraction. Protocol specific sequences are built up from these. Sequence items that employ also data abstraction are marked with white. Design specific sequences are built up from these as well (at the same conceptual level of hierarchy as the protocol specific sequences). All of the above are then be used to build up even higher sequences, which will also not be reusable.

4. Reuse from TLM to RTL Verification

Sequences from TLM verification have great potential of reuse for RTL verification. What is missing is the conversion from the TLM agent output (usually a TLM 2.0 generic payload) to the signal protocol level. This could be done in one adapter component. But assuming that the VIP for RTL verification already exists, a converter from the TLM agent's output to the RTL agent's driver sequence item is required. Such a conversion is easy to do, as both items sit at the same level of abstraction.

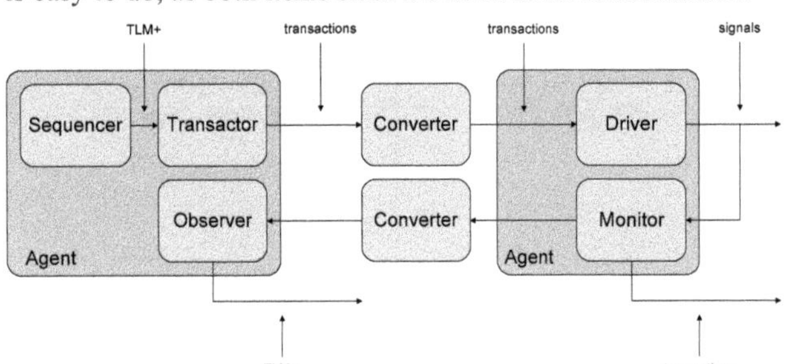

Figure 6 - Mixed TLM/RTL agent

In Figure 6, the converter between the transactor and the driver handles the conversion between the output format of the TLM agent (generic payload) and the sequence item of the RTL agent. To be able to provide monitoring, a converter doing the opposite must be placed between the monitor and the observer. This is only required if the reference model would be a TLM+ model. If using the previously verified TLM model as a reference model, this can be skipped.

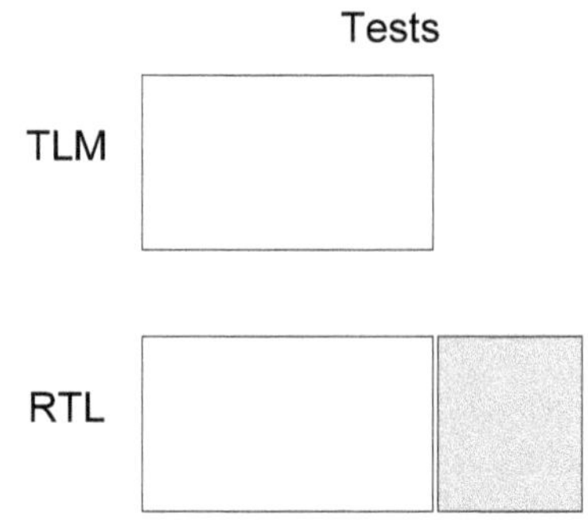

Figure 7 - Test hierarchy

The drawback with this approach is that the stimulus will all have to be written at the TLM+ level, because the VIP only has a TLM+ interface. The timing achievable with such sequences might be too coarse and RTL DUT's interesting stimulus scenarios might not be reachable. As RTL includes more detail than TLM, it will almost surely be the case that additional tests will have to be performed to validate the extra features. In Figure 7, such a test hierarchy is presented. The tests that compose the light gray suite are enough to verify the TLM model. The RTL model, providing additional levels of details in terms of bit and cycle accuracy, will require extra tests to verify these, pictured in the white test suite. Another drawback is that the source code for the RTL agent has to be modified, which is undesirable.

In Figure 8, a more advanced version of a mixed TLM/RTL agent is presented. The main difference here is that the RTL agent's sequencer is still present. The converter starts items on this sequencer, which will eventually get to the driver. In this case, the VIP can be stimulated using either the sequences developed for TLM verification (through the TLM agent sequencer) or with newly written sequences written at the TLM level of abstraction (through the RTL agent sequencer). This allows implementing the test hierarchy in Figure 7, while maximizing reuse.

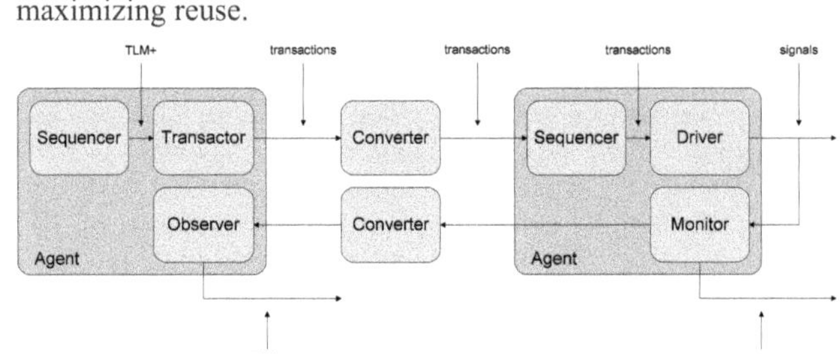

Figure 8 - Mixed TLM/RTL agent (advanced)

5. Summary and Outline

We presented a novel testbench structure supporting top down verification of a TLM DUT by using TLM+ abstraction in the testbench's agents and the scoreboards. Further on, this structure is extended to support reuse of testcases as well as addition of new testcases for an RTL DUT. It is important to mention, that this concept follows the OVM methodology and could also be implemented in SystemVerilog.

When available, we will move the testbench structure to a UVM [2] SystemC implementation. Finally, we plan a generator for basic testbench structures to simplify the use of the concept.

ACKNOWLEDGMENTS
This work has been partially funded as part of the funded Project SANITAS (01M3088) by the Federal Ministry of Education and Research.

6. REFERENCES
[1] Accellera Organization Inc. Open Verification Methodology (OVM). (2009,May). Available at: http://www.accellera.org/activities/ovm/

[2] Accellera Organization Inc. Universal Verification Methodology (UVM), May 2012. www.uvmworld.org

[3] IEEE Computer Society. Standard for the Functional Verification Language e. IEEE Std 1647-2011, 2011.

[4] IEEE Computer Society. IEEE Standard for SystemVerilog - Unified Hardware Design, Specification, and Verification Language - IEEE Std 1800-2009, 2009.

[5] Glasser, M.; Bergeron, J.:TLM-2.0 in SystemVerilog. Proceedings of the DVCON2011. Available at: events.dvcon.org/2011/proceedings/.../04_2.pdf

[6] C. Kuznik and W. Müller. Functional Coverage-driven Verification with SystemC on Multiple Level of Abstraction. Proceedings of DVCON, 2011.

[7] M. F. S. Oliveira, C. Kuznik, W. Mueller, W. Ecker, and V. Esen. A SystemC Library for Advanced TLM Verification. In Proceeding of Design and Verication Conference (DVCON), Mar. 2012.

[8] W. Ecker, V. Esen, M. Hull, T. Steininger, M. Velten: Requirements and Concepts for Transaction Level Assertions. International Conference on Computer Design, 2006. ICCD 2006.

[9] F. Haedicke, H. M. Le, D. Große, and R. Drechsler. CRAVE: An advanced constrained random verification environment for SystemC. In International Symposium on System-on-Chip (SoC), 2012. Available at www.systemc-verification.org.

[10] W. Ecker, V. Even, R. Schwencker, and M. Velten, "Defining TLM+," in *Design & Verification Conference & Exhibition (DVCON)*, San Jose, USA, February 2010.

[11] Accellera Organization Inc. SystemC 2.3 (Includes Transaction-level Modeling). Available at: www.accellera.org/downloads/standards/systemc

The System Verification Methodology for Advanced TLM Verification

Marcio F. S. Oliveira[1]
Christoph Kuznik[1]
Wolfgang Mueller[1]

Finn Haedicke[2]
Hoang M. Le[2]
Daniel Große[2]

Rolf Drechsler[2,3]
Wolfgang Ecker[4]
Volkan Esen[4]

[1]C-LAB, University of Paderborn, 33102 Paderborn, Germany
{marcio, kuznik, wolfgang}@c-lab.de
[2]Institute of Computer Science, University of Bremen, 28359 Bremen, Germany
{finn, hle, grosse, drechsle}@informatik.uni-bremen.de
[3]Cyber-Physical Systems, DFKI GmbH, 28359 Bremen, Germany
[4]Infineon Technologies AG, 85579 Neubiberg, Germany
{Wolfgang.Ecker, Volkan.Esen}@infineon.com

ABSTRACT

The IEEE-1800 SystemVerilog [20] system description and verification language integrates dedicated verification features, like constraint random stimulus generation and functional coverage, which are the building blocks of the *Universal Verification Methodology* (UVM) [3], the emerging standard for electronic systems verification. In this article, we introduce our *System Verification Methodology* (SVM) as a SystemC library for advanced *Transaction Level Modeling* (TLM) testbench implementation. As such, we first present SystemC libraries for the support of verification features like functional coverage and constrained random stimulus generation. Thereafter, we introduce the SVM with advanced TLM support based on SystemC and compare it to UVM and related approaches. Finally, we demonstrate the application of our SVM by means of a testbench for a two wheel self-balancing electric vehicle.

Categories and Subject Descriptors

J.6 [**Computer-Aided Engineering**]: [Computer-Aided Design (CAD)]

General Terms

Verification, Standardization

Keywords

UVM, SystemVerilog, SystemC, Functional Coverage, Constrained Random Stimulus Generation

1. INTRODUCTION

As electronic systems grow in complexity, verification activities have started to dominate the design effort. Today, verification accounts for more than 70% of the total development effort [27] with the trend to an exponential growth [15]. To cope with that increasing complexity and to boost productivity at *Electronic System Level* (ESL), more efficient verification languages and technologies have been introduced. Today, advanced verification languages like IEEE-1800 SystemVerilog [20] and IEEE-1647 *e* [22] support features like assertion specification to define behavioral properties, constrained random stimulus generation to generate directed randomized testbench input, and functional coverage definitions to determine the verification closure.

For the structured implementation of testbenches, the *Universal Verification Methodology* (UVM) [3] with the *Open Verification Methodology* (OVM) [8] as a predecessor is well accepted for ESL testbench implementation. UVM is a methodology with a complementary library for RTL and ESL verification, at which the full feature set comes as a SystemVerilog and *e* implementation only.

On the other hand, IEEE 1666 SystemC is widely accepted for description and simulation of mixed HW/SW systems at higher levels of abstraction. For instance, the TLM 2.0 library has already been introduced in 2007 [4] and is meanwhile integrated in the IEEE 1666-2011 SystemC standard [21]. However, in contrast to SystemVerilog, the support of dedicated verification features is very limited in SystemC. This is an obstacle for adapting verification library concepts like UVM to SystemC. For instance, SystemC has no built-in language construct for functional coverage specification such as the `covergroup` metric of SystemVerilog. Therefore, there exists an OVM implementation in SystemC (OVM-SC) [10], which is limited to an OVM subset and lacks various important modeling and verification features like domain specific components, random stimulus generation facilities, sequence library management, sequence arbitration, response to request routing, command-line processor, and a register abstraction layer. Nevertheless, the

SystemC Verification (SCV) library [31] can be used as an alternative for random stimulus generation and constraint solving. However, it has several drawbacks: poor dynamic constraint support, no constraint specification for dynamic data-structures, low constraints specification usability for composed data structures, insufficient information in case of over-constraining, and substantial limits in constraints complexity.

This paper presents the *System Verification Methodology* (SVM) for SystemC, which is based on the OVM-SC [10] implementation and incorporates verification best practices and standards from OVM and partly UVM, such as factory and configuration facilities and stimulus sequence generation and management. The SVM library integrates functional coverage and advanced constraint solving and constrained random stimulus generation as mandatory features to SystemC for true testbench support.

The remainder of this paper is organized as follows. The next section presents related work in the areas of verification tools and methodologies for the SystemC ecosystem. Section 3 introduces our contributions to improve the SystemC verification feature set. In Section 4 we present the SVM, which integrates the two previous contribution in a feature rich library to boost the verification in SystemC environments. In Section 5 we apply our SVM library to a high level control model of a two wheel self-balancing electric vehicle. Finally, Section 6 closes with conclusions and future directions.

2. RELATED WORK

For testbench implementation, several verification methodologies were developed such as the *Universal Reuse Methodology* (URM) [9] from Cadence, the *Advanced Verification Methodology* (AVM) [28] from Mentor Graphics, and the *Verification Methodology Manual* (VMM) [5] from Synopsys. Cadence and Mentor Graphics first joined efforts to the *Open Verification Methodology* (OVM) [8] with a later unification to the Universal Verification Methodology (UVM) [3] with Synopsys. Additionally, the *Open Verification Library* (OVL) [2] was developed by Accellera. OVL provides means that may work as assertion, assumption, or coverage point checkers. All verification methodologies came with a handbook and a complementary SystemVerilog library for testbench implementation. There is no SystemC support except an OVM implementation published by Accellera which implemented a very limited OVM subset in SystemC, i.e., OVM- SC [10], which was the starting point for our SVM implementation.

More precisely, our SVM SystemC library is based on the concepts of OVM multiple languages SystemC package v2.1.1 and OVM for SystemVerilog v2.1.1 where its base package was refactored to reflect the improvements from the transition of OVM to UVM additionally improved by callbacks, transaction routing, and recording facilities. We also included a package with crucial structural components to build the verification environment. For example, we implemented stimulus sequences, sequence scheduler facilities, as well as a command-line processor.

All of those libraries are based on dedicated verification features from languages like IEEE-1800 SystemVerilog [20] and IEEE-1647 *e* [22]. Therefore, a direct conversion of those verification libraries to SystemC is not possible. Thus, we first had to extend SystemC by functional coverage and advanced constrained random stimulus generation, which we presented in [26] and [19].

For SystemC functional coverage, [34] presents a vendor-specific functional coverage implementation in SystemC. The author of [33] uses the callback facility of the SCV library to achieve functional equivalent of SystemVerilog value and (simple) transition coverpoints. Moreover, the SCV introspection facility and smart pointer callbacks are used to tie variables to coverpoints. This leads to automatic sampling of coverpoints, which is often not intended. Furthermore, this approach does not include advanced features such as cross coverage with select operators, illegal bins or default bin declaration. Moreover, various vendors provide commercial products for SystemC code, and limited functional and transition coverage such as [23, 29].

For constrained random stimulus generation, the SCV library [31] provides a SystemC implementation. However, it has limits in dynamic constraint support, dynamic data structures, composed data structures, over-constraining, and the complexity of constraints. Therefore, several improvements for the SCV library have been introduced. In [16] bit vector operators have been added and the uniform distribution among all constraint solutions is ensured in all cases. An approach to determine the exact reasons in case of over-constraining has been presented in [17]. In [37] the BDD-based constraint-solver is replaced by a method which uses a generalization of *Boolean Satisfiability* (SAT).

In contrast to our implementation, all these approaches compensate only some of the SCV weaknesses. In particular, no constraints on dynamic data structures can be specified, constraints cannot be controlled dynamically during run-time, references to the state of constraints are not available, and no inline constraints are possible limiting the usability. In addition, the integration of different constraint solvers working in parallel is mandatory to reduce the time for stimulus generation to a minimum.

3. SYSTEMC EXTENSIONS FOR VERIFICATION

Before we introduce our *System Verification Methodology* (SVM) library, we first present SystemC verification extensions, which are required as a basis for SVM, i.e., functional coverage and advanced constrained random stimulus generation.

3.1 Functional Coverage

Functional coverage is a user-defined metric that measures how many percentages of the verification objectives are met by the test plan. It can be, for instance, used to measure if interesting scenarios, corner cases or specification invariants have been observed, validated, and tested by means of covergroups and coverpoints. The coverage of a group C_g is the weighted average of the coverage of all items i defined in the group. It is computed by the following equation:

$$C_g = \frac{\sum_i W_i \cdot C_i}{\sum_i W_i},$$

whereas W_i is the weight associated with item i and C_i is the coverage of item i. The remainder of this section outlines details of the functional coverage implementation of the SVM as a SystemC library, which is based on the following assumptions:

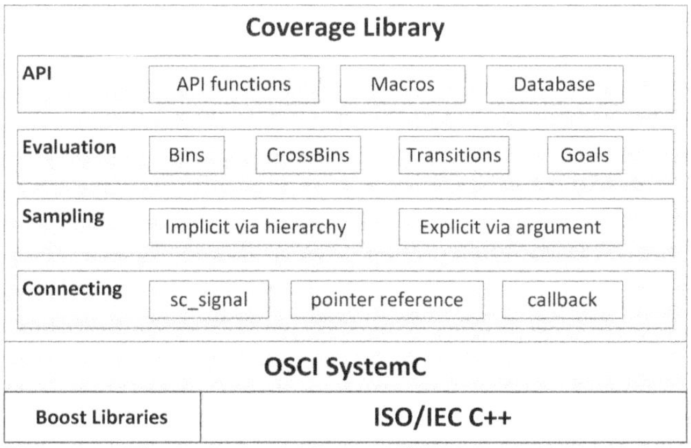

Figure 1: Elements according to IEEE-1800 **covergroup** concept.

- Metric Expressiveness
  A structured hierarchical composition of a functional coverage metric shall be enabled. The metric elements shall allow the capturing of coverage information in fine-grained fashion, e.g., like the concept of covergroups, coverpoints and bins in SystemVerilog.

- Interoperability
  To collect and evaluate functional coverage no modifications of the SystemC kernel are permitted.

- Build Environment Dependencies
  The functional coverage facility shall not rely on the SystemC Verification Library (SCV). Moreover, it may only use header file includes of third-party libraries such as the boost library.

- Advanced TLM Verification
  Multiple explicit samplings per delta cycle shall be supported to allow coverage of pre and post transaction event coverage.

The main facility of the functional coverage library is a single factory class providing all necessary setup and management API calls for the creation and administration of the implemented coverage metric elements. Moreover, the factory handles the administration of the coverage database, which stores collected functional coverage information **(i)** to capture already sampled coverage information prior to the next run and **(ii)** to save this data after the test, which is simplified by a set of convenience API functions. This allows temporal merging of coverage results from independent simulation runs of the same coverage metric.

3.1.1 Functional Coverage Metric

The library is organized in different layers, as given in Figure 1. Besides explicit sampling, a connection layer allows the binding of coverpoints to `sc_signals`, variables or callback functions of the DUT (Design under Test). The evaluation layers provide the implementation of the SystemVerilog metric elements such as covergroups, coverpoints, and bins as well as the definition of associated goals and weights for the overall functional coverage computation.

3.1.2 Coverage Features

As such, the coverage library implements covergroups, coverpoints, and coverpoints. Each coverpoint may contain an arbitrary number of (normal) bins, illegal bins, ignore bins, and an optional default bin. A default bin contains all non-specified intervals of a data type. Default bins, one per coverpoint, and their corresponding intervals can be generated for integer data types. Once an illegal bin is hit, the library notifies and halts the simulation. The hits of ignore bins will be counted but ignored for the overall coverage percentage calculation of bins and coverpoints, respectively. Each bin may also have numerous integer intervals assigned. A coverpoint can contain transition bins, which may be associated with an arbitrary number of integer sequences to implement simple successional value transition coverage. Allowing multiple samplings within one SystemC simulator delta cycle, we do not rely on `SC_MODULE`s and clock sensitive `SC_METHOD`s within the implementation. The sampling process can be triggered from the outside in a method call fashion.

3.2 Advanced Constrained Random Stimulus Generation

Constrained random verification applies stimuli to the DUT that are solutions of constraints. These solutions are determined by a constraint solver. Thereby, the generated stimuli are much more likely to hit corner cases. This is due to the fact that scenarios are simulated which the verification engineer might have not thought of. Furthermore, the stimulus generation process is automated and hence a huge set of scenarios can be executed leading to higher coverage. Hence, for large and complex systems the confidence in the correct functionality significantly increases.

In the following we describe our developed constrained random stimulus generation library.

3.2.1 Features

Our constrained random stimulus generation is based on CRAVE [19], an advanced *C*onstrained *RA*ndom *V*erification *E*nvironment for SystemC. CRAVE provides the following features:

- New Constraint Specification API
  An intuitive and user-friendly API to specify random variables and random objects has been developed.

- Dynamic Constraints and Data Structures
  Constraints can be controlled dynamically at run-time. Moreover, constraints for elements of dynamic data structures like STL vectors can be specified.

- Improved Usability
  Inline constraints can be formulated and changed incrementally at run-time. Furthermore, automatic debugging of unsatisfiable constraints is supported.

- Parallel Constraint Solving
  BDD-based and SAT/SMT-based techniques have been integrated for constraint solving. A portfolio approach is used to enable very fast generation of constraint solutions.

Those features are supported as follows, where we take the example in Figure 2 for further outlines.

```
1   struct packet : public rand_obj {
2     randv< unsigned int > src_addr;
3     randv< sc_uint<16> > dest_addr;
4     rand_vec< char > data;
5
6     packet(int &expected_max_size) : src_addr(this),
            dest_addr(this), data(this) {
7      constraint(src_addr() <= 0xFFFF);
8      constraint("diff", src_addr() != dest_addr());
9      soft_constraint(dest_addr() % 4 == 0);
10
11     constraint( data().size() % 4 == 0 &&
          data().size() < reference(expected_max_size) );
12     constraint.foreach( data, _i, IF_THEN( _i == 0,
          'A' <= data()[_i] && data()[_i] <= 'Z') );
13     constraint.foreach( data, _i, IF_THEN( _i != 0,
          'a' <= data()[_i] && data()[_i] <= 'z') );
14     constraint.soft_foreach( data, _i, data()[_i] +
          data()[_i-1] > 'a' + 'b');
15    }
16  };
```

Figure 2: Constrained Packet.

3.2.2 Constraint Specification

We first introduce the APIs for the creation of the elementary entities: random variables and constrained random objects.

Random Variable.

The template class *randv<T>* represents a random variable of the C/C++ or SystemC built-in type *T*. All standard applicable operators (arithmetic, comparison, logical, etc.) are overloaded so that an instance *x* of *randv<T>* behaves as if it were a variable of type *T*. A call *x.next()* assigns a random value in the range of *T* to *x*. While the focus of CRAVE is on complex constraints with many variables, it also supports simple constraints on a single variable. Two member functions *addRange* and *addWeightedRange* can be used to refine the distribution of *x.next()*. Furthermore, *x()* returns a symbolic link to the value of *x* to be used to specify constraints in conjunction with other instances of *randv<T>* as shown hereafter.

Random Object and Constraint Inheritance.

Complex constrained random objects can also be specified. They must inherit from the class *rand_obj* provided by CRAVE. Such an object can contain several instances of *randv<T>* and *rand_obj*. Constraints for each of these instances as well as constraints between them can be specified in a constructor of the object. For the instance *x* of *rand_obj*, *x.next()* randomizes all belonging instances of *randv<T>* and *rand_obj*, respecting the specified constraints. The inheritance/reuse of constraints in CRAVE is straightforward. The user can add more fields and constraints to an existing random constrained object by using C++ class inheritance.

The following example outlines the application of CRAVE features. The constrained packet in Figure 2 inherits from *rand_obj* and consists of a source address as *randv<unsigned int>*, a destination address as *randv<sc_uint<16>>*, a data field as a randomized vector (see Section 3.2.3), and a set of constraints. The source address is constrained to be in the range [0x0, 0xFFFF] (Line 7) and the both addresses must not be the same (Line 8). Both constraints are so-called hard constraints, i.e., they must be satisfied otherwise *next()* fails. The second constraint is also a named constraint, which enables dynamic management of constraints as described later in Section 3.2.3. Line 9 shows a soft constraint stating that the destination address should be a multiple of four. Soft constraints can be ignored by the constraint-solver if they cannot be satisfied in conjunction with the specified hard constraints. As it can be seen in all constraints, the symbolic links to the actual instances of *randv* are used. Line 11-14 declare constraints related to the randomized vector, which will be explained in the next section.

3.2.3 Dynamic Data Structures and Constraints

This section introduces vector constraints, references, and dynamic constraint management as three distinctive features of CRAVE, which are not supported by the SCV library.

Vector Constraints.

The SCV library offers no direct support for the constrained randomization of dynamic data structures such as vectors. The user must mimic dynamic data structures by using arrays of fixed-size. This is inconvenient and not memory-efficient. Furthermore, the upper bound on size of dynamic data structures might not be known at the time of constraint specification. CRAVE offers a template class *rand_vec<T>* for the constrained randomization of vectors, where currently C/C++ and SystemC built-in data types are supported as template parameter *T*.

The class *rand_vec<T>* also implements the APIs of the STL class *vector* and thus behaves as if it is an STL vector. Similar to *randv<T>*, for an instance *v* of *rand_vec<T>*, *v* refers to the actual vector while *v()* is the symbolic vector used to specify constraints. For the symbolic vector *v()*, *v().size()* refers to the size, *v()[_i]* to a symbolic vector element, and *v()[_i - c]* to a previous element relative to *v()[_i]* (*_i* is a predefined constant in CRAVE and *c* is a positive constant). The symbolic elements *v()[_i]* and *v()[_i - c]* are used in a *foreach* constraint.

Back to the example shown in Figure 2. The vector constraints can now be explained: Line 12 and 13 ensure that the first element is capitalized and the remainder is in lower case letters, respectively. Both are hard constraints. The last constraint is a soft *foreach* constraint: two consecutive elements cannot be *aa*, *ab* or *ba*. The first one (Line 11) forces the size of the vector to be a multiple of four and strictly less than an upper bound. This upper bound can change dynamically depending on *max_expected_size*. This is captured by the concept of *references* introduced next.

References.

In many cases, the randomization depends on the dynamically changing state of the verification environment. To include the state in the constraints using the SCV library, the user must use additional variables to save the state and to update them manually whenever the state is changed. For this purpose, CRAVE provides references as a convenient shortcut. A reference in CRAVE basically links a "real" variable with a symbolic variable, which can be used during constraint specification. Before the constraints are solved, the value of this symbolic variable is fixed to the actual value of the linked variable.

Dynamic Constraint Management.

During the verification process, it is very useful that the user can enable/disable specific constraints of a random object. With the SCV library, the user has to mimic the feature by adding an auxiliary variable and constrain this variable in an implication with the constraints to be enabled/disabled, which is inconvenient and inefficient. CRAVE's constraint management APIs of *rand_obj*: *enable_constraint(name)* and *disable_constraint(name)* allow to directly enable/disable named constraints. Note that the vector constraint *foreach* can also be named and intentionally soft constraints cannot be enabled/disabled.

Where the previous features demonstrated different use cases where CRAVE offers clear advantages over the SCV library, the next paragraphs discuss important usability enhancements of CRAVE compared to the SCV library.

3.2.4 Usability

Inline and Incremental Constraints.

Constraints in CRAVE can be specified without a formal constraint class. A standalone constrained random generator can be created anywhere and used with arbitrary variables and constraints. In practice, this reduces the effort when coding non-trivial testbench environments. A generator can use all features of CRAVE except for inheritance. However, incremental constraint specification is supported. This feature is very helpful for dynamic testbenches. After the generator has been executed for a certain set of constraints, new constraints can arbitrarily be added, e.g., to generate more general values first and more specific ones later. The use of inline constraints will be demonstrated later in the case study.

Debugging Constraint Contradictions.

The composition of constraints to large sets can easily give contradiction(s) in the global constraint. The manual debugging of such a contradiction is very time-consuming. Therefore, CRAVE can automatically identify which named constraints are part of a conflict. This is completely done on a formal level. Therefore, all minimal subsets of the constraints that form a conflict will be reported.

3.2.5 Parallel Constraint Solving

Various alternatives to BDD-based constraint solving have been studied, see e.g. [25]. Approaches based on *Boolean Satisfiability* (SAT) [32, 24] or *Satisfiability Modulo Theories* (SMT) [37] gave very good results for constraints, which are hard to be solved by BDDs. However, in general it is not possible to know in advance which type of constraint solver will show the best performance. Therefore, CRAVE uses a portfolio approach. Instead of running a specific constraint solver, an SMT-based constraint solver as well as a BDD-based constraint-solver are executed in parallel for the same set of constraints. We use *metaSMT* [18] for implementing the constraint solving in CRAVE. Essentially, *metaSMT* allows engine independent programming by providing a unified interface to different solvers, e.g., CUDD [35], Z3 [11], Boolector [7], MiniSAT [12], PicoSAT [6], SWORD [36], and AIGER [1]).

Overall, solutions for complex constraints can be generated very fast.

4. SYSTEM VERIFICATION METHODOLOGY

For the seamless integration of the presented functional coverage and advanced constrained random stimulus generation techniques an appropriate integration within a verification methodology is essential. For this, we introduce the *System Verification Methodology* (SVM) library for RTL and TLM [30]. The SVM library provides the building blocks for efficient testbench modeling with integrated functional coverage and constrained random stimulus libraries for SystemC verification extension as introduced before. The building blocks of the SVM library include base classes, utilities, and macros, which support the engineer to construct disciplined artefacts improving the reuse of verification components and stimuli.

Taking advantages from SystemC abstract modeling and refinement features, the methodology used in SVM follows the principles of OVM and UVM. In this sense, SVM is developed in compliance with OVM and UVM, thus keeping the best possible interoperability between these libraries.

4.1 Verification Methodology for SystemC

SVM was designed to be compatible with the standard IEEE SystemC simulators. Its packages are defined for a seamless integration of the library into different verification flows, as well as legacy verification environments. Assertions, randomization/constraint solver, and coverage packages implement dedicated TLM verification features. The SVM base, components, and sequences packages will be further outlined in the next subsections.

4.1.1 Base Package

This package is an extension to the OVM multiple languages release v2.1.1, a donation of Cadence to the OVM community, which includes a SystemC implementation. Originally, this package contained elements for factory automation, environment configuration, simulation control, and a root component, which is the base for all other verification components. We additionally included a callback facility, a command-line processor, and a transaction routing and recording feature and moved the base component to the component package, which reflects the alignment to UVM.

The verification methodology implementation follows the factory design pattern, which introduces higher abstraction in the process of instantiating components/objects. In this context, it is possible to change object behavior by providing different implementations with same interface without changes in the object itself that applies that interface. Examples of the application of the factory in the verification process are when it is required to change stimuli, e.g., using a stimulus generator with more constraints, or providing a different driver to adapt the way data is sent to the DUT, e.g., considering a refinement from TLM to RTL. The factory implementation provides facilities to overwrite types and to control the effect of object creation in the entire environment or to a specific object.

The library also provides a configuration facility, which allows the registration of a configuration to affect the entire environment or a specific object. By registering a configuration, a verification component/object queries for an existing configuration that applies to it and performs the required adaptation. The configuration can adapt the component topology - the types and number of subcomponents, and its fields. For example, one can consider a component reading from its configuration table, the name of the input file to read stimuli, or the number and type of components, which are instantiated and bound to a communication bus. Although automatic configuration is provided by the latest OVM SystemVerilog version, due performance and reusability problems [13], we decided not to support this feature in the current SVM release.

On top of that, SVM supports a transaction facility as transactions represent important flows of data object, such as instructions, pixels and data items. The transaction facilities allow users to record transactions, route response to specific requests, and to control timing information for a transaction.

SVM also comes with a callback facility. A callback is an extension mechanism used in complement to the factory, which allows changing the behavior of components without change of the component itself. It can be used to modify the component parameter definition during generation of a testbench or to provide flexible mechanism to allow execution of personalized behavior before or after executing an arbitrary function. One obstacle in the direct conversion of testbenches between SystemC and SystemVerilog is that their simulation kernels perform different execution phases. They must be harmonized in order to change the environment, the configuration of objects, start multiple sections, etc. On top of that, OVM defines multiple phases, improving the simulation phases as given by the SystemVerilog simulation standard. We started with the phase implementation from OVM-SC as it is aligned with the OSCI SystemC simulator and already widely accepted. Although there is a basic alignment in OVM-SC between the phases of OVM and SystemC, some further adaptation is still required due the different between construction and connection performed in SystemC and OVM. Since most of the construction of the OVM hierarchy is performed in the Build Phase, the Connection Phase is required so that all components are created in the time of connection. Although the Connect Phase callback is available in the OVM-SC, it is not automatically called by SystemC kernel, so that a binding has to be performed inside of the Build Phase. However, in order to improve the conformance to OVM, we implemented the automatic call to the Connection Phase after the execution of the Build method of each component. Note that it still executes in the Build Phase and full hierarchical names cannot be used in this phase. However, by using this two distinguished phases, i.e., Build and Connection, the code for connect components can be easily identified and is ready to be used in an SystemC Connection Phase, in the case of potential future SystemC extensions.

4.1.2 Components

OVM-SC provides one verification component, which must be used as base class for all other components. In comparison to OVM-SC, we add an additional package with structural components, which support the development of verification environments and tests in a well-structured way. It includes classes, such as Agents, Drivers, Monitors, etc. These components allow the construction of a topology easy to use, to understand, and to reuse. They reduce some implementation details, improve automation and are the base for future improvements. Currently, SVM provides the following components:

Test: This module has to be extended by the user in order to generate a self-contained test for the DUT. Instances of different Test modules can be used to perform a set of tests, which can be executed in batch mode. Each test can contain one or more Environments in order to verify multiple properties or views.

Environment: This module encapsulates the configuration and instantiation of the topology of verification components. It may contain Agents, Monitors, Scoreboards, etc. that are configured for different environments.

Agent: This module is an abstract container for Driver, Monitor and Sequencer. It is used to emulate the DUT or a functional behavior of components that must be connected to the DUT. Active Agents emulate devices connected to the DUT and passive Agents are used to monitor DUT activity.

Driver: This module drives the signal to the DUT ports. Drivers receive SequenceItems (transaction data) and pass them to DUT. It has detailed information about the DUT interface and its logic and can be used to refine or adapt SequenceItems to a DUT interface.

Monitor: This module extracts transactions, signals and other information from DUTs and makes them available to other components. Typically, a monitor is a subcomponent of an Agent, so that it checks only data relevant for the parent Agent.

Subscriber: This module is used to perform coverage analysis and check the information from DUT provided by Monitors. Multiple Subscribers can be connected to a Monitor. Each Subscriber is responsible to encapsulate different coverage and verification logic.

Scoreboard: Scoreboards may receive different pieces of information from different Monitors for self-checking Environments. Additionally, it can provide coverage information and verify the design at the functional level.

4.1.3 Sequences

The central task in the verification process is to generate and coordinate the stimuli for the DUT. Beyond standard stimuli generation technologies, such as constrained random stimulus generation, the management and arbitration of generated stimuli require special attention to create reusable stimuli. For this purpose, we add a package in our SVM library that contains classes, which support the definition of stimuli and sequences of stimuli. These classes encapsulate the procedure to generate data for the DUT and allow the organization of different data in sequences of stimuli, which can be hierarchically or sequentially organized in libraries. Moreover, different arbitration modes are available to provide the right sequence distribution.

SequenceItem: SequenceItem represents data for stimulus and response of the DUT. It may represent a command, a bus transaction, or a protocol package. The fields in a SequenceItem may be randomized to generate different stimuli in different runs.

Sequence: Sequence implements the procedure to create SequenceItems. Sequences can be reused or combined hierarchically to generate complex stimuli. When Sequences are used sequentially they can represent the different phases of a stimulus, such as configuration phase prior to a communication phase. Additionally, Sequences may be combined, in order to create a hierarchy of stimuli or to generate stimuli in parallel to multiple interfaces of a DUT. They are denoted as Virtual Sequences, which are associated to Virtual Sequencers, containing subsequences to coordinate the flow of stimuli. This feature allows users to generate complex stimuli combining Sequences from a library.

Sequencer: Sequencers are used to generate and to coordinate the Sequences submitted to the Driver or the response to it. Using Sequencers, the user may model time in different scenarios and call the randomization mechanism in Sequences and Sequence Items to generate stimuli. They provide different arbitration modes to select the next Sequence in the library: FIFO, Weighted Priority Distribution, Random, Strict FIFO, Strict Random, and a user implemented arbitration comparison.

4.2 OVM, UVM, and SVM Comparison

The status of our current SVM library (including functional coverage and constraint random stimulus generation) can be classified best when we compare it with OVM and UVM as given in Table 1.

The basis for comparison with OVM is the OVM version 2.2.1, as OVM is the first standardized verification methodology library. After its publication, OVM incorporated some features from UVM 1.1. The most prominent is the UVM Register Abstraction Layer, supported by the UVM Register Kit for OVM, which originates from Synopsys VMM and joined work from Synopsys and Mentor Graphics. However, to use this feature some UVM components must be used together with the OVM library.

As the first UVM release was comparable the latest version of OVM, they show not much difference. Later UVM releases included new features, mainly a command-line processor, a Register Abstraction Layer, an improved simulation control (Phasing), and with general improvements of the API.

In February 2009, Cadence donated the OVM-ML package to ovm-world.org including the OVM-SC. At the same time, a functionally equivalent UVM for SystemC (UVM-SC) version, with minor changes, was donated by Cadence to uvmworld.org under the UVM multiple-languages package umbrella.

Table 1 highlights the main differences between UVM-SC and UVM, the original version for SystemVerilog. It can easily be seen there that UVM-SC lacks most of the features provided by UVM, which are mandatory to perform coverage-driven and constrained-random verification.

The SVM library supports almost all missing features missing of OVM/UVM for SystemC, by adding features based on the OVM for SystemVerilog version 2.2.1. Additionally, we integrated the libraries for the functional coverage and stimulus generation features of SystemC. Moreover, SVM is complemented with a powerful assertion language for SystemC, which was first introduced in [14].

Therefore the set of libraries tailored for advanced TLM verification, which integrates SVM provides powerful tools to develop CDV and CRV testbenches for SystemC environments using TLM and RTL models.

5. CASE STUDY

Our case study implements a high-level control model of a two wheeled self-balancing electric vehicle. The closed-loop control model, a classic inverted pendulum control, receives its driving commands from the user's balance and through a vertical steering axis with immediate impact of the driving motors.

We created a virtual platform, which runs the control algorithms wrapped in SystemC components as given in Figure 3. The virtual platform is composed of one CPU, sensors and actuators, communicating through a TLM2 bus. A command interface receives commands from the steering axis and forwards it to the CPU component using the TLM2 bus.

The testbench consists of a `SVM Test` component that is

Table 1: Comparison of OVM, UVM and SVM.

Feature	OVM	UVM	UVM-SC	SVM
Call-backs	Yes	Yes	No	Yes
Comparison	Yes	Yes	No	No
Command-Line Processor	No	Yes	No	Yes
Configuration	Yes	Yes	Yes	Yes
Factory	Yes	Yes	Yes	Yes
Methodological Components	Yes	Yes	Yes	Yes
Objection	Yes	Yes	No	No
Packing	Yes	Yes	Yes	Yes
Simulation Control and Phasing	Yes	I	Yes	Yes
Polices	Yes	Yes	No	No
Recording	Yes	Yes	SCV	Yes
Register Abstraction Layer	Yes	Yes	No	YES
Reporting	Yes	Yes	SC	SC
Routing	Yes	Yes	No	Yes
Sequencing	Yes	Yes	No	Yes
Synchronization	Yes	Yes	SC	SC
Assertion	SV	SV	No	I
Coverage	SV	SV	SCV	I
Constrained Random Stimuli	SV	SV	SCV	I

Yes - The library provides the feature; No - The library does not provide the feature; I - Improved feature; SC - Feature from the SystemC Language; SV - Feature provided by SystemVerilog language; SCV - Feature provided by SystemC Verification Library.

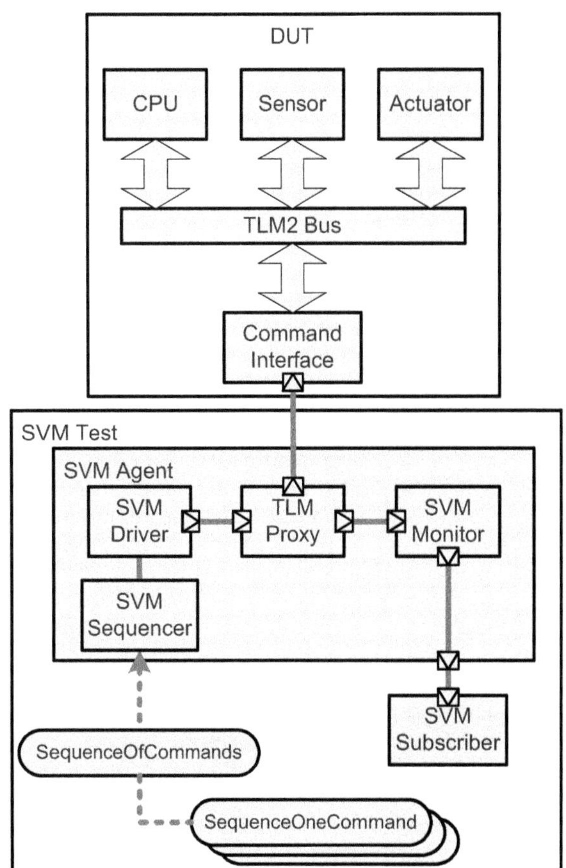

Figure 3: Verification testbench structure.

```
1  class SVMAgent : public svm_agent {
2  public:
3    tlm::tlm_analysis_port<tlm::tlm_generic_payload > aport;
4    SVMDriver *pDriver;
5    SVMMonitor *pMonitor;
6    SVMSequencer *pSequencer;
7
8    SVMAgent(sc_core::sc_module_name name);
9
10   SVM_COMPONENT_UTILS(SVMAgent)
11
12   void SVMAgent::build(){
13     svm_agent::build();
14     get_config_int("debug", debug);
15     pSequencer = DCAST<SVMSequencer*>(
           svm_factory::create_component( "SVMSequencer",
           "","pSequencer" ) );

16   }
17 };
18 SVM_COMPONENT_REGISTER(ActorAgent);
```

Figure 4: Partial code showing the SVMAgent structure.

```
1  constraint(0 <= degree() && degree() <= 36);
2  constraint(0 <= percent() && percent() <= 100);
3  constraint(IF_THEN(command() != ifx::IFX_TURN_LEFT
       && command() != ifx::IFX_TURN_RIGHT, degree() ==
       0));
4  constraint(IF_THEN(command() !=
       ifx::IFX_INCREASE_SPEED && command() !=
       ifx::IFX_DECREASE_SPEED, percent() == 0));
```

Figure 5: Constraints for One Command Item.

```
BIN: IFX_ACTOR_CMD:TURN_LEFT::: 2014 Hits
BIN: IFX_ACTOR_CMD:TURN_RIGHT::: 1965 Hits
BIN: IFX_ACTOR_CMD:INCREASE_SPEED::: 1985 Hits
BIN: IFX_ACTOR_CMD:DECREASE_SPEED::: 2068 Hits
BIN: IFX_ACTOR_CMD:STOP::: 1968 Hits
BIN: IFX_ACTOR_DEGREE:DEGREE::: 3979 Hits
BIN: IFX_ACTOR_PERCENT:PERCENT::: 4053 Hits

BIN: SEQ_LENGTH:0-15::: 1908 Hits
BIN: SEQ_LENGTH:16-30::: 57 Hits
BIN: SEQ_LENGTH:31-..::: 3 Hits
```

Figure 6: `IXF_ACTOR` transaction coverage.

the main container for the testbench. The `SVM Test` contains one `SVM Agent` that replaces the steering axis and is composed by one TLM2 `SVM Driver` and one TLM2 `SVM Monitor`. The `SVM Agent` contains a `SVM Sequencer`, which receives sequences of stimuli from the `SVM Test` and schedules it to the `SVM Driver`, which drives the stimuli for the DUT interface. Figure 4 shows an excerpt of the `SVM Agent` code. At Line 18 SVM defined macros are used to register components within the factory, the creation of component using the factory at line 15 as well as the acquisition of configuration values at Line 14.

When it comes to the stimulation of TLM2 interfaces, the question of how to organize a driver and a monitor is important. In RTL verification, this separation is fairly simple since a RTL driver is connected via signals to the DUT. A RTL monitor, hence, needs to be connected to the same signals for observing the behavior. At TLM, however, a connection is usually done on a port-to-port basis, i.e., initiator to target connections. Hence, it was necessary to incorporate a so called "`TLM-Proxy`". This proxy broadcasts any incoming transaction to both the monitor and towards the DUT. However, the broadcast to the monitor happens twice - once at the beginning of the transaction and once when the transaction call has returned from the DUT. This allows a monitor to observe pre- and post-conditions of a transaction.

The connection to the DUT is established through a regular SystemC TLM2 initiator to target binding. Hence, a delta-free connection could be established between the DUT and the verification component. This also enables the verification environment to perform tests, which check the behavior of the TLM model by performance optimization techniques such as the Quantum Keeping mechanism.

Extending the `svm_sequence_item` class we defined the `Command Item` class, which holds the stimuli generated for the DUT command interface. Each `Command Item` to the DUT can either make it turn left/right by a given angle or increase/decrease its speed by a given percentage, or simply stop the vehicle. Therefore, the `Command Item` contains three fields: the *command*, the given *degree*, and the given *percent*. The constraints for each `Command Item` are shown in Figure 5. As can be seen at Line 3 and 4, *degree* and *percent* are constrained to be zero if *command* does not indicate a turn or a change of speed, respectively.

The DUT is stimulated by two hierarchical sequences, which define how the `Command Items` are driven to the command interface. At high level, we define one `Sequence of Commands`, which is the main container for the generated sequences. It creates sets of `Sequence One Command`, so that pattern of commands can be generated and grouped, building a library of stimuli. Finally, each `Sequence One Command` holds an `Command Item`, which is randomized and is ready to be driven to the DUT. For this, one `Command Item` is pushed by the `SVM Sequencer` to the driver. Following that, the `SVM Driver` interprets the `Command Item` and executes two transactions in the command interface - one for the command and one for the parameter. In order to investigate the verification closure of the simulation runs, we monitor the received transactions within the `SVM Monitor` component. A `SVM Subscriber` is connected to `SVM Monitor` and implements a functional coverage metric with four coverpoints as follow:

IFX_ACTOR_CMD has bins corresponding to `command` values. This allows checking the distribution of the generated commands during the simulation.

IFX_ACTOR_DEGREE which implements bins for `degree` values, therefore keeping track of the path.

IFX_ACTOR_PERCENT which collects coverage of the altering of the speed, expressed in percentage ranging from 0 to 100.

SEQ_LENGTH which covers the number of consecutive commands before a STOP command occurs.

In the first run of stimuli, we send 10,000 random `Command Items` to the DUT. As shown by the first seven lines of the collected coverage. in Figure 6, the first run examines the design thoroughly. However, the main shortcoming is that the STOP command was executed too often. That means, that long sequences of turns and speed changes before stop are not sufficiently considered. This is visible in the last three lines in Figure 6: most considered sequences have only between 0 and 15 commands.

Therefore, in the second run, we send several constrained sequences of commands to the DUT. The constraints for the

```
1  Generator<Context> inline_constraints;
2  rand_vec<IfxCommandValT> commands;
3  randv<int> tmp;
4
5  inline_constraints(25 <= tmp() && tmp() <= 40);
6  inline_constraints(commands().size() == tmp());
7  inline_constraints.foreach(commands, _i, IF_THEN(_i == 0,
       commands()[_i] == ifx::IFX_INCREASE_SPEED));
8  inline_constraints.foreach(commands, _i, IF_THEN_ELSE(_i <
       reference(tmp) - 1, commands()[_i] != ifx::IFX_STOP,
       commands()[_i] == ifx::IFX_STOP));
9  inline_constraints.foreach(commands, _i, (commands()[_i] !=
       commands()[_i - 1]) || (commands()[_i] !=
       commands()[_i - 2]) || (commands()[_i] !=
       commands()[_i - 3]));
10
11 while (sequenceCount-- > 0) {
12   inline_constraints.next();
13   // generate each individual command item and deliver it
         to the DUT
14   ...
15 }
```

Figure 7: Constraints for One Command Sequence.

sequences are captured using inline constraints on a random vector of CRAVE as depicted in Figure 7. The first two constraints ensure that each sequence contains between 25-40 commands. The third constraint forces the first command to be an increase of speed. The fourth constraint specifies that all commands should not be a stop command with the exception of the last command. Finally, no four consecutive commands in a sequence should be equal. After the generation of a vector of commands (Line 12), each individual command item is generated respecting the constraints in Figure 5 with the *command* field being fixed to the corresponding value in the generated vector.

We defined also a similar set of constraints in the SCV library using fixed size array of commands. However, even for only 25 commands, the SCV library has not been able to generate a single sequence after several hours. This result is consistent with the experimental comparison of CRAVE and SCV reported in [19].

6. CONCLUSIONS

In this paper we presented the *System Verification Methodology* (SVM) as a set of SystemC libraries for TLM testbench implementation. SVM combines missing building blocks for advanced functional verification with SystemC. The combination of advanced constraint solving and random stimulus generation capabilities with a functional coverage facility under the umbrella of a verification methodology allows building highly modular testbenches in a standardized, structured, efficient, and reusable way. The SVM is completely compliant to existing standards as it is based on the concepts of OVM Multiple-Languages - SystemC package v2.1.1 and OVM for SystemVerilog v2.1.1 that has been refactored for UVM.

We successfully applied our methodology to a high level control model of a two wheel self-balancing electric vehicle and performed regression tests within larger case studies. At this point, a pretty stable implementation of SVM is apparently achieved as it has also been applied to more complex industrial designs. The next step will be the completion towards complete UVM. This is mainly the support of the register abstraction layer.

7. ACKNOWLEDGMENTS

This work was partly funded by the German Ministry of Education and Research (BMBF) through the project SANITAS (01M3088), the DFG SFB 614, the ITEA2 projects VERDE (01S09012) and TIMMO-2-USE (01IS10034), and the DFG Reinhart Koselleck project DR 287/23-1. We greatly appreciate the cooperation with the project partners.

8. REFERENCES

[1] Aiger. http://fmv.jku.at/aiger/.
[2] Accellera Organization, Inc. Open Verification Library (OVL), May 2009.
[3] Accellera Organization, Inc. Universal Verification Methodology (UVM), May 2012.
[4] J. Aynsley. *OSCI TLM-2.0 LANGUAGE REFERENCE MANUAL*. Open SystemC Initiative (OSCI), 2009.
[5] J. Bergeron. Writing Testbenches: Functional Verification of HDL models. Kluwer Academic Publishers, 2003.
[6] A. Biere. Picosat essentials. *JSAT*, 4(2-4):75–97, 2008.
[7] R. Brummayer and A. Biere. Boolector: An efficient SMT solver for bit-vectors and arrays. In *Tools and Algorithms for the Construction and Analysis of Systems*, pages 174–177, 2009.
[8] Cadence Design Systems, Inc. Open Verification Methodology Multi-Language (OVM-ML).
[9] Cadence Design Systems, Inc. Universal Reuse Methodology (URM).
[10] Cadence Design Systems, Inc. OVM-SC Library Reference Version 2.0.1, February, 2009.
[11] L. de Moura and N. Bjørner. Z3: An efficient SMT solver. In *TACAS*, pages 337–340, 2008.
[12] N. Eén and N. Sörensson. An extensible SAT-solver. In *SAT*, pages 502–518, 2003.
[13] A. Erickson. Are OVM & UVM Macros Evil? A Cost-Benefit Analysis. In *Proceeding of Design and Verification Conference (DVCON)*, Mar. 2011.
[14] V. Esen. *A new assertion language covering multiple levels of abstraction*. PhD thesis, 2008.
[15] H. Foster. Redefining Verification Performance (part 2), August 2010.
[16] D. Große, R. Ebendt, and R. Drechsler. Improvements for constraint solving in the SystemC verification library. In *ACM Great Lakes Symposium on VLSI*, pages 493–496, 2007.
[17] D. Große, R. Wille, R. Siegmund, and R. Drechsler. Contradiction analysis for constraint-based random simulation. In *Forum on Specification and Design Languages*, pages 130–135, 2008.
[18] F. Haedicke, S. Frehse, G. Fey, D. Große, and R. Drechsler. metaSMT: Focus on your application not on solver integration. In *DIFTS'11: 1st International workshop on design and implementation of formal tools and systems*, pages 22–29, 2011.
[19] F. Haedicke, H. M. Le, D. Große, and R. Drechsler. CRAVE: An advanced constrained random verification environment for SystemC. In *International Symposium on System-on-Chip (SoC)*, 2012. Available at www.systemc-verification.org.

[20] IEEE Computer Society. IEEE Standard for System Verilog-Unified Hardware Design, Specification, and Verification Language - IEEE 1800-2009. 2009.

[21] IEEE Computer Society. IEEE 1666-2011 Standard SystemC Language Reference Manual. *IEEE Std 1666-2011*, 2011.

[22] IEEE Computer Society. Standard for the Functional Verification Language e. *IEEE Std 1647-2011 (Revision of IEEE Std 1647-2008)*, pages 1 –495, 26 2011.

[23] JEDA Technologies, Inc. JEDA ESL Validation Solution.

[24] H. Kim, H. Jin, K. Ravi, P. Spacek, J. Pierce, B. Kurshan, and F. Somenzi. Application of formal word-level analysis to constrained random simulation. In *Computer Aided Verification*, 2008.

[25] N. Kitchen and A. Kuehlmann. Stimulus generation for constrainted random simulation. In *International Conference on Computer-Aided Design*, pages 258–265, 2007.

[26] C. Kuznik and W. Müller. Functional Coverage-driven Verification with SystemC on Multiple Level of Abstraction. *Proceedings of DVCON*, 2011.

[27] W. K. Lam. *Hardware Design Verification: Simulation and Formal Method-Based Approaches (Prentice Hall Modern Semiconductor Design Series)*. Prentice Hall PTR, Upper Saddle River, NJ, USA, 2005.

[28] Mentor Graphics, Inc. Advanced Verification Methodology (AVM).

[29] NextOp Software, Inc. NextOp assertion-based verification.

[30] M. F. S. Oliveira, C. Kuznik, W. Mueller, W. Ecker, and V. Esen. A SystemC Library for Advanced TLM Verification. In *Proceeding of Design and Verification Conference (DVCON)*, Mar. 2012.

[31] Open SystemC Initiative. SystemC Verification Library v1.0p2, 2006.

[32] S. M. Plaza, I. L. Markov, and V. Bertacco. Random stimulus generation using entropy and XOR constraints. In *Design, Automation and Test in Europe*, pages 664–669, 2008.

[33] K. Schwartz. A technique for adding functional coverage to SystemC. In *DVCON 2007*. Willamette HDL Inc., 2007.

[34] R. Siegmund, U. Hensel, A. Herrholz, and I. Volt. A functional coverage prototype for SystemC-based verification of chipset designs. In *9th European SystemC User Group Meeting at Design, Automation and Test in Europe*, 2004.

[35] F. Somenzi. *CUDD: CU Decision Diagram Package Release 2.4.1.* University of Colorado at Boulder, 2009.

[36] R. Wille, G. Fey, D. Große, S. Eggersglüß, and R. Drechsler. Sword: A SAT like prover using word level information. In *VLSI of System-on-Chip*, pages 88–93, 2007.

[37] R. Wille, D. Große, F. Haedicke, and R. Drechsler. SMT-based stimuli generation in the SystemC verification library. In *Forum on Specification and Design Languages*, pages 1–6, 2009.

Generation of TLM Testbenches Using Mutation Testing

Marcelo Sousa
Dept. of Information Computing Sciences
Utrecht University, Netherlands
marceloabsousa@gmail.com

Alper Sen
Dept. of Computer Engineering
Bogazici University, Turkey
alper.sen@boun.edu.tr

ABSTRACT

Testbench development is a major component of simulation based verification, which is the de-facto verification technique used in the industry. Verification of a TLM design is not complete without a measure of the effectiveness of its testbenches. We devise a coverage driven testbench generation technique where the coverage metric uses that of a fault insertion based approach, namely mutation testing. Mutation testing is a commonly used software testing technique to measure the quality of testbenches. In mutation testing, the goal is to insert mutations (syntactic changes) into the program and check whether the impact of these mutations on the program can be detected by the available testbenches. If the testbenches cannot detect the impact of these inserted mutations then one can potentially add new testbenches to detect these changes. In this work, we automate the process of mutation testing based testbench generation exploiting the properties of concurrent TLM designs. Our framework is novel in that it uses the byte code representation of SystemC TLM models using Low Level Virtual Machine (LLVM) framework. Furthermore, these testbenches can detect concurrency related defects such as deadlocks or race conditions. We perform experiments on TLM models to demonstrate the effectiveness of our test bench generation approach.

Categories and Subject Descriptors

D.2.4 [**Software Engineering**]: Software/Program Verification; D.2.5 [**Testing and Debugging**]: Testing tools

Keywords

SystemC, TLM, verification, mutation testing, LLVM

1. INTRODUCTION

The increasing complexity of System-on-Chips (SoCs) exposed limitations of standard Register Transfer Level (RTL) simulations. The main limitation is related to the low level nature of RTL originating simulations with poor performance. Furthermore, the costs of debugging and validation of RTL simulations reached levels unbearable to the industry.

Transaction Level Modeling (TLM) is an approach that overcomes the RTL scalability problem by operating at a higher level of abstraction. The basic idea of TLM is to model hardware components as modules that communicate with *transactions*. Due to its higher abstraction level, TLM allows fast simulations that can be used by designers in an early stage of the design cycle to obtain various performance results and discover potential errors of the real system.

In recent years, SystemC became a de-facto standard for simulation of SoCs using TLM designs. SystemC [1] is an IEEE standard C++ library composed of an event scheduler and constructs to represent the concurrent behavior of hardware. The SystemC TLM [1] standard enables system level verification and debugging as well as hardware/software co-design, architectural exploration, and power/performance analysis.

Automated verification of SystemC TLM designs is valuable since the verification phase can potentially consume a substantial part of the design cycle. Although formal verification of TLM designs are emerging, simulation remains the most popularly used verification technique in the industry. Nevertheless using this approach, verification of a TLM design is not complete without a measure of the effectiveness of its testbenches. Hence, it is crucial to aid hardware designers with methods that automatically generate testbenches based on a coverage criteria to guarantee that the generated testbench is effective with respect to the criteria.

Mutation testing is a commonly used software testing technique to measure the quality of testbenches. Mutation testing consists of inserting errors, known as mutations, into the program and checking if the testbenches detect the inserted mutations. If the testbenches cannot detect the impact of a set of mutations, then one can argue that new testbenches need to be added to detect these changes and improve the overall testbench quality.

In this paper, we devise an automated hybrid coverage driven testbench generation technique based on mutation testing. We base our fault model in the hypothesis that a suitable testbench for a concurrent program should reach the maximum number of synchronization operations possible. We are interested in exploring the effects of mutated synchronization operations in fault identification and resolution.

The problem of whether a test case can reach a point in a

program is undecidable [34]. We apply static analysis techniques to generate constraints over the input variables from a bounded version of the original program. Our method exploits the properties of concurrent TLM designs and the deterministic semantics of the SystemC scheduler. From the generated constraints, we obtain concrete input tests using a Satisfiability Modulo Theories (SMT) solver, an efficient constraint-satisfaction problem solver [4]. Finally, we dynamically generate oracles that encapsulate the impact of the mutations based on execution trace comparison. Hence, we achieve testbenches with high ratio of detected mutants.

Our framework is novel in that it uses the byte code representation of SystemC TLM models using the Low Level Virtual Machine (LLVM) framework [22]. LLVM is a compiler framework designed for aggressive multistage optimizations over a well-defined intermediate representation. The main advantage of this approach is that we lift the lack of formal semantics of the high-level language C++ that represents one of the current problems of SystemC TLM design validation [28]. Hence, by using LLVM Intermediate Representation (IR) we leverage its formal semantics to apply formal methods such as SAT/SMT solvers or theorem proving.

We also show with a complete example of our approach that we can detect concurrency related defects such as deadlocks or lost notifies. We perform initial experiments on TLM models to demonstrate the effectiveness of our test bench generation approach.

The rest of the paper is organized as follows. Section 2 describes related work in SystemC mutation testing and test case generation using mutation analysis. Section 3 details the background on mutation testing, SystemC TLM and LLVM. Section 4 describes our mutation framework for SystemC that operates at the LLVM byte code level. Section 5 describes our testbench generation flow with details of our algorithms for input generation. Section 6 presents a dynamic approach for oracle generation and Section 7 describes our experiments. We conclude with a discussion of our current limitations to be left as future work and conclusions.

2. RELATED WORK

Mutation testing is an approach based on software testing to assess the quality of test suites [8, 31, 32]. It has been defined for programming languages such as Java [27, 7], state machines [33] and hardware description languages such as Verilog [15]. A detailed survey on applications of mutation testing can be found in [20].

Mutation testing has been widely applied in exploiting the correlation between the fault model and real faults [3]. The standard mutation testing approach is to inject mutations into the program one at a time, and check whether the test suite can identify the fault introduced. Hence, it helps to strengthen the quality of test suites by providing information related to tests cases that should complement the test suite. Mutation testing has proven more powerful than other coverage criteria such as statement, branch, and all-use dataflow [13, 39, 26].

Standard mutation frameworks implement optimization to reduce the high number of mutants generated. Prior work on mutant equivalence [36] and higher order mutation testing [19] have tackled this problem.

A mutation model for SystemC TLM 2.0 communication interfaces have been defined in [5, 6] and this has been extended to all SystemC concurrency constructs in [37]. Our work implements a mutation framework that supports the latter mutation model. We do not require any modification of the SystemC libraries, hence our mutation framework is scalable and transparent to the user.

Automated test case generation is a natural application of mutation testing. Early research on mutation testing [30] developed methods based on constraint solving to solve the input-mutant reachability problem. In [12], this work is extended with a necessity condition encoding the mutant effects on states of the program. Moreover, [10, 18] have used fault models for test generation.

μTest [14] applies a genetic algorithm to generate unit tests for object-oriented classes in Java based on mutation analysis. The framework generates oracles to increase mutation coverage by comparing execution traces of a test case on a program and its mutants. Our approach focuses on the domain of concurrent programs and uses a byte code representation that supports a wider range of programming languages.

SymBMC [34] uses SMT/bounded model checking approach using mutation analysis to generate test cases from ANSI-C programs. KLEE [9] and KLOVER [24], perform symbolic execution of sequential C and C++ programs represented with the LLVM byte code for automatic test suite generation. Recently, GKLEE [25], a tool based on KLEE, applies concolic execution to CUDA programs for test generation. The tools of the KLEE family require manual instrumentation from the user and all except GKLEE do not handle concurrent programs. Our approach is more transparent to the user and supports a better integration since we do not require any user modification on the source code.

3. BACKGROUND

In this section, we provide background on Mutation Testing, SystemC TLM and LLVM.

3.1 Background on Mutation Testing

Mutant testing is based on a fault model represented as a set of mutation operators. A mutation operator MO is a non-deterministic rewrite system.

Example Mutation operator MO for *wait(e)*:

wait(e) $\rightarrow$ wait(1,SC_NS);
wait(e) $\rightarrow$ e.notify();
wait(e) $\rightarrow$ ϵ;

The example above is composed of three rewrite rules. The left hand-side of a rule represents the operation to be mutated, and by definition in a mutation operator, the left hand-side of all rules is the same. The first rule mutates the argument of *wait* to a value of a different type. The second rule applies the dual relation between *wait* and *notify* and the third rule removes the operation.

A mutant P' of a program P is the program generated by one reduction of the mutation operator MO. In the previous example, MO can potentially generate three mutants. Following the definition of *mutant*, we can define *killed* and *live mutant*.

DEFINITION 1. *A mutant P' of a program P is said to be* killed *by a test t if and only if there are observable differences between $P'(t)$ and $P(t)$.*

Algorithm 1 Mutation Coverage Algorithm

Input: a program P, a testbench T.
Output: mutation coverage.

```
1: generate a metamutant MP from P;
2: for each mutation operator MO in MP do
3:    generate a mutant P' from MO and P;
4:    for each test t ∈ T do
5:       execute P' with t;
6:       check if P' is killed by t;
7:    end for
8: end for
9: compute mutation coverage;
```

Definition 2. *A mutant P' of a program P is said to be* live *if and only if there is no test t in the testbench T that kills the mutant.*

Using mutation testing we can compute a new coverage metric, *mutation coverage*, that is useful to assess the quality of a testbench.

Definition 3. *The* mutation coverage *of a testbench T for a program P is the ratio of the number of killed mutants to the number of all mutants.*

Mutation coverage is a useful metric since it identifies errors, encoded as mutants, that are not tested in the testbench T. Therefore, mutation coverage of T can be improved by extending the testbench with new test cases that kill live mutants.

Algorithm 1 describes a general mutation coverage algorithm. In line 1, we generate a metamutant MP by inserting mutation operators into P. A metamutant captures all possible mutations and supports a mechanism that allows dynamic activation of one mutation operator. This strategy is popular for mutant testing since it is more efficient than generating a compiled version of the program for each mutation. In line 3, we generate a mutant from the original program using the mutation operator as described above. Then, in line 4, we iterate over the test suite and execute the mutant with every test (line 5) and check if the mutant is killed by the test using Definition 1 (line 6). Finally, we compute the mutation coverage rate using Definition 3. A mutation coverage rate of 1 may no be possible due to equivalent mutants.

The complexity of the algorithm can reach $M \times T \times C_t$, where M is the number of inserted mutations, T is the size of the test suite and C_t is the execution cost of one test. Since the number of mutations can be high, mutation analysis suffers from a scalability problem so mutation coverage can be an expensive metric to compute.

3.2 Background on SystemC TLM

SystemC [1] models hardware components as modules. Modules are composed of processes which encode the concurrent behavior of the component, and ports that are used for interprocess communication. Although processes run concurrently, their execution is sequential. The SystemC scheduler is non-preemptive; hence, a process has to voluntarily yield control for another process to be executed. The scheduler chooses non-deterministically exactly one process at a time to be executed. It implements an event-based simulator similar to VHDL by handling event notifications and managing updates to channels. Hardware parallelism is abstracted with the notion of delta cycle.

SystemC supports method processes and thread processes. A method executes atomically and cannot explicitly suspend itself. The simulator regains control after the entire method has been executed. Threads are run exactly once by the scheduler and are typically enclosed by a loop that keeps them alive for the duration of the simulation. The program-flow control remains with the thread till it explicitly yields by calling $wait()$ or finishing its execution. In the former case, the thread stays in a $wait$ state until some event $triggers$ it, and it resumes execution from the next statement after $wait$.

Processes are triggered and synchronized with respect to its sensitivity on events. A SystemC event is the occurrence of an *sc_event* notification and happens at a single point in time. An event has no duration or value. Events are controlled via $wait$, $next\_trigger$ and $notify$ functions of the *sc_event* class. A $wait$ function changes dynamic sensitivity of a thread process and suspends its execution. For example, $wait(SC\_ZERO\_TIME)$ delays the process by one delta cycle, a process waits on event e with $wait(e)$, and with $wait(e1|e2|e3)$ a process waits on event $e1, e2$, or $e3$.

Events occur explicitly by using the $notify$ function, and the scheduler resumes execution of a thread or method process by executing the $trigger$ function. For example, $e.notify()$ is called an immediate notification since processes sensitive to event e will run in the current evaluation phase or delta cycle. Using $e.notify(SC\_ZERO\_TIME)$ processes sensitive to event e will run in the evaluation phase of the next delta-cycle. Using $e.notify(t)$ processes sensitive to event e will run during the evaluation phase of some future simulation time.

Process synchronization also occurs with the usage of channels, interfaces, and ports. These constructs are the core of SystemC Transaction Level Model (TLM) based methodology [1]. The basic idea of TLM is to model hardware components as modules that communicate with transactions. TLM provides interoperability layer for bus modeling through generic payloads and phases that in turn get used through initiator and target sockets. These sockets can use blocking and non-blocking transport interfaces. Different levels of model abstraction is provided in TLM through different coding styles such as loosely-timed (used by blocking transport interface) and approximately-timed (used by non-blocking transport interface). Loosely-timed is more suitable for software development, whereas approximately-timed is more suitable for performance analysis or architectural exploration. Some of the TLM synchronization functions are $b\_transport$ (blocking transport), $nb\_transport\_fw$ (non-blocking transport forward path), and $nb\_transport\_bw$ (non-blocking transport backward path). Note that, in SystemC, communication between processes is established either by explicit concurrency functions or by shared variables.

The following displays the steps of the simulation scheduler in more detail. The first phase of a SystemC simulation, the elaboration phase, consists of describing an architecture by registering the processes in the scheduler and defining constructs for module interconnection.

1. *Initialization:* All processes are made executable in an unspecified order.
2. *Evaluate:* Select a ready-to-run process and resume its

execution. This may result in more processes ready for execution in this same phase due to immediate notification. Signals and channels may invoke a request for update in the update phase.

3. Repeat Step 2 until no more processes are ready-to-run.
4. *Update:* Execute all pending update requests due to calls made in Step 2.
5. If Steps 2 or 4 resulted in delta event notifications, go back to Step 2.
6. If there are no more events, simulation is finished for current time.
7. Advance to next simulation time that has pending events. If none, exit simulation.
8. Go back to Step 2.

The SystemC scheduler is not preemptive, that is, a process runs without interruption until it explicitly gives control back with a wait statement. In [17], the authors show that a non-preemptive scheduler introduces implicit atomic sections (a wait-to-wait block in a process) hiding most of the issues regarding concurrent accesses to shared resources.

3.2.1 SystemC Example

Figure 1 illustrates a SystemC design. We will use this example throughout this paper to demonstrate our methodology. The code in Figure 1 declares a SystemC module $M1$ where internal processes, threads $T1$ and $T2$, communicate through a SystemC event e and two shared variables $cs1$ and $cs2$.

In this example, the synchronization of the event e is guarded by two booleans $cs1$ (line 17) and $cs2$ (line 26) assigned in the constructor of $M1$. The values of $cs1$ and $cs2$ are assigned to arguments of the constructor. Therefore, both threads $T1$ and $T2$ are open programs. The input-synchronization dependency of the threads presents an interesting case study since the presence of synchronization errors is not uniquely dependent on the SystemC scheduler. This behavior is similar to synchronization events generated by other processes through interprocess communication. In this paper, we are interested in an automatic method for generation of unit tests that explore different SystemC simulations.

```
1  SC_MODULE(M1)
2  {
3    sc_event e;
4    bool cs1, cs2;
5
6    SC_HAS_PROCESS(M1);
7
8    M1(sc_module_name name, bool x,
       bool y)
9    {
10     SC_THREAD(T1);
11     SC_THREAD(T2);
12     cs1 = x;
13     cs2 = y;
14   }
15
16   void T1() {
17     if(cs1){
18       wait(e);          // Mutation #1
19       cs2=false;
20     }
21     wait(10,SC_NS);     // Mutation #2
22     cs2=true;
23   }
24
25   void T2(){
26     if(cs2){
27       cs1=false;
28       e.notify();       // Mutation #3
29     }
30     wait(10,SC_NS);     // Mutation #4
31     cs1=true;
32   }
33 };
```

Figure 1: A SystemC Design

3.3 Background on LLVM

LLVM is a popular and steadily growing compiler framework that supports aggressive multistage optimizations with competitive results against industrial compilers. The framework was initially designed to be a flexible, well-documented and transparent infrastructure for research projects in the compiler domain [22].

LLVM supports reusable back-end components that simplify the compiler construction process since, out of the box, compiler implementors can reuse several optimizations and analysis already implemented. Hence, the main compiler construction step is the front-end implementation. Moreover, LLVM provides code generation for several architectures, and although primarily focused on C and C++, other programming language front-ends have been implemented.

In LLVM, every optimization or transformation is performed over LLVM Intermediate Representation (IR) code. The LLVM IR language implements an unbounded register machine. The instruction set is composed of RISC-like three address code instructions in Single Static Analysis (SSA) form [35] with high level type information. The SSA representation form and the combination of low-level and high-level information translate in a well-defined and target-independent semantics. Hence, LLVM IR is suitable for analysis and, in theory, is capable of representing 'all' high-level languages cleanly [2, 23].

In Figure 2, we describe some of the productions that compose the implemented LLVM IR grammar. We describe a simplified grammar since we are not interested in attributes such as linkage, section or garbage collection.

An LLVM IR ⟨module⟩ is composed of a list of named types, global variables and functions. A named typed, ⟨nmd-ty⟩, binds an identifier to a type. In line 1 of Figure 3, %"*class.std* :: *ios_base* :: *Init*" is defined as the integer type of one byte. A global variable ⟨global⟩ is represented by an identifier, a type and an optional value if the variable is initialized. Line 2 of Figure 3, defines "@M1" as a constant with the value "M1".

Function definitions are composed of a declaration (identifier ⟨ident⟩, type ⟨ty⟩ and parameters ⟨param⟩*) and a list of basic blocks. Each basic block ⟨bb⟩ is represented by a label identifier, a list of ⟨phi⟩ instructions, a list of instructions and a final terminator ⟨tmn⟩ instruction such as an unconditional *branch* (line 4). A *phi* instruction represents a choice between several basic blocks.

Instructions are grouped into binary ⟨bop⟩, bitwise ⟨bwop⟩,

$$
\begin{array}{rl}
\langle\text{module}\rangle \models & \langle\text{nmd-ty}\rangle^* \ \langle\text{global}\rangle^* \ \langle\text{fn}\rangle^* \\
\langle\text{nmd-ty}\rangle \models & \%\ \langle\text{ident}\rangle \ \langle\text{ty}\rangle \\
\langle\text{global}\rangle \models & @\ \langle\text{ident}\rangle \ \langle\text{ty}\rangle \ \langle\text{val}\rangle? \\
\langle\text{fn}\rangle \models & \text{fun-decl} \ \langle\text{ident}\rangle \ \langle\text{ty}\rangle \ \langle\text{param}\rangle^* \\
 & \mid \ \text{fun-def} \ \langle\text{ident}\rangle \ \langle\text{ty}\rangle \ \langle\text{param}\rangle^* \ \langle\text{bb}\rangle^+ \\
\langle\text{param}\rangle \models & \langle\text{ident}\rangle \ \langle\text{ty}\rangle \\
\langle\text{bb}\rangle \models & \langle\text{label}\rangle \ \langle\text{phi}\rangle^* \ \langle\text{instr}\rangle^* \ \langle\text{tmn}\rangle \\
\langle\text{phi}\rangle \models & \text{phi} \ \langle\text{value}\rangle \ \langle\text{ty}\rangle \ (\langle\text{value}\rangle \ \langle\text{label}\rangle)^+ \\
\langle\text{tmn}\rangle \models & \text{unreachable} \mid \langle\text{br}\rangle \mid \langle\text{ret}\rangle \\
\langle\text{instr}\rangle \models & \langle\text{bop}\rangle \mid \langle\text{bwop}\rangle \mid \langle\text{vop}\rangle \\
 & \mid \langle\text{aop}\rangle \mid \langle\text{mop}\rangle \mid \langle\text{cop}\rangle \mid \langle\text{oop}\rangle \\
\langle\text{value}\rangle \models & \langle\text{ident}\rangle \mid \langle\text{const}\rangle \\
\langle\text{ty}\rangle \models & \text{void} \mid \text{i} \ \langle\text{int}\rangle \mid \langle\text{float}\rangle \\
 & \mid [\ \langle\text{int}\rangle \times \langle\text{ty}\rangle\ ] \mid \langle\ \langle\text{int}\rangle \times \langle\text{ty}\rangle\ \rangle \\
 & \mid \langle\text{ty}\rangle{*} \mid \langle\text{ty}\rangle^* \rightarrow \langle\text{ty}\rangle \mid \{\ \langle\text{ty}\rangle^*\ \}
\end{array}
$$

Figure 2: LLVM IR Grammar

```
%"class.std::ios_base::Init" = type { i8 }
@M1 = linkonce_odr constant [2 x i8] c"M1"
%.0 = phi i8* [%.pre1, %bb1],[%tmp8, %bb4]
br label %bb14
```

Figure 3: LLVM IR example

vector ⟨vop⟩, aggregate ⟨aop⟩, memory access and addressing ⟨mop⟩, conversion ⟨cop⟩ and other ⟨cop⟩ operations.

LLVM IR is equipped with a type system that adds extra expressive power to the language. Every LLVM IR ⟨value⟩, either an identifier ⟨ident⟩ or a constant ⟨const⟩ has a type ⟨ty⟩. LLVM IR supports primitive types: void, integers with a specified bit width i⟨int⟩ or ⟨float⟩; and derived types for arrays, vectors, structs, pointers and functions.

4. MUTATION FRAMEWORK

In this section, we describe our SystemC metamutant generation flow illustrated in Figure 4. It is an instance of our mutation framework that operates at the LLVM IR level, since we can potentially mutate programs of all programming languages supported by LLVM.

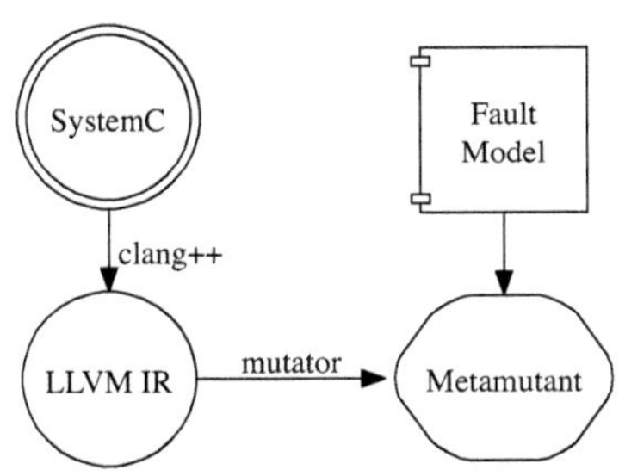

Figure 4: Metamutant Generation Flow

Given a SystemC program, we use clang++ [11], a C++ compiler front-end for LLVM, to generate LLVM IR byte

Algorithm 2 Meta Mutant Generation

Input: LLVM IR Module M.
Output: Metamutant, Number c of mutation operators.

1: initialize counter c to 0;
2: **for** each function F in M **do**
3:   **for** each basic block BB in F **do**
4:     **for** each instruction I in BB **do**
5:       **if** $isSync(I)$ **then**
6:         $I' = mutate(I, c)$;
7:         increment c;
8:       **end if**
9:     **end for**
10:   **end for**
11: **end for**

code. Then we apply Algorithm 2 based on a fault model for SystemC through an LLVM pass to generate a metamutant.

Algorithm 2 describes our metamutant generation procedure. In line 1, we initialize the integer c to 0. This integer serves as a counter that represents the number of instructions mutated so far and also is an argument to a new mutate function in our mutation library. The mutate function implements a mutation operator. Then, we iterate over all instructions (lines 2 to 4) and check if the current instruction is a call to a relevant SystemC synchronization function (line 5). In that case, in line 7, we mutate the callee of the instruction to point to our mutation library.

We currently explore a simple fault model that implements mutation operators that remove synchronization functions related to SystemC events and time. Nevertheless, our framework is easily extensible to a complete set of SystemC constructs and richer mutation operators.

```
void T1()
{
  if(cs1){
 // wait(e);
    cs2=false;
  }
  wait(10,SC_NS);
  cs2=true;
}
```

```
void T2()
{
  if(cs2){
    cs1=false;
    e.notify();
  }
  wait(10,SC_NS);
  cs1=true;
}
```

Figure 5: Mutant Example for SystemC Design in Figure 1

Previous work [37] have investigated the relationship between SystemC TLM synchronization operations and common concurrent error patterns such as deadlocks, lost notifies or data races. Figure 5 shows an example of a mutant generated from the SystemC design in Figure 1. In this case, *Mutation #1* was enabled and the mutation operator removed the call to $wait(e)$. Independent of the scheduling order, this mutant has a lost notify in thread $T2$ if the value of $cs2$ is $true$. This information is useful for testers in fault identification and resolution.

5. TESTBENCH GENERATION FLOW

We explore the dependency relation between input variables and synchronization operations following the hypothesis that a suitable testbench for a concurrent program should reach all possible synchronization operations. Although the reachability problem for a general program is undecidable, we use a bounded version of the original program to partially solve this problem. Therefore, we only support SystemC designs that have free variables in at least one of their processes and support a mechanism such that testing different values for those free variables is possible. Also, note that although in this section we motivate our techniques through SystemC models our results are applicable to SystemC TLM models as well.

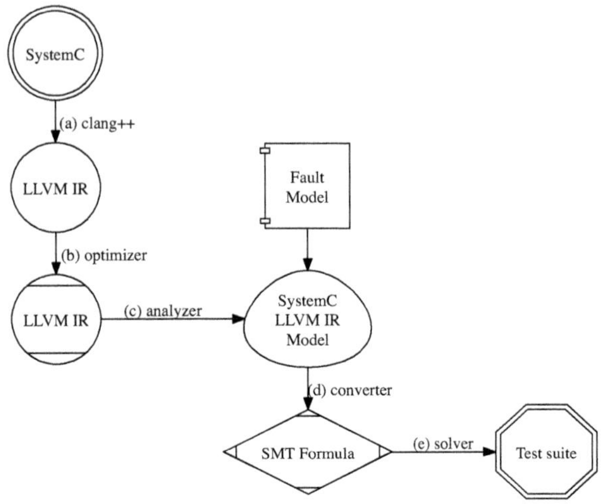

Figure 6: Testbench Generation Flow

In Figure 6, we present our automatic test generation flow. Given a SystemC design we start by generating LLVM byte code with clang++. Since the implementation of SystemC and other C++ libraries is heavily based on template programming, we apply various optimizations to obtain more compact byte code modules.

In phase (b), we use the optimizer to transform the current byte code into a form that is suitable for our analysis. In total, we apply 18 LLVM passes (optimizations, transformations) achieving considerable byte code reduction. For the design in Figure 1, we achieve a 80% reduction between the byte code bounded version and an unoptimized version. We describe some of these passes now. We divide the set of transformations applied into decidability and simplification categories. Decidability transformations aim at generating a bounded version of the program such that the reachability problem becomes decidable. For the purpose of our analysis we want to obtain byte code that has no cycles in the basic block graph. Simplification transformations aim at simplifying our formalization. We further reduce the byte code size eliminating LLVM IR constructs not supported by our analysis such as invoke or switch instructions. Also, we leverage the LLVM IR unbounded number of registers to promote the stack to registers and we name all nameless identifiers.

In phase (c), we extract a SystemC model that contains information about the architecture and the behavior of the processes. We describe this method in detail in Section 5.1.

In Section 5.2, we describe our conversion function from a SystemC model to an SMT formula, phase (d), exploiting the deterministic implementation of the SystemC scheduler. Finally, in phase (e), described in Section 5.3, we use an SMT solver to generate a test case.

5.1 SystemC Model Extraction

We have formalized the LLVM IR language with the Utrecht Attribute Grammar System (uuagc) [38]. Our representation of LLVM IR is similar to the one in Figure 2. We use a binding library for Haskell [21], a general purely functional language, to retrieve information from LLVM byte code modules. Our main motivation for this approach is a combination of the advantages of Haskell as a prototyping language with an expressive type system and equational reasoning, and the similarities between LLVM IR and functional languages. *uuagc* is a framework suitable for analysis of functional programming languages that generates optimized Haskell programs.

```
int sc_main(int argc , char *argv[])
{
  // Initialize cs1 and cs2 with argv

  M1 M1("M1", cs1 , cs2);
  sc_start();

  return 0;
}
```

Figure 7: *sc_main* of SystemC design in Figure 1

In Figure 7, we present a simple example of a simulation model for the SystemC design in Figure 1. In *sc_main*, we start by assigning $cs1$ and $cs2$ with the user input arguments. Then, we create an instance of the SystemC module $M1$ with $cs1$ and $cs2$. Finally, we start the simulation with a call to *sc_start*.

```
1
2  %struct.M1 = type { %"class.sc_core::sc_module", %"
         class.sc_core::sc_event", i8, i8 }
3   @.str = private unnamed_addr constant [3 x i8] c"M1\00"
         , align 1
4   define i32 @sc_main(i32 %argc, i8** nocapture %argv)
         uwtable {
5     ; ...
6     %M1 = alloca %struct.M1, align 8
7     %tmp1 = alloca %"class.sc_core::sc_module_name",
         align 8
8     ; %tmp5 ~= argv[1], %tmp9 ~= argv[2]
9     call void @_ZN7sc_core14sc_module_nameC1EPKc(%"
         class.sc_core::sc_module_name"* %tmp1, i8*
         getelementptr inbounds ([3 x i8]* @.str, i64 0,
         i64 0))
10    call void @_ZN2M1C2EN7sc_core14sc_module_nameEbb(%
         struct.M1* %M1, %"class.sc_core::sc_module_name"
         * undef, i1 zeroext %tmp5, i1 zeroext %tmp9)
11    call void @_ZN7sc_core14sc_module_nameD1Ev(%"
         class.sc_core::sc_module_name"* %tmp1)
12    call void @_ZN7sc_core8sc_startEv()
13
14  ; ...
15  }
```

Figure 8: LLVM IR of *sc_main*

Figure 8 lists the LLVM byte code relevant to *sc_main*, and in Figure 9 we present its formalization as Haskell *data*. The [ ] notation is the Haskell representation for lists. The model represented in Figure 9 is a simplified, structured and readable version of the actual LLVM byte code of Figure 8.

The *sc_main* byte code starts by allocating a struct $M1$ (line 6). The definition of the named type *struct.*$M1$ is listed in line 2. Note that it contains information about the class variables of $M1$. In line 9, there is a call to the constructor of *sc_module_name*. Then, in line 10, an instance of $M1$ is defined with a call to the constructor. Finally, *sc_start* is called (line 12) after the call for the destructor of *sc_module_name* (line 11).

```
Module
 [NmdTy (Local "struct.M1") TyStruct (Local "struct.M1"
     ) [SyscMod, SyscEv, (TyI 8), (TyI 8)]]
 [Global (Global ".str") (TyArray 3 (TyI 8)) (Const (
     CString "M1\00"))]
 [FunctionDef (Global "sc_main") (TyI 32) [Param (Local
      "argc") (TyI 32), Param (Local "argv") (TyPtr (
     TyPtr (TyI 8)))]
  [BasicBlock
   [Alloca (Local "M1") (TyStruct (Local "struct.M1")
       ...)
   ,Alloca (Local "tmp1") (TyStruct (Local "class.
       sc_core::sc_module_name") ...)
   ,...
   ,Call TyVoid (Global "sc_core::sc_module_name::
       sc_module_name") [Ident (Local "tmp1"), Ident (
       Global ".str"), Const (CInt (TyI 64) 0), Const
       (CInt (TyI 64) 0)]
   ,Call TyVoid (Global "M1::M1") [Ident (Local "M1"),
       Const UndefC, Ident (Local "tmp5"), Ident (
       Local "tmp5")]
   ,Call TyVoid (Global "sc_core::sc_module_name::~
       sc_module_name()") [Ident (Local "tmp1")]
   ,Call TyVoid (Global "sc_core::sc_start()") []
   ]
  ]
 ]
```

Figure 9: *sc_main* Model

We apply static analysis techniques to analyze the elaboration phase of a SystemC simulation model. Our method iterates over all instructions in the *sc_main* function and checks for calls to *sc_module* constructors until it reaches the call to *sc_start*. In case of a call to a *sc_module* constructor we retrieve the module information. This function analyzes the named type to retrieve the class variables and inspects the constructor to gather information about the module processes and communication.

```
SysC
  [ScMod (Id "M1")
         (Vars [ScEvent, TyI 8, TyI 8])
         (ScProcs [ScThread (Id "T1")
                    (..)
                  ,ScThread (Id "T2")
                    (..)
                  ]
         )
  ]
```

Figure 10: SystemC Model in Haskell

We generate a SystemC model with the architecture as in Figure 10. The model is represented by a list of modules. Each module is composed of an identifier, a list of class variables and a list of processes that respect the same declaration order as in the original constructor. A process is either a thread or a method. They are represented by an identifier and the LLVM byte code model of their function bodies.

5.2 SystemC Model Encoding

In this section, we present an encoding function to generate an SMT closed quantifier-free formula with bit-vectors from a SystemC model. Given a mutated instruction i in a basic block β_i, and a SystemC model M, as the one in Figure 10, we generate the following SMT formula:

$$\Psi(i, M) = \overbrace{\otimes(i, M)}^{\text{inter } \beta_i \text{ analysis}} \wedge \underbrace{\oplus(i, M)}_{\text{intra } \beta_i \text{ analysis}} \tag{1}$$

Formula 1 encodes the reachability problem for LLVM IR with concurrent constructs. We model this problem as a conjunction of the predicates given by operators $\otimes$ (otimes) and $\oplus$ (oplus).

$\otimes$ encodes the constraints related to local identifiers to reach the basic block of instruction i and is formally defined as follow.

$$\otimes(i, M) = \bigvee_{\beta' \in \Pi(\beta_i)} \odot(\llbracket \tau_{\beta'},\ \beta_i \rrbracket,\ \Pi(\tau_{\beta'}),\ M) \wedge \overbrace{\otimes(\tau_{\beta'},\ M)}^{\text{recursion}} \tag{2}$$

To reach the mutated basic block β_i, we iterate over its direct basic block predecessors and for each basic block the operator $\odot$ (odot) encodes the reachability constraints. $\odot$ performs an intra basic block backwards analysis with an initial predicate that represents the reachability path to β_i. The initial predicate is given by $\llbracket \tau_{\beta'},\ \beta_i \rrbracket$ (Formula 3), where $\tau_{\beta'}$ is the terminator instruction of the basic block β'.

Finally, we reach the entry basic block by recursion, and guarantee termination based on the assumption that there are no cycles in the basic block graph.

Note that Π is a polymorphic function; $\Pi(\beta_i)$ computes the direct predecessor set of basic blocks and $\Pi(\tau_{\beta'})$ computes the predecessor set of instructions.

$$\llbracket \tau_{\beta'},\ \beta_i \rrbracket = \begin{cases} \mathit{true}, & (\tau_{\beta'} = \text{br } \beta_\kappa) \wedge \beta_i \equiv \beta_\kappa \\ \nu \equiv 1, & (\tau_{\beta'} = \text{br } \nu, \beta_t\ \beta_f) \wedge \beta_i \equiv \beta_t \\ \nu \equiv 0, & (\tau_{\beta'} = \text{br } \nu, \beta_t\ \beta_f) \wedge \beta_i \equiv \beta_f \\ \mathit{false}, & \text{otherwise} \end{cases} \tag{3}$$

$\odot$ is defined based on set induction. The base case, Formula 4, is the head of the basic block and since there are no more instructions to interpret, we return the predicate. In the induction step, Formula 5, we interpret the instruction ϵ with the current predicate ψ. The interpretation function $\llbracket\ \rrbracket$ encodes the instruction in a simple flat memory model supported by SMT solvers and applies logical conjunction with the current predicate. We have extended the encoding provided in [29] to support synchronization operations. In that case, we apply function Ψ to retrieve the SMT formula generated. Since such operations are also mutated, we can use memoisation techniques to optimize our implementation.

$$\odot(\psi,\ \emptyset,\ M) = \psi \tag{4}$$

$$\odot(\psi,\ \epsilon \cup \Upsilon,\ M) = \odot(\llbracket \epsilon,\ \psi,\ M \rrbracket,\ \Upsilon,\ M) \tag{5}$$

When reasoning about sequential programs at the LLVM byte code level we can assume reachability of any instruction in a basic block if we reach the entry point of the basic block. However, in a concurrent program reachability from the head of the basic block to the current mutated instruction is not guaranteed. The operator $\oplus$ (oplus) defined in Formula 6, encodes the constraints for the current thread to be enabled (operator $\uplus_i$, uplus) and also considers previous deadlock scenarios in the mutated basic block β_i (operator $\uplus$). The function $\Lambda(i)$ returns the set of predecessor operations in the basic block that may lead to a deadlock situation.

$$\oplus(i, M) = \uplus_i(i, M) \bigwedge_{i' \in \Lambda(i)} \uplus(i', M) \tag{6}$$

We exploit the deterministic implementation of the SystemC scheduler to fix a scheduling order. In a SystemC model M, we define a poset $\prec_{proc}$ composed of the processes in the model. We build this relation based on the declaration order in the original program. For the SystemC design in Figure 1, $T1 < T2$.

$$\uplus_i(i, M) = \begin{cases} true & , T_i \text{ minimal } \prec_{proc} \\ \bigvee_{T<T_i} \Psi(i^{-1}, M) & , \text{ otherwise} \end{cases} \quad (7)$$

Operator $\uplus_i$ in Formula 7, checks if the thread executing instruction i, T_i is the minimal element of $\prec_{proc}$. In that case we can assume that T_i will be the first thread to be executed. To guarantee reachability of i if T_i is not the minimal element of $\prec_{proc}$, at least one of the previously executed threads has to reach an instruction i^{-1} that gives control to the scheduler. The operator $\uplus$ in Formula 8, encodes the constraints for previous i^{-1} instructions in the basic block.

$$\uplus(i, M) = \bigvee_{T<T_i} \Psi(i^{-1}, M) \quad (8)$$

5.3 Testbench Generation

We pass the generated SMT formula to a solver to generate a set of assignments. It is not guaranteed that the formula generated will be satisfiable. This means that the mutated instruction might be dead or that for that scheduling a deadlock occurs.

In the final step of test generation we map the thread local identifiers to user input arguments of *sc_main*. The method described in Section 5.2 can be applied to the constructor instruction of the SystemC module. If the formula contains are free variables, the SMT solver will choose a default value according to its type.

5.3.1 SystemC Model Encoding Example

We demonstrate our method with the mutant of Figure 5. In Figure 11, we provide the relevant LLVM byte code instructions of thread $T1$.

```
1  bb:
2    %tmp = alloca %"class.sc_core::sc_time", align 8
3    %tmp1 = getelementptr inbounds %struct.M1* %this, i64
         0, i32 2
4    %tmp2 = load i8* %tmp1, align 1, !tbaa !6, !range !7
5    %tmp3 = icmp eq i8 %tmp2, 0
6    br i1 %tmp3, label %._crit_edge, label %bb4
7
8  bb4:                                          ; preds = %
       bb
9    %tmp5 = getelementptr inbounds %struct.M1* %this, i64
         0, i32 1
10   %tmp6 = getelementptr inbounds %struct.M1* %this, i64
         0, i32 0, i32 0, i32 1
11   %tmp7 = load %"class.sc_core::sc_simcontext"** %tmp6,
         align 8, !tbaa !0
12   call void
         @_ZN7sc_core4waitERKNS_8sc_event_13sc_simcontextE
         (%"class.sc_core::sc_event"* %tmp5, %"
         class.sc_core::sc_simcontext"* %tmp7)
```

Figure 11: LLVM byte code for *T1*

In this example, the mutated instruction i is the $wait(e)$ in line 12, and we use the extracted model M in Figure 10.

$$\Psi(\text{wait(e)}, M) = \otimes(\text{wait(e)}, M) \wedge \oplus(\text{wait(e)}, M)$$

Since the basic block predecessor of *bb4* is the entry basic block *bb*, the operator $\otimes$ is reduced to:

$$\otimes(\text{wait(e)}, M) = \odot([\![\tau_{\text{bb}}, \text{ bb4}]\!], \ \Pi(\tau_{\text{bb}}), \ M)$$

Then, we use the interpretation function in Formula 3 to further reduce $\otimes$ to:

$$\odot(\text{tmp3} = 0, \ \Upsilon, \ M) = \text{struct.M1[2]} \neq 0$$

Υ is the set of instructions from lines 5 to 2.

The $\oplus$ operator is reduced to *true* since $T1$ is the minimal element of M_T and there is no more *call wait* instructions before line 12. The simplified SMT expression generated is:

$$\Psi(\text{wait(e)}, M) = \text{struct.M1[2]} \neq 0 \wedge \text{true}$$

Table 1 shows a test suite for M using four mutants. In this case, we achieve total input coverage. Note that some formulas can generate the same test case. This information could be used as a heuristic to reduce the number of mutants.

M#	Simplified SMT Formula	Input
M1	$\text{argv}[1] = \text{t}$	(t,f)
M2	$\text{argv}[1] = \text{f} \vee (\text{argv}[1] = \text{t} \wedge \text{argv}[2] = \text{t})$	(f,f)
M3	$\text{argv}[2] = \text{t}$	(f,t)
M4	$\text{argv}[1] = \text{t} \wedge \text{argv}[2] = \text{t}$	(t,t)

Table 1: Test suite generated for SystemC in Figure 1

6. ORACLE GENERATION

A test oracle is a mechanism that determines the program correctness with respect to a test [40]. We modify this notion of test oracle for our mutation testing based technique as follows. Using the testbenches generated with our method, we produce oracles that represent the differences between a program and its mutant by instrumenting the program with observers for all variables. The observers dump an internal state triggered by any synchronization operation. Our state representation is the thread identifier and the values of all variables in scope. We use execution trace comparison as observable differences to obtain a complete definition of *killed mutant*. Note that an assertion could also be an oracle for our technique.

Table 2 lists two execution traces generated when executing the original design in Figure 1 and Mutant #1 with the input generated (t,f) from Table 1. Both the original and mutant program start executing $T1$ with the initial input (t,f). The original program will reach $wait(e)$ and suspend itself. Then $T2$ will not call notify since $cs2$ is false and wait 10 simulation time units. Since $T1$ is waiting for the notification of the event, the scheduler will update the time to enable $T2$, which will then execute $cs1 = true$ and terminate leading to a deadlock. Mutant #1 starts executing $T1$ and skips the operation $wait(e)$. The second line of the trace corresponds to the dump of the assignment $cs2 = false$. Then both threads will wait 10 simulation time units. The fourth line of the trace corresponds to the assignment $cs2 = true$ and finally, $T2$ will reach the assignment $cs1 = true$.

Oracles provide useful information to find synchronization errors. Table 3 lists all the schedulings for the test suite generated in Table 1. We can use the execution traces for

Original Trace	Mutant #1 Trace
T1:(t,f)	T1:(t,f)
T2:(t,f)	T2:(t,f)
Time Elapse	Time Elapse
T2:(t,f)	T1:(t,t)
Deadlock	T2:(t,t)

Table 2: Execution Trace Comparison.

fault localization to explain why the program deadlocks in the original version and not the mutant.

M#	Input	Original Schedule	Mutant Schedule
M1	(t,f)	T1; T2; TE; T2 (DL)	T1; T2; TE; T1; T2
M2	(f,f)	T1; T2; TE; T1; T2	T1; T2; TE; T2
M3	(f,t)	T1; T2; TE; T1; T2 (LN)	T1; T2; TE; T1; T2
M4	(t,t)	T1; T2; T1; TE; T1; T2	T1; T2; TE; T1

Table 3: Schedulings.
(TE = time elapse, DL = deadlock, LN = lost notify)

7. EXPERIMENTS

We have conducted initial experiments with 5 SystemC designs. We have modified for our analysis four test cases from the SCRV [16] test suite and implemented an instance of the producer consumer example. In Table 4, we present our results. The second column of the table represents the size of the optimized LLVM byte code in number of lines. In the third column and fourth columns we present the number of generated mutants and test cases generated, respectively. Note that the number of test cases is smaller or equal to the number of mutants, since we generate at most a single test case for each mutant. The same test case can kill multiple mutants. The last column presents our mutation coverage results. Although we generated test cases that reached all mutations, the mutation coverage scores were not always 100%. The reason is that some mutations do not produce any observable effects in the traces, e.g., Mutation #2 in Table 3. Also in the case of *prodcod*, the original program contains redundant synchronization mechanisms, hence mutation these does not produce any observable effect.

Design	# Lines	# Mutants	# Test cases	MC
indexer	1077	5	3	80%
sirac	1110	9	4	89%
fiveteen	1226	4	4	100%
prodcon	1229	5	3	40%
srX	1781	5	2	100%

Table 4: Mutation Coverage Results

8. CONCLUSIONS AND FUTURE WORK

In this work, we have introduced a complete testbench generation flow for concurrent SystemC programs based on mutation testing. Our framework operates at the LLVM byte code level, leveraging its formal semantics that lifts previous limitations of SystemC analysis. Our implementation operates at the domain of functional languages which are known to provide useful abstraction patterns for program analysis. We generate formal models that have wider applicability in other formal verification fields. Our experiments show that we can automatically generate testbenches with high mutant coverage ratio. In the future, we plan to use the Just In Time (JIT) compiler in LLVM for dynamic compilation of the elaboration phase in SystemC model generation.

9. ACKNOWLEDGMENTS

This work was supported in part by Marie Curie European Reintegration Grant within the 7th European Community Framework Programme, Semiconductor Research Corporation under task 2082.001, Bogazici University Research Fund 5483, and the Turkish Academy of Sciences.

10. REFERENCES

[1] IEEE Standard for Standard SystemC Language Reference Manual. *IEEE Std 1666-2011 (Revision of IEEE Std 1666-2005)*, pages 1 –638, jan 2012.

[2] V. Adve, C. Lattner, M. Brukman, A. Shukla, and B. Gaeke. LLVA: A Low-level Virtual Instruction Set Architecture. In *Proceedings of the 36th annual ACM/IEEE international symposium on Microarchitecture (MICRO-36)*, San Diego, California, Dec 2003.

[3] J. H. Andrews, L. C. Briand, and Y. Labiche. Is Mutation an Appropriate Tool for Testing Experiments? In *Proceedings of the 27th International Conference on Software Engineering (ICSE)*, pages 402 – 411, 2005.

[4] C. Barrett, R. Sebastiani, S. Seshia, and C. Tinelli. Satisfiability Modulo Theories. In *Handbook of Satisfiability*, pages 737–797. IOS Press, Amsterdam, The Netherlands, 2009.

[5] N. Bombieri, F. Fummi, and G. Pravadelli. A Mutation Model for the SystemC TLM 2.0 Communication Interfaces. In *Proceedings of the Conference on Design Automation and Test in Europe (DATE)*, pages 396–401. ACM, 2008.

[6] N. Bombieri, F. Fummi, G. Pravadelli, M. Hampton, and F. Letombe. Functional Qualification of TLM Verification. In *Proceedings of the Conference on Design Automation and Test in Europe (DATE)*, pages 190–195. ACM, 2009.

[7] J. Bradbury, J. Cordy, and J. Dingel. Mutation Operators for Concurrent Java (J2SE 5.0). In *Workshop on Mutation Analysis*, page 11, Nov. 2006.

[8] T. A. Budd. Mutation analysis: Ideas, examples, problems and prospects. In *Computer Program Testing*, pages 129–148. North-Holland, 1981.

[9] C. Cadar, D. Dunbar, and D. R. Engler. Klee: Unassisted and automatic generation of high-coverage tests for complex systems programs. In *OSDI*, pages 209–224, 2008.

[10] D. V. Campenhout, H. Al-Asaad, J. P. Hayes, T. Mudge, and R. B. Brown. High-level Design

Verification of Microprocessors via Error Modeling. *ACM Transactions on Design Automation of Electronic Systems*, 3(4):581–599, 1998.

[11] clang: a C language family frontend for LLVM, http://clang.llvm.org/, 2012.

[12] R. A. DeMillo and A. J. Offutt. Constraint-based automatic test data generation. *IEEE Trans. Softw. Eng.*, 17(9):900–910, Sept. 1991.

[13] P. G. Frankl, S. N. Weiss, and C. Hu. All-uses vs Mutation Testing: an Experimental Comparison of Effectiveness. *Journal of Systems and Software*, 38(3):235–253, September 1997.

[14] G. Fraser and A. Zeller. Mutation-driven generation of unit tests and oracles. In *Proceedings of the 19th international symposium on Software testing and analysis*, ISSTA '10, pages 147–158, New York, NY, USA, 2010. ACM.

[15] M. Hampton and S. Petithomme. Leveraging a commercial mutation analysis tool for research. In *Testing: Academic and Industrial Conference Practice and Research Techniques - MUTATION, 2007*, pages 203–209, Sept. 2007.

[16] C. Helmstetter, F. Maraninchi, and L. Maillet-Contoz. Full Simulation Coverage for SystemC Transaction-Level Models of Systems-on-a-Chip. *Formal Methods in System Design*, 35(2):152–189, 2009.

[17] C. Helmstetter and O. Ponsini. A Comparison of Two SystemC/TLM Semantics for Formal Verification. In *Proceedings of the International Conference on Formal Methods and Models for Co-Design (MEMOCODE)*, pages 59–68, 2008.

[18] M. S. Hsiao, E. M. Rudnick, and J. H. Patel. Dynamic State Traversal for Sequential Circuit Test Generation. *ACM Trans. Des. Autom. Electron. Syst.*, 5(3):548–565, 2000.

[19] Y. Jia and M. Harman. Higher order mutation testing. *Inf. Softw. Technol.*, 51(10):1379–1393, Oct. 2009.

[20] Y. Jia and M. Harman. An Analysis and Survey of the Development of Mutation Testing. *Software Engineering, IEEE Transactions on*, PP(99):1, 2010.

[21] S. P. Jones, editor. *Haskell 98 Language and Libraries: The Revised Report*. http://haskell.org/, September 2002.

[22] C. Lattner. LLVM: An Infrastructure for Multi-Stage Optimization. Master's thesis, University of Illinois at Urbana-Champaign, 2002.

[23] C. Lattner and V. Adve. Architecture for a Next-Generation GCC. In *Proc. First Annual GCC Developers' Summit*, Ottawa, Canada, May 2003.

[24] G. Li, I. Ghosh, and S. P. Rajan. Klover: a symbolic execution and automatic test generation tool for c++ programs. In *Proceedings of the 23rd international conference on Computer aided verification*, CAV'11, pages 609–615, Berlin, Heidelberg, 2011. Springer-Verlag.

[25] G. Li, P. Li, G. Sawaya, G. Gopalakrishnan, I. Ghosh, and S. P. Rajan. Gklee: concolic verification and test generation for gpus. In *Proceedings of the 17th ACM SIGPLAN symposium on Principles and Practice of Parallel Programming*, PPoPP '12, pages 215–224, New York, NY, USA, 2012. ACM.

[26] N. Li, U. Praphamontripong, and J. Offutt. An Experimental Comparison of Four Unit Test Criteria: Mutation, Edge-Pair, All-Uses and Prime Path Coverage. In *IEEE International Conference on Software Testing Verification and Validation Workshop*, pages 220–229, 2009.

[27] Y.-S. Ma, J. Offutt, and Y. R. Kwon. MuJava: An Automated Class Mutation System: Research Articles. *Software Testing, Verification and Reliability*, 15(2):97–133, 2005.

[28] F. Maraninchi, M. Moy, J. Cornet, L. Maillet-Contoz, C. Helmstetter, and C. Traulsen. SystemC/TLM Semantics for Heterogeneous System-on-Chip Validation. In IEEE, editor, *2008 Joint IEEE-NEWCAS and TAISA Conference*, page unknown, Montréal, Canada, June 2008.

[29] F. Merz, S. Falke, and C. Sinz. Llbmc: Bounded model checking of c and c++ programs using a compiler ir. In *VSTTE*, pages 146–161, 2012.

[30] J. Offutt. *Automatic Test Data Generation*. PhD thesis, Georgia Institute of Technology, Atlanta, USA, 1988.

[31] J. Offutt, P. Ammann, and L. Liu. Mutation Testing implements Grammar-Based Testing. In *Workshop on Mutation Analysis, 2006*, pages 12–12, 2006.

[32] J. Offutt and R. H. Untch. *Mutation 2000: Uniting the Orthogonal*. Kluwer Academic Publishers, 2001.

[33] S. P. F. Fabbri, M. Delamaro, J. Maldonado, and P. Masiero. Mutation Analysis Testing for Finite State Machines. In *5th International Symposium on Software Reliability Engineering*, pages 220–229, Nov 1994.

[34] H. Riener, R. Bloem, and G. Fey. Test case generation from mutants using model checking techniques. In *Proceedings of the 2011 IEEE Fourth International Conference on Software Testing, Verification and Validation Workshops*, ICSTW '11, pages 388–397, Washington, DC, USA, 2011. IEEE Computer Society.

[35] B. K. Rosen, M. N. Wegman, and F. K. Zadeck. Global value numbers and redundant computations. In *Proceedings of the 15th ACM SIGPLAN-SIGACT symposium on Principles of programming languages*, POPL '88, pages 12–27, New York, NY, USA, 1988. ACM.

[36] D. Schuler, V. Dallmeier, and A. Zeller. Efficient mutation testing by checking invariant violations. In *ISSTA '09: Proceedings of the 18th International Symposium on Software Testing and Analysis*, pages 69–80, July 2009.

[37] A. Sen. Concurrency-oriented verification and coverage of system-level designs. *ACM Trans. Des. Autom. Electron. Syst.*, 16(4):37:1–37:25, Oct. 2011.

[38] S. D. Swierstra, P. R. A. Alcocer, and J. Saraiva. Designing and implementing combinator languages. In *Advanced Functional Programming*, pages 150–206, 1998.

[39] P. J. Walsh. *A Measure of Test Case Completeness (software, engineering)*. PhD thesis, State University of New York at Binghamton, Binghamton, NY, USA, 1985.

[40] E. J. Weyuker. On Testing Non-Testable Programs. *The Computer Journal*, 25(4):465–470, 1982.

A Testbench Specification Language for SystemC Verification

Giuseppe Di Guglielmo, Graziano Pravadelli
University of Verona
Strada Le Grazie 15, Verona, Italy
{name.surname}@univr.it

ABSTRACT

Testing of embedded systems, operating in the real environment, is generally performed by using an industrial test bench that stimulates the system through sensors and human-machine interfaces. The test bench provides the engineers with a set of tools for reproducing the environmental conditions which may affect the system. On the contrary, a different approach is adopted at the early stages of the design flow, when system level languages, like SystemC, are used to describe the functionality of the design. At this level, stimuli for testing the design are traditionally generated in a random or statistical way, which makes more difficult to capture well-specific behaviors of the considered environment, thus decreasing the effectiveness and the efficiency of the verification. This is particularly evident for dynamic assertion-based verification where, to avoid vacuous passes of assertions, stimuli must reflect specific scenarios to activate the assertions.

In this work, we propose a graphical framework to automatically generate stimuli, particularly suited to be used for dynamic ABV of embedded SW. The framework relies on the definition of a Testbench Specification Language (TSL) that allows to formally capture the behavior of the real environment where embedded SW is intended to be executed, i.e., how input values evolve on time intervals. Then, the framework allows to automatically synthesize TSL descriptions into SystemC-based stimuli generators, which exploit and extend the functionality of the SystemC Verification Library.

Categories and Subject Descriptors

D.2.4 [**Software Engineering**]: Software/Program Verification; D.2.5 [**Software Engineering**]: Testing and Debugging—*testing tools, data generators*

Keywords

Testbench Specification Language, Embedded Software, Stimuli Generation, SystemC Verification Library

1. INTRODUCTION

With the increasing complexity of embedded systems and, in particular, of the Embedded Software (ESW) [23], the need arises to improve the verification of the software components at the early stages of the design cycle.

Two main classes of approaches exist for ESW verification: *structural code analysis*, i.e., testing based on coverage metrics [25], and *specification conformance*, i.e., functional verification, for example, by means of Assertion-based Verification (ABV) [5].

Testing based on coverage metrics, also known as white-box testing, concentrates on checking that all structural items, e.g., executable statements, branches, and paths, within the ESW application have been exercised. If there is a portion of code that has never been exercised, then there is a high possibility that it could contain an error that will remain undetected; or it identifies "dead code" that is a not correct implementation of the specifications. Thus, aim of structural code analysis is to raise the designer's confidence level that the code does not contain any untested areas. Structural testing can therefore be considered as concentrating on checking that the ESW control logic operates correctly.

Functional verification, also known as black-box testing, ensures that "correct results at the correct time" are obtained when "good inputs" are applied, and the design operates in a predictable manner when "bad inputs" are applied. Functional verification can therefore be considered as concentrating on checking that the ESW applications respect the requirements and specifications. Functional verification is inherently concerned with behavioral or functional aspects, that are orthogonal to the structural code analysis.

If, nowadays, the coverage-based testing approaches are fully automated, functional verification is still relying on human-based process which are only partially supported by semi-automatic methodologies [13, 8] . Indeed, the de-facto approach to guarantee the functional correctness of ESW is monitoring the application execution: verification teams are responsible of putting the application into appropriate states by generating the required stimuli, judging when stimuli should be executed, manually simulating environment and user interactions, and, finally, analyzing the results to identify unexpected behaviors [28]. In this case, the engineers follow *test scenarios* that are documents describing both typical and atypical situations that may occur in the use of ESW application. Scenarios define test conditions, data to be used for testing, and the expected results [18].

ABV [10] aims at providing verification engineers with a way for formally capturing the intended specifications and checking their compliance with the implemented design, i.e., it automates the scenarios defined in the traditional approach. In ABV, specifications are expressed by means of temporal assertions, that, to overcome the ambiguity of natural languages, are defined according to formal assertion languages, like, for example, the Property Specification Language (PSL) [16]. Such assertions can be verified by using formal methods, i.e., model checking, or dynamically through simulation. In the hardware domain, dynamic ABV affirmed as a leading strategy in industry to guarantee fast and high-quality verification of hardware components [4, 26] and several verification approaches have been proposed [10, 9]. More recently, dynamic ABV have been extended to ESW verification [5]. In dynamic ABV, PSL assertions are compiled into executable checkers, i.e., software modules that constantly monitor design behavior during execution under a specific set of stimuli.

Thus, the effectiveness of dynamic ABV depends on the quality of the stimuli that exert the ESW implementation. In particular, the stimuli should try to stress the ESW functionalities to fully exercise the checkers and avoid vacuous passes of the corresponding assertions. However, stimuli generated by means of Automatic Test Pattern Generators (ATPGs) addressing structural-coverage metrics are targeted to cover statements/conditions disregarding the real behavior of the implementation. This can cause assertions are trivially satisfied, e.g., antecedent always false, or false positives, e.g., either a liveness property that appears to be false just because simulation stops before reaching the right activation state, or a safety property failing due to the generation of stimuli which do not respect the behavior of the real environment where the ESW is expected to operate. Let us think for example to an assertion checking if the temperature of an oven reaches the target temperature after the desired time. While checking such a scenario, the input controlling the target temperature must remain stable. However, a structural-code oriented ATPG could freely change the value of such an input at each simulation run, thus preventing the assertion to be correctly satisfied. Indeed, coverage metrics measure how well code is exercised, rather than how well design functionalities are exercised.

This work is intended to present a way to complement stimuli generated by structural-code oriented ATPGs such that the desired test scenario is simulated to correctly activate assertions and effectively verify their satisfiability during simulation.

In particular, the paper proposes a framework based on a Testbench Specification Language (TSL) for modeling the behavior of the input stimuli that should represent the real environment during the ESW execution. The developed framework permits to mimic the physical testbench (e.g., temperature probes, variable resistors, etc.) applied to the board executing ESW and the test scenarios defined from the specifications. This automated approach allows engineers to express high-level intentions and it allows testbench-automation tool to create various stimuli that manifest those intentions. For example, the engineer can specify simple stimuli generators addressing weighted and constrained randomization, e.g., uniform distribution on a range of integers. Or more complex generators that provides input stimuli following a specific trend, e.g., trends that investigate the behavior of the system into/outside specific ranges of the input domains. Finally, TLS permits to specify commonly-used linear filters in few lines of code, that traditionally requires knowledge and programming efforts.

In this context, the main contributions of this work are:

- definition of a new language, the Testbench Specification Language. TSL is used to formally specify constraints on inputs of the ESW to model test scenarios that reflect the intent of the verification engineer in reproducing real-environment behaviour;
- implementation of generators that create sequences of stimuli according to the constraints defined by means of the TSL; such generators are defined upon the SystemC Verification Library (SCV);
- definition of a graphical editor that allows verification engineers to create the desired test scenario by graphically composing TSL elements and automatically synthesizing the corresponding stimuli generators;
- integration of the proposed environment into an off-the-shelf design and verification tool for ESW, i.e., radSuite [2] to improve its capability in generating stimuli that effectively represent the desired test scenarios.

The rest of the paper is structured as follows. Section 2 summarizes the state of the art. Section 3 provides and overview of the proposed environment. Section 4 describes the stimuli editor. Section 5 defines the TSL and makes some example of use. Section 6 describes how the stimuli generators are synthesized from TSL descriptions. Section 7 describes the radSuite framework that integrates the proposed methodology. Section 8 deals with experimental results. Finally, Section 9 is devoted to concluding remarks.

2. RELATED WORKS

Actual-value inputs may be either automatically generated or developed by engineers as stimuli suites, for example, exploiting the SCV library. In both the cases, the main purpose of dynamic verification is increasing the confidence of designers in the ESW behavior by creating stimuli and evaluating them in terms of adequacy criteria, e.g., coverage metrics.

In particular, there are three main categories for classifying stimuli-generation techniques for (embedded) software: *concrete execution*, *symbolic execution*, and *concolic execution*. The concrete execution is based on random, probabilistic, or genetic techniques [25]. It is considered a narrow-width and long-range exploration method, since it reaches deep states of the system space by executing a large number of long paths, but it is not an exhaustive approach. The symbolic execution [19] represents an alternative for overcoming concrete execution limitations, where an executable specification is simulated using symbolic variables and a decision procedure is used to obtain concrete values for inputs. However, such approaches suffer the solver limitations in handling the complexity of either the formulas or the data structures or the surrounding-execution environment.

Such limitations have been recently addressed by proposing *concolic execution* [30, 24]. In concolic approaches, concrete and symbolic executions run together, and, when necessary, symbolic constraints are simplified by using the corresponding concrete values. However, a concolic engine still represents the module execution as a symbolic-execution tree. Thus, state space explosion can still be a problem, since the size of the execution tree grows exponentially in the number of the maintained paths, states, and conditions.

Several tools on the market adopt these approaches and provide the user with automatic stimuli generation addressing coverage metrics in embedded software [21, 27, 33, 29, 35].

In particular, DART [12] is a tool for generating stimuli for C programs that are able to trigger errors such as crashes. It combines random stimuli generation with symbolic reasoning to keep track of constraints for executed control-flow paths. CUTE [30] is a variation on the DART approach addressing complex data structures and pointer arithmetic. KLEE [3] is a framework for symbolically executing LLVM [22] byte-code. PEX [31] is an automated structural-testing generation tool for .NET code developed at Microsoft Research. In [24] the authors describe a hybrid-concolic stimuli generation approach for C programs. It interleaves random stimuli generation with bounded exhaustive symbolic exploration to achieve better coverage. However, it cannot selectively and concolically execute symbolic paths in a neighborhood of the corner cases. Nevertheless stressing structural entities of an application does not guarantee to observe and achieve specification conformance and vice versa [15].

2.1 SystemC Verification Library

In the context of verification of SystemC descriptions, the SCV library [17] has been introduced for constraint-based random stimulus generation.

SCV library is built on top of the system description language SystemC and adds tightly integrated verification capabilities to SystemC. The main features of the SCV library are the *data introspection for SystemC and C++ data types*, the *transaction API*, and the *constraint-based stimulus generation for SystemC and C++*. In particular, the SCV library provides high-quality pseudo-random generators and an integrated constraint solver based on BDDs.

Randomization allows a large amount of stimulus to be generated with less manual effort than user-defined stimuli. In order to improve coverage and focus on specific aspects of the design, constraints or weights are typically used in randomization. While the most-used approach for stimuli generation is based on *rand()* function from the C library to generate a random integer, SCV library supports randomization of any data type through the use of the data introspection facility. Boolean predicates can be used as a constraint, and weights can be used as a distribution from which values are selected.

Some works exist in literature that extend the SCV library due to its limitations. In [14], the authors address some practical restriction of the library: the absence of support of bit operators in SCV constraints and absence of guarantee of uniform distribution of the constraint solutions. Similarly, in [34], the authors pinpoint the memory problems of the SCV underlying constraint-solver based on Binary Decision Diagrams. They substitute it with a SMT-solver that allows the exploitation of additional information due to the high-level representation of SystemC descriptions. In [11], the authors overcome the limitations of the SystemC data introspection borrowed from the underlying C++ structures and data types. Some other works use the SCV library for improving the quality of verification based on ABV [32, 20]. But none of these work aim at defining a new language and a graphical interface for abstracting the problem of the SCV testbench specification for ESW application, as the present work does. In particular, the proposed TSL-based approach allows complex generators to be synthesized from concise representations of the stimuli.

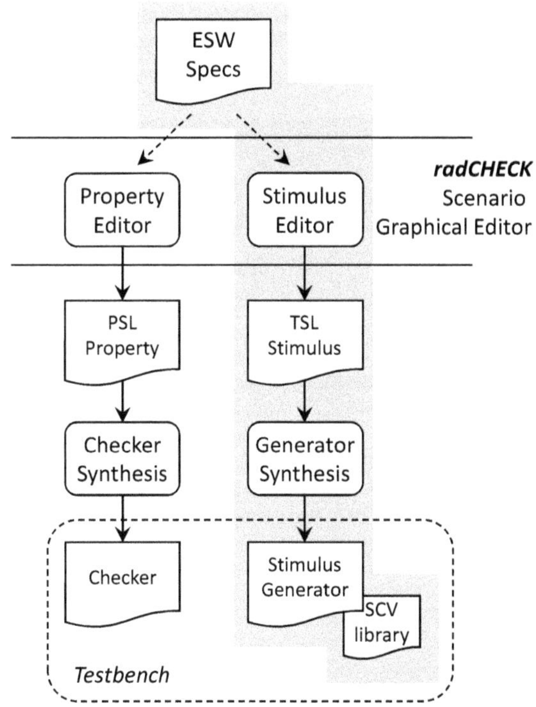

Figure 1: An overview of the modeling and synthesis of stimuli generator based on TSL.

3. FRAMEWORK OVERVIEW

Commonly, scenarios are described by using natural languages. As a consequence, due to the ambiguity of such languages, misinterpretation can happen and the assertions and stimuli defined by the verification engineers may differ from the intended ones. Besides, scenarios must be implemented as testbenches, i.e., checkers and stimulus generators, in order to use them for the verification purpose. For these reasons, a formal approach for defining scenarios and an automatic way for implementing them is required.

The proposed approach is depicted in Figure 1. The flow on the left, which is out of the scope of this paper, is related to the definition of assertions and synthesis of the related checker and it has already been implemented in radCHECK [7, 5]. This paper focuses on the flow on the right, which adopts a graphical-modeling paradigm to define stimuli compliant with the desired test scearnios.

The Stimulus Editor aims at raising the level of abstraction of the stimuli that must be applied to the ESW appli-

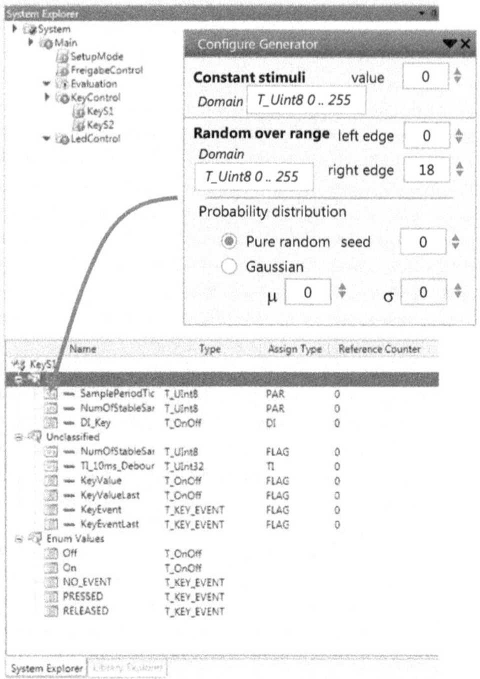

Figure 2: An overview of the Stimulus Editor.

cation. It describes the stimuli in terms of abstract characterization, attempting to be generic not only in the choice of the target application, but even in the choice of execution and interaction semantics. A TSL description of the desired intent is then generated and the corresponding stimuli generator is automatically synthesized. The gain offered by the adoption of such an abstraction is the capability of generating the source code implementing the Stimulus Generator in a systematic way, i.e., it avoids the need of manual writing, analyzing and modifying the code.

4. STIMULUS EDITOR

To address the limitations of natural languages, we propose a formal notation for stimuli specification, both graphical and language-based. The focus of the graphical Stimulus Editor is to elevate the development of stimulus generators to a higher level of abstraction than that provided by programming languages and text notations. Indeed, they are awkward to use especially for verification engineers that are not necessary programmers. Moreover, the abstract characterization of stimuli separates "what" the stimuli should do, from "how" they need to be implemented on the target technology.

The Stimulus Editor provides general-purpose graphic elements to create visual models of Stimulus Generators. It allows to drag-and-drop pre-defined generators and combining them in more complex ones. It provides support for representing time and time-dependent behaviors of stimuli. In particular, the use of an interface semantic allows clean separation between stimulus implementation and semantic. Such interface notably simplifies definition of stimuli. The user needs only to understand the semantics of the interface and to replace parameters with the intended values.

As an example, Figure 2 shows the configuration interface for generating constant or random values on a user-defined interval. The user can specify the edges of the interval, seed, mean (μ), standard deviation (σ) of the final Stimulus Generator.

The Stimulus Editor provides a graphical user interface that is characterized by the four main frames: *System Data*, *Generator rules*, *Timeline*, and *Generator list*.

The *System Data* frame shows information to the user about the structure of the ESW applications and provides references to the input variables the user can use to define generators. In particular, by choosing a module, the graphical interface retrieves (i) its hierarchical structure, that is the set of submodules that are instantiated in that specific module, and (ii) its set of input variables that are characterized by their own identifier and the associated data type.

The *Generator Rules* frame stores the list of the Generators (listed in Section 5.1) that the user can combine and nest to define new Generators. Once a generator is selected, the user can substitute its parameters with appropriate values. Moreover, generator can be nested each other on the Timeline.

The *Timeline* frame shows the components of a (composite) generator, i.e., other generators, in the order and timing that they operate. Adjustments to the length of each generator affect the duration of sequence of stimuli associated to the generator. Moreover, the user can specify a sample rate for generating the stimuli over the select time interval.

Once the generator is completely defined, the user can save it. The generator will be stored into the project file as a TSL description and a reference will be added into the *Generator List* frame. Such a frame does not provide a static list of generator. In fact, the user can select/modify/delete them in case of errors, or copy them for deriving other generators.

Once generators are defined, the Stimulus Editor automatically generates the TSL description that is synthesized into Stimulus Generators. The so generated Stimulus Generator is strictly related to the ESW application, e.g., it involves application variables.

5. TESTBENCH SPECIFICATION LANGUAGE

TSL is proposed to exceed the limits of natural languages and to provide well-defined specifications of stimuli to be applied. On the experience of test engineers, some input behaviors may more easily highlight weaknesses and errors during ESW simulation. For this reason testbenches reproducing such behaviours must be defined. For example, some general trends, depicted in Figure 3, are hereby listed.

- *Tracking trends* model the measurement of physical parameters, e.g., temperature, that are vertically shifted; see, for example, waveforms $ln_1, \ldots, ln_n$ in Figure 3.a.
- *Crossing trends* model the measurement of physical parameters that avoid to follow an existing variation pattern (Figure 3.b); both this and the previous trend try to investigate the input state space of the application.
- *Inside- and outside-hysteresis-range trends* investigate the behavior of the system into/outside specific range of the input domains (Figure 3.c).

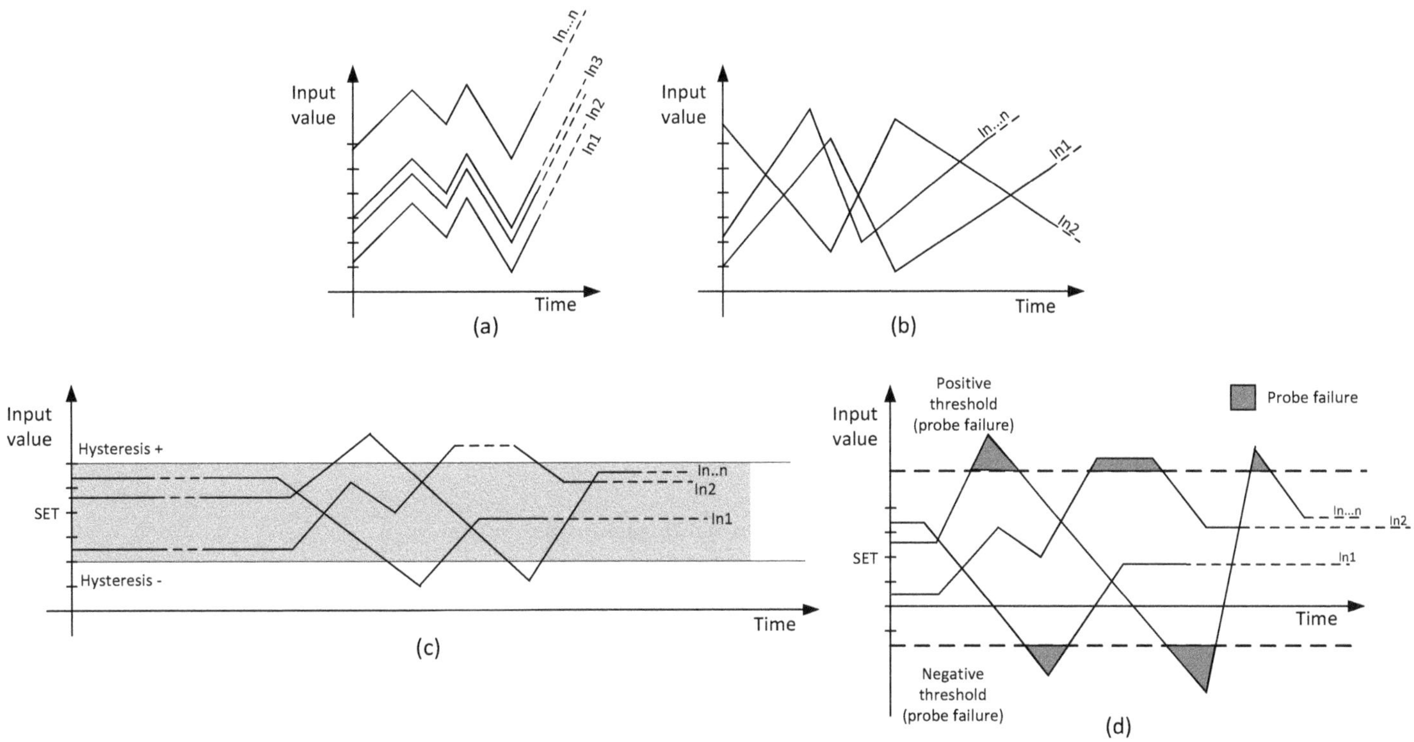

Figure 3: Examples of input behaviors. (a) Tracking trend. (b) Crossing trend. (c) Inside and outside hysteresis ranges. (d) Out of legal ranges.

- *Out-of-legal-range trends* investigate the behavior of the system when non-expected stimuli are applied (Figure 3.d).

Note that the waveforms in Figure 3 are triangle waves, but any other waveform is allowed, e.g., sine, square, etc. TSL has been defined keeping these general trends in mind. In first instance, it should permit to describe the behavior of digital/analog inputs from environmental probes which typically equip embedded systems.

Moreover, TSL permits to define a library of generators to solve recurring patterns of use. For example, the use of linear filters is quite common, however, their specifications are not so simple for most of the programmers. As a consequence, it may be useful to define them once and then reuse them. Some examples of usage are provide in Section 5.2. Finally, aim of this work is to introduce a language for specifying the testbench behavior spreading across time in a concise and unambiguous manner. Indeed, TSL has been defined for describing temporal behaviors of stimuli as PSL does for behaviors of designs.

5.1 The grammar

The BNF grammar in Listing 1 describes the abstract syntax tree of the TSL used to define custom generators. In particular:

- A **Named** generator provides a name and a type to a generator. Other generators can then refer to an existing named generator by its name. A named generator can be:
  1. an `INPUT` element of the interface. In this case the name of the generator matches the name of an input port of the design;
  2. a `TEMP`, that is a *local* name, used to define other generators. Local generators are not displayed in the generated sequences, but may contribute to the definition of generators associated with input ports.
- **Generator** is a type used to describe objects that can generate a stream of data.
  - A **Constant** generator produces always the same specified value.
  - A **Uniform** generator produces a values uniformly distributed in a range `[range_min, range_max]`.
  - A **Sequence** generator g consists of a non-empty list of pairs $[< g_1, d_1 >, ..., < g_n, d_n >]$, where each g_k is a generator and d_k a duration. When the end of the list is reached, depending on the value of a boolean flag `do_loop`, the above evaluation may be repeated, or g_n, the last generator of the list, may be evaluated indefinitely.
- **Sum** and **Product** generators implement the addition and multiplication operations, respectively, between two generators.
- The **Uminus** generator computes the negation of the argument generator.
- The **Range_Restrict** generator truncates the values of the argument generator to a given range `[min_range,`

```
<Named_Generator> ::= <kind> <name> <type> <Generator>
             <kind> ::= 'INPUT' | 'TEMP'
        <Generator> ::= <Constant> | <Uniform> | <Sequence>
                      | <Sum> | <Product> | <Uminus> | <Range_Restrict>
                      | <Time_Expand>
                      | <Reference> | <Delay>
         <Constant> ::= 'constant ' <value>
          <Uniform> ::= 'uniform ' <range_min> <range_max>
         <Sequence> ::= 'sequence ' <do_loop> '[' <Sequence_Pair_List> ']'
<Sequence_Pair_List> ::= <Sequence_Pair>
                      | <Sequence_Pair_List> ',' <Sequence_Pair>
    <Sequence_Pair> ::= '<' <Generator> ',' <duration> '>'
              <Sum> ::= 'sum' <Generator> <Generator>
          <Product> ::= 'product ' <Generator> <Generator>
           <Uminus> ::= 'uminus' <Generator>
   <Range_Restrict> ::= 'range_restrict ' <range_min> <range_max> <Generator>
        <Reference> ::= 'reference ' <name>
            <Delay> ::= 'delay ' <initial_value> <delay_amount> <Generator>
      <Time_Expand> ::= 'time_expand ' <factor> <Generator>
```

Listing 1: TSL grammar.

max_range]. Precisely, said $g = range\_restrict f$, then $g(t)$, the value of the generator g at time t, is:

  - **min_range** if $f(t) < min\_range$,
  - **max_range** if $f(t) > max\_range$,
  - f(t), otherwise.

- The **Reference** generator takes the same values of the named generator identified by the argument *name*. This construct can be used to build dependencies among different generators.

- The **Delay** generator shifts horizontally the argument generator by a given constant k. Said $g = delay\ k\ f$, if we look at the generators g and f as functions of time, then we have:

  - if $t < k$, then $g(t)$ is equal to the given *initial* value.
  - otherwise, $g(t) = f(t - k)$.

- The **Time_Expand** generator stretches horizontally the argument generator by a given factor k. Said $g = time\_expand\ k\ f$, if we look at the generators g and f as functions of time, then we have: $g(t) = f(t/k)$.

5.2 Examples

Listing 2 describes the generator associated with the graphic element of the Stimulus Editor shown in Figure 2. The values are uniformly distributed on the range from 0 to 18.

The generator in Listing 3 builds a linear filter element_02 on a uniform generator element_01 in the range $[-1, 1]$. The formal expression of the filter is:

- $element\_02(0) = 0$

- $element\_02(t + 1) = 0.75 * element\_02(t) + 0.25 * elemen\_01(t)$.

The generator in Listing 4 defines an initial uniform distribution element_01 in the range [-2, 2]. Then element_02 truncates element_01 in the range $[-1, 1]$. Notice that said $g = range\_restrict\ a\ b\ f$, then $g(t) = min(b, max(a, f(t)))$.

```
INPUT UINT8 uniform_generator Uniform 0 18
```

Listing 2: TSL Uniform Generator associated with the graphic element in Figure 2.

```
TEMP FLOAT 0 filter_parameter Constant 0.75
TEMP FLOAT 0 uniform_generator Uniform −1 1
INPUT element_01 Reference
    uniform_generator
INPUT element_02
  Sum
    Product
      Sum
        Constant 1
        UMinus Reference filter_parameter
      Reference uniform_generator
    Product
      Reference filter_parameter
      Delay 1 0 end Reference element_02
```

Listing 3: Linear filter.

```
INPUT element_01 Uniform −2 2
INPUT element_02 Range_Restrict −1 1
    Reference element_01
```

Listing 4: Truncated distribution.

The generator in Listing 5 is defined as a sequence that assumes the value 0 for the first 5 time units, then the value 2 for the next 5, and again the value 0 for the next 5 time units. After this, the generator becomes constant with value -1.

In Listing 6, the generator element_02 presents the same plot of element_01 but shifted to the right of 3 units on the x-axis.

Finally, in Listing 7, the generator description element_02 presents the same plot of element_01 stretched along the y-axis of a 0.7 factor. Similarly, *element_03* presents the same plot of *element_01* shifted along the y-axis of a 0.7 offset.

```
INPUT element_01
  Sequence 0
    Constant 0 5
    Constant 2 5
    Constant 0 5
    Constant -1 1
  end
```

Listing 5: Sequence of generators.

```
INPUT element_01 Uniform -1 1
INPUT element_02 Delay 3 0 end Reference
   element_01
```

Listing 6: Time shifting.

```
INPUT element_01 Uniform -1 1
TEMP INT16 1 scale_param Constant 0.7
INPUT element_02
  Product
    Reference scale_param
    Reference element_01
INPUT element_03
  Sum
    Constant 1
    Reference element_01
```

Listing 7: Time stretching.

6. SCV-BASED STIMULI GENERATOR

In the presented approach, TSL descriptions are automatically synthesized into stimulus generators. Listing 8 reports the (simplified) code associated with the Uniform Generator described in Listing 2. As shown in lines 1-7, the implementation of such a generator layers on top of SCV library and it exploits its constrained randomization capabilities. The generators extends a base class `Generator` (line 10) that provides an uniform interface, e.g., `generate()` function (line 21). Given a time interval and a time step, stimuli are uniformly generated and stored into a sequence.

As shown for this simple example, TSL allows complex generators to be synthesized from a concise representation of the stimuli. The programmer using either the graphical Stimulus Editor or the TSL language is completely unaware of the final implementation.

7. RADSUITE

Our approach has been contextualized on radSUITE, a design and verification framework composed of two environments: radCASE and radCHECK (Figure 4). radCASE is a UML-modeling and development environment for ESW supporting model-driven design. radCHECK is a dynamic ABV environment that supports assertion definition, automatic synthesis of the corresponding checkers, stimuli generation and simulation.

Starting from the informal specifications and requirements, the designer, with the Model Editor of radCASE, defines the ESW model using an UML-based approach. Concurrently, with the Property Editor of radCHECK, he/she defines a set of PSL assertions that the application must fulfil. Then, radCASE automatically translates the UML specifications in the ESW C-code implementation. At the same time, radCHECK can be used to automatically generate executable checkers from the defined PSL assertions. Checkers are executable components that monitor the evolution of the ESW during dynamic ABV. The dynamic ABV is guided by stimuli automatically generated. Previously, the stimuli were generated by adopting a Montecarlo approach and hybrid-symbolic simulation [6]. Both these approaches aim at improving coverage metrics. Thus, the verification phase is performed by using the generated stimuli on top of an ESW simulator or on the application running on the target hardware. The checkers execute within the ESW and monitor if the state of the application causes an assertion to falsify. The designer uses the resulting information, i.e., failed requirements, for refining the UML specifications incrementally and in an iterative fashion.

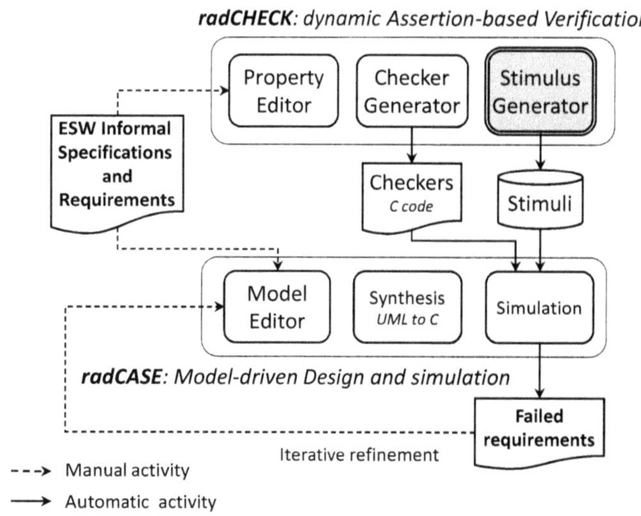

Figure 4: The radCASE and radCHECK model-driven design and verification framework.

The paper described how the Stimulus Generator integrated into radCHECK has been extended to allow the engineers to define test scenarios. Such scenarios encompass both the assertions and the stimuli aiming at exercise the assertions themselves.

8. EXPERIMENTAL RESULTS

The proposed TSL-based framework for stimuli generation has been integrated in radSUITE and tested on an industrial case study. The considered case study is a control application for an automatic bread making machine for domestic usage developed by STMProducts s.r.l. [1]. It is composed of three main modules: Thermostat, Mixer, and Breadmaker, and a set of periodic tasks that monitor the environment and periodically acquire sensory data.

Verification engineers derived a set of 16 safety temporal assertions[1] starting from the design test scenarios. The assertions were defined in PSL and compiled into checkers by using the checker generator included in radSUITE.

[1]A safety assertion specifies something bad must never happen

```
// Define a simple constraint on top of SCV library
struct contraint : public
  scv_constraint_base {
    scv_smart_ptr< sc_uint<32> > a;
    SCV_CONSTRAINT_CTOR( g_constraint )
    { SCV_CONSTRAINT( a() >= 0 && a() <= 18 ); }
};


class Uniform : public Generator {

  Uniform( Stimuli_Sequence& ss, // Stimuli sequence to be expanded
  int unsigned sample_rate_ms,       // Chosen time step
  int unsigned duration_ms )         // Chosen time interval
    : stimuli_sequence (ss), sample_rate_ms (sr), duration_ms (d) {

      // Use the defined constraint
      constraint cnst(''cnst'');
  }

  void generate () {
    // Itialize sequence timing
    int unsigned curr_timestamp = 0;
    if ( !ss.empty() )
      curr_timestamp = ss.back().timestamp + sample_rate_ms;
    int unsigned const last_timestamp = curr_timestamp + duration_ms;

    // Iterate over the time interval by using the chosen time step
    for ( ; curr_timestamp <= last_timestamp; curr_timestamp += sample_rate_ms ) {

      // Generate a new value in the sequence
      sc_uint< 32 > value = cnst.next();
      ss.push_back( value );

      // Keep trace of the time for the current
      ss.back().timestamp = curr_timestamp;
    }
}
```

Listing 8: Synthesized code for the Uniform Generator. The associated TLS description is reported in Listing 2.

		STRUCTURE-ORIENTED		TSL-BASED	
Ass. num.	CHECKED FUNCTIONALITY	Act.	Vect. #	Act.	Vect. #
1	Clockwise (cw) and counter clockwise (ccw) never active same time	ok	–	ok	–
2	when cw and ccw are off, the motor is off	ok	1	ok	1
3	doFast works with either cw or ccw	no	5000	ok	32
4	mixing	ok	10	ok	10
5	kneading	no	5000	ok	309
6	proving	no	5000	ok	909
7	baking	no	5000	ok	1219
8	thermostat inactive, heating off	ok	3	ok	3
9	fast - to change motor from ccw to cw 2s pause necessary	no	5000	ok	225
10	fast cycle	no	5000	ok	152
11	slow cycle	no	5000	ok	594
12	fast - to change motor from cw to ccw 2s pause necessary	no	5000	ok	153
13	slow - to change motor from cw to ccw 10s pause necessary	no	5000	ok	510
14	slow - to change motor from ccw to cw 10s pause necessary	no	5000	ok	774
15	heating on when temp < set - hyst	no	5000	ok	322
16	heating off when temp >= set	no	5000	ok	324

Table 1: Activation of assertions defined for the breadmaker case study by using stimuli generated by a code structure-oriented ATPG and the proposed TLS-based framework.

Experimental results are reported in Table 1. We simulated the breadmaker application to check the correctness of assertions, first by using the original stimuli generator of radSUITE, which is code structure-oriented (Column *Structure-oriented*), then by using the stimuli generators defined by means of the TSL-based framework proposed in this work (Column *TSL-based*). The table shows the checked functionality in the second column. Then it shows if assertions have been activated during simulation of generated stimuli (Column *Act.*) and the length of the stimuli sequence that activates and verifies the assertion (Column *Vect.#*). In particular, we were interested in finding an activation sequence (i.e., a sequence that satisfies the antecedent). In several cases, the code-structure oriented ATPG fails to find such an activation sequence and it reaches the size limit imposed for the length of the sequence (5000 test vectors) without verifying the assertion. On the contrary, our TSL-based generators, reproducing real testing scenarios, is able to activate all assertions. Please note that for assertion 1 no data is reported since it is an invariant that does not require any activation sequence.

The code structure-oriented ATPG is unable to find the most of activation sequences because the breadmaker requires some conditions are preserved for many simulation cycles. A simple example is represented by the necessity that the start/stop button is not continuously switched on and off. A more complex situation refers to the need that the temperature monitored by the sensor internal to the bread making machine continuously increases till the target threshold. Such conditions cannot be easily met by code structure-oriented ATPG and they require constraints are specified by the verification engineers to model significant scenarios. The proposed TSL-based framework has shown to effectively help verification engineers by providing both an intuitive graphical approach for composing such constraints and the related stimuli generators, providing a significant time saving.

9. CONCLUDING REMARKS

In this paper the Testbench Spercification Language has been define as a way to formally describe sequence of stimuli that reflect the behavior of the real environment where embedded SW is intended to be executed. Moreover, a graphical editor, implemented upon TSL, has been presented to help verification engineers in defining the stimuli behavior without directly writing TSL descriptions, and to automatically synthesize the corresponding stimuli generators. These generators are defined by exploiting the SystemC Verification Library. Experimental results showed that stimuli generated by the proposed environment are more suited than stimuli generated by a code structure-oriented ATGP for dynamic assertion-based verification, where precise test scenarios must be simulated to activate and verify assertions.

A limitation of the current version of the framework is that the stimuli generation phase is off-line with respect to the ESW execution. That is, once the generator is synthesized, the generator is executed and a file containing the traces of the input signals is created. In many situations it would be useful to express the value of an input signal as a function of an output signal of the design, that is, to have feed-backs between the generator and the application. Future work will investigate in this direction.

10. REFERENCES

[1] http://www.stm-products.com/en/index.html.

[2] http://www.verificationsuite.com.

[3] C. Cadar, D. Dunbar, and D. Engler. KLEE: Unassisted and Automatic Generation of High-Coverage Tests for Complex Systems Programs. In *Proc. of USENIX Symposium on Operating Systems Design and Implementation (OSDI)*, 2008.

[4] Cadence. Assertion-based Verification, 2012.

[5] G. Di Guglielmo, L. Di Guglielmo, F. Fummi, and G. Pravadelli. Enabling dynamic assertion-based verification of embedded software through model-driven design. In *Proc. of ACM/IEEE Design, Automation and Test in Europe*, pages 212–217, 2012.

[6] G. Di Guglielmo, M. Fujita, F. Fummi, G. Pravadelli, and S. Soffia. Efsm-based model-driven approach to concolic testing of system-level design. In *Formal Methods and Models for Codesign (MEMOCODE), 2011 9th IEEE/ACM International Conference on*, pages 201–209. IEEE, 2011.

[7] L. Di Guglielmo, F. Fummi, N. Orlandi, and G. Pravadelli. Ddpsl: An easy way of defining properties. In *Computer Design (ICCD), 2010 IEEE International Conference on*, pages 468–473. IEEE, 2010.

[8] C. Ebert and C. Jones. Embedded software: Facts, figures, and future. *Computer*, 42(4):42–52, 2009.

[9] L. Ferro and L. Pierre. ISIS: runtime verification of TLM platforms. *Advances in Design Methods from Modeling Languages for Embedded Systems and SoCs*, 63:213–226, 2010.

[10] H. Foster, A. Krolnik, and D. Lacey. *Assertion-based design*. Springer Netherlands, 2004.

[11] C. Genz and R. Drechsler. Overcoming limitations of the SystemC data introspection. In *Proceedings of the Conference on Design, Automation and Test in Europe*, pages 590–593. European Design and Automation Association, 2009.

[12] P. Godefroid, N. Klarlund, and K. Sen. DART: Directed Automated Random Testing. In *Proc. of ACM SIGPLAN Conference on Programming Language, Design, and Implementation (PLDI)*, pages 213–223, 2005.

[13] B. Graaf, M. Lormans, and H. Toetenel. Embedded Software Engineering: The State of the Practice. *IEEE Software*, 20(6):61–69, 2003.

[14] D. Große, R. Ebendt, and R. Drechsler. Improvements for constraint solving in the SystemC verification library. In *ACM Great Lakes symposium on VLSI*, pages 493–496. ACM, 2007.

[15] M. P. E. Heimdahl, D. George, and R. Weber. Specification Test Coverage Adequacy Criteria = Specification Test Generation Inadequacy Criteria? In *Proc. of IEEE International High Assurance Systems Engineering Symposium (HASE)*, pages 178–186, 2004.

[16] IEEE Computer Society. IEEE Standard for Property Specification Language (PSL) (IEEE Std 1850-2010), 2010.

[17] O. Initiative. Systemc verification library, 2006.

[18] C. Kaner. An introduction to scenario testing. *Lecture Notes, Center for Software Testing Education and Research, Florida Institute of Technology*, 2003.

[19] J. C. King. Symbolic Execution and Program Testing. *Communications of the ACM*, 19(7):385–394, 1976.

[20] Y. Lahbib, O. Missaoui, M. Hechkel, D. Lahbib, B. Mohamed-Yosri, and R. Tourki. Verification flow optimization using an automatic coverage driven testing policy. In *Design and Test of Integrated*

Systems in Nanoscale Technology, 2006. DTIS 2006. International Conference on, pages 94–99. IEEE, 2006.

[21] K. Lamberg, M. Beine, M. Eschmann, R. Otterbach, M. Conrad, and I. Fey. Model-based testing of embedded automotive software using mtest. In *SAE World Congress*, 2004.

[22] C. Lattner and V. Adve. The LLVM Compiler Framework and Infrastructure Tutorial. In *Proc. of International Workshop on Languages and Compilers for High Performance Computing (LCPC)*, pages 15–16. Springer, 2005.

[23] E. Lee. Embedded software. *Advances in computers*, 56, 2002.

[24] R. Majumdar and K. Sen. Hybrid Concolic Testing. In *Proc. of IEEE International Conference on Software Engineering (ICSE)*, pages 416–426, 2007.

[25] P. McMinn. Search-based software test data generation: A survey. *Software Testing, Verification and Reliability*, 14(2):105–156, 2004.

[26] Mentor Graphics. Assertion-based Verification, 2012.

[27] W. Mueller, A. Bol, A. Krupp, and O. Lundkvist. Generation of Executable Testbenches from Natural Language Requirement Specifications for Embedded Real-Time Systems. *Distributed, Parallel and Biologically Inspired Systems*, pages 78–89, 2010.

[28] A. Piziali. *Functional verification - Coverage measurement and analysis*. Springer, 2004.

[29] Razorcat Development GmbH. Classification Tree Editor (CTE) for Embedded Systems, 2012.

[30] K. Sen and G. Agha. CUTE and jCUTE: Concolic unit testing and explicit path model-checking tools. In *Proc. of International Conference on Computer Aided Verification (CAV)*, pages 419–423. Springer, 2006.

[31] N. Tillmann and J. De Halleux. Pex: White Box Test Generation for. NET. In *Proc. of ACM International Conference on Tests and Proofs (TAP)*, pages 134–153, 2008.

[32] K. Tomasena, J. Sevillano, J. Perez, A. Cortes, and I. Velez. A Transaction Level Assertion Verification Framework in SystemC: An Application Study. In *International Conference on Advances in Circuits, Electronics and Micro-electronics*, pages 75–80. IEEE, 2009.

[33] J. Wegener, R. Pitschinetz, K. Grimm, and M. Grochtmann. TESSY - Yet Another Computer-Aided Software Testing Tool. In *Proc. of European International Conference on Software Testing, Analysis and Review (EuroSTAR)*, 1994.

[34] R. Wille, D. Große, F. Haedicke, and R. Drechsler. Smt-based stimuli generation in the systemc verification library. *Advances in Design Methods from Modeling Languages for Embedded Systems and SoCŠs*, pages 227–244, 2010.

[35] G. Williams, M. Karlesky, and M. VanderVoord. Unity - Compact Test Framework for C, 2012.

SystemC Simulation on GP-GPUs: CUDA vs. OpenCL *

Nicola Bombieri
Dip. Informatica
Università di Verona, Italy
nicola.bombieri@univr.it

Sara Vinco
Dip. Informatica
Università di Verona, Italy
sara.vinco@univr.it

Valeria Bertacco
EECS Department
University of Michigan, USA
valeria@umich.edu

Debapriya Chatterjee
EECS Department
University of Michigan, USA
dchatt@umich.edu

ABSTRACT

SystemC is a widespread language for developing SoC designs. Unfortunately, most SystemC simulators are based on a strictly sequential scheduler that heavily limits their performance, impacting verification schedules and time-to-market of new designs. Parallelizing SystemC simulation entails a complete re-design of the simulator kernel for the specific target parallel architectures. This paper proposes an automatic methodology to generate a parallel SystemC simulator kernel, exploiting the massive parallelism of GP-GPU architectures. Our solution leverages static scheduling to reduce synchronization overheads. The generated simulator code targets both CUDA and OpenCL libraries, to boost scalability and provide support for multiple GP-GPU architectures. Finally, the paper compares the performance of our solution on CUDA vs. OpenCL platforms, with the goal of investigating advantages and drawbacks that the two thread management libraries offer to concurrent SystemC simulation.

Categories and Subject Descriptors

C.3 [**Special-Purpose and Application-Based Systems**]: Real-time and embedded systems

General Terms

Design, Performance

Keywords

Parallel SystemC, simulation acceleration, CUDA, OpenCL

1. INTRODUCTION

SystemC is the de-facto standard language for system-level modeling, architectural exploration, performance analysis, software development, and functional verification of embedded systems [1].

*This work has been partially supported by EU project FP7-ICT-2011-7-288166 (TOUCHMORE) and the Gigascale Systems Research Center, one of six research centers funded under the Focus Center Research Program (FCRP), a Semiconductor Research Corporation entity.

CODES+ISSS'12, October 7-12, 2012, Tampere, Finland.

It supports modeling and simulation of designs at different abstraction levels, from register transfer level (RTL) to electronic system level (ESL) through the transaction level modeling (TLM) [6].

Such a flexibility to model from the most accurate to the most abstracted description level simplifies system design, as well as verification, by providing a simpler, more powerful way to verify complex systems. Moreover, by exploiting reuse-based methodologies, IP cores, complete of their verification infrastructure, can be re-deployed across several abstraction levels, thus enabling shorter design cycles [2, 3, 11].

Nevertheless state-of-the-art SystemC simulation kernels rely on application-level threading (co-operative threads) forcing the execution to be intrinsically sequential, since the operating system cannot dispatch co-operative threads to different processing elements. Such inability of SystemC kernels to exploit parallel processing architectures has been addressed only recently. Several works in the literature have attempted to parallelize SystemC simulation, targeting heterogeneous architectures to reduce synchronization overheads [5, 9, 12].

Concurrently, general purpose graphics processing units (GP-GPUs) have been explored in the past few years as a new general purpose computing paradigm for accelerating computation-intensive EDA applications, such as gate-level fault simulation [6], fault table computation [7], and logic simulation [8]. SystemC simulation on GP-GPUs has been explored very recently, and it is proving to be a promising match between the most widespread system-level design language and these up-and-coming low cost devices [13, 19]. Early experimental results have shown SystemC simulation speed-ups from 3x to 2,000x, depending on testbench design and GP-GPU board model. Nevertheless, all these works target CUDA [14] GP-GPUs, thus limiting their applicability to only the NVIDIA family of many-core devices.

To allow execution of parallel programs across various platforms, the Khronos Group [17] has established an open standard, known as OpenCL. OpenCL is a framework for writing programs that execute across heterogeneous platforms consisting of CPUs, GPUs, and other processing elements. As a result, OpenCL provides software developers with portable and efficient access to the power of diverse processing platforms.

An open question on this front is whether portability in OpenCL impacts application's perfomance, as it is often the case for languages and middlewares that target portability across different platforms [18]. If performance were to suffer significantly on OpenCL platforms, their suitability would be limited.

To investigate the tradeoff between performance and portability of OpenCL, we present a detailed analysis using a range of SystemC designs and compare simulation performance of CUDA vs. OpenCL running on several NVIDIA's devices.

The remainder of this paper is organized as follows. Section 2 reports the related work. Section 3 summarizes and compares CUDA and the OpenCL programming models. Section 4 discusses the implementation of a C++ SystemC kernel for CUDA and OpenCL, by comparing different scheduling solutions. Section 5 presents compares simulation performance on CUDA and OpenCL. Finally, experimental results are reported in Section 6, while Section 7 concludes our work.

2. RELATED WORK

SystemC uses an event-based architecture, where a centralized scheduler controls the execution of processes based on events (synchronizations, time notifications or signal value changes).

Within each simulation cycle, there is first an *evaluation phase*, during which all runnable processes are executed. Signals are updated at the end of the execution of each process. If a signal value change occurs, all processes sensitive to that signal are added to the runnable queue (this is called *signal and event update phase*). Finally, during the *time update phase*, the time of the next simulation cycle is determined by setting it to the earliest of (i) the time at which the simulation ends, (ii) the next time at which an event occurs, or (iii) the next time at which a process is scheduled to resume. If simulation time is not increased, the next simulation cycle will be a delta cycle.

In SystemC, the order of process execution within an evaluation phase does not affect simulation output since the simulator presents the same system status to all those processes. Thus, processes activated within a same evaluation phase can be naturally executed in parallel, either by using multiple threads or by designing a distributed scheduler.

Several works in the literature suggest taking advantage of this inherent parallelism to speedup simulation [7, 9, 15, 20]. In [15], SystemC processes are executed as distinct threads on multiple CPUs. However, the overall simulation platform (ArchSim) introduces heavy overhead, thus making this approach ineffective overall. In [7], each processing node includes a copy of the scheduler and it simulates a subset of the application modules. All scheduler copies must synchronize at each signal and event update phase, to update the value of shared signals and of simulation time, thus generating many synchronization events among the separate processors. A different approach is proposed in [15]. The methodology analyzes SystemC modules and it divides all processes into blocks of operations that are executed consecutively. Then, blocks are scheduled according to their data and control dependencies, parallelizing those blocks that can be executed during the same simulator phase In summary, all these solutions rely on SystemC source code modifications or introduce overhead.

SystemC simulation on CUDA GP-GPUs has been proposed for the first time in [13]. In that work, independent SystemC processes are mapped into parallel threads that synchronize at each iteration of a delta cycle, through a barrier synchronization, to maintain the correct producer-consumer relation among threads. The same authors then proposed [16], a methodology that parallelizes the simulation of mixed-abstraction level SystemC models across multi-core CPUs and GPUs. Given a SystemC description, the methodology partitions the model into processes suitable for GPU and CPU execution. Then, it converts the processes identified for GPU execution into GPU kernels with additional wrapper processes to invoke those kernels. The wrappers enable seamless bi-directional communication of events between GPUs and CPUs. The authors reworked the OSCI SystemC simulation kernel to allow parallel execution of processes.

A framework for simulating SystemC code on CUDA GP-GPUs has been also proposed in [19]. The framework fully exploits the intrinsic parallelism of RTL SystemC descriptions, by limiting synchronization events with ad-hoc static scheduling and separate independent dataflows. Finally, SystemC simulation on CUDA has been proposed in [4], where the authors propose a framework for functional verification of RTL designs. The framework translates the RTL code into C code targeting NVIDIA GPUs, thus allowing fast parallel automatic test pattern generation and fault simulation.

All the previous works applied SystemC simulation to CUDA GP-GPUs, while, to the best of our knowledge, there is no work that has analyzed the performance of SystemC simulation by adopting OpenCL.

3. GP-GPU PROGRAMMING

The following Sections present CUDA and OpenCL (Section 3.1 and 3.2). Then, Section 3.3 compares platform models, memory models, execution models and programming models of the two frameworks.

3.1 CUDA

NVIDIA's Compute Unified Device Architecture (CUDA) [14] has been proposed to facilitate GP-GPU programming with a general purpose interface. In the CUDA execution model, the GP-GPU is a co-processor capable of executing many threads in parallel, following the single instruction multiple data (SIMT) model of execution. A data parallel computation process, known as a kernel, can be offloaded to the GP-GPU for execution. The collection of threads represented by a kernel is divided into a grid of thread-blocks.

The CUDA architecture (Figure 1) consists of a number of multiprocessors within a single GP-GPU chip. Multiprocessors are responsible for the execution of the thread-blocks mapped to each of them. Each multiprocessor comprises multiple stream processors with common instruction fetching and support for a large number of concurrent threads. Thus, each multiprocessor executes several groups of threads at a time (known as a *warp*) in a time-multiplexed fashion, with frequent context-switches from one warp to another. Because of the shared fetch unit, execution path divergence between threads in a same warp is detrimental to performance as only one branch path can be executed at a time. Thus, if threads in a same multiprocessors must execute different code paths, the least penalizing solution is to map them to different warps.

Each multiprocessor has access to low latency scratchpad memory, divided between local registers and shared memory. All multiprocessors also have access to a region of global memory called device memory, which has higher access latency. Communication with the host CPU's main memory is achieved via lower bandwidth direct memory access (DMA) transfers. Thus, it is important to keep communication between the host and the GP-GPU to the bare minimum.

3.2 OpenCL

OpenCL is a standard for general purpose programming across heterogeneous processors developed by the Kronos group since 2008. OpenCL supports vendor-independent architectures, ranging from CPUs to GP-GPUs and matching the OpenCL platform structure.

An OpenCL program is divided into host code and device code. The host program prepares the device execution and it transfers data to the device. The device code is structured in *kernels*, pro-

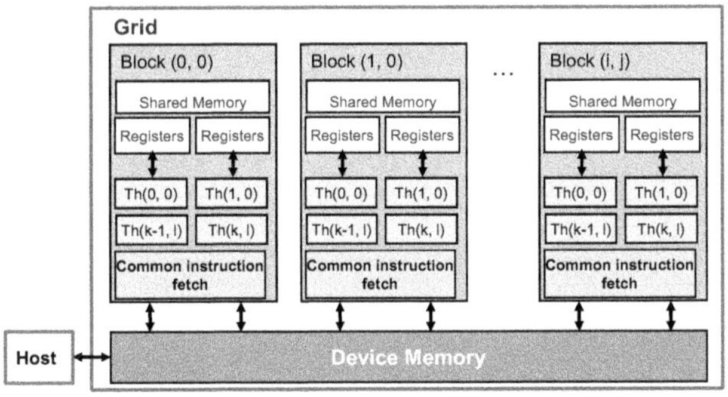

Figure 1: NVIDIA CUDA architecture

grams that perform the functionality of the target application. Each thread is associated with an instance of the kernel, called work-item, and is identified by an ID. Work-items are grouped into work-groups, that execute concurrently on the processing elements of a single compute unit. As a result, threads belonging to the same work-group execute the same instruction, in a SIMD flavor.

When offloading code to the device, the host must define a *context*. Each context is made of a set of devices where execution occurs and by the kernel that must be executed. Furthermore, a context contains a reference to the program source code and to the memory objects that are visible from both the host and the devices. A command queue is created to coordinate execution among contexts on the devices.

Each compute unit has access to low latency memory, that can be shared between the different processing elements. In addition, there is a region of memory, called global memory, that can be accessed by all multiprocessors. Communication with the host CPU's main memory is achieved by means of data transfers (added to the command queue) or shared pointers. However, data sharing with the host introduces a heavy overhead, and thus communication between host and device must be minimized.

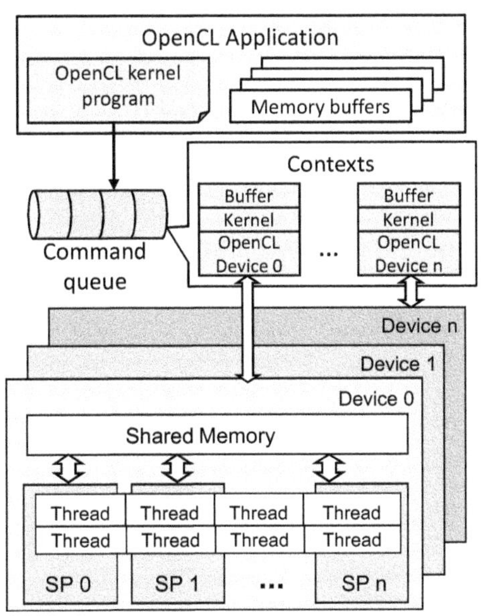

Figure 2: Typical OpenCL architecture

3.3 CUDA-OpenCL comparison

As outlined in the previous sections, OpenCL and CUDA share their core ideas as they have similar platform models, memory models, execution models and programming models. To the programmer, the computing system consists of a host (e.g., a typical CPU) and one or more devices that are massively parallel processors equipped with a large number of arithmetic execution units.

However, OpenCL targets a wider range of architectures, while CUDA is restricted to NVIDIA devices. This implies that OpenCL must be more flexible and it can not take into account specific properties of the architecture, such as the availability of read-only memory. This consideration impacts execution performance and thus a number of aspects should be taken into account to achieve a fair comparison:

- CUDA provides optimization pragma directives to automatically improve the code. An example is the *unroll* pragma, that applies unrolling to loops, thus reducing branch prediction failures and the presence of dynamic instructions. Once again, OpenCL can not exploit such optimizations. When removing pragma support, CUDA code may become slower than OpenCL [10];

- CUDA assumes the availability of fast-access read-only memory, such as texture memory and constant memory. Applications can exploit this architectural characteristics to reduce memory access overhead [10]. On the other hand, OpenCL can not make assumptions on the underlying platform and thus memory handling is less optimized;

- CUDA compilers are more mature than OpenCL ones. As a result, OpenCL compilers generate up to two times more arithmetic instructions than their CUDA counterpart [10]. This difference can not be eliminated and it is implied by the open source nature of OpenCL;

- Unlike CUDA, OpenCL requires environmental setup before launching the kernels on the GP-GPU. This process includes selecting the target device, by querying the available resources, and compiling the kernels at runtime. As a result, OpenCL's initialization cost includes compilation cost and lead to kernels setup taking longer than kernels execution [8]. However, OpenCL set up costs are fixed and thus it can be amortized on complex applications.

We took the above into consideration, and strove to create a fair comparison between the two platforms. We do not use pragma optimizations, nor read-only memory accesses in our analysis. However, the OpenCL simulator is still penalized by initialization overhead and less optimized compilers.

4. SYSTEMC TO C++ TRANSLATION TARGETING GP-GPUs

Mapping of SystemC applications to GP-GPU architectures is a non trivial task, since it requires scheduling support and the ability to preserve correct simulation outputs, even when the processes are executed in parallel. In the literature, two main approaches have been proposed to address this issue. [13] applies dynamic scheduling to the GP-GPU framework, by executing individual threads in parallel only when the testbench structure allows it and by synchronizing after each simulation step. On the other hand, [19] proposes a static scheduling approach that avoids frequent synchronization steps by partitioning the starting SystemC processes into independent sets that execute on different multiprocessors. The proposed techniques are outlined in Section 4.1 and Section 4.2 respectively, while Section 4.3 compares the two.

4.1 Dynamic scheduling

The work proposed in [13] maps SystemC processes to a model of concurrent threads that synchronizes after each simulation step. Each SystemC process is assigned to one thread and all threads belong to the same thread block, to gain fast synchronization. In this way, barriers can be exploited to synchronize threads, to update memory and to maintain the correct producer-consumer relation among threads. An example of this approach is shown in Figure 3. Grey-colored threads are those performing meaningful computation. White-colored threads are waiting on a barrier for the other threads to complete their job.

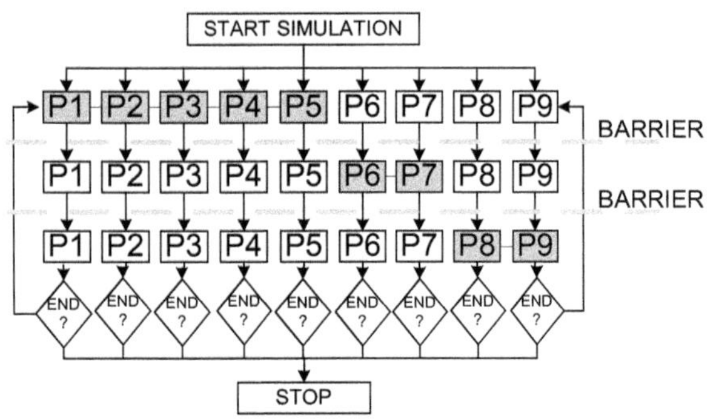

Figure 3: Scheduling example based on SCGPSim

4.2 Static scheduling

SAGA [19] proposes a different approach based on static scheduling. The read-write dependencies between the starting SystemC processes are analyzed to generate a dependency graph of the processes (left hand side of Figure 4). The graph is then topologically sorted and partitioned into independent dataflows, i.e., portions of the process graph that can be executed independently (right hand side of Figure 4). Such dataflows are then mapped to distinct multiprocessors for concurrent execution. When necessary, some portions of the process graph may be replicated to attain independence among dataflows (as happened to processes $P3$, $P4$ and $P7$ in Figure 4).

The dataflows built in the previous step are process dependency trees, that must be executed level-by-level to respect the internal dependency constraints. Thus, for each dataflow obtained in the previous step, a total serial order of processes must be built, with the goal of satisfying the level-to-level dependencies.

Processes in each dataflow are serialized, starting from the lower levels up to the root processes of the dependency graph (processes at the same level can be executed in any sequential order). Such sequential order eliminates the need of frequent synchronization after each level. An example timeline obtained from this example is shown on the right hand side of Figure 5.

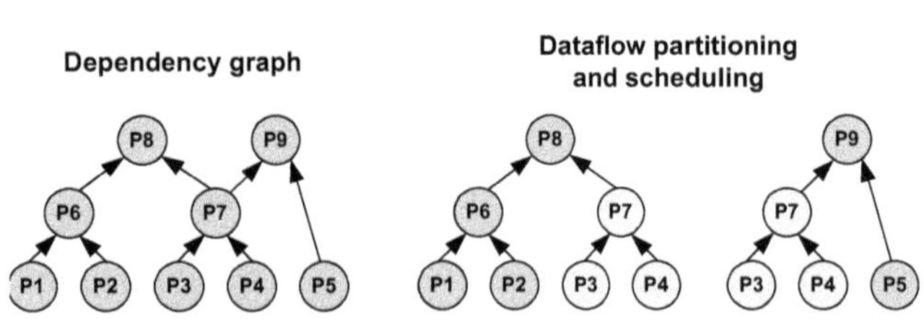

Figure 4: Application of the SAGA methodology to the same example testbench of Figure 3

4.3 Dynamic vs. static scheduling comparison

The proposed approaches to SystemC simulation on GP-GPU architectures have many differences that affect overall performance.

The dynamic scheduling approach of SCGPSim [13] implies an overhead for both handling of events and frequent synchronization barriers. The left hand side of Figure 5 highlights the frequency and the overhead induced by dynamic scheduling, with respect to the static approach (right hand side of Figure 5). Static scheduling has been adopted in SAGA to avoid such synchronization issues, while still preserving the dependencies between processes. The static approach was shown to be more efficient also on complex designs [19].

Both the scheduling approaches have also a heavy impact on thread management, as outlined in Figure 5. Dynamic scheduling requires fast synchronization primitives called barriers, available only when the synchronizing threads belong to the same thread block. However, if this is the case (as in SCGPSim), processes are serialized (as highlighed on the left hand side of Figure 5). Indeed, SystemC processes tend not to share the same code, generating a path divergence in the instructions executed by each thread. On the other hand, static scheduling can adopt heavier synchronization mechanisms, due to less frequent synchronization. Thus, the executing threads can belong to different blocks and still achieve concurrent execution (as highlighed on the right hand side of Figure 5).

As a result, static scheduling is a winning approach to speed up simulation, both for better thread management and reduced need for synchronization. Thus, we adopt static scheduling in our solution.

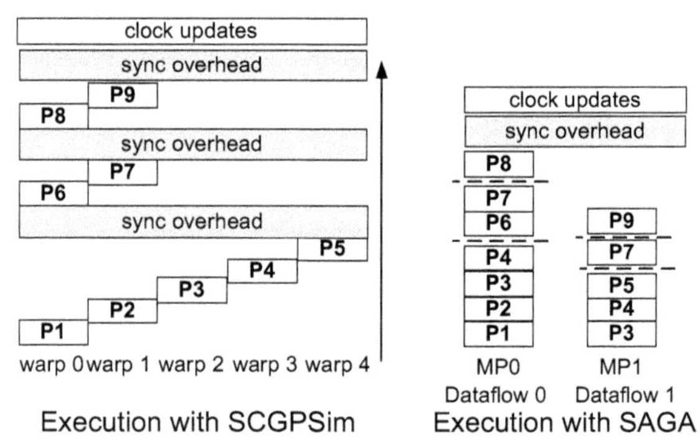

Figure 5: Comparison of actual execution schedule when using SCGPSim (on the left) vs. SAGA (on the right)

5. PARALLEL EXECUTION ON GP-GPUs

In this paper, we adopt SAGA to determine the static scheduling and to generate the target code. Both OpenCL and CUDA maintain the same code structure, with two separate kernels executed on the GP-GPU. A *simulation kernel* manages dataflow execution, and it is generated by listing all the dataflows and predicating each by a thread-block ID condition, so that only a specific thread-block is responsible for executing a certain dataflow. The simulation kernel alternates execution with a *value-update kernel*, responsible for transferring next-state values into the corresponding present-state values and performing testbench actions. A simulation cycle is completed by one execution of the simulation kernel followed by one execution of the value-update kernel.

Since device memory accesses are particularly slow, only variables written by synchronous processes are allocated in global memory, while all other variables can be declared as local variables mapped to registers.

The following sections discuss the differences in the code generated for OpenCL frameworks (Section 5.2) with respect to CUDA frameworks (Section 5.1). The main differences deal with memory handling and with kernel management on the device.

5.1 Execution on CUDA frameworks

A pseudo-code of the host code generated for CUDA frameworks is outlined in Figure 6. In CUDA, kernels are invoked by the host and they result in the activation of a high number of parallel threads that perform computation (line 8). Host and devices have separate memory spaces. Thus memory must be allocated separately on the host (line 2) and the device (line 4). When memory must be shared between the host and the device (e.g., to pass inputs or return the result of computation to the host), all memory transfers must be explicit (line 10). Since such transfers are time-consuming operations, they must be reduced to the bare minimum.

```
1: // allocation of memory on the host
2: host_m = malloc(size);
3: // allocation of memory on the device
4: cudaMalloc((void**)&device_m, size);
5: // memory transfer to provide inputs
6: cudaMemcpy(device_m,host_m,size,cudaMemcpyHostToDevice);
7: // kernel invocation
8: kernel_f«< block_number, thread_number »>(device_m);
9: // memory transfer to get results
10: cudaMemcpy(device_m,host_m,size,cudaMemcpyDeviceToHost);
```

Figure 6: Example of host code for CUDA frameworks

5.2 Execution on OpenCL frameworks

OpenCL management of GP-GPU execution requires an initialization phase to set up the GP-GPU and the code. Figure 7 outlines the code and the operations that are necessary for the setup. The host queries the system to get a reference to the device (line 2-3). Since OpenCL supports a wide range of devices, the device type must be provided (e.g., GP-GPU). Then, this information is used to setup the context (line 5) and the command queue used to communicate with the device (e.g., to transfer data or activate kernels, line 7). The command queue is necessary since kernel invocations and memory transfers are not directly invoked by the host. On the contrary, they are added to the command queue of each device.

Finally, the host must configure the program that runs on the GP-GPU, perform runtime compilation (line 9-10) and initialize kernel functions (line 12). All such operations are not necessary in CUDA, since CUDA targets exclusively NVIDIA GP-GPU.

```
1: // get information about the platform and the GP-GPU
2: status = clGetPlatformIDs(1, &platform, NULL);
3: status = clGetDeviceIDs(platform, device_type, 1, &device, NULL);
4: // initialize the context
5: context_properties = CL_CONTEXT_PLATFORM, platform, 0 ;
6: // create the command queue
7: clCreateCommandQueue(context, device, 0, &status);
8: // setup and compile the program
9: clCreateProgramWithSource(context, 1, &source, size, &status);
10: status = clBuildProgram(program,1,&device,options,NULL,NULL);
11: // initialize the kernel
12: initialize = clCreateKernel(program, "kernel_f", &status);
```

Figure 7: Example of host code to initialize execution on OpenCL frameworks

Once initialization and platform configuration have been executed, the host code must manage memory and kernel invocations. A simple outline of the host code generated for OpenCL frameworks is shown in Figure 8. In OpenCL, kernels and memory transfers are added to the command queue initialized during the initialization phase (Figure 7). When launching a kernel, parameters are explicitly set and then the kernel can be queued for execution (line 9-10), leading to parallel execution on the device.

Memory management in OpenCL is more flexible. The programmer may decide to make memory locations visible only from the device or available to the host as well. Such configurations are set during memory allocation, by passing the desired configuration as a parameter (line 4). Performance of memory transfers between the device and the host are heavily affected by the selection of such parameters (line 6 and line 11).

```
1: // allocation of memory on the host
2: host_m = malloc(size);
3: // allocation of memory on the device
4: device_m = clCreateBuffer(context,OPENCL_CONFIG,size,NULL,
   &status);
5: // memory transfer to provide inputs
6: clEnqueueWriteBuffer(commandQueue, device_m, CL_TRUE, 0, size,
   host_m, 0, NULL, NULL);
7: // kernel setup and invocation
8: clSetKernelArg(kernel_f,n,size,parameter);
9: clEnqueueNDRangeKernel(commandQueue,kernel_f, 1, NULL,
   &thread_number, &grid_number, 0, NULL, NULL);
10: // memory transfer to get results
11: clEnqueueReadBuffer(commandQueue, device_m, CL_TRUE, 0, size,
   host_m, 0, NULL, NULL);
```

Figure 8: Example of host code for OpenCL frameworks

6. EXPERIMENTAL RESULTS

This section evaluates the performance of the generated code for SystemC simulation on GP-GPUs. Furthermore, we provide a detailed comparison between CUDA and OpenCL frameworks, to highlight their strengths and drawbacks when simulating SystemC RTL code.

6.1 Experimental setup

All the experiments have been carried out on two different GP-GPUs: NVIDIA GeForce GTX 460 and NVIDIA GeForce GTX 570. The main characteristics of such platforms are outlined in Table 1.

Characteristics	NVIDIA GTX460	NVIDIA GTX570
CUDA Version	4.2	4.2
OpenCL Version	1.1	1.1
Cores (#)	336	480
Core clock (MHz)	1350	1464
Memory clock (MHz)	1800	1900
Memory bandwidth (GB/s)	115.2	152.0
Compute capability	2.1	2.0

Table 1: Characteristics of the GP-GPU platforms

The designs used in the experiments are part of a complex embedded platform that was developed in the context of a European project together with silicon vendor industry partners:

- ClockGen, ResGen, Sync and RegCtrl are part of a complex DSPI system. ClockGen is a multiple clock generator. ResGen transforms and outputs the computed results in the specified format. Sync is a specialized synchronization function among a number of components. RegCtrl is a register controller for a set of registers.
- 8b10b is a module encoding and decoding byte-wide data according to the 8b/10b protocol.

- Ecc is an error correction code device.
- System is a complex platform integrating all the designs previously discussed.

For each design, Table 2 reports the number of processes in the original SystemC description (*Processes (#)*), the lines of code (*SystemC (loc)*), the number of dataflows extracted (*Dataflows (#)*) while building the static scheduling and the number of thread blocks launched on the GP-GPU(*Thread block (#)*).

Design	Processes(#)		SystemC	Dataflows	Thread
	Synch.	Asynch.	(loc)	(#)	block (#)
ClockGen	6	15	741	12	12
ResGen	3	6	478	9	9
Sync	4	22	641	23	23
RegCtrl	18	32	2677	43	43
8b10b	7	30	799	7	7
ECC	4	7	582	4	4
System	42	112	5643	98	98

Table 2: Characteristics of the testbench designs

6.2 Compilation costs

Table 3 compares the cost of compilation for the generated code. Column *CUDA comp. (ms)* contains the compilation time for the CUDA version of each design, including compilation of the device code. Column *OpenCL comp. (ms)* details the time spent during the offline and runtime compilation phases by the OpenCL implementation.

Design	CUDA	OpenCL comp. (ms)	
	comp. (ms)	Offline	Runtime
ClockGen	5,170	270	8.42
ResGen	5,230	270	11.75
Sync	6,220	270	9.95
RegCtrl	4,920	280	11.27
8b10b	5,740	260	11.67
Ecc	4,500	290	7.09
System	16,080	290	17.37

Table 3: Comparison of compilation times for the sequential SystemC simulator and the CUDA and OpenCL versions executed on the NVIDIA GTX 570 GP-GPU.

OpenCL offline compilation cost is much smaller than CUDA compilation cost (avg. 270 ms vs 6,380 ms), since it consists only of the host code compilation and of the generation of an intermediate representation for the device code. On the other hand, OpenCL code initialization includes runtime compilation, consisting in the generation of the actual device code binary, starting from the intermediate representation (as explained in section 3.2). This last compilation step can be performed only at runtime, since it depends on the device chosen at initialization time for the execution. As a result, the runtime compilation cost for OpenCL is bigger and it depends on the size of the design (avg. 11.07 ms).

These GP-GPU experiments have been conducted on the NVIDIA GTX 570 GP-GPU. However, similar times apply to the NVIDIA GTX 460 GP-GPU.

6.3 Performance

Table 4 reports the execution time for the CUDA and OpenCL versions of each testbench example on the NVIDIA GTX 570 and NVIDIA GTX 460 GP-GPU, respectively. The table highlights that execution is faster on the GTX 460 architecture, even if the HW architecture of the NVIDIA GTX 570 GP-GPU is more optimized and contains more computing units. This behavior is strictly due to a more optimized version of the NVIDIA framework running on the NVIDIA GTX 460 architecture, including support SW and compilers. This shows that performance is heavily affected by both the underlying architecture and the support SW framework. Section 6.4 will show that the impact of each operation on the overall performance is similar on both the architectures, and thus the considerations made for the GTX 570 GP-GPU will apply also to the GTX 460 GP-GPU.

Design	NVIDIA GTX 570 (ms)		NVIDIA GTX 460 (ms)	
	OpenCL	CUDA	OpenCL	CUDA
ClockGen	1,011.0	1,317.0	210.2	420.3
ResGen	15,675.0	72,343.0	16,953.2	90,739.0
Sync	1,013.4	1,159.1	186.9	443.4
RegCtrl	1,046.8	1,450.0	235.6	637.1
8b10b	20,610.0	82,594.0	23,445.9	90,739.0
Ecc	1,055.8	1,181.1	183.3	402.1
System	61,995.7	227,142.0	71,720.4	201,379.0

Table 4: Execution time for the CUDA and OpenCL versions of each testbench example on the NVIDIA GTX 570 and NVIDIA GTX 460 GP-GPU

6.4 Performance analysis

Table 5 analyzes the performance of the generated code on the NVIDIA GTX570 GP-GPU, deepening the timing results reported in table 4. Column *(Real time (ms))* reports the execution time on CUDA and OpenCL frameworks, respectively. Then, the execution time is divided into the different operations:

- *initialization*: initialization phase that includes GP-GPU and memory setup and (for OpenCL frameworks) runtime compilation;
- *initialization kernel*: execution of the initialization kernel;
- *simulation kernel*: execution of the simulation kernel, to execute the dataflows;
- *value-update kernel*: execution of the value-update kernel;
- *DH memory transfer*: transfer of data from the device memory to the host memory;
- *HD memory transfer*: transfer of data from the host memory to the device memory.

For each operation, the table shows time spent on the CPU (Column *CPU (ms)*) and the time spent on the GPU (Column *GPU (ms)*). CPU time includes the host overhead to launch functions, kernel setup and memory setup. GPU time includes kernel execution and memory transfer execution. Furthermore, Column *Operation overhead (%)* shows the overhead of each operation on overall execution, thus allowing to analyze the performance of each operation on both the frameworks.

Figures 9 to 13 highlight the most relevant aspects of the table. As shown in Figure 9, *real time* is always faster for the CUDA version of each testbench design. This is easily explained when considering the analysis in section 3.3. SystemC simulation on GP-GPUs does not exploit architecture peculiarities such as read-only memory or loop unrolling pragmas. However, CUDA is more mature and its compilers are more optimized for the NVIDIA GP-GPU architectures than the OpenCL counterpart. This speeds up execution of the CUDA versions, to the detriment of the OpenCL implementations.

Design	Real time (ms)		Operation	Invocations	CPU (ms)		GPU (ms)		Operation overhead (%)	
	CUDA	OpenCL		(#)	CUDA	OpenCL	CUDA	OpenCL	CUDA	OpenCL
ClockGen	1,011	1,317	initialization	1	1.00	8.42	0.00	0.00	2.12	10.14
			initialization kernel	1	0.02	0.03	0.00	0.00	0.04	0.04
			simulation kernel	3,300	5.48	8.74	5.84	4.56	24.01	16.01
			value-update kernel	3,300	6.19	8.09	4.41	3.59	22.49	14.06
			DH memory transf.	3,300	15.32	32.98	2.06	4.90	36.86	45.61
			HD memory transf.	3,300	5.55	10.41	1.27	1.35	14.47	14.15
ResGen	15,675	72,343	initialization	1	0.80	11.75	0.00	0.00	0.00	0.04
			initialization kernel	1	0.02	0.03	0.00	0.00	0.00	0.00
			simulation kernel	1,000,000	3,675.34	6,625.11	2,594.11	2,296.28	23.66	31.28
			value-update kernel	1,000,000	3,381.12	5,305.48	1,953.26	2,002.04	20.13	25.62
			DH memory transf.	1,000,000	9,530.30	1,974.81	1,305.40	3,113.09	40.89	17.84
			HD memory transf.	1,000,000	3,245.82	6,354.84	813.44	835.60	15.32	25.21
Sync	1,013	1,159	initialization	1	0.99	9.95	0.00	0.00	2.57	11.67
			initialization kernel	1	0.01	0.04	0.01	0.00	0.05	0.05
			simulation kernel	1,300	4.85	14.07	3.76	3.30	22.45	20.36
			value-update kernel	1,300	4.47	9.00	4.58	3.85	23.57	15.07
			DH memory transf.	1,300	12.67	31.31	1.63	3.96	37.29	41.34
			HD memory transf.	1,300	4.38	8.77	1.01	1.05	14.07	11.51
RegCtrl	1,046	1,450	initialization	1	1.09	11.27	0.00	0.00	1.07	4.37
			initialization kernel	1	0.01	0.03	0.01	0.00	0.02	0.01
			simulation kernel	6,600	11.97	60.78	10.37	9.01	22.00	27.07
			value-update kernel	6,600	10.90	30.60	14.55	14.58	25.05	17.52
			DH memory transf.	6,600	35.00	90.66	4.25	9.96	38.64	39.03
			HD memory transf.	6,600	10.88	28.30	2.56	2.62	13.23	11.99
8b10b	20,610	82,594	initialization	1	0.98	11.67	0.00	0.00	0.00	0.02
			initialization kernel	1	0.01	0.03	0.00	0.00	0.00	0.00
			simulation kernel	1,000,000	3,602.43	5,904.27	5,904.27	5,203.65	26.44	21.52
			value-update kernel	1,000,000	3,269.76	4,356.19	4,217.16	3,579.21	20.82	16.28
			DH memory transf.	1,000,000	12,881.70	21,872.60	1,230.69	2,984.38	39.25	51.00
			HD memory transf.	1,000,000	3,186.54	4,646.12	1,659.49	798.13	13.48	11.17
Ecc	1,056	1,181	initialization	1	1.01	7.09	0.00	0.00	3.16	10.18
			initialize kernel	1	0.01	0.03	0.00	0.00	0.06	0.04
			simulation kernel	1,026	3.49	7.64	4.14	3.78	22.80	16.40
			value-update kernel	1,026	3.88	11.40	3.40	2.75	22.72	20.31
			DH memory transf.	1,026	10.63	25.42	1.28	3.06	37.18	40.86
			HD memory transf.	1,026	3.39	7.69	0.80	0.82	13.08	12.21
System	61,996	227,142	initialization	1	1.36	17.37	0,00	0,00	0,00	0,01
			initialization kernel	1	0.01	0.03	0.01	0.01	0,00	0,00
			simulation kernel	2,200,002	7,190.06	15,237.60	11,255.20	9,755.01	16.53	16.76
			update kernel	2,200,002	7,854.85	25,732.20	27,430.70	23,973.40	31.63	33.34
			DH memory transf.	2,200,002	45,820.00	50,841.90	2974.18	7,104.37	43.73	38.86
			HD memory transf.	2,200,002	7,348.70	14,517.30	1,697.00	1,917.47	8.11	11.02

Table 5: Comparison of execution times for the CUDA and OpenCL versions executed on the NVIDIA GTX570 GP-GPU and analysis of the overhead of the single operations on overall performance

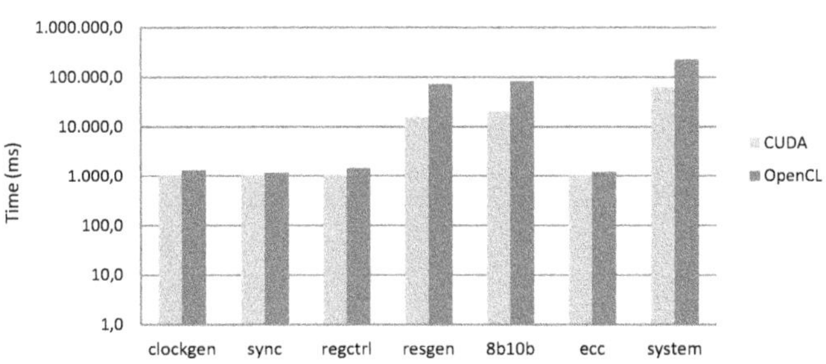

Figure 9: Comparison of simulation performance (real time) for the CUDA and OpenCL simulation of each design

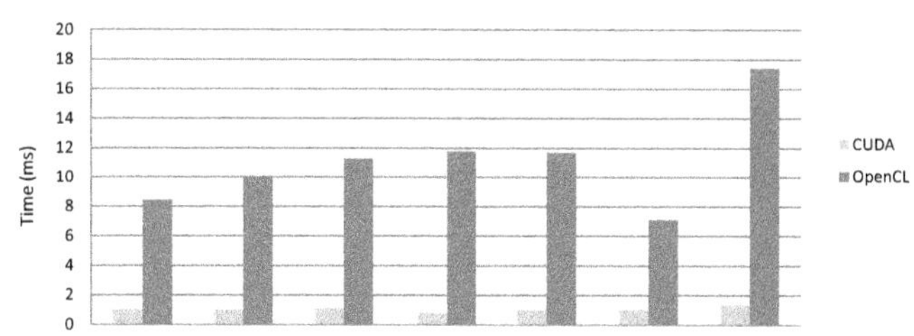

Figure 10: Initialization overhead of the CUDA and OpenCL implementations for all testbench designs

Figure 10 shows the time devoted to *initialization* in the CUDA and OpenCL code. The CUDA version has an almost constant initialization time, that results in being faster than the OpenCL version. Indeed, OpenCL initialization includes runtime compilation costs that strictly depend on the device code and on the kernel's size (as explained in section 3.2 and shown in section 6.2). As a result, a more optimized OpenCL compiler would enhance initialization and reduce its impact on performance.

Then, it is important to evaluate the overhead of each *operation* on the execution time. The analyzed operations are: initialization (including runtime compilation for OpenCL), device kernels (initialization kernel, simulation kernel and value-update kernel) and memory transfers (DH if the transfer is from device to host, HD for the other direction). Figures 11, 12 and 13 highlight the impact of each operation on the RegCtrl example. However, similar considerations apply to all testbench designs.

Figure 11 shows the average *CPU time* necessary to perform

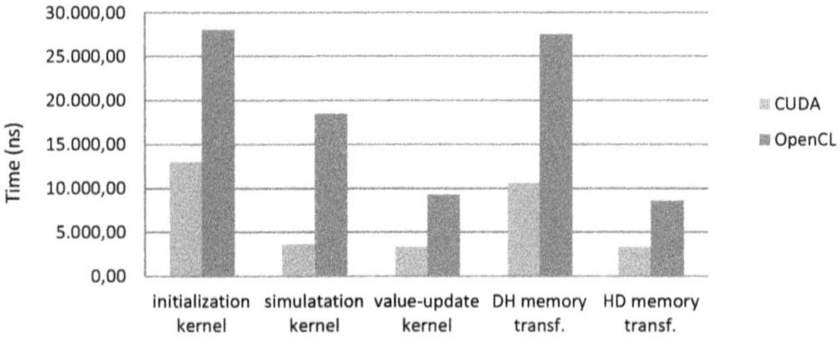

Figure 11: Comparison of average CPU time of each operation for CUDA and OpenCL implementations of the RegCtrl example

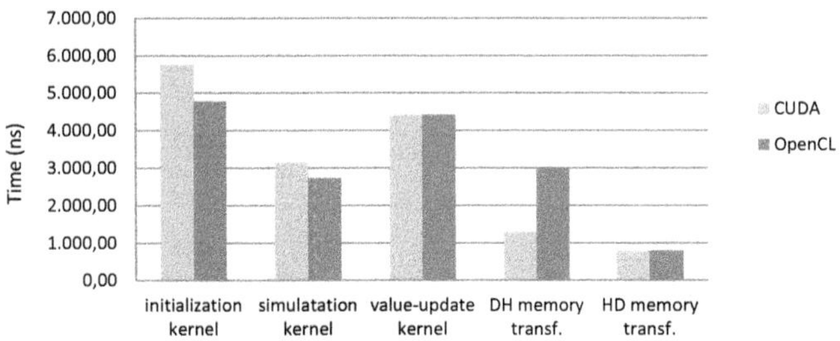

Figure 12: Comparison of average GPU time of each operation for CUDA and OpenCL implementations of the RegCtrl example

each operation. The figure highlights that CPU time is always higher for OpenCL versions. Indeed, kernel management and memory handling imply a heavier overhead for OpenCL. On the other hand, Figure 12 shows the average *GPU time* necessary to perform each operation. Kernel execution is faster on OpenCL, while memory transfers are more optimized and, thus, faster for the CUDA version. The difference on memory handling is explained by the different nature of CUDA and OpenCL. CUDA targets specific GP-GPU architectures, thus it can efficiently exploit the architecture characteristics (e.g., read-only memory). On the other hand, OpenCL must be more flexible and it can make no assumption on the underlying architecture, leading to an heavy impact on memory operations.

Finally, Figure 13 depicts the *impact of each operation* on execution performance for both the CUDA and the OpenCL versions of the examples. CUDA and OpenCL have similar behaviors. Initialization and the initialization kernels have a low impact on performance (0.02% and 1.07% on CUDA, 0.01% and 4.37% on OpenCL, respectively). Furthermore, the more complex funtionality execution is, the less impact initialization has.

A percentage comprised between the 40% and the 50% of the execution time is occupied by execution of the kernels that are necessary for simulation in both the CUDA and OpenCL versions. Indeed, the simulation and value-update kernels occupy the 22% and 27.07% on CUDA, and the 25.05% and 17.52% on OpenCL, respectively.

Finally, memory management has a heavy impact on the performance. Copy of data from the device memory to the host memory is up to 3x slower than transfers in the opposite direction, for both the CUDA and the OpenCL version. Indeed, it requires an average of 38.83% of overall execution time (38.64% on CUDA and 39.03% on OpenCL), while memory transfers from the host memory to the device memory require an average of the 12.61% (13.23% on CUDA and 11.99% on OpenCL). As a result, memory transfers dominate both CUDA and OpenCL execution performance.

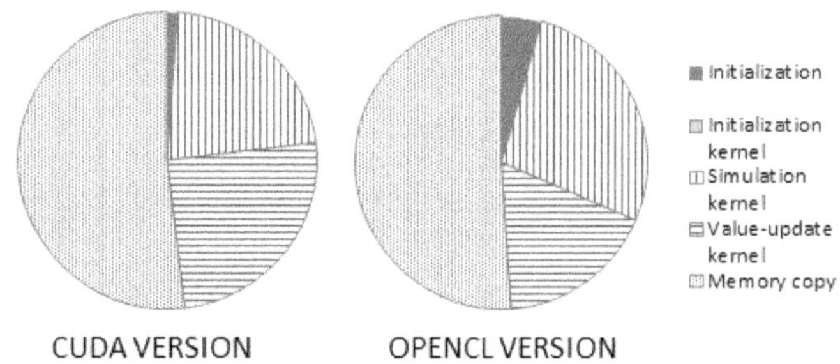

Figure 13: Overhead of the individual operations for the RegCtrl example, applied to the CUDA (on the left) and to the OpenCL version (on the right) on the NVIDIA GTX570 GP-GPU.

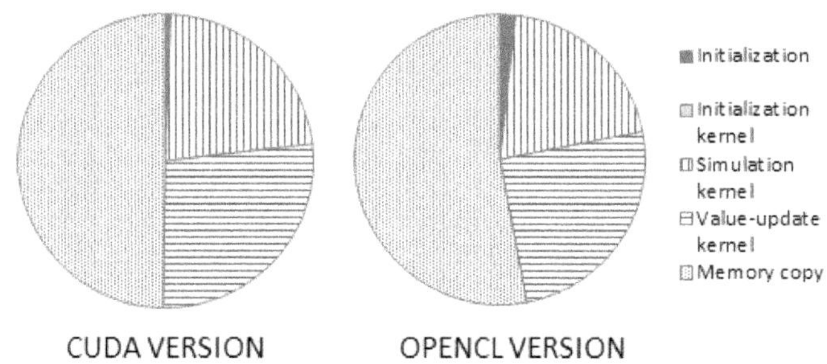

Figure 14: Overhead of the individual operations for the RegCtrl example, applied to the CUDA (on the left) and to the OpenCL version (on the right) on the NVIDIA GTX460 GP-GPU.

The above considerations justify the overall performance trends shown in Figure 9. OpenCL versions are faster only in kernel execution. On the contrary, all management tasks (kernel activation and synchronization and memory transfers) are faster on CUDA. Figure 14 highlights that the comments made for the GTX 570 architecture apply also to the GTX 460 GP-GPU. Indeed, each operation has the same impact on the execution for both the CUDA and the OpenCL version, despite of the more optimized compute capability support.

All the former considerations highlight how the OpenCL performance is affected by non optimized compilers. This is highlighted also by the comparison between the NVIDIA GTW 460 and 570 architectures, where a more optimized SW framework makes execution faster on the less performing architecture (the GTX 460). OpenCL is less mature that CUDA, thus affecting execution management and memory handling costs. However, former development of OpenCL may improve performance and management, reaching the performance of CUDA still preserving the higher degree of portability.

7. CONCLUSION

This paper presented an analysis of SystemC simulation on GP-GPU architectures, targeting both CUDA and OpenCL frameworks. The analysis is enriched with a detailed analysis of the performance differences between the two frameworks, highlighting strengths and drawbacks. We found that OpenCL is slower that the corresponding CUDA version, due to a less optimized management of the underlying architecture. However, OpenCL is less mature than CUDA and the analysis conducted in the paper showed that the SW framework has a heavy impact on performance. Thus, future development may lead to more optimized compilers and to overcome the limitations of OpenCL portability.

8. REFERENCES

[1] Accellera Systems Initiative. *SystemC*. `http://www.accellera.org`.

[2] F. Balarin and R. Passerone. Functional verification methodology based on formal interface specification and transactor generation. In *Proc. of IEEE/ACM DATE*, pages 1013–1018, 2006.

[3] N. Bombieri, A. Fedeli, F. Fummi, and G. Pravadelli. Hybrid incremental ABV for functional validation in TLM design flows. *IEEE Design and Test of Computer*, 24(2):140–152, 2007.

[4] N. Bombieri, F. Fummi, and V. Guarnieri. FAST-GP: An RTL functional verification framework based on fault simulation on GP-GPUs. *Proc. of ACM/IEEE DATE*, pages 562–565, 2012.

[5] R. Buchmann and A. Greiner. A fully static scheduling approach for fast cycle accurate SystemC simulation of MPSoCs. In *Proc. of IEEE ICM*, pages 101 –104, 2007.

[6] L. Cai and D. Gajski. Transaction level modeling: An overview. In *ACM/IEEE CODES+ISSS*, pages 19–24, 2003.

[7] P. Combes, E. Caron, F. Desprez, B.Chopard, and J. Zory. Relaxing synchronization in a parallel SystemC kernel. In *Proc. Of ISPA*, pages 180–187, 2008.

[8] P. Du, R. Weber, P. Luszczek, S. Tomov, G. D. Peterson, and J. Dongarra. From CUDA to OpenCL: Towards a performance-portable solution for multi-platform GPU programming. *Parallel Computing*, 38(8):391–407, 2012.

[9] P. Ezudheen, P. Chandran, J. Chandra, B. Simon, and D. Ravi. Parallelizing SystemC kernel for fast hardware simulation on SMP machines. In *Proc. of ACM/IEEE PADS*, pages 80–87, 2009.

[10] J. Fang, A. L. Varbanescu, and H. Sips. A Comprehensive Performance Comparison of CUDA and OpenCL. In *Proc. of ICPP*, pages 216–225, 2011.

[11] R. Jindal and K. Jain. Verification of transaction-level SystemC models using RTL testbenches. In *Proc. of ACM/IEEE MEMOCODE*, pages 199–203, 2003.

[12] A. Mello, I. Maia, A. Greiner, and F. Pecheux. Parallel simulation of SystemC TLM 2.0 compliant MPSoC on SMP workstations. In *Proc. of ACM/IEEE DATE*, pages 606–609, 2010.

[13] M. Nanjundappa, H. D. Patel, B. A. Jose, and S. K. Shukla. SCGPSim: A fast SystemC simulator on GPUs. *Proc. of ACM/IEEE ASP-DAC*, pages 149–154, 2010.

[14] NVIDIA. *NVIDIA CUDA Compute Unified Device Architecture - Programming Guide*, 2008. http://developer.download.nvidia.com.

[15] N. Saviou, S. Shukla, and R. Gupta. *Design for Synthesis, Transform for Simulation: Automatic Transformation of Threading Structures in High Level System Models*. University of California at Irvine, 2008. Technical Report TR-01-58.

[16] R. Sinha, A. Prakash, and H. D. Patel. Parallel simulation of mixed-abstraction systemc models on GPUs and multicore CPUs. In *Proc. of ACM ASP-DAC*, pages 455–460, 2012.

[17] The Khronos OpenCL Working Group. *OpenCL - The open standard for parallel programming of heterogeneous systems*, 2011. http://www.khronos.org/opencl/.

[18] R. Tsuchiyama, T. Nakamura, T. Iizuka, A. Asahara, and S. Miki. *The OpenCL Programming Book*. Fixstars Corporation, 2010.

[19] S. Vinco, D. Chatterjee, V. Bertacco, and F. Fummi. SAGA: SystemC Acceleration on GPU Architectures. In *Proc. of ACM/IEEE DAC*, 2012.

[20] H. Ziyu, Q. Lei, L. Hongliang, X. Xianghui, and Z. Kun. A parallel SystemC environment: ArchSC. In *Proc. of ICPADS*, pages 617–623, 2009.

DevScope: A Nonintrusive and Online Power Analysis Tool for Smartphone Hardware Components

Wonwoo Jung, Chulkoo Kang, Chanmin Yoon, Dongwon Kim, Hojung Cha
Department of Computer Science
Yonsei University
Seoul, Korea
{wwjung, ckkang, cmyoon, dwkim, hjcha}@cs.yonsei.ac.kr

ABSTRACT
Smartphone power modeling is an important technique for users, application developers, and hardware manufacturers to build energy-aware systems. Compared to traditional offline techniques that use external power measurement devices, the online approach uses a built-in BMU (Battery Monitoring Unit), which has the advantage of generating a dynamic power model. However, the very low update rate of a BMU is an issue for online power modeling. In this paper, we introduce an autonomous power modeling tool for smartphones called DevScope, which overcomes the limitations of BMU-based online power modeling. DevScope controls components according to the BMU update rate, and derives the component power model automatically by analyzing the changes of power state. With DevScope, we construct an online and automatic power modeling that reflects both the diversity of users' environments and smartphone hardware complexity. By evaluating the scheme with various smartphones and configurations, we show that DevScope, indeed, generates a flexible and accurate power model.

Categories and Subject Descriptors
C.4 [Performance of Systems]: Modeling techniques

General Terms
Measurement, Experimentation.

Keywords
Smartphone Power Analysis, Power Modeling, Battery Monitoring Unit

1. INTRODUCTION
With the increasing number of smartphones, the energy usage of applications and hardware components has become a major issue for smartphone users. In addition to the users' concern, researchers and application developers are interested in optimizing their applications in terms of energy consumption. There has been a great deal of research to deal with this problem. Previous work is generally categorized into two groups: modeling and estimation of power consumption [1, 2], and policy development to reduce the power consumption of smartphones [3, 4]. Accurate power estimation helps end users construct a personalized energy-efficient smartphone system. The estimation result is used as a guideline to choose the applications to install, or to determine the usage patterns of smartphones. Application developers use the result to estimate the energy consumption of their programs and help developing energy efficient applications. Smartphone vendors use the estimation result as a guideline to select hardware components and to optimize the system software in an energy efficient way. Moreover, researchers can use the results to find the energy bottleneck in the system and develop solutions [3, 4]. For these reasons, we say that power modeling and estimation is an important technique that is necessary for constructing energy efficient smartphone systems.

Active work has recently been devoted to constructing an accurate power model. The research usually uses the offline method to measure and analyze power consumption patterns [1, 5-7]. Power consumption patterns are even different for the same device due to operating temperature or some other reasons [1]. The operating system or updating device driver may also affect the patterns. The power models for smartphones should therefore be constructed for each device individually, and updated with the changes of the external factors. Meanwhile, an offline method is often used under laboratory conditions and uses external measurement tools to understand power usage. With this method it is practically very hard to construct individual power models for each device. Additionally, dynamic update of the model is not possible.

The limitation of the offline method can be overcome by using an online approach that employs a Battery Monitoring Unit (BMU) [1, 2]. The BMU is a hardware component, equipped in most recent smartphones, that provides information such as supply voltage, current, and battery temperature. These features would enable the implementation of an online power model that automatically constructs a power model for each device. The scheme enables the reconstruction of the model dynamically at any time, providing flexibility to adapt to changes of external factors, such as software updates. Zhang et al. [1] used an offline method as default, and an online method to compensate for the limitation of offline method. However, they did not consider the detailed properties of a BMU that affect the accuracy; thus, we may not expect accuracy of their online model although their offline model is very accurate. Dong et al. [2] analyzed the properties of BMU and constructed an online power consumption model. Their model did not, however, provide information for each hardware component. In general, to employ a BMU as an online power measurement tool for accurate power modeling, we should consider two factors that are inherent in the properties of BMU. First, online measurement may not be precise compared to offline measurement. This is because the information update rate of a BMU is noticeably lower than external measurement tools. Second, since user is not able to intervene in the process of constructing a model, it is difficult to figure out the exact relationship between system activities and power consumption.

In this paper, we propose the solutions for each problem and validate them with experiments. The low update rate of the BMU is overcome by a well-refined measurement scenario. In our solution, the scenario is determined after going through an automatic analysis on the update rate of the BMU as well as on the characteristics of each hardware component equipped in the device. To understand the relationship between system activity and power consumption in online power models, we control the hardware activities in the scenario being synchronized with an update rate of the BMU. In other words, we set aside the relationship in advance by using the method to trigger the hardware activities related to power consumption only at the point that we can measure the device.

The technical contribution of our work is summarized as follows:

- We propose a detailed solution to overcome the limitations of using BMU and dynamically generate accurate power model. The solution is validated with the construction of an accurate power model for smartphone hardware.
- We provide an individual power model for each hardware component of smartphone. To the best of our knowledge our work is the first to construct a power model for each component automatically only using BMU.

The rest of this paper is constructed as follows. In Section 2, we describe the technical challenges of online power modeling. In Section 3, we propose our solution for overcoming these challenges. We describe the detailed mechanism for each hardware component and evaluate it with some smartphones in Section 4. Section 5 presents related works, and we conclude the paper in Section 6.

2. ONLINE POWER MODELING: THE CHALLENGES

2.1 Battery Monitoring Unit (BMU)

A BMU monitors discharge voltage curve, battery temperature, discharging current, and so on. The unit periodically stores the values in registers. Two methods are available to measure the power consumption of a smartphone: (1) using voltage curve and (2) sensing the value of discharging current. Using voltage value is an estimating technique that is available for every BMU but the scheme is prone to generate a significant amount of errors. Sensing the current is an accurate scheme, but the scheme is only available for BMU that is equipped with the current sensors. In our research, we consider BMUs that can measure the discharging current directly. The accuracy of a current value provided by a BMU is reasonable enough to be used for the current measurement of smartphone components. In the case of DS2784 [8], a BMU that is equipped on Google Nexus One (N1) [9], the sensing resolution is about 104 uA, and the measurement range is between -3430 mA and 3430 mA, with the measurement error of ±1%. The BMU monitors the discharging current levels with high sampling rate, and reports its average with low update rate. In the case of DS2784, the sampling rate is 18.6 KHz and the update rate is lower than 0.28 Hz (1 time per 3.52 s).

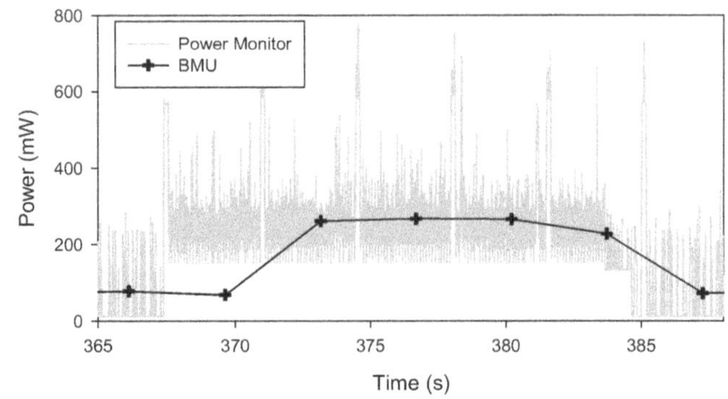

Figure 1. Offline measurement Vs. online measurement.

2.2 Challenges

Due to the low update rate (i.e., reporting rate) of BMU, it is difficult to determine the power states of system components. While the update rate of the external measurement tool is 5 KHz [11], the update rate of a BMU (in the case of DS2784) is lower than 0.28 Hz. That is, the external tool is more precise than the internal one in the same measurement scenario. In the case of power state changes within a very short time, we cannot pick up these changes with a BMU. Figure 1, for example, shows the result of power consumption of a WiFi interface card that is measured with external and internal tools. We transmitted 50 MTU sized packets per second in this experiment with N1. The sampling rate of the BMU is high enough (18.6 KHz) to trust the measurement result. However, its update rate is very low, so the power consumption pattern (i.e., power state changes) of the WiFi interface card is hard to grasp with BMU. Note that the pattern can easily be obtained with the use of external measurement tools. Since a power model should provide the power consumption pattern as well as the power consumption value, we should somehow overcome the limitation of the BMU to maximize the advantages of internal measurement.

The online method has to perform the analysis, as well as the measurement, online. The system should therefore recognize the relationship between power consumption and system activity in order for accurate analysis. For example, the first rise in Figure 1 represents the start of sending packets. For humans this is simple to recognize, but the fact is hard to be detected automatically by the system. We need a mechanism to recognize the relationship autonomously and accurately.

3. NONINTRUSIVE POWER MODELING

In this paper, we define the nonintrusive power modeling as a system modeling technique that is conducted automatically and at run-time without external devices or any artificial intervention. Without any modification of the operating system, we developed an application, called DevScope, which analyzes and models the smartphone power consumption.

In line with the previous research [1, 2, 6, 7], the system power consumption model (P) is presented as a first-order polynomial regression function:

$$P = \Sigma_i(\beta_i \times u_i),$$

where u_i is individual component utilization and β_i is power coefficient value of component i.

Some hardware components have multiple terms (i.e., combinations of β_i and u_i) in this equation. For example, most of modern CPU has multiple operating frequencies. To determine the necessary terms for the power model equation, we pre-analyzed each component by investigating the general characteristics of power state transitions. In a practical situation, the detailed operating characteristic of each component depends on hardware and configuration. Therefore, for a flexible power model, the number of terms should be determined dynamically during the modeling process.

DevScope is an automatic and online training tool to generate a power model. The tool first probes the operating systems to find information about the individual component types and its configuration (e.g., available CPU frequency levels). Additionally, by monitoring the update activity of BMU, DevScope figures out the update rate automatically. According to individual component types, system configuration, and BMU update rate, DevScope dynamically creates a component control scenario to perform power analysis. Hence, even though the device (i.e., smartphone) model is identical, the scenario might be different by each configuration. DevScope performs the test scenario, and automatically classifies the results into each terms of the power model. Finally, DevScope analyzes the classified data to find power coefficients that are required in modeling the system power.

Figure 2 shows the overview of the DevScope framework. The tool consists of four parts: Component Controller, Timing Controller, BMU Event Monitor, and Power Model Generator. The BMU Event Monitor is a module to monitor the discharging current data from the BMU. The Timing Controller calculates the BMU update rate and generates a control signal which triggers the actions of the Component Controller. The Component Controller constructs test scenarios for individual components and performs the actions according to control triggers, which are generated by the Timing Controller. All the test results are analyzed by the Power Model Generator to obtain power coefficients. These four modules collaborate to overcome the challenges discussed in the previous section.

3.1 Update Event-based Component Control

The solution to overcoming the very low update rate of BMU is to control individual components thoroughly, according to the update rate while conducting test scenarios. This solution has two problems. First, the update rates of the built-in BMU depend on the type of hardware. Second, the BMU update rate cannot be controlled at run-time. Due to these problems, it is hard to synchronize the component behavior with BMU update rates

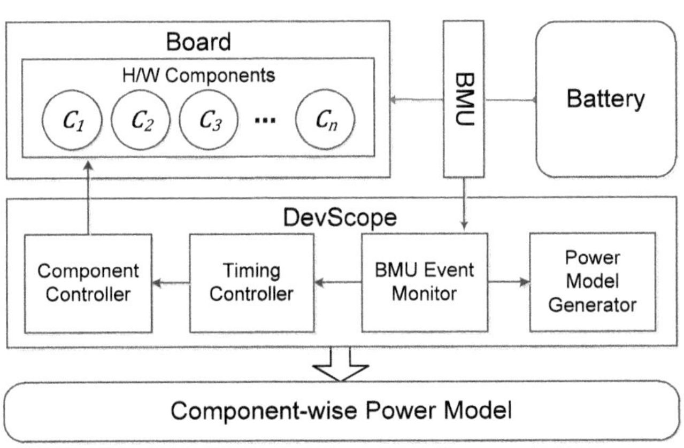

Figure 2. The overview of DevScope framework.

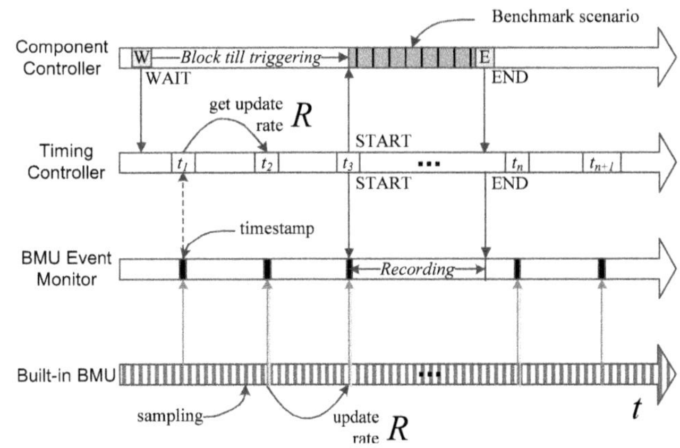

Figure 3. BMU update event based timing controlled component job processing to benchmark its power consumption.

dynamically. To handle this, DevScope adopts an event-driven method that regards the BMU update as an event and monitors the update events continuously. Test scenario for individual component should be performed depending on the BMU update events. Figure 3 describes how DevScope performs the test scenarios based on the event-driven method. The BMU Event Monitor puts a timestamp on each discharging current data whenever an update occurs. Every test scenario has WAIT and END messages. If a scenario is ready to perform, the Component Controller sends WAIT message to the Timing Controller, then blocks every operation until it is triggered by the Timing Controller. A WAIT message is received; the Timing Controller reads the timestamp multiple times to calculate the BMU update rate *R*. The BMU update rate in the application level has a little delay compared to the actual update rate in the hardware level; hence, *R* should be re-calculated before the test scenario is performed to redeem the delay between actual update and triggering time. After re-calculating, the Timing Controller triggers the Component Controller to release a blocked scenario when the next update event occurs. Accordingly, this event-driven component control method can synchronize individual test scenarios with the BMU update.

3.2 Update Rate-aware Workload Allocation

Even if each component behavior is synchronized with the BMU update, the power state transition cannot be recognized online, without considering the duration of each power state and the BMU update period. Moreover, some components (e.g., WiFi interface) have different power states depending on the workload size for the same operation. In this case, the test scenario should be designed with a proper workload size to keep power state stable long enough to cover the BMU update period. Consequently, DevScope should consider not only the power state duration but also the workload size to successfully conduct the test scenario.

Figure 4 represents the examples of BMU measurement results with update rate *R* according to the power states change. Note that the updated value from the BMU is an average value during one update period. The top two graphs show the case of power state change from base to active, and the bottom two graphs show the opposite case. In Figure 4(a), it is easy to recognize power state changes because the active power state is longer than *R*. Note that the start of component operation is synchronized with the BMU update by DevScope (See Section 3.1). However, if the duration

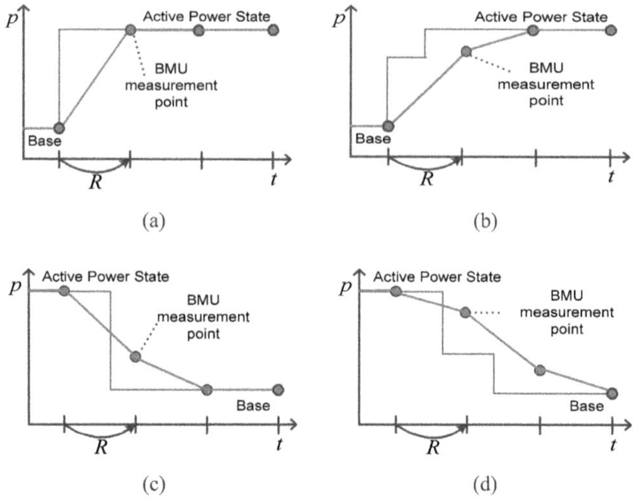

Figure 4. Examples of BMU measurement result by component power state transition. The blue line represents real power states and the red line represents the measurement result of BMU.

of state is shorter than R, the state cannot be defined and often called a hidden state. With hidden states, the BMU measurement result would have multiple slopes, as illustrated in Figure 4(b). Thus, we need at least $3R$ duration to recognize the hidden state by observing slopes of the BMU measurement result.

On the other hand, it is not possible to halt component behavior intrusively, at the exact update moment of the BMU, without any effect on power state stability (See Figure 4(c) and (d)). Accordingly, we cannot predict a timing of power state change from active to base state. In Figure 4(c) and (d), similar to the above method, DevScope recognizes the power state changes with at least $4R$ duration for both cases. DevScope assigns sufficient duration for component control and allocates workload to keep every power state longer than $5R$, as a default, to recognize power states more accurately.

Unfortunately, the duration of some power states cannot be controlled. For instance, the WiFi interface has multiple power states, depending on workload size, during the data sending operation; hence, DevScope finds the threshold workload size, which triggers the power state change, by conducting the tests repeatedly by increasing the workload size gradually. Indeed, the corresponding workload for WiFi interface is the number of packets transmitted per second (See Section 4.4).

As discussed above, DevScope recognizes the transition in component power state by adjusting the duration of power states. Nevertheless, for some components, duration adjustment is insufficient or impossible to recognize because of its fundamental power characteristics. Considering this, DevScope conducts a preliminary test to find the adequate factors, such as the packet rate of the WiFi interface.

In the following section, we describe the preliminary testing and detailed power consumption analysis method for each component, and discuss the power measurement result. We also show the evaluation results with experimentation.

4. COMPONENT POWER ANALYSIS

With DevScope, we analyze the power characteristic of major hardware components in a smartphone: CPU, Display, WiFi, Cellular, and GPS. Previous research [6] directly measured the power consumption of hardware components. Their evaluation showed that most of the power consumption of smartphones is caused by CPU, Display, and Network. Considering that many applications are based on location-based services, we additionally analyzed the GPS. In this section, we describe the specific policy for these five hardware components.

Unlike other hardware components, the CPU cannot be turned off unless the smartphone is off. Therefore, we cannot independently measure the power consumption of the other four components. We calculate the power consumption of hardware components by subtracting the power consumption of the CPU, as illustrated in (1).

$$P_{Component} = P_{Measured} - P_{CPU}, \quad (1)$$

where $P_{Component}$ is the power consumption of hardware component, $P_{Measured}$ the total power consumption of smartphone that is measured by the BMU, and P_{CPU} the power consumption of the CPU. For estimating P_{CPU} , we used the CPU power model computed by DevScope. The CPU power model should therefore be generated ahead of the other hardware components. To minimize the error caused by the CPU, we set the CPU frequency to the highest performance, and the CPU state to idle.

In the following, we describe the technique for measuring and analyzing power consumption of hardware components. We evaluate the model using two smartphones: Google Nexus One (N1) and Sony-Ericsson Xperia Arc (Arc) [10]. Note that either device has different types of BMUs, that is to say their update rates are different. To validate the analysis, we also conducted the analysis with the Monsoon Power Monitor [11] in off-line using the same scenario.

4.1 CPU

Modern processors of mobile devices are able to adjust the frequency automatically to conserve power. This technique is commonly known as DVFS (Dynamic Voltage and Frequency Scaling). According to the CPU frequency governor, DVFS sets the CPU frequency, depending on the predefined frequency-voltage table. The frequency-voltage table is defined by the policy of kernel, thus the power consumption of identical CPUs can differ as a result of each system policy.

The CPU cannot be independently turned off; therefore, the power consumption of the CPU must be subtracted in the power consumption of other components. For this, DevScope analyzes the frequency-voltage table ahead of anything else, and generates the discrete power model. The CPU power model is as follows:

$$P_{CPU} = \beta_{freq_i} \times u + \beta_{idle_i}, 0\% \leq u \leq 100\%, \ i = 0,1,2 \cdots, n, \quad (2)$$

where i is the index of the frequency-voltage table, β_{freq_i} is the power consumption of the CPU in the i-th CPU frequency, u is the CPU utilization, and β_{idle_i} the idle power consumption of the i-th frequency. The number of available frequency is dynamically determined by DevScope which looks up the frequency-voltage table.

To determine β_{freq_i} and β_{idle_i} with frequency-voltage table, DevScope measures the power consumption after setting the

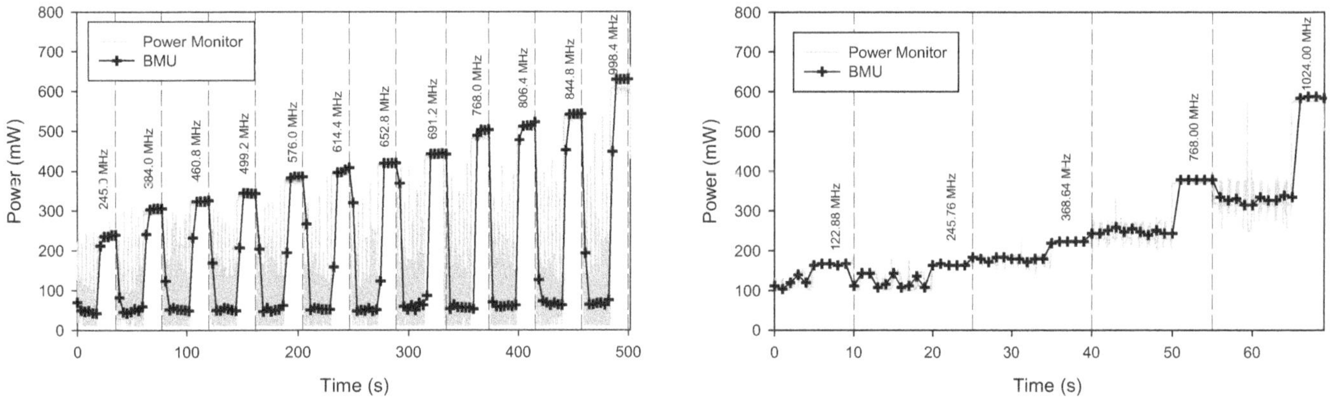

(a) Google Nexus One

(b) Sony-Ericsson Xperia Arc

Figure 5. The power consumption measurement result for CPU by DevScope.

frequency to every value in the table. To compute β_{idle_i}, DevScope first induces the utilization of the CPU to zero. Second, DevScope leads the utilization of the CPU to the maximum value, then computes β_{freq_i}. DevScope repeats this operation with every frequency in the table. In this operation, the Component Controller must recognize the state transitions of the CPU to precisely measure the power consumption. To generate the precise coefficients, DevScope keeps the CPU power states stable for $5R$ which we consider an adequate period.

Figure 5(a) shows the power consumption traces of CPU with N1 by the Monsoon Power Monitor and BMU. Since the frequency-voltage table of N1 is classified with twelve (i.e., 12 different settings), the figure shows the power consumption within twelve types of frequency. In each frequency level, the low power consumption is in an idle state, the high power consumption is in the maximum working status. The idle state defined is the complete idle because of the CPU usage by kernel. In our work, the necessary power consumption required by the system is considered as the base power, and is included in β_{idle}. Figure 5(b) shows the power trace with Arc. The device has five types of frequency level, and the power consumption of the base power is sharply changed at different frequencies. Since R of Arc is 1 second, the scale of the x-axis is different.

4.2 Display

The display type of recent smartphone is usually LCD or OLED. The power consumption of OLED is changed by the color of the screen [3]. Since the analysis on color change is not in the scope of this paper, we only analyze the LCD display in the current work.

The power consumption of LCD varies with the brightness level of the screen. The relationship is not completely linear [6], hence, DevScope generates the power model by considering every possible brightness level.

$$P_{Display} = \beta_{brightness_B},\ 0 \le B \le 255, \qquad (3)$$

where B means the brightness level of display backlight, and $\beta_{brightness_B}$ is the power consumption of display when the brightness level is B.

DevScope dynamically generates the table which contains the coefficients for each brightness level. To reduce the overhead, DevScope does not measure the power consumption of every brightness level; instead, a set of brightness level is measure and the rest are interpolated. Like other components, DevScope measures the power consumption at update timing of the BMU with a fixed brightness level, and the duration of the state is $5R$. At each brightness level, DevScope averages the sampled data and considers this value as the power consumption of display.

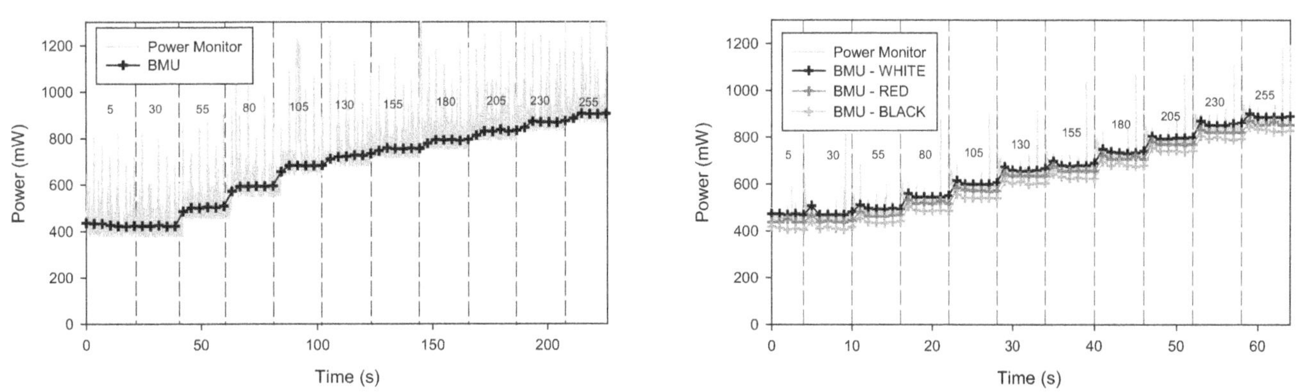

(a) Google Nexus One

(b) Sony-Ericsson Xperia Arc

Figure 6. The power consumption measurement results for LCD display by DevScope.

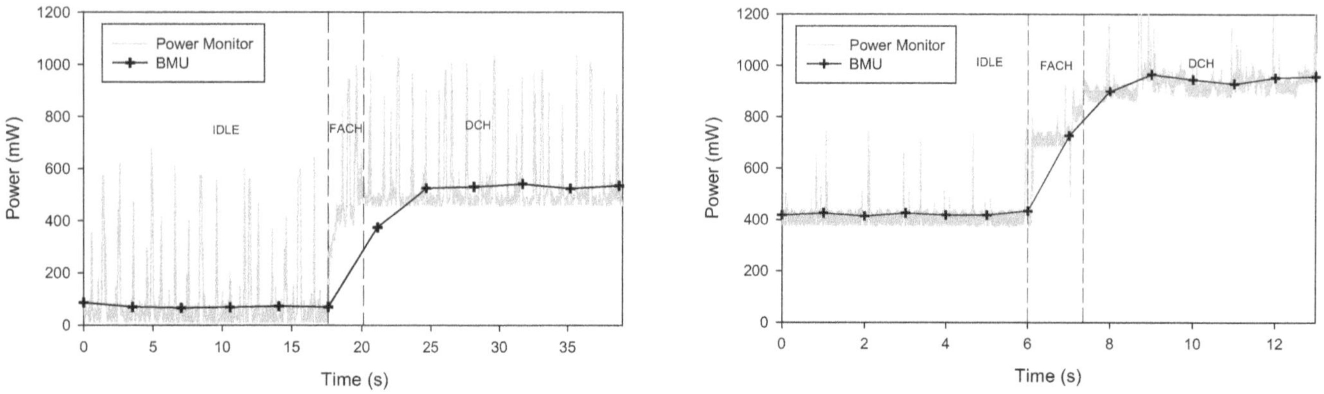

(a) Google Nexus One

(b) Sony-Ericsson Xperia Arc

Figure 7. The power consumption measurement graph for Cellular by DevScope.

Figure 6 shows the measurement results according to the brightness level. Similar to other components, the scale of the x-axis is different by the BMU update rate. The indicated value at the top is the brightness level. Figure 6 shows that the power consumption of the display is not linear with the brightness level. Arc in Figure 6(b) uses the LCD display, but uses the LED type as backlight. This display adjusts the backlight by the color of the frame buffer. Thus, when the screen color is black, red, or white, the power consumption differs in Figure 6(b). The difference in the power consumptions for each color is, however, very small. In this paper, DevScope fixes the color as white and considers the brightness level only.

4.3 Cellular

The Cellular has three types of RRC (Radio Resource Control) states, which are IDLE, FACH, and DCH, according to energy-awareness policy in mobile networks [12]. The power consumption of Cellular interface does not depend on the packet rates as opposed to WiFi (See Section 4.4), but only depends on the power state transitions. We model the Cellular power consumption, $P_{Cellular}$ as follows:

$$P_{Cellular} = \beta_{rrc}, rrc \in \{IDLE, FACH, DCH\}, \qquad (4)$$

where rrc is one of the RRC state, and β_{rrc} is the power coefficient.

To analyze the power state transition, the test scenarios for Cellular are performed by controlling data traffic. First of all, DevScope waits until the RRC state becomes IDLE without any data transmission. After detecting the IDLE state, DevScope sends HTTP requests immediately. At this time, the IDLE state transits to DCH. There indeed exists FACH state in this transition. However, the FACH state cannot be recognized directly by the BMU. We define the unrecognizable states, such as the FACH state, as the hidden state (See Section 3.2). In the DCH state, DevScope sends the HTTP requests periodically to keep the DCH state stable for $5R$.

Figure 7 shows the measurement results of N1 and Arc while running DevScope for Cellular. DevScope clearly distinguishes IDLE and DCH states. To find the power coefficients of the FACH state, DevScope uses a heuristic method. In Figure 7(a), the FACH state duration is shorter than R(=3.52 s), thus the FACH state could not be monitored by BMU. If there exists a FACH state as a hidden state, such as Figure 7(a) (Refer to Figure 4(b)), DevScope estimates the power coefficient, β_{FACH}, by approximation between IDLE and DCH state power consumption. We represent the β_{FACH} function as follows:

$$\beta_{FACH} = \frac{P_{component} \times R - \beta_{DCH} \times \Delta t_{DCH}}{\Delta t_{FACH}}, \qquad (5)$$

where $P_{component}$ is the result of subtracting CPU power consumption from the measured power consumption at the first-detected DCH state by BMU, and Δt_{DCH} and Δt_{FACH} are the amounts of time staying in the corresponding power states within R. On the other hand, in Figure 7(b), the FACH state duration is similar to Figure 7(a), but the update rate of Arc (R =1.00 s) is much shorter than N1. Thus, the FACH state is not a hidden state but its duration is insufficient to estimate the power consumption automatically. DevScope figures out β_{FACH} of Arc in the same way as N1.

4.4 WiFi

Depending on the amounts of outgoing packets, the WiFi power states are classified into four states [1, 2, 7]: L_IDLE, H_IDLE, L_TRANSMISSION, H_TRANSMISSION. Both L_IDLE and H_IDLE states are the states in which outgoing packets do not exist, whereas outgoing packets are available in L_TRANSMISSION and H_TRANSMISSION. The power consumption pattern of WiFi differs according to the specific packet rate (i.e., threshold workload size) [1, 2]. Figure 8(a) and Figure 8(b) represent the WiFi power consumption. The results do not include the power consumption of the CPU. The power pattern of WiFi is separated by the threshold. The threshold of N1 and Arc is 20 packets/sec and 25 packets/sec, respectively. If the packet rate is less than threshold, WiFi is in the L_TRANSMISSION; otherwise in the H_TRANSMISSION. Based on this fact, we model the power consumption of WiFi as follows:

$$P_{WiFi} = \begin{cases} \beta_{LT} \times p + \beta_{LT\,Base} & if\ p \le Threshold \\ \beta_{HT} \times p + \beta_{HT\,Base} & if\ p > Threshold \end{cases}, \qquad (6)$$

where β_{LT} and $\beta_{HT}$are the rate of increase in power consumption in the L_TRANSMISSION and H_TRANSMISSION, p is the packet rate, and $\beta_{LT\,Base}$ and $\beta_{HT\,Base}$ are the base power consumptions of WiFi in the L_IDLE and H_IDLE, respectively. The parameters are constant with packet rate. The H_IDLE state is a hidden state that cannot be monitored by the BMU. Considering that the BMU provides power consumption of the WiFi as the average power consumption for the BMU sampling period, we assume that the power consumption of the H_IDLE is included in the computation of H_TRANSMISSION and it is not computed separately.

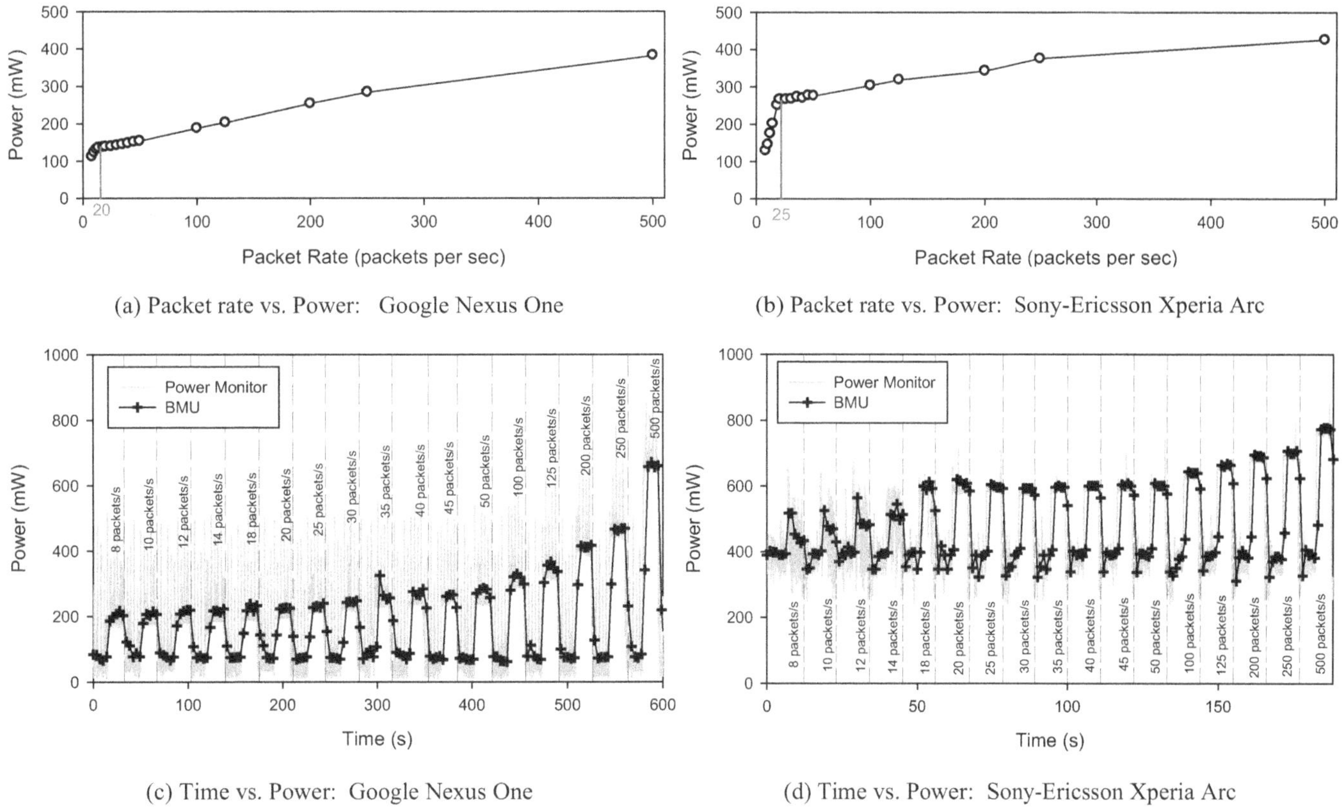

(a) Packet rate vs. Power: Google Nexus One

(b) Packet rate vs. Power: Sony-Ericsson Xperia Arc

(c) Time vs. Power: Google Nexus One

(d) Time vs. Power: Sony-Ericsson Xperia Arc

Figure 8. The power consumption measurement result for WiFi by DevScope.

DevScope automatically calculates the threshold, the coefficients, and the constants mentioned in (6). Figure 8(c) and Figure 8(d) show the overall change in power consumption with the increasing packet rate. As the packet rate continuously increases, we observe that the power obtained with DevScope also increases. The pattern of increase in power consumption slightly differs due to the devices used in the experiment. The major difference in base power, when outgoing packets do not exist, is caused by the CPU power consumption. Because the CPU frequency is set to the highest, the value of the base power is different. The starting time of the workload is the same as the update timing of the BMU, and the state duration is $5R$. Since the device's BMU sampling frequency is different, DevScope obtains a different number of samples in a given time. Therefore, the scale of x-axis is different in Figure 8(c) and Figure 8(d). Because the threshold is generally a small value, in order to increase the accuracy of threshold detection, DevScope runs with higher granularity in the lower packet rates.

4.5 GPS

GPS consumes most of the power in the process of communicating with satellites. The power states of GPS are defined into three states: OFF, SLEEP, ACTIVE. GPS does nothing in OFF state. In SLEEP state, GPS waits to connect with satellites. In ACTIVE state, GPS communicates with satellites. Even though ACTIVE consumes more power than SLEEP, the duration of ACTIVE is very short; hence, it is a hidden state to the BMU. Since it has a small effect in power consumption, we regard SLEEP and ACTIVE states as ON states. Based on these two states, we model the power consumption of GPS as follows:

$$P_{GPS} = \beta_{GPS}, \qquad (7)$$

where β_{GPS} is the power coefficients.

If GPS receives the request for updating location, it keeps in the ON state until GPS fixes the current location or the request is canceled. DevScope should maintain the ON state until receiving a sufficient number of samples. Thus we designed a method to keep GPS in the ON state. If GPS fixes the current location in the time shorter than the sampling interval of BMU, GPS once again updates its current location. Figure 9(a) and Figure 9(b) represent the power change by GPS. The difference of base power for each device is caused by different power consumption of each CPU. After repeating to turn ON and OFF state, DevScope calculates the difference of power consumption as β_{GPS}.

4.6 Summary

We empirically characterized the component power characteristics and described power analysis methods to derive power models for each component. Based on the component power characteristics, DevScope dynamically devises the test scenario in accordance with the update rate-event based control methods and the update rate-aware workload allocation rules.

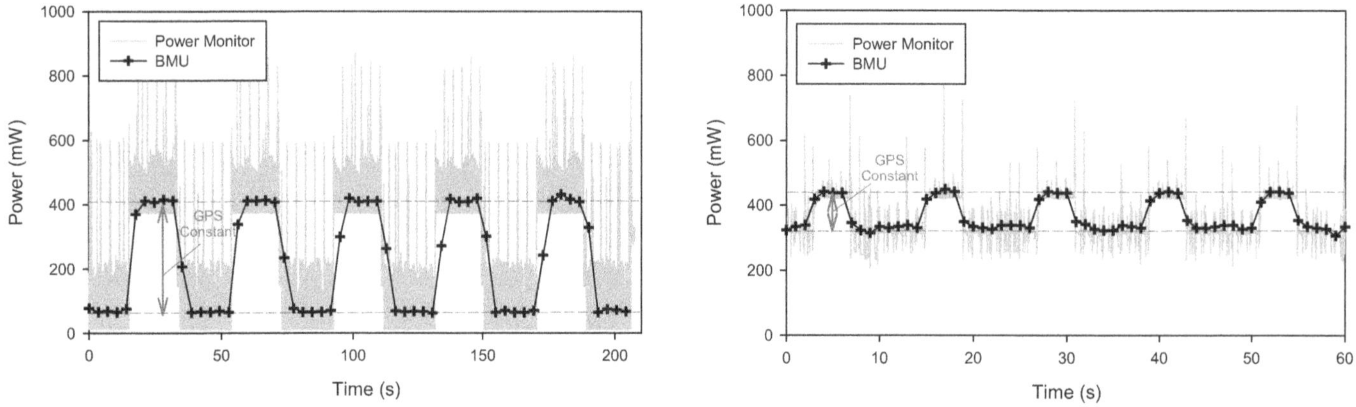

(a) Google Nexus One (b) Sony-Ericsson Xperia Arc

Figure 9. The power consumption measurement graph for GPS by DevScope.

Table 1 summarizes the results of the power coefficients and other constants, which are found by DevScope on two smartphones. For the relative comparison between online modeling results with offline one, we have also derived offline power models using Monsoon instead of built-in BMU. As shown in Figure 5, 6, 7, 8, 9, the BMU power measurement results were reliable compared to external measurement results. The online results which have 5 samples total are the average of 3 nearest values (i.e., KNN with k=3). Accordingly, the results show that the BMU measurements filter out fluctuations on each power state by the update rate-aware workload allocation mechanisms. This filtering effect makes it easy to analyze the component power states automatically. DevScope keeps observing slopes of the result to detect the power state transitions. Obviously, the hidden power states exist. Finding accurate power coefficients of the hidden states is difficult. DevScope classifies the hidden power states into two types. The FACH state of Cellular, for instance, exists at the beginning of the power state transition from base to active power state. Depending on the BMU update rate, the FACH state could be hidden. In this case, DevScope detects the existence of the hidden state and estimates its coefficient by approximation. Comparing to the FACH state, the High Idle state of WiFi exists at the end of power transition from active to base. This case is, in fact, a remaining issue in modeling component power characteristics with online measurement.

Table 2 shows the error rates. We calculated the error rate E_{β_x} which is related to coefficient β_x as follows:

$$E_{\beta_x} = \left|\frac{\beta_{x\_monsoon} - \beta_{x\_bmu}}{\beta_{x\_monsoon}}\right|, \tag{8}$$

where $\beta_{x\_monsoon}$ is the coefficient value obtained with Monsoon, and β_{x_bmu} the one with BMU. As shown in the table, the measurement results of DevScope are similar to the offline results.

Table 1. Power Coefficient Values.

Comp.	Index	N1-Monsoon		N1-BMU (R=3.52 s)		Arc-Monsoon		Arc-BMU (R=1.00 s)	
CPU	i	β_{freq_i}	β_{idle_i}	β_{freq_i}	β_{idle_i}	β_{freq_i}	β_{idle_i}	β_{freq_i}	β_{idle_i}
	0	193.8	41.5	197.1	39.2	47.9	118.9	50.8	115.9
	1	254.5	41.9	258.3	39.6	42.5	122.4	41.8	122.9
	2	276.4	43.8	278.9	43.5	42.9	176.8	46.3	177.1
	3	296.2	43.6	298.1	43.9	127.9	242.9	130.7	247.7
	4	327.4	45.0	330.5	43.6	251.8	325.6	264.6	323.0
	5	347.1	46.0	351.7	43.1	N/A			
	6	365.7	49.9	370.6	46.3				
	7	391.6	47.4	390.0	50.2				
	8	436.6	46.9	438.4	47.1				
	9	461.1	47.7	459.9	49.9				
	10	488.2	47.6	491.6	46.0				
	11	553.6	53.7	552.6	55.6				
GPS		β_{GPS}		β_{GPS}		β_{GPS}		β_{GPS}	
	ON	346.9		330.0		108.0		113.0	

Comp.	Index	N1-Monsoon		N1-BMU (R=3.52 s)		Arc-Monsoon		Arc-BMU (R=1.00 s)	
Display	B	$\beta_{brightness_B}$		$\beta_{brightness_B}$		$\beta_{brightness_B}$		$\beta_{brightness_B}$	
	5	351.6		359.9		147.9		148.4	
	55	427.6		435.1		172.1		171.1	
	105	628.1		614.3		276.0		278.5	
	155	686.3		686.8		354.1		357.3	
	205	770.9		764.8		469.6		473.2	
	255	835.3		837.5		559.5		564.5	
Cellular	rrc	β_{rrc}		β_{rrc}		β_{rrc}		β_{rrc}	
	IDLE	76.9		69.2		85.0		96.4	
	FACH	461.5		321.8		393.0		403.0	
	DCH	551.1		531.4		619.0		623.4	
WiFi		β_{LT}	β_{HT}	β_{LT}	β_{HT}	β_{LT}	β_{HT}	β_{LT}	β_{HT}
	Transmit	2.0	0.7	2.0	0.6	4.1	0.3	3.8	0.3
	Base	110.0	140.7	110.0	140.7	166.2	250.3	173.1	251.4
	Threshold	20		20		25		25	

Table 2. Error Rate (%)

Comp.	Index	N1		Arc	
CPU	i	β_{freq}	β_{idle}	β_{freq}	β_{idle}
	0	1.8	5.5	6.1	2.7
	1	1.5	5.7	1.7	0.4
	2	0.9	0.7	8.0	0.2
	3	0.7	0.7	2.2	2.0
	4	1.0	3.1	5.1	0.8
	5	1.3	6.1	N/A	
	6	1.4	7.3		
	7	0.4	6.0		
	8	0.4	0.4		
	9	0.3	4.5		
	10	0.7	3.4		
	11	0.1	3.6		
GPS		β_{GPS}		β_{GPS}	
	ON	4.9		4.7	

Comp.	Index	N1		Arc	
Display	B	$\beta_{brightness}$		$\beta_{brightness}$	
	5	2.4		0.3	
	55	1.8		0.6	
	105	2.2		0.9	
	155	0.1		0.9	
	205	0.8		0.8	
	255	0.3		0.9	
Cellular	rrc	β_{rrc}		β_{rrc}	
	IDLE	10.1		13.4	
	FACH	30.3		2.5	
	DCH	3.6		0.7	
WiFi		β_{LT}	β_{HT}	β_{LT}	β_{HT}
	Transmit	0.3	7.4	6.5	0.4
	Base	0.1	0.0	4.2	0.4
	Threshold	0.0		0.0	

In the case of Cellular, the power coefficient β_{FACH} of N1 has bigger difference between online and offline models than other cases. This is because the FACH state is a hidden state as we described in Section 4.4. In summary, the results, indeed, validate the accuracy and effectiveness of the proposed scheme.

5. RELATED WORK

Power modeling on smartphones is an important research topic. The power model for each component is used to analyze the application power consumption [1, 18]. The model is used as a guideline for power management research for hardware component [3, 4, 13, 14]. The technique also provides important information for energy-efficient operating systems [15, 16].

Power modeling is accomplished with the information about the hardware activities, and also with information on the actual power consumption related to the activities. The information on hardware activities is generally provided by the operating system. The OS provides information about utilization for each hardware component, and power modeling is based on this. This approach is generally called utilization-based approach [1, 6, 7]. One difficulty of this approach is that every power state of a component is represented only with this information. That is, it is not possible to construct an accurate power model for the hardware components (e.g., WiFi) that have several power states based on the size of the workload. Pathak et al. [5] proposed an approach, called the syscall-based approach, based on the system call to overcome the limitation of utilization-based approach. They analyzed the system calls to get the status and the workload of each component, then constructed finite state machines based on them. This approach is interesting, but in-depth study and measurements on target devices should be required *a priori* to obtain detailed power states.

Power measurement methods are categorized into offline and online methods. Carroll and Heiser [6] measured the actual power consumption with a specific device of which electric schematic was open. However, it is not practical to apply this approach to commercial smartphones that have complex and closed circuit structures. Many researchers proposed one-time modeling with an external measurement tool in a laboratory environment [1, 5, 7]. However, the power consumption pattern of a smartphone is changing dynamically by external factors such as operating temperature or system software updates. One-time power models based on offline methods are static, so they cannot be adapted to the dynamic properties. There has been research that overcomes the weaknesses of offline methods with online methods. Dong and Zhong [2] proposed an accurate self-modeling mechanism based on online measurement method. However, the model targets the whole smartphone systems, and unlike ours, each component of smartphone cannot be analyzed with their approach. Zhang et al. [1] proposed an online measurement method using discharge voltage curve to make up for the weaknesses of offline measurement. However, the discharge voltage curve can be altered by external factors such as operating temperatures. Kj□rgaard et al. [17] proposed a power profiling technique using an online measurement method based on a genetic algorithm. However, the scheme requires additional resources to execute the algorithm, and the utilization factor which governs the power consumption of some hardware components (e.g., CPU) is not considered.

6. CONCLUSION

In this paper, we demonstrated automatic and online smartphone power modeling techniques, based on the use of BMU, which provides component power analysis and generates power model. We proposed a synchronization technique between update rate and component control for overcoming the limitations of online power modeling using BMU. Furthermore, we proposed an autonomous method for power state analysis to generate component power model for five components: CPU, LCD, WiFi, Cellular, and GPS. Through an extensive evaluation using the Android smartphones, we showed that DevScope derives component power models dynamically and nonintrusively, regardless of the BMU update rate, device models, and configurations. In summary, we proposed a practical smartphone power modeling technique to reflect both the diversity of the user environment and smartphone hardware complexity by implementation. The result of our research is expected to contribute to the development of energy-aware smartphone systems. For instance, the power model generated by DevScope is currently used for AppScope [18, 19], which is a framework to meter application energy consumption for Android smartphones.

7. ACKNOWLEDGEMENT

This work was supported by a grant from the National Research Foundation of Korea (NRF), funded by the Korean government, Ministry of Education, Science and Technology under Grant (No.2012-0005522).

8. REFERENCES

[1] Zhang, L., Tiwana, B., Qian, Z., and Wang, Z. 2010. Accurate Online Power Estimation and Automatic Battery Behavior Based Power Model Generation for Smartphones. In *Proceedings of the 8th IEEE/ACM/IFIP International Conference on Hardware/Software Codesign and System Synthesis* (Scottsdale, AZ, USA, October 24 – 29, 2010). CODES+ISSS'10. ACM, New York, NY, 105-114. DOI= http://dx.doi.org/10.1145/1878961.1878982.

[2] Dong, M. and Zhong, L. 2011. Self-Constructive High-Rate System Energy Modeling for Battery-Powered Mobile Systems. In *Proceedings of the 9th International Conference on Mobile Systems, Applications, and Services* (Washington, D.C, USA, June 28 – July 1, 2010). MobiSys'11. ACM, New York, NY, 335-348. DOI= http://dx.doi.org/10.1145/1999995.2000027.

[3] Dong, M. and Zhong, L. 2011. Chameleon: A Color-Adaptive Web Browser for Mobile OLED Displays. In *Proceedings of the 9th International Conference on Mobile Systems, Applications, and Services* (Washington, D.C, USA, June 28 – July 1, 2010). MobiSys'11. ACM, New York, NY, 85-98. DOI= http://dx.doi.org/10.1145/1999995.2000004.

[4] Anand, B., Thirugnanam, K., Sebastian, J., Kannan, P. G., Ananda, A. L., Chan, M. C., and Balan, R. K. 2011. Adaptive Display Power Management for Mobile Games. In *Proceedings of the 9th International Conference on Mobile Systems, Applications, and Services* (Washington, D.C., USA, June 28 – July 1, 2010). MobiSys'11. ACM, New York, NY, 57-70. DOI= http://dx.doi.org/10.1145/1999995.2000002.

[5] Pathak, A., Hu, Y. C., Zhang, M., Bahl, P., and Wang, Y. – M. 2011. Fine-grained Power Modeling for Smartphones Using System Call Tracing. In *Proceedings of the ACM European Conference on Computer Systems* (Salzburg, Austria, April 10 – 13, 2011). EuroSys'11. ACM, New York, NY, 153-167. DOI= http://dx.doi.org/10.1145/1966445.1966460.

[6] Carroll, A. and Heiser, G. 2010. An Analysis of Power Consumption in a Smartphone. In *Proceedings of the 2010 USENIX Annual Technical Conference* (Boston, MA, USA, June 23 – 25, 2010). USENIX ATC'10. USENIX Association, Berkeley, CA.

[7] Shye, A., Scholbrock, B. and Memik, G. 2009. Into the Wild: Studying Real User Activity Patterns to Guide Power Optimizations for Mobile Architectures. In *Proceedings of the 42nd IEEE/ACM International Symposium on Microarchitecture* (New York, NY, USA, December 12 – 16, 2009). MICRO'09. ACM, New York, NY, 168-178. DOI= http://dx.doi.org/10.1145/1669112.1669135.

[8] DS2784 Datasheet, http://pdfserv.maxim-ic.com/en/ds/DS2784.pdf retrieved on 3/20/2012

[9] Google Nexus One Specification, http://www.htc.com/us/support/nexus-one-google/tech-specs/ retrieved on 3/20/2012

[10] Sony Ericsson Xperia Arc, http://www.sonymobile.com/gb/products/phones/xperia-arc/specifications/ retrieved on 3/20/2012

[11] Monsoon Solutions, Inc., http://www.msoon.com/LabEquipment/PowerMonitor/ retrieved on 3/20/2012

[12] Qian, F., Wang, Z., Gerber, A., Mao, Z. M., Sen, S., and Spatscheck, O. 2010. Characterizing Radio Resource Allocation for 3G Networks. In *Proceedings of the 10th ACM Internet Measurement Conference* (New York, NY, USA, November 1 – 3, 2010). IMC'10. ACM, New York, NY, 137-150. DOI= http://dx.doi.org/10.1145/1879141.1879159.

[13] Haverinen, H., Siren, J. and Eronen, P. 2007. Energy Consumption of Always-On Applications in WCDMA Networks. In *Proceedings of the IEEE 65th IEEE Vehicular Technology Conference* (Dublin, Ireland, April 22 – 25, 2007). VTC'07. IEEE, 964-968. DOI= http://dx.doi.org/10.1109/VETECS.2007.207.

[14] Qian, F., Wang, Z., Gerber, A., Mao, Z. M., Sen, S., and Spatscheck, O. 2011. Profiling Resource Usage for Mobile Applications: A Cross-layer Approach. In *Proceedings of the 9th International Conference on Mobile Systems, Applications, and Services* (Washington, D.C, USA, June 28 – July 1, 2010). MobiSys'11. ACM, New York, NY, 321-334. DOI= http://dx.doi.org/10.1145/1999995.2000026.

[15] Roy, A., Sumble, S., and Stutsman, R. 2011. Energy management in mobile devices with the Cinder operating system. In *Proceedings of the ACM European Conference on Computer Systems* (Salzburg, Austria, April 10 – 13, 2011). EuroSys'11. ACM, New York, NY, 139-152. DOI= http://dx.doi.org/10.1145/1966445.1966459.

[16] Vallina-Rodrigues, N. and Crowcroft, J. 2011. ErdOS: Achieving Energy Savings in Mobile OS. In *Proceedings of the ACM 6th International Workshop on Mobility in the Evolving Internet* (Washington, D.C., USA, June 28, 2011). MobiArch'11. ACM, New York, NY, 36-42. DOI= http://dx.doi.org/10.1145/1999916.1999926.

[17] Kj□rgaard, M. B. and Blunck, H. 2011. Unsupervised Power Profiling for Mobile Devices. In *Proceedings of the 8th International ICTS Conference on Mobile and Ubiquitous* (Copenhagen, Denmark, December 6 – 9, 2011). MobiQuitous'11.

[18] Yoon, C., Kim, D., Jung, W., Kang, C. and Cha, H. 2012. AppScope: Application Energy Metering Framework for Android Smartphone using Kernel Activity Monitoring. In *Proceedings of the 2012 USENIX Annual Technical Conference* (Boston, MA, USA, June 13 – 15, 2012). USENIX ATC'12. USENIX Association, Berkeley, CA.

[19] AppScope, http://mobed.yonsei.ac.kr/~appscope/ retrieved on 7/25/2012

ADEL: An Automatic Detector of Energy Leaks for Smartphone Applications

Lide Zhang† Mark S. Gordon† Robert P. Dick†
Z. Morley Mao† Peter Dinda⋆ Lei Yang∘

†EECS Department,
University of Michigan
Ann Arbor, MI, USA
{lide,msgsss,dickrp,zmao}
@umich.edu

⋆ EECS Department,
Northwestern University
Evanston, IL, USA
pdinda@northwestern.edu

∘ Google Inc.
Mountain View,
CA, USA
leiyang@google.com

ABSTRACT

Energy leaks occur when applications use energy to perform useless tasks, a surprisingly common occurrence. They are particularly important for mobile applications running on smartphones due to their energy constraints. Energy leaks are difficult to detect and isolate because their negative consequences are often far removed from their causes. Few tools are available for addressing this problem. We have therefore developed ADEL (Automatic Detector of Energy Leaks). ADEL consists of taint-tracking enhancements to the Android platform. It detects and isolates energy leaks resulting from unnecessary network communication by tracing the direct and indirect use of received data to determine whether they ever affect the user. We profiled 15 applications using ADEL. In six of them, energy leaks detected by ADEL and verified by us account for approximately 57% of the energy consumed in communication. We identified four common causes of energy leaks in these applications: misinterpretation of callback API semantics, poorly designed downloading schemes, repetitive downloads, and aggressive prefetching.

Categories and Subject Descriptors

D.2 [**Software Engineering**]: Design Tools and Techniques

General Terms

Design

Keywords

Energy leaks, energy bugs, mobile applications

1. INTRODUCTION

Energy is a scarce resource for smartphone users. Available energy is constrained by limits on battery size and weight, and improvements in battery technology have historically been slow. Moreover, energy demands often increase with the addition of new hardware and software features. To make matters worse, operating systems and applications frequently consume energy to perform tasks that are ultimately useless, a phenomenon we call *energy leaks*. Smartphone users commonly complain about the effects of energy leaks. For example, many iPhone users reported a sudden drop in battery life from 100 hours standby to 6 hours standby due to new energy leaks in Apple's iOS 5 [1]. Android users also experienced bad battery life on various type of devices [2].

Energy leaks are in general difficult to detect and isolate [3]. There are two main reasons for this difficulty. First, it is much more difficult to determine how much energy an application leaks than to determine how much energy it uses because some applications necessarily consume a lot of energy while wasting little, e.g., Google Maps. Second, there can be a wide range of causes for unintended energy use, e.g., incorrect API use or poor application design. As we will demonstrate in Section 7, even mature and carefully developed operating systems or applications can contain energy leaks.

An energy leak is the use of energy on activities that never directly or indirectly influence the user-observable output of the smartphone. More specifically, if removing a task from the application never directly or indirectly changes any output presented to users, the task is unnecessary and the energy consumed by it is wasted. We consider energy leaks with two sources. The first source is unambiguous programming errors, e.g., frequently accessing sensor data without using it. The second source is reliance on predictions that have the potential to be too inaccurate for their intended purposes, as can happen with applications that use aggressive prefetching. In addition to identifying unambiguous energy bugs, our work can also determine the percent of energy wasted as a result of prefetching misprediction and identify the particular prefetched data elements that are not ultimately used, thereby supporting improvements to predictors or adaptation of prefetching aggressiveness.

We now describe the design, implementation, and evaluation of ADEL (Automatic Detector of Energy Leaks). ADEL is an extension of the Android platform that tracks the information flow of network traffic through applications. We focus on detecting and isolating energy leaks in network communication for mobile applications. We choose to focus on network communication because network communication, including both Wi-Fi and 3G interface, accounts for 39% of system-wide energy consumption. More importantly, developers have a hard time optimizing for network energy efficiency, resulting in substantial energy waste [4]. By tracking all the computations that depend on each network packet, ADEL

This work was supported in part by the NSF under awards CNS-1059372 and CNS-0720691 and in part by Google.

CODES+ISSS'12, October 7–12, 2012, Tampere, Finland.

is able to determine whether or not a packet's transmission constitutes an energy leak. ADEL helps developers isolate the causes of energy leaks by showing them the arrival times and contents of unused packets. ADEL uses dynamic taint-tracking analysis to detect energy leaks. It automatically labels each data object with a tag when it is first downloaded, then follows and propagates the tag when new data objects are derived from the tainted object. Thus, system outputs can be associated with the downloaded data that influenced them. ADEL further provides developers with insight on the use of each packet, associated with the packet arrival time and its content, allowing design flaws resulting in energy waste to be more easily detected and isolated.

We evaluated the effectiveness of ADEL by using it to profile five open source applications and three closed source applications. For the open source applications, we confirmed the wasted network communication by manually checking the source code to determine whether ADEL correctly labeled each packet. For the closed source applications, we manually correlated the network packet labeled by ADEL with the displayed content.

Our ADEL-supported analysis of 15 applications revealed four categories of energy leaks.

1. Misinterpretation of callback APIs that results in wasteful downloads. For example, an application containing a separate downloading thread might not kill the thread properly, allowing the download to continue after the application exits the foreground.

2. Inefficient data refreshing behavior that ignores the application and device status. For example, a widget might be updated whether or not the display is currently on.

3. Repetitive downloads. For example, an application might download the same content every time it updates because it fails to cache downloaded content.

4. Aggressive prefetching. For example, the prefetching scheme of an application can be so aggressive that significant energy is wasted without improving the user's experience.

Eliminating energy leaks of the first three kinds reduces the network energy consumption by approximately 62.1% while reducing energy leaks in prefetching can potentially reduce the network energy consumption by 52.7%. In summary, ADEL helps identify and isolate communication energy leaks.

This work makes the following contributions.

- We provide a definition of *energy leaks*: the energy consumed by actions that never influence any output produced by a system.
- We describe ADEL, a dynamic taint-tracking infrastructure that identifies network energy leaks. ADEL tracks data originating at the network interface through applications to their eventual use or deletion. Automatically determining whether particular network data are ever used can help applications developers and users identify, isolate, and fix energy leaks. ADEL is the first system that uses taint-tracking for energy efficiency analysis.
- We used ADEL to profile 15 applications. Six of them have energy leaks that account for more than 57% of their communication energy use. By further examining these leaky applications, we identified four common causes. Our analysis may be useful for both application and platform developers.

The rest of the paper is organized as follows. Section 2 describes related work. Section 3 formally defines *energy leak* and describes the problem ADEL seeks to solve. Section 4 gives an illustrative example of ADEL's use and explains its design challenges. Section 5 describes the implementation of ADEL in detail. Section 6 explains our efforts to validate ADEL and points out its limitations. Section 7 describes our analysis of energy leaks in 15 applications and indicates major classes of design characteristics resulting in energy leaks. Section 8 concludes the paper.

2. RELATED WORK

We use dynamic taint analysis to identify energy leaks due to network communication. This section summarizes prior work on the following related topics: energy debugging, network energy reduction, and taint analysis.

Energy debugging is an emerging research area, with few prior publications. The work by Pathak et al. [3, 5] is closest to ours. They first provide a taxonomy of energy bugs based on posts to mobile user forums and operating system bug repositories. They recognize four classes of energy bugs: hardware-related, software-related, external-condition-triggered, and those of unknown cause [3]. They also provide an automatic method to detect no-sleep bugs, which arise from mishandling power control APIs by applications or the operating system, resulting in significant and unexpected energy drainage [5]. Our work differs by detecting and isolating energy leaks, a different class of energy bugs.

There has been prior research on reducing energy consumption due to network communication. This work can be divided into two major categories: (1) adapting power management schemes to network traffic [6, 7, 8] and (2) adapting network traffic to power management schemes [9, 10, 11, 4]. In the first category, Krashinsky and Balakrishnan [6] propose to adapt network interface sleep durations depending on past application network activity. This allows the network interface to sleep for longer periods of time when there is no activity, thereby reducing the energy consumed receiving beacons sent from the access point. In the second category, Armstrong et al. [9] propose to shift polling responsibility from mobile clients to a proxy server so that network traffic can be batched. This approach prevents the network card from frequently transitioning among power states, allowing it to sleep longer. However, most prior work assumes that all transmitted data are useful. We question this assumption and detect network energy waste due to transmission of useless data. Existing network energy consumption optimization techniques can be applied together with our work: they are orthogonal or synergistic.

Our energy leak detections and isolation framework uses dynamic taint analysis. In particular, we build upon TaintDroid [12], an extended Android platform that supports system-wide taint tracking through the Dalvik Virtual Machine and persistent storage, e.g., in files. TaintDroid detects security flaws in mobile applications by associating tags with sensitive information, e.g., location information or phone contacts. Information leaks are detected when sensitive information leaves the mobile devices, e.g., via the network interface. Our work differs by solving the problem of identifying communication energy leaks. This new problem definition requires changes in the representation of tags and method of tracking information flow (from network interfaces to eventual display or deletion). To the best of our knowledge, this is the first time taint tracking analysis has been used to identify energy leaks.

There are other methods of dynamic taint analysis in virtual machine and interpreter environments [13, 14, 15]. Haldar et al. [13] instrumented the Java String class with taint tracking. Xu et al. [14] instrumented the PHP interpreter source code for dynamic information tracking. Both of these papers have the goal of preventing SQL injection attacks. Chandra and Franz [15] proposed to instrument Java byte-code to aid control flow analysis in additional to fine-grained information flow tracking within the Java virtual machine. These papers all solve security problems. They do not focus on improving energy efficiency, but their implementations are related because all use taint tracking.

3. PROBLEM DEFINITION

We define an *energy leak* as *energy consumed that never influences the outputs of a computer system, e.g., through display interface, audio interface, or network interface.* In other words, any energy consumed by actions that never change system outputs, directly or indirectly, is wasted. Eliminating such waste cannot cause observable changes in application behavior. For example, the widget of a news application might frequently update the latest news regardless of whether it is currently visible to the users, e.g., whether the display is even on or off. From the user's perspective, these downloads are useless and waste energy. Eliminating these extra downloads (e.g., by only downloading when the widget is visible to users) will not degrade the user's experience. Prefetching is more subtle, and we will address it in Section 7.4.

Automatic Detector of Energy Leaks (ADEL) system detects smartphone application energy leaks due to network downloads by tracking network data in order to determine which downloads ever have user-observable effects. We focus on network downloads for two main reasons. First, network devices, including 802.11 card and cellular devices, are power-hungry; the two devices together consume 39% of smartphone. Among the network transmissions, 70% of energy is due to downloads. This is estimated by aggregating 137 users' over a month of traces. The traces were generated by PowerTutor [16], an Android-based power estimation tool that estimates power consumption every 1 second. Second, application developers have an especially difficult time optimizing applications for network energy efficiency due to the complicated power management characteristics of the network interface [4]. As a result, a significant amount of energy is wasted in network communication [4].

The definition of *energy leak* is general. In practice, it is difficult to track accurately, as we explain in Section 6.1. However, we believe it is an appropriate goal to proceed toward.

4. ILLUSTRATIVE EXAMPLE AND DESIGN CHALLENGES

We designed and implemented a system supporting on-line analysis of transitive use of downloaded data objects. We anticipate that this work will be most useful to developers attempting to improve the energy efficiency of their applications. In this section, we will first use a simple example to explain the use of our infrastructure. We will then discuss design challenges.

4.1 Illustrative example

Consider a game that downloads crossword puzzles and displays them to users. As shown in Figure 1, the game has two major threads: one downloading puzzles from the Internet and one managing the user interface (UI), including showing the puzzle and taking user inputs. The downloading thread receives network packets that contain the grid layout for each game, the hints to each word, and the solution to each game. It then parses the contents of different packets and passes them as messages to the UI thread. The UI thread first displays the grid based on the messages from the downloading thread. Then it displays hints when the user clicks on the corresponding grid element. When the user finishes and submits the game, it shows the solution.

To track the use of the downloaded data objects in the crosswords game, the system first identifies them in the network interface where a *tag* is associated with each object at the packet level. These network interfaces are *taint sources* and the downloaded objects are *tainted.* As shown in Figure 1, each type of data object is associated with a unique *tag*. During the propagation of the *tainted* object, the system passes on a *tag* when one data object is derived from a *tainted* one. The shaded area represents the functions the *tainted* objects pass through. Finally when tainted objects reach the *taint sink* (e.g., the display) they are detected and the *tags* representing the original downloaded data objects are recorded.

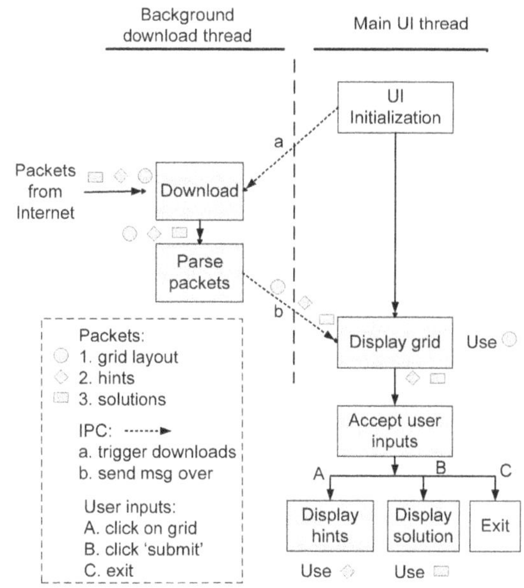

Figure 1: Crosswords game has two major threads: downloading and user interface. Tags of packets are propagated to derived data objects. Eventual use of packets depends on user inputs.

4.2 Design challenges

When designing a system to track the use of data objects, we were faced with the following challenges.

- *Downloaded data objects are not necessarily used immediately.* In the above example, the hints and solution of each game may be stored in memory for a long time before the user requires them. This delay between downloading and use prevents some alternative approaches. For example, tracking data use by first monitoring both the network and display interface simultaneously, then comparing downloaded content and displayed content is infeasible due to the time lag. As a result, the monitoring system must be able to trace data objects through memory until they are used or deleted.
- *Data objects can be parsed or processed before they are displayed.* For example, the grid color can be specified using strings in an XML file. Although the strings are not displayed, they will influence the color of the output grid. Transitive use of downloaded data must be considered.
- *The use of data objects depends on the dynamic environment of the application.* For example, a valid code path that leads to the display of the downloaded data objects might rarely or never be executed during a particular run of the application. As a result, static analysis of application source code is insufficient to determine the application's run-time use of objects. Therefore, we focus on dynamic analysis.
- *The use of data objects depends on the dynamic environment of the application, e.g., user behavior.* As shown in Figure 1, the use of hints and solutions to the game depend on user behavior. As a result, static analysis of application source code is insufficient to fully understand the application's real-world data use.
- *It is necessary to identify the original data object when a derivative is displayed.* Our goal is to help developers to (1) understand the use of each downloaded data object and (2) identify

potential bugs in their code that produce unnecessary data transmission. Therefore, it is necessary to trace downloaded data objects and their derivatives for their entire lifespans so that if they are ultimately displayed, the original downloaded data objects can be identified. To achieve this, the system needs to associate a unique ID with each data object and propagate this ID to all its transitive derivatives.

- *Mobile devices are resource constrained.* Limits on smartphone CPU speed, memory size, and energy capacity makes high-overhead techniques such as instruction-level taint tracking [17] less practical than lower-overhead techniques.

5. SYSTEM ARCHITECTURE OF ADEL

The challenges described in the previous section motivate us to use dynamic taint tracking analysis of downloaded data objects. The closest existing implementation we found is TaintDroid [12], an extended Android platform for improving security by identifying the flow of private information. This section first presents background information on Android that is necessary to understand ADEL, our taint tracking infrastructure. It then provides an overview of the ADEL system architecture. Finally, we explain each component of ADEL in detail.

5.1 Background: Android

Android is a Linux-based operating system for mobile devices such as smartphone and tablets developed by Google. It differs from other Linux distributions due to an additional layer of abstraction between user applications and Linux system library, called the application framework layer. The four major differences between Android and other Linux distributions follow.

Dalvik virtual machine, Java Native Interface (JNI), and native interface: Android is composed of a modified Linux kernel written and compiled to native machine code, with middleware, libraries, and APIs written in both Java and native code. Although development of applications using native machine code is allowed, most Android applications are written in Java.

Each Java application is compiled to bytecode and runs in the Dalvik virtual machine (VM) and each Dalvik VM instance contains only one application. The Dalvik VM has its own instruction set. An interpreter converts Java bytecode into Dalvik code at run time. ADEL consists of taint tracking code inserted into the interpreter.

There are two types of native methods that can be accessed by Android applications: (1) native methods in the Android framework or system library such as WebKit or SQLite and (2) native methods stored in shared objects in the application package. All native methods accessed from a Java-based application must be called through JNI methods. Application packages containing native methods account for 5% of applications according to a survey of the Android market [12] and handling taint tracking through native code would substantially complicate the taint tracking infrastructure. Therefore, ADEL does not cover application-specific native methods in the taint tracking flow. Note, however, that it can do information flow tracking in the Java portions of applications that contain JNI methods as explained in Section 5.3.

Binder: Binder is a specially customized kernel mechanism for Android to do Inter Process Communication (IPC). In the core of binder, messages are passed between processes using *parcel*, a container of serialized data objects.

Shared memory: A shared memory region in the Android framework allows sharing between different processes. Note that reference counting in the shared memory region to prevent deletion of live objects.

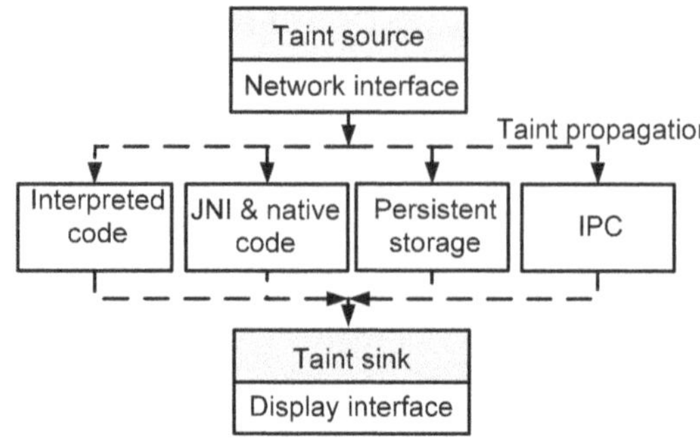

Figure 2: ADEL architecture.

Zygote process: Zygote is the first application process loaded by the Dalvik VM when the system boots. It maintains memory regions that are shared by multiple applications and spawns all other Android applications via fork().

5.2 Architecture overview

We now provide an overview of the ADEL system architecture. ADEL provides on-line monitoring of the use of downloaded objects by applications. It uses dynamic taint tracking to follow the information flow during the entire lifespan of the downloaded object, from download to use or deletion. As shown in Figure 2, the taint flow can be decomposed into three phases: *taint source*, *taint propagation*, and *taint sink*.

Taint source: The network interface is a *taint source*. We detect all downloaded data objects and associate a unique *tag* with each at packet-level. Each *tag* is a 32-bit integer that indirectly indicates (indexes) the size of the packet. Note that packet size is needed to determine the number of bytes of network transmission associated with energy leaks. A hash table is used to map tags to packet sizes. The table is kept in shared memory region and maintained by Zygote. To store tags, we instrument the Dalvik VM to change the memory allocation and Java class data structures in order to store an indexing tag adjacent to its corresponding data object.

Taint propagation: During *taint propagation*, tags are propagated to new variables when they are derived from tainted variables. Taint propagation happens at variable-level, method-level, file-level, and message-level. These levels correspond to four sources for which tags are propagated: interpreted code, JNI and native code, persistent storage, and IPC. For interpreted code, an alternative design is instruction-level taint tracking [17]. However, this fine-grained approach imposes up to 20× performance overhead for workstations: it is contradicted for resource-constrained mobile platforms. For JNI and native code, the system retrieves the tags of the inputs to invoked methods and propagates them to the return value. This heuristic is used to prevent the overhead of monitoring native code. For persistent storage, each file is associated with a tag. Any write of the tainted data will taint the tag of the file and any data read from the file will be tainted with the same tag. Finally for IPC propagation, we associate a tag with the message passed between processes. File-level and message-level propagation permits false positive. By propagating the tag at multiple levels, we are able to achieve system-wide taint tracking.

Taint sink: At the *taint sink*, the output of tainted data is identified. Every time a tainted object is detected, the original downloaded object(s) that influenced the tainted object is logged, based on its tag. Mobile computers may have multiple output device, e.g., video and audio displays. Currently ADEL only supports the video display interface taint sink, as it was used for displaying the most network-tainted data in the applications we are aware of. However, the approach could be easily extended to handle other output

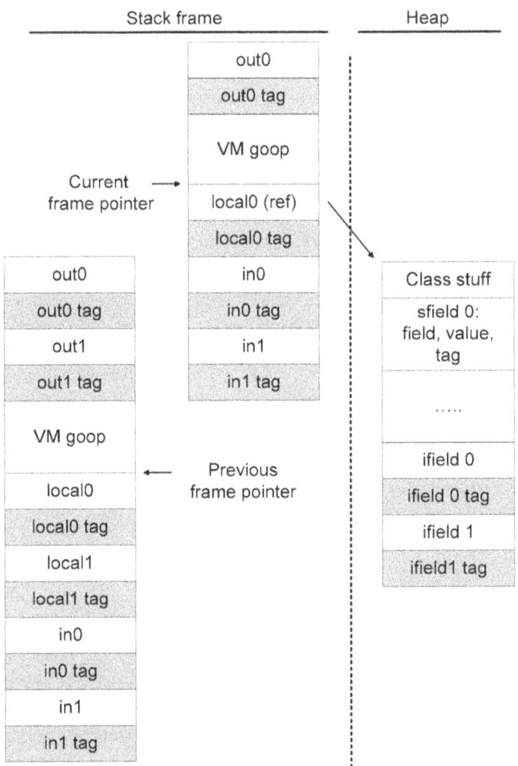

Figure 3: Taint tags are stored adjacent to their data objects in both stack and heap.

devices. For example, the audio interface can be added by instrumenting the audio API in the Java framework.

5.3 Implementation

We implemented ADEL on top of TaintDroid [12] with 2,414 lines of code modifications. The adaptation of this infrastructure for use in energy leak detection required changes to taint tag representation, taint propagation rules, taint source, and taint sink.

Tag storage

Figure 3 shows how ADEL stores taint tags in the Dalvik VM. Tags are associated with five types of data: local variables in method, method arguments, method return value, class static fields, and class instance fields. Whenever a new method is invoked, a new stack frame containing local variables, method arguments, and return values is constructed. To store their tags, the size of the stack frame is doubled. This allows us to store an additional 32-bit tag for each data object. Tags must be retrieved whenever the corresponding data object is operated upon. Therefore, they are stored adjacent to their corresponding data objects. As shown in Figure 3, the shaded area represents the added memory for tags. For class static fields and instance fields stored in the heap, additional memory is used. A taint tag field is added for static fields while each instance field is extended by adding a 32-bit tag space adjacent to it. In the case of arrays and strings, only one tag is associated with the whole class object. That is to say, any value coming out of a tainted array or string is tainted. This decision was made to avoid the overhead of having multiple tags, each associated with one data element.

Tag representation and propagation logic

In order to determine the presence and causes of energy leaks, we need to track the flow of each network packet and record the contribution of tainted variables to each newly derived variable. In this case, ADEL can work backwards to determine whether each

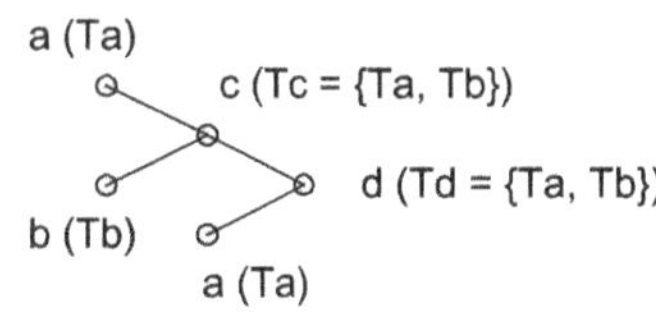

Figure 4: Example of correct taint tag propagation.

Algorithm 1 Copy taint tag

Require: *SrcTag*

Increase the ref_count of *SrcTag*

DestTag ⇐ *SrcTag*

return *DestTag*

packet ultimately influences displayed content. One common solution in security research is to use each bit to represent a unique type of tainted variable and use a bitwise OR operation when merging variables. Unfortunately, this solution is infeasible for our application because it requires one bit for each new tainted variables. Recall that each packet represents a new tainted variable. In ADEL, each tag represents a set of packets that have been used to derive the corresponding variable as shown in Figure 4. Each packet is represented by a unique ID, packet_tag. Every time a new variable is derived from multiple tainted variables, the union of all sets is taken to derive the new tag.

We use two hash tables in ADEL. One maps packet_tag, the packet ID, to packet size. The other maps tag to the set of packet_tag as shown below.

```
map<int packet_tag, int size> packet_map;
map<int tag, set<int packet_tag>> tag_map;
```

A new tag is generated if any of the following conditions holds: (1) a new data object is downloaded or (2) a new variable is derived from more than one tainted variable. The allocation of a new tag is controlled by a unique sequence number. Note that these two maps are global data structures containing all the tags for any application. Consequently, we place them in shared memory and modify Zygote to insert new tags and propagate existing tags.

Taint tags are propagated using the following rules.

- Copy taint tag: When only one tainted object is used to derive a new variable, e.g., move and single-input instructions, we copy the taint tag to the newly derived variable so that both variables have identical sets of packet_tags. Meanwhile, each tag is associated with a reference counter to record the number of variables associated with that tag. That reference counting is needed for copy-on-write when merging taint tags. This algorithm is shown in Algorithm 1.

- Merge taint tags: When more than one tainted object is used to derive a new variable, we must take the union of the sets. This is required for any two-input instructions, e.g., add. As shown in Algorithm 2, copy-on-write is used to reduce memory overhead. A new tag and set are only constructed if both of the source variable's tag have multiple references.

Tag sources and sinks

To determine the percentage of energy leaked, ADEL needs to track the network packet from downloaded until display. Therefore, we identify the network interface as the taint source and video display interface as the taint sink. Because taint tags are stored only in the interpreted code as explained in Figure 5.3, we instrument the Java side of the library instead of the native side of the library.

We instrument the receive function in the network Java library to implement network taint sources. The granularity of tag association determines the trade-off between tracking accuracy and memory overhead. Packet-level tracking is chosen over byte-level tracking

Algorithm 2 Merge taint tag

```
Require: Src1Tag, Src2Tag, tag_map
  {Update an old tag or merge to create a new one}
if any of Src1Tag or Src2Tag has only one reference count then
    DestTag ⇐ the one in Src1Tag and Src2Tag that has one tag
    update the set of DestTag by inserting the set of the other
    source tag
    increase the ref_count of DestTag
else
    DestTag ⇐ a newly created tag
    new_set ⇐ union of sets of both Src1Tag and Src2Tag
    insert (DestTag, new_set) into tag_map
    initialize ref_count of DestTag
end if
return DestTag
```

to control overhead. Fortunately, despite of the inaccuracy induced by this granularity, ADEL still identifies numerous energy leaks in real applications as explained in Section 7.

The display interface is instrumented as the taint sink, i.e., tainted objects are logged when they are rendered to the display. We determine which network packets are useful by tracking the tainted objects backwards through packet_tags. It is challenging to identify all tainted object accurately because Android provides application developers multiple ways to render the display. By performing a survey of the network-intensive applications in the Android Market, we determined that the Canvas class in graphic interface and LoadListener in Webkit are the two most frequent APIs for eventual rendering use by other graphics display APIs. We therefore use these two APIs as taint sinks in ADEL. Note that WebKit is a complicated rendering engine in which data objects are passed between native methods and Java methods before display. Our Dalvik-based taint tracking framework cannot trace through native methods. We instead use the following heuristic to approximate taint tracking through native graphics display routines: data objects being passed to the native WebKit rendering engine will be displayed. We have not found contradictory examples in the applications we examined; please note that perfect accuracy is not necessary to achieve our goal of identifying and isolating energy leaks.

Tag propagation

Taint tags are propagated through four paths: interpreted code, JNI and native code, persistent storage and IPC.

To track tags through interpreted code, we modify the native code interpreter in the Dalvik VM to realize the propagation logic. The native code interpreter is one of two interpreters in the VM. We modified the native code interpreter because it can be used on any Android system supporting native code. An alternative would have been to modify the assembly code interpreter. This interpreter has the advantage of higher performance but the greater disadvantage of only being available on a few phone models.

JNI and native code taint tag propagation is handled by manually instrumenting methods that are necessary for APIs in taint sink and source or selected benchmark applications. This is mainly because all taint tags are stored in the interpreted code stack and therefore once a native method is invoked, the tags cannot be accessed any more. To handle taint propagation through native code, we instrument code to guarantee one postcondition: if the arguments accessed are tainted, the return value of native methods is associated with the new tag that follows the propagation logic. 1098 out of 3024 native methods in Android source code, which do not use object references, are covered by this heuristic. Other native methods are instrumented as needed.

Persistent storage taint tag propagation is handled by associating each file with one taint tag. This is achieved by using the extended attribute of the Android file system. That is to say, any byte read from a tainted file will be tainted with the same tag. This results in false positives, especially if the file is big, e.g., database. Ideally we would like byte-level filesystem taint propagation logic. However, this would greatly increase implementation complexity or require modification of database implementation [18]. This is an area for future work. Despite the false positives resulting from course-grained file taint tracking, the impact on accuracy was negligible for the applications we studied: only 0.26% of network traffic ended up in files such as database in these applications.

Message-level taint tag propagation is implemented for IPC in ADEL. This is achieved by instrumenting the *parcel* in binder as explained in Section 5.1.

6. VALIDATION

We next examine the accuracy of ADEL and the overhead incurred by ADEL. The experiment is done on a Nexus One phone running Android 2.1 and ADEL.

6.1 Accuracy and limitations

We examine the accuracy of ADEL by evaluating 8 applications, 5 of which are open-source and three of which are closed-source. Table 1 lists all the application names and corresponding functionalities. Note that we include three closed-source applications for validation because we found a limited number of open-source Android applications. By analyzing each application with ADEL, we produced profiles of all network packets. This profile contained each packet's content, its arrival time, and whether the packet ultimately influenced outputs to the user. Packets (transitively) reaching the taint sink were flagged as used while the rest were considered unused. We read the source code of the open-source applications, then manually examined all the network packets and used our understanding of the code to determine whether ADEL correctly labeled each. Analysis of closed-source applications required less direct confirmation. We compared the profile generated by ADEL with the content observed on the display. For example, we manually compared the content of each network packet with the news stories displayed on the user interface for ABC news application. We identified the following types of the packet classification errors.

- **False negatives** are useful network transmissions that are incorrectly identified as useless. ADEL tracks data flow, not control flow. This is mainly because control flow tracking either requires static analysis [19] of application source code, which would undermine on-line use, or incurs heavy overhead [17]. One example of a false positive due to neglecting control flow follows. Many applications contain some empty HTTP responses that contain only headers and codes, e.g., "200 OK". These responses are indeed useful, e.g., the status code determines which branch to execute. However, because the influence on application behavior is a result of control flow, ADEL neglects it. Luckily, the size of such packets is usually very small, resulting in only minor errors in network energy leaks. In the applications we study in Section 7, these empty HTTP responses account for only 0.52% of the total traffic.

- **False positives** are useless network transmissions that are falsely identified as used. Another limitation of ADEL is the false positives induced during tag propagation, including packet-level, array-level, message-level, and file-level tag propagation. One example we found in our experiment results from packet-level association. For applications in which the data unit is large, e.g., a whole news article for news application, using packet-level association does not influence accuracy. However, in applications like "Busmap", each data unit contains the text information for one bus

Table 1: Applications for Validation

Application			Functionality
Open source	Real-world apps	Crossword	A game application that downloads crossword from multiple online sources
		Read for speed	An application that downloads book and display it word by word for speed reading
		BusMap	A map-based application that shows the incoming buses for all bus stops
		Photostream	A sample application that downloads and displays picture from Flikr
	Syn. app	Taint test	A self-written application that downloads and displays specific webpages
Closed source	ABC, Stock quote, and CNN		Refer to the Android Market

Table 2: Performance Overhead

Benchmark	ADEL (ms)	Android (ms)	Slow down (×)
Download	1285	1055	1.21
Inter. code	43	4	10.75
IPC	15	4	3.25
File	233	139	1.67
Read	204	503	2.46
Xwords	442	4565	10
P stream	641	6091	9.5
BusMap	2083	8745	4.19

Table 3: Applications Studied

Category	Applications
News and Weather	CNN, ABC, World News, News and Weather
Transportation	Google Maps, BusMap
Game	Crossword, Read for Speed
Social	Facebook
Photography	Photostream
Sports	ESPN Score Center
Finance	Stock Quote
Widgets	ABC widget, Facebook widget
Other	Taint test

stop and 2 to 3 data units are packed in the same packet. As a result, information for unused bus stops is falsely identified as used if any bus stop in the packet was used. These false positives could potentially be reduced by fine-grained propagation at the cost of performance overhead.

We should comment at this point that unlike the use of taint tracking in security applications, misclassification of some network traffic does not necessary prevent ADEL from fulfilling its design objective: to help application developers identify and isolate programming and design flaws accounting for most energy leaks. ADEL allowed the identification and isolation of numerous large energy leaks in real-world energy leaks as described in Section 7.

6.2 Overhead analysis

The performance overhead of ADEL results from additional computation and storage necessary for tracking taint tags. We have two goals when designing the experiments. First, we want to understand the average slowdown when ADEL is used on real-world applications. Second, we want to examine all taint propagation paths to understand their overheads, allowing us to determine what sorts of slow-downs can be expected for applications with particular behaviors. To achieve these goals, we conduct two sets of experiments: one with real-world applications and one with synthetic applications that stress particular propagation paths.

We use two Nexus one phones, one of which runs the stock Android 2.1 operating system, and one of which is equipped with ADEL. The portable interpreter was used on both phones (recall that ADEL is only implemented in the portable interpreter for the Dalvik VM).

Real-world applications: As shown in Table 2(down), ADEL incurs 6.14× slow down on average for real-world applications. We notice that for both application "Cross words" and "Photo stream", where tainted objects are intensively propagated between download and display, ADEL incurs roughly 10× overhead. For applications like "Read for speed" and "Busmap" where tainted objects are displayed immediately after being downloaded, ADEL incurs less than 4× slow down. Note that the past works on taint tracking generally reports significant overhead, e.g., 20× [17] slowdown. Despite the slowdown, ADEL adds at most 8 seconds to the time for real-world applications to load. We consider this to be a tolerable but annoying latency because ADEL is designed mainly for use by application developers during testing.

Synthetic applications: To cover all possible taint propagation paths, we construct synthetic benchmarks to intensively exercise specific paths in the taint flow. For example, intensive downloading exercises operations in the taint source. Intensive tag propagations through interpreted code, inter-process communication (IPC), and files are also exercised. Table 2(up) demonstrates the performance overhead of ADEL for these synthetic applications. Intensive tag propagation through interpreted code incurs the most overhead (10.75× slowdown). This benchmark approaches the worst-case situation: every instruction involves tag merging. This also explains the slowdown of "Cross words" and "Photo stream". There are two main causes of the overhead: context switches due to IPC and lock acquisition due to shared memory access. Both of these result from storing tags in a shared memory region and managing them with Zygote as explained in Section 5. The slowdown of all other benchmarks is less than 5×.

The overhead imposed by ADEL does not contradict its use in helping developers find energy inefficiencies at design time; its intended purpose. One major concern about overhead is that changes in performance might change the application behavior and hence prevent us from finding energy leaks. For example, an application that uses a timer to control downloads might potentially have different behavior if latencies were to change. This concern is legitimate. However, we have not encountered such cases in our study.

7. APPLICATION STUDY

This section describes ADEL-assisted study of network energy efficiency for 15 Android applications. Seven of these applications are suspected to contain substantial energy leaks and we were able to manually verify the presence of significant ADEL-detected leaks in six of these. For the leaky applications, approximately 57% of network energy consumption was the result of energy leaks. We explain four root causes for the detected energy leaks. Our findings illustrate the value of ADEL and reveal opportunities for improving application and Android framework API energy efficiency.

7.1 Experimental setup

We study the 15 applications summarized in Table 3. These applications are chosen based on two criteria: (1) there is intensive network activity and (2) there is limited database usage in the application. We use the second criteria because database use results in false positives as mentioned in Section 6. The closed-source applications are popular applications with more than 100,000 downloads in the Android Market.

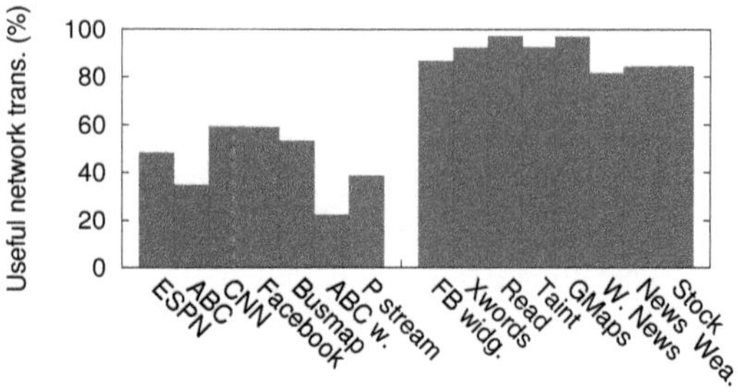

Figure 5: Percent of useful network transmissions for applications separated by efficiencies, for leaky (left) and efficient (right) applications.

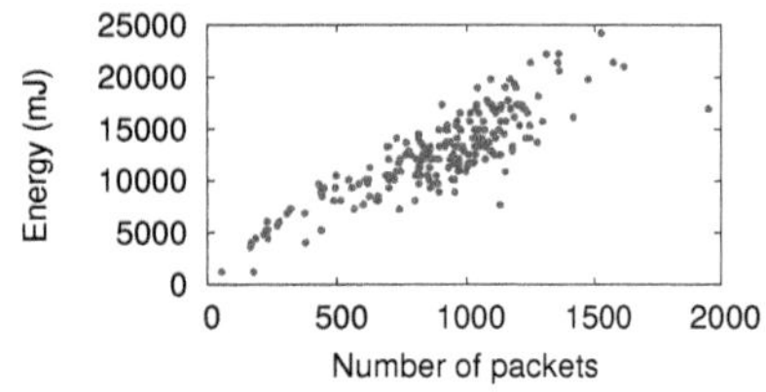

Figure 6: Correlation between network energy and transmission.

We used ADEL to identify (and isolate) network energy leaks in each application. We are aware of two possible sources of bias in our experiments.

- *Whether an application generates energy leaks is dependent on the application's active session length.* For example, an application may download a significant amount of content right after it is launched. These downloads are energy leaks if the user exits the application immediately after launch. However, they can be useful if application runs longer. To eliminate this bias, we emulate an average application session by spending more than 250 seconds in each application before exit. 250 seconds is reported to be the average application session duration [20]. During the application session, we manually exercise application functions. One exception for typical use cases is widget applications. Widgets typically stay active without exiting. We therefore attempt to approximate typical use of two widget applications by placing them on the home screen, reading updates from them every five to ten minutes, and monitoring their activities for 30 minutes for each application.

- *The propensity of an application to leak energy might depend on whether it is in its initialization or normal use phase.* Imagine a news application that downloads latest articles during the first time it is used during a day and stores them for later use. During a single session, a user might not read all the articles, making the unused articles appear useless. However, the user might ultimately read these articles in a later session. As a result, analysis of the first session alone might result in overestimation of energy leaks. To solve this problem, we run each application three times, with a five-hour intervals between runs.

To understand the root causes of the suspected energy leaks, first we examine the network packet usage profile generated by ADEL for each leaky application. The profile contains each network packet's taint tag, packet content, packet arrival time, and whether the packet ultimately influences displayed content. By doing this, we are able to identify suspected energy leak causes. We then manually examine application source code, if available, to confirm our suspicions.

7.2 Findings

Figure 5 shows the percentage of *useful network transmissions* for each application, i.e., packets that ultimately influence the content displayed. We derive this ratio for each application by averaging traces from three runs. A higher percent of useful transmissions suggests a more efficient design. As shown in Figure 5, the applications with lower bars on the left are suspected to have more serious energy leaks. Interestingly, there is a clear division between the suspected leaky applications and efficient applications at 60%.

Table 4: Root Causes for Leaks

Causes		Applications
Design flaws	Misinterp. API	Photo Stream
	Download scheme	BusMap, and ABC widget
	Repetitive download	ABC widget
Aggressive prefetching		ESPN, ABC, CNN, and Facebook

To determine the amount of energy saved by eliminating these energy leaks, we must understand the relationship between energy and total number of packets transmitted. Figure 6 shows the relationship between network energy and total number of packets for one phone user. The correlation coefficient between energy and number of packets is 0.79. We obtained this data by analyzing a month of network communication quantity and energy consumption logs for 51 Nexus One phone users [16]. Note that these energy use logs capture the real-world impact of time-dependent wireless interface power management state changes. Given this correlation, we claim that reducing the energy leaks detected by ADEL will save approximately 56.5% of the energy used in network communications for the detected leaky applications.

By exploring the network packet usage profile and source code, we identify four major reasons for energy leaks: (1) misinterpretation of callback API semantics, (2) poorly designed downloading schemes, (3) repetitive downloads, and (4) aggressive prefetching. We associate applications with their causes of energy leaks in Table 4. Note that a single application may have multiple types of energy leaks. We categorize the first three causes as design flaws and the last as aggressive prefetching.

7.3 Application design flaws

This subsection, expands on the three types of unambiguous design or programming errors that resulted in network energy leaks. Section 7.4 will deal with energy leaks caused by aggressive predictive prefetching.

Misinterpretation of callback API semantics: We find that the application "Photostream" incorrectly uses APIs, leading to substantial network energy leaks. "Photostream" is a sample application written by Google that intends to show beginner developers how to use specific APIs. The application allows users to retrieve other user's pictures from Flickr. As shown in Figure 5, only 38.6% of network transmissions ultimately influence the display.

Investigating the content and timing of unused network packets reveals that the "PhotoStream" application downloads many unused packets even when the application is put into the background. By exploring the source code, we confirm that the background downloading thread is stopped in *onDestroy()*, a callback method that is not guaranteed to be called after the application is put into background. As a result, the application continues downloading objects that cannot ever be displayed, resulting in network energy leaks.

This bug can influence many applications due to misunderstanding of the documentation. Android SDK clearly suggests that developers clean up threads in the *onDestroy()* callback method before the application is about to be killed. This suggestion is reasonable for handling threads in general because it reduces the cost of initializing a new thread when the application is resumed. However, in this particular case, it produces energy leaks because the thread continues downloading (useless) data. To make things worse, the source code of "PhotoStream" was provided as an example application for use by beginner Android developers, potentially prop-

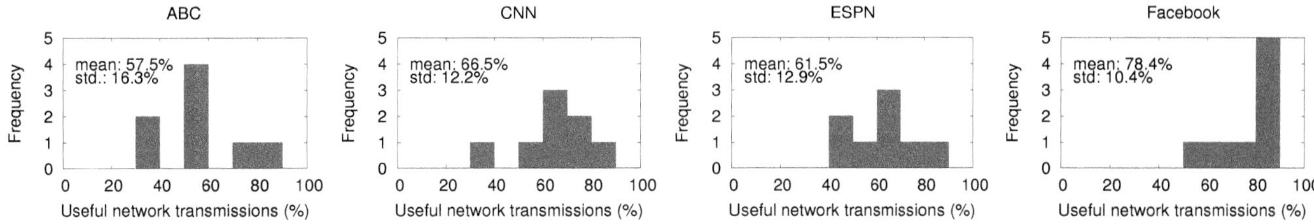

Figure 7: Histogram of percent of useful network transmission from user study for suspected leaky applications.

agating the design error into other applications. This bug could be fixed by stopping the thread in *onPause()*, which is guaranteed to be called after the application is placed in the background.

Poorly designed downloading scheme: In this case, the network device is frequently used to update data objects without considering either device state (e.g., whether the screen is on or off) or user input. We identify two applications with this problem: "ABC widget" and "BusMap". The first wastes 78.0% of network transmissions and the second wastes 46.9% of network transmissions.

"ABC widget" is a news widget application that can be placed on home screen. Surprisingly, by examining the timing of unused network packets, we find that the widget keeps updating news article every 5 minutes, regardless of whether the widget is being shown or even whether the display is on or off. This poorly designed downloading scheme is detrimental to smartphone battery life as it not only wastes communication energy and CPU when the phone is active, but also causes the phone to wake up every 5 minutes even when it is idle.

More interestingly, further exploration on the widget related APIs in Android leads us to believe that the Android framework fails to provide a good mechanism for widgets to stop updating when not visible. There are three scenarios when a widget is not visible: the display is off, the widget is placed on another home screen that is not displayed, or another application is running in the foreground. Android's API provides an indirect way to help the widget to identify the first scenario [21], but it is impossible for the latter two. Apparently, "ABC widget" even fails to identify the first one. This finding suggests improvements in the Android framework API, e.g., provide widget applications notifications when they are not visible or stop sending the update notifications when widgets are not visible.

"BusMap" contains another example of a poorly designed downloading scheme. It is a map-based application that informs users to the next three school buses to arrive at bus stops. A user selects a specific stop to view its bus schedule. The schedule for only a single stop can be examined at any particular time. Examination of the timing and content of unused network packets reveals a cause for energy leaks: regardless of which stop the user selects, the application downloads schedules for all stops, even those that are not visible on the current map. To eliminate the inefficiency, developers should design downloading schemes that take possible (and ideally common) user input into consideration.

Repetitive downloads "ABC widget" application is found to have repetitive downloads, e.g., packets containing identical content are downloaded but never used. By examining the content of its unused network packets, we discover that every time the application updates, it downloads all recent news articles, even when they have not been updated. Clearly, this observation suggests that the application naïvely fetches the latest news articles from the Internet without caching any of the downloads. In order to fix this bug, application developers could add an expiration time for each article or have the application server notify the client of new updates.

7.4 Aggressive prefetching

Prefetching has been used extensively in both desktop and mobile environments to improve user satisfaction by eliminating download delays for data that are expected to be required soon. It generally uses prediction, often of future user actions. Such predictions cannot be perfectly accurate. Therefore, even a well-developed predictive prefetching application will download some objects that are never used. In order to enable a rational understanding of the trade-off between response latency and unused transmission, developers must first understand the percentage of unused transmissions by the target application. ADEL helps to provide this number and hence also assists developers to determine when it would improve application energy efficiency by adjusting prefetch aggressiveness and/or improving prefetching predictor accuracy. As shown in Table 4, four out of seven suspected leaky applications we studied have inappropriate prefetching settings.

Whether a significant portion of prefetching wastes energy cannot be determined by a single user's trace. This is mainly because an unnecessary packet for one user may be useful for another user due to varying use patterns. Hence, to capture the prefetching aggressiveness of an application, it is necessary for us to study the applications with different usage patterns.

We conducted a small-scale user study with 8 graduate students who are regular smartphone users running applications on top of ADEL. To avoid bias, none of the users were told the intention of the experiment until after it was completed. Each participant was asked to use the four leaky applications as they would in daily life; each application was run three times. There was no time constraint for any particular application. After gathering user traces for one application, the percent of *useful network transmissions* is derived from each trace. Note that this percentage is inversely related to prefetching aggressiveness. Figure 7 summarizes the distribution of the percent of *useful network transmission* for each application.

We can draw two conclusions from Figure 7.

- The percent of *useful network transmissions* for one application varies significantly across users due to variation in user behavior. As shown in Figure 7, the percent of *useful network transmission* spans a range of more than 40%. Note that each sample represents the average *useful network transmission* of three runs. The average variation of a particular user across runs is 4.2%. This substantial variation across users suggests that the optimal prefetching aggressiveness depends on the user; it suggests that a static prefetching scheme is unlikely to be optimal for all users.

- "Facebook" is more efficient than the other three suspected leaky applications. For example, more than 80% of the network transmissions are useful for 5 of the 8 users. What's more, the mean of the distribution is 78.4%, indicating that 78.4% the downloaded content turns out to be useful for an average user. As a result of this, we find that "Facebook" is not leaky, despite of our previous suspicion.

Based on our observations, the applications the energy efficiency of "ABC", "CNN", and "ESPN" can be improved by reducing prefetching aggressiveness, at some possible cost to user-observed performance.

ADEL's ability to determine unused prefetched content enables three additional use scenarios in addition to detecting energy bugs. First, developers can use ADEL to learn the effectiveness of the application's prefetching scheme and adjust it during application design. Second, users can occasionally use ADEL to determine whether an application is prefetching with appropriate aggressiveness and adjust this parameter within the application or operating system. Third, with performance optimizations, ADEL could potentially be used within the operating system to provide applications with a real-time feedback on prefetching energy waste for one particular user. Applications could then adjust their prefetching aggressiveness to customize the user's current behavior.

7.5 Discussion

The above findings indicate that ADEL can help application developers to find the root causes of energy leaks in their applications. One may argue that a simpler approach can also detect such bugs. For example, repetitive downloads can be detected by simply checking the timing of the download pattern. However, without ADEL, the application developers do not even know the specific problems that should be tested for. For example, the developers may not know that the timing of download pattern is the most promising place to look for problems. ADEL makes it really easy for application developers to find where energy leaks occur.

Eliminating energy leaks detected by ADEL can improve energy efficiency. However, some leaks can be difficult to eliminate. For example, it is quite easy to fix the first three types of leaks in Section 7.2: the incorrectly used API can be fixed by changing API use; the widget that downloads data ignoring device state can be fixed by checking device state before download; and the repetitive downloads can be eliminated by caching. In contrast, it may not always be possible to develop a prefetching scheme that is both energy efficient and maintains adequate user performance because the very concept of prefetching relies on prediction, which is by nature imperfect. Therefore, it should be up to the developers to determine whether the potential energy saving suggested by ADEL justify the extra implementation effort.

8. CONCLUSION

In this work, we provided a definition of *energy leaks*: common but hard to detect energy waste resulting from useless activities in smartphone applications. We have described the design and implementation of ADEL, an Automatic Detector for Energy Leaks. ADEL identifies unnecessary network communication and its root causes via dynamic taint tracking. ADEL incurs 21.8% performance overhead on average.

We studied 15 real-world applications using ADEL and found that 6 of these have significant energy leaks. Eliminating these energy leaks results in an average 56.5% reduction in energy consumption due to network communication. Our study revealed four common causes for energy leaks: misinterpretation of callback API semantics, poorly designed downloading scheme, repetitive downloads, and aggressive prefetching. Both ADEL and our study of network energy leaks in Android applications have the potential to help application developers improve energy efficiency.

9. REFERENCES

[1] "iPhone battery life flaw confirmed by Apple," http://www.huffingtonpost.com/.

[2] "Android battery life: terrible, or just plain bad?" http://reviews.cnet.com/8301-19736_7-20058834-251.html.

[3] A. Pathak, Y. C. Hu, and M. Zhang, "Bootstrapping energy debugging on smartphones: a first look at energy bugs in mobile devices," in *Proc. Wkshp. Hot Topics in Networks*, Nov. 2011.

[4] F. Qian, et al., "Profiling resource usage for mobile applications: a cross-layer approach," in *Proc. Int. Conf. on Mobile Systems, Applications, and Services*, June 2011.

[5] A. Pathak, et al., "What is keeping my phone awake? characterizing and detecting no-sleep energy bugs in smartphone apps," in *Proc. Int. Conf. Mobile Systems, Applications And Services*, June 2012, pp. 267–280.

[6] R. Krashinsky and H. Balakrishnan, "Minimizing energy for wireless web access with bounded slowdown," in *Proc. Int. Conf. Mobile Computing and Networking*, Sept. 2002, pp. 135–148.

[7] M. Anand, E. Nightingale, and J. Flinn, "Self-tuning wireless network power management," in *Proc. Int. Conf. Mobile Computing and Networking*, Sept. 2003, pp. 176–189.

[8] D. Qiao and K. Shin, "Smart power-saving mode for IEEE 802.11 wirelss LANs," in *Proc. Int. Conf. Computer Communications*, Mar. 2005, pp. 1573–1583.

[9] T. Armstrong, et al., "Efficient and transparent dynamic content updates for mobile clients," in *Proc. Int. Conf. Mobile Systems, Applications And Services*, June 2006, pp. 56–68.

[10] B. Housel and D. Lindquist, "WebExpress: a system for optimizing web browsing in a wireless environment," in *Proc. Int. Conf. Mobile Computing and Networking*, June 1996, pp. 108–116.

[11] M. C. Rosu, et al., "PAWP: A power aware web proxy for wireless lan clients," in *Workshop on Mobile Computing Systems and Applications*, Dec. 2004, pp. 206–215.

[12] W. Enck, et al., "TaintDroid: An information-flow tracking system for realtime privacy monitoring on smartphones," in *Proc. Int. Symp. Operating Systems Design and Implementation*, Oct. 2010.

[13] V. Haldar, D. Chandra, and M. Franz, "Dynamic taint propagation for Java," in *Proc. Annual Computer Security Applications Conference*, 2005, pp. 303–311.

[14] W. Xu, S. Bhatkar, and R. Sekar, "Taint-enhanced policy enformacement: a practical apporach to defeat a wide range of attacks," in *Proc. USENIX Conf.*, 2006, pp. 121–136.

[15] D. Chandra and M. Franz, "Fine-grained information flow analysis and enforcement in a Java Virtual Machine," in *Proc. Annual Computer Security Applications Conference*, Dec. 2007, pp. 463–475.

[16] PowerTutor, "PowerTutor," 2009, http://powertutor.org.

[17] H. Yin, et al., "Panorama: capturing system-wide information flow for malware detection and analysis," in *Proc. Conf. on Computer and Communications Security*, Oct. 2007, pp. 116–127.

[18] B. Davis and H. Chen, "DBTaint: cross-application information flow tracking via databases," in *Proc. USENIX Conf.*, June 2010, pp. 12–12.

[19] A. C. Myers, "JFlow: practical mostly-static information flow control," in *Proc. of the ACM Symp. on principles of Programming Languages*, Jan. 1999, pp. 228–241.

[20] H. Falaki, et al., "Diversity in smartphone usage," in *Proc. Int. Conf. Mobile Systems, Applications And Services*, June 2010, pp. 179–194.

[21] "Android SDK reference," http://developer.android.com/reference/packages.html.

Don't burn your mobile! Safe Computational Re-Sprinting via Model Predictive Control

Andrea Tilli, Andrea Bartolini, Matteo Cacciari, Luca Benini
University of Bologna, DEIS
via Risorgimento 2, 40136 Bologna, Italy
Email: andrea.tilli,a.bartolini,matteo.cacciari,luca.benini@unibo.it

ABSTRACT

Computational sprinting has been recently proposed as an effective solution to mitigate the upcoming dark silicon utilization wall problems. As most applications do not require constantly the maximum performance level and parallelism, computational sprinting uses the intrinsic thermal capacitance of the heat dissipation system, possibly augmented with Phase Change Materials, as heat buffer for tolerating bursts of intensive computational resource usage largely exceeding the steady-state thermal design power. It is clear that sprinting poses peculiar challenges on the dynamic thermal control policy. In this paper we introduce and evaluate an innovative and low-overhead hierarchical model-predictive controller that enables thermally-safe sprinting while guaranteeing a predictable re-sprinting rate.

Categories and Subject Descriptors

C.1.4 [**Computer Systems Organization**]: Processor Architectures—*Parallel Architectures, Mobile processors*; B.8.0 [**Hardware**]: Performance and Reliability—*General*

Keywords

Dark Silicon, Computational Sprinting, Thermal Control, Thermal Model

1. INTRODUCTION

The race for increasing CPU performance has seen as collateral effect the rapid increase of power consumption. This has been the main wall for sequential execution speed scaling across the whole spectrum of computing systems [1]. In the era of power-limited computing, performance is scaled by parallelizing execution on multiple cores. Multi-core architectures can effectively leverage Moore's law [2], by packing more cores in the same silicon area, thereby achieving higher parallel computational density as silicon technology keeps improving with the pace dictated by Moore's law. Unfortunately, parallelism is not a panacea: it is now accepted that in upcoming and future technology nodes (22nm and beyond) all the units on a die cannot be continuously switched on at the same time, as their total power consumption would exceed the maximum Thermal Design Power (TDP): leading to thermal run-out [8]. Cooling solutions, needed to remove the heat from the silicon die, are limited by cost or by physical constraints: in data centers approximately 50% of the energy consumed is used for powering the cooling infrastructure [16], whereas in embedded/mobile platforms the cooling system is constrained by form factor and packaging cost [13]. Dark Silicon has been estimated to be the 21% at 22nm and 50% at 8nm [8]: practically limiting the maximum parallelism achievable by future many-cores. In future mobile platforms this problem is even more serious since active cooling cannot be easily implemented without compromising battery lifetime, form factor, user experience [27].

Applications that run on these power-bound systems are typically composed of alternating sequences of parallel and sequential sections [14] and thus they do not exploit constantly the underling HW parallelism (parallel tasks are also characterized by different computational phases [26]). This is exacerbated in mobile platform where applications are often triggered by the users and differently from batch jobs, their Quality of Service (QoS) does not depend on average throughput, but on users experience and response time. Studies demonstrate that an average user perceives a response time below 150ms as crisp, noticeable within 1s, annoying in 2s and not acceptable in the 2-5s range [24]. Moreover accordingly to the usage scenario, the user needs to share its cognitive resources with the perception of the external environment. The minimum continuous span of attention to the mobile device is 4s in a busy street whereas the maximum switch-back duration (the time spent on attending the environment before switching back to the mobile device) is 7-8s [15]. As a consequence, mobile platform are often response-time constrained and they need to provide fast bursts of computation on demand.

Fortunately, we can turn this requirement to our advantage to cut some slack on thermal design. Traditional Thermal Design Power is defined statically on the worst case power consumption, considering only the package thermal resistance [5]. As consequence, packages are optimized for minimizing their resistance with the ambient temperature neglecting the heat storage capabilities of the different package materials, associated with their thermal capacitance. In a regime where classical TDP cannot ensure the power on all the integrated cores, but maximum performance is needed mainly in short bursts, the heat buffer associated with the thermal capacitance can be sufficient to run all the cores at the maximum performance for short time windows, ideally triggered on-demand whenever peak parallel workload phases and user interaction occur. These Computational Sprints [17] can be lengthened by increasing the thermal capacitance of the package. Phase Change Material that are solid at ambient temperature, can store extra heat during the melting process, releasing it to the ambient later on, during solidification. As consequence of that, PCM allows packing in a small volume and within a small temperature gap a large thermal capacitance placed close to the silicon die [17]. Embedding the correct PCM quantity and material can enable longer sprints (e.g. 1s), suitable for periodically speed-ups and can improve the QoS of interactive tasks.

From the above considerations, clear advantages can be achieved by exploiting silicon/package thermal capacitance, PCM or other materials as "heat tanks" to be filled along sprinting phases. However, these tanks are finite, then only limited sprinting intervals are sustainable. Suitable "rest intervals" are, then needed to let the tanks to release heat in the external ambient. This is necessary to keep cores temperatures below their critical values and to restore sprinting capabilities. Such intrinsically-dynamic thermal behavior requires a suitable run-time temperature management to guarantee safe working, even under variable and possibly uncertain conditions.

Once a sprinting architecture has been defined with a reliable and effective thermal control, one has to cope with another crucial challenge, not yet deeply considered in literature. That is *how to exploit limited sprinting capabilities, when different tasks are running together with different QoS requests or criticality features.* As a matter of facts, rest intervals are a sort of blanking periods w.r.t. possible sprinting requests, then their durations and placement along time will affect the actual QoS of different applications. In the mobile domain, different APPs/tasks can be executed at the same time with different QoS requirements (e.g. video encoding/decoding [18], driving augmented reality[19] and health monitoring [20], phone call and text message). Moreover, in other domains as automotive embedded control, mixed criticality scenarios will take place with hard real-time and even safety-critical tasks running along with soft real-time applications. A suitable run-time control policy is clearly needed to tackle such heterogeneous workload scenarios. Sprinting capabilities have to be exploited or reserved to favor, or even guarantee, the execution and the QoS of most critical tasks. Summing up, sprinting time is a shared, limited and dynamical resource which needs dynamical restore time. Then, whenever a sprint is launched, the system should preserve a suitable "room" for subsequent sprints, according to a policy defined for managing different task criticalities. We refer such a feature as *Re-sprinting* management.

1.1 Related Work

A seminal work on Computation Sprinting has been published recently by Ragavan et. al. [17]. It demonstrates the feasibility and the benefits of this approach in a 16 cores multicore model, with a sustainable TDP of 1W equal to the power consumption of just one core. From the architecture perspective the authors first show that dangerous power-grid drops and ripples caused by the transitioning into and out the sprint mode can be effectively mitigated by introducing a gradual core activation scheduling with 128us total duration. Second, they show that high peak power phases, required by the sprint mode can be effectively delivered using Li Polymer battery [11] and ultra capacitors [21]. Moreover the 16A peak current is not typical in mobile packages and would require a large number of pins to be delivered, this cost can be mitigated by using higher pin voltages combined with an on-chip voltage regulator. Intrinsic package thermal capacitance would not be enough to sustain sprint periods that covers the entire execution of image processing applications on HD images [7]. In the paper authors use 150g of PCM material to substitute the heat-spreader, augmenting its thermal capacitance to sustain 1s of continuous sprint. It is shown that the heat stored during the sprint requires a cooling period of 25s to repristinate the initial sprinting capability. For these materials, phase change happens at constant temperature reflecting in a complex non-linear thermal model [25] not directly applicable in state-of-the-art thermal simulators [10]. In [17], the PCM material is modelled with a variable capacitance and both the PCM layer and the silicon one are modelled as isothermal blocks. Whereas this is a reasonable assumption for small volumes of PCM, it does not account for the effect of thermal gradients in the silicon die. In the same paper the authors quantify the performance gain during sprinting phases, in average benchmarks achieved a 10.2x speed-up compared to single-core execution time. The same thermal capacitance can be exploited by voltage/turbo-boosting, common in today high-end multi-processors [6]. Indeed voltage/turbo boosting allows to speed-up the performance of single-threaded workload by increasing for a short time period the supply voltage of the core and consequently its clock frequency. The voltage supply-frequency relation is almost linear whereas dynamic power depends on the square of supply voltage and linearly with the frequency. As consequence of that in [17] the authors demonstrate that with the same 16x sprint power budget a single-core that uses voltage-boosting can only achieve an average 2.5x speed-up on the same benchmarks [7]. This is 8x slower than the computational sprint one.

For what concerns thermal management, the following approach is proposed in [17]. If the sprinting applications execute enough to completely melt the PCM, the sprint is stopped by a threshold-based feedback thermal controller when the critical junction temperature is reached; above this value the HW could be severely damaged. Safe thermal stop are enabled architecturally with fast cache flush and tasks migration, ensuring the correct software execution. Nonetheless, no possible performance optimization or re-sprinting requests are taken into account in such approach. On the one hand, whenever the critical junction temperature is reached, sprint is stopped without seeking for profitable intermediate solutions, exploiting DVFS. On the other hand, in the above stop policy, only thermal issues are taken into account, without considering which room has been left for a subsequent re-sprint.

In order to tackle thermal constraints giving the best possible performance, predictive thermal controls have been shown to be capable of ensuring better results when compared to standard reactive ones [28]. Moreover Model Predictive Controllers (MPCs) have been recently shown to be capable of tackling workload variability, optimizing the multicore run-time thermal evolution while ensuring a hard bound on the run-time temperature of the cores. Indeed, this is done by exploiting a thermal predictor embedded in the MPC for choosing run-time core frequencies that minimize a cost function (i.e. overall performance degradation, hot-spots and thermal gradients occurrence), providing hard bound on the maximum core temperature [28, 3, 4]. The computational complexity of both the thermal prediction and the optimization step increases with the number of cores. Bartolini et. al [3, 4] present a distributed model predictive controller in which a local MPC runs on each core. Each of these controllers uses only neighbours temperature information to predict future temperature. As consequence of that, the complexity of each controller is lowered and does not depend on the number of cores integrated in the system.

The above MPC approaches look a natural choice for dynamical performance optimization and effective thermal capping in sprinting architectures. Nevertheless, even in these solutions, peculiar re-sprinting capabilities are not taken into account directly. Additional run-time control functions are required to manage the heat buffer properly, providing room for prescribed re-sprinting.

1.2 Contribution

The main contribution of this paper is a novel closed-loop control solution to guarantee thermally-safe and run-time optimal sprinting and re-sprinting. We exploit Model Predictive Control (MPC) to design a two-layer hierarchical and scalable run-time controller. The proposed solution dynamically maximizes the sprinting performance and guaranties prescribed re-sprinting capability, according to the physical properties and the current conditions of the target system.

In the path toward the main result, "formal" definition of the re-sprinting requirement is introduced, first, referring to a mixed criticality scenario. Then, a simplified modelling is proposed to map such requirement, for a given system, into a suitable time-varying constraint on the amount of energy stored in the "heat buffer" (usually PCM).

Drawing upon these results and the considerations reported in Subsection 1.1, the main elements of the two layers constituting the proposed hierarchical MPC are defined as follows. The lower layer manages optimization of the current core computation powers and effective capping of core temperatures, taking advantage of the distributed and scalable MPC solution presented in related work [3]. At the top layer we propose a novel centralized MPC solution to manage the heat buffer (PCM, in this paper) maximizing sprinting time, while guaranteeing re-sprinting performance for the considered system. The higher level interacts with the lower one by tuning the computational power requested for sprinting. For the PCM management, we leverage energy-based modelling [23], which allows a simple handling of PCM variable thermal capacitance. This gives a simple representation of the coupling between the thermal models considered in the lower MPC layer and in the higher one.

The proposed solution can effectively tackle heterogeneous tasks with different criticality levels by giving guaranteed re-sprinting rooms. In addition, when no guaranteed re-sprinting is needed, the proposed system can be easily "downgraded" to such simpler condition by just turning off the higher layer of the proposed controller. This can be useful when a generic taskset have to be served according to a best effort approach. It is worth noting that this transition between "guaranteed" and "non-guaranteed" re-sprinting, and even the opposite, can be handled dynamically at run time.

Along this paper a 16 cores embedded device equipped with PCM is considered as a target platform. Nevertheless, the considered approach can be applied to any system for re-sprinting capability definition, translation of such requirement into a time-varying constrain for the heat buffer and effective run-time control.

The proposed MPC solution is compared to state-of-the-art run-time thermal management exploiting threshold-based controllers, as defined in [17]. Tests with and without guaranteed re-sprinting specifications are carried out to represent both heterogeneous and homogeneous QoS tasks scenarios. Relevant performance improvement is obtained under non-guaranteed re-sprinting thanks to the optimality of thermal MPC in exploiting the "available thermal room". When guaranteed re-sprinting request is considered, standard threshold-based controllers cannot meet such specification under critical conditions, whereas the proposed solution is always able to guarantee it, minimizing the total performance loss.

The remainder of the paper is organized as follows. In Section 2 we present the benchmark embedded device, equipped with PCM. Its thermal model is defined and benefits of PCM in giving a larger room for sprinting are briefly highlighted. Rigorous definition of re-sprinting capability is given and motivated; then a simplified, but significant model, is derived to translate such requirements in time-varying bounds for the energy stored in PCM. In Section 3, the proposed MPC solution with PCM energy management capabilities is presented. In Section 4, simulations are reported to compare standard solution reported in literature with the proposed MPC under different scenarios, particular attention is paid to mixed periodic/aperiodic computational loads to highlight re-sprinting properties. Non-nominal working conditions are considered as well. Finally, in Section 5 some conclusions and issues for future works are drawn.

2. SPRINTING ARCHITECTURE

In this Section a PCM-based sprinting architecture for an embedded device is presented. We define the main properties of a realistic platform to derive a thermal model to test our sprinting controller. A multicore with 16 cores is considered, the die area is $6.8mm \times 6.8mm$ with a thickness of $350\mu m$. Per-core DVFS is assumed and the maximum power dissipated by each core under maximum frequency and worst load conditions is set to $P_{c,max}=1W$ (i.e. the chip maximum dissipated power is P_{max}=16W). Maximum frequency, corresponding to maximum power is set to 1.5Ghz and minimum one is set at 500Mhz, with a per core power equal to $P_{c,min}$=150mW under worst load conditions.

In sprinting conditions, all the cores are requested to work with maximum frequency and full utilization. In rest conditions, only one core is assumed to run at full frequency and utilization (i.e. at full power), while all of the others are assumed to be in idle status with an equivalent power of $P_{c,idle}$=50mW each (i.e. a chip power of P_{rest}=1.75W is assumed). This characterization of computational/power traces is simplified, but significant to represent relevant thermal issues. Indeed, actual sprinting traces are expressed in terms of high frequency (and voltage) pulses, while the actual power consumption also depends on current workload characteristics. Nevertheless, in this work, to simplify the discussion, sprinting traces will be represented in terms of power (P_{max} along sprints and P_{rest} in rest conditions), assuming worst workload conditions. This does not give a relevant generality loss, when focusing on thermal issues.

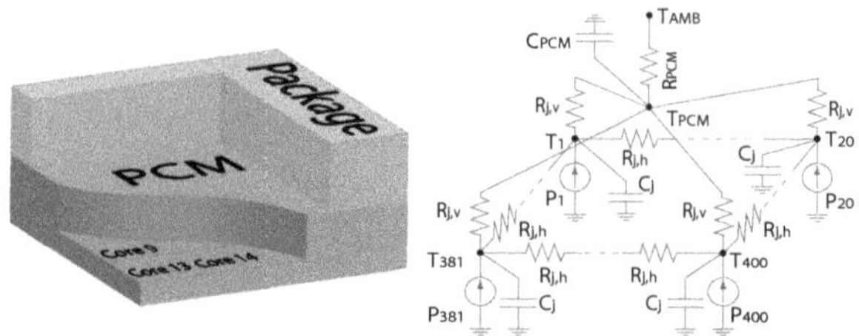

Figure 1: The considered sprinting architecture and the adopted thermal modelling

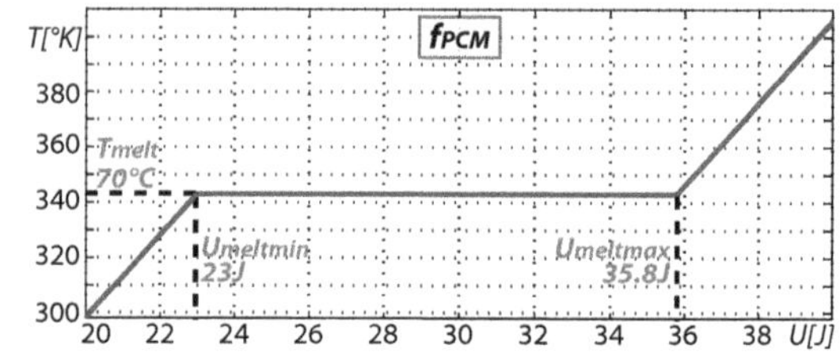

Figure 2: Internal Energy to Temperature nonlinear function

Thermal stability is obviously guaranteed in rest condition, while the system cannot sustain permanent sprinting; the maximum admissible Silicon temperature is T_{max}= 360°K, while the considered maximum ambient temperature is T_{AMBmax}=318°K. As reported on the left of Fig. 1 a layer of PCM with physical properties similar to commercial Climsel-C70 [22] is interposed in between the Silicon die and the device case. The thickness of such layer is $410\mu m$. According to common mobile and embedded applications, no heat-sink is considered [13]. A Copper based thermal conductivity enhancer is assumed inside the PCM layer to improve conductivity and speed up heat charging and discharging during the melting phase. This mixture can be seen as an homogeneous material with both high thermal conductivity and high heat capacity [17].

2.1 Thermal Modeling

A lumped thermal model is proposed for the considered device, according to the equivalent electric network reported on the right of Fig. 1. Each core has been split into single-layer 25 cells, each one modeled by a current generator representing the power dissipated by the cell, a resistor and a capacity. As in previous work [17], the PCM layer and conductivity enhancer have been modeled by a single large cell assuming a uniform distribution of the heat. The resulting model is,

$$\begin{aligned} \dot{T}_k &= \frac{P_k}{C_j} + \frac{T_{PCM} - T_k}{C_j \cdot R_{j,v}} + \sum_{i=1}^{\#neighbors} \frac{T_{neigh,i} - T_k}{2 \cdot C_j \cdot R_{j,h}} \\ \dot{U} &= \sum_{k=1}^{16} \frac{T_k - T_{PCM}}{R_{j,v}} - \frac{T_{PCM} - T_{AMB}}{R_{PCM}} \end{aligned} \quad (1)$$

where T_k, P_k are respectively the temperature and the power dissipated by the k-th Silicon cell, $T_{neigh,i}$ are the neighbor cells temperatures, T_{PCM} is the temperature of the PCM, T_{AMB} is the ambient temperature and U is the internal energy of the PCM layer. It is worth noting that, in (1), the first equation is obtained by standard space-discretization of the well-known Heat Equation. In contrast, for the second equation, according to [23], an energy-based model has been exploited for PCM to handle its nonlinear phase-changing behavior. The PCM temperature can be easily derived from U by a nonlinear map, $T_{PCM} = f_{PCM}(U)$, to represent monotonic increasing behavior in solid and liquid condition, while constant temperature will be given in the melting phase, see Fig. 2. The first term in the top equation represents the contribution of the power consumption in each cell, whereas the last two, according to Fourier Law, are the effects of heat flow entering in the cell k from PCM and neighbor cells, respectively. Similarly, in the bottom equation, the first term is the heat flow from all of the silicon cells to PCM, whereas the second gives the heat flow from PCM to the external environment; no direct thermal path is assumed between the silicon cells and the ambient. The following values for cell capacitance and thermal resistances are assumed, $C_j = 6.6e-5J/°K$, $R_{j,h} = 22.9°K/W$, $R_{j,v}$=215°K/W and R_{PCM}=7.9°K/W. The latter two resistances, linking the PCM layer to the others elements, benefit from the Copper conductivity enhancer, in particular in $R_{j,v}$ contact resistance between Silicon and PCM layer has been considered. Parameters of the adopted PCM are melting temperature, T_{melt}=70 ℃, density, $1700Kg/m^3$, specific latent heat, $396KJ/Kg$, latent heat of the whole volume $12.8J$ and differential thermal capacitance in solid and liquid condition, $3.52J/(°K\,\mu m^3)$. These parameters will characterize the whole "PCM + conductivity enhancer layer", since Copper thermal capacitance does not affect relevantly the PCM thermal inertia. All these leads to a maximum internal energy for solid phase $U_{meltmin} = 23J$ and a minimum internal energy for liquid phase $U_{meltmax} = 35.8J$, in between melting phase will take place.

In Fig. 3 the effectiveness of the PCM with conductivity enhancer is highlighted. A constant full power working condition is considered and the adopted device is compared with two variants where the PCM+enhancer is replaced by a $2mm$ thick heat spreader or by a pure PCM layer, respectively. By observing the time when core temperatures reach T_{max}, it can be noted that the considered architecture enables larger sprinting room w.r.t. the others.

2.2 Guaranteed re-sprinting definition

In this Subsection, we provide and motivate a "formal" definition of Guaranteed Re-sprinting capability, then we translate it in a clear requirement for PCM energy management by exploiting a simplified, but effective, thermal model of the given system.

As stated in Section 1, the concept of Re-sprinting management has been introduced to handle heterogeneous tasks

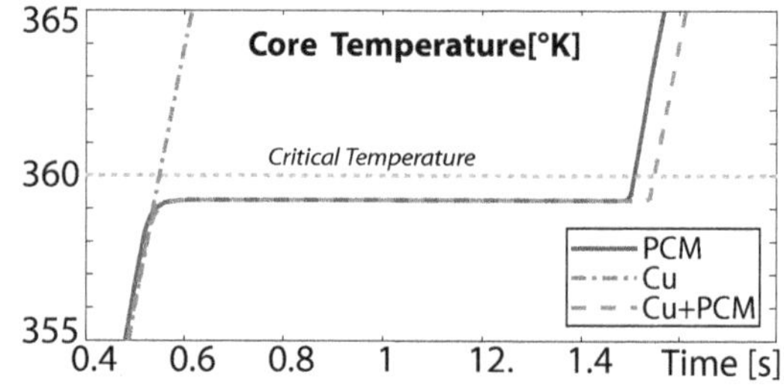

Figure 3: Comparison among sprinting architectures

with different QoS requests or criticality levels. In particular, limited sprinting capability have to be spent or preserved according to a policy which favors, or even guarantees, most critical or QoS-demanding task space. Toward this goal, we consider the following scenario. We suppose to have two main task groups, both requiring full-power sprinting, critical hard real-time periodic and predictable tasks and non-critical aperiodic tasks. For the first group, the total fulfillment of the sprinting requests has to be guaranteed, while, for the second one, best effort is admissible; we refer those groups as *Guaranteed Group* and *Best Effort Group*, respectively. For the Guaranteed Group a known periodicity of M is assumed, while the total time needed to execute all these tasks together at full power is assumed equal or lower than a given bound equal to N. This kind of information is usually available when dealing with real-time critical tasks. Differently, for the Best Effort Group no information is assumed. Under the considered condition, it is clear that the sprinting and rest intervals need to be dynamically arranged not only to maximize service of generic sprinting providing thermal capping, but N-long sprinting windows must be guaranteed every M seconds to serve the Guaranteed Group. We formalize such requirement in the following definition of N-M Guaranteed Re-sprinting.

N-M Guaranteed Re-sprinting for a computing system is the capability of guaranteeing a sprint at full power of duration N, as soon as a time M ($M > N$) has elapsed from the starting of the previous guaranteed sprinting.

From the above definition, it is clear that whenever a sprint has been launched, the runtime control system has to limit the sprint period not only taking into account maximum temperature bounds, but also considering that the system needs some rest time to cool down properly and get ready for a possible new sprinting request of N seconds, after M seconds from the beginning of the previous one. Such behavior requires a suitable sizing and management of the PCM heat tank which provides room for sprinting according to its "charge level". In the following an explicit and treatable relation is determined to link PCM energy condition with re-sprinting requirements. Toward this goal, we consider a simplified, but effective, thermal model by collapsing all the Silicon cells into a single cell with temperature T_{Si}. Summing up all the cells capacitors and power sources (neglecting horizontal resistances $R_{j,h}$), and by parallel compositions of all the $R_{j,v}$, we can define the total approximated Silicon capacitance, C_{Si}=$26mJ/^{\circ}K$, and the total approximated Silicon-to-PCM thermal resistance, $R_{Si-PCM} = 0.6^{\circ}K/W$. Then the following approximated model can be drawn.

$$\begin{aligned} \dot{T}_{Si} &= \frac{P_{tot}}{C_{Si}} - \frac{T_{Si} - T_{PCM}}{C_{Si} \cdot R_{Si-PCM}} \\ \dot{U} &= \frac{T_{Si} - T_{PCM}}{R_{Si-PCM}} - \frac{T_{PCM} - T_{AMB}}{R_{PCM}} \end{aligned} \quad (2)$$

where $P_{tot} = \sum P_k$. In common sprinting time-scale, usually in the range of 1-10s, the effect of the Silicon inertia can be neglected with respect to PCM and enhancer dynamics, therefore a static relation between T_{Si} and P_{tot} can be exploited to revise (2) leading to

$$\begin{aligned} T_{Si} &= T_{PCM} + R_{Si-PCM} \cdot P_{tot} \\ \dot{U} &= P_{tot} - \frac{T_{PCM} - T_{AMB}}{R_{PCM}} \end{aligned} \quad (3)$$

With this model at hand, the re-sprinting requirement can be easily translated in a time-varying constraints on the PCM internal energy U according to the time diagram of Fig. 4. Let assume a guaranteed sprinting has been issued at time t_i, then according to the prescribed N-M Guaranteed Re-sprinting between time t_i+M and time t_i+M+N the PCM is expected to be able to store $P_{max} \cdot N$ energy without violating Silicon temperature bounds. That means $U(t_i+M+N) \leq U_{MAX}$, where U_{MAX} can be easily defined, using (3), as

$$U_{MAX} = max\{U \mid f_{PCM}(U) = T_{max} - R_{Si-PCM} \cdot P_{max}\} \quad (4)$$

In the considered 16-cores case, we have $T_{melt} < T_{max} - P_{max} \cdot R_{Si-PCM}$. That means we can run a sprinting up to a $T_{PCM} > T_{melt}$ and a corresponding $U > U_{meltmax}$, where PCM is totally liquid. Nevertheless, we simply assume $U_{MAX} = U_{meltmax}$, this saves some margin and mitigates thermal cycles caused by the on-off computational paradigm. Having defined U_{MAX}, we can compute U_N reported in Fig. 4 as follows,

$$U_N = U_{MAX} - \left(P_{max} - \frac{T_{PCM} - T_{AMBmax}}{R_{PCM}}\right) \cdot N \quad (5)$$

U_N in (5) is the maximum admissible energy at time t_i+M which guarantees that a sprint at full power can be sustained in the following N seconds. Therefore, whatever the previous sprint requests are, N-M Guaranteed Re-sprinting asks for an $U(t_i+M) \leq U_N$. It is worth noting that, in (5), U_N derivation is carried out assuming that PCM melting condition is preserved, i.e. $U_N > U_{meltmin}$ but can be easily extended to more general condition. Now, moving back along time from (t_i+M, U_N), we can derive the time-varying $U_b(t)$ taking into account the maximum cooling capabilities of chip under T_{AMB}=T_{AMBmax}. These are achieved when all the cores but one are in idle conditions (i.e. the system is in a rest phase). Hence, in a generic time instant $t < t_i+M$, the maximum admissible internal energy $U_b(t)$ is the maximum one which can be steered to (t_i+M, U_N) exploiting the maximum cooling capability of the system. At the same time, the bound $U<U_{MAX}$ has to be considered, then $U_b(t)$ can be computed as follows $\forall t \in [t_i, t_i+M[$, leading to the line reported in Fig. 4.

$$U_b(t) = max\{U_{MAX}, \; U_N + \left(\frac{T_{PCM} - T_{AMBmax}}{R_{PCM}} - P_{rest}\right) \cdot ((t_i+M) - t)\} \quad (6)$$

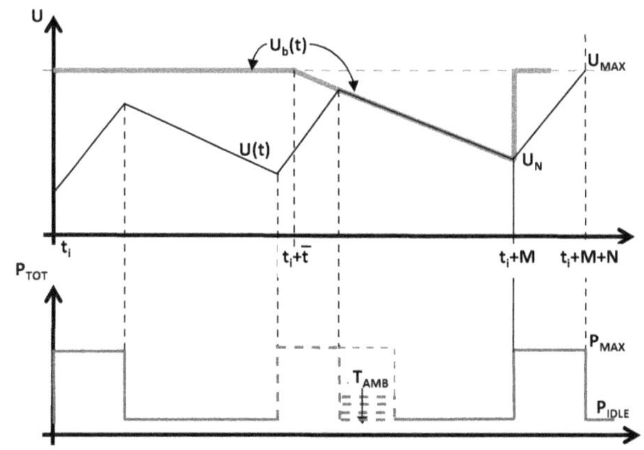

Figure 4: Translation of the N-M Guaranteed Re-sprinting objective in a time-varying constraint on PCM internal energy, U

where obviously $\frac{T_{PCM}-T_{AMBmax}}{R_{PCM}} - P_{rest} > 0$, otherwise the system is not thermally balanced (i.e. is not sized correctly). In addition, the instant $\bar{t}$ where $U_N + \left(\frac{T_{PCM}-T_{AMBmax}}{R_{PCM}} - P_{rest}\right) \cdot ((t_i + M) - \bar{t}) = U_{MAX}$ has to be greater than $t_i + N$, otherwise the N-M Guaranteed Re-sprinting is not sustainable by the system owing to its physical properties (i.e. a suitable resizing is needed).
Finally, summing up all of the previous considerations, the N-M Guaranteed Re-sprinting request can be effectively translated into a time-varying bound on the internal energy U of the PCM by using, in each M interval, the $U_b(\cdot)$ profile derived in (6).

In Fig. 4 a typical P_{tot} profile is also reported to highlight sprinting from both Guaranteed (continuous line) and Best Effort Groups (dashed line). It is worth noting as the sprinting for the Best Effort Group will be affected by the time varying bound $U_b(\cdot)$. In addition, it is possible to figure out that, whenever the bound is reached, the control system will enforce a power consumption that makes the PCM internal energy U to slide along $U_b(\cdot)$. The power giving such a behavior is the rest power with $T_{AMB} = T_{AMBmax}$, according to (6), but it can be larger whenever $T_{AMB} < T_{AMBmax}$. This degree of freedom can be effectively used to maximize the integral of the sprinting power.

For the considered sprinting architecture, a 0.2-4s *Guaranteed Re-sprinting* is requested. By applying (5) and (6) it can be noted that this kind of Re-sprinting is effectively sustainable with $U_{MAX} = U_{meltmax}$, $U_N = 33.2$ and $\bar{t} = t_i + 2.23s$. In addition, it can be verified that, according to the system sizing, this re-sprinting capability requirement for Guaranteed Group leaves a significant room for Best Effort Group. Detailed computations for such issue, and sizing procedure in general, are not reported here since this is not the main focus of this work (nevertheless, some hints on such topic have been already depicted while discussing the feasibility issues in (5) and (6)).

3. TWO-LAYER MODEL PREDICTIVE CONTROLLER

In this Section we propose a closed-loop controller based on MPC approach that provides effective and reliable thermal capping and achieves optimal management of various and dynamics sprinting scenarios. Workload with mixed-criticality heterogeneous tasks are considered, then Guaranteed Re-sprinting requirements, defined in Subsection 2.2, are tackled directly. In addition, the proposed solution is designed to handle as well situations where just best effort approach is needed, with no re-sprinting guarantees.
For each core, the PCM layer and the ambient, a temperature sensor is assumed; their readings are $T_{c,i}$, with $i = 1..16$, T_{PCM} and T_{AMB}, respectively.

We use a two-layer hierarchical approach. In the lower layer, we address the core thermal management exploiting a distributed scheme. In the higher one, a suitable centralized algorithm is defined to manage Guaranteed Re-sprinting requirements, if any, according to PCM status. The general architecture of the proposed approach is reported in Fig. 5

3.1 Lower-layer thermal controller

In the lower layer we take advantage of [3] to define a distributed scalable solution. For each i-th core the following

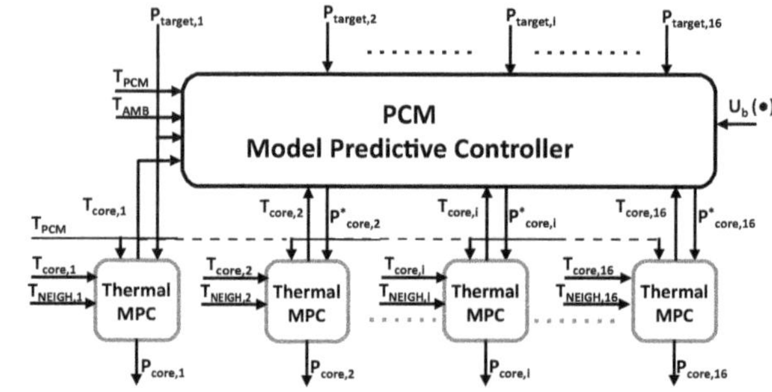

Figure 5: Structure of the proposed controller

discrete-time local MPC problem is set,

$$\begin{aligned} &\min_{P_{c,i}} (P_{c,i}(k|k) - P^*_{c,i}(k))^2 \\ &\text{subject to } T_{c,i}(k+1|k) \leq T_{max} \end{aligned} \tag{7}$$

$P^*_{c,i}$ are the core power references. Their values for $i = 2..16$ are determined by the higher level controller as highlighted in the next Subsection, while for the core 1, $P^*_{c,1} = P_{c,max}$ at any time, according to sprinting architecture described in Section 2. $P_{c,i}$, are the actual core powers (i.e. the sum of the powers dissipated in cores areas). They are assumed as control knobs. Actually, only the core frequencies are directly controllable. As reported in [3], a suitable power-to-frequency model needs to be adopted. This can be effectively implemented using performance counters readings, accounting for the different workload to frequency sensitivities. T_{max} is the maximum admissible temperature for the cores as defined in Section 2. The general idea driving such control approach is to keep the power of each core as close as possible to the requested one, complying with hard thermal bounds. As long as no thermal issue occurs, the power will be equal to the requested one, otherwise temperature limitation will be enforced with minimum performance penalty. This will provide optimal power performance combined with reliable temperature capping. The distributed setting of such MPC problem allows one to obtain linear complexity w.r.t. the number of cores and to split the implementation on all of the cores [3]. The simplified discrete-time single-core models adopted for prediction purposes are represented by the following equations, with sampling time T_{sT}.

$$\begin{aligned} T_{c,i}(k+1|k) = T_{c,i}(k) + T_{sT}\Bigg(&\frac{P_{c,i}(k)}{C_c} + \\ &+ \frac{T_{PCM}(k) - T_{c,i}(k)}{C_c \cdot R_{c,v}} + \sum_{i=1}^{\#neigh} \frac{T_{c\,neigh,i}(k) - T_{c,i}(k)}{2 \cdot C_c \cdot R_{c,o}}\Bigg) \end{aligned} \tag{8}$$

where $C_c = 1.65mJ/°K$, $R_{c,o} = 4.6°K/W$, $R_{c,v} = 9.6°K/W$ are given by straightforward parallel composition of capacitances and resistances of the cells belonging to a core. Note that in these single core models the interaction with the reminder of the chip is taken into account by means of the neighbor cores and PCM temperatures, acting as uncontrollable but measurable inputs. An additional positive effect of such feature is that the model (8) is Linear Time-Invariant, despite of the large nonlinearity characterizing PCM. Thanks to the use of the simplified, but effective, first-order model (8), the MPC problems (7) can be solved explicitly, leading to the following algorithm for the thermal controller of each core,

$$P_{c,i}(k) = \begin{cases} P^*_{c,i}(k) & if\ P^*_{c,i}(k) \le \bar{P}_{c,i}(k) \\ \bar{P}_{c,i}(k) & if\ P^*_{c,i}(k) > \bar{P}_{c,i}(k) \end{cases} \quad (9)$$

where

$$\bar{P}_{c,i}(k) = \frac{C_c}{T_{sT}}\left(\bar{T}_{max} - T_{c,i}(k) + -T_{sT}\left(\frac{T_{PCM}(k)-T_{c,i}(k)}{C_c \cdot R_{c,v}} + \sum_{i=1}^{\#neigh} \frac{T_{c\,neigh,i}(k)-T_{c,i}(k)}{2 \cdot C_c \cdot R_{c,o}}\right)\right) \quad (10)$$

$\bar{P}_{c,i}(k)$ in (10) represents the maximum sustainable power at the instant k preventing violation of the thermal bound T_{max} at $k{+}1$. This expression is derived from the simplified model (8), taking into account the current temperature sensor readings. $\bar{T}_{max}$, lower than T_{max}, is adopted in (10) to save some margin and take into account model approximations and parameters uncertainty. A reliable $\bar{T}_{max}$ can be derived empirically with simulation tests or formally with more complex computations. For the sake of brevity, details on such issue are not reported in this work. In the considered benchmark, we have $\bar{T}_{max}$= $359.9°K$, while T_{max}= $360°K$. This testifies the good approximation given by simplified models (8), when no parameter uncertainties are accounted. In the actual implementation of algorithm (9)-(10) a deadzone will be added collapsing to $P_{c,idle} = 50mW$ all values of $P_{c,i}(k)$ lower than $P_{c,min}$=$150mW$. This item represents the discontinuity in DVFS between minimum frequency and idle condition, as stated at the beginning of Section 2. It is worth underlining that the MPC approach can be effectively adopted even with more complex models replacing (8). In general, when linear models are adopted, problems (7) could be translated into a equivalent *Quadratic Programming (QP)* problems. Then, for each core, the adopted runtime controller could be a standard *Active Set* algorithm exploited to solve the optimization problem with the current samplings. In these cases, run time observers could be exploited to recover states of the considered models when they are not directly available from sensor readings and/or relevant measurement noises are present [3].
We use a sampling time of $T_{sT} = 2.5ms$, thus computational time of the MPC routine can be neglected $\sim 5\mu s$ [4]. In general, sampling time is related to the physical properties of the considered system. A rule-of-thumb for its selection in such kind of applications is 1/3-1/5 of the smallest time constant characterizing the uncontrolled system [29].

3.2 Higher-layer PCM controller

Once thermal capping with minimum performance degradation is guaranteed by the lower-layer MPC, in the higher level one it is possible to manage the PCM to ensure guaranteed re-sprinting performance, whenever needed to tackle heterogeneous tasks with different QoS requirements or criticalities. According to Subsection 2.2, we consider two tasks groups; the Best Effort Group and the Guaranteed Group, with a *N-M* Guaranteed Re-sprinting requirement (0.2s-4s for the considered benchmark). Taking the cue from Fig. 4 and (6), the idea is to enable every sprinting request until the PCM internal energy, U, approaches the bound U_b, then a suitable sprinting reduction has to be taken to preserve $U(k) = U_b(k)$, i.e. to preserve the requested re-sprinting room for the Guaranteed Group. Moving from these considerations, we propose the following centralized MPC problem to tackle PCM management.

$$\min_{P^*_{c,i}} \sum_{i=2}^{16} (P^*_{c,i}(k|k) - P_{t,i}(k))^2 \quad \text{subject to } U(k+1|k) \le U_b(k+1) \quad (11)$$

where $P^*_{c,i}$, $i = 2..16$ are the control knobs of such controller, representing the power references delivered to distributed thermal controllers as reported in Fig. 5 and in Subsection 3.1. Differently, $P_{t,i}(k)$, $i = 1..16$ are the original computational power targets for the cores; they are equal to $P_{max}/16 = P_{c,max} = 1W$, when a sprinting request is running; whereas, in rest conditions, $P_{t,1} = P_{c,max} = 1W$ and $P_{t,i} = P_{c,idle} = 50mW$ for the other cores. The rationale of this approach is to let the power references $P^*_{c,i}$, for lower level MPC, to be close to $P_{t,i}(k)$, whenever the PCM energy is clearly far from the time-varying repetitive bound U_b (see Fig. 4). Differently, when the prediction of the internal energy $U(k+1|k)$ approaches $U_b(k+1)$, power references are decreased. A one-step-ahead preview is assumed on the bound $U_b(\cdot)$, this is admissible according to strategy adopted to derive it in (6).
The approximated discrete-time model adopted for prediction purposes, with sampling time T_{sP}, is

$$U(k+1|k) = U(k) + +T_{sP}\left(\frac{T_{PCM}(k)-T_{AMB}(k)}{R_{PCM}} + \sum_{k=1}^{16} \frac{T_{c,i}(k)-T_{PCM}(k)}{R_{c,v}}\right) \quad (12)$$

It is worth noting that, since T_{PCM} is available from measurements, it can be used as an input and the energy-based model (12) will be Linear Time-Invariant, despite the nonlinearity of the PCM behavior.
The PCM internal energy, $U(k)$ adopted in (12) is not directly available, an observer is actually used for such variable, exploiting temperature measurements. Some attention has to be paid along the melting condition since the internal energy becomes unobservable from the PCM temperature. Details on that are not reported here for the sake of brevity.
In the prediction model proposed in (12), the control knobs $P^*_{c,i}$ are not directly available. In order to apply standard MPC solutions a more complex model would be necessary to highlight the relationships among the control knobs and the internal energy. In addition, this would involve lower-layer thermal controllers, too. To prevent such heavy modelling and to save the separation among the control layers, the simplified model proposed in (3) is exploited and the following non-conventional approximated model predictive controller is derived

$$P^*_{c,i}(k) = \begin{cases} P_{t,i}(k) & if\ \bar{U}_b(k+1) > U(k+1|k)\ \textit{from (12)} \\ \bar{P}_{t,i}(k) & if\ \bar{U}_b(k+1) \le U(k+1|k)\ \textit{from (12)} \end{cases} \quad (13)$$

where $i = 2..16$ and $\bar{P}_{t,i}(k) = \bar{P}_{tot}(k)/15$ with,

$$\bar{P}_{tot}(k) = \frac{\bar{U}_b(k+1)-\bar{U}_b(k)}{T_{sP}} + \frac{T_{PCM}(k)-T_{AMB}(k)}{R_{PCM}} - P_{t,1}(k) \quad (14)$$

With such a solution, (12) is used to predict $U(k{+}1|k)$, while (14), directly derived discretizing (3), is adopted to compute the power references when $U(k{+}1|k)$ hits the bound $\bar{U}_b(k{+}1)$. Similarly to the lower layer thermal controller case, the bound $U_b(k)$ is replaced with $\bar{U}_b(k){<}U_b(k)$ to save some margin and to compensate for the approximations of the adopted models. Computations and simulations tests can be

carried out to derive a reliable bound $\bar{U}_b(k)$. For the considered benchmark, under 0.2-4s Guaranteed Re-sprinting requirement, $\bar{U}_b(k) = U_b(k) - 0.25J$. Details on such part are skipped, since this is not the main focus of this work.
Focusing on $\bar{P}_{t,i}(k)$, it can be shown with straightforward computations that, according to the definition of $U_b(k)$ in (6), $\bar{P}_{t,i}(k) = P_{c,idle}$ when $T_{AMB}(k) = T_{AMBmax}$, but it can be larger whenever $T_{AMB} < T_{AMBmax}$. This behavior has been already highlighted at the bottom of Fig. 4 and can be effectively exploited to improve sprinting performance.
It is worth noting that the proposed control approach is valid for every $U_b(\cdot)$, computed according to (6), and, then, for every N-M Guaranteed Re-sprinting request or even for more involved scenarios. Moreover, as already anticipated, this control layer can be easily and dynamically enabled/disabled according to the current re-sprinting requirement. Whenever no guaranteed re-sprinting is needed, the following power references will be simply set $P_{c,i}(k) = P_{t,i}(k)$ for $i = 2..16$ and only the lower layer will be active. Finally, the adopted sampling time for the considered benchmark is $T_{sP} = 10ms$.

4. RESULTS

We compare our solution, described in Section 3, with a Threshold-based solution as defined in [17], where each sprinting request is executed at maximum speed, until each core, but the #1, is forced to shutdown once the temperature reaches T_{max}. We have used Matlab/Simulink environment for simulations and the plant is the one described in Subsection 2.1.

Before showing the results it is worth to stress that, according to Section 2 and to simplify the discussion, the sprinting traces used in simulations are represented in terms of power. Constant workload instruction characteristics are assumed, then power consumption can be seen as proportional to the adopted frequency. In addition, those traces are assumed fixed, even though, in real reactive applications, the sprinting request trace is dynamically affected by the actual responsiveness of the device. This effect has been disregarded here to make the results easier to be interpreted.

Tests can be split into three macro groups. The first shows the behavior of our solution respect to the Threshold-based one when generic workload is applied and no guaranteed re-sprints are needed. In the second, critical periodic tasks are introduced to evaluate the performance of our solution when N-M Guaranteed Re-sprinting are required. Finally, to show the reliability of our solution, we applied non-nominal working conditions to the controlled system.

4.1 Generic workload

When no guaranteed re-sprints are needed the higher-layer controller (namely PCM Model predictive controller in Fig. 5) can be disabled. As consequence of that, only the lower-layer (namely thermal MPC in Fig. 5) is active and $P_{c,i} = P_{t,i}$. In Fig. 6 we compare the performance of our solution against the Threshold-based one when a sprint of 1s is requested every 2s. Differently from the threshold one, our solution is not purely on/off and is capable of finding an optimal intermediate operating mode (i.e. operating frequency and voltage, implying a particular core power consumption level) for each core, that maintains the cores temperatures close to the limit. This optimal value is inversely proportional to the ambient temperature. Indeed in

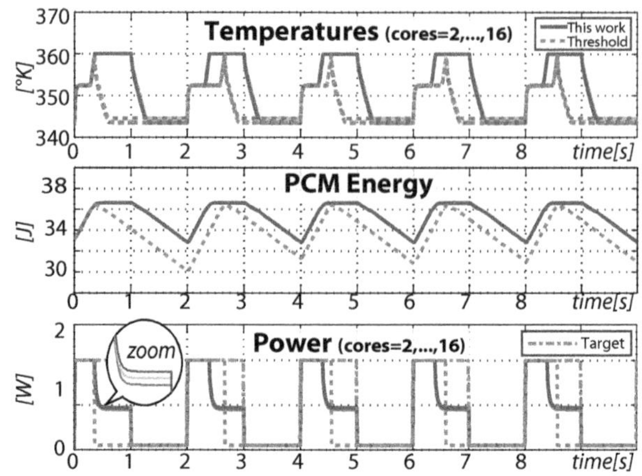

Figure 6: Typical non guaranteed trace response

	tasks Gaussian mean value			
	μ=1	μ=1.5	μ=2	μ=2.5
This work	97.4	93.4	91.8	81.0
Threshold	95.5	88.5	85.8	68.0

Figure 7: Non guaranteed performance comparison

a colder environment, the heat is dissipated to the ambient faster, allowing higher cores frequencies (power). Moreover, compared to [17] our distributed controller solution does not assume isothermal silicon temperature and thus can exploit the different core thermal dissipation efficiency[1] as shown in the zoomed area. Threshold-based solution puts all cores to idle (except #1) when any core first crosses T_{max}, our solution instead decreases frequency (power) independently for each core. From the same figure we can notice that our solution leads to a more regular sprinting duration profile, whereas for the threshold one it depends strongly on the previous sprint duration and in the internal energy level.

As consequence of that to quantify the improvement obtained with our solution we built 4 sprinting traces of 200s constituted by tasks with duration distributed with Gaussian probability (standard deviation 0.5 and mean value respectively 1s, 1.5s, 2s, 2.5s) and separated from each other with a rest time generated using a Poisson cumulative distribution function ($\lambda = 10$). The table in Fig. 7, collects the percentage of the total operating frequencies (computed integrating on time the operating frequencies of all cores) normalized with respect to the requested one: $\frac{\int \sum_i f_{c,i}(\tau)d\tau}{\int \sum_i f_{t,i}(\tau)d\tau} \cdot 100$; where $f_{c,i}$ and $f_{t,i}$ are the i-th controlled and target core frequencies respectively. Our solution outperforms the Threshold-based one reaching a 19% of improvements when tasks have mean value equal to 2.

4.2 Guaranteed re-sprints

As previously discussed when the system executes both critical and sporadic non-critical tasks a guaranteed re-sprint needs to be ensured. In the second set of tests we evaluated the performance of our solution comparing it to the state-of-the-art threshold one. Fig. 8 refers to a 0.2-4s Guaranteed Re-sprinting scenario and shows in order the tem-

[1]boundary cores are colder than the center one, since they have lower thermal resistance with the PCM layer

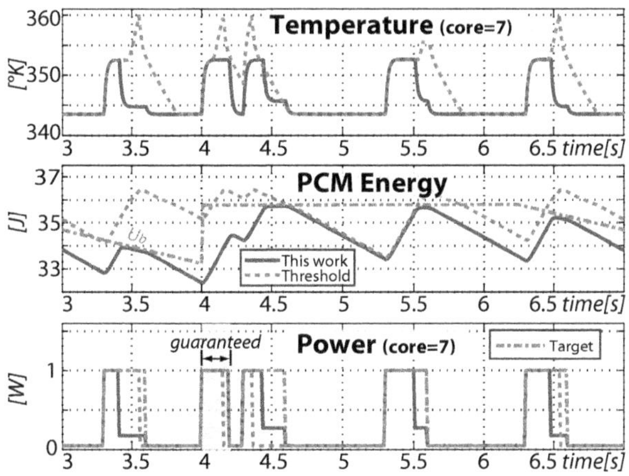

Figure 8: Typical guaranteed trace response

Guaranteed tasks mean value		% Guaranteed λ=3	λ=6	λ=9	λ=12	% Total λ=3	λ=6	λ=9	λ=12
μ=0.175	This work	100	100	100	100	74.2	76.8	75.6	76.1
	Threshold	94.4	82.4	76.2	70.6	76.6	80.6	80.2	80.7
μ=0.125	This work	100	100	100	100	76.4	77.0	78.3	77.9
	Threshold	98.3	91.4	82.9	79.9	79.0	81.2	83.1	83.0
μ=0.075	This work	100	100	100	100	78.0	80.5	79.4	81.7
	Threshold	99.9	98.9	95.1	92.8	80.4	84.4	84.4	86.7
μ=0.025	This work	100	100	100	100	83.0	80.8	83.4	82.6
	Threshold	100	100	99.6	99.2	84.9	84.3	87.6	87.3

(λ: Non guaranteed number of tasks)

Figure 9: Guaranteed performance comparison

perature, the PCM internal energy and the P_t and P_c of the core #7. In the top subplot we can first notice that Threshold-based solution runs the tasks until the temperatures reach the T_{max}, while in our solution, for a design decision (see Subsection 2.2), the PCM cannot cross T_{melt}, and then cores are actually bounded to a temperature a little bit lower than T_{max}. This gives an extra heat storage room to the Threshold-based controller but on the contrary leads to crisper thermal cycles. The internal energy of the system is shown in the central subplot. Whereas our solution keeps the energy below U_b, limiting non guaranteed tasks to have enough energy to run the hard real-time task at time 4s, the Threshold-based solution is not so far-seeing. In fact, it cannot ensure a predefined internal energy level at the beginning of a guaranteed task. This leads to an unpredictable and variable duration of the guaranteed sprint phase, that strongly depends on the previous sporadic computation.

To quantify the benefit of our approach in a realistic scenario we performed a set of tests under different stochastic workloads. Fig. 9 shows the results. In these tests, the guaranteed tasks duration is determined using a uniform probability distribution function, while the non guaranteed total tasks duration (1.4s) of each period (4s) has been split into a number of equal parts dependent on a Poisson probability distribution function. Each part constitutes the mean value of a Gaussian distribution with standard deviation $0.3/\#tasks$. Each trace differs from the other for the characteristic number λ of the Poisson function and the mean value of the uniform distribution. The ambient temperature is set to $25\,°C$ and the metrics used to evaluate the performance are $\frac{\int \sum_i f_{c,i}(\tau)d\tau}{\int \sum_i f_{t,i}(\tau)d\tau} \cdot 100$ and $\frac{\int \sum_i f^G_{c,i}(\tau)d\tau}{\int \sum_i f^G_{t,i}(\tau)d\tau} \cdot 100$, called respectively $\%Total$ and $\%Guaranteed$ in Fig. 9, where $f^G_{c,i}$ and $f^G_{t,i}$ differently from the previously defined total controlled and target frequencies of the i-th core ($f_{c,i}$ and $f_{t,i}$ respectively) are assumed not zero only in guaranteed windows. This two metrics are proportional to the effective throughput. As it is clear from the table our solution guarantees the execution of all hard real-time tasks, whereas the Threshold-based does not. From the same figure we can notice that the operating frequency percentage is slightly higher for the Threshold-based approach. This was expected since our solution does not exploit the core temperature up to T_{max} and because of the hard constraint U_b, adopted in our solution to preserve guaranteed re-sprinting room.

In Fig. 10 we repeat the previous tests by considering a

Guaranteed tasks mean value		% Guaranteed λ=3	λ=6	λ=9	λ=12	% Total λ=3	λ=6	λ=9	λ=12
μ=0.175	This work	100	100	100	100	74.2	76.8	75.6	76.1
	Threshold	92.9	79.4	73.7	68.8	74.4	77.0	75.8	76.4
μ=0.125	This work	100	100	100	100	76.4	77.0	78.3	77.9
	Threshold	97.2	89.0	80.4	77.4	76.5	77.2	78.6	78.2
μ=0.075	This work	100	100	100	100	78.0	80.5	79.4	81.7
	Threshold	99.7	97.8	93.1	90.3	78.2	80.8	79.7	82.0
μ=0.025	This work	100	100	100	100	83.0	80.8	83.4	82.6
	Threshold	100	100	99.2	98.7	83.3	81.0	83.6	82.9

(λ: Non guaranteed number of tasks)

Figure 10: Guaranteed performance comparison ($T_{max} = T_{melt}$)

Threshold-based solution which switches off the cores when the PCM shows $T_{PCM} > T_{melt}$. In this way we remove the advantage for such solution in exploiting the cores up to T_{max}. In this case, the performance loss of our solution for total operating frequency is below the 0.3% (see Fig. 10). This is the actual cost of guaranteed re-sprinting rooms.

4.3 Non-nominal conditions

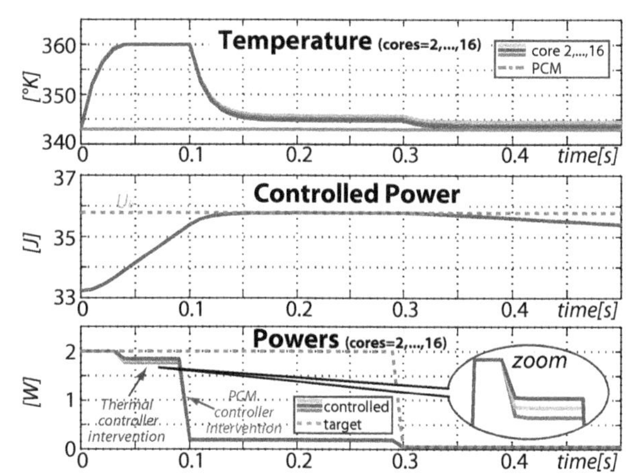

Figure 11: Non-nominal workload system response

Finally, we have tested our solution with non-nominal working conditions with mixed-criticality workload. Since a well suited chip thermal design should prevent critical temperatures when nominal operating frequencies are provided, we set the ambient temperature to $40\,°C$ (i.e. "phone on the beach") and we increased the power consumption of each core (i.e. $2W$ per core instead of $1W$). This emulates a possible leakage power increase due to higher ambient temperatures, aging and process variation. As shown in Fig.11 cores thermal controllers must intervene to reduce power. Power reduction is different from each core and optimized to maximize performance maintaining the temperature close to T_{max}.

5. CONCLUSION

In this paper, we have presented a novel thermal controller infrastructure for efficiently managing at run-time the heat buffer and the run-time temperature of computational sprinting architectures. This novel controller enables the system to optimally managing at run-time the sprint phase and the rest phase duration to ensure a well defined sprinting rate and QoS.

We first introduce the re-sprinting problem in mobile system where workload with heterogeneous QoS requirements coexist and we described a methodology to turn a specified N-M Guaranteed Re-sprinting rate into a time-varing bound for the PCM internal energy. We then present a novel thermal controller architecture that can exploit these information to control at run-time the sprint and the restore phase duration. This is based on a model predictive and hierarchical approach.

The presented new controller topology enables to maximize, with low-overhead, the sprint efficiency both when mix-critical and generic workload are executed. In both of the situations, the presented controller solution outperforms state-of-the-art thermal controller for computational sprinting: it is the only one capable to ensures the 100% of guaranteed re-sprints and extends the sprints duration up to the 20% when no guaranteed re-sprints are required. The presented solution allows the higher software layers to specify the safe-resprint requirements according to the user needs, ensures them effectively and, last but not least, *"does not burn your mobile!"*

6. ACKNOWLEDGMENTS

This work was supported, in parts, by the EU FP7 ERC Project MULTITHERMAN (GA n. 291125) and the EU FP7 Project Therminator (GA n. 248603). Technical support from Intel Labs. Braunschweig is also acknowledged.

7. REFERENCES

[1] S. Borkar Design challenges of technology scaling. *IEEE Micro*, vol. 19, no. 4, pp. 23–29, 1999.

[2] K. Asanovic et al., The landscape of parallel computing research: a view from Berkeley, *Technical Report UCB/EECS-2006-183*, EECS Department, University of California, Berkeley, December 2006.

[3] A. Bartolini, M. Cacciari, A. Tilli, and L. Benini. A distributed and self-calibrating model-predictive controller for energy and thermal management of high-performance multicores. *Proc. of DATE*, 2011.

[4] A. Bartolini, M. Cacciari, A. Tilli, and L. Benini. "Thermal and energy management of high-performance multicores: Distributed and self-calibrating model-predictive controller", *IEEE T. Parall.Distr.*, PP(99):1, 2012.

[5] J. Benson. Thermal characterization of packaged semiconductor devices, 2002.

[6] J. Charles et al. Evaluation of the Intel Core i7 Turbo Boost feature. *Proc. of IISWC*, 2009.

[7] J. Clemons, H. Zhu, S. Savarese, and T. Austin. Mevbench: A mobile computer vision benchmarking suite. *Proc. of IISWC*, pages 91 –102, nov. 2011.

[8] H. Esmaeilzadeh, E. Blem, R. St. Amant, K. Sankaralingam, and D. Burger. Dark silicon and the end of multicore scaling. *SIGARCH Comput. Archit. News*, 39(3):365–376, June 2011.

[9] J. Howard et al. A 48-Core IA-32 message-passing processor with DVFS in 45nm CMOS. *Proc. of ISSCC*, pages 108–109, Feb. 2010.

[10] W. Huang, S. Ghosh, and S. Velusamy. HotSpot: A compact thermal modeling methodology for early-stage VLSI design. *IEEE Trans. on VLSI*, 14(5):501–513, 2006.

[11] B. Kang and G. Ceder. Battery materials for ultrafast charging and discharging. *Nature*, 458(7235):190–193, Mar. 2009.

[12] S. Li et al. Mcpat: an integrated power, area, and timing modeling framework for multicore and manycore architectures. *Proc. of MICRO 42*, pages 469–480, 2009.

[13] Z. Luo, H. Cho, X. Luo, and K. il Cho. System thermal analysis for mobile phone. *Applied Thermal Engineering*, 28(14Ű15):1889 – 1895, 2008.

[14] A. Marongiu and L. Benini. An openmp compiler for efficient use of distributed scratchpad memory in mpsocs. *Computers, IEEE Transactions on*, 61(2):222 –236, feb. 2012.

[15] A. Oulasvirta, S. Tamminen, V. Roto, and J. Kuorelahti. Interaction in 4-second bursts: the fragmented nature of attentional resources in mobile hci. *Proc. of CHI '05*, pages 919–928, 2005.

[16] A. Power. Data center thermal runaway. a review of cooling challenges in high density mission critical environments, 2007.

[17] A. Raghavan et al. Computational sprinting. *Proc. of HPCA*, Feb. 2012.

[18] Apple iMovie http://itunes.apple.com/en/app/-imovie/id377298193?mt=8

[19] iOnRoad http://www.ionroad.com/

[20] B. Gyselinckx, C. Van Hoof, J. Ryckaert, R.F. Yazicioglu, P. Fiorini and V. Leonov. Human++: autonomous wireless sensors for body area networks. *Proc. of CICC*, pages 13- 19, Sept. 2005

[21] J. Schindall. The charge of the ultracapacitors. *IEEE Spectrum*, 44(11):42 – 46, Jan. 2007.

[22] Climator. *www.climator.com.*

[23] A. Tilli and R. Diversi. A modular approach to dynamic modelling of heat exchangers in vapor compression cycles. *Proc. of IFAC*, Sept. 2011.

[24] N. Tolia, D. Andersen, and M. Satyanarayanan. Quantifying interactive user experience on thin clients. *Computer*, 39(3):46 – 52, Mar. 2006.

[25] V. R. Voller, C. R. Swaminathan, and B. G. Thomas. Fixed grid techniques for phase change problems: A review. *International Journal for Numerical Methods in Engineering*, 30(4):875–898, 1990.

[26] K. Wonyoung, G. M.S., W. Gu-Yeon, and D. Brooks. System level analysis of fast, per-core dvfs using on-chip switching regulators. *Proc. of HPCA*, pages 123–134, feb. 2008.

[27] R. Yavatkar and M. Tirumala. Platform wide innovations to overcome thermal challenges. *Microelectronics Journal*, 39(7):930 – 941, 2008.

[28] F. Zanini, D. Atienza, L. Benini, and G. De Micheli. Thermal-aware system-level modeling and management for multi-processor systems-on-chip. *Proc. of ISCAS*, pages 2481 –2484, may 2011.

[29] G. F. Franklin, J. D. Powell, M. L. Workman. Digital Control of Dynamic Systems. *Addison-Wesley*,1997.

Concurrent Architecture and Schedule Optimization of Time-triggered Automotive Systems

Martin Lukasiewycz
TUM CREATE
Singapore
martin.lukasiewycz@tum-create.edu.sg

Samarjit Chakraborty
TU Munich
Munich, Germany
samarjit.chakraborty@rcs.ei.tum.de

ABSTRACT

This paper presents a methodology for the concurrent optimization of the architecture and scheduling of upcoming synchronous time-triggered automotive systems. A fully synchronous time-triggered system is highly predictable and therefore the best candidate for safety and drive-by-wire functions with strict real-time constraints. While the architecture of these systems has to be optimized in terms of resource allocation, task mapping, and message routing by taking multiple conflicting objectives into account, the scheduling has to be carried out such that application deadlines are satisfied. In case of stringent real-time constraints, available approaches that treat architecture optimization and scheduling as separate problems become inapplicable as most architectures do not permit a feasible schedule. As a remedy, a novel and efficient approach based on conflict refinement is presented. For a given architecture, either a schedule might be obtained or a conflict refinement is performed to determine and exclude the architecture decision that prevents a feasible schedule. In this paper, an extended architecture model is presented and the scheduling and refinement approaches are given for time-triggered architectures based on the FlexRay protocol. This approach can be extended to other protocols and scenarios. A case study of a realistic time-triggered system gives evidence of the efficiency of the proposed approach, solving a large design problem from the automotive domain.

Categories and Subject Descriptors

C.3 [**Special-purpose and application-based systems**]: Real-time and embedded systems

General Terms

Algorithms, Design

Keywords

Architectural Design Space Exploration, Synchronous Scheduling, Conflict Refinement

This publication is made possible by the Singapore National Research Foundation under its Campus for Research Excellence And Technological Enterprise (CREATE) programme.

1. INTRODUCTION

Modern automotive systems consist of dozens of Electronic Control Units (ECUs) interconnected by a set of different buses. With a growing degree of freedom introduced by software component concepts like AUTomotive Open System ARchitecture (AUTOSAR) [1], the optimization of these automotive systems becomes a challenging task due to the very large design space. Often multiple conflicting objectives have to be considered like monetary costs, reliability, or energy consumption. The goal of the architectural optimization is the determination of the resource allocation and configuration, task mapping, and message routing for the entire system. Finally, an appropriate scheduling has to be applied such that each application satisfies its stringent deadline constraints.

Since the first broad introduction of automotive electronics in the 1980s, many automotive systems are based on event-triggered systems. These systems are using priority-based operating systems like OSEK [17] and the priority-based Control Area Network (CAN) bus [2] for the communication. Event-triggered systems have the advantage of being very flexible and easily extensible with the goal of a very high utilization. This is a reasonable approach in case the computational power is a restrictive factor and the number of functions that require very short execution and communication latencies is low. In case functions have stringent latency and jitter constraints, these systems require often a complex validation of end-to-end timing behavior using tools like Symbolic Timing Analysis for Systems (SymTA/S) [20] or Modular Performance Analysis (MPA) [3]. This is becoming a challenging design task and often leads to high over-approximations which are not acceptable.

With a growing number of passive and active safety functions in the automotive domain as well as the introduction of drive-by-wire functions for electric vehicles, predictability of the entire system becomes a major design goal. Therefore, the design paradigm in the automotive domain is changing towards synchronous time-triggered systems. The main component for such a system is a communication bus like FlexRay [7] or Precision Time Protocol (PTP) Ethernet [21] that allows a synchronization of the ECUs. Additionally, the ECUs require a time-triggered operating system that is either non-preemptive using for instance eCos [5] or preemptive using operating systems like OSEKtime [17]. These time-triggered systems enable the design of predictable systems with guaranteed end-to-end latencies. Thus, very short end-to-end latencies can be achieved with no jitter. This enables the design of very robust applications and control func-

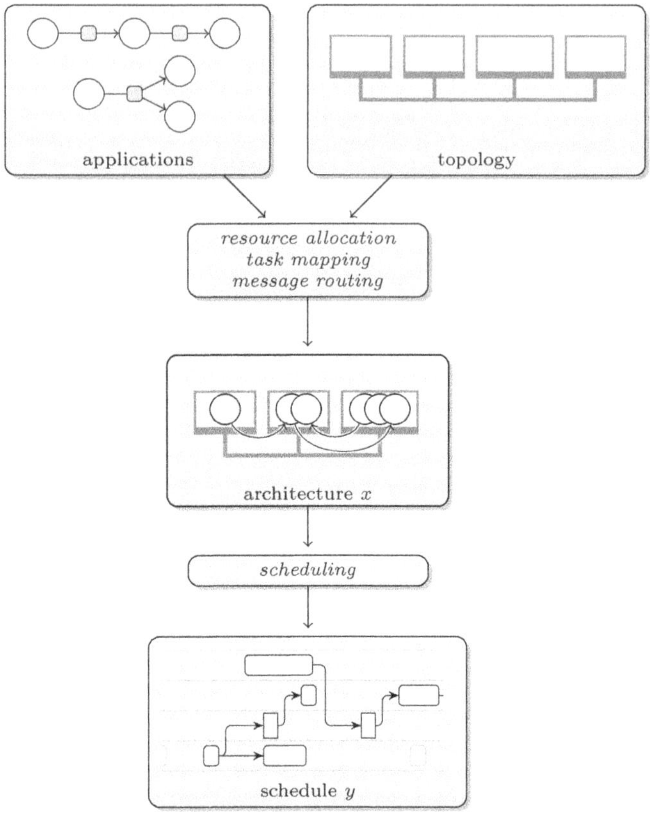

Figure 1: Y-chart approach for the design of time-triggered automotive systems. An architecture x is obtained from the mapping of the applications to a topology of hardware resources. In a second step, a scheduling has to be performed to obtain a schedule y.

tions without any oversampling which is often necessary for event-triggered systems. Besides a significant reduction of the computational demands, this enables the implementation of functions with stringent real-time constraints.

In order to enable a full optimization of time-triggered systems at system-level, both the architecture optimization and scheduling have to be performed. A general y-chart approach is illustrated in Figure 1. Here, first an architectural exploration is carried out that maps the applications to a hardware topology, followed by a scheduling that determines a feasible schedule. In particular for time-triggered systems, the scheduling is a complex design task that has to determine offset times for processes on ECUs and appropriate bus schedules. For complex systems not every architecture permits a feasible schedule. Therefore, a concurrent optimization of the architecture and scheduling becomes necessary. In this paper, this methodology is presented for the first time to perform this complex optimization efficiently within a proposed framework.

Contributions of the paper. This paper proposes a methodology for the optimization of time-triggered automotive systems, taking architecture and scheduling decisions *concurrently* into account. To cope with the inherent problem complexity, the architecture optimization and schedule determination are separated into two coupled tasks. In case no feasible schedule exists for a given architecture, a conflict refinement [9, 16] and justification deduction are performed. This approach effectively prunes the search space and enables an efficient optimization, considering multiple objectives. In case the objectives are linear, an iterative optimization is performed until the optimal system architectures with feasible schedules are obtained. In case at least one objective is non-linear, an iterative heuristic approach is suggested to enable an efficient optimization. In this paper, the methodology is applied to time-triggered systems in the automotive domain that are based on the FlexRay [7] protocol. The methodology might be extended to support other protocols and might be also applied in other domains like avionics or automation technology.

Besides the novel approach to use conflict refinement for concurrent architecture and scheduling optimization, the contributions are the following:

- An extended architecture model is presented that takes resource configuration, resource utilization, and path delays concurrently into account. This enables a very efficient exploration by pruning already a large fraction of the search space.
- For the scheduling, an Integer Linear Programming (ILP) formulation is defined to determine the FlexRay bus scheduling and offsets for the non-preemptive task scheduling on an eCos-based [5] operating system. Here, a hierarchical approach for each cluster of applications is proposed that significantly improves the scalability of the synchronous scheduling.
- A group-based conflict refinement strategy is proposed that takes domain knowledge of the architecture model into account. This enables a very efficient determination of architecture decisions which prevent a feasible schedule.

Finally, the methodology is applied to a large case study from the automotive domain. A realistic case study of an automotive subsystem is presented to give evidence of the efficient multi-objective optimization in terms of RAM size and flash memory size of program code.

Organization of the paper. The remainder of the paper is organized as follows: Section 2 discusses related work. Section 3 introduces the optimization scheme, using conflict refinement. In Section 4, the architecture model is presented and extended by additional constraints to restrict the search space. In Section 5, the scheduling model for time-triggered systems and a hierarchal scheduling approach are proposed. Moreover, a justification scheme and a problem-specific group-based refinement strategy are presented. Section 6 presents experimental results, before the paper is concluded in Section 7.

2. RELATED WORK

In embedded system design, many optimization problems are highly complex such that multi-step optimization approaches are applied, see [8, 15]. In a combined architecture and scheduling optimization, first an optimal architecture is obtained followed by a scheduling. For the event-triggered scheduling, heuristic strategies for priority optimization [11] and exact approaches for period optimization [4] exist. For time-triggered systems, a synchronous scheduling [22] of all components has to be obtained which might be a very complex design task. In case a feasible schedule cannot be obtained, a different architecture has to be found, making the optimization approach very time-consuming and unpredictable if stringent real-time constraints are existent. In [18, 19], a strategy is proposed that combines the architecture and scheduling model for event-triggered systems by a pruning approach based on SMT solvers. This approach finds a feasible system if one exists, but is not used for the optimization in terms of system objectives. Moreover, it is restricted to event-triggered systems which can be expressed by a binary formulation. In contrast, the proposed approach in this paper is flexible in terms of the scheduling and is highly scalable by separating the optimization problems into coupled tasks using a conflict refinement feedback. Thus, a time-triggered scheduling within an architectural optimization becomes efficiently applicable for the first time.

The proposed work is based on previous work in [14] and [13]. The work in [14] presents the basic model for the architecture exploration. In the work at hand, this model is appropriately adapted and extended by additional configuration constraints, utilization constraints, and path delay constraints that help to prune a large fraction of the search space. The work in [13] presents a basic scheduling framework for time-triggered automotive systems. In this paper, it is extended by a proposed hierarchical scheduling scheme to improve the scalability significantly. Moreover, a problem-specific conflict refinement and justification deduction for the scheduling are introduced to enable the concurrent architecture and scheduling optimization.

3. OPTIMIZATION SCHEME

In the following, the optimization problem for systems that require a concurrent architectural optimization and scheduling is defined. An efficient optimization flow that separates the architecture optimization and scheduling with an appropriate feedback method is proposed. This optimization is using conflict refinement which constitutes a novel approach for multi-layered design space exploration problems that consider the architecture and scheduling concurrently.

3.1 Problem Definition

The concurrent optimization of the architecture and scheduling is a challenging *design space exploration* task. While the architectural optimization comprises the optimization of the resource allocation and configuration, task mapping, and message routing, the scheduling has to be performed such that all applications fulfill their end-to-end latency constraints. For time-triggered systems, the scheduling is defined by process task offsets and appropriate bus schedules. The determination of these offsets and schedules is a complex design task due to the large search space.

The design space exploration task is formulated as the following multi-objective optimization problem:

DEFINITION 1 (DESIGN SPACE EXPLORATION).
optimize $f(x)$
subject to:
x is a feasible *architecture*
there exists a feasible *schedule* y for *architecture* x

In real-world problems, the objective function f consists of multiple functions (sometimes also including non-linear calculations). In general, the principal design objectives depend on the architecture x while the schedule y has to be determined such that all deadline constraints are fulfilled. The proposed optimization scheme in this paper allows a primary optimization of the objectives f in terms of the architecture x and for each x a secondary optimization of the schedule y in terms of a single objective like the minimization of the end-to-end application latencies or the minimization of used communication slots.

3.2 Optimization Flow

The proposed optimization scheme is based on the separation of the architecture optimization problem C and scheduling problem C_x for each architecture x. An efficient feedback between the scheduling and architecture optimization is incorporated by using *conflict refinement* and *justification deduction* when no feasible schedule exists for a given architecture x. This avoids the formulation of a large common optimization problem that comprises both the architecture and scheduling problem which becomes too complex to be solved efficiently.

The proposed optimization flow is illustrated in Figure 2. First, an architecture x is determined from an architecture specification that is formulated as a set of constraints C. If no feasible architecture x exists (denoted as $\forall x : x \nvDash C$)[1], the optimization is stopped, otherwise the optimization is continued. Based on a feasible architecture x (denoted as $x \vDash C$), a scheduling problem C_x is defined that is specifically formulated for the architecture x. The scheduling problem C_x is used to determine a schedule y.

In case no feasible schedule y exists (denoted as $\forall y : y \nvDash C_x$), a conflict refinement on C_x is carried out to determine the reason for the conflict, i.e., a subset of constraints $\tilde{C}_x \subseteq C_x$. This reduced set of constraints $\tilde{C}_x$ is known as Irreducible Infeasible Subsets (IIS) [9] or Minimally Unsatisfiable Subformula (MUS) [16], respectively. For all $\tilde{c} \in \tilde{C}_x$ the reduced set of constraints $\tilde{C}_x \backslash \{\tilde{c}\}$ is satisfiable while $\tilde{C}_x$ is unsatisfiable. A conflict refinement might be done using several techniques, see [9, 16], and is part of each modern ILP solver [10].

Based on $\tilde{C}_x$, a justification c (an additional constraint) for the architecture constraints C is determined and added to the architecture model. The justification ensures that the architecture x as well as all other architectures that contain the design decisions that prohibit a feasible schedule are pruned in the ongoing optimization. Since the conflict refinement finds a minimal reason for the deadline violation in the scheduling model C_x, often a large part of the search space C might be pruned by adding the constraint c.

In case a feasible architecture x and a feasible schedule y are found, an appropriate optimization strategy is carried out. Note that determining the schedule y can also be defined as an optimization problem such that for a given architecture x the optimal schedule y is determined. If the optimization problem is linear, i.e., all objective functions are linear, an exclusion of all sub-optimal solutions is done as follows:

$$C = C \cup \bigcup_i (f_i(x) < v_i + M \cdot \mathbf{z_i}) \cup \sum_i (\mathbf{z_i} \leq n - 1) \quad (1)$$

This additional constraint ensures that dominated solutions are excluded from the search space. Here, v_i is the

[1] $x \vDash C$ is read as x *satisfies* C. $x \nvDash C$ is read as x *does not satisfy* C.

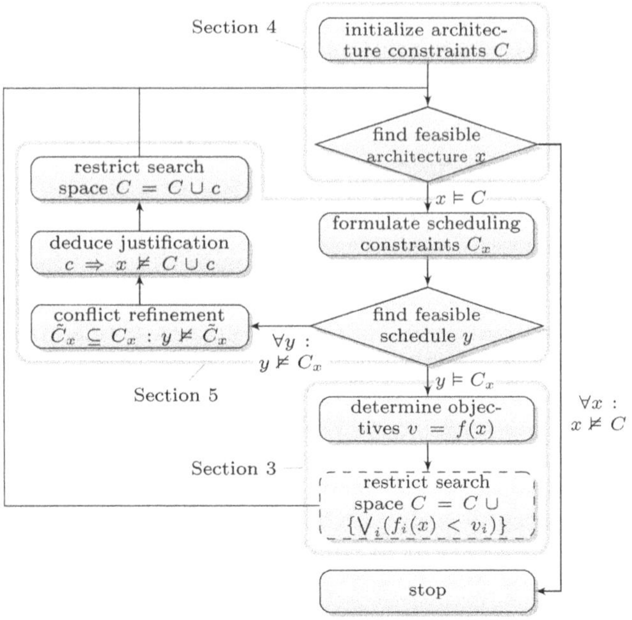

Figure 2: The proposed optimization flow. An architecture x and schedule y are determined separately. In case a feasible schedule y exists, an optimization is performed. Otherwise a conflict refinement is carried out and the search space for the architecture is efficiently pruned. The figure denotes in which sections the specific parts of the optimization flow are discussed in this paper.

objective value of the current objective value determined by f_i for an architecture x. The switch variables $\mathbf{z_i}$ ensure that at least one of n objectives is better than the value of the current obtained architecture x. Here, the constant M represents a very large number such that all constraints except one might be relaxed.

In case the problem is non-linear, a heuristic search as presented in [12] might be applied to optimize the architecture x. This is achieved by an appropriate randomized variation of x, guided by a heuristic to optimize multiple objectives.

4. ARCHITECTURE MODEL

In the following, the model for the architecture exploration and an encoding of the architecture constraints C are presented. First, the exploration model is introduced and the basic constraints are presented. In order to enable different configuration of ECUs, additional configuration parameters are introduced. Moreover, to exclude a large fraction of architectures that do not permit a feasible schedule from the search space, additional utilization constraints and path delay constraints are proposed.

4.1 Exploration Model

The architectural exploration is defined by a *specification*, consisting of a set of *applications* and the target *topology*. From this specification, an architecture x is defined by the allocation of target resources, mapping of process tasks, and routing of messages. An example of a specification and architecture x is given in Figure 3.

In the following, the exploration model is defined formally. The specification consists of a *topology graph* G_R and an *application graph* G_T :

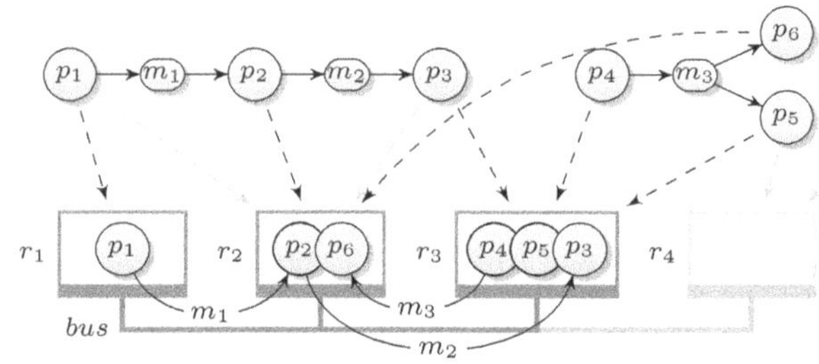

Figure 3: Illustration of a architecture specification and one possible architecture implementation. In the implementation, two applications are mapped to a topology with three allocated ECUs.

- The topology graph $G_R(R, E_R)$ consists of a set of resources R such as ECUs, buses, or gateways. The undirected edges E_R indicate that two resources are connected, i.e., a communication is possible.
- The application graph $G_T(T, E_T)$ is a directed acyclic graph and consists of a set of tasks $T = T_p \cup T_m$ which are either processes (T_p) or messages (T_m). The directed edges in E_T depict data-dependencies, i.e., sending of messages or receiving of messages, respectively. For each $t \in T$, the resources $R_t \subseteq R$ define the possible target resources of task t, i.e., where t might be mapped to or routed, respectively.

Given the exploration model, an architecture x is defined by the allocation of resources in the topology graph and the mapping of the application graph by an appropriate selection of target resources for each task:

- The allocation is an induced subgraph $G_R^x \subseteq G_R$ that consists of all resources that are used in the architecture implementation.
- The application graph is mapped to the allocated resources as follows: Each process task $t \in T_p$ is mapped to exactly one resource $R_t^x \in R_t$. Each message $t \in T_m$ is mapped to a routing tree on the set of allocated resources $R_t^x \subseteq R_t$. The mapping of processes and routing of messages has to be carried out such that all data-dependencies are satisfied, i.e., sent messages start at the resource of the sending task and received messages pass the resource of the receiving tasks, respectively.

4.2 Encoding C

Basic constraints. In the following, a set of linear constraints C is defined such that a solution $x \vDash C$ corresponds to a *feasible* architecture, i.e, the allocation of resources, the mapping of processes, and the routing of messages fulfill the data-dependencies. The symbolic encoding comprises the following binary variables:

- $\mathbf{r} \in \{0, 1\}$ - 1 if resource $r \in R$ is allocated, 0 otherwise
- $\mathbf{t_r} \in \{0, 1\}$ - 1 if task $t \in T$ and is mapped to resource $r \in R_t$, 0 otherwise
- $\mathbf{t_{r,n}} \in \{0, 1\}$ - 1 if message $t \in T_m$ is routed on resource $r \in R_t$ in communication step $n \in \mathbb{N}$, 0 otherwise

The linear constraints are formulated as follows:
$\forall t \in T_p$:

$$\sum_{r \in R_p} \mathbf{t_r} = 1 \qquad (2)$$

$\forall t \in T_m$:

$$\sum_{r \in R_t} \mathbf{t_{r,o}} = 1 \tag{3}$$

$\forall t \in T_m, \tilde{t}$ with $(\tilde{t}, t) \in E_T, r \in R_t$:

$$\mathbf{t_r} - \mathbf{\tilde{t}_{r,o}} = 0 \tag{4}$$

$\forall t \in T_p, \tilde{t}$ with $(\tilde{t}, t) \in E_T, r \in R_t$:

$$\mathbf{\tilde{t}_r} - \mathbf{t_r} \geq 0 \tag{5}$$

$\forall t \in T_m, r \in R_t$:

$$\sum_{i=1}^{n} \mathbf{t_{r,i}} \leq 1 \tag{6}$$

$$\sum_{i=1}^{n} \mathbf{t_{r,i}} - \mathbf{t_r} \geq 0 \tag{7}$$

$\forall t \in T_m, r \in R_t, i = \{1, ..., n\}$:

$$\mathbf{t_r} - \mathbf{t_{r,i}} \geq 0 \tag{8}$$

$\forall t \in T_m, r \in R_t, i = \{1, ..., n-1\}$:

$$-\mathbf{t_{r,i+1}} + \sum_{\tilde{r} \in R_t \wedge e = (\tilde{r}, r) \in E_R} \mathbf{t_{\tilde{r},i}} \geq 0 \tag{9}$$

$\forall t \in T, r \in R_t$:

$$\mathbf{r} - \mathbf{t_r} \geq 0 \tag{10}$$

$\forall r \in R$:

$$-\mathbf{r} + \sum_{t \in T \wedge r \in R_t} \mathbf{t_r} \geq 0 \tag{11}$$

Constraint (2) ensures that each process task is mapped to exactly one resource. Constraints (3) and (4) imply that each message has exactly one source that equals the used resource of the preceding process. Analogously for each process, the received messages have to be routed on the corresponding resources as stated in Constraint (5). Constraint (6) ensures that a message can pass a resource at most once such that no routing cycles exist. A message has to be existent in one communication step on a resource in order to be correctly routed on this resource as implied by Constraints (7) and (8). Constraint (9) states that a communication is only possible between adjacent resources. Constraint (10) implies that a process or message, respectively, is mapped or routed on an allocated resource only. On the other hand, Constraint (11) states that a resource is only allocated if at least one task is mapped or routed on this resource.

Configuration constraints. The architecture exploration might be extended by additional parameters. In our experimental results, the resources can have different configurations (V_r) in terms of available flash memory and RAM. For this purpose, binary variables $\mathbf{r_v} \in \{0, 1\}$ are introduced to indicate whether resource r is in configuration $v \in V_r$. Additionally, a load function l and capacity function c for each dimension is defined. Here, $l : T \times R \to \mathbb{R}$ defines the load that is generated by task t on resource r and $c : R \times V_r \to \mathbb{R}$ defines the capacity of the resource r in configuration v.
$\forall r \in R$:

$$\sum_{t \in T} l(t, r) \cdot \mathbf{t_r} \leq \sum_{v \in V_r} c(r, v) \cdot \mathbf{r_v} \tag{12}$$

$$\sum_{v \in V_r} \mathbf{r_v} = 1 \tag{13}$$

Constraint (12) defines the capacity constraint. Constraint (13) states that each resource is in exactly one configuration state.

Utilization constraints. In order to avoid unsatisfiable schedules if the load on a resource is above 1, the following constraint is added:
$\forall r \in R$:

$$\sum_{t \in T} \frac{e_t(r)}{h_t} \cdot \mathbf{t_r} \leq 1 \tag{14}$$

This constraint ensures that the sum of processing load from each process t on a resource r is below 1. Here, $e_t(r)$ is the worst-case execution time of task t on resource r and h_t is the period of task t.

Path delay constraints. It is further necessary to exclude those architectures where the execution time of tasks along a path $\pi \in \Pi$ in the application graph G_T exceeds the deadline $\tau_\pi \in \mathbb{R}$. Since the introduced model allows multi-cast communication, a consideration of each separate communication path becomes necessary. For this purpose, the introduction of the following additional variables is required:

- $\mathbf{t_r^{\tilde{t}}} \in \{0, 1\}$ - 1 if message $t \in T_m$ and is routed to the task $\tilde{t} \in T_p$ over the resource $r \in R_t$, 0 otherwise
- $\mathbf{t_{r,n}^{\tilde{t}}} \in \{0, 1\}$ - 1 if message $t \in T_m$ is routed to the task $\tilde{t} \in T_p$ on resource $r \in R_t$ in communication step $n \in \mathbb{N}$, 0 otherwise

The constraints are defined as follows:
$\forall t \in T_m, (t, \tilde{t}) \in E_T, r \in R_t$:

$$\mathbf{t_{r,o}} = \mathbf{t_{r,o}^{\tilde{t}}} \tag{15}$$

$\forall t \in T_m, (t, \tilde{t}) \in E_T, i = \{1, ..., n\}$:

$$\sum_{r \in R_t} \mathbf{t_{r,i}^{\tilde{t}}} \leq 1 \tag{16}$$

$\forall t \in T_m, (t, \tilde{t}) \in E_T, r \in R_t, i = \{1, ..., n\}$:

$$\mathbf{t_r^{\tilde{t}}} - \mathbf{t_{r,i}^{\tilde{t}}} \geq 0 \tag{17}$$

$$\mathbf{t_{r,i}} - \mathbf{t_{r,i}^{\tilde{t}}} \geq 0 \tag{18}$$

$\forall t \in T_m, (t, \tilde{t}) \in E_T, r \in R_t, i = \{1, ..., n-1\}$:

$$\sum_{\tilde{r} \in R_t, (r, \tilde{r}) \in E_R} \mathbf{t_{\tilde{r},i+1}^{\tilde{t}}} + \mathbf{\tilde{t}_r} - \mathbf{t_{r,i}^{\tilde{t}}} \geq 0 \tag{19}$$

The Constraints (15)-(19) define routing of messages $t \in T_m$ from the sender to a dedicated receiver task $t \in T_p$ by setting the $\mathbf{t_r^{\tilde{t}}}$ variables. Constraint (15) defines that each separate routing path starts at the same source resource as the routing of the corresponding message. Constraint (16) ensures that the routing path from t to $\tilde{t}$ is a path, i.e., not a tree. Here, a message is routed at most on one single resource at a communication step. Constraint (17) sets the $\mathbf{t_r^{\tilde{t}}}$ variables while Constraint (18) ensures that the separate routing paths are only mapped on the original routings of the messages. Constraint (19) states that a message is either forwarded to an adjacent resource or it is terminated at the target resource of the receiver task $\tilde{t}$.

With the additional variables, each path of the application is constrained as follows:

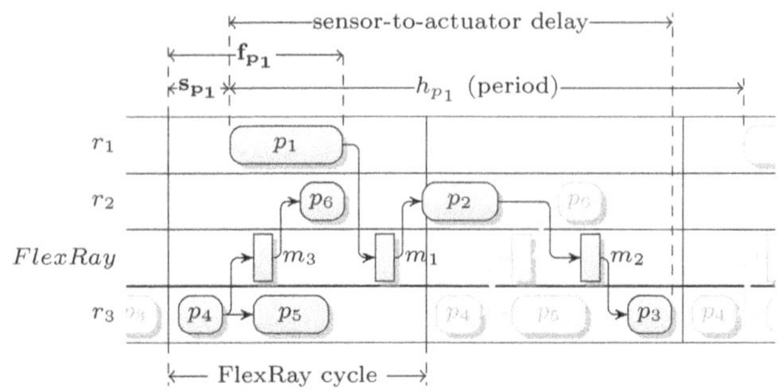

Figure 4: Illustration of a time-triggered schedule for the architecture in Figure 3. For each task, a start and finish time has to be defined. The tasks have to be executed with their period and end-to-end deadlines constraints have to be satisfied.

$\forall \pi \in \Pi$:

$$\sum_{t \in \pi \cap T_p, r \in R_t} e_t(r) \cdot \mathbf{t_r} + \sum_{(t,\tilde{t}) \in \pi, t \in T_m, r \in R_t} e_t(r) \cdot \mathbf{t_r^{\tilde{t}}} \leq \tau_\pi \quad (20)$$

Here, each process task in T_p and each message in T_m along the path π is considered. $e_t(r)$ is the execution time or transmission time, respectively, of a task t on the resource r. Thus, all architectures are excluded where the execution times along a path exceed the maximal delay.

5. SCHEDULING MODEL

In the following, the model for the scheduling is presented. Given an architecture x, the encoding of C_x is proposed for time-triggered systems using a synchronization via the FlexRay bus. Moreover, a hierarchical approach is proposed that improves the runtime of the conflict refinement. Finally, the justification deduction from a unsatisfiable scheduling problem is presented that prunes the infeasible search space of the architectural optimization problem. For this purpose, a fast conflict refinement strategy is proposed, using an elastic and deletion filter with domain knowledge to group the constraints that affect same tasks.

Many real-world applications have strict end-to-end timing delays. In this paper, it is assumed that each application and task $t \in T$ is executed with a fixed period $h_t \in \mathbb{R}$. Moreover, for each task t, a worst-case execution time e_t is given for the current task mapping. These upper bounds for execution times might be estimated using approaches like presented in [6]. A schedule has to be obtained that executes the tasks with the given period and satisfies all deadline constraints. The end-to-end timing constraints might be defined on each path $\pi \in \Pi$ in the application graph G_T by a deadline $\tau_\pi \in \mathbb{R}$.

5.1 Time-triggered Scheduling C_x

The time-triggered scheduling in this paper is assuming that all ECUs are using a non-preemptive operating system as well as the FlexRay static segment for the communication. The schedule y is determined by the offset/start time of each task in the system. For the architecture in Figure 3, an appropriate scheduling is illustrated in Figure 4.

For the determination of a feasible schedule y that considers all platform constraints, we propose an ILP formulation that determines the following variables:

- $\mathbf{s_t} \in \mathbb{R}_{[0,h_t]}$ - start time of task $t \in T$
- $\mathbf{f_t} \in \mathbb{R}_{[0,h_t]}$ - finish time of task $t \in T$

In the following the separate ILP formulation for the components are presented. First, the scheduling constraints of the ECUs using an eCos-based operating system without preemption are defined. The static segment of a FlexRay bus is used for the bus system. Finally, the end-to-end timing constraints are defined.

ECU Scheduling. The tasks on each ECU have to be scheduled in compliance with the used operating system scheduler. Here, the processes $T_r = \{t | r \in R_t^x, t \in T_p\}$ are scheduled on each ECU $r \in R$ where $r \in R_t^x$ determines the target resource for each process task in the architecture x.

The formulation for the eCos operating system requires the following additional variables:

- $\mathbf{of_t} \in \{0, 1\}$ - offset for finish time $t \in T_p$
- $\mathbf{y_{t,\tilde{t}}^{i,j}} \in \{0, 1\}$ - 1 if job i of task $t \in T_p$ finished before job j of task $\tilde{t} \in T_p$

The constraints are determined as follows:
$\forall t \in T_r$:

$$\mathbf{f_t} + h_t \cdot \mathbf{of_t} = \mathbf{s_t} + e_t \quad (21)$$

$\forall t, \tilde{t} \in T_r, t \neq \tilde{t}, i = \{0, .., \frac{2 \cdot H_r}{h_t} - 1\}, j = \{0, .., \frac{2 \cdot H_r}{h_{\tilde{t}}} - 1\}$:

$$i \cdot h_t + \mathbf{s_t} + e_t \leq j \cdot h_{\tilde{t}} + \mathbf{s_{\tilde{t}}} + 2 \cdot H_r \cdot (1 - \mathbf{y_{t,\tilde{t}}^{i,j}}) \quad (22)$$

$$j \cdot h_{\tilde{t}} + \mathbf{s_{\tilde{t}}} + e_{\tilde{t}} \leq i \cdot h_t + \mathbf{s_t} + 2 \cdot H_r \cdot \mathbf{y_{t,\tilde{t}}^{i,j}} \quad (23)$$

Constraint (21) determines the finish time of each task. In case the process finishes in the next cycle, the finish time is smaller than the start time. In this case, the variable $\mathbf{of_t}$ becomes 1 to fulfill Constraint (21). Constraints (22) and (23) ensure that two tasks never preempt each other within two hyper-periods ($2 \cdot H_r$ with $H_r = \underset{t \in T_r}{lcm}(h_t)$). The variable $\mathbf{y_{t,\tilde{t}}^{i,j}}$ is used for switching, i.e., one of the Constraints (22) or (23) is trivially satisfied depending on $\mathbf{y_{t,\tilde{t}}^{i,j}}$.

FlexRay Scheduling. The FlexRay bus is used as a central communication bus in the proposed architecture. This bus system enables a synchronization of the ECUs and, thus, a fully time-triggered system. For message scheduling, here the static segment of FlexRay is used. The static segment of FlexRay is organized in $n_{fx} \in \mathbb{N}$ static slots with each slot having a duration of $e_{fx} = e_t \in \mathbb{R}$ and available payload of $l_{fx} \in \mathbb{N}$ bytes. The static segment is transmitted in the beginning of each FlexRay cycle which has a duration of $h_{fx} \in \mathbb{R}$. A message is defined by the repetition that is deduced from the period $r_t = \frac{h_t}{h_{fx}} \in \mathbb{N}$, the execution time that equals the slot duration, and the size in bytes $l_t \in \mathbb{N}$.

For each message, a slot and base cycle have to be determined. From this value, the assignments of slots to ECUs is deduced implicitly. The slot and base cycle are encoded in the binary variable $[\mathbf{s}, \mathbf{b}]_\mathbf{t}$ such that the following variables are required:

- $[\mathbf{s}, \mathbf{b}]_\mathbf{t} \in \{0, 1\}$ - 1 if message $t \in T_m$ is sent in slot $s \in \{0, .., n_{fx} - 1\}$ at base cycle $b \in \{0, .., r_t - 1\}$, 0 otherwise
- $\mathbf{s_r} \in \{0, 1\}$ - becomes 1 if slot s is assigned to ECU r and 0 otherwise

These constraints are defined as follows:
$\forall t \in T_m$:

$$\sum_{s\in\{0,..,n_{fx}-1\}} \sum_{b\in\{0,..,r_t-1\}} [\mathbf{s},\mathbf{b}]_\mathbf{t} = 1 \quad (24)$$

$$\mathbf{s_t} = \sum_{s\in\{0,..,n_{fx}-1\}} \sum_{b\in\{0,..,r_t-1\}} (s \cdot e_{fx} + b \cdot h_{fx}) \cdot [\mathbf{s},\mathbf{b}]_\mathbf{t} \quad (25)$$

$$\mathbf{f_t} = \mathbf{s_t} + e_{fx} \quad (26)$$

$\forall s \in \{0, .., n_{fx} - 1\}, b \in \{0, .., \frac{\underset{t\in T_m}{lcm}(h_t)}{h_{fx}} - 1\}$:

$$\sum_{t\in T_m} l_t \cdot [\mathbf{s}, \mathbf{b}\%\mathbf{r_t}]_\mathbf{t} \leq l_{fx} \quad (27)$$

$\forall s \in \{0, .., n_{fx} - 1\}$:

$$\sum_{r\in R} \mathbf{s_r} \leq 1 \quad (28)$$

$\forall t \in T_m, s \in \{0, .., n_{fx} - 1\}, b \in \{0, .., r_t - 1\}, r \in R_t^x$:

$$[\mathbf{s},\mathbf{b}]_\mathbf{t} \leq \mathbf{s_r} \quad (29)$$

Constraint (24) states that each message is scheduled in exactly one slot at a specific base cycle. Constraint (25) determines the start time of a message transmission based on the slot and base cycle. Constraint (26) defines the finish time of a message transmission depending on the duration of the transmission of a static slot. Constraint (27) ensures that the capacity of a slot is not exceeded. Constraint (28) states that a slot can be assigned to at most one ECU. Constraint (29) ensures that if a message is sent in a specific slot, the slot is assigned to the sending ECU.

Sensor-to-Actuator Delay. The end-to-end delay is determined in an additive manner as follows. Along the paths, the delay is determined by the sum of the execution and transmission times, respectively, of all tasks as well as the waiting time between the data-dependent tasks, respectively. To constrain the end-to-end delay, the following variables are required:

- $\mathbf{w_{t,\tilde{t}}} \in \mathbb{R}_{[0,h_t]}$ - waiting time between the finish of $t \in T$ and start of $\tilde{t} \in T$
- $\mathbf{ow_{t,\tilde{t}}} \in \{0, 1\}$ - 0 if $t \in T$ starts before $\tilde{t} \in T$, 1 otherwise

The constraints are defined as follows:
$\forall \pi \in \Pi, (t, \tilde{t}) \in \pi$:

$$\mathbf{w_{t,\tilde{t}}} = \mathbf{s_{\tilde{t}}} - \mathbf{f_t} + h_t \cdot \mathbf{ow_{t,\tilde{t}}} \quad (30)$$

$\forall \pi \in \Pi$:

$$\tau_\pi \geq \sum_{t\in\pi} e_t + \sum_{(t,\tilde{t})\in\pi} \mathbf{w_{t,\tilde{t}}} \quad (31)$$

Constraint (30) determines the waiting time between data-dependent tasks. The binary variable $\mathbf{ow_{t,\tilde{t}}}$ ensures that the waiting time is always within the predefined bounds, i.e., not negative. Constraint (31) determines the end-to-end delay of a function. The end-to-end delay is defined as the maximal latency along all paths of a function.

5.2 Hierarchical Scheduling

To reduce the time to perform the scheduling, a hierarchical approach is proposed. Subproblems of the complete scheduling problem are solved iteratively to search for trivially unsatisfiable sub-formulas of C_x. For this purpose, domain knowledge is used as proposed in the following. If one of these subproblems is already unsatisfiable, the scheduling can be stopped and conflict refinement on the sub-formula can be performed more efficiently. The iterative search is defined as follows:

1. Schedule each ECU $r \in R$ separately.
2. Schedule each application (weakly connected component in the application graph G_T) separately.
3. Schedule each cluster (set of weakly connected components in the application graph G_T) separately.
4. Schedule the whole system.

A cluster $D \in \mathcal{D}$ defines a subset of tasks ($D \subseteq T$). For two clusters $D, \tilde{D} \in \mathcal{D}$, none of the process tasks from different clusters are mapped to the same ECU:

$$(\bigcup_{t\in D\cap T_p} R_t^x) \cap (\bigcup_{\tilde{t}\in \tilde{D}\cap T_p} R_{\tilde{t}}^x) = \{\} \quad (32)$$

Moreover, each cluster D defines a set of weakly connected components in the application graph G_T.

In order to minimize the time to obtain a schedule of a whole system, a combination of cluster schedules is proposed. This approach is applied if each cluster has a feasible schedule. By definition, the scheduling of each cluster on the ECUs does not influence the ECU scheduling in another cluster. Therefore, the task in combining cluster schedules is to find a feasible bus schedule. Each cluster D is using the the slots $S_D = \{s | t \in T_m, [\mathbf{s},\mathbf{b}]_\mathbf{t} = 1, s = \{0, .., n_{fx} - 1\}, b = \{0, .., r_t - 1\}\}$. In order to combine the schedules of all clusters, it has to be ensured that a slot is never used by two clusters. To avoid conflicting slots, the schedule of each cluster can be shifted by h_{fx}/e_{fx} steps of the size of one slot e_{fx}. Thus, if a schedule is shifted by i slots, the required slots are $S_{D,i} = \{(s + i)\%(h_{fx}/e_{fx}) | s \in S_D\}$. In the following, an ILP formulation is given that determines the shifting of each cluster that allows to combine cluster schedules. The ILP determines the binary offset variables:

- $\mathbf{o_{D,i}} \in \{0, 1\}$ - 1 if cluster D is scheduled with offset $i \cdot e_{fx}$, 0 otherwise

The constraints are formulated as follows:
$\forall D \in \mathcal{D}$:

$$\sum_{i=0}^{\frac{h_{fx}}{e_{fx}}-1} \mathbf{o_{D,i}} = 1 \quad (33)$$

$\forall D, \tilde{D} \in \mathcal{D}, i, j \in \{0, .., \frac{h_{fx}}{e_{fx}} - 1\}, S_{D,i} \cap S_{\tilde{D},j} \neq \{\}$:

$$\mathbf{o_{D,i}} + \mathbf{o_{\tilde{D},j}} \leq 1 \quad (34)$$

$\forall D \in \mathcal{D}, i \in \{0, .., \frac{h_{fx}}{e_{fx}} - 1\} \exists s \in S_{D,i} : s \geq n_{fx}$:

$$\mathbf{o_{D,i}} = 0 \quad (35)$$

Constraint (33) states that each cluster has exactly one offset. Constraint (34) ensures that offsets for two clusters are not possible if there is at least one common slot that would have to be equal for both clusters. Constraint (35) sets each offset to 0 for each cluster if a slot would not be mapped to the static segment which is in the beginning of the FlexRay cycle and has a duration of $n_{fx} \cdot e_{fx} \leq h_{fx}$.

5.3 Justification Deduction

Given an unsatisfiable scheduling formula C_x, a conflict refinement is applied to determine the subset $\tilde{C_x} \subseteq C_x$. Using the hierarchical approach, the set of unsatisfiable scheduling constraints from C_x might be already significantly minimized. From the reduced scheduling formula $\tilde{C_x}$, a justification c (an additional constraint) for the architectural optimization problem C has to be deduced. This is done by analyzing which tasks are part of $\tilde{C_x}$. The tasks that are considered are defined as

$$T_c = \{t | t \in T, \tilde{c} \in \tilde{C_x}, \mathbf{s_t} \in \tilde{c}\}. \qquad (36)$$

Thus, the additional constraint c that extends the architecture problem C is defined as follows:

$$\sum_{t \in T_c} \sum_{r \in R_t^x} (1 - \mathbf{t_r}) \geq 1 \qquad (37)$$

This constraint ensures that at least one mapping or routing decision that caused the conflict $\tilde{C_x}$ is changed in the ongoing architectural optimization.

5.4 Conflict Refinement

In general it is possible to use the default conflict refinement of a state-of-the-art ILP solver. However, we suggest to use a group-based approach to significantly speed-up the conflict refinement. In the following it is shown that a fine-grained conflict refinement over all constraints in C_x is not necessary to determine the smallest set T_c as defined in Equation (36).

In the following, it is outlined how to define the groups of constraints that will be used for the problem-specific conflict refinement. Let a function map define the mapping in Equation (36) such that $T_c = map(\tilde{C_x})$. For a given $\tilde{C_x}$, T_c is invariant to constraint $\tilde{c} \in \tilde{C_x}$ if $map(\tilde{C_x}) = map(\tilde{C_x} \backslash \{\tilde{c}\})$. This means that removing the constraint $\tilde{c}$ does not change the justification. A set of constraints C_t for each task $t \in T$ is defined as follows: It holds $\tilde{c} \in C_t$ if and only if $\mathbf{s_t} \in \tilde{c}$, i.e., each constraint $\tilde{c} \in C_t$ influences the starting time of task t. Let the groups be defined by $\mathcal{C}_T = \{C_t | t \in T\}$. It holds that $map(\tilde{C_x}) = \{t | C_t \in \mathcal{C}_T, C_t \cap \tilde{C_x} \neq \{\}\}$. Thus, it is sufficient to define the irreducible inconsistent set (IIS) over the groups $\mathcal{C}_T$ instead of over all constraints in C_x. Since the cardinality of the $\mathcal{C}_T$ is significantly smaller than the number of constraints in C_x, this reduces the complexity of the IIS determination.

In the following, an approach to determine the IIS based on the set of constraint groups $\mathcal{C}_T$ is proposed. First, a deletion filter is presented that is capable of determining this IIS in an iterative manner. In order to quickly reduce the set of relevant constraints, additionally an elastic filter is presented.

Deletion filter. The deletion filter removes iteratively sets of constraints, ensuring that the remaining constraint are still unsatisfiable. It is presented in Algorithm 1.

The algorithm starts with the initial assumption that the IIS are all constraints in C_x. The algorithms removes the groups of constraints that affect one task iteratively (line 2). If the reduced set of constraints remains unsatisfiable (line 3), the group of constraints is permanently removed from the irreducible set $\tilde{C_x}$ (line 4), otherwise the group is not removed from the IIS $\tilde{C_x}$.

Algorithm 1 Deletion filter for conflict refinement based on the set of constraint groups $\mathcal{C}_T$. Given a set of constraints C_x, the irreducible inconsistent set of constraints with respect to the groups $\mathcal{C}_T$ is defined as $\tilde{C_x}$.

1: $\tilde{C_x} = C_x$
2: **for** $C_t \in \mathcal{C}_T$ **do**
3:     **if** $\forall x : x \nvDash (\tilde{C_x} \backslash C_t)$ **then**
4:         $\tilde{C_x} = \tilde{C_x} \backslash C_t$
5:     **end if**
6: **end for**

In contrast to the IIS deletion approach known from literature that requires $|C_x|$ iterations, the proposed approach requires only $|T|$ iterations. In the proposed design space exploration, this approach significantly reduces the runtime since the number of tasks is much smaller than the number of constraints.

Elastic filter. The elastic filter quickly identifies a subset of constraints that is unsatisfiable. However, this subset does not have to be necessarily irreducible such that an additional application of the deletion filter becomes necessary afterwards. The elastic filter that considers the sets $\mathcal{C}_T$ is presented in Algorithm 2.

Algorithm 2 Elastic filter for conflict refinement based on the set of constraint groups $\mathcal{C}_T$. Given a set of constraints C_x, the irreducible inconsistent set of constraints with respect to the groups $\mathcal{C}_T$ is defined as $\tilde{C_x}$.

1: $C'_x = \{c' |$ create elastic constraint c' for $c \in C_x$
2:             with variable $\mathbf{e_c}\}$
3: **for** $t \in T, c \in C_t$ **do**
4:     $C'_x = C'_x \cup \{\mathbf{e_t} \geq \mathbf{e_c}\}$
5: **end for**
6: $T' = T$
7: **while** $\exists x : x \vDash C'_x$ **do**
8:     min $\sum_{t \in T'} \mathbf{e_t}$
9:     $T' = T' \backslash \{t | \mathbf{e_t} > 0\}$
10:     **for** $c \in C_x$ with $\forall C_t \cap \{c\} \neq \{\} : t \in T \backslash T'$ **do**
11:         $C'_x = C'_x \cup \{\mathbf{e_c} = 0\}$
12:     **end for**
13: **end while**
14: $\tilde{C_x} = C_x \backslash \bigcup_{t \in T'} C_t$

The conflict refinement based on an elastic filter requires to add an elastic variable $\mathbf{e_c}$ to each constraint c (line 1). Here, each linear constraint c is transformed to the form $g(x) \geq b$ and extended to $g(x) \geq b - \mathbf{e_c}$ with $\mathbf{e_c} \geq 0$. Thus, the constraint c is made elastic with the variable $\mathbf{e_c}$. In order to make equality-constraints elastic, they have to be converted to two corresponding $\geq$-constraints ($g(x) = b$ equals $g(x) \geq b$ and $-g(x) \geq -b$). In the next step (line 3), the elastic variables $\mathbf{e_c}$ are constrained by variables $\mathbf{e_t}$ which are defined for each $t \in T$ or $C_t \in \mathcal{C}_T$, respectively. The elastic constraints and the constraints for the bounds $\mathbf{e_t}$ are defined as C'_x. It is checked iteratively whether the constraints C'_x are satisfiable (line 7). If this is this case, a feasible solution is searched that minimizes the bounds $\mathbf{e_t}$ (line 8), i.e., a solution that tries to tighten as many elastic constraints as possible. In case the solution does require a variable $\mathbf{e_t}$ to be greater than 0, the corresponding tasks t are removed from

ECU	MHz	flash [kB] / RAM [kB]
MPC560xB (e200z0)	64	256/24, 384/28, 512/32, 768/64, 1024/80, 1536/96
MPC564xB (e200z4)	120	1536/128, 2048/160, 3072/192
MPC560xP (e200z0)	64	192/12, 256/20, 384/36, 512/40
S12XFxxx (S12(X))	50	128/16, 256/20, 384/24, 512/32
MPC560xS (e200z0)	64	256/24, 512/48, 1024/48
MPC5645S (e200z4)	125	2048/64
MPC564xF (e200z4)	150	2048/128, 3072/192, 4096/192
MPC567xF (e200z7)	200	3072/192, 4096/256

Table 1: Used ECUs for the experimental results. Each ECU might be configured with a specified flash memory size and RAM.

the set T' (line 9). In the following, all elastic variables $\mathbf{e_c}$ are set to 0 where the corresponding constraint c does only contain $\mathbf{s_t}$ variables for those tasks t that have been removed from T' (line 10-11). This ensures that these constraints are tightened in the next iteration. This approach is carried out until there exists no feasible solution and the algorithm is aborted. The subset of unsatisfiable constraints $\tilde{C}_x$ is defined by reducing the set C_x by the constraints C_t where the corresponding tasks $t \in T'$ did not need to be tightened (line 14). As mentioned before, the application of the deletion filter on the reduced set $\tilde{C}_x$ is necessary to prove or define the IIS, respectively.

6. EXPERIMENTAL RESULTS

In the following, experimental results based on a case study give evidence of the applicability of the proposed methodology. The case study models a realistic problem from the automotive domain. All experiments were carried out on an Intel Xeon CPU @3.20 GHz (QuadCore) with 12 GB RAM using the GUROBI ILP solver [10].

Case study. The case study is based on ECUs with 16-bit S12(X) microcontrollers and 32-bit PowerPC microcontrollers as given in Table 1. For the PowerPC architectures, three different cores are considered: e200z0, e200z4, e200z7. Each ECU has a specific clock speed and might be configured with a given flash memory size and RAM. For the FlexRay bus, a configuration with $n_{fx} = 60$ static slots with a duration of $e_{fx} = 0.0666$ms is chosen such that the length of the static segment is 4ms. The cycle duration of the FlexRay bus is $h_{fx} = 5$ms.

For the proposed case study, two linear objectives were considered: The overall flash size and overall RAM size. This is a common approach since the memory size is often an indicator for the monetary costs of a system in the automotive domain where high quantities are produced and delivered. Moreover, memory components for vehicles have to fulfill strict requirements regarding heat, cold, and vibration tolerances and are therefore significantly more expensive than consumer electronics.

For the time-triggered case study, a FlexRay-based system with ten ECUs is used as outlined in Table 2. Three body applications are mapped to one MPC564xB and one MPC560xB. Four chassis applications are mapped to two S12XFxxx and one MPC560xP. Four information applications are mapped to one MPC560xS and one MPC564xS. Three applications for hybrid and electric auxiliaries are mapped to two MPC567xF and one MPC564xF. The applications consist overall of 66 process tasks and 43 messages. The detailed number of process tasks and messages as well as the periods and deadlines, respectively, are given in Table 3. The mappings of the process tasks are in total 111, resulting in a very large search space for the architectural exploration with $1.98 \cdot 10^{13}$ possible task mappings. The periods for the applications range between 5ms and 80ms, while the deadlines equal the periods.

cluster	ECU	flash [kB] / RAM [kB] opt1	opt2
body	MPC560xB	512/32	512/32
	MPC564xB	1536/128	1536/128
chassis	MPC560xP	256/20	192/12
	S12XFxxx	256/20	384/24
	S12XFxxx	256/20	256/20
information	MPC560xS	512/48	512/48
	MPC5645S	2048/64	2048/64
electric	MPC567xF	3072/192	3072/192
	MPC567xF	3072/192	4096/256
	MPC564xF	3072/192	2048/128

Table 2: Information about the ECUs of the case study and the optimal solution. The case study is using four clusters and ten ECUs. Two optimal results were obtained by the proposed optimization approach.

cluster	tasks	messages	period [ms]/deadline [ms]
body	4	1	10.0
	5	4	10.0
	5	3	20.0
chassis	6	5	20.0
	4	2	20.0
	4	3	20.0
	4	4	20.0
information	4	2	80.0
	7	4	80.0
	4	2	40.0
	5	5	40.0
electric	6	3	10.0
	4	2	5.0
	4	3	5.0

Table 3: Information about the applications that are used in the case study. Given is the number of process tasks and messages for each application as well as the period and deadline, respectively.

Results. The results of the iterative optimization process using the proposed framework are illustrated in Figure 5. The optimal results with feasible schedules were obtained after 77 iterations and 602 seconds. Finally, two optimal results were obtained as outlined in Table 2. The first optimal solution (opt1) requires 14592 kB flash memory and 908 kB RAM. The second optimal solution (opt2) requires 14656 kB flash memory and 904 kB RAM. Note that both objectives are strongly correlated and, therefore, the number of optimal solutions is low.

Within the optimization process, 38 architectures were obtained that allow a feasible scheduling while 39 architectures prohibited a feasible scheduling. However, the first feasible solution was obtained after 19 iterations. Until then, the conflict refinement and justification effectively removed infeasible solutions. The small size of the justification constraints ($|c|$) indicates that a very large part of the architectural design space is pruned. The results show that the proposed approach is capable of optimizing even large problems efficiently and is applicable to realistic problems from the automotive domain.

For 10000 randomly generated architectures for the given case study, all of these architectures prohibit a feasible schedul-

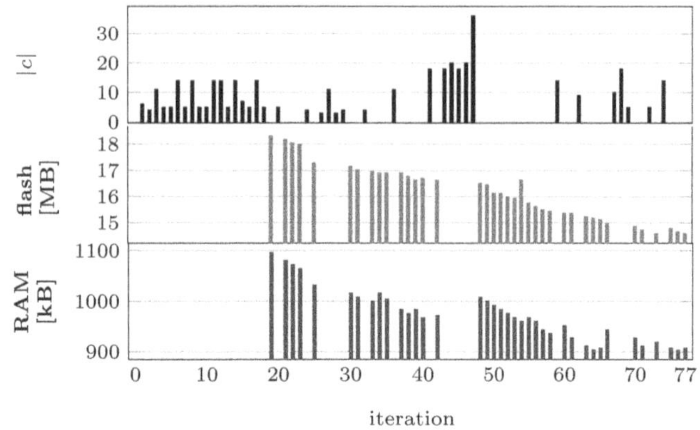

Figure 5: Illustration of the optimization process for the case study. The optimal results were obtained after 77 iterations. Illustrated is the size of the justifications c in terms of variables in the constraint ($|c|$), the flash size, and the RAM size.

ing. Thus, with known multi-step approaches from literature, the case study could not be optimized appropriately.

Scalability. Compared to other case studies in other concurrent optimization approaches such as [18, 19], the proposed case study is significantly larger. In particular, the number of tasks and messages in the used case study is very high compared to the number of ECUs. This leads to a very large search space for the scheduling. Nevertheless, the optimization runtime is very low with approximately only 10 minutes.

The scalability of the proposed approach depends on the scalability of the architecture exploration, the scheduling, and the combination of both, i.e., the conflict refinement and justification deduction. The architecture exploration is based on [14] which has been shown to be capable of handling very large problems. The architecture model is further extended by several constraints such as utilization and path delay constraints to restrict the search space. Moreover, the hierarchical scheduling approach allows the separate scheduling of different clusters, leading to a very scalable approach. Finally, the group-based conflict refinement shows a very good behavior for also very large problems.

Moreover, very often complex systems like automotive systems can be clustered into subsystems which can be designed separately. Thus, the proposed approach can be used iteratively for each subsystem as it is shown in the proposed case study.

7. CONCLUSION

This paper proposed a concurrent architecture and scheduling optimization for time-triggered automotive systems based on conflict refinement. In an iterative process, for each architecture, a time-triggered scheduling is carried out. In case no feasible schedule exists for a given architecture, a conflict refinement and justification deduction are performed to find the minimal architectural decision that prohibits a feasible schedule. This approach is incorporated into a global optimization framework. In particular, for systems with stringent timing constraints, the proposed approach is capable of finding optimal architectures in a short amount of time. The proposed approach is applicable beyond the automotive domain where complex optimization problems might be separated into subproblems accordingly to the proposed approach.

8. REFERENCES

[1] AUTOSAR. AUTomotive Open System ARchitecture. http://www.autosar.org.

[2] CAN. Controller Area Network. http://www.can.bosch.com/.

[3] S. Chakraborty, S. Kunzli, and L. Thiele. A General Framework for Analysing System Properties in Platform-based Embedded System Designs. In *Proc. of DATE 2003*, pages 190–195, 2003.

[4] A. Davare, Q. Zhu, M. Di Natale, C. Pinello, S. Kanajan, and A. Sangiovanni-Vincentelli. Period Optimization for Hard Real-time Distributed Automotive Systems. In *Proc. of DAC 2007*, pages 278–283, 2007.

[5] eCos. embedded Configurable operating system. http://ecos.sourceware.org/.

[6] H. Falk. WCET-aware Register Allocation Based on Graph Coloring. In *Proc. of DAC 2009*, pages 726–731, 2009.

[7] FlexRay Consortium. FlexRay Communications Systems - Protocol Specification. http://www.flexray.com.

[8] A. Gerstlauer, J. Peng, D. Shin, D. Gajski, A. Nakamura, D. Araki, and Y. Nishihara. Specify-Explore-Refine (SER): From Specification to Implementation. In *Proc. of DAC 2008*, pages 586–591, 2008.

[9] O. Guieu and J. W. Chinneck. Analyzing Infeasible Mixed-Integer and Integer Linear Programs. *INFORMS Journal on Computing*, 11:63–77, 1999.

[10] Gurobi Optimizer. Gurobi 4.6. http://www.gurobi.com.

[11] A. Hamann, M. Jersak, K. Richter, and R. Ernst. Design Space Exploration and System Optimization with SymTA/S–Symbolic Timing Analysis for Systems. In *Proc. of RTSS 2004*, pages 469–478, 2004.

[12] M. Lukasiewycz, M. Glaß, C. Haubelt, and J. Teich. SAT-Decoding in Evolutionary Algorithms for Discrete Constrained Optimization Problems. In *Proc. of CEC 2007*, pages 935–942, 2007.

[13] M. Lukasiewycz, R. Schneider, D. Goswammi, and S. Chakraborty. Modular Scheduling of Distributed Heterogeneous Time-triggered Automotive Systems. In *Proc. of the ASP-DAC 2012*, pages 665–670, 2012.

[14] M. Lukasiewycz, M. Streubühr, M. Glaß, C. Haubelt, and J. Teich. Combined System Synthesis and Communication Architecture Exploration for MPSoCs. In *Proc. of the DATE 2009*, pages 472–477, 2009.

[15] B. Meyer and D. Thomas. Simultaneous Synthesis of Buses, Data mapping and Memory Allocation for MPSoC. In *Proc. of CODES+ISSS 2007*, pages 3–8, 2007.

[16] Y. Oh, M. Mneimneh, Z. Andraus, K. Sakallah, and I. Markov. Amuse: a minimally-unsatisfiable subformula extractor. In *Proc. of DAC 2004*, pages 518–523, 2004.

[17] OSEK. OSEK VDX Portal. http://www.osek-vdx.org/.

[18] F. Reimann, M. Glaß, C. Haubelt, M. Eberl, and J. Teich. Improving Platform-based System Synthesis by Satisfiability Modulo Theories Solving. In *Proc. of CODES+ISSS 2010*, pages 135–144, 2010.

[19] F. Reimann, M. Lukasiewycz, M. Glass, C. Haubelt, and J. Teich. Symbolic System Synthesis in the Presence of Stringent Real-time Constraints. In *Proc. of DAC 2011*, pages 393–398, 2011.

[20] K. Richter, D. Ziegenbein, M. Jersak, and R. Ernst. Model Composition for Scheduling Analysis in Platform Design. In *Proc. of the DAC 2002*, pages 287–292, 2002.

[21] White Paper. Ethernet Time Synchronization, 2008. http://www.broadcom.com/collateral/wp/StrataXGSIV-WP100-R.pdf.

[22] H. Zeng, W. Zhengzheng, M. Di Natale, A. Ghosal, P. Giusto, and A. Sangiovanni-Vincentelli. Scheduling the FlexRay bus Using Optimization Techniques. In *Proc. of DAC 2009*, pages 874–877, 2009.

A SAFE Approach towards Early Design Space Exploration of Fault-tolerant Multimedia MPSoCs

Peter van Stralen, Andy Pimentel
Department of Computer Science
University of Amsterdam, The Netherlands
{p.vanstralen,a.d.pimentel}@uva.nl

ABSTRACT

With the reduction in feature size, transient errors start to play an important role in modern embedded systems. It is therefore important to make fault-tolerance a first-class citizen in embedded system design. Fault-tolerance patterns are techniques to make an application fault-tolerant. Not only do fault-tolerance patterns affect the quality of the embedded system (like performance, energy and cost), but there also are many ways of applying them. In this paper, we present the SAFE simulation framework that supports the early exploration of the different possibilities to apply fault-tolerance patterns to MPSoC-based embedded multimedia systems. The SAFE model incorporates fault injection, detection and correction. As a result, a Pareto front can be obtained that not only shows the trade-off between metrics like performance, energy, cost, but also captures reliability metrics like frame drops due to soft errors and the number of unresolvable faults.

Categories and Subject Descriptors

J.6 [**Computer-aided Engineering**]: Computer-aided design

Keywords

MPSoC, Design Space Exploration, Simulation, Fault-Tolerance

1. INTRODUCTION

The design of Multi-Processor System-on-Chip (MPSoC) based embedded systems deals with many objectives. One of them is reliability. An MPSoC design needs to be able to cope with soft and hard errors. Soft errors are transient errors that cause a temporal malfunction in the system. There are multiple sources of soft errors. Examples are single upset events (SUE) [23] caused by high energy neutrons resulting from cosmic rays colliding with particles in the atmosphere, and negative bias temparature instability (NBTI) [1]. In general, soft errors are failures in processor execution due to electrical noise or external radiation. Traditionally, soft errors were only an issue in electronic circuits used in space. However, due to the reduction in feature size and voltage levels, MPSoCs are becoming more susceptible to soft errors [23]. Therefore, an MPSoC-based embedded system needs to be able to cope with these errors.

Fault-tolerance patterns allow an MPSoC to deal with system errors. One of the possible fault-tolerance patterns is active redundancy in space and/or time. If active redundancy is used in the space domain, different resources are used to run the same tasks by means of task replication. Another possibility is to run the task multiple times on the same resource (time domain). The outcomes of the different runs are collected (no response within a certain time frame is also a response) and compared. Based on these results, majority voting can be applied to detect and handle faults.

When mapping an application onto an MPSoC, there are many ways of applying fault-tolerance patterns to the application. This procedure of applying fault-tolerance patterns to an application is called *patternization*. The type of patternization that is applied (like the granularity of the patterns and the number of task replicates used) directly influences the quality of the design in terms of performance, energy and cost. As the effect is hard to predict, it is important to be able to reason about the effects of patternization, right from the start of the design process. Therefore, the patternization should be part of the early design space exploration (DSE) of MPSoC-based embedded systems.

To explore different patternizations, we present the Sesame Automated Fault-tolerance Explorer (SAFE). SAFE provides a novel and generic framework for the early design space exploration of realtime multimedia applications where the effects of implementing fault-tolerance are taken into account. In other words, it aims at making fault-tolerance a first class citizen in early design space exploration. SAFE provides early feedback on the effects of making multimedia MPSoCs fault-tolerant, thereby enabling better decision taking as compared to an approach where fault-tolerance is only addressed in the later design phases. In the latter case, any fault-tolerance measure may invalidate all the decisions taken earlier. Moreover, SAFE provides a simulation-based evaluation, which allows for more detailed architecture models compared to the analytical models often deployed in this domain. As a result, SAFE can produce important metrics like frame drop ratio for dynamically scheduled applications for a wide range of (mixed) fault-tolerance patterns. In this paper, we only focus on active redundancy and soft errors, but SAFE also allows for deploying other types of

CODES+ISSS'12, October 7Ð12, 2012, Tampere, Finland.

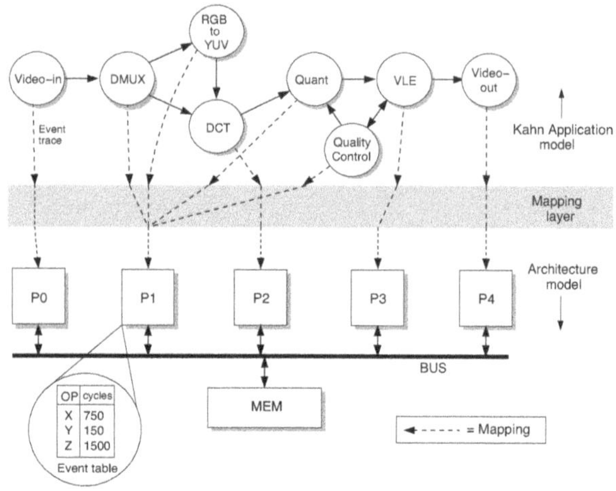

Figure 1: High level MPSoC simulation.

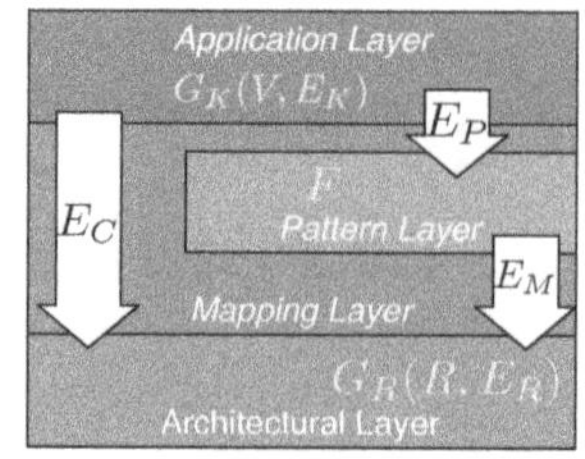

Figure 2: System model with integrated fault-tolerance patterns.

fault-tolerance patterns, like (low overhead) assertion based techniques, as well as for addressing permanent faults.

This paper is organized as follows: the next section describes Sesame, a high level framework on which SAFE is based. Next, the fault-tolerance integration in the MPSoC model is described. The extension of the Sesame simulation model is described in Section 4. Section 5 describes a number of experiments performed with SAFE. Finally, Section 6 describes related work and Section 7 concludes the paper.

2. THE SESAME ENVIRONMENT

For SAFE, we are building upon the Sesame framework for high-level simulation of multimedia MPSoCs [20]. The advantage of high-level modeling is that it allows for a quick pruning of the space of possible MPSoC designs. The Sesame framework, which is illustrated in Figure 1, enables fast performance evaluation using separate application and architectural models with a typical accuracy of 5% compared to a prototype implementation [17]. An application model is built using a Kahn Process Network (KPN) [13], while the architecture model models the MPSoC architecture in a cycle-approximate fashion. Subsequently, there is a mapping of the application model(s) onto the architecture model, implemented using trace-driven co-simulation of the two aforementioned models. Mapping solves two aspects concurrently: 1) *allocation* and 2) *binding*. Allocation selects the architectural components used in the MPSoC platform, whereas the binding defines on which architectural component the application tasks and communications are executed. During the evaluation of a mapping, each process in an application model generates a trace of application events, representing the workload at a high level of abstraction (like read/write a chunk of data, or execute a particular function). These event traces are simulated by the architecture model to obtain metrics like execution time and energy consumption.

Since the applications that need to be mapped on MPSoCs become more and more dynamic, SAFE uses the concept of scenario based design [19]. More precisely, SAFE is based on the scenario-based version of Sesame [24], deploying workload scenarios [8] to model dynamic application workloads. Where Sesame uses absolute metrics for an application workload, like total execution time and energy consumption, SAFE uses the notion of frames. As a result, SAFE considers metrics like frame rate and average power usage. For this purpose, we assume that a single scenario of an application is equivalent to the handling of a single frame. That is, frames are the elementary unit of work performed by an application. For a video application this is the decoding of a single image, whereas the frame of an MP3 application is a single block of sound. Important to notice is that between scenarios application processes do not have any implicit state. As will be explained later on, this simplifies the implementation and modeling of fault-tolerance.

3. FAULT-TOLERANCE INTEGRATION

In this section, a description is given of how fault-tolerance is integrated in SAFE. The first subsection specifies the integration of the fault-tolerance patterns in the system model. Next, the mapping procedure is described. Finally, the fault-tolerance aware mapping process is illustrated using a motion-JPEG (MJPEG) application.

3.1 System model

Figure 2 shows the SAFE system model that integrates fault-tolerance. Apart from the layers that were already mentioned in Section 2 (application, mapping and architecture), the system model also contains a pattern layer. The pattern layer consists of all the possible fault-tolerance patterns that can be used to make an application fault-tolerant. In the following, we will describe the layers in more detail:

Application layer Applications are represented by a directed graph $G_K(V, E_k)$ with $V = V_{\mathrm{N}} \cup V_{\mathrm{OWP}}$ and $V_{\mathrm{N}} \cap V_{\mathrm{OWP}} = \emptyset$. Vertices represent the Kahn Process nodes. To make the external I/O with respect to the complete application explicit, a distinction is made between two type of nodes. Normal process nodes (V_{N}) do not have any interaction with the outside world, whereas *outside world processes* (V_{OWP}) exclusively model the interaction with the world externally to the application. Actions taken by normal process nodes should not affect anything externally to the application. This means that they also cannot write to memory that is accessible by components that are not part of the embedded system. As a result, normal process nodes can be replicated without any side-effects to the application output. Directed edges $E_k = V \times V$ represent communications links to pass messages between process nodes. It is not allowed for OWP processes to communicate directly with eachother:

$$\forall v_1, v_2 \in V_{\mathrm{OWP}} : (v_1, v_2) \notin E_k$$

Architecture layer The architecture is described by the undirected graph $G_R(R, E_R)$. R represents architectural resources like processors, communication buses, splitters, majority voters and buffers. There are some special architectural elements that need to be mentioned specifically. Architectural processors $R_P \subset R$ are the elements capable of executing normal process nodes. OWP processes, on the other hand, are handled by I/O elements $R_I \subset R$. Majority voters $R_V \subset R$ are special architectural resources for implementing active redundancy. They split messages to send them to the different replicas and do a majority voting on outgoing messages. The edges in $E_R = R \times R$ describe the communication links in the architecture.

Pattern layer There are many approaches to make the application fault-tolerant. The collection F represents the possible fault-tolerance patterns. In this paper, we focus on active redundancy [6], but in principle more approaches are possible. A fault-tolerance pattern $f \in F$ contains a description of how the active redundancy is implemented. Examples are double modular redundancy (DMR) and triple modular redundancy (TMR). The fault-tolerance pattern also includes policies like what to do on the detection of a fault and the frequency of checkpoints (see Section 4.3). The function $n_{\text{proc}}(f)$ specifies the number of processors required for the fault-tolerance pattern $f \in F$. For the DMR pattern, this is two processors (possibly the same processor).

Mapping layer Patternization edges E_P describe the manner in which the application is made fault-tolerant. Each edge $(v, f) \in E_P$ represents a possible appliance of the fault-tolerance pattern $f \in F$ for the process node $v \in V_N$.

Mapping edges E_M assign architectural resources to the fault-tolerance pattern. More precisely, the edge $(f, r) \in E_M$ assigns processor $r \in R_P \cup R_V$ to pattern $f \in F$. Next, the I/O edges (E_{IO}) bind the I/O processes. An edge $c = (v, i)$ assigns the OWP processes $v \in V_{\text{OWP}}$ to an I/O component $i \in R_I$ in the architecture.

A final step in the mapping layer is the message dispatch. E.g., there may be multiple process replicas that generate different copies of the same data for a particular destination. Similarly, data may need to be sent to multiple processes Let $M = V_{\text{N}} \times V \times R$ be the set of messages. A message $m = (v_s, v_d, r) \in M$ is data sent from normal process node v_s from resource r such that $(v_s, v_d) \in E_k \vee (v_d, v_s) \in E_k$.

Dispatch edges E_D specify the target of the messages. When $(m, r) \in E_D$, message $m \in M$ needs to be sent to architectural resource $r \in R$.

3.2 Mapping procedure

During DSE, different design instances are created from the system model. To achieve this, a Y-chart approach [14] is used. Figure 3 shows the modification to the Y-chart to integrate fault-tolerance in the DSE. The inputs to our DSE are the applications, the architecture and the fault-tolerance patterns. With these inputs, the mapping procedure can synthesize a design instance. This instance is used in the SAFE simulation framework to obtain performance numbers, after which the DSE process uses these numbers to optimize the application, architecture or mapping.

The mapping procedure maps the application onto the fault-tolerant architecture and is divided into three steps: patternization, binding and message dispatch. Patternization selects the fault-tolerance patterns that will be used in the application. The binding step binds the application onto the architectural resources. Finally, the dispatch specifies the destination of the messages which are sent between the architectural resources. The complete procedure is as follows:

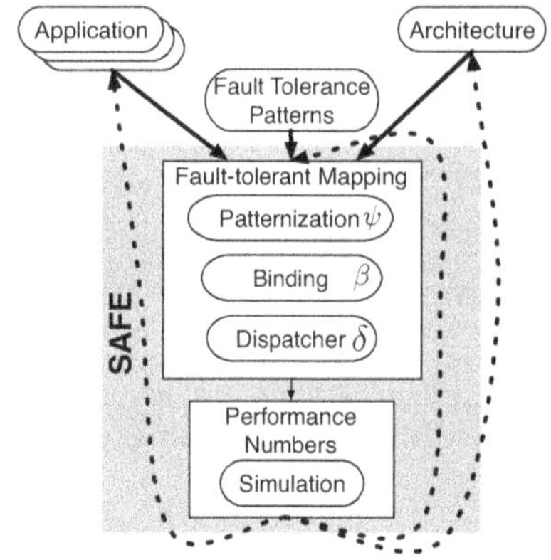

Figure 3: The modified Y-chart for synthesis with fault-tolerance support.

Patternization The first step in our fault-tolerant mapping is patternization ψ. The patternization ψ contains one edge for each node in V_{N} such that $\psi \subseteq E_P$:

$$\forall v \in V_{\text{N}} : |\{f|(v, f) \in \psi\}| = 1$$

The complete patternization ψ describes the used fault-tolerance patterns in the MPSoC design and the process nodes that are assigned to them. Processes that are connected to a pattern $f \in F$ are called a *fault-tolerant subnetwork* (G_f):

$$G_f := \{v|(v, f) \in \psi\}$$

Computational Binding Computational binding β_x maps the fault-tolerant subnetworks onto the architecture such that $\beta_x \in E_M$. In case a fault-tolerant pattern is used it must be assigned to a voter and a set of processors:

$$\forall f \in F : G_f = \emptyset \vee (|\{r|(f, r) \in \beta_x \wedge r \in R_V\}| = 1 \wedge |\{p|(f, p) \in \beta_x \wedge p \in R_P\}| = n_{\text{proc}}(f))$$

The implication of this constraint is that all the processes in a replica of a subnetwork are mapped onto the same processor. This is useful for minimizing the overhead of explicit checkpoints (as described in Section 4.3.2) as the checkpoint can be taken locally at the processor. Each voter may only be used by one pattern:

$$\forall r \in R_V : |\{f|(f, r) \in \beta_x\}| \leq 1$$

I/O binding I/O binding β_{io} maps the OWP processes onto the architecture such that $\beta_{io} \in E_{IO}$:

$$\forall v \in V_{\text{OWP}} : |\{i|(v, i) \in \beta_{io}\}| = 1$$

Each OWP process must be mapped on exactly one I/O component.

Message Dispatch After binding, a message dispatch δ must be generated. The dispatch δ defines the target of each message such that $\delta \in E_D$. Additionally, the routing between the processors, voters and I/O elements is determined. Currently, this routing is fixed and is not part of the mapping procedure.

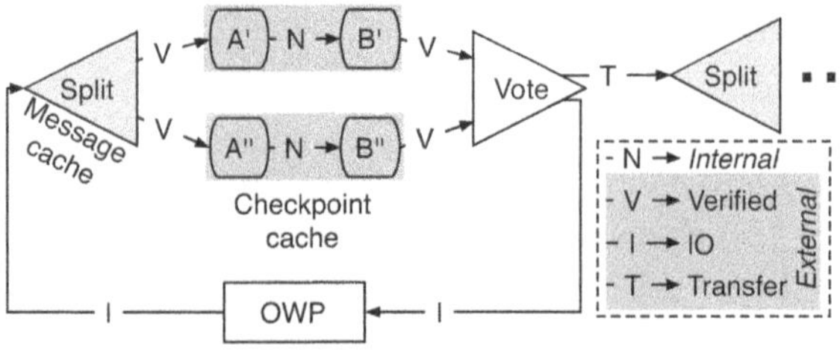

Figure 4: The different types of communication and the required caching for enabling restarting.

In order for the dispatch to be valid, two requirements must be met: 1) the process must be mapped on the resource the message is sent from and 2) each message has at most one destination resource.

$$\forall((v_s, v_d, r), r_d) \in \delta : \exists f \in F \mid ((v_s, f) \in \psi \wedge (f, r) \in \beta_x)$$
$$\forall m \in M : |\{r | (m, r) \in \delta\}| \leq 1$$

The dispatch must also be complete. For each link $e \in E_k$, the message dispatch must specify the destination resource of all the messages:

$$\forall(v_s, v_d) \in E_k : \begin{cases} Intern(v_s, v_d, f) & \exists f \in F : v_s, v_d \in G_f \\ Extern(v_s, v_d, f) & \nexists f \in F : v_s, v_d \in G_f \end{cases}$$

There are two types of communication: internal and external communication. Figure 4 shows the communication types.

Internal communication is communication between two process nodes in the same fault-tolerance subnetwork (in the example between processes A and B). This communication is handled internally by the processor and is unverified (recall that the computational binding enforces that processes on the same subnetwork are mapped onto the same processor). For each of the replicated processes, a message dispatch entry must be present:

$$Intern(v_s, v_d, f) := |\{r | ((v_s, v_d, r), r) \in \delta \wedge r \in R_P\}| = n_{\text{proc}}(f)$$

If the processes of the link are not in the same subnetwork, the communication is external. *External communication* passes the majority voter and consists of two steps:

$$Extern(v_s, v_d, f) := \mathrm{V}(v_s, v_d, f) \wedge \begin{cases} IO(v_s, v_d) & v_d \in V_{\text{OWP}} \\ T(v_s, v_d) & v_d \in V_N \end{cases}$$

The first step is *verified communication* (V). This is communication from the replicated process to the majority voter. The majority voter will collect the messages of the different replicas of v_s and will verify the message that is passed on to the destination process v_d:

$$V(v_s, v_d, f) := |\{r | ((v_s, v_d, r), r_d) \in \delta \wedge r \in R_P \wedge r_d \in R_V \wedge (f, r_d) \in \beta_x\}| = n_{\text{proc}}(f)$$

The second step of external communication depends on the type of the process node v_d. If the destination process is a normal process node ($v_d \in V_{\text{N}}$), there will be a *transfer* (T) of the message to the subnetwork of v_d. In the case of an OWP process ($v_d \in V_{\text{OWP}}$), *IO* is performed:

$$IO(v_s, v_d) := |\{r | ((v_s, v_d, r), r_d) \in \delta \wedge r \in R_V \wedge (v_d, r_d) \in \beta_{io} \wedge r_d \in R_I\}| = 1$$
$$T(v_s, v_d) := |\{r | ((v_s, v_d, r), r_d) \in \delta \wedge r, r_d \in R_V \wedge (v_d, f_d) \in \psi \wedge (f_d, r_d) \in \beta_x\}| = 1$$

This second step only needs to be done once. For a transfer, the destination resource must be the voter on which the subnetwork of v_d is mapped. The message will be split by a splitter (which is physically part of a voter component, see Figure 5b) for use by the replicated processes of v_d. In case of I/O, the destination resource must be the I/O element on which process v_d is mapped.

Besides writing data, read requests are issued by process nodes. These read requests are passed on to a voter element or an I/O element. The completeness requirements are similar to those of writing data, except that the reading node is the sending process and the writing node is the receiving process:

$$\forall(v_s, v_d) \in E_k : \begin{cases} Intern(v_d, v_s, f) & \exists f \in F : v_s, v_d \in G_f \\ Extern(v_d, v_s, f) & \nexists f \in F : v_s, v_d \in G_f \end{cases}$$

A design instance is feasible if and only if all the constraints during the patternization, computational binding, I/O binding and message dispatch are fulfilled.

3.3 An MJPEG Example

To illustrate the fault-tolerance aware mapping in SAFE, an example mapping of an MJPEG encoder is given in Figure 5. First, the application model is illustrated in Figure 5a. All the processes are normal (V_{N}), apart from the OWP process. As discussed in the previous section, the OWP is part of V_{OWP} to make those actions explicit that can have side-effects external to the specific application. As the OWP is aware of the arrival times of frames, as well as their output times, we can determine if a certain frame rate is met.

DMR-A and DMR-B are the fault-tolerance patterns that are used in our example application. DMR is a type of *active redundancy* [6] that uses two processors (not necessarily different). The active redundancy subnetwork is duplicated in time or space ($n_{\text{proc}}(\text{DMR}) = 2$) among the processor(s) to be able to compare the different outgoing messages. An architectural majority voter (VOTER-A or VOTER-B) takes care of the splitting of incoming messages to the replicas and the verification of outgoing messages using majority voting. The complete description of the mapping procedure is as follows:

The first step of the mapping is the patternization. Most fault-tolerant exploration frameworks are fixated on a single fault-tolerance pattern: replicate the complete application or replicate each single process. The SAFE model is, however, not limited to a fixed pattern. In our example (Figure 5a), the MJPEG encoder is split into two fault-tolerant subnetworks: $G_{f,\text{DMR-B}} = \{\text{DMUX}, \text{RGB2YUV}, \text{DCT}\}$ and $G_{f,\text{DMR-A}} = \{\text{Control}, \text{Q}, \text{VLE}\}$.

$$\psi = \{(\text{DMUX}, \text{DMR-B}), (\text{Control}, \text{DMR-A}), (\text{RGB2YUV}, \text{DMR-B}), (\text{DCT}, \text{DMR-B}), (\text{Q}, \text{DMR-A}), (\text{VLE}, \text{DMR-A})\}$$

A next step is to perform the binding (see Figure 5b). During the communication binding, the OWP process is

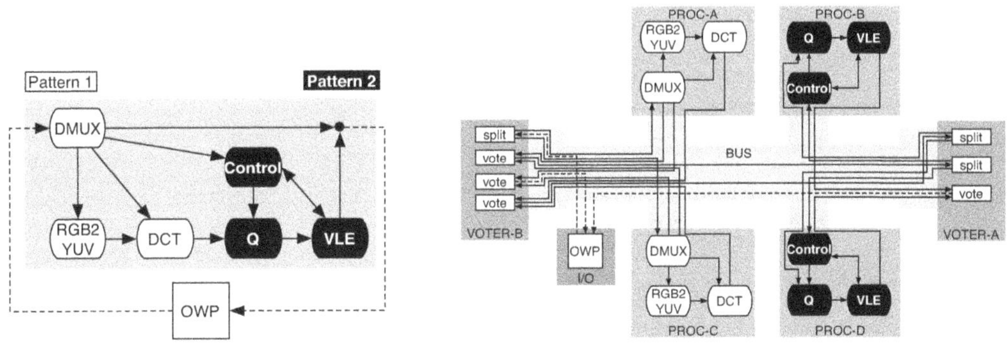

(a) Patternized Application

(b) Synthesized design with two DMRs

Figure 5: MJPEG application synthesized with two active redundancy networks.

bound onto the I/O module. As the DMR pattern of subnetwork $G_{f,\text{DMR-A}}$ requires two processors, subnetwork $G_{f,\text{DMR-A}}$ is bound to processors PROC-B and PROC-D. Similarly, subnetwork $G_{f,\text{DMR-B}}$ is bound to PROC-A and PROC-C. In this example, all the replicas are mapped to different processors. The SAFE model does not require this and all the replicas could e.g. also have been mapped to PROC-A.

$$\beta_{io} = \{(OWP, I/O)\}$$
$$\beta_x = \{(\text{DMR-A}, \text{PROC-B}), (\text{DMR-A}, \text{PROC-D}), (\text{DMR-A}, \text{VOTER-A}), (\text{DMR-B}, \text{PROC-A}) (\text{DMR-B}, \text{PROC-C}), (\text{DMR-B}, \text{VOTER-B})\}$$

The final step is generating the dispatch of the messages. In this example, we will discuss messages from four links: (VLE, OWP), (Q, VLE), (DCT, Q) and (OWP, DMUX). For each link, multiple messages need to be dispatched: one message per replicated process and possibly a verified message after majority voting. For the replicated processes, the communication is internal or verified. (Q, VLE) is internal because Q and VLE are on the same subnetwork $G_{\text{DMR-A}}$. That is why Q on PROC-B can directly write a message to VLE on PROC-B without any dependency on the Q process that is running on PROC-D.

For (VLE, OWP), (DCT, Q) and (OWP, DMUX) the communications (read/write) are external. For the DMR pattern, this means that for written data the messages of all the replicas must be compared before a message is passed on. Take for example (DCT, Q). Both the DCT processes on PROC-A and PROC-C must write a message after which they are processed (i.e., voting) and a single message is passed on. As the destination of the message is located in another subnetwork ($G_{f,\text{DMR-A}}$), the resulting messages are transferred to VOTER-B. Whenever one of the Q processes does a read request on (DCT, Q), it receives a copy of the message from VOTER-B. The OWP process is passive. Incoming frames for the MJPEG application, i.e. (OWP, DMUX), are handled by sending the data to the voter belonging to the subnetwork of the target process (VOTER-B for (OWP, DMUX)). Whenever a voter has a message for an OWP process (outgoing I/O) it will be sent to the I/O element.

4. SIMULATION MODEL

After a design instance is generated using the mapping procedure, a SAFE simulation model is used to obtain its performance numbers. This section describes the different aspects of this fault-tolerant aware model. The first subsection discusses the fault injection, followed by a description of the fault detection. To facilitate fault correction, restarting and checkpointing is introduced in the simulation model. This is elaborated in the third subsection. Finally, the last subsection describes the obtained performance metrics.

4.1 Fault Injection

To be able to reason about the trade-off between objectives like reliability and performance, faults must be simulated in our model. First, we make the assumption that the communication network is fault-tolerant. Therefore, the only source of error is at the processor level. Potentially, all the different processor components can be affected by an error [3]. Examples are the register file, the logical units and the on-chip memories. As SAFE models a processor at a high level of abstraction, we only know what function an application is executing and when it reads or writes data. Therefore, we use the SoftWare Initiated Fault Injection (SWIFI) method [22]. In principle, both permanent and transient errors can be modeled. In this paper, however, we limit ourselves to transient errors.

The processor models the occurrence of faults using an exponential random distribution. An exponential distribution describes the time between events in a Poisson process, which occur continuously and independently at a constant average rate. This is very suitable for modeling fault injection times [7] as transient errors are infrequent and independent of earlier errors. During the simulation, the processor model iteratively injects transient faults based on the exponential distribution. Here, it depends if the transient error affects the execution of the application. The fault does not have any consequences when no process is active at the time the fault occurs. However, in case a process is active, it will invalidate all future output of the process. In reality, it may be the case that the fault does not affect the output, but in our high-level approach we cannot know the exact effect. Therefore, we take the most pessimistic assumption.

4.2 Fault Detection

A fault injected into an application will be propagated until it is detected by one of the fault-tolerant subnetworks. When a fault-tolerant subnetwork detects an error, there are two possible responses: fault masking and fault correction. *Fault masking* is applied when there is a clear majority for the data values among the different replicates. The execution can be continued by passing on the data value of the majority. The corrupt replicate is allowed to continue its execution. As there is no implicit state between frames in our KPN applications (see Section 2), the next frame is processed with clean data again.

If there is no majority, then only *fault detection* can be performed. On the detection of a non-maskable fault, there are two options: *skipping* and *restarting*. In case of skipping, the current frame is dropped and the processing of the next frame is started.

4.3 Fault Correction

If the number of skipped frames becomes too large, then the quality of service (QoS) of the application significantly deteriorates. In this case, restarting the frame processing can improve the QoS. To facilitate such restarting, *checkpointing* must be part of the SAFE model.

4.3.1 Checkpoint budget

As illustrated in Figure 6, there are two types of checkpoints: implicit and explicit. *Implicit checkpoints* are located at the frame barriers. In the example of Figure 6 checkpoints $C_{A.3.0}$ and $C_{B.3.0}$ form the implicit checkpoint at frame 3. Notice that an implicit checkpoint is not taken at once. Process A reaches the barrier of frame 3 much earlier than process B. The complete implicit checkpoint is available once every process in the subnetwork has reached the specific frame barrier. A complete implicit checkpoint does not require storage (as there is no implicit state between frame barriers), but it allows us to perform message cleanup as will be discussed in Section 4.3.2.

As will also be detailed in the next subsection, the restart from an implicit checkpoint is trivial because no state needs to be restored for the processes. Still, restarting from an implicit checkpoint has some disadvantages. Not only needs the complete frame to be recalculated, but it can also be the case that the application is not started at its full capacity. Take the simple application in Figure 6. On a restart from an implicit checkpoint at the end of frame 2, both processes start at the barrier of frame 2. In this case process B needs to wait for output of process A before it can do any work.

To resolve this, explicit checkpoints can be taken during the lifetime of an application. *Explicit checkpoints* are initiated by the voter and store the state of all the processes in the active redundancy network and their internal communication channels at a specific point in time. In contrast

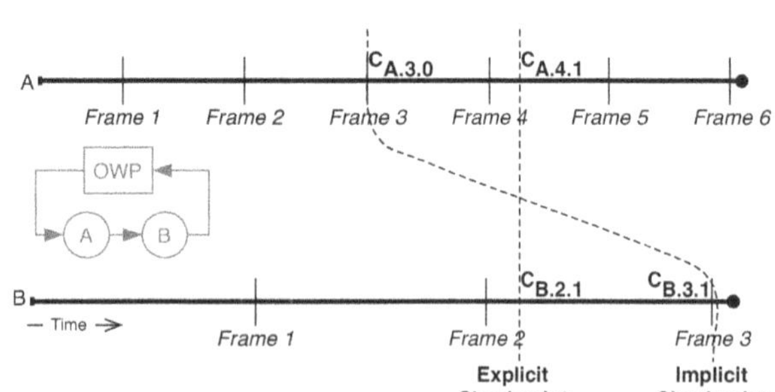

Figure 6: Implicit versus explicit checkpoints as illustrated by a timeline of a simple application.

to implicit checkpoints, the complete subnetwork is halted to capture the state of the current processes and the internal communication channels. To obtain a consistent explicit checkpoint, the voter will ensure that all the replicas stop at the same point in the application. One of the processes in the subnetwork will be responsible for collecting and sending the checkpoint. This results in a checkpoint for each replica, which will be compared by the voter. In Figure 6, $C_{A.4.1}$ and $C_{B.2.1}$ are illustrations of an explicit checkpoint.

Implicit and explicit checkpoints can also enhance each other. Take for example the checkpoints in Figure 6. If there is a restart just after the checkpoint of $C_{B.3.1}$, the restart can take place from a combination of the explicit checkpoint $C_{*.*.1}$ and the implicit checkpoint $C_{*.3.*}$. This means that process A starts from $C_{A.4.1}$ and process B starts from $C_{B.3.1}$. Without the presence of explicit checkpoints, process A should have processed frame 3 again. Similarly, with only explicit checkpoints, process B would have been required to process frame 2 again.

For each fault-tolerant subnetwork, a *checkpoint budget* is defined. The checkpoint budget determines the checkpointing granularity by describing the number of explicit checkpoints per frame (possibly 0). The size, and thus the overhead, of the checkpoint is dependent on the application processes and the amount of data in the internal communication channels. This also means that the voting time of a checkpoint is variable. That is, the explicit checkpoints of the different replicas in a subnetwork must be verified against each other to ensure that on a restart the process state is valid. After verification by the voter, the explicit checkpoint is stored locally at the processor.

Explicit checkpoints are not only useful to minimize the amount of work that has to be redone, but they also allow to implement fault-tolerant techniques like Roll Forwarding Checkpointing Schemes [21] or assertion based techniques [11] where a fault is corrected by reprocessing the frame. This is, however, beyond the scope of the current paper.

4.3.2 Restart budget

Fault correction is not simply the case of enabling or disabling the possibility to restart the processing of a corrupted frame. As restarting requires some overhead, it cannot be done unlimitedly. Therefore, a restarting budget is specified. The restarting budget defines the number of times a restart may be done during the processing of a frame. In case the restart budget is zero, no restarting is performed at all and the fault-tolerant subnetwork will skip corrupted frames.

When restarting is enabled, some data must be cached (see Figure 4). The explicit checkpoints must be stored locally at each of the processors on which the fault-tolerant subnetwork is mapped. Moreover, messages need to be cached at the splitter. Without caching the incoming messages of the subnetwork, it cannot be guaranteed that input data is still available. On top of that, it must be possible to restart subnetworks without the need of restarting other networks to regenerate the incoming data. The caches can be protected from errors in several ways, but as SAFE is currently only targeted towards transient errors a memory with ECC should be sufficient.

The splitter model incorporated in SAFE models a limited amount of cache capacity. Therefore, a policy is required for *message cleanup*. There are two moments for cleaning up messages: during explicit checkpoints and during implicit checkpoints. During explicit checkpoints all the messages in the cache may be discarded. At implicit checkpoints, all the input messages of earlier frames may be removed.

If a corrupted frame is encountered then there are two possibilities. When the restart budget is empty, the current frame is dropped. Otherwise, the restart budget is decreased by one and the subnetwork is restarted from the most recent checkpoint. Two things need to be done during a restart: 1) extract the process states from the checkpoint (not necessary in the case of an implicit checkpoint) and 2) restoring the externally incoming messages at the splitter.

To conclude, checkpointing involves overhead (in space and time), but it tries to avoid skipping frames on faulty processors. The usage of checkpoints depends on the application and the failure rate of the processors. The higher the failure rate of processors, the higher the fraction of skipped frames will be. Additionally, the type of application determines the fraction of skipped frames that can be tolerated. For a safety critical application, none of the frames may be skipped. Multimedia applications typically allow for a small fraction of the frames to be skipped, as long as it is unnoticeable to the user. All these trade-offs can be explored automatically by SAFE.

4.4 Performance metrics

All the techniques described in the previous subsections have been implemented in an extension of the Sesame environment [20]. As the external I/O is made explicit by the use of OWP processes, SAFE allows for obtaining metrics like frame rate in the presence of transient faults. Moreover, since the modeled architectural elements include fault-tolerance components such as majority voters, the overhead of applying active redundancy (or any other fault-tolerance implementation technique) is part of the analysis. Besides the frame rate, other metrics can be obtained as well, such as frame miss ratio, the number of unrecoverable faults and the number of frames that are skipped because the incoming I/O is not available anymore.

We should note, however, that our simulation-based approach is not able to provide guarantees for the realtime behavior. Its goal is not to make the system reliable, but to identify the most reliable design in the design space taking all the other system objectives into account. SAFE is thus able to prune the design space such that only a limited number of designs need to be studied in more detail during later design phases.

5. EXPERIMENTS

In this section, a use case for fault-tolerant DSE with SAFE will be presented. For this purpose, three different applications are used: an MJPEG encoder, a sobel edge detector (to detect edges for each image in a video stream) and an MP3 decoder. All of these applications are individually mapped onto an MPSoC, which somewhat resembles the architecture in Figure 5b. The only difference is that for our experiments, 6 voters are available. To reduce the probability of a communication bottleneck, there are two buses to which all the processors are connected. The voters, however, are distributed: 3 voters are connected per bus.

All the processors have the same failure rate: 10^{-6} FIT. This is a rather conservative choice based on logic implemented in a 180nm technology [23]. Our focus will be on exploring the trade-offs of implementing fault-tolerance. Therefore, the computational binding will be fixed: processors A, B and C will be used to for the first, second and third instance of each replicated process.

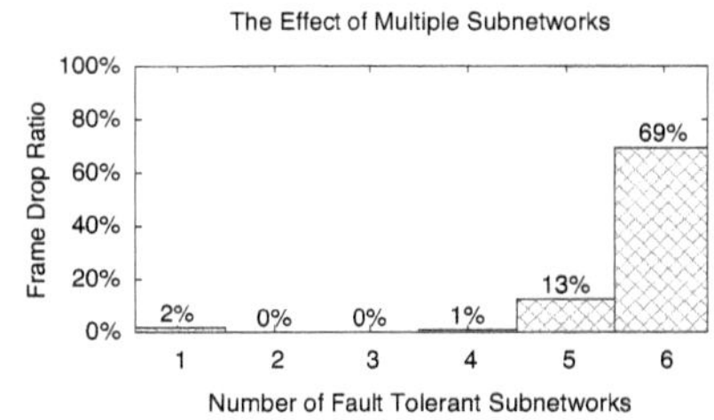

Figure 8: Different subnetworks and their effect on frame drop ratio of the MJPEG application.

We have performed two experiments. In the first experiment, the MJPEG application is revisited. Here, we will scrutinize the process of patternization, and in particular, the identification of several optimal patternizations. Subsequently, SAFE is used for a fault-tolerant DSE on the three test applications individually.

5.1 MJPEG Patternization

To study the process of patternization, we performed an exhaustive patternization for the MJPEG application and an MPSoC where only triple modular redundancy (TMR) patterns are used. There are multiple instances of the TMR in the set of fault-tolerance patterns, involving different choices for the restart budget and the checkpoint budget.

Figure 7 shows the optimal patternization for a different number of fault-tolerant subnetworks. In this case, we have taken frame drop ratio as a primary objective and power consumption as a secondary objective. A first observation is that in this design space the patternization is incremental. By adding an additional subnetwork, one of the processes is moved into the new subnetwork. In the case of two subnetworks, the application is split into two equally sized subnetworks. Not only are these subnetworks equally sized, but also the number of external communication channels is kept minimal. Apart from the I/O communication channels (which are external by definition), only the channels (DCT, Q) and (DMUX, Control) are external. Due to this minimum of external channels, the amount of majority voting (only done on external communication) is minimized.

When increasing the number of subnetworks to three, the DCT process is put into a separate subnetwork. The rationale is not the minimization of external communication, but the guarding of the compute intensive tasks. As the DCT is the most computationally expensive operation, it is beneficial to ensure that verified data is used in the computation. If it would have been unverified, it can be the case that unnecessary computation will be done. The same is true for the optimal patternization with four subnetworks. In this case, the quantization (Q) process is separated, being the second most compute intensive operation in MJPEG.

Having more fault-tolerant subnetworks may increase the quality of the application (with respect to frame drop ratio). However, it also increases overhead. This can be seen in Figure 8. Up to four subnetworks, the frame drop ratio reduces to 0 percent. With five or more subnetworks, the frame drop ratio quickly climbs up to 69 percent when each process is placed in a separate subnetwork.

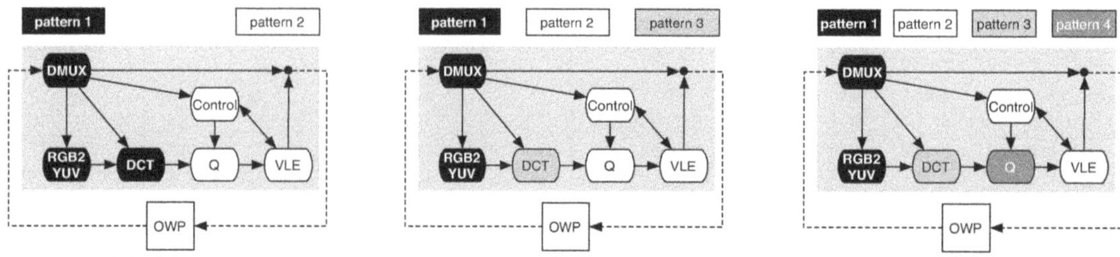

(a) 2 subnetworks (b) 3 subnetworks (c) 4 subnetworks

Figure 7: Optimal patterns for a different number of fault-tolerance subnetworks.

5.2 Fault-tolerant DSE

To further illustrate the potentials of SAFE, three test applications are mapped using a fault-tolerant DSE: MJPEG, sobel and MP3. To keep the experiment feasible, we performed a partial search of the design space. To achieve this, we explored all the mappings with at most six fault-tolerant subnetworks. Each of the subnetworks is implemented using the same type of fault-tolerance pattern. The explored fault-tolerance types are DMR and TMR, and for the restart budget and the checkpoint budget (only relevant when the restart budget is nonzero) the complete range between 0 and 6 is covered. Our model is only able to make explicit checkpoints between communication events. Because the MP3 application is too coarse grained as it has at most two communication events per frame, the fault tolerance patterns with an explicit checkpoint budget larger than 0 are not explored for the MP3 application.

5.2.1 Power and Frame Drop Ratio

Figure 9a shows the frame drop ratio and power consumption trade-off for all of the design points. The design points are differentiated based on the type of fault-tolerant pattern: 1) DMR or TMR and 2) restarting enabled or not. A first and straightforward observation is that for our experiment DMR takes less power than TMR. The overhead of executing an additional replica, is clearly larger than the restarting overhead, since DMR with restarting takes less power than TMR without restarting.

Therefore, for this experiment, it depends on the application if it makes sense to use TMR. Figure 9a also shows the Pareto front of non-dominated solutions. For MJPEG and MP3, DMR dominates all the design instances with TMR. The reason is that DMR is already capable of achieving a frame drop ratio close to or equal to zero. However, for the sobel application, DMR cannot obtain a frame drop ratio below 5 percent. With TMR, sobel can achieve a frame drop ratio of 1.4 percent. Similarly, it depends on the application if restarting is required. The MP3 application is quite lightweight and can already achieve a frame drop ratio of 0.1 percent without restarting. Heavier applications like sobel and MJPEG cannot go below a frame drop ratio of 16 and 31 percent respectively without restarting.

More unexpected are the two clusters of design instances for the MJPEG application. For each experiment instance (DMR, TMR, with and without restarting), there are roughly two clusters: a large drop ratio and a low one. Further investigation showed that once the frame drop ratio is above a certain threshold ($\pm 50\%$) the MJPEG application cannot keep up pace with the incoming frames from the OWP process. As a result, many frames are skipped (e.g., not processed at all) due to deadline misses and the frame drop ratio is drastically increased. The higher number of unprocessed input images has a side effect: less power is required.

Also interesting to notice is the shape of the front of the MP3 application. Increasing power consumption of the system (e.g., making it more fault-tolerant), makes the frame drop ratio even higher. This is caused by the fault tolerance overhead as will be discussed in the next subsection.

5.2.2 Breakdown of Frame Drop Ratio

Dropping a frame can have several causes, which is illustrated in Figure 9b. First, there are corrupted frames. In these frames, a fault is detected (due to a transient error), but the restart budget was too small to correct these faults. Second, there are deadline misses. In these cases, the application is too late to retrieve or deliver a frame from/to the OWP process. For the experiment in Figure 9b, we have taken all the design points of the previous experiments where the explicit checkpoint budget was 0. These design points are differentiated by restart budget and for each category the average frame drop ratio is given. Not only the total drop ratio is given, but also the fractions that are due to corrupt frames and deadline misses.

A larger restart budget can both improve the frame drop ratio (less corrupted frames) and degrade the frame drop ratio (more deadline misses). The more effort is put in fault correction the lower the number of corrupted frames. However, the effort has a negative effect on the number of deadline misses. The optimal restart budget is thus application dependent. For all our applications, the gain in the reduction of corrupted frames is overshadowed by the increase of deadline misses at about 1 or 2 restarts per frame. However, the MP3 application is not influenced anymore once the restart budget is above 3. In this case, the MP3 application is already able to circumvent corrupted frames and the additional restarts will not be used.

5.2.3 Buffer Requirements

We have already shown that restarting and checkpointing have a positive effect on the frame drop ratio. A next question is what the effect of the additional checkpointing is on the buffer requirements. For this purpose, we studied the MJPEG and the sobel applications and selected the best design points for a checkpoint budget between 0 and 6. The results are illustrated in Figure 10. The left vertical axis represents the normalized buffer size, whereas the right vertical axis shows the frame drop ratio.

The checkpoint budget has a positive effect on the buffer

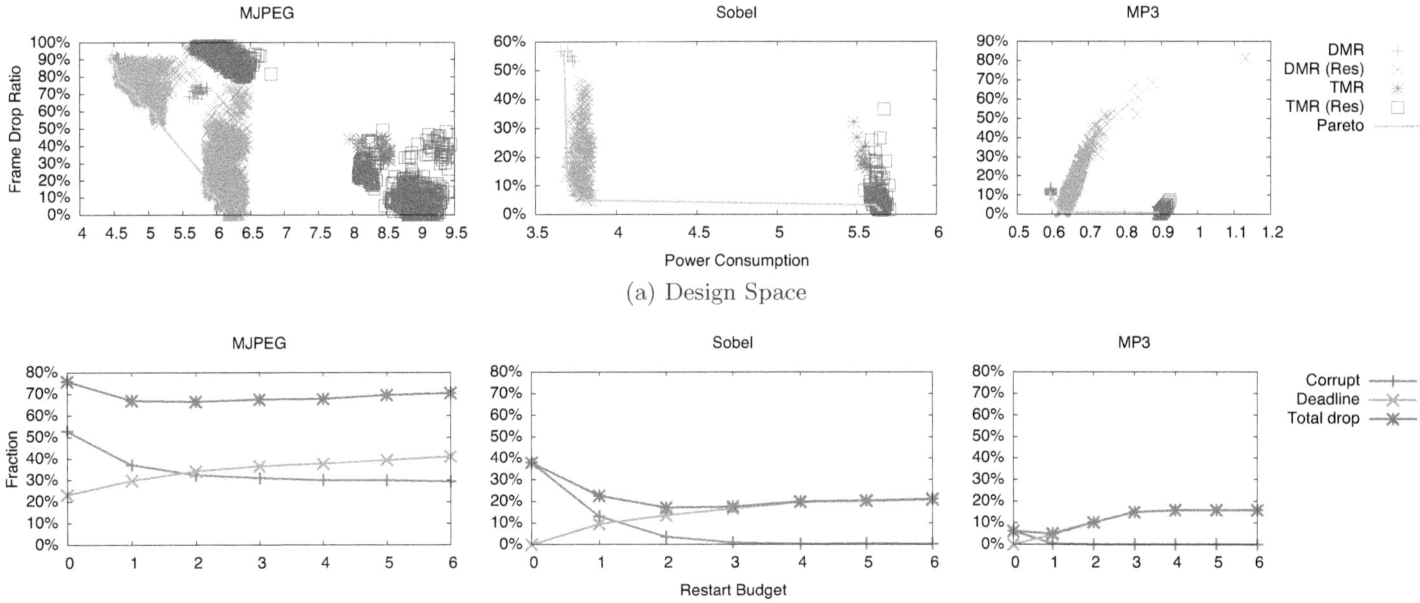

(a) Design Space

(b) Breakdown of Frame Drops

Figure 9: The results of the fault-tolerant DSE of the 3 test applications: MJPEG, sobel and MP3.

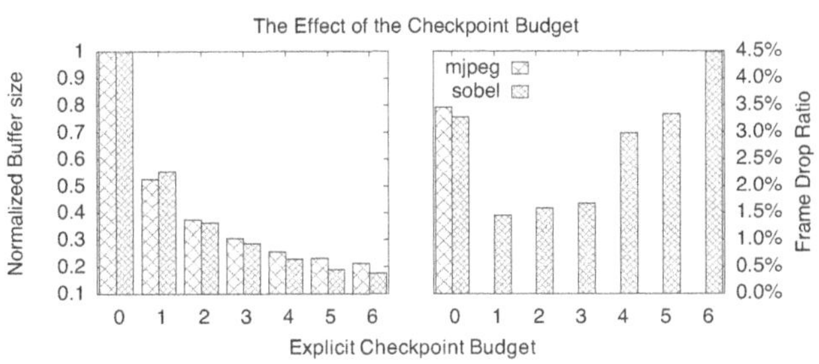

Figure 10: Varying the checkpoint budget of an MJPEG application with restarting enabled.

requirements. When the checkpoint budget increases, the required size of the message cache decreases. The reason is that the message cache can be flushed whenever an explicit checkpoint is taken (see Section 4.3.2). The more often a checkpoint is taken, the fewer messages are simultaneously cached. The storage requirements of the explicit checkpoints, however, are less influenced by the frequency of checkpointing (not shown in the graph).

Still, a checkpoint has its overhead. It depends on the application if it can be tolerated or not. The sobel application cannot tolerate the overhead and with a checkpoint budget above 1, the frame drop ratio is increasing due a larger number of deadline misses. The MJPEG application, on the other hand, can take up to 6 checkpoints per frame without any deadline misses.

6. RELATED WORK

A lot of research effort has been spent on the early DSE of embedded systems [10]. Recently, workload scenarios [8] have been introduced to make the embedded system design scenario aware [19, 18, 24]. Our work is based on [24], and extends this into the direction of fault-tolerance aware DSE. This is because reliability becomes a major design objective [23, 16] and has a major effect on other objectives. It is therefore important that this objective is explored as a separate design objective [9] and not hierarchically.

Many of the reliability aware DSE environments [2, 5, 12, 11, 6] are based on a static scheduling of application tasks. COFTA [5] aims at minimizing the overhead of fault-tolerance measures using replication and assertion. The analysis only takes the performance and failure rate of the final application into account. It provides exploration of the placement of the assertion and replication patterns. COFTA misses the ability to reason about handling multiple frames and their throughput. The methods in [12, 11] provide fault-tolerance in realtime embedded systems using re-execution of tasks. For this purpose, a sanity check determines if the task is executed correctly. In case of a fault, a special time slot can be used to re-execute a task. As all of these approaches use static scheduling, they are based on worst case execution time. The method in [2] tries to resolve this by using a hyperperiod instead of a fixed time. Still, it does not allow for modeling the full dynamism within applications.

Bolchini [4] provides an analysis framework that performs reliability analysis for an embedded system with dynamic scheduling. The framework injects faults into the system during execution and classifies the effect on the system (like silent, detected and failure).

The novelty of SAFE is that it not only provides exploration on the placement of fault-tolerance patterns, but it is also capable to fully simulate realtime embedded systems with dynamic scheduling at a high abstraction level. On top of that, it provides a unique fine-grained and parametrized checkpointing model. Most fault-tolerant aware DSE frameworks only take implicit checkpoints into account [15] that are strictly taken in between frames. As a result, SAFE provides more detailed insight into the consequences of fault-tolerant design. By using the patternization approach, different fault-tolerance patterns can be applied to different parts of the same application. Finally, the explicit modeling of transient errors allows us to not only model the effects of the (mixed) fault-tolerance patterns on the system performance, but also to gain insight into the number of missed frames (due to a late arrival or an unrecoverable fault).

7. CONCLUSION

In this paper, we have argued that fault-tolerance should become a first class citizen in the early design space exploration of MPSoCs. To this end, we have presented SAFE, a simulation environment to explore the different implementation strategies for realizing fault-tolerance in MPSoC-based embedded multimedia systems.

Our experiments show that it is beneficial to explore all the possible ways of implementing fault-tolerance. A custom patternization allows to leverage fault handling capabilities and reducing performance overhead by minimizing the amount of verified communication and to assure that the input of compute intensive tasks is correct. As a consequence, an automated way of exploring all these possible fault-tolerant implementation variants is crucial to make the correct decisions during the early design stages.

Future work will focus on large-scale DSE in which mixed techniques (not only active redundancy, but also assertion-based techniques) are explored for fault-tolerant MPSoC-based embedded systems.

8. REFERENCES

[1] M. Agostinelli et al. Random charge effects for PMOS NBTI in ultra-small gate area devices. In *IEEE Int. Symp. on Reliability Physics*, pages 529–532, 2005.

[2] P. Axer, M. Sebastian, and R. Ernst. Reliability analysis for MPSoCs with mixed-critical, hard real-time constraints. In *Proc. of the 9th Int. Conf. on Hardware/Software Codesign and System Synthesis (CODES+ISSS)*, pages 149–158, October 2011.

[3] C. Bolchini et al. A model of soft error effects in generic IP processors. In *Defect and Fault Tolerance in VLSI Systems, 2005. DFT 2005. 20th IEEE Int. Symposium on*, pages 334 – 342, October 2005.

[4] C. Bolchini and A. Miele. An application-level dependability analysis framework for embedded systems. In *IEEE Int. Symposium on Defect and Fault Tolerance in VLSI and Nanotechnology Systems (DFT)*, pages 171–178, October 2011.

[5] B. Dave and N. Jha. COFTA: hardware-software co-synthesis of heterogeneous distributed embedded systems for low overhead fault tolerance. *IEEE Trans. on Computers*, 48(4):417–441, April 1999.

[6] O. Derin, E. Diken, and L. Fiorin. A middleware approach to achieving fault tolerance of kahn process networks on networks on chips. *International Journal of Reconfigurable Computing*, 2011:15, 2011.

[7] F. Faure et al. Single-event-upset-like fault injection: a comprehensive framework. In *IEEE Transactions on Nuclear Science*, volume 52, pages 2205–2209, December 2005.

[8] S. V. Gheorghita et al. System-scenario-based design of dynamic embedded systems. *ACM Trans. on Design Automation of Electronic Systems*, 14(1):1–45, 2009.

[9] M. Glass et al. Reliability-aware system synthesis. In *Design, Automation Test in Europe Conference Exhibition 2007 (DATE '07)*, April 2007.

[10] M. Gries. Methods for evaluating and covering the design space during early design development. *Integration, the VLSI Journal*, 38(2):131–183, 2004.

[11] J. Huang et al. Reliability-aware design optimization for multiprocessor embedded systems. In *14th Euromicro Conf. on Digital System Design (DSD)*, pages 239–246, September 2011.

[12] V. Izosimov et al. Design optimization of time-and cost-constrained fault-tolerant distributed embedded systems. In *Proc. of the conf. on Design, Automation and Test in Europe (DATE)*, pages 864–869, 2005.

[13] G. Kahn. The semantics of simple language for parallel programming. In *IFIP Congress*, pages 471–475, 1974.

[14] B. Kienhuis et al. A methodology to design programmable embedded systems: the Y-chart approach. *LNCS - Embedded Processor Design Challenges*, 2268:18–37, 2002.

[15] K. Lee et al. Mitigating the impact of hardware defects on multimedia applications: a cross-layer approach. In *Proc. of the 16th ACM int. conf. on Multimedia*, pages 319–328, 2008.

[16] S. Mitra et al. Robust system design with built-in soft-error resilience. *IEEE Computer*, 38(2):43–52, February 2005.

[17] H. Nikolov et al. Daedalus: toward composable multimedia MP-SoC design. In *Proc. of the Design Automation Conf. (DAC)*, pages 574–579, 2008.

[18] G. Palermo, C. Silvano, and V. Zaccaria. Robust optimization of SoC architectures: A multi-scenario approach. In *Proceedings of ESTIMedia 2008 - IEEE Workshop on Embedded Systems for Real-Time Multimedia. Atlanta, Georgia, USA*, October 2008.

[19] J. M. Paul, D. E. Thomas, and A. Bobrek. Scenario-oriented design for single-chip heterogeneous multiprocessors. *IEEE Trans. Very Large Scale Integr. Syst.*, 14(8):868–880, August 2006.

[20] A. D. Pimentel, C. Erbas, and S. Polstra. A systematic approach to exploring embedded system architectures at multiple abstraction levels. *IEEE Trans. on Computers*, 55(2):99–112, 2006.

[21] D. Pradhan and N. Vaidya. Roll-forward checkpointing scheme: a novel fault-tolerant architecture. *IEEE Trans. on Computers*, 43(10):1163–1174, October 1994.

[22] A. Rohani and H. Kerkhoff. A technique for accelerating injection of transient faults in complex SoCs. In *14th Euromicro Conf. on Digital System Design (DSD)*, pages 213–220, September 2011.

[23] P. Shivakumar et al. Modeling the effect of technology trends on the soft error rate of combinational logic. In *Proc. of the Int. Conference on Dependable Systems and Networks (DSN'02)*, pages 389 – 398, 2002.

[24] P. van Stralen and A. D. Pimentel. A trace-based scenario database for high-level simulation of multimedia MP-SoCs. In *Proc. of the Int. Conference on Embedded Computer Systems: Architectures, MOdeling and Simulation (SAMOS '10)*, Samos, Greece, July 2010.

Synthesis of Optimized Hardware Transactors from Abstract Communication Specifications

Dongwook Lee
dongwook.lee@utexas.edu

Hyungman Park
hyungman@utexas.edu

Andreas Gerstlauer
gerstl@ece.utexas.edu

Electrical and Computer Engineering
University of Texas at Austin
Austin, Texas, U.S.A.

ABSTRACT

Increasing system complexity and heterogeneity make system integration and communication synthesis a growing concern. Even with transaction-level modeling and high-level synthesis of hardware, communication interfaces still have to be manually designed at a low protocol level. To address this challenge, we present a design flow for automatic synthesis of hardware transactors, which realize abstractly specified communication semantics on top of protocol-level transactions. Transactor synthesis is tightly coupled with high-level synthesis of computation for integrated computation/communication co-design of complete hardware processors, thus establishing a seamless path from abstract system specifications down to hardware implementations in synthesizable RTL. The flow supports a generic set of communication semantics and target implementations, where transactors are custom-generated for a specific application and architecture combination. Furthermore, we develop protocol stack optimizations that reduce the area and performance overhead of synthesized communication interfaces. We have applied our synthesis flow to several industrial-strength examples under various communication settings. Results show that synthesized interfaces are comparable to manual designs in terms of area and latency, where protocol stack optimizations can reduce area and latency overhead by up to 77% and 21%, respectively.

Categories and Subject Descriptors

J.4 [**Computer-Aided Engineering**]: CAD

General Terms

Design, Algorithm

Keywords

transactor, hardware synthesis, interface synthesis

1. INTRODUCTION

Addressing ever-increasing complexity and heterogeneity of Multi-Processor Systems-on-Chip (MPSoCs), Transaction-Level Models (TLMs) have emerged to raise the design abstraction to higher levels [3]. Fundamentally, this is achieved by a separation of computation and communication, which enables independent design space exploration [13]. In a TLM methodology, communication details are abstracted away to the level of protocol transactions. This makes simulations faster and, on the computation side, a High-Level Synthesis (HLS) tool can be used to refine C descriptions into RTL, enhancing design productivity as compared to a traditional design flow. However, communication interfaces still have to be designed manually at a low, detailed protocol level. Furthermore, their separation does not allow for optimizations across computation and communication boundaries.

Low-level system integration is a tedious, time-consuming bottleneck in the MPSoC design process. What is lacking are approaches that raise communication design to the same level as C-based computation, where system interactions of hardware components are abstractly specified using message-passing, queue, semaphore or other communication primitives, and *hardware transactors* are automatically synthesized to realize high-level semantics over protocol-level transactions while applying computation/communication co-design optimizations. Over the years, several approaches for system-level communication synthesis have been proposed. However, existing solutions are mostly library- or template-based and as such either limited to a single, canonical target architecture or to a generic implementation that comes with high overhead. By contrast, we aim to provide a synthesis flow that is (a) general in supporting a wide range of communication semantics and target implementations, while (b) able to custom generate communication interfaces optimized for a specific application and architecture.

In this paper, we present an approach for automatic synthesis of optimized hardware transactors from high-level communication specifications. The approach is tightly integrated with high-level synthesis of computation. Combined, this enables efficient, fully automated system integration including automatic generation of optimized bus-based communication interfaces and protocol stacks. Fig. 1 illustrates how the approach integrates into a typical system design flow based on standard system-level design languages (SLDLs), such as SpecC [7] or SystemC [10]. Starting from an architecture model in which the desired network topology and interactions between system components are specified using abstract SLDL channels, communication synthesis takes

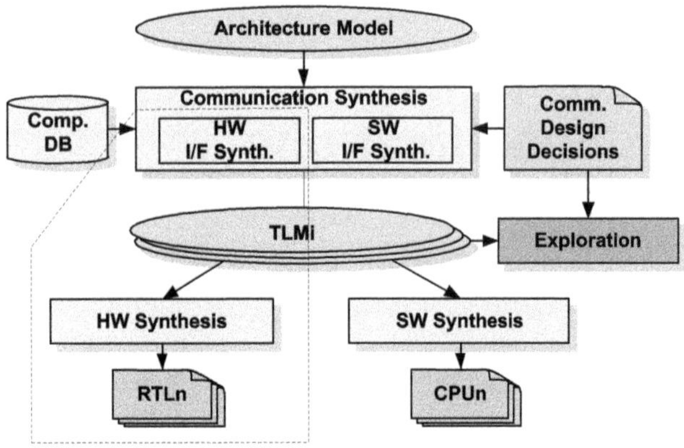

Figure 1: System design flow.

user decisions on targeted communication mechanisms and refines communication channels into a protocol-level TLM. The TLM can be used to explore the design space of possible communication implementations. In the TLM, components communicate over actual system busses using internally generated hardware or software transactor stacks. In this paper, we specifically focus on the hardware side. Synthesis of protocol stacks for hardware components is integrated with back-end hardware synthesis to automatically generate final RTL descriptions of complete hardware processors, which include all computation, transactors and external bus interfaces. In the process, hardware-specific protocol stack optimizations are applied to reduce area and communication overhead of the final RTL design.

The rest of the paper is organized as follows: following a discussion of related work and an overview of our synthesis flow, Sections 2, 3 and 4 elaborate on each step of our methodology. Section 5 shows experimental results of applying the flow to a set of industrial-strength design examples. Finally, Section 6 concludes the paper with a summary and an outlook on future work.

1.1 Related Work

Many communication synthesis approaches aim to provide integrated environments for design space exploration and mapping of applications onto custom or generic network-on-chip type of system architectures [9, 18, 15]. In almost all cases, complete system implementations are composed out of a fixed library of communication components, often limited to a single, canonical target architecture template that is proprietary and custom-designed [22] or based on an industry standard [14, 17]. Solely targeting design space exploration, several approaches support the automatic generation of TLMs for early prototyping and validation, but without the capability to generate actual implementations [20, 1, 19].

The focus in synthesis of component interfaces has been mainly on automatic generation of bridges or transducers that translate between protocols of incompatible cores. Several approaches [22, 12, 21] propose a generic architecture of the interface as a wrapper that connects processors to a common bus network. All of these approaches allow modularity in the design. However, they do not address the vertical integration path to bridge the semantic gap between abstract, high-level communication primitives and RTL. By contrast, our approach can synthesize communication from user-level channels at a range of abstraction levels.

Only recently have approaches emerged that try to synthesize communication implementations from higher-level TLMs. Cho et al. [5] describe a tool for synthesizing a TLM into a universal RTL bridge that translates the canonical TLM interface into a target bus protocol using platform definitions and protocol libraries. The bridge contains a FIFO and a dedicated controller for each bus protocol. Hatami et al. [11] and Bombieri et al. [2] propose a similar approach but with the interfaces written in SystemC TLM-2.0. Moss et al. [16] utilize communication refinement and HLS tools to generate a data slicing transactor that realizes pin-level interfaces down to a final RTL bus adapter. Beyond academia, several commercial HLS tools [4, 6] have started to integrate similar capabilities of synthesizing interface functions written in TLM form. In all cases, however, synthesis is only supported from TLMs at a low protocol level. Designers are still required to manually implement transactors that translate from abstract communication semantics down to a protocol- or cycle-accurate level. Furthermore, existing approaches are purely database-, IP- or transducer-based, where a generic architecture template can add overhead in terms of area and latency. Our approach, on the other hand, supports tight integration with computation to synthesize a custom, application- and target-specific implementation of optimized bus transactors on top of a thin realization of the basic bus protocol taken out of a pre-designed RTL database.

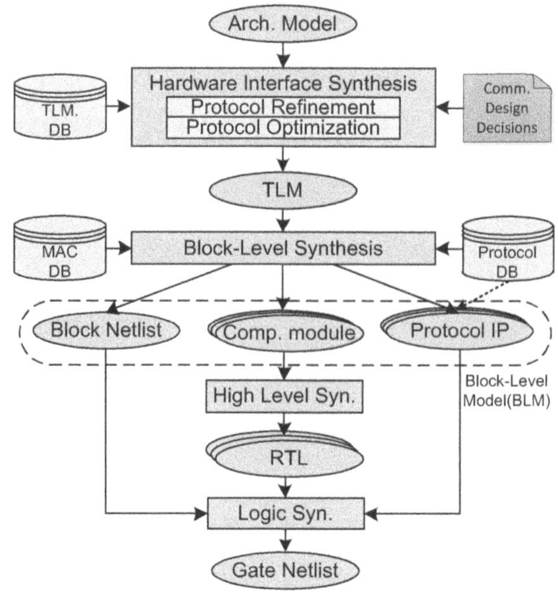

Figure 2: Hardware synthesis flow.

1.2 Hardware Synthesis Flow

Our flow supports hardware synthesis from models at varying levels of abstraction (Fig. 2). Starting from an untimed architecture model, we follow a four-step methodology to synthesize communication down to a protocol-level TLM, transform the TLM into a block-level model (BLM), further synthesize block modules down to cycle-accurate RTL using a traditional HLS tool, and perform logic synthesis to generate a final gate-level netlist. The design flow utilizes databases in various forms through which the synthesis process can be adapted to different targets and HLS backends.

The architecture model describes the desired system topology, as well as its functional behavior. Computation is mapped to Processing Elements (PEs) that interact through

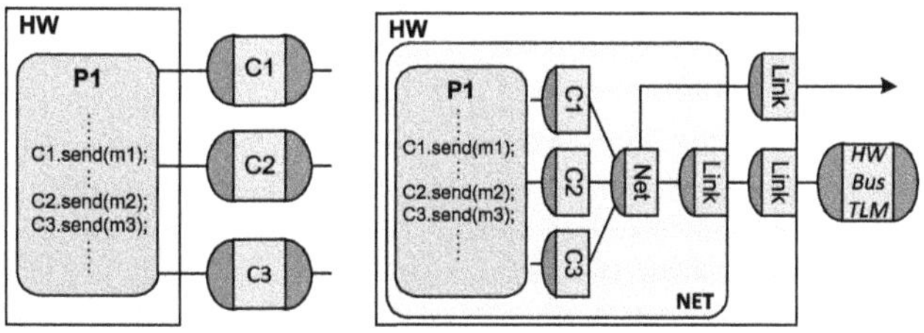

(a) Arch. model (b) TLM

Figure 3: Protocol refinement.

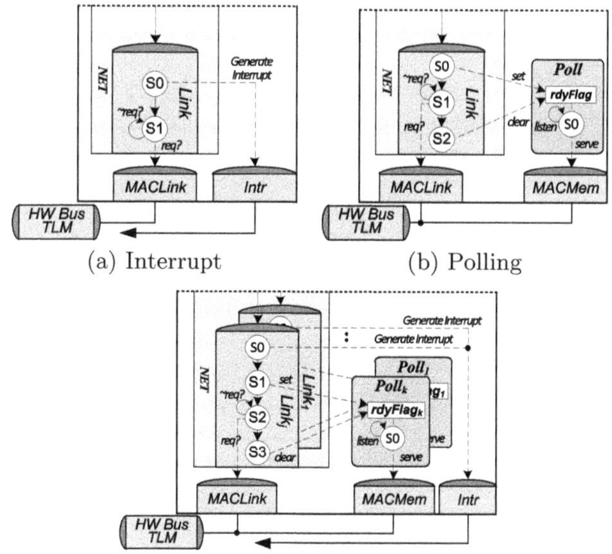

(a) Interrupt (b) Polling

(c) Interrupt Sharing

Figure 4: Message-passing protocol stack.

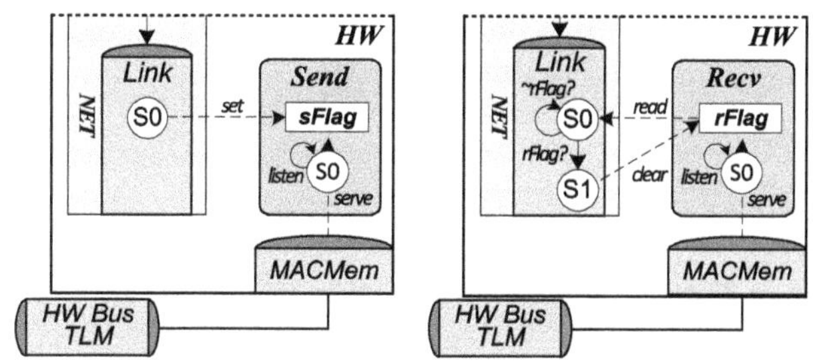

(a) Polled send (b) Receive

Figure 5: Event transfer protocol stack.

logical point-to-point links. Communication is specified in abstract form, where links are user-defined through untimed channels of specific semantics, such as message-passing transfers, shared memory accesses, and event notifications.

Hardware interface synthesis uses the architecture model as input and generates the TLM. In the protocol refinement step, layers of protocol transactors are synthesized and inserted into PEs to implement communication following user-defined specifications, which include a given address map and the choice between interrupt- and polling-based synchronization mechanisms. As a result, message-passing channels of the architecture model are refined down to bus protocol transactions on top of loosely- or approximately-timed TLMs of busses brought in from a database. In the process, generated protocol stacks are flattened and optimized. Protocol optimizations are specifically developed to target synthesis of transactors down to efficient hardware.

Finally, the TLM is converted into a BLM. Block-level synthesis generates synthesizable C++/SystemC code for each computation module in a hardware PE. It thereby extracts single-threaded processes and merges them with generated code for protocol transactors. In the process, thin media access (MAC) layer implementations taken out of a database translate a canonical MAC interface targeted by code generation into bus- and HLS-specific code required for further synthesis. Finally, block-level synthesis uses lightweight templates stored in a protocol database to generate both SystemC models and RTL implementations of interface IPs realizing external bus state machines. To form the BLM, generated computation blocks are combined with bus protocol IPs and a pin-level netlist that connects all blocks and external bus interface IPs.

Computation blocks are further synthesized down to cycle-accurate RTL descriptions using an external HLS tool, which transforms combined block-level computation and communication code into a merged RTL implementation of each hardware block. Generated RTL blocks, RTL bus protocol IPs, and the SystemC module netlist converted into RTL form can then be synthesized into a gate-level netlist using a traditional logic synthesis tool.

2. PROTOCOL REFINEMENT

We utilize an existing communication synthesis engine for generation of basic protocol stacks. In the following, we briefly summarize its operation, further details of which can be found in [8].

In the architecture model, hardware PEs are described in the form of C-based computation processes that communicate externally through a user-defined set of abstract, untimed messaging channels (Fig. 3(a)). We support both synchronous message-passing (double-handshake) and pure event synchronization (single-handshake). Double-handshake channels implement a synchronous, buffer-free, two-way blocking transfer of typed data streams from a sender to a receiver. By contrast, single-handshake channels perform asynchronous, data-less event notifications where the receiver blocks until the sender invokes the event. Protocol refinement then generates necessary transactor stacks to implement high-level semantics down to protocol-level transactions. In the TLM (Fig. 3(b)), protocol layers are inserted into an additional network level of the PE hierarchy to realize channel communication over external busses. Inserted layers include a presentation layer for data conversion, a network layer for packeting and routing, a link layer for synchronization, and a MAC layer for data slicing, alignment and media access.

Both message-passing and event communication require synchronization between slaves and masters, where we support interrupt- and polling-based mechanisms. Both types of channels can be synthesized into either implementation. Without loss of generality, we assume for the following discussions that the hardware processor is a bus slave communicating with a software processor acting as bus master.

Interrupt- and polling-based implementations of message-passing communication are shown in Fig. 4. In all cases, a link adapter is responsible for synchronizing with the external communication partner, either by generating an interrupt (Fig. 4(a)) or by setting a separate polling flag that can

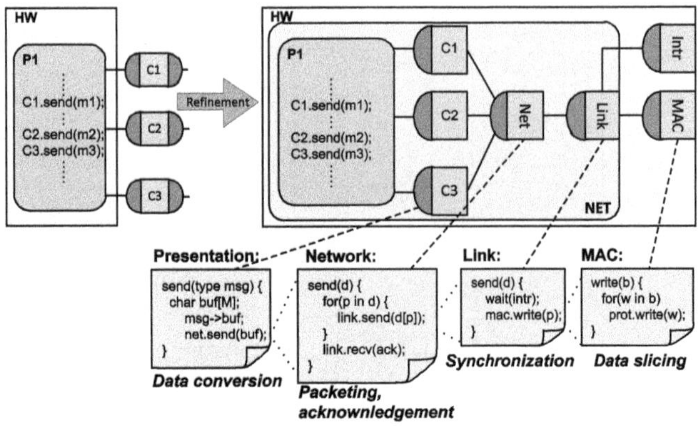

(a) Unoptimized layer-based code.

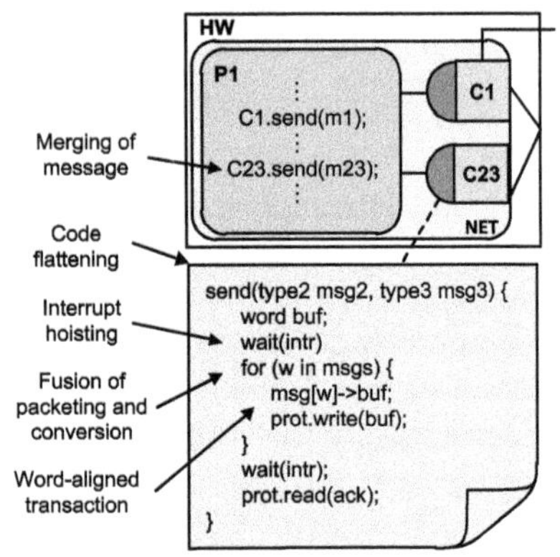

(b) Hardware-optimized transactor.

Figure 6: Protocol stack optimizations.

be accessed by the master (Fig. 4(b)). After synchronization, the actual data transfer is performed via MAC layer operations. Sharing of interrupts among multiple channels also requires a polling flag in addition to interrupt generation (Fig. 4(c)). In both cases, flags are cleared once the transaction is completed.

Pure event transfer channels are synthesized as buffered event notifications. As shown in Fig. 5, their implementation is a variant of the message-passing synchronization scheme. Depending on the event direction, either master or slave can be sender or receiver. When sending an event from slave to master, the link adapter realizes interrupt, interrupt-sharing or polling-based synchronization. In a pure polling case (Fig. 5(a)), a separate *Send* process serves an event mailbox that is set by the link layer to indicate event availability to the master. When receiving an event from the master, neither interrupts nor polling can be utilized. Instead, the link layer blocks on an event flag in a separate *Recv* process, which serves the flag to be written and set by the master over the bus (Fig. 5(b)). In all cases, the *Send* behavior or link adapter will clear the flag once it has been consumed.

3. PROTOCOL STACK OPTIMIZATIONS

Basic protocol refinement generates unoptimized code for protocol stacks following a strict layer-based organization. For efficient backend synthesis, protocol code needs to be further optimized across layer boundaries.

In an unoptimized TLM (Fig. 6(a)), protocol code inserted into the PEs during basic refinement consists of four stacked adapter channels realizing layers of communication. The presentation layer converts abstract data types in application messages to untyped blocks of bytes transferred over the network layer following a canonical data layout between PEs. The network layer then optionally packetizes byte blocks into smaller chunks (packets) that are routed and transferred from PE to PE over bridges and transducers in the network. In case of synchronous message-passing over more than one hop, the network layer also performs end-to-end synchronization via acknowledge packets to restore barrier synchronicity and confirm successful completion of each message transfer. Finally, the link layer realizes point-to-point synchronization using one of the mechanisms described in Section 2, while the MAC layer slices data packets into external protocol transactions as supported by the underlying bus.

Protocol stack optimizations flatten basic communication layers and apply hardware-specific cross-layer optimizations for message merging, protocol fusion and interrupt hoisting (Fig. 6(b)). In addition, protocol coupling supports application-specific co-optimization of protocol stacks and bus protocol state machines. Each of these optimizations can be selectively enabled or disabled during synthesis. In the following, we describe optimizations in more detail.

3.1 Message Merging

Message merging combines consecutive messages transferred over one or more channels between two PEs into a single message over a common channel. This reduces the total number of channels and messages in the system. Consequently, overall resource demands are minimized.

Messages of different channels can generally be re-mapped onto a single logical link if they are exchanged between the same two partners and if channels are accessed sequentially on both sides. For example, if sequential application processes exchange messages over separate application channels, and if there is no overlapped sending or receiving of such messages, the applications channels can be merged. As shown in Fig. 6(a), after conversion of data types to a canonical byte layout, this is achieved by multiplexing presentation layers to access a single untyped lower-layer stream. Overall, the number of network- and link-level streams is reduced, which in turn can lead to reduced hardware area requirements, e.g. for bus address decoding.

On top of basic channel merging, further message merging is applied (Fig. 6(b)). An analysis of data dependencies determines if two or more messages are sent (sequentially) over the same (merged) network-/link-level stream and are independent, i.e. can be considered logically consecutive with no intermediate computations. Such consecutive messages are then combined into a single, larger message. This eliminates the need for synchronization of each individual message. As such, message merging can reduce the total number of synchronization points and hence lead to less synchronization overhead in the system.

3.2 Protocol Fusion

After flattening of protocol stacks, a fusion of presentation, network and MAC layers is performed to interleave data conversion, packetizing and slicing. Protocol fusion can significantly reduce memory and area requirements, as well as generally unlock opportunities for optimization and scheduling in following high-level synthesis steps. Note that many HLS tools can internally perform loop fusion/merging.

P1

```
struct my_st {
  char len;
  short a[4];
} m2;
int m3;

    :

C23.send(m2,m3);

    :
```

C23

```
void send(struct my_st d, int dl)
{
   unsigned char buf[4];
   char temp_0;
   short temp_1;
   int temp_2;

   intr.receive();
   temp_0 = d.len;
   buf[0] = temp_0;
   for (int i = 0; i < 4; i+=2) {
      temp_1 = d.a[i];
      htonshort(&buf[2],&temp_1);
      bus.write(&buf[0], 4);
      temp_1 = d.a[i+1];
      htonshort(&buf[0],&temp_1);
   }
   bus.write(&buf[0], 2);
   temp_2 = dl;
   htolong(&buf[0], temp_2);
   bus.write(&buf[0],4);
}
```

Figure 7: Example code after protocol fusion.

However, without further application-level knowledge, backend tools can not perform such optimizations across multiple layers of functionality in all cases.

In the unfused case, the presentation layer first converts a complete message into a block of bytes, the link layer then packetizes each byte block and the MAC layer finally slices each packet into bus words/frames. This requires buffering of complete messages and packets between layers. By contrast, protocol fusion merges the loops of different layers and reschedules processing steps such that messages are processed on a word by word or frame by frame basis (Fig. 6(b)).

Within the protocol fusion process, proper alignment of message members to bus word or frame boundaries has to be considered. If even supported by the backend synthesis tool, misaligned accesses to data in PE buffers, registers or memories can lead to significant hardware and latency overhead. To combat inefficiencies, we implement an alignment algorithm in the synthesis tool. However, aligning of transactions can require padding of bus words and non-optimal utilization of available bus bandwidth, i.e. increased bus traffic. As an alternative, synthesis tools support tight packing, in which basic data members may be partially split across two bus transactions if there is leftover space in the current bus word. This is a trade-off between bus utilization and data alignment overhead. Typically, however, bandwidth losses will be smaller than the cost for restoring alignment.

Fig. 7 shows an example of protocol code after flattening and fusion, where chars and shorts are aligned and packed into half-word units while the trailing integer is aligned to the next full word boundary. In the optimized code, individual message elements of basic data type are converted into network byte format (e.g. using *hton*-type macros for endianess conversion) until enough bytes are available to fill the next bus word. Once a word is complete, it is sent or received over the bus using a protocol-level transaction. This process is repeated, possibly in a looped and hierarchical fashion, over all basic data members in a message.

All protocol fusion algorithms are realized in the synthesis tools based on PE- and bus-specific size and alignment information. Corresponding tables with size and alignment for each basic data type are stored in TLM and MAC databases. By modifying these tables, the fusion process can be adapted to different target architectures, system configurations and backend HLS/memory technology combinations. To create fused code, messages are recursively decomposed into basic data types, which are individually converted, aligned and assembled into bus words or frames. Calls to trigger bus transactions are further inserted at appropriate points in the code whenever a word/frame is complete. In the process, code optimizations are applied to maximally utilize looping structures and hence reduce overall code size.

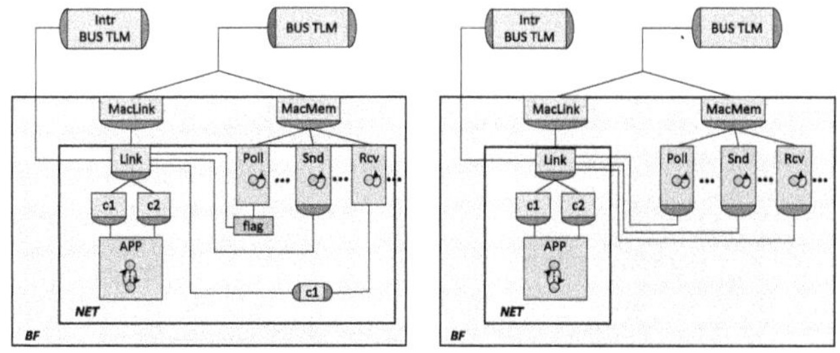

(a) Non-Coupled TLM (b) Coupled TLM

Figure 8: TLM coupling variants.

Protocol fusion significantly reduces physical storage requirements and hence hardware overhead. Instead of buffering a complete message for conversion and packeting, the optimized code only requires a single word-sized buffer. Furthermore, interleaving across layers may lead to better opportunities for pipelining during high-level synthesis. Overall, protocol fusion is a process that can lead to significant gains, but is tedious and error-prone to perform manually.

3.3 Interrupt Hoisting

Interrupt hoisting is aimed at minimizing synchronization overhead. It is performed as a post-optimization to remove side effects of protocol fusion, and to restore synchronization points as defined after message merging. Protocol fusion effectively removes the packeting layer, which results in synchronizations being pushed down to a word or frame level. During interrupt hoisting, synchronization points are elevated up to as high a level as possible, without violating required system-wide synchronization semantics. As a result, synchronization code is hoisted to the packet or message level, and synchronization overhead is minimized.

3.4 Protocol Coupling

Protocol coupling optimizations support a tighter integration of application-specific high-level protocol stacks with synthesis of custom low-level bus protocol implementations. Link-level synchronization behaviors are either coupled with the protocol implementation or synthesized as separate computation blocks. As a result, one of two types of TLMs is generated (Fig. 8). In both cases, the TLM is hierarchically partitioned into a bus functional (BF) and a network layer. During hardware synthesis, the BF layer will be replaced with a custom IP that is generated as part of block-level synthesis (see Section 4.4). The network layer will be converted into synthesizable hardware modules that are passed through the HLS tool. In the uncoupled case (Fig. 8(a)), flag and polling behaviors are part of the network layer, where they become separately synthesized hardware blocks. By contrast, in a coupled TLM (Fig. 8(b)), synchronization functionality is tightly integrated with the protocol layer implementation, which is custom synthesized to provide a minimal set of required flags and synchronization services.

Traditional library- or transducer-based communication synthesis approaches follow an uncoupled approach in which computation blocks are integrated with general bus proto-

```
DESIGN-UNIQUIFY (t):
1  visited[t] ← True
2  ENQUEUE (Q, t)
3  while u ← DEQUEUE(Q)
4    for each i ∈ Instances[u]
5        v = FIND-TYPE(i)
6        if visited[v] = True
7           then v = COPY(v)
8                SET-TYPE(i, v)
9           visited[v] = True
10          ENQUEUE(Q, v)
```

(a) Isolation

```
UPDATE (t):
1 ENQUEUE (Q, t)
2 while u ← DEQUEUE(Q)
3   for each i ∈ Instances[u]
4      v = FIND-TYPE(i)
5      ENQUEUE(Q, v)
6      for each p ∈ Ports[i]
7         m ← GET-MAP(p)
8         w = FIND-TYPE(m)
9         SET-TYPE(p, m)
```

(b) Updating

Figure 9: Pseudo-code for inlining algorithm.

col implementations through a generic protocol-level interface. By contrast, a coupled implementation allows us to support joint co-optimization and co-synthesis of custom-generated protocol/synchronization state machines, as will be described in the following sections.

4. BLOCK-LEVEL SYNTHESIS

Block-level synthesis refines the TLM down to block-level modules, protocol IPs, and a block-level netlist. Computation and synchronization behaviors in the network layer of the TLM are divided into single-threaded modules that are merged with communication adapters to become synthesizable hardware blocks. In addition, adapters and behaviors in the BF layer are combined with and transformed into custom-generated protocol IP components. Finally, pin-level connections between synthesized blocks and protocol IPs are translated into a corresponding HDL netlist.

4.1 Block Module Code Generation

A module code generator performs the necessary conversion of the TLM network layer into C++ or SystemC code that can be synthesized by a following HLS tool. In the process, it subdivides the TLM into behavioral block-level modules, inlines communication layers, and converts communication calls at block boundaries into MAC ports.

Most HLS tools can synthesize multiple single-threaded C++/SystemC modules with the capability to stitch blocks together. However, they can not automatically partition pre-existing code. Furthermore, multi-block synthesis is not universally supported and syntax and semantics vary. In order to provide a general approach that can be easily adapted to different HLS backends, we partition the code into separately synthesized modules that are integrated through our own netlisting engine. In the process, each computation or synchronization behavior in the TLM network layer is converted into a separate, synthesizable hardware block.

After block partitioning, transactor protocol stacks are inlined into each accessing computation block. This is done in such a way as to enable computation/communication co-optimizations in the following high-level synthesis step, with the scheduling freedom to overlap computation with communication and to perform general, joint optimizations, such as resource sharing or parallelization.

In the TLM, computation behaviors connect to communication adapters via an interface mechanism. Interfaces define a base signature of methods that a behavior can access without having to know the method realizations, which are provided by separate adapter channels. During block synthesis, however, interface calls need to be resolved and

```
sc_module(MacLink) {
public:
   sc_port<sc_signal_in<...> > listen;
   sc_port<sc_signal_out<..> > serve;
   ...
   uint_t Listen(uint_t addr, bool read) {
      do { sc_bv<...> bus = listen.read();
      } while (!checkRW(bus,read) && !checkAddr(bus, addr));
      return getRdata(bus);
   }
   void Serve(uint_t data) { serve.write(data); }

   void slaveRead(uint_t addr, uint_t* data, uint_t len) {
      for( ; len; len--, data++) {
         *data = Listen(addr, false);
         Serve(0);
      }
   }
   void slaveWrite(uint_t addr, uint_t* data, uint_t len) {
      for( ; len; len--, data++) {
         Listen(addr, true);
         Serve(*data);
      }
   }
};
```

Figure 10: MAC database protocol wrapper.

adapters inlined to establish the true caller-callee relationship and allow for joint high-level synthesis. Since static code analysis in most HLS tools cannot natively handle dynamic interface binding, we perform a preprocessing step to resolve interfaces and any associated polymorphism.

The inlining algorithm in Fig. 9 traverses the module hierarchy and replaces interfaces with direct, statically bound calls to the connected adapter channel. Multiple instances of the same module type that connect to different channels are isolated into unique instance types, which include appropriate target calls. Given a top module t, the algorithm in Fig.9 (a)) visits all module classes in the TLM layer hierarchy in a breadth-first manner. For each class type u, all of its children are examined and the type v of each child instance i is determined. If another instance of v has already been encountered, i is replaced with an instance of a copy of v (lines 7 and 8). After all child instances have been examined and isolated, their types are guaranteed to be unique. In a second UPDATE algorithm, (Fig. 9 (b)) the class hierarchy is traversed again to remove all interfaces and update all port types to directly point to the connected channel instead. For each child instance in each visited class, the list of ports is traversed (line 6), the target m of the port's mapping is determined (line 7) and the port type is set to the class w of the connected instance m (lines 8-9).

4.2 MAC Layer Insertion

At the lowest level of the adapter hierarchy, behavioral interface or variable ports between blocks and bus protocol IPs have to be converted into wire-level register or FIFO interfaces as supported by the underlying HLS engine. The challenge is in providing an interfacing mechanism that is general in supporting a wide range of pre-defined bus targets while allowing for customization and co-optimization of low-level protocol implementations based on application requirements. For this purpose, MAC implementations inserted from a database provide the glue logic between application and target specifics. MAC database implementations convert functional into HLS-specific low-level interfaces. They thereby replace MAC adapters in the TLM with code that

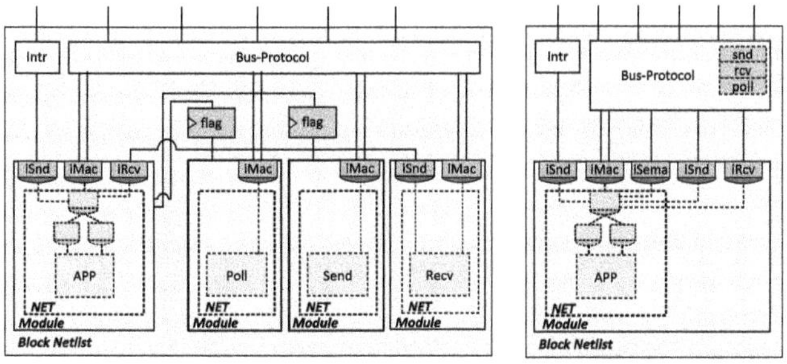

(a) Non-coupled BLM (b) Coupled BLM

Figure 11: Block-level model.

provides equivalent, canonical protocol-level TLM bus interfaces while internally translating each transaction into corresponding pin- and wire-level interactions with a target-specific bus protocol IP component. For coupling-driven optimizations, the MAC database also contains adapters that are inserted to replace synchronization behaviors in the BF layer with equivalent interfaces to flag and polling functionality directly synthesized into the protocol IP.

Fig. 10 shows an example of MAC database code for a slave protocol wrapper. The MAC adapter communicates with the protocol IP through primitive ports, which will be synthesized into a corresponding pin-level interface by the HLS tool. At the other end, it provides a TLM-equivalent, functional *Read()/Write()* interface to the calling module in which it is inlined. Internally, the MAC adapter contains functionality to translate between the two sides. In case of a bus protocol MAC adapter as shown here, this includes slicing of data packets into individual protocol transactions. To enable interleaving of communication and computation, and to expose corresponding parallelism to the HLS tool, protocol transactions are split into separate *Listen()* and *Serve()* methods. Furthermore, part of the protocol layer address decoding functionality is merged into the *Listen()* method. Combined, this provides the HLS tool the scheduling freedom to overlap computation with communication and to hide communication delays.

4.3 Protocol IP Generation

Each protocol adapter in the BF layer is synthesized into a protocol IP. Based on parameters, such as the type and number of adapters, a protocol generator creates a custom IP block from SystemC and RTL templates stored in the protocol database. The database templates are pre-written to model and implement external bus protocol and interrupt control logic. Their internal interface is designed to match associated protocol wrappers in the MAC database, which, when synthesized into other blocks, will realize appropriate pin- and wire-level interactions with the generated IP.

In a coupled model, additional parameters, such as address mapping and number and type of synchronization flags are used to synthesize custom synchronization functionality directly into the generated protocol IP. This allows for sharing of address decoding logic between synchronization and data transfers. Based on provided parameters, a protocol IP generator creates the required template instantiations, re-configures the address decoder, and provides necessary internal MAC interfaces to computation blocks.

4.4 Bus-Functional Synthesis

Bus-functional synthesis transforms the BF layer of the TLM into a final netlist to connect synthesized blocks and protocol IPs. As shown in Fig. 11, the resulting BLM combines modules to be synthesized by the HLS tool with custom-generated protocol-level IPs. As described above, application and, in the uncoupled case, synchronization behaviors are converted into synthesizable modules, where communication adapters are inlined and external interfaces are replaced with MAC implementations from the database. In a coupled model (Fig. 11(b)), synchronization functionality is realized directly in the generated protocol IP, and thin MAC wrappers are inserted to replace original synchronization behaviors with corresponding protocol IP interfaces.

Finally, the connectivity of all blocks, IPs and external ports is converted into a block-level netlist. In the process, variables and channels between modules are converted into registers and logic connecting the pin-level FIFO ports of synthesized blocks and protocol IPs. Fig. 12 shows the resulting RTL model after high-level synthesis. Protocol IPs realize state machines for driving and sampling of external bus and interrupt wires. The sampled external bus signals are passed on to MAC implementations synthesized into computation and synchronization blocks. A listen port thereby broadcasts the contents of an IP-internal bus sampling register. Synthesized MAC implementation in each block decode the listen addresses and communicate input data to the computation. The protocol IP in turn receives acknowledgements and output data from the MAC layers over a custom-generated number of serve ports. In a coupled

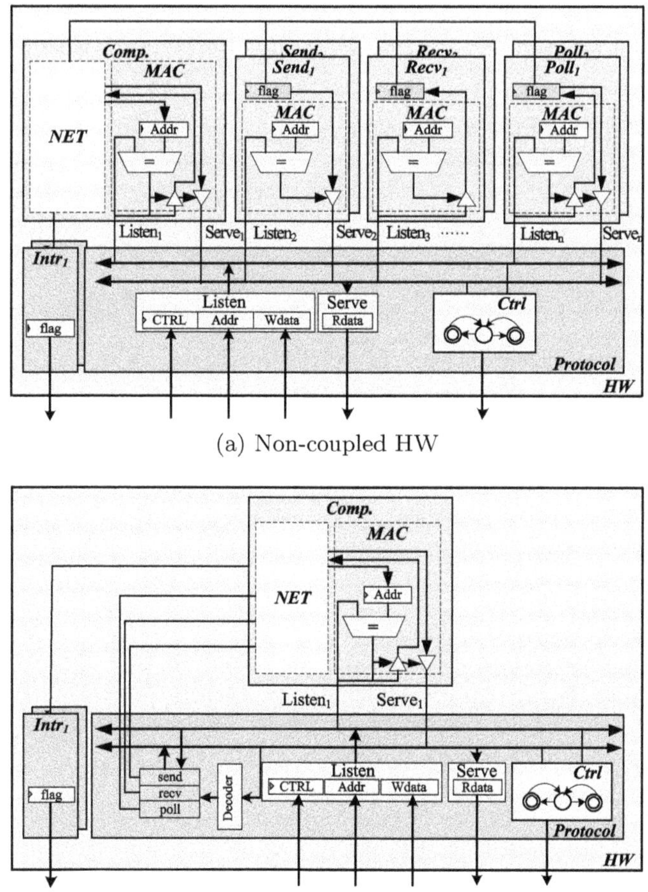

(a) Non-coupled HW

(b) Coupled HW

Figure 12: Synthesized hardware processor.

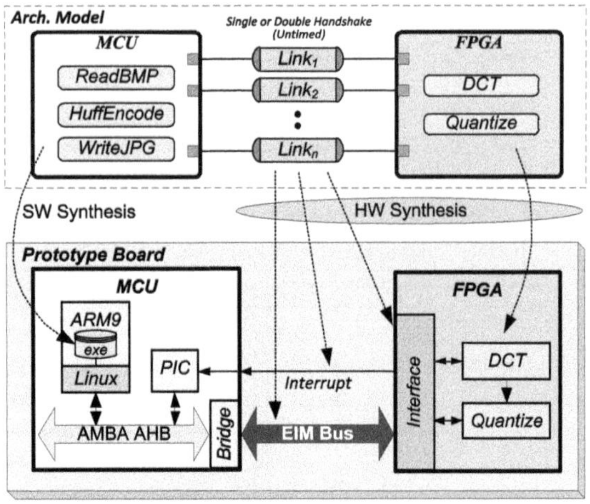

Figure 13: JPEG Encoder mapping.

model (Fig. 12(b)), the generated protocol IP provides additional interfaces to access synchronization flags over matching thin MAC wrappers synthesized into each computation block. By contrast, in the uncoupled case (Fig. 12(a)), each separately synthesized synchronization block includes its own address decoders and tristate drivers that interface with the internally shared bus IP on a generic protocol level.

5. EXPERIMENTS AND RESULTS

We have implemented communication and block-level synthesis tools for our proposed approach and integrated them into an overall flow that utilizes Calypto Catapult [4] as HLS backend. Without loss of generality, we use the SpecC language to describe TLMs throughout the flow, and C++ and Verilog as input and output of the HLS tool, respectively. To demonstrate the benefits of our approach, we have applied the flow to synthesis of JPEG encoding and AC3 decoding applications onto an ARM-based target platform consisting of a Freescale i.MX21 applications processor (MCU) and a Xilinx Spartan-3 FPGA communicating over Freescale's proprietary EIM bus. The MCU contains an ARM9 that runs a Linux kernel and an EIM module that bridges between the AMBA AHB and EIM busses. We prepared database components for each tool in the flow, including TLMs of AHB and EIM busses, models of MCU and FPGA PEs, and EIM MAC layers and custom RTL bus protocol IPs.

We created architecture models for JPEG and AC3 examples with different mappings and communication semantics. As shown in Fig. 13 for the JPEG design, selected computation processes are mapped onto the FPGA while the rest of the application functionality executes on the ARM in the MCU. In the JPEG case, DCT and Quantize (Q) blocks are mapped into hardware. For the AC3, either the inverse modified discrete cosine transform (IMDCT) or the mantissa unpacking (MANT) process is in the FPGA. In both cases, the two PEs communicate through double-handshake (DH) message and single-handshake (SH) event channels. For every double-handshake channel, we configured associated implementation parameters (bus addresses and synchronization mechanism) to synthesize a polling, interrupt, or interrupt-sharing scheme for synchronization. For single-handshake channels, we applied polling for slave-to-master and master-to-slave notifications. Input architecture model configurations are summarized in Table 1.

Using our fully automated flow, we were able to synthesize input architecture models into correct RTL ready for further FPGA download within minutes, yielding substantial productivity gains compared to a manual design process. High-level synthesis was performed using Catapult's default optimization settings. Generated RTL was synthesized down to an FPGA bit file using Mentor Precision and Xilinx ISE. Designs were synthesized for target FPGA clock frequency of 50MHz. Area and latency results of synthesizing computation processes alone are summarized in Table 2. On the MCU side, software was synthesized, combined with manually written driver code, and cross-compiled into a Linux executable. The same firmware code was used for all designs. In all cases, we have successfully validated the functionality on the board. We evaluated end-to-end hardware latency by instrumenting the JPEG encoder and AC3 decoder software to record the average turnaround times over 180 DCT-Q, 1740 IMDCT or 1740 MANT invocations, including all communication and synchronization overhead.

We synthesized variants of each design mapping all double-handshake message-passing channels into polling (POLL) or interrupt (INTR) implementations. In all cases, we applied message merging (MM), protocol fusion (PF), protocol coupling (PC), or all optimizations combined (ALL), and we compared FPGA resource usage and hardware latency against an unoptimized design (NOPT) and a manual implementation (MAN). The unoptimized, non-coupled implementations replicate traditional library- or transducer-based communication synthesis approaches, as realized by others and discussed in the related work. For a fair comparison, the manual design utilizes the same computation block synthesized by Catapult and the same firmware code to access hardware.

Table 3 compares designs in terms of their communication statistics and communication overhead as determined, respectively, by the number of synchronization behaviors in the TLM and by additional latency and FPGA resources of communication interfaces. Transactor overhead was measured as area and latency on top of basic computation requirements, i.e. by subtracting results in Table 2 from the final area and latency of the complete FPGA hardware.

We can observe that in all cases, the latency of final, optimized transactors synthesized with our flow is always significantly less than in a manual design. In contrast to a manual design in which transactors and computation blocks are designed separately to manage complexities, our approach is able to perform co-optimizations across computation and communication boundaries, e.g. to overlap and hide communication latency behind computation delays. In the DCT-Q case, data is processed strictly in the order it is received and sent. This allows computation and com-

Table 1: Input architecture models.

Application	FPGA process	DH Chs.	SH Chs.
Jpeg Encoder	DCT-Q	4	2
AC3 Decoder	IMDCT	5	0
	MANT	8	0

Table 2: Computation synthesis results.

Setup	LUTs	FFs	Muls	Memory	Latency
DCT-Q	3298	2121	16	512 bytes	6.25ms
IMDCT	6661	3673	28	11,264 bytes	1.57ms
MANT	6853	4158	1	0 bytes	0.697s

Table 3: **Transactor synthesis results.**

Setup	Opt	TLM				Communication overhead (% difference vs. unoptimized)				
		Intr	Poll	Send	Recv	LUTs	FFs	Logic score	Mem [bytes]	Latency
DCT-Q-INTR	NOPT	2	2	1	1	2036	1076	3112	512	53.6ms
	MM	2	2	1	1	2036	1076	3112 (0.0%)	512 (0.0%)	53.6ms (0.0%)
	PF	2	2	1	1	2091	1171	3262 (4.8%)	512 (0.0%)	53.6ms (0.0%)
	PC	2	2	1	1	827	287	1114 (-64.2%)	512 (0.0%)	53.3ms (-0.5%)
	ALL	2	2	1	1	793	-75	718 (-76.9%)	512 (0.0%)	53.4ms (-0.4%)
	MAN	NA				-14	61	47 (-98.5%)	512 (0.0%)	71.4ms (33.1%)
DCT-Q-POLL	NOPT	0	4	1	1	2109	1181	3290	512	3.15ms
	MM	0	4	1	1	2109	1181	3290 (0.0%)	512 (0.0%)	3.15ms (0.0%)
	PF	0	4	1	1	2093	1161	3254 (-1.1%)	512 (0.0%)	3.15ms (0.1%)
	PC	0	4	1	1	810	264	1074 (-67.4%)	512 (0.0%)	3.08ms (-2.2%)
	ALL	0	4	1	1	835	220	1055 (-67.9%)	512 (0.0%)	3.50ms (11.2%)
	MAN	NA				-17	58	41 (-98.8%)	512 (0.0%)	13.5ms(329.1%)
IMDCT-INTR	NOPT	3	2	0	0	5035	2445	7480	41984	6.59ms
	MM	2	2	0	0	4239	1733	5972 (-20.2%)	41984 (0.0%)	6.50ms (-1.8%)
	PF	3	2	0	0	3767	1536	5303 (-29.1%)	21504(-48.8%)	6.24ms (-5.2%)
	PC	3	2	0	0	3858	1342	5200 (-30.5%)	41984 (0.0%)	6.60ms (0.4%)
	ALL	2	2	0	0	2574	699	3273 (-56.2%)	21504(-48.8%)	5.60ms(-14.8%)
	MAN	NA				522	322	844 (-88.7%)	25600(-39.0%)	6.27ms (-4.7%)
IMDCT-POLL	NOPT	0	5	0	0	4874	2181	7055	41984	5.76ms
	MM	0	4	0	0	4239	1733	5972 (-15.4%)	41984 (0.0%)	5.74ms (-0.4%)
	PF	0	5	0	0	3687	1485	5172 (-26.7%)	21504(-48.8%)	5.54ms (-3.8%)
	PC	0	5	0	0	3933	1452	5385 (-23.7%)	41984 (0.0%)	5.74ms (-0.4%)
	ALL	0	4	0	0	2463	622	3085 (-56.3%)	21504(-48.8%)	5.61ms (-2.6%)
	MAN	NA				540	319	859 (-87.8%)	25600(-39.0%)	5.82ms (1.0%)
MANT-INTR	NOPT	6	2	0	0	9164	3232	12396	23552	5.54ms
	MM	2	2	0	0	6032	4906	10938(-11.8%)	19456(-17.4%)	4.97ms(-10.2%)
	PF	6	2	0	0	8912	2987	11899 (-4.0%)	7168 (-69.6%)	5.01ms (-9.5%)
	PC	6	2	0	0	7462	3000	10462(-15.6%)	23552 (0.0%)	5.20ms (-6.1%)
	ALL	2	2	0	0	6911	3830	10741(-13.4%)	7168 (-69.6%)	4.36ms(-21.2%)
	MAN	NA				2254	2990	5244 (-57.7%)	13312(-43.5%)	4.62ms(-16.5%)
MANT-POLL	NOPT	0	8	0	0	9851	3622	13473	23552	4.41ms
	MM	0	4	0	0	6743	2640	9383 (-30.4%)	19456(-17.4%)	4.00ms (-9.2%)
	PF	0	8	0	0	7860	5543	13403 (-0.5%)	7168 (-69.6%)	3.89ms(-11.7%)
	PC	0	8	0	0	7184	3034	10218(-24.2%)	23552 (0.0%)	3.64ms(-17.4%)
	ALL	0	4	0	0	5724	1438	7162 (-46.8%)	7168 (-69.6%)	3.66ms(-17.0%)
	MAN	NA				2280	2992	5272 (-60.9%)	13312(-43.5%)	3.88ms(-11.8%)

munication to be pipelined and scheduled in parallel. By contrast, non-sequential data access patterns in the IMDCT and MANT blocks result in less latency improvements than in the DCT-Q. In both cases, computation/communication co-optimizations are also only enabled after exposing them to the following HLS tool through a protocol fusion step, as will be described below. In all cases, however, a naive, unoptimized realization of such computation/communication co-design can lead to a large increase in logic complexity, memory size and hence total area.

The proposed protocol stack optimizations prove to be efficient in reducing this area overhead as well as in further improving latency. Message merging can improve both. In the complex MANT design with a large number of messages, message merging can achieve up to 30.4% logic and 9.2% latency reduction by removing four out of eight interrupt or polling synchronizations. In the IMDCT, only one channel can be optimized away. As such, latency improvements are small but up to 29.1% less logic is required. No improvements can be seen for the simple DCT-Q design, in which only one message is exchanged at a time.

As expected, protocol fusion eliminates the need for large buffer memory between communication layers that a naive computation/communication co-design approach requires. Instead of buffering complete messages and packets, the optimized code only requires a single word-sized flip-flop. Additionally, protocol fusion can lead to latency improvements of up to 11.7% due to better interleaving and pipelining across layers during high-level synthesis. Note that in the simple DCT-Q case, Catapult is able to perform loop merging by itself. Hence, protocol fusion is not effective in optimizing the code further. However, this is not the case for more complex MANT and IMDCT designs, in which multiple levels of loop hierarchy need to be exposed for merging.

Finally, protocol coupling paired with custom-generation of protocol IP can significantly reduce resource utilization and latency. In uncoupled implementations reminiscent of traditional library- or transducer-based approaches, generality comes with high overhead and subsequent loss in optimality. By contrast, resource sharing in the coupled design results in up to 67.4% logic and 17.4% latency reduction.

Fig. 14 plots communication overhead in terms of area, memory and latency, normalized to the unoptimized case. After applying all protocol stack optimizations, logic, memory and latency overheads are reduced by up to 77%, 70% and 21%, respectively. Overall quality of results is comparable to a manual design, where on average a 21% improvement in latency can be achieved. Note that in the manual

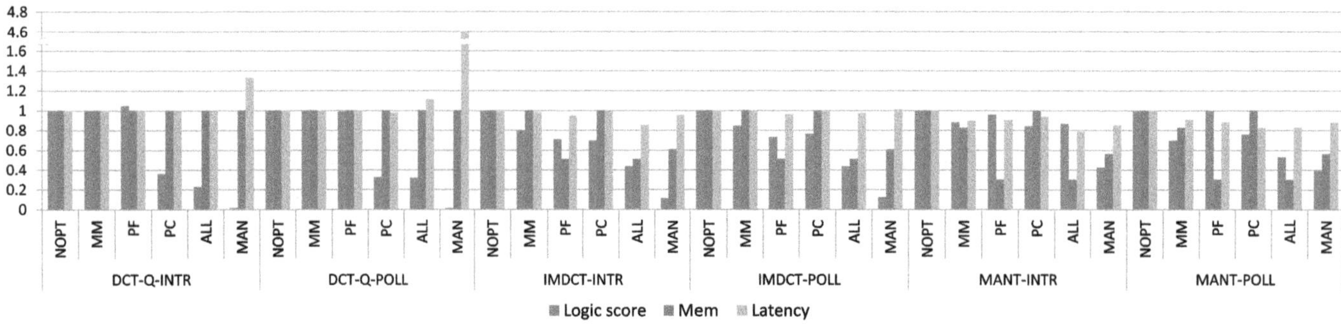

Figure 14: Comparison of communication overheads.

case, logic complexity is decreased at the expense of a higher memory requirement. This is due to less opportunities for sharing of memory among different message members. In summary, when including computation and communication, the total latency, logic score and memory size of our complete design is on average 16% faster, 20% larger and 19% smaller, respectively, than a complete hardware processor with a manually designed communication interface.

6. SUMMARY AND CONCLUSIONS

We have presented a systematic design approach to automatically synthesize custom, application- and target-specific bus-based hardware interfaces. Utilizing tools and databases along with a HLS engine, we provide a seamless flow from abstract specifications of desired communication functionality and topology down to cycle-accurate RTL. The approach supports various synchronization schemes and by replacing databases, it can be easily adapted to different HLS backends and synthesis targets. Experiments demonstrate that significant productivity gains can be achieved. Moreover, the quality of result is comparable to area and latency of manual designs, where a set of novel protocol optimizations can provide significant area and latency gains. In the future, we plan to extend our work to synthesize a wider range of communication primitives and styles (e.g. shared variables, hardware queues, master interfaces and transducers), including further optimizations of synthesized transactors. We also intend to expand support for SystemC TLM-2.0 interfaces and for utilizing other HLS backend tools.

7. REFERENCES

[1] S. Abdi et al. Automatic TLM generation for early validation of multicore systems. *IEEE D&T*, 28(3), 2011.

[2] N. Bombieri, F. Fummi, and V. Guarnieri. Automatic synthesis of OSCI TLM-2.0 models into RTL bus-based IPs. In *HLDVT*, 2010.

[3] L. Cai and D. Gajski. Transaction level modeling: An overview. In *CODES+ISSS*, 2003.

[4] Calypto Design Systems. Catapult C. http://www.calypto.com.

[5] H. Cho, S. Abdi, and D. Gajski. Interface synthesis for heterogeneous multi-core systems from transaction level models. In *LCTES*, 2007.

[6] Forte Design System. Forte Cythesizer. http://www.forteds.com.

[7] D. Gajski et al. *SpecC: Specification Language and Methodology.* Kluwer Academic Publishers, 2000.

[8] A. Gerstlauer et al. Automatic layer-based generation of system-on-chip bus communication models. *TCAD*, 26:1676–1687, 2007.

[9] J. Gladigau et al. Automatic system-level synthesis: From formal application models to generic bus-based MPSoCs. *Transactions on HiPEAC*, 5(4), 2011.

[10] T. Grotker et al. *System Design with SystemC.* Kluwer Academic Publishers, 2002.

[11] N. Hatami, P. Prinetto, and A. Trapanese. Hardware design methodology to synthesize communication interfaces from TLM to RTL. In *AQTR*, May 2010.

[12] Y.-T. Hwang and S.-C. Lin. Automatic protocol translation and template based interface synthesis for IP reuse in SoC. In *APCCAS*, 2004.

[13] K. Keutzer et al. System level design: Orthogonalization of concerns and platform-based design. *TCAD*, 19, 2000.

[14] G. Lee et al. Automatic bus matrix synthesis based on hardware interface selection for fast communication design space exploration. In *SAMOS*, 2007.

[15] H. G. Lee et al. On-chip communication architecture exploration: A quantitative evaluation of point-to-point, bus, and network-on-chip approaches. *TODAES*, 12(3), 2007.

[16] L. Moss et al. Automation of communication refinement and hardware synthesis within a system-level design methodology. In *RSP*, 2008.

[17] S. Pasricha et al. CAPPS: A framework for power-performance trade-offs in bus matrix based on-chip communication architecture synthesis. *TVLSI*, 18(2), 2010.

[18] A. Pinto, L. Carloni, and A. Sangiovanni-Vincentell. COSI: A framework for the design of interconnection networks. *IEEE D&T*, 25(5), 2008.

[19] K. Popovici and A. Jerraya. Flexible and abstract communication and interconnect modeling for MPSoC. In *ASPDAC*, Jan. 2009.

[20] D. Shin et al. Automatic generation of transaction level models for rapid design space exploration. In *CODES+ISSS*, 2006.

[21] S. Watanabe et al. Automatic protocol transducer synthesis aiming at facilitating IP-reuse. In *IWLS*, 2006.

[22] N.-E. Zergainoh, A. Baghdadi, and A. Jerray. Hardware/software codesign of on-chip communication architecture for application-specific multiprocessor system-on-chip. *JES*, 1:112–124, 2005.

Fast Online Synthesis of Generally Programmable Digital Microfluidic Biochips

Daniel Grissom, Philip Brisk
Department of Computer Science and Engineering
University of California, Riverside
{grissomd, philip}@cs.ucr.edu

ABSTRACT

We introduce an online synthesis flow for digital microfluidic biochips, which will enable real-time response to errors and control flow. The objective of this flow is to facilitate fast assay synthesis while minimally compromising the quality of results. In particular, we show that a virtual topology, which constrains the allowable locations of assay operations such as mixing, dilution, sensing, etc., in lieu of traditional placement, can significantly speed up the synthesis process without significantly lengthening assay execution time.

Categories and Subject Descriptors

B.7.2 [**Integrated Circuits**]: Design Aids – *Placement and routing.*

General Terms

Algorithms, Design, Performance.

Keywords

Microfluidics, Laboratory-on-Chip (LoC), Electrowetting-on-Dielectric (EWoD), Synthesis.

1. INTRODUCTION

With the emergence of novel, scalable, flexible digital microfluidic biochips (DMFBs) [15], new features such as end-user programmability and online synthesis will revolutionize microfluidic applications. Instead of application-specific DMFBs, low-cost, general-purpose DMFBs will provide a reusable, flexible, programmable platform. With the notion of end-user programmability being introduced to DMFBs, control-flow constructs present exciting, new possibilities for microfluidic applications. Consequently, when control-flow is introduced, synthesis (**Figure 2**) will need to be performed online since the order of *assays* (biochemical reactions) to be executed is no longer deterministic, but instead dependent on live-feedback from the DMFB [2][13].

In contrast to *offline compilers*, which synthesize assays as deterministic state-machines, an *online interpreter* will act more like a virtual machine which manages the DMFB's resources and interprets assays on-the-fly. **Figure 1** shows the tradeoffs that need to be made when moving synthesis online. During offline compilation, optimized designs are created with little concern to runtime since the synthesis process is run once and the compiled

CODES+ISSS'12, October 7–12, 2012, Tampere, Finland.

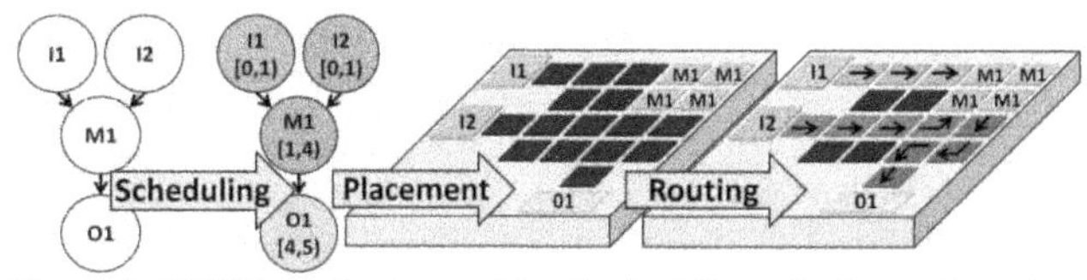

Figure 2. DMFB synthesis consists of ***scheduling, placing*** **and** ***routing*.**

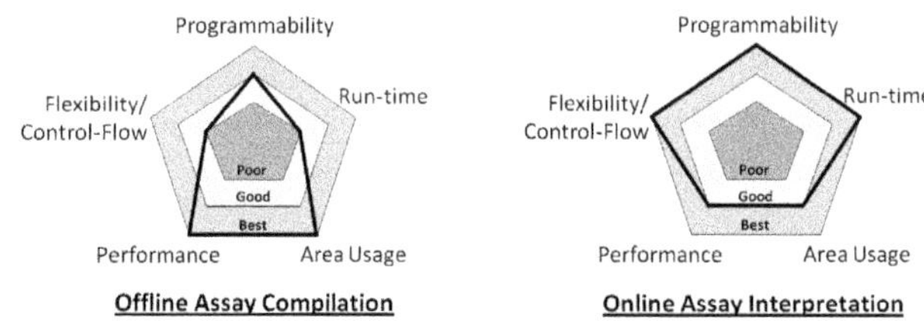

Figure 1. Offline vs. online synthesis tradeoffs.

"executable binary" is packaged into an application-specific device. With a programmable DMFB, the end-user will have to wait each time a programmed assay is synthesized. Furthermore, each time a branch is taken, the user will have to wait as the target assay of the branch is interpreted online. Thus, new synthesis methods are needed that concede optimality in performance and area to reduce algorithmic runtimes from seconds/minutes to milliseconds and achieve a greater amount of flexibility [13].

1.1 Motivation

We motivate the need for fast, online synthesis methods with an example that is either impossible without this feature, or requires unreasonably complex solutions. Consider a drug-discovery application where a DMFB executes an assay, measures the result and then automatically executes a new assay (or batch of assays) with different concentrations, based on the previous result. This process is repeated thousands of times until a set of concentrations yielding the desired result is discovered.

With offline compilation, a single DAG must be created that details every possible execution path, which quickly becomes intractable as the compiler must account for numerous paths that will never be taken [2]. Instead, upon completion of one assay, an online interpreter could immediately interpret and execute the next assay with only milliseconds of downtime between assays.

Although synthesis has been performed entirely offline up to this point, Ho, Chakrabarty and Pop suggest that online systems are forthcoming with the development of "specialized heuristics" which can perform synthesis in milliseconds [10]; Luo Chakrabarty, and Ho [13] have implemented one such specialized heuristic for an error detection and recovery scheme based on checkpointing: at each checkpoint, a droplet is routed to a sensor that detects whether its concentration is satisfactory; if not, the assay is re-synthesized on-the-fly to repeat the sequence of operations that produced the droplet, interleaving the schedule of these newly-introduced operations with concurrent operations that do not depend on the droplet that failed the checkpoint.

1.2 Contribution

Assays are synthesized by computing solutions for three NP-complete problems, as seen in **Figure 2**. Before synthesis, an assay is modeled as a directed acyclic graph (DAG), where the nodes and edges represent operations and operation dependencies, respectively. Each assay operation is then assigned start/stop times during resource-constrained scheduling [19]. During the placement stage, the scheduled operations are assigned specific locations, called *modules*, on the array [25]. Finally, the routing stage computes droplet paths between subsequent modules and I/O ports so droplets arrive safely at each destination [27].

We present an online synthesis flow that can interpret assays and map them onto a cross-referenced, fully-addressable or active-matrix DMFB [15] in milliseconds, making it appropriate for both offline and online synthesis. Our key contribution is a virtual topology that defines distinct regions for module placement and droplet routing. With our topology in mind, list scheduling [24] is used to quickly produce schedules. Placement, which has been solved in the past by iterative improvement algorithms [25][32] or integer linear programming (ILP) [12], is simplified to a binding problem, which can be solved efficiently in polynomial-time [11]. The placement defined by the virtual topology provides dedicated routing cells which ease the router's job. We simplify an existing router [20] to compute droplet paths very quickly.

1.3 DMFB Technology Overview

A DMFB manipulates discrete droplets of fluid on a 2D array of electrodes (**Figure 3(a)**) through electrowetting, a process that induces droplet motion [18]. **Figure 3(b)** shows a droplet sandwiched between a ground electrode and a set of independent control electrodes. The droplet is centered over one electrode (CE2), but overlaps adjacent electrodes CE1 and CE3. If a voltage is applied to CE1 or CE3, the surface energy gradient induces motion and the droplet will move to the center of the newly activated electrode(s). During each droplet-actuation *cycle*, a set of electrodes is activated which moves droplets from electrode to electrode. Basic assay operations such as transport, mixing, merging and splitting are performed through the appropriate sequence of electrode activations over a number of cycles.

There are several classes of DMFBs that provide varying levels of droplet control. Typical *direct-addressing* (*fully-addressable*) DMFBs have one control pin for each electrode (i.e. $(M \times N)$ control pins for an $(M \times N)$ array of electrodes) so each electrode (droplet) can be independently controlled at all times. However, the wiring cost of independently controlled electrodes, especially as array sizes grow, has motivated cheaper designs [29].

Cross-referencing DMFBs use $(M + N)$ control pins to control an $(M \times N)$ array of electrodes [5]. In this scheme, each row and each column has a single control pin; when a particular column m and row n are activated, the electrode at (m, n) is activated. Multiple columns and rows can be simultaneously activated, but may cause superfluous electrode activation, yielding undesired droplet movement [28]. Thus, once a route for a direct-addressing DMFB is computed, each droplet-actuation cycle is serialized across multiple droplet-actuation cycles, resulting in prolonged routing times and increased algorithmic complexity.

Pin-constrained DMFBs represent another addressing scheme. An assay is first synthesized as if on a direct-addressing DMFB; then, special heuristics attempting to solve the clique partitioning problem (NP-Hard) are used to minimize the total number of

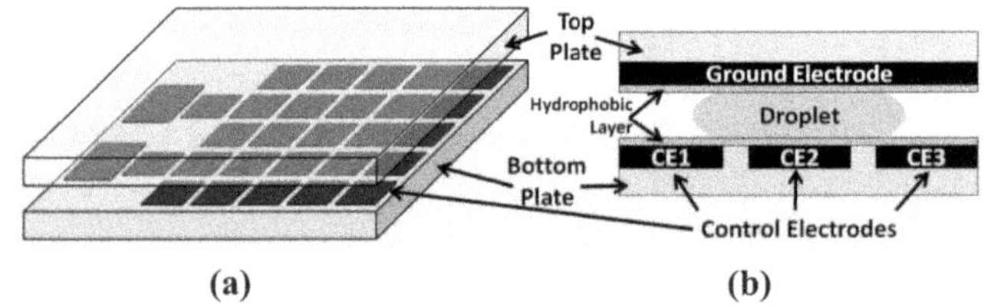

Figure 3. (a) DMFB with a 2D array of electrodes; (b) DMFB cross-section.

control pins, based on which electrodes can be activated together without causing undesired droplet movement [29].

To summarize, pin-constrained designs offer minimal product costs, are inflexible and cannot be reprogrammed after being manufactured; cross-referencing DMFBs are reprogrammable, but add another layer of complexity that must be handled to serialize droplet motion [28].

Fortunately, *active-matrix addressing* designs are emerging which give independent control of $(M \times N)$ electrodes while using only $(M + N)$ control pins [15]. Active matrix addressing can scale without growing prohibitively expensive, while maintaining the maximum level of flexibility and control so that assays can be programmed with minimal levels of algorithmic complexity. *The online synthesis flow presented in this paper is compatible with direct, cross-referencing, and active-matrix addressing DMFBs.*

2. RELATED WORK

Here, we highlight some of the previous work in DMFB synthesis for scheduling, placement and routing.

2.1 Scheduling

Su and Chakrabarty present modified list scheduling (MLS) and genetic algorithm (GA) heuristics, as well as an optimal integer linear programming (ILP) model for scheduling microfluidic operations onto a DMFB [24]. As expected, the ILP implementation consumes a large amount of time to compute optimal solutions. Although the GA finds optimal or near-optimal results in much less time than ILP, its iterative nature still results in large computation times. MLS produces schedules comparable to GA in much less time. Other scheduling algorithms such as Ricketts' hybrid genetic algorithm [19] and Maftei's tabu search scheduler [14] are iterative improvement algorithms which spend anywhere from 4 seconds to 1 hour computing schedules. We chose list scheduling as the base scheduler for our framework, but other fast schedulers being developed now [8][16] or in the future could be used as well.

2.2 Placement

At the physical level, all electrodes are equally capable of performing the basic microfluidic operations (i.e. merging, mixing, splitting, transport, storage); hence, basic operations can be performed anywhere on a DMFB array. The objective for most placers is to pack as many concurrent operations/modules into as little area as possible. Several direct-addressing placement and unified scheduling-placement algorithms [25][26][30][32] use simulated annealing, which run in minutes or tens of seconds; in contrast, our online flow completes in tens of milliseconds.

Griffith et al. [6] place a virtual topology onto the DMFB, which dictates separate regions for assay operations and droplet routing; however, they only present results for one assay, and their implementation suffers from deadlocks during droplet routing. Our approach is similar, but does not suffer from deadlock; in the absolute worst case, our router will transport one droplet at a time;

however, we include a compaction step to transport multiple droplets concurrently.

2.3 Routing

Böhringer [3] modeled droplet routing as an A* search, similar to path planning in robotics, achieving an optimal-length solution, when routable. Su et al. route droplets sequentially and redo placement when routing fails [27]. BioRoute [31] uses a min-cost max-flow algorithm to compute several routes at once, followed by negotiation-based detailed routing. Cho and Pan [4] route droplets one-by-one and sort them based on a *bypassability* metric; if a deadlock occurs, droplets are moved to *concession zones* to break the deadlock. Huang and Ho [9] construct a system of global routing tracks, which are aligned in the same direction as the majority of droplets traveling on that tract. They use an entropy-based equation to determine the order in which droplets are routed, and finally, compact the routes using dynamic programming. Since the aforementioned methods were designed for offline routing, few mention runtimes [3][4][27]. BioRoute [31] and Huang's algorithm [9] both report runtimes below 1s on a desktop PC. The router used in our online flow, in contrast, achieves comparable runtimes on an Intel Atom™ processor.

2.4 Combined Methods

Most work on synthesis has focused on the scheduling, placement or routing problems in isolation. Several papers, however, solve some of these problems together, using iterative improvement heuristics [13][25][26][30][32], whose runtime is prohibitive. These approaches address problems that can arise when one stage of synthesis does not consider the next. For instance, a placer can generate a valid placement that is unroutable. Our virtual topology ensures routability by leaving room for droplets to pass between adjacent "modules" where mixing, storage, and other assay operations are performed.

3. VIRTUAL TOPOLOGY

Our online interpreter utilizes a virtual topology, as seen in **Figure 4**, and takes advantage of its order and structure to yield fast algorithmic runtimes for scheduling, placement and routing. First, we define a *cell* as the 2D area covering an electrode. The virtual topology shows evenly spaced modules (3x3 squares of cells) where basic droplet operations (i.e. merge, mix, split, store) are performed. If at least one of a module's cells is augmented with an external detector or heater, the module can also perform detect or heat operations, respectively. The white cells indicate the area of the DMFB array used explicitly for routing droplets between modules and I/O ports (not pictured); however, any cell can be used for routing if a module is not in use. Dedicated routing cells ensure there is a valid path between any source-destination pair. A perimeter of *interference region (IR) cells* surrounds each module [27], so that interference-free droplet routes can be computed easily; this topology ensures that there is at least one path between all DMFB inputs, modules, and outputs. The inputs and outputs, (not shown in **Figure 4**), are on the perimeter of the chip.

3.1 Module Topology and Synchronization

To help prevent droplet deadlock, droplets have well-defined module entrance and exit locations, as seen in the 3x3 module of **Figure 5(a)**. The two entrances are in the northwest and southwest corners, while the exits are in the northeast and southeast corners. By providing distinct entrances and exits, we prevent droplet deadlock by allowing droplets leaving a module to wait safely in their exit cells as long as necessary to avoid deadlock in the routing cells. **Figure 5(b)** and **Figure 5(c)** show

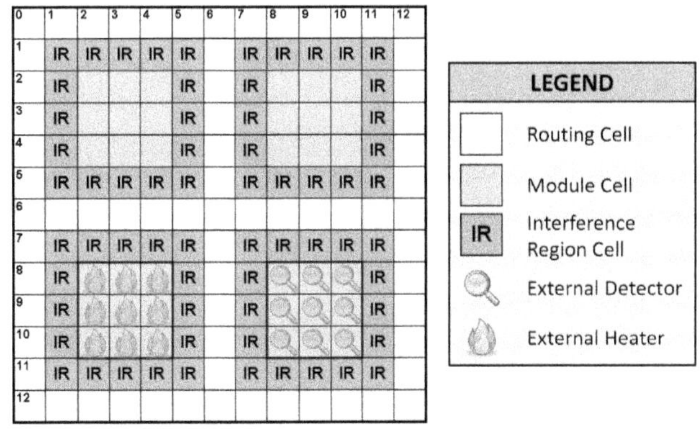

Figure 4. Virtual topology imposed onto a DMFB.

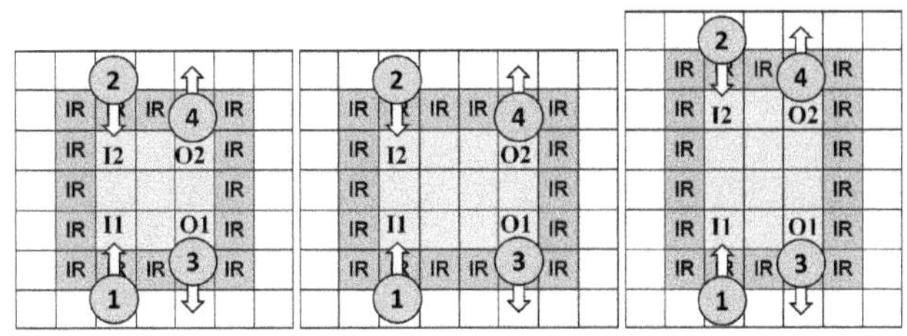

(a) (b) (c)

Figure 5. The entrance cells (I1/I2) and exit cells (O1/O2) of (a) a 3x3 module, (b) a 4x3 module and (c) a 3x4 module.

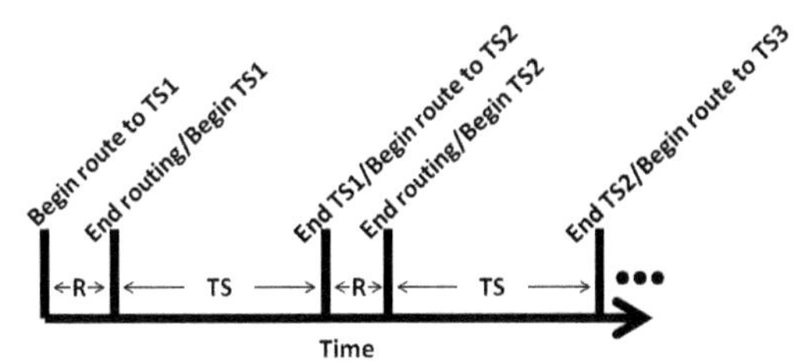

Figure 6. An assay time-line showing that each fixed time-step (TS) is interleaved with a variable-length routing phase (R).

that modules can be elongated along the X- or Y-axis to accommodate larger 2x4 mixers, often used in literature [17][19].

As seen in **Figure 6**, time-step stages of assay operations are interleaved with routing stages until the entire schedule has been processed. A *time-step* is the basic, minimum-resolution unit of time used to schedule microfluidic operations; time-steps usually last one or two seconds and are fixed in length for the duration of the assay. The routing stages are variable in length, depending on the routes that are generated, and can even be instantaneous if no droplets are being routed between time-steps.

Droplets are required to enter/exit a module at one of the two entrances/exits. When a droplet travels to a new module, it must enter the module during the routing phase at one of the module-entrance cells and wait until the time-step officially begins. The droplet is then processed (e.g. split, mixed, stored) during the time-step phase. If a droplet leaves the module after the current time-step, it must position itself at one of the module-exit cells before the end of the time-step. In **Figure 5(a)** droplets 1 and 2 (D1/D2) enter a module to be processed while droplets 3 and 4 (D3/D4) exit to be processed elsewhere. If D1 and D2 arrive before D3 and/or D4 exit, there will be no conflict since the entrance and exit cells are sufficiently spaced to avoid droplet interference. When the time-step begins, D1 and D2 can move freely within the module, as D3 and D4 are at their respective

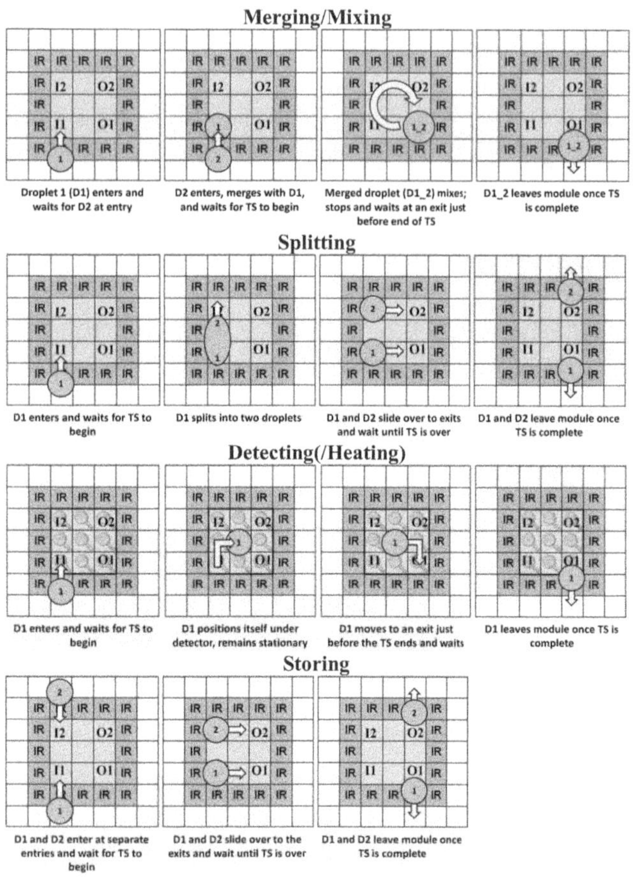

Figure 7. Intra-module droplet processing/routing for microfluidic operations.

destinations. This synchronization scheme prevents inter-module deadlocks because there is always an open spot at the destination module's entrances for every incoming droplet at every module.

Figure 7 shows how a module can perform each assay operation. For each operation, the droplet(s) enters at one of the entrance cells and then waits for the time-step to begin. When the time-step begins, any droplets that were waiting in the exit cells are now gone, and thus, any remaining droplets in the module are free to move about the entire module to perform an operation. If the droplet(s) leaves the module at the end of the time-step, it moves to an exit cell before the time-step ends. Once the time-step is complete, during the subsequent routing stage, the droplet(s) exits the module. If a droplet is scheduled to begin a new operation in the same module at the next time-step, it maneuvers itself to an entrance cell before the time-step ends (not shown in **Figure 7**); this eliminates the need for a droplet to exit and then re-enter the same module.

4. FAST ONLINE SYNTHESIS

In this section, we show how the virtual topology presented in Section 3 can be leveraged to create fast online synthesis methods for scheduling, placement and routing.

4.1 Scheduling

We use list-scheduling (LS) [24] with several extensions to schedule assays. LS is a greedy, constructive algorithm in which each operation (node) in an assay (DAG) is scheduled exactly once. LS is much faster than iterative improvement algorithms, which randomly compute numerous schedules [14][19][24] or

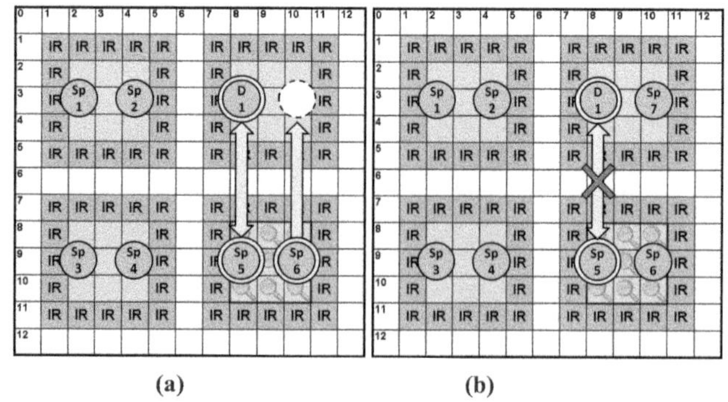

Figure 8. Two DMFB scenarios with droplets that are going to be split (Sp) or detected (D) during the next time-step. In (a), Sp6 can move and occupy the open space in another module, allowing D1 and Sp5 to swap so D1 can be detected in the detect-module. In (b), there is no way to isolate a single droplet and since no droplets will be mixed next time-step, the assay cannot continue.

optimal algorithms based on integer linear programming [24]; however, these approaches generally do produce higher quality schedules than LS.

4.1.1 *Definitions and Constraints*

As mentioned in Section 1.2, an assay is given to the scheduler in the form of a DAG, $G = (V, E)$, where the vertices (V) and edges (E) represent assay operations and operation dependencies, respectively. If the given DMFB is an $a_x \times a_y$ array of cells and each module is $m_x \times m_y$ cells, then the total number of modules, N_m, can be calculated as seen in **Equation 1**. We add 3 to the module dimensions to encapsulate the IR cells on all sides and the routing cells to the right (for the X dimension) and bottom (for the Y dimension) of each module (see **Figure 4**).

$$\left\lfloor \frac{(a_x-1)}{(m_x+3)} \right\rfloor \times \left\lfloor \frac{(a_y-1)}{(m_y+3)} \right\rfloor = N_m \qquad (1)$$

Once the virtual topology is placed, modules with external devices above their cells are considered to be *special modules* (e.g. detect module, heat module); all other modules are considered to be *basic modules*. The array is initially populated based on the virtual topology. An array called $availMods[\,]$ contains the number of modules of each module-type (e.g. basic module, detect module, etc.), and satisfies the following condition:

$$\sum_{i=1}^{numModTypes} availMods[i] = N_m \qquad (2)$$

We define s_m to be the number of droplets a module can store and d_{max} to be the maximum number of droplets we allow on the DMFB during any time-step. Since each module has 2 entrance and 2 exit cells, a module can store 2 droplets during a time-step (i.e. $s_m = 2$). Consider **Figure 8(a)** in which all but one of the modules is at maximum capacity. Since the northeast module has room for one droplet, droplets can be shuffled around so that any single droplet on the array can be isolated in any chamber, allowing the assay to continue. However, if all modules are at maximum capacity (**Figure 8(b)**), then deadlock may arise because it is impossible to process more operations unless some of the droplets are scheduled to output or mix with each other next time-step. To reduce the likelihood of scheduling deadlock, we set the maximum number of droplets permitted on the DMFB during any time-step (d_{max}) as follows:

$$d_{max} = (N_m \times s_m) - 1 \qquad (3)$$

Lastly, I is a set of all the input ports and keeps track of when input ports have been scheduled for dispensing.

```
1  Given sequencing graph: G = (V,E)
2  Given resource constraints: availMods[numModTypes], I, s_m, d_max
4  Assign priorities for all nodes: v ∈ V ∀v based on CPP
5  Find candidate operations: C = {v_i ∈ V: Type(v_j) = input, ∀j: (v_j, v_i) ∈ E}
6  Unfinished operations: UF = ∅
7  TimeStep ts = 0;
8
9  while (all candidate operations are scheduled: C = ∅) {
10   if (uf.endTS = ts, ∀uf : uf ∈ UF)
11     Remove uf from unfinished ops UF;
12     availMods[uf.modType]++;
13   end if
14
15   Sort candidate ops C in ascending order of CPP;
16   for (∀c : c ∈ C)
17     if (CanSchedule(c) = true)
18       Add c to unfinished ops UF, remove from candidate ops C;
19       c.SetAsScheduled(ts, ts + c.duration, SelectModType(c));
20       availMods[c.ModType]--;
21
22       for (∀p : p ∈ c.parents)
23         if (Type(p) = input)
24           SetAsScheduled(ts − dispenseTime, ts, SelectInput(p));
25         else if (p.end < ts)
26           Create new storage node s;
27           s.SetAsScheduled(p.end, ts, NULL);
28           Insert s between p and c in G;
29       end ∀p for
30
31       for ( ∀cc: cc ∈ c.children)
32         if (ccp.scheduled = true, ∀ccp: ccp ∈ cc.parents)
33           Add cc to candidate ops C;
34     end canSchedule(c) if
35   end ∀c for
36
37   for (int i = 0; i < ⌈dropsBeingStored(ts) ÷ s_m⌉ )
38     Create new storage-holder node sh;
39     sh.SetAsScheduled(ts, ts + 1, SelectModType(sh));
40     availMods[sh.ModType]--;
41   end for
42   ts++;
43 end while
```

Figure 9. Pseudocode for our list scheduler algorithm.

4.1.2 Scheduling Algorithm

We present pseudocode for our list-scheduling (LS) algorithm in **Figure 9**. Before scheduling begins, LS assigns a priority to each node (V) in the assay (G) based on that node's critical path length. The *critical path priority* (CPP) for any node n is the largest summation of time-steps from n (including n) to any output in n's fan-out. Finally, before LS begins scheduling, all nodes with only dispense (input) parents are added to the candidate list and the scheduling time-step is set to 0.

Lines 9-43 describe the main scheduling loop which continues until all operations are scheduled; each iteration through this loop, as many operations as possible are scheduled for the current time-step before incrementing to the next scheduling time-step (*Line 42*). As mentioned in the previous section, $availMods[\,]$ holds the available number of free modules for the current time-step. As a new time-step begins, operations that are finishing relinquish the modules they were using to the scheduler (*Lines 10-13*).

Next, the candidate nodes are sorted (*Line 15*) so that they are examined in ascending order (*Lines 16-35*) based on their CPP. Each candidate is checked to see if it can be scheduled by the $CanSchedule(\,)$ function in *Line 17*. $CanSchedule(c)$ returns true if (1) all $c's$ dispense parents have free input ports of the proper fluid-type in the previous time-steps, (2) all $c's$ non-dispense parents have been scheduled to complete before the current time-step, (3) there is a free module to process c, and (4) processing c does not violate **Equation 3**. If c can be scheduled, it

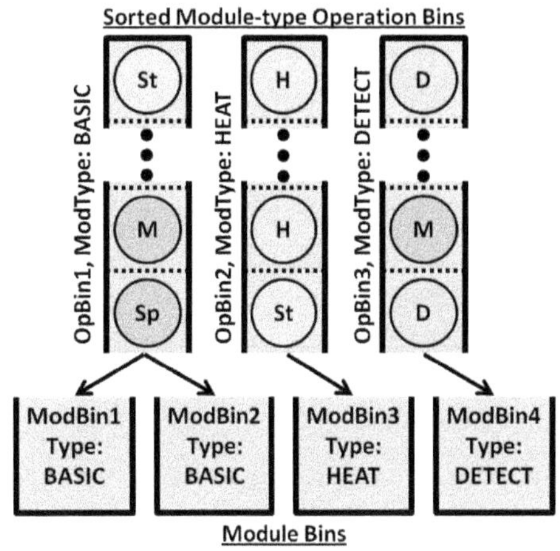

Figure 10. Left-edge algorithm binding operations to modules.

is $SetAsScheduled(\,)$ with a starting and ending time-step and module-type. $SelectModType(c)$ selects a module type based on $c's$ operation-type and always selects a basic module, if possible, to conserve the special modules.

Once c is scheduled, *Lines 22-29* examine $c's$ parents. If a parent is an input, it is scheduled (inputs are not scheduled until a non-input child is scheduled). For non-dispense parents, a storage node is created and inserted between the parent (p) and child (c) if the parent was scheduled to complete more than one time-step before c was scheduled to begin. In *Lines 31-33*, any of $c's$ children whose parents are all scheduled are added to the candidate list.

Lastly, since s_m storage nodes (each node represents 1 droplet) can be stored in a single module, a storage-holder node is added to G for each set of s_m droplets being stored at the current time-step. Each storage-holder node is scheduled for 1 time-step, even if the droplets they are storing are stored for a longer period of time. This is done to prevent specialized modules from storing droplets for long periods of time; this way, a droplet stored in a specialized module can be moved to a basic module if a specialized operation (e.g., heat or detect) requires the specialized module.

4.2 Placement

Microfluidic placement is NP-complete [25]; the virtual topology limits the reconfigurable capabilities of the DMFB by pre-placing the location of modules. In our framework, operations are bound to pre-placed modules in accordance with the schedule that has been computed a-priori. The scheduler assigns operations to module types (e.g., basic or specialized), but does not select a specific module for each operation; this is the job of the binder.

4.2.1 Binding Algorithm

Our binder is based on the left-edge algorithm, which has been used in the past for register allocation and track assignment in channel routing [11]. The left-edge algorithm has an $O(|V|^2)$ time complexity, where $|V|$ is the number of assay operations.

Figure 10 shows how the left-edge algorithm binds operations to modules for the DMFB shown in **Figure 4**. **Figure 11** provides pseudocode for our binding algorithm and can be followed (up to *Line 20*) in the example. A *fixed-module bin* is created (*Line 2*) for each module in the virtual topology; $N_m = 4$ for this example. Then, each operation is placed into an *operation-bin* based on the module-type it was assigned during scheduling (*Lines 9-11*). Next, the operations in each bin are sorted in ascending order based on their start time (*Lines 13*).

```
1  Given a scheduled sequencing graph: G = (V,E)
2  Given a list of fixed module schedules: fixedMods : |fixedMods| = N_m
3
4  Operations by module-type: opsByModType[numModTypes] = ∅
5  Storage operations: storageOps = V.storageOps
6  Storage-holder operations: sHoldsOps = V.storageHolderOps
7
8  // Put operations in bins by module-type
9  for (∀v : v ∈ V)
10   if (Type(v) ≠ (storage OR input OR output))
11     Add v to opsByModType[Type(v)];
12
13 Sort storageOpsand all lists in opsByModType[ ], ascending by start time;
14 Sort sHoldsOps, first by fixed-module location, then ascending by start time;
15
16 // Left-edge bind the modules
17 for (∀m : m ∈ fixedMods)
18   for (∀o : o ∈ opsByModType[ModType(m)])
19     if (o.start > m.LastOp.end)
20       Add o to end of m, remove o from opsByModType[ModType(m)];
21
22 // Bind storage into storage-holders
23 for (∀s : s ∈ storageOps)
24   int curEnd = 0;
25   for (∀sh : sh ∈ sHoldsOps)
26     if (Status(s) ≠ bound AND s.start = sh.start AND sh.size < s_m)
27       BindStorageToHolder(s,sh);
28       Set curEnd = sh.end;
29     else if (Status(s) = bound)
30       if (curEnd = sh.start AND sh.size < s_m AND s.Mod = sh.Mod)
31         BindStorageToHolder(s,sh);
32         Set curEnd = sh.end;
33      else
34         Split s at curEnd to form s2, add s2 to front of storageOps;
35         Return to outer ∀s  for loop;
36
37     if (curEnd = s.end)
38       Remove s from storageOps and return to outer ∀s for loop;
39   end ∀sh for
40 end ∀s for
```

Figure 11. Pseudocode for our left-edge-based binding algorithm. NOTE: Only module binding is shown; input and output binding is left out for brevity.

Lines 17-20 perform the actual binding process. The first module, *ModBin1*, finds the operation bin matching its module-type (*OpBin1*). The binding method then examines each operation in *OpBin1*, in order of start time, to ensure it will not conflict with any other operation already assigned to *OpBin1* (i.e. that the start time of the operation in question is later than the end time of the last operation assigned to *ModBin1*). If an operation is placed in *ModBin1*, it is removed from *OpBin1*; otherwise, it remains in *OpBin1* to be bound to another module. This process is repeated for the remaining three bins; when the last module (*ModBin4*) has examined its corresponding operation bin (*OpBin3*), all operations will have been bound to a module.

Lines 23-40 describe how storage operations are bound. Note that storage operations are not placed into the operation bins in *Lines 9-11*, and thus, were not bound to specific modules; however, the storage-holder nodes were bound in *Lines 17-20*. As mentioned in Section 4.1.2, a storage-holder node was created in the scheduling phase for each set of s_m droplets being stored each time-step (i.e. $\lceil st_t / s_m \rceil$ 1-time-step storage-holder nodes are created at time-step t, where st_t is the number of droplets being stored at t). Storage-holder nodes are created so that storage nodes can be broken into a number of smaller, contiguous storage nodes to prevent rare modules (e.g. detect modules) from being tied up as storage.

Each storage node is examined and assigned to one or more storage-holder nodes (*Lines 23-40*) since storage-holders are always one time-step. If storage node s has not yet been bound (*Line 26*), a suitable storage-holder is one that shares the same starting time as s and is not yet storing its maximum capacity of droplets (s_m). If this criteria is met by a storage-holder node sh, then $BindStorageToHolder(s, sh)$ (*Line 27*) marks s as bound, assigns it to the same module sh is bound to and updates the number of droplets sh is storing. A variable named $curEnd$ is then updated to keep track of how much of s has been bound (for storage nodes larger than one time-step).

Once s has been initially bound (i.e. the first time-step of s), the algorithm attempts to bind the rest of the storage node to the same module location (*Lines 30-32*). It is possible to do this by iterating to (*Line 25*) and examining the next storage-holder in the storage-holders list since the storage-holders were sorted by their module-location and start-time, as seen in *Line 14*. If the next sh shares the same module as s, has the same start-time as our running end ($curEnd$) and is not at maximum capacity, we bind s to sh to update $sh's$ storage count and update $curEnd$. If the condition in *Line 30* cannot be met, s is split at $curEnd$ because it cannot be stored in the same module any longer. The new module is inserted into the storage list to be bound later. If $curEnd$ equals $s's$ end time (*Line 37*), then s has been completely bound and the algorithm can return to *Line 23* to bind the next storage node.

4.3 Routing

To complete the synthesis flow, we use a simplified version of an existing droplet router by Roy [20]. We created a number of routing methods that restricted routes to the cells in between modules, but found that Roy's maze-routing approach produced shorter routes in only a few more milliseconds of computation time compared to the alternatives. As in Roy's router, we use Soukup's fast maze router [21] to produce sequential routes for droplets and then compact the routes together, adding stalls in the middle of the routes to avoid droplet interference.

We do modify Roy's router, however, taking advantage of the virtual topology to avoid deadlock (i.e. when droplets form a dependency cycle and cannot move forward until one of the droplets in the dependency cycle concedes). We describe this optimization step in the following subsections.

4.3.1 Routing Algorithm Overview

We provide pseudocode for the simplified Roy routing algorithm in **Figure 12** and **Figure 13**. The router receives a scheduled and placed DAG, G, from the placer. Throughout the routing process, all droplets in motion must maintain static and dynamic spacing constraints to prevent interference, as shown in **Figure 14**.

Instead of having a module-type or fluid-type (for dispense nodes), each node now has a reference to a specific module or I/O port. An empty set of routes is created which holds a separate route for each droplet (*Line 3*). A *route* is composed of a set of *routing points* that specify the droplet's location each cycle. The operations of G are copied into a new list, *ops*, and sorted first by ascending start time; operations with the same start time are then sorted by ascending end time (*Line 5*).

Starting at time-step 0 (*Line 6*), droplet routes are computed one routing sub-problem at a time. As seen in **Figure 6**, a *routing sub-problem* (or phase) is the problem of routing a number of droplets from their source (input or module) to their destination (module or output); routing sub-problems occur between the end of one time-step and the beginning of the subsequent time-step. Each iteration of the loop in *Lines 8-15* computes one routing sub-problem.

For a specific sub-problem, individual routes are first computed for each droplet using Soukup's fast maze routing algorithm (*Line*

```
1  Given a scheduled and placed sequencing graph G = (V, E)
2  Assay operations: ops = V
3  List of routes for each droplet for entire assay: routes = ∅
4
5  Sort ops by start time first, by stop time second, in ascending order;
6  TimeStep ts = 0;
7
8  while (!ops.empty)
9     subProbRoutes = GetIndivSoukupRoutes(ops, ts);
10    CompactRoutes(subProbRoutes);
11    Append routes in subProbRoutes to routes;
12    ts++;
13    if (o.end ≤ ts, ∀o : o ∈ ops)
14       Remove o from ops;
15 end while
```

Figure 12. Pseudocode for the simplified Roy routing algorithm.

```
1  Given list of individual routes for each sub-problem droplet: subProbRoutes
2  List of compacted routes: compactedRoutes = ∅
3  Sort subProbRoutes in descending order by length;
4
5  for (∀r : r ∈ subProbRoutes)
6     bool routeMustWait = false;
7     RouteCycle i = 0;
8     while (i < r.size AND r.size > 0)
9        for (∀cr : cr ∈ compactedRoutes)
10          if(IRV(r[i], cr[i − 1]) OR IRV(r[i], cr[i + 1]) OR
11             IRV(cr[i], r[i − 1]) OR IRV(cr[i], r[i + 1]) OR
12             IRV(r[i], cr[i]) OR IRV(r[i − 1], cr[i − 1]))
13             routeMustWait = true, jump to line 17;
14          end if
15       end ∀cr for
16
17       if (routeMustWait = true)
18          Add a single-cycle stall to r at r[i − 2];
19          routeMustWait = false;
20       else
21          i++;
22       end if
23    end while
24    Add r to compactedRoutes;
25 end ∀r for
```

Figure 13. Pseudocode for the CompactRoutes( ) function.

9) [21]. Soukup's maze router works by routing around blockages; it routes straight to its destination until it hits a blockage, at which point it attempts to route around it.

A *persisting module* is defined as a module that starts before and ends after time-step ts. For the entire sub-problem at time-step ts, ts's persisting modules (including interference regions) are marked as blockages for Soukup's algorithm. Let us define D_{ts} as the set of droplets to be routed during the sub-problem at time-step ts. Then, for each sub-problem droplet $d_i \in D_{ts}$, the algorithm sets the source and destination cells, along with an 8-cell interference region surrounding them, as blockages for each sub-problem droplet $d_j \in D_{ts}, d_j \neq d_i$. The blockages from the persisting modules remain persistent throughout the sub-problem, whereas, the blockages from sources and destinations vary depending on which droplet is currently being routed.

The result of Soukup's routing (*Line 9*) is a list containing a route for each droplet. The routes have no stalls and are not concurrent (i.e. the droplets may interfere with each other if routed at the same time). Thus, once the individual, sequential routes are computed, they are *compacted* so droplets can be routed concurrently (*Line 10*, explained in the next subsection). Once the sub-problem routes are compacted, they are appended to the matching droplet routes for the entire assay (*Line 11*). Finally, the time-step (ts) is incremented (*Line 12*) and any operations finished before ts are removed (*Lines 13-14*). When there are no more operations to route to, routing is complete.

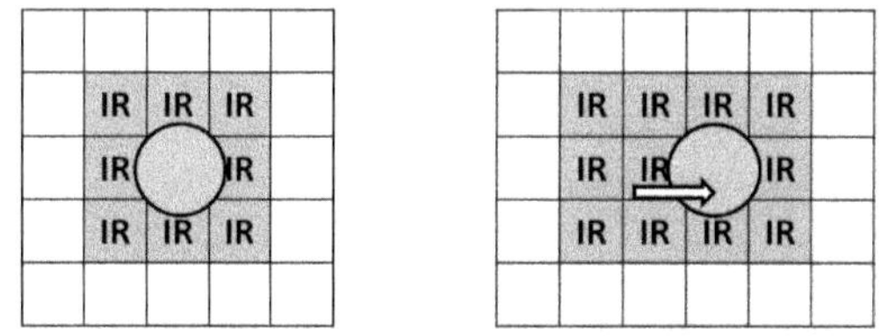

(a) (b)

Figure 14. The interference region (IR) for a droplet at (a) the beginning and (b) end of a droplet-actuation cycle.

4.3.2 Route Compaction

Route compaction is the process of taking a number of sequential routes and causing the droplets to move in parallel at the same time; however, the original routes are not created with concern to other droplet routes and caution must be taken when compacting to prevent routes from intersecting in time and space. When compacting routes, droplets may not enter any cell that is adjacent to any other droplet or the droplets will interfere (merge) with one another. To prevent this, a static interference region (IR) is created around each droplet at the beginning of each droplet-actuation cycle, as seen in **Figure 14(a)**. As a droplet moves from one cell to the next, the IR is stretched dynamically to include the union of the static IRs of the beginning and end cells (see **Figure 14(b)**). In general, a droplet may not enter any other droplet's IR while routing. Static and dynamic droplet interference rules are formally defined in ref. [27].

Figure 13 shows pseudocode for the $CompactRoutes(\,)$ function (**Figure 12**, *Line 10*). It receives the list of individual routes ($subProbRoutes$) as described in the last section. The routes are sorted in descending order so that the longest route is processed first. *Lines 5-25* proceed to compact these routes one-at-a-time. The index of a route now represents time (i.e. $r[0]$ describes the xy-coordinate of a droplet during the first cycle of this routing phase). Thus, when determining if route r can be compacted, we check each cycle i of r's route against any previously-compacted route, cr, at cycle i. *Lines 10-12* compute the dynamic and static droplet restraints described in **Figure 14** and ref. [27]. If an interference region violation (IRV) is found between the two routes, then r cannot be compacted as is. To remedy this, a single stall is added (*Line 18*) 2 routing cycles before the IRV is discovered until the algorithm can successfully compact r.

It is possible, however, that deadlock may occur if two (or more) droplets are waiting for each other to move. In this case, stalling cannot resolve the deadlock (e.g. consider the case where two droplets are attempting to enter the same cell but cannot because it would cause a head-on collision).

Roy's router attempts to recover from deadlock by moving one of the droplets backward [20]. We simplify the process by taking advantage of our virtual topology. With our module synchronization, described in Section 3.1, droplets have designated sources (module exits) and destinations (module entries) that do not interfere with any other sources and destinations in a given time-step (i.e. a droplet source will never interfere with another droplet's destination). Thus, a droplet can stay at its source as long as necessary, until all other droplets are safely off its path, and then commence its route. By employing this method, we are guaranteed to avoid deadlock.

With this in mind, the router keeps track of the number of stalls added to any route r. If the number of stalls added to route r reaches some threshold, $stallThresh$, all of the stalls added to

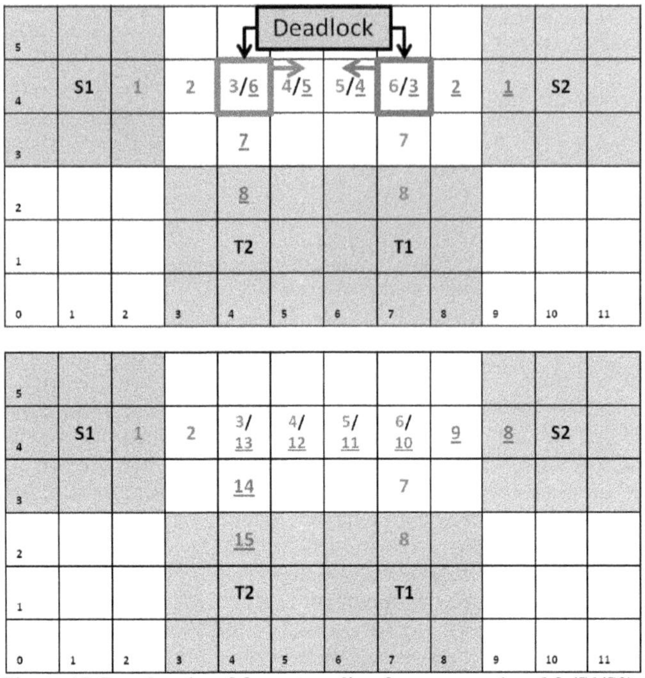

Figure 15. Droplets 1 and 2 are traveling from source 1 and 2 (S1/S2) to target 1 and 2 (T1/T2), respectively. The red and blue (blue also underlined for clarity) numbers are time-stamps for droplets 1 and 2, respectively). The top scenario shows that deadlock can occur when routes 1 and 2 are compacted and stalls are added mid-route. The bottom scenario shows that both routes are safely completed if droplet 2 stalls at its source location until droplet 1 is safely out of the way.

any route thus far in the sub-problem are removed. Then, the entire sub-problem is compacted again, except this time, stalls are added to the beginning of the routes instead of the middle (i.e. the compaction algorithm in **Figure 13** is applied, except *Line 18* adds a stall at $r[0]$ instead of $r[i-2]$). In this case, droplets do not leave the safety of their source cell until they are guaranteed an unobstructed path in space and time to their destination.

Consider **Figure 15** in which droplets 1 and 2 are being routed from their sources (S1 and S2) to their target cells (T1 and T2). As seen in the top scenario, if the routes start at the same time, deadlock will occur at cycle 3 as droplet 1, at cell (4, 4), and droplet 2, at cell (7, 4), cannot move forward without merging. No amount of mid-route stalls will resolve this deadlock since they are heading straight toward each other; it is not a matter of allowing one droplet to pass. The bottom scenario shows that if droplet 2 is allowed to stay in its source until droplet 1 is safely off its route, droplet 1 can reach its target. Since the cells around S2 are considered as blockages to droplet 1, droplet 2 is safe to wait at S2 as long as necessary because droplet 1 will never attempt to pass through that area, even if its destination is to the east of S2.

Adding stalls to the beginning of a path will always work and will never result in deadlock, as can occur when inserting stalls mid-route; however, we discovered empirically that inserting stalls mid-route tends to yield shorter routes, and rarely results in deadlock. Thus, we employ the mid-route-stall compaction method first and revert to the pre-route-stall compaction method only when a deadlock occurs.

5. EXPERIMENTS

Our experiments compare the online DMFB synthesis flow described in this paper, with a prototypical offline synthesis flow based on algorithms described in prior literature. The goal of this experiment is to demonstrate that our online flow can achieve competitive solutions in terms of total assay execution time, while maintaining a low algorithmic runtime overhead.

5.1 Benchmarks

We used three standard benchmarks: PCR, in-vitro diagnostics, and a protein assay, whose DAGs have been made publicly available by researchers at Duke University [23]; we also used the provided module libraries to obtain operation timings. We used a 2x4 mixer (3s) for all PCR mixing operations. For the protein assay, we used a 2x4 diluter (5s) and 2x4 mixer (3s) for all dilute and mixing operations, respectively; all 2-input, 2-output dilute operations in the protein assay were implemented using a mix operation, followed by a split operation, which took 5s in total.

In-vitro diagnostics is actually a family of assays that mixes and detects up to 4 samples with 4 reagents (e.g., up to 16 mix-and-detect operations). We use the 5 in-vitro assays, along with mixing and detection times, as listed in Table 1 of ref. [22].

We assume a droplet actuation frequency of 100 Hz [31].

5.2 Offline Synthesis Flow (Baseline)

Our offline synthesis flow is based on algorithms that have been published previously for DMFB synthesis; these algorithms have generally been optimized for solution quality, not for runtime. We used a genetic algorithm to perform scheduling [24], simulated annealing to perform module placement [25] and our implementation of Roy's algorithm for droplet routing [20]. We chose Roy's algorithm for droplet routing because it achieved short routes and never failed for any of the routing test cases. Roy's router did not fail in any of our experiments. The offline algorithms mentioned in this section are freely available as open source [1].

5.3 Online Synthesis Flow

The online synthesis flow is described in Section 4 of this paper. The use of the virtual topology eliminates the need for a placer. The flow includes three main steps: scheduling, binding, and routing; the same router was used in both the online and offline flow, as it obtained good quality results and fast runtimes. The online algorithms described in this paper are freely available as open source [1].

5.4 Implementation Details

The offline and online synthesis flows were implemented in C++ using the University of California, Riverside's (UCR's) DMFB Synthesis Framework [7]. We evaluated their performance on two computers available in our laboratory. The first is an Inforce SYS9402-01 development board, with a 1GHz Intel Atom™ E638 processor and 512MB RAM, running TimeSys 11 Linux. This is a relatively low-end embedded system that could be integrated to control a DMFB, e.g., to provide a platform for portable healthcare diagnostics.

The second is a 64-bit Windows 7 desktop PC, with 4GB of RAM and an Intel Core i7™ CPU operating at 2.8GHz. This platform represents a typical use case for a controlled laboratory setting.

5.5 Results and Discussion

Table 1 compares the genetic scheduler and list scheduler; consistent with prior work [24], the list scheduler produces schedules that are several time steps longer than the genetic algorithm in most cases; however, this comes at a significant overhead in terms of runtime. On both platforms, the list scheduler was able to schedule all assays in less than 30ms.

Table 1. Results showing the schedule lengths and computation times (on Intel i7 and Atom processors) for genetic and list scheduling.

Genetic Scheduling vs. List Scheduling						
Benchmark	Genetic Scheduling			List Scheduling		
	i7 (ms)	Atom (ms)	Sched (s)	i7 (ms)	Atom (ms)	Sched (s)
PCR	395	2,621	12	1	1	12
InVitro_1	665	4,475	15	0	2	15
InVitro_2	1,293	8,122	17	0	5	19
InVitro_3	1,990	13,156	19	1	13	23
InVitro_4	3,541	22,376	23	1	17	26
InVitro_5	5,744	39,410	31	2	27	35
Protein	3,297	22,334	110	3	14	116

Table 2. Results showing computation times (on Intel i7 and Atom processors) for simulated annealing and module binding.

Placement vs. Binding						
Benchmark	Simulated Annealing Placer			Module Binder		
	i7 (ms)	Atom (ms)	%Cells Used	i7 (ms)	Atom (ms)	%Cells Used
PCR	16	200	16	0	0	20
InVitro_1	621	12,843	16	0	0	24
InVitro_2	105,138	141,177	21	0	0	28
InVitro_3	72,311	506,767	29	0	0	36
InVitro_4	19,789	3,317,571	32	0	0	45
InVitro_5	74,899	1,399,936	36	0	0	48
Protein	4,867,220	79,531,695	29	0	4	46

Table 3. Results showing route lengths and computation times (on Intel i7 and Atom processors) for the classic offline flow (GA/SA) and our proposed online flow (List/Binding).

Simplified Roy Routing						
Benchmark	GA Scheduling - SA Placement Flow			List Scheduling - Module Binding Flow		
	i7 (ms)	Atom (ms)	# Routing Cycles / # Sub-problems	i7 (ms)	Atom (ms)	# Routing Cycles / # Sub-problems
PCR	0	2	78 / 4	0	6	56 / 4
InVitro_1	0	2	135 / 9	0	3	111 / 9
InVitro_2	0	4	180 / 11	0	7	167 / 12
InVitro_3	0	10	207 / 15	0	12	209 / 16
InVitro_4	0	7	234 / 15	1	19	299 / 19
InVitro_5	1	9	342 / 22	1	26	351 / 24
Protein	5	32	1212 / 71	3	76	638 / 45

Table 2 compares the simulated annealing-based placer to the online binder proposed in this paper. The binder runs several orders of magnitude faster than the placer on both platforms; in most cases, the runtime of the binder was faster than the resolution of the function that we use to measure execution time (e.g., faster than 0.5 ms). As we will see shortly, the impact on total assay execution time is negligible.

Table 3 reports the results of the router; due to inferior schedule qualities, the online synthesis flow has more routing sub-problems to solve than the offline flow. **Table 3** sums the total number of cycles (1 cycle = .01s with 100Hz droplet-actuation frequency) required for droplet routing across all sub-problems. It is important to note that even when the schedules are identical, the placer will yield a different sub-problem than the virtual topology. We ignore sub-problems where all droplet routes start and stop at the same module; this explains, for example, why the online flow has 45 sub-problems for Protein, while the offline router has 71.

Table 3 shows that the runtimes of the router are a little bit slower for our virtual topology, compared to the placer; however, the algorithmic runtime advantages of the list scheduler and binder compared to the genetic scheduler and placer far outweigh the disparity between the runtimes of the routers.

Table 4. Results showing the assay time (AT, i.e. the schedule and route lengths) and computation times (CT) for the entire offline flow on the Intel Atom processor.

GA Scheduling - SA Placement - Simp. Roy Routing Offline Flow						
Benchmark	Schedule		Placement	Routing		Total
	AT (s)	CT (s)	CT (s)	AT (s)	CT (s)	(AT + CT) (s)
PCR	12	3	0	1	0	16
InVitro_1	15	4	13	1	0	34
InVitro_2	17	8	141	2	0	168
InVitro_3	19	13	507	2	0	541
InVitro_4	23	22	3,318	2	0	3,365
InVitro_5	31	39	1,400	3	0	1,474
Protein	110	22	79,532	12	0	79,676

Table 5. Results showing the assay time (AT, i.e. the schedule and route lengths) and computation times (CT) for the entire online flow on the Intel Atom processor.

List Scheduling - Module Binding - Simp. Roy Routing Online Flow						
Benchmark	Schedule		Placement	Routing		Total
	AT (s)	CT (s)	CT (s)	AT (s)	CT (s)	(AT + CT) (s)
PCR	12	0	0	1	0	13
InVitro_1	15	0	0	1	0	16
InVitro_2	19	0	0	2	0	21
InVitro_3	23	0	0	2	0	25
InVitro_4	26	0	0	3	0	29
InVitro_5	35	0	0	4	0	39
Protein	116	0	0	6	0	122

Tables 4 and **Table 5** compare the total computation time (CT) and the assay execution time (AT) for both flows on the Intel Atom™ processor; please note that the times reported here are in seconds (s), whereas the times reported in **Tables 1-3** are in milliseconds (ms). We can see that the total runtime, AT+CT, is significantly lower for the online flow than for the offline flow, except for PCR, which is a very small benchmark. The most dramatic results that favor the online synthesis flow are for the largest benchmarks, InVitro_4 and 5 and Protein, where the runtimes are reduced by two orders of magnitude.

6. CONCLUSION

The online synthesis flow introduced in this paper can run in real-time on a low-cost embedded processor, as typified by the Intel Atom™ used in our experiments. Empirically, this work has shown that a virtual topology coupled with a simple binding algorithm can be nearly as effective as longer-running placement algorithms based on simulated annealing. Using this approach, the synthesis flow spends most of its time on scheduling, which is the step that has the most significant impact on assay execution time.

Our future work will extend the online synthesis flow to account for control flow operations that cannot be predicted at compile-time, including variable-latency assay operations, and runtime fault detection and recovery; of particular interest is the ability to dynamically reconfigure the virtual topology when permanent errors are detected; when this occurs, the online flow will be invoked to re-synthesize the assay at runtime.

7. ACKNOWLEDGMENTS

This work was supported in part by NSF Grant CNS-1035603. Daniel Grissom was supported by an NSF Graduate Research Fellowship.

8. REFERENCES

[1] www.microfluidics.cs.ucr.edu

[2] M. Alistar, E. Maftei, P. Pop, and J. Madsen, "Synthesis of biochemical applications on digital microfluidic biochips with operation variability," in *Proc. DTIP MEMS/MOEMS*, Sevilla, Spain, 2010, pp. 350-357.

[3] K. F. Böhringer, "Modeling and controlling parallel tasks in droplet-based microfluidic systems," *IEEE Trans. Comput.-Aided Des. Integr. Circuits Syst.*, vol. 25, no. 2, pp. 334-344, Feb. 2006.

[4] M. Cho and D. Z. Pan, "A high-performance droplet routing algorithm for digital microfluidic biochips," *IEEE Trans. Comput.-Aided Des. Integr. Circuits Syst.*, vol. 27, no. 10, pp. 1714-1724, Oct. 2008.

[5] S-K. Fan, C. Hashi, and C-J. Kim, "Manipulation of multiple droplets on NxM grid by cross-reference EWOD driving scheme and pressure-contact packaging," in *Proc. IEEE MEMS*, Kyoto, Japan, 2003, pp. 694-697.

[6] E. J. Griffith, S. Akella, and M. K. Goldberg, "Performance characterization of a reconfigurable planar-array digital microfluidic system," *IEEE Trans. Comput.-Aided Des. Integr. Circuits Syst.*, vol. 25, no. 2, pp. 345-357, Feb. 2006.

[7] D. Grissom, et al., "A digital microfluidic biochip synthesis framework," in *Proc. VLSI-SOC*, Santa Cruz, CA, 2012.

[8] D. Grissom and P. Brisk, "Path scheduling on digital microfluidic biochips," in *Proc. DAC*, San Francisco, CA, 2012, pp. 26-35.

[9] T. Huang and T. Ho, "A fast routability- and performance-driven droplet routing algorithm for digital microfluidic biochips," in *Proc. IEEE ICCD*, Lake Tahoe, CA, 2009, pp. 445-450.

[10] T. Ho, K. Chakrabarty, and P. Pop, "Digital microfluidic biochips: recent research and emerging challenges," in *Proc. CODES+ISSS*, Taipei, Taiwan, 2011, pp. 335-343.

[11] F. J. Kurdahi and A. C. Parker, "REAL: a program for REgister ALlocation," in *Proc. ACM/IEEE DAC*, Miami, FL, 1987, pp. 210- 215.

[12] C. Liao and S. Hu, "Multiscale variation-aware techniques for high-performance digital microfluidic lab-on-a-chip component placement," IEEE Trans. Nanobioscence, vol. 10, no. 1, pp. 51-58, March 2011.

[13] Y. Luo, K. Chakrabarty, and T. Ho, "A cyberphysical synthesis approach for error recovery in digital microfluidic biochips," in *Proc. DATE*, Dresden, Germany, 2012, pp. 1239-1244.

[14] E. Maftei, P. Pop, and J. Madsen, "Tabu search-based synthesis of dynamically reconfigurable digital microfluidic biochips," in *Proc. CASES*, Grenoble, France, 2009, pp. 195-203.

[15] J.H.Noh, J. Noh, E. Kreit, J. Heikenfeld, and P. Rack, "Toward active-matrix lab-on-a-chip: programmable electrofluidic control enabled by arrayed oxide thin film transistors," *Lab Chip*, vol. 12, no. 2, pp. 353-360, Dec. 2011.

[16] K. O' Neal, D. Grissom, and P. Brisk, "Force-directed list scheduling for digital microfluidic biochips," in *Proc. VLSI-SOC*, Santa Cruz, CA, 2012.

[17] P. Paik, V. Pamula, and R. Fair, "Rapid droplet mixers for digital microfluidic systems," *Lab Chip*, vol. 3, no. 4, pp. 253-259, Sep. 2003.

[18] M. G. Pollack, A.D. Shenderov, and R. B. Fair, "Electrowetting-based actuation of droplets for integrated microfluidics," *Lab Chip*, vol. 2, no. 2, pp. 96-101, 2002.

[19] A. J. Ricketts, K. Irick, N. Vijaykrishnan, and M. J. Irwin, "Priority scheduling in digital microfluidics-based biochips," in *Proc. DATE*, Munich, Germany, 2006, pp. 329-334.

[20] P. Roy, H. Rahaman, and P. Dasgupta, "A novel droplet routing algorithm for digital microfluidic biochips," in *Proc. GLSVLSI*, Providence, RI, 2010, pp. 441-446.

[21] J. Soukup, "Fast maze router," in *Proc. DAC*, Las Vegas, NV, 1978, pp. 100-102.

[22] F Su and K. Chakrabarty, "Architectural-level synthesis of digital microfluidics-based biochips," in *Proc. ICCAD*, San Jose, CA, 2004, pp. 223-228.

[23] F. Su and K. Chakrabarty, "Benchmarks for digital microfluidic biochip design and synthesis," *Duke Univ. Dept. ECE*, 2006: http://www.ee.duke.edu/~fs/Benchmark.pdf

[24] F. Su and K. Chakrabarty, "High-level synthesis of digital microfluidic biochips," *ACM J. Emerging Tech. Comput. Syst.*, vol. 3, no. 4, pp. 16.1-16.32, Jan. 2008.

[25] F. Su and K. Chakrabarty, "Module placement for fault-tolerant microfluidics-based biochips," *ACM Trans. on Design Automation of Electronic Systems*, vol. 11, no. 3, pp. 682-710, Jul. 2006.

[26] F. Su and K. Chakrabarty, "Unified high-level synthesis and module placement for defect-tolerant microfluidic biochips," in *Proc. DAC*, Anaheim, CA, 2005, pp. 825-830.

[27] F. Su, W. Hwang, and K. Chakrabarty, "Droplet routing in the synthesis of digital microfluidic biochips," in *Proc. DATE*, Munich, Germany, 2006, pp. 323-328.

[28] Z. Xiao, and E. F. Y. Young, "Placement and routing for cross-referencing digital microfluidic biochips," *IEEE Trans. Comput.-Aided Des. Integr. Circuits Syst.*, vol. 30, no. 7, pp. 1000-1010, Jul. 2011.

[29] T. Xu and K. Chakrabarty, "Broadcast electrode-addressing for pin-constrained multi-functional digital microfluidic biochips," in *Proc. DAC*, Anaheim, CA, 2008, pp. 173-178.

[30] T. Xu and K. Chakrabarty, "Integrated droplet routing in the synthesis of microfluidic biochips," in *Proc. DAC*, San Diego, CA, 2007, pp. 948-953.

[31] P-H. Yuh, C-L. Yang, and Y-W. Chang, "BioRoute: a network-flow-based routing algorithm for the synthesis of digital microfluidic biochips," *IEEE Trans. Comput.-Aided Des. Integr. Circuits Syst.*, vol. 27, no. 11, pp. 1928-1941, Nov. 2008.

[32] P-H. Yuh, C-L. Yang, and Y-W. Chang, "Placement of defect-tolerant digital microfluidic biochips using the T-tree formulation," *ACM J. Emerging Tech. Comput. Syst.*, vol. 3, no. 3, pp. 13.1-13.32, Nov. 2007.

An Intelligent Compaction Technique for Pin Constrained Routing in Cross Referencing Digital Microfluidic Biochips

Pranab Roy [1], Rupam Bhattacharjee[2], Modud Sohid[3], Sudipta Chakraborty[4], Hafizur Rahaman[5]
School of VLSI Technology
Bengal Engineering and Science University, Shibpur,India

Parthasarathi Dasgupta[6]
Indian Institute of Management, Calcutta, India
Email – [1]ronmarine14@yahoo.co.in ,[2]thrup@gmail.com, [3]himaddy08@gmail.com, [4]sudipta1755@gmail.com, [5]rahaman_h@yahoo.co.in, [6]partha@iimcal.ac.in

ABSTRACT

The recent advances in microfluidic technology have resulted in the emergence of commercially successful lab-on-chip systems that manifested as applicable devices in the wide range of areas e.g. high-throughput DNA sequencing, immunoassays and clinical chemistry, environmental toxicity monitoring and point of- care diagnosis of diseases. The current generation of microfluidic devices termed as digital microfluidic biochips (DMFB) are capable of manipulating individual droplets of chemicals on a 2D planar array of electrodes. A special class of DMFB classified as Cross-referencing biochip has currently drawn major attention for targeted integration of multiple bioassay protocols. However, for parallel execution of multiple bioassays within a single array - these chips face a serious issue of electrode interference during simultaneous routing of droplets. In this paper, we propose a routing-aware zone-based detailed placement and compaction technique that reorients the droplet locations on a pre-synthesized Bioassay schematic fulfilling the requisite dependency constraints necessary for efficient execution# of the specified bioassay protocols. The focus for the proposed scheme include (i)enhanced routing in respect of less overall and average routing time, optimum cell utilization (ii)minimum or no crossover with intelligent collision avoidance, and (iii) optimized pin utilization with intelligent pin clustering and hence overcoming the major issue of electrode interference for Cross referencing biochips. Simulations are carried out on three test benches of Benchmark suite III, and the results obtained are encouraging..

Categories and Subject Descriptors

J.6 [Computer application]: Computer Aided Engineering Electronics, Medical Information Systems.

Keywords

Algorithms, placement, routing, pin constraint, Cross referencing, Digital microfluidics, Biochips, sample droplets, EWOD.

1. INTRODUCTION

Modern day microfluidic technology provides the key to miniaturization in biochemical and biomedical processes that lead to chip based application both for continuous flow and discrete droplet based platforms.

CODES+ISSS'12, October 7–12, 2012, Tampere, Finland.

The term *microfluidics* refers to devices, systems, and methods for the manipulation of fluid flows with characteristic volume scales in the nanoliter range. The emergence of so-called "lab-on-a-chip" or miniaturized total analysis system (μ-TAS) offer chemical and biological analyses in miniaturized small chips with faster analysis times, smaller reagent consumptions, and higher level of throughput, using parallel analyses than their macroscale counterparts. Several procedures such as sample preparation, dispensing, separation, mixing and detection are typically incorporated into a system to perform and complete the required analyses on asingle chip.

A popular class of microfluidic biochip is based on continuous fluid flow in permanently-etched microchannels.[1] Such devices require networks of microchannels and valves combined with pressure sources, resulting in complicated fabrications and component integrations, reduced portability, and considerable volumes of samples required for analysis [20]. An alternative approach for manipulation of liquid as unit-sized discrete microdroplets termed as ''digital'' microfluidics has come into focus in recent days. These digital microfluidic systems provide a more scalable architecture that is easier to fabricate as compared to its continuous flow counterparts. The reconfigurable nature of droplet transportation and mixing offers major benefits such as the estimation and selection of path by a droplet at any given time can be determined by an external microcontroller that can be programmed for dynamic accessibility and movement to and from individual locations within the stipulated 2D planar grid. The microcontroller can be reprogrammed later if a better schedule can be accomplished or even can be updated itself after detecting a fault.

Discrete droplet transportation in DMFBs are based on two major variety of droplet/particle transport mechanisms (usually involving surface tension modulation) namely electrowetting on dielectric (EWOD) and dielectrophoresis (DEP). Electro wetting based devices control the modulation of the interfacial tension between a conductive fluid and a solid electrode by applying an electric field between them. The basic cell of a DMFB consists of two plates, and the filler medium, i.e., the silicone oil, with the droplets being sandwiched between the plates; shown in Figure 1.The bottom plate contains a patterned array of individually controllable electrodes, whereas the top plate is coated with a continuous ground electrode.

Digital Microfluidic biochips are categorized into two major types based on their electrode control schemes. In the simplest and most common droplet control scheme, each electrode is directly addressed and controlled by a dedicated control pin, which allows each electrode to be individually activated. These are termed as Direct addressing Biochips. Although this architecture provides large flexibility for droplet movement, it suffers from the major drawback of having the number of control pins being increased rapidly with increasing system complexity. This large number of control pins significantly surmounts the manufacturing cost and the control wire routing problem complicates the overall design process [2]. For large scale integration a new architecture has been proposed. This uses a set of electrodes in one row/column being connected to a single control pin, leading to considerable reduction of the number of control pins. This number is proportional to half of the perimeter of the chip instead of the area of the chip. This scheme is referred as cross-referencing biochips. Having the major advantage of pin reduction, the architecture introduces an additional complexity of droplet movement namely interference of electrodes. As the electrode for initiating a droplet movements activated by the row column intersection of two pins, there is a possibility of unintentional initiation of another droplet. This imposes an additional constraint in routing of droplets in cross referencing DMFB which makes the routing problem to be more complex and error prone. To make matters worse for concurrent routing of droplets - this may result in frequent deadlock as well as abrupt increase in latest arrival time.

In this paper we propose a route-aware finer placement algorithm of the nets(i.e. source, target location for each droplet) for cross-referencing DMFBs. The scheme primarily handles only the rearrangement of the droplet locations (source, target and mixer) in relation to the modules, without altering the locations of the pre-synthesized modules. Later it computes the interdependency between individual modules and based on such interdependency the reorientation of modules can be incorporated (without violation of the presynthesized schedule) and both nets and modules can be rearranged in altered location to accomplish intelligent compaction.

The rest of the paper is arranged as follows. Section 2 provides the relevant literature survey. The formulation of the droplet routing problems and the related constraints for cross referencing Biochips are stated in Section 3. Section 4 discusses the preferable as well as forbidden routing options in cross referencing biochips. Motivation and contribution of the proposed work have been described in Section 5. In Section 6 the route aware zone based net placement algorithm is discussed. It further defines module interdependency followed by its application for further compaction for same subproblem. An example illustrating the proposed approach is elaborated in Section 7. The routing algorithm that follows the route-aware net placement is described in Section 8. Section 9 summarizes the simulation results on three test benches in benchmark suite III and compares them with other recent reports. Finally Section 10 analyses the results along with the concluding remarks.

2. RELATED WORKS

The droplet routing problem is primarily combined with accomplishment of multiple objectives, namely the latest arrival time of all droplets from source to target, the total transport time of all the droplets, the overall resource utilization, as well as optimization of the pin numbers. Initially most of the methods were targeted for solving the routing problems in direct addressing platforms. A direct addressing method is used in [5] where the droplet routing problem is mapped into a graph clique model. An integer linear programming (ILP) formulation based on direct addressing mode is reported in [4]. This appears to be the first major attempt to address the droplet routing problem in cross referencing DMFBs. The movement of droplets at each time step is determined by solving an ILP. A 'droplet movement cost' is used as a heuristic to evaluate congestion when solving the ILP. This method works directly on cross-referencing biochip, and hence better results can be obtained. In [7], dynamic reconfigurability of the microfluidic array is exploited during run-time. A high performance droplet routing algorithm using grid-based representation is reported in [8]. In [9], a network flow-based approach is proposed for droplet routing. The proposed method is based on non-intersecting bounding box technique. An A^* search algorithm is proposed in [10]. A recent work based on Soukup's routing algorithm [12] for concurrent path allocation to multiple droplets appears in [13]. This scheme uses stalling, and possible detouring of droplets in cases of contentions. A partition-based algorithm for pin-constraint based design is proposed in [3]. Another fast routability and performance-driven droplet router for DMFBs has been proposed in [15]. Next attempt for addressing the droplet routing issue of cross-referencing DMFBs has been made in [6] where a droplet manipulation method has been proposed by mapping the droplet movement problem to the clique partitioning problem which in turn facilitates high-throughput applications on a pin-constrained biochip. In [16] a new method has been proposed that solves the droplet routing problem on cross-referencing biochip directly. The proposed method uses 2 colouring approach to address the electrode constraint issue. [17] presents a broadcast-addressing based design technique for pin constrained multi-functional biochips. The proposed method provides high throughput for bioassays and it reduces the number of control pins by identifying and connecting control pins with "compatible" actuation sequences. Finally a pre-placement based routing method is proposed in [18] that provides much improved results. The method used in [18] directly starts with a given Bioassay protocol and performs architectural level synthesis that addresses the placement issues for modules as well as resource binding of droplets. In our method the algorithm starts with this synthesis result and perform finer optimization and compaction for the droplet samples together with modules maintaining the necessary dependency constraints as defined in Section IV. The resultant placement provides a highly optimized routing performance both in terms of Arrival time, total time, cell utilization and pin optimization.

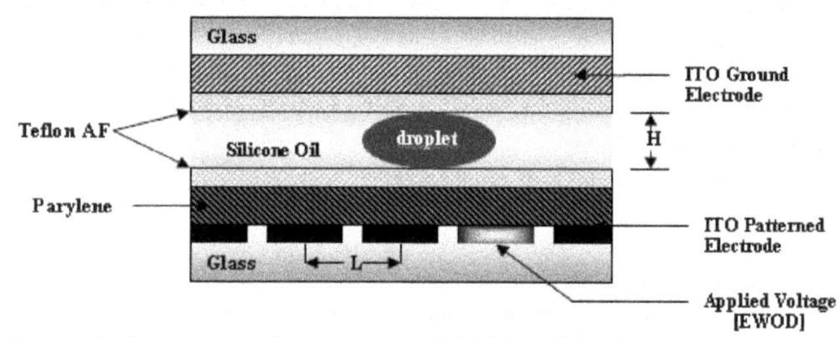

Figure 1: Schematic diagram of a DMFB (EWOD Based)

3. ROUTING PROBLEM IN DMFBS (CROSS REFERENCING)

The DMFB is represented as a 2D square grid array of given dimension in terms of number of cells .Each cell of a $m \times n$ array represents an electrode. A droplet is placed on a hydrophobic surface over an electrode Droplets are routed to a pre-determined location where fluorescently-labelled library of probes are preplaced for mixing. In addition to the 2D microfluidic array, there are on-chip reservoirs or dispensing ports and optical detectors. The dispensing Port/ reservoirs perform the task of droplet generation while the optical detectors are used for droplet detection. Electrodes are connected to control pins for electrical actuation. Therefore, by controlling voltage to each electrode in the bottom glass plate with control pins, it is possible to manipulate the direction of droplet movements. For applications in cross-referencing platforms, there are two separate sets of electrodes: one arranged in rows along the *X*-axis and the other arranged in columns along the *Y*-axis. They are assigned either a driving (High) or reference (Low) voltage. A grid point or cell is "addressed" if a potential difference is developed between the upper and lower electrodes. This causes a droplet at a neighbouring cell to move into this location (Figure 2).The activation of necessary electrode and deactivation of the neighbouring ones are shown in Figure 3 for a single as well as multiple droplet movement (simultaneous) through a single cell. However the corresponding pin sequences for multiple droplet movements are shown in Figure 4.

Hence an efficient schedule (virtual route) is often required to be developed to provide an optimal routing solution with objectives such as latest arrival time, total electrodes utilization as well as pin optimization. The major advantages of cross referencing is to use only (x+y) number of pins instead of (x*y) pins as in cases of direct addressing biochips. This in turn reduces the fabrication and packaging costs making it feasible for integration of large number of bioassays in a single substrate.

The routing problem is typically modelled in terms of a 2D grid. For each droplet, there exists a set of source grid locations, a set of target grid locations, and (optionally) a set of mixers. Each source, target combination is defined as a *net*. A 2-pin net has a single source and single target. Multiple sources, mixers and a single target form a multi-pin net. A combination of two Sources, one Mixer and one Target is a 3-pin net.

In cases of 3-pin or multi-pin nets, droplet merging is desired at specific locations called mixers. Several microfluidic modules may exist concurrently for mixing, splitting, storage, dispensing and other operations is also placed on the array. These are considered as the *Hard Blockage* or *Obstacle*. In order to avoid conflicts between droplet routes and assay operations, a segregation region is defined around the functional region of such microfluidic modules to isolate the droplets from active microfluidic modules during routing. Moreover, there are possibilities of intersection or overlapping of droplets during their concurrent routing in time-multiplexed manner. Also application of a given high or low voltage at any pin may result in unintentional movements of any other droplet which is not scheduled for that undesired movement at that timestamp. In order to avoid such unusual behavior three major constraints have been identified:

3.1 Timing Constraints

A predetermined time limit called the *Timing Constraint* defines the maximum allowed transportation time for a given set of droplets. All droplets are to be routed within this specified time.

3.2 Fluidic Constraints

Let d_i at (x^t_i, y^t_i) and d_j at (x^t_j, y^t_j) denote two independent droplets at any given timestamp t. Then, the following constraints, called *Fluidic Constraint*s should be satisfied for any time t during routing [19]:

Static constraint: $|x^t_i - x^t_j| > 1$ *or* $|y^t_i - y^t_j| > 1$

Dynamic constraint: $|x^{t+1}_i - x^t_j| > 1$

or, $|y^{t+1}_i - y^t_j| > 1$

or, $|x^{t+1}_j - x^t_i| > 1$ *or* $|y^{t+1}_j - y^t_i| > 1$

This implies that for any droplet at location ***(x, y)***, the locations ***(x+1, y), (x-1, y), (x, y+1), (x, y-1), (x+1, y+1), (x+1, y-1), (x-1, y-1),*** and ***(x-1, y+1)*** are prohibited for any other droplet to enter at timestamps t and $t+1$ in order to maintain these fluidic constraints. Hence, all the locations adjacent to ***(x, y)*** as stated above form *Critical Zone* for any droplet at ***(x, y)*** at timestamp *t*.

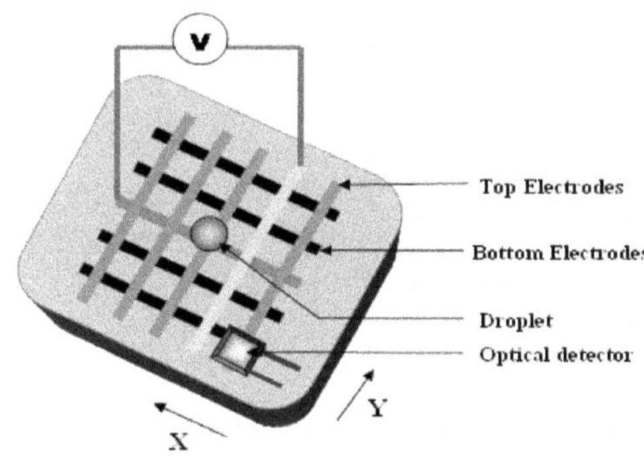

Figure 2: Top view of a cross-referencing Biochip

3.3Electrode Interference Constraint

When moving multiple droplets simultaneously, we must set potential levels on multiple rows or columns as driving electrodes. However each associated pin of a row/column involves all the electrodes in the same row/column -setting electrode-voltage values to move a set of droplets may result in inadvertent and wrong movement of some other droplets. Figure 4(a) indicates a case of wrong movement of droplet B while attempting to move droplets A and C concurrently. Figure 4(b) shows the correct electrode sequence for the concurrent movements of droplets A, B and stalling of C. The green circles indicate blockage at cell having Low-Low or High-High intersection.

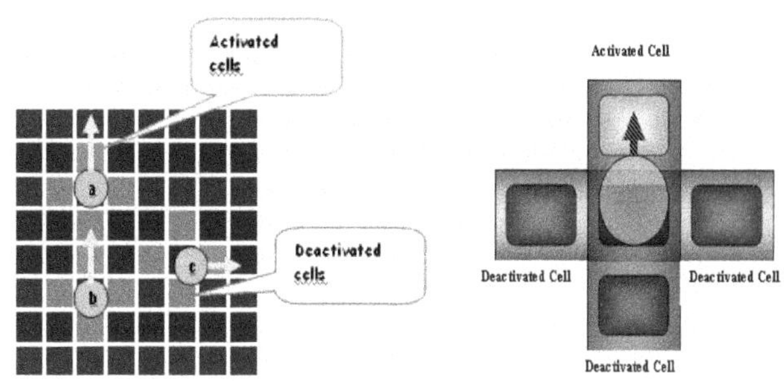

a) b)

Figure 3. a) Schematic for activation sequence of cells for parallel movement of droplets b) Individual movement and detailed neighboring cell activation for a single droplet

4. ROUTING OPTIONS IN CROSS REFERENCING BIOCHIPS

If two droplets arrives at the critical zone of one another at the same time – they are said to be under collision(due to violation of fluidic constraints).Hence both for direct addressing as well as cross referencing biochips stalling or detouring of droplets are necessary to avoid collision. However another major issue in droplet routing is electrode interference as stated in section 3.3 and the consequence of accidental droplet actuation or stalling is shown in figure 5.

In order to avoid the electrode interference constraint as well as to continue with routing without violation of fluidic constraints we define certain type of concurrent droplet movement as permissible movements – and consider movements of certain other types as Forbidden ones(because of resulting collision or accidental droplet actuation). Figure 6 represents types droplet transportation along with the respective voltage assignment at the vertical and horizontal electrodes - that represents permissible movements both

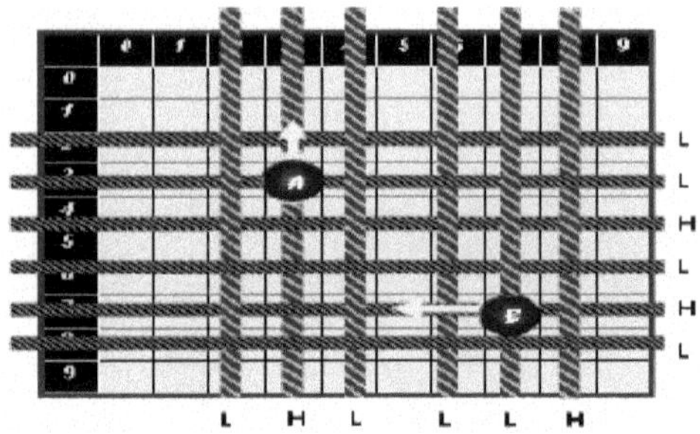

Figure 4: Pin voltage sequences to be employed for movement of droplets; droplet A vertically upwards and droplet B horizontally left. **L**-Low Voltage and **H** – High voltages.

in terms of fluidic constraints and electrode interference constraints. Whereas Figure 7 represents types of droplet transportation that causes violation in fluidic constraints and/or electrode interference constraints and hence considered to be forbidden.

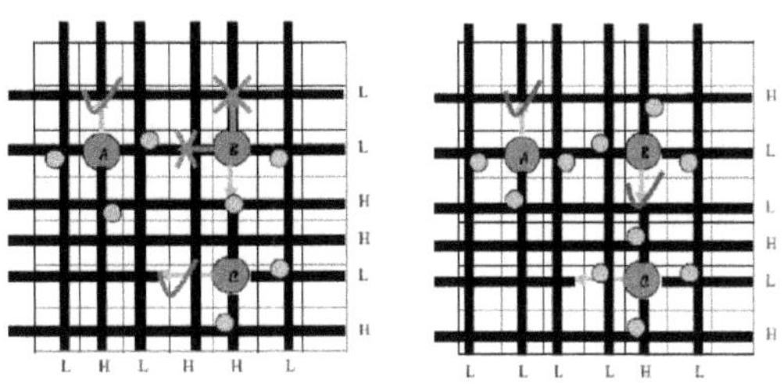

Figure: 5 a) A wrong voltage assignment causing Erroneous movement of droplet B. b) A correct voltage assignment causing correct movement of A and B and stalling of C; L-Low ,H-High (small circles show deactivated cells)

Observations from the following cases (figure 6 and figure 7) lead to the following conclusions:

1. For movement in the opposite direction in the same row or column – minimum difference of Two cell locations between two droplets are sufficient – both to avoid electrode interference as well as fluidic constraints.
2. For movement in the same direction along the same row or column – minimum difference of two cells are necessary in order to avoid electrode interference.
3. For parallel movement along the same direction or in the opposite direction – minimum difference of two row/column (if permitted to sustain fluidic constraints) is necessary to avoid electrode interference.
4. For mixed away movement (one vertical and other horizontal)—minimum difference of Two cells are necessary to avoid electrode interference.(refer to figure 7 a),7b) and 6 h).)
5. For mixed inwards movements (one vertical inward and other horizontal inward)—minimum difference of Two cells between destinations are necessary to maintain fluidic constraint, although electrode interference is sustainable. (refer to figure 7 c)).

Accordingly in the following sections we attempt to allow certain types of droplet movement for routing and design techniques in order to arrange the nets to favor these types of movements – that do not violate any constraints and result in optimized routing. The droplet movement types are as follows:

1. Unidirectional or away movement of multiple samples along same row or column with difference greater than *Two* between consecutive locations.
2. Parallel movement (both vertical and horizontal) difference between consecutive locations should be greater than *One.*
3. For Mixed away movement (One horizontal and other vertical) difference between corresponding locations of two droplets should be greater than *Two*.
4. For Mixed inward movement (One horizontal and other vertical) difference between corresponding locations of two droplets should be greater than *Two*.
5. No movements of droplets towards each other(resulting in cross overs) in the same row or column are allowed.

Finally these results in revised constraints for allowable droplet movements stated above. The constraints turn out to be as follows:

Static constraint: $|x^t_i - x^t_j| > 2$ *or* $|y^t_i - y^t_j| > 2$

Dynamic constraint: $|x^{t+1}_i - x^t_j| > 2$ *or,* $|y^{t+1}_i - y^t_j| > 2$

However in cases of violation – an unavoidable state arises termed as collision .This may result in stalling or detouring or a trade off between the two droplet movements – which may affect the final routing performance.

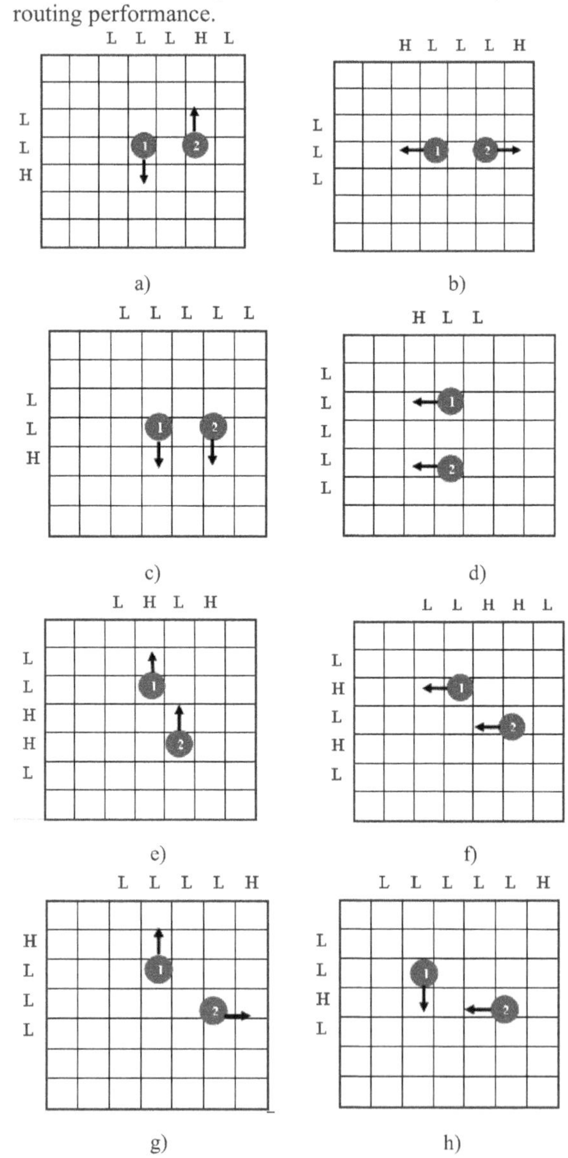

Figure 6: Permissible movements in Cross referencing DMFBs. a),c)e) represents parallel vertical movements; b),d),f) represents parallel horizontal movements; g),h)represents mixed movements

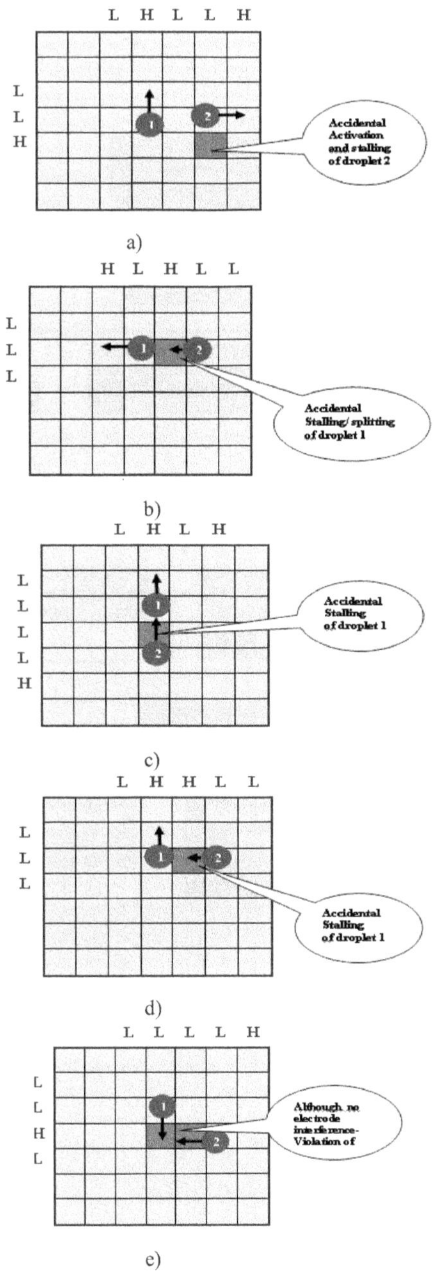

Figure 7: Movements causing violation of constraints in Cross referencing DMFBs a),d) mixed movements causing electrode interference .e) mixed movement causing violation in Fluidic constraints. c) vertical movement causing electrode interference

5. MOTIVATION

Numerous techniques have been proposed so far to resolve the problem of concurrent routing in both direct addressing and cross-referencing DMFBs. Some of them tackled the problem using partial concurrency, where simultaneous routing has been attempted for all those nets having disjoint paths in the first phase, with droplets with conflicting paths being routed next. Some other methods attempted total concurrency, using a trade-off between droplet stalling and detour to optimize the overall route time and the latest arrival time. In this paper, for the same objective of maximizing concurrency in routing of several droplets, we explore an alternative scheme of appropriately refining the placement of the source and target locations for each droplet keeping the module locations intact.

We propose to start with a given schedule of placement of modules along with source and target locations for the different nets as obtained from architectural level synthesis. This synthesis result provides information about locations of the modules and the locations for source, target and mixers (if any) for every sample in a subproblem. We attempt initially to rearrange the locations of corresponding source, target and mixers keeping the module locations intact. We define and use the notions of *module dependency* and *I/O dependency* (see Section 6) to maintain the order for the original schedule. Thereby we attempt to iteratively place the source, target and mixer locations maintaining the above dependency constraints for each droplet so as to minimize the chance of droplet collisions during routing. Next we tried to identify the modules that are interdependent. Thereby we rearrange the location of modules marinating the interdependency in terms of related source target locations within the module. This route-aware net and module placement and compaction technique results in optimized routing. This type of placement is termed as *detailed placement* of nets (maintaining the global placement of modules and its relative dependency intact). Proposed algorithm is tested on three testbenches of benchmark suite III, each testbench comprising multiple subproblems and each subproblem comprising numerous 2-pin and 3-pin nets. The hierarchy is illustrated with a Venn Diagram in Figure 8. Experimental simulation has shown large improvement in results in terms of latest arrival time, resource utilization for number of cells and total number of pins utilized (by clustering) for every testbench compared to the contemporary algorithms.

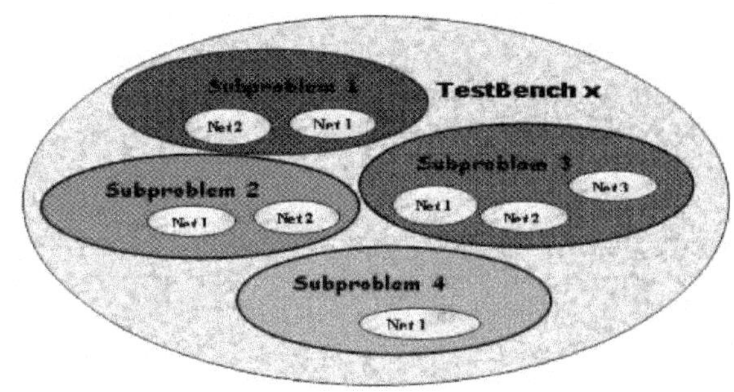

Figure 8: Venn diagram representing a test bench containing multiple subproblems with each subproblem containing multiple nets.

5.1 Brief summary of the work

- First identify the source and target locations for the different nets with dependencies.
- Form rectangular routing zone covering each source target mixer combination for a given sample.
- Draw a zone intersection graph representing intersection of routing zones.
- Start zone compaction by rearranging the location for each net iteratively until the number of zone intersections is minimal (maintaining the dependency constraints).
- Identify interdependency between the modules already placed as per schedule of the Bioassay protocol during synthesis. Form module interdependency zones in the form of rectangle that covers the corresponding interdependent modules.
- Draw a module interdependency graphs showing connection of respective dependent droplets with corresponding modules.

- For such interdependent modules identify the module dependent locations for sample droplets within Module interdependency zones .
- Attempt to rearrange such interdependent modules using compaction within the interdependency zones that enhances more permissible movements with shortened routing distances among source, mixer and target locations for each droplet.
- Attempt further rearrangement of the relative locations of source and target to comply with symmetrical movements (see Section 6) to avoid electrode interference as well as to obtain similar electrode sequence that promotes pin sharing.
- Define routing of the droplets using line probing algorithm with routes with larger Manhattan distance between source and target having higher preference in the events of collision (if any).

The overall process is further depicted in a flowchart (Figure 9).

6. PROPOSED METHOD FOR ROUTE AWARE NET PLACEMENT

6.1. Definitions

1. Zone of a net (*ZP*) - defined as the minimal rectangle bounding a source-target pair (for 2-pin nets) or Two source and One Mixer (for 3-pin droplets) or Mixer and target (for 3-pin droplets) for a given droplet location representing a 2-pin or 3-pin net in a given subproblem.

2. Module Dependency – If any source, target or mixer location for a droplet lies on the boundary of any preplaced module in a 2D grid, the location is defined as module dependent. This implies that either it is generated from or directed to that particular module (as per the schedule obtained from architectural level synthesis) for performing functions e.g. splitting, merging, mixing, storage or buffering etc. and are considered to be bound to that module. These locations are considered to be fixed and can not be rearranged during net placement. In order to avoid crossover between the zones, their orientation can be changed to another symmetric location bound with the same module without violating the module dependency.

3. I/O Dependency – If any source or target location for a droplet lies on the boundary of the 2D grid, it is considered as I/O dependent. This implies that it is either generated from some reservoir or scheduled to be dispensed to some well (as per the schedule developed from architectural level synthesis). These locations are considered to be bound to the particular row or column at the boundary where they are preplaced. However, they can be relocated to any position along the same row or column to avoid zone crossover or for final routing compaction. If the location happens to be at the intersection of a boundary row and a boundary column (termed as diagonal points), it can be relocated along either of the row or column, according to the demand for the zone compaction requirement. (stated later).

4. Interdependency between modules- If two source and target location for a given droplet is found to be bound with two different modules – the corresponding modules are said to be interdependent. The rectangle drawn for binding the two interdependent modules is termed as module interdependent zones (M.I.Z).Module interdependency indicates that the interdependent modules perform scheduled operation in consecutive sequence.

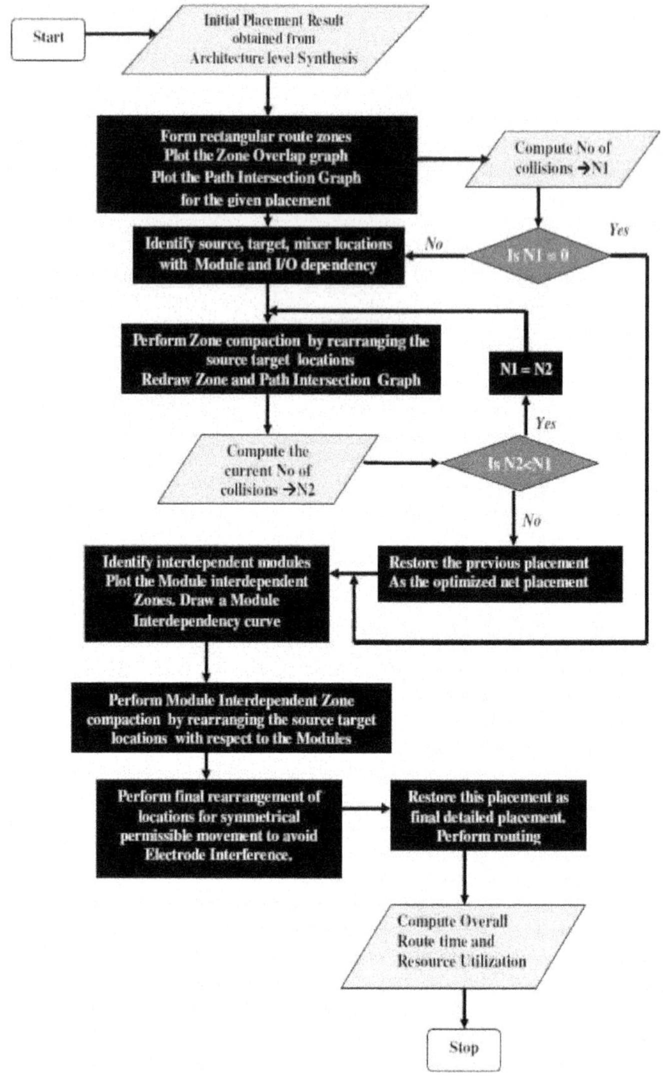

Figure 9: Flowchart for the overall scheme

6.2. The Proposed Algorithm

***Input*:** placement information obtained as an output of architectural level synthesis. All the sources and targets and mixers (if any) for each droplet as well as the functional modules are preplaced according to the schedule obtained from architectural level synthesis. We assume that the microfluidic modules already placed as per schedule are fixed within the layout.

1. For the given problem, identify the set of source and targets which are module dependent. Initially consider the locations of these source and targets as fixed relative to the preplaced functional modules.
2. For the given problem, identify the set of source and targets that are I/O dependent. Movements of these source and targets are restricted within the row or column in which they are preplaced respectively.
3. For each droplet in a given subproblem the minimum Manhattan distance between the source to target, source to mixer (if any) and mixer to target (if any) are computed as the initial route path. Identify the *ZP*s

based on this computed route paths associated with each set of source, targets, and mixer (if any).

4. Construct a zone graph G_z =(V,E) showing the intersection of the ZPs. Each vertex of the graph represents a zone of a problem, and an edge between two vertices implies that the corresponding ZPs are mutually intersecting.
5. Based on the given placement draw a Path intersection Graph G_p =(V,E) where each vertex v ϵ V represents a droplet and an edge e ϵ E exists between vertices v_i and v_j -if there is a cross over between the routing paths of the two droplets. The point at which the paths meet are termed as *Crossover point C.* The distance d_i between source of v_i and C and the distance d_j between source of v_j and C are computed. The difference ($d_i \sim d_j$) is computed and assigned as weight w_{ij} of edge $e(v_i, v_j)$. If this weight $w_{ij} <= 2$, it implies a probable collision either due to electrode interference or violation of fluidic constraints (as stated in Sections 3 and 4).
6. For each droplet representing a net, relocate the corresponding source and target within their respective *ZPs* so as to minimize the routing distance between them, maintaining the dependency constraints. (refer to lemma 2. for timing analysis in the next subsection). In case of 3-pin droplets attempt to relocate two sources symmetrically on both side of the mixers along the same row or column (if permissible).This prevents unwanted stalling of any of the source droplets on arrival to the mixer location.
7. During this relocation – if either of the source or target for a given net is found to be module dependent – it is kept fixed at the same location and its corresponding counterpart is relocated to the nearest possible cell location relative to the fixed one.
8. However if this non-fixed counterpart is I/O dependent – it can be relocated along the corresponding row or column so that distance between the two is minimum. But if both the source and target are found to be module dependent no relocation is allowed.
9. Identify the modules for interdepency in terms of module dependent source and target locations assigned for the same droplet. Draw Module interdependent zones (binding rectangles) for each pair of interdependent modules.
10. Plot G_m= (M,E) a module interdependency graph where each vertex m_i indicated by a square represents a module and an edge $e_{ij}(m_i,m_j)$ ϵ E exists if modules m_i and m_j are interdependent. Droplets (shown as round vertices) are connected to each respective module indicating their module dependencies.
11. Attempt to rearrange such interdependent modules using compaction within the M.I.Zs that enhances more permissible movements with shortened routing distances among source, mixer and target locations for each droplet.
12. Redraw the zone graph and the Path intersection Graph with the new placement. Find the number of zone intersections and the number of collisions (if any, remaining after relocation.)
13. Repeat Steps 5 to 13 iteratively until no further reduction in number of zone intersections as well as number of collisions are found to be possible. The corresponding zone intersection graph, Z_p, say, is the one associated with maximum possible compaction, such that functionalities of the problems are all preserved.
14. Clearly, droplets associated with non-overlapping zones can be concurrently routed without any collision. For droplets associated with overlapping zones, there is a possibility of collision based on the routing times, fluidic constraints and electrode interference. In such cases, techniques of stalling or detour for the corresponding droplets need to be applied for routing.
15. Now a placement obtained with minimum collision ensures minimum violation of fluidic constraints. However in order to take care of electrode interference it becomes necessary to check for permissible movements for each droplet as stated in section 4 based on the routing path of the droplets computed after step 13.Hence it becomes necessary to explore the possibility of further rearrangement of locations (if permitted without violation of constraints) for those droplets that are not following the path complying with permissible movements.
16. Check for possible rearrangement of the relative locations of source and target to comply with symmetrical movements either in horizontal or vertical or both directions to avoid electrode interference as well as to obtain similar electrode sequences that promotes pin sharing.
17. Identify all those droplets violating the permissible routing paths. If the source or target or both are module dependent try to relocate either of them symmetrically at other location adjacent to the module. For droplets whose source or target or both are not constrained by module dependency or I/O dependency, try to interchange the source and target locations if it provides an arrangement that allows the permissible movements.
18. Compute the Final Zone intersection and Path intersection graph for this finer compaction in order to make sure that this does not result in an increase in number of collisions. However if it has been found that number of collisions is increased after this final compaction, retrench back to the older arrangement for the droplets involving the collision.
19. However once detailed placement of nets is done it may be possible to result in a final placement where a small number of unavoidable collisions are involved. It becomes necessary to continue with these unavoidable cases that results in stalling or detour and hence affecting the routing performance.

6.3. Analysis

Lemma 1. The net time necessary for identifying the ZPs is proportional to the sum of total number of 2-pin droplets and twice the number of 3-pin droplets contained in the subproblem.

Proof. Let X_a is the average time to identify a zone. Let N1 is the number of 2-pin droplets. Each such droplet contributes to the formation of One zone based on the minimal bounding rectangle.

Let N2 represents the number of 3-pin droplets. Now for each such droplet two source and one mixer forms the first zone and the mixer and the corresponding target form the second one. Hence number of zones formed by 2-pin droplets is N1 and that by 3-pin droplets are 2 x N2. Thus, the total time necessary for Zone identification is given by X_a * (N1 + 2 * N2).

Lemma 2. The total time necessary for zone compaction is directly proportional to the number of zones formed.

Let X_c is the time for checking each zone for possible compaction. Let X_{avg} be the average time for compaction of each zone and X_{max} be the maximum time required for compaction among all the zones. Let Z be the total number of zones identified. Hence, in the worst possible case, if each zone takes time X_{max} for compaction, total time for zone compaction is given as

$$T_{max} = (X_c + X_{max}) * Z \;..... \text{(i)}$$

For the best case no compaction is necessary for any zone, and hence the total time for Zone compaction is $T_{min} = X_c * Z$ [only checking time for each zone is necessary] .... (ii)

For the average case the total zone compaction time is given by

$$T_{avg} = (X_c + X_{avg}) * Z. \;.... \text{(iii)}$$

X_c, X_{avg}, X_{max} are found to be constant for a given subproblem. Thus the total compaction time is proportional to the number of zones evident from Equations (i), (ii) and (iii).

7. AN ILLUSTRATIVE EXAMPLE

Here we are showing a given test case comprising Four 2-pin droplets namely a, b, c and d forming respectively zones A, B, C, D. Initially the zones for each droplet are all mutually intersecting The corresponding zone intersection graph and path intersection graphs are plotted in figure 11 a) and b).

In the next step zone compaction is carried out. The initial placement and respective iterations are shown in fig 10 a) and b). It has been found that after relocation number of crossover has been reduced to just One – between zone B and zone D.[figure 10 b)].

The module interdependency zones are identified and displayed using rectangles in figure 10 c) .The corresponding Module intersection graphs are plotted in figure 11 c). The direction of module rearrangement in terms of module reallocation is shown with arrows. The final placement of modules and the corresponding M.I.Z s are shown in figure 10 d) . Finally a symmetrical rearrangement without violation of module or I/O dependency constraints are carried out in zone D for droplet d to allow for simultaneous permissible movement as identified in section 4.The final arrangement after module reallocation and compaction is displayed in figure 10 e).

The corresponding final zone intersection , path intersection and module interdependency graphs are plotted in figure 11 d).The path intersection graph represents the possible collision edge shown by Red color – between droplet b and d and each box connected to each droplet represents the corresponding source to target routing zones. Here the collision edge between b and d has weight = 0 computed according to step 5 of the algorithm.(this initiates collision and invites necessary stalling). In the path intersection graph edges marked red indicates collision.

The corresponding routing sequence assigning Low(0) and High(1) to the respective pins are shown in figure 12. The result gives latest arrival time =3 ,cells Utilization = 9 ,Ratio of shared pins to available pins = 3/9.

8. THE ROUTING PROCEDURE

Hightower line probe based routing algorithm [16] is applied to compute the shortest distance termed as H-distance between each source and target and (for a 3-pin net) between the mixer and the target. If for a 3-pin net *p* is the distance between the source Sx and mixer and *q* is the distance between source Sy and mixer and r is the distance between the mixer and the target, the total distance is computed as(maximum of p and q) + r. This maximum distance serves as an estimate of the droplet route length, and helps to resolve conflicts in concurrent routing of nets.

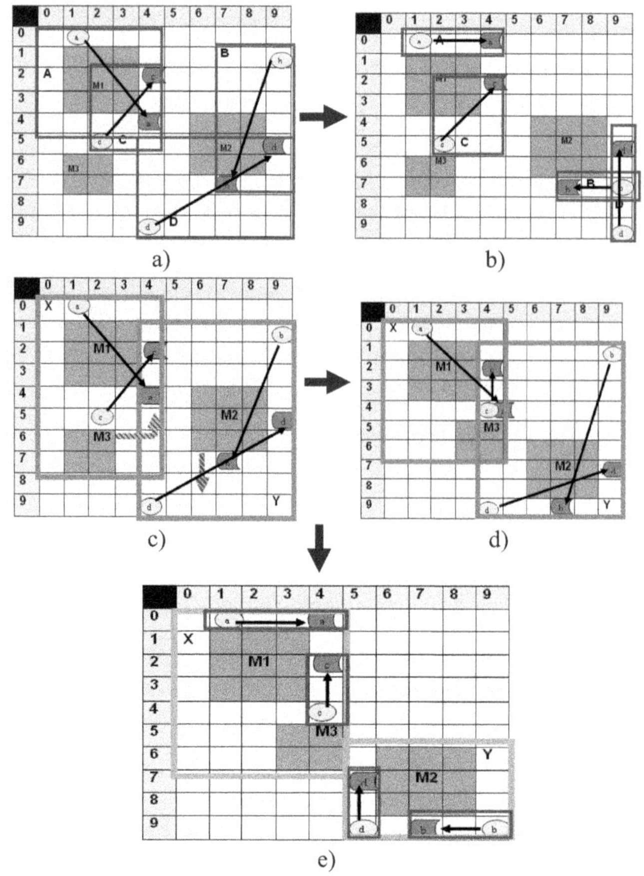

Figure 10. a) Rectangular Zone formation for a given module and net placement. b) Final Zone formation after rearrangement of nets based on Module dependency and I/O dependency. c) Module dependent zone formation for the modified net placement. d) Module dependent zone formation after rearrangement of modules e) Final Module dependent zone formation after symmetrical rearrangement of nets (droplet d is symmetrically rearranged).

1. For every source, the start time is initialized to zero. A time stamp increment of one is considered for each transition from one cell to next adjacent cell.

2 each droplet within the subproblem is started to be routed concurrently along their respective H-distance computed earlier. The droplets are sorted in descending order on the basis of their computed H-distance.

3. During concurrent routing of several droplets, there is a possibility of collision or overlap of paths of multiple droplets. In such a case, conflicts are resolved in favour of the droplets with larger *H*-distance.

4. For 2-pin nets, however, each droplet is routed directly from its source to its target. For 3-pin (multi-pin) nets, routing from each of the sources *Sx* and *Sy*, say, to the mixer (*M*) is done concurrently. This part of routing is referred to as the 1st Generation route. The largest arrival time *TSM* among (*Sx* →*M*) and (*Sy* → *M*) is noted. The final mixed droplet from *M* is next routed to Target *T*.

5. If a deadlock situation arises during droplet routing, at least one droplet has to be retreated. Consider a droplet Sx stalled due to possible contamination with another droplet Sy that has a higher routing priority (based on the group it belongs to). However, *Sy* may be stalled due to the movement of a 3rd droplet *Sz* that in turn

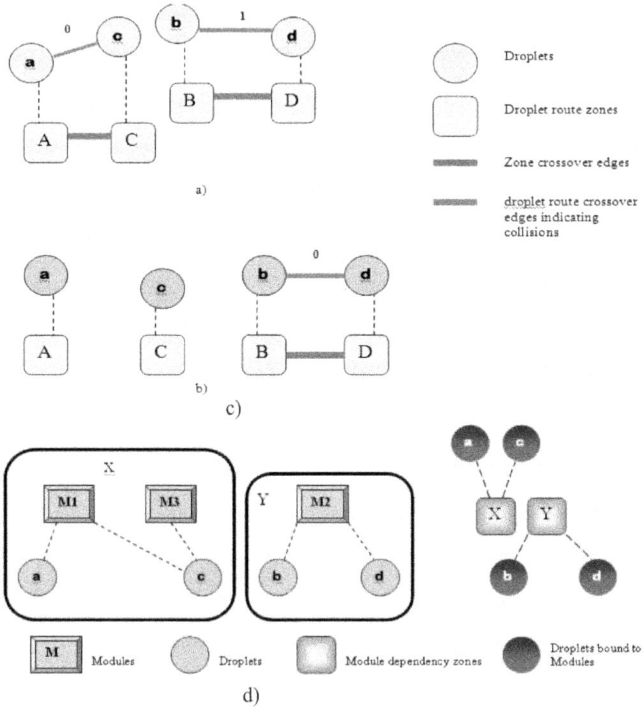

Figure 11 .a) zone intersection graph and path intersection graph combined diagram for initial placement. b) Final zone and path intersection graph after readjustment of source and target locations for adjustable droplets .c) The module interdependency graph with MIZ droplet binding graph for the configuration obtained in figure 9. b. d) Module dependency graph together with MIZ binding graph after final adjustment of nets and modules.

cannot move due to current position of *Sx* or *Sy*. In such cases, it is necessary to identify the specific droplet, which is responsible for the deadlock, and move it to a safe position. This phenomenon is known as *Retreat.* It is stalled at the new position for some time, allowing other two droplets to steer clear towards their respective destinations. Subsequently, the retreated droplet is rerouted to its earlier position and routed finally along its predetermined path.

6. Finally in order to avoid electrode interference we define zones for each droplet. For a droplet moving vertically along a column- the row comprising the next cell ahead is termed as Look ahead row and the row comprising the next cell behind to be deactivated is termed as Look back row. Similarly for horizontal movement we define Look ahead column and Look back column. Now we follow following routing regulations for intelligent avoidance of electrode interference:

a) If two droplets in the same timestamp have their look ahead zones coinciding with each other, proceed with normal pin voltage assignment (Figure 5. b) and 5 .d)).

b) if two droplets in the same timestamp have one's look ahead zone intersection with others Look behind zone maintain same voltage on the overlapped row (or column)pin but other corresponding column (or row)pins assigned for respective droplets must be assigned opposite voltage that enables concurrent movement of droplets in opposite direction.[figure 5 .a),c)].

c) If three droplets are placed such that one lies in the intersection of row and column of the other two at the same timestamp – stalling of any one of the three droplets is necessary to allow others to steer clear.[refer to figure 4.b)].

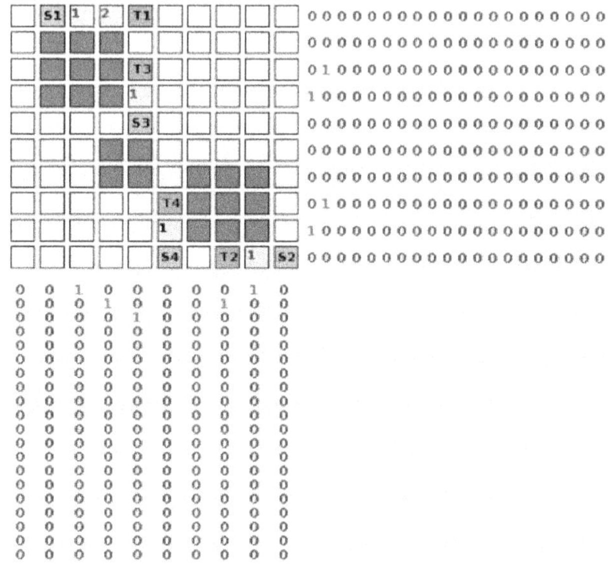

Figure 12 The optimized routing of the final configuration after final placement and compaction together with voltage sequences at each electrode. Latest arrival time -3,Cells used – 9,Pins used overall -9.Actual pins required after grouping – 3.Sx – source,Tx-Target , yellow cells – cells used for routing.

9. EXPERIMENTAL RESULTS

The route aware detailed placement algorithm and the consequent routing is tested on Benchmark suite III comprising of three testbenches namely In-Vitro_1, In-vitro_2 and Protein_2 comprising 11, 15 and 78 subproblems respectively. The detailed results for each subproblem in In-vitro 1 are given in table 1.Table 2 gives pin utilization and sharing details for each testbench. Here pin sharing implies that when identical sequences are generated on multiple electrodes using symmetrical movements, it reduces the electrode interference as droplet movements takes place along parallel vertical or horizontal lines at the same timestamps. This further allows grouping of multiple electrode connections to a single pin, which helps not only in wire planning but also in saving of energy and process cost (cost of applying separate sequences to separate electrodes through separate pins).On connecting multiple electrodes with a single pin there is an overall improvement in the required number of pins as shown in Table 2 Table 3 and 4 gives the comparative results with other existing algorithms stated in section 2 in terms of average time, total time and cells utilization. Major improvement has been noticed in the comparative results. However main reason for cross-referencing biochip results are found to be better in comparison to the direct addressing ones – because routing is performed after route aware placements using our algorithm which was not the case for the other direct addressing ones. If this technique is applied to direct addressing DMFBs results are expected to be even better than the cross referencing DMFBs.

10. CONCLUSION

In this paper we propose a heuristic for route-aware finer net placement and compaction method that (i) identifies each routing zone for any given droplet in a subproblem, and (ii) using a graph based method iteratively compact the zones by relocating for the respective nets(if applicable) as well as the interdependent modules and (iii) optimizes the routing performance through intelligent zone based collision avoidance. Results obtained show remarkable improvements in comparison to the contemporary methods proposed earlier. Further scope of improvement includes the reorientation of module location based on given bioassay protocol. Another issue regarding minimization of cross contamination between two consecutive subproblem executions in the same bioassay needs to be worked out in future.

Table 1 – detailed routing result for test bench In-Vitro 1

Subproblem no	Latest arrival time	Cell used	Pin used (Clustered)	Pin used (Non-clustered)
Subprob 1	16	40	21	47
Subprob 2	16	20	17	25
Subprob 3	15	20	17	47
Subprob 4	1	1	1	1
Subprob 5	8	20	13	24
Subprob 6	3	3	5	7
Subprob 7	1	2	1	2
Subprob 8	1	2	1	2
Subprob 9	1	2	1	2
Subprob 10	1	1	1	1
Subprob 11	1	1	1	1
Final Results	Average Time- **5.9** Max. Time **- 16**	**112**	**79**	**159**

Table2 – pin utilization and sharing details

Test bench	Size	Pins available /subproblem	Pins used (clustered)	Pins Used (total)	Improvement
In-Vitro 1	16 x 16	256	79	159	50.31 %
In-Vitro 2	14 x 14	196	70	127	44.88 %
Protein 2	13 x 13	169	445	669	33.48 %

Table 3 – comparison of the proposed method in terms of maximum to average arrival time with other algorithms

Maximum time /Average Time Comparison								
Test bench	No of probs	Progress-ive ILP [4]	Cho & Pan [8]	Network flow[9] + Broadcast Addr [17]	Cross Router [16]	Hwang & Ho [15]	Xiao Young [18]	Our Algorithm
In-Vitro 1	11	24/13.09	19/14.30	20/13.00	20/12.00	18/12.4	16/9.64	16/5.90
In-Vitro 2	15	22/11.00	20/12.00	17/11.33	19/10.70	17/10.4	17/6.40	13/3.94
Protein 2	78	26/10.23	20/12.19	20/10.51	20/9.86	20/10.04	20/9.87	15/5.385

Table 4 – comparison of the proposed method in terms of cell /Resource utilization with other algorithms

Cell Utilization comparison								
Test bench	Grid size	Progres sive ILP [4]	Cho & Pan [8]	Network flow[9] + Broadcast Addr [17]	Cross Router [16]	Hwang & Ho [15]	Xiao Young [18]	Our Algorithm
In-Vitro 1	16 x 16	231	258	237	246	231	246	**112**
In-Vitro 2	14 x 14	231	246	236	250	229	250	**88**
Protein 2	13 x 13	927	963	939	952	923	974	**510**

11. ACKNOWLEDGEMENTS

This work is supported partially by Special manpower development project, Dept. of Information Technology, Government of India and partially by VLSI Design Centre Project, Dept. of Information Technology, Government of West Bengal, India.

12. REFERENCES

[1] E. Verpoorte and N. F. De Rooij, "Microfluidics meets MEMS", *Proc. IEEE*, 2003, vol. 91, pp. 930-953.

[2] T. Xu and K. Chakrabarty." Droplet-trace-based array partitioning and a pin assignment algorithm for the automated design of digitalmicrofluidic biochips." In *CODES+ISSS*, pages 112–117, Oct. 2007.

[3] K. Chakrabarty,"Design, Testing, and applications of Digital Microfluidics-Based Biochips"In Proceedings of the18th International Conference on VLS Design held jointly with 4th International Conference on Embedded Systems Design (VLSID'05).

[4] P. Yuh, S. Sapatnekar, C. Yang, and Y. Chang, "A progressive ILP based routing algorithm for cross refere -ncing biochips," *Design Automation Conference*, pp. 284–289, 2008.

[5] S. Akella , E. J. Griffith and M. K. Goldberg. "Performance characterization of a reconfigurable planar-array digital micro fluidic system", IEEE Transactions Computer-Aided Design of Integrated Circuits and Systems, 25(10):340-352, Feb, 2006.

[6] T. Xu and K. Chakrabarty, "A cross-referencing-based droplet manipulation method for high-throughput and pin-constrained digital microfluidic arrays." In *Proceedings of Design Automation and Test in Europe*, pp.552 - 557, April 2007.

[7] W.Hwang, F. Su and K.Chakrabarty, "Droplet routing in the synthesis of digital microfluidic biochips." In Proc. *of Design Automation & Test in Europe*, 2006.

[8] M. Cho and D. Z. Pan ,"A high-performance droplet routing algorithm for digital microfluidic biochips." *IEEE Transactions Computer-Aided Design of Integrated Circuits and Systems*,27(10):406-419, October 2008.

[9] C.L .Yang, P.H. Yuh and Y.W. Chang. "Bioroute: A network flow based routing algorithm for digital micro fluidic biochips." In *Proceedings of IEEE/ACM International Conference on Computer-Aided Design*,pages 752-757, 2007.

[10] K. F. Boehringer. "Modeling and controlling parallel tasks in Droplet based microfluidics" *Computer Aided Design of Integrated Circuits and Systems*, 25(2):334- 344, February 2006.

[11] T. Xu and K. Chakrabarty, "Integrated Droplet Routing in the Synthesis of Microfluidic Biochips", Design AutomationConference, San Diego, California, U.S.A, June 4-8, 2007.

[12] J. Soukup, "Fast Maze Router" *Proceedings of the 15thACM Design Automation Conference,* Pages 100-102,1978.

[13] P Roy, H Rahaman, P Dasgupta, "A Novel Droplet Routing Algorithm for Digital Microflluidic Biochips", GLSVLSI, 2010, Providance, Rhode Island, USA.

[14] D. H. Hightower, "A generalized Channel router" "Proceedings of 17th ACM/IEEE Design Automation conference, pages 12 – 21,1980.

[15] T.-W.Huang, T.Y. Ho, "A Fast Routability- and Performance-driven droplet routing algorithm for digital Microfluidic biochips"- Computer Design, 2009. ICCD 2009. IEEE International Conference 4-7, Oct.2009, pages 445-450 Lake Tahoe,

[16] Z.Xiao, E. F.Young,**"**CrossRouter: a droplet router for cross-referencing digital micro fluidic biochips", ASPDAC '10 Proceedings of the 2010 Asia and South Pacific Design Automation Conference,Taipei,Taiwan,2010,pp 187-192.

[17] T. Xu and K. Chakrabarty," Broadcast Electrode-Addressing for Pin Constrained Multi-Functional Digital Microfluidic Biochips",Design Automation Conference,June,Anaheim,California USA,2008pp 173 – 178.

[18] Z. Xiao, E. F. Y. Young," Droplet-Routing-Aware Module Placement for Cross-Referenc -ing Biochips",ISPD 2010,SanFransisco,California, USA,17th March,2010.

[19] Y Zhao, K Chakraborty, "Cross Contamination, avoidance of Droplet routing in Digital microfluidic biochips"—Procedure of the Design and Automation Test in Europe, 2009.

[20] D. Erickson and D. Li, "Integrated microfluidic devices," ***Anal.*** Chim. Acta., 507, 11-26 (2003).

Enabling Ultra-Low Power Operation in High-End Wireless Sensor Networks Nodes

Carlo Brandolese, William Fornaciari, Luigi Rucco, Federico Terraneo
Politecnico di Milano - P.zza Leonardo da Vinci, 32 - 20133 - Milano (Italy)
{brandole,fornacia,rucco,terraneo}@elet.polimi.it

ABSTRACT

This paper presents a prototype hardware/software architecture for minimizing energy consumption on high-end microcontrollers, while simplifying the development of applications providing a general-purpose-like programming environment. The key features enabling this twofold goal are operating system support to processes, optimized sensing and hibernation of the system state. To balance performance offered by high-end microcontrollers with the need for ultra-low power operation—especially required by WSNs—it is essential to minimize the duty cycle by keeping the microcontroller in a low-power state as long as possible, without affecting the performance required by the application. To cope with the increasing leakage current observed in today's microcontrollers a software-based hibernation mechanism has been implemented to transparently save the memory of processes in a non-volatile memory, allowing to completely switch off the microcontroller. To further avoid costly process loading overheads during the sleeping periods, we devised a smart sensing mechanism capable of gathering data from peripherals without restoring the state of processes. Preliminary results show that the lifetime of the proposed node architecture is of the same order of magnitude of that of ultra low-power nodes and significantly better than that of high-end ones.

Categories and Subject Descriptors

D.4.1 [**Operating Systems**]: Process Management; C.2.4 [**Computer-Communications Networks**]: Distributed Systems—*Network operating systems*; B.8.2 [**Performance and Reliability**]: Performance Analysis and Design Aids

General Terms

Design, Performance

Keywords

Power Optimization, Wireless Sensor Networks

CODES+ISSS'12, October 7-12, 2012, Tampere, Finland.

1. INTRODUCTION

The goal of this work is to bring some of the features of general-purpose systems, such as multitasking, memory protection, dynamic loading, standard programming languages and libraries, into wireless sensor networks. Such features are, in fact, expected to significantly increase the capabilities of wireless sensor networks, allowing for more complex tasks on-node, reducing radio transmission, running multiple isolated tasks on the same node and simplifying code development by leveraging on standard libraries and APIs. Moreover, this approach enables code mobility, useful to dynamically reconfigure nodes both to add applications while the network is operating and to distribute the power consumption over nodes [1]. From this point of view, ultra-low power microcontrollers used for WSN nodes are seen as a stopgap to their evolution. This stimulated experimenting the use of high-end microcontrollers while at the same time optimizing their duty cycle to minimize the power consumption. The paper is organized as follows. Section 2 provides an overview of wireless sensor nodes and operating systems, in the light of which the positioning of the proposed approach is motivated in Section 3; Section 4 presents the hardware and software architectures that have been developed; Section 5 describes the energy model adopted to compare against existing nodes; Section 6 presents and discusses the quantitative results obtained. Finally, Section 7 summarizes the achievements of the present work.

2. RELATED WORK

Many sensor nodes are currently available off-the-shelf of two main classes: small, cheap and ultra-low power sensor nodes, on one hand, and costly, powerful high-end nodes, on the other. Within each family, the general structure of the hardware, as well as the average power consumption profile, do not vary significantly. Moreover, depending on the node characteristics, different operating systems are available: from small OS suitable for ultra-low power motes, to full-fledged embedded versions of general purpose operating systems like Linux. Each presents some advantages and disadvantages, depending on the goal being pursued: ultra-low power performances rather then flexibility and easiness of programming and development.

2.1 WSNs nodes

One of the best known nodes of the ultra-low power family is the Berkeley TelosB [2]. This node is provided with an MSP430 microcontroller, the internal memory of which is composed of 10KB of RAM and 48KB of Flash. Older nodes, also well known, belongs to the MICA[3] family, in particular Mica, Mica2Dot and Mica2: all of them integrate an ATmega128 microcontroller, with 4KB of internal RAM and 128KB of Flash. Power consumption figures for these nodes are reported in Table 3, Section 6. Other nodes with similar characteristics are Firefly [4], with camera-enabled features (so more power consuming), WiSMote, devised by LCIS (Grenoble), and others.

Slightly more powerful architectures are the BTnode, developed at ETH Zurich, which does integrate larger memories (64KB of RAM, 128KB of Flash, 4KB of EEPROM and 180KB of external SRAM), but consuming 100–200mW in full active state. Another node in this class is Egs [5], based on a Cortex-M3 Atmel SAM3U2C μC, whose maximum operating frequency scales up to 96MHz and whose internal memory is composed by 36KB of RAM and 128KB of Flash, plus an external 2Gb NAND Flash. The microcontroller consumes 48mA in active state, while in wait mode (a sort of deep sleep) its consumption decreases to 15μA.

Among the high-end and powerful architectures, two of the most widespread platforms are the IMote nodes by Intel and the SunSpot, by Oracle Sun. The IMote2.0 [6],integrates a PXA271 XScale processor, whose operating frequency can range from 13MHz to 416MHz and is equipped with 32MB of SDRAM and 32MB of Flash, with additional 256KB of SRAM. The current absorption in active state and radio off are considerably high, and are reported as well in Table 3, Section 6. Previous versions of this node, i.e. IMote and IMote1.0, are both based on ARM architectures, with 64KB of RAM and 512KB of Flash. SunSpot[7] is another example of powerful and energy-consuming device: these nodes use an ARM920T core operated at up to 180MHz, and are provided with 512KB of RAM and 4MB of Flash memory. The current consumption reaches 98mA with processor in active state and radio on and 80mA with radio off. In sleep mode, the current consumption is 24mA, while in deep-sleep it decreases to 33μA.

2.2 WSNs Operating Systems

Because of the different amount of memory and computing power available in the two classes of nodes, also the operating systems and the services offered at system level considerably vary. Many operating systems have been proposed for low-end nodes, all of them having in common the need for small footprint (10KB or less) and low processing overheads. These operating systems can be divided in three main categories with respect to their architecture [8]: *monolithic* (TinyOS, MagnetOS, etc.), *modular* (Contiki, Mantis OS, SOS, Bertha, CORMOS, Kos, etc.) and *virtual machines* (Maté, ContikiVM, MagnetOS JVM, VM*, SwissQM, etc.). Some of the above-cited systems fall into the paradigm of pure event-driven (e.g. TinyOS and SOS), other into pure thread-based (e.g. MantisOS) and others are hybrid and incorporate both the aspects (e.g. Contiki and kOS). Besides this very fundamental distinction, the various operating systems differs for the way they support scheduling, memory management, dynamic reprogramming, power management and network protocol stack(s). Due to the resource-constrained hardware, hardly any small operating system of this family really provide complete functional coverage for a general-purpose like programming to the end-user, such as standard libraries, standard system call, standard executable format and reprogramming mechanisms, standard programming languages and so on. On this last point, it is worth noting that many operating systems have been developed in lightweight variants of C language, e.g. TinyOS in NesC or LiteOS in LiteC++. Other, like Contiki and Mantis, have been written in C, but the programming style needs to be adapted to specific features of the systems Some virtual machines try to emulate a subset of the Java instruction set, e.g. SwissQM[9].

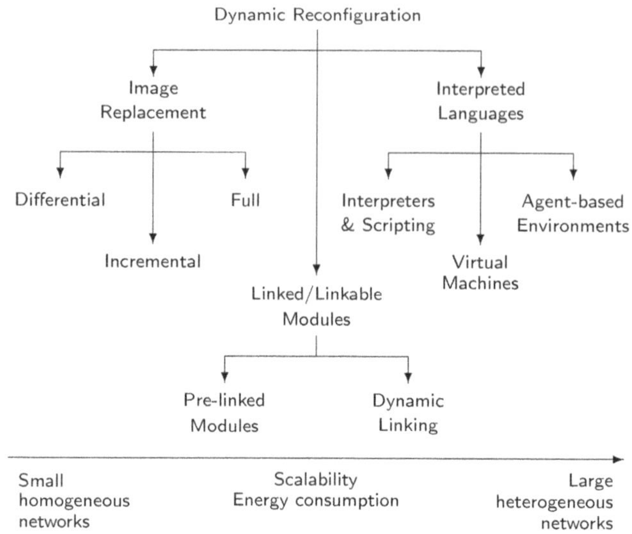

Figure 1: Reconfiguration techniques overview

The reprogramming mechanism is one of the features with greater impact on the user-level development process. Virtual machines well fit with the need for dynamic reconfiguration of the networks, but usually require very high run-time costs. Similar advantages and problems arise in other interpreted environments, like run-time script interpreters (e.g. SensorWare [10], COMIS [11], SpatialProgramming [12] or DeepPython [13]) or distributed agent-based approaches (e.g. Agilla [14]). Besides raw image replacement techniques (native in TinyOS, MantisOS, NutOS and others), some distributed mechanisms have also been devised to make network-wide reconfiguration more efficient. The most notable examples are XNP [15], MOAP [16] and Deluge[17, 18]. In addition to theses monolithic approaches, some *binary differential* solutions have been proposed (Koshy and Pandey [19], Reijers & Langendoen [20], Jeong & Culler [21]), which are very energy efficient, but not scalable.

Many operating systems support pre-linked modules, for example Contiki, SOS, Bertha, and other like Impala for Zebranet [22] or ScatterWeb [23]. Lightweight variants of dynamic linkers have also been proposed in FlexCup [24] and Contiki [25]. A synopsis of the reprogramming approaches is presented in Figure 1.

Power management service are offered by various small WSN operating systems like TinyOS [26] and SenOS [27], while dedicated APIs are provided in NanoRK and PEEROS.

In small WSN operating systems, there is no isolation among running programs because of the lack of real processes, mainly due to the absence of a MPU or a MMU on the microcontroller. Very few proposals have been presented for managing a sort of virtual memory in MMU-less platforms at software-level. SNACK-pop [28] implements a form of compiler-assisted paging. The t-kernel [29] operating system provides MMU virtual memory management and memory protection for `text` and `data` segments. A proposal for paging only the `data` segment, by enforcing virtual memory through application-level library and VM-aware assembler can be found in [30], while software-level memory expansion techniques can be found in MEMMU [31] and Enix [32]. To the best of our knowledge, none except isolated cases of commercial operating systems for embedded devices, like Micrium, have modules to support processes, while standard C libraries are available, often in a reduced version, in very few operating systems such as Enix. New proposals like MansOS [33] claim to offer some principles of Unix operating systems like sockets, threads and device managers, with plain C programming.

More powerful nodes, like Imote2, can run embedded Linux releases like μCLinux, while the SunSpot mounts the Squawk Virtual Machine [34], a full-fledged micro-edition Java virtual machine. Clearly, such a virtual machine has very high energy costs, reducing the estimated lifetime of a node in active state to 23 hours only [7]. These systems, designed for high-end and energy-consuming platforms, have a footprint in the order of megabytes, so they are unportable to the small *ultra-low* power nodes. On the contrary, however, they provide to the end-user a development environment similar to that of general-purpose platforms, at the expense of a lifetime significantly shorter.

Some other operating systems and middleware layers for WSNs have been proposed, supporting real-time applications and other special use cases, but they fall beyond the objectives of the present work.

3. PROPOSED APPROACH

As seen, a myriad of operating systems have been proposed for small nodes, each with particular features which aim at providing to the developer services to cope with the high complexity of a WSN. None of them, however, seems to reach a reasonable level of completeness and generality to avoid a programmer to be acquainted with a lot of specific issues of the OS and of the hardware underneath. High-end nodes and operating systems, on the contrary, succeed in the purpose of furnishing to the end-user ease of programming and general-purpose like environments, but show unacceptable power consumption and thus do not fit for application which require long lifetime and cheap hardware devices. The solution appears to place in the balance between the low-power features offered by small nodes and operating systems, with the abstraction level offered by high-end ones, but this clearly leads to a trade-off.

A possible solution to manage this trade-off is to take advantage from the newest and next-generation microcontrollers, which offer a good amount of memory and computing resources and have been designed to provide different operating states with different profiles of power consumption. Unfortunately, increasing leakage current due to the reduction to nanometer scale of newest high-end microcontrollers seems to be an harsh barrier to the development of hardware/software WSN architectures based on these devices. On the other hand, the multiple operating points offered by these microcontrollers constitutes a foremost opportunity to cope with the problem of leakage by optimizing the duty cycle, exploiting the possibility of switching from high-performance to low-power states and taking advantage from the high scalability in operating frequency. The lowest power consumption states, however, often require the internal memory to be switched off, maintaining in active state only a small portion of backup memory (usually less than 10KB). Thus the possibility of adopting this new class of microcontrollers, making the most of their duty cycle optimization, passes through the need of *hibernating* the system state on an external memory. High frequency of swapping operations does not fit well with the usage of Flash or EEPROM memories, which have a limited number of write cycles and need expensive wear-leveling at software-level. This limitation can be overcome thanks to emerging magneto-resistive, ferro-electric and phase-changing RAM, which have unlimited number of write cycles, retain their state even when switched-off and have comparable energy consumption figures. Optimization of swap-in/swap-out operations must then be performed by the operating systems to reduce hibernation overheads to an acceptable level.

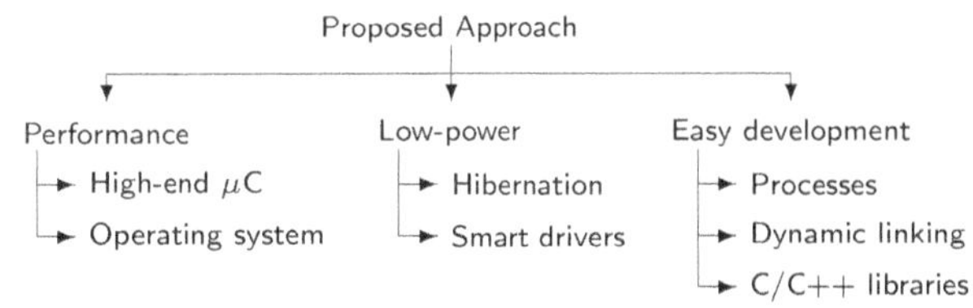

Figure 2: Goals of the proposed approach

In conclusion, a possible effective way for enforcing the adoption of these new microcontrollers and memory devices in WSNs seems to be a joint development of both the hardware and the operating systems architecture, eventually extending an existing small operating systems with a proper power-management layer, which should enforce, in particular, an efficient management of the system hibernation as well as a smart usage of peripherals drivers, to maximize energy saving during idle and purely sampling periods. Moreover, the superior resources made available by new generation high-end μC can lead to the implementation of operating system features typical of general purpose systems, with which many programmers are familiar, eventually promoting a wider adoption of WSNs outside highly-specialized fields. Among these general features, some of the most important to make the development phase easier are the availability of standard Libraries, support for full-fledged processes as well as Dynamic Linking and Reprogramming (Figure 2).

4. HW/SW ARCHITECTURE

This section describes the architecture of the PoliNode and Miosix operating system. First, the hardware architecture will be discussed, whose distinguishing feature is the presence of a high-end microcontroller and a non-volatile memory for performing process hibernation. Then, the software architecture is discussed, detailing the implementation of processes, hibernation and smart drivers. It should be noted that while we focused our choices on a specific hardware implementation and operating system, the concept of combining processes, hibernation and smart drivers constitute a general methodology useful for a wider range of energy critical and reconfigurable systems. Such concepts, not only can be implemented also on different microcontrollers and

Transceiver	
Operating state	Current drawn
Deep sleep	900 nA
Receive	13.1 mA
Transmit (0dBm)	11.3 mA
Microcontroller	
Operating state	Current drawn
Running at 60MHz	12 mA
Sleeping at 60MHz	5 mA
Running at 16MHz	4 mA
Sleeping at 16MHz	2.1 mA
Sleep, unclocked	300 μA
Deep sleep, unpowered and unclocked	4.8 μA
Magnetoresistive RAM	
Operating state	Current drawn
Quiescent	7 μA
Reading at 15MHz	3.75 mA
Writing at 15MHz	13.4 mA

Table 1: Power consumption summary

with different operating systems, but can also be proficiently used outside of the area of wireless sensor networks.

4.1 Hardware architecture

An high-level sketch of the PoliNode architecture is shown in Figure 3. The sensor node is divided into five functional units, each serving a well defined purpose.

The *Communication unit* integrates a power optimized wireless transceiver operating at 2.4GHz—a frequency commonly used by many WSN nodes, including the TelosB and the IMote— and a PCB antenna, which, again, is a common choice to minimize production costs. A summary of the transceiver power consumption figures is reported in top part of Table 1.

The *Processing Unit* is composed of an ARM Cortex-M3 based microcontroller providing hardware memory protection and integrating 128KB of RAM and 1MB of Flash memory. The core can operate at up to 120MHz, but in the current implementation it is used at 60MHz. The core also features a low-power operating mode in which it can be clocked by an internal 16MHz oscillator. This shortens the startup time from the Deep Sleep mode, since it is not necessary to wait for the external oscillator and internal PLL to settle. Concerning sleep modes, it is possible to have the whole processor powered but unclocked (except for the RTC), guaranteeing RAM data retention, or shut down the internal voltage regulator, losing the content of the internal RAM, except for a small 4KB portion and maintaining the RTC active. As the power figures in the middle part of Table 1 show, the power consumptions is significantly different in these two modes. This microcontroller has been selected to provide enough computational power and memory to both be able to perform complex on-node tasks, accommodate applications making use of C/C++ standard libraries, as well as running multiple processes concurrently.

A key component of the node is the magneto-resistive RAM (MRAM) used to save the data image of the running processes while the node is in deep sleep mode. The use of an external non-volatile memory coupled with hibernation support allows to write applications that are programmed as if they were always resident in memory, relying on hibernation activated by the operating system during deep sleep

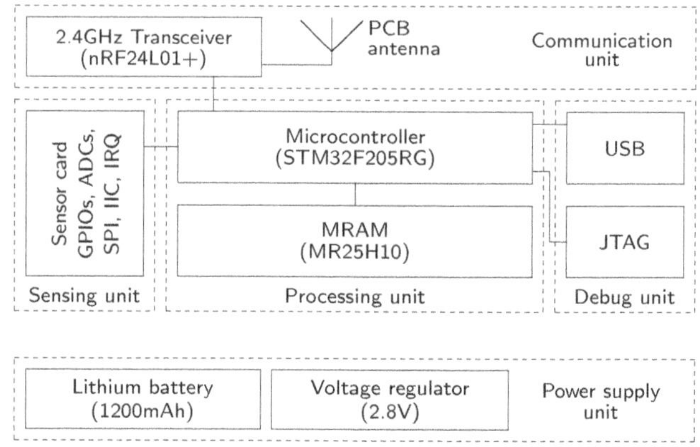

Figure 3: Architecture of the PoliNode

periods. The lack of such a feature would have prevented the microcontroller from entering its lowest power state of operation, and is therefore a key component of the node. A 1 Mbit MRAM memory has been selected instead of a Flash memory both due to its lower power consumption and for having a virtually unlimited number of write cycles. The MRAM is connected to the microcontroller through an SPI bus operating at 15MHz. A DMA channel of the microcontroller is used to ensure that the required speed is actually achieved when copying the data image of processes. A summary of the power consumption information for the MRAM is reported in the bottom part of Table 1. Note that when the MRAM is not used, i.e. during deep sleep periods, the microcontroller can switch it off, bringing its power consumption from 7μA of the quiescent state to zero.

The *Sensors card* collects specific sensing devices and is strongly application dependent. Therefore the node, instead of integrating specific sensors, provides a connector for a custom sensor daughter-board. The connector provides a number of analog channels connected to the ADC, SPI and I^2C interfaces for digital sensors, as well as some GPIOs. One of the GPIOs is configured to generate an interrupt, used to wake the processor from deep sleep when specific sensors generate an event. Furthermore, additional circuitry allows switching sensors on and off by means of a subset of the GPIOs available in the daughter-board connector. Efficient policies can be designed both at application and operating system level to exploit this feature to further reduce the overall power consumption.

The *Power Supply Unit* hosts a 1200mAh lithium battery and integrates a 2.8V voltage regulator ensuring that the voltage used to power the processor, the transceiver, the sensors and the MRAM remains constant throughout the battery's lifetime. Finally, a *Debug Unit* provides an USB connector to load the operating system to the board, and a JTAG header is for in-circuit debugging during the development phase. It must be noted that once the sensor is operating, new applications can be downloaded over-the-air, as explained in more detail when discussing processes.

4.2 Software architecture

The software architecture adopted for the node is based on the Miosix operating system (previously developed by one of the authors). A simplified view of its structure is shown in Figure 4. It is composed of a board support package that collects low-level, architecture dependent code, a kernel

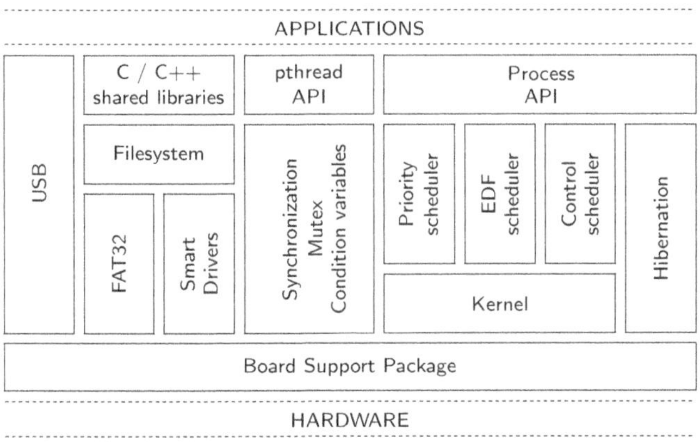

Figure 4: Architecture of Miosix

providing scheduling and synchronization primitives, as well as an support for the C/C++ standard libraries. Multi-threading is also available through the standard POSIX API. Extensions to this base system are described in the following.

4.2.1 *Processes*

Processes are a key feature of the proposed architecture, and their introduction allows the implementation of *run-time application loading* onto the sensor nodes without affecting the operation of other running processes. In addition, processes—differently from threads—provide *memory isolation* and simplify the implementation of the hibernation functionality. A process is an independent instance of a program running on a node, with its own *data image* composed of a stack, optionally a heap, and some global variables. Multiple processes can run in the system, and preemptive multitasking is used to schedule them.

Program loading starts by allocating a suitably sized RAM area to store the process data image. Then, global variables are initialized and—if needed—relocated, since no MMU is available and addresses of data are not known until run-time. Relocation of program code, on the other hand, is not necessary, as the microcontroller and toolchain allow for efficient Position-Independent Code (PIC). The resulting process image is therefore composed of two non-contiguous memory areas, one in Flash memory, containing the program code, and one in RAM, hosting process data. This arrangement simplifies memory isolation, obtained by means of the Memory Protection Unit (MPU) configured to set permissions for read, write and execute operations on selected memory regions, according to the process memory layout. The operating system, at every context switch, configures two areas of the MPU with the actual memory positions of the program code and the data of the process that is about to execute. Any attempt to access locations outside these memory areas or to violate access permissions results in an hardware interrupt that the operating system uses to terminate the process, preventing run-time errors in one program from affecting other software running on the same node.

Since processes cannot access other memory areas, including the operating system code, a general-purpose *system calls* mechanism has also been implemented.

It is worth comparing the presented approach with similar proposals used in thread-based operating system supporting dynamic linking. As a reference we consider Contiki

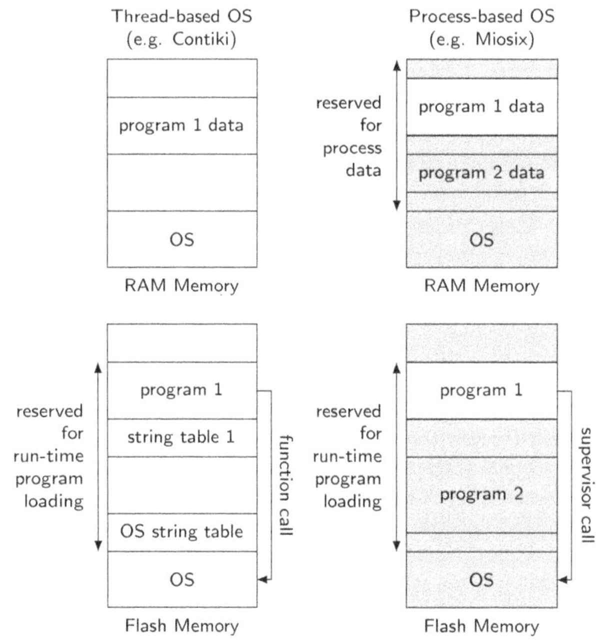

Figure 5: Memory layouts and system calls

[35]. Figure 5 shows the memory layout and system call approaches in the two cases. Miosix provides memory protection (grayed-out areas) and system calls, while Contiki, lacking any form of protection, can use regular function calls.

Both these approaches allow to execute programs loaded at run-time, thus enabling an efficient reprogramming mechanism for remote nodes. However, while in Contiki and other similar embedded operating systems there is no clear separation between system and user addressing space, a process-based execution model enforces memory isolation, thus providing a secure environment for testing applications and preventing malicious software from untrusted sources to affect the functionality of the system.

4.2.2 *Program file format*

The program format chosen for dynamic loading is the standard ELF format. As noted in previous works [35], the ELF format has a non negligible size overhead (meta-data), resulting in an increase of the energy required to transfer a program over the network. The cited authors reduced the ELF size by replacing 32bit addresses in the meta-data with 16bit ones, but this approach is only suitable for 16bit microcontrollers. While the meta-data found in *sections* is vital for compilers, loaders do not need it, and the ELF specification do not mandate their presence in executable files. We have thus completely removed section information. In addition, the *symbol table* and *string table* have been removed as well, since calls into the operating system are not made through function calls—which would require relocation—but via system calls. The resulting ELF structure is still compliant to the standard, but only consists of the minimal information required by the loader.

4.2.3 *Hibernation*

As already discussed, the lowest power state of high-end microcontrollers, differently from ultra-low power ones, can be achieved by powering off the processor core, therefore losing the content of the internal RAM memory. This would not allow saving the data of running processes, therefore hibernation was implemented. When all processes are either waiting for data from the smart drivers or sleeping, and the closest wakeup time is greater than a certain threshold, the operating system performs an hibernation operation. This consists in: i) saving the RAM data image of each running process in the external non-volatile memory, ii) configuring the RTC to wakeup the processor at the required time, and, iii) entering deep sleep mode. On the other hand, the operating system data image is not saved, and a new boot is performed when the RTC interrupt occurs. This is made possible by the very short boot time of Miosix ($144\mu s$) combined with a minimal set of information (mainly the process descriptors) stored in the microcontroller's backup RAM. After booting, thus, the operating system restores the state of processes from the backup RAM, swaps-in their data image from the external memory and restarts them.

A number of optimizations can be adopted to minimize the overhead of swap operations. A first improvement consists in limiting the data to be swapped to the portion of the RAM image actually used (the operating system knows about the actual heap and stack usage), while an even more aggressive approach would postpone swapping-in processes with longer sleep times to the moment they are strictly required to be executed.

4.2.4 *Smart drivers*

While the aforemetioned optimizations reduce the overhead of swapping processes in and out, the need for an application to perform periodic measurements results in a particularly inefficient situation where a process wakes up only to perform a very short operation, such as doing a single measurement from a sensor for later processing. In such cases the time and energy to swap-in and swap-out the process data image is much higher than that strictly required to perform actual work.

To solve this issue, *Smart Drivers* have been conceived and introduced. A smart driver is an enhanced peripheral driver within the operating system, that offloads the burden of periodically performing measurements from the applications. Accessing a smart driver from a process, in fact, causes the process itself to be blocked and to be awakened only after a predefined *measurement batch* is completed, i.e. when a queue allocated for storing samples is full. Individual measurements are then performed by the kernel, without the need of swapping-in and awakening any process. For example, the smart driver for performing ADC sampling has the following interface:

```
int adc_sample( int channel, int *queue, int size,
                int period, int min, int max );
```

where the function arguments have the following meaning: `channel` specifies which ADC channel to sample, `queue` points to a queue where samples are stored, `size` is the queue size, and `period` is the time between two samples. Finally, `min` and `max` are parameters used to wakeup the process earlier, should a sample fall out of the specified range. This allows awakening the process as soon as an anomaly is detected.

The operation of the smart driver depends on the type of measurement requested, which can either be periodic or event-driven. In case of periodic sensing, the smart driver works by configuring the internal RTC to wakeup the processor at regular intervals to perform measurements, while in case of event-driven operation sensors themselves are responsible to wake the processor up by means of an interrupt. In both cases, the processor and the internal RAM are powered-off in the waiting periods, while only the internal 4KB backup RAM is active and retains the queues for the smart drivers. In such a way the overall power consumption profile in the sleeping period is lowered to a level typical of ultra-low power systems.

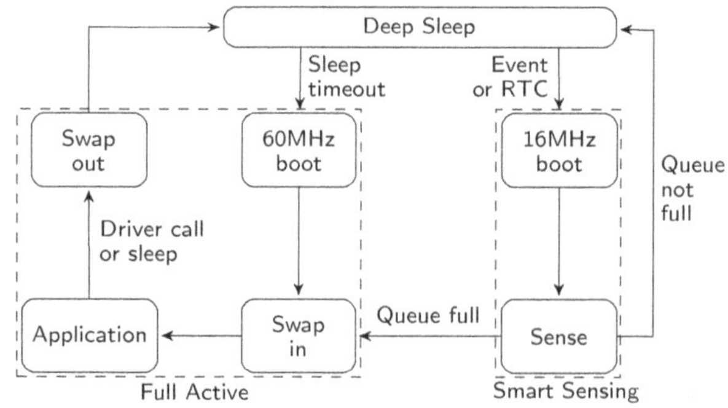

Figure 6: Operating model of the system

When an RTC or an event occurs, the processor is awakened and clocked by internal low-power 16MHz oscillator. At this frequency, the operating system boots in $540\mu s$[1], then the actual *sensing* phase begins. In this phase the sensor data is retrieved and the result pushed in the queue associated to the process requiring the measurement. If the queue is not full the processor goes back to deep sleep, otherwise it immediately loads the calling process performing a swap-in operation and enters full active state. After an entire measure batch is completed, the queues in the backup RAM are elaborated by the processes, minimizing the full active duty cycle and reducing the overhead of frequent processing and related swapping operations. Figure 6 shows the different phases of this mechanism.

4.3 Operating model

The overall mode of operation of the proposed solution is summarized in Figure 6, where are three main states are highlighted, *Full Active*, *Deep Sleep* and *Smart Sensing*, each characterized by a specific power consumption profile (see Section 5 for details). The transitions among the various states follow the logic described in previous sections.

5. ENERGY MODEL

In this section we derive a first energy and timing characterization of the different operating states with the goal of building a simplified overall non-functional model of the entire system. Such a model will be used in the next section as a basis to obtain the presented results. Timing figures used in the models are derived from direct measurement on the hardware using an oscilloscope. Energy consumption data, on the other hand, are all average values derived from the data-sheets. The reason is that the current hardware

[1]The sum of the time required by the microcontroller voltage regulator startup and OS boot poses a lower bound of approximately 1ms on the node response latency, limiting its adoption for tight real-time applications.

implementation of the node does not provide probes and dedicated circuitry for current sensing.

5.1 Full Active mode

As discussed, the Full Active mode is always preceded by a startup phase, which in turns is composed of three steps. A pictorial view of these phases is provided in Figure 7, where the contributions of the microcontroller, the external magneto-resistive non-volatile RAM and the radio transceiver are shown separately.

As far as the microcontroller is concerned, the first step requires waiting the internal voltage regulator to stabilize. At this point the microcontroller is clocked at 16MHz and waits for the internal PLL to lock at a frequency of 60MHz, which is the frequency we have chosen for normal operation. Once the PLL is stable, the operating system starts booting, which requires 144μs. The system is then ready to start the execution of one or more processes. This requires (apart from the very first time) swapping-in the process data section from the external memory into RAM before starting the execution of the processes. The number of processes n_p that need to be loaded is, in general, a time varying value as different processes may have different sleep and sensing cycles, and those still sleeping or waiting on smart drivers do not have to be loaded. The time needed to load a process is bound by the size of its data image (8KB in the current implementation) and the data rate of the SPI bus (15MHz, in our setting) connecting the microcontroller with the MRAM. Once the process image has been loaded, the operating system schedules processes and remains in this state for a time τ_{app} that, depending on the specific application, is left as a parameter of the models. The energy consumption for this phase is expressed as average power and is 34nJ/μs.

When the application terminates its time slot, the updated data images in RAM are swapped-out. Reading and writing magneto-resistive memories requires the same time, thus the duration of this phase is exactly the same as the swap-in. It must be noted, though, that if one or more processes are not scheduled during the application time period, its data will have undergone no changes and thus needs not to be swapped out. Summarizing these contributions leads to the equations (units are μs and μJ):

$$\tau_{\mu C,fa} = 944 + 8740 \cdot n_p + \tau_{app} \quad (1)$$
$$E_{\mu C,fa} = 15 + 188 \cdot n_p + 0.034 \cdot \tau_{app} \quad (2)$$

In addition to the microcontroller, the Full Active phase requires access to the MRAM, with an additional energy consumption contribution, shown in the middle diagram of Figure 7. The specific components used in the current implementation requires a power-on phase during 400μs but having a negligible energy contribution of 100nJ. Reading and writing require the same time but consume different energies. The swap-in phase absorbs 46μJ, while the swap-out phase consumes 164μJ. While the application is running, the memory is kept in its quiescent state, with a power consumption of 20pJ/μs. Compared to energies involved in the other phases this last contribution can be neglected. The resulting models are the following:

$$\tau_{mram,fa} = 400 + 8740 \cdot n_p + \tau_{app} \quad (3)$$
$$E_{mram,fa} = 210 \cdot n_p \quad (4)$$

Finally, while in Full Active mode, the radio transceiver is powered on to perform two main operations: synchronization and data exchange. The synchronization phase requires receiving a specific packet at predefined time intervals. To compensate for drifts of the interval duration two slack periods, one before and one after the actual receive phase, are needed and the interval duration itself is adjusted at runtime using an integral regulator. As far as the data exchange phase is concerned, we suppose that its duration is 25% of τ_{app}, avalue compatible with a wide spectrum of ambient intelligence applications. Th resulting models are:

$$\tau_{tsc,fa} = 2870 + \tau_{app}/4 \quad (5)$$
$$E_{tsc,fa} = 50 + 0.036 \cdot \tau_{app}/4 = 50 + 0.009 \cdot \tau_{app} \quad (6)$$

The complete Full Active mode model is thus:

$$\tau_{fa} = 944 + 8740 \cdot n_p + \tau_{app} \quad (7)$$
$$E_{fa} = 65 + 398 \cdot n_p + 0.043 \cdot \tau_{app} \quad (8)$$

where $\tau_{fa} = \max(\tau_{\mu C,fa}, \tau_{mram,fa})$, while the total energy is simply the sum of the three contributions.

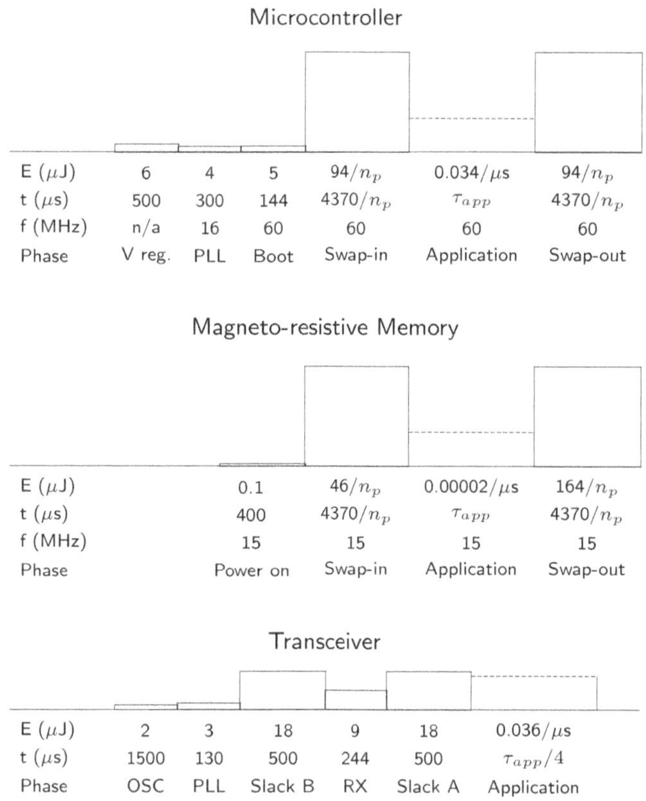

Figure 7: Full Active mode characterization

5.2 Smart Sensing mode

Smart Sensing is performed totally by the operating system and does not require executing the application code of the processes. Smart sensing begins with a startup phase similar to that of the Full Active mode, except that the operating frequency is set to 16MHz instead of 60MHz. This choice is mainly motivated by the fact that smart drivers only need to perform simple operations—basically register/ memory transfers—and thus do not require the core to be running at an higher frequency. At this frequency, though the operating system boot takes 540μs and consumes 12μJ

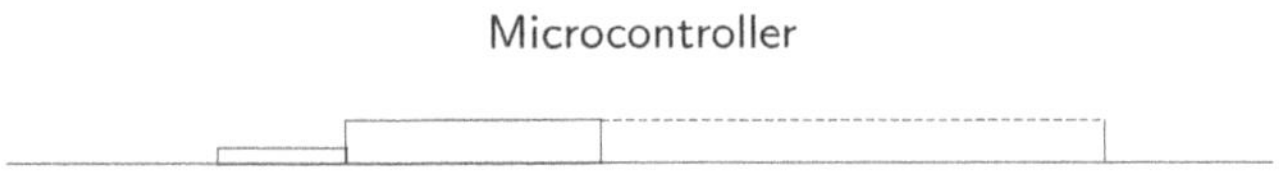

E (μJ)	6	6	0.011/μs
t (μs)	500	540	τ_{drv}
f (MHz)	n/a	16	16
Phase	V reg.	Boot	Smart sensing

Figure 8: Smart Sensing mode characterization

of energy. After the operating system boot is complete, actual sensing operations are performed and require a time that, again, is application dependent and is thus left as a parameter in the model, namely τ_{drv}. The average power consumption of the microcontroller in this state is 11nJ/μs. The model is expressed by the following equations:

$$\tau_{ss} = 1040 + \tau_{drv} \quad (9)$$
$$E_{ss} = 12 + 0.011 \cdot \tau_{drv} \quad (10)$$

Sensing time and current consumption strongly vary depending on the type of sensor as well as on the specific device. Accounting also for this contribution, hardly fit with the need of comparing the proposed approach with previous architectures, since each of them integrates different sensors with different power consumption figures. For this reason we omitted sensors' contributions to E_{ss}, being possible at any time to account for it.

5.3 Deep Sleep mode

In Deep Sleep mode, the node is almost completely powered off. In particular, the MRAM is totally switched off, while the microcontroller is forced into its low-power state, with a current consumption of 4.8μA. This accounts for the internal RTC used to wake the microcontroller up to perform smart sensing, and the small 4KB of backup RAM used to temporarily store the data acquired by smart sensors as well as network topology information. Thus:

$$E_{\mu C,ds} = 14 \times 10^{-6} \cdot \tau_{off} \quad (11)$$
$$E_{mram,ds} = 0 \quad (12)$$
$$E_{tsc,ds} = 2.5 \times 10^{-6} \cdot \tau_{off} \quad (13)$$

5.4 Complete model

To derive the complete model, in addition to the contributions considered in the three previous sections, it is necessary also to account for the energy absorbed by the ancillary circuitry, mainly the voltage regulator. A rough estimate of this contribution yields a value below 12μW, i.e. 12pJ/μs. It is worth noting that this contribution is only significant during the Deep Sleep phase, while is negligible in the Full Active and Smart Sensing phases.

Summarizing the parameters of the complete model are the number of processes n_p, the application time τ_{app}, the sensing time τ_{ss}, the time for which the system is kept in Deep Sleep mode τ_{off} and the number of times n_{ss} the system enters the smart sensing mode while in one period of Deep Sleep. Figure 9 shows the relation among these times. In particular, recalling Equation (1), it turns out that:

$$\tau_{on} = 944 + 8740 \cdot n_p + \tau_{app} \quad (14)$$

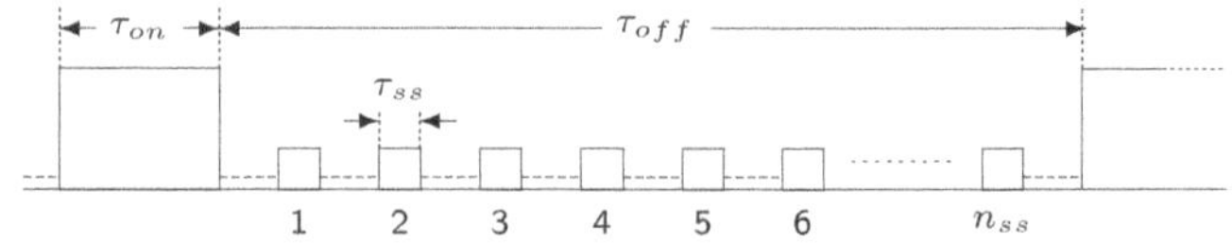

Figure 9: Timing parameters for characterization

while the time the system is in Deep Sleep mode is given by:

$$\tau_{ds} = \tau_{off} - n_{ss}\tau_{ss} \quad (15)$$

The overall energy consumption for one period is thus:

$$E_{on} = 65 + 398 \cdot n_p + 0.043 \cdot \tau_{app} + n_{ss}(12 + 0.011\tau_{ss}) \quad (16)$$
$$E_{off} = 29 \times 10^{-6} \cdot \tau_{ds} \quad (17)$$
$$E_{tot} = E_{on} + E_{off} \quad (18)$$

and the effective duty cycle, including smart sensing, is:

$$DC = (\tau_{on} + n_{ss}\tau_{ss}) / (\tau_{on} + \tau_{off}) \quad (19)$$

6. EXPERIMENTAL RESULTS

The proposed approach has been assessed against both high-end and ultra-low power architectures in order to determine the power consumption trend, and consequently the expected lifetime, by varying the duty cycle, the sampling rate and the number of running processes.

To perform time measurements for the phases described in Section 5 we used a Tektronix TDS2014B oscilloscope with 100 MSa/s, relying also on data-sheet values for a few time measures, such as the PLL lock-time. For current consumption figures we used data provided by device manufacturers, since the board did not permit an accurate direct detection of the current, especially in lowest power states. For timing and energy figures for the architectures we compare against we relied on components data-sheets and reference literature on specific nodes.

A first result concerns the executable programs footprint. Far from being a secondary aspect, the size of the binaries has a significant impact both at the application level—a high number of available processes improves the overall flexibility—and on the energy efficiency of the entire network. Spawning and moving programs across the nodes, in fact, requires transmitting binary images over the wireless interface, and thus impacts the total power consumption.

The reduction of the size of the ELF images, obtained as discussed in Section 4.2.2, thus, is a first step towards energy optimization. Table 2 shows a comparison between the size we obtained for ELF images and that of images produced by the Contiki dynamic linker, as reported in literature [35]. This required minor adaptations of the code examples to fit the Miosix application interface. It should be noted that the resulting code size slightly differs for the two systems due to differences of the instruction sets of the two processors and APIs of the two operating systems. The table reports the code size (in bytes), the standard ELF size and the reduced ELF size, referred to as SELF for Miosix and CELF for Contiki. The introduction of processes carries along an unavoidable overhead due to context switching, again resulting in a potential loss of energy efficiency. To quantitatively evaluate such an overhead we have directly measured the context

	Miosix			Contiki		
Name	Code	ELF	SELF	Code	ELF	CELF
Blinker	98	1154	340	130	1056	361
Tracker	334	1456	548	344	1668	758

Table 2: ELF size reduction (bytes)

Parameter	TelosB	Mica2	Imote2.0
Processor/μC	MSP430	ATmega128L	PXA271
Frequency	8 MHz	8 MHz	13–416 MHz
DeepSleep/Standby	5.1 μA	19.0 μA	387 μA
Active	1.8 mA	8 mA	53 mA
Active+Radio(RX)	21.8 mA	15.1 mA	66 mA
Active+Radio(TX)	19.5 mA	25.4 mA	66 mA

Table 3: Characteristics of the benchmark nodes

switch and scheduling time which turned out to be approximately of 5μs. Assuming time slots of 5ms, the average overhead is between 0.1% and 0.2%, resulting in a negligible energy increase.

The results discussed in the following are based on the energy model presented in Section 5, considering a typical ambient intelligence application collecting environmental measures with a specific *sensing period*. Samples are then aggregated, processed and transmitted with a longer period, referred to in the following as *processing period*. Referring to Figure 9, the sampling period equals τ_{off}/n_{ss}, while the processing period is simply $\tau_{on} + \tau_{off} \approx \tau_{off}$.

To evaluate the energy efficiency of our approach we compared against an ultra-low power node (TelosB), a low-power node (Mica2) and an high-end node (Imote2.0). Figures characterizing the electrical and functional parameters of these benchmark nodes are reported in Table 3, where the current values for the Imote2.0 refer to an operating frequency of 104MHz, used in our evaluation. It should be noted that none of the nodes is characterized considering the power consumption of sensors. This is the most reasonable approach, since sensors can significantly vary from application to application and even different devices for the same physical measure show a very wide spectrum of electrical characteristics. By neglecting such contributions, the lifetimes reported in the following are necessarily overestimates of the actual operating times, but, on the other hand, have the advantage that can be directly compared, since are guaranteed to be as homogeneous as possible.

Though the energy consumed by the sensor themselves is omitted from all models, the time τ_{ss} required for sensing must be considered. During this time, in fact, the microcontroller, though in low-power mode, is active and thus contributes to the overall energy. While in the model the time τ_{ss} has been left as a parameter, to perform quantitative comparison we have set it to 3ms, since analog sensors exist that can reach a steady state condition within this time. It should also be noted that increasing this time to 10ms, i.e. more than three time as much, increases the overall energy consumption of less the 27%.

The time the system remains fully active performing actual processing has been scaled according to the operating frequency of the four architectures as well as the data transmission rate of the related transceivers. We roughly estimated the total amount of data exchanged through the radio channel during one active period in 8Kbit, accounting also for forwarding operations as well as possible packet retransmission due to collisions, delays or obstacles in the broadcast radio channel.

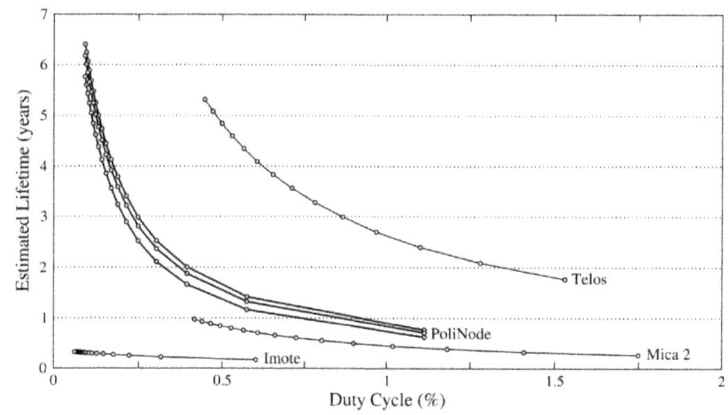

Figure 10: Lifetime versus duty cycle

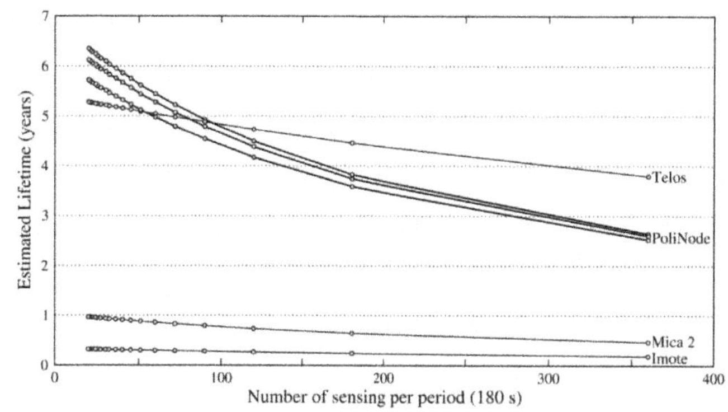

Figure 11: Lifetime versus number of samples

Figure 10 shows the resulting lifetime for a test case with fixed sensing period and varying processing period. The effect of changing the processing period and consequently the number of samplings in one such period can be summarized by the overall duty cycle. It must be noted that the PoliNode performs sensing operations by means of smart drivers, while the other nodes resort to the typical approach that requires bringing them to the normal active mode[2] The figure reports three sets of data for the PoliNode corresponding to applications with 1, 2 and 4 processes, the lower curve referring to the case of 4 processes. The difference between the three data sets, as can be deduced from the model, is essentially related to energy contributions for swapping in and out the data images of the processes. Since other nodes do not support hibernation, no swapping is necessary and the energy does not vary with the number of running tasks.

A different view of the energy performance of the proposed solution is to set the processing period to a fixed value and changing the sampling period. The chart in Figure 11 refers to a 180s processing time and shows the lifetimes estimated varying the number of samples per processing period from 20 to 360, that is considering sampling period from 500ms to 9s. Again, the three data sets for the PoliNode refer to 1, 2 or 4 processes. As the estimates show, for a number of samples between 50 and 90 the proposed approach reaches

[2]For this reason, fixing the parameters of the application results in different duty cycles for the different platforms.

the same energy efficiency of an ultra-low power node and outperforms it for an even lower number of samples. Increasing the number of samples, on the other hand, the ultra-low power solution shows its superior performance.

Far from trying to reach such a performance level, the proposed solution demonstrated reasonably close to ultra-low power nodes and much more efficient than low-power and high-end ones. It is worth noting that the developed hardware/software architecture offers functional and high-level features such as reprogramming, code mobility and ease of development that are typical of high-end nodes.

7. CONCLUSIONS

This paper presented an hardware/software architecture for enabling ultra-low power performances on scalable and reasonably powerful WSN nodes. A WSN node and operating system have been implemented according to the proposed approach to evaluate its feasibility and the associated energy and functional performance. It should be noted though, that the same approach is also suited for developing general embedded system platforms. Experimental results demonstrated that the proposed architecture shows energy consumptions and lifetime values in the same order of magnitude of those of ultra-low power architectures, but providing, at the same time, enough memory and computational resources to enable a general-purpose like programming and development style, typical of high-end powerful and power-consuming nodes.

8. REFERENCES

[1] C. Brandolese and L. Rucco. Optimization of functional allocation to maximize the lifetime of wireless sensor networks. In *Wireless Communication and Sensor Networks (WCSN), 2010 Sixth International Conference on*, pages 1 -6, dec. 2010.

[2] J. Polastre et al. Telos: enabling ultra-low power wireless research. In *IPSN 2005, ACM/IEEE*, pages 364 – 369, april 2005.

[3] J.L. Hill and D.E. Culler. Mica: a wireless platform for deeply embedded networks. In *Micro, IEEE*, volume 22, pages 12 – 24, nov/dec 2002.

[4] A. Rowe et al. Firefly mosaic: A vision-enabled wireless sensor networking system. In *IEEE RTSS 2007*, pages 459 -468, dec. 2007.

[5] JeongGil Ko et al. Egs: A cortex m3-based mote platform. In *IEEE SECON 2010*, pages 1 -3, june 2010.

[6] Crossbow. Imote2 hardware reference manual, 2007.

[7] Oracle-Sun. Sun small programmable object technology (sun spot) owner' s manual release 3.0, October 2007.

[8] Adi Mallikarjuna V. Reddy et al. Wireless sensor network operating systems: a survey. In *Int. J. Sen. Netw.*, volume 5, pages 236–255, August 2009.

[9] René Müller et al. Swissqm: Next generation data processing in sensor networks. In *Proc. of CIDR 2007*, pages 1–9, 2007.

[10] A. Boulis and M.B. Srivastava. A framework for efficient and programmable sensor networks. In *Proc. of IEEE OPENARCH 2002*, pages 117 – 128, 2002.

[11] D. Janakiram et al. Comis: Component oriented middleware for sensor networks. In *Proc. of LANMAN '05*. IEEE Computer Society, 2005.

[12] Liviu Iftode et al. Programming computers embedded in the physical world. In *International Standard ISO*, volume 8327, 1987.

[13] J. Lilius and I. Paltor. Deeply embedded python, a virtual machine for embedded system. Technical report, Turku Centre for Computer Science.

[14] Chien-Liang Fok et al. Rapid development and flexible deployment of adaptive wireless sensor network applications. In *Proc. of ICDCS '05*, pages 653–662. IEEE Computer Society, 2005.

[15] J. Jeong et al. Network reprogramming. In *Berkeley University, at http://webs.cs.berkeley.edu/tos/tinyos-1.x/doc/NetworkReprogramming.pdf.*

[16] T. Stathopoulos et al. A remote code update mechanism for wireless sensor networks. Technical report, 2003.

[17] Jonathan W. Hui and David Culler. The dynamic behavior of a data dissemination protocol for network programming at scale. In *Proc. of SenSys '04*, pages 81–94. ACM, 2004.

[18] Prabal K. Dutta et al. Securing the deluge network programming system. In *Proc. of IPSN '06*, pages 326–333. ACM, 2006.

[19] J. Koshy and R. Pandey. Remote incremental linking for energy-efficient reprogramming of sensor networks. In *Wireless Sensor Networks, 2005. Proceeedings of the Second European Workshop on*, pages 354 – 365, jan.-2 feb. 2005.

[20] Niels Reijers and Koen Langendoen. Efficient code distribution in wireless sensor networks. In *Proc. of WSNA '03*, pages 60–67. ACM, 2003.

[21] Jaein Jeong and D. Culler. Incremental network programming for wireless sensors. In *IEEE SECON 2004*, pages 25 – 33, oct. 2004.

[22] Ting Liu et al. Implementing software on resource-constrained mobile sensors: experiences with impala and zebranet. In *Proc. of MobiSys '04*, pages 256–269. ACM, 2004.

[23] Jochen Schiller et al. Scatterweb - low power sensor nodes and energy aware routing. In *Proc. of HICSS '05*, page 286.3. IEEE Computer Society, 2005.

[24] Pedro José Marrón et al. Flexcup: A flexible and efficient code update mechanism for sensor networks. In *Proc. of EWSN 2006*, pages 212–227, 2006.

[25] Adam Dunkels et al. Contiki - a lightweight and flexible operating system for tiny networked sensors. In *Proc. of IEEE LCN'04*, pages 455–462. IEEE Computer Society, 2004.

[26] Philip Levis et al. The emergence of networking abstractions and techniques in tinyos. In *Proc. of NSDI'04 - Volume 1*, pages 1–1. USENIX Association, 2004.

[27] A. Sinha and A. Chandrakasan. Dynamic power management in wireless sensor networks. In *Design Test of Computers, IEEE*, volume 18, pages 62 -74, mar/apr 2001.

[28] Chanik Park et al. Compiler-assisted demand paging for embedded systems with flash memory. In *Proc. ACM EMSOFT '04*, pages 114–124. ACM, 2004.

[29] Lin Gu and John A. Stankovic. t-kernel: providing reliable os support to wireless sensor networks. In *Proc. of SenSys '06*, pages 1–14. ACM, 2006.

[30] Siddharth Choudhuri and Tony Givargis. Software virtual memory management for mmu-less embedded systems. Technical report, 2005.

[31] Lan S. Bai et al. Memmu: Memory expansion for mmu-less embedded systems. In *ACM Trans. Embed. Comput. Syst.*, volume 8, pages 23:1–23:33. ACM, April 2009.

[32] Yu-Ting Chen et al. Enix: a lightweight dynamic operating system for tightly constrained wireless sensor platforms. In *Proc. of ACM SenSys '10*, pages 183–196. ACM, 2010.

[33] Girts Strazdins et al. Mansos: easy to use, portable and resource efficient operating system for networked embedded devices. In *Proc. of SenSys '10*, pages 427–428. ACM, 2010.

[34] Doug Simon and Cristina Cifuentes. The squawk virtual machine: Java on the bare metal. In *Conference on Object Oriented Programming Systems Languages and Applications*, page 150, 2005.

[35] Adam Dunkels et al. Run-time dynamic linking for reprogramming wireless sensor networks. In *ACM SenSys '06*, pages 15–28. ACM Press, 2006.

Reducing NBTI-induced Processor Wearout by Exploiting the Timing Slack of Instructions

Fabian Oboril, Farshad Firouzi, Saman Kiamehr and Mehdi B. Tahoori
Chair of Dependable Nano Computing (CDNC), Karlsruhe Institute of Technology (KIT)
Haid-und-Neu-Str. 7
76131 Karlsruhe, Germany
fabian.oboril@kit.edu, firouzi@ira.uka.de, kiamehr@kit.edu, mehdi.tahoori@kit.edu

ABSTRACT

Transistor aging due to Negative Bias Temperature Instability (NBTI) is a major reliability challenge for embedded microprocessors at nanoscale. It leads to increasing path delays and eventually more failures during runtime. In this paper, we propose a novel microarchitectural approach combining aging-aware instruction scheduling with specialized functional units to alleviate the impact of NBTI-induced wearout. To achieve this, the instructions are classified depending on their worst-case delay into critical (i.e. the instructions whose delay is close to the cycle boundary) and non-critical instructions (i.e. those instruction with larger timing slack). Each of these classes uses its own (specialized) functional unit(s). By that means it is possible to increase the idle ratio of the units executing the critical instructions, which can be used to extend lifetime by up to 2.3x in average compared to the usually used balanced scheduling policy.

Categories and Subject Descriptors

B.8.1 [**Performance and Reliability**]: Reliability, Testing, and Fault-Tolerance

Keywords

instruction scheduling, NBTI, functional unit, transistor aging, microarchitecture

1. INTRODUCTION

Aggressive transistor scaling of CMOS technology over the past decades allowed increasing transistor counts and by this means the implementation of more and more features in modern microprocessors. This also enabled the successful entrance of embedded systems in almost all areas of our daily life. Though, many of these systems have very tight reliability constraints. However, with decreasing feature sizes to nanoscale dimensions, reliability is threatened by various challenges. Thereby, a major reliability issue of nanoscale embedded processors is fast transistor aging [6, 10, 24].

Among several phenomena *Negative Bias Temperature Instability* (NBTI) is the dominant transistor wearout effect [6, 32]. It leads to a shift of the threshold voltage V_{th} of the affected transistors, which manifests in an increasing switching delay of these transistors. Over the time, this results in increasing path delays, which can lead to timing violations.

To combat these runtime degradation issues manufacturers are currently adding *guardbands* to their designs, to ensure that the chips will be functional for a certain lifetime. However, this overdesign increases development and manufacturing costs, which is crucial for the embedded segment where low costs are a primary target. Hence, new approaches are necessary to take further advantage of scaled technology nodes. Therefore, a lot of research is done at various design levels. To name just a few, special NBTI-resilient circuits [3], input vector control [15, 16, 33], power gating [12], adaptive body biasing [29], dynamic voltage and frequency scaling (DVFS) [5, 26] and enhanced instruction and application scheduling techniques [28, 29] are some of the existing aging mitigation methods. The last two techniques try to balance the necessary calculations on the available units (cores) to achieve equal wearout states on all units (cores), which should guarantee a longer lifetime of these parts.

Our investigation of various (embedded) microprocessors shows that the execution stage (i.e. the functional units) in a pipelined microprocessor is among the most timing-critical stages and hence to improve the overall lifetime of the microprocessor, the execution stage must be dealt with. However, as we will show in this paper, balancing the number of executed instructions (workload) over several functional units is not always the best aging mitigation strategy. This is mainly due to the fact that within the same clock cycle boundaries, different instructions executed by the same functional unit have different timing criticality and consequently different time slacks. Although all instructions executed in an ALU have an execution time of one cycle, there are some instructions whose delay is close to one cycle (e.g. arithmetic operations with long operands), while others need much less time (e.g. simple logic operations). Hence, the first group of instruction is called *timing-critical (TC)*, the other one is named *non-timing-critical (NTC)*. In fact, this makes no difference from the performance point of view (always one cycle). However, in terms of aging, when the path delay of the circuit increases, the TC instructions start to fail (i.e. have timing delays) while NTC instructions will continue to be executed correctly for a much longer time. This observation is the main motivation behind the technique presented in this work and illustrated in Figure 1. We plan to ex-

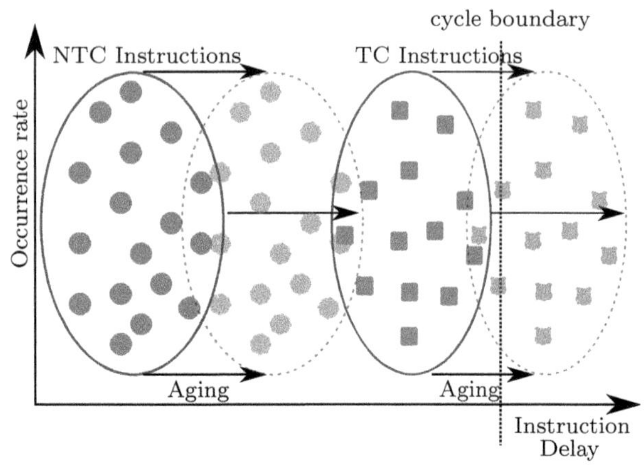

Figure 1: Illustration of TC and NTC instructions

ploit this information for aging-aware scheduling of different instruction classes on different functional units.

If an embedded microprocessor with two functional units of the same type (e.g. ALU) uses a balanced instruction scheduling technique, both units will fail almost after the same time. Now imagine, that one unit is used only for the TC instructions and the other one just for the NTC instructions. Since the latter have a delay which is far less than the TC instructions, the first unit will always fail first and hence determines the lifetime. In addition, as long as the fraction of TC instructions is less than 50 %, the critical unit will execute less instructions than in the first case. Hence, the idle ratio of this unit is increased. This can be used in combination with various architectural techniques such as power gating [12] or input vector control for NOP-operations [16] to reduce the NBTI effect and hence, to increase the lifetime of this unit.

Based on this idea, in this paper we propose a novel microarchitectural approach combining aging-aware instruction scheduling with specialized functional units to alleviate the impact of NBTI-induced wearout. In our proposed microarchitecture, the instructions are categorized depending on their worst-case delays into classes of critical and non-critical instructions. Each of these classes uses its own (specialized) functional unit(s). By that means it is possible to increase the idle ratio of the units executing the critical instruction, which can be used to extend lifetime of the functional units by applying special mitigation techniques. Our simulation results show that the proposed scheduling technique can achieve this goal and can yield improvements in terms of *Mean Time to Failure (MTTF)* of 1.5x (for power gating) and 2.3x (for input vector control) in average, compared to the standard (i.e. balanced) scheduling.

The rest of this paper is organized as follows. In Section 2 the NBTI phenomenon is introduced followed by the presentation of two special aging mitigation techniques in Section 3. Our proposed microarchitectural solution is provided in Section 4. Afterwards we present in Section 5 the simulation framework we use to investigate the proposed methodology. Also the simulation results will be shown in this section. Finally, the paper is concluded in Section 6.

2. PRELIMINARIES ON NBTI-INDUCED AGING

NBTI occurs in PMOS transistors when the transistor is under negative gate-source bias i.e., $V_{gs} = -V_{dd}$, (stress mode). When a PMOS transistor experiences the stress mode, some Si-H bonds break at the interface $Si - SiO_2$ due to the presence of holes in the channel. The resulting H diffuses away and as a result some positive traps (Si^+) are left causing the magnitude of transistor threshold voltage V_{th} to increase [7]. When the stress mode is removed (recovery mode i.e. $V_{gs} = 0$) some of the created interface traps are healed, and the threshold voltage shift can be partially recovered [7]. This process is shown in Figure 2.

The long-term NBTI-induced threshold voltage shift, ΔV_{th}, can be modeled by the following equation [32]:

$$\Delta V_{th} = A(T)Y^n t^n, \tag{1}$$

where $A(T)$ is a technology dependent function of temperature T, n is a fabrication process dependent constant, t is the total time, and Y is the duty cycle. The duty cycle represents the ratio between stress to total time. To calculate the delay degradation of a gate due to ΔV_{th} imposed by NBTI, the alpha power model can be used [11]:

$$\tau = \frac{K}{(V_{gs} - V_{th})^\alpha}. \tag{2}$$

Here K is a technology dependent factor, V_{gs} is the gate-source voltage, and α represents the velocity saturation. If ΔV_{th} is small, by using first order Taylor expansion, the following equation for NBTI-induced delay degradation can be derived from Equation (2):

$$\Delta\tau = \frac{\alpha \Delta V_{th}}{V_{gs} - V_{th0}} \times \tau_0. \tag{3}$$

where ΔV_{th} is the NBTI-induced threshold voltage change, V_{th0} is the original transistor threshold voltage, and τ_0 is the pre-aging delay of the gate. By using Equations (1) and (3), the total NBTI-induced delay degradation can be estimated as follows:

$$\Delta\tau = \frac{A(T)\alpha Y^n t^n \tau_0}{V_{gs} - V_{th}}. \tag{4}$$

It should be noted that, this equation is valid for a simple inverter, which has one transistor in each pull-up/pull-down network. For other gates (e.g. NAND and NOR) the stacking effect has to be considered as well. In stacked structures, the delay of each gate is affected by the threshold voltage change of all the internal transistors. Moreover, the duty

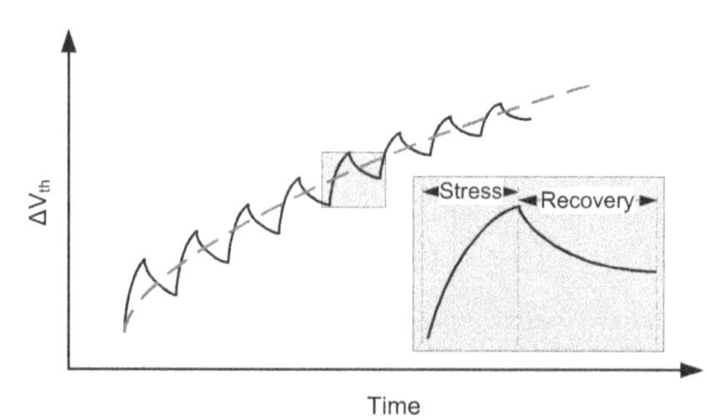

Figure 2: The conceptual illustration of V_{th} change under stress and recovery conditions

cycle of each transistor depends not only on the state of its input, but also on the state of upper and lower transistors [35].

Beside NBTI also *Positive Bias Temperature Instability* (PBTI) is an emerging reliability problem due to the introduction of high-k gate oxides [27]. However, the impact of PBTI on the behavior of NMOS transistors is very similar to the NBTI effect on PMOS transistors and hence our proposed technique can be used for PBTI mitigation as well.

3. SPECIAL AGING MITIGATION TECHNIQUES

The main goal of this work is to increase the idle ratio of the functional units executing aging critical instruction by applying a novel instruction scheduling policy in combination with special aging mitigation techniques. In the following we will introduce two approaches namely input vector control and power gating, that can be used during idle phases of functional blocks to alleviate their NBTI-induced wearout by increasing their relaxation phases.

3.1 Input Vector Control

Duty cycle (the time ratio which transistor is in stress mode to the total time) has a strong impact on NBTI induced wear out. Moreover, the duty cycle of each transistor in the circuit is determined by the input vector and the state of the gate inputs. Therefore, the input vector can affect the NBTI-induced delay degradation and by that means Input Vector Control (IVC) can be used during the standby mode (when the circuit does not perform any operation) to reduce the NBTI effect without any performance degradation.

IVC is a well known technique which has been used for leakage power reduction in conjunction with clock gating [23]. In this approach, the clock of a unit which does not perform any operation is disabled, to avoid dynamic power dissipation due to switching activity. IVC is also combined with other techniques such as Dual V_{th} assignment to minimize the static leakage power [36].

There is also some work to minimize the NBTI effect by exploiting IVC techniques. In the following we briefly present a few of them. The authors in [32] have investigated that the input vector has a strong effect on NBTI and proposed an IVC method based on random vector simulation to mitigate the NBTI effect. IVC in conjunction with internal node control is used in [8] for minimizing the effect of NBTI. This approach uses a concept similar to test point insertion. A linear programming approach to find the best NBTI-aware input vector to be applied during standby is proposed by the authors of [15]. Furthermore, a microarchitectural IVC study using special No-Operations as input vectors for an ALU is presented in [16].

NBTI-induced circuit degradation and leakage power are both strongly dependent on the input vector but in different directions. Two different methods are proposed in [33] to find the best input vector resulting in the minimum NBTI-induced wearout and/or leakage power: exhaustive search and probability based algorithm. In the exhaustive method the random input vectors are generated and the best input vector resulting in the minimum NBTI-induced delay degradation is chosen. In the probability based method, first a number of input vectors are generated. Then the best set of input vectors with the minimum wearout due to NBTI is chosen. Based on the 0/1 probability of each input obtained from the selected set, the new random inputs are generated until a convergence is obtained. In [34], IVC is combined with gate replacement technique using a dynamic programming algorithm to co-optimize leakage power and NBTI-induced degradation.

3.2 Power Gating

Power gating is another technique to mitigate NBTI [12, 13]. Since it reduces the power consumption, temperature decreases which in turn alleviates the NBTI effect. Furthermore, the stress time of PMOS transistors is reduced and thereby duty cycle, since a power gated PMOS transistor is in recovery mode ($V_{gs} = 0$). However, it takes some time to power down or up a block of a processor, whereby the time periods depend on the size and amount of the power gate transistors as well as the size of the power-gated block. Recent work has shown, that an ALU can have a wake up time of 3 ns to 10 ns [20, 30]. Hence, the power gated block is not available for a certain amount of time, which can lead to performance losses. Due to the implied performance penalty, power gating is nowadays mainly used in multi-core processors to switch off unused cores to reduce power consumption [21]. However, it also becomes more and more popular in low-power embedded systems [4, 19].

4. AGING-AWARE INSTRUCTION SCHEDULING

In this section we describe our microarchitectural approach to mitigate the impact of NBTI using enhanced instruction scheduling and specialized functional units.

Based on the observations described in Section 2, temperature and duty cycle are two of the key aspects that influence the NBTI effect. Hence, to slow down wearout due to NBTI, it is mandatory to reduce temperature and duty cycle. In a functional unit like an ALU, these two parameters strongly depend on the sequence of executed instructions. Especially the idle periods between two instructions can be used to mitigate the impact of NBTI, for example by applying power gating or input vector control (IVC) for NOP-operations [12, 16]. However, these techniques can only be used efficiently, if the idle periods between two instructions are very long, which is often not the case. Our envisioned microarchitectural technique aims at increasing the idle periods between two instructions using an enhanced instruction scheduler. By that means the benefit that can be taken from power gating or IVC can be increased. In the following we introduce our idea using an exemplary ALU. However, the idea is also applicable to other functional units.

4.1 Instruction Classification

By investigating the delay of various paths in a functional unit such as an ALU in detail, it is observed that different instructions have different execution times (path delays). Some instructions need just a small fraction of a clock cycle to complete, while others need almost the entire clock cycle. The real execution time (i.e. delay) thereby strongly depends on the instruction and the applied operands. For the ALU of IVM [31] synthesized using the Synopsys Design Compiler and the SAED 90 nm library, the worst-case delay for each instruction is depicted together with the occurrence rate of the instructions in Figure 3.

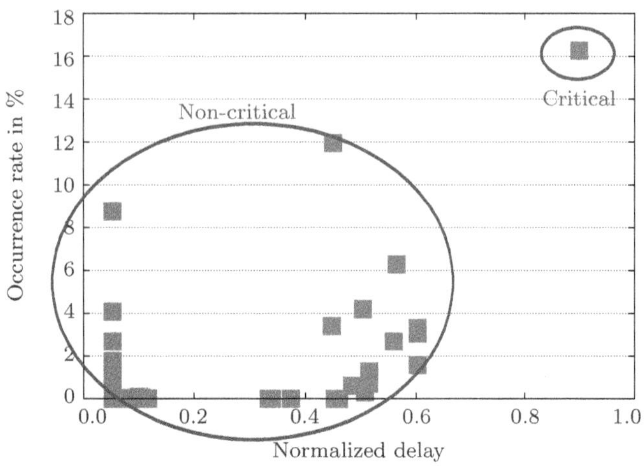

Figure 3: Worst-Case delay distribution and occurrence rate of ALU instructions

From timing perspective, the delay of a functional unit is determined by its longest path delay (slowest instruction) which is obtained from static timing analysis. Once the clock period is set accordingly, from the performance perspective at microarchitecture level, all instructions are considered the same. However, due to aging effects, the delay of various paths in the circuit increases. Finally for some instructions the (intermediate) result will not be computed within the given timing boundaries, i.e. one clock cycle. Thereby, the instructions whose timing slack is very small are the first ones that start to fail. This means that the *timing critical (TC) instructions* (the ones with a real delay close to one cycle) determine the lifetime of the ALU. Moreover, the critical instructions (here it is ADDQ, i.e. add for 64 bit operands) occur much less frequent than the non-critical instructions. Using the performance simulator gem5 [9] we observed that just 16 % of all instructions of various SPEC2000 benchmarks (compiled with GCC 4.3 and *-O3*-optimization) that are executed in the ALU(s) belong to the critical category, while 84 % are *non-timing critical(NTC) instructions* as detailed in Table 1. Based on this observation, our key idea to increase the lifetime of the functional units is to use dedicated unit(s) for each of the two instruction classes, instead of executing both classes in the same unit(s).

Please note that for another ALU or functional unit with a different set of instructions and/or different implementation the timing distribution of various instructions and their occurrence rate will change from what is shown in Figure 3, but the overall classification will still be valid. For instance, logic operations will have less delay than arithmetic operations (with wider word sizes and more sophisticated bit operations). This observation, which basically tells different instructions have different *aging-criticality* can be used for aging-aware scheduling. For example, a functional unit might be aged in a way that it can no longer be used for TC instructions, but it still can execute NTC instructions with no timing failures.

Workload	Instructions	NTC [%]	TC [%]
applu	160,614,011	63.4	36.6
bzip2	293,455,843	80.9	19.1
equake	459,022,375	87.5	12.5
gcc	502,540,388	85.7	14.3
gzip	558,920,018	80.8	19.2
lucas	163,374,308	86.2	13.8
mcf	75,321,231	87.5	12.5
mesa	564,352,647	87.8	12.2
mgrid	80,766,502	93.5	6.5
parser	351,760,701	90.8	9.2
swim	93,599,572	66.7	33.3
twolf	365,459,289	84.8	15.2
wupwise	418,895,837	87.8	12.2
average	**314,467,902**	**83.7**	**16.3**

Table 1: Workloads and their instruction ratios (execution time = 0.5 seconds)

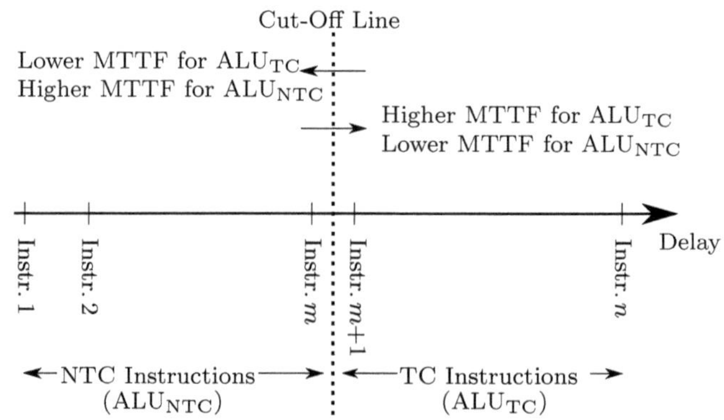

Figure 4: Classification of instructions into TC and NTC and its impact on MTTF

4.1.1 *Optimal cut-off line between TC and NTC instructions*

In the following we present a general approach to find the cut-off line to obtain the highest MTTF considering all units. This approach works for any delay distribution of various instructions and occurrence rates. For simplicity, lets consider that there is one functional unit for the TC instructions (ALU$_{TC}$) and another one for the NTC instructions (ALU$_{NTC}$). As illustrated in Figure 4, the placement of the cut-off line is crucial. If the cut-off line is shifted to the right, more instructions are considered as NTC. Hence MTTF of ALU$_{NTC}$ will decrease (more instructions lead to a lower idle ratio which lowers MTTF; in addition the worst-case delay increases and hence MTTF decreases). However, at the same time MTTF of ALU$_{TC}$ will be improved (less instructions lead to a higher idle ratio and hence higher MTTF). If the cut-off line is moved to the left, MTTF of ALU$_{NTC}$ will increase (less instructions, lower worst-case delay), but MTTF of ALU$_{TC}$ will decrease (more instructions). Hence, finding the right placement of the cut-off line is an optimization problem.

The algorithm, to find the optimal solution is described in Algorithm 1. First, only the instruction with the highest worst-case delay (instruction n) is considered as TC instruction (Step 1). Then, simulations are processed and MTTF of ALU$_{NTC}$ and ALU$_{TC}$ is evaluated (Step 2). Afterwards, the set of TC instructions is expanded by instruction $n-1$ (Step 5) and again MTTF of both units is evaluated (Step 6). This process is continued until the highest MTTF considering both units is found. In our cases the algorithm yielded the result depicted in Figure 3.

4.2 Delay-Aware Scheduling

Normally the information about the instruction delay is not used by the instruction scheduler (or the unit which de-

Algorithm 1 Finding the optimal cut-off line between NTC and TC instructions

// List all instructions according to their worst-case delay,
// i.e. $\text{delay}_{\text{Instruction } 1} \leq \cdots \leq \text{delay}_{\text{Instruction } n}$
1. TC = {Instruction n}
2. Run simulations with this setting and extract:
   $\text{MTTF}_0 = \min(\text{MTTF}_{\text{ALU}_{\text{TC}}}, \text{MTTF}_{\text{ALU}_{\text{NTC}}})$
3. $i = 0$

Do
   4. $i = i + 1$
   5. TC = TC $\cup$ {Instruction $n - i$}
   6. Run simulations with this setting and extract:
      $\text{MTTF}_i = \min(\text{MTTF}_{\text{ALU}_{\text{TC}}}, \text{MTTF}_{\text{ALU}_{\text{NTC}}})$

While ($\text{MTTF}_i > \text{MTTF}_{i-1}$)

cides which functional unit will be used). Instead, if two ALUs are available, the scheduler will balance the workload, so that both ALUs will execute roughly 50% of all the instructions, which is mainly due to performance reasons. Also some previous work on aging-aware instruction scheduling [28], that considers the delay of all instructions to be the same (i.e. 1 clock cycle), shows that the balanced technique is better than unbalanced ones in terms of MTTF. However, as we discussed before, if the accurate timing of instructions is taken into account, a balanced scheduling is not the best choice from the aging perspective. Hence, in our proposed microarchitecture each instruction class has its own dedicated ALU, i.e. one ALU just for the TC instructions and one ALU just for the NTC ones, although this can lead to an unbalanced load among the two ALUs.

The scheduler (or the unit which decides which functional unit will be used) selects the unit, which corresponds to the actual instruction based on the instruction opcode. Hence, no extra bits to encode the classification are necessary. For example in our evaluated scenario the critical ADDQ instruction has the opcode 1020h. Whenever this opcode is detected, the corresponding instruction (ADDQ) is sent to the corresponding ALU, while all other instruction will be sent to the other ALU. However, due to this additional classification of instructions (TC ALU instructions, NTC ALU instructions) a small hardware overhead comes along with our proposed technique. Using this approach the first ALU executes only 16 % of all the instructions, while the other ALU handles the other 84 %. This means, that the first ALU, which deals with the critical instructions, is idle most of the time, which is also shown in Figure 5. Hence, this unit can be power gated very efficiently and also IVC can be applied most of the time. *Please note that the "critical ALU" is the one which determines the lifetime, since the non-critical instructions have a delay which is much smaller than the delay of the critical instructions and even with aging included never surpasses the delay of the critical ones, before these will start to fail.*

Of course, this unbalanced load can lead to a performance loss compared to an architecture with two "full" functional units of the same type. However, the performance loss is relatively small, as we will explain in the next section. Moreover, the functional units in the first case can be more specialized, hence they can be smaller. By this means die size and manufacturing costs can by saved. Furthermore, smaller units will consume less power and by that means stay cooler. This again will help to slow down wearout.

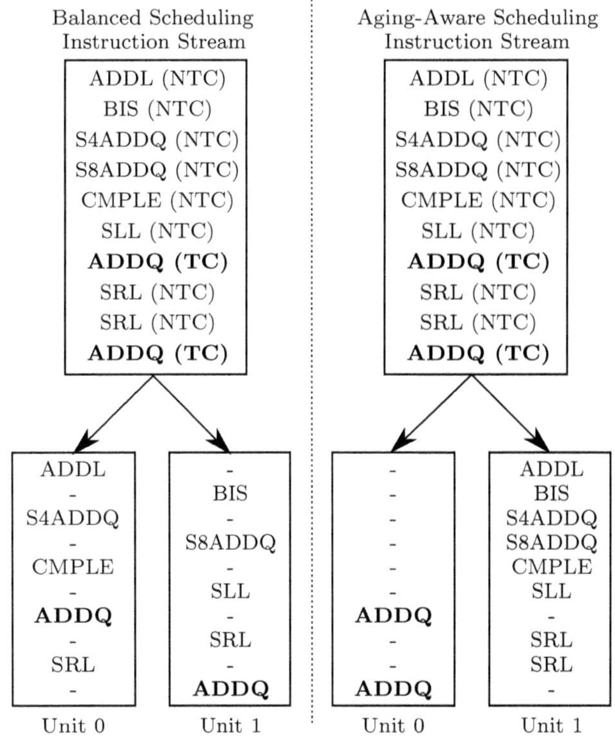

Figure 5: Assignment of instructions to functional units for balanced and aging-aware scheduling

In our case, the specialized critical-ALU needs just to support the ADDQ-instruction (ADD instruction for three 64 bit operands a+b = c). Hence, the feature set can be heavily reduced for this specialized ALU, resulting in a very small size. Using Synopsys Design Compiler and the SAED 90 nm library we found out that the size for such a specialized ALU is just 8 % of a normal, general purpose ALU. This means that using one specialzed ALU together with a normal ALU (aging-ware) results in only 54 % of the size of two normal ALUs (balanced) as it is shown in Table 2. Furthermore, we also investigated the power consumption of these two configurations using Synopys PrimeTime. For this purpose we extracted the instruction sequences for each ALU using the simulation framework detailed in Section 5 and various SPEC2000 workloads. With ModelSim the switching activity behavior for each benchmark and each ALU was extracted and afterwards PrimeTime was used to calculate the power consumption of each ALU for each application. Using the specialized ALU in our proposed microarchitecture, the power consumption of the two ALUs (critical +

Scheduling	normal ALU(s)	special ALU(s)	Area [um^2]	Avg. Power [uW]
Balanced	2x	0	91790 (100 %)	296 (100 %)
Aging-Aware	1x (NTC)	1x (TC)	49546 (54 %)	160 (54 %)
Aging-Aware (Enhanced)	2x (NTC)	1x (TC)	95441 (104 %)	307 (104 %)

Table 2: Different scheduling techniques and combinations of ALUs (normal once and specialized once for TC instructions)

non-critical) can be reduced to 54 % (extracted with Synopsys PrimeTime using real switching activity values) for all executed SPEC200 benchmarks (see Table 2). Due to the performance loss, the small size and the low power consumption of the specialized ALU, another option beside using one critical and one non-critical ALU is to feature two non-critical ALUs and one critical. This will eliminate the performance penalty, as we will show later and the area as well as power overhead is negligible compared to the entire embedded processor.

If an embedded processor uses only one ALU, our proposed technique leads to a small area and power overhead, since a second ALU has to be implemented. However, due to its small size and power consumption both overheads are very minimal. In addition, lifetime will be greatly improved (see Section 5).

4.3 Further Extensions

Beside for a simple ALU, the proposed scheduling technique is also applicable to much more sophisticated functional units such as floating point units or vector execution units. Also these units will feature some instructions (typically multi-cycle instructions) that have a slack close to zero in one of their execution cycles.

Moreover, the concept can be also extended to handle process variation as well. If two functional units of the same type are available, one can be faster than the other one due to process variation, i.e. the timing slack of an instruction executed in the faster unit is larger than in the slower unit. In that case, the TC instructions should be scheduled to the faster unit, while the NTC instructions should use the slower unit.

5. EXPERIMENTAL RESULTS

5.1 Simulation Setup

To validate our microarchitectural approach and to investigate the advantages as well as disadvantages, we used our microarchitectural framework ExtraTime [25]. It is based on the cycle-accurate microarchitectural performance simulator gem5 [9] and includes models for power (based on McPAT [22]), temperature (based on HotSpot [18]) and aging, so that these parameters can be observed during the execution of typical applications. The temperature information in conjunction with information about the usage/activity of different microarchitectural blocks is used by our microarchitectural aging model for NBTI. This is based on the transistor-level model explained in Section 2. For each microarchitectural block (e.g. ALU, instruction decoder, etc.) it is assumed that all transistors behave similarly (i.e. have the same temperature, aging rates, etc.). Hence, a representative transistor can be chosen, for which the current and future V_{th} shift is estimated. Based on that the delay increase using an alpha power law can be calculated and so the current and future delay change of the entire block can be determined. We have validated this representative transistor model with accurate circuit-level implementation and the results show a high accuracy (< 3 % difference).

Processor	Single-core @ 3 GHz, out-of-order, 4-issue
L1-Cache	64 KByte, 3 cyc latency
L2-Cache	2 MByte, 15 cyc latency
Execution Units	2x ALU, 2x CALU, 2x FPU
Expected wearout	$\Delta^{rel}d$ = 10 % in 3 years, i.e MTTF = 3 years (90 °C)
Conditions	T_{start} =57 °C, V_{dd} = 1.0 V, V_{th} = 0.21 V
SPEC2000 benchmarks	applu, bzip2, equake, gcc, gzip, lucas, mcf, mesa, mgrid, parser, swim, twolf, wupwise
Runtime	0.5 seconds excluding initialization

Table 3: Configuration details for the experiments

Details on the processor configuration modeled and the simulated workloads (SPEC2000 benchmarks) can be found in Table 3. As functional unit we have again chosen the ALU detailed in the previous section.

As said before, our proposed scheduling technique aims at increasing the idle ratio of the ALU executing the TC instructions. By that means it is possible to increase the Mean Time To Failure (MTTF) of these functional units by exploiting NBTI mitigation techniques. Please note that it is always the ALU executing the TC instructions, which will fail first. Hence this unit is mainly responsible for the achieved MTTF values. Moreover, it is worth to note that usually the execution stage is the pipeline stage with the smallest timing slack, i.e. highest delay. This means that a lifetime extension of the functional units which are part of the execution stage is crucial, if lifetime of the entire microprocessor should increase. The aging mitigation techniques for the functional units we used in this paper are input vector control and power gating. The details for both are provided in the following subsections.

5.1.1 Applied Input Vector Control Technique

Usually input vector control (IVC) is used at gate-level to mitigate the influence of NBTI and/or leakage (see Section 3). However, IVC can be also used at microarchitecture-level. At that level, input vectors are applied at the primary inputs of the entire microarchitectural blocks, such as functional units. For an ALU, the input vector consists of an instruction opcode and two instruction operands. Since, the NBTI-minimizing input vector should not affect the program execution running on the processor, it has to be a No-Operation (NOP) [17]. In the selected superscalar out-of-order processor the NBTI-minimizing input vector can be applied at the ALU inputs every cycle the ALU is idle, i.e. not executing an instruction. Since it takes some time, until all internal gates of the functional unit are in the state resulting in the minimal NBTI-induced wearout, the first cycle in every idle period is considered as a normal operational cycle with higher degradation rate.

To identify the aging rates of the ALU, when the NBTI-minimizing input vector is applied, we did the following: First, the gate-level description of the IVM processor [31] (similar to the core modeled in gem5) is extracted using Synopsys Design Compiler and the SAED 90 nm library. In the same step, all critical paths of the functional units are extracted as well. Afterwards, the signal probabilities (probability of a signal being 1) of all internal nodes are obtained with Modelsim. Using these signal probabilities the duty cycle of all transistors inside the ALU can be derived and by that means the aging rate of these transistors (Equation 4). Then, a linear programming solver is used to extract the input vector resulting in the minimum NBTI-induced degradation similar to [16]. Finally, the wearout rate for

	Balanced 2x normal ALU		Aging-Aware 1x TC ALU, 1x or 2x NTC ALU	
	power gating	input vector	power gating	input vector
applu	4.5	5	8.5	11
bzip	5	5.5	5	13
equake	5	5	7	10.5
gcc	4	5.5	6.5	14
gzip	4.5	4.5	4.5	13
lucas	4.5	5.5	4.5	12.5
mcf	5	5	8	10
mesa	5	5	5.5	9
mgrid	4.5	5	13	8.5
parser	4	5.5	8	14.5
swim	5	4.5	6	11
twolf	4.5	5.5	7.5	14
wupwise	4	5	4.5	12.5
Average	**4.6 (+1.5x)**	**5.1 (+1.7x)**	**7 (+2.3x)**	**11.8 (+3.9x)**

Table 4: MTTF in years for several SPEC2000 benchmarks (with power gating or input vector control)

this NBTI-minimizing input vector is calculated and used in our microarchitectural aging model for the representative transistor. For the normal ALU of IVM our extracted input vector resulting in the minimum NBTI-induced degradation leads to a relative delay increase of 6.25 % in 3 years. This means, that the duty cycle of our representative transistor in case this special input vector is applied (i.e. in idle cycles) is just 0.15 (see Equation 4). In non-idle cycles, i.e. in cycles the ALU is executing "normal" operations, the duty cycle of the representative transistor estimates the average duty cycle of the transistors in the critical paths [25].

5.1.2 *Applied Power Gating Technique*

The chosen power gating technique is relatively simple. After an idle period of at least 200 cycles a functional unit can be power gated. The following power down time until the ALU is completely power gated is set to 3 ns [20, 30]. Until no new instruction is incoming, the unit then remains power gated. When a new incoming instruction is detected, the unit is woken up. The wake up time is set to 7 ns [20, 30] and afterwards it can execute the new instruction(s). In our microarchitectural simulations only in the period, in which the unit is completely power gated, the duty cycle of all transistors in this block is considered as 0. In the other cycles the duty cycle of the representative transistors estimates the average duty cycle of the transistors in the critical paths [25].

5.2 Results

As said before, our proposed scheduling technique aims at increasing the idle ratio of the ALU executing the TC instructions. By that means it is possible to increase the Mean Time To Failure (MTTF) of these functional units by exploiting NBTI mitigation techniques such as power gating or input vector control. Since the units executing the TC instructions, are the ones that will fail first, these functional units also determine the lifetime of the entire processor. The corresponding MTTF and performance results for these techniques can be found in Table 4 and Table 5.

The previously introduced power gating scheme can greatly improve MTTF. Using power gating in combination with the aging-aware scheduling, MTTF can be increased to 7 years in average as shown in Table 4. Since the standard scheduling policy yields only 4.6 years, this translates into a benefit of 52 % of the aging-aware scheduling over the standard policy. However, in some cases, both approaches deliver comparable results. This is due to the fact. that a unit cannot be power gated in every idle period. Compared to the situation without power gating, in which MTTF is just 3 years, the improvements are even better and underline the efficiency of our proposed scheduling technique.

Beside power gating, also input vector control (IVC) can be very helpful to mitigate NBTI-induced aging as explained before (see Table 4). If this special input vector is applied at the primary inputs of the investigated ALU in all idle cycles

	Balanced 2x normal ALU		Aging-Aware 1x TC ALU, 1x NTC ALU		Aging-Aware (Enhanced) 1x TC ALU, 2x NTC ALU	
	w/o power gating	w/ power gating	w/o power gating	w/ power gating	w/o power gating	w/ power gating
applu	0.93	0.93	0.93	0.92	0.93	0.92
bzip2	0.78	0.77	0.74	0.73	0.77	0.76
equake	0.74	0.74	0.74	0.73	0.74	0.74
gcc	0.83	0.83	0.80	0.79	0.83	0.82
gzip	1.25	1.25	1.20	1.20	1.26	1.25
lucas	0.72	0.72	0.71	0.71	0.72	0.72
mcf	0.24	0.24	0.24	0.24	0.24	0.24
mesa	1.18	1.18	1.15	1.15	1.18	1.17
mgrid	0.67	0.67	0.67	0.67	0.67	0.67
parser	0.70	0.70	0.68	0.67	0.70	0.68
swim	0.22	0.22	0.22	0.22	0.22	0.22
twolf	0.68	0.68	0.67	0.65	0.68	0.66
wupwise	1.05	1.05	1.02	0.99	1.05	1.03
Average	**0.77 (100 %)**	**0.77 (100 %)**	**0.75 (97 %)**	**0.74 (96 %)**	**0.77 (100 %)**	**0.76 (99 %)**

Table 5: Performance (IPC) evaluation of different scheduling techniques

MTTF can be extended to 12 years using the aging-aware scheduling. This is an improvement of almost 4x compared to the case without IVC and still 2.3x compared to the standard scheduling policy with IVC.

In addition, the performance penalty of the proposed scheduling technique is almost negligible. As it is illustrated in Table 5, the average performance loss of the aging-aware instruction scheduling using a (non)-critical classification is 4 % in average and at most 5 %. In case the performance impact is not acceptable, we suggest to use two normal ALUs, which handle the NTC instructions according to a balanced workload distribution and add a third specialized ALU, which deals only with the TC instructions. Since the specialized ALU is very small (see Section 4.2), the additional overhead is negligible and hence the additional manufacturing costs. In addition, this approach does not just incur any performance overhead compared to the standard technique, but it can also further reduce the aging rates in the "normal" ALUs, due to a lower load (i.e. more idle cycles). Please note that the performance results for IVC are not presented in Table 4, since IVC has no impact on performance. Hence, performance with IVC is the same as the performance without power gating.

Now, the important question is whether the applied approach can improve the lifetime of the entire microprocessor. In other words, the key question is whether the lifetime of the entire microprocessor is determined by the lifetime the functional unit due to time criticality of the execution unit compared to the other stages. To answer this question, we synthesized various processor cores using the SAED 90 nm library and Synopsys Design Compiler. For IVM [31] and FabScalar [14] (both superscalar, out-of-order) as well as OpenRisc 1200 [2] and miniMIPS [1] (both in-order), we investigated the delay of each pipeline stage. The results confirm that the execution stage always contains the longest paths, i.e. has the highest delay. That means the wearout of the functional units has to be addressed in order to extend the lifetime of the entire microprocessor. Hence, our proposed technique which extends the lifetime of the functional units can help to increase the MTTF of the entire processor as well.

6. CONCLUSION

Embedded microprocessors at nanoscale are exposed to various reliability issues, which include a more rapid aging of all components. This will eventually reduce the Mean Time to Failure (MTTF), a crucial point for embedded systems that have often very tight reliability constraints (e.g. long mission times). To alleviate the impact of transistor aging due to Negative Bias Temperature Instability (NBTI) we proposed a new delay-aware scheduling methodology in this paper. Instructions are categorized dependent on their timing slacks within clock cycle boundaries and then scheduled to separate functional units. In combination with specialized functional units and efficient mitigation techniques MTTF can be extended in average by 1.5x using power gating and 2.3x using input vector control compared to the standard (i.e. balanced) scheduling approach. At the same time performance is not compromised.

7. REFERENCES

[1] miniMIPS. Opencores: `http://opencores.org/project,minimips`. [Online; accessed July 2012].

[2] OpenRisc 1200. Opencores: `http://opencores.org/project,or1200_hp`. [Online; accessed July 2012].

[3] J. Abella, X. Vera, and A. Gonzalez. Penelope: The NBTI-Aware Processor. In *Proc. of the Int'l Symp. on Microarchitecture*, pp. 85–96, Dec. 2007.

[4] ARM Limited. *Cortex-A8 Technical Reference Manual*, 2010.

[5] M. Basoglu, M. Orshansky, and M. Erez. NBTI-Aware DVFS: A New Approach to Saving Energy and Increasing Processor Lifetime. In *Proc. of the Int'l Symp. on Low Power Electronics and Design*, pp. 253–258, Aug. 2010.

[6] K. Bernstein, D. J. Frank, A. E. Gattiker, W. Haensch, B. L. Ji, S. R. Nassif, E. J. Nowak, D. J. Pearson, and N. J. Rohrer. High-performance CMOS variability in the 65-nm regime and beyond. *IBM Journal of Research and Development - Advanced silicon technology*, 50, pp. 433–449, July 2006.

[7] S. Bhardwaj, W. Wang, R. Vattikonda, Y. Cao, and S. Vrudhula. Predictive modeling of the NBTI effect for reliable design. In *Proc. Custom Integrated Circuits Conf.*, pp. 189–192, 2006.

[8] D. Bild, G. Bok, and R. Dick. Minimization of NBTI performance degradation using internal node control. In *Proc. of the Conf. on Design, Automation and Test in Europe*, pp. 148–153, Mar. 2009.

[9] N. L. Binkert, R. G. Dreslinski, L. R. Hsu, K. T. Lim, A. G. Saidi, and S. K. Reinhardt. The M5 Simulator: Modeling Networked Systems. *IEEE Micro*, 26(4), pp. 52–60, July 2006.

[10] S. Borkar. Designing Reliable Systems from Unreliable Components: The Challenges of Transistor Variability and Degradation. *IEEE Micro*, 25(6), pp. 10–16, Nov. 2005.

[11] K. A. Bowman, B. L. Austin, J. C. Eble, X. Tang, and J. D. Meindl. A Physical Alpha-Power Law MOSFET Model. In *Proc. of the Int'l Symp. on Low Power Electronics and Design*, pp. 218–222, Aug. 1999.

[12] A. Calimera, E. Macii, and M. Poncino. NBTI-Aware Power Gating for Concurrent Leakage and Aging Optimization. In *Proc. of the Int'l Symp. on Low Power Electronics and Design*, pp. 127–132, Aug. 2009.

[13] T. Chan, J. Sartori, P. Gupta, and R. Kumar. On the Efficacy of NBTI Mitigation Techniques. In *Proc. of the Conf. on Design, Automation and Test in Europe*, pp. 1–6, Mar. 2011.

[14] N. Choudhary, S. Wadhavkar, T. Shah, H. Mayukh, J. Gandhi, B. Dwiel, S. Navada, H. Najaf-abadi, and E. Rotenberg. FabScalar: Automating Superscalar Core Design. *IEEE Micro*, 32(3), pp. 48–59, May 2012.

[15] F. Firouzi, S. Kiamehr, and M. B. Tahoori. A Linear Programming Approach for Minimum NBTI Vector Selection. In *Proc. of the Great Lakes Symp. on VLSI*, pp. 253–258, May 2011.

[16] F. Firouzi, S. Kiamehr, and M. B. Tahoori. NBTI Mitigation by NOP Assignment and Insertion. In

Proc. of the Conf. on Design, Automation and Test in Europe, pp. 218–223, Mar. 2012.

[17] J. L. Hennessy, D. A. Patterson, and D. Goldberg. *Computer Architecture: A Quantitative Approach.* Morgan Kaufmann, 2003.

[18] W. Huang, S. Ghosh, S. Velusamy, K. Sankaranarayanan, K. Skadron, and M. R. Stan. HotSpot: A Compact Thermal Modeling Methodology for Early-Stage VLSI Design. *Trans. on Very Large Scale Integration Systems*, 14(5), pp. 501–513, May 2006.

[19] R. Islam, A. Sabbavarapu, and R. Patel. Power Reduction Schemes in Next Generation Intel ATOM Processor Based SoC for Handheld Applications. In *Symp. on VLSI Circuits*, pp. 173–174, June 2010.

[20] S. Kim, S. V. Kosonocky, and D. R. Knebel. Understanding and Minimizing Ground Bounce During Mode Transition of Power Gating Structure. In *Proc. of the Int'l Symp. on Low Power Electronics and Design*, pp. 22–25, Aug. 2003.

[21] R. Kumar and G. Hinton. A Family of 45nm IA Processors. In *Proc. of the IEEE Int'l Solid-State Circuits Conf.*, pp. 58 –59, Feb. 2009.

[22] S. Li, J. H. Ahn, R. D. Strong, J. B. Brockman, D. M. Tullsen, and N. P. Jouppi. McPAT: An Integrated Power, Area, and Timing Modeling Framework for Multicore and Manycore Architectures. In *Proc. of the Int'l Symp. on Microarchitecture*, pp. 469–480, Dec. 2009.

[23] S. Naidu and E. Jacobs. Minimizing Stand-by Leakage Power in Static CMOS Circuits. In *Proc. of the Conf. on Design, Automation and Test in Europe*, pp. 370–376, Mar. 2001.

[24] V. Narayanan and Y. Xie. Reliability Concerns in Embedded System Designs. *Computer*, 39(1), pp. 118–120, Jan. 2006.

[25] F. Oboril and M. B. Tahoori. ExtraTime: Modeling and Analysis of Wearout due to Transistor Aging at Microarchitecture-Level. In *Proc. of the Int'l Conf. on Dependable Systems and Networks*, June 2012.

[26] F. Oboril and M. B. Tahoori. Reducing Wearout in Embedded Processors using Proactive Fine-Grained Dynamic Runtime Adaptation. In *Proc. of the European Test Symp.*, pp. 68–73, May 2012.

[27] S. Pae, M. Agostinelli, M. Brazier, R. Chau, G. Dewey, T. Ghani, M. Hattendorf, J. Hicks, J. Kavalieros, K. Kuhn, M. Kuhn, J. Maiz, M. Metz, K. Mistry, C. Prasad, S. Ramey, A. Roskowski, J. Sandford, C. Thomas, J. Thomas, C. Wiegand, and J. Wiedemer. BTI Reliability of 45 nm High-K + Metal-Gate Process Technology. In *Int'l Reliability Physics Symp.*, pp. 352–357, May 2008.

[28] T. Siddiqua and S. Gurumurthi. A Multi-Level Approach to Reduce the Impact of NBTI on Processor Functional Units. In *Proc. of the Great Lakes Symp. on VLSI*, pp. 67–72, May 2010.

[29] A. Tiwari and J. Torrellas. Facelift: Hiding and slowing down aging in multicores. In *Proc. of the Int'l Symp. on Microarchitecture*, pp. 129–140, Nov. 2008.

[30] K. Usami, T. Shirai, T. Hashida, H. Masuda, S. Takeda, M. Nakata, N. Seki, H. Amano, M. Namiki, M. Imai, M. Kondo, and H. Nakamura. Design and Implementation of Fine-Grain Power Gating with Ground Bounce Suppression. In *Int'l Conf. on VLSI Design*, pp. 381–386, Jan. 2009.

[31] N. J. Wang, J. Quek, T. M. Rafacz, and S. J. patel. Characterizing the Effects of Transient Faults on a High-Performance Processor Pipeline. In *Proc. of the Int'l Conf. on Dependable Systems and Networks*, pp. 61–71, June 2004.

[32] W. Wang, S. Yang, S. Bhardwaj, S. Vrudhula, F. Liu, and Y. Cao. The Impact of NBTI Effect on Combinational Circuit: Modeling, Simulation, and Analysis. *IEEE Trans. on Very Large Scale Integration Systems*, 18(2), pp. 173–183, Feb. 2010.

[33] Y. Wang, X. Chen, W. Wang, V. Balakrishnan, Y. Cao, Y. Xie, and H. Yang. On the efficiancy of Input Vector Control to mitigate NBTI effects and leakage power. In *Proc. of the Int'l Symp. on Quality of Electronic Design*, pp. 19–26, Mar. 2009.

[34] Y. Wang, X. Chen, W. Wang, Y. Cao, Y. Xie, and H. Yang. Leakage Power and Circuit Aging Cooptimization by Gate Replacement Techniques. *IEEE Trans. on Very Large Scale Integration Systems*, (99), pp. 1–14, 2011.

[35] K. Wu and D. Marculescu. Joint Logic Restructuring and Pin Reordering against NBTI-induced Performance Degradation. In *Proc. of the Conf. on Design, Automation and Test in Europe*, pp. 75–80, Mar. 2009.

[36] L. Yuan and G. Qu. Simultaneous Input Vector Selection and Dual Threshold Voltage Assignment for Static Leakage Minimization. In *Proc. of the Int'l Conf. on Computer-Aided Design*, pp. 548–551, 2007.

LRCG: Latch-based Random Clock-Gating for Preventing Power Analysis Side-Channel Attacks

Kazuyuki Tanimura
Department of Computer Science
University of California, Irvine
Irvine, CA 92697 USA
ktanimur@uci.edu

Nikil D. Dutt
Department of Computer Science
University of California, Irvine
Irvine, CA 92697 USA
dutt@uci.edu

ABSTRACT

This paper proposes a new ASIC design flow using latch retiming and random clock-gating to cope with power analysis side-channel attacks. We cast the side-channel attack problem as a combination of retiming and clock-gating problems and solve the problems using only existing EDA tool chains. In particular, we achieve light weight time-shifting obfuscation against DPA (Differential Power Analysis) and CPA (Correlation Power Analysis) attacks by changing when to latch randomly. Our proposed LRCG (Latch-based Random Clock-Gating) method incurs only 13% of hardware area overhead that is significantly smaller than other balancing and masking countermeasures which require 100% and 294% overhead, respectively. Our experimental results show that LRCG incurs only negligible performance and energy consumption penalty, while successfully preventing DPA and CPA attacks in all cases.

Categories and Subject Descriptors

B.6 [**Hardware**]: LOGIC DESIGN

General Terms

DESIGN

Keywords

Retiming, Clock-Gating, DPA, CPA

1. INTRODUCTION

Latch-based circuit, retiming, and clock-gating are traditionally used for performance and low power design. This paper, in fact, shows the possibility of utilizing these design approaches as a light weight countermeasure for preventing side-channel power analysis attacks.

Side-channel attacks discover the secret key embedded in crypto-hardware by finding correlation between the key and leaking hardware information such as power consumption.

CODES+ISSS'12, October 7—12, 2012, Tampere, Finland.

DPA (Differential Power Analysis) was proposed by Kocher et al.[10] and is now one of the most well researched side-channel attacks. DPA overcomes some drawbacks of SPA (Simple Power Analysis) that traces the absolute value of power consumption. SPA compares the traced power consumption data and corresponding input data and finds the correlation between them. By the nature of probing errors, the result of SPA attacks is easily distorted by power noise from environment and/or the countermeasures that consumes extra power and introduces noise.

In contrast, DPA suppresses the power noise influence (from surrounding environment, measurement errors, etc.) by calculating the differential power that is an absolute difference between the two mean values. The each mean value is calculated from arbitrary-grouped power-consumption data of a circuit. Since both mean values are assumed to carry the same amount of noise, taking their difference cancels out the noise with an adequate number of power trace data. Thus, the Differential Power of DPA finds better correlation between the power consumption and the input data compared to SPA in practice.

CPA (Correlation Power Analysis) was introduced by Brier et al.[3] extending the idea of DPA. CPA uses correlation coefficients for observed power groups in order to filter out noise, and CPA is recognized as a stronger attack method than DPA.

No perfect countermeasure against DPA and CPA attacks has been proposed that has a good balance of overhead and resistivity to the best of the authors' knowledge. Of course, countermeasures with higher overhead have better resistivity in general. The challenge is how to achieve higher resistivity with smaller overheads.

Meanwhile, there are only a few power analysis countermeasures integrated into the traditional EDA/CAD circuit design flow due to that they are too side-channel attack specific. Ghavami et al.[6] proposed an automation flow; however, we believe that introducing a new tool for power analysis attacks or modification of tools takes too many efforts to be adopted. Therefore, we propose, from synthesis point of view, a new design flow that uses only existing EDA tools with a minor modification of the usage to prevent power analysis attacks.

This paper has two main contributions.

Problem Conversion –
We cast the problem of power analysis attacks as a retiming problem of circuits. We do not only simply retime the circuit but also employ latch-based design and randomly change the clock timing using clock-gating

techniques to obfuscate the power signature of crypto-hardware, which falls into the classification of a time-shifting obfuscation. Due to its simplicity, the time-shifting idea requires low hardware overhead. Moreover, this approach is applicable to any block-based crypto algorithm including AES.

New Design Flow –
We solve this problem and introduce how to design the latch-based circuit with random clock-gating using only existing EDA tools. The designed circuit is only a first step, leaving plenty of room for improvement and optimization; however, the experimental results show that the circuit with random clock-gating successfully obfuscates all the cases against DPA and CPA attacks.

The proposed LRCG (Latch-based Random Clock-Gating) method is significantly light weight (only 13% area overhead compared to other conventional countermeasures that incur ~294% based on our experimental results). Moreover, it prevented all the DPA and CPA attacks that we conducted. Therefore, we believe that the proposed method is a promising approach for block-based cipher hardware implementation.

2. RELATED WORK

There are mainly three categories of countermeasures against power analysis attacks. The first category is minimizing the differential power, namely power balancing such as WDDL (Wave Dynamic Differential Logic)[31, 27, 30, 29, 24, 23] and other full-custom and transistor level countermeasures[9, 25, 26, 22, 28, 8, 21]. Placing complementary cell or transistor balances power consumption and de-emphasize the trait of power signature. However, these countermeasures require to make physically uniform hardware for both original and complementary circuits, which is prohibitively difficult to achieve in practice. Process variations adversely affects the hardware implementation of power balancing, thus the power analysis resistivity heavily depends on the manufacturing. Furthermore, these techniques incur additional area, power, and sometimes performance penalties in order to complement the power imbalance resulting in more than doubled area and energy overheads. In order to reduce the burden of physical design effort, we need structural and architectural countermeasures to mitigate power analysis attacks.

The second category is randomization countermeasures[1, 4, 5, 7, 15, 16, 18, 14] that use randomly generated signals to mask power consumption patterns of the crypto data path. By the nature of randomness, the power signature alters every time even if the input sequences are the same. In order to inject more random power, Sui et al.[20] employed an asynchronous circuit incorporating dynamic voltage scaling techniques. This approach requires more engineering efforts than designing a general synchronized circuit. Yang et al.[32] proposed dynamic voltage and frequency switching approach to do more randomization; however, it still incurs delay overhead (the area overhead was not discussed in the paper). Due to the randomly injected noise, the randomization countermeasures increases the number of power probing data to detect the correct secret key. At the same time, those countermeasures sacrifices performance and/or incur significant area and power overheads in order to produce jamming power.

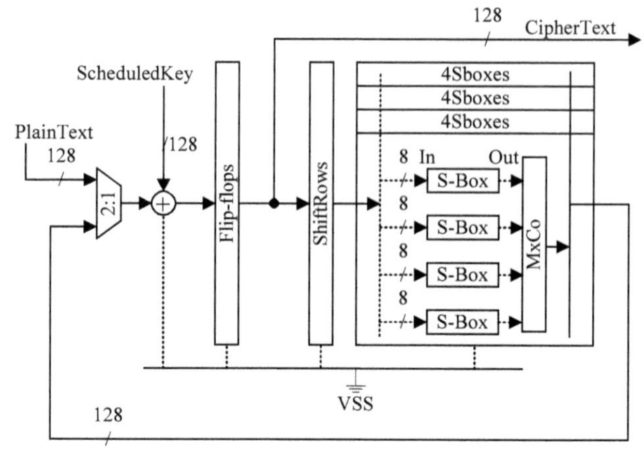

Figure 1: AES Data Path of Power Analysis Target

The third approach is time-shifting obfuscation. Time-shifting techniques have not been explored much since they have been mainly proposed for software crypto-application implementation on/with general purpose processors/ASIPs[2]. Re-ordering or changing the timing of encryption instructions obfuscate when to observe power consumption. This approach is non-trivial to apply to ASIC designs since all gates are hardwired in the ASIC.

This paper is the first work that overcomes the limitation of the third approach, the time-shifting obfuscation, and demonstrates how to seamlessly co-opt it into ASIC designs and the EDA flow. Thus, we believe that our approach is promising for embedded systems. Furthermore, the advantage of this strategy is that it requires less extra hardware and energy overheads. We cast the power analysis problem as a retiming problem and solve it using widely used EDA tools. We introduce a new extra step into the conventional hardware design flow to realize the light weight latch random clock-gates method. Our simulation-based experimental results showed that this approach successfully prevented DPA and CPA attacks in all cases.

Note that the simulation-based experiments are accurate enough so as to validate our random clock-gating method, since the core idea of our method relies on the randomly time-shifted power obfuscation ability rather than power balancing ability. Conducting DPA or CPA is not a simple task. Significant amounts of noise prevent accurate probing of the power rail in real experiments. Since the simulation-based experimental data is ideal for adversaries (=no noise disturbance), preventing DPA or CPA attacks on the simulation results implies that attacking on real hardware implementation is even more difficult to conduct.

3. DPA AND CPA FORMULATION

This paper focuses on the original (first-order) DPA attack[10] and CPA[3] formulated as follows. Readers who are not familiar with these attacks can proceed to the next section in order to catch the main idea of this paper and come back to this section later. Let Fig. 1 be the power analysis attack target. Fig. 1 is an exemplar of an AES encryption data path; however, the same formulation is equally applicable to any other block-based symmetric cryptographic hardware.

Fig. 1 has two inputs labeled as `PlainText` and `Scheduled-Key` and one output labeled as `CipherText`. In addition, all combinational logic share the same `VSS`. Refer to the work of Sugawara et al.[19] for the entire AES architecture. Based on the measured `VSS` current of the circuit and 8-bit `Out` from one of the S-Box in Fig. 1, adversaries attempt to conjecture the corresponding secret 8-bit `Key` that is not observable from outside. Adversaries observe the `Out` and `VSS` as many times as possible. The more observed data, the more accurate is the `Key` estimation from noisy `VSS` data. An AES circuit has more than 16 copies of S-Boxes. For instance, a 128-bit AES circuit depicted in Fig. 1 takes 128-bit vectors of plain text and scheduled key, consisting of 16 8-bit `Ins` to S-Boxes and 16 corresponding 8-bit secret `Keys`, respectively. According to Morioka et al.[13], S-Boxes account for 75% of energy consumption of an AES circuit. Thus, adversaries have high incentive to conduct power analysis attacks over the components that include S-Boxes. AES performs 10 Rounds (cycles) of S-boxes calculations to finish the operation.

Adversaries group the observed `VSS` into either G_0 or G_1 referring to a selection function D in Eq. (1). D returns 8-bit a value[33].

$$D = Sbox^{-1}(c \oplus k_{est.}) \tag{1}$$

c, $k_{est.}$, and $Sbox^{-1}$ are 8-bit cipher text, estimated 8-bit sub secret key, and inverse AES S-Box function, respectively. Moreover, c is equivalent to `Out` in Fig. 1. The returned D value equals to `In` in Fig. 1 iff 8-bit $k_{est.}$ =`Key`.

A_0 and A_1 in Eqs. (3) and (4) are the average of `VSS` current values in G_0 and G_1, respectively.

$$0 \leq \quad t \quad < \text{clock period} \tag{2}$$

$$A_0(t) \quad = \quad \frac{1}{|G_0|} \sum_{D(c,k_{est.}) \in G_0} p_c(t) \tag{3}$$

$$A_1(t) \quad = \quad \frac{1}{|G_1|} \sum_{D(c,k_{est.}) \in G_1} p_c(t) \tag{4}$$

$$\tag{5}$$

t is the time `VSS` current is sampled. $p_c(t)$ is the measured `VSS` current with respect to cipher text c at time t. Every $p_c(t)$ has to belong to either G_0 or G_1. $|G_0|$ and $|G_1|$ are the number of $p_c(t)$ in the group.

There are two well-known grouping methods for making G_0 or G_1. One refers to the ith bit of the 8-bit D value. In this method, $p_c(t)$ is grouped into

$$\left.\begin{array}{l} G_0 \text{ when } D[i] = 0 \\ G_1 \text{ when } D[i] = 1 \end{array}\right\} \tag{6}$$

The other one refers to Hamming weight of the D[12]. In this method, $p_c(t)$ is grouped into

$$\left.\begin{array}{l} G_0 \text{ when } 0 \leq \text{Hamming weight of} D < 4 \\ G_1 \text{ when } 4 < \text{Hamming weight of} D \leq 8 \end{array}\right\} \tag{7}$$

When $k_{est.} \neq$`Key`, the absolute difference between A_0 and A_1 is expected to be close to zero, meaning no correlation between `Key` and observed `VSS` data. In contrast, when $k_{est.}$ =`Key`, the absolute differential power between A_0 and A_1 is expected to become the largest (high correlation between `Key` and `VSS`) amongst all $2^8 = 256$ candidates of 8-bit $k_{est.}$. This largest differential power is denoted as DP and

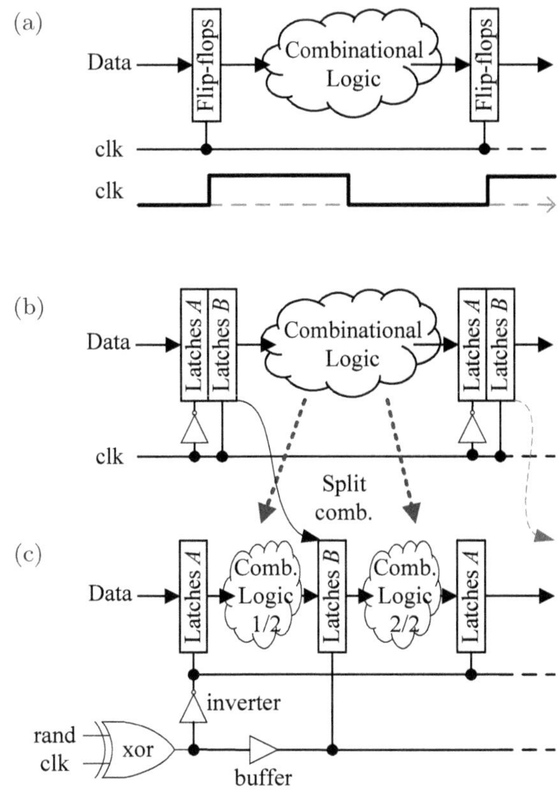

Figure 2: LRCG Procedure (a) Regular Flip-Flop based Clocking (b) Replacing Flip-Flops with Master and Servant Latches (c) Split the Combinational Logic between Latches for Obfuscating Power Information

formulated as follows.

$$DP \quad = \quad \arg\max_t |A_0(t) - A_1(t)| \tag{8}$$

Finding the maximum DP amongst all estimated `Keys` ($k_{est.}$) is called DPA attack. Although adversaries have to examine the DP of every 256 $k_{est.}$ candidate for a single S-Box DPA attack, DPA is much faster than exhaustive search. The total search space of DPA is $2^8 \times 16$ (128-bit AES uses 16 S-Boxes) whereas an exhaustive search has to examine all 2^{128} candidates of 128-bit `ScheduledKey`.

CPA is also formulated in a similar manner. Instead of using DP, the largest correlation power is denoted as CP and formulated as follows[3].

$$CP \quad = \quad \arg\max_t \left| \frac{Cov(p_c(t), \text{Hamming weight}(D))}{\sigma_{p_c(t)} \cdot \sigma_{\text{Hamming weight}(D)}} \right| \tag{9}$$

Finding the maximum CP amongst all $k_{est.}$ is called CPA attack.

4. LRCG

4.1 Latch Design Conversion and Retiming

4.1.1 Preparation

Fig. 2 shows the general design flow of generating the proposed LRCG (Latch-based Random Clock-Gating) obfuscation. First, Fig. 2 (a) shows a conventional register (flip-flop)

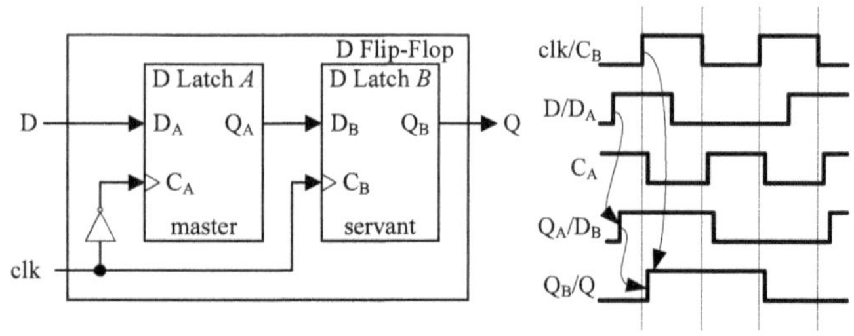

Figure 3: Master-Servant Combination of Latches Functionally Equals a Flip-flop

based sequential circuit design comprising and connecting combinational logic in between. All data traveling from the left flip-flops go through the combinational logic to perform the necessary calculations. The result will be stored in the right flip-flops (and wait for the next clock cycle). The clock signal drives and determines when to capture the result from the combinational logic. The length of one clock cycle limits how long the combinational logic has to perform the calculation and the frequency of the circuit. For positive-edge triggered flip-flops, all signal from the previous flip-flops are required to arrive at the next flip-flop stage before the next positive clock edge (and stable during the range of hold and setup time).

4.1.2 Conversion to Latch-Based Design

Recalling logic design textbooks (Fig. 3), two level-sensitive latches conform to an edge triggered flip-flop. Fig. 2 (b) shows the functionally same diagram as (a) except that flip-flips are comprised with two (master and servant) Latches labeled and B. Aside from clock timing problems, it should function properly even if combinational logic resides between the master and servant latches (between Q_A and D_B in Fig. 3).

4.1.3 Random Clock-Gating

Fig. 2 (c) shows the incorporation of the proposed random clock-gating obfuscation method onto Fig. 2 (b). The combinational logic is split into two parts and the Latches B was moved to the middle using retiming techniques.

Now, the clock is gated by *rand*, and we can determine which latches to clock-gate. If *rand*=0, Fig. 2 (c) functionally operates the same as (b). I.e., clk' and clk are passed to Latches and B, respectively. In contrast, the clock phase becomes inverted when *rand*=1. As a result, clk is fed to Latches and clk' goes to Latches B. When *rand*=1, the new clock cycle starts from the Latches B placed in the middle. The Latches B now behave as a master latches, which were originally the servant latches, and now the first and last Latches , which were originally master latches, serve as servant latches instead. By secretly changing the value of *rand* (i.e., connecting an internal random number generator but not the part of AES circuit), Fig. 2 (c) obfuscates the timing of clocking. This behavior change is what we propose as randomized clock-gating. Assuming that adversaries cannot estimate the *rand* value[1], the circuit becomes dynamically retimed and has randomized power signature since the DP/CP defined in Eqs. (8) and (9) are sensitive to the parameter t that is the time power samples are probed.

[1]The random number generator has to be cryptographically safe and cannot be observed from outside of the chip. Physical true random number generator is preferable.

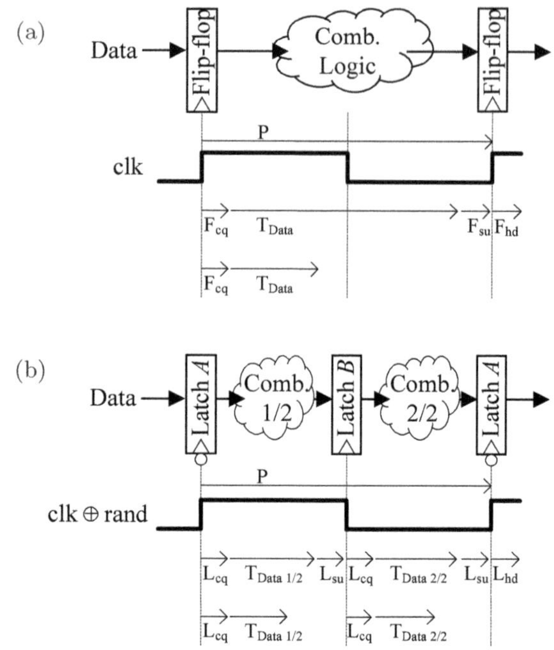

Figure 4: Setup and Hold Time Constraints (a) Conventional Flip-Flop Based Circuit (b) Latch-Based Circuit with Clock-Gating

4.2 Timing Constraints

4.2.1 Conventional Flip-Flop Based Circuit

The conventional flip-flop based sequential circuit has the following timing constraints. Fig. 4 (a) shows two positive edge-triggered flip-flops with a block of combinational logic in between. P is the clock period, and T_{Data} is the delay of the combinational logic. F_{cq} is clk-to-Q (Fig. 3) delay of the flip-flop. F_{su} and F_{hd} are the setup time and hold time, respectively[11].

In Fig. 4 (a), the delay timed from the clock of the left flip-flop propagated through the Q to the end of the combinational logic has to arrive at the right flip-flop earlier than its setup time before the next rising edge of the clock. Thus, the longest delay of the combinational logic is constrained as

$$F_{cq} + T_{Data} \leq P - F_{su} \tag{10}$$

In contrast, the delay has to last later than the hold time of the starting flip-flop after the current rising edge of the clock in order to maintain the current value of the right flip-flop. Hence, the shortest delay of the combinational logic is constrained as

$$F_{cq} + T_{Data} \geq F_{hd} \tag{11}$$

4.2.2 Latch-Based Circuit with Clock-Gating

The proposed latch-based random clock-gating sequential circuit has similar constraints. Fig. 4 (b) shows two negative level-sensitive Latches and one positive level-sensitive

Latch B interposing halved[2] combinational logic 1/2 or 2/2. $T_{Data\ 1/2}$ and $T_{Data\ 2/2}$ are the delay of the combinational logic. L_{cq} is the latch delay of clk-to-Q_A (or Q_B) in Fig. 3. For simplicity, let the delay of clk-to-Q_A and clk-to-Q_B be the same. L_{su} and L_{hd} are the setup time and hold time, respectively.

In Fig. 4 (b), the delay timed from the clock of the left Latch propagated through the Q_A to the end of the combinational logic 1/2 has to arrive at the Latch B earlier than its setup time before the next rising edge of the clock. Similarly, the delay timed from the clock of the Latch B propagated through the Q_B to the end of the combinational logic 2/2 has to arrive at the right Latch earlier than its setup time before the next rising edge of the clock. Thus, the longest delay of the combinational logic is constrained as

$$L_{cq} + T_{Data\ 1/2} \leq P/2 - L_{su} \quad (12)$$
$$L_{cq} + T_{Data\ 2/2} \leq P/2 - L_{su} \quad (13)$$

In contrast, the delay has to arrive to the next latch later than their hold time after the current rising edge of the clock in order to maintain the current value of the Latches B and . Hence, the shortest delay of the combinational logic is constrained as

$$L_{cq} + T_{Data\ 1/2} \geq L_{hd} \quad (14)$$
$$L_{cq} + T_{Data\ 2/2} \geq L_{hd} \quad (15)$$

Even though we now have more latches in the proposed method than the number of flip-flops, the delay of latches is smaller than that of flip-flops (58% of the flip-flop delay for the technology that we used in this paper).

Note that once entire circuit starts operating, *rand* is not changed in order to maintain the clock frequency (but *rand* is set when the circuit itself is reset or between operations). More details will be explained in the next subsection.

We can observe that the proposed latch-based circuit with random clock-gating has similar longest timing constraints to the constraint of the conventional flip-flop based design based on Eq. (10) and Eqs. (12) and (13). In the same manner, the proposed latch-based circuit with random clock-gating and conventional flip-flop based design have similar shortest timing constraints based on Eq. (11) and Eqs. (14) and (15). **Therefore, we are able to treat the retimed latch-based circuit as flip-flop based circuit and utilize conventional synthesis tools to generate a netlist with slight modifications of their usage.** Section 4.4 will describe how to synthesize the latch-based retiming circuit and clock-gating using only existing EDA tools.

It is also worthwhile to mention that the constraints discussed above can be relaxed for further optimization using the notion of latch time-borrowing. It would be an interesting research direction; however, it is beyond the scope of this paper at this point.

4.3 AES with LRCG

Let us apply the latch retiming technique to the AES circuit. Fig. 5 shows the circuits before and after applying the proposed latch retiming method. Let us assume that we do not pipeline the AES circuit in this case for simplicity. Fig. 5 (a) is the original AES circuit. The combinational

[2]Ideally the delays of both Comb. Logic 1/2 and 2/2 are the same, which is approximately the half of the clock period, but they do not have to be exactly the same.

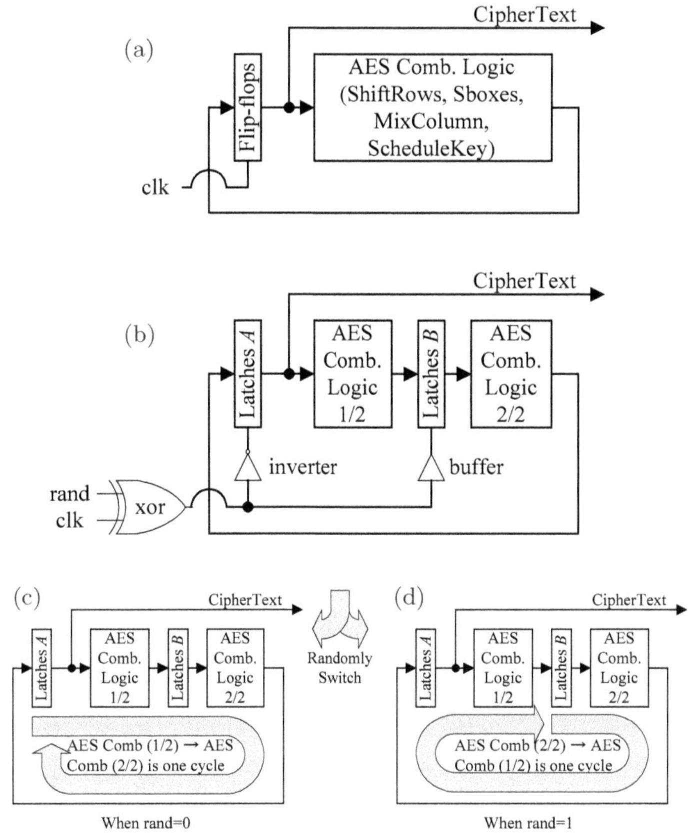

Figure 5: LRCG on AES (a) The Original AES Circuit Combinational and Flip-Flops Separation (b) After Applying the Latch-based Random Clock-Gating Obfuscation Design (c) When *rand*=0, One Cycle Starts from Latch A (d) When *rand*=1, One Cycle Starts from Latch B

part and the flip-flops are depicted separately. Following the proposed procedure, in Fig. 5 (b), the flip-flops are separated into two Latches and B, and the *rand* was added to the clock line. The place of Latches B can be determined by general synthesis or retiming tools. The more balanced delay between AES Comb. Logic 1/2 and 2/2, the better obfuscation. Of course, the number of Latches and B can be different as well.

Figs. 5 (c) and (d) show that the starting and ending points of one cycle when *rand*=0 and *rand*=1, respectively. When the Latches are holding the previous values (either $\{clk{=}0,\ rand{=}1\}$ or $\{clk{=}1,\ rand{=}0\}$), the Latches B are transparent and passing through the new value. In contrast, when the Latches B are holding the previous values (either $\{clk{=}0,\ rand{=}0\}$ or $\{clk{=}1,\ rand{=}1\}$), the Latches are transparent and passing through the new value. Mixing those two states, the power signature of the AES circuit becomes obfuscated. Additionally, we can, of course, generate more latching stages for better obfuscation if necessary.

During the operation of AES rounds, *rand* is not changed in order to maintain the clock frequency but the *rand* is renewed for every new `PlainText` data. ASIC designers also may place output registers to `CipherText` to prevent data arrival time analysis.

Table 1: Preliminary Experimental Setup

Target Design	AES Combinational Logic
Synthesis Tool	Synopsys Design Compiler C-2009.06
Fast-Spice	Synopsys NanoSim C-2009.06
Standard Cell Library	SAED_EDK 90nm

4.4 Design Flow for Latch-based Countermeasure Design and Retiming

An additional goal of the proposed LRCG approach is to use existing EDA tools that will allow ease of incorporation into a standard synthesis-based design flow; therefore, designers will not need to redesign/respecify RTL code for DPA/CPA countermeasures, which also makes this approach amenable for use of other crypto-algorithms. Towards this end, we propose the following EDA tool usage scenario.

We use Synopsys Design Compiler (DC), an industrial standard synthesis tool, in order to implement the latch-based random clock-gating countermeasure. Ideally, synthesis tools are able to handle master-servant latch retiming and move the servant latch into the middle of combinational logic. However, DC does not support[3] retiming in such a way. In order to enable use of this tool, we make the following modifications.

First, we design a regular flip-flop based synchronous RTL and synthesize it with a reasonable clock period constraint. Second, we add another flip-flop right after every original flip-flop. This set of original and secondly-added flip-flops are nominally used for retiming in DC. Since DC has register-register retiming capability, we let it run with the retiming option and try to balance the delay between the flip-flops, constraining it with the half of the previous clock period. The generated netlist from DC contains flip-flops. We then replace all those flip-flops with latches.

Thus, we can utilize existing EDA tools to design the proposed latch retiming countermeasure. The clock-gating cells can be inserted onto the clock line during the retiming procedure of the proposed method.

5. EXPERIMENTAL RESULTS

We compare the proposed LRCG (Latch-based Random Clock-Gating) with other three designs including "Baseline" (without countermeasures) and two most cited countermeasures. One is "WDDL"[31, 27, 30, 29, 24, 23] on behalf of the balancing countermeasures, and other one is "Random Mask" proposed by Akkar et al.[1] on behalf of the randomization category. Table 1 shows the experimental setup. We use the composite field architecture for S-Boxes proposed by Satoh et al.[17] and deploy cells from the Synopsys 90nm generic library (SAED_EDK 90nm). The clock period constraint is 5ns (200MHz). NanoSim measures the `VSS` current of each design every 10ps. As we mentioned earlier, the simulation-based experiments are suitable to compare this work with other countermeasures since the fast-spice we use simulates at transistor-level accuracy and takes care of the cell-delay information and glitch cases. It does not take the environmental power noise into account; however, noiseless data is more preferable for adversaries. Therefore, preventing attacks with the fast-spice data means it is generally even more difficult to attack on the real environment.

[3]To the best knowledge of the authors. Some latch retiming commands did not properly function due to memory-related problems.

Table 2: Comparison* in Area and Energy

	Area	Energy
Baseline	100.0%	100.0%
WDDL	200.1%	316.9%
Random Mask	393.8%	480.2%
RSM**	128%~	172%~
LRCG (This Work)	**113.3%**	**100.5%**

*Normalized by the Baseline **Estimated from the literature

5.1 Area, Energy, Performance Overheads

First, we compare the overheads between the proposed method and other countermeasures. The area overhead of the proposed LRCG over the Baseline is only 13%. In contrast, WDDL and Random Mask incur much more area overhead: 100.1% and 293.8%, respectively. Table 2 shows the comparison in area and energy consumption of each target design. Thus, the proposed LRCG can be implemented with significantly smaller overheads compared to other countermeasures.

In addition, the proposed LRCG requires only 0.5% energy overhead. This is because we use a latch-based design. The reduction of flip-flop energy compensates for the increased energy of the additional latches. In comparison, WDDL and Random Mask incur 216.9% and 380.2% of additional energy overhead, which is significantly more expensive than our approach.

Moreover, the delay overhead of the proposed LRCG is only 123ps that is the delay for additional latches and still fits in the 200MHz frequency constraint. In contrast, WDDL slows down the clock speed 2x in order to wait for the entire circuit to be pre-charged to 0, which also increases the energy consumption. The power consumption penalty of WDDL is approximately 58%; however, since the clock period of WDDL is doubled, the energy overhead becomes 216.9%, which is more than the amount of its area overhead. Random Mask also incurs considerably high (215%) delay overhead that violates the delay constraint.

Even the newest countermeasure, RSM, proposed by Nassar et al.[14] that incurs the smallest are overhead amongst all the literature still requires more than 28% of area overhead and 72% (estimation) of energy overhead.

5.2 DPA and CPA Obfuscation

Second, we evaluate DPA and CPA obfuscation ability of LRCG. The `VSS` current of AES that includes all 16 AES S-Boxes is measured. We use the data of Round 10 (the last cycle) since `CipherText` at Round 10 is visible from outside of the circuit. We collected `VSS` current traces corresponding to 1024, 2048, 4096, and 8192 inputs. Those inputs are randomly generated 128-bit numbers and injected from `PlainText` of Fig. 1. We calculate DP (Differential Power defined in Eq. (8)) and CP (Correlation Power defined in Eq. (9)) for all possible candidates `Keys` ($k_{est.}$), rank the `Keys`' DP/CP in descending order, and observe how the ranks of the correct `Key` vary.

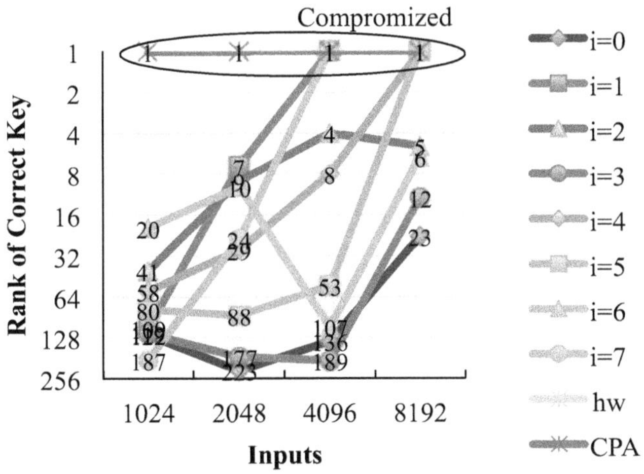

Figure 6: Ranks of Correct Key = 0x7F for Baseline

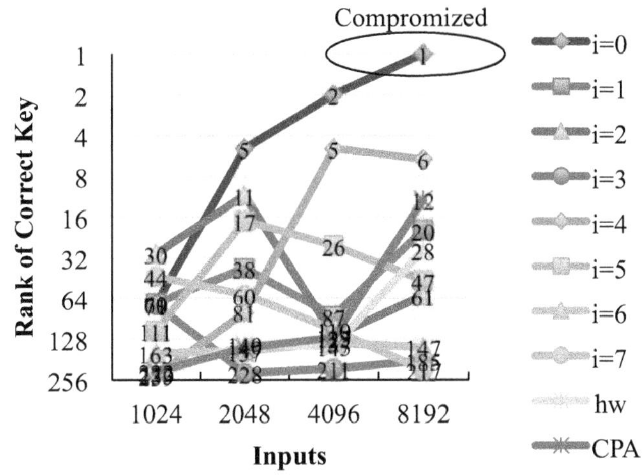

Figure 7: Ranks of Correct Key = 0x7F for WDDL

Figs. 6, 7, 8, and 9 show[4] the ranks of the correct Key = 0x7F amongst all possible Key candidates ($k_{est.}$) for the four target designs: Baseline, WDDL, Random Mask, and the proposed LRCG (Latch-based Random Clock-Gating), respectively. The correct Key is randomly selected[5]. The vertical axes represent the ranks of the correct Key amongst other Key candidates in log scale. The horizontal axes are the number of inputs. The experimental results cover all the grouping cases denoted in Eqs. (6) and (7) with 1024, 2048, 4096, and 8192 inputs. The "i=0, 1 ..., 7" in the legend represent the groupings denoted in Eq. (6) of DPA. Also, the "hw" in the legend represents the grouping denoted in Eq. (7) of DPA. The "CPA" in the legend is CPA attacks denoted with Eq. (9).

Indeed, Figs. 6, 7, 8, and 9 visualize the general tendency of the results: the larger DP/CP, the higher rank denoted with smaller number. If the DP/CP of the correct Key is blended within the range of other DPs/CPs of wrongly estimated $k_{est.}$, the rank of the correct Key is also placed somewhere in the middle of the ranking so that the adversaries cannot confidently determine which Key candidate is the correct one. In contrast, if the rank of the $k_{est.}$ is 1 (or constantly ranked at a particular position), there is a higher chance that the $k_{est.}$ is the correct Key by the definition of DPA/CPA. In such cases, adversaries have more confidence that they only need to check the highest ranked $k_{est.}$ to find the correct Key.

As the input number of power samples increases; the Baseline, WDDL, and Random Mask are compromised with rank=1 with various groupings. In Fig. 6, Baseline is compromised with six grouping cases. Moreover, in Fig. 7, WDDL is compromised when i=0 with 8192 input PlainText data. In Fig. 8, Random Mask is also compromised when i=1 and i=5 with 8192 input PlainText data. In contrast, LRCG is still intact against both DPA and CPA as discussed in the next paragraph.

Fig. 9 shows that the ranks of the proposed latch random clock-gating DO NOT become 1 or stay at the same

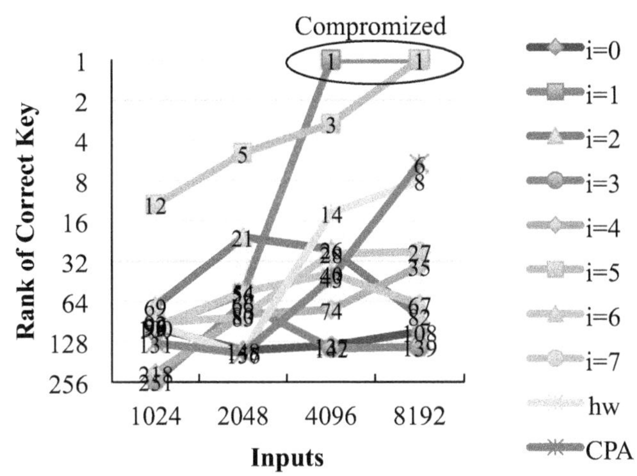

Figure 8: Ranks of Correct Key = 0x7F for Random Mask

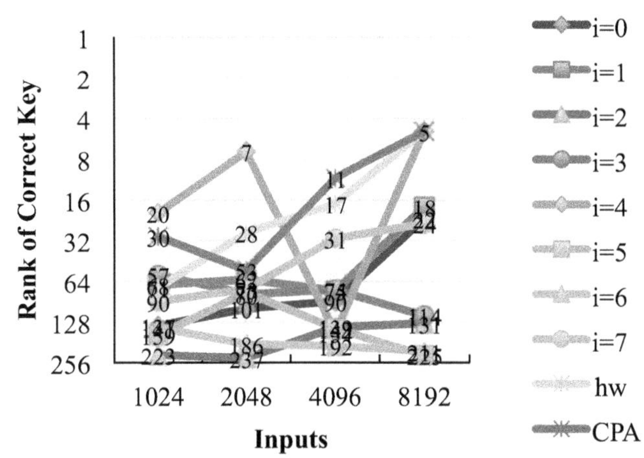

Figure 9: Ranks of Correct Key = 0x7F for LRCG (This Work)

[4] Best viewed in color.

[5] We observed similar results for other keys as well. See Appendix.

rank. For example, the rank of the grouping i=4 becomes higher when there are 2048 inputs than 4096 inputs[6]. In contrast, the rank of the same grouping and the same `Key` with 4096 inputs is lower than the one with 8192 inputs. Hence, adversaries are unable to confidently determine that what $k_{est.}$ (highly or lowly ranked) is the correct `Key`. Accordingly, LRCG has more resistivity against both DPA and CPA compared to Baseline, WDDL, and Random Mask.

Note that we conducted more experiments using other randomly chosen `Keys` and observed similar results. Refer to Appendix for more detailed results.

In summary, our experimental results demonstrate that the proposed LRCG successfully repels the DPA and CPA attacks and achieves higher resistivity with smaller area and energy overheads compared to WDDL and Random Mask.

6. CONCLUSIONS

In this work, we proposed LRCG (Latch-based Random Clock-Gating), a simple, yet effective time-shifting approach to prevent power analysis attacks. This method converts the power analysis problem to a retiming problem so as to obfuscate the power information. This paper is the first step in realizing the idea of the time-shifting countermeasure with the technique of circuit retiming and clock-gating that are traditionally used for performance and low power design. The experimental results show that the AES circuit designed with the proposed LRCG flow successfully prevented DPA and CPA attacks with only 13% of area overhead and 0.5% of energy overhead. We also demonstrated how this approach can be seamlessly implemented within a standard commercial EDA synthesis flow.

Future work will consider further optimization of LRCG with respect to the timing constraints of latch-based circuit and circuit design itself. We will also investigate variations of LRCG for better performance and resistivity against power analysis attacks. Future work could also consider evaluations of LRCG using different variety of side-channel attacks such as EM analysis.

7. ACKNOWLEDGMENTS

The authors thank Dr. Morioka, NEC Lab. for his courtesy in providing the composite field AES S-Box Verilog code.

8. REFERENCES

[1] M.-L. Akkar and C. Giraud. An implementation of DES and AES, secure against some attacks. In *roc CH*, pages 309–318, 2001.

[2] J. Ambrose, R. Ragel, and S. Parameswaran. RIJID: Random code injection to mask power analysis based side channel attacks. In *roc C*, pages 489–492, June 2007.

[3] E. Brier, C. Clavier, and F. Olivie. Correlation power analysis with a leakage model. In *roc CH*, pages 16–29, 2004.

[4] J.-S. Coron and L. Goubin. On boolean and arithmetic masking against differential power analysis. In *roc CH*, pages 231–237, 2000.

[6]The same information represented in a Table format is available in Appendix.

[5] C. Gebotys. A table masking countermeasure for low-energy secure embedded systems. *I Trans I yst*, 14(7):740–753, July 2006.

[6] B. Ghavami and H. Pedram. An automatic design flow for implementation of side channel attacks resistant crypto-chips. In *T*, pages 330–339, 2007.

[7] J. D. Golic and C. Tymen. Multiplicative masking and power analysis of AES. In *roc CH*, pages 198–212, 2003.

[8] S. Guilley, P. Hoogvorst, Y. Mathieu, R. Pacalet, and J. Provost. CMOS structures suitable for secured hardware. In *roc T*, pages 1414–1415, 2004.

[9] M. Khatir, A. Moradi, A. Ejlali, M. T. M. Shalmani, and M. Salmasizadeh. A secure and low-energy logic style using charge recovery approach. In *roc I*, pages 259–264, 2008.

[10] P. C. Kocher, J. Jaffe, and B. Jun. Differential power analysis. In *roc C Y T*, pages 388–397, 1999.

[11] H. Lee, S. Paik, and Y. Shin. Pulse width allocation with clock skew scheduling for optimizing pulsed latch-based sequential circuits. In *roc ICC*, pages 224–229, Nov. 2008.

[12] T. S. Messerges, E. A. Dabbish, and R. H. Sloan. Investigations of power analysis attacks on smartcards. In *roc NIX Wor s op on martcard Tec nology*, page 17, Berkeley, CA, USA, 1999. USENIX Association.

[13] S. Morioka and A. Satoh. An optimized S-Box circuit architecture for low power AES design. In *roc CH*, pages 172–186, 2002.

[14] M. Nassar, Y. Souissi, S. Guilley, and J.-L. Danger. RSM: a small and fast countermeasure for AES, secure against 1st and 2nd-order zero-offset SCAs. In *roc T*, pages 1173–1178, Mar. 2012.

[15] T. Popp and S. Mangard. Masked dual-rail pre-charge logic: DPA-resistance without routing constraints. In *roc CH*, pages 172–186, 2005.

[16] M. Saeki, D. Suzuki, K. Shimizu, and A. Satoh. A design methodology for a DPA-resistant cryptographic LSI with RSL techniques. In *roc CH*, pages 189–204, 2009.

[17] A. Satoh, S. Morioka, K. Takano, and S. Munetoh. A compact rijndael hardware architecture with S-Box optimization. In *roc I C Y T*, pages 239–254, 2001.

[18] P. Schaumont and K. Tiri. Masking and dual-rail logic don't add up. In *roc CH*, pages 95–106, 2007.

[19] T. Sugawara, N. Homma, T. Aoki, and A. Satoh. Differential power analysis of AES ASIC implementations with various S-box circuits. In *roc CCT*, pages 395–398, Aug. 2009.

[20] C. Sui, J. Wu, Y. Shi, Y.-B. Kim, and M. Choi. Random dynamic voltage scaling design to enhance security of NCL s-box. In *roc I International id est ymposium on Circuits and ystems*, pages 1–4, Aug. 2011.

[21] K. Tanimura and N. Dutt. ExCCel: Exploration of complementary cells for efficient DPA attack resistivity. In *H T*, pages 52–55, Jun. 2010.

[22] K. Tiri, M. Akmal, and I. Verbauwhede. A dynamic and differential CMOS logic with signal independent

power consumption to withstand differential power analysis on smart cards. In *roc CI C*, pages 403–406, Sept. 2002.

[23] K. Tiri, D. Hwang, A. Hodjat, B. Lai, S. Yang, P. Schaumont, and I. Verbauwhede. Prototype ic with wddl and differential routing - DPA resistance assessment. In *roc CH* , pages 354–365, 2005.

[24] K. Tiri, D. Hwang, A. Hodjat, B. Lai, S. Yang, P. Schaumont, and I. Verbauwhede. A side-channel leakage free coprocessor IC in 0.18um CMOS for embedded AES-based cryptographic and biometric processing. In *roc C*, pages 222–227, June 2005.

[25] K. Tiri and I. Verbauwhede. Securing encryption algorithms against DPA at the logic level: Next generation smart card technology. In *roc CH* , pages 125–136, 2003.

[26] K. Tiri and I. Verbauwhede. Charge recycling sense amplifier based logic: securing low power security ICs against DPA. In *roc CI C*, pages 179–182, Sept. 2004.

[27] K. Tiri and I. Verbauwhede. A logic level design methodology for a secure DPA resistant ASIC or FPGA implementation. In *roc T* , volume 1, pages 246–251 Vol.1, Feb. 2004.

[28] K. Tiri and I. Verbauwhede. Design method for constant power consumption of differential logic circuits. In *roc T* , pages 628–633, 2005.

[29] K. Tiri and I. Verbauwhede. A vlsi design flow for secure side-channel attack resistant ICs. In *roc T* , volume 3, pages 58–63, Mar. 2005.

[30] K. Tiri and I. Verbauwhede. A digital design flow for secure integrated circuits. *I Trans Comput - ided esign Integr Circuits yst* , 25(7):1197–1208, July 2006.

[31] I. Verbauwhede, K. Tiri, D. Hwang, and P. Schaumonr. Circuits and design techniques for secure ICs resistant to side-channel attacks. In *roc ICIC T*, pages 1–4, 2006.

[32] S. Yang, W. Wolf, N. Vijaykrishnan, D. Serpanos, and Y. Xie. Power attack resistant cryptosystem design: a dynamic voltage and frequency switching approach. In *roc T* , volume 3, pages 64–69, Mar. 2005.

[33] P. Yu and P. Schaumont. Secure FPGA circuits using controlled placement and routing. In *roc C +I* , pages 45–50, 2007.

APPENDIX

A. ADDITIONAL EXPERIMENTAL DATA

A.1 Ranks of Correct `Key` = 0x94

Figs. 10, 11, 12, and 13 show the ranks of the correct `Key` = 0x94 amongst all possible `Key` candidates ($k_{est.}$) for Baseline, WDDL, Random Mask, and the proposed LRCG, respectively. Baseline (Fig. 10) is compromised with many cases. WDDL (Fig. 11) is also compromised when i=0,4 with 8192 input `PlainText` data. Moreover, Random Mask (Fig. 12) is also compromised when i=5 with 8192 input `PlainText` data. In contrast, the proposed LRCG (Fig. 13) is NOT compromised with any groupings even when `Key` = 0x94. Thus, the resistivity advantage of the proposed LRCG is still the same for the different key.

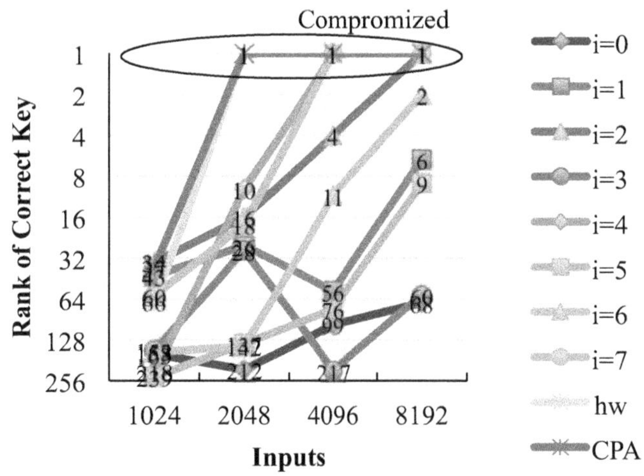

Figure 10: Ranks of Correct `Key` = 0x94 for Baseline

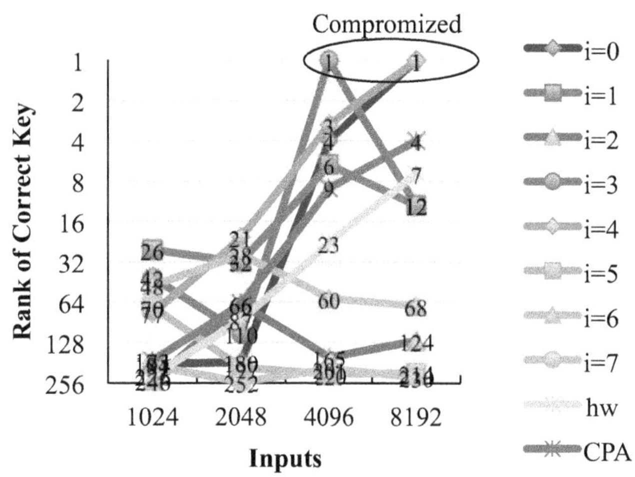

Figure 11: Ranks of Correct `Key` = 0x94 for WDDL

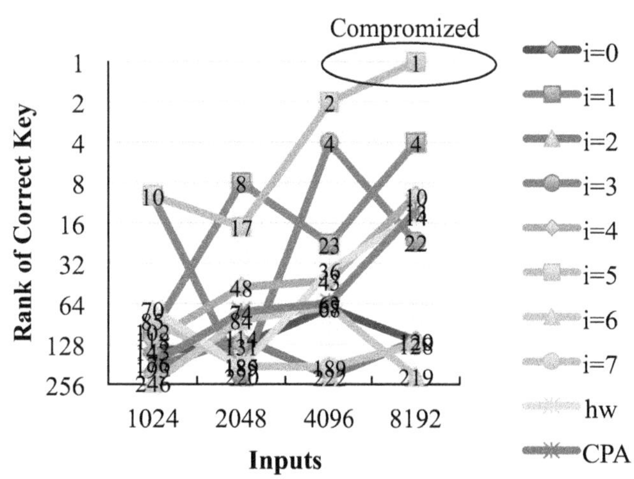

Figure 12: Ranks of Correct `Key` = 0x94 for Random Mask

A.2 Ranks of Correct Key in Tables

Tables 3, 4, 5, and 6 summarize the ranks of the correct Key amongst all possible Key candidates ($k_{est.}$) for Baseline, WDDL, Random Mask, and LRCG, respectively. These Tables and Figs. 6, 7, 8, 9, 10, 11, 12, and 13 are representing the same experimental results; however, these Tables provide more readable values of the ranks, which the Figs. cannot show due to the overlaps.

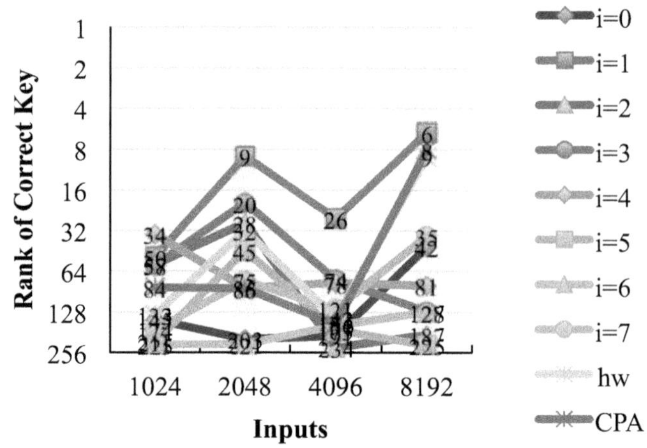

Figure 13: Ranks of Correct Key = 0x94 for LRCG (This Work)

Table 3: Ranks of Correct Key for Baseline

Attack Method (Grouping)	Key = 0x94										Key = 0x7F									
	DPA									CPA	DPA									CPA
	Eq. (6)								Eq. (7)	Eq. (9)	Eq. (6)								Eq. (7)	Eq. (9)
	i=0	i=1	i=2	i=3	i=4	i=5	i=6	i=7			i=0	i=1	i=2	i=3	i=4	i=5	i=6	i=7		
1024 inputs	163	43	34	153	218	239	158	60	66	37	122	109	41	119	58	80	20	187	1	1
2048 inputs	212	26	16	28	10	137	142	18	1	1	223	7	9	177	29	88	10	24	1	1
4096 inputs	99	56	4	217	1	76	11	1	1	1	136	1	4	189	8	53	107	1	1	1
8192 inputs	68	6	1	60	1	9	2	1	1	1	23	1	5	12	1	1	6	1	1	1

Table 4: Ranks of Correct Key for WDDL

Attack Method (Grouping)	Key = 0x94										Key = 0x7F									
	DPA									CPA	DPA									CPA
	Eq. (6)								Eq. (7)	Eq. (9)	Eq. (6)								Eq. (7)	Eq. (9)
	i=0	i=1	i=2	i=3	i=4	i=5	i=6	i=7			i=0	i=1	i=2	i=3	i=4	i=5	i=6	i=7		
1024 inputs	184	26	246	42	77	70	48	191	226	173	70	69	30	71	239	111	163	44	233	222
2048 inputs	180	32	66	110	21	197	28	252	87	66	5	38	11	228	81	17	157	60	140	149
4096 inputs	4	6	165	1	3	220	60	201	23	9	2	87	123	211	5	26	137	110	145	125
8192 inputs	1	12	124	12	1	214	68	230	7	4	1	20	61	185	6	47	147	217	28	12

Table 5: Ranks of Correct Key for Random Mask

Attack Method (Grouping)	Key = 0x94										Key = 0x7F									
	DPA									CPA	DPA									CPA
	Eq. (6)								Eq. (7)	Eq. (9)	Eq. (6)								Eq. (7)	Eq. (9)
	i=0	i=1	i=2	i=3	i=4	i=5	i=6	i=7			i=0	i=1	i=2	i=3	i=4	i=5	i=6	i=7		
1024 inputs	143	102	193	10	118	10	246	85	70	176	100	98	69	251	218	12	99	92	96	131
2048 inputs	131	8	114	220	48	17	84	185	189	74	148	56	21	66	80	5	54	83	157	156
4096 inputs	68	23	222	4	43	2	67	189	36	63	137	1	26	142	74	3	40	28	14	43
8192 inputs	120	4	120	22	10	1	219	128	14	13	108	1	82	139	35	1	67	27	8	6

Table 6: Ranks of Correct Key for LRCG (This Work)

Attack Method (Grouping)	Key = 0x94										Key = 0x7F									
	DPA									CPA	DPA									CPA
	Eq. (6)								Eq. (7)	Eq. (9)	Eq. (6)								Eq. (7)	Eq. (9)
	i=0	i=1	i=2	i=3	i=4	i=5	i=6	i=7			i=0	i=1	i=2	i=3	i=4	i=5	i=6	i=7		
1024 inputs	145	50	57	58	34	211	225	174	133	84	137	68	223	57	20	159	141	90	71	30
2048 inputs	203	9	28	20	85	45	221	75	32	86	101	62	237	80	7	77	186	73	28	53
4096 inputs	191	26	234	74	78	173	161	121	143	156	90	75	139	74	154	143	192	31	17	11
8192 inputs	42	6	187	127	81	225	128	35	9	8	22	18	131	114	5	225	211	24	5	5

Worst-case Throughput Analysis of Real-time Dynamic Streaming Applications

Firew Siyoum[1] Marc Geilen[1] Orlando Moreira[2] Henk Corporaal[1]

[1] Eindhoven University of Technology [2]ST-Ericsson, Eindhoven
Eindhoven, The Netherlands
{f.m.siyoum, m.c.w.geilen, h.corporaal}@tue.nl orlando.moreira@stericsson.com

ABSTRACT

Wireless embedded applications have stringent temporal constraints. The frame arrival rate imposes a throughput requirement that must be satisfied. These applications are often dynamic and streaming in nature. The FSM-based Scenario-Aware Dataflow (FSM-SADF) model of computation (MoC) has been proposed to model such dynamic streaming applications. FSM-SADF splits a dynamic system into a set of static modes of operation, called *scenarios*. Each scenario is modeled by a Synchronous Dataflow (SDF) graph. The possible scenario transitions are specified by a finite-state machine (FSM). FSM-SADF allows a more accurate design-time analysis of dynamic streaming applications, capitalizing on the analysability of SDF. However, existing FSM-SADF analysis techniques assume 1) scenarios are *self-timed bounded*, for which strong-connectedness is a sufficient condition, and 2) inter-scenario synchronizations are only captured by initial tokens that are common between scenarios. These conditions are too restrictive for many real-life applications. In this paper, we lift these restrictive assumptions and introduce a generalized FSM-SADF analysis approach based on the $(max, +)$ linear systems theory. We present both exact and conservative worst-case throughput analysis techniques that have varying levels of accuracy and scalability. The analysis techniques are implemented in a publicly available dataflow analysis tool and experimentally evaluated with different wireless applications.

Categories and Subject Descriptors

C.4 [**Performance of Systems**]: Modeling Techniques; F.1.1 [**Computation by Abstract Devices**]: Models of Computation

General Terms

Theory, Performance, Verification, Algorithms

Keywords

Synchronous Dataflow, Generalized Eigenmode, $(max, +)$ Algebra, Scenario-aware Dataflow, Self-timed Boundedness, Worst-case Throughput

1. INTRODUCTION

Modern embedded wireless applications have strict real-time requirements. The throughput requirement is imposed by the frame arrival rate that must be satisfied to comply with standards. The design of these applications relies on worst-case temporal analysis to ensure that real-time requirements are satisfied at all operating conditions. These applications typically run on heterogeneous multi-processor systems-on-chip (MPSoC). MPSoC platforms have limited resources that must be efficiently utilized.

Dataflow Models of Computation (MoCs) are widely used to analyze streaming applications running on a MPSoC [18]. A dataflow model is a directed graph that consists of *actors* as vertices and FIFO buffer *channels* as edges. Actors conservatively model different system properties, such as computation, resource arbitration and synchronization. In data-driven *self-timed* execution of such graphs, an actor starts execution as soon as all input data have arrived. After the actor takes a finite time to execute, it produces output data.

The dataflow modeling of modern-day streaming applications is challenging due to their dynamically changing workload. Dynamic models such as Dynamic Dataflow (DDF) [4] are expressively Turing-complete, but formal properties such as deadlock-freedom are undecidable. On the other hand, static models such as Synchronous Dataflow (SDF) [14] are sufficiently analysable, but they have limited expressiveness. SDF actors consume and produce fixed number of data *tokens* per execution. Hence, SDF cannot effectively express dynamic mode switchings. A conservative SDF model, if it exists, is pessimistic and results in over-allocation of scarce MPSoC resources [19].

The FSM-based Scenario-Aware Dataflow (FSM-SADF) MoC has been proposed to improve the expressiveness of SDF, while allowing for design-time analysability [5]. FSM-SADF splits the dynamic data processing behavior of an application into a group of static modes of operation. Each static mode of operation, referred to as *scenario*, is modeled by a SDF. The possible orders of executions of these scenarios are specified by a finite state machine (FSM).

An execution of FSM-SADF is an execution of the possible scenario sequences specified by the FSM. In a distributed implementation, the execution of scenarios is pipelined. As a result, multiple scenarios may be concurrently active. This poses a challenge to analyse scenario sequences. The techniques in [5,6] analyse each scenario first individually. Then, they derive performance guarantees for a sequence compositionally. However, these techniques require two conditions.

1) Scenarios must be *self-timed bounded*. A scenario is self-timed bounded if the number of tokens in every channel is bounded in a self-timed execution [7], where an actor executes as soon as all of its input data have arrived.

2) All inter-scenario synchronizations (data dependencies between scenarios) must be captured by initial tokens that are common between scenarios. An initial token is common between two scenarios if it is located on the same channel in both scenarios.

These two conditions are too restrictive for many real-life application graphs. In this paper, we present a generalized FSM-SADF analysis approach based on the $(max, +)$ linear systems theory. The paper has three main contributions. 1) It presents a technique to analyse a SDF scenario that is not necessarily self-timed bounded. The technique is based on the concept of *generalized eigenmode* from $(max, +)$ algebra. 2) It introduces *initial token labeling* to flexibly specify scenario dependencies. 3) It presents exact and conservative worst-case throughput analysis techniques for FSM-SADFs that possibly have non-self-timed bounded scenarios.

The remainder of this paper is organized in nine sections. Section 2 highlights the contributions of this work with a simple motivational example. Section 3 discusses related work. Section 4 recaps basic dataflow and $(max, +)$ algebra concepts. Section 5 elaborates the problem addressed in this paper. Section 6 characterizes a SDF scenario in terms of its self-timed components. This is followed by the analysis of a scenario and a set of scenarios in Section 7 and Section 8, respectively. Experimental results are presented in Section 9. The paper concludes in Section 10.

2. MOTIVATIONAL EXAMPLE

FSM-SADF can sufficiently express dynamic streaming applications while lending itself to design-time analysability [17]. However, restrictions on existing analysis techniques limit its applicability for many application graphs. A simple example is the baseband processing of Long Term Evolution (LTE). LTE is a recent (pre-4G) standard in cellular wireless communication. LTE's downlink frame consists of 10 sub-frames. Each sub-frame has 14 OFDM symbols. These symbols are allocated to data and control channels. The three possible allocations are 1, 2 or 3 control channels, followed by 13, 12, or 11 data channels, respectively.

Figure 1 shows a simplified FSM-SADF model of LTE's baseband processing. This model is adopted from the discussion in [17]. In Figure 1, black dots represent *initial tokens* that are available in channels at the start of a scenario. The model has five scenarios, which are labeled $\mathbf{s}_1$ to $\mathbf{s}_5$. Scenario $\mathbf{s}_1$ decodes a control format indicator channel that is allocated at symbol 1. Scenario $\mathbf{s}_2$ decodes a control channel that is allocated at symbols 2 and 3. Scenarios $\mathbf{s}_3, \mathbf{s}_4$ and $\mathbf{s}_5$ decode a data channel that is allocated from symbol 2 to 14, 3 to 14, and 4 to 14, respectively. This results in three possible scenario sequences (and hence, three different sub-frame types), as shown by the FSM of Figure 1.

Sub-frames are decoded by executing the possible scenario sequences specified by the FSM. An example scenario sequence is $\langle \mathbf{s}_1, \mathbf{s}_3, \mathbf{s}_1, \mathbf{s}_2, \mathbf{s}_2, \mathbf{s}_5, \mathbf{s}_1, \mathbf{s}_3, \mathbf{s}_1, \mathbf{s}_2, \mathbf{s}_4, \cdots \rangle$ and the corresponding sub-frame type sequence is $\langle 1, 3, 1, 2, \cdots \rangle$. Sub-frame types are detected by scenario $\mathbf{s}_1$. At the end of scenario $\mathbf{s}_1$, a mode detection actor (*md*) dispatches the type of sub-frame to be decoded. This requires synchronization so that some sub-frame-specific actors of successive scenarios (i.e. $\mathbf{s}_2$ and $\mathbf{s}_3$) do not start execution before the sub-frame type is detected. This synchronization is modeled by the initial token t_1 and the data dependency actor (*dda*). t_1 is like a common variable (flag) that is read and written by actors *md* and *dda*. Actor *dda* has zero execution time. Thus, in scenario transitions from $\mathbf{s}_1$ to $\mathbf{s}_2$ ($\mathbf{s}_3$), actor *cdmp* (*ddmp*) of $\mathbf{s}_2$ ($\mathbf{s}_3$) cannot start execution before *md* of $\mathbf{s}_1$ has finished.

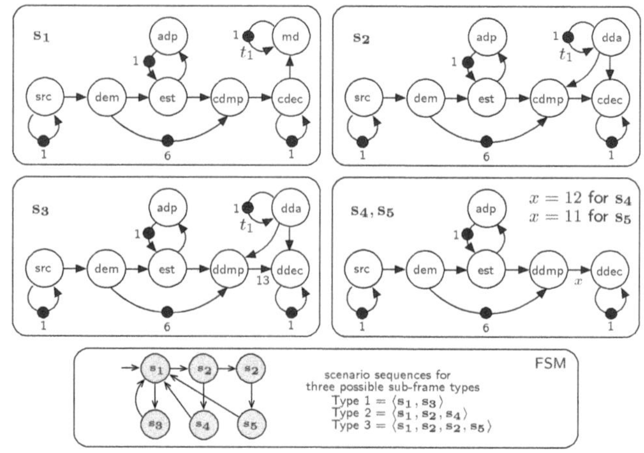

Figure 1: FSM-SADF model of LTE

Modeling sub-frame detection in LTE violates the two analysis conditions, discussed in Section 1. First, scenarios $\mathbf{s}_2$ and $\mathbf{s}_3$ are not self-timed bounded. Self-timed executions of these scenarios result in a continuously increasing accumulation of tokens in outgoing channels of actor *dda* (since *dda* has zero execution time). Second, initial token t_1 is not a common initial token between $\mathbf{s}_1$ and $\mathbf{s}_2$ ($\mathbf{s}_3$). Initial token t_1 in $\mathbf{s}_1$ and initial token t_1 in $\mathbf{s}_2$ ($\mathbf{s}_3$) are two independent initial tokens. Thus, synchronization is not enforced. Consequently, existing techniques are not immediately applicable to analyse the FSM-SADF of Figure 1.

3. RELATED WORK

Due to its analyzability, Synchronous Dataflow (SDF) [14] has been widely used to model and schedule real-time streaming applications onto a MPSoC [3,15]. The throughput of a self-timed bounded SDF graph is analyzed by state-space exploration [8] or $(max, +)$ spectral analysis [5]. A SDF graph is self-timed bounded if the number of tokens in every channel is bounded in a self-timed execution. Self-timed execution is of special interest as it gives the maximum achievable throughput of a SDF graph [7]. Sufficient and necessary conditions for deadlock-free execution of SDF as well as schedulability with bounded buffer size are studied in [7, 13, 14]. However, SDF is too static to capture the dynamic behavior of modern-day multimedia and wireless applications. This may result in unnecessary resource over-allocation [19].

Different dataflow models are proposed that enhance the expressiveness of SDF [4,9,11,12,15,16,20–23]. The majority of these dataflow models, however, are either not sufficiently analysable or do not have known design-time temporal analysis techniques. In expressively Turing-complete dataflow models, such as Dynamic Dataflow (DDF) [4], Khan Process Network (KPN) [11], Boolean Dataflow (BDF) [12] and Core-Function Dataflow (CFDF) [16], deadlock-freedom is an undecidable property. Parameterized Polyhedral Process Networks (P^3N) [23] also offer considerable freedom of expressiveness. However, it requires a run-time consistency check, which is not affordable in embedded baseband MPSoCs. Variable Rate Dataflow (VRDF) as well as its cyclo-static variant Variable Phased Dataflow (VPDF) [22] express application dynamism by allowing a port rate to vary arbitrarily within a specified range. However, existing analyses of VRDF and VPDF are limited to conservative buffer size computations. Heterochronous Dataflow (HDF) [9] does not also have known performance analysis techniques.

Scenario-Aware dataflow (SADF) [20] improves the expressiveness of SDF while allowing for design-time analysability. It identifies different static modes of operations (called scenarios) at design time and uses a stochastic approach to model the order in which scenarios occur. Similar to SADF, Mode-Controlled Dataflow (MCDF) [15] also allows design-time analysis by identifying different static modes. MCDF particularly has appealing constructs from dataflow programming/implementation perspective. However, MCDF currently supports only single-rate modes, which are basically Homogeneous SDF (HSDF) graphs whose main downside is scalability.

FSM-SADF is a version of SADF, where scenario transitions are non-deterministically specified by a finite-state-machine. Its applicability to model and analyse embedded wireless applications is studied in [17]. Performance analysis techniques for FSM-SADF are presented in [5, 6]. However, these techniques require scenarios to be self-timed bounded. Moreover, they implicitly define inter-scenario synchronizations through common initial tokens.

In this paper, we analyse FSM-SADF without requiring self-timed boundedness of scenarios. Unlike SDF, this is essential since an unbounded scenario does not necessarily make a scenario sequence unbounded. In addition, we use identifiers of initial tokens, instead of positions of initial tokens, to explicitly define data dependencies between scenarios. Section 5 later discusses these topics in more detail.

4. PRELIMINARY

This section defines basic dataflow concepts and recaps the $(max, +)$ algebra. It is organized in three sections. Section 4.1 briefly introduces the $(max, +)$ algebra. Section 4.2 gives formal definitions of SDF and FSM-SADF. Section 4.3 revises the $(max, +)$ characterization of SDFs.

In this paper, we use $\mathbb{R}$ for real numbers, $\mathbb{N}$ for natural numbers and $\mathbb{N}^0$ for natural numbers with zero. We use $A \rightarrow B$ and $A \leftrightarrow B$ to denote injective and bijective relations, respectively. In addition, we use $|A|$ to denote the cardinality of a set, sequence or vector.

4.1 $(max, +)$ Algebra

We first briefly introduce basic $(max, +)$ algebra notation. Define $\mathbb{R}_{\max} = \mathbb{R} \cup \{-\infty\}$, the set of real numbers extended with $-\infty$. For elements $a, b \in \mathbb{R}_{\max}$, $(max, +)$ algebra defines $a \oplus b \overset{\text{def}}{=} \max(a, b)$ and $a \otimes b \overset{\text{def}}{=} a + b$. In this paper, we use the standard max and addition notation for the sake of readability. For $a \in \mathbb{R}_{\max}$, $\max(-\infty, a) = \max(a, -\infty) = a$ and $a + -\infty = -\infty + a = -\infty$.

The algebra is extended to vectors and matrices as follows. For $n \in \mathbb{N}$, define $\underline{n} \overset{\text{def}}{=} \{1, 2, \cdots, n\}$. An n dimensional vector is an element of the set $\mathbb{R}^n_{\max}$. For vector $\gamma \in \mathbb{R}^n_{\max}$, the entry at row $i \in \underline{n}$ is denoted as $[\gamma]_i$. For $c \in \mathbb{R}_{\max}$, vector $\mathbf{u}[c] \in \mathbb{R}^n_{\max}$ is such that for any $i \in \underline{n}$, $[\mathbf{u}[c]]_i = c$. In addition, scalar to vector addition and multiplication are given as $[c + \gamma]_i = c + [\gamma]_i$ and $[c\gamma]_i = c[\gamma]_i$, respectively.

The set of $m \times n$ matrices is denoted as $\mathbb{R}^{m \times n}_{\max}$. Row $i \in \underline{m}$ is denoted as $[M]_{i:}$ and column $j \in \underline{n}$ as $[M]_{:j}$. An entry at row $i \in \underline{m}$ and column $j \in \underline{n}$ is denoted as $[M]_{ij}$.

Given vectors $\gamma, \theta \in \mathbb{R}^n_{\max}$, we have the following properties. Vector addition, subtraction and max operation are element-wise operations, i.e. $[\gamma \pm \theta]_i = [\gamma]_i \pm [\theta]_i$ and likewise $[\max(\gamma, \theta)]_i = \max([\gamma]_i, [\theta]_i)$. The *norm* of vector γ is the maximum entry of the vector, denoted as $\|\gamma\| = \max_i [\gamma]_i$. For vector γ with $\|\gamma\| > -\infty$, the normalized vector is denoted as $\bar{\gamma}$, where $[\bar{\gamma}]_i = [\gamma]_i - \|\gamma\|$.

We write $\gamma \preceq \theta$ if $\forall i \in \underline{n}, [\gamma]_i \leq [\theta]_i$. Similarly, $\gamma \succeq \theta$ if $\theta \preceq \gamma$. Vector dot-product $\gamma \cdot \theta$ is max of sums, which is analogous to sum of products of standard algebra: I.e. $\gamma \cdot \theta = \max_i([\gamma]_i + [\theta]_i)$.

Given matrix $M \in \mathbb{R}^{m \times n}_{\max}$ and matrix $N \in \mathbb{R}^{n \times o}_{\max}$, matrix multiplication is defined using vector dot-products as $[MN]_{ij} = [M]_{i:} \cdot [N]_{:j}$. Similarly, matrix-vector product is given as $[M\gamma]_i = [M]_{i:} \cdot \gamma$. Two interesting properties of matrix multiplication are *linearity* and *monotonicity*. Monotonicity says if $\gamma \preceq \theta$, then $M\gamma \preceq M\theta$. With linearity, $M(c + \gamma) = c + M\gamma$ and $M(\max(\gamma, \theta)) = \max(M\gamma, M\theta)$.

4.2 Synchronous Dataflow Scenarios

A Synchronous Dataflow Graph (SDFG) [14] is a directed graph that consists of *actors* as vertices and FIFO buffer *channels* as edges. Actors communicate by sending *tokens* through their *ports*. Definition 1 formally defines SDFGs.

DEFINITION 1 (SDFG). *A SDFG $g = (A, C, I, \mathcal{X}, \mathcal{R}, \mathcal{I})$ is a tuple, comprising a set A of actors, a set $C \subseteq A \times A$ of channels , a set I of initial tokens, the worst-case execution time of an actor in time-unit $\mathcal{X} : A \rightarrow \mathbb{N}^0$, the source and destination port rates of a channel $\mathcal{R} : C \rightarrow \mathbb{N} \times \mathbb{N}$ and initial token placement $\mathcal{I} : I \rightarrow C \times \mathbb{N}$.*

A SDFG actor *fires*, i.e. starts execution, by consuming from each of its input ports as many tokens as the port rate. After a delay, given by the actor's execution time, it produces at each of its output ports as many tokens as the port rate. In SDFG schematics, black dots represent initial tokens available in channels at the start. The set of actor firings that restores the graph back to its initial token distribution is called an *iteration*. The number of actor firings in one iteration is given by the *repetition vector*, as defined in Definition 2.

DEFINITION 2 (REPETITION VECTOR). *The repetition vector of a SDFG $g = (A, C, I, \mathcal{X}, \mathcal{R}, \mathcal{I})$ is the mapping $\mathcal{V} : A \rightarrow \mathbb{N}$ such that $\mathcal{V}(a)$ is the number of firings of actor $a \in A$ within one iteration of execution of g.*

A SDFG $g = (A, C, I, \mathcal{X}, \mathcal{R}, \mathcal{I})$ is said to be *strongly connected* if there is a *path* between any two actors of g. A path is a sequence of actors $\langle a_0, a_1, \cdots a_n \rangle$ such that for $\forall i < n$, $(a_i, a_{i+1}) \in C$. A non-strongly connected SDFG consists of more than one *strongly connected component (SCC)* (defined in Definition 3).

DEFINITION 3. (STRONGLY CONNECTED COMPONENT) *A strongly connected component of SDFG $g = (A, C, I, \mathcal{X}, \mathcal{R}, \mathcal{I})$ is a maximal sub-graph of g that has a connecting path between any two actors $a, b \in A$. The set of SCCs of g is denoted as $\mathcal{C}(g)$.*

SDFGs are too static to model modern-day dynamic streaming applications, such as wireless radios. These applications have varying computation and communication characteristics that changes with the processed data. As a result, they go through different operating modes, called *scenarios* [20], depending on the input stream. However, the possible scenarios and the scenario sequences for input streams are mostly known at design time. Definition 4 defines a finite state machine on infinite words that captures all possible scenario sequences for a given set of scenarios.

DEFINITION 4 (FINITE-STATE MACHINE (FSM)). *Given a set S of scenarios, a finite state machine f on S is a tuple $f = (Q, q_0, \delta, \Psi)$. Q is a set of states, $q_0 \in Q$ is an initial state, δ is a transition between two states, $\delta \subseteq Q \times Q$, and Ψ is scenario labeling, $\Psi : Q \rightarrow S$.*

When an application operates at a given scenario, its characteristics mostly remain static. Hence, a SDFG can be used to effectively model and analyze it. A dynamic dataflow modeling approach, based on SDFG scenarios and their FSM is referred to as *FSM-based scenario-aware dataflow (FSM-SADF)* [5], as defined in Definition 5. In this paper, we use the terms scenario and SDFG interchangeably.

DEFINITION 5. (FSM-SADF) *FSM-SADF F is a tuple $F = (S, f)$. S is a set of scenarios and f is an FSM on S.*

An example FSM-SADF that consists of three scenarios is shown in Figure 2. Numbers written inside actors are worst-case execution times (WCETs). Port rates are assumed to be 1, unless otherwise indicated. While scenario $\mathbf{s}_0$ is strongly connected, $\mathbf{s}_1$ and $\mathbf{s}_2$ are not. The dashed boxes of Figure 2 show the SCCs of each scenario: $\mathcal{C}(\mathbf{s}_0) = \{\mathbf{s}_0^0\}$, $\mathcal{C}(\mathbf{s}_1) = \{\mathbf{s}_1^0, \mathbf{s}_1^1\}$ and $\mathcal{C}(\mathbf{s}_2) = \{\mathbf{s}_2^0, \mathbf{s}_2^1, \mathbf{s}_2^2\}$. SCCs are further discussed in Section 6.

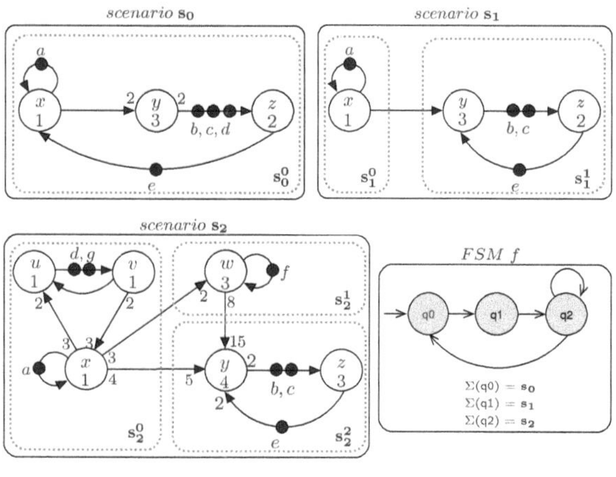

Figure 2: Example FSM-SADF

4.3 $(max, +)$ Characterization of a Scenario

The completion time of an iteration is obtained from the production times of the latest tokens at the end of the iteration. This collection of tokens is the same as the initial tokens. A **time-stamp vector** $\gamma \in \mathbb{R}^n_{\max}$ is used to record the production times of initial tokens after each iteration. Each initial token has exactly one entry in this vector.

The $(max, +)$ algebra [2] is a useful tool to compute the production times of tokens. In self-timed execution of a scenario, an actor fires as soon as all input tokens have arrived. Thus, the firing time of an actor is determined by the last arriving token, i.e. the *maximum* of the production times of all input tokens. The completion time of an actor's firing is obtained by *adding* its execution time to its start time. As a result, the entire timing behavior of a self-timed execution of a SDFG can be analyzed using $(max, +)$ expressions.

We show this with an example. Scenario $\mathbf{s}_1$ of Figure 2 has four initial tokens: $I = \{a, b, c, e\}$. We represent the time-stamp vector of iteration $k \geq \mathbb{N}^0$ of scenario $\mathbf{s}_1$ symbolically as $\gamma_k = [t_a, t_b, t_c, t_e]$. The repetition vector of scenario $\mathbf{s}_1$ equals $[1, 1, 1]$. Hence, in a single iteration, each actor fires once. After the firing of actor x, the time-stamp of token a becomes $t'_a = t_a + 1$. This can also be written as a $(max, +)$ vector dot-product as $t'_a = [1, -\infty, -\infty, -\infty] \cdot \gamma_k$. After firing of actor y, we get $t'_b = \max(t'_a + 3, t_e + 3) = \max(t_a + 4, t_e + 3)$. In vector dot-product, this becomes $t'_b = [4, -\infty, -\infty, 3] \cdot \gamma_k$. After the firing of actor z, we get $t'_e = t'_c + 2 = [-\infty, -\infty, 2, -\infty] \cdot \gamma_k$. Token b is not consumed in this iteration and at the end of the iteration this token becomes token c. Thus, $t'_c = t_b = [-\infty, 0, -\infty, -\infty] \cdot \gamma_k$. The time-stamp vector of the $(k+1)^{th}$ iteration is then given as $\gamma_{k+1} = [t'_a, t'_b, t'_c, t'_e]$, where

$$\begin{aligned} t'_a &= [1, -\infty, -\infty, -\infty] \cdot \gamma_k, \\ t'_b &= [4, -\infty, -\infty, \quad 3] \cdot \gamma_k, \\ t'_c &= [-\infty, 0, -\infty, -\infty] \cdot \gamma_k \text{ and} \\ t'_e &= [-\infty, -\infty, 2, -\infty] \cdot \gamma_k. \end{aligned}$$

This relationship between two consecutive iterations is conveniently expressed by the recurrence relation of Equation (1).

$$\gamma_{k+1} = \mathbf{M} \cdot \gamma_k \qquad (1)$$

$\mathbf{M} \in \mathbb{R}^{n \times n}_{\max}$ is referred to as the *matrix* of the scenario and has a size of $|\gamma| \times |\gamma|$. The matrix of $\mathbf{s}_1$ is given by Equation (2).

$$\mathbf{M} = \begin{bmatrix} 1 & -\infty & -\infty & -\infty \\ 4 & -\infty & -\infty & 3 \\ -\infty & 0 & -\infty & -\infty \\ -\infty & -\infty & 2 & -\infty \end{bmatrix} \qquad (2)$$

Every initial token $i \in I$ has a distinct *index* in the recurrence relation of Equation (1), as given in Definition 6.

DEFINITION 6 (INITIAL TOKEN INDEX). *Initial token index is a bijection $\zeta : I \leftrightarrow \underline{n}$, where $n = |I|$ such that for $i \in I$, $\zeta(i)$ is a row index in γ_k and a row/column index in $\mathbf{M}$.*

The matrix of a scenario is computed with a single iteration of the scenario through symbolic simulation (Algorithm 1 of [5]). An entry $[\mathbf{M}]_{\zeta(i)\zeta(j)}$ of the matrix gives the minimum timing distance between the time-stamp of token i of iteration $k+1$ and token j of iteration k; i.e. $[\mathbf{M}]_{\zeta(i)\zeta(j)} \leq [\gamma_{k+1}]_{\zeta(i)} - [\gamma_k]_{\zeta(j)}$. $[\mathbf{M}]_{\zeta(i)\zeta(j)} = -\infty$ implies there is no dependency between the two initial tokens.

5. PROBLEM DESCRIPTION

In this paper, we study the analysis of the worst-case throughput (WCT) of FSM-SADF. The analysis of FSM-SADF is challenged by three issues. 1) In distributed implementations, such as in MPSoCs, scenario executions are pipelined. Thus, multiple scenarios are concurrently active. 2) Scenarios have data dependencies between each other. This requires inter-scenario synchronization. 3) If a scenario is not *self-timed bounded*, different components of the scenario execute at different rates of iteration. This section discusses these three issues and outlines how we intend to address them. The main contributions of this paper are on the second and the third issues.

5.1 Pipelined Execution of Scenarios

For the first issue, we follow a similar strategy as in existing approaches. The techniques introduced in [5] and [6] analyse pipelined scenario executions by executing scenario sequences, specified by the FSM. The FSM can possibly specify infinitely many state sequences. An example state sequence for Figure 2 is $\tilde{q} = \langle q0, q1, q2, q2, q2, q0, q1, \cdots \rangle$.

In a sequence $\tilde{q}$, scenarios are executed one after the other. The scenario of each FSM state $q \in \tilde{q}$, i.e. $\Psi(q)$, is executed for one iteration. During the execution of a scenario, all data needed for synchronization are time-stamped with their production times. Then, the next scenario is executed, starting from these time-stamps. Therefore, data dependencies between these two consecutive scenarios are captured by the time-stamps of the synchronization data.

Figure 3 illustrates an example pipelined (overlapping) execution of a sequence that involves three scenarios $\mathbf{s}_1, \mathbf{s}_2, \mathbf{s}_3$. At time t all the three scenarios are concurrently active. The sequence has a length of 7 iterations: $\mathbf{s}_1\mathbf{s}_3\mathbf{s}_1\mathbf{s}_2\mathbf{s}_3\mathbf{s}_1\mathbf{s}_2$.

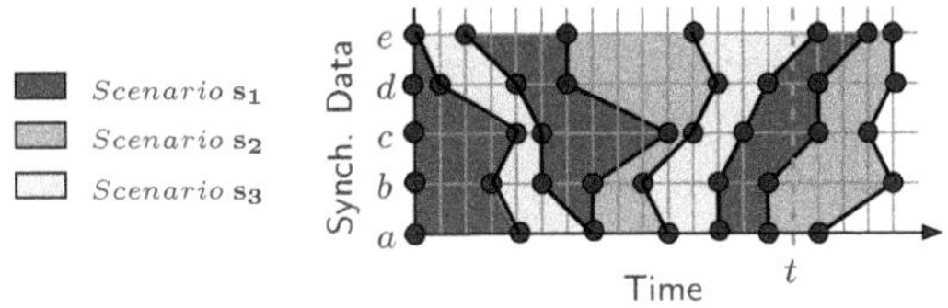

Figure 3: Example scenario sequence: $\mathbf{s}_1\mathbf{s}_3\mathbf{s}_1\mathbf{s}_2\mathbf{s}_3\mathbf{s}_1\mathbf{s}_2$

A sequence is basically formed by concatenation of cycles of the FSM. For example, the FSM of Figure 1 has three cycles. Any scenario sequence specified by this FSM is made up of the three fragments $\langle \mathbf{s}_1, \mathbf{s}_3 \rangle$, $\langle \mathbf{s}_1, \mathbf{s}_2, \mathbf{s}_4 \rangle$ and $\langle \mathbf{s}_1, \mathbf{s}_2, \mathbf{s}_2, \mathbf{s}_5 \rangle$, one for each sub-frame type.

We define the throughput of a sequence as the long-run average of completed *iterations per time-unit.* However, this long-run average does not necessarily exist for all sequences. Instead, it may bounce within a superior and inferior limiting bounds. We take the limit inferior as the WCT of a sequence. Then, we define the WCT of FSM-SADF as the minimum among the WCTs of all scenario sequences, as given by Definition 7.

DEFINITION 7. (WORST-CASE THROUGHPUT) *The worst-case throughput ρ of FSM-SADF $F = (S, f)$ is given as*

$$\rho = \min_{\forall \tilde{q}} \liminf_{k \to \infty} \frac{\tilde{q}^k}{c_{\tilde{q}^k}} \tag{3}$$

where $\tilde{q}$ is a sequence specified by FSM f, $\tilde{q}^k$ is the first $k \in \mathbb{N}$ elements of $\tilde{q}$ and $c_{\tilde{q}^k} \in \mathbb{N}$ is the completion time of $\tilde{q}^k$.

We say a computed WCT ρ_c is *conservative* if $\rho_c < \rho$ and *exact* if $\rho_c = \rho$. In Section 8, we present both exact and conservative WCT computation techniques. These techniques can also be used to derive conservative throughput bounds for sequences of finite length. In addition, the analysis approaches can be straightforwardly adapted to other definitions of throughput, such as average number of firings of a particular actor [5].

5.2 Inter-scenario Synchronization

Existing analysis techniques implicitly assume that the synchronization data between two scenarios are the *common initial tokens* they have. An initial token is common between two scenarios if it is in a *common channel.* A channel is common if it has the same source and destination actor in both scenarios. Synchronization through common initial tokens requires that 1) common channels must exist to enforce synchronization and 2) a common channel must have the same number of initial tokens in all scenarios. These are restrictive requirements for many real-life application graphs.

A simple example is the modeling of sub-frame detection in LTE (Figure 1), as discussed in Section 1. Synchronization is required to stall subsequent scenarios until the sub-frame type is detected. We cannot enforce this synchronization, since the mode detection actor (actor *md* of scenario $\mathbf{s}_1$) does not exist in other scenarios.

In this paper, we use initial token labeling to model inter-scenario synchronization. Common initial tokens are explicitly defined by their identifier (name). Two initial tokens of two different scenarios are common only if they have the same identifier. With this approach, common channels need not to have equal number of initial tokens.

5.3 Self-timed Boundedness

In compositional FSM-SADF analysis approaches, each scenario is first analysed individually. Then, performance guarantees are given for a sequence of scenarios compositionally (as also discussed in Section 8). To analyse scenarios individually, existing analysis techniques [5,6] assume scenarios are self-timed bounded. A self-timed bounded scenario requires bounded buffer sizes in a self-timed execution [7]. The time-stamp vector of a self-timed bounded scenario becomes periodic after a finite number of transient iterations. E.g. the matrix of scenario $\mathbf{s}_0$ of Figure 2 is given by Equation (4). The time-stamp vectors of the first 5 iterations are shown by the black solid lines of Figure 4, computed using the relation $\gamma_{k+1} = \mathbf{M} \cdot \gamma_k$, where $\gamma_0 = \mathbf{u}[0]$ is a zero vector.

$$\mathbf{M} = \begin{bmatrix} 2 & -\infty & -\infty & 3 & 2 \\ 5 & -\infty & -\infty & 6 & 5 \\ 5 & -\infty & -\infty & 6 & 5 \\ -\infty & -\infty & 0 & -\infty & -\infty \\ -\infty & 2 & -\infty & -\infty & -\infty \end{bmatrix} \tag{4}$$

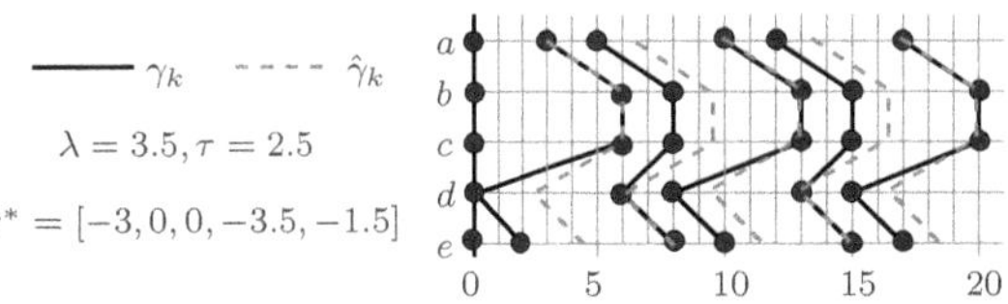

Figure 4: Time-stamp vectors of $\mathbf{s}_0$ of Figure 2

This graph becomes periodic after γ_2. The shape of the vector ($\overline{\gamma}_k$) repeats with *cyclicity* $\sigma = 2$ (i.e. every 2 iterations). In the periodic phase, it completes 2 iterations every 7 time-units. Hence, the average duration of an iteration is $\lambda = 3.5$. λ is referred to as the *period.* This periodicity is crucial to simplify the analysis into an entirely periodic pattern. The idea is to find a *delay* $\tau \in \mathbb{R}$, and a vector $\gamma^* \in \mathbb{R}^n_{\max}$, such that $\gamma_k \preceq \hat{\gamma}_k = \tau + \gamma^* + \lambda k$ for any $k > 0$. The vector $\hat{\gamma}_k$ is a **conservative linear upper-bound** to γ_k, as shown by the red dashed lines in Figure 4. An example delay τ and vector γ^* for scenario $\mathbf{s}_0$ are shown in Figure 4.

However, this periodic behavior does not hold for non-self-timed bounded scenarios. Consider scenario $\mathbf{s}_1$ of Figure 2. The token production rate of channel (x, y) is faster than the consumption rate. Thus, the self-timed execution leads to an increasing accumulation of tokens in channel (x, y). Figure 5 shows the time-stamp vectors for the first 10 iterations of scenario $\mathbf{s}_1$. Scenario $\mathbf{s}_1$ has two SCCs, as shown in Figure 2. SCC $\mathbf{s}_1^0$ runs at 1 iteration/time-unit, whereas SCC $\mathbf{s}_1^1$ runs at 0.6 iteration/time-unit. This difference causes the time-stamps of tokens b, c, e to continuously diverge from token a. Thus, the different components of the scenario run at different rates of iterations. As a result, a recurrent vector does not exist and the algorithms of [5] cannot find parameters for linear upper-bound characterization.

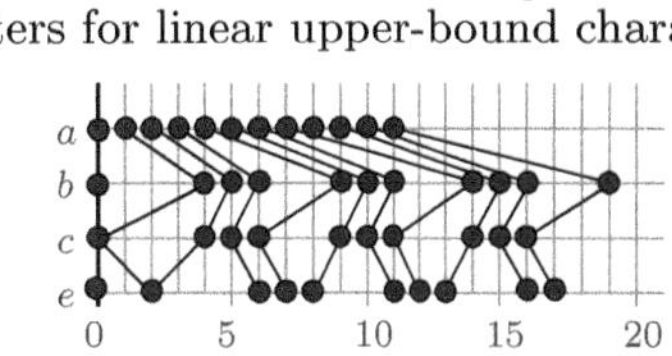

Figure 5: Time-stamp vectors of $\mathbf{s}_1$ of Figure 2

Limiting FSM-SADF analysis only to self-timed bounded scenarios is restrictive. Though strong-connectedness is a sufficient condition for self-timed boundedness [7], FSM-SADF scenarios of many applications are non-strongly connected (cf. LTE in Section 1 and WLAN in Section 9).

These scenarios can potentially be non-self-timed bounded. Unlike SDF, a non-self-timed bounded scenario is not necessarily a problem to unbounded buffering in FSM-SADF. A channel with faster production rate in one scenario may be compensated by a faster consumption rate in another scenario, resulting in the net effect of a bounded channel.

One solution to the self-timed boundedness issue is converting scenarios to strongly connected graphs. However, adding extra channels and initial tokens without compromising the temporal and functional behavior of the FSM-SADF is not trivial. Scenarios of an *architecture-aware* FSM-SADF may also be non-strongly connected. An architecture-aware FSM-SADF captures architectural aspects of a system, such as buffer sizes of channels, in the application model [19]. Buffer-size modeling introduces a backward channel with initial-tokens between actors [18]. However, dataflow components that model other system aspects such as inter-scenario synchronization [17] do not need such backward channels. Therefore, buffer-size modeling does not always guarantee strong-connectedness. Besides, no solution exists to date for analyzing buffer-sizing in FSM-SADF [19].

In this work, we analyse scenarios without requiring strong-connectedness. In the remainder of this paper, we present FSM-SADF analysis in three steps. 1) Section 6 characterizes a scenario in terms of SCCs. 2) Section 7 computes the completion times of iterations of a scenario. 3) Section 8 generalizes the single scenario solution to a set of scenarios.

6. CONDENSATION GRAPH

Each SCC of a scenario is self-timed bounded. Hence, the conservative upper-bound characterization, discussed in Section 5.3, is applicable. Thus, each SCC $\mathbf{c}$ has a distinct period $\lambda_{\mathbf{c}} \in \mathbb{R}_{\max}$. If each SCC of scenario $\mathbf{s}$ is contracted into a single node, a directed acyclic graph (DAG) is obtained. Each node of the DAG is then associated with a SCC. Define the period of node n of the DAG as $\lambda_n \stackrel{\text{def}}{=} rep(\mathbf{c}) \times \lambda_{\mathbf{c}}$, where $\mathbf{c}$ is the SCC of node n and $rep(\mathbf{c})$ is the **repetition** of SCC $\mathbf{c}$, defined as the number of iterations of $\mathbf{c}$ within one iteration of scenario $\mathbf{s}$.

Repetition is given as $rep(\mathbf{c}) = \frac{\mathcal{V}_{\mathbf{s}}(a)}{\mathcal{V}_{\mathbf{c}}(a)}$, where $\mathcal{V}_{\mathbf{s}}$ is the repetition vector of scenario $\mathbf{s}$, $\mathcal{V}_{\mathbf{c}}$ is the repetition vector of $\mathbf{c}$ and a is any actor of $\mathbf{c}$. E.g. the repetition vector of scenario $\mathbf{s}_2$ of Figure 2 is $\mathcal{V} = \{(u, 15), (v, 15), (w, 15), (x, 10), (y, 8), (z, 16)\}$. The repetition vector of SCC $\mathbf{s}_2^0$ is $\mathcal{V}_{\mathbf{c}} = \{(u, 3), (v, 3), (x, 2)\}$. Hence, $\mathbf{s}_2^0$ has a repetition of 5.

We next partition a scenario into a set of maximal *self-timed bounded components (STBCs)*. We achieve this through repetitive SCC grouping. A STBC is not necessarily strongly-connected but it is always self-timed bounded.

Consider an edge (m, n) of the DAG. The maximum rate at which the SCC of node n completes iterations of the scenario is $\frac{1}{\lambda_n}$ iterations per time-unit. However, if $\lambda_m \geq \lambda_n$, the SCC of n cannot run faster than the SCC of m in the execution of the scenario. This is because the SCC of n consumes input tokens that are produced by the SCC of m. As a result, the SCC of node n runs at the same rate as the SCC of node m. Combining these two SCCs, as per their original connections in the scenario, gives a STBC $\mathbf{c}_{mn}$. We group the two nodes m and n into one node mn. Node mn is now associated with the STBC $\mathbf{c}_{mn}$. The period of node mn is the slower of the the two SCCs, hence $\lambda_{mn} = \lambda_m$.

Repetitive grouping of nodes in such a manner terminates when $\lambda_m < \lambda_n$ for any edge (m, n) of the DAG. This operation partitions the scenario into a set of STBCs. We denote the set of STBCs of scenario $\mathbf{s}$ as $\mathcal{BC}(\mathbf{s})$.

After such node grouping, some channels of the scenario are left that are not part of any STBC but only connect the different STBCs. We refer to such channels as *feed-forward channels*, denoted as $\mathcal{F}(\mathbf{s})$. The resulting DAG after the repetitive node grouping is referred to as *condensation graph*, as defined in Definition 8.

DEFINITION 8 (CONDENSATION GRAPH). *Condensation graph of SDFG* $\mathbf{s}$ *is the tuple* $\mathcal{CG}(\mathbf{s}) = (V, E, \Gamma, \Pi)$, *where* V *denotes a set of vertices,* $E \subseteq V \times V$ *denotes a set of edges between vertices,* $\Gamma : V \leftrightarrow \mathcal{BC}(\mathbf{s})$ *is vertex labeling and* $\Pi : E \leftrightarrow \mathcal{F}(\mathbf{s})$ *is edge to feed-forward channel labeling.*

The feed-forward channels and condensation graphs of the FSM-SADF scenarios of Figure 2 are shown in Figure 6.

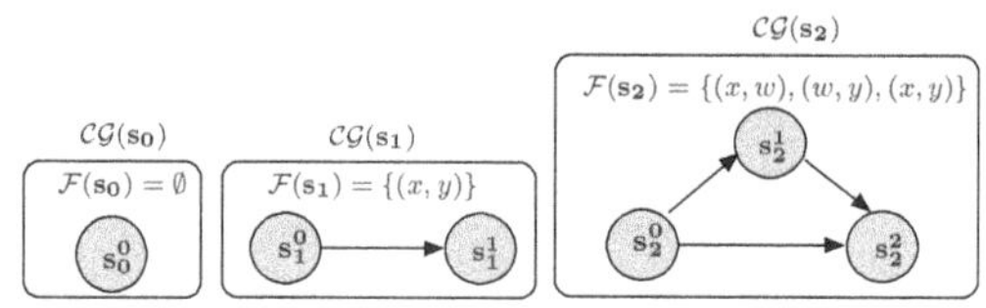

Figure 6: Condensation graphs of Figure 2

We say initial token $t \in I$ belongs to vertex v_t iff t is either in STBC $\Gamma(v_t)$ or is on an outgoing feed-forward channel of $\Gamma(v_t)$. We use the *levels of vertices* to determine dependencies between initial tokens. The level of a vertex is defined inductively as follows: for a root vertex, $level(v) = 0$ and for any other vertex, $level(v) = 1 + \max_{v \in v^-} level(v)$, where v^- is the set of all direct predecessors of v.

If $level(v_t) < level(v_u)$ then initial token t has no dependency from initial token u. Hence, the $(max, +)$ matrix of the scenario has $[\mathbf{M}]_{\zeta(t)\zeta(u)} = -\infty$, as discussed in Section 4.3. The levels of vertices are also used to construct a *topological order* of the condensation graph, as defined by Definition 9.

DEFINITION 9. (TOPOLOGICAL ORDER) *A topological order of* $\mathcal{CG}(\mathbf{s})$ *is a linear ordering of its vertices* $\langle v^1, v^2, \cdots, v^n \rangle$, *such that* v^i *comes before* v^j *only if* $level(v^i) \leq level(v^j)$, *where for* $i \in \mathbb{N}$, v^i *denotes the* i^{th} *vertex in the order.*

We use topological order of vertices to present the matrix of a scenario in a lower triangular form. Shuffle time-stamp vector γ_k and matrix $\mathbf{M}$ based on a given topological order: I.e. for any two initial tokens t and u in two different STBCs, assign $\zeta(t) < \zeta(u)$ only if $level(v_t) \leq level(v_u)$. As a result, the indices of those initial tokens that belong to the same vertex becomes consecutive. Hence, we can partition γ_k into a set of n disjoint sub-vectors $\langle \gamma_k^1, \gamma_k^2, \cdots, \gamma_k^n \rangle$, where γ_k^i denotes the sub-vector of vertex v^i. Similarly, matrix $\mathbf{M}$ is also partitioned into $n \times n$ sub-matrices. The resulting matrix has a triangular form, as shown in the recurrence relation of Equation (5).

$$\begin{bmatrix} \gamma_{k+1}^1 \\ \gamma_{k+1}^2 \\ \vdots \\ \gamma_{k+1}^n \end{bmatrix} = \begin{bmatrix} \mathbf{M}^{11} & -\infty & \cdots & -\infty \\ \mathbf{M}^{21} & \mathbf{M}^{22} & \cdots & -\infty \\ \vdots & \vdots & \ddots & \vdots \\ \mathbf{M}^{n1} & \mathbf{M}^{n2} & \cdots & \mathbf{M}^{nn} \end{bmatrix} \cdot \begin{bmatrix} \gamma_k^1 \\ \gamma_k^2 \\ \vdots \\ \gamma_k^n \end{bmatrix} \quad (5)$$

The dimension of sub-matrix $\mathbf{M}^{ij}$ is $m \times n$ where $m = |\gamma_k^i|$ and $n = |\gamma_k^j|$. In Equation (5), $-\infty$ represents a sub-matrix whose entries are all $-\infty$. Sub-matrices on the diagonal, i.e. $\mathbf{M}^{ii}$, can be computed from the matrices of the STBCs of the scenario. Given matrix $\mathbf{M}_{\mathbf{c}_i}$ of STBC $\mathbf{c}_i = \Gamma(v^i)$, $\mathbf{M}^{ii}$ is computed by multiplying $\mathbf{M}_{\mathbf{c}_i}$ with itself $rep(c_i)$ times so that it accounts for a complete iteration of the scenario.

E.g. the partitioning of scenario $\mathbf{s}_1$ of Figure 2 (whose matrix discussed in Section 4.3) is given in Equation (6).

$$\begin{bmatrix} t'_a \\ t'_b \\ t'_c \\ t'_d \end{bmatrix} = \begin{bmatrix} 1 & -\infty & -\infty & -\infty \\ 4 & -\infty & -\infty & 3 \\ -\infty & 0 & -\infty & -\infty \\ -\infty & -\infty & 2 & -\infty \end{bmatrix} \cdot \begin{bmatrix} t_a \\ t_b \\ t_c \\ t_d \end{bmatrix} \quad (6)$$

Any sub-vector γ^i_{k+1} is related to other sub-vectors as given by Equation (7), derived directly from Equation (5).

$$\begin{aligned} \gamma^i_{k+1} &= \max\left(\mathbf{M}^{i1} \cdot \gamma^1_k,\ \mathbf{M}^{i2} \cdot \gamma^2_k,\ \cdots,\ \mathbf{M}^{in} \cdot \gamma^n_k\right) \\ &= \max\left(\max_{j=1}^{i-1}\left(\mathbf{M}^{ij} \cdot \gamma^j_k\right),\ \mathbf{M}^{ii} \cdot \gamma^i_k\right) \quad (7) \end{aligned}$$

The term $\max_{j=1}^{i-1}\left(\mathbf{M}^{ij} \cdot \gamma^j_k\right)$ of Equation (7) represents the data dependencies of vertex v^i with all its predecessors in the topological order. Equation (7) is a valuable relation to explain a periodic behavior in non-self-timed bounded scenarios, discussed next in Section 7.

7. ANALYZING A SINGLE SCENARIO

In this section, we derive conservative upper-bounds to iterations of a scenario ($\hat{\gamma}_k$), as discussed in Section 5.3. We present a generalized approach that allows analysing any arbitrary scenario, without requiring self-timed boundedness. A valuable concept in our approach is the *periodicity* of a (non-strongly connected) scenario in a self-timed execution.

The self-timed execution of a SDFG $g = (A, C, I, \mathcal{X}, \mathcal{R}, \mathcal{I})$ enters a periodic phase after a finite number of transient iterations. In the periodic phase, the timing distance between consecutive time-stamp vectors $\Delta_{k+1} = \gamma_{k+1} - \gamma_k$ becomes periodic; I.e. Δ_{k+1} repeats every $\sigma \in \mathbb{N}$ iterations. This periodic behavior is intuitively explained as follows.

Any vertex of the condensation graph $\mathcal{CG}(g)$ is slower than any of its predecessors. This implies that in a self-timed execution of the scenario, tokens increasingly accumulate in all feed-forward channels. Such token accumulations decouple the executions of consecutive vertices. Consequently, the STBC of each vertex executes independently, after a finite number of transient iterations.

When a vertex v_i enters the independent execution phase, it has no dependencies with its predecessor vertices. Therefore Equation (7) becomes $\gamma^i_{k+1} = \mathbf{M}^{ii} \cdot \gamma^i_k$. Eventually, the entire γ_k attains periodicity as given by Equation 8.

$$\forall k \geq p, \quad \gamma_{k+\sigma} = \gamma_k + \sigma\eta. \quad (8)$$

where $p \in \mathbb{N}$ is the first iteration of the periodic phase, $\sigma \in \mathbb{N}$ is the LCM of the cyclicities of the STBCs and vector $\eta \in \mathbb{R}^n_{\max}$ is the collection of the periods of the vertices of the condensation graph, as given by Equation (9), where v_i is the vertex of initial token $i \in I$.

$$[\eta]_{\varsigma(i)} = \lambda_{v_i} \quad (9)$$

The vector η is called *cycle-time vector* in $(max, +)$ algebra [10]. It indicates the growth rate of a vector in a recurrence relation of the form of Equation 1. The cycle-time vector of a regular matrix is unique and finite [10]. The maximum entry of η, $\|\eta\|$ is the period of the slowest vertex. Hence, the worst-case throughput of a scenario is given as $\frac{1}{\|\eta\|}$ iterations/time-unit. E.g. scenario $\mathbf{s}_1$ of Figure 2 has $\eta = [1, 1.667, 1.667, 1.667]$. The maximum entry $\|\eta\| = 1.667$ is the period of vertex $\mathbf{s}^1_1$, which is the slowest of the two vertices of scenario $\mathbf{s}_1$.

As in the case of self-timed bounded scenarios (Section 5.3), a conservative upper-bound $\hat{\gamma}_k$ can also be computed for non-self-timed bounded scenarios, as given by Equation (10). With such conservative characterization, we can derive a bound to the finishing time of any iteration $k > 0$.

$$\gamma_k \preceq \hat{\gamma}_k = \mathbf{u}[\tau] + \gamma^* + k\eta \quad (10)$$

We refer to $\tau \in \mathbb{R}$ as *delay* and $\gamma^* \in \mathbb{R}^n_{\max}$ as *initial vector.* To compute these two parameters, we use the concept of *generalized eigenmode* from $(max, +)$ algebra [10], defined in Definition 10. Generalized eigenmode is a generalization of eigenvectors to reducible $(max, +)$ matrices, which are matrices of non-strongly connected graphs.

DEFINITION 10. (GENERALIZED EIGENMODE) *Given the cycle-time vector η of matrix $\mathbf{M}$, a generalized eigenmode of $\mathbf{M}$ is a pair $(\eta, \nu) \in \mathbb{R}^n_{\max} \times \mathbb{R}^n_{\max}$ such that for any $p \in \mathbb{N}^0$, $\mathbf{M}(p\eta + \nu) = (p+1)\eta + \nu$.*

The generalized eigenmode implies that if we execute the recurrence relation $\gamma'_k = \mathbf{M}\gamma'_{k-1}$ starting from $\gamma'_0 = \nu$, the vectors advance exactly by η, i.e. $\gamma'_{k+1} - \gamma'_k = \eta$. This makes ν a suitable candidate for initial vector γ^*, because the average difference between consecutive iterations in the periodic phase is also equal to η (cf. Equation (8)). Thus, these vectors (γ'_k) can be upper-bounds to γ_k if shifted sufficiently. Delay τ is such a shifting distance, i.e. $\gamma_k \preceq \tau + \gamma'_k$. A tight delay, however, is key to avoid overly pessimistic analysis.

The generalized eigenvector of a matrix is not unique. Lemma 1 presents one approach for computing ν using any σ consecutive iterations in the periodic phase.

LEMMA 1. (GENERALIZED EIGENVECTOR) *Let γ_k where $1 \leq k \leq \sigma$ be a time-stamp vector in the periodic phase, i.e. $\gamma_{\sigma+1} = \gamma_1 + \sigma\eta$. Then $\nu = \max_{1 \leq k \leq \sigma}(\gamma_k - k\eta + \sigma\eta)$ is a generalized eigenvector.*

PROOF. Define $x \stackrel{\text{def}}{=} \mathbf{M}(p\eta + \nu)$. Then, substitute the term $\nu = \max_{1 \leq k \leq \sigma}(\gamma_k - k\eta + \sigma\eta)$ in x. Applying multiplication linearity gives $x = \max_{1 \leq k \leq \sigma} \mathbf{M}(\gamma_k - k\eta + \sigma\eta + p\eta)$. This evaluates to $x = \max_{1 \leq k \leq \sigma} \mathbf{M}\gamma_k - k\eta + \sigma\eta + p\eta$, since if $i < j$ then $c[\eta]_i \leq c[\eta]_j$ for any $c \in \mathbb{N}^0$, and in the periodic phase, $\max_{j=1}^{i-1}[\mathbf{M}]_{ij} \cdot \gamma^j_k \preceq [\mathbf{M}]_{ii} \cdot \gamma^i_k$. We then get $x = \max_{1 \leq k \leq \sigma} \gamma_{k+1} - k\eta + \sigma\eta + p\eta$, using recurrence relation of Equation (1). Adding $\eta - \eta$ and following basic algebric steps gives $x = (p+1)\eta + \max_{1 \leq k \leq \sigma} \gamma_{k+1} - (k+1)\eta + \sigma\eta$. Then, $x = (p+1)\eta + \max_{1 \leq k \leq \sigma} \gamma_k - k\eta + \sigma\eta$, using the periodic property $\gamma_{\sigma+1} = \gamma_1 + \sigma\eta$. This gives $x = (p+1)\eta + \nu$ and hence, (η, ν) is a generalized eigenmode by Definition 10. □

Algorithm 1 Compute delay τ

```
ComputeDelay(η, γ_0, γ*)
k := 0, τ := −∞, γ̃ := ∅,
(γ_k, δ_k) := (γ_0, u[−∞])
loop
    γ̃ := γ̃ ∪ {(γ_k, δ_k)}, k := k + 1
    γ_k := M · γ_{k−1}
    δ_k := γ_k − γ_{k−1}
    τ := max(τ, ||γ_k − γ* − kη||)
    if ∃(γ_m, δ_m) ∈ γ̃ : δ_k = δ_m then
        if γ_k − γ_m = (k − m) · η then
            return τ
        end if
    end if
end loop
```

An algorithm for computing a delay τ from a given γ^* and η is given in Algorithm 1. It finds a delay $\tau \in \mathbb{R}$ that satisfies Equation (11) that is derived from Equation (10).

$$\mathbf{u}[\tau] \succeq \gamma_k - \gamma^* - k\eta \tag{11}$$

The algorithm executes the recurrence relation (line 6) of Equation (1) until the periodic phase is detected (lines 9-10). It tracks the difference vector (line 7) to detect the periodic phase. After the periodic phase is reached, τ does not change and therefore, the algorithm stops.

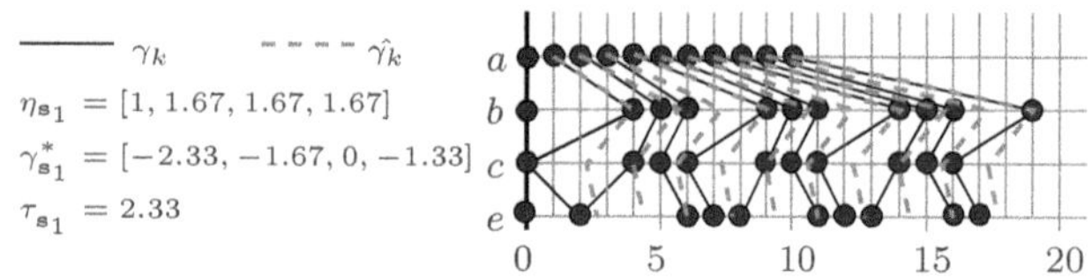

Figure 7: Time-stamp vectors of $\mathbf{s}_1$ of Figure 2

Figure 7 shows the conservative upper-bounds ($\hat{\gamma}_k$) of time-stamp vectors of Figure 5 (scenario $\mathbf{s}_1$). The initial vector $\gamma^*_{\mathbf{s}_1}$ and delay $\tau_{\mathbf{s}_1}$ are computed by Lemma 1 and Algorithm 1, respectively. Using such conservative upper-bounds for every individual scenario, we can reason about completion times of iterations irrespective of the scenario sequence they are executed in, as discussed next in Section 8.

8. FSM-SADF THROUGHPUT ANALYSIS

Execution of FSM-SADF is execution of the possible scenario sequences specified by the FSM. In the execution of a sequence, each scenario is executed for one iteration. The end of the kth iteration is marked by time-stamp vector γ_k, which is used as a starting vector for the $(k+1)^{th}$ iteration. This means, $\gamma_{k+1} = \mathbf{M_s} \cdot \gamma_k$ where $\mathbf{M_s}$ is the $(max, +)$ matrix of the scenario at the $(k+1)^{th}$ iteration. In this section, we analyse the worst-case throughput of FSM-SADF, as given by Definition 7. Section 8.1 defines time-stamp vector of FSM-SADF. Section 8.2 and 8.3 present conservative and exact analysis techniques, respectively.

8.1 Time-stamp Vector of an FSM-SADF

The scenarios of an FSM-SADF can have different sets of initial tokens (i.e. I of Definition 1). If so, their respective matrices have inconsistent dimensions for the recurrence relation, $\gamma_{k+1} = \mathbf{M_s} \cdot \gamma_k$. Hence, we need to extend the matrix of each scenario $\mathbf{s}$ to accommodate those initial tokens that exist in other scenarios but not in $\mathbf{s}$.

Denote the set of initial tokens of scenario $\mathbf{s}$ as $I_\mathbf{s}$. Denote the set of initial tokens of FSM-SADF $F = (S, f)$ as $I_F = \bigcup_{\forall \mathbf{s} \in S} I_\mathbf{s}$. Similar to Definition 6, associate indices to initial tokens; $\zeta_F : I_F \leftrightarrow \underline{n}$, where $n = |I_F|$. The time-stamp vector of F is then the vector $\gamma_k \in \mathbb{R}^n_{\max}$ that has exactly one row for every initial token $i \in I_F$ at index $\zeta_F(i)$.

A *super-matrix* of scenario $\mathbf{s}$, $\mathbf{M}^F_\mathbf{s} \in \mathbb{R}^{n \times n}_{\max}$, is constructed from the original $(max, +)$ matrix of $\mathbf{s}$, $\mathbf{M_s}$, as given by Equation (12). $\mathbf{M}^F_\mathbf{s}$ accommodates every initial token $i \in I_F$. When scenario $\mathbf{s}$ is executed at some iteration k, the super-matrix $\mathbf{M}^F_\mathbf{s}$ enables to preserve the time-stamps of every initial token $i \in I_F \backslash I_\mathbf{s}$ for subsequent iterations (beyond k).

$$[\mathbf{M}^F_\mathbf{s}]_{\zeta_F(i)\zeta_F(j)} = \begin{cases} [\mathbf{M_s}]_{\zeta_\mathbf{s}(i)\zeta_\mathbf{s}(j)} & i, j \in I_\mathbf{s} \\ 0 & i = j \wedge i, j \in I_F \backslash I_\mathbf{s} \\ -\infty & i \neq j \wedge i \in I_F \backslash I_\mathbf{s} \vee j \in I_F \backslash I_\mathbf{s} \end{cases} \tag{12}$$

E.g. the initial tokens of the scenarios of Figure 2 are $I_{\mathbf{s}_0} = \{a, b, c, d, e\}$, $I_{\mathbf{s}_1} = \{a, b, c, e\}$ and $I_{\mathbf{s}_2} = \{a, b, c, d, e, f, g\}$. Therefore, $I_F = \{a, b, c, d, e, f, g\}$.

Extending the matrix of scenario $\mathbf{s}_1$ (Equation 2) to accommodate initial tokens $I_F \backslash I_{\mathbf{s}_1} = \{d, f, g\}$ yields matrix $\mathbf{M}^F_{\mathbf{s}_1}$ of Equation (13). The indices of initial tokens of $\mathbf{M}^F_{\mathbf{s}_1}$ are $\zeta_F = \{(a, 1), (b, 2), (c, 3), (d, 4), (e, 5), (f, 6), (g, 7)\}$. Executing scenario $\mathbf{s}_1$ (i.e $\gamma_{k+1} = \mathbf{M}^F_{\mathbf{s}_1} \cdot \gamma_k$) preserves the time-stamps of tokens $\{d, f, g\}$, as $[\gamma_k]_i = [\gamma_{k+1}]_i$ for $i \in \{4, 6, 7\}$.

$$\mathbf{M}^F_{\mathbf{s}_1} = \begin{bmatrix} 1 & -\infty & -\infty & -\infty & -\infty & -\infty & -\infty \\ 4 & -\infty & -\infty & -\infty & 3 & -\infty & -\infty \\ -\infty & 0 & -\infty & -\infty & -\infty & -\infty & -\infty \\ -\infty & -\infty & -\infty & 0 & -\infty & -\infty & -\infty \\ -\infty & -\infty & 2 & -\infty & -\infty & -\infty & -\infty \\ -\infty & -\infty & -\infty & -\infty & -\infty & 0 & -\infty \\ -\infty & -\infty & -\infty & -\infty & -\infty & -\infty & 0 \end{bmatrix} \tag{13}$$

8.2 Conservative Worst-Case Throughput

In this section, we present three different conservative WCT analysis techniques. The WCT of FSM-SADF is the minimum among the WCTs of the possible scenario sequences, as given by Definition 7. The WCT of a sequence is defined as the minimum long-run average of completed iterations per time-unit. The FSM can potentially specify infinitely many scenario sequences. However, all sequences are basically formed by concatenation of the cycles of the FSM. Hence, a conservative WCT of FSM-SADF can be computed by a maximum cycle mean (MCM) analysis on the FSM. For this purpose, each FSM state $q \in Q$ is assigned a weight $w_{\Psi(q)} \in \mathbb{N}$. A valid weight is a conservative bound to the duration of one iteration of the scenario of q.

This narrows down the WCT analysis problem to finding such conservative bounds of scenarios. One simple approach is to abstract from scenario transitions; i.e to derive a bound for one iteration of a scenario, regardless of other scenarios in the FSM-SADF.

Evaluating Equation (10) for the first iteration ($k = 1$) gives $\gamma_1 = \mathbf{M}^F_\mathbf{s} \gamma_0 \preceq \mathbf{u}[\tau_\mathbf{s}] + \gamma^*_\mathbf{s} + \eta_\mathbf{s}$, where $\gamma_0 = \mathbf{u}[0]$ and $\eta_\mathbf{s}$, $\gamma^*_\mathbf{s}$ and $\tau_\mathbf{s}$ are the cycle-time vector, the generalized eigenvector and delay of scenario $\mathbf{s} \in S$, computed by Equation 9, Lemma 1 and Algorithm 1, respectively. Let scenario $\mathbf{s}$ is executed at iteration k of a scenario sequence specified by the FSM. Generally, $\bar{\gamma}_{k-1} \preceq \gamma_0$ since all entries of the normalized vector $\bar{\gamma}_{k-1}$ are less than or equal to 0. From monotonicity, we have $\mathbf{M}^F_\mathbf{s} \bar{\gamma}_{k-1} \preceq \mathbf{M}^F_\mathbf{s} \gamma_0$. Thus, $\mathbf{M}^F_\mathbf{s} \bar{\gamma}_{k-1} \preceq \mathbf{u}[\tau_\mathbf{s}] + \gamma^*_\mathbf{s} + \eta_\mathbf{s}$. Thus, the maximum entries are related as $\|\mathbf{M}^F_\mathbf{s} \bar{\gamma}_{k-1}\| \leq \|\mathbf{u}[\tau_\mathbf{s}] + \gamma^*_\mathbf{s} + \eta_\mathbf{s}\|$.

The duration of iteration k (i.e. the distance between the finishing times of iteration k and $k-1$) equals $\|\mathbf{M}^F_\mathbf{s} \bar{\gamma}_{k-1}\|$. As a result, the bound to the first iteration of scenario $\mathbf{s}$ i.e. $w_\mathbf{s} = \|\mathbf{u}[\tau_\mathbf{s}] + \gamma^*_\mathbf{s} + \eta_\mathbf{s}\|$ is a bound to an iteration of scenario $\mathbf{s}$ at any iteration k, in any scenario sequence (since we have no assumptions regarding the scenario of iteration $k-1$).

The inverse of the maximum among all such weights is a valid WCT of FSM-SADF. We refer to this technique as the *scenario graph* approach and the WCT ρ_{sg} is given as $\rho^{-1}_{sg} = \max_{\mathbf{s} \in S} w_\mathbf{s}$. We choose this simple computation, instead of a MCM analysis, as it scales very well for large graphs, as shown later in Section 9.3. However, this may make the analysis overly pessimistic.

A more accurate analysis is obtained if conservative bounds of scenarios are computed, tailored to the scenarios in the FSM-SADF. Define a global initial vector $\gamma^*_S = \max_{\mathbf{s} \in S} \gamma^*_\mathbf{s}$, where $\gamma^*_\mathbf{s}$ is the generalized eigenvector of scenario $\mathbf{s} \in S$, computed by Lemma 1. For each scenario $\mathbf{s}$, compute delay $\tau_\mathbf{s}$ (Algorithm 1) using the cycle-time vector of the scenario

$\eta_{\mathbf{s}}$ and γ^*_S. Following a similar argument as in the scenario graph approach, we get that $w_{\mathbf{s}} = \|\mathbf{u}[\tau_{\mathbf{s}}]+\gamma^*_S+\eta_{\mathbf{s}}\|$ is a bound to a single iteration of scenario $\mathbf{s}$ at any iteration k, in any scenario sequence. The MCM of the FSM gives a valid WCT ρ_{gv}, referred to as *global initial vector* approach, as given by Equation (14). C denotes the set of cycles of FSM f. A cycle $c \in C$ is a sequence of states $\langle q_{i+0}, q_{i+1}, \cdots, q_{i+n}, q_{i+0}\rangle$, such that there exits a transition between consecutive states and no state appears more than once.

$$\frac{1}{\rho_{gv}} = \max_{c \in C} \frac{1}{|c|} \sum_{\forall q \in c} w_{\Psi(q)} \tag{14}$$

The global initial vector approach can also be further refined by computing local vectors $\gamma^*_{\mathbf{rs}} = \max(\gamma^*_{\mathbf{r}}, \gamma^*_{\mathbf{s}})$ between every FSM transition $(p, q) \in \delta$, where $\mathbf{r} = \Psi(p)$ and $\mathbf{s} = \Psi(q)$. For FSM transition (p, q), compute delay $\tau_{\mathbf{rs}}$ (Algorithm 1) using cycle-time vector $\eta_{\mathbf{s}}$ and $\gamma^*_{\mathbf{rs}}$. Hence, $w_{\mathbf{rs}} = \|\mathbf{u}[\tau_{\mathbf{rs}}] + \gamma^*_{\mathbf{rs}} + \eta_{\mathbf{s}}\|$ is a bound to a single iteration of scenario $\mathbf{s}$ in any scenario transition $\mathbf{r}$ to $\mathbf{s}$, in any scenario sequence. The MCM of the FSM gives a valid WCT referred to as *local initial vector* approach, as given by Equation (15), where p is the preceeding FSM state of q in cycle c.

$$\frac{1}{\rho_{lv}} = \max_{c \in C} \frac{1}{|c|} \sum_{\forall q \in c} w_{\Psi(p)\Psi(q)} \tag{15}$$

8.3 Exact Worst-Case Throughput

Two exact WCT computation techniques for FSM-SADF, whose scenarios are all self-timed bounded, are presented in [6]. In this section, we show that one of these techniques is applicable to compute the exact WCT of FSM-SADF whose scenarios are possibly non-self-timed bounded. This technique is known by the name $(max, +)$ *automaton*. It is based on *timed-event graphs* of the scenarios of the FSM-SADF.

A timed-event graph (TEG) is a weighted directed graph representation of a $(max, +)$ matrix. It depicts the timing distance between initial tokens. It is also known as *communication graph* in $(max, +)$ literature [10]. The TEG of an $n \times n$ matrix has n nodes. The graph has an edge from node i to node j if $[\mathbf{M}]_{ij} \neq -\infty$ and the weight of the edge equals $[\mathbf{M}]_{ij}$. The TEG of Equation (2) is shown in Figure 8.

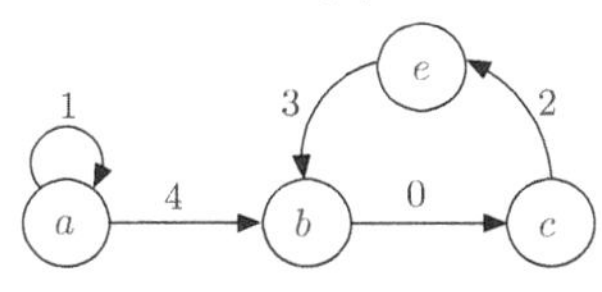

Figure 8: Timed-event graph of Equation (2)

According to the $(max, +)$ automaton technique, the worst-case throughput of an FSM-SADF is equal to the MCM of the *throughput graph* of the FSM-SADF. The throughput graph $\mathbf{G} = (V, E)$ is a weighted directed graph that is constructed from the TEGs of the scenarios and the FSM of the FSM-SADF.

First, for each FSM state $q \in Q$, place the TEG of its scenario, $\Psi(q)$. Then, for every fsm transition $(p, q) \in \delta$, add edge from node i of the TEG of $\Psi(p)$ to node j of the TEG of $\Psi(q)$ if $[\mathbf{M}^F_{\Psi(q)}]_{\zeta_F(j)\zeta_F(i)} \neq -\infty$. Set the weight of edge $e = (i, j)$ to $w(e) = [\mathbf{M}^F_{\Psi(q)}]_{\zeta_F(j)\zeta_F(i)}$.

The weight of an edge is the minimum timing distance between two initial tokens in consecutive iterations. Hence, it gives the length of an iteration relative to these two dependent initial tokens. For infinitely long execution of the FSM-SADF (as in streaming applications), almost all such distances reside within the cycles of the throughput graph. Therefore, the inverse of the maximum average weight among all cycles gives the exact WCT as defined in Definition 7.

The exact WCT of FSM-SADF is then given by the MCM of the throughput graph as given in Equation 16, where C denotes the set of all cycles in the throughput graph and E^c denotes the set of edges in a cycle.

$$\frac{1}{\rho_{ma}} = \max_{c \in C} \frac{1}{|E^c|} \sum_{\forall e \in E^c} w(e) \tag{16}$$

Unlike the conservative approaches of Section 8.2, Equation 16 gives the exact WCT that may occur in the execution of the FSM-SADF. The improvement in accuracy, however, comes at a price of run-time, as discussed next in Section 9.

9. EXPERIMENTAL RESULTS

We have implemented the presented analysis techniques in the publicly available dataflow toolset, SDF3 [1]. In this section, we demonstrate the applicability of these techniques and evaluate their scalability. We present the FSM-SADF model of a radio application in Section 9.1. We discuss the conservativeness of the analysis techniques in Section 9.2. We evaluate their scalability for large graphs in Section 9.3. Finally, we summarize main observations in Section 9.4.

9.1 Wireless LAN (WLAN)

Figure 9 depicts an FSM-SADF model of WLAN 802.11a baseband (physical layer) processing. This model is based on the discussion in [15]. The packet decoding consists of 4 scenarios. Once a packet is received, scenario $\mathbf{s}_1$ executes repeatedly until synchronization succeeds. Then, scenario $\mathbf{s}_2$ decodes the packet header to determine the size of the payload. The payload can vary from 1 to 256 OFDM symbols. After header decoding, scenario $\mathbf{s}_3$ is executed as many times as the number of OFDM symbols. The FSM approximates this conservatively by allowing an arbitrary number of payload symbols. Finally, scenario $\mathbf{s}_4$ preforms cyclic redundancy check and sends an acknowledgement. In Figure 9, all port rates are equal to one. Actors *dda*3 and *dda*4 model inter-scenario synchronizations.

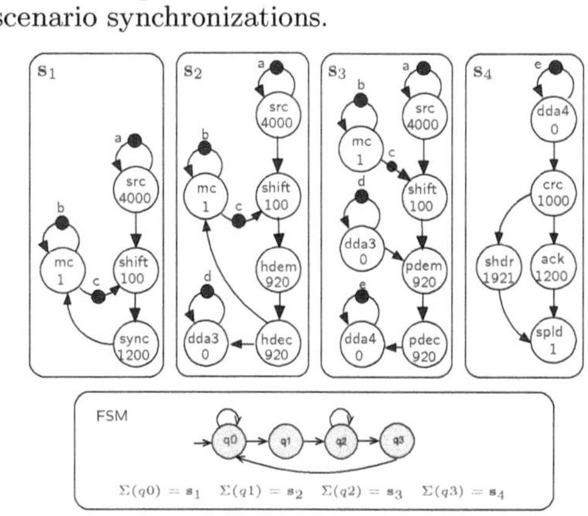

Figure 9: FSM-SADF of WLAN 802.11a baseband

9.2 Conservativeness

Table 1 shows the worst-case throughputs (WCTs) of the FSM-SADF models of WLAN (Figure 9) and LTE (Figure 1), according to the different analysis techniques presented in Section 8. The $(max, +)$ automaton ρ_{ma} gives the exact WCT of the FSM-SADF model and hence it is the most accurate result. As a result, we use it as reference

Table 1: WCT($\times 10^{-4}$ iterations/time-unit)

Application	ρ_{sg}	ρ_{gv}	ρ_{lv}	ρ_{ma}
WLAN	1.7	1.7	2.5	2.5
LTE	4.8	8.1	9.9	11.1

to compare the relative conservativeness (accuracy) of the other three techniques. Table 1 shows that ρ_{lv} gives better results than the other two and ρ_{gv} is better than ρ_{sg}. This observation also holds in general. ρ_{sg} does not consider scenario transitions and hence, it is the least accurate. ρ_{lv} gives better result than ρ_{gv} as it computes transition delays locally. However, such accuracy improvements come at a price of the run-times of the analyses, as discussed next in Section 9.3.

9.3 Scalability

If a dynamic application is modeled in detail, the number of scenarios may substantially increase. As a result, the size of the FSM may also increase. Figure 10 shows how the run-times of the different analysis techniques scale with increase in number of FSM states. The SDF3 [1] dataflow tool is used to generate random graphs for this experiment.

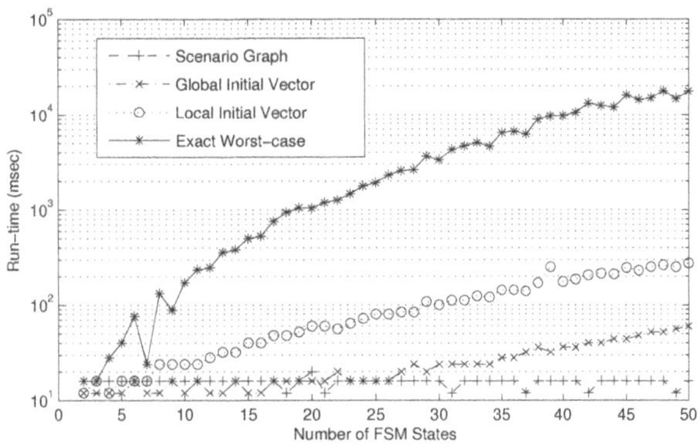

Figure 10: Scalability relative to FSM states

Conservative techniques perform MCM analysis on the FSM, whereas the exact technique performs MCM analysis on the throughput graph. The MCM analysis on the FSM has an order of complexity $\mathcal{O}(Q^3)$, since the FSM has $|Q|$ states and at most $|Q|^2$ edges. The MCM on the throughput graph, on the other hand, has an order of complexity $\mathcal{O}(V^3)$, where V is the number of vertices of the throughput graph. $V = |Q| \times |I_F|$, where I_F is the number of initial initial tokens of the FSM-SADF. Hence, conservative techniques scale better than the exact technique, as shown in Figure 10. Nevertheless, graphs with a large number of initial tokens mostly have sparse $(max, +)$ matrices (populated primarily with $-\infty$). Thus, the number of edges of the throughput graph is much less than the maximum connection. As a result, the actual run-time of the exact technique is in order of tens of seconds for graphs with hundreds of scenarios.

9.4 Summary

FSM-SADF scenarios of real-life streaming applications are not necessarily strongly-connected. The different analysis techniques, presented in Section 8, can be directly applied in such graphs. These techniques have different levels of accuracy and run-time. The conservative techniques are generally faster and more scalable than the exact technique. However, they give only an upper-bound WCT whereas the exact technique gives the actual WCT that may occur in the execution of the FSM-SADF.

10. CONCLUSION

The frame arrival rate of wireless and multimedia embedded applications imposes a throughput requirement that must be satisfied. The analysis of these applications is challenged by their dynamism. The finite-state machine based Scenario-Aware Dataflow (FSM-SADF) allows analysis of dynamic streaming applications by isolating different static *scenarios*. Existing FSM-SADF analysis techniques, however, are limited to 1) self-timed bounded scenarios and 2) inter-scenario synchronizations only through common initial tokens. This work lifts these restrictive assumptions and presents a generalized approach to analyse the worst-case throughput of an arbitrary set of SDF scenarios.

11. REFERENCES

[1] SDF3 - Synchronous Dataflow for Free. http://www.es.ele.tue.nl/sdf3/.

[2] F. Baccelli *et. al.* *Synchronization and Linearity: An Algebra for Discrete Event Systems.* 1993.

[3] A. Bonfietti *et. al.* An efficient and complete approach for throughput-maximal SDF allocation and scheduling on multi-core platforms. In *DATE*, 2010.

[4] J. Buck. A dynamic dataflow model suitable for efficient mixed hardware and software implementations of dsp applications. In *CODES*, 1994.

[5] M. Geilen. Synchronous dataflow scenarios. *ACM Transactions on Embedded Computing Systems*, 2011.

[6] M. Geilen and S. Stuijk. Worst-case performance analysis of synchronous dataflow scenarios. In *CODES/ISSS*, 2010.

[7] A. Ghamarian *et. al.* Liveness and boundedness of synchronous data flow graphs. *FMCAD*, 2006.

[8] A. Ghamarian *et. al.* Throughput analysis of synchronous data flow graphs. In *ACSD*, 2006.

[9] A. Girault *et. al.* Hierarchical finite state machines with multiple concurrency models. *IEEE Trans. on CAD of ICs and Systems*, 1999.

[10] B. Heidergott *et. al.* *Max Plus at Work: Modeling and Analysis of Synchronized Systems.* Princeton University Press, 2006.

[11] G. Khan. The semantics of a simple language for parallel programming. In *IFIP*, 1974.

[12] E. Lee. Consistency in dataflow graphs. *IEEE Trans. on Parallel and Distributed Systems*, 1991.

[13] E. Lee and D. Messerschmitt. Static scheduling of synchronous data flow programs for digital signal processing. *IEEE Transactions on Computers*, 1987.

[14] E. Lee and D. Messerschmitt. Synchronous dataflow. *IEEE Proceedings*, 1987.

[15] O. Moreira. *Temporal Analysis and Scheduling of Hard-Real Time Radios on a Multi-processor.* PhD thesis, TU Eindhoven, 2011.

[16] W. Plishker *et. al.* Functional dif for rapid prototyping. In *IEEE/IFIP*, 2008.

[17] F. Siyoum *et. al.* Analyzing Synchronous Dataflow Scenarios for Dynamic Software-defined Radio Applications. In *SOC*, 2011.

[18] S. Sriram and S. S. Bhattacharyya. *Embedded Multiprocessors: Scheduling and Synch.* 2009.

[19] S. Stuijk *et. al.* Scenario-aware dataflow: Modeling, analysis and implementation of dynamic applications. In *IC-SAMOS*, 2011.

[20] B. Theelen *et. al.* A scenario-aware data flow model for combined long-run average and worst-case performance analysis. In *MEMOCODE*, 2006.

[21] P. Wauters *et. al.* Cyclo-dynamic dataflow. *IEEE Transactions on Signal Processing*, 1996.

[22] M. Wiggers *et. al.* Buffer capacity computation for throughput-constrained modal task graphs. *ACM Trans. Embed. Comput. Syst.*

[23] J. Zhai *et. al.* Modeling adaptive streaming applications with parameterized polyhedral process networks. In *DAC*, 2011.

Synthesis of Communication Schedules for TTEthernet-Based Mixed-Criticality Systems

Domiţian Tămaş–Selicean
Technical University of Denmark
Kongens Lyngby, Denmark
dota@imm.dtu.dk

Paul Pop
Technical University of Denmark
Kongens Lyngby, Denmark
paul.pop@imm.dtu.dk

Wilfried Steiner
TTTech Computertechnik AG
Vienna, Austria
wilfried.steiner@tttech.com

ABSTRACT

In this paper we are interested in safety-critical distributed systems, composed of heterogeneous processing elements interconnected using the TTEthernet protocol. We address hard real-time mixed-criticality applications, which may have different criticality levels, and we focus on the optimization of the communication configuration. TTEthernet integrates three types of traffic: Time-Triggered (TT) messages, Event-Triggered (ET) messages with bounded end-to-end delay, also called Rate Constrained (RC) messages, and Best-Effort (BE) messages, for which no timing guarantees are provided. TT messages are transmitted based on static schedule tables, and have the highest priority. RC messages are transmitted if there are no TT messages, and BE traffic has the lowest priority. TT and RC traffic can carry safety-critical messages, while BE messages are non-critical. Mixed-criticality tasks and messages can be integrated onto the same architecture only if there is enough spatial and temporal separation among them. TTEthernet offers spatial separation for mixed-criticality messages through the concept of virtual links, and temporal separation, enforced through schedule tables for TT messages and bandwidth allocation for RC messages. Given the set of mixed-criticality messages in the system and the topology of the virtual links on which the messages are transmitted, we are interested to synthesize offline the static schedules for the TT messages, such that the deadlines for the TT and RC messages are satisfied, and the end-to-end delay of the RC traffic is minimized. We have proposed a Tabu Search-based approach to solve this optimization problem. The proposed algorithm has been evaluated using several benchmarks.

Categories and Subject Descriptors

B.4.4 [**Input/Output and Data Communications**]: Performance Analysis and Design Aids; C.2.2 [**Computer-Communication Networks**]: Network Protocols

Keywords

mixed-criticality; real-time systems; optimization of communication configuration; network protocol; partitioned architectures; TTEthernet

1. INTRODUCTION

Depending on the particular application, an embedded system has certain requirements on performance, cost, dependability, size etc. In a *hard real-time* application the correctness depends not only on the logical results of the computations, but also on the physical instant at which these results are produced [21]. *Safety* is a property of a system that will not endanger human life or the environment. *Safety-Integrity Levels* (SILs) capture the required protection against failure when building a safety-critical embedded system, and will dictate the development processes and certification procedures that have to be followed.

There are two basic approaches for handling real-time applications [21]. In the *Event-Triggered* (ET) approach, activities are initiated whenever a particular event is noted. In the *Time-Triggered* (TT) approach, activities are initiated at predetermined points in time. There has been a long debate in the real-time and embedded systems communities concerning the advantages of each approach [7, 21, 39]. Several aspects have been considered in favor of one or the other approach, such as flexibility, predictability, jitter control, processor utilization, testability etc. However, the consensus is that the right approach depends on the particularities of the application, as it has been shown in an automotive context [23]. This means not only that there is no single "best" approach to be used, but also that within a system the two approaches can be used together, some tasks and messages being TT and others ET.

This duality is also reflected at the level of the communication infrastructure, where communication activities can be triggered either dynamically, in response to an event, as with the Controller Area Network (CAN) bus [2], or statically, at predetermined moments in time, as in the case of Time-Division Multiple Access (TDMA) protocols such as the Time-Triggered Protocol (TTP) [21]. The trend is towards bus protocols that support both static and dynamic communication [4, 5].

Many safety-critical real-time applications, following physical, modularity or safety constraints, are implemented using distributed architectures, composed of heterogeneous processing elements (PEs), interconnected in a network. Initially, each function was implemented in a separate PE, which has led to a large increase in the number of PEs. The current trends are towards *integrated architectures* where several functions are integrated onto the same PE. Mixed-criticality applications, i.e., applications with different SIL levels, as well as non-critical applications, can be integrated onto the same architecture only if there is enough spatial and temporal separation among them.

In the avionics area, the PE-level separation mechanisms are provided by implementations of the ARINC 653 standard, also called *Integrated Modular Avionics* (IMA) [31]. ARINC 653 consists of hardware-mediated operating system-level spatial and temporal partitioning [31] mechanisms. Similar PE-level separation mechanisms are available in other industries [15, 22]. At the communication level, there are also several partitioning solutions, such as SAFEBus [19], ARINC 664 Specification Part 7 (ARINC 664p7, for short) [3] and TTP [21]. In this paper we are interested in the TTEthernet [5] protocol, which provides both spatial and temporal partitioning, and can handle both TT and ET communication.

There is a large amount of research on hard real-time systems [21]. At the PE-level, researchers have addressed systems with mixed time-criticality requirements, showing how TT/ET tasks [29] or hard/soft real-time tasks [20, 33] can be integrated onto the same platform. Researchers have also started to address the integration of mixed safety-criticality tasks onto the same platform [8, 9, 10, 37]. In [37], researchers have proposed an optimization approach to determine the mapping of tasks to PEs, the assignment of tasks to partitions, the sequence and size of the time slots on each PE and the schedule tables, such that all the applications are schedulable and the development costs are minimized. In that work, communications were ignored, and a simple un-partitioned statically scheduled shared bus was used.

The problem of the optimization of time-partitions has been addressed at the bus level. Researchers have shown how a TDMA bus such as the TTP [26] and a mixed TT/ET bus such as FlexRay [30] can be optimized to decrease the end-to-end delays. FlexRay allows the sharing of the bus among ET and TT messages, thus offering the advantages of both worlds. In [30], an optimization approach for determining a FlexRay bus configuration is proposed, which is adapted to the particular features of an application and guarantees that all time constraints are satisfied.

Our focus in this paper is on the optimization of the TTEthernet protocol [5], which is a deterministic, synchronized and congestion-free network based on the IEEE 802.3 Ethernet standard and compliant with the ARINC 664p7The widespread Ethernet protocol is known to be unsuitable for real-time or safety-critical applications [3]. For example, in half-duplex implementations, frame collision is unavoidable, leading to unbounded transmission times. The ARINC 664p7 specification [3] is a full-duplex Ethernet network, which emulates point-to-point connectivity over the network by defining *virtual links*, tree-like structures with one sender and one or several receivers (see Section 2). ARINC 664p7 provides predictable event-triggered communication suitable for hard real-time applications, and separation of safety-critical messages through the concept of virtual links. In addition to the functionality offered by Ethernet and ARINC 664p7, TTEthernet supports time-triggered communication based on static communication schedules which rely on a synchronization time base. Such time-triggered static scheduling approach is especially suitable for applications with highest criticality requirements in both temporal and safety domains.

TTEthernet supports applications with mixed-criticality requirements in the temporal domain, as it provides three types of traffic: TT traffic and ET traffic, which is further subdivided into Rate Constrained (RC) traffic that has bounded end-to-end latencies, and Best-Effort (BE) traffic, for which no timing guarantees are provided. TT messages are transmitted based on static schedule tables and have the highest priority. RC messages are transmitted if there are no TT messages, and BE traffic has the lowest priority. TTEthernet is highly suitable for applications of different safety criticality levels, since it offers spatial separation for mixed-criticality messages through the concept of virtual links. For more details on the traffic classes, protocol services and separation mechanisms, see Section 5.

In this paper we are interested in mixed-criticality applications (both in the safety and time domains) implemented using heterogeneous processing elements interconnected using TTEthernet. We consider that the architecture, the topology of the virtual links and the assignment of messages to virtual links is given. Furthermore, we assume that the designer has decided the partitioning of messages into TT, RC or BE, depending on the particularities of the application. We are interested in synthesizing the static communication schedules for the TT messages, such that the TT and RC messages are schedulable, and the end-to-end delay of RC messages is minimized. We have proposed a Tabu Search-based metaheuristic to solve this optimization problem.

There is very limited work in this area. Steiner proposes in [34] an approach for the synthesis of static TT schedules, where he ignored the RC traffic and used a Satisfiability Modulo Theory (SMT)-solver to find a solution which satisfies an imposed set of constraints. The same author has proposed an SMT-solver approach to introduce periodic evenly-spaced slots into the static schedules to help reduce RC delays in [35]. Our Tabu Search-based metaheurstic does not restrict the space inserted into the TT schedules to evenly-spaced periodic slots and is able to take into account the RC end-to-end delays during the design space exploration, and not only as a post-synthesis check.

The paper is organized as follows: after we introduce the architecture model in Section 2 and the application model in Section 3, we present the problem formulation in Section 4. Section 5 describes how the TTEthernet protocol works. Section 6 presents a motivation example to better understand the problem, and the proposed solution is described in Section 7. The proposed Tabu Search-based approach is evaluated in Section 8.

2. ARCHITECTURE MODEL

A TTEthernet network is composed of a set of clusters. Each cluster consists of a set of End Systems (ESes) interconnected by links and Network Switches (NSes). The links are full duplex, allowing thus communication in both directions, and the networks can be multi-hop. An example cluster is presented in Fig. 1, where we have 4 ESes, ES_1 to ES_4, and 2 NSes, NS_1 and NS_2.

Each cluster has its own separate clock synchronization domain, hence the TT schedules are derived per cluster. The problem of optimizing the TT schedules addressed in this paper is performed at the cluster-level. Each ES consists of a processing element containing a CPU, RAM and non-volatile memory, and a network interface card (NIC), see Fig. 1.

We model a TTEthernet cluster as an undirected graph $\mathcal{G}(\mathcal{V},\mathcal{E})$, where $\mathcal{V} = \mathcal{ES} \cup \mathcal{NS}$ is the set of end systems ($\mathcal{ES}$) and network switches ($\mathcal{NS}$) and $\mathcal{E}$ is the set of physical links. For Fig. 1, $\mathcal{V} = \mathcal{ES} \cup \mathcal{NS} = \{ES_1, ES_2, ES_3, ES_4\} \cup \{NS_1, NS_2\}$, and the physical links $\mathcal{E}$ are depicted with thick, black, double arrows.

The space partitioning between messages of different criticality transmitted over physical links and network switches is achieved through the concept of *virtual link*. Virtual links are defined by ARINC 664p7 [3], which is implemented by the TTEthernet protocol, as a "logical unidirectional connection from one source end system to one or more destination end systems". Virtual links connect one sender to multiple receivers. Each virtual link carries a single message.

Let us assume that in Fig. 1 we have two applications, $\mathcal{A}_1$ and $\mathcal{A}_2$. $\mathcal{A}_1$ is a high criticality application consisting of tasks τ_1 to τ_3 mapped on ES_1, ES_3 and ES_4, respectively. $\mathcal{A}_2$ is a non-critical application, with tasks τ_4 and τ_5 mapped on ES_2 and ES_3, respectively. τ_1 sends message m_1 to τ_2 and τ_3. Task τ_4 sends message m_2 to τ_5. The flow of these messages will intersect in the physical links and switches. Virtual links are used to separate the highly critical message m_1 from the non-critical message m_2. Thus, m_1 is transmitted over virtual link vl_1, which is isolated from virtual link vl_2, on which m_2 is sent, through protocol-level temporal and spatial mechanisms (which are briefly presented in Section 5).

We denote the set of virtual links in a cluster with $\mathcal{VL}$. A virtual link $vl_i \in \mathcal{VL}$ is a directed tree, with the sender as the root

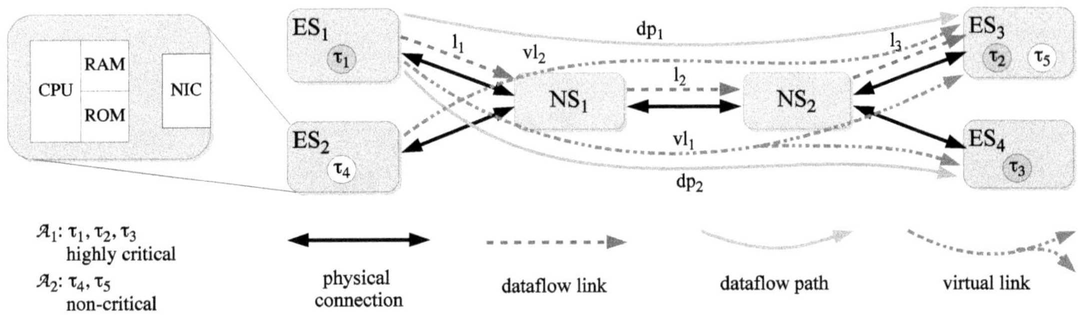

Figure 1: TTEthernet cluster example

and the receivers as leafs. For example, vl_1, depicted in Fig. 1 using dot-dash red arrows, is a tree with the root ES_1 and the leafs ES_3 and ES_4. Each virtual link is composed of a set of dataflow paths, one such dataflow path for each root-leaf connection. More formally, a *dataflow path* dp_i is an ordered sequence of dataflow links connecting one sender to one receiver. For example, in Fig. 1, $vl_1 = dp_1 \cup dp_2$, and dp_1 connects ES_1 to ES_3, while dp_2 connects ES_1 to ES_4 (the dataflow paths are depicted with green arrows). A *dataflow link* $l_i = [\nu_j, \nu_k] \in \mathcal{L}$, where $\mathcal{L}$ is the set of dataflow links in a cluster, is a directed communication connection from ν_j to ν_k, where ν_j and $\nu_k \in \mathcal{V}$ can be ESes or NSes. Using this notation, a dataflow path such as dp_1 in Fig. 1 can be denoted as $[[ES_1, NS_1]$, $[NS_1, NS_2]$, $[NS_2, ES_3]]$.

For a given application, with tasks mapped to ESes and exchanging messages over the network, there are several possible virtual link configurations, depending on how senders and receivers are grouped. In this paper, we assume that the virtual links are given. Determining the set of virtual links for a given application has been studied in the context of Steiner trees [16, 17].

3. APPLICATION MODEL

In [37] researchers have proposed an application model for mixed-criticality applications composed of interacting tasks, which communicate using messages. The proposed model can capture aspects specific to mixed-criticality applications, e.g., higher criticality tasks cannot receive messages from lower criticality tasks (because these messages could be corrupted) and additional task-level separation requirements, preventing certain tasks to share the same partition on an ES.

In this paper we focus only on messages. There are several approaches to integrate task and message scheduling, see [25] for a survey. Each message m_i transmitted using TTEthernet is packed into a frame f_i. In this paper we assume that a frame carries only one message, and that messages are not split into packets. The issue of frame packing [28] is orthogonal to our problem.

We assume that the topology of virtual links and the assignment of frames to virtual links are given. This assignment is captured by the function $\mathcal{M}(f_i) = vl_i, \mathcal{M} : \mathcal{F} \rightarrow \mathcal{VL}$, where $\mathcal{F}$ is the set of all frames in the cluster.

As mentioned, TTEthernet supports three traffic classes: time-trig- gered (TT), rate constrained (RC) and best effort (BE). A bit pattern specified in the frame header identifies the traffic class. We assume that the designer has decided the traffic classes for each frame, and we define the sets $\mathcal{F}^{TT}$, $\mathcal{F}^{RC}$ and $\mathcal{F}^{BE}$, respectively, with $\mathcal{F} = \mathcal{F}^{TT} \cup \mathcal{F}^{RC} \cup \mathcal{F}^{BE}$.

The size $f_i.size$ for each frame $f_i \in \mathcal{F}$ is given. In addition, for the TT and RC frames we know their periods and deadlines, $f_i.period$ and $f_i.deadline$, respectively. RC frames are not necessarily periodic, but have a minimum inter-arrival time f_i. We define the rate of an RC frame f_i as $f_i.rate = 1/f_i.period$. Knowing the size of a frame f_i and the given speed of a dataflow link $[\nu_j, \nu_k]$, we can determine the transmission duration $C_i^{[\nu_j,\nu_k]}$ of f_i on $[\nu_j, \nu_k]$.

4. PROBLEM FORMULATION

The problem we are addressing in this paper can be formulated as follows: given (1) the topology of the network $\mathcal{G}$, (2) the set of TT and RC frames $\mathcal{F}^{TT} \cup \mathcal{F}^{RC}$, (3) the set of virtual links $\mathcal{VL}$, (4) the assignment of frames to virtual links $\mathcal{M}$ and (5) for each frame f_i the size, the deadline and the period, we are interested to find the set of TT schedules $\mathcal{S}$ such that the deadlines for the TT and RC frames are satisfied. Once both TT and RC frames are schedulable several optimization objectives can be tackled. In this paper we are interested to synthesize the schedules $\mathcal{S}$ such that the end-to-end delay of RC frames is minimized. Section 7.1 presents the cost function used for the optimization. In this paper we ignore the BE traffic, but a quality-of-service measure for the BE traffic could easily be added to the objective function, if desired. The problem is illustrated in Section 6 using a motivational example.

5. TTETHERNET PROTOCOL

Let us illustrate how the TTEthernet protocol works using the example in Fig. 2, where we have two end systems, ES_1 and ES_2, and three network switches, NS_1 to NS_3. Task τ_2 on ES_1 sends the TT message m_2 to task τ_4 mapped on ES_2, while task τ_1 on ES_1 sends the RC message m_1 to task τ_3 on ES_2. Let us assume that tasks τ_1 and τ_3 are part of application $\mathcal{A}_1$ and tasks τ_2 and τ_4 belong to application $\mathcal{A}_2$. Furthermore, $\mathcal{A}_1$ and $\mathcal{A}_2$ are of different safety criticality. The separation of the applications is achieved at the CPU-level through partitioning. Thus, tasks τ_1 and τ_3 are placed in partitions $\mathcal{P}_{1,1}$ and $\mathcal{P}_{2,2}$, respectively, while tasks τ_2 and τ_4 are assigned to partitions $\mathcal{P}_{1,2}$ and $\mathcal{P}_{2,1}$, see Fig. 2.

Message m_1 is sent within application $\mathcal{A}_1$ and packed in frame f_1. m_2 is sent within $\mathcal{A}_2$ and packed into the frame f_2. The different criticality frames are separated by assigning them to two different virtual links, vl_1 and vl_2 (not depicted in the figure). Frames f_1 and f_2 have to transit the switch NS_1, which also forwards frames f_3 and f_4, from NS_2 and NS_3, respectively, see Fig. 2.

5.1 Time-Triggered Transmission

In this section we present how TT frames are transmited by TTEthernet, using the example of the TT message m_2 sent from task τ_2 on ES_1, to task τ_4 on ES_2. We depict each step of the TT transmission on Fig. 2 and mark it with a letter from (a) to (m) on a blue background.

Thus, in the first step denoted with (a), task τ_2 packs m_2 into frame f_2 and in the second step (b), f_2 is placed into buffer $B_{1,Tx}$ for transmission. Conceptually, there is one such buffer for every

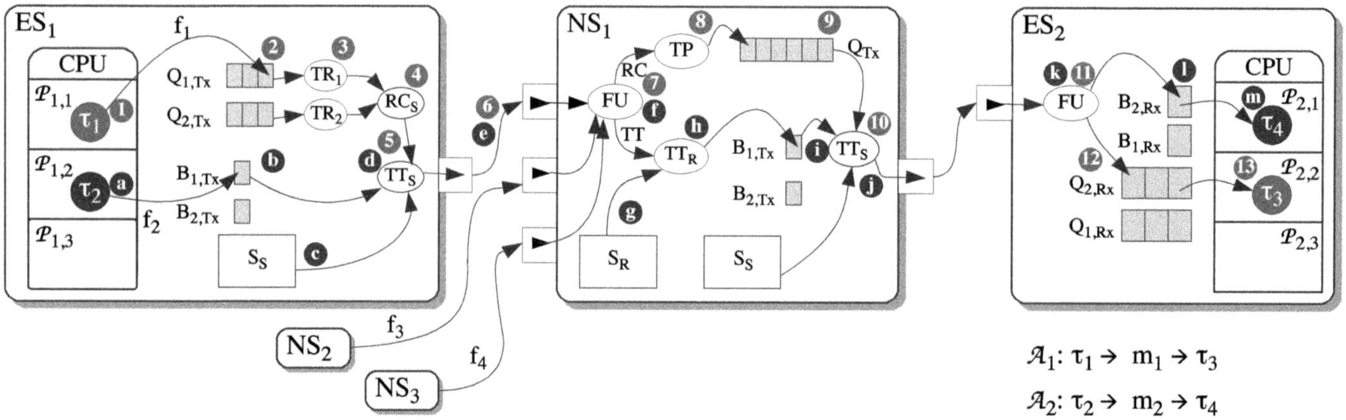

Figure 2: TT and RC message transmission example

TT message sent from ES_1. TT communication is done according to static communication schedules determined offline and stored into the ESes and NSes. The complete set of local schedules in a cluster are denoted with $\mathcal{S}$. The schedules $\mathcal{S}$ are derived by our optimization approach. Thus, in step (d), the scheduler task TT_S will send f_2 to NS_1 at the time specified in the send schedule S_S stored in ES_1 (c). There are several approaches to the synchronization of tasks (which could be TT or ET) and TT messages [25]. Often, TT tasks are used in conjunction with TT messages, and the task and message schedules are synchronized such that the task is scheduled to finish before the message is scheduled for transmission.

Next, f_2 is sent on a dataflow link to NS_1 (e). The computational logic of the TTEthernet protocol is implemented in hardware and, conceptually, consists of several hardware tasks working in parallel to implement the protocol services. Such is the case of the Filtering Unit (FU) task, which is invoked every time a frame is received by an NS. The FU checks the integrity and validity of frame f_2 (see step (f)) and forwards it to the TT receiver task TT_R (h), which copies it into the sending buffer $B_{1,Tx}$ for later transmission.

The separation mechanisms implemented by TTEthernet to isolate mixed-criticality frames, such as f_1 and f_2 in our example, are spread across several hardware tasks. In addition, TTEthernet provides fault-tolerance services, such as fault-containment, to the application level. For example, if a task such as τ_2 becomes faulty and sends more messages than scheduled (called a "babbling idiot" failure), the TT sender task TT_S on ES_1 will protect the network as it will only transmit messages as specified in the schedule table S_S.

Also, a TT receiver task TT_R in an NS will rely on a receive schedule S_R (g) stored in the switch to check if a TT frame has arrived within a specified receiving window. This window is determined based on the sending times in the send schedules (schedule S_S on ES_1 for the case of frame f_2), the precision of the clock synchronization mechanism and the "integration policy" used for integrating the TT traffic with the RC and BE traffic (see next subsection for details). TT message frames arriving outside of this receiving window are considered faulty. In order to provide virtual link isolation and fault-containment, a TT receiver task TT_R will drop such faulty frames.

The schedules $\mathcal{S}$ contain the sending times and receiving windows for all the frames transmitted during an application cycle, T_{cycle}. A periodic frame f_i may contain several instances (a *frame instance* is the equivalent of the periodic *job* of a task) within T_{cycle}. We denote the *x-th* instance of frame f_i with $f_{i,x}$. The sending time of a frame f_i relative to the start time of its period is called the *offset*, denoted with $f_i.offset$. Within an application cycle, the offset of a frame may vary from period to period. However, a particular TTEthernet implementation may restrict the sending times such that the offset of a frame is identical in all the periods (which has the advantage of reducing the size needed to store the schedules). Our implementation considers the general case, and such constraints can be easily added to our optimization approach. Also, a restricted TTEthernet implementation can "emulate" the general case by assigning a message to multiple virtual links.

Let us continue to follow the transmission of f_2 in Fig. 2. The frame has arrived in NS_1 and has been placed in $B_{1,Tx}$ (h). Next, f_2 is sent by the TT sender task TT_S in NS_1 to ES_2 at the time specified in the TT send schedule S_S in NS_1. When f_2 arrives at ES_2 (k), the FU task will store the frame into a dedicated receive buffer $B_{2,Rx}$ (l). Finally, when task τ_4 is activated, it will read f_2 from the buffer (m).

5.2 Rate Constrained Transmission

This section presents how RC traffic is transmitted using the example of frame f_1 sent from τ_1 on ES_1 to τ_3 on ES_2. Similarly to the discussion of TT traffic, we mark each step in Fig. 2 using numbers from (1) to (13), on a green background.

Thus, τ_1 packs message m_1 into frame f_1 (1) and inserts it into a queue $Q_{1,Tx}$ (2). Conceptually, there is one such queue for each RC virtual link. RC traffic consists of event-triggered messages. The separation of RC traffic is enforced through "bandwidth allocation". Thus, for each virtual link vl_i carrying an RC frame f_i the designer decides the Bandwidth Allocation Gap (BAG). A BAG is the minimum time interval between two consecutive instances of an RC frame f_i. The BAG is set in such a way to guarantee that there is enough bandwidth allocated for the transmission of a frame on a virtual link, with $BAG_i \leq 1/f_i.rate$.

The BAG is enforced by the Traffic Regulator (TR) task. Thus, TR_1 in ES_1 in Fig. 2 will ensure that each BAG_1 interval will contain at most one instance of f_1 (3). Therefore, even if a frame is sent in bursts by a task, it will leave the TR task within a specified BAG. Thus, the maximum bandwidth used by a virtual link vl_i which transmits an RC frame f_i is $BW(vl_i) = f_i.size/BAG_i$. In this paper we assume that the BAG for each RC frame is given by the designer.

Several messages will be sent from an ES. Let us first discuss how RC messages are *multiplexed*, and then we will discuss the *integration* with the TT traffic.

In an ES, the RC scheduler task RC_S (such as the one in ES_1) will multiplex several RC messages (4) coming from the traffic regulator tasks, TR_i, such as TR_1 and TR_2 in ES_1. Fig. 3 depicts how this multiplexing is performed for the frames f_x and f_y with the sizes and BAGs as specified in Fig. 3(a) and (b), respectively. Fig. 3(c) shows how the two frames will be sent on the outgoing dataflow link $[ES_1, NS_1]$ by the RC_S task. In the case several TRs attempt to transmit messages at the same time, due to the multiplexer, the frames waiting to be transmitted will be affected by jitter. This

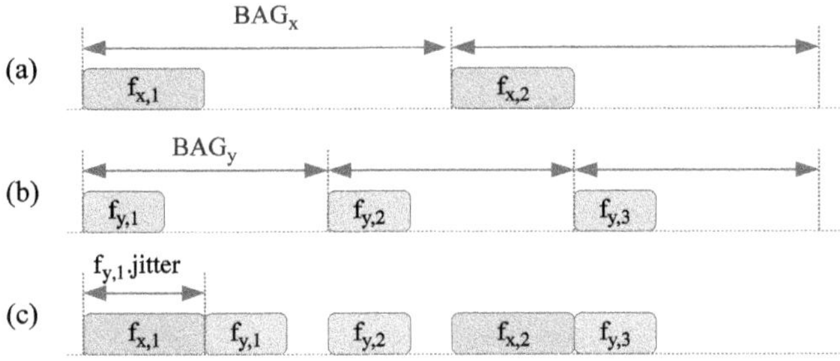

Figure 3: Multiplexing two RC frames

is the case of f_y in Fig. 3(c), which is delayed to allow for the transmission of f_x. Thus, the $f_{y,1}.jitter$ jitter for $f_{y,1}$ equals to the transmission duration of f_x.

RC traffic also has to be integrated with TT traffic, which has higher priority. Thus, RC frames are transmitted only when there is no TT traffic on the dataflow link. Hence, for our example on ES_1, the TT_S task on ES_1 will transmit frame f_1 (5) to NS_1 on the dataflow link $[ES_1, NS_1]$ only when there is no TT traffic (6). With integration, contention situations can occur when a TT frame is scheduled for transmission, but an RC frame is already transmitting.

There are three approaches in TTEthernet to handle such situations [5, 36]: (i) shuffling, (ii) pre-emption and (iii) timely block. (i) With *shuffling*, the higher priority TT frame is delayed until the RC frame finishes the transmission. Thus, in the worst-case scenario, the TT frame will have to wait for the time needed to transmit the largest Ethernet frame, which is 1542 Bytes. In the case (ii) of *timely block*, the RC frame is blocked (postponed) from transmission on a dataflow link if a TT frame is scheduled to be sent before the RC frame would complete its transmission. In the case (iii) of *pre-emption*, the RC frame is pre-empted, and its transmission is restarted after the TT frame finished transmitting. Note that, as discussed in the previous subsection, the integration approaches have an impact on the receiving window of a TT frame, which has to account for the delays due to shuffling, for example.

When the RC frame f_1 arrives at NS_1, the Filtering Unit task (7) will check its validity and integrity. As mentioned, TTEthernet provides services to separate the mixed-criticality frames, such that a faulty transmission of a lower-criticality frame will not impact negatively a higher-criticality frame. Fault-containment at the level of RC virtual links is provided by the Traffic Policing (TP) task, see NS_1 in Fig. 2. TP implements an algorithm known as *leaky bucket* [3, 5], which checks the time interval between two consecutive instances on the same virtual link. If this interval is shorter than the specified BAG, the frame instance is dropped. Thus, the TP function prevents a faulty ES to send faulty RC frames (more often than allowed) and thus to disturb the network.

After passing the checks of the TP task (8), f_1 is copied to the outgoing queue Q_{Tx} (9). In this paper we assume that all the RC frames have the same priority, thus the TT_S (10) will send the RC frames in Q_{Tx} in a FIFO order, but only when there is no scheduled TT traffic. At the receiving ES, after passing the FU (11) checks, f_1 is copied in the receiving $Q_{2,Rx}$ queue (12). Finally, when τ_3 is activated, it will take f_1 (13) from this queue.

6. MOTIVATIONAL EXAMPLE

Let us illustrate the schedule synthesis problem presented in Section 4 using the setup from Fig. 4, where we have an architecture model for a cluster composed of three ESes, ES_1 to ES_3 and a network switch NS_1 (see Fig. 4a) and an application model with three frames, see the table in Fig. 4b. We have three virtual links, vl_1, vl_2 and vl_3 one for each frame, f_1, f_2 and f_3, respectively, as captured by the function $\mathcal{M}$ in the table. The periods $f_i.period$, deadlines $f_i.deadline$ and transmission times C_i on a dataflow link are given in the table for each frame. The dataflow links have the same speed, hence the C_i of a frame f_i is the same for each link. For this example we consider that the RC and TT traffic are integrated using a timely block policy, i.e., an RC frame will be delayed if it could block a scheduled TT frame.

Our problem is to determine the TT schedules $\mathcal{S}$ such that all the TT and RC frames are schedulable. The schedulability of a TT frame f_i is easy to determine: we just have to check the schedules $\mathcal{S}$ to see if the times are synthesized such that the TT frame f_i is received before its deadline $f_i.deadline$. To determine the schedulability of an RC frame f_j we have to compute its worst-case end-to-end delay, from the moment it is sent to the moment it is received. We denote this worst-case delay with R_{f_j}. Section 7.2 will present a schedulability analysis technique for determining the worst-case end-to-end delay of an RC frame, which can then be compared to the deadline $f_j.deadline$ to determine if the RC frame f_j is schedulable.

Fig. 5 presents two possible solutions for synthesizing the TT schedules $\mathcal{S}$. In both cases, Fig. 5a and 5b, instead of presenting the actual schedule tables, we show a Gantt chart, which shows on a timeline from 0 to 600 μs what happens on the three dataflow links, $[ES_1, NS_1]$, $[ES_2, NS_1]$ and $[NS_1, ES_3]$. For the TT frames f_2 and f_3 the Gantt chart captures their sending times (the left edge of the rectangle) and transmission duration (the length of the rectangle).

Since the transmission of RC frames is not synchronized with the TT frames, there are many scenarios that can be depicted for f_1, depending on when f_1 is sent in relation to the schedule tables. Because we are interested in the schedulability of RC frames, for the RC frame f_1 we show in both cases (a) and (b) in Fig. 5 the worst-case scenario, i.e., the situation which has generated the largest (worst-case) end-to-end delay. The two TT frames are schedulable in both cases. In Fig. 5a the TT schedules are constructed such that the end-to-end delay of TT frames is minimized, i.e., the TT frames arrive at their destination as soon as possible. In this case, the worst-case end-to-end delay of the RC frame f_1, namely R_{f_1}, is 470 μs, which is greater than its deadline of 300 μs, hence f_1 is not schedulable. This worst-case for f_1 happens for the first frame instance $f_{1,1}$, see Fig. 5a, when $f_{1,1}$ happens to be sent by ES_1 at 105 μs. In this case, as the network implements the *timely block* integration algorithm, the frame cannot be forwarded by NS_1 to ES_3 until there is a big enough time interval to transmit the frame without

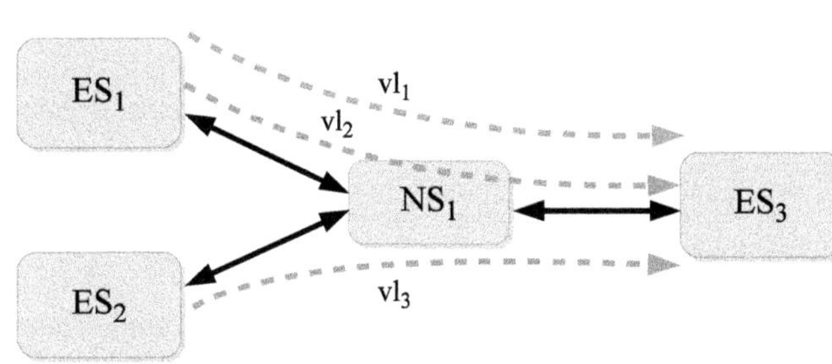

(a) Example architecture model

	period (μs)	deadline (μs)	C_i (μs)	$\mathcal{M}$
$f_1 \in \mathcal{F}^{RC}$	300	300	75	vl_1
$f_2 \in \mathcal{F}^{TT}$	200	200	50	vl_2
$f_3 \in \mathcal{F}^{TT}$	300	300	50	vl_3

(b) Example application model

Figure 4: Example system model

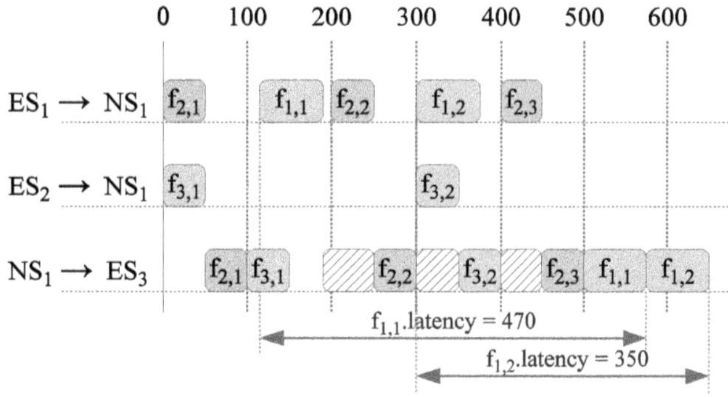

(a) Initial TT schedule

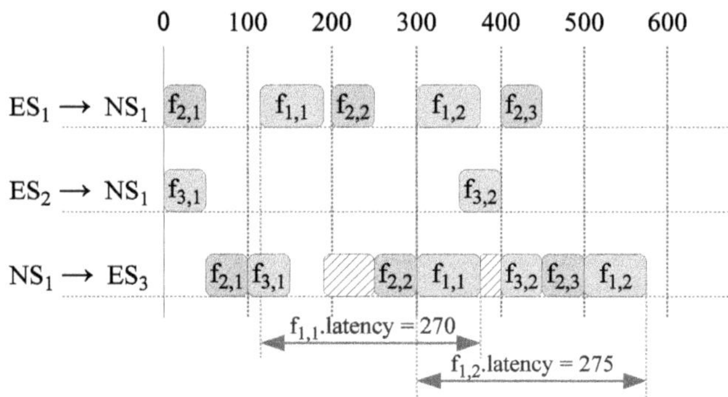

(b) Optimized TT schedule

Figure 5: Worst-case scenario for RC frame f_1

disturbing the scheduled TT frames. We denote these "blocked" time intervals with hatched boxes. The first big enough interval starts only at time 500, right after $f_{2,3}$ is received by ES_3, which is too late.

However, if we instead schedule the TT frame f_3 such that its second instance $f_{3,2}$ will be sent by ES_2 to NS_1 at 350 μs, the worst case end-to-end delay for f_1 is reduced to 275, hence f_1 is schedulable. Such a solution is depicted in Fig. 5b, where we also depict the worst-case scenario for f_1.

This example shows that by considering the RC traffic when scheduling the TT frames, the impact of the TT schedule on the latency of the RC frames can be greatly reduced.

7. SCHEDULE OPTIMIZATION

The problem presented in Section 4 is NP-complete [38]. In order to solve this problem, we will use the "TTEthernet Schedule Optimization" (TTESO) strategy from Fig. 7. TTESO takes as input the topology of the network $\mathcal{G}$, the set of TT and RC frames $\mathcal{F}^{TT} \cup \mathcal{F}^{RC}$ (including the size, period/rate and deadline), the set of virtual links $\mathcal{VL}$ and the mapping of frames to virtual links $\mathcal{M}$, and returns the schedules $\mathcal{S}$ for the TT frames.

Our synthesis strategy uses a tree model to represent each frame f_i. Each frame f_i is assigned to a virtual link vl_i. A virtual link is a tree structure, where the sender is the root and the receivers are the leafs. In the case of a virtual link, the ESes and NSes are the nodes, and the dataflow links are the edges of the tree. However, in our tree model of a frame, the dataflow links are the nodes and the edges are the precedence constraints. A periodic frame f_i has several frame instances. We denote with $f_{i,x}$ the xth instance of frame f_i, and with $f_{i,x}^{[\nu_j,\nu_k]}$ the instance sent on the dataflow link $[\nu_j,\nu_k]$. Fig. 6 presents the tree model of a frame instance $f_{1,1}$ transmitted on virtual link vl_1, from ES_1 to ES_3 and ES_4 considering the topology from Fig. 1. Naturally, frame instance $f_{1,1}$ on dataflow link $[NS_2,ES_3]$ cannot be sent before it is transmitted on $[NS_1,NS_2]$ and received in NS_2. Such a precedence constraint is captured in the model using an edge, e.g., $f_{1,1}^{[NS_1,NS_2]} \rightarrow f_{1,1}^{[NS_2,ES_3]}$.

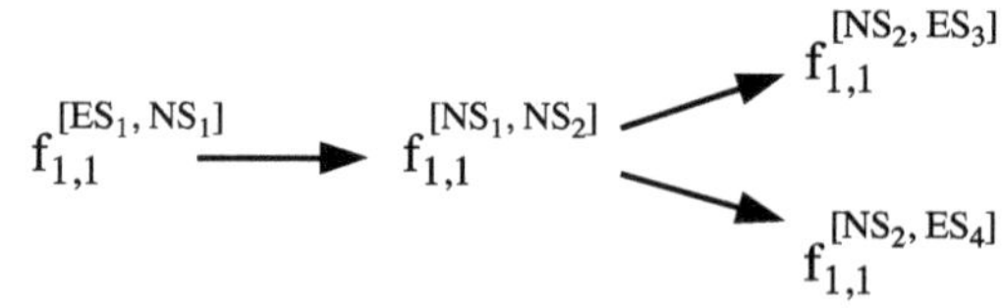

Figure 6: Representation of a frame as a tree

We denote with $pred(f_{i,x}^{[\nu_j,\nu_k]})$ the set of predecessor frame instances of the frame instance $f_{i,x}$ on dataflow link $[\nu_j,\nu_k]$. In Fig. 6, $pred(f_{1,1}^{[NS_2,ES_3]}) = \{f_{1,1}^{[ES_1,NS_1]}, f_{1,1}^{[NS_1,NS_2]}\}$. We denote with $succ(f_{i,x}^{[\nu_j,\nu_k]})$ the set of successor frame instances of the frame instance $f_{i,x}^{[\nu_j,\nu_k]}$. In Fig. 6, $succ(f_{1,1}^{[NS_1,NS_2]}) = \{f_{1,1}^{[NS_2,ES_3]}, f_{1,1}^{[NS_2,ES_4]}\}$.

Our strategy has 2 steps:

(1) In the first step, we determine an initial set of TT schedules $\mathcal{S}^{\circ}$, line 1 in Fig. 7. The initial schedules $\mathcal{S}^{\circ}$ are built without using the analysis of RC traffic, and with the goal of minimizing the end-to-end response time of the TT frames. In this step we use a List Scheduling (LS) based heuristic to construct the static schedules $\mathcal{S}^{\circ}$. Before LS is called, we merge [27] all the trees representing the frames (which can have different periods) into a single graph covering the least common multiple of all the periods. The graph has a dummy source node to which all root nodes are connected, and a dummy sink node to which all leafs are predecessors. LS schedules this graph onto the given architecture considering the given virtual link topology. The ESes, NSes and dataflow links are considered the resources onto which the frame instances have to "execute".

(2) In the second step, we use a Tabu Search meta-heuristic (see Section 7.1) to determine the TT schedules $\mathcal{S}$, such that the TT and RC frames are schedulable, and the end-to-end delay of RC frames is minimized.

7.1 Tabu Search

Tabu Search (TS) [18] is a meta-heuristic optimization, which sear- ches for that solution which minimizes the *cost function*. Tabu Search takes as input the topology of the network $\mathcal{G}$, the set of TT and RC frames $\mathcal{F}^{TT} \cup \mathcal{F}^{RC}$ (including the size, period/rate and deadline), the set of virtual links $\mathcal{VL}$ and the mapping of frames to virtual links $\mathcal{M}$, and returns at the output the best TT schedules $\mathcal{S}$ found during the design space exploration, in terms of the cost function. We define the cost function of an implementation as:

$$Cost = w_{TT} \times \delta_{TT} + w_{RC} \times \delta_{RC} \quad (1)$$

where δ_{TT} is the "degree of schedulability" for the TT frames and δ_{RC} is the degree of schedulability for the RC frames. These are summed together into a single value using the weights w_{TT} and w_{RC}, given by the designer. In case a frame is not schedulable, its corresponding weight is a very big number, i.e., a "penalty" value. This allows us to explore unfeasible solutions (which correspond to unschedulable frames) in the hope of driving the search towards

TTESO($\mathcal{G}$, $\mathcal{F}^{TT} \cup \mathcal{F}^{RC}$, $\mathcal{VL}$, $\mathcal{M}$)
1 $\mathcal{S}^{\circ}$ = InitialSolution($\mathcal{G}$, $\mathcal{F}^{TT} \cup \mathcal{F}^{RC}$, $\mathcal{VL}$, $\mathcal{M}$)
2 $\mathcal{S}$ = TabuSearch($\mathcal{G}$, $\mathcal{F}^{TT} \cup \mathcal{F}^{RC}$, $\mathcal{VL}$, $\mathcal{M}$, $\mathcal{S}^{\circ}$)
3 **return** $\mathcal{S}$

Figure 7: TTEthernet Schedule Optimization strategy

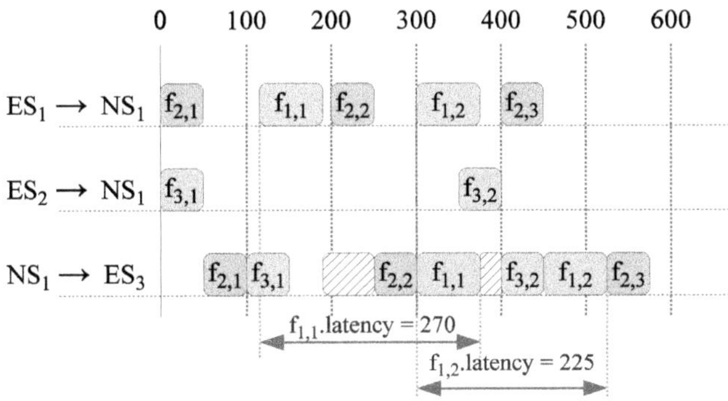

(a) *Postpone* move on $f_{2,3}^{[NS_1,ES_2]}$ from Fig. 5b

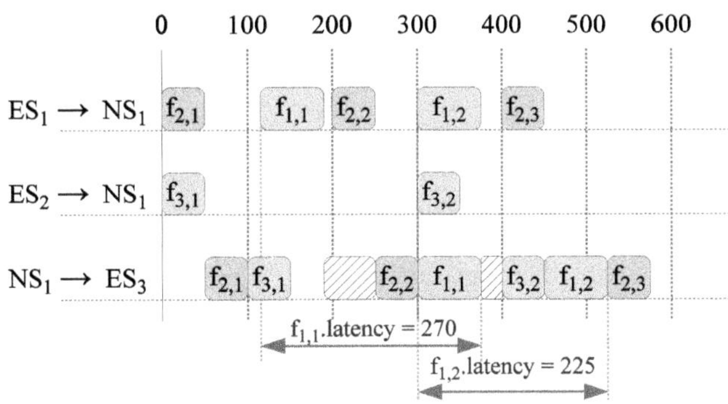

(b) *Advance* move on $f_{3,2}^{[ES_2,NS_1]}$ from Fig. 8a

Figure 8: Moves for TT traffic

a feasible region. Once the TT frames are schedulable we set the weight w_{TT} to zero, since we are interested to minimize the end-to-end delays for the RC frames. The degree of schedulability is calculated as:

$$\delta_{TT/RC} = \begin{cases} c_1 = \sum_i \max(0, R_{f_i} - f_i.deadline) & \text{if} c_1 > 0 \\ c_2 = \sum_i (R_{f_i} - f_i.deadline) & \text{if} c_1 = 0 \end{cases} \quad (2)$$

If at least one frame is not schedulable, there exists one R_{f_i} greater than the deadline $f_i.deadline$, and therefore the term c_1 will be positive. However if all the frames are schedulable, this means that each R_{f_i} is smaller than $f_i.deadline$, and the term c_1 = 0. In this case, we use c_2 as the degree of schedulability, since it can distinguish between two schedulable solutions.

Tabu Search explores the design space by using design transformations (or "moves") applied to the current solution in order to generate neighboring solutions. As it is practically impossible to exhaustively evaluate the whole design space, in order to increase the efficiency of the Tabu Search, and to drive it intelligently towards the solution, these "moves" are not performed random, but chosen based on a *candidate list* of moves that may improve the search. Each candidate is evaluated. If the currently explored solution is better than the best known solution, it is saved as the "best-so-far" solution. To escape local minima, TS incorporates an adaptive memory (called "Tabu list"), to prevent the search from revisiting previous solutions. Thus, moves that improve the search are saved as "Tabu". In case there is no improvement in finding a better solution for a number of iterations, we use *diversification*, i.e., we visit previously unexplored regions of the search space. In case the search diversification is unsuccessful, we *restart* the search from the best known solution.

We use four types of moves applied to TT frame instances: *advance*, *advance predecessors*, *postpone* and *postpone successors*. The *advance* move will advance the scheduled send time of a TT frame instance $f_{i.x}$ from a node ν_j on a dataflow link $[\nu_j, \nu_k]$ to an earlier moment in time. The *advance predecessors* applied to a frame instance $f_{i.x}^{[\nu_j,\nu_k]}$, will advance the scheduled send time for all its predecessors, $pred(f_{i.x}^{[\nu_j,\nu_k]})$. Similarly the *postpone* move will postpone the schedule send time of a TT frame instance from a node, while *postpone successors* will postpone the send time for all the successors of that frame instance.

The maximum amount of time a frame instance is advanced or postponed at a node $\nu_j \in \mathcal{V}$ is computed such that the frame instance will not be sent before it is received, or sent too late to meet its deadline. Also, after each move we may need to adjust the schedules (move other frame instances later or earlier) to keep the solution valid, i.e., the schedules respect the precedence and resource constraints.

Let us illustrate these moves using the example presented in Section 6. The setup from Fig. 4 shows the architecture model in Fig. 4a and the application model in Fig. 4b. Fig. 5a presents a possible solution for synthesizing the TT schedule. In this case, the worst-case end-to-end delay R_{f_1} for the RC frame f_1 is 470 μs. Fig. 5b shows the result of a *postpone successors* move applied to the frame instance $f_{3,2}$ from Fig. 5a on dataflow link $[ES_2, NS_1]$. Consequently, frame instance $f_{3,2}^{[NS_1,ES_3]}$ is also postponed, thus creating sufficient space for $f_{1,1}$ to execute. The latency of frame instance $f_{1,2}$ can be further reduced by applying a *postpone* move to $f_{2,3}^{[NS_1,ES_3]}$ from Fig. 5b, as shown in Fig. 8a. Fig. 8b presents the result of an *advance* move applied to $f_{3,2}$ from Fig. 8a on dataflow link $[NS_1, ES_3]$, with no effect on the latencies of any of the frames involved.

For situations when there are several TT frames scheduled for transmission back-to-back on a dataflow link $[\nu_j, \nu_k]$ which may lead to large delays for RC frames, our optimization applies an *add blank* move, which adds a blank interval $bi_i^{[\nu_j,\nu_k]}$ on dataflow link $[\nu_j, \nu_k]$, which is reserved for RC traffic. Blank spaces will also be introduced by advance/postpone moves. The difference between an *add blank* and these moves is that the blank interval introduced through advance/postpone may be used by other TT frames, while the space introduced by an *add blank* move is reserved for RC frames only. In case a TT frame instance misses its deadline due to a certain blank interval $bi_i^{[\nu_j,\nu_k]}$ on dataflow link $[\nu_j, \nu_k]$, the optimization will either remove or resize the blank interval, by performing a *remove blank* move or a *resize blank* move, respectively.

Let us consider the situation presented in Fig. 9. We assume the topology presented in Fig. 4a, and we consider dataflow links $[ES_1, NS_1]$ and $[NS_1, ES_2]$. We assume that the dataflow links have equal transmission speeds. For this example, we have one RC frame, f_{10} sent by ES_1 to ES_2, with the transmission duration $C_{f_{10}} = 100$ μs, and 5 TT frames f_1 to f_5 to be forwarded by NS_1 to ES_2. The transmission durations for the TT frames f_1 to f_5 are 100 μs, 75 μs, 100 μs, 50 μs and 125 μs, respectively. Let us consider the TT schedule presented in Fig. 9a, where the TT frames are scheduled back-to-back on dataflow link $[NS_1, ES_2]$, starting at time 150 μs. In this case, the worst-case delay for the RC frame f_{10} is 725 μs. The network implements the *timely block* approach (see Section 5.2), and we represent with a hatched box the time interval RC frame is blocked to transmit so it does not disturb the TT frames.

For situations such as the one presented in Fig. 9a, where an RC frame is blocked from transmission due to TT frames scheduled back-to-back, the *candidate list* will contain an *add blank* move to reduce the delay of the RC frame. By applying an *add blank* move to dataflow link $[NS_1, ES_2]$, as shown in Fig. 9b, the algorithm reserves a time interval of 175 μs for RC traffic, marked by a green box on the schedule. In this case, the worst-case delay for f_{10} is of only 550 μs.

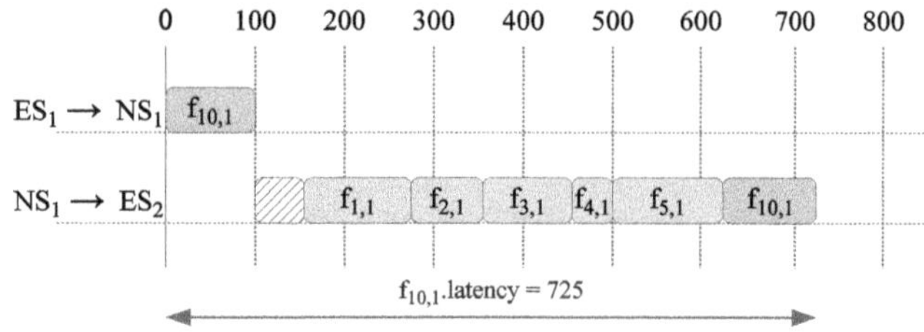

(a) Initial TT schedules

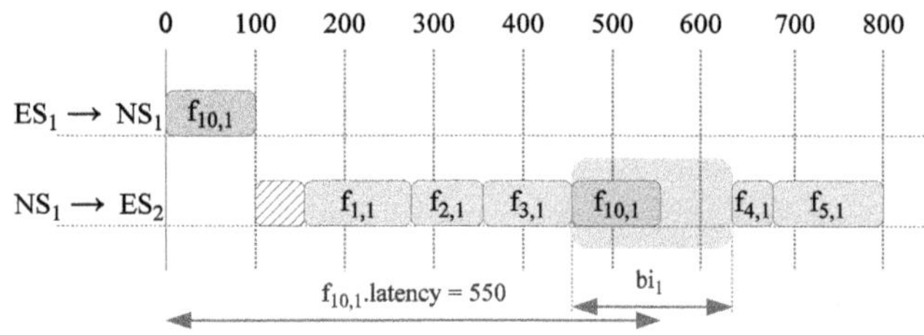

(b) The *add blank* move reduces the latency for $f_1 0$

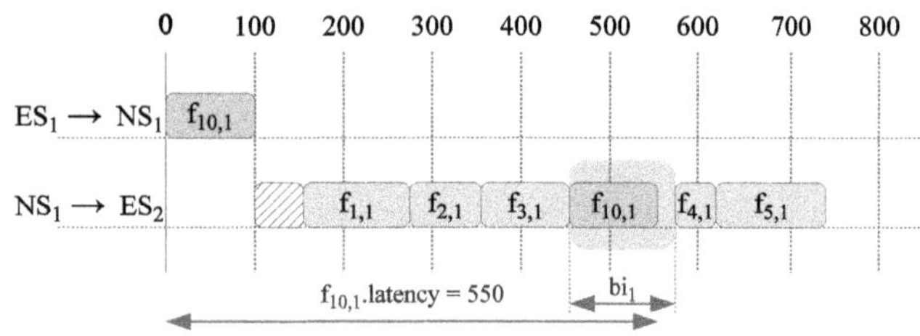

(c) The *resize blank* move reduces the latency for f_4 and f_5

Figure 9: Moves for RC traffic

Let us assume frame f_5 has a deadline of 775 μs. In case a frame instance misses its deadline due to a blank interval $bi_i^{[\nu_j,\nu_k]}$ on dataflow link $[\nu_j,\nu_k]$, the algorithm can apply either a *remove blank* or a *resize blank* move to the blank interval. In Fig. 9c we apply a *resize blank* move on the blank interval bi_1 on dataflow link $[NS_1,ES_2]$. Thus, we resize bi_1 from 175 μs to 100 μs, which allows us to advance the scheduled send time for frames f_4 and f_5, and consequently, allows frame f_5 to be delivered before its deadline.

7.2 RC frame end-to-end delay analysis

The worst-case end-to-end delay R_{f_i} of an RC frame $f_i \in \mathcal{F}^{RC}$ sent on a virtual link $vl_i = \mathcal{M}(f_i)$ is the sum of the worst-case queueing delays $Q_{f_i}^{[\nu_j,\nu_k]}$ on each network node (ES or NS) $\nu_j \in \mathcal{V}$ (which is the source of a dataflow link $[\nu_j,\nu_k] \in vl_i$) and the transmission duration $C_{f_i}^{[\nu_j,\nu_k]}$ for each dataflow link $[\nu_j,\nu_k] \in vl_i$ the frame transits:

$$R_{f_i} = \sum_{\substack{\nu_j,\nu_k \in \mathcal{V} \\ [\nu_j,\nu_k] \in vl_i}} (Q_{f_i}^{[\nu_j,\nu_k]} + C_{f_1}^{[\nu_j,\nu_k]}) \quad (3)$$

The worst-case queueing delay $Q_{f_i}^{[\nu_j,\nu_k]}$ of frame $f_i \in \mathcal{F}^{RC}$ transmitted on dataflow link $l_l = [\nu_j,\nu_k]$ is given by the following equation:

$$Q_{f_i}^{[\nu_j,\nu_k]} = Q_{f_i,[\nu_j,\nu_k]}^{TT} + Q_{f_i,[\nu_j,\nu_k]}^{RC} + Q_{\nu_j}^{TL} \quad (4)$$

where $Q_{f_i,[\nu_j,\nu_k]}^{TT}$ is the queueing delay due to the transmission of TT frames scheduled to be sent between the moment f_i arrives at the network node ν_j and the moment the frame instance is sent, $Q_{f_i,[\nu_j,\nu_k]}^{RC}$ is the delay caused by the RC frames that can arrive, in

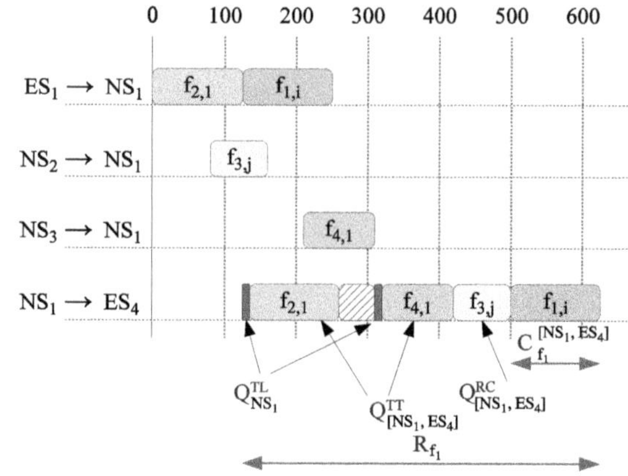

Figure 10: Worst-case end-to-end analysis for frame f_1

the worst-case, before f_i at the node and thus are placed before f_i into the outgoing queue. $Q_{\nu_j}^{TL}$ is the technical latency introduced by the network node for frame f_i, due to the hardware tasks implementing the TTEthernet protocol functionality, other than the latency resulting from queueing effects.

Let us illustrate in Fig. 10 these sources of delay for an RC frame at a network node considering the topology example presented in Fig. 2. There are 4 frames, with frames f_1 and f_2 sent from ES_1 to ES_2 and frames f_3 and f_4 forwarded by NS_2 and NS_3, respectively, to ES_2, with $f_1, f_3 \in \mathcal{F}^{RC}$ and $f_2, f_4 \in \mathcal{F}^{TT}$. All the dataflow links have the same speed, hence the transmission duration for the frames are $C_1 = 120$ μs for f_1, $C_2 = 125$ μs for f_2, $C_3 = 80$ μs for f_3 and $C_4 = 100$ μs for f_4. The RC frame under analysis is $f_{1,1}$. We consider the technical latency introduced by NS_1 to be $Q_{NS_1}^{TL} = 5$ μs. The network implements the timely block approach.

Fig. 10 presents the worst-case scenario for frame f_1, i.e., the case in which the end-to-end response time R_{f_1} is the largest. This happens for the frame instance $f_{1,i}$, which is delayed by frame instance $f_{2,1}$, $f_{4,1}$ and $f_{3,j}$. Thus, the TT frames $f_{2,1}$ and $f_{4,1}$ are scheduled for transmission on dataflow link $[NS_1, ES_4]$ at 130 μs and 310 μs, respectively, according to the TT schedules determined at design time. In the worst-case scenario, frame $f_{1,i}$ arrives at NS_1 at time moment 250 μs. Note that the RC frames are not synchronized with the TT schedules, so they can arrive at any time. The network implements the timely block algorithm, hence frame $f_{1,i}$ cannot be dispatched as soon as it arrives at NS_1, as it would interfere with the transmission of the scheduled TT frame $f_{4,1}$. We marked this blocking time of 60 μs in Fig. 10 with an hatched box. In this case, $Q_{f_1,[NS_1,ES_4]}^{TT} = 265$ μs, and it includes the blocking time.

In the worst-case scenario for $f_{1,i}$, the RC frame instance $f_{3,j}$ arrives at NS_1 before $f_{1,i}$, hence, $f_{3,j}$ will be sent to ES_4 before $f_{1,i}$. Consequently, $Q_{f_1,[NS_1,ES_4]}^{RC} = 80$ μs. The worst-case queueing delay for $f_{1,i}$ in NS_1, using Eq. 4, is $Q_{f_1}^{[NS_1,ES_4]} = Q_{f_1,[NS_1,ES_4]}^{TT} + Q_{f_1,[NS_1,ES_4]}^{RC} = 265 + 80 = 345$ (μs). Thus, we can compute the worst-case end-to-end delay for $f_{1,i}$ using Eq. 3 as $R_{f_1} = C_{f_1}^{[ES_1,NS_1]} + Q_{f_1}^{[NS_1,ES_4]} + C_{f_1}^{[ES_1,NS_1]} = 120 + 345 + 120 = 485$ (μs).

Researchers have proposed several worst case end-to-end delay analyses for the traffic in an ARINC 664p7 network, including analyses based on Network Calculus [14, 13], Finite State Machine [32], Timed Automata [6] or Trajectory Approach [11, 12]. However, none of these analysis methods are applicable to TTEthernet, since they do not consider the impact of TT messages on the schedulability of RC messages. In this paper we use the TTEther-

Set	Test case	ES	NS	Messages	Frame instances	Load [%]	Δ_{cost} [%]
1	11	13	4	80	12593	50	2.58
	12	25	6	88	1787		24.44
	13	35	8	103	2285		20.06
	14	45	10	165	3299		11.90
2	21	11	4	115	16904	70	9.17
	22	25	6	179	2523		20.61
	23	35	8	154	3698		39.34
3	31	25	6	76	1387	40	37.97
	32			88	1787	50	24.44
	33			115	2503	60	40.47
	34			179	2523	70	20.61
	35			155	2960	80	32.10
4	41	35	8	65	1976	40	38.75
	42			103	2285	50	20.06
	43			89	2801	60	12.73
	44			176	3856	70	12.75
	45			135	3490	80	20.23
5	automotive	15	3	170	38305	80	50.88

Table 1: Experimental results

net analysis from [35], which shows how to consider TT messages. In our future work, we plan to extend the Trajectory Approach [12] to consider TT messages, with the aim to reduce the pessimism of the analysis from [35]. However, note that the analysis used for RC frames is orthogonal to our optimization problem.

8. EXPERIMENTAL EVALUATION

For the evaluation of our proposed optimization approach, "TTEthernet Schedules Optimization" (TTESO), we used 17 synthetic benchmarks and one real-life case study. The TTESO algorithm was implemented in Java (JDK 1.6), running on SunFire v440 computers with UltraSPARC IIIi CPUs at 1.062 GHz and 8 GB of RAM.

The results are presented in Table 1. For the synthetic benchmarks, we have used 6 network topologies, and we have randomly generated the parameters for the frames, taking into account the details of the TTEthernet protocol. All the dataflow links have a transmission speed of 100 Mbps. In columns 3–7, we have the details of each benchmark, the number of ESes, NSes, number of messages, the number of frame instances and the load on the network, respectively. The load within an application cycle T_{cycle} is calculated as the ratio of the sum of the sizes of all frame instances divided by the network speed (in our case 100 Mbps).

For all experiments, we have compared TTESO with a baseline solution, namely the Straightforward Solution (SS), which builds the TT schedules with the goal of minimizing the end-to-end response time of the TT frames without using the analysis of RC traffic. The comparison between SS and TTESO, Δ_{cost}, is shown in the last column in the table as a percentage improvement of TTESO over SS, in terms of the cost function (Eq. 1).

In the first two sets of experiments, labeled "Set 1" and "Set 2" in Table 1, we were interested to evaluate the quality of the results obtained with TTESO as the size of the system increases. Thus, we have used 7 synthetic benchmarks, with the number of network nodes ranging between 16 and 55 nodes. The first set of 4 benchmarks have a load of 50%, and the second set of benchmarks have a load of 70%. As we can see, TTESO is able to significantly improve the cost function over SS, even as the size of the system increases. We used a time limit of 45 minutes for the first set and 90 minutes for the second set.

In the third sets of experiments, labeled "Set 3" were interested on how TTESO performs as the load of the network increases from 40% to 80%. As we can see, TTESO is able to significantly improve on the the solution provided by SS. These results were obtained using a time limit of 30, 45, 70, 90 and 120 minutes for the test cases with a load of 40%, 50%, 60%, 70% and 80%, respectively. A similar evaluation was performed in the case of experimental "Set 4", with the difference that we considered a larger architecture.

Finally, we used one real-life benchmark derived from [24], based on the SAE automotive communication benchmark [1]. In this benchmark we have 18 network nodes (ESes and NSes), and 83 frames (with the parameters generated based on the messages presented in [24]). Table 1 contains the results for this benchmark—the last line labeled with "Set 5". The results obtained for the real-life benchmark confirms the results of the synthetic benchmarks.

9. CONCLUSIONS

In this paper we have addressed the optimization of the TTEthernet protocol. TTEthernet is very suitable for mixed-criticality systems, both in the temporal and safety domain. In the temporal domain, TTEthernet offers three types of traffic classes, Time-Triggered, Rate Constrained and Best Effort. In the safety domain, the protocol offers separation between mixed-criticality frames using the concept of virtual links, and protocol-level specialized dependability services.

We have considered mixed-criticality hard real-time applications implemented on distributed heterogenous architectures. Given the sets of TT and RC frames and the topology of the virtual links to which they are assigned, we have proposed a Tabu Search optimization strategy for the synthesis of the TT schedules. The synthesis is performed such that the frames are schedulable, and the degree of schedulability is improved. The results on several synthetic benchmarks and a real-life case study show that through the careful optimization of TT static schedules, significant improvements can be obtained.

10. ACKNOWLEDGEMENTS

This work has been funded by the Advanced Research & Technology for Embedded Intelligence and Systems (ARTEMIS) within the project 'RECOMP', support code 01IS10001A, agreement no. 100202.

11. REFERENCES

[1] SAE Technical Report J2056/1. Technical report, SAE International.

[2] *ISO 11898: Road Vehicles – Controller Area Network (CAN)*. International Organization for Standardization (ISO), Geneva, Switzerland, 2003.

[3] *ARINC 664P7: Aircraft Data Network, Part 7, Avionics Full-Duplex Switched Ethernet Network*. ARINC (Aeronautical Radio, Inc), 2009.

[4] *ISO 10681: Road vehicles – Communication on FlexRay*. International Organization for Standardization (ISO), Geneva, Switzerland, 2010.

[5] *AS6802: Time-Triggered Ethernet*. SAE International, 2011.

[6] M. Adnan, J.-L. Scharbarg, J. Ermont, and C. Fraboul. Model for worst case delay analysis of an AFDX network using timed automata. In *Proceedings of the Conference on Emerging Technologies and Factory Automation*, pages 1 –4, 2010.

[7] N. Audsley, K. Tindell, and A. Burns. The end of the line for static cyclic scheduling. In *Proceedings of Euromicro Workshop on Real-Time Systems*, pages 36–41, 1993.

[8] S. Baruah and G. Fohler. Certification-Cognizant Time-Triggered Scheduling of Mixed-Criticality Systems.

Proceedings of the Real-Time Systems Symposium, pages 3–12, 2011.

[9] S. Baruah, H. Li, and L. Stougie. Towards the design of certifiable mixed-criticality systems. In *Proceedings of the Real-Time and Embedded Technology and Applications Symposium*, 2010.

[10] S. K. Baruah, A. Burns, and R. I. Davis. Response-Time Analysis for Mixed Criticality Systems. *Proceedings of the Real-Time Systems Symposium*, pages 34–43, 2011.

[11] H. Bauer, J.-L. Scharbarg, and C. Fraboul. Applying and optimizing trajectory approach for performance evaluation of AFDX avionics network. In *Proceedings of the Conference on Emerging Technologies Factory Automation*, pages 1 –8, 2009.

[12] H. Bauer, J.-L. Scharbarg, and C. Fraboul. Worst-case end-to-end delay analysis of an avionics AFDX network. In *Proceedings of the Conference on Design, Automation and Test in Europe*, pages 1220–1224, 2010.

[13] A. Bouillard, L. Jouhet, and E. Thierry. Tight Performance Bounds in the Worst-Case Analysis of Feed-Forward Networks. In *Proceedings of INFOCOM*, pages 1–9, 2010.

[14] M. Boyer and C. Fraboul. Tightening end to end delay upper bound for AFDX network calculus with rate latency FIFO servers using network calculus. In *Proceedings of the International Workshop on Factory Communication Systems*, pages 11 –20, 2008.

[15] R. Ernst. Certification of Trusted MPSoC Platforms. 10th International Forum on Embedded MPSoC and Multicore, 2010.

[16] R. N. et al. Steiner tree based distributed multicast routing in networks. In X. Cheng and D.-Z. Du, editors, *Steiner Trees in Industry*. Springer, 2002.

[17] E. N. Gilbert and H. O. Pollak. Steiner minimal trees. *SIAM Journal on Applied Mathematics*, 16(1):1–29, 1968.

[18] F. Glover and M. Laguna. *Tabu Search*. Kluwer Academic Publishers, Norwell, MA, USA, 1997.

[19] K. Hoyme and K. Driscoll. SAFEbus. *IEEE Aerospace Electronic Systems Magazine*, 8:34–39, 1993.

[20] V. Izosimov, P. Pop, P. Eles, and Z. Peng. Scheduling of fault-tolerant embedded systems with soft and hard timing constraints. In *Proceedings of the Conference on Design, Automation and Test in Europe*, pages 915–920, 2008.

[21] H. Kopetz. *Real-Time Systems: Design Principles for Distributed Embedded Applications*. Springer, 2011.

[22] B. Leiner, M. Schlager, R. Obermaisser, and B. Huber. A Comparison of Partitioning Operating Systems for Integrated Systems. *Computer Safety, Reliability, and Security*, pages 342–355, 2007.

[23] H. Lonn and J. Axelsson. A comparison of fixed-priority and static cyclic scheduling for distributed automotive control applications. In *Proceedings of the Euromicro Conference on Real-Time Systems*, pages 142–149. IEEE, 1999.

[24] U. Mohammad, N. Al-holou, and P. D. Development of an automotive communication benchmark. *Canadian Journal on Electrical and Electronics Engineering*, 1(5):99–115, 2010.

[25] R. Obermaisser. *Time-Triggered Communication*. CRC Press, Inc., 2011.

[26] P. Pop, P. Eles, and Z. Peng. Scheduling with optimized communication for time-triggered embedded systems. In *Proceedings of the International Workshop on Hardware/Software Codesign*, pages 178–182, 1999.

[27] P. Pop, P. Eles, and Z. Peng. *Analysis and Synthesis of Communication-Intensive Heterogenous Real-Time Systems*. Kluwer Academic Publishers, 2004.

[28] P. Pop, P. Eles, and Z. Peng. Schedulability-driven frame packing for multicluster distributed embedded systems. *ACM Transactions on Embedded Computing Systems (TECS)*, 4(1):112–140, 2005.

[29] T. Pop, P. Pop, P. Eles, and Z. Peng. Analysis and Optimisation of Hierarchically Scheduled Multiprocessor Embedded Systems. *International Journal of Parallel Programming*, 36(1):37–67, feb 2008.

[30] T. Pop, P. Pop, P. Eles, Z. Peng, and A. Andrei. Timing analysis of the FlexRay communication protocol. In *Proceedings of the Euromicro Conference on Real-Time Systems*, pages 11 pp. –216, 2006.

[31] J. Rushby. Partitioning for Avionics Architectures: Requirements, Mechanisms, and Assurance. NASA Contractor Report CR-1999-209347, NASA Langley Research Center, 1999.

[32] I. Saha and S. Roy. A Finite State Modeling of AFDX Frame Management Using Spin. In L. Brim, B. Haverkort, M. Leucker, and J. van de Pol, editors, *Formal Methods: Applications and Technology*, volume 4346 of *Lecture Notes in Computer Science*, pages 227–243. Springer, 2007.

[33] P. K. Saraswat, P. Pop, and J. Madsen. Task Mapping and Bandwidth Reservation for Mixed Hard/Soft Fault-Tolerant Embedded Systems. *Proceedings of the Real-Time and Embedded Technology and Applications Symposium*, pages 89–98, 2010.

[34] W. Steiner. An Evaluation of SMT-based Schedule Synthesis For Time-Triggered Multi-Hop Networks. In *Proceedings of the Real-Time Systems Symposium*, pages 375–384, 2010.

[35] W. Steiner. Synthesis of Static Communication Schedules for Mixed-Criticality Systems. In *Proceedings of the International Symposium on Object/Component/Service-Oriented Real-Time Distributed Computing Workshops*, pages 11 –18, 2011.

[36] W. Steiner, G. Bauer, B. Hall, M. Paulitsch, and S. Varadarajan. TTEthernet Dataflow Concept. In *Proceedings of the International Symposium on Network Computing and Applications*, pages 319 –322, 2009.

[37] D. Tămaş-Selicean and P. Pop. Design Optimization of Mixed-Criticality Real-Time Applications on Cost-Constrained Partitioned Architectures. In *Proceedings of the Real-Time Systems Symposium*, pages 24–33, 2011.

[38] J. D. Ullman. NP-complete scheduling problems. *J. Comput. Syst. Sci.*, 10(3):384–393, 1975.

[39] J. Xu and D. L. Parnas. On Satisfying Timing Constraints in Hard-Real-Time Systems. *IEEE Transactions on Software Engineer*, 19(1):70–84, 1993.

A Hierarchical Control Scheme for Energy Quota Distribution in Hybrid Distributed Video Coding

Muhammad Usman Karim Khan, Muhammad Shafique, Jörg Henkel
Karlsruhe Institute of Technology (KIT), Chair for Embedded Systems, Karlsruhe, Germany
{muhammad.khan, muhammad.shafique, henkel} @ kit.edu

ABSTRACT

Hybrid Distributed Video Coding (HDVC) has emerged as an attractive solution for energy and resource constrained video processing systems in different domains like distributed video sensors, mobile devices with dynamically varying energy levels, or hybrid paradigms where mobile devices are communicating with high-end servers. In this paper, we present a hierarchical control scheme for determining and distributing the energy quota in HDVC encoder and decoder under scenarios of dynamically varying energy levels and user constraints. The energy quotas are computed and controlled online at various hierarchical levels (like group of frames, frames, and macroblocks), while jointly accounting for the computation and transmission energy. For energy reduction, the processing of selective regions is intelligently distributed at both encoder and decoder sides, considering the texture and motion properties of different video regions and available spatial/temporal correlations. Experimental results demonstrate that our scheme provides on average 20%-25% reduced energy consumption compared to state-of-the-art HDVC schemes. The key to high energy efficiency is to leverage the video content properties.

Categories and Subject Descriptors: C.3 [**Special-Purpose and Application-Based Systems**]: Real-time and embedded systems; I.4.2 [**Compression (Coding)**]: Approximate Methods

General Terms: Algorithms, Design, Management, Performance

Keywords: Video Coding, Distributed Video Coding (DVC), Hybrid Distributed Video Coding (HDVC), Motion Estimation, Low-Power, Adaptivity, Energy Budgeting

1. INTRODUCTION & RELATED WORK

The high compression efficiency of the H.264/AVC [2] advanced video coding standard has enabled a wide range of applications like video sensors under low-bandwidth constraints, surveillance with smart cameras, entertainment, mobile multimedia, etc. To achieve high compression, H.264 employs variable block-sized motion estimation, deblocking filter, and context-adaptive entropy coding [3]. This results in a significantly increased computational complexity and energy consumption (~10x relative to MPEG-4 ASP [4][11]). H.264/AVC follows the predictive video coding (PVC) model where the prediction (motion estimation, motion compensation, etc.) is performed at the encoder side. In this scenario, computational requirements of the H.264 decoder are 10x-20x lesser compared to that of the H.264 encoder [1][4]. However, due to high compression efficiency, the transmission power for PVC is quite low. Therefore, PVC is typically well-suited for scenarios where encoding devices have high computational power available, while decoders are resource-/power-constrained devices, like video streaming for mobile devices, etc.

Recently, Distributed Video Coding (DVC) has been emerged as an attractive solution for scenarios where the *encoding devices are resource-constrained* requiring low-complexity encoding (like in-field wireless video sensor nodes, small autonomous flying robots, mobile devices with low processing capabilities, etc.), while the *decoding devices have high computational power* and can execute high-complexity decoding (like servers, high-end transmission head) [13][6][15][27][28][23][12]. DVC paradigm provides means to *shift/offload the computational workload from encoder to decoder*. A DVC encoder typically consumes only 7% of the total power consumed by a PVC H.264 encoder (see Fig. 1a) [16][17]. In DVC paradigm, instead of the encoder, the decoder performs the Motion Estimation (ME) with interpolation, extrapolation, and upsampling, while exploiting the inter-frame correlation in order to generate an estimate of the input video sequence. At the DVC decoder side, Slepian-Wolf decoder and ME with interpolation contribute towards 90% of the total decoding complexity [15] (see DVC details in Section 1.1). To improve the estimation quality, the DVC decoder demands auxiliary information from the encoder (i.e. parity bits generated by turbo coding), which results in a much higher transmission power compared to the PVC case (see Fig. 1b; [16]). More are the parity bits, higher is the video quality at the decoder side and higher is the transmission energy at the encoder-side [29][30].

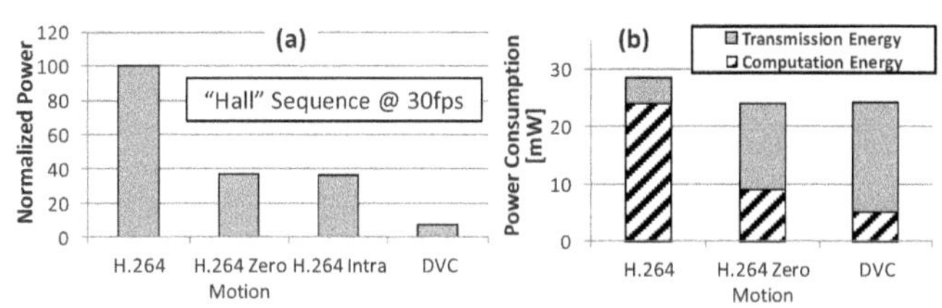

Fig. 1 (a) Relative computation power comparison for different coding systems; (b) Comparing the computation and transmission power for an ASIC-based video sensor [16]; wireless transmitter of [18]; H.264 implementation of [17]

Fig. 1b shows that for the "Hall" test video sequence, the transmission power of a DVC-based system is about 4x more than that of the PVC-based H.264 coding system for a 65 nm ASIC-based video sensor node [13]. Note, although in this example of "Hall" sequence, the power of three codecs is almost similar, the power consumption of PVC and DVC can significantly vary depending upon the video sequence properties[1] (see case study in Section 2) [11][16]. The major drawback of DVC is lower video quality compared to that provided by PVC [25]. **In short,** DVC is beneficial in scenarios, where the encoder-side devices are computation-constrained and have sufficient transmission power, while the decoder-side devices have sufficient computational power available.

[1] For surveillance type sequences with low motion, DVC power consumption is lower than PVC; while for entertainment quality sequences with hectic motion, PVC power consumption is lower than DVC.

Issues with PVC and DVC: Both PVC and DVC individually become power-/energy-wise inefficient in scenarios where both encoder- and decoder-side devices are resource-constrained and/or subjected to run-time varying conditions of available energy levels and computational resources. In such scenarios, only one or neither of encoder-/decoder-side devices has sufficient computational and/or transmission power to deliver the required quality of service (frame rate, etc.). Examples of such scenarios are: (1) collaborative distributed video sensor networks for smart energy-aware surveillance; (2) mobile devices – with dynamically varying battery energy levels – communicating with each other or with high-end power-constrained laptops/servers; (4) heterogeneous communicating devices from different vendors with distinct energy consumption properties, etc.[13][18][31]; see Fig. 2.

Hybrid Distributed Video Coding (HDVC) as an Emerging Coding Paradigm: To cope with the energy-related issues for video coding in such dynamic scenarios, *Hybrid Distributed Video Coding (HDVC)* has emerged as an attractive solution [24][25][10]. HDVC aims at combining the positive aspects of both PVC and DVC, i.e. providing high encoded video quality close to PVC and low computational power close to DVC. In HDVC, the decoder-side ME complexity is relaxed at the cost of partial ME at the encoder side. The partial ME at the encoder side results in better reconstruction of frames at the decoder side, that corresponds to a high video quality and low energy consumption at the decoder side. However, it incurs high energy consumption at the encoder side due to ME processing. Note, ME is the most energy consuming functional block and may consume up to 65% of the total encoding energy [5][11]. *Better ME at the HDVC encoder side also reduces the number of parity bits that results in low transmission energy* [8]. However, this depends upon the amount of ME to be performed at the encoder side (see Section 2 for detailed analysis). Complex motion sequences may require more ME at the HDVC encoder side to meet the quality of service requirements, which may not be feasible due to the unavailability of sufficient computational and battery energy resources at the HDVC encoder side.

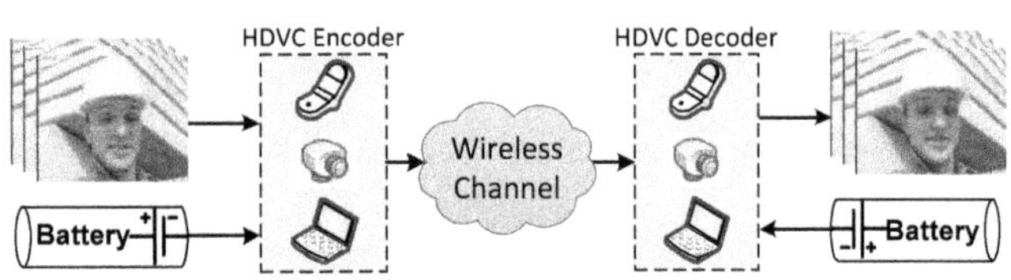

Fig. 2 Video capture and wireless transmission scenario with resource constrained encoder and decoder

Challenging Problem: In order to realize HDVC in resource- and energy-constrained devices subjected to dynamically varying scenarios, *an adaptive energy quota distribution scheme is required.* Such a scheme needs to compute and control the energy quota for determining the ME effort at both HDVC encoder and decoder sides, such that overall energy (considering computation and transmission) is minimized, while satisfying the user constraints.

Prominent state-of-the-art techniques in low-power HDVC (like [9][21][22]) determine the number of Macroblocks (MB: 16x16 pixel blocks) to be processed at the encoder side in a *raster scan order*, use global motion models, send a low quality reference, or process it at the encoder side based upon MB's motion intensity. Our experiments in Section 2 illustrate that objects in video sequences typically consist of MBs that do *not* occur on the raster scan order [39]. Moreover, selection of the MBs with high motion intensity cannot cope with constant camera motion and panning. Therefore, an inexpert selection of MBs in the raster scan order or based on mere motion intensity may lead to inefficient energy distribution in HDVC. As a result, these state-of-the-art techniques may quickly exhaust the available energy quotas for the ME of non-important MBs. In general, state-of-the-art techniques in HDVC and DVC may not be energy efficient as they do not exploit (i) video content properties (like texture, motion, etc.); (ii) the relationship between video content properties and the ME effort and parity bits produced; and (iii) correlation of MBs. Therefore, the energy quota distribution and control scheme need to perform intelligent partitioning of ME in HDVC by exploiting the video content properties while minimizing the overall energy.

Our Novel Concept and Contributions in a Nutshell: To address the above-discussed challenges, we propose a *novel hierarchical control scheme for HDVC that performs video content-aware adaptive energy quota distribution and control at multiple hierarchical levels (i.e. group of frames, frame, and MB) for both HDVC encoder and decoder.* Our scheme reduces the overall energy consumption by jointly considering for the computation and transmission energy under scenarios of dynamically varying energy levels and user constraints. Our scheme accounts for video content properties (i.e. texture and motion) for selecting MBs from the regions of interest (ROIs) to perform selective ME, while efficiently utilizing the allocated energy quotas. Fig. 3 shows an overview of our HDVC codec with novel contributions in colored filled-blocks.

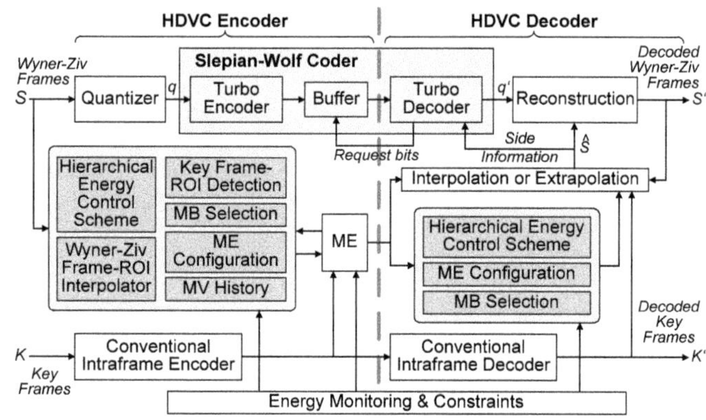

Fig. 3 Our HDVC system with hierarchical control scheme for run-time adaptive energy quota distribution and control

Our scheme employs:

1) **A group-of-frame-level energy control algorithm (Section 3.1)** that computes the target energy quota for a complete group of frames depending upon the battery level and user-defined coding duration constraints. It then controls the target quota of the subsequent group-of-frames in a feedback loop.

2) **A frame-level control energy algorithm (Section 3.2)** that adaptively distributes the group-level energy quota among different frames depending upon their temporal distances. It thereby, accounts for the changing temporal correlation among different frames. The energy quota among different frames is controlled to avoid violation of group-level quota.

3) **An ROI-identification and extrapolation algorithm (Section 3.3)** that detects the ROIs by evaluating the motion properties of different MBs w.r.t. their spatial and temporal neighboring MBs. A ranking mechanism is used to select important ROI-MBs for HDVC encoder-side ME depending upon the frame-level energy quota.

4) **An MB-level energy control algorithm (Section 3.4)** that distributes the frame level energy quota among the selected ROI-MBs starting from the highest *rank* value. It controls the MB-level energy quota by back-propagating the weighted error between consumed and target MB energy.

At the encoder side, the MB-level energy quota is used to determine the ME configuration of the selected MBs. At the decoder side, the allocated energy quota is used for determining the ME/SI configuration for the MBs that are not selected for the encoder-side ME.

Paper Organization: Section 1.1 presents an overview of PVC, DVC, and HDVC. Section 2 presents a motivational analysis of HDVC for energy and correlation. Our novel hierarchical control scheme for energy quota distribution is presented in Section 3. Section 4 presents the results followed by conclusion in Section 5.

1.1 DVC/HDVC: Terminology and Basics

The DVC concept originated from the works of Slepian-Wolf [14] and Wyner-Ziv [6]. Prominent research projects are DISCOVER [19][13][20]. Due to resource constraints, the DVC encoder only performs spatial predictions, i.e. so-called Intra-frame encoding of Key-Frames (denoted as I-frames in this paper). Other video frames between two I-frames are called Non-Key-Frames or Wyner-Ziv frames (denoted as W-frames in this paper). For W-frames, encoder only sends the auxiliary information, i.e. parity bits generated using turbo coding. The decoder reconstructs the W-frames using decoder-side ME and interpolation and uses parity bits to correct the estimates. The basic principle of decoder-side reconstruction is to exploit the correlation between two I-frames. The decoder-side estimate of W-frames is called *Side Information* (SI). This estimate is improved by requesting more parity bits from the encoder side. See more details on SI generation mechanisms in [8][32]. Note that a better estimate of SI at the decoder implies better reconstructed video quality and lesser transmission of parity bits from the encoder, thus reducing the transmission energy. HDVC extends the concepts of DVC and PVC by adaptively distributing the ME at both encoder and decoder sides [24]. It is beneficial in scenarios, where both encoding and decoding devices are resource-/power-constrained. The group of W-frames and preceding I-frame is called the Group of W-frames (GOW); see Fig. 4. The number of frames in a GOW is denoted as size of GOW ($S_{GOW}=m+1$); *'m'* is the number of W-frames and *'1'* is the I-frame.

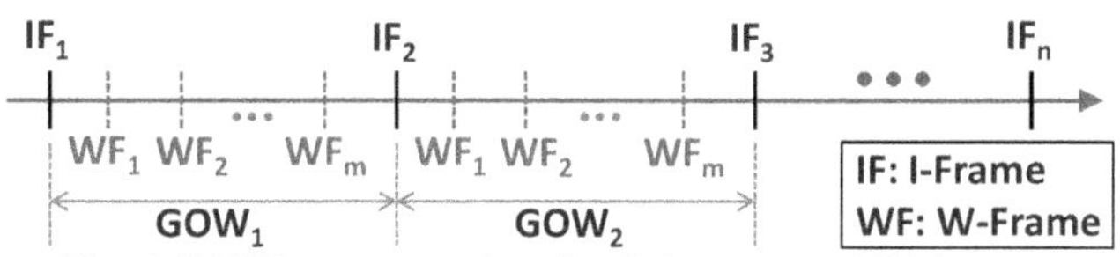

Fig. 4 GOW structure showing I-frames and W-frames

Before proceeding to the details of our novel scheme, we present an experimental case study to accentuate the research challenges and issues related to the energy quota distribution problem in HDVC. This analysis provides the foundation for this work.

2. MOTIVATIONAL CASE STUDY: HDVC ENERGY AND CORRELATION ANALYSIS

We have performed an experimental case study for the scenario shown in Fig. 2, where two energy-constrained mobile devices are communicating with each other over wireless network using an HDVC video codec; see experimental setup in Section 4. This case study demonstrates the impact of diverse video properties on the distribution of computation and transmission energy. Additionally, we have implemented the approach of [9] to illustrate the limitations of state-of-the-art that allocates the energy quota for ME of the MBs in the raster scan order, i.e. ignoring the video content properties.

Fig. 5 shows varying distribution of computation and transmission energy for different test video sequences with diverse texture and motion properties. Note that for a given number of MBs for which ME has to be processed at the HDVC encoder side, there is an increase in the ME energy due to extensive ME search for fast moving MBs. Moreover, since for the remaining MBs decoder may not get accurate matches, it results in increased transmission energy of encoder due to more parity bits. Such an increase in the computation and transmission energy can be seen in the "Coastguard" sequence (Fig. 5a), which contains river water with ripples and moving boats that are hard to predict. Due to low texture/motion, "Mother and Daughter" and "Hall" sequences have reduced transmission and computation energy compared to the other two sequences with same Peak Signal to Noise Ratio (PSNR)=36 dB; see Fig. 5a.

Hint-1: More energy quota should be allocated for encoder side ME in case of video scenes with high texture and motion. Higher energy savings for computation and transmission at the encoder-side can be obtained for the low-texture and low-motion video scenes, as the decoder – with a high probability – generates good quality reconstructed video frames. *The key is to leverage the video content properties during the energy quota distribution in order to balance the ME computation energy and the parity bit transmission energy at the encoder side, such that the video quality achieved at the decoder side is high.*

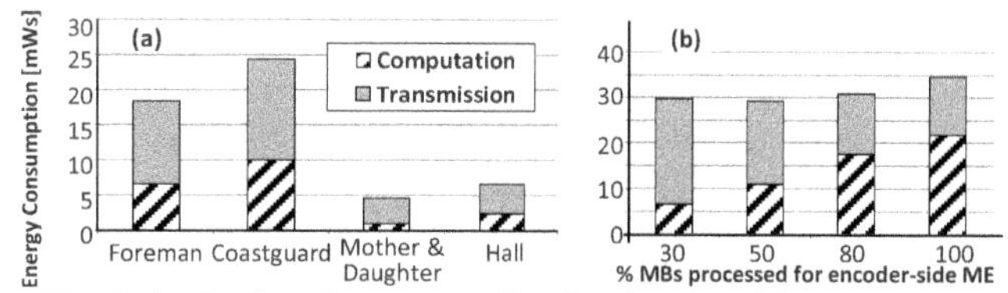

Fig. 5 Analyzing the energy distribution for different video sequences and different number of MBs processed for ME

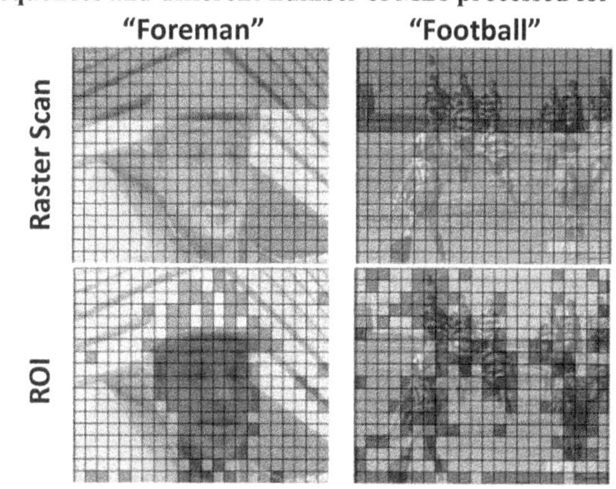

Fig. 6 Selected MBs in raster scan order and in ROI

Even within a video scene, due to their diverse texture and motion properties, it is important to study that which MBs have the highest impact on the computation and transmission energy. For this, we have performed experiments with different number of MBs processed for encoder-side ME. More encoder-side ME leads to high ME computation energy, but reduced transmission energy (see Fig. 5b). However, for a given number of MBs to be processed for ME, the energy consumption highly depends upon which MBs are selected for encoder-side ME. State-of-the-art techniques in HDVC (like [9]) select MBs in the raster select for ME processing. Since MBs of ROI typically do not lie on the raster scan order (see "Foreman" and "football players" in see Fig. 6), such techniques may lead to high transmission energy in case of few MBs processed for encoder-side ME; see Fig. 5b. Moreover, ME of background MBs (low-texture/motion, static MBs; see Fig. 6) may not provide effective reduction in the parity bits, thus leading to higher transmission energy (see Fig. 5b). Since such MBs can be easily regenerated at the decoder side, there is no need to waste energy for encoder-side ME of such MBs. Furthermore, ME of many complex MBs of background regions may quickly exhaust the available energy quotas for the ME. Therefore, it is beneficial to

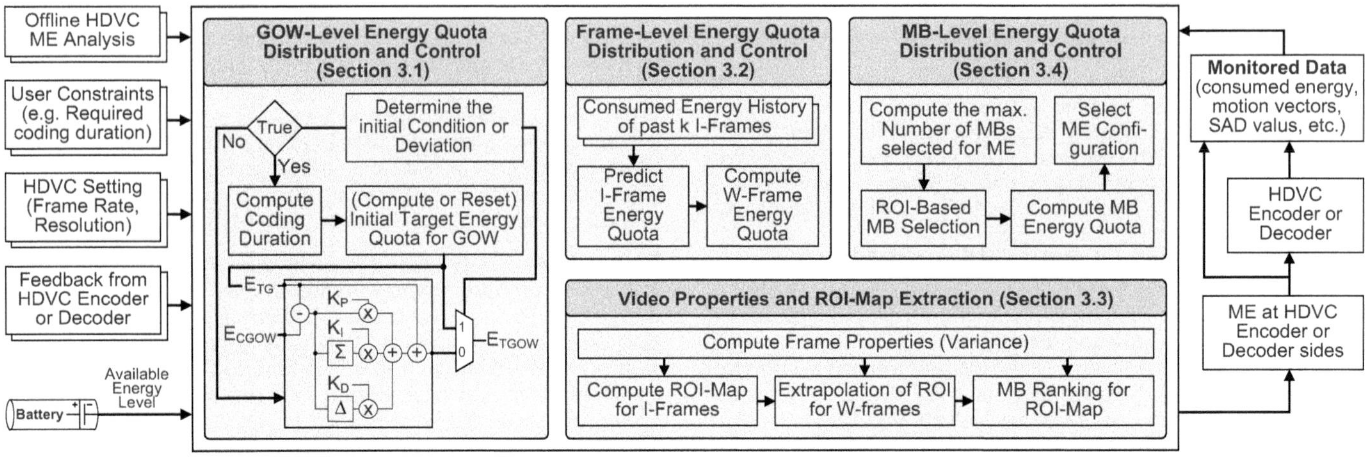

Fig. 8 Detailed operational flow of our hierarchical control scheme for energy quota distribution

spend encoder-side energy in the ME of the complex MBs of the ROI, because in this case, the decoder will have difficulty in estimating such MBs (as our results illustrate in Section 4).

Hint-2: Computation and transmission energy in HDVC highly depends upon the MB types selected for the encoder-side ME. Higher overall energy savings and better video quality can be achieved if the MBs of objects in ROI are selected for encoder-side ME processing. Such knowledge needs to be incorporated during the energy quota distribution. *The key challenges are low-overhead ROI identification, ROI-based MB selection for different video scenes, and adaptive energy quota distribution considering this knowledge.*

Fig. 7 demonstrates that there is extensive *spatial* and *temporal correlation* between the MBs of the same frame and neighboring frames, respectively. Typically MBs of objects with low variance have high spatial correlation [36][37][38][39]. Similarly slow-moving MBs have high temporal correlation. Fig. 7 shows motion vector drift (motion vector difference of spatial neighbors) and motion vector difference between the current and collocated MBs (i.e. temporal neighbors). This correlation can be used to efficiently predict the important MBs for which encoder performs the ME to reduce the prediction error at the decoder-side. However, the highly-correlated MBs are left for the decoder, as decoder has a high probability to find a good approximation for such spatially and temporally correlated MBs, thus resulting in less number of parity bits.

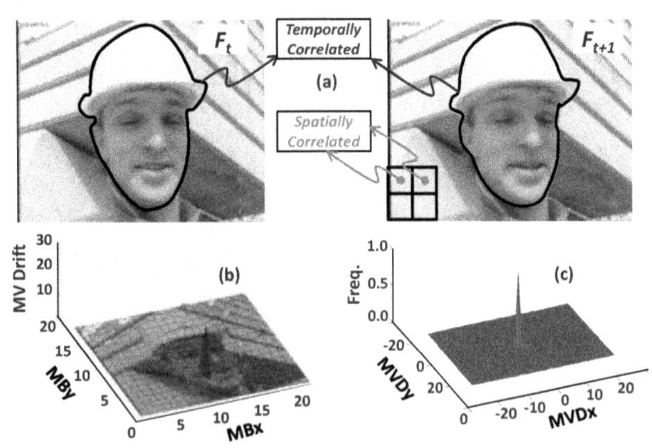

Fig. 7 Spatial and temporal correlation in "Foreman" sequence

Hint-3: The match of the MBs with high spatial and temporal correlation can be accurately predicted at the decoder-side without excessive decoder-side ME. MBs with high spatial and temporal correlation need not to be processed for encoder-side ME, thus using the encoder-side energy quota for more important MBs. *The key challenge is to account for motion vector drift for ROI identification and ranking ROI-MBs.*

Summarizing the motivational analysis: *the key research challenges* for reducing the energy consumption of HDVC are:

a) *Adaptive energy quota distribution and control* at various levels under dynamically varying scenarios;
b) *Leveraging video content properties* to enable efficient control on energy distribution and to achieve high energy reduction
c) *Low-overhead Region of Interest (ROI) identification* and *ROI-based MB selection* depending upon MB properties,
d) *Motion-based ranking of MBs* for efficient MB selection;

3. HIERARCHICAL CONTROL SCHEME FOR ENERGY QUOTA DISTRIBUTION

Fig. 8 illustrates the detailed operational flow of our hierarchical control scheme that adaptively distributes and controls the energy quota of HDVC encoder and decoder at various hierarchical levels, i.e. GOW, frame, and Macroblock (MB) levels. The inputs to our scheme are (i) offline energy analysis of HDVC ME at both encoder and decoder sides; (ii) user constraints (like required coding duration); and (iii) HDVC configurations (like resolution, frame rate, S_{GOW}). The output is the list of selected MBs with their allocated energy quota. The MB-level energy quota is used to obtain an appropriate ME configuration for the selected MBs. Afterwards, the consumed energy during encoding and decoding are monitored and fed back to the scheme along with the motion statistics (like motion vectors). Our scheme operates in four major steps:

Step-1) GOW-Level Energy Quota Distribution and Control (Section 3.1): First, user defined constraints and available energy from the battery level are used to determine the potential coding duration. If the potential coding duration is less than the user-defined constraint, the frame rate and GOW size are re-adjusted to fulfill the user constraints in the available battery level. This coding duration along with the offline ME energy analysis is used to derive the initial target energy quota for each GOW. Since the consumed energy of a GOW may differ from the allocated energy quota, the target of the upcoming GOW is recomputed using a feedback control mechanism. Our scheme employs a simple PID controller to control the target of the upcoming GOWs. In case of a deviation (i.e. a significant change between two I-frames, for instance, due to a scene cut), the initial target for a GOW is reset for the controller. The GOW-level energy quota is forwarded to the frame-level energy quota distributor.

Step-2) Frame-Level Energy Quota Distribution and Control (Section 3.2): At the frame level, the energy quota is distributed among the I-frame and *'m'* W-frames. The energy quota of the I-frame is computed by performing a history-based prediction using the energy consumption of *'k'* previous I-frames. Afterwards, the energy quota of *'m'* W-frames is obtained. This quota is distributed among *'m'* W-frames considering the temporal distance of a given W-frame from the preceding I-frame and relative variance difference of two I-frames at the borders of the current GOW. The temporal distance based energy quota distribution accommodates the changing temporal correlation inside a given GOW due to the longer temporal distance. At the decoder side, the energy quota distribution primarily focuses on the bi-directional ME between two I-frames, which are used for motion interpolation for different W-frames.

Step-3) ROI Identification and Extrapolation (Section 3.3): In order to intelligently distribute the frame-level energy quota among different MBs of a frame, our scheme employs a ROI-based MB selection and ROI-driven energy quota distribution. The ROI is identified for I-frames considering the motion drift of a given MB w.r.t. its neighboring MBs. Since MBs in the object/ROI have high spatial and temporal correlation, our scheme selects the ROI-MB with high *rank* value, which is quantified as the motion vector drift. It is based on the analysis of Section 2, that decoder can generate the estimates for W-frames for highly-correlated MBs. Typically, MBs at the object boundaries are selected by our scheme. An ROI map containing the ROI-MBs sorted w.r.t. their *rank* values in a descending order (starting with the highest *rank* value). This facilitates generating a high-quality SI at the decoder side that leads to reduced energy at the encoder side. Note, our scheme does not waste energy for the homogeneous and slow-moving MBs, because decoder can estimate these MBs with a high probability. Instead the energy is spent on complex MBs with high texture and fast motion, such that the SI generation at the decoder side can be improved that leads to less parity bits and consequently low transmission energy. In order to reduce the ROI overhead, the I-frame ROI-MBs are extrapolated for W-frames. The extrapolation is considered by fitting the projected ROI-MB location to the nearest MB boundary.

Step-4) MB-Level Energy Quota Distribution and Control (Section 3.4): First the maximum number of selected MBs is computed based on the available frame-level energy quota and best case ME (i.e. ME configuration with the least energy). Since in a resource-constrained scenario, sufficient processing power may not be available to meet the throughput constraints, the number of selected MBs is readjusted. For the number of selected MBs, ROI-MBs from the ROI map are extracted starting from the highest *rank* value. The energy quota of each MB is computed and controlled in a feedback manner. Depending upon the allocated energy quota, an appropriate ME configuration is selected and ME is performed. The consumed energy is monitored. This consumed energy may differ from the allocated energy quota. Therefore, the target of the subsequent MB is adjusted by back-propagating the error between the consumed and target MB energy in a weighted fashion. The total consumed energy is fed back for controlling the frame-level and GOW-level energy quota distribution.

In the following, we present detailed algorithms of different operational steps of our scheme.

3.1 GOW-Level Energy Quota Distribution & Control

Fig. 9 illustrates the pseudo-code for computing the GOW-level target energy quota for both encoder and decoder sides. Each GOW has *'m=*S_{GOW}*-1'* W-frames and *'1'* I-frame (see Section 1.1). When the HDVC is initialized the encoder and decoder side target GOW energy quotas ($E_{TGOW(Enc,Dec)}$) are computed considering the available battery levels and user constraints; lines 2-13. First the potential encoding or decoding durations are computed considering the available battery levels (line 4; Eq. 1) and minimum of two is selected to determine the overall potential coding duration; line 5. Note, E_{IAvg} and E_{WAvg} are the average energy consumption of I-frames and W-frames that are obtained using an offline analysis for various test video sequences [33].

```
1.  GOW_EnergyControl ( ): Input: Initialization Signal Init;
    Deviation Signal Dev; User defined duration D_U, Battery levels
    BL_Dec, BL_Enc, Frame rate FR; Size of GOW S_GOW; Consumed
    GOW energy E_CGOW(Enc,Dec);
    Output: Target energy of GOW E_TGOW(Enc,Dec); Adjusted frame
    rate and GOW size FR', m, S_GOW
2.  if(Init OR Dev)     { // (Re)compute Duration; see Eq. 1, Eq. 3
3.    m ← S_GOW − 1;  S_GOW' ← S_GOW;  FR' ← FR;  sumE_i ← 0;
4.    ∀i∈{Enc,Dec} D_i ← getDur(BL_i, m, FR, E_IAvgi, E_WAvgi);
5.    D ← min(D_Enc, D_Dec);
6.    D_Req ← max(D, D_U);
7.    if(D_U > D)     {
8.      FR' ← ⌊(FR × D)/D_U⌋;
9.      S_GOW' ← ⌊(S_GOW × FR')/FR⌋;
10.     m ← S_GOW' − 1;     }
11.   ∀i∈{Enc,Dec} E_TGi ← (BL_i × (m+1))/(D_Req × FR);
12.   ∀i∈{Enc,Dec} E_TGOWi ← E_TGi;
13. }  else
14. ∀i∈{Enc,Dec}  {
15.   ΔE_i ← E_i − (E_TGi − E_CGOWi);
16.   E_i ← E_TGOWi − E_CGOWi;
17.   sumE_i ← sumE_i + E_i;
18.   E_TGOWi ← E_TGi + ((K_P × E_i) + (K_I × sumE_i) + (K_D × ΔE_i));
19. }
20. return (E_TGOW(Enc,Dec), FR', m, S_GOW');
```

Fig. 9 Pseudo-code for computing and controlling the target energy quota at the GOW level for both encoder and decoder

If the potential coding duration is less than the user-defined coding duration constraint, the required duration is set (line 6) and the frame rate (*FR*) and GOW size (S_{GOW}) are readjusted to accommodate the required coding duration in the available battery levels; lines 7-10. Afterwards, the target GOW energy quotas are computed; lines 11-12. Since the consumed energy of a GOW may differ from the target GOW energy quota, our scheme adapts the target GOW energy quotas in a feedback control mechanism; lines 14-19. The error between the consumed energy and target energy quota is computed after for each GOW. Our scheme employs a simple PID controller to control the target energy quota of the next GOW. K_P, K_I, and K_D are the proportional, integral, and derivative gains. K_P reduces the error, K_I eradicates the steady error effects, and K_D ameliorates the stability. These gains are computed using the Ziegler-Nichols Method [26] using the settings given in Eq. 2 ($K_{PC}=0.8;\ T_C=2$).

$$D = \left(BL \times (m+1)\right) / \left(\left(E_{IAvg} + m \times E_{WAvg}\right) \times FR\right) \qquad (1)$$

$$K_P = 0.6 \times K_{PC};\ K_I = K_P / \left(0.5 \times T_C\right);\ K_D = K_P \times \left(0.125 \times T_C\right); \qquad (2)$$

Line 2 shows that in case of a *deviation* (Dev; line 2), the target GOW quota is reset and forwarded to the controller. The (Dev) is denoted as a significant change between two I-frames, such that the decoder cannot create a high quality estimate of the W-frames. It is typically due to a scene cut or significant texture difference ($\xi_{IFt}-\xi_{IFt+1}$) between two consecutive I-frames IF_t and IF_{t+1}. The deviation signal is computed using Eq. 3, where ξ_{TH} denotes the texture threshold.

$$Dev = \begin{cases} 1; & if\ \left((sceneCut)\ OR\ \left((\xi_{IFt} - \xi_{IFt+1}) > \xi_{TH}\right)\right) \\ 0; & Otherwise \end{cases} \qquad (3)$$

3.2 Frame-Level Energy Quota Distribution and Control

The GOW-level energy quota is distributed among the I-frames (E_{TIF}) and the W-frames (E_{TWF}) depending upon S_{GOW}.

Encoder-Side Energy Quota Distribution: The energy quota is distributed to the I-frame for intra encoding and ROI identification ($E_{TIF}=E_{IF}+E_{ROI}$), and to the W-frames for selective ME, transmission, channel coding, and ROI extrapolation: $E_{TWF}=E_{ME}+E_{Tx}(d)+E_{CC}+E_{ROIex}$.

E_{TIF} Prediction: The energy quota for the I-frame in the ith GOW is allocated based on the consumed energy of the previous 'k' I-frames (E_{CIF}) using Eq. 4. In order to avoid noise in the energy consumption median operator is used for 'k-1' I-frames in the history, while the immediately previous I-frame's energy is used to compensate for the sudden error effects.

$$E_{TIFi} = \underset{\forall j \in [1...k]}{pred}\left(E_{CIF(i-j)}\right) = \frac{E_{CIF(i-1)} + median\left(E_{CIF(i-2)},\cdots,E_{CIF(i-k)}\right)}{2} \quad (4)$$

E_{TWF} Prediction: The total target energy quota for 'm' W-frames ($E_{TWFi}=E_{TGOWi}-E_{TIFi}$) is computed and distributed among individual W-frames considering their temporal distance (see Eq. 5).

$$E_{TWFj} = \left(\frac{(1-\upsilon)}{m-(j-1)} + \frac{\upsilon}{\sum_{l=1}^{m-(j-1)} l}\right) \times \left(E_{TWFi} - \sum_{k=1}^{j-1} E_{CWFk}\right) \quad (5)$$

$$such\ that,\ \ \upsilon = \left(1-\min\left(\upsilon_{IFi},\upsilon_{IFi-1}\right)/\max\left(\upsilon_{IFi},\upsilon_{IFi-1}\right)\right)$$

The amount of temporal correlation for a given W-frame w.r.t. its preceding I-frame decreases depending upon its temporal distance. It is due to the fact that objects in farther video frames have more temporal distance that may not be captured by ME under a given search range and energy quota constraints. Therefore, extensive search is required for farther W-frames, and less motion search may be sufficient for the closer W-frames. To facilitate this, our scheme adaptively distributes the E_{TWFi} energy quota among W-frames depending upon their temporal distance from the preceding I-frame and variance difference (υ) between the bordering I-frames; see Eq. 5.

The variance difference υ of two consecutive I-frames hints towards the quality of the temporal correlation. Depending upon the variance difference, a part of E_{TWFi} (first addend without υ in Eq. 5) is equally distributed in order to keep the fairness of allocation in order to compensate for the energy consumption other than ME computations, like $E_{Tx}(d)$, E_{CC}, and E_{ROIex}. However, the other part (second addend with υ in Eq. 5) is distributed based on the temporal distance to compensate for the temporal correlation changes.

After the encoding of each W-frame, the energy quota of the next W-frame is controlled depending upon the consumed energy of the previous W-frames (E_{CWF}); see Eq. 5. For instance, for $m=4$, the energy quota of WF_1, WF_2, WF_3, and WF_4 can be computed as follows:

$$E_{TWF1} = \left((1-\upsilon)/4 + \upsilon/10\right) \times \left(E_{TWFi}\right)$$
$$E_{TWF2} = \left((1-\upsilon)/3 + \upsilon/6\right) \times \left(E_{TWFi} - E_{CWF1}\right)$$
$$E_{TWF3} = \left((1-\upsilon)/2 + \upsilon/3\right) \times \left(E_{TWFi} - \left(E_{CWF1} + E_{CWF2}\right)\right)$$
$$E_{TWF4} = \left(E_{TWFi} - \left(E_{CWF1} + E_{CWF2} + E_{CWF3}\right)\right)$$

Decoder-Side Energy Quota Distribution: At the decoder side, the energy quota is mainly distributed among the key I-frames in order to perform the bi-directional ME. For W-frames an average quota based on the history is reserved considering the energy consumption for SI generation/interpolation and Slepian-Wolf decoder. The size of history is 'l' previous GOWs each having 'm' W-frames; see Eq. 6. The remaining quota of the ith GOW is allocated to the decoding of I-frames E_{CD} and bi-directional ME E_{ME}; Eq. 7.

$$E_{TWFi} = m \times \left(\underset{\substack{\forall j \in [1...l] \\ \forall k \in [1...m]}}{AVG}\left(E_{CWF(i-(j,k))}\right)\right); \quad (6)$$

$$E_{TIFi} = E_{TGOWi} - E_{TWFi};\ \ E_{TIFi,ME} = \left(E_{TIFi} - E_{CD}\right)/2 \quad (7)$$

3.3 ROI Identification and Extrapolation

As previously discussed, HDVC encoder-side ME of selective MBs in ROI may lead to significant energy reduction due to improved SI and parity bits reduction. Typically, the decoder cannot perform a good estimation for the MBs with high motion and/or variance, especially at the object boundaries. Therefore, it is of key importance in HDVC to spend energy at the encoder side to perform ME of the ROI-MBs. Note, if the boundary of the moving region is extracted, the HDVC decoder can exploit the correlation of MBs belonging to the same object to predict the other MBs of the moving objects/regions. Therefore, the key focus of our scheme is to accurately extract the ROI-MBs at the object boundaries (see Fig. 10). Our scheme exhibits an integrated motion-based algorithm for ROI identification and ROI-MB selection; see Fig. 11. For a low-overhead scheme, the ROI map is generated only at key frames and extrapolated for all the W-frames see Fig. 12. The ROI map is regenerated when decoder requests the ROI re-computation due to significant degradation in the SI-quality as a result of accumulation of prediction error; Fig. 12. For each frame, the extrapolation is done considering the ROI in the immediately preceding frame (see later in this section).

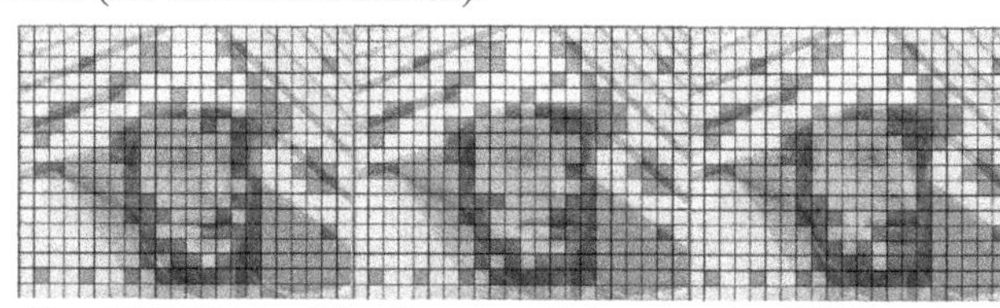

Fig. 10 ROI identification at an I-frame using MVD and extrapolation for 2 W-frames of foreman sequence

MVD	Accumulator	List
0	3	(16,16), (16,32), (48,208)
1	2	(32, 48), (96, 128)
2	4	(96,96),(352, 64),(208, 80),(128, 154)

Table I: An example hash table used as an ROI-Map

The ROI-MBs are identified based on the Motion Vector Drift (MVD; Eq. 8) of given MBs w.r.t. their neighboring MBs; see lines 2-5. Note, this MVD is also denoted as *"rank"* value to perform ROI-based MB selection at the encoder side. Higher is the MVD of an MB, higher the *rank* it gets, i.e. more energy needs to be spent for this MB to perform extensive ME in order to obtain a good match. Note, MVD already denotes an inverse function of correlation in the neighborhood. Therefore, selecting highest *rank* MBs as ROI-MBs complies with the motivational study of Section 2, where we discussed that the HDVC decoder can regenerate/estimate the highly-correlated MBs (i.e. low-ranked) without requesting a large number of parity bits from the HDVC encoder.

$$\overrightarrow{mvd} = \left(\sum_{i=-1}^{1}\sum_{j=-1}^{1}\left\|\overrightarrow{mv}_{(x,y)} - \overrightarrow{mv}_{(x+i,y+j)}\right\|\right) \times SAD_{(x,y)} \quad (8)$$

(x,y) are the location coordinates of a given MB and $SAD_{(x,y)}$ is the best matching cost in terms of Sum of Absolute Difference (SAD) of the current MB w.r.t. the best matching MB in the previous frame. MVD value ensures that only the MBs at the high MV gradient and with high motion cost are included in the ROI. This means that for a moving object, only the MBs at the object boundaries are selected as ROI-MBs. The MVD acts as an index to a hash table, which stores the accumulated number of MBs having the same MVD and their coordinates; see Table I. This list is referred as the ROI map which is *rank-wise sorted* in a descending order, i.e. starting from the ROI-MB with the highest *rank* value. An example ROI identification procedure is shown in Fig. 10 for the "Foreman" test video sequence, where only the boundaries of the moving regions are detected.

```
GenerateROI-MAP(Input: Previous reconstructed I-frame
    IFp, Motion Vector and SAD arrays from ME mv, SAD, Current Frame CF; Output: rank-wise sorted ROI map ROI)
∀MB ∈ CF    {
    mvd(x,y) ← ComputeMVD(mv,SAD);
    IncrementHashTable(mvd(x,y));
    AddtoList(mvd(x,y),(x,y));    }
counter ← 0;
∀i ∈ Last index of HashTable to 0    {
    counter ← counter + HashTable(i);
    if (counter ≥ Th) {λ ← i;  break;}
}
ROI ← getMBList(λ, last);
return(ROI);
```

Fig. 11 Pseudo-code for extracting the ROI of a frame

Extrapolation of the ROI Map for W-frames: First, the reflected location vector (*reflectLoc*) is computed by subtracting the motion vector of an ROI-MB to obtain a potential extrapolation of its motion. Afterwards, a fitting to the MB boundary is performed by comparing the ROI-MB with extrapolated motion to the neighboring MB boundaries; as shown in Fig. 13. The vector *r* is computed to locate the nearest MB boundary using Eq. 9. *Minimum* denotes a function that returns the vector corresponding to the minimum magnitude out of r_1, r_2, r_3, r_4. The *r* vector is added in the reflected location to determine the extrapolated ROI-MB.

$$\overrightarrow{reflectedLoc} = \overrightarrow{ROIMB_{(Ft)}} - \overrightarrow{mv}_{MB(Ft)}$$
$$\vec{r} = Minimum\left(\vec{r}_1, \vec{r}_2, \vec{r}_3, \vec{r}_4\right) \quad (9)$$
$$ROIMB_{(Ft+1)} = \overrightarrow{reflectedLoc} + \vec{r}$$

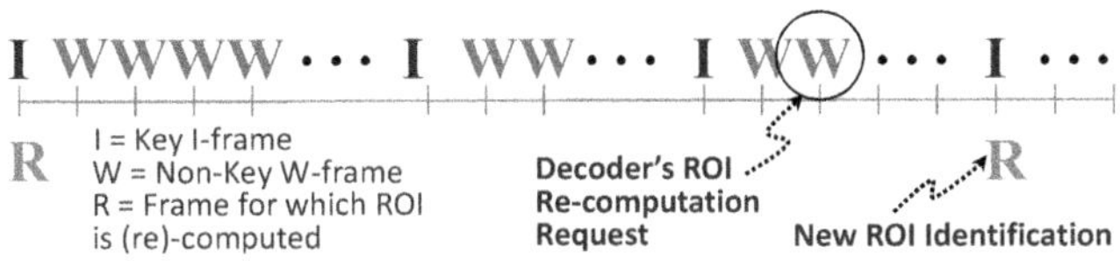

Fig. 12 ROI identification and extrapolation within a sequence

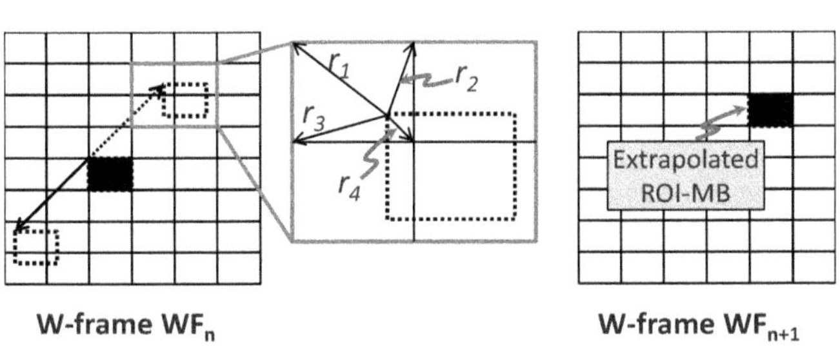

Fig. 13 ROI-MB extrapolation between two W-frames (the dark-filled boxes represent the ROI-MBs)

3.4 MB-Level Energy Quota Distribution and Control

Fig. 14 shows the ROI-driven MB selection and energy distribution. The input is the frame-level energy quota of the W-frame and the ROI map sorted w.r.t. the rank values of the MBs in a descending order. First, the maximum number of selected MBs (N_{Emax}) that need to be considered for encoder-side ME is computed using the frame-level energy quota and the energy required for transmission, channel coding, and ROI extrapolation; line 2. Note, the transmission energy is a function of the transmission distance '*d*' [34]. Since in several cases, the underlying platform may not be able to provide the required throughput due to limited computational resources and/or limited processing power. Therefore, the maximum number of MBs (N_{Tmax}) that can be processed by the underlying platform are computed in line 3. The maximum number of selected MBs *'N'* is determined as the minimum of N_{Emax} and N_{Tmax}; line 4. Afterwards, *'N'* MBs are extracted from the ROI map starting from the highest *rank* value; lines 5-7. If *N* is greater than the number of MBs in the ROI, additional MBs are extracted from the non-ROI map; line 8-9.

```
1.  ROI-DrivenMB_EnergyDistribution( ): Input: Hardware
        throughput constraint T_HW; rank-wise sorted map of ROI
        ROI, List of MBs outside the ROI nonROI, Energy quota of
        the current W-frame E_TWF, Energy for transmission for a given transmission distance 'd' E_Tx(d); Energy of channel coding
        E_CC; Energy of extrapolating ROI E_ROIex;
        Output: Consumed Energy of W-frame, E_CWF
2.  NEmax ← (ETWF − ETx(d) − ECC − EROIex) / getAvgMBEnergy(lowQuality, ME);
3.  NTmax ← THW/FR;
4.  N ← min(NEmax, NTmax);
5.  NROI ← getNumMBs(ROI);
6.  if(N = NROI)  ListMBs ← ROI;
7.  if(N < NROI)  ListMBs ← getMBs(ROI, N);
8.  if(N > NROI)
9.      ListMBs ← getMBs(ROI, N) + getMBs(nonROI,(N − NROI));
10. ET ← (EWF − ERes − ETx(d) − ECC − EROI)/N;
11. ECWF ← 0;   ETMB ← ET;
12. ∀mbi∈ListMBs  { // loop over all MBs in the list of selected MBs
13.     configME ← getMEconfig(ETMB);
14.     EMB ← performME(configME,mbi);
15.     ECWF ← ECWF + EMB;
16.     ΔE ← ET − EMB;
17.     ETMB ← ET + α×ΔE;
18. }
19. return(ECWF);
```

Fig. 14 Pseudo-code for ROI-driven MB selection and MB-level energy distribution and control

The target energy quota for one MB is computed depending upon the number of selected MBs; line 10. Afterwards, all the MBs in the selected MB list are processed for ME starting from the highest *rank* MBs first; lines 12-18. An appropriate ME configuration is selected considering various ME configurations that provide energy vs. quality tradeoffs; line 13. Multiple ME configurations can be formulated depending upon the search window size, search pattern types, termination rules, initial search point prediction, etc. Note, ME configuration is not the contribution of this paper. In this paper, we deployed the ME configuration technique of [11] since we consider it crucial to deploy a state-of-the-art ME configuration technique to evaluate the quality of our work in a fair way.

After the ME is completed for the MB, the consumed energy (E_{MB}) is monitored; line 14. The consumed energy can be different from the target energy or the average energy of the selected ME configuration. Therefore, we adapt the energy quota of the MB and the average energy value of the ME configuration in order to have a better ME configuration selection for the subsequent MBs. Depending upon the error between the target and the consumed energies (see line 16), the target of the next MB is readjusted by back-propagating the energy error; line 17. The weighting factor 'α' controls the strength of back-propagation. The total consumed energy of the W-frame is returned to control the frame-level energy quota (line 15, 19); see Section 3.2.

Note, the decoder-side MB-level energy distribution and ranking are very similar to that at the encoder side, except that the energy quota for the I-frame includes the energy for forward and backward ME.

4. RESULTS AND EVALUATION

4.1 Experimental Setup

In order to evaluate the energy efficiency of our scheme, we have developed a complete HDVC system with 5 different ME configuration classes at encoder and 2 ME configuration classes at encoder. The configuration of ME classes are borrowed from the work of [11]. The Intra-frame encoder for I-frame coding is based on H.264/AVC standard. For W-frame coding and estimation, the algorithms for side information, parity-bits generation, and the quality matrix Q4 are based on [35]. For transmission energy estimation, the model of [34] is employed. For transmission energy estimation, the distance of 100 meters is assumed. Based on this model, the energy for one bit transmission is given as ≈1µJ/bit. The computation energy results are obtained from the synthesis results using a 90 nm technology.

We have compared our ROI-based energy quota distribution and control scheme with Raster-scan based scheme of [9]. For fairness of comparison, we have employed the same I-frame coding algorithm, same ME algorithm, and same SI generation unit. The coding is performed under the similar target PSNR constraints. The energy results illustrate the benefit of our energy distribution and control scheme and ROI-based decisions. Note, the overhead of our scheme is included in the energy results. Detailed discussion on the overhead results can be found in Section 4.4.

4.2 Comparison with State-of-the-Art

Experiments in Fig. 15 illustrate the energy consumption comparison of our scheme with state-of-the-art for different video sequences. Fig. 15 shows that our scheme provides on average 20% energy reduction (maximum 25%) compared to state-of-the-art. Higher savings are obtained for "Coastguard", "Foreman" and "Hall" sequences, as they exhibit more motion. Note, the savings for "Mother & Daughter" and "News" sequences are relatively less due to limited motion content in the sequences. In such scenarios, adaptive ME already terminates earlier as it quickly determines the best match. This result also demonstrates that in case of high-motion and high-texture, our scheme exhibits a higher potential for energy savings compared to state-of-the-art.

Fig. 16 shows detailed energy consumption comparison between our scheme and state-of-the-art at MB-level for "Foreman" sequence. It is noteworthy in Fig. 16 that our scheme has allocated more energy quota to the Foreman face as it is detected as ROI. However, due to the raster scan nature, state-of-the-art only captures the moving hat of the "Foreman" object, while the significant energy quota is wasted on the background wall MBs (marked with circles), which could have been easily generated by the HDVC decoder. As a result, our scheme also provides PSNR improvement even under same quality constraints, because the decoder has a much better match of the "Foreman" face in the case of our scheme compared to that of the state-of-the-art. This implies that to achieve the quality comparable to that of our scheme, state-of-the-art will have to spend even more energy. However, due to the video dynamics, only a controlled rate based encoding is possible and a controlled quality based encoding is typically not possible.

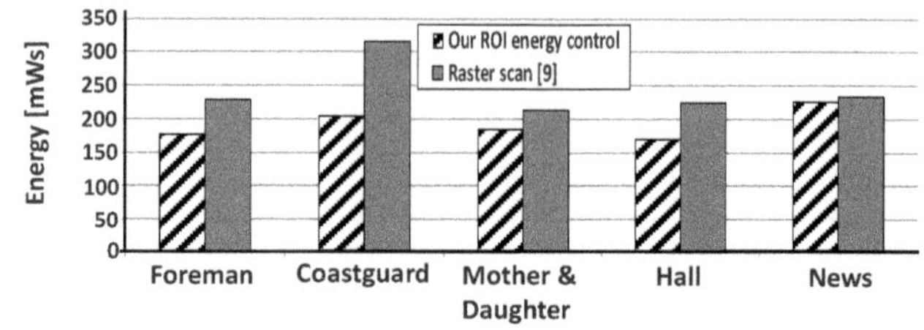

Fig. 15 Energy consumption of our HDVC configurations compared with [9] for CIF sequences

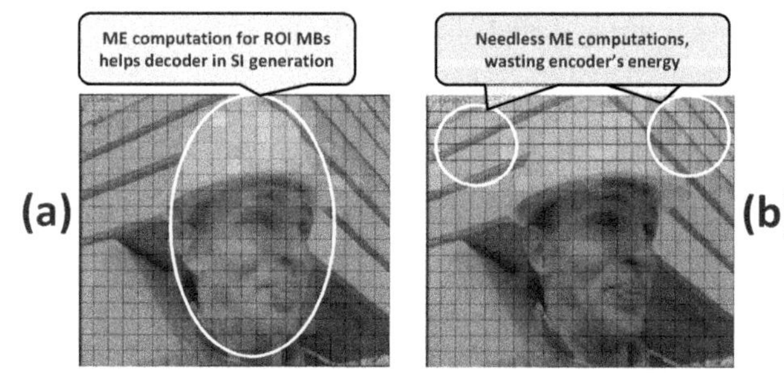

Fig. 16 Energy distribution per MB of (a) proposed ROI-based scheme and (b) Raster-scan scheme

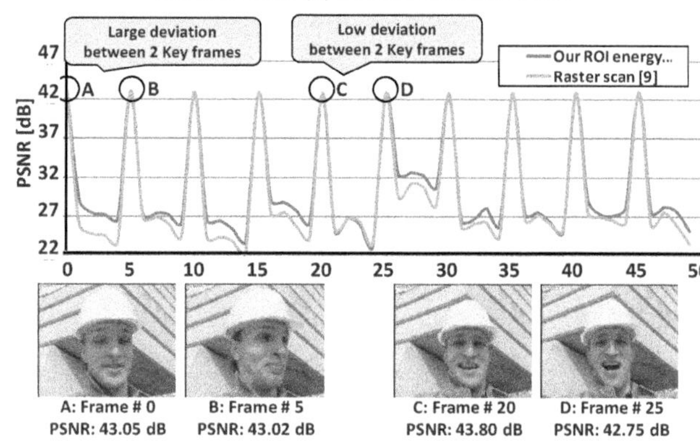

Fig. 17 PSNR comparison for our proposed scheme energy budgeting with raster-scan ordering for m=4 and same transmission energy

Fig. 17 depicts the quality (PSNR) comparison on frame-level between the two schemes for the cases of same transmission energy. For the frames at labels A and B, the deviation between the two key-frames is high, thus resulting in a higher variance between the two frames. Our scheme allocates more energy to the frame farther away from the key-frame A and thus provides better PSNR compared to state-of-the-art. The raster-scan based scheme fails to allocate energy quota to important blocks, thus the results in PSNR loss. Our scheme achieves 2 dB higher PSNR in these cases. For low variance key-frames (i.e. frames at labels C and D in Fig. 17), the energy distribution among the non-key frames is nearly constant and therefore, the PSNR difference between C and D is less between the two schemes. Note, both schemes achieve the same quality at the I-frames, as we provide the same I-frame coding algorithms to both schemes and the difference only lies in the energy quota distribution and control for W-frames. Therefore, the PSNR for I-frames is same for both schemes, while PSNR difference only occurs for W-frames in this case. This is to ensure a high fairness in the comparison to highlight the benefits of only our scheme.

4.3 Detailed Experimental Evaluation

Fig. 18 and Fig. 19 illustrate the detailed observations for quality and energy consumption when using our scheme. Fig. 18 shows that our scheme tends to increase the relative quality if the value of *m* increases, where *m* is the number of W-frames between two I-frames. This observation is shown for "Foreman" sequence encoded with QP=18 and QP=36 for the I-frames. The later W-frames in the GOW are usually of lower quality compared to the earlier W-frames because of the increased temporal de-correlation with the I-frames. Since our approach allocates these later W-frames a higher energy quota, a better estimate (or match) of the current MB in I-frames can be found. This leads to a quality increase even for these frames, which will not be possible when allocating energy without consideration of temporal distance, i.e. equally allocating energy to all W-frames.

Fig. 19 shows the energy quota adaptation at the (a) frame-level; and (b) GOW-level (see Section 3.1and 3.2 for algorithms). Fig. 19 shows that our scheme keeps the energy quota distribution close to the target energy; thus leading to a reduced controller error. An interesting observation in Fig. 19b is that the error between the target and consumed energy at the GOW-level is almost insignificant. This is due to the hierarchical control of the target energy quota which minimizes the risk of target energy quota violations. Fig. 19a shows that over the period, the controller error (i.e. difference between the target and consumed energy) is reducing. This is due to the adaptation of the controller output. Note that in Fig.19a, results for only W-frames are shown, because the variance in the energy consumption for I-frames insignificant and are adapted using a different equation; Eq. 4.

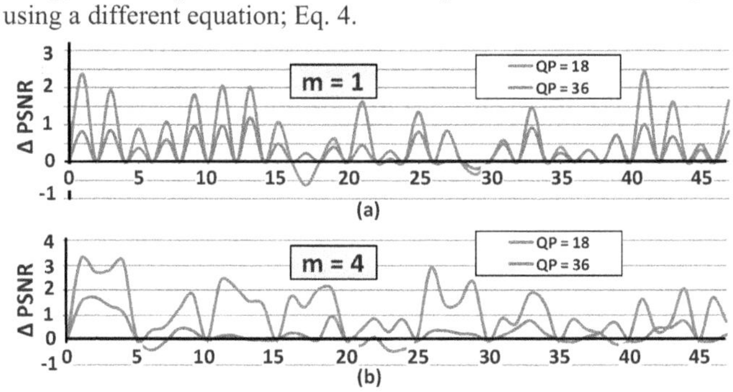

Fig. 18 Difference in PSNR for the proposed ROI and raster-scan approaches at (a) m=1 and (b) m=4.

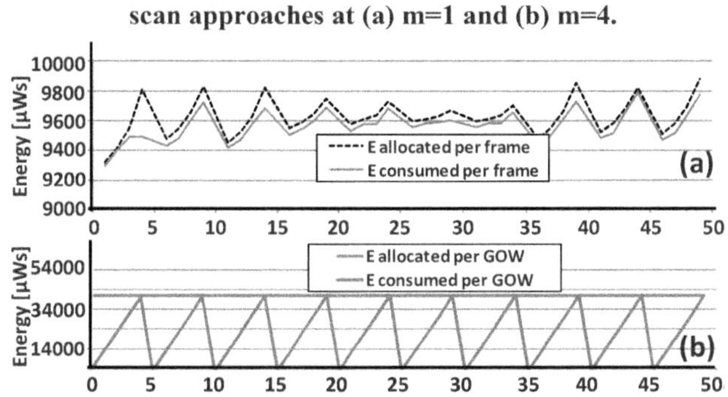

Fig. 19 (a) Proposed and consumed energy per frame (b) proposed and consumed energy per GOW

Fig. 20 shows the overall percentage error between the target and the consumed energy quota, on frame and GOW level. It is noteworthy that the error is hardly 1% for both GOW and frame-level energy quota allocation.

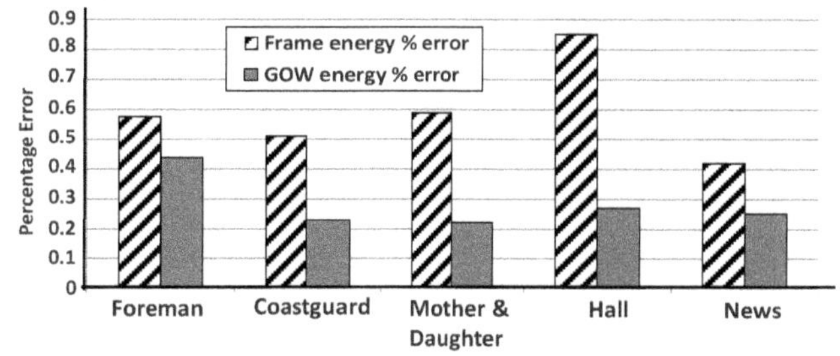

Fig. 20 Percentage error between energy quota allocation and energy consumption

4.4 Overhead

Table II shows the performance, area and energy overhead of the proposed scheme after synthesis and place&route results for a 90nm technology. The implementation includes one *divider* and three *multipliers*, which are shared among the different calculation steps. For the GOW-, Frame- and MB-Level calculations 4cycles/23cycles (depending on init/dev in Fig. 9), 2+2*m+4cycles and 6+3*N_{ROI} cycles are required, respectively (see parameters in the algorithm shown in Fig. 14). Table II shows that the energy overhead is insignificant compared to the savings of our scheme.

Moreover, the ROI extrapolation requires only 2 additions and a search for minimum magnitude vector within 4 vectors. This is a negligible overhead compared to the encoding process and our energy savings.

		Synthesis results for 90 nm Technology	
	Latency	**Area**	**Energy**
	[Cycles]	GE	[nWs]
GOW-Level	5/23	11,103	18.4
Frame-Level	2+12	8,327	11.1
MB-Level	6+360	14,238	292.2
Total	1501	62,638	1211.2

Table II: Performance, area and energy overhead of our scheme (m=4, k=5, N_{ROI}=120)

5. CONCLUSION

We have presented a hierarchal control scheme for adaptive energy quota distribution and control for HDVC. Our scheme controls the distribution of energy quota at various levels namely: (i) GOW-level; (ii) Frame-level; and (iii) MB-level. To achieve high energy distribution efficiency, our scheme exploits the video content properties and region of interest. An intelligent MB selection for ME leads to reduced transmission energy. Overall, our scheme provides on average 20% energy reduction compared to state-of-the-art energy management scheme for HDVC. Consideration of ROI and video content properties in the HDVC paradigm facilitates a high-quality SI generation at the decoder-side in addition to efficiently distributing energy at both encoder and decoder sides. Due to its high energy efficiency and adaptivity to provide higher quality for ROIs, our scheme enables HDVC in resource- and energy-constrained devices subjected to dynamically varying scenarios, involving complex motion and longer GOW lengths.

6. ACKNOWLEDGMENT

We would like to thank Mr. Florian Kriebel, Karlsruhe Institute of Technology (KIT), for his contribution to the hardware implementation.

7. REFERENCES

[1] M. Ravasi, M. Mattavelli, C. Clerc, "A Computational Complexity Comparison of MPEG4 and JVT Codecs", Joint Video Team (JVT) of ISO/IEC MPEG & ITU-T VCEG (ISO/IEC JTC1/SC29/WG11 and ITU-T SG16 Q.6), 2002.

[2] H.264 Codec: http://iphome.hhi.de/suehring/tml/index.htm

[3] T. Wiegand et al., "Overview of the H.264/AVC video coding standard", IEEE TCSVT, vol. 13, pp. 560-576, 2003.

[4] J. Ostermann, et. al., "Video coding with H.264/AVC: Tools, Performance, and Complexity", IEEE Circuits and Systems Magazine, vol. 4, no. 1, pp. 7-28, 2004.

[5] S. Yang, et al., "Power and performance analysis of motion estimation based on hardware and software realizations", IEEE Trans. on Computers, vol.54, no.6, pp. 714- 726, 2005.

[6] A. Wyner, J. Ziv, "The rate-distortion function for source coding with side information at the decoder", IEEE Transaction on Information Theory, vol. 22, pp. 1–10, 1976.

[7] B. Girod, et al., "Distributed Video Coding". IEEE Proceedings, 93(1), pp. 71-83, 2005.

[8] B. Macchiavello, et al., "Side-Information Generation for Temporally and Spatially Scalable Wyner-Ziv Codecs", EURASIP JIVP, 2009, 1-11, 2009.

[9] D. Forte, A. Srivastava, "Energy and Thermal-Aware Video Coding via Encoder/Decoder Workload Balancing", IEEE ISLPED, pp. 207-212, 2010.

[10] A. Aaron, S. Rane, B. Girod, "Wyner-ziv video coding with hash-based motion compensation at the receiver", IEEE ICIP, 2004.

[11] M. Shafique, L. Bauer, J. Henkel, "enBudget: A Run-Time Adaptive Predictive Energy-Budgeting Scheme for Energy-Aware Motion Estimation in H.264/MPEG-4 AVC Video Encoder", IEEE DATE, pp. 1725-1730, 2010.

[12] D. Sejdinovic, R. J. Piechocki, A. Doufexi, "Rateless distributed source code design", ICST Mobile Multimedia Communications Conference, 2009.

[13] Distributed Coding for Video Services (DISCOVER). Application scenarios and functionalities for DVC; Online: http://www.discoverdvc.org/deliverables/.

[14] D. Slepian and J. Wolf, "Noiseless coding of correlated information sources," IEEE Trans. Inf. Theory, vol. 19, no. 4, pp. 471–480, Jul. 1973.

[15] Girod, B., Aaron, a. M., Rane, S., & Rebollo-Monedero, D. Distributed Video Coding. Proceedings of the IEEE, 93(1), pp.71-83, 2005

[16] S.-yi Chien, et al., "Power Optimization of Wireless Video Sensor Nodes in M2M Networks", ASP-DAC, pp. 401-405, 2012.

[17] Y.-W. Huang et al., "A 1.3TOPS H.264/AVC single-chip encoder for HDTV applications", ISSCC, pp. 128-588, 2005.

[18] C.-C. Chiu et al., "Distributed video coding: a promising solution for distributed wireless video sensors or not?", Visual Communications and Image Processing (VCIP), 2011.

[19] X. Artigas et al., "The DISCOVER codec: Architecture, techniques and evaluation", PCS, 2007.

[20] Puri, R., Majumdar, A., & Ramchandran, K."PRISM: A video coding paradigm with motion estimation at the decoder", IEEE transactions on image processing : a publication of the IEEE Signal Processing Society, 16(10), pp. 2436-2448, 2007.

[21] Dufaux, F., & Ebrahimi, T.. "Encoder and decoder side global and local motion estimation for Distributed Video Coding", 2010 IEEE International Workshop on Multimedia Signal Processing, pp. 339-344, 2010

[22] Martinian, E., Vetro, A., Yedidia, J. S., Ascenso, J., Khisti, A., & Malioutov, D.. "Hybrid distributed video coding using SCA codes", Multimedia Signal Processing, 2006 IEEE 8th Workshop on pp. 258–261, IEEE, 2006

[23] Tseng, H.-yun, Shen, Y.-chung, & Wu, J.-ling.. "Distributed Video Coding with Compressive Measurements", MM '11 Proceedings of the 19th ACM international conference on Multimedia pp. 1273-1276, 2011

[24] Jrgen Slowack, Jozef Skorupa, Stefaan Mys, Peter Lambert, Christos Grecos, and Rik Van de Walle, "Flexible distribution of complexity by hybrid predictive-distributed video coding," Signal Processing: Image Communication, vol. 25, no. 2, pp. 94 – 110, 2010.

[25] Hu Chen and E. Steinbach, "Flexible distribution of computational complexity between the encoder and the decoder in distributed video coding," in Multimedia and Expo, 2008 IEEE International Conference on, Hannover, June/Apr., pp. 801–804, 2008.

[26] M. A. Johnson. M. H. Moradi, "PID Control: New Identification and Design Methods", Springer, 2005.

[27] Puri, R.; Ramchandran, K.; , "PRISM: an uplink-friendly multimedia coding paradigm," Acoustics, Speech, and Signal Processing, 2003. Proceedings. (ICASSP '03). 2003 IEEE International Conference on , vol.4, no., pp. IV- 856-9 vol.4, 6-10 April 2003

[28] Chen, J.; Khisti, A.; Malioutov, D.M.; Yedidia, J.S.; , "Distributed source coding using serially-concatenated-accumulate codes," Information Theory Workshop, 2004. IEEE , vol., no., pp. 209- 214, 24-29 Oct. 2004

[29] Elamin, A.; Jeoti, V.; Belhouari, S.; , "Feed back channel usage reduction in distributed video coding," Intelligent and Advanced Systems (ICIAS), 2010 International Conference on , vol., no., pp.1-4, 15-17 June 2010

[30] Pedro, J. Q., Brites, C., Ascenso, J., & Pereira, F.. "Studying the feedback channel in transform domain wyner-ziv video coding". 6th Conference on Telecommunications - ConfTele, pp. 1-4, 2007

[31] C. Brites and F. Pereira, "Distributed Video Coding: Bringing New Applications to Life", 5th Conference on Telecommuni- cations - ConfTele, Tomar, Portugal, April 2005.

[32] J. Ascenso, C. Brites, and F. Pereira, "Improving frame interpolation with spatialmotion smoothing for pixel domain distributed video coding," in Proceedings of the 5th EURASIP Conference on Speech and Image Processing, Multimedia Com- munications and Services, pp. 1–6, Smolenice, Slovakia, June- July 2005.

[33] JVT video sequence archive. Online: http://wftp3.itu.int/av-arch/video-site/sequences/

[34] Heinzelman, W. R., Chandrakasan, A., & Balakrishnan, H. "Energy-Efficient Communication Protocol for Wireless Microsensor Networks". 33rd Hawaii International Conference on System Sciences Vol. 0, pp. 1-10, 2000

[35] C. Brites, J. Ascenso and F. Pereira, "Improving Transform Domain Wyner-Ziv Coding Performance", IEEE International Conference on Acoustics, Speech and Signal Processing, Tou- louse, France, May 2006.

[36] M. Shafique, B. Molkenthin, J. Henkel, "An HVS-based Adaptive Computational Complexity Reduction Scheme for H.264/AVC Video Encoder using Prognostic Early Mode Exclusion," IEEE DATE, 2010.

[37] B. Zatt, M, Shafique, F. Sampaio, L. Agostini, S. Bampi, J. Henkel, "Run-time adaptive energy-aware motion and disparity estimation in multiview video coding", IEEE DAC, pp. 1026-1031, 2011.

[38] B. Zatt, M, Shafique, S. Bampi, J. Henkel, "A Low-Power Memory Architecture with Application-Aware Power Management for Motion & Disparity Estimation in Multiview Video Coding", IEEE ICCAD, pp. 40-47, 2011.

[39] M, Shafique, B. Zatt, F. L. Walter, S. Bampi, J. Henkel, " Adaptive Power Management of On-Chip Video Memory for Multiview Video Coding ", IEEE DAC, pp. 866-875, 2012.

Working-Set-Based Address Mapping for Ultra-Large-Scaled Flash Devices *

Ming-Chang Yang
Graduate Institute of Networking and Multimedia
National Taiwan University
Taipei 106, Taiwan (R.O.C.)
r99944005@csie.ntu.edu.tw

Yuan-Hao Chang
Institute of Information Science
Academia Sinica
Taipei 115, Taiwan (R.O.C.)
johnson@iis.sinica.edu.tw

Po-Chun Huang
Department of Computer Science and Information Engineering
National Taiwan University
Taipei 106, Taiwan (R.O.C.)
f95070@csie.ntu.edu.tw

Tei-Wei Kuo
Department of Computer Science and Information Engineering
National Taiwan University
Taipei 106, Taiwan (R.O.C.)
ktw@csie.ntu.edu.tw

ABSTRACT

Address mapping for flash devices has been a challenging design problem for controllers because of the rapidly growing device capacity. Different from the past work, a capacity-independent address mapping scheme that only depends on users' access data set, referred to as working set, is proposed. As a result, fine-grained address mapping is achieved with significant performance boosting, compared to the past work. In addition, a simple but practical wear-leveling design is proposed with the capability in lifetime estimation of flash devices. The proposed scheme was evaluated by a series of experiments with encouraging results.

Categories and Subject Descriptors

D.4.2 [**Operation Systems**]: Storage Management—*Allocation/deallocation strategies, Garbage collection, Secondary storage*

General Terms

Design, Experimentation, Management, Measurement, Performance, Reliability

*This work was supported in part by the National Science Council under Grant Nos. 98-2221-E-002-120-MY3, 100-2628-E-027-008-MY2, and 101-2220-E-001-001, and by the Excellent Research Projects of National Taiwan University under Grant No. 10R80919-2 and 101R890822.

Keywords

Flash memory, storage systems, working set, march operation

1. INTRODUCTION

Flash storage devices have gained their momentum in the storage market because of the booming markets in mobile electronics such as digital cameras, smart phones, tablets, and laptops. Well-known device examples are solid-state drives (SSDs) and SD cards. Even though the markets of flash storage devices grow rapidly, serious threats keep building upon the design to map the logical addresses of requests into their physical addresses over flash chips, due to the limited amount of RAM in device controllers. Such observations motivate this work in the proposing of a new address mapping scheme to release the dependency between the RAM space usage and the device capacity without sacrificing the performance of the storage devices.

A flash storage device usually contains multiple NAND flash chips, each of which consists of at least one plane. Each plane is composed of many blocks, each of which is the basic unit for erase operations. A block is made up of a fixed number of pages, and a page is the basic unit for read and write operations. Each page is partitioned into the data area and the spare area, where the data area and the spare area are for the storage of user data and the house-keeping information such as error correction codes and status flags, respectively. Due to the *write-once property*, a page could not be overwritten unless its residing block is erased first. As a result, data are usually updated over free pages so as to improve the write performance (referred to as *out-place update*). Pages with the latest version of data (i.e., valid data) are called *valid pages* or *live pages*, and pages with the old versions of data (i.e., invalid data) are considered as *invalid pages* or *dead pages* and must be reclaimed by erasing their residing blocks when their device runs out of free pages.

In the past decade, researchers have proposed different excellent system architectures and layer designs for flash storage devices. In particular, address mapping has received lots of attention in flash management. The flash translation layer (FTL) [3] is among the first few ones proposed to maintain the address mapping information for read/write requests with a page-level (or fine-grained) mapping table. As the capacity of flash storage devices grows, the huge RAM space usage for the fine-grained mapping table makes FTL infeasible, and many excellent management designs, e.g., NFTL [1], were thus proposed to trade the device performance with the RAM space demand with a block-level (or coarse-grained) address mapping table. With the objective to balance the RAM space demand and device performance, various excellent hybrid address mapping designs were proposed to manage frequently-accessed addresses with a fine-grained mapping table and less-frequently-accessed addresses with a coarse-grained mapping table. Excellent example designs are AFTL, BAST, FAST, and KAST [6, 15, 17, 24]. To further solve the scalability issue imposed by the limited RAM space and the growing capacity of flash storage devices, some recent studies, e.g., DFTL and CFTL [21, 10], proposed to save fine-grained mapping information in flash memory with a tradeoff in extra flash-memory accesses and management/performance overheads to load/store mapping information between flash memory and RAM in the flash storage device. In another direction, some researchers proposed an on-board cache or write buffer to improve the write performance of flash storage devices, e.g., [2, 11, 14, 12, 23], and some paid their attention to the reliability and endurance enhancement of flash storage devices, e.g., [4, 5, 9, 13, 18, 20], because the number of erases per block is limited so that erases over blocks should be evenly distributed (referred to as *wear leveling*).

Different from the past work, we are interested in fine-grained address mapping without the restrictions due to the huge capacity of a flash storage device. The rationale behind our design is that the RAM space needs of a flash storage device should depend on the access data sets of users, referred to as their *working sets*, instead of the capacity of a flash storage device. In other words, our design is not confined to the constraint of many existing designs, in which the RAM space needs of an address mapping scheme is related to the amount of the total mapping information. In this paper, a working-set-based address mapping scheme is proposed with fine-grained address mapping, and it is not hijacked by the rapidly increasing capacity of flash storage devices (that is doubled for every 18–24 months in a way similar to many storage media). The proposed scheme comes with a simple but practical wear-leveling design based on the idea in utilizing flash chips in a more exhaustive way from one end to the other end. The wear-leveling design could not only provide good lifetime estimation of flash storage devices but also get even better and better in reliability enhancement when the capacity of a flash storage device grows over time. A series of experiments based on realistic workloads was conducted to evaluate the capability of the proposed scheme. We show that the write performance of the proposed scheme is at least 1.96 times of many other existing coarse-grained address mapping methods and nearly achieves the performance of fine-grained address mappings in most evaluated cases.

The rest of this paper is organized as follows: Section 2 presents the system architecture and the motivation of this work. In Section 3, a working-set-based address mapping scheme is proposed. Section 4 summarizes the experiment results. Section 5 is the conclusion.

2. SYSTEM ARCHITECTURE AND MOTIVATION

NAND flash memory could be classified into two types: Single-level-cell (SLC) and multiple-level-cell (MLC) flash memory. Each SLC flash cell could store one-bit information, while each $MLC_{\times n}$ flash cell could contain n-bit information. An SLC(/MLC) block usually consists of 64(/128) pages, each of which could usually store 2KB(/4KB) user data and 64B(/224B) spare information. As shown in Table 1, MLC flash memory has lower cost than SLC flash memory does, but it has worse endurance and read-write performance than SLC flash memory does. In addition, MLC flash memory is associated with two write constraints: No page could be partially programmed, and pages of a block must be written sequentially from the first one to the last.

Cell type	SLC	$MLC_{\times 2}$	$MLC_{\times 3}$
Price (USD/32Gbs)	25.1	4.08	3.87
Page size (KBs)	4	8	8
Block size (pages)	128	256	384
Page read time (μsec.)	35	75	100
Page write time (msec.)	0.3	1.3	2.5
Block erase time (msec.)	0.7	3.8	3
Endurance (P/E cycles)	≥ 10000	≈ 3000	≤ 1000

Table 1: Comparisons of flash chips.

As shown in Figure 1, a flash storage device usually includes two software layers, i.e., the flash translation layer (FTL) driver and the memory technology device (MTD) driver. The MTD driver controls the flash chips and provides primitive operations. The FTL driver is named after its provided functionalities and usually contains an *allocator*, a *garbage collector*, and a *wear-leveler*. The allocator manages the flash-memory space and does the address translation from logical block addresses (LBAs) to the physical addresses of their corresponding valid data because multiple data versions of an LBA could coexist in flash memory, where each LBA represents the address of a sector. The garbage collector is to reclaim the space of invalid pages by erasing their residing blocks when there is not enough free space over flash memory, where "live-page copying" should be performed to copy live pages to free space before their residing block is erased. The wear-leveler is an optional component so as to evenly distribute erases over blocks to enhance the endurance of flash memory.

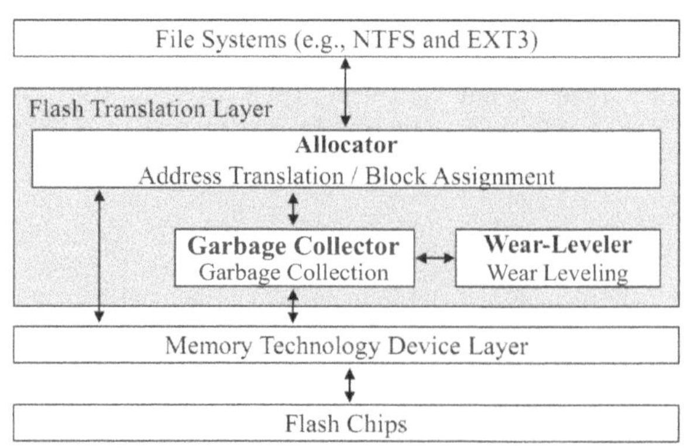

Figure 1: A typical flash system architecture.

Most of the FTL designs store the mapping information in the RAM space of their controllers. A design proposed by Intel and also referred to as "FTL" was among the first few being proposed to perform address translation for read-write requests at the page level. Because this design is a page-level mapping method, it has the minimal management overheads, the best access performance, and the highest space utilization on flash management in most cases [3]. However, as the capacity of flash storage devices grows, the required size of the address mapping table of page-level designs, including FTL, grows proportionately and is eventually too large to fit in the limited RAM space of the flash storage devices. To resolve this issue, coarse-grained designs, such as BL, were proposed to reduce the table size by adopting various block-level address mapping mechanisms. For example, BL maps each given LBA to a physical block and an offset in the block [16]. However, the BL design could result in excessive live-data copyings when data updates of strong LBA locality occur. It is because the out-place-update nature of flash memory would require BL to allocate a free block for every update and trigger live-data copyings from the corresponding previous block to the free block. NFTL is another block-level translation design that could reduce such overheads [1]: With an extra physical block, referred to as a *replacement block* (in addition to the corresponding physical block under BL), subsequential writes of the same LBA are written to any free pages of the replacement block if data of the same LBA was already written to the BL-mapped *data block* (with the mapped page offset). The tradeoff between page-level and block-level address mapping mechanisms is mainly on the address mapping table size and performance (and indirectly on the space utilization, endurance, garbage collection overheads, etc).

In order to have a good compromise, various hybrid mapping mechanisms, such as AFTL, BAST and FAST, were proposed. In particular, FAST and BAST store data in the *data blocks* and try to manage translation information at the block level, while updated data are stored in *log blocks* and are temporarily managed with a page-level translation mechanism [15, 17]. AFTL dynamically switches between page-level and block-level mapping by favoring hot-data access with page-level address mapping [24]. CFTL provides a configurable mechanism and can handle address translation with adaptive translation granularities [21]. Due to the fast growing capacity of flash storage devices, the RAM space might not be sufficient for coarse-grained mapping because the mapping information size is still proportional to the device capacity. Methodologies are needed to save mapping information, as needed, on flash memory, such as the approach by DFTL [10]. Moreover, the saving of mapping information on flash memory would inevitably result in performance degradation and raise the challenges on endurance, especially when the access patterns of requests from the host are not carefully tackled. Such observations motivate this work in the proposing of "fine-grained" address mapping methodologies with limited run-time overheads in the RAM space and less extra flash access for mapping information. We refer astute readers to Table 2 for the comparison of different approaches.

This work is inspired by the needs of the virtually "page-level" address mapping methodology for ultra-large scale MLC-based flash storage devices but with very limited RAM space. Our goal is to propose an address mapping methodology to achieve the performance of fine-grained address mappings with very small RAM space usage and less extra flash access for mapping information. The technical problem is how to decouple the capacity of flash storage devices and the required mapping information size and read-write performance overheads. The proposed address mapping scheme should be scalable to the capacity of flash storage devices and be adaptive to different access patterns with wear leveling supports.

Attribute	FTL	BL	NFTL	FAST	AFTL	DFTL
Table Granularity	Fine	Coarse	Coarse	Hybird	Hybrid	Fine
RAM Size	Large	Small	Small	Median	Median	Small
Translation Time	Short	Long	Long	Median	Median	Short
Space Utilization	High	High	Low	High	Median	High
GC Overhead	Less	More	More	More	Median	More
System Overhead	Less	Median	Less	More	More	More

Table 2: Comparisons of FTL designs.

3. A WORKING-SET-BASED ADDRESS MAPPING SCHEME

3.1 Overview

In this section, a working-set-based address mapping scheme for ultra-large-scaled MLC-based flash storage devices is proposed to achieve or approximate the performance of fine-grained address mapping methods. In this scheme, the RAM space requirement for address mapping is very small and is independent of the storage device capacity and the amount of data in the storage. As shown in Figure 2, the proposed scheme partitions the physical space of the flash memory into a large *in-place area* and a small *out-place area*. The in-place area is the data storage area for in-place updates, and the out-place area is a fixed-size over-provision area (or the extra area) to contain hot data (i.e., data that are updated recently and frequently) for out-place updates, where the size of the out-place area is nearly independent of the storage device capacity but is determined according to the working set size of data accessed by the system. In practice, data in the working set are mostly hot data that usually account for a small ratio of (the data stored on) a storage device and the ratio keeps decreasing due to the increasing capacity of flash storage devices, so that the size of the out-place area is usually multiple times of (or much larger than) the size of hot data or working set. On the other hand, the logical space is composed of consecutive logical addresses (i.e., LBAs) that are partitioned into consecutive fixed-size virtual blocks and each virtual block is divided in a fixed number of virtual pages, where the size of a virtual block(/page) equals to that of a flash physical block(/page), where a physical page could store data of multiple LBAs. For example, a 4KB physical page could store data belonged to eight 512B LBAs. *In the in-place area, no address mapping information needs to be maintained because there is an one-to-one mapping from the logical space to the physical space.* That is, each virtual block is mapped to a physical block, and consecutive virtual blocks are mapped to consecutive physical blocks. Each virtual page of a virtual block is sequentially mapped to a physical page of its corresponding physical block. Thus, the virtual block size equals to the physical block size and the virtual page size equals to the physical page size. As the example in Figure 2 shows, physical blocks 10-90009 are in the out-place area so that virtual blocks 0-9 are mapped to physical blocks 0-9, virtual block 10 is mapped to physical block 90010, and so on. In contrast, the out-place area needs address mapping information from the logical space to the physical space because the out-place update is adopted to enhance the efficiency on handling read/write requests to hot data.

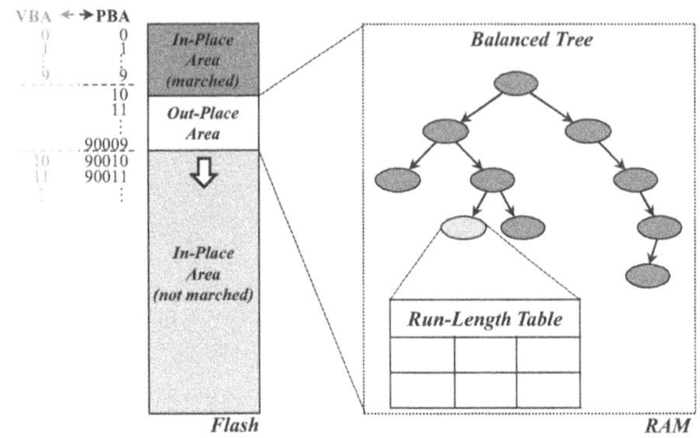

Figure 2: Working-set-based address mapping scheme.

For the write requests, they could be classified into *sequential updates* and *random updates*. In practice, sequential updates usually update cold data (i.e., infrequently updated data) and random updates usually update hot data, where most write requests are random updates to small part of data in the storage device [8]. With the consideration of reliability and endurance, the proposed scheme adopts a comparatively conservative rule for write requests: Both types of updates are written to the out-place area to avoid wearing out any physical blocks of the in-place area excessively, even though it is more efficient to directly write data of sequential updates to their corresponding physical blocks in the in-place area. Based on the above rule to write requests, when a read request is received, the out-place area should be checked first. If the requested data are not in the out-place area, the in-place area is then checked.

In order to achieve the performance of fine-grained address mapping with limited RAM space, a *run-length address mapping structure* (see Section 3.2) is proposed to manage the address mapping of the data stored in the out-place area, where the mapping information of a set of consecutive virtual pages is maintained by only one run-length record. Meanwhile, because the access pattern might change as time elapses and a few randomly updated data might be in fact cold data, we propose a *marching-based hot data gathering policy* (see Section 3.3) to gather hot data together and write the cold data back to the in-place area during garbage collection with the consideration of wear leveling. Before physical blocks in the out-place area are worn out, the out-place area is moved or marched forward by excluding physical blocks in the beginning of the out-place area and including the physical blocks right after the end of the out-place area. For example, the out-place area in Figure 3.2 is marched to contain physical blocks 11-90010 after physical block 10 is excluded and physical block 90010 is included. When the out-place area reaches the end of the physical space, the flash storage device should be replaced because most of the physical blocks have endured excessive erases.

3.2 Run-Length Address Mapping Structure for Out-Place Area Management

To achieve the performance of page-level address mapping inside the out-place area with limited RAM space, we need a space-efficient data structure to manage the data stored in the out-place area efficiently. Different from the traditional page-level mapping methods that keep the address mapping information for each (virtual) page, we propose a *run-length tree* to maintain the mapping information of multiple virtual pages with one run-length record so as to reduce the memory footprint size of the address mapping information. The rationale behind this is that a write request usually involves the data update to multiple physical pages so that multiple physical pages usually store data of consecutive LBAs (or virtual pages) whose mapping information could be compressed with the run-length encoding.

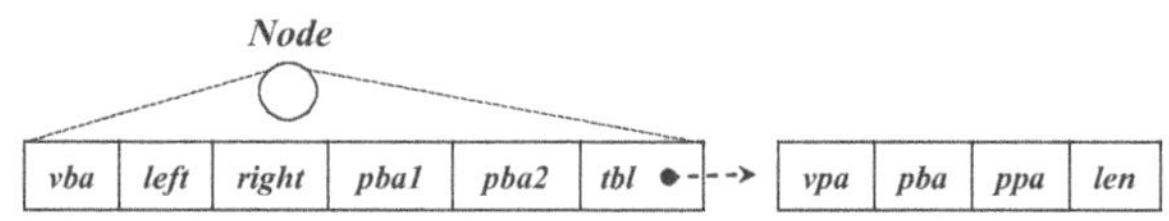

Figure 3: The fields of a node and its run-length table.

The run-length tree is a balanced binary search tree to facilitate the average performance on address translation. In this tree, *each node corresponds to a virtual block to maintain the mapping information of the virtual pages of this virtual block when the up-to-date data of these virtual pages are stored in the out-place area.* Thus, as shown in Figure 3, each node has six fields: The "vba" field is the address of its corresponding virtual block and serves as its key for key searching, and the "left" and "right" fields denote its left child and right child nodes respectively; the "pba1" and "pba2" fields point to its corresponding two physical blocks, and the "tbl" field points its corresponding *run-length table* that maintains the mapping information of its corresponding virtual block. In the run-length table, each entry is a *run-length record* to maintain the mapping information of one or more virtual pages that are mapped to consecutive physical pages. Thus, each entry needs to include four fields: The "vpa" field denotes the address (or the offset) of the first virtual page that is mapped to the physical page whose address is denoted by the "pba" and "ppa" fields, and the "len" field is the number of consecutive virtual pages that are mapped to consecutive physical pages sequentially in a one-to-one fashion[1]. Based on our observations, most run-length tables contain a small number of run-length records because random updates usually update a small part of data of a virtual block frequently. Thus, the run-length table is very space-efficient in practice, compared to the page-level address mapping table. For example, as shown in Figure 4(a), Node N_A corresponds to virtual block 39 and the first entry of its run-length table denotes that consecutive 6 virtual pages from virtual page 2 of virtual block 39 are one-to-one mapped to 6 consecutive physical pages from physical page 5 of physical block 8. That is, virtual pages 2-7 of virtual block 39 are mapped to physical pages 5-10 of physical block 8 one after another.

Figure 4 shows an example of how the run-length tree is

[1] In this paper, we use a virtual page as the mapping unit to simplify the explanation on address mapping. This could be easily revised to use an LBA as the mapping unit so as to reduce the read-merge-write overheads when partial data of a physical page are updated by a write request.

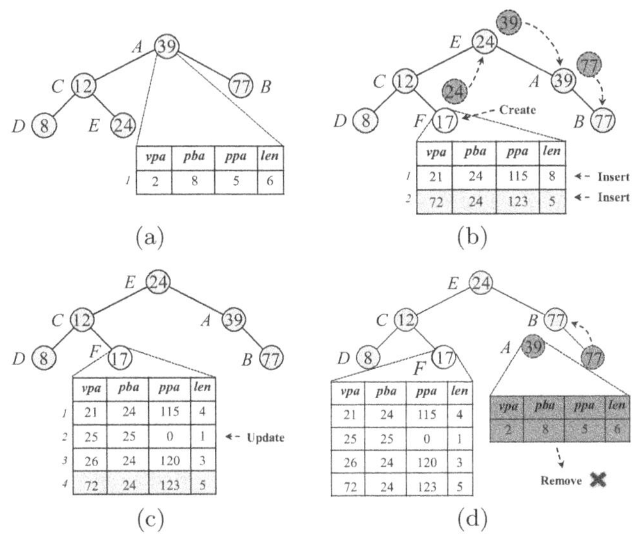

Figure 4: An example of the run-length table maintentance.

maintained. Suppose that each virtual block contains 128 virtual pages, each of which consists of one LBA[2]. As shown in Figure 4(a), the balanced run-length tree initially maintains the mapping information of five virtual blocks, i.e., nodes N_A, N_B, N_C, N_D and N_E for virtual blocks 39, 77, 12, 8 and 24 respectively. When a random update is received to update data of LBAs 2197-2204, the run-length tree is searched for the node with key 17 because the updated 8 consecutive LBAs are mapped to virtual pages 21-28 (i.e., the remainders of 2197 to 2204 divided by 128) of virtual block 17 (i.e., the quotient of 2197 to 2204 divided by 128). Since the node with key 17 is not found in the run-length tree, the node with key 17 (i.e., Node N_F) is created and inserted into the proper position to maintain the mapping information of the updated data, and the run-length tree is re-balanced according to the rules of the binary search trees such as the AVL tree. As shown in Figure 4(b), the updated data are stored in consecutive 8 physical pages of physical block 24 from physical page 115 (see Section 3.3 for the space allocation), and the mapping information of the subsequent random update to virtual pages 72-76 of virtual block 17 without overlapping any existing run-length record is maintained in a new record of the same run-length table. However, as shown in 4(c), the next random update to virtual page 25 of virtual block 17 overlaps with the logical range of the first run-length record of Node N_F and is stored in physical page 0 of physical block 25. As a result, the original run-length record should be separated into three run-length records: the first and third ones for the original data and the second one for the updated data caused by the random update to virtual page 25 of virtual block 17. After a series of random updates, there might not have enough RAM space to maintain the new mapping information introduced by a new random update. When such a situation occurs, the mapping information of the node with the least-recently-updated data in the out-place area is reclaimed, and all of the data corresponding to this node are written back to their corresponding physical block in the in-place area.

[2]Each LBA represents the address of a sector. The traditional sector size is 512B, but the new sector size is 4KB or even larger in the future.

As shown in Figure 4(d), Node N_A containing the least-recently-updated data is removed from the run-length tree for the RAM space reclamation, followed by the operations to re-balance the tree. Note that the operation to release RAM space in the unit of one physical block (or one virtual block) minimizes the number of affected physical blocks in both in-place area and out-place area, and is beneficial to the performance on garbage collection and hot-data gathering in the out-place area (see Section 3.3 for the detail).

3.3 Marching-Based Hot Data Gathering Strategy

In order to improve the performance and endurance of ultra-large-scaled flash storage devices, a marching-based hot data gathering strategy is proposed to ease the complexity on free block management/allocation, to reduce the overheads on garbage collection, and to prevent wearing out any specific block excessively. This strategy consists of a block status table (*BST*) and four procedures: *ReqHandler*, *MarchingBlkAlloc*, *OldBlkRecycle* and *March*. When a request is received, *ReqHandler* (see Algorithm 1) is invoked to handle the request. This procedure would invoke *MarchingBlkAlloc* (see Algorithm 2) to allocate free blocks when needed. If there are not enough free physical blocks in the out-place area, *OldBlkRecycle* (see Algorithm 3) is invoked to reclaim the less-recently-used physical blocks by looking up *BST*. The process to look up *BST* is very efficient because *BST* keeps the status of the physical blocks in the out-place area. To avoid erasing some physical blocks in the out-place area excessively, *March* (see Algorithm 4) is regularly activated to move (or march) the out-place area forward such that most physical blocks can be evenly used when the out-place area goes through every physical block and reaches the last one in the flash memory.

3.3.1 *The Handling of Read/Write Requests*

The purpose of this section is to explain how to handle read/write requests. Based on the policies for handling read/write requests mentioned in Section 3.1, updated data of write requests are written to the out-place area to enhance the endurance of physical blocks in the in-place area. Thus, when a read request is received, the run-length tree of the out-place area is first searched for the requested data. If not found, the requested data are directly read from their corresponding physical pages and blocks in the in-place area. When a write request is received, the run-length tree is searched for the mapping information of the virtual block(s) corresponding to the updated data of the write request, and then the updated data are written to the physical block(s) corresponded to the virtual block(s).

To accelerate the performance on handling (updated) data of write requests, each node of the run-length tree could be mapped to at most two physical blocks in the out-place area through its "pba1" and "pba2" fields that point to its *current physical block* and *previous physical block* respectively. When data of a virtual block are updated, they are sequentially written to the current physical block of the node corresponding to this virtual block. *Hereafter, we use the physical block of a node and the physical block of a virtual block interchangeably.* Once the current physical block is full, it is replaced by a free physical block[3] that becomes the new "current physical block". Among the original current and previous physical blocks of this node, the one with more valid pages becomes the new "previous physical block", and

[3]A *"free physical block"* is a physical block that has not been written with any data and is not mapped to any node.

the one with fewer valid pages is reclaimed and erased after its valid pages are copied to the new current physical block. The reason of maintaining two physical blocks for each node (or each virtual block) is that based on our observations, updates with higher frequency usually update the same part of data of a virtual block repeatedly, so that the previous physical block of a node usually contains no valid page or a small number of valid pages when both of the two physical blocks of the node are full. That is, "hot data" are automatically gathered in the current physical block and should not be forcibly migrated or copied to other physical block.

Algorithm 1 illustrates the handling of a read/write request: First, the type of the received request is checked. If the received request is a read request, the requested virtual pages ("*vpa*" to "*vpa* + *length*") are read from the out-place area through searching the run-length tree or from the corresponding pages in the in-place area (Steps 1-6). Otherwise, the received request is a write request, and the run-length tree is searched to find the node N_v that corresponds the virtual block v of the updated *data* so that the updated *data* of the write request could be stored in the proper physical block(s) (Steps 7-23). If the node N_v corresponding to the virtual block v cannot be found in the run-length tree, the node N_v is created and inserted into the run-length tree, and a free physical block blk_{free} in the out-place area will be allocated as the current physical block of this new node N_v by invoking procedure *MarchingBlkAlloc* (Steps 8-11). Then, the current physical block of node N_v is checked whether it has enough free pages to store the updated *data*. If the current physical block has not enough free pages, a new free physical block blk_{free} is allocated for virtual block v (or node N_v) to replace the physical block with fewer valid pages between the physical blocks pointed by *pba*1 and *pba*2 (i.e., the two physical blocks of node N_v). That is, data of the valid pages in the physical block (i.e., blk_{less}) with fewer valid pages are copied to the free physical block blk_{free} and this new free physical block blk_{free} becomes the current physical block of node N_v while the physical block (i.e., blk_{more}) that is not replaced becomes the previous physical block of node N_v, so that the overheads on copying live pages could be minimized (Steps 12-18). Besides, the corresponding bit of blk_{less} in *BST* should be reset to 0 to indicate that blk_{less} is no longer mapped to any virtual block (Step 19). Then the updated *data* are sequentially written to the current physical block from its first free page $page_{free}$, and the *record* is created to maintain the mapping information of the updated *data* and is inserted into the run-length table of node N_v directly as we illustrated in Section 3.2 (Steps 20-23). This procedure could be demonstrated in Figure 5 when physical block 24 is full and physical block 25 is allocated/mapped to the node with key 17 on receiving a random update to update data of virtual page 25 of virtual block 17 (see Figures 4(b) and 4(c) for the procedure to update the run-length table).

For the ease of the free block allocation, physical blocks in the out-place area are considered a circular queue by connecting its last physical block to its first physical block. Two pointers *head* and *tail* are maintained to index the head and the tail of the queue respectively, where *head* points to the first non-free physical block (i.e., the first physical block that is not free) and *tail* points to the first free physical block. Thus, every physical block in the out-place area is free (or the circular queue is empty) when *head* = *tail*, and only one physical block in the out-place area is free (or the circular queue is full) when *head* = *tail* + 1. Initially, all of the physical blocks in the out-place area are free, so

Algorithm 1: ReqHandler

Input: *type*, *vpa*, *length*, *data*, *BST*
Output: *null*

1 **if** $type = Read$ **then**
2   **for** $i \leftarrow 1;\ i \leq length;\ i \leftarrow i+1$ **do**
3   **if** $page_{vpa+i} \in$ *out-place area* **then**
4   Read $page_{vpa+i}$ from out-place area;
5   **else**
6   Read $page_{vpa+i}$ from in-place area;
7 **else if** $type = Write$ **then**
8   **if** $N_v \notin$ *run-length tree* **then**
9   Create N_v and insert it into run-length tree;
10     $blk_{free} \leftarrow MarchingBlkAlloc()$;
11     $pba1 \leftarrow blk_{free}$;
12   **if** *there is not enough free pages in* blk_{pba1} **then**
13     $blk_{less} \leftarrow MIN(blk_{pba1}, blk_{pba2})$;
14     $blk_{more} \leftarrow MAX(blk_{pba1}, blk_{pba2})$;
15     $blk_{free} \leftarrow MarchingBlkAlloc()$;
16   Copy valid pages from blk_{less} to blk_{free};
17     $pba1 \leftarrow blk_{free}$;
18     $pba2 \leftarrow blk_{more}$;
19   BST[Addr[blk_{less}]] $\leftarrow 0$;
20   $page_{free} \leftarrow$ The first free page of blk_{pba1};
21   Sequentially write *data* to blk_{pba1} from $page_{free}$;
22   $record \leftarrow (vpa, pba1, \text{Addr}[ppa_{free}], length)$;
23   Create *record* and insert it into the run-length table of N_v;

that both *head* and *tail* point to the first physical block in the out-place area. When the node of the run-length tree needs a free physical block, the free physical block pointed by *tail* is allocated to the node and is enqueued by letting *tail* point to the next physical block that must be a free physical block. When there are not enough free physical blocks in the out-place area, the procedure *OldBlkRecycle* is activated to reclaim the non-free physical block pointed by *head* so as to release a free physical block. Then, this physical block is dequeued by moving *head* to the next physical block that must be a non-free physical block. To avoid wearing out the physical blocks in the out-place area excessively, the out-place area would be marched by triggering the procedure *March* when *tail* touches or reaches the right boundary of out-place area. The process of free block allocation is summarized in procedure *MarchingBlkAlloc* (see Algorithm 2), and the procedure *OldBlkRecycle* (see Algorithm 3) and *March* (see Algorithm 4) will be explained in Section 3.3.2.

Figure 5 shows a practical example to explain the procedure *MarchingBlkAlloc*. As the example in Figure 5 shows, the out-place area is composed of 90,000 physical blocks (i.e., blocks 10-90,009) and forms a circular queue by connecting physical block 90,009 to physical block 10. In this figure, *head* points to physical block 36 and *tail* points to physical block 26, so that physical blocks 36-90009 and physical blocks 10-25 are non-free physical blocks, and physical blocks 26-35 are free physical blocks. Meanwhile, physical blocks 24 and 25 are the latest two physical blocks allocated to the node with key 17 because of the random updates to update data of virtual block 17. Suppose that the least number of free physical blocks in the out-place area is 11, the

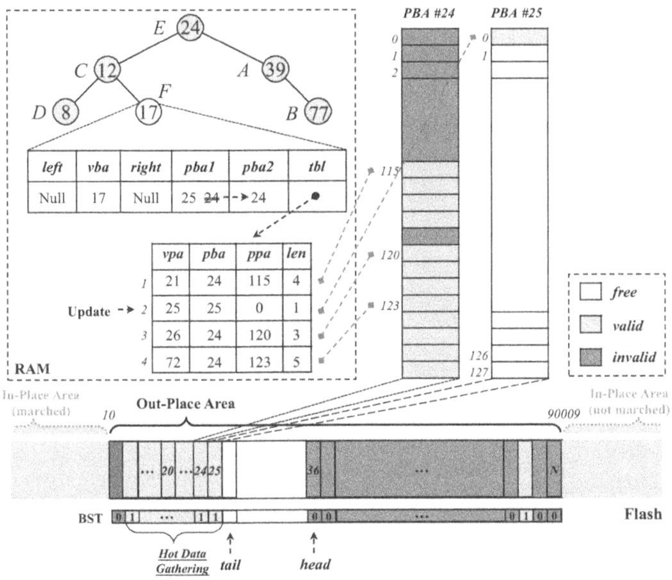

Figure 5: The marching-based hot data gathering policy.

Algorithm 2: MarchingBlkAlloc

Input: *head*, *tail*, *BST*
Output: blk_{new}

1 **while** *there are not enough free physical blocks* **do**
2   OldBlkRecycle();

3 **if** *tail touches the right boundary of out-place area* **then**
4   March();

5 $tail \leftarrow (tail + 1)\%SIZE_{out-place}$;
6 $BST[tail] \leftarrow 1$;
7 Return blk_{tail};

---

garbage collection should be activated to reclaim non-free physical blocks after physical block 25 is allocated.

3.3.2 Marching-Based Garbage Collection

In order to accelerate the performance on garbage collection without searching physical blocks for a proper one to reclaim, a block status table (BST) is maintained to keep the status of the physical blocks in the out-place area. The status list is a bit-array, and each bit is a flag to indicate the status of one physical block. For a free physical block, its corresponding bit flag is ignored because the garbage collection always selects the physical block pointed by *head* to reclaim and *head* never points to a free physical block. For a non-free physical block, its corresponding bit flag is set to "1" if it is mapped to a node of the run-length tree, and is set to "0" if it is not mapped to any node. Meanwhile, a non-free physical block is referred to as a *valid physical block* if its corresponding bit flag is set to "1" and is referred to as an *invalid physical block* if its corresponding bit flag is set to "0", as shown in Figure 5. Thus, when a free physical block is allocated/mapped to a node of the run-length tree for the data storage of random updates, it becomes a valid physical block with its corresponding bit flag set to "1"; a valid physical block turns into an invalid physical block with its corresponding bit flag set to "0" when 1) it is removed from its corresponding node or 2) its corresponding node is removed from the run-length tree. However, if a valid physical block is removed from its corresponding node, all of its valid data are written to the free physical block that replaces it (see Step 16 of Algorithm 1); if the node of a valid physical block is removed from the run-length tree due to the limited RAM space, all of the valid data corresponding to the node should be written back to their corresponding physical block in the in-place area (see Step 2 of Algorithm 3). As a result, an invalid physical block does not have any valid data and can be erased without any overheads on copying live pages, yet a valid physical block might contain some valid data.

Algorithm 3: OldBlkRecycle

Input: *head*, *tail*, *BST*
Output: *null*

1 **if** $BST[head] = 1$ **then**
2   Merge blk_{head} to in-place area;

3 Erase blk_{head};
4 Remove blk_{head} from its corresponding node;
5 $BST[head] \leftarrow 0$;
6 $head \leftarrow (head + 1)\%SIZE_{out-place}$;

Algorithm 3 shows procedure *OldBlkRecycle* for the garbage collection to reclaim one physical block: When procedure *OldBlkRecycle* is activated by procedure *MarchingBlkAlloc* to performance garbage collection, the physical block pointed by *head* is considered the victim physical block. If the bit flag is "1", the spare area of the first page in the physical block is checked to see which virtual block is mapped to this victim physical block because the spare area of each physical page stores the address of its corresponding virtual page or LBAs. Then the derived virtual block address is used as the index to search the run-length tree for the node corresponding to the virtual block so as to derive the address mapping information. With the mapping information, valid data in the victim physical block are merged with the physical block of the same virtual block in the in-place area (Steps 1-2). The reason to write the valid data back to their corresponding physical block in the in-place area is that valid data in a victim physical block must be cold data and haven't been updated for a long time even though they might be initially hot data. Then the victim physical block is erased directly (Step 3) because there are no valid data in the victim physical block after merging valid data back to the in-place area in Step 2. After the victim physical block is erased, it should be removed from its corresponding node, its corresponding bit flag in the status list should be reset to "0", and *head* should move to the next physical block (Steps 4-6). Note that the bit flag of a free physical block could be ignored. This procedure is repeated called repeatedly by procedure *MarchingBlkAlloc* until there are enough free physical blocks in the out-place area or the total RAM space consumption meets the system constraint. *It is worth noting that most hot data are gathered in the physical blocks close to tail* because hot data are frequently updated and stored in the current physical blocks of their corresponding nodes and the current physical block of a node is usually a newly allocated free physical block if the virtual block of the node keeps being updated. As a result, the garbage collection overheads such as live-page copyings could be minimized because most data stored in the physical blocks close to *head* were invalidated before these physical blocks are pointed by *head* and reclaimed, as shown in Figure 5.

Algorithm 4: March

Input: *remained_step*
Output: *null*

1 **if** *remained_step* > 0 **then**
2 Migrate $blk_{boundary_{left}+1}$ to $blk_{boundary_{left}}$;
3 $boundary_{left} \leftarrow boundary_{left} + 1$;
4 $boundary_{right} \leftarrow boundary_{right} + 1$;
5 $remained\_step \leftarrow remained\_step - 1$;
6 **else if** *remained_step* $= 0$ **then**
7 $remained\_step \leftarrow N_m$;

The garbage collection of the proposed policy achieves the wear leveling through the procedure *March* (see Algorithm 4). Initially, the out-place area consists of a fixed number of physical blocks in the beginning of the flash memory. When there are not enough free physical blocks, the physical block pointed by *head* is reclaimed. Then *head* moves forward to reclaim the next physical block. When *tail* reaches the last physical block (i.e., $blk_{boundary_{right}}$ in Algorithm 4) in the out-place area and reclaims it, the proposed policy checks whether the out-place area should be moved forward and what is the least march distance N_m to move forward in terms of the number of physical blocks such that each physical block could be evenly erased and be seriously worn during the time period of staying in the out-place area. When the out-place area reaches the end of the flash memory and rolls back to the beginning of the flash memory, most physical blocks are seriously worn but have not reached their erase limit. At this moment, the flash storage device should be replaced to prevent data loss. As for the least march distance N_m, suppose that the out-place area consists of N_o physical blocks, each physical block could endure N_e erases, and $N_o > N_e$. The least march distance N_m is $\lceil \frac{N_o}{N_e} \rceil$ in each run when *head* reaches the end of the out-place area. When *head* reaches the last physical block in the out-place area and reclaims it, the first N_m physical blocks in the out-place area are switched with the first N_m physical blocks that are right after the out-place area. The switch operation could be separated into N_m steps and each step only switches one physical block in the out-place area with one physical block in the in-place area. After the march operation, *head* rolls back to the first physical block (i.e., $blk_{boundary_{left}}$ in Algorithm 4) in the new out-place area. This procedure repeats until the out-place area reaches the end of the flash memory and rolls back to the beginning of the flash memory. We summarize procedure *March* of the march operation in Algorithm 4. When the march operation is activated because *head* reaches the last physical block in the out-place area (see Steps 3-4 of Algorithm 2), procedure *March* will be invoked or activated for N_m times. On each activation, this procedure only march the out-place area with the distance of one physical block (Steps 1-5). After the out-place area has marched forward with the distance of N_m physical blocks, the variable (i.e., *remained_step*) to maintain the remaining march distance is reset to N_m and the pointer *tail* will be moved back to the first physical block of the out-place area (see Step 5 of Algorithm 2) so as to stop the march operation (Steps 6-7). Note that after a physical block leaves the out-place area, any writes to the physical block should be supported by a stronger error correction code or followed by a read operation to verify the correctness of the written data because the physical block has endured a lot of erases and is less reliable[4].

As the example in Figure 5 shows, the out-place area consists of 90,000 (i.e., 90,009-10+1) physical blocks. Suppose that each physical block could endure 10,000 erase cycles, and we hope to preserve 10% of the erase cycles for each physical block such that physical blocks could, on average, endure 1,000 erase cycles when they are not in the out-place area. Thus, when physical block 90,009 in the out-place area is reclaimed, the out-place area should be marched forward for 10 (i.e., $\lceil \frac{90,000}{10,000\times(1-10\%)} \rceil$) physical blocks. That is, physical blocks 90,010-90,019 are included into the out-place area, and physical blocks 10-19 becomes part of the in-place area. The virtual blocks that were originally mapped to physical blocks 90,010-90,019 are now mapped to physical blocks 10-19. Of course, physical blocks 10-19 should be reclaimed, followed by copying data in physical blocks 90,010-90,019 to physical blocks 10-19 respectively. After the out-place area is marched forward, the new out-place area contains physical blocks 20-90,019 and then *tail* is rolled back to the first physical block (i.e., physical block 20) of the new out-place area (as shown in Figure 6) .

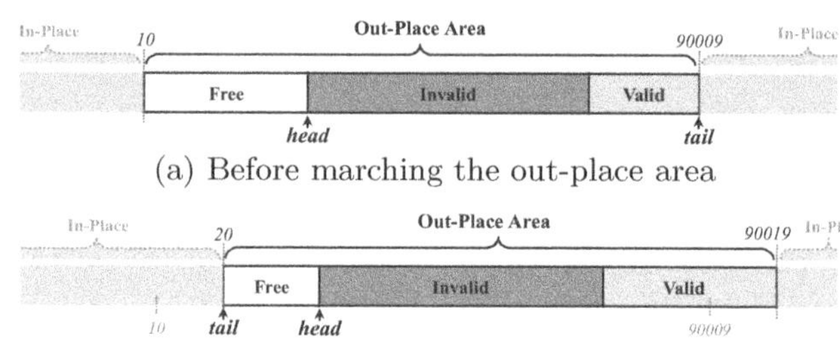

(a) Before marching the out-place area

(b) After marched the out-place area

Figure 6: An example of the procedure March.

4. PERFORMANCE EVALUATION

4.1 Metrics and Experiment Setup

The purpose of this section is to evaluate the capability of the proposed working-set-based address mapping scheme (referred to as WSB) with existing popular FTL strategies, in terms of access performance and reliability. The access performance was evaluated based on the average response time per read/write request. The reliability evaluation was evaluated in terms of the first failure time, where the first failure time is the first time that an error can not be corrected.

The proposed WSB was compared to FTL, BL, NFTL and FAST management strategies. FTL and NFTL adopted a greedy policy for the garbage collection: That is, blocks in the flash memory are circularly scanned to find the victim block to reclaim, and a block is considered as a victim when the number of invalid pages is larger than the number of valid pages in the block. BL does not have to do garbage collection because the original block is erased immediately after all valid data are copied to the block that replaces the original block. FAST circularly reclaims the space of its log blocks by merging the valid pages in the to-be-erased log block with the valid pages in its corresponding data blocks

[4]In practice, some marched physical blocks might be eventually worn out in extreme cases, so some spare physical blocks should be reserved for the worn-out block replacement.

into a free block, and then the to-be-erased log block and its corresponding data blocks are erased. Note that the total numbers of log blocks used in NFTL and FAST are limited by the size of main-memory in this experiment. As shown in Table 3, a 256GB four-chipped MLC-based flash storage device with 4MB main-memory space was under investigation, and 80% of the storage device excluding the over-provision space was initially stored with data. Without loss of generality, we assign extra 20% capacity as its over-provision space. The capability of the management strategies was evaluated through three realistic traces: "file server", "proxy server" and "web server". They are public one-week traces collected from an enterprise data center and could be obtained from the SINA IOTTA Repository [19].

# of chips	4	Write	$800\mu s$
Chip size	64GB	Erase	$1.5ms$
Over-Provision Size	Extra 20% per chip	Random read	$60\mu s$
RAM size	4MB	Serial access	$25ns/B$ ($52.8\mu s/page$)
Block size	256KB (128 pages)	Erase cycles	500

Table 3: The evaluated MLC flash-memory storage system [7, 22].

4.2 Experimental Results

4.2.1 Performance

Figure 7 shows that WSB could greatly improve the access performance of the flash storage device compared to BL, NFTL and FAST, and almost achieve the access performance of fine-grained address mappings compared to FTL, where the x-axis denotes the request type (i.e., read or write), and the y-axis denotes the average response time of each request. Although FTL has the best performance on handling both read and write requests, its huge page-level address mapping table makes it infeasible for large-scaled flash storage devices. In our estimation, FTL needs about 44MB RAM space to manage a flash device with 256GB capacity. As shown in Figure 7, the proposed WSB has similar performance to FTL, BL, and FAST on handling read requests, but outperforms the read performance of NFTL for more than 94%, 91% and 18% under the file server trace, proxy server trace and web server trace respectively. This is because NFTL needs to sequentially search pages of replacement blocks for the latest version of data. On the other hands, the write performance of the proposed WSB is at least 1.99, 2.08, and 1.96 times of those of BL, NFTL and FAST under the file server trace, proxy server trace and web server trace respectively. This is because the proposed WSB gathers hot and valid data together near the tail of the out-place area naturally so as to reduce the garbage collection overheads when reclaiming blocks near the head of the out-place area. It is interesting to see that FAST has poor performance under both proxy server trace and web server trace. This is because only limited number of blocks in the storage device is preserved as log blocks for data updates in FAST in this experiment because of the limited RAM space to maintain the page-level address mapping for log blocks. In addition, because a log block in FAST usually contains valid data of multiple data blocks, the reclaiming of one log block could trigger a large overheads on block erases and live-page copies when the log block and its corresponding data blocks are merged. It is worth noting that FTL could only outperform the proposed WSB for no more than 15% in terms of write performance.

4.2.2 Reliability

Figure 8 shows the reliability of the simulated flash device using the proposed WSB and other FTLs, in terms of the first failure time, where x-axis indicates the input trace, and the y-axis denotes the first failure time (in a logarithmic scale). The first failure time of the proposed WSB is longer than those of BL and FAST under the file server trace and proxy server trace, and is longer than that of NFTL under the web server trace. The rational behind this is that in a read-intensive trace such as web server trace, the working set is possibly contained in the out-place area so that the frequency to write data back to the in-place area is significantly reduced. However, the first failure time of the proposed WSB is at most 74% that of FTL under all traces. In an environment with high requirement to reliability, the first failure time could be effectively extended by replacing those fast worn out blocks with the good blocks in the un-marched in-place area.

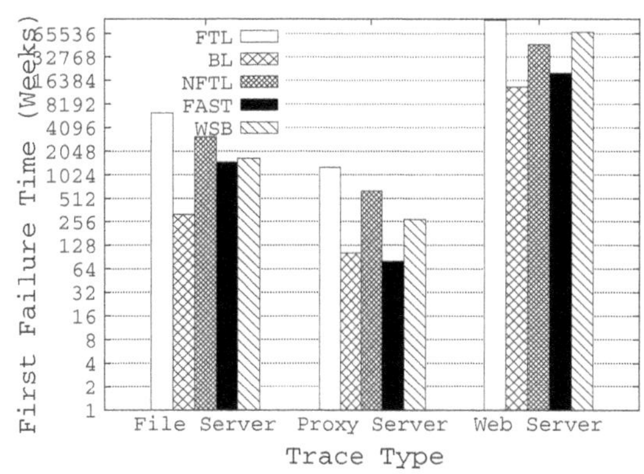

Figure 8: First failure time over different FTLs.

5. CONCLUSION

This work is motivated by the challenging issue on the address mapping design due to the fast-growing capacity and limited RAM space of flash storage devices. In this paper, a working-set-based address mapping scheme is proposed to solve the address mapping issue with the considerations of the system performance, wear leveling, RAM space usage, and storage space utilization. The proposed scheme has better performance as the capacity of flash storage devices increases, and demands RAM space related to the access patterns and the working sets of users, instead of the device capacity. In the proposed scheme, a marching-based hot data gathering policy is proposed to reduce the overheads on garbage collection by gathering hot data together and preventing from scanning the whole flash memory for the victim block, and to improve the system endurance by wearing blocks in the out-place area evenly and marching the out-place area forward regularly. A series of experiments is conducted based on realistic workloads. We show that the write performance of the proposed scheme is at least 1.96 times of other existing coarse-grained address mapping methods and nearly achieves the performance of the fine-grained address mappings in most cases, while the required RAM space is no more than 2MB based on our observation.

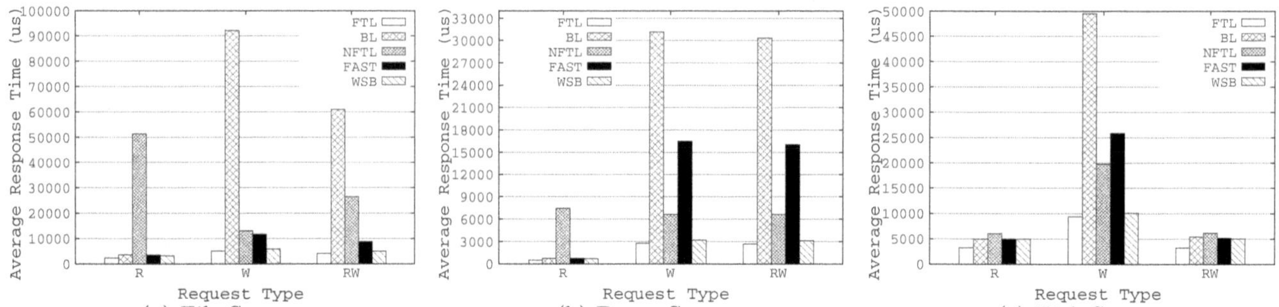

(a) File Server (b) Proxy Server (c) Web Server

Figure 7: Average response time of requests.

In our future research, we shall investigate flash storage devices with more diversified access patterns to examine the effectiveness of the proposed address mapping scheme. We shall also explore the possibility to extend the proposed scheme to cooperate with the new 3D flash chips and new architecture designs for the next-generation flash storage devices.

6. REFERENCES

[1] Flash-memory Translation Layer for NAND flash (NFTL). *M-Systems*, 1998.

[2] N. Agrawal, V. Prabhakaran, T. Wobber, J. D. Davis, M. Manasse, and R. Panigrahy. Design Tradeoffs for SSD Performance. In *the USENIX Annual Technical Conference*, pages 57–70, June 2008.

[3] A. Ban. Flash File System. US Patent 5,404,485. In *M-Systems*, April 1995.

[4] L.-P. Chang. On Efficient Wear Leveling for Large-scale Flash-memory Storage Systems. In *the 2007 ACM symposium on Applied computing (SAC)*, 2007.

[5] Y.-H. Chang and T.-W. Kuo. A Commitment-based Management Strategy for the Performance and Reliability Enhancement of Flash-memory Storage Systems. In *the 46th ACM/IEEE Design Automation Conference (DAC)*, 2009.

[6] H. Cho, D. Shin, and Y. Eom. KAST: K-Associative Sector Translation for NAND Flash Memory in Real-Time Systems. In *DATE*, 2009.

[7] R. Dan and R. Singer. *Implementing MLC NAND Flash Memory for Cost-Effective, High-capacity Memory*. M-Systems, September 2003.

[8] A. P. Ferreira, M. Zhou, S. Bock, B. Childers, R. Melhem, and D. Moss. Increasing PCM Main Memory Lifetime. In *the ACM/IEEE Design, Automation and Test in Europe (DATE)*, 2010.

[9] B. Godard, J.-M. Daga, L. Torres, and G. Sassatelli. Evaluation of Design for Reliability Techniques in Embedded Flash Memories. In *the ACM/IEEE Design, Automation and Test in Europe (DATE)*, 2007.

[10] A. Gupta, Y. Kim, and B. Urgaonkar. DFTL: a flash translation layer employing demand-based selective caching of page-level address mappings. In *ASPLOS*, 2009.

[11] H. Jo, J.-U. Kang, S.-Y. Park, J.-S. Kim, and J. Lee. FAB: flash-aware buffer management policy for portable media players. *IEEE Trans. Consum. Electron.*, 52(2):485–493, May 2006.

[12] S. Kang, S. Park, H. Jung, H. Shim, and J. Cha. Performance trade-offs in using nvram write buffer for flash memorybased storage devices. *IEEE Trans. Comput.*, 58(6):744–758, Jun 2009.

[13] Y. Kang and E. L. Miller. Adding Aggressive Error Correction to a High-Performance Compressing Flash File System. In *the ACM International Conference on Embedded Software (EMSOFT)*, 2009.

[14] H. Kim and S. Ahn. BPLRU: a buffer management scheme for improving random writes in flash storage. In *USENIX Conference on File and Storage Technologies (FAST)*, 2008.

[15] J. Kim, J. M. Kim, S. H. Noh, S. L. Min, and Y. Cho. A Space-Efficient Flash Translation Layer For CompactFlash Systems. *IEEE Transactions on Consumer Electronics*, Nov 2002.

[16] T.-W. Kuo, Y.-H. Chang, P.-C. Huang, and C.-W. Chang. Special Issues in Flash. In *the IEEE/ACM International Conference on Computer-Aided Design (ICCAD)*, 2008.

[17] S.-W. Lee, D.-J. Park, T.-S. Chung, D.-H. Lee, S. Park, and H.-J. Song. A log buffer-based flash translation layer using fully-associative sector translation. *ACM Transactions on Embedded Computing Systems*, 6(3), July 2007.

[18] M. Murugan and David.H.C.Du. Rejuvenator: A static wear leveling algorithm for nand flash memory with minimized overhead. In *MSST*, 2011.

[19] D. Narayanan, A. Donnelly, and A. Rowstron. Write Off-Loading: Practical Power Management for Enterprise Storage. *ACM Transactions on Storage*, 4:10:1–10:23, November 2008.

[20] V. Papirla and C. Chakrabarti. Energy-Aware Error Control Coding for Flash Memories. In *the ACM/IEEE Design Automation Conference (DAC)*, July 2009.

[21] D. Park, B. Debnath, and D. Du. CFTL: A Convertible Flash Translation Layer Adaptive to Data Access Patterns. In *SIGMETRICS*, pages 14–18, June 2010.

[22] Samsung Electronics. *K9GAG08U0M 2G x 8bit NAND Flash Memory Data Sheet*, September 2006.

[23] A. Smith. Disk cache–miss ratio analysis and design considerations. *ACM Transactions on Computer Systems (TOCS)*, 3(3):161–203, Aug 1985.

[24] C.-H. Wu and T.-W. Kuo. An Adaptive Two-level Management for the Flash Translation Layer in Embedded Systems. In *the IEEE/ACM Iinternational Conference on Computer-Aided Design (ICCAD)*, pages 601–606, 2006.

An Exploration Methodology for a Customizable OpenCL Stereo-Matching Application Targeted to an Industrial Multi-Cluster Architecture

Edoardo Paone, Gianluca Palermo, Vittorio Zaccaria, and Cristina Silvano
Politecnico di Milano - Dipartimento di Elettronica e Informazione, Milano, Italy
{paone, gpalermo, zaccaria, silvano}@elet.polimi.it

Diego Melpignano, Germain Haugou, and Thierry Lepley
STMicroelectronics, Grenoble, France
{diego.melpignano, germain.haugou, thierry.lepley}@st.com

ABSTRACT

Open Computing Language (OpenCL) is emerging as a standard for parallel programming of heterogeneous hardware accelerators. With respect to device specific languages, OpenCL enables application portability but does not guarantee performance portability, eventually requiring additional tuning of the implementation to a specific platform or to unpredictable dynamic workloads.

In this paper, we present a methodology to analyze the customization space of an OpenCL application in order to improve performance portability and to support dynamic adaptation. We formulate our case study by implementing an OpenCL image stereo-matching application (which computes the relative depth of objects from a pair of stereo images) customized to the STMicroelectronics Platform 2012 many-core computing fabric. In particular, we use design space exploration techniques to generate a set of *operating points* that represent specific configurations of the parameters allowing different trade-offs between performance and accuracy of the algorithm itself. These points give detailed knowledge about the interaction between the application parameters, the underlying architecture and the performance of the system; they could also be used by a run-time manager software layer to meet dynamic Quality-of-Service (QoS) constraints.

To analyze the customization space, we use cycle-accurate simulations for the target architecture. Since the profiling phase of each configuration takes a long simulation time, we designed our methodology to reduce the overall number of simulations by exploiting some important features of the application parameters; our analysis also enables the identification of the parameters that could be explored on a high-level simulation model to reduce the simulation time. The resulting methodology is one order of magnitude more efficient than an exhaustive exploration and, given its randomized nature, it increases the probability to avoid sub-optimal trade-offs.

Categories and Subject Descriptors

C.3 [**Special-Purpose and Application-Based Systems**]: Real-time and embedded systems

Keywords

Design Space Exploration, OpenCL, Runtime Monitoring

1. INTRODUCTION

As a cross-platform open standard, OpenCL is used today for programming heterogeneous systems with hardware accelerators, from high-end multi-core CPUs and GPUs, to System-on-Chip (SoC) architectures for embedded devices and even Field Programmable Gate Arrays (FPGAs) [1]. Although OpenCL provides functional portability over a wide range of computing devices, it does not guarantee performance portability. OpenCL applications then require additional design-time and run-time tuning for achieving best performance on each target platform, as well as for addressing potential unpredictable workloads of the application itself. This can be done by exploiting application-level parameters and OpenCL structuring parameters such as the *workgroup size* [16].

In this paper we present a novel OpenCL design approach targeting the stereo-matching algorithm [30] and exploiting a design space exploration (DSE) methodology for application customization. The main goal consists of improving performance portability on the STMicroelectronics Platform 2012 (P2012) architecture [4] by customizing application parameters. The stereo-matching algorithm computes pixel *disparity* from a pair of stereo-images captured by two cameras. The disparity information is then used to generate the relative distance of the objects in the scene from the cameras: the result is a depth map represented in gray-scale bitmap format.

To address run-time adaptation, the stereo-matching application was designed to expose as many configuration parameters as possible, so that optimization for a specific OpenCL platform can be done by selecting the Pareto-optimal set of parameter values at run-time. This choice can be done either by the application designer at deployment time or by a suitable run-time layer that, given the actual goals of the system, can trade off *Quality of Service* with respect to performance [20].

Our methodology has been validated on a cycle-accurate simulation model of P2012. This tool provides an accurate profiling of OpenCL kernel execution time on P2012 processing cores; however, the simulation is relatively slow (around 30 minutes for simulating one configuration on one input pair of stereo images). To address this problem we developed an efficient, design-time analysis and optimization heuristic to efficiently navigate over the design options of the stereo-matching application. The output of this multi-objective optimization step is a list of optimal *operating points* to be used by a run-time manager and a detailed knowledge about the interactions between the application parameters, the underlying architecture, the performance of the system (*throughput*) and the quality of the results (*disparity error*, a measure of result accuracy with respect to a reference scenario).

To summarize, the main contributions of this paper are:

- A new customizable OpenCL implementation of the stereo-matching algorithm [30] that applies the principle of *software pipelining* to improve the usage of asynchronous memory transfers.
- An innovative exploration-based methodology to support the customization of applications, which allows for a reduction of the overall number of simulations by exploiting relations between parameters as they are discovered and unfolded during the exploration.
- A technique exploiting a fast high-level simulation model to further reduce the exploration time, which allows for an overall speed-up of 16x with respect to an exhaustive exploration of the entire design space.

The remainder of this paper is organized as follows. In Section 2 we describe the implementation of the Stereo-Matching OpenCL application while in Section 3 we describe the design space exploration methodology proposed in this paper. In Section 4 we present the experimental results while in Section 5 we describe the state-of-the-art methodologies used to address design space exploration.

2. THE OPENCL CUSTOMIZABLE STEREO-MATCHING APPLICATION

Stereo-matching is used in image-processing to compute disparities between a pair of stereo images (the same scene observed by two cameras). The disparity information can then be processed to calculate the depth of the objects in the scene, given that objects close to the cameras are characterized by a higher disparity. In this section, we assume that the reader has basic familiarity with the OpenCL framework and terminology.

The stereo-matching application has been implemented primarily targeting STMicroelectronics P2012 [4], thus some design choices address specific features of a multi-cluster architecture.

P2012 consists of a Globally Asynchronous Locally Synchronous (GALS) fabric of clusters, connected through an asynchronous global Network-on-Chip (GANOC). The P2012 cluster is composed of a multi-core computing engine, called ENCore, and a cluster controller. The ENCore cluster (Fig. 1) can host a number of processors (processing elements – PEs) that can be varying, at design-time, from 1 to 16; the base processing element of the ENCore engine is a STxP70-V4 processor, a dual-issue customizable 32-bit RISC core of STMicroelectronics with a 32-bit floating-point unit.

The processing elements do not have private data caches to avoid maintaining memory coherency across cores. Nevertheless, they share a L1, 256-KB multi-banked tightly coupled data memory (TCDM): this memory is mapped as *local memory* by the STMicroelectronics's OpenCL toolchain. A DMA engine allows for efficient asynchronous memory transfers between external memory (referred to as *global* in OpenCL) and local memory: this mechanism – exploited by the OpenCL asynchronous copies – allows hiding the latency of accesses to the external memory, which can be several hundreds of clock cycles.

Two aspects have primarily been addressed in the design of our stereo-matching application:

- The latency of accesses to external memory represents a bottleneck for OpenCL applications on P2012. Thus, a lot of effort has been spent to reduce the number of read/write operations and to exploit asynchronous transfers. In particular, *software pipelining* has been used to write the core application kernel: this allows for asynchronously fetching next data with DMA while elaborating current data.

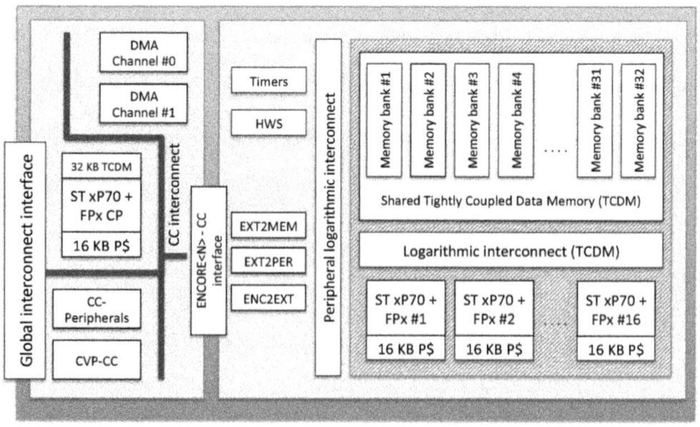

Figure 1: P2012 cluster architecture overview

- One workgroup is executed on one cluster and each one of its work-items is mapped to a processing element, to exploit the computational power at the cluster level. Work-items have access to the 256 KB local memory and to the synchronization module available on ENCore that provides a hardware-supported accelerated synchronization. Parallelism between workgroups can only be exploited on a multi-cluster configuration and it is anyway limited by the number of clusters.

The application has been designed to exploit the parallelism within a workgroup, but still leaves the possibility, by means of a *resource parameter*, to change the number of workgroups depending on the number of available clusters.

Our implementation of the application is inspired by the algorithm proposed in [30]. This algorithm uses adaptive-shape local support windows for each pixel that are based on color similarity: pixels with similar color are, in fact, likely to belong to the same object surface. Support windows are represented by means of a *cross*-like structure for each pixel, whose arms extend to cover any irregular shape in the image (see Fig. 2).

Given the stereo-image pair as input, we assume that each considered pixel on the right image ('anchor') has a corresponding position in the left image. We assume that images have been captured by cameras with the same vertical position, thus **the search can be limited to the same row**. The difference between the horizontal position in the left image and the position in the right image is called *disparity* and it is inversely proportional to the distance of the point with respect to the cameras. To compute the disparity for each pixel, the algorithm proceeds by formulating *disparity hypotheses* to be validated through the support regions that are built for each pixel.

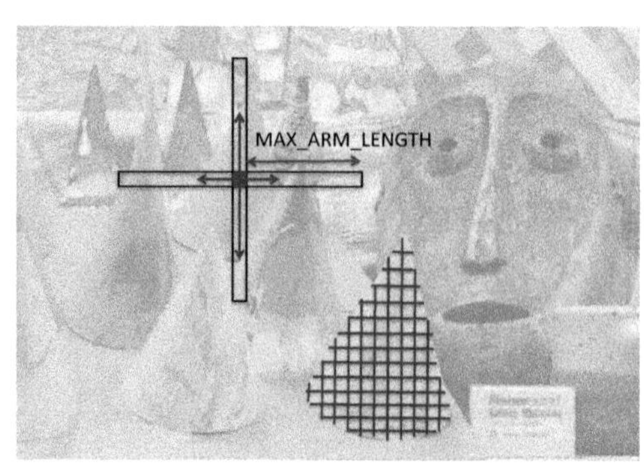

Figure 2: Construction of shape-adaptive support windows.

To check the validity of a hypothesis, the algorithm has to first find a match of the 'anchor' pixel in the left image and then compute the distance it actually moved. For example, in Fig. 3 we have for the anchor pixel **R** (in the right image) two hypotheses to be tested for matching: either pixel **R** has moved to **A** (disparity hypothesis 1) or it has moved to **B** (disparity hypothesis 2). When comparing the *difference* between the support region of **R** and those associated with **A** and **B**, it turns out that the lowest difference (matching cost) is for pixel **B**, thus hypothesis 2 wins. The disparity is then computed as the distance between the specular pixel **R'** in the left image and **B**. The disparity information for each pixel of the right image is typically stored as a gray-level bitmap file, where higher-intensity pixels represent higher disparity values.

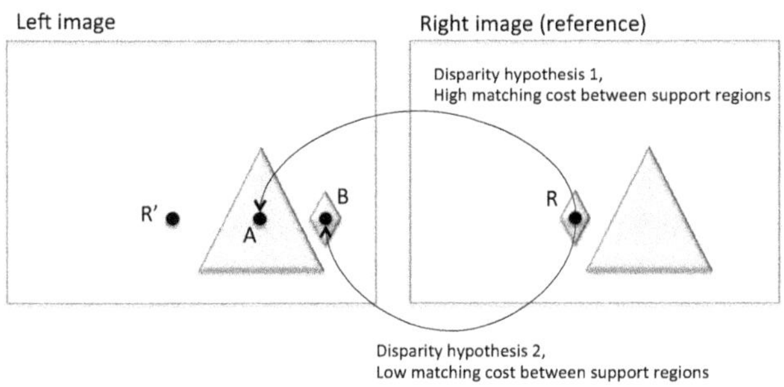

Figure 3: Examples of disparity hypotheses with triangular and quadrangular support regions.

2.1 Description of the application parameters

Some parameters are application-specific and were already used in [30]. These parameters will be referred to as *application parameters* in the rest of the paper and they are listed below.

Confidence: defines a threshold for color similarity with respect to the anchor pixel when building a support region.

Max_arm_length: the support region for each pixel is encoded in a cross structure and all pixels covered by the cross arms (left, right, up and down) are similar in color to the anchor pixel: this parameter represents the maximum arm length and can thus limit the size of support windows (see Fig. 2).

Max_hypo_value and **hypo_step**: these parameters define the set of integer disparities that the algorithm should test for each pair of pixels. Each disparity value is a 'hypothesis' that is actually evaluated by the algorithm. The disparity hypotheses (in pixels) will range from 0 to *max_hypo_value*, with a given *hypo_step* step. The latter parameter acts as the 'resolution' of the algorithm, by setting the step between consecutive disparity hypotheses.

Match_limit: controls the truncation limit of matching cost.

2.2 Structure of the OpenCL kernels

The structure of the application is described in Fig. 4. For each pair of stereo images, the following five OpenCL kernels are executed.

WinBuild (left and right cameras): two instances of the same OpenCL kernel (one for the left and one for the right image) can be submitted in parallel to the OpenCL command queue to build the local support regions for each pixel in the image. Fig. 2 shows an example of the construction of the cross arms (a 4 byte structure, each arm encoded on one byte): the search span is limited by the application parameter *max_arm_length* and the arms cover all the pixels that satisfy the condition of color similarity specified by *confidence*.

Matching-cost aggregation: this kernel evaluates all the disparity hypotheses by computing the matching-cost associated with support regions of pixels on the same line in the two reference images. A Winner-Takes-All (WTA) decision is then taken for selection of the 'cheapest' disparity hypothesis in terms of matching-cost.

FinalDecision: this kernel simply considers the results of all the workgroups involved in the previous step and decides the global disparity result. It can be seen as a reduction step.

Refinement: it performs a regularization (*smoothing*) of disparities in the support region.

The profiling percentages reported in Fig. 4 show that *Matching-Cost Aggregation* kernel is the most computational-intensive. As proposed in [30], for each disparity hypothesis d this kernel performs two orthogonal integration steps over the raw matching-costs on the aggregation region. As expressed by (1), the result is the disparity hypothesis d_p^0 that minimizes the aggregation cost $E_d(p)$:

$$d_p^0 = \arg\min_d E_d(p), d \in [0, d_{max}] \quad (1)$$

Since different disparity hypotheses can be considered independently, it is possible to distribute the workload over several workgroups, each workgroup working on a different range of disparities (see Fig. 5). The WTA decision is first taken at the workgroup level, on the local range of disparity hypotheses; then *FinalDecision* kernel selects the final disparity that minimizes the aggregation cost over all the workgroups. This solution has been designed for multi-cluster architectures with a shared-memory model such as P2012.

2.3 Resource parameters

In order to explore different platform configurations, the following *resource parameters* have been introduced.

Number of workgroups in WTA stage (*nb_wta_workgroups*). In our implementation, data-parallelism is mainly exploited by work-items within a workgroup; however different workgroups can work in parallel if more clusters are available. This parameter allows setting the number of workgroups for *Matching-Cost Aggregation* kernel, enabling concurrent execution on several clusters. Each workgroup will thus process a different range of disparity hypotheses (see Fig. 5). The maximum allowed number of workgroups is the number of disparity hypotheses to be evaluated divided by the

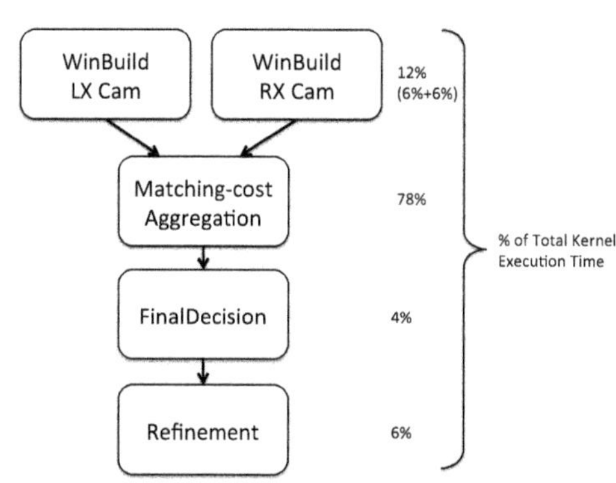

Figure 4: Execution flow of the OpenCL kernels described in Par. 2.2 and related percentages of execution time.

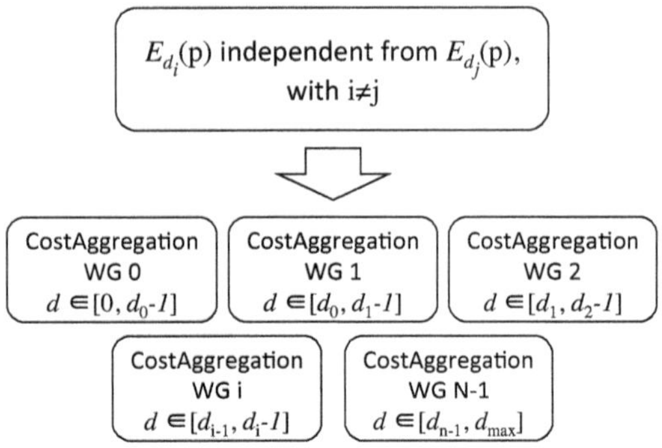

Figure 5: Parallelization of Matching-cost Aggregation over several workgroups.

number of hypotheses evaluated in one cycle by each workgroup (*nb_hypo_per_wg*, described later):

$$num\_disparities_{tot} = \frac{max\_hypo\_value}{hypo\_step} + 1 \quad (2)$$

$$nb\_wta\_workgroups_{max} = \lceil \frac{num\_disparities_{tot}}{nb\_hypo\_per\_wg} \rceil \quad (3)$$

Workgroup size (*nb_wi_per_wg*). This parameter specifies the workgroup size: by reducing the workgroup size, it becomes possible to schedule several workgroups on the same cluster. We have set *nb_wi_per_wg* to 16 (the number of available PEs on one cluster) given the current features of the SDK we have used. However, this parameter must be tuned according to the accelerator architecture: other platforms might provide a lower parallelism within the workgroup, in this case it is important to reduce the workgroup size and to exploit the parallelism between workgroups.
In our application, the work-items work on different image rows, each one processing a number of pixels specified by *wg_col_pixel_-width*. Fig. 6 shows the execution model for *Matching-cost Aggregation* kernel: this kernel is slightly different from the other ones,

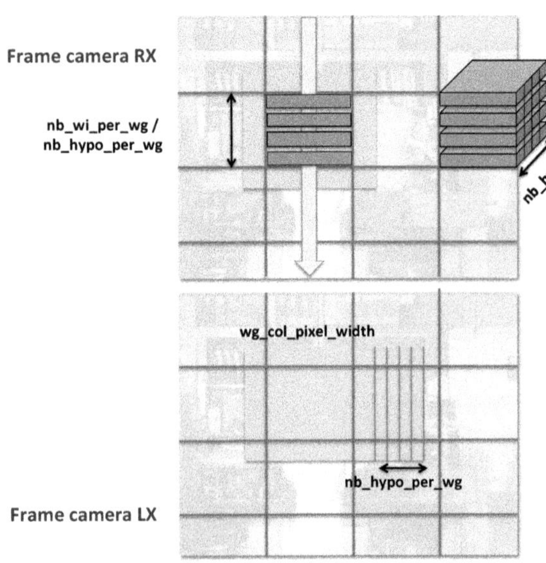

Figure 6: Matching-cost Aggregation OpenCL kernel.

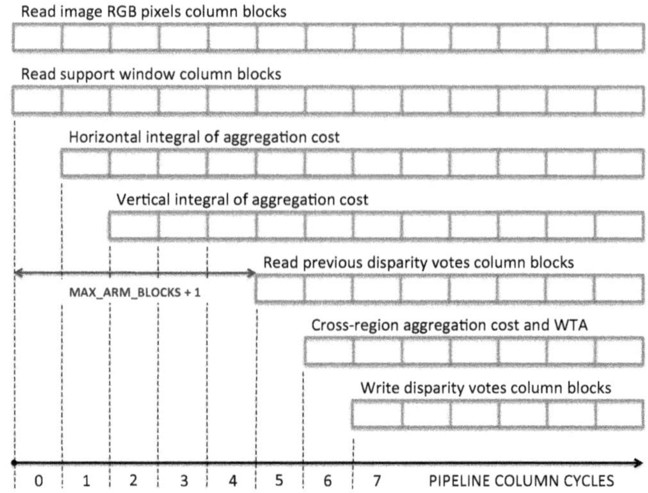

Figure 7: Software pipeline for Matching-cost Aggregation kernel, with max_arm_blocks=4 (e.g. *nb_wi_per_wg*=16, *nb_-hypo_per_wg*=4 and *max_arm_length*=16).

since there might be more than one PE working on the same image row but with a different disparity value (see *nb_hypo_per_wg*).

Number of pixels processed per work-item (*wg_col_pixel_-width*). Our OpenCL kernels never access external memory directly, data is first copied to local memory (L1, 256 KB on cluster) by means of asynchronous DMA transfers at workgroup level. In order to compensate for the DMA latency, we have implemented a software pipeline (Fig. 7) so that asynchronous memory transfers – global-to-local (read) and local-to-global (write) – are executed in parallel to data processing. The application also exploits FIFO buffers allocated in local memory to pipeline different stages of data processing, for example horizontal integration, vertical integration, and cross-region aggregation.
The parameter *wg_col_pixel_width* allows to indirectly control the size of DMA transfers. As shown in Fig. 6, *wg_col_pixel_width* specifies the length of the row of pixels to be processed by one work-item: thus, tuning of this parameter makes it possible to compensate the DMA latency with the processing time in the pipeline stage.
The configuration of application parameters changes the pipeline properties: not only the stage duration, as explained before, but also the latency (*max_arm_blocks*, as shown in Fig. 7). The relation between *max_arm_blocks* and *application parameters* is described below:

$$block\_size = \frac{nb\_wi\_per\_wg}{nb\_hypo\_per\_wg} \quad (4)$$

$$max\_arm\_blocks = \lceil max\_arm\_length/block\_size \rceil \quad (5)$$

Number of disparity hypotheses for each workgroup (*nb_-hypo_per_wg*). This parameter introduces a third dimension in *Matching-cost Aggregation* kernel (see Fig. 6). *block_size* in Eq. 4 is the number of pixel rows processed within one pipeline stage; however, there might be more than one work-item processing the same line but evaluating different disparity hypotheses (as many as specified by *nb_hypo_per_wg*). For some configurations of the parameters (as we will show in Section 4), increasing *nb_hypo_-per_wg* might give better results in terms of both performance and memory utilization.

3. THE DSE METHODOLOGY FOR APPLICATION CUSTOMIZATION

The goal of the *Design Space Exploration* (DSE) is to analyze and tune application-specific parameters and resource parameters to minimize the *disparity error* and maximize the application *throughput*, also taking into account the variability on input data and runtime workload.

The *disparity error* is defined as the error of the algorithm in computing the actual depth of the points in a scene. To evaluate the *disparity error*, we used a set of seven bitmap image-pairs (three color components per pixel, encoded on 24bit) chosen from the Middlebury stereo datasets [26, 27]. Each reference image-pair has a corresponding *truth* disparity map which is used to compute the *disparity error* as the *average intensity difference per pixel* in the seven disparity maps.

Since we have to deal with a minimization problem, the other objective was set to *delay per pixel* (execution time divided by the number of pixels processed by the application), that is the inverse of *throughput*. This metric is computed as the geometric average value of *delay per pixel* over the seven images in the set.

The output of the methodology is a set of **operating points**, i.e., tuples composed of application-specific parameter and resource parameter values providing optimal *disparity error* and *delay per pixel*. Since there are two target objectives, the definition of optimality is not unique [11]; thus the final output of our methodology is a Pareto-set of configurations.

Finally, the Pareto-set of operating points can be used by either the application designer, at deployment time, or by a suitable run-time management layer to trade off *Quality of Service* (QoS) with performance [20]. In fact, the original parameter space is too wide to make accurate decisions about the optimal configurations, both for the developer or the run-time layer. Moreover, workloads or QoS requirements (such as the *disparity error*) can change dynamically, requiring a new parameter configuration. Our methodology prunes the parameter space to identify only those important to make this decision.

An operating point for the stereo-matching application can be formally defined by a tuple:

$$c = \langle \boldsymbol{\alpha}, \boldsymbol{\rho}, \delta, \epsilon \rangle \tag{6}$$

where:

- $\boldsymbol{\alpha}$ and $\boldsymbol{\rho}$ are two arrays of values, the first one for application parameters and the second one for resource parameters.

$$\boldsymbol{\alpha} = \begin{bmatrix} confidence \\ max\_arm\_length \\ hypo\_step \\ max\_hypo\_value \\ match\_limit \end{bmatrix} \in A \tag{7}$$

$$\boldsymbol{\rho} = \begin{bmatrix} nb\_wta\_workgroups \\ nb\_wi\_per\_wg \\ wg\_col\_pixel\_width \\ nb\_hypo\_per\_wg \end{bmatrix} \in R \tag{8}$$

  where both A and R are finite, discrete domains: $A \subset N_0^5$, $R \subset N_0^4$ (the possible values are reported in Table 1).

- δ is the *delay per pixel*, which depends on both $\boldsymbol{\alpha}$ and $\boldsymbol{\rho}$:

$$\delta = f_1(\alpha, \rho) \tag{9}$$

- ϵ is the *disparity error*, which only depends on $\boldsymbol{\alpha}$:

$$\epsilon = f_2(\alpha) \tag{10}$$

The multi-objective optimization is thus defined as a set of two objective functions to be minimized:

$$\min_{\boldsymbol{\alpha} \in A, \boldsymbol{\rho} \in R} \boldsymbol{f}(\boldsymbol{\alpha}, \boldsymbol{\rho}) = \begin{bmatrix} f_1(\boldsymbol{\alpha}, \boldsymbol{\rho}) \\ f_2(\boldsymbol{\alpha}) \end{bmatrix} \in R^2 \tag{11}$$

However, each configuration of parameters $c = \langle \boldsymbol{\alpha}, \boldsymbol{\rho} \rangle$ requires the allocation of a certain amount of buffers when deployed on the device. Thus, the choice of $\boldsymbol{\alpha}$ and $\boldsymbol{\rho}$ is also subject to the following constraint:

$$m(\boldsymbol{\alpha}', \boldsymbol{\rho}') \leq M \ with \ \boldsymbol{\alpha}' \subseteq \boldsymbol{\alpha}, \boldsymbol{\rho}' \subseteq \boldsymbol{\rho} \tag{12}$$

where M is the size of local memory available on the device and the function m quantifies the memory usage for a given configuration of parameters.

In this paper we propose a DSE methodology based on a parameter inter-dependency model [10], aiming at reducing the space of application configurations by exploiting relations between parameters. Eq. 12 points out that **the size of local memory poses a constraint on the feasible solutions** for the stereo-matching implementation proposed in this paper. In particular, it creates inter-dependencies among application and resource parameters that should be taken into account. This also means that the multi-dimensional subspace of feasible solutions has an irregular shape (e.g., Fig. 9).

The methodology consists of three main phases, presented below.

Phase 1: Random sampling of design space. We first apply a random sampling over all parameters on the complete reference dataset. In this phase we apply a preliminary analysis of the results:

- **Analysis of correlation:** we calculate the correlation between input parameters and measured metrics. A high value of correlation often means that there is some kind of dependency: this analysis provides an estimate of the impact of parameters on the metrics.

- **Analysis of standard deviation:** the standard deviation is a measure of variability. We are mostly interested in the variability of metrics *disparity error* and *delay per pixel* with respect to the input data. This information is used to determine if the image pairs in the dataset can be pruned by using only one representative image pair.

Phase 2: Exploration of resource parameters and inter-dependent parameters. According to Eq. 10, the *disparity error* is independent of the resource parameters (i.e., the quality of the result does not depend, in our implementation, on the configuration of the workgroups). By exploiting this property, the goal of this phase is to identify the configuration of the *resource parameters* that minimizes the *delay per pixel* metric.
We manually identify the dependencies between parameters and draw a dependency graph (Fig. 8) where nodes represent the input parameters and edges the inter-dependencies[1]. As expressed by Eq. 12, not all parameters necessarily impact on the memory usage: thus, the set of inter-dependent parameters consists of the subset $\boldsymbol{\alpha}' \cap \boldsymbol{\rho}'$. For all the inter-dependent parameters a full combinatorial search is needed. The other parameters can be considered separately in the next phase since their choice is not constrained by the memory size. Besides, we explore the configurations of inter-dependent parameters on the single representative image pair identified in phase 1. Eventually, this phase allows for identification of the best configuration of *resource parameters* for each configuration of inter-dependent *application parameters*.

[1]"A path from node A to a node B and back to A, which forms a cycle, indicates that the Pareto-optimal configurations of all the parameters on the cycle need to be calculated simultaneously" [10]

Phase 3: Refinement of application parameters on a high-level simulation model. We refine the Pareto-optimal solutions found at step 2 by considering all the image-pairs in the reference data-set and by exploring the values of the remaining independent application parameters. Since they impact mainly on the *disparity error*, we show that it is possible to refine the analysis by using a fast simulation model instead of the ISS-based one. Although this introduces some approximation, this optimization technique provides a significant speedup that will be quantified in Section 4. The resulting operating points are Pareto-filtered leaving a set of trade-offs in terms of *throughput* and *disparity error*.

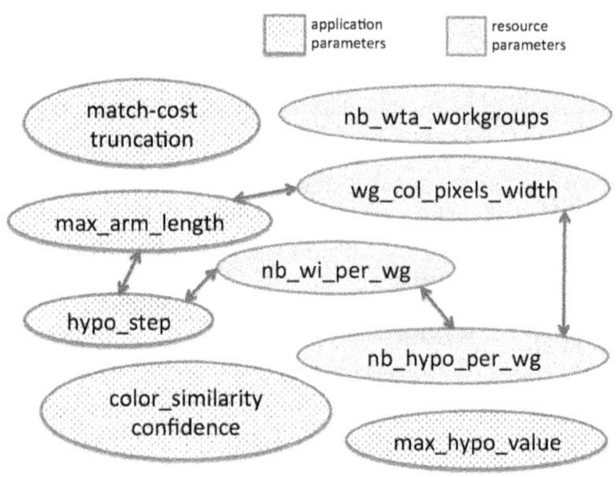

Figure 8: Inter-dependency graph of application parameters due to the constraint of local memory size.

4. EXPERIMENTAL RESULTS

In this section we apply the methodology described in Section 3 to the OpenCL stereo-matching application: the goal is to optimize the application targeted to P2012 by customizing application parameters. In particular, we follow the three phases described in Section 3 to efficiently derive a set of Pareto-optimal operating points in terms of *disparity error* and *delay per pixel*.

Table 1 describes the design space of our stereo-matching application: an important preliminary task, actually, is to define the design space. We have assigned a constant value to the parameters *match_limit* and *max_hypo_value*, based on the characteristics of input data (seven images from the Middlebury stereo dataset). Indeed, the experimental results have been generated by using a single-cluster configuration for the P2012 simulator (multi-cluster is not supported by the SDK version we have used): for this reason, parameter *nb_wta_workgroups* has not been explored (fixed to 1); since the provided SDK does not allow multiple workgroups to be executed concurrently on the same cluster, also parameter *nb_wi_per_wg* is constant, fixed to the number of PEs available on the cluster.

Considering all possible values for each parameter in our design space, the total number of potential configurations is 3888. Since these configurations must be profiled on a dataset consisting of 7 images, 27216 ISS-based simulations are required for an exhaustive exploration of the application parameters. This is a very large number considering that it would have required approximately 1.5 years by using the cycle-accurate simulator on a modern workstation (around 30 minutes for each simulation). We will show that our methodology allows to reduce the time associated with the exploration to derive a Pareto-approximate set of configurations.

4.1 Phase 1: Random sampling of design space

We first consider a Design-of-Experiments (DoE) consisting of a random sampling of the entire design space; these configurations

parameter	min	max	step
hypo_step	1	3	1
confidence	14	64	10
max_arm_length	1	18	1
match_limit	60	60	–
max_hypo_value	200	200	–
nb_wi_per_wg	16	16	–
nb_hypo_per_wg	1	4	exp2
nb_wta_workgroups	1	1	–
wg_col_pixel_width	64	96	16

Table 1: Design space for the stereo-matching OpenCL application.

are explored on the cycle-accurate simulation model for P2012 considering all images in the dataset. The sample was sized in order for the exploration to satisfy a given temporal constraint (100 configurations, so that this task did not require longer than two weeks on a modern workstation). Then, we perform the following analyses:

Analysis of correlation. A first analysis of the correlation values in Table 2 points out the parameters that mostly affect the metric *delay per pixel*: *hypo_step* and *wg_col_pixel_width*. We can also see that *confidence* has almost no impact on the execution time, while there is a significant correlation between *confidence* and *disparity error* (this result will be useful in the third exploration phase). The correlation value between parameter *wg_col_pixel_width* and metric *disparity error* is due to the irregular shape of the space of feasible solutions (Fig. 9), since the resource parameters do not change the accuracy of results (see Par. 2.3). For example, it might not be possible to execute on P2012 a configuration of the stereo-matching application with a high value for both parameters *max_arm_length* and *wg_col_pixel_width*. As a consequence, the feasible solutions with high *wg_col_pixel_width* must have low values of *max_arm_length*, thus the accuracy of results will be low because of the strong negative correlation (-38.0%) between *max_arm_length* and *disparity error*.

Parameters/Objectives	*delay per pixel* (μs)	*disparity error*
hypo_step	-76.5%	57.4%
confidence	1.6%	-12.1%
max_arm_length	12.9%	-38.0%
nb_hypo_per_wg	-13.3%	1.0%
wg_col_pixel_width	-47.2%	23.9%

Table 2: Phase 1, correlation analysis after random sampling.

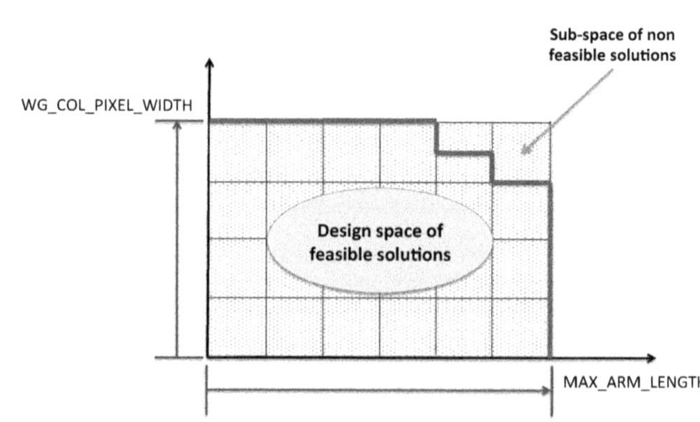

Figure 9: Irregular space of feasible solutions due to the constraint of local memory size.

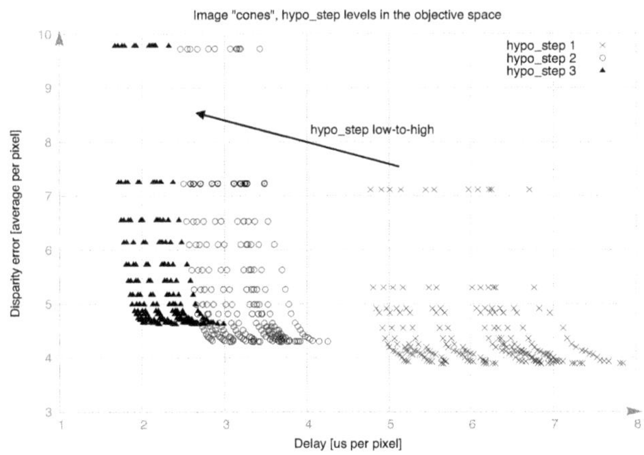

Figure 10: Phase 2, objectives space for *hypo_step*

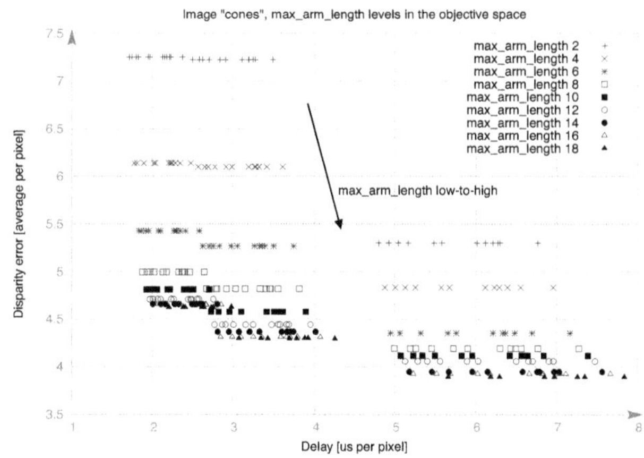

Figure 11: Phase 2, objectives space for *max_arm_length*

Analysis of standard deviation. Table 3 shows the average coefficient of variation (also known as Relative Standard Deviation – RSD) of metrics *delay per pixel* and *disparity error* over all random configurations of parameters for each image in the dataset; the last row reports the RSD of the average value of application metrics considering the whole set of seven images. The image with average RSD closest to the average RSD of the dataset is "*cones*", thus this image was selected as representative of the dataset in phase 2.

Image/RSD	*delay per pixel*	*disparity error*
baby	1.55×10^{-2}	0.88
barn	1.69×10^{-2}	0.73
cones	2.20×10^{-2}	0.63
sawtooth	1.19×10^{-2}	0.47
tsukuba	1.30×10^{-2}	0.46
teddy	1.72×10^{-2}	0.47
venus	0.81×10^{-2}	0.30
dataset	1.79×10^{-2}	0.61

Table 3: Phase 1, relative standard deviation (RSD) for the dataset.

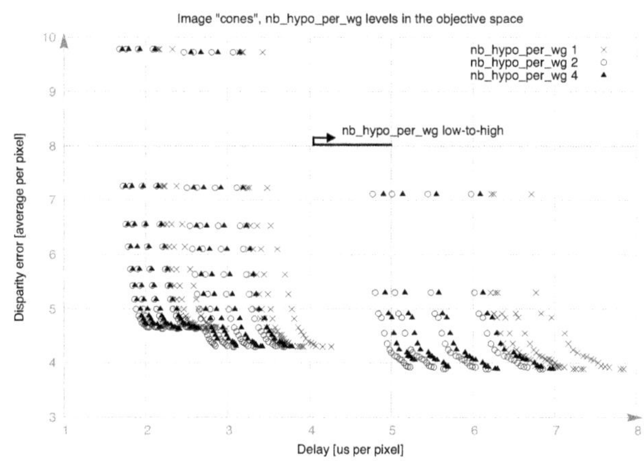

Figure 12: Phase 2, objectives space for *nb_hypo_per_wg*

4.2 Phase 2: Exploration of resource parameters (and other inter-dependent parameters)

As we noted above, the *disparity error* is independent from the resource parameters. Since resource parameters have some impact only on the *delay per pixel*, the goal of this phase is to identify the configuration of the *resource parameters* that minimizes the *delay per pixel*. However, we should consider the memory constraint on the feasible solutions. In particular, it creates inter-dependencies among application and resource parameters that should be taken into account (see Fig. 8) to trade-off *disparity error* and *delay per pixel*.

Among the parameters selected by the inter-dependency analysis, we have:

- application parameters: *hypo_step*, *max_arm_length*
- resource parameters: *nb_hypo_per_wg*, *wg_col_pixel_width*.

In this way the number of simulations has been reduced to 648. Note that in our exploration *nb_wi_per_wg* is not considered: its value is kept constant to 16, the number of processing elements on the P2012 ENCore (at the moment the provided SDK does not support two kernels on the same cluster).

As said above, the configurations must be profiled with the cycle-accurate simulator. We observe from Table 3 that *delay per pixel* does not vary significantly with the input image set (average RSD 1.8%). Since in this phase we are mainly interested in optimizing *delay per pixel*, we use a single representative image (*cones*) for the whole dataset.

Fig. 10 to 14 present the results in the *disparity error* vs *delay per pixel* objective space with reference to the values of different parameters. Whenever a clear behavior can be noticed, an arrow has been plotted: in these cases, it is possible to infer that a dependence exists between the parameter and the measured metrics.

Fig. 10 focuses on *hypo_step* levels: this parameter is the most significant for the stereo-matching application because it enables the identification of three clusters of operating points. This also means that any change to *hypo_step* has a direct effect on the measured metrics (as highlighted by the arrow).

Within each cluster of configurations defined by *hypo_step*, parameter *max_arm_length* allows for additional fine-tuning of the trade-off between *delay per pixel* and *disparity error*: in particular, *disparity error* decreases with higher values of *max_arm_length*. Indeed, in Fig. 11 we can notice different horizontal rows of configurations, each one characterized by a certain configuration of *application parameters* (*hypo_step* and *max_arm_length*).

The points belonging to the same horizontal row have the same value of metric *disparity error*, so only the configuration of *resource*

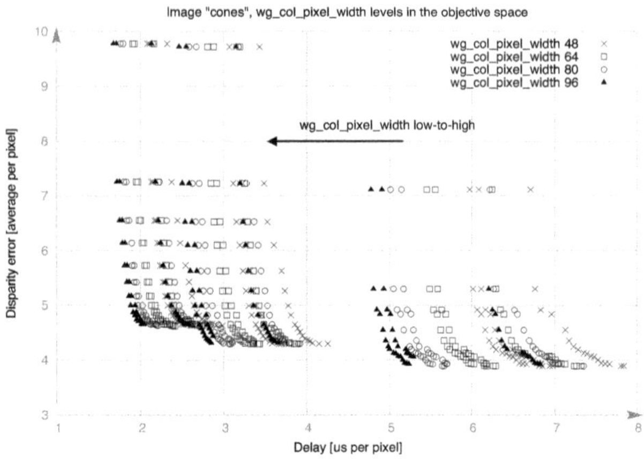

Figure 13: Phase 2, objectives space for *wg_col_pixel_width*

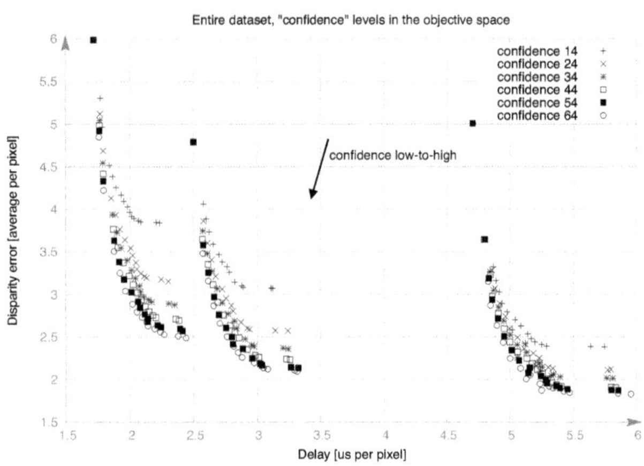

Figure 14: Phase 3, objectives space for *confidence*

parameters changes. Fig. 12 and 13 show the objective space for parameters *nb_hypo_per_wg* and *wg_col_pixel_width* respectively: the best configuration of *resource parameters* is *nb_hypo_per_wg*=2 and *wg_col_pixel_width*=96, independently from the configuration of the inter-dependent *application parameters*.

However, the choice of *nb_hypo_per_wg*=2 and *wg_col_pixel_width*=96 does not represent a feasible solution (see Fig. 9) together with some values of *max_arm_length* (17 and 18); thus, for these configurations we select a smaller value of *wg_col_pixel_width* (80).

4.3 Phase 3: refinement of application parameters on a high-level simulation model

This phase is aimed at identifying the configurations of application parameters that optimize both the *disparity error* and the *delay per pixel* (*confidence*, *max_arm_length* and *hypo_step*). For this reason, we include in the DoE also those parameters not considered in the previous phase (*confidence*), i.e. the parameters independent from the design constraint (the size of local memory in our implementation).

In principle, this could be done by just exploring all the configurations on the cycle-accurate simulator for the entire dataset: this means 324 configurations for each image. However, the results of the correlation analysis in Table 2 show that *confidence* almost has no impact on the *delay per pixel*.

Thus, we split this exploration in the following sub-phases:

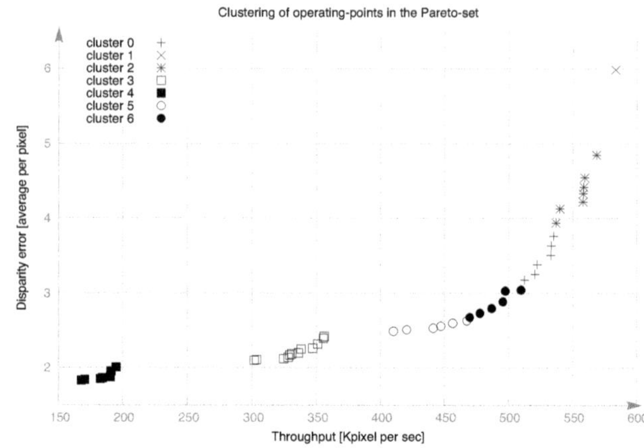

Figure 15: Clustering of Pareto-solutions for generation of operating points (listed in Table 4).

1. we use the cycle-accurate simulator to profile the average *delay per pixel* δ for one value of *confidence* (54 configurations $\times$ 7 images);
2. we use a high-level simulation model[2] to derive the *disparity error* and the *delay per pixel* for all the combinations of *confidence*, *max_arm_length* and *hypo_step*.
3. we scale the *delay per pixel* computed in the previous step according to δ.

Fig. 14 shows the levels of parameter *confidence* in the objective space. It is still possible to identify three clusters of configurations corresponding to the three values of *hypo_step*. Within each cluster it is possible to achieve different trade-offs between throughput and accuracy by fine-tuning *confidence* and *max_arm_length*.

By Pareto-filtering the final points, we find the optimal solutions represented in Fig. 15. In order to be able to quantify the loss in accuracy caused by introducing the high-level model, we have also run phase 3 entirely on the cycle-accurate simulator. This approach gives us accurate profiling information for the execution time of all configurations: the Pareto-optimal solutions calculated on this database will be referred to as reference Pareto set in the following.

To quantify the loss in accuracy, we use the ADRS metric to measure the distance between the exact Pareto set $\Pi = \Psi(\Phi)$ and the approximate Pareto set $\Lambda = \Psi(\Omega)$ as defined in [8]:

$$\text{ADRS}(\Pi, \Lambda) = \frac{1}{|\Pi|} \sum_{\boldsymbol{x}_R \in \Pi} \left(\min_{\boldsymbol{x}_A \in \Lambda} \{\delta(\boldsymbol{x}_R, \boldsymbol{x}_A)\} \right) \quad (13)$$

where δ is a measure of the normalized distance in the objective function space of two configurations:

$$\delta(\boldsymbol{x}_R, \boldsymbol{x}_A) = \max_{j=1,\ldots,m} \left\{ 0, \frac{f_j(\boldsymbol{x}_A) - f_j(\boldsymbol{x}_R)}{f_j(\boldsymbol{x}_R)} \right\} \quad (14)$$

The ADRS is usually measured in terms of percentage; the higher the ADRS, the worst is Λ with respect to Π.

[2]The high-level simulation model is based on the native ATI-Stream OpenCL runtime of a 4-cluster Non-Uniform-Memory-Access (NUMA) AMD machine. OpenCL being a cross-platform standard, the stereo-matching application can be compiled and executed on this machine. While it is not needed to change the application implementation, the configuration of parameters must be modified in order to meet a tighter constraint of local memory size (32KB).

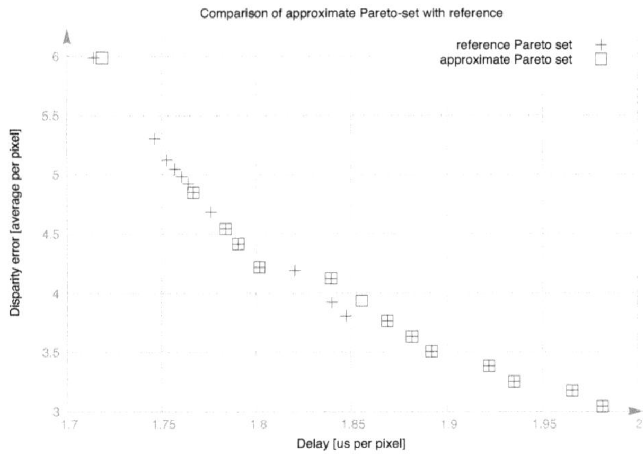

Figure 16: Phase 3, comparison of Pareto frontier on a region of the design space.

h	c	m	n	w	*disparity error*	*throughput* (Kpixel/sec)
1	64	18	2	80	1.83	167.88
2	64	18	2	80	2.09	301.72
3	64	18	2	80	2.49	410.11
3	64	12	2	96	2.67	469.76
3	64	7	2	96	3.25	520.62
3	64	4	2	96	4.22	557.93
3	54	2	2	96	5.99	583.29

Table 4: List of operating points for stereo-matching on P2012 with single-cluster configuration. Parameters are *hypo_step* (h), *confidence* (c), *max_arm_length* (m), *nb_hypo_per_wg* (n), *wg_-col_pixel_width* (w).

We calculate the ADRS between the approximate Pareto set obtained with the high-level simulation model (black triangles in Fig. 16) and the reference Pareto set obtained with the cycle-accurate simulator (empty circles): the ADRS is smaller than 0.3%.

4.4 Generation of operating points from the Pareto-set

The approximate Pareto-set obtained in Phase 3 has been used to generate a set of configurations for the stereo-matching application. We decided to cluster the configurations into 10 possible sets and to identify one configuration representative of each cluster (centroid) (see plot in Fig. 15 and the list of operating points in Table 4).

The different symbols in Fig. 15 represent different clusters, plotted on the objective space of *disparity error* and *throughput* (Kpixel/s). The operating points in Table 4 are sorted by *disparity error*. In this case, it also happens that they are sorted by *throughput*, so that it is easy to identify different trade-offs between performance and QoS.

The operating points identified by our methodology allow to optimize the application targeted to P2012, thus the first result achieved is **performance portability**. The same methodology could be used to customize the application for a different device, in which case the operating points would probably have different configurations of parameters depending on the platform architecture.

However, the operating points could also be exploited by a software Runtime Monitor as described in [20] in order to provide **application auto-tuning**: this allows for reconfiguration of the application – by changing operating point – in presence of variable QoS requirements or unpredictable workloads.

4.5 Final considerations

Our methodology provides a speed-up by reducing the overall number of simulations and exploiting a fast high-level simulation model. An exhaustive exploration of the entire design space would have required 27216 simulations on the cycle-accurate simulator. With our methodology, we only need 1672 cycle-accurate simulations, while the simulation time on the high-level model can be neglected. In conclusion, the overall speed-up is 16x.

The exploration time could be further reduced a) by executing simulations in parallel on a cluster (linear speed-up with the number of nodes), and b) by replacing the cycle-accurate simulator with a cycle-approximate one (but with a decreased accuracy of results).

5. BACKGROUND

Conventional *Design Space Exploration* (DSE) is used to tune the hardware/software parameters of a platform to achieve a desired power/performance trade-off. It generally consists of a multi-objective optimization problem whose domain is composed of parameters of a microprocessor-based platform (and all integrated IPs) and/or application parameters while the objective functions are, typically, the overall performance and power consumption [15]. The solution of the optimization problem is a set of candidate points termed *Pareto set* [11].

The emphasis on the efficiency of the DSE algorithms is due to the fact that in computer architecture research and development, simulation still represents the main tool to predict performance of alternative architectural design points. If we consider a full cycle-accurate system-level simulation, even the most simple workload requires a significant time to be analyzed, thus a comprehensive exploration of the design alternatives can exceed practical limits [24]. The overall goal is thus to minimize the number of simulations to be executed during the exploration phase. A common approach to solve this problem is to use Design of Experiments (DoEs) and Response Surface Modeling (RSM) techniques [25] combined with suitable multi-objective minimization or maximization techniques. An alternative approach is based on meta-heuristics (such as Simulated Annealing and Genetic Algorithms) that provide more accurate results but in the long term considering simulation time.

The DoE is typically used to identify an initial plan of simulations to provide the designer a coarse grained view of the architectural design space; consolidated approaches are either based on random sampling or more sophisticated techniques like Box-Behnken and Latin Hypercube designs [24, 14]. RSM techniques are usually introduced after the initial experimental design to analyze the system response of unknown configurations without incurring into additional delay due to simulation. They can be used to derive main and interaction effect analysis [13, 18] or to extend traditional optimization (as in *meta-model assisted optimization*). In particular, they can be used in *iterative refinement* approaches [24], as a filtering criterion which excludes from the optimization the worst configurations [9] and even by identifying the best experiments to be done to improve the model itself [17].

Analytical RSM models might vary from simple or piecewise linear regression [13, 18], radial basis functions [14, 24], artificial neural networks [24, 12], Kriging interpolation [21] or fuzzy algebra [2]. The selection of a specific type of RSM (*model selection*) has been addressed by means of data mining [19], genetically evolved neural networks [5] and genetically evolved linear models [6].

Design-time decisions might obviously be sub-optimal with respect to the actual deployment scenario, especially concerning application performance portability. It is a common procedure to adjust the platform resource usage and/or allocation at run-time (such as the platform processors) to meet the actual application needs. Heuristics have thus been developed to achieve sustained performance by keeping power consumption under a pre-determined constraint [23]. On-line RSMs have been used to improve run-time management by either using piecewise linear regression [3], artificial neural networks and Q-learning [22] or other predictive/adaptive models [7]. Design-time exploration is increasingly used as an alternative technique to provide simple guidelines for run-time management for small eco-systems [29, 20] or to support more complex and versatile *composite* approaches [28].

6. CONCLUSIONS

The paper proposes an innovative customizable OpenCL implementation of the stereo-matching algorithm and a methodology to efficiently derive the optimal customization options (*operating points*) for Platform 2012 in the form of a Pareto-set of configurations. The methodology is general enough to be reproduced for customizing a different OpenCL application on another type of platform, provided that the application exposes a set of parameters to control both the QoS/performance trade-offs and the usage of platform resources. Our methodology reduces up to 16x the overall number of simulations for exploration of the stereo-matching application: this speed-up is achieved by exploiting relations between parameters as they are discovered and unfolded during the exploration and by accelerating one phase of the exploration on a fast high-level simulation model.

7. ACKNOWLEDGMENTS

This work has been partially funded by the European Commission under the projects FP7-ICT-248716-2PARMA and ARTEMIS-100230-SMECY.

8. REFERENCES

[1] Altera. Implementing fpga design with the opencl standard, November 2011. http://www.altera.com/literature/wp/wp-01173-opencl.pdf.

[2] G. Ascia, V. Catania, A. G. D. Nuovo, M. Palesi, and D. Patti. Efficient design space exploration for application specific systems-on-a-chip. *Journal of Systems Architecture*, 53(10):733–750, 2007.

[3] S. Banerjee, G. Surendra, and S. K. Nandy. On the effectiveness of phase based regression models to trade power and performance using dynamic processor adaptation. *Journal of Systems Architecture*, 54(8):797–815, 2008.

[4] L. Benini, E. Flamand, D. Fuin, and D. Melpignano. P2012: Building an ecosystem for a scalable, modular and high-efficiency embedded computing accelerator. In *Design, Automation Test in Europe Conference Exhibition (DATE), 2012*, pages 983–987, 2012.

[5] P. A. Castillo, A. M. Mora, J. J. M. Guervós, J. L. J. Laredo, M. Moretó, F. J. Cazorla, M. Valero, and S. A. McKee. Architecture performance prediction using evolutionary artificial neural networks. In *EvoWorkshops*, pages 175–183, 2008.

[6] H. Cook and K. Skadron. Predictive design space exploration using genetically programmed response surfaces. In *DAC '08: Proceedings of the 45th annual Design Automation Conference*, pages 960–965, New York, NY, USA, 2008. ACM.

[7] M. Curtis-Maury, F. Blagojevic, C. D. Antonopoulos, and D. S. Nikolopoulos. Prediction-based power-performance adaptation of multithreaded scientific codes. *IEEE Trans. Parallel Distrib. Syst.*, 19(10):1396–1410, 2008.

[8] J. A. Czyzak P. Pareto simulated annealing - a metaheuristic technique for multiple-objective combinatorial optimisation. *Journal of Multi-Criteria Decision Analysis*, 7(7):34–47, April 1998.

[9] M. Emmerich, K. Giannakoglou, and B. Naujoks. Single- and multiobjective evolutionary optimization assisted by gaussian random field metamodels. *Evolutionary Computation, IEEE Transactions on*, 10(4):421–439, Aug. 2006.

[10] T. Givargis, F. Vahid, and J. Henkel. System-level exploration for pareto-optimal configurations in parameterized systems-on-a-chip. In *Computer Aided Design, 2001. ICCAD 2001. IEEE/ACM International Conference on*, pages 25 –30, 2001.

[11] Hwang, C. L. and Masud, A. S. M. . *Multiple Objective Decision Making – Methods and Applications: A State-of-the-Art Survey*, volume 164. Lecture Notes in Economics and Mathematical Systems, Springer-Verlag, Berlin–Heidelberg, 1979.

[12] E. Ipek, S. A. McKee, R. Caruana, B. R. de Supinski, and M. Schulz. Efficiently exploring architectural design spaces via predictive modeling. *Proceedings of the 12th international conference on Architectural support for programming languages and operating systems*, 40(5):195–206, 2006.

[13] P. J. Joseph, K. Vaswani, and M. J. Thazhuthaveetil. Construction and use of linear regression models for processor performance analysis. In *Symposium on High Performance Computer Architecture*, pages 99–108, Austin, Texas, USA, 2006. IEEE Computer Society.

[14] P. J. Joseph, K. Vaswani, and M. J. Thazhuthaveetil. A predictive performance model for superscalar processors. In *MICRO 39: Proceedings of the 39th Annual IEEE/ACM International Symposium on Microarchitecture*, pages 161–170, Washington, DC, USA, 2006. IEEE Computer Society.

[15] K. Keutzer, A. Newton, J. Rabaey, and A. Sangiovanni-Vincentelli. System-level design: orthogonalization of concerns and platform-based design. *Computer-Aided Design of Integrated Circuits and Systems, IEEE Transactions on*, 19(12):1523–1543, Dec 2000.

[16] Khronos Group. The opencl specification, version 1.1, June 2011. http://www.khronos.org/registry/cl/specs/opencl-1.1.pdf.

[17] J. Knowles. Parego: a hybrid algorithm with on-line landscape approximation for expensive multiobjective optimization problems. *Evolutionary Computation, IEEE Transactions on*, 10(1):50–66, Feb. 2006.

[18] B. C. Lee and D. M. Brooks. Accurate and efficient regression modeling for microarchitectural performance and power prediction. *Proceedings of the 12th international conference on Architectural support for programming languages and operating systems*, 40(5):185–194, 2006.

[19] B. Li, L. Peng, and B. Ramadass. Accurate and efficient processor performance prediction via regression tree based modeling. *Journal of Systems Architecture*, 55(10-12):457 – 467, 2009.

[20] G. Mariani, P. Avasare, G. Vanmeerbeeck, C. Ykman-Couvreur, G. Palermo, C. Silvano, and V. Zaccaria. An industrial design space exploration framework for supporting run-time resource management on multi-core systems. In *Proc. Design, Automation & Test in Europe Conf. & Exhibition (DATE)*, pages 196–201, 2010.

[21] G. Mariani, A. Brankovic, G. Palermo, J. Jovic, V. Zaccaria, and C. Silvano. A correlation-based design space exploration methodology for multi-processor systems-on-chip. In *Proc. 47th ACM/IEEE Design Automation Conf. (DAC)*, pages 120–125, 2010.

[22] J. Martinez and E. Ipek. Dynamic multicore resource management: A machine learning approach. *Micro, IEEE*, 29(5):8 –17, sept.-oct. 2009.

[23] V. Nollet, D. Verkest, and H. Corporaal. A safari through the mpsoc run-time management jungle. *Journal of Signal Processing Systems*, 60:251–268, 2010. 10.1007/s11265-008-0305-4.

[24] G. Palermo, C. Silvano, and V. Zaccaria. ReSPIR: A Response Surface-based Pareto Iterative Refinement for application-specific design space exploration. *IEEE Transactions on Computer Aided Design of Integrated Circuits*, 28(12):1816–1829, Dec. 2009.

[25] T. J. Santner, W. B., and N. W. *The Design and Analysis of Computer Experiments*. Springer-Verlag, 2003.

[26] D. Scharstein and R. Szeliski. A taxonomy and evaluation of dense two-frame stereo correspondence algorithms. *Int. J. Comput. Vision*, 47(1-3):7–42, Apr. 2002.

[27] D. Scharstein and R. Szeliski. High-accuracy stereo depth maps using structured light. In *Computer Vision and Pattern Recognition, 2003. Proceedings. 2003 IEEE Computer Society Conference on*, volume 1, pages I–195 – I–202 vol.1, june 2003.

[28] H. Shojaei, A. Ghamarian, T. Basten, M. Geilen, S. Stuijk, and R. Hoes. A parameterized compositional multi-dimensional multiple-choice knapsack heuristic for cmp run-time management. In *DAC '09: Proceedings of the 46th conference on Design automation*, New York, NY, USA, 2009. ACM.

[29] C. Ykman-Couvreur, V. Nollet, F. Catthoor, and H. Corporaal. Fast multidimension multichoice knapsack heuristic for mp-soc runtime management. *ACM Trans. Embed. Comput. Syst.*, 10:35:1–35:16, May 2011.

[30] K. Zhang, J. Lu, and G. Lafruit. Cross-based local stereo matching using orthogonal integral images. *Circuits and Systems for Video Technology, IEEE Transactions on*, 19(7):1073 –1079, july 2009.

A Case of System-level Hardware/Software Co-design and Co-verification of a Commodity Multi-Processor System with Custom Hardware

Sungpack Hong*
Oracle Labs
sungpack.hong@oracle.com

Tayo Oguntebi
Stanford University
tayo@stanford.edu

Jared Casper
Stanford University
jaredc@stanford.edu

Nathan Bronson*
Facebook, Inc.
nbronson@stanford.edu

Christos Kozyrakis
Stanford University
kozyraki@stanford.edu

Kunle Olukotun
Stanford University
kunle@stanford.edu

ABSTRACT

This paper presents an interesting system-level co-design and co-verification case study for a non-trivial design where multiple high-performing x86 processors and custom hardware were connected through a coherent interconnection fabric. In functional verification of such a system, we used a processor bus functional model (BFM) to combine native software execution with a cycle-accurate interconnect simulator and an HDL simulator. However, we found that significant extensions need to be made to the conventional BFM methodology in order to capture various data-race cases in simulation, which eventually happen in modern multi-processor systems. Especially essential were faithful implementations of the memory consistency model and cache coherence protocol, as well as timing randomization. We demonstrate how such a co-simulation environment can be constructed from existing tools and software. Lessons from our study can similarly be applied to design and verification of other tightly-coupled systems.

Categories and Subject Descriptors

B.4.4 [**Performance Analysis and Design Aids**]: Simulation, Verification

Keywords

Co-Verification, Co-Simulation, Bus Functional Model, FPGA Prototyping, Transactional Memory

1. INTRODUCTION

Modern digital systems are moving increasingly towards heterogeneity. Today, many digital systems feature multiple (heterogeneous) processors, advanced interconnect topologies beyond simple buses, and often specialized hardware to improve the performance-per-watt for specific tasks [5].

Development of such heterogeneous systems, however, requires intensive system-level verification. System-wide co-design and co-verification of hardware and software components [16] is especially essential for systems where multiple heterogeneous components are executing a single task in a tightly-coupled manner, orchestrated by the software. In such systems, for example, data races between multiple computational components should be thoroughly verified since they can induce various unexpected system behaviors.

In this paper, we present our experiences designing and verifying a tightly-coupled heterogeneous system in which multiple x86 processors are accompanied by specialized hardware that accelerates software transactional memory (Section 2.1). We discuss which among the many conventional co-design/verification methods would best serve our purposes and why. Our chosen method was one which combined an un-timed software model with cycle-accurate interconnection and HDL simulation through a processor bus functional model (BFM), since this provided sufficient visibility and simulation speed (Section 2.2). However, we found that *when using a BFM for verification, conventional methodology needs to be significantly extended* in order to capture data-race corner cases induced by modern multi-processor architectures. Especially crucial were correct implementations of memory consistency and cache coherence as well as a need to introduce timing randomization (Section 3.1). This paper also demonstrates how such a co-simulation environment can be constructed on top of existing tools and software (Section 3.2). We show the effectiveness of our methodology and draw out general lessons from it (Section 4), before we conclude in Section 5.

Our contributions can be summarized as follows:

- We present a non-trivial system-level co-design and co-verification experience with x86 processors connected to custom hardware. In this scenario, we found that combining the software model with an interconnection simulator and HDL simulator via a processor BFM is the most effective method for functional verification.
- We also explain, however, that conventional ways of constructing a processor BFM should be revised in accordance with modern multi-core processors and inter-

*This work was done when the authors were at Stanford

CODES+ISSS'12, October 7-12, 2012, Tampere, Finland.

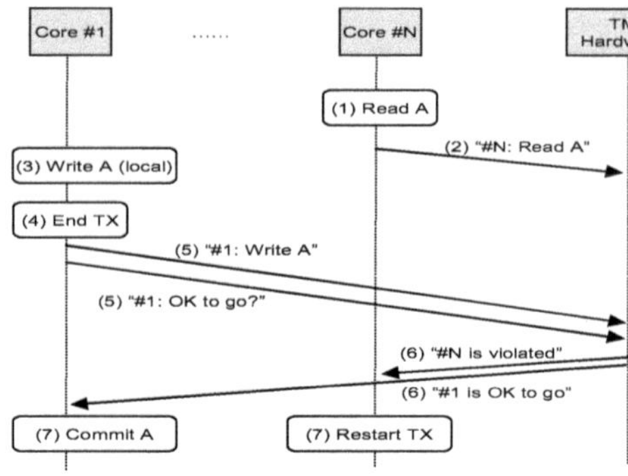

Figure 1: Outline of the STM acceleration protocol.

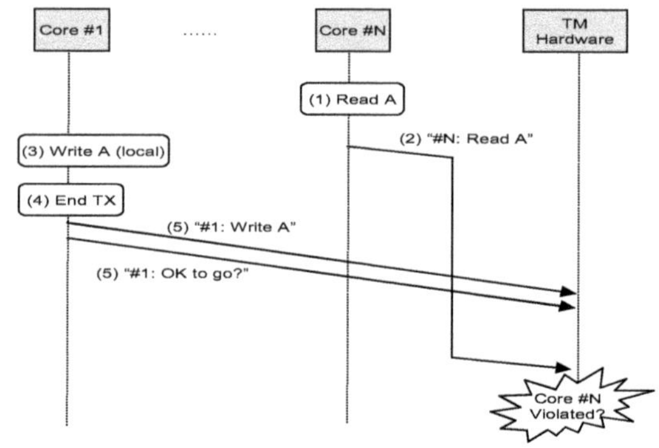

Figure 2: A failure case in our first design.

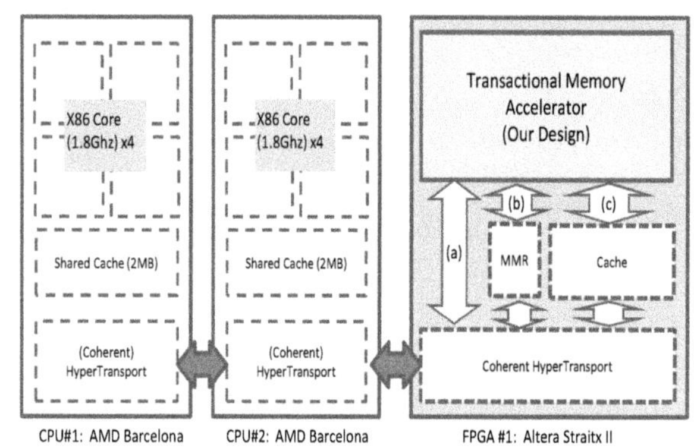

Figure 3: Block Diagram of Implementation Environment: Our design is connected to the rest of the system via (a) non-coherent interface, (b) memory-mapped register interface, and (c) coherent cache interface.

connection architecture; it is especially important to accurately implement the memory consistency model and cache coherence protocol. Introducing timing randomization is also very important.

2. DESIGN AND VERIFICATION

2.1 Target Design

This section outlines the design of our system for the sake of providing sufficient background context for one to understand our co-design and co-verification issues, while the detailed design of the system is outside scope of this paper.

Transactional Memory (TM) [9] is an abstract programming model that aims to greatly simplify parallel programming. In this model, the programmer declares atomicity boundaries (transactions), while the runtime system ensures a consistent ordering among concurrent reads and writes to the shared memory. However, a typical software transactional memory (STM), an implementation of such a runtime system solely with software, tends to exhibit huge performance overhead.

Our system is composed of specialized hardware which is externally connected to commodity CPUs and accelerates an STM system [2]. The motivation was reduction of the performance overhead generally experienced by STM systems without modifying the core and thus increasing processor design complexity. The TM abstraction is enforced through the following protocol, which is outlined in Figure 1:

(1) Whenever a core reads a shared variable, (2) the core fires a notification message to the TM hardware. (3) Writes to shared variables are kept in a software buffer, and are not visible to other cores until (4) execution reaches the end of a transaction. At this point, the core (5) sends the addresses of all the writes that it wants to commit to the hardware and waits for a response. (6) The TM hardware, based on all the read/write address received from all the cores, now determines which cores(transactions) have conflicting read and writes and sends out the requisite messages to those cores. (7) Depending on these messages, each core proceeds to commit or restart its current transaction from the beginning.

The above protocol is implemented as a tightly-coupled software and hardware system. Software sends messages and manages the local write buffer, while the external hardware accelerator performs fast conflict detection. For our development environment, we used an instance of an FPGA-based rapid prototyping system [14]. Figure 3 illustrates the block diagram of the prototyping system. The system is composed of two quad-core x86 CPUs and an FPGA that is connected coherently via a chain of point-to-point links. We implemented our custom hardware (TM Accelerator) on the FPGA of the system (Figure 3). Messages from the CPU are sent to our HW via a non-coherent interface, while responses to the CPU go through the coherent cache. Note that the former non-coherent mechanism enables hiding communication latency between the CPU and FPGA while the latter coherent communication avoids interrupts and long-latency polling.

2.2 Our Initial Failure and Issues with Co-Verification

Since our system was composed of tightly coupled hardware and software, we had to deal with a classic chicken-and-egg co-verification problem: How can we verify the correctness of the hardware without the correctly-working software and vice versa? Our initial approach was to decouple hardware and software verification; we verified the software with an instruction set simulator (ISS) and virtual hardware model while targeting the hardware using unit-level HDL simulation and direct debugging on the FPGA.

It was only after the simulation in our ISS environment

Method	Strength	Weakness
(A) Prototyping	Fastest execution on real HW	Limited visibility regarding hardware status
(B) Full HW simulation	Full visibility and control	Extremely low simulation speed
(C) ISS + HW simulation [15, 12]	Faster simulation than (B)	Waste of simulation cycles for unrelated instructions
(D) ISS + Virtual HW model [7, 18]	Faster simulation than (C); Can predate HDL development	Same issues as (C); Fidelity of virtual HW model; Requires a separate HW verification step
(E) SW model + HW sim. [20, 17, 21] (possibly through BFM)	Verification of target HDL with real SW execution	Overhead of SW re-writing; Lack of timing information for SW execution
(F) Emulation [13, 1]	Fast execution of target HDL	Cost of the systems; Limited support of core types
(G) Binary Translation [10]	Fast SW execution on host HW	Lack of deterministic replay of concurrent execution.

Table 1: Comparisons of HW-SW co-verification methods.

and unit tests in FPGA environment had all passed successfully, but the whole system was tested altogether for the first time, when we realized that there was a flaw in our original design. The specific error scenario is shown in Figure 2. The figure depicts the same read-write sequence as in Figure 1 except that in this case, the delivery of the read message from core N is delayed until after delivery of the commit message from core 1. As there was no consideration of such case in our original design, the software execution was simply crashed after a failure of consistency enforcement. Note that since the ISS assumed in-order instruction execution and the HW model assumed in-order packet delivery, our environment was not able to generate the scenario described in Figure 2. As it happened, this scenario occurred quite frequently in real HW.[1]

That being said, we had spent a significant amount of engineering efforts to confirm that Figure 2 is really the reason of the observed failure. Single-threaded SW executions never failed, while multi-threaded ones crashed occasionally but *non-deterministically.* A logic analyzer, tapped onto our FPGA, was not very helpful because a typical execution involves billions of memory accesses, each access generating tens of memory packets – it was extremely hard to identify which of those packets were relevant to the error and how those are related to SW execution. For example, a crash observed after one last memory access from one core (e.g. de-referencing a dangling pointer), could be a result of a write, falsely allowed to commit, from another core millions of cycles before. Simple step-by-step execution of a single processor was not helpful either due to our parallel execution requirement. As a matter of fact, we identified this issue through a deep speculation on our initial design, which was confirmed later only after adapting another co-design/co-verification methodology (Section 3).

Fixing up this issue, we properly augmented the protocol in Figure 1 and re-designed our hardware and software accordingly. This time, however, in order to save ourselves from repeating the same mistake, we considered applying other methodologies and tools proposed for HW/SW co-design and co-verification [16, 1, 18, 12, 20, 15, 7, 17, 13] Our requirements could be summarized as follows:

- The new STM software needed to be intensely validated (with the new hardware), especially under the assumption of parallel execution, variable latency and out-of-order message delivery as shown in Figure 2. Such an intensive SW validation naturally demanded fast execution.
- We were more interested in functional verification of the new hardware rather than architecture exploration. Furthermore, as our new hardware was becoming available soon (after small modification from the initial version), we wanted direct verification of target RTL as well.
- We wanted a mechanism for error analysis better than manual inspection of GBs of logs/waveforms from simulation or logic analyzer. At a minimum, we wanted to associate such logs with software execution context.

[1]There are two major reasons for this. (1) The underlying network enforces no delivery ordering between different cores. (2) We used a non-temporal x86 store instruction to implement asynchronous message transmission; however the semantics of the instruction allowed the message to stay in the store-buffer for an indefinite amount of time.

Table 1 summarizes the advantages and disadvantages of conventional approaches that we considered. Our initial approach used prototyping (Method A in Table 1) and ISS combined with virtual models (Method D), but as described previously failed to serve our purpose. Full simulation (Method B) was never an option since we didn't have access to the HDL source of the CPUs and it would have surely failed to meet the fast execution requirement. We have already described how ISS (Method C) initially failed to find the erroneous case in the first place. An alternative was to use a detailed architecture simulator (e.g. [22]) but its simulation speed was insufficient. Also, there were no emulators (Method F) available to us which supported our core (AMD x86) and interconnection type (HyperTransport). Finally, we were not able to use fast software simulation techniques based on binary instrumentation (Method G), because it is not trivial with this method, to replay every load/store instruction of every processors in exact same order. Note that such a feature is crucial for verifying multi-processor systems like ours by nature.

The only remaining option was to construct a model that faithfully reflected the behavior of the software while interfacing with the HDL simulation (Method E). However, this method brought its own challenges which we discuss in detail in the following section.

3. APPLYING SW MODEL-BASED CO-SIMULATION

3.1 General Issues and Solutions

In this section, we discuss general issues that arise when using a software model for HW/SW co-verification and how we overcame those issues. For each issue, we either introduce lessons learned from previous research or discuss how they were not applicable in our case.

(Issue #1) Software has to be re-written into a form that can interface with HDL simulation.

The first issue can be minimized by using the BFM of the processor [17] (also known as processor abstraction with transaction-level (TL) interface) which works as a bridge between software execution and hardware simulation. Specifically, instead of creating a separate software model, the whole software is executed natively; however every *read* and *write* instruction that may potentially affect the target hardware is replaced with a `simul_read()` and `simul_write()` function call. These function calls invoke data transfers in simulation, suspending the software context until the underlying hardware simulation finishes processing the requested data transfer (in a cycle-accurate way). In the worst case, every load and store should be replaced; in most cases, it is enough to change only the Hardware Abstraction Layer (HAL), a small well-encapsulated portion of software [21, 6].

Hardware simulation can consist of two different components: a cycle-accurate interconnection network simulation and HDL simulation. The interconnection simulator can easily interact with HDL through simple function-to-signal translators [3] as long as the simulation is packet-wise accurate. This decoupled approach provides more flexibility and better simulation speed than doing whole HDL simulation [19].

In our case, only a small portion of code inside the STM was identified as HAL – the user application was entirely built upon the STM interface. For the interconnect, we used a cycle-accurate HyperTransport simulator, developed by AMD, which can interact with the HDL simulator (e.g. ModelSim) via PLI.

(Issue #2) The multi-threaded software should be executed concurrently, but also be re-playable in a determistic manner.

The second issue arises because we are combining execution of multi-threaded software with a simulator which is executed sequentially by nature. Note that we cannot let each thread in the original application freely interact with the simulator for the purpose of deterministic re-execution, i.e. simulators based on binary instrumentation such as Pin [10] cannot be used. Instead, we rely on the single-threaded simulator to interleave multiple software execution contexts.

SystemC [8] is a standard simulation engine that can handle multiple execution contexts for such use cases [21, 17]; SystemC allows for trivial implementation of blocking calls. Unfortunately, there are still plenty of (in-house) simulators which do not adhere to the SystemC standard, including popular CPU simulators [22] and interconnection simulators [4]. Our interconnection simulator[2] was not compliant with SystemC, either. We therefore implemented our own blocking-call mechanism using co-routines, or fibers.

(Issue #3) Software models lose timing information.

Being natively executed, software models lose timing information – they simply continuously inject read/write requests to the BFM simulator. The conventional solution is to insert `delay` calls explicitly before each call-site of `simul_read` and `simul_write` in the user application, which compensates for the CPU cycles between the previous blocking call and the current one [21, 6].

[2]The simulator is a proprietary implementation by AMD and requires an NDA to access.

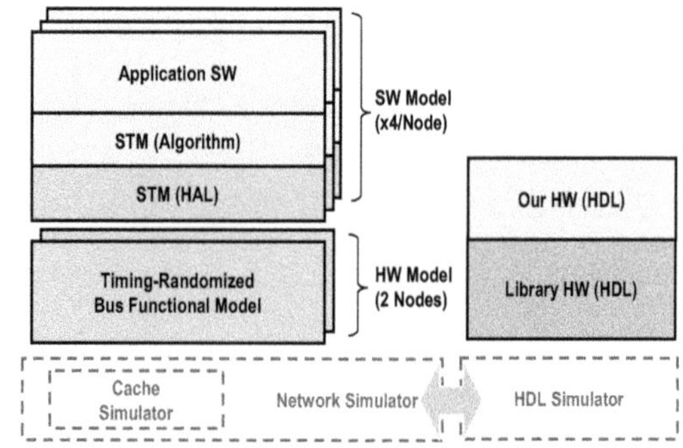

Figure 4: Block diagram of our co-simulation environment.

Our approach differs from the conventional solution in two ways: (1) we insert the delay inside the `simul_read` method rather than at the call-sites in the user-application code, and (2) we (pseudo-)randomize the delay values. We justify this for the following reasons: First, our method requires no further modification of the user application code. Second, user-provided delay information at the call-sites is already inaccurate. For instance, CPU cycles between two call-sites cannot be accurately compensated if there are (exponentially) many execution paths between them. Finally, for the purpose of functional verification, the exact number of execution cycles for non-relevant SW sections is of little interest. Rather, for functional verification, we want to interleave packet injection from multiple cores in varying orders as much as possible.

(Issue #4) The memory consistency model must be carefully considered.

This is one issue that has *not* been discussed extensively in the literature. In previous studies [17, 21, 6], the BFM simply injected network packets to the interconnection network in the order requested by the software as is the behavior in classic embedded processors. However, this does not closely approximate the memory packet generation pattern of our modern x86 processor; it fails to account for the aggressive reordering of memory requests.

Instead, we implement a more realistic memory consistency model in our processor BFM, namely Total Store Ordering (TSO) [11]. This is the model on which many modern processors (e.g. x86 and SPARC) are based. To ensure TSO, we keep a per-core store buffer inside our BFM. The write request goes to the buffer without injecting a packet into the network as long as there is an available slot in the buffer. On a read request, we first search for the target address in the store buffer. If not found, a new (read-request) packet is injected into the network. Otherwise, the contents in the store buffer, up to the entry that has been matched, are flushed before the new packet is injected. The store buffer is always flushed in FIFO order.

In addition, cache coherency should be implemented correctly as well, simply for the sake of correct parallel execution. However, we were able to leverage the cache simulator already embedded in our network simulator.

(Issue #5) There should be an easy way of error analysis.

In previous section, we explained how painful and unsuc-

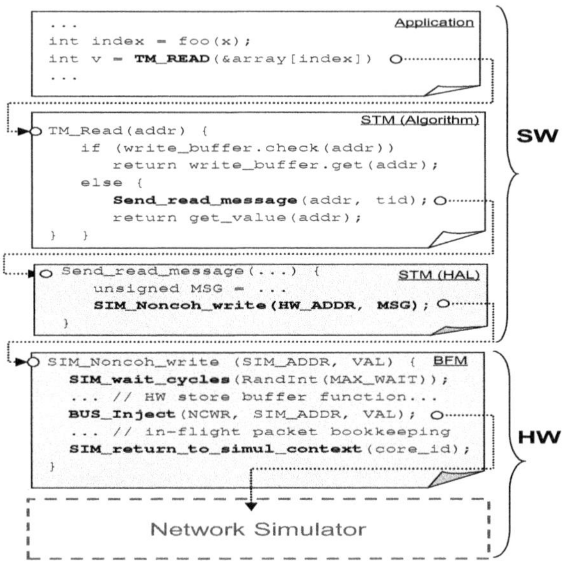

Figure 5: Execution sequence: From SW-context to simulator context.

cessful it was manually inspecting massive amounts of logs that are blindly generated by logic analyzer (or simulator), when identifying breach of consistency protocol.

To the contrary, our BFM-based approach enabled a better scheme for an off-line analysis; we exploit the facts that (1) the multi-processor simulation is actually being executed single-threaded on a workstation, that (2) the simulated address space is separated from simulator's address space, and that (3) simulated execution context and native execution context are also clearly divided. In specific, we further instrumented the STM (i.e. our HAL) such that we add a log entry in a global shadow data structure whenever there is a relevant activity from the current core, such as transactional memory access or commit request. Whenever a new entry is appended to the shadow data structure, a global check on consistency protocol is performed as well – for instance, if the log indicates that the current transaction has a conflicting memory access with another transaction but both are allowed to commit, the simulation immediately reports an error with accurate conflict information. Note that the global shadow data structure is kept inside simulator's context, and therefore such a error check is thread-safe and does not consume any simulation cycle.

3.2 Our Co-simulation Environment: Implementation

This subsection details the implementation of our co-simulation environment where all the issues discussed in previous subsections are resolved. Figure 4 depicts the block diagram of our co-simulation environment. Our HDL design is simulated alongside the library HDL of our FPGA framework, whose interconnect pin-outs are connected to the network simulator through the PLI mechanism. Our BFM implementation is treated as a traffic generator by the interconnection network simulator, which is dynamically linked at runtime. The BFM module, network simulator and HDL simulator represent the hardware part of the system in this simulation environment. The software part is the whole

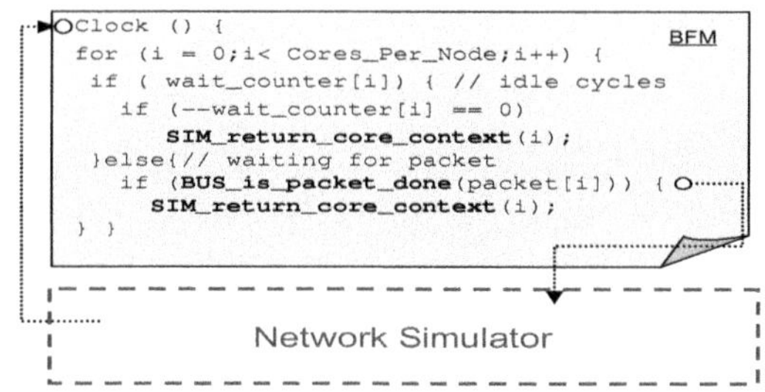

Figure 6: Execution sequence: From simulator context to SW-context.

application and STM software that are unmodified except HAL, which is now built upon BFM API (Table 2). Each application thread is implemented as a fiber (co-routines) whose context switching is managed by BFM. Specifically, we used the POSIX `makecontext(3)` and `swapcontext(3)` mechanisms for fiber implementation. We instantiate two BFM modules (CPU nodes) on the simulator with each BFM module executing four SW threads (CPU cores) at a time, which faithfully models our system configuration (see Figure 3).

Table 2 summarizes the API of our processor BFM, which is called by the software model. Noticeably, the API provides separate methods for normal (cached), non-coherent, and uncached accesses as well as flush and atomic operations. Separation of these methods is required for accurate implementation of TSO memory consistency as explained in the previous subsection.

Figure 5 shows how execution flows from a SW context (i.e. a fiber executing the SW model) to the simulator context (i.e. the main fiber for simulation). As in normal execution, whenever the user application reads a shared variable, the code jumps to and executes the `TM_READ` function in the STM library. Note that the application has executed natively up to this point and has not yet consumed a single simulation cycle. However, instead of actually sending a transactional read message to the FPGA, the HAL part of the STM calls into the BFM API (`SIM_Noncoh_write`) which eventually injects a packet into the simulator (`BUS_Inject`) and switches context to simulator execution (`SIM_return_simulator`). However, before injecting each packet, the BFM adds random idle cycles (`SIM_wait_cycles`).

Figure 6 shows execution flow from the simulator context to SW context. The network simulator, which performs simple cycle-based simulation, calls `clock()` function for each BFM at each simulation cycle. Since the software context is either idle-waiting or waiting for packet transfer, the BFM checks those conditions and resumes any software model that is ready by context-switching back to the software model (`SIM_return_core_context`).

4. RESULTS AND DISCUSSION

Our new co-simulation environment (Section 3.2), was extremely useful for verifying the functional correctness of our system. With this environment, we first simulated our old design and confirmed that the old system fails at cases like Figure 2. Note that the new environment is able to generate such cases, while our previous ISS-based simulation wasn't; also it is easy to track down errors in this environment, which

Method Name	Description
SIM_write/read	Normal cacheable memory accesses.
SIM_noncoh_write/read	Memory accesses bypass cache but stay in store-buffer.[a]
SIM_uncached_write/read	Memory accesses bypass cache and store-buffer[b]
SIM_memory_fence	Flush pending memory accesses
SIM_atomic_cas	Atomic compare and swap
SIM_wait_cycles	Insert idle cycles

[a] We keep two separate store-buffers; one for cacheable accesses and the other for non-coherent ones.

[b] An uncached access flushes all pending memory accesses.

Table 2: API of our processor BFM.

was nearly impossible in our previous FPGA execution. Afterwards, we used this co-simulation environment intensively to validate functional correctness of the new design.

The merits of this BFM-based software model approach can be summarized as follows. First, it enabled us to execute the application software compiled with the entire STM library in conjunction with the target hardware simulation. We remind the readers that our STM library itself is a very complicated piece of software which orchestrates the correct execution of our tightly-coupled HW-SW system. In other words, there was *no* way of writing *simple test-bench* for our system level simulation but executing the whole software.

Second, the co-simulation environment could generate many variations of overlapped transactions. On one hand, randomized timing helped to explore corner cases in data-race conditions. Note that this randomized timing does not accurately reflect actual software execution timing at all. However, for the purpose of functional verification, this is better than an un-timed or even ISS-based approach that does not provide for such variation. This is analogous to the usefulness of a random-based test bench in unit-level hardware verification.

On the other hand, accurate implementation of the memory consistency model was another key factor in successful test-pattern generation. For example, our `stm_read` instruction is composed of an actual memory read followed by a message passed to the FPGA – the race between the read request packet and the message created many interesting corner cases in our design. Note that in-order packet generation, as used in previous studies [21, 6, 17], is not able to capture such cases. Overall, the consistency model creates interleaving of data accesses from a single core; timing randomization among multiple cores.

Third, we were able to execute many different simulations in a relatively short time. The absolute simulation speed was still dominated by the HDL simulator and its PLI interface. However, since most of the software model was executed natively, there was no waste of valuable simulation cycles to execute instructions that were not necessary for functional verification. Table 3 compares the performance of all of our co-verification environments. We remind the users that SW-model based approach only consumes simulation cycles for required instructions, i.e. shared memory access; other instructions, such as local memory access, branches, and arithmetic operations are executed natively at the speed of underlying workstation.

Fourth, the co-simulation environment provided a very helpful error detection mechanism, which was impossible in native execution on FPGA. Figure 7 displays an example of an error-identified log generated by our simulation environment. Note that the last row points out which address

Environment	Speed (cycles/secs)	Time[b]
Prototype	1.8 (GHz)	< 1 ms
(SW-model[a]+ HDL sim)	~ 400	< 15 mins
(SW-model[a]+virtual model)	~ 3M	< 100 ms
ISS[a]+virtual model	~ 50K	< 1.5 hrs

(a) Simulation time was measured on a 2.3Ghz Nehalem machine.
(b) Time to execute our small application.

Table 3: Simulation Speed of our Verification Environments

cycle	T_1	T_2	...
...		...	
1048976	– TX Begin –		
1048990		W 1000786h	
1059102	R 1000786h		
1070428		– TX commit –	
1078824		C 1000786h	
1081034		– TX end –	
1081106	– TX commit –		
1081300	Error: T_1 got Commit Okay.		
1081300	It should be violated by 100786h		

Figure 7: Example log and error detection from our simulation.

is violating serialize-ability From this log, we were able to relate SW context and HW status, since the simulation cycle is shared by both SW simulation and HDL simulation. The ability of deterministic re-play of problematic execution was also crucial for debugging. As a result, we found bugs not only in HW, but also in SW or in protocol with this environment.

The lessons from our case study can be summarized as follows: (a) It is beneficial to combine a SW model with an interconnection simulator and an HDL simulator for functional verification, as it enables fast simulation. This combination can be easily realized through a BFM processor model. (b) In such an environment, it is essential to accurately implement the memory consistency model and cache coherency in order to capture corner cases induced by data races. Adding timing randomization is also important. (c) Keeping a shadow log in the (non-simulated) memory can help track down data race-induced errors by exploiting the fact that the simulation is being sequentially executed.

In a sense, the above lessons are a minimal simulation abstraction for fast functional co-verification of tightly coupled HW-SW systems, where data race between multiple computation units becomes an issue. We believe these lessons are also valuable to other designers since the trend of modern digital system is to introduce more and more parallelism and heterogeneity in it; our prototype was an exemplar instance of such systems.

5. CONCLUSION

In this paper, we presented our HW/SW co-verification experience on a commodity multi-processor system with custom hardware. For the sake of functional verification of such a system, it was most effective to combine native SW execution with cycle-based interconnect simulation and HDL simulation by means of a processor BFM. However, our experiences showed that such BFMs should faithfully reflect the memory consistency models of their target processors and would benefit greatly from randomized packet injection timing in their network simulations. These requirements enable the co-simulation to generate a wide variety of data access interleavings, which is essential for co-verification of modern multi-processor systems.

6. ACKNOWLEDGEMENTS

This paper was supported by DOE contract, Sandia order 942017; Army contract AHPCRC W911NF-07-2-0027-1; DARPA contract, Oracle order US1226344; NSF grant CCF-0546060; DARPA Contract, SEEC: Specialized Extremely Efficient Computing, Contract # HR0011-11-C-0007; NSF grant, SHF: Large: Domain Specific Language Infrastructure for Biological Simulation Software, CCF-1111943; Stanford PPL affiliates program, Pervasive Parallelism Lab: Oracle, AMD, Intel, and NVIDIA. Authors also acknowledge additional support from Oracle.

7. REFERENCES

[1] Cadence, Inc. Palladium series. `http://www.cadence.com/products/sd/palladium_series/pages/default.aspx`.

[2] J. Casper, T. Oguntebi, S. Hong, N. G. Bronson, C. Kozyrakis, and K. Olukotun. Hardware acceleration of transactional memory on commodity systems. ASPLOS '11. ACM, 2011.

[3] J. Cornet, F. Maraninchi, and L. Maillet-Contoz. A Method for the Efficient Development of Timed and Untimed Transaction-Level Models of Systems-on-Chip. In *DATE*, 2008.

[4] W. Dally and B. Towles. *Principles and practices of interconnection networks.* Morgan Kaufmann, 2004.

[5] R. Hameed, W. Qadeer, M. Wachs, O. Azizi, A. Solomatnikov, B. Lee, S. Richardson, C. Kozyrakis, and M. Horowitz. Understanding sources of inefficiency in general-purpose chips. In *ISCA*, 2010.

[6] S. Honda, T. Wakabayashi, H. Tomiyama, and H. Takada. RTOS-centric hardware/software cosimulator for embedded system design. In *CODES+ISSS*. ACM, 2004.

[7] S. Hong, S. Yoo, S. Lee, S. Lee, H. Nam, B. Yoo, J. Hwang, D. Song, J. Kim, J. Kim, et al. Creation and utilization of a virtual platform for embedded software optimization:: an industrial case study. In *CODES+ISSS*, 2006.

[8] O. S. Initiative. Systemc. `http://www.systemc.org`.

[9] J. Larus and R. Rajwar. *Transactional Memory.* Morgan Claypool Synthesis Series, 2006.

[10] C. Luk, R. Cohn, R. Muth, H. Patil, A. Klauser, G. Lowney, S. Wallace, V. Janapa, and R. Hazelwood. Pin: building customized program analysis tools with dynamic instrumentation. In *PLDI*, 2005.

[11] P. McKenney. Memory ordering in modern microprocessors, part I. *Linux Journal*, 2005(136):2, 2005.

[12] Mentor Graphics, Inc. seamless. `http://www.mentor.com/products/fv/seamless/`.

[13] Y. Nakamura, K. Hosokawa, I. Kuroda, K. Yoshikawa, and T. Yoshimura. A fast hardware/software co-verification method for system-on-a-chip by using a C/C++ simulator and FPGA emulator with shared register communication. In *DAC*, 2004.

[14] T. Oguntebi, S. Hong, J. Casper, N. Bronson, C. Kozyrakis, and K. Olukotun. FARM: A prototyping environment for tightly-coupled, heterogeneous architectures. In *FCCM*, 2010.

[15] M. Reshadi, P. Mishra, and N. Dutt. Instruction set compiled simulation: a technique for fast and flexible instruction set simulation. In *DAC*, 2003.

[16] J. Rowson. Hardware/software co-simulation. In *DAC*, 1994.

[17] L. Séméria and A. Ghosh. Methodology for hardware/software co-verification in C/C++. In *ASP-DAC*, 2000.

[18] Sysnopsys, Inc. Virtual prototyping solutions. `http://http://www.synopsys.com/Systems/VirtualPrototyping/Pages/default.aspx`.

[19] J. Um, W. Kwon, S. Hong, Y. Kim, K. Choi, J. Kong, S. Eo, and T. Kim. A systematic IP and bus subsystem modeling for platform-based system design. In *DATE*, 2006.

[20] Xilinx, Inc. Bus functional model (bfm) simulation of processor intellectual property. `http://www.xilinx.com/support/documentation/application_notes/xapp516.pdf`.

[21] S. Yoo, I. Bacivarov, A. Bouchhima, Y. Paviot, and A. Jerraya. Building fast and accurate SW simulation models based on hardware abstraction layer and simulation environment abstraction layer. In *DATE*, 2003.

[22] M. Yourst. PTLsim: A Cycle Accurate Full System x86-64 Microarchitectural Simulator. In *ISPASS*. IEEE, 2007.

A Configurable Test Infrastructure using a Mixed-Language and Mixed-Level IP Integration IP-XACT Flow

Erwin de Kock
NXP Semiconductors
High Tech Campus 46
5656 AE Eindhoven
The Netherlands
erwin.de.kock@nxp.com

Jos Verhaegh
NXP Semiconductors
High Tech Campus 46
5656 AE Eindhoven
The Netherlands
jos.verhaegh@nxp.com

Serge Amougou
Magillem Design Services
4 rue de la pierre levée
75011 Paris
France
amougou@magillem.com

ABSTRACT

We present a reusable test infrastructure for RTL designs as an application of mixed-level and mixed-language integration using the IP-XACT standard. The test infrastructure is configurable, meaning that specific configurations can be generated from a template. The main part of the components in the test infrastructure is implemented using the SystemC TLM2 standard. A small part is implemented in VHDL. The design technology to generate configurations uses the IP-XACT standard. We present an application of the reusable test infrastructure for randomized IC verification. To this end, a specific test configuration is integrated with additional stubs and a DUT which are described in Verilog and VHDL. Software images are executed both on the test bench and the DUT. Our results demonstrate an efficient integration flow for mixed-language and mixed-level IPs through flow automation.

Categories and Subject Descriptors

B.7.2 [**Design aids**]: Simulation and Verification.

General Terms

Design; standardization; languages; verification.

Keywords

IP-XACT; SystemC; TLM; FastModel; RTL; mixed-language; mixed-level; randomized verification.

1. INTRODUCTION

The goal of this paper is to demonstrate application of a mixed-language and mixed-level IP integration flow using IP-XACT-based design technology. Furthermore, we demonstrate IP and subsystem configurability using a configurable Test Bench. We show that a large part of this flow can be automated using the IP-XACT standard and IP-XACT tooling. Another contribution of this paper is the use of software for system-level verification.

A key issue for system integration companies is the ability to separate IP models from tools that work with IP models. IP models should work in a variety of tools and tools should work with a variety of IP models. The IP-XACT standard [10] enables this by standardizing IP meta-data descriptions and tool interfaces to operate on meta-data. IP-XACT 1.4 and later versions support both RTL and TLM IP models. There are few integration and simulation tools that support this combination in an IP neutral way. We have used Magillem IP-XACT tools [7] for integration and Cadence Incisive simulator [3] for simulation. Furthermore, we have used the ARM FastModel tools [1] to generate an instruction-accurate Cortex-M3 processor model. These technologies have been used to generate a system-level test bench. On top of this test bench we developed software for randomized verification.

Related work in the area of randomized verification is the Universal Verification Methodology (UVM) [16]. This approach has proven itself for IP verification, also in earlier incarnations such as OVM and *e*. We argue that our approach can be combined with existing IP verification methodologies such as UVM. This is enabled by Software-Driven Verification IP. Related work in the area of IP integration often splits in RTL IP integration and TLM IP integration. For RTL IP integration there are tools such as Mentor HDL Designer [8] and Synopsys Core Assembler [14]. For TLM IP integration there are tools such as ARM FastModels [1], Carbon SOC Designer [4], Mentor Vista [9], and Synopsys Virtualizer [15]. Some tools support co-simulation, for instance in Synopsys Virtualizer, but a true mix of RTL and TLM is rare.

The outline of this paper is as follows. In Section 2 we provide a short introduction to IP-XACT technology. In Section 3 we present our Reusable Test Infrastructure. In Section 4 we apply this infrastructure for randomized verification of a microcontroller IC. In Section 5 we present our results. We conclude in Section 6.

2. IP-XACT Design Technology

We make use of design technology that is based on the IP-XACT standard IEEE 1685-2009. This standard provides a way to describe meta-data of hardware IP components and designs as well as a tool interface to operate on the meta-data. IP component meta-data that can be described are hardware interfaces, software interfaces, and file sets. Hardware interface descriptions include pinning, bus interfaces, and instantiation information. Software interface descriptions include address spaces, memory maps, registers, and bit fields. File set descriptions contain files and options needed for compilation. Design meta-data that can be described are component instances, connections between component instances, and connections between component instances and design boundaries.

Our design technology includes commercial tooling from Magillem Design Services. This tooling includes support for IP

CODES+ISSS'12, October 7–12, 2012, Tampere, Finland.

packaging, platform assembly, netlisting, and generator development and execution. IP packaging is the generation of meta-data for components. Platform assembly is the generation of meta-data for designs. Netlisting is the generation of code for design structures in SystemC, VHDL, or Verilog. Generator development is the development of software tools that operate on the meta-data database in order to produce meaningful output or to generate additional meta-data. We have developed in-house generators for HDL build flow generation, SystemC IP template model generation, and hardware-dependent software generation. These generators have been used for DUT integration in earlier projects. In this paper, we re-use this flow for test bench integration.

3. Reusable Test Infrastructure

Our Reusable Test Infrastructure (RTI) is a configurable SystemC-based Test Bench. In Figure 1 the template for this infrastructure is shown.

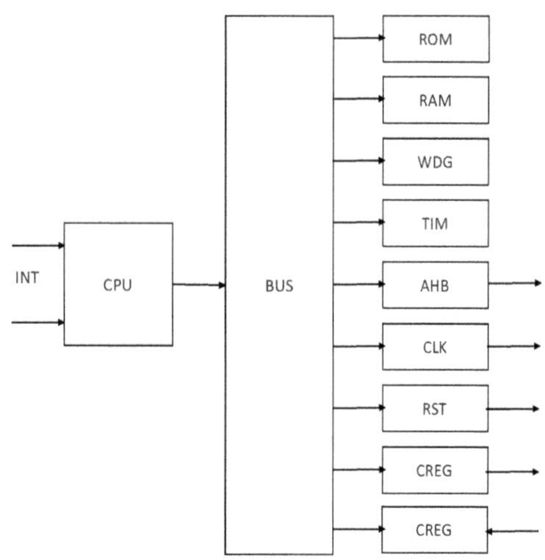

Figure 1. Reusable Test Infrastructure template.

3.1 RTI Components

We use an ARM FastModel Cortex-M3 processor model (CPU) for software execution in the RTI. This is an instruction-accurate model. Furthermore, we make use of the Nested Vector Interrupt Controller (NVIC) in the processor model to support interrupts (INT) in RTI. We wrap the FastModel in a SystemC TLM2 [13] wrapper using generic payloads.

The processor is connected to a generic SystemC TLM2 bus (BUS). The number of masters and slaves that can be connected to the bus are C++ template parameters of the bus model.

Furthermore, we have a generic TLM2 memory model that we use to model ROM and RAM. This model has a special member function that can be called from the Cadence IUS Tcl command line for preloading binary files in memory instances.

Next, we have peripheral models. All these models have a TLM2 target interface that is connected a register set. To model the registers, we make use of the SystemC Modeling Library version 2 (SCML) [11]. There is timer model that we use both as watchdog timer (WDG) and normal timer (TIM). It can be used to implement a software wait function, to abort simulation in case of time outs, and to get the actual simulation time in software. There are models for clock generation (CLK) and reset generation (RST). The shape of clock and reset pulse can be controlled via register settings. Also, there are peripheral models for register input and output (CREG). The initial values of all peripheral registers can be set via SCML properties.

Finally, we have a TLM2-to-AHBlite signal-level transactor (AHB). This transactor translates TLM2 generic payload transactions into AHBlite slave signal-level transactions. This translation is implemented in Esterel [6] from which synthesizable VHDL code is generated. The transactor can be used to connect an AHBlite slave component to a TLM2 bus. This enables us to connect RTI instances to signal-level DUTs.

All RTI components have been described in IP-XACT XML documents, except for the TLM2 bus. The bus is configurable in terms of the number of masters and slaves that can be connected. This type of configurability cannot be described in IP-XACT documents. For this reason, we generate IP-XACT XML documents for specific TLM2 bus configurations when needed, as explained in the next section.

For the RTI peripheral components, part of the implementation can be generated automatically from the IP-XACT description. First, SCML register descriptions can be generated from the IP-XACT register descriptions. They are part of a self-contained SystemC module from which we inherit to implement callback functions on the register accesses. Next, software register access functions can be generated from the IP-XACT register description. To this end, first a register hardware abstraction layer is generated, called vHAL, based on C macros. The vHAL format is described in [5]. A vHAL has the following content.

- A set of macros that define the offset of the registers relative to the instance base address.
- A set of macros that define register characteristics regarding read, write and POR (Power-On Reset).
- A set of bit field macros that define location identifiers of register bit fields.

Finally, get and set functions are generated which are implemented on top of the vHAL. On top of these get and set functions we have implemented a software API similar to the vHAPI functions described in [5] manually. Here we list some examples of such functions.

- Generating clock and reset pulses.
- Registering of interrupt service routines.
- Printing strings and values.
- Sleeping of CPU.
- Resetting of RTI configuration.

3.2 Configurability

3.2.1 RTI Configuration Options

The RTI is configurable. Configuration options include the number of interrupts, the number of AHB interfaces, the number of clock generators, the number of reset generators, and the number of register inputs and outputs. For each AHB interface, the address offset and the address range can be specified such that the user can control the AHB addresses that are generated from the RTI configuration.

Additional configuration options are the ROM and RAM sizes, the address offset of the heap in the RAM, and the size of the heap and stack. Also the watchdog has configuration options to control the time out functionality. Finally, there are configuration options for the ARM FastModel processor including options for the processor frequency, the quantum value, and the enabling and disabling of the CADI interface for debugger connections.

3.2.2 RTI Configuration Generation

The above-mentioned configuration options are supplied by users in a text file. We parse this text file using a bash script and we configuration options in the IP-XACT database as generator parameter values using the command line interface of the commercial IP-XACT tools. Next, the commercial netlister and in-house generators are called to generate the RTI configuration. These generators make use of a software interface to operate on the IP-XACT database that is similar to IP-XACT Tight Generator Interface, but this software interface adds more functionality. Specifically, we make use of IP-XACT component editing functionality, for instance, to generate specific IP-XACT TLM2 bus descriptions. The RTI configuration generation process contains three steps.

In Step 1, additional meta-data is generated to describe the TLM2 bus configuration and RTI configuration. The TLM2 bus configuration depends on the number of interfaces specified in the configuration options. In the meta-data, the correct number of transactional ports, bus interfaces, and corresponding address spaces with offsets and ranges is generated. Subsequently, an IP-XACT design is generated containing the desired component instances and interconnect. This design is encapsulated as a hierarchical view in an IP-XACT component that reflects the RTI configuration. All relevant signals are exported from the RTI design to the RTI component.

In Step 2, files are generated that are needed at build time of the RTI configuration. For hardware, these files include a SystemC netlist for the implementation of the RTI configuration and a VHDL wrapper for the usage of the RTI configuration in a signal-level environment. Furthermore, a list of files for compilation is generated that can be used as input for the Cadence irun tool in order to build a mixed-language and mixed-level simulation. For software, these files include a C/C++ description of the system memory map similar to the chip context format that is described in [5]. For each bus interface of each component instance, a base address is generated that reflects the position of that interface in the memory map.

In Step 3, an SCML property file is generated which is needed at run-time. This file contains configuration options that can be set at start of simulation.

Users can control which steps in the RTI configuration are executed. This avoids re-building their system if they only change values of run-time configuration options.

4. Case Study

We have applied RTI for randomized verification of a microcontroller IC. The IC contains an ARM Cortex-M3 processor and it has I2C, SPI, and UART interfaces. Our goal was to verify correct functioning of the IC when streaming data over these interfaces. Also DMA capabilities and power-down modes of the IC had to be verified. The acceptance criteria for randomized verification have been captured by 15 test cases which had to run continuously with different seeds for a period of at least two weeks without failures. Randomized verification is the last part in a hardware integration verification flow including formal interconnection verification using PSL assertions and directed tests for basic interoperability using verification software as targeted in the Hardware Verification Software Standard [5].

Figure 2 shows an overview of the Test Bench and DUT integration setup. The DUT is the IC. It is connected to the Test Bench via Test Bench pads. These pads are connected to I2C, SPI, and UART subsystems. These subsystems are connected to an RTI configuration via an AHB connection. For I2C there are two pads, namely serial clock SCL and serial data SDA. For SPI there are four pads, namely master-out-slave-in MOSI, master-in-slave-out MISO, serial clock SCK, and slave select (SSEL). For UART there are three pads, namely transmit data TXD, receive data RXD, and serial clock SCK for synchronous mode. The Test Bench contains four SPI subsystems but for simplicity these are not shown in Figure 2. Each SPI subsystem has its own Test Bench pads which are directly connected to the IC SPI pads. The SPI slave select signal is routed from the IC via one additional GPIO pad per SPI subsystem. These are also not shown in Figure 2. The DUT contains a single SPI interface. In SPI master mode, the DUT selects the corresponding SPI slave via the additional GPIO slave select connections.

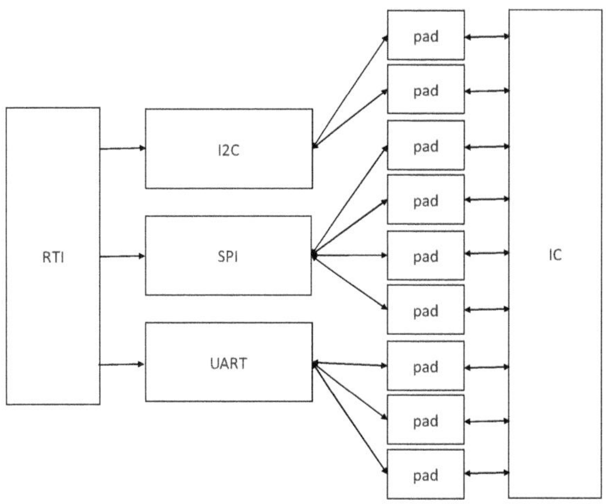

Figure 2. Test bench and DUT integration.

This system has been integrated using an IP-XACT-based flow. The IC has been handled as a black box IP. The Test Bench top-level and the I2C, SPI, and UART sub-systems have been integrated manually using the IP-XACT-based flow. The RTI subsystem has been generated automatically.

4.1 RTI Configuration

Table 1 shows the RTI configuration values for our case study which are input for Step 1. Row 1 and 2 specify which environment variables should be used.

Row 3 specifies the location of the RTI configuration that will be generated.

Row 4 specifies the HDL path of the RTI configuration instance. This path is needed to generate the SCML property file content.

Table 1. RTI configuration values for case study.

	Configuration option	Configuration value
1	projectWork	PROJECT_WORK
2	projectName	PROJECT_RTIGEN
3	cell	$PROJECT_WORK/data/ssd_chip_tb_lib/ssd_chip_tb_rti
4	hdlPath	.u_rti
5	vendor	nxp.com
6	library	ssd
7	name	ssd_chip_tb_rti
8	version	1.0
9	enable_debug	false
10	arm_frequency	100000000
11	quantum_value	0.00001
12	app_file_name	../VERIFICATION/apps/rtiSsd_clock_gen_basic/rtiSsd_clock_gen_basic.axf
13	timeOutEnable	true
14	timeOutUnit	1
15	timeOut	20000
16	romSize	0x20000000
17	ramSize	0x20000000
18	heapBaseAddress	0xFF00000
19	heapSize	0xE0000
20	stackSize	0x20000
21	numberOfInterrupts	26
22	numberOfAhbs	6
23	numberOfClocks	5
24	numberOfResets	2
25	numberOfCregOuts	10
26	numberOfCregIns	6
27	baseAddressesAhbs	"0x40000000 0x50000000 0x60000000 0x50000100 0x50000200 0xB0000000"
28	baseAddressesClocks	"0x70000000 0x70000200 0x70000400 0x70000600 0x70000800 0xC0000000 0x80000000 0x80000200 0x80000400 0x80000600 0x80000800"
29	baseAddressesResets	"0x70000100 0x70000300 0x70000500 0x70000700 0x70000900 0xC0000100 0x80000100 0x80000300"
30	baseAddressesCregOuts	"0x90000000 0x90000100 0x90000200 0x90000300 0x90000400 0x90000500 0x90000600 0x90000700 0x90000800 0x90000900"
31	baseAddressesCregIns	"0xA0000000 0xA0000100 0xA0000200 0xA0000300 0xA0000400 0xA0000500"
32	addressSpacesAhbs	"0x0 0x100 0x0 0x100 0x0 0x100 0x0 0x100 0x0 0x100 0x0 0x1000"

Rows 5-8 specify the IP-XACT Vendor, Library, Name, and Version of the IP-XACT component that will be generated for the RTI configuration.

Rows 9-12 specify the settings for the ARM FastModel Cortex-M3 model.

Rows 13-15 specify settings for the watchdog. The time out unit indicates the unit of the time out value (1 means nanoseconds). The given time out value is small to support license check out failures. In the software running on the processor we reprogram the watchdog for a larger time out value. If the processor does not start executing software because of a license check out failure, then the simulation is stopped early because of the small time out value.

Rows 16-20 specify the memory configuration. These values are used to configure the TLM memories and to generate a scatter file for the ARM linker.

Rows 21-26 specify the interfaces of the RTI configuration. For each AHB interface also a clock and reset component is generated. So the total number of clock and reset components in this example is 6+5=11 and 6+2=8, respectively.

Rows 27-31 specify the base addresses for the RTI component instances. Users can control these explicitly as in this example or they can leave that implicit in which case the RTI configuration process will automatically assign base addresses.

Finally, Row 32 specifies the AHB address offsets and ranges for each of the AHB interfaces. In this example, an access at address 0x40000000 by the Cortex-M3 model will result in an AHB address of 0x0 on the first AHB interface of the RTI configuration.

The configuration options are parsed and the information is used to generate an IP-XACT database. To this end, we have developed in-house generators. An IP-XACT TLM2 bus component is generated and an IP-XACT component, design, and design configuration are generated. The IP-XACT design configuration contains generator chain configurations with parameter values that are derived from the RTI configuration options. The IP-XACT database also contains IP-XACT component descriptions of the other RTI components. This database is the starting point for the source code generation in Steps 2 and 3 as described in Section 3.2.2.

4.2 Test Bench Integration

The next phase was to integrate the complete Test Bench. The RTI configuration from the previous section has become available as a VHDL signal-level IP block. We integrated it with the peripheral I2C, SPI, and UART RTL IP blocks to form the complete Test Bench show in Figure 2. Again, we used an IP-XACT approach. We used IP-XACT descriptions of the peripheral IPs which were either supplied by the IP provider or generated using our commercial packaging tool. IP-XACT design integration is a straightforward job using our commercial assembly tool. Figure 3 shows a schematic view of the top-level Test Bench. The I2C, SPI, and UART blocks are sub-systems containing the respective IP blocks and AHB-to-APB bridges. The DUT was handled as a black box meaning that we only described the pin interface and file set in IP-XACT. After IP-XACT design integration, the VHDL netlist generation is again straightforward using a commercial netlister.

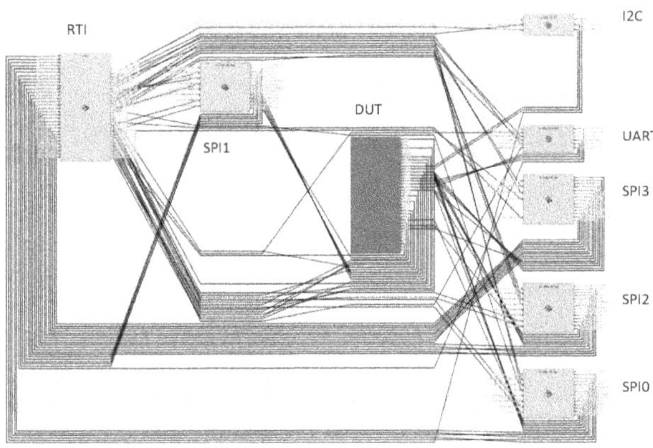

Figure 3. Schematic view of top-level Test Bench IP-XACT design.

4.3 Embedded Software Development

The final phase was to develop software for the Test Bench and for the DUT. Both contain a Cortex-M3 processor so we can re-use software on both ends. In the setup we ran independent software images. There is one Test Bench image and one DUT image.

The software architecture is based on queues. Each peripheral IP has a software TX queue and a software RX queue. Each queue element can contain a message which is a pointer to a stream of bytes. A stream of bytes has a certain structure: there is a header and a payload. The header contains the following elements:

- size (Byte 0), i.e., the number of bytes in the message,
- id (Byte 1), i.e., the id of the message,
- command1 (Byte 2), i.e., the source (Bit 0-2) and destination (Bit 3-5) IP in the Test Bench,
- command2 (Byte 3), i.e., the commands to be executed by the IC which are DMA memory copies to be done (Bit 0-1), DMA channels to be used (Bit 2-4), and power-down modes to be entered (Bit 5-7).
- source address (Byte 4-7), i.e., the start address of the message in the memory space of the DUT, and
- destination address (Byte 8-11), i.e., the start address of the message in the memory space of the DUT after a memory copy of the message by the DUT DMA.

The payload of the message is a sequence of upper case character byte values of random length. Also message headers are randomized. In this way, sequences of messages are streamed in and out of the DUT, verifying peripheral operations, processor operations, DMA operations, memory operations, and power-down modes. In the Test Bench, a shadow memory of the DUT memory is maintained such that it knows which memory locations are in use at any time. This is needed to constrain the randomization of the source and destination addresses. The Test Bench transmits and receives messages from and to the DUT and it verifies correctness by comparing transmitted and received messages.

The processors in the Test Bench and in the DUT execute read and write operations as well as full and empty checks on the queues of their peripherals. A key issue is that these queue operations are protected in critical regions such that the queue operations are atomic and the queue administration remains consistent. To this end, we disable and enable the relevant interrupts for each queue before and after each queue operation by means of the CMSIS NVIC disable and enable operations [2]. On the Test Bench side, the processor adds random messages to the transmit queues and removes messages from the receive queues. On the DUT side, the processor moves messages from receive queues to transmit queues after processing the commands in the messages.

The software on the Test Bench side has been developed on top of the register get and set functions that have been generated automatically from the IP-XACT register description.

4.4 Randomized Verification

The randomized verification setup consisted of 15 test setups which match with the 15 test cases defined in the acceptance criteria. Test cases specify amongst others the following items.

- The interfaces used to stream data to the DUT.
- The interfaces used to stream data from the DUT.
- The amount of DMA copies to be executed by the DUT.
- The power-down and wake-up sequence of the DUT.

On the Test Bench side we developed 15 software images to constrain the randomization process according the specifications of the 15 test setups. On the DUT side we developed 6 software images to program the DUT in different modes. The DUT images control whether the I2C and SPI interfaces run in master or slave mode (resulting in 4 different images). In 2 of these 4 images, we needed to control the activation of the serial interfaces from the Test Bench using GPIO events for some test setups. This results in a total of 6 images. Both on the Test Bench side and on the DUT side a large part of the code base is shared between the setups. The randomization only occurs on the Test Bench side. The DUT side is deterministic. The random seed is loaded into a designated ROM address before simulation start and it is pickup by the software to initialize the random number generator.

The random verification setup has run continuously for 4 weeks. In this period, 45000 seeds have been simulated while running the 15 test setups in parallel jobs. During these weeks, all tests have been developed further continuously. We spent 3 weeks developing the complete setup, without the RTI development time, before we were able to start running seeds continuously.

Figure 4 shows simulation results for one of the test setups. In this setup messages are streamed from the Test Bench UART into the DUT. After a DMA memory copy, the messages are streamed back to the Test Bench via SPI. One of the four SPI slaves is randomly selected for each message via four separate connections. The Test Bench compares the incoming messages with the outgoing messages to implement automated functional pass/fail checking.

Furthermore, the simulations provide performance numbers on throughput and latency of the messages. Simulations have shown that message streaming across the serial interfaces continues to function correctly with acceptable throughput and latency when DMA activity consumes an increasing amount of memory bandwidth inside the DUT.

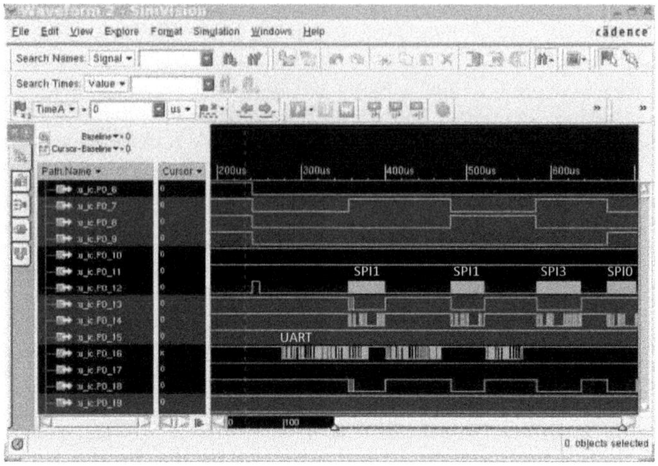

Figure 4. Waveforms showing streaming from TB UART (P0_16) via DUT back to TB SPI blocks (P0_14). The TB contains 4 SPI blocks numbered SPI0 to SPI3. Pins P0_6 to P0_9 are used as slave select for these blocks, respectively.

4.5 Summary

Here we summarize the flow that we used in our case study. First, we have generated an RTI configuration using Table 1 as input. For this RTI configuration the following data was generated automatically.

Meta-data

- IP-XACT component for the SystemC TLM2 bus, and
- IP-XACT component, design, and design configuration for the RTI configuration.

Hardware integration

- SystemC netlist for the RTI configuration,
- VHDL wrapper for the RTI configuration,
- SCML property file for the RTI configuration,
- Address decoding file for the SystemC TLM2 bus, and
- File set with SystemC and VHDL files for hardware compilation using irun.

Hardware component

- SystemC module with SCML register description for RTI clock generator, reset generator, timer, and register input and output.

Software integration

- C/C++ files describing the RTI system memory map,
- ARM scatter file, and
- Makefile for software compilation.

Software component

- C/C++ macros in vHAL format for register and bit field access on RTI clock generator, reset generator, timer, and register input and output, and
- C/C++ get and set functions for register and bit field access on RTI clock generator, reset generator, timer, and register input and output.

Documentation

- Data sheets for the RTI configuration and RTI components.

Second, we have integrated the test bench using IP-XACT technology, i.e., we have used our commercial GUI to generate IP-XACT components, designs, and design configurations for the test bench and the peripheral subsystems. From this IP-XACT database the following files were generated automatically.

Hardware integration

- VHDL entity, architecture, package, and configuration for the test bench top-level and peripheral subsystems.
- File set with SystemC, VHDL, and Verilog files for compilation of the complete test bench using irun.

Software integration

- C/C++ files describing the test bench system memory map including peripheral I2C, SPI, and UART base addresses.
- ARM scatter file for the complete test bench, and
- Makefile for software compilation.

Software component

- C/C++ macros in vHAL format for register and bit field access on I2C, SPI, and UART peripherals.
- C/C++ get and set functions for register and bit field access on I2C, SPI, and UART peripherals.

Documentation

- Data sheets for the I2C, SPI, and UART peripherals.

Third, we have developed embedded software for randomized verification on top of the automatically generated software. This includes drivers for I2C, SPI, and UART which are programmed on top of the generated register get and set functions.

5. RESULTS

One of the benefits of using IP-XACT is that all views for RTI configurations are generated using our existing IP integration flow. The work for generating specific RTI configurations was to script the generation of meta-data. All other views are generated using our existing IP integration flow. The development of the RTI components was additional work. Another benefit of using IP-XACT is that this standard is supported by EDA vendor tools which increase the productivity of flow automation as presented in this paper a lot.

The case study presented in this paper has taken 7 weeks by 2 persons. After 1 week, first results were presented showing streaming between UART and I2C. After 3 weeks, 15 test setups were started running continuously for 4 weeks. In these four weeks, the test setups have been refined further and have been debugged. A large part of the time has been spent on developing and debugging the message streaming software and programming of the peripherals because this was not available from earlier work. Test bench integration has been very efficient. As a result of this case study we can add I2C, SPI, and UART interfaces to the RTI infrastructure, such that they can be used immediately in future test benches. In 4 weeks, more than 45000 seeds have been simulated using 15 parallel jobs. This averages to 15 minutes per seed. Simulation speeds are identical to RTL simulation speeds.

Another observation is that the presented test infrastructure easily accommodates integration of software-driven verification IP.

Such verification IPs typically have register interfaces via bus connections. The ARM FastModel can be used to run software that drives the verification IPs. This approach combines IP and system-level verification.

6. CONCLUSIONS

In this paper, we have demonstrated efficient test bench integration that can be achieved using IP integration and flow automation using IP-XACT technology. Also we have applied IP-XACT technology for configuration of test benches. The same technology can be applied to configure systems and subsystems. The configurability has been implemented at the IP-XACT meta-data level. The configuration process produces a configured IP-XACT design. On this configured design, a "traditional" IP-XACT flow is executed producing the relevant implementation views.

7. REFERENCES

[1] ARM FastModels, http://www.arm.com/products/tools/models/fast-models.php

[2] ARM Cortex Microcontroller Software Interface Standard, http://www.arm.com/products/processors/cortex-m/cortex-microcontroller-software-interface-standard.php

[3] Cadence Incisive Enterprise Simulator, www.cadence.com/products/sd/enterprise_simulator

[4] Carbon SOC Designer, http://www.carbondesignsystems.com/soc-designer-plus/

[5] CoReUse 4.6, Hardware Verification Software Standard, http://www.ip-extreme.com/MediaFiles/ebooks/26.pdf

[6] Esterel, http://www.esterel-technologies.com/

[7] Magillem Design Services, http://www.magillem.com/eda/

[8] Mentor HDL Designer, http://www.mentor.com/products/fpga/hdl_design/hdl_designer_series/

[9] Mentor Vista, http://www.mentor.com/esl/vista/upload/vista-architect-ds.pdf

[10] IP-XACT, Standard Structure for Packaging, Integratimg, and Reusing IP within Tool Flows, IEEE 1685-2009, http://standards.ieee.org/getieee/1685/download/1685-2009.pdf

[11] SystemC Modeling Library, http://www.synopsys.com/cgi-bin/slcw/kits/reg.cgi

[12] SystemC, Open SystemC Language Reference Manual, IEEE 1666-2011, http://standards.ieee.org/getieee/1666/download/1666-2011.pdf

[13] SystemC TLM2, http://www.accellera.org/downloads/standards/systemc/tlm

[14] Synopsys Core Assembler, http://www.synopsys.com/dw/ipdir.php?ds=core_assembler

[15] Synopsys Virtualizer, http://www.synopsys.com/systems/virtualprototyping/Pages/default.aspx

[16] Universal Verification Methodology, http://www.uvmworld.org/

A MDD Methodology for Specification of Embedded Systems and Automatic Generation of Fast Configurable and Executable Performance Models

Fernando Herrera, Hector Posadas, Pablo Peñil and Eugenio Villar
University of Cantabria
ETSIIT, Av. Castros sn Santander
Spain, 39009
00 34 942 20 08 78
{fherrera,posadash, pablop,evillar}@teisa.unican.es

Francisco Ferrero, Raúl Valencia
GMV Aerospace and Defense S.A.U.
Isaac Newton 11 P.T.M. Tres Cantos
Spain, 28760
00 34 91 807 75 11
{fferrero,rvalencia}@gmv.com

ABSTRACT
This paper presents the COMPLEX UML/MARTE modeling methodology and its related framework for automatic generation of executable performance models. The modeling methodology supports Model-Driven Development (MDD), required by industrial flows, and a novel set of modeling features specifically suitable for Design Space Exploration (DSE), a crucial design activity. The COMPLEX framework has other advantages for DSE. The COMPLEX tooling enables the automatic generation of an executable and configurable model for fast performance analysis without requiring engineering effort. The COMPLEX tooling automates the production of an easily portable text-based representation of the UML/MARTE model. This representation is read by the underlying simulation infrastructure, which automatically builds a fast performance model supporting the evaluation of different configurations of the system. An important aspect of this performance analysis framework is that it supports a system-level text-based front-end, which is produced from the COMPLEX UML/MARTE model, and which avoids the development of SW implementations, HW refinements, or the implementation of HW/SW interfaces. Moreover, neither code regeneration, nor recompilation is required for any DSE iterations, and thus, the time taken in the exploration is mostly due to model simulation.

Categories and Subject Descriptors
D.2.2 **[Design Tools and Techniques]**: Languages, Methodologies, Tools; D.2.10 **[Design]**: Methodologies.

General Terms
Design, Performance, Standardization, Languages.

Keywords
Electronic System-Level (ESL), Design Space Exploration (DSE), Model-Driven Development (MDD), Component-Based Design (CBD), UML, MARTE, SystemC.

1. INTRODUCTION
Modern electronic systems are increasingly complex. This complexity is due to growing integration capabilities, which enable the addition of new functionalities and the improvement of performance capabilities. As a result, system designers must take decisions with a large potential impact in the system performance very early in the design process. In order to ensure the competitiveness of the system as a product, these early design decisions must be optimum or nearly optimum. At the same time, these decisions have to be made quickly, in order to achieve a short time to market. This poses a big challenge to system designers. In fact, the design of a medium size system may easily offer thousands or millions of design alternatives as a result of considering many different feasible platform architectures (including different types of processors and accelerators, many memory architectures and dimensions, several working frequencies, etc), followed by the consideration of the alternatives in the software architecture and the architectural mapping. The generation and exploration of each design alternative may require an unaffordable time. First, each design alternative might require the development of a Platform-Specific Model (PSM) for performance assessment. In addition, the time for the simulation and analysis of the PSM may require a non-negligible time. This time depends on the accuracy vs. analysis time trade-off, so the use of traditional, detailed techniques such as RTL or Instruction Set Simulators and even, virtualization are unsuitable for design space exploration (DSE). Finally, throughout the exploration, one could find that some parameters have more impact on performance than others, making an exhaustive exploration very inefficient.

A better approach is to enable the generation of a performance model able to efficiently capture all the relevant functional and non-functional characteristics of the embedded system. This model should be configurable and easy to analyze in order to allow efficient DSE. This paper presents the COMPLEX (COdesign and power Management in PLatform-based design space EXploration [1]) UML/MARTE methodology and its associated Eclipse-based ESL design framework, integrated with a simulation infrastructure, specifically designed to tackle the previously discussed challenges.

2. PROPOSED METHODOLOGY
The proposed methodology is depicted in Figure 1. The first step is shown at the top of Figure 1, and it consists of the specification

of the system and of the environment model. In this phase the user employs the UML language and the MARTE profile to create a standardized way to describe a set of design solutions of the system and a variety of stimuli environments, which reflect a bounded set of common and feasible extreme working conditions. Since the model represents a set of alternative designs and not a single one, the model captures a *design space*, so it is suitable for a DSE flow. Capturing in the model different stimuli environments reflecting feasible use cases, it is possible to ensure sufficient representativeness in the results obtained from the application of dynamic techniques for performance assessment.

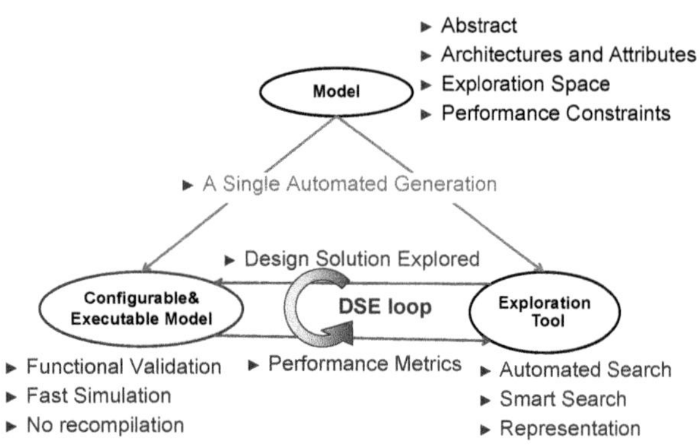

Figure 1. Generic UML/MARTE COMPLEX DSE flow.

A second step of the flow consists of the automatic generation of a fast performance model, which reflects an executable counterpart of the UML/MARTE model plus the set of C/C++ code referenced by the UML/MARTE model. This model provides the main features required for DSE: simulation speed, low engineering effort and estimation accuracy.

In order to ensure reduced simulation times and good accuracy, the methodology relies on fast simulation and performance estimation technology based on native simulation, called SCoPE+. This kind of simulation allows speeds near functional execution speeds to be achieved with sufficient accuracy, which is optimal for DSE [6]. Additionally, this generation step needs to be done only once for each DSE iteration, which speeds up the DSE loop. This is feasible since, on the one hand,, the modeling methodology supports the representation of a design space, and, on the other, the generation process produces an automatically configurable simulation model, by relying on dynamic libraries and on the passing of architectural parameters to the executable performance model through XML files.

Another factor contributing to a fast DSE loop and reduced effort is the full automation of the exploration. The UML/MARTE framework enables the user to configure and trigger the exploration independently from any specific exploration tool. Once the exploration tool is triggered, it automatically decides on the different design solutions, and automatically launches the executable model.

3. MODELING METHODOLOGY

As mentioned, in the COMPLEX UML/MARTE flow, the user can specify:

- A specification of the system including relevant aspects in terms of performance, such as the application architecture, platform architecture, architectural mapping, etc;
- The design space, covering the system configurability;
- Environment models describing the actors interacting with the system and the way they interact with the system.

3.1 System Specification

The COMPLEX UML/MARTE modeling methodology adopts Model-Driven Development (MDD) principles making it possible to raise the abstraction level. The modeling methodology enables the capture of the functional structure (interfaces and classes) of the system, and the way it is split into components [2] to describe the architecture of the application. The platform architecture and the architectural mapping are also described. The proposed system modeling methodology is specifically suitable for DSE [3] since it makes it possible to describe a design space. That is, instead of a single system, the model represents the set of design alternatives to be explored. This is done through DSE parameters, and by enabling a compact way to specify a set of architectural mappings. Moreover, the design space can be bound by means of DSE rules, and also by means of constraints on performance metrics. Moreover, the modeling methodology supports the description of the environment [4], in order to describe the expected scenarios which will exercise the system. The framework uses Papyrus- MDT (http://www.eclipse.org/modeling/mdt/papyrus/) for the capture of the model, and provides the profile infrastructure as a set of installable plug-ins.

The system modeling methodology described in this paper follows a component-oriented approach and applies Model-Driven Architecture (MDA) principles in the development of HW/SW embedded systems. Moreover, the proposed approach makes this methodology software centric as it enables the description of a platform-independent model (PIM) which can be fully allocated to a SW implementation, and thus can be considered as an application model. However, the methodology also enables the HW implementation of application components to be considered.

In Component-based Software Engineering (CBSE), the system is built as a composition of application components interacting with each other only through well-defined interfaces. Components are software units that exhibit their interfaces (provided or required). Thus, the application can be split into clearly separable and reusable blocks, improving the organization of the product as well as its reusability and modularity.

The COMPLEX methodology supports the separation of concerns. This separation is achieved by providing distinct system views to the designer, in the form of UML packages, each one for each relevant aspect:

- **Data View:** captures the relevant data types of the system, i.e., types of data exchanged at interfaces.
- **Functional View:** captures the functional structure of the system, as a set of interfaces and a set of classes implementing and using those interfaces.
- **Communication and Concurrency (CC) View:** captures the application architecture, enclosing classes into components. It also captures the non-functional aspects of system functionality related to the application behavior, such as concurrency and real-time constraints.
- **Platform Description View:** describes both software and hardware resources of the platform.

- **Architectural View:** describes the platform architecture and the architectural mapping of the application components to the processing resources of the platform. It also captures DSE parameters, rules and constraints which specify the different architectural solutions, that is, the design space.
- **Verification View:** is devoted to the definition of the system stimuli environment. The Stimuli modeling is explained in detail in [5].

3.1.1 Description of the Application (PIM)

The initial steps in the methodology consist of identifying the system functions, modeled through the Data model and Functional View. System functions are captured by means of the use of UML use cases and the relations between them. The UML use cases will allow the designer to identify the UML interfaces that model the system functions and create the UML classes that will implement them. System functions are modeled by means of UML interfaces stereotyped with the MARTE <<ClientServerSpecification>> stereotype. The operations of the <<ClientServerSpecification>> interfaces might have parameters whose types should have been defined in the Data Model.

In the CC view, the application components are defined. The CC view contains components with the MARTE <<RtUnit>> and <<PpUnit>> stereotypes. The former stereotype identifies a component which can have its own execution thread, providing/requiring services to/from other components by means of its provided and required interfaces. The latter represents a non-active component, which provides services, such as giving access to shared data, as a reaction to active component demands. The functional behavior of the UML components is defined by adding instances of functional classes. They are captured as UML properties of the UML component. Property type is one of the classes defined in the Functional View. UML Components use UML Ports stereotyped with the MARTE <<ClientServerPort>> and <<RtFeature>> stereotypes for defining the interfaces which are used for communicating with other components, and specifying real-time behavior. In order to complete all the necessary information for the CC View, the user will add an additional UML component with the COMPLEX <<system>> stereotype. This component represents the PIM and captures the software architecture. It includes application component instances, captured as UML properties typed as any of the <<RtUnit>> or <<PpUnit>> components declared in the CC view with UML connectors for their interconnection.

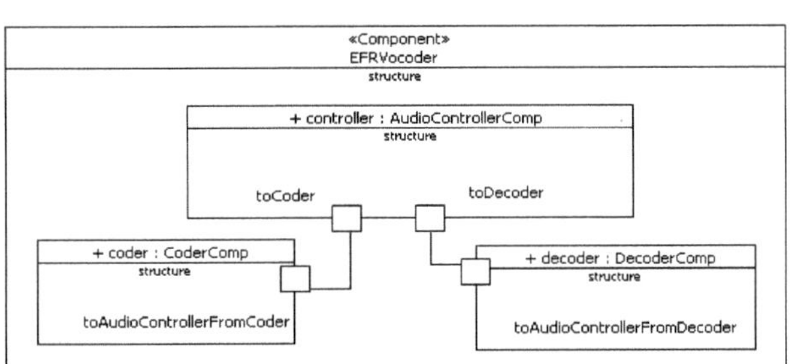

Figure 2. Architecture of the ER vocoder Application.

The composite diagram in Figure 2 shows the SW architecture of an EFR vocoder system, within a <<system>> component of the CC view. It encloses three component instances ("coder", "controller" and "decoder"). Each instance (e.g. "coder") is an UML property typed as a component previously defined in the CC view (e.g. "CoderComp"). Such a component, in turn, encloses an instance of a functional class defined within the functional view (e.g., "Coder").

3.1.2 Platform and Architectural Mapping (PSM)

The proposed modeling methodology supports the description of the HW/SW platform within two views, the Platform view and the Architectural view. SW and HW components are declared in the Platform view. An RTOS is declared as a component with the MARTE <<Scheduler>> stereotype. Declaration of HW components relies on the MARTE Hardware Resource Modeling (HRM) sub profile (i.e. <<HwProcessor>>, <<HwBus>>, <<HwCache>>, <<HwRAM>>,…).

The architecture of the platform is captured within the Architectural view, specifically within a UML component ("archi_system" in Figure 3), stereotyped with the COMPLEX <<system>> stereotype again. This component contains SW component instances and the hardware platform architecture, as reflected in Figure 3. Figure 3 also shows how a fixed architectural mapping can be specified. Application component instances (the three at the top in Figure 3) captured in the CC view are referenced in the Architectural view (to do this, first, the <<system>> component of the Architectural view is captured as an extension of the <<system>> component of the CC view). Then, associations with the MARTE <<Allocate>> stereotype, which reflect a spatial allocation, map application components onto instances of platform components with computation capabilities.

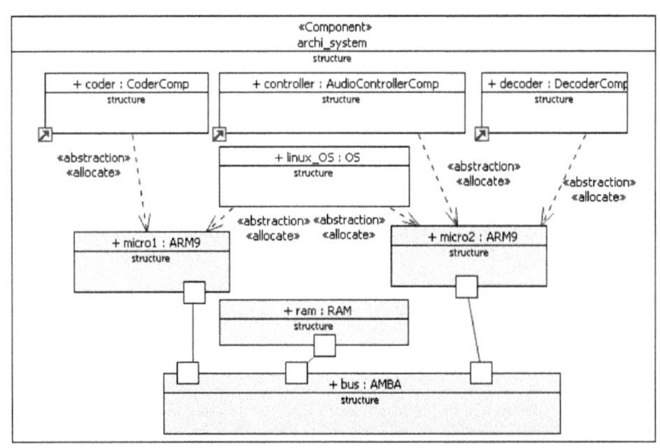

Figure 3. Architecture of the EFR vocoder system.

The diagram in Figure 3 models a single implementation since it shows a fixed architecture, a single architectural mapping, and fixed attributes for platform components. The COMPLEX UML/MARTE modeling methodology provides features for enabling the specification of a design space, that is, a set of design alternatives. This enables the generation of a configurable executable counterpart in order to obtain performance estimates. This way neither model modification, nor performance model regeneration is required. This makes the methodology suitable for DSE flows.

3.2 Design Space Specification

The COMPLEX UML/MARTE modeling methodology enables the specification of a design space which can consist of (a) a set of architectural mappings (allocation space); (b) a range of values for platform attributes (attribute value space); and (c) a set of platform architectures (architecture space). Moreover, the design space can be shaped and constrained through the definition of DSE constraints and rules. Finally, the methodology also enables the definition of the output metrics to be considered for the goal functions used in the exploration. A dedicated UML profile, the COMPLEX profile, has been created to add the necessary semantics that are missing in the MARTE profile with regard to the aforementioned features. Therefore, this UML profile complements MARTE for DSE. Four elements have been created to represent the necessary concepts: *Exploration parameters*, of three possible types (allocation parameters, scalar parameters and vector parameters); DSE *Rules*; *Constraints* and *Estimation parameters* (for defining output metrics).

1) Description of the Architectural Mapping Space

Architectural mapping is a factor with a big impact on performance. This methodology enables the description of a set of architectural mappings. This set is captured through one or more UML comment placed in the Architectural view, and stereotyped with the MARTE *<<Assign>>* stereotype (to specify the allocation itself) and with the COMPLEX *<<DseAllocationParameter>>* (which provides a name to the allocation).

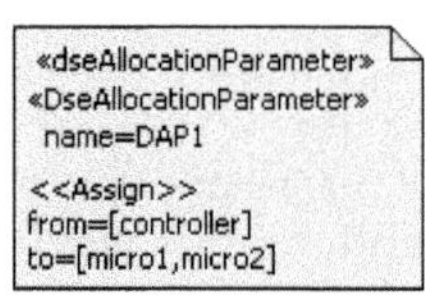

Figure 4. Specification of a set of architectural mappings.

Figure 4 shows an example for the EFR vocoder model where 2 feasible allocations (controller to micro1 and controller to micro2) are expressed in a single construct.

2) Specification of a Configurable Attribute Values

Many platform attributes can have a significant impact on system performance (cache sizes, core and bus frequencies, etc). The proposed methodology enables the association of a range of values to specific attributes of platform components for exploring their impact on performance. This is done by capturing DSE parameters, specified as UML comments associated with the component containing the explored attributes, and with the application of either a *<<DseScalarParameter>>* or a *<<DseVectorParameter>>* COMPLEX stereotype. *DSE scalar parameters* specify a sequential progression associated with a specific non-functional property. The designer can specify either minimum, maximum and step values to define possible values or annotate a specific sequence of values. *DSE vector parameters* enable the modeling of vector parameters with constraints on the possible combinations of the elements.

Figure 5 shows the modeling of the platform parameter space for the EFR Vocoder model. This space is defined by the possible values of data and instruction cache memories (2K, 4K and 8K for ARM920T cores); by using either a 32 or 16 bit (ARM thumb instruction set) bus; and by the consideration of 4 core frequencies. This space is specified through four DSE scalar parameters related to components of the Platform view. Thus, the size of the space of platform attribute values is 4 (core frequencies) x 3 (data cache sizes) x 3 (instruction cache sizes) x 2 (data bus word) = 72 design alternatives.

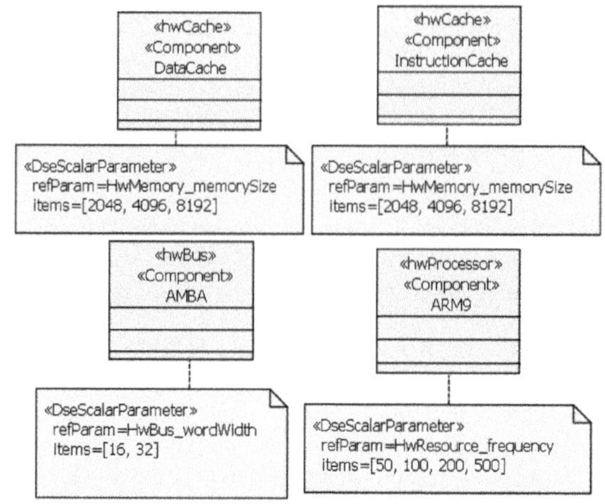

Figure 5. Attribute value space for the EFR Vocoder model.

3) Specification of the Architecture Space

DSE parameters and *<<Assign>>* comments widen the design space without changing the platform architecture. However, the user might be interested in exploring the impact on performance of different platform architectures. The COMPLEX UML/MARTE modeling methodology supports the specification of different architectures in the same model. This is done by enabling the specification of several architectural views, in a similar way as several architectures can be associated with an entity in VHDL. This way the designer's DSE can include loop solutions in which the platform architecture is very different and thus the alternatives cannot be represented by means of a parameterized template. Additionally, it is also possible to capture a cluster of processors through a single component instance, whose multiplicity is associated with a DSE parameter.

3.2.1 DSE Rules

The proposed modeling methodology enables delimitation of the size of the design space by means of DSE rules. It is useful since the design space can exponentially grow, making the exploration unaffordable. Moreover, all possible solutions might not be feasible, e.g., all platforms modeled might not be available. DSE rules are specified as comments with the COMPLEX <<DseRule>> stereotype, and they can refer to one or more DSE parameter included in the model. DSE rules create a logical condition that in case of not being fulfilled discards the design point from the set of solutions to be explored.

3.2.2 Estimation Parameters

The methodology allows the designer to state in the model which output metrics have to feed the exploration loop. They are called estimation parameters in the sense that, in a DSE context, performance metrics are obtained by means of a performance estimation technology. There are two types of DSE estimations. DSE Application Estimations refer to non-functional attributes corresponding to the application components, e.g. the minimal inter-arrival time of a sporadic service. DSE Platform Estimations refer to the performance metrics on the platform resources, e.g. load of CPU, power consumption, etc. The estimation parameters are defined in the Architectural View by means of UML comments stereotyped with the COMPLEX *<<DseAppEstimation>>* and *<<DsePlatformEstimation>>* stereotypes.

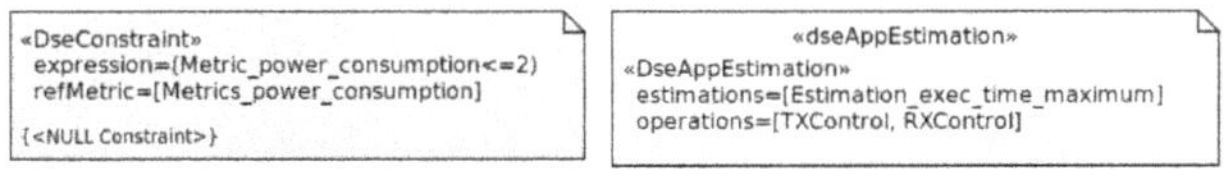

Figure 6. DSE constraints and estimations.

Estimation parameters, that is, output metrics to be used by the exploration tool, can also be referenced in the methodology to define DSE rules and constraints. The right hand side of Figure 6 shows how the model declares the export of two application performance metrics of the EFR vocoder for their consideration in the exploration loop: the maximum execution time of the *TXControl* and of the *RXControl* operations (within the "controller" module). These metrics can be used for the definition of the objective function(s), which are tool-dependent and managed by the COMPLEX toolset.

3.2.3 DSE Constraints

DSE constraints are logic expressions referring to one or more estimation parameters (that is, output metrics). When the simulation of an exploration cycle finishes, the COMPLEX toolkit reads the output performance metrics and evaluates the logic expression to check the validity of the design point. If the logic expression is proved to be false, the exploration tool discards this design point from the analysis space, since required constraints are not accomplished. For instance, the DSE constraint on the left hand side of Figure 6 states that the system power consumption, a platform performance metric, has to be fed to the DSE loop and that any design solution involving power consumption over 2W has to be discarded.

3.3 Environment Specification

The user can develop the environment model at the same abstraction level, clearly separating the system from the verification environment. Specifically, the user will enclose all UML elements modeling the environment within a specific view of the COMPLEX model: the *Verification view*.

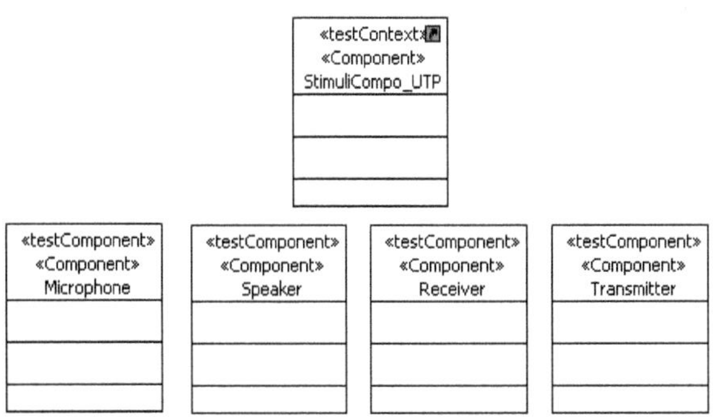

Figure 7. Declaration of Environment and test components in the Verification view.

As with other views of the COMPLEX modeling methodology, the verification view is modeled as a UML package, which, in this case, has the COMPLEX <<*VerificationView*>> stereotype applied. Using a UML element (i.e., a package), facilitates tool-independent separation of system and verification elements. The verification view declares the whole set of environment actors as a set of UML components with the UTP <<*testComponent*>> stereotype applied (bottom part of Figure 7).

An additional UML component, with the UTP <<*testContext*>> stereotype is used for the declaration of a verification environment (*StimuliCompo_UTP* in Figure 7).

The internal structure of this component, depicted in the composite diagram in Figure 8, reflects the interconnection among the system and environment component instances. Environment component instances are captured as UML properties typed as <<*testComponent*>> components. The system component is captured as a UML property typed as the system component of the architectural view of the COMPLEX methodology. Moreover, the system component instance has to be stereotyped with the UTP <<*SUT*>> (system under test) stereotype. Through this scheme a clear separation is established between the system element and the environment elements.

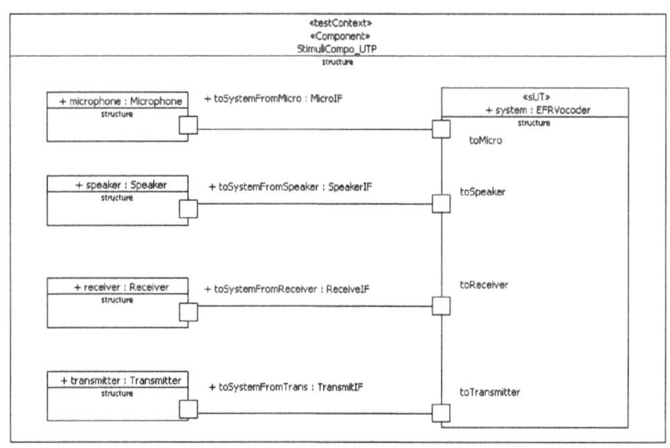

Figure 8. Environment structure for the EFR vocoder.

The composite diagram also shows the port-to-port connection. This interconnection defines which environment components provide the services required by the system. Similarly, it also serves to model which environment modules require the services provided by the system.

3.3.1 Modeling a Scenario

Relevant information about the environment includes how the environment elements are interconnected with the system, how the environment elements communicate with the system, that is, in which order and/or when services are called, and whether the system and environment are synchronized. The proposed methodology assumes separation of communication and computation, and the inclusion of functional behavior, more practical at the SystemC level, where the user can simply encrust functionality, e.g. by means of calls to functions of a reused library or by typing the algorithm within the automatically produced SystemC code. For the capture of this relevant information, the proposed methodology enables the specification of:

- A scenario which covers all the relevant interactions among the system and the whole environment for a given use case.
- Each interaction between an environment component and the system, as a totally ordered sequence of service calls, which can be synchronous or asynchronous.
- Compact specification of the interactions between the system and the components of the environment, indicating the physical ports supporting these interactions
- Ability to fix order relationships among messages exchanged by one or several environment components.

The scenario packages all the interactions over time between the system component and the environment components. A scenario is captured as a UML package stereotyped with the COMPLEX <<scenario>> stereotype. A <<scenario>> package has to be a child element of the verification view, that is, of the <<VerificationView>> package. In turn, the scenario package must include a UML component with the UTP <<testContext>> stereotype applied.

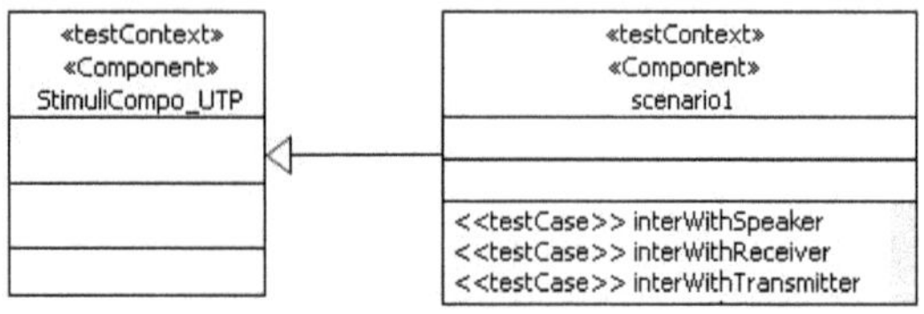

Figure 9. Generalization for referencing environment components in the modeling of each scenario.

As shown in Figure 9, this component must be declared as a specialization of the <<testContext>> component which reflects the generic structure of the system-environment interconnection (shown in Figure 8). In this way, environment component instances can be accessed and associated with UML lifelines, which are the UML elements used for specifying scenario interactions.

Moreover, Figure 9's inheritance relationship allows a future extension of the methodology, where the inheriting <<testContext>> component can redefine system-environment interconnection structure.

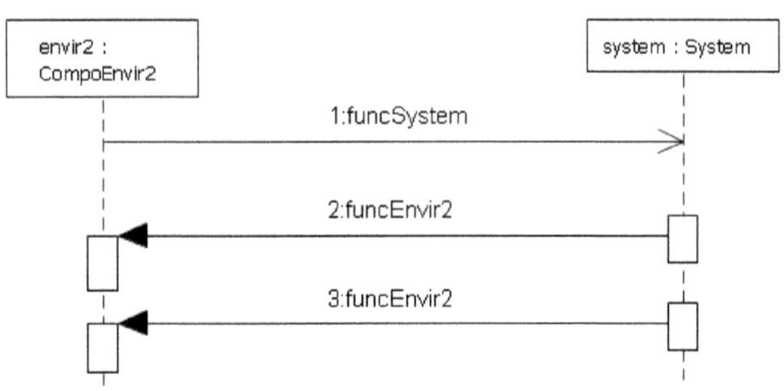

Figure 10. Sequence diagram for a port-to-port interaction.

Figure 10 shows a sequence diagram capturing the interaction between an environment component and the system component. One *lifeline* references the instance of the system component, while the other lifeline references an instance of one environment component. As explained, these references are feasible thanks to the specialization shown in Figure 9.

As well as the lifelines, the interaction diagram shows the set of UML messages exchanged between the system and the environment component. These messages represent function calls, such as services provided either by the system or by the environment. The sense of the messages (captured through the "from" and "to" attributes of the UML messages) state whether the system calls a function provided by the environment ("from=system") or, on the contrary, the environment requires a service provided by the system ("to=system").

Two different types of UML messages are used: synchronous messages and asynchronous messages. They enable the specification of synchronous and asynchronous services. Synchronous services require the return of the function call, e.g. because the client expects some output data from the service call. However, it might be interesting to specify service calls which just provide input data for the triggered service, and which immediately return to let either the system or the environment component go on executing. An UML synchronous message is represented by a bold arrow head (see Figure 10). UML asynchronous messages are shown by the other arrow heads.

The name of the message identifies which function is called. For instance, in the example in Figure 10, firstly the environment component calls a "funcSystem" service, provided by the System component. Next, the system calls twice the funcEnvir2 function provided by the system component. These functions must be part of the interface accessed through any of the environment component ports.

Although the sequence diagram graphically reflects a total order in the exchange of messages, this information is not contained in the UML interaction. Diagrams provide a graphical representation, but not all this graphical information is contained in the UML model (contained in a ".uml" file). This means that the .uml file read for SystemC code generation lacks information about the order of messages in a local interaction. Local interaction here refers to interaction between the system and a single environment component. Therefore, in the proposed methodology, a unique order identifier ("i:") prefixes the names of the messages exchanged at local level.

The user can specify all the interactions in a compact way. The messages in a sequence diagram can refer to functionalities of different ports in the environment component, and thus in the system. Moreover, one UML interaction can be used for specifying the interaction of the system with more than one environment component. Figure 11 shows a sequence diagram that specifies the communication between the system and two environment components.

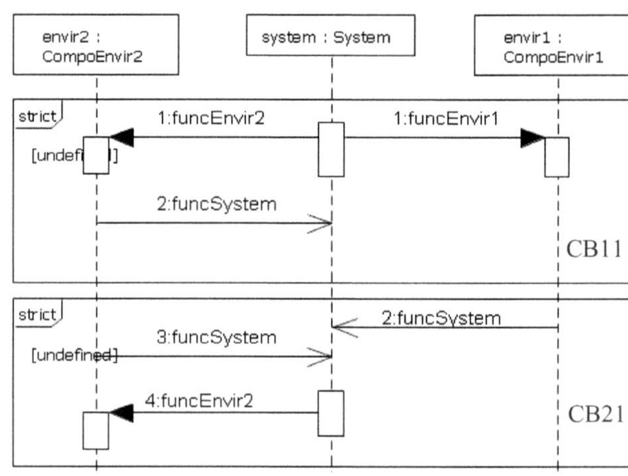

Figure 11. Two interactions in a single sequence diagram.

If the strict labeled boxes shown in the diagram in Figure 11 are removed, then the sequence of messages exchanged between the system and one environment component is not related to the sequence of messages exchanged between the system and another environment component. In other words, there are no order relationships among messages between the system and envir2 lifelines or messages between system and envir1 lifelines. That is, the i-th message in system-envir2 communication might happen before, at the same time, or after the j-th message in *system-envir1* communication.

However, many use cases will require environments with order constraints among interactions. In the proposed methodology, the user can specify order relationships among the messages exchanged by different environment components and the system. This is done by using UML CombinedFragments, shown as boxes in Figure 11. In this example a strict combined fragment is used for this purpose. The strict combined fragment groups the execution of the set of the messages it covers, so that all these messages have to be executed before or after the messages grouped in a different combined fragment. The execution of combined fragments has to be coherent with the total order specified for each interaction. Thus, local orders impose an order in the execution of the combined fragments.

For instance, in the example in Figure 11, the order of the envir2-system interaction messages implies that the strict combined fragment CB2 has to be executed after the strict combined fragment CB1. This, in turn, involves a partial order of messages, which includes ordering relationships among messages belonging to different interactions. In the diagram in Figure 11, "1:funcEnvir2" and "2:funcSystem" messages function calls will take place before the "2:funcSystem" call. Similarly, the diagram in Figure 11b) defines that "3:funcSystem" and "4:funcEnvir1" will always take place after 1:funcEnvir1.

The methodology also supports another two types of combined fragments. The "loop" combined fragment (loop) is used for specifying repetitive sequences of message exchanges. Thus, for instance, in the example in Figure 8, a "loop" combined fragment is used for specifying that the Microphone environment component sends a fixed number of frames (N) corresponding to a standard test. The "parallel" combined fragment (par) is used to model that certain groups of services either provided or required by the same environment component can be executed in parallel.

3.3.2 Modeling several scenarios

The proposed methodology supports the modeling of several scenarios. This support enables the capture in a single model of the stimuli associated with different use cases. As a result, it is possible to perform a DSE exploration for a specific use case or a set of use cases, and to tailor the design for this use case(s). Complementarily, a wide range of scenarios can be used to validate a single design for different use cases.

In order to specify several scenarios, the user only needs to specify a new scenario package, containing a test case component. This test case component generalizes the test case component and contains as many interactions as the user requires to describe the new scenario.

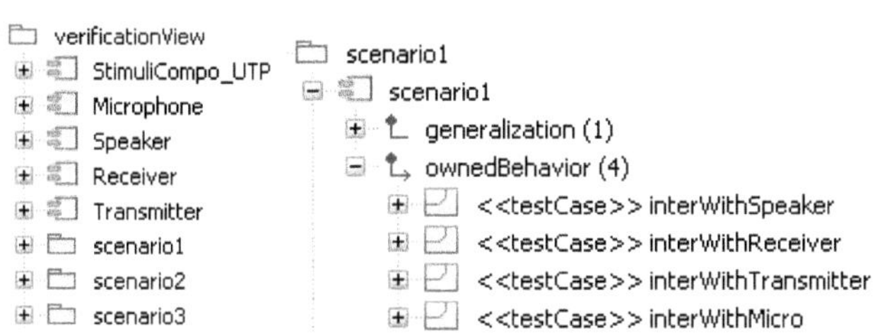

Figure 12. Several scenarios are supported.

3.3.3 Modeling physical time information

The features presented up to now enable the specification of a partial order of service calls in the environment. Formally speaking, this is the most abstract way to specify time constraints in the environment model. Furthermore, the proposed methodology enables the association of physical time information with the environment model. Specifically, the initiation of each service call can be placed in a specific physical time stamp. In order to specify it, the MARTE <<timedProcessing>> stereotype is used. This stereotype is applied to the UML message resembling the service call placed in physical time. The stereotype provides the attribute "start", which denotes a UML Time Event, which in turn, is placed in physical time through a UML Time Expression.

4. COMPLEX ECLIPSE APPLICATION

4.1 Introduction

The COMPLEX modeling methodology is supported by the COMPLEX Eclipse application (CEa) tool which provides an integrated framework for HW/SW co-design and design exploration (Figure 13). This tool is integrated within the Eclipse framework and makes extensive use of the Eclipse Modeling Framework (EMF) and Model-to-Text facilities.

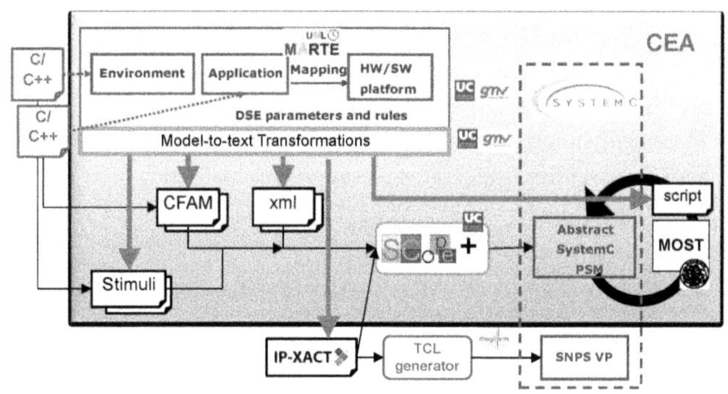

Figure 13. Sketch of the framework for the generation of the performance model from the UML/MARTE model.

This section aims to provide a summary of the most important features of the CEa tool for supporting the COMPLEX modeling methodology.

4.2 Main Features

The CEa tool is based on open-source standards and tools so it guarantees its compatibility with other existing development environments on the market. Interoperability, configurability and extendibility are the main features that drove the development of the tool.

The tool is built around the PapyrusMDT modeling environment. The COMPLEX Eclipse Application provides a set of features to support the COMPLEX methodology in:

- the development of the model and its compliance with the COMPLEX modeling rules;
- the generation and simulation of the executable model for performance analysis;
- a smooth integration with exploration tools, and the tool-independent configurability of the DSE.

Additionally, the tool affords analysis and transformation extension points by using the existing Eclipse features so that third party developers may add new analysis or transformation engines to the existing ones. This feature improves the extendibility of the tool by allowing new functions to be added to interface with other tools or methodologies.

Figure 13 shows the design flow in which the CEa tool is used. The UML/MARTE model is produced through the PapyrusMDT editor. The model describes the PIM, the PDM, the allocation of the application components into the existing computational resources, and the stimuli environment. Additional C/C++ source code can be used as input to the application and stimuli environment in the UML/MARTE model.

If the analysis engines installed in the tool do not trigger any errors, the tool generates the executable and configurable performance SCoPE+ model. The SCoPE+ simulation is triggered by the exploration tool (MOST), which collects the performance metrics and decides on the design alternatives to be explored.

4.3 Modeling Support Tools

As mentioned, Papyrus MDT is used as a UML (graphical) model editor with a set of interesting features:

- Support for editing any model compatible with the Eclipse Modeling Framework (EMF) model, in particular UML2 models and SysML
- Support for UML profiling by providing extensions to register UML-based profiles, such as the MARTE profile or the COMPLEX profile
- High customizability, in particular the modeling palette, feature highly appreciated by users

The CEa tool provides additional support for modeling:

- Automatic generation of the COMPLEX project structure (i.e. creating COMPLEX views)
- Implementation of a customized modeling palette that limits the set of the UML/MARTE design entities to a COMPLEX defined sub-set for the given model viewpoint and UML diagram type

Furthermore, model analyzers are provided, in order to check the correction of the model. Their need comes from the fact that the COMPLEX methodology makes use of a sub-set of the UML modeling entities and MARTE stereotypes for specifying the system and the stimuli environment. Then, the UML meta-model implemented using the EMF only validates the UML model checking its conformance with the OMG UML standard, so it is necessary to enforce that the given UML/MARTE model follows the modeling rules and constraints specified in the COMPLEX modeling.

By means of the CEa extension points for analysis, the CEa tool implements a set of analysis engines that focus their model checks on specific aspects of the system:

- Compliance of the UML/MARTE model with the COMPLEX component model
- Enforcement of the separation of concerns concept by verifying that all views define the right design entities
- Verification of the model consistency
- Identification of potential problems during the model-to-text transformation

Prior to the generation of the different output artifacts produced by the application in Figure 13, designers should execute each of the existing analysis engines. If any error is triggered by the tool, the transformation of the model is disabled.

4.4 Generation of the Performance Model

As shown in Figure 13, the process required to obtain the executable model able to produce the performance metrics is broken down into two main stages. In the first stage, a set of model-to-text transformation tools produce a text-based representation of the COMPLEX UML/MARTE model. In the second stage, a framework called SCoPE+, an evolution of SCoPE [6], reads the text-based description and generates the executable and configurable performance model.

4.4.1 COMPLEX Code Generation tools

COMPLEX code generators are integrated with the CEa tool through the existing transformation extension point. The transformation is performed using the *Acceleo* model-to-text transformation engine (http://www.acceleo.org). This code generates a set of files, containing the following artifacts:

- The application source code skeletons, in C/C++, which can be completed by the user with the actual implementation code. Note that the tool generates the necessary stub code to simulate the actual code with the non-functional information included in the model.
- The application component containers and connectors, supported by the *CFAM* simulation infrastructure (see section 4.4.1) that wraps the application functional code and implements the non-functional concerns of the provided operations of the application component (i.e. cyclic execution of the application functions, service dispatching).
- The *XML* files that configure the analysis tool (i.e. SCoPE+). These files contain different sections, including the description of the hardware architecture and the architectural mapping. The design space is also described by means of XML files.
- The C/C++ source code skeletons of the functionality of the stimuli environment and component structure of the *stimuli* environment in SystemC.
- The IP-XACT specification of the hardware platform description that will serve as input to generate the virtual platform on which the application will be executed.

The usage of the different formats for describing the different aspects of the model, including the system and the environment, makes the CEa application portable to different performance analysis frameworks.

4.4.2 SCoPE+

In COMPLEX, an extension of the previous SCoPE infrastructure has been developed in order to provide all the features required to support all the DSE possibilities covered by the UML/MARTE modeling methodology. The resulting simulation framework, used to obtain the performance metrics has been called SCoPE+.

The original SCoPE infrastructure [6][7][8] is a framework able to perform fast co-simulation of complex HW/SW embedded systems based on native simulation technology and able to estimate a wide set of performance figures. SCoPE relies on native simulation technology. It is able to consider SW and HW layers of a complex platform. It handles an abstract model with both the CPUs and the RTOS, and it internally builds a TLM2 model of the platform, which can cover MPSoC with NoC architectures. This abstraction enables native simulation achieving performance metrics faster than other simulation technologies, such as RTL, ISS or virtualization approaches (i.e., QEMU is about 5 to 20 times slower than native code execution [9]), and still provides accurate results (error less than 10%). This makes native simulation suitable for time-approximate functional validation and fast exploration of a wide design space, while other simulation techniques can be exploited in later design phases, e.g. for SW debugging and design verification. Furthermore, high-level HW component models can be included to take into account

HW/SW interaction. In [7], the XML front-end is presented. An XML structure file is defined to completely describe embedded systems, automatically generating an adequate native simulation model. Moreover, SCoPE executables do not require recompilation between iterations of the design exploration loop [8]. All these features make SCoPE a suitable basis for a performance analysis technique for DSE.

However, current native simulation techniques, including SCoPE, still present important issues in order to enable estimation and exploration of platform-independent codes.

The first main issue is the lack of a system-level front-end which avoids implementation refinements in the DSE loop. Most of these refinements might not be used in later implementation phases, which would make the DSE loop inefficient and slow. When the DSE flow relies on performance estimation technologies, a non-negligible refinement effort is required. Most of the refinement effort is related to communication codes, which explicitly handles peripheral memory addresses, and OS services for communication. Therefore, the first main requirement to enable fast native simulation tools for a system-level performance estimation methodology is to provide a high-level implementation-independent front-end to describe the PIM.

The second issue is related to the generation of a single static object code in native simulation technology. In native simulation, the annotations of the performance impacts associated with a specific piece of code are integrated together with the same code in the object file. This object file models only an allocation, that is, an implementation of the functionality. However, DSE needs to explore the effects of executing a single functionality on different processing resources (e.g. different processor types, or a custom HW implementation).

Additionally, the third issue is related to the need to simulate a performance model build of a component-based PIM, where PIM components can be allocated to different platform resources. The component-based PIM enables a client-server communication which, at a platform-independent level, means a chaining of function calls which can traverse different components. That is, an execution flow can correspond to different components allocated to different resources. The modeling of the performance impact of this is not supported by the usual OS models developed for native simulation.

SCoPE+, the simulation and performance estimation infrastructure developed in COMPLEX has features for covering these limitations.

4.4.2.1 High-Level Component-based Modeling
SCoPE+ provides the CFACM (Concurrent Functional Application Component Model) front end. The CFACM front end is a layer which is on top of the SCoPE simulation kernel and enables text-based and component-based description of the PIM. The CFAM infrastructure also implements all non-functional properties declared in the component interfaces.

As mentioned in section 4.4.1, the CFAM code is automatically produced from the COMPLEX UML/MARTE model. This code calls and hides the code of the simulation infrastructure which models and takes into account the performance impacts of the interactions among components, which depend on the platform and architectural mapping modeled. This is combined with simulation and estimation of the performance impacts of the user-provided functional codes, as was already possible in SCoPE.

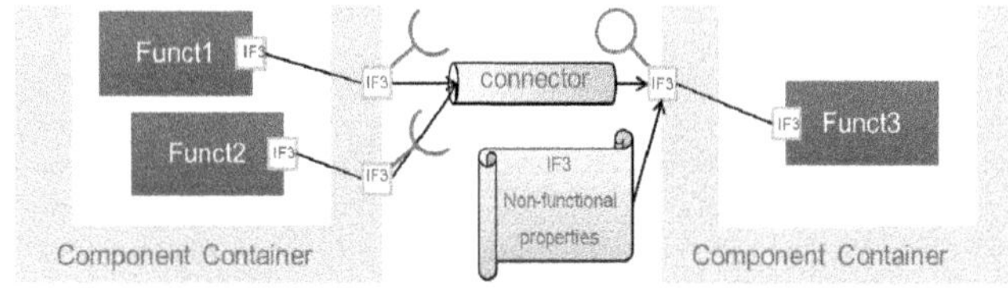

Figure 14. The CFAM API enables a Component-based description of the SCoPE+ performance model.

4.4.2.2 Integration of different annotations
SCoPE+ automatically builds interconnection wrappers for the components. For each component, a set of protected dynamic libraries (i.e., using the –fvisibility=protected gcc flag) is produced. Each dynamic library reflects a possible allocation of the component to a processing resource (e.g., an allocation to a processor reflecting a SW solution, or an allocation to an FPGA reflecting a HW refinement). The dynamic library to be loaded and simulated depends on the allocation described by the simulated design solution. Each dynamic library contains object code with the annotations accounting for the performance impact of the given allocation. SW simulation is done through existing SCoPE native simulation. HW allocation is estimated through a novel HW estimation technique [11]. As a result, instead of a static executable, the executable performance model is composed of precompiled dynamic libraries. This makes it possible to perform the compilation of the annotated code once, and carry out the generation of the executable performance model used during each iteration of the DSE as a load of dynamic libraries, which is significantly faster, as well as allowing different implementation solutions (allocations) of the same component to be explored.

4.4.2.3 Communication Modeling
In the client-server methodology proposed, communications among different resources are generated to support all possible resource allocations. Communication modeling is divided into three steps: detection of the time when the communication is performed; identification of the communication path through the HW resources involved; and estimation of the amount of information transferred. Communication wrappers are automatically generated from the UML model. These wrappers indentify the client and server resources involved and start the communication modeling procedure if required. Finally, the communication path is automatically extracted from the HW platform description, and modeled as accesses to the SystemC code which model communication resources. Thus, delays and bottlenecks are modeled and can be identified.

4.4.2.4 Modeling of Execution flows
Since platform-independent functional codes are used in the simulation, we have to consider that the execution flows (threads or processes) resulting in the simulation and the final implementation are different. As a result, the same execution flow can execute chained function calls that can be allocated to different HW resources. Thus, execution flows can traverse different HW resource models and even OS models. To support this, SCoPE+ provides a simulation engine which works as a global operating system model, controlling all the system resources (processors and programmable HW). This global OS contains all the system resources (processes, threads, OS services,

etc) used by the application. Additionally, thread and processes have an affinity mask that indicates in which resources the element can run. This mask is automatically changed when a function allocated to a different resource is requested.

4.5 Integration with Exploration Tools

As a result of all the new features presented in the previous sections, it is possible to use the automatically generated SCoPE+ model to automatically explore different allocations of components considering the processors and operating systems in the model using pure algorithmic codes, without requiring any intervention from the designer. Moreover, the CEa framework facilitates full automation of the DSE loop. It integrates the SCoPE+ model and the exploration tool by means of several features:

- Configuration of the Exploration from the GUI
- Automated generation of the corresponding scripts from the COMPLEX Eclipse Application.
- Triggering from the CEa menu of the Exploration
- Communication between the underlying exploration tool (MOST [10]) and the performance analysis tool (SCoPE+) through an XML based interface

The CEa application enables a novel user perspective for the configuration of the exploration, e.g. selecting the metrics used in the optimization functions, and describing the optimization goals. Additionally, it also enables an advanced mode, where the user can directly edit the exploration script. CEa lets the full DSE loop be run through a menu option. It calls the scripts which trigger the MOST exploration tool. No further user intervention is required for the execution of the DSE loop. As shown in Figure 13, the exploration tool (MOST) takes over the exploration, decides on the design points explored, launches the SCoPE+ model and collects the resulting performance figures.

SCoPE+ supports an XML interface in which the exploration tool has been extended. Through this XML front-end, a SCoPE executable performance model can (a) receive system configurations as a set of parameters decided by the exploration tool, which takes over Design of Experiments (DoE), and (b) return information to the exploration tool for Response Surface Modeling (RSM). The XML based interface has been kept simple from the exploration perspective; the configuration of the model only requires sweeping through configuration parameters. This provides the generality of the XML interface and thus the portability of the CEa application to other exploration tools. At the same time, in the COMPLEX framework, not only can attributes be swept (such as memory sizes, work frequencies, etc), but so too can sweeps through different architectural mappings or different scenarios.

5. CONCLUSIONS

This paper has presented a COMPLEX UML/MARTE-based methodology, which demonstrates that a fast and sufficiently accurate assessment of the design solutions of a system is possible, starting from a high-level model which can later be reused for other design activities, e.g., verification and implementation. The solution described relies on a novel UML/MARTE specification methodology, which supports the description of a space of design solutions, and moreover, different environment conditions. An automated, tool-assisted and portable flow enables the generation of fast and configurable performance models, which can be driven by exploration tools.

6. ACKNOWLEDGMENTS

This work has been supported by the 247999 COMPLEX FP7 European Integrated Project [1], and the Spanish TEC2011-28666-C04-02 MCI project.

7. REFERENCES

[1] The COMPLEX project (247999), "Codesign and power management in platform-based design space exploration," http://complex.offis.de.

[2] E. Alana, F. Ferrero, A. I. Rodriguez, R. Valencia, E. Conquet, J. Puente, J. Zamorano, F. Herrera, and R. Varona, "Component-based technologies for HW/SW co-design," in Embedded Real Time Software and Systems- ERTS2. Toulouse. France, February 2012.

[3] F.Herrera, P. Peñil, E. Villar, F. Ferrero, and R.Valencia, "An embedded system modeling methodology for design space exploration," in III Jornadas de Computacion Empotrada, I Jornadas SARTECO, Oct 2012.

[4] F.Herrera, P. Peñil, H. Posadas, and E. Villar, "A model-driven methodology for the development of SystemC executable environments," in Proceedings of Forum of Design Languages, FDL'2012, Sept 2012.

[5] F.Herrera, P. Peñil, E. Villar, and D. Calvo, "Enhanced ip-xact platform descriptions for automatic generation from UML/MARTE of fast performance models for DSE," in 15th Euromicro Conference on Digital System Design, DSD'2012, Sept 2012.

[6] H. Posadas, S. Real, E. Villar: "M3-SCoPE: Performance Modeling of Multi-Processor Embedded Systems for Fast Design Space Exploration", in C. Silvano, W. Fornaciari & E. Villar (Eds.): "Multi-objective Design Space Exploration of Multiprocessor SoC Architectures: the MULTICUBE Approach", Springer, 2011.

[7] P. Botella, P. Sánchez and H. Posadas: "Automatic Generation of SystemC SMP Models for HW/SW Co-Simulation". In proc. of XXV Conf. on Design of Circuits and Integrated Systems, DCIS'10, 2010.

[8] H. Posadas, G. de Miguel, E. Villar: "Automatic generation of modifiable platform models in SystemC for Automatic System Architecture Exploration ", In Proc. of Design of Circuits and Integrated Systems, DCIS' 2009, Zaragoza, Spain. 2009-11.

[9] M. Becker, T. Xie, W. Mueller, G. Di Guglielmo, G. Pravadelli and F. Fummi: "RTOS-Aware Refinement for TLM2.0-Based HW/SW Designs", in proc. of DATE'10, IEEE, 2010.

[10] G. Palermo, C. Silvano, and V. Zaccaria, "Respir: a response surface-based Pareto iterative refinement for application-specific design space exploration," Trans. Comp.-Aided Des. Integ. Cir. Sys., vol. 28, no. 12, pp. 1816–1829, Dec. 2009. Available in http://dx.doi.org/10.1109/TCAD.2009.2028681.

[11] P. González, P. Sánchez, J. González. "Hardware Performance Estimation by Dynamic Scheduling". In Proc. Of FDL'2011. Sept., 2011.

Software Energy Optimization Through Fine-Grained Function-Level Voltage and Frequency Scaling

Carlo Brandolese
Politecnico di Milano
P.zza L. da Vinci, 32 – Milano (Italy)
brandole@elet.polimi.it

William Fornaciari
Politecnico di Milano
P.zza L. da Vinci, 32 – Milano (Italy)
fornacia@elet.polimi.it

ABSTRACT

This paper presents a methodology and a toolchain to perform estimation and optimization of the energy consumption associated to software execution on tiny embedded systems. The estimation phase is based on an ISA-level characterization of the target processor, while the optimization phase is made combining the estimation process with design space exploration in order to exploit fine-grained dynamic voltage and frequency scaling. The proposed approach operates at compile-time, with the granularity of single C functions and almost automatically augments the source code.

Categories and Subject Descriptors

C.4 [**Computer Systems Organization**]: Performance of systems; C.3 [**Computer Systems Organization**]: Special-Purpose and Application-Based Systems; C.0 [**Computer Systems Organization**]: Modeling of computer architecture; B.8.2 [**Performance and Reliability**]: Performance Analysis and Design Aids

General Terms

Design, Performance

Keywords

Power Optimization, Embedded Systems

1. INTRODUCTION

Traditionally, software consumption estimation is performed with energy- and cycle-accurate instruction-set simulators. These simulators are precise, but very computationally demanding and not useful to determine the consumption information of source-level entities. A first attempt to raise the abstraction level of the estimates [6] is made by coupling an ISS with coarse-grained estimates obtained with `gprof`, a profiling tool based on program counter sampling. This can resolve costs at the function level, but not at finer elements. The approach is good for obtaining rough estimates or comparing strongly different algorithms, but not helpful for optimization: experience shows that most of the time is spent inside loops entirely contained in one function, and the approach cannot resolve at that resolution. Splitting critical loops in functions just to allow measurement is not a solution because it seriously perturbs the estimates.

Another approach is the so-called compilation-based performance estimation. It exploits a real compiler (namely `gcc`) to obtain the control flow graph (CFG) of the code. The CFG is then annotated with information useful to derive a cycle-accurate model. SoftExplorer and similar tools implement a fast technique to estimate the consumption of data-dominated loops directly from the C source, based on functional-level modeling of the architecture and statistical parameters extracted from the assembly code. SIT is the first real 2-way source-level technique that redistributes estimates onto source-level entities, for the help of the developer. Here, like in our proposed approach, the source code is conceptually instrumented, though in a different way. More precisely, the input C code is promoted to C++ and overloaded instrumented versions of all the operators are provided. The estimation approach proposed in this this paper is an evolution of a methodology and its related toolchain already presented by the authors in a previous work [4]. Two are the major novelties of the models and of the toolchain described in this paper:

- The new methodology expresses the energy costs of the basic entities of the intermediate representation in term of effective capacitance, rather than as average current absorptions per clock-cycle. This choice allows accumulating energy figures independently from the actual clock frequency and core supply voltage. This approach is crucial for exploring different voltage/frequency operating modes, since it decouples the process of capacitance and timing characterization of individual functions from the actual computation of overall energy and time figures.

- The toolchain totally decouples the the estimation of the effective capacitance and the number of clock cycles for the execution of individual functions from the overall voltage and frequency dependent time and energy figures. In this way capacitance and number of clock cycles associated to the execution of a function operating on fixed data can be calculated once and for all in a first phase, while leaving to a second post-processing step the actualization of such figures for function-specific frequencies and voltages.

CODES+ISSS'12, October 7-12, 2012, Tampere, Finland.

The core part of this paper concerns energy optimization, and in particular a methodology to exploit voltage and frequency scaling capabilities of the target core. The proposed approach is targeted to small, constrained embedded application built in absence of an operating system and combines the estimation methodology described so far—implemented by the SWAT toolchain—with an optimization tool for design space exploration—the MOST optimization engine—both developed at Politecnico di Milano.

The key idea is to explore possible assignments of operating modes to individual functions, find the optimal assignment, and (almost) automatically augment the source code of the functions in such a way that mode switching is performed by the function themselves.

2. MODELS

2.1 Estimation model

The basic ideas supporting the proposed approach have been explored by the authors in previous works [3] and finalized in [4]. The new approach described in this paper uses an intermediate representation based on the assembly-level LLVM code produced by the open-source project *LLVM Compiler Infrastructure* [2]. The modeling approach described in the following mimics the methodology proposed in [4], but uses the concept of effective capacitance to express the basic energy figures on which the estimation is founded. The estimation is decomposed in three subsequent phases:

1. *Source code modeling.* This first modeling phase decouples the influence of the *static structure* of the source code from the specific target architecture, from its dynamically varying operating conditions (voltage and frequency) and from the input runtime data.
2. *Dynamic behavior modeling.* The dynamic behavior is introduced in the model through basic-block profiling at intermediate-representation level (i.e., LLVM code). Such a profiling can be accomplished by executing the code on a host machine, possibly resorting to some support libraries that model hardware devices.
3. *Target machine modeling.* Finally, the actual timing and energy characteristics of the target architecture are combined with static and dynamic models to derive the final estimate. To this purpose it is necessary to derive a target-specific cost model of the LLVM instruction set and characterize the voltage and frequency transitions supported by the core under consideration.

2.1.1 Source code and dynamic models

Given a *program run*, that is the combination of a program and a specific set of input stimuli, let $c^{(e)}$ and $c^{(t)}$ be consumed energy and the time necessary for its execution. The LLVM intermediate representation can be seen as a list of basic-blocks, each constituted by LLVM instructions of different types. Let B be number of basic blocks and L be the number of instructions composing the pseudo-assembly LLVM instruction set. The *representation matrix* $\mathbf{R} = [R_{i,j}]$ describes the combination of instructions belonging to each basic block. More precisely, $R_{i,j} = n$ means that the i-th basic block contains n LLVM instructions of type j. The matrix $\mathbf{R}$ is thus a *static representation* of the source code. Note that, for the purpose of this model, the ordering of instructions within a basic block is not relevant. More accurate models proposed in literature also account for inter-instruction effects, and thus require to know the exact ordering of instructions in the program. In order to be as independent as possible from the actual target processor and instruction set, the approach described here operates directly on the LLVM intermediate code, which will be translate into the target code in a subsequent phase. This prevents obtaining information about the actual ordering of target instructions. Inter-instruction effects at the LLVM level are thus irrelevant since show extremely limited correlation—if any—with the effect associated to the final translation. The instrumentation process is performed by adding suitable tracing function calls to each basic-block. The instrumented program is then compiled, linked and run on the host machine. As a result, a profile $p = [\, p_1\, p_2\, \ldots\, p_B \,]$ is generated. In such a profile p_i indicates the execution count of the i-th basic-block. Combining the profile p and the representation matrix $\mathbf{R}$, the vector of execution counts of all instruction types is obtained. Mathematically:

$$s = p \cdot \mathbf{R} = [\, s_1\; s_2\; \ldots\; s_L \,] \tag{1}$$

where s_j is the overall execution count of the instruction of type j in the specific program run under consideration. Since each instruction of the intermediate language corresponds to one ore more assembly instructions executed by the target architecture, the evaluation of the overall cost of a program run requires decomposing the intermediate instructions into such elementary contributions. The elementary operations considered at this stage depend on the target architecture model and more precisely on the target assembly language. Let K be the number of instructions of the target assembly language and $\mathbf{T} = [T_{i,j}]$ be the *translation matrix* with L rows corresponding to the types of LLVM instructions, and K columns corresponding to the different target assembly instructions. The element $T_{i,j} = n$ models the fact that the LLVM instruction of type i requires n instruction of type j of the target assembly. Of course, the exact form of the target code resulting from the translation of an LLVM instruction cannot be known in advance. This is due to two main reasons. First of all, the LLVM code is in static single assignment (SSA) form, and thus uses an unlimited number of virtual registers, while the actual code will be limited by the number of register available on the target architecture. This limitation of the available registers will result in memory spilling, that is, additional load/store instructions. Secondly, even though the first pass of the LLV-to-target code translation is deterministic and template-based, the subsequent optimization pass will strongly modify the code. For these reasons, the translation matrix has a statistical meaning only. This matrix is the result of the characterization phase, described in in Section 2.1.2 and can be also viewed as a collection of L row vectors T_i. Each vector represents the *statistical translation model* of a specific LLVM instruction. Indicating with $\mathcal{L}_m$ the LLVM instruction of type m and with $\mathcal{T}_i$ the target assembly instruction of type i, the cost of $\mathcal{L}_m$ for the specific target architecture is:

$$\text{cost}(\mathcal{L}_m) = \sum_{i=1}^{K} T_{m,i} \cdot \text{cost}(\mathcal{T}_i) \tag{2}$$

The target processor is supposed to be characterized in terms of execution time and energy consumption with the granularity of single assembly instruction. It is worth noting that, while the actual average execution time of each instruction in generally known and publicly available, the energy consumption is often not known or not available for single instructions. In this case, accepting a loss of accuracy, average energy consumption figures can also be used. The proposed model, in fact, only accounts for such figures in the final phase. This decouples the formal static and dynamic modeling phases from the final physical characterization.

Each target instruction $\mathcal{T}_i$ is thus characterized by its average execution time n_i, expressed in clock cycles, and its effective capacitance c_i, expressed in farad. Furthermore, the instantaneous operating conditions of the microprocessor—referred to as *mode* in the following—is characterized by the power supply voltage and the clock frequency. Indicating with $\mathcal{M}_j$ a mode of the core, let V_j and f_j be the corresponding voltage and frequency respectively. The execution time and energy of instruction $\mathcal{T}_i$ in mode $\mathcal{M}_j$ are thus:

$$K_{i,j}^{(t)} = \frac{n_i}{f_j} \qquad K_{i,j}^{(p)} = \frac{1}{2} c_i V_j^2 f_j \tag{3}$$

Combining these expressions, finally, gives the energy consumption f instruction $\mathcal{T}_i$ in mode $\mathcal{M}_j$:

$$K_{i,j}^{(e)} = K_{i,j}^{(p)} K_{i,j}^{(t)} = \frac{1}{2} c_i V_j^2 n_j \tag{4}$$

Timing and energy figures for each target instruction i and each processor mode j are thus collected into two matrices $\mathbf{K^{(t)}}$ and $\mathbf{K^{(e)}}$. The current operating mode m of the processor is represented by means of the *mode selection* vector $M_m = [\ \mu_{m,j}\ ]$, where $\mu_{m,j} = 1$ if $m = j$ and 0 otherwise. Combining all equations derived so far gives the total execution time and energy consumption of the task:

$$c_m^{(e)} = p \cdot \mathbf{R} \cdot \mathbf{T} \cdot \mathbf{K^{(e)}} \cdot \text{diag}(M_m) \tag{5}$$

$$c_m^{(t)} = p \cdot \mathbf{R} \cdot \mathbf{T} \cdot \mathbf{K^{(t)}} \cdot \text{diag}(M_m) \tag{6}$$

These equations summarize our estimation methodology.

2.1.2 *Target Architecture Characterization*

The model described in the previous section relies on several matrices that need to be determined by means of a suitable procedure, in particular:

- **R**. The representation matrix is determined by the front-end portion of the toolchain described in Section 4. The source code is compiled into LLVM code, which is in turn transformed into a model file describing the mix of LLVM instructions per each basic block.

- **T**. The translation matrix is constructed by juxtaposition of the translation model vectors T_i for each LLVM instruction. Such vectors express the static correlation between the mix of instructions used by the LLVM compiler and the actual mix of assembly instructions generated by the target compiler. The procedure adopted to determine the individual translation model vectors is the core topic of this section.

- n_i, c_i. These figures are provided by the target architecture manufacturer. They express, for each instruction of the target assembly, the average execution time in clock cycles and the effective capacitance.

- p. The profile vector models the dynamic behavior of an application run, i.e. a program and a specific set of input data. It is derived by the back-end portion of the toolchain, as described in Section 4.

In this section we shortly describe the methodology used to determine the translation vectors for each LLVM instruction $\mathcal{L}_m$. This procedure has been described in detail in [4].

The key idea of the methodology consists in computing the correlation between the counts of each LLVM instruction of the LLVM-compiled code and the counts of the target instructions of the same code compiled with the target compiler. This requires first identifying a suitable, large enough, set $\mathcal{S} = \{S_0, S_1, \ldots, S_N\}$ of simple but varied source codes to be used for learning. Let then $L_{i,j}$ be the number of LLVM instructions of type j in the LLVM code corresponding to the source code S_i and $D_{i,k}$ be the number of target instructions of type k in the destination assembly code corresponding to the same source code S_i. The analysis of all source codes for each instruction leads to the over-constrained system:

$$L_{i,j} = \sum_{k=1}^{K} D_{i,k} \cdot x_{j,k} \tag{7}$$

in the $N \times K$ unknowns $x_{j,k}$. This set of equations can be rewritten in in matrix form as $\mathbf{L}_j = \mathbf{D}\mathbf{x}_j$ where $\mathbf{L}_j$ and $\mathbf{x}_j$ are vectors representing the LLVM instruction count and the coefficient of the desired model, respectively, and $\mathbf{D}$ is the matrix of target instruction counts over the entire set of source codes. Since it is not realistic to assume that *all* target instructions will participate in the translation of each single LLVM instruction, we restrict the set of target instructions that can contribute to the model of each specific LLVM instruction by defining an *initial model vector* $\mathbf{M_j} = \{m_{j,1}, m_{j,2}, \ldots, m_{j,K}\}$ of coefficients $m_{j,p} = \{0, 1\}$. A value $m_{j,p} = 1$ indicates that the target instruction of type p participates to the model of the LLVM instruction of type j. The general equation $\mathbf{L}_j = \mathbf{D}\mathbf{x}_j$ can be modified to include the initial model vector by simply transforming the vector $\mathbf{M_j}$ into a diagonal matrix and multiplying it by the coefficient matrix $\mathbf{D}$, that is:

$$\mathbf{L}_j = \mathbf{D}\,\text{diag}(\mathbf{M}_j)\,\mathbf{x}_j = \mathbf{D}_j'\mathbf{x}_j \tag{8}$$

A further restriction necessary to preserve the *physical* meaning of the mode is that the coefficients $\mathbf{x}_j$ must be positive. This requirement implies solving the problem of Equation 8 in *non-negative least-square sense*, that is:

$$||\mathbf{D}_j'\mathbf{x}_j - \mathbf{L}_j||_2^2 \quad \text{with} \quad \mathbf{x}_j \geq 0 \tag{9}$$

To this purpose, we adopted the method described in [1], Ch. 23, p. 161. Once the system has been solved, the translation matrix can be built as $T = [x_0^T\ x_1^T\ \cdots\ x_L^T]$.

2.2 Operating modes model

The target processors, as anticipated in Section 2.1, provides a set of operating modes, which will be referred to in the following as *explicit modes*. Each function can be assigned a specific explicit mode and, as a consequence, the toolchain will augment the C source code by inserting platform-specific library function calls devoted to switch to the selected mode on entering the function and back to the previous mode, on exiting. In addition to the explicit modes, we define the two *implicit modes* referred to as *force* and *inherit*, as described in the following.

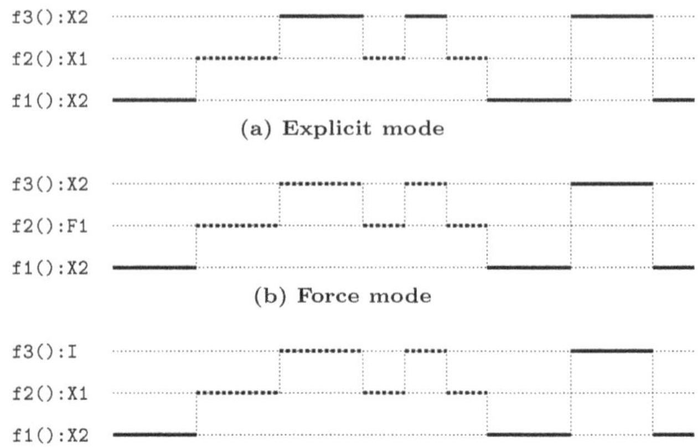

(a) Explicit mode

(b) Force mode

(c) Inherit mode

Figure 1: Mode assignment effects

Force. When the mode of a function is set to force to a specific explicit mode, all its callees will be executed in the same operating condition as the caller, regardless of their specific explicit assignments.

Inherit. The inherit mode has, in a sense, a dual meaning. It specifies that the mode of a function is not explicitly set, but is rather inherited from its caller.

These special modes provide a simple yet powerful means to have a function being executed in different modes, depending on its context, thus providing more flexibility to the approach. Let us consider, as an example, a task constituted by three functions `f1()`, `f2()` and `f3()` and target processor with two modes only: 1 and 2. The timing diagram of Figure 1 shows the effects of three different mode assignments on the processor operating conditions. In the figure, the labels `X1` and `X2` indicate explicit mode assignments, `F1` the force mode, and `I` the inherit mode. Furthermore, the solid line, indicates that a function is executed in mode 2 while the dotted line represents execution in mode 1.

A part from the obvious effects of explicit assignments shown in Figure 1-(a), it is interesting to observe the behavior resulting from forcing and inheriting modes. To this purpose we concentrate the attention on function `f3()`. When `f2()` forces the mode 1 and calls `f3()`, Figure 1-(b) shows that the explicit mode assignment of `f3()` is ignored. On the other hand, when called directly from `f1()`, `f3()` is executed in mode 2, as specified by its explicit assignment. Furthermore, observing the diagram in Figure 1-(c), it can be noted that the operating mode in which `f3()` is executed is always that of its caller. Though the behavior in these two last cases is the same, it is obtained in two dual ways: in the first case the caller imposes its mode to all callees, while in the second is the callee that delegated the decision on the operating mode to its caller.

3. OPTIMIZATION MODEL

The goal of the optimization is to find the assignment of a mode to each function in such a way to minimize the overall energy of a program run with a constraint on the maximum allowed time for the task. Let us now consider a call of function F_j from function F_i. Given a specific mode assignment $\mathcal{M}$, function F_i will be executed in mode m_i and function F_j in mode m_j. In the following we will indicate such a call with the notation:

$$[i, m_i] \rightarrow [j, m_j] \tag{10}$$

Section 2.1 provides the background for the estimation of an entire program run, but the same model, methodology and toolchain can be used to obtain cost estimates for individual functions. Let thus denote with $c^{(e)}_{k,m}$ and $c^{(t)}_{k,m}$ the energy and execution time of function F_k with the processor in operating mode m. Furthermore, let denote with $\tau^{(e)}_{m_i,m_j}$ and $\tau^{(t)}_{m_i,m_j}$ the energy and time associated with the transition from mode m_i to mode m_j. The total execution time and energy consumed for the execution of the call $[i, m_i] \rightarrow [j, m_j]$ with the mode assignment $\mathcal{M}$ can thus be expressed as:

$$T([i, m_i] \rightarrow [j, m_j], \mathcal{M}) = c^{(t)}_{j,m_j} + \tau^{(t)}_{m_i,m_j} + \tau^{(t)}_{m_j,m_i} \tag{11}$$

$$E([i, m_i] \rightarrow [j, m_j], \mathcal{M}) = c^{(e)}_{j,m_j} + \tau^{(e)}_{m_i,m_j} + \tau^{(e)}_{m_j,m_i} \tag{12}$$

Adding such total costs for all the calls executed by the task $\mathcal{T}$ gives the total execution cost of the task run, that is:

$$T(\mathcal{M}) = \sum_{[i,m_i]\rightarrow[j,m_j]\,\in\,\mathcal{T}} T([i, m_i] \rightarrow [j, m_j]) \tag{13}$$

$$E(\mathcal{M}) = \sum_{[i,m_i]\rightarrow[j,m_j]\,\in\,\mathcal{T}} E([i, m_i] \rightarrow [j, m_j]) \tag{14}$$

The optimization goal can now be formally stated as finding an assigmant $\mathcal{M}_{opt}$ such that:

$$E(\mathcal{M}_{opt}) = \min_{\mathcal{M} \in \mathcal{M}^*} E(\mathcal{M}) \quad \wedge \quad T(\mathcal{M}) < T_{max} \tag{15}$$

where $\mathcal{M}^*$ is the set of all possible assignments and T_{max} is the maximum execution time allowed for the task.

Considering N_M possible processor operating modes and N_F functions, the exact solution of the problem requires examining $N_M^{N_F}$ assignments. Given the exponential complexity, this problem becomes soon intractable. For 4 modes and 20 functions, for example, the number of assignments is close to 3.5 billions, which makes using a heuristic design space exploration approach necessary.

4. TOOL FLOW

This section describes the estimation and optimization flows. The former is detailed in [4], while the exploration methodology is described in [5].

4.1 Estimation

The implemented estimation flow is based on the LLVM compiler infrastructure, upon which a completely custom toolset called SWAT (*SoftWare Analysis Toolset*) has been developed. A simplified view of the portion of the flow strictly related to the estimation process necessary for the problem being studied in this paper is outlined in Fig. 2. The input is the set of C source files (`*.c`) collecting the code of task being considered, a model of the target CPU (`cpu.lib`) and an assignment of modes to functions (`task.modes`). Performing a sequence of transformations the flow produces the energy and time estimates T and E. Note that the mode assignment and the target processor model files are fixed.

The transformation performed by the tools of the flow have been collected into four *phases*, indicated by numbered black boxes, and are detailed in the following.

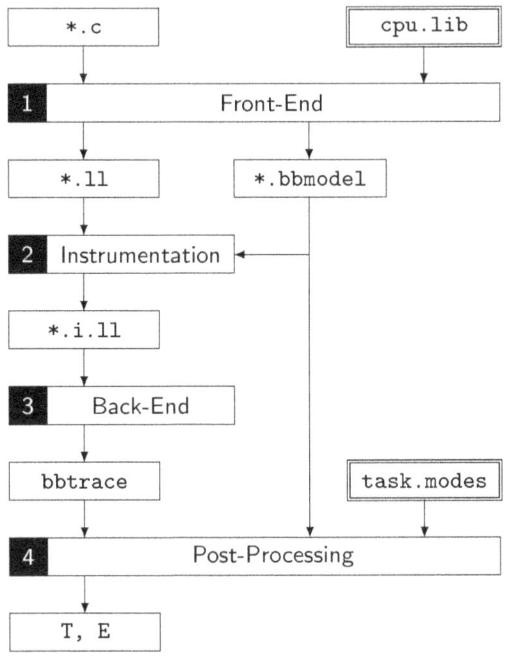

Figure 2: Simplified SWAT estimation flow

1. *Front-End.* This phase compiles each source file into architecture-independent LLVM assembly code, which is then used to build a model (`*.bbmodel`) of each basic block consisting of the list of op-codes, functions called, size, execution time in clock cycle and effective capacitance. Data for timing and energy characterization is in the *target CPU library* (`cpu.lib`), which is the result of characterization (Section 2.1.2).

2. *Instrumentation.* Instrumentation is performed by first enriching each basic block of the LLVM code with all the relevant figures in the form of a special comment (*meta-instrumentation*), then by translating the comments into actual calls to tracing functions based on *expansion rules* collected into an instrumentation library. The output of this phase is a new, instrumented, LLVM assembly file (`*.i.ll`).

3. *Back-End.* The back-end of the SWAT flow performs two main operations. First, it translates all the instrumented LLVM files into host assembly code, which is then assembled and linked into an executable program. Secondly, it runs the executable and collects the execution trace (`bbtrace`) consisting of a list of the identifiers of the basic blocks that have been executed.

4. *Post-Processing.* The post-processing phase analyzes the execution trace and combines the dynamic information with the static costs models, accounting for the specific operating modes specified in the allocation file (`task.modes`). This produces the total timing and energy of the specific run of the task.

This estimation flow is then combined with the optimization engine MOST that performs design space exploration over the possible mode assignment. It is worth noting that steps 1–3 of the estimation flow need not to be repeated for each and every assignment. They are, in fact, performed only

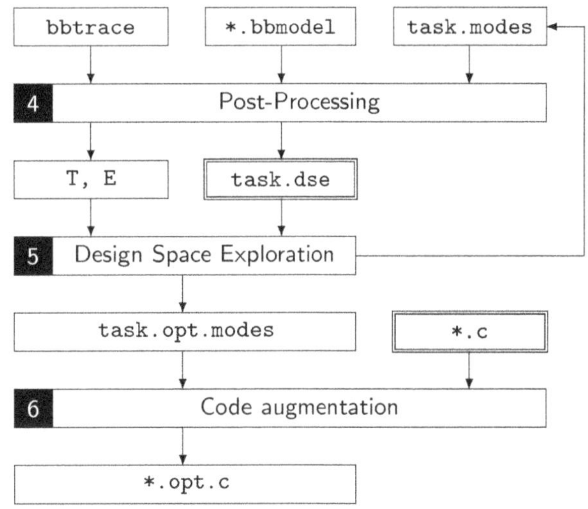

Figure 3: SWAT / MOST optimization flow

once with the goal of producing an execution trace and a set of cost models. Steps 1–3 (and in particular step 3, that involves task execution) are much more time-consuming than the post-processing phase only. The proposed toolchain is thus efficient enough to enable design space exploration with simulation-in-the-loop.

4.2 Optimization

The optimization flow, sketched in Fig. 3, is built around the design exploration engine MOST.

5. *Design Space Exploration.* This tool requires a configuration file (`task.dse`) specifying which are the parameters and which values each parameter can assume. In our case the parameter are the modes m_i of each functions and the values are integers in the range $[1; N_M]$ corresponding to the target processor modes. Based on this configuration, the DSE engine generates a specific mode assignment (`task.modes`) which is fed as input, together with the execution trace and the basic block models, to the SWAT post-processor. The execution time and energy estimated by SWAT are used by MOST to selects a new, potentially better, assignment. This loop is repeated until a satisfactory assignment (`task.opt.modes`) is found.

6. *Code augmentation.* Using a set of predefined macros and a simple code generator, this tool adds to the original source code, at the beginning and at the end of each functions, the suitable code performing mode switching. The augmentation mechanism is described in further detail in Section 4.3.

The two toolchains depicted in Fig. 2 and 3 have been used to produce the experimental results described in Section 5.

4.3 Code generation

The code generation is the last step of the optimization flow and its goal is to augment the original source code with calls to suitable—and user-definable—APIs devoted to changing the operating mode of the processor on entry and/or on exit of a function.

This process is currently semi-automated, as it requires adding two macros at the beginning and at the exit of each function that is considered in the exploration process. Considering, for example, a function:

```
int foo( int x, int y ) {
  // --------------------------
  // Declarations
  // --------------------------
  // --------------------------
  // Function body
  // --------------------------
  return some_var;
}
```

and assuming that the function as a single exit point, the only task left to the programmer is to modify the function definition as follows:

```
int foo( int x, int y ) {
  // --------------------------
  // Declarations
  // --------------------------
  VFS_ENTER(foo)
  // --------------------------
  // Function body
  // --------------------------
  VFS_EXIT(foo)
  return some_var;
}
```

The expansion of the two macros generates new code that depends in turn on other macros built based on the function name passed as argument, which, in our example, would be `VFS_MODE_foo`. Since functions can not only be assigned explicit modes, but also can be defined as forcing or inheriting the operating mode of caller/callee, it is necessary to implement a sort of *mode stack* where to save the mode of the current function before entering one of its callees and restore this mode on exit. Rather than using a separate stack, our mechanism is based on four entities, namely:

- A global variable `vfs_cm` storing the current mode. The variable is static in a support library that need to be compiled along with the application.
- A global variable `vfs_fm` indicating whether the current mode is being forced or if it is explicit/inherited. This variable is also static in the support library.
- A variable `vfs_sm`, local to each function, holding the saved mode, i.e. the current mode upon function entry.
- A macro `VFS_SET_MODE(m)` that is platform specific and will be expanded to a call to the suitable function exposed by the target API and responsible of changing the operating mode. Such a function will usually write the relevant CPU registers.

Thanks to the local variable added to each function, a separate stack for modes is not necessary as it is distributed into the activation frames of the function themselves. Using these variables and exploiting the macros, the code of the original function is transformed into that shown in Figure 4.

It is worth noting that, since macros are expanded before compile time, only one of the branches of the conditional constructs in the preamble will actually be compiled, the other being dead code. Although a minimal overhead is introduced by this mechanism, the macro-based approach tends to limit it to a minimum.

```
int foo( int x, int y ) {
  // --------------------------
  // Declarations
  // --------------------------
  int vfs_sm = vfs_getcm();
  if( VFS_MODE_foo > 0 ) {
    // Explicit mode
    if( vfs_getfm() == 0 ) {
      // Mode not being forced from caller
      vfs_setcm( VFS_MODE_foo );
    }
  } else if( VFS_MODE_foo < 0 ) {
    // Forces the mode to calless
    vfs_setcm( -VFS_MODE_foo );
    vfs_setfm( 1 );
  } else {
    // Inherits the mode of the caller
  }
  VFS_SET_MODE( vfs_getcm() )
  // --------------------------
  // Function body
  // --------------------------
  vfs_setcm( vfs_sm );
  VFS_SET_MODE( vfs_getcm() )
return some_var;
}
```

Figure 4: Example of augmented code

Parameter	Range
Number of functions	5 – 12
Average execution time of function (cycles)	5K – 50K
Average direct calls per function	5 – 10
Average calls in a loop per function	1 – 3
Average iterations of loops	10 – 50
Average conditional calls per function	1 – 5
Average probability of conditional calls	50% – 90%

Table 1: Synthetic code parameters

5. EXPERIMENTAL RESULTS

The experimental results presented here refer to a specific target processor, namely the STMicroelectronics ultra low power core ReISC 4. Since this core is still in development, timing and energy characterization is not yet publicly available. It has been disclosed to Politecnico di Milano under the agreement of the COMPLEX Project. For this reason, energy and timing figures appearing in the graphs of this section have been scaled by a constant factor in order not to disclose proprietary information. The ReISC 4 core provides dynamic voltage and frequency scaling capabilities over three different modes.

In order to validate the approach on a large number of differently structured tasks, synthetic code has been used. To this purpose a parametric tool for code generation has been developed. It can generate random programs based on the parameters summarized in Table 1 along with the ranges used to generate the specific tasks for which results are reported.

Let us start considering a simple example, with three functions only. In this case the possible assignments are $5^3 = 125$. Since the exploration engine do not perform an exhaustive analysis, much fewer assignments have been generated, as shown in the plot of Figure 5. As it can be noted, to a reduction of the execution time corresponds an increase in the energy consumption. In this example the execution

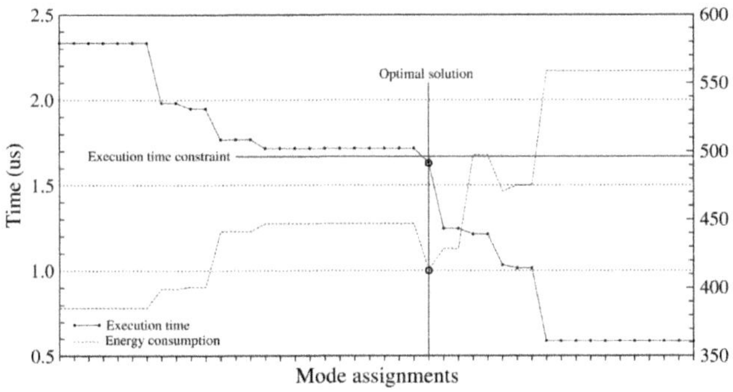

Figure 5: Energy and time for a 3-functions task

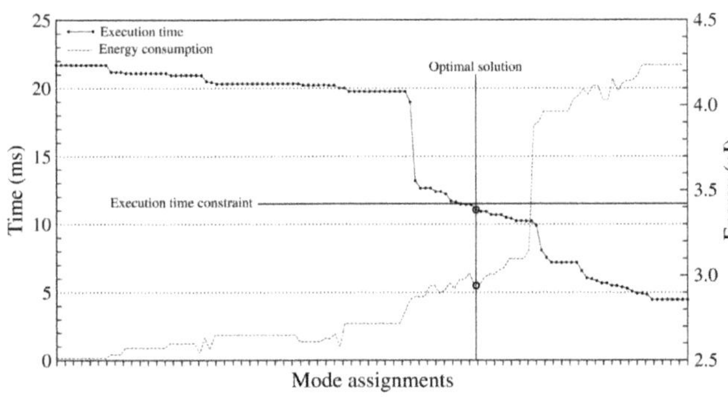

Figure 6: Average power for a 5-functions task

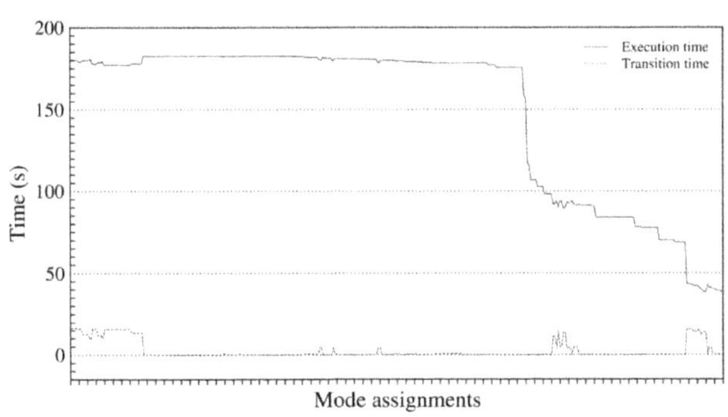

Figure 7: Execution and transition times

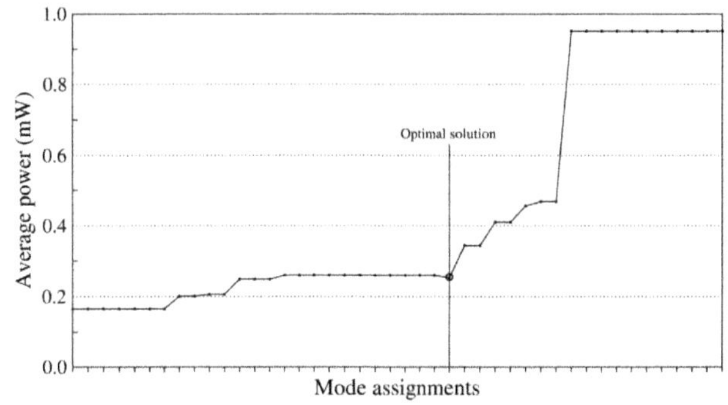

Figure 8: Average power for a 3-functions task

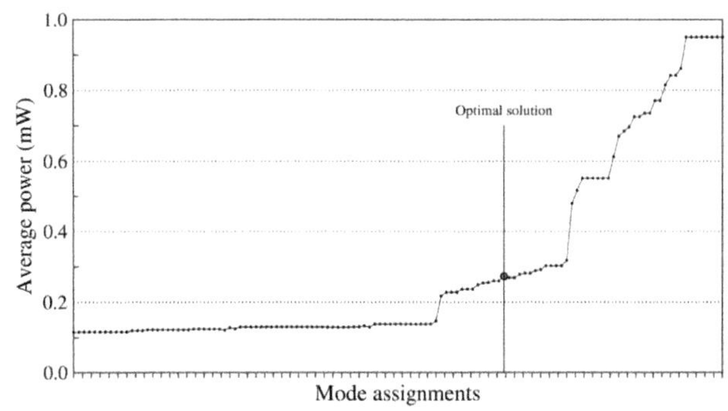

Figure 9: Average power for a 5-functions task

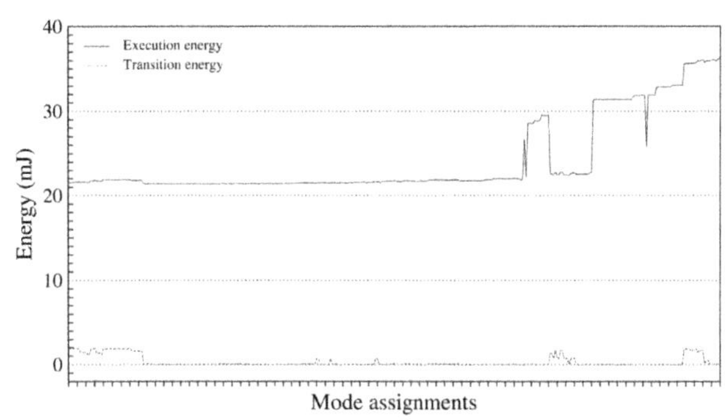

Figure 10: Execution and transition energies

time constraint was set to 1.65 μs. The solution found, highlighted in the plot was characterized by an execution time of 1.626 μs and an energy consumption of 412 nJ. This correspond to an average power consumption of 253 μW, as the plot of Figure 8.

The results of exploration applied to a more complex task are reported in Figures 6 and 9. The task analyzed is composed of 5 functions for an overall dynamic call count of 9782. In this case the time constraint was set to 11.5 ms and the optimal solution found has an energy consumption of 2.94 μJ and corresponds to an execution time of 11.15 ms.

The last results reported in detail refers to a much more complex task with 20 functions and an overall dynamic call count slightly greater than 1.49 million. It must be noted that in this case the portion of the design space of all possible assignments has been explored in a minimal part, that is in 3800 points out of the possible 9.53×10^{13}. As Figures 7 and 10 show for execution time and energy consumption, the overhead introduced by the operating mode transitions, though much smaller than the the figures associated to the actual execution of the task, cannot be neglected. In the worst cases, in fact, the timing overhead impacts on the overall execution time for 27.9%, while for the energy the impact in worst case is limited to 8.1%.

Finally, the results obtained applying the proposed optimization methodology to a set of 33 randomly generated tasks are reported in Figure 11. The plot shows the energy consumption of the optimized task (black bars) with that obtained maintaining the system either in the highest voltage/frequency mode (white bars) or in its deepest low-power modes. It must be noted that the optimized tasks—and of course the tasks run in full active mode—do respect their deadlines, while the tasks run in the lowest power mode do not. The energy gains obtained by the mode allocation tech-

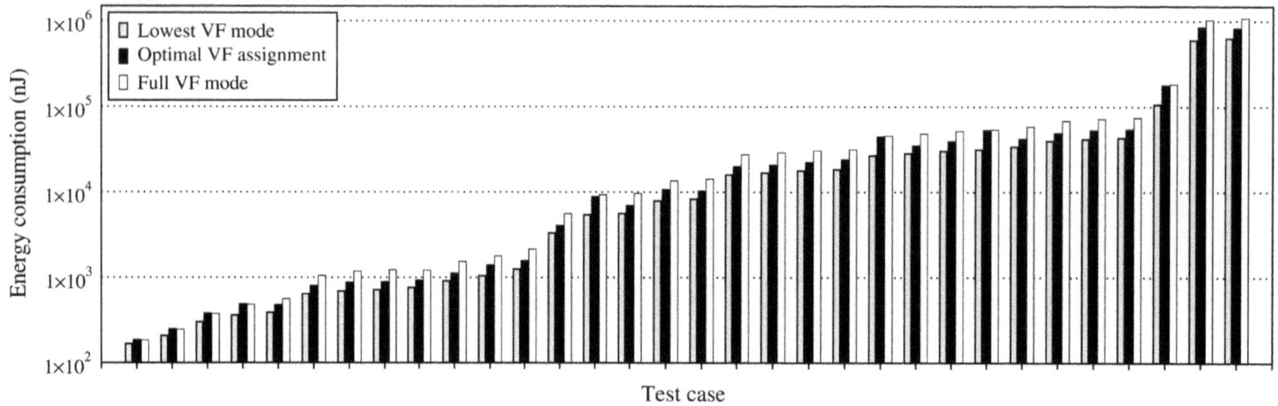

Figure 11: Absolute energy consumption comparison

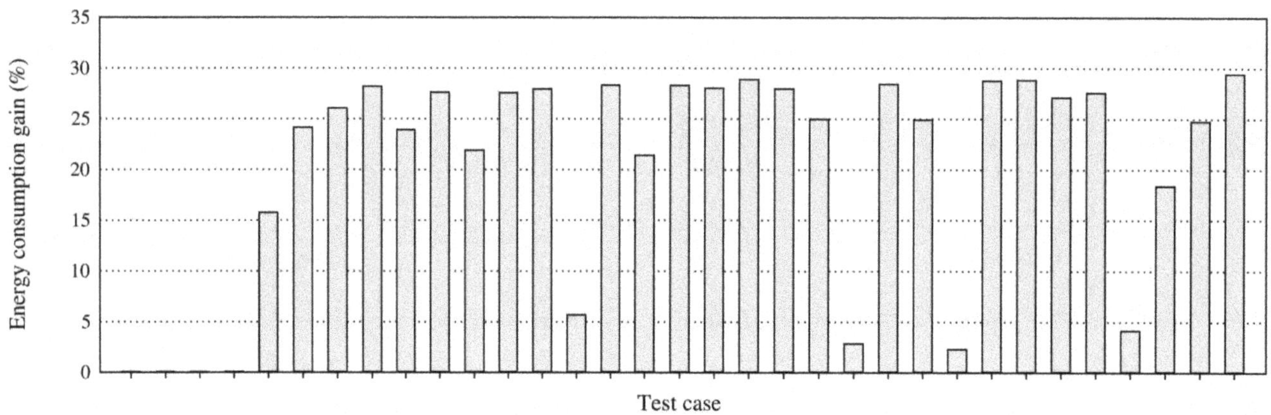

Figure 12: Energy consumption gains w.r.t full votage/frequency mode

nique with respect to the full active mode of the processor are shown in Figure 12, where a maximum energy saving of 29.4% can be observed. The average gain for the test cases considered is 20.1%.

6. CONCLUSIONS

This paper extended and adapted a previous estimation methodology to allow the analysis of execution time and energy consumption of software for processors supporting dynamic voltage and frequency scaling. The methodology has been implemented in the SWAT toolchain and integrated with the design exploration engine MOST to minimize the execution energy of a task under timing constraints by finding a sub-optimal assigments of operating modes to individual functions. The experimental results obtained on a large number automatically generated tasks show that an average 20% energy saving can be obtained, with only a trivial manual intervention on the source code.

Acknowledgements

This work has been partially supported by the EU integrated project COMPLEX under grant FP7-247999.

7. REFERENCES

[1] C. L. Lawson, R. J. Hanson, Solving Least-Squares Problems, Prentice-Hall, 1974.

[2] The LLVM Compiler Infrastructure, *http://www.llvm.org.*

[3] C. Brandolese, W. Fornaciari, D. P. Scarpazza, Source-Level Energy Estimation and Optimization of Embedded Software, *IEEE Latin America Symposium on Circuits and Systems, (LASCAS'10),* Foz do Iguazu, Paranà, Brazil, February 2010.

[4] C. Brandolese, S. Corbetta, W. Fornaciari, Software Energy Estimation Based on Statistical Characterization of Intermediate Compilation Code, *International Symposium on Low Power Electronics and Design, (ISLPED'Š11),* Fukuoka, Japan, August 2011.

[5] G. Palermo, C. Silvano, V. Zaccaria. Multi-Objective Design Space Exploration of Embedded Systems, In Journal of Embedded Computing. IOS Press, 1(3), January, 2006, pp. 305-316.

[6] T. Simunic, L. Benini and G. De Micheli, Energy-efficient design of battery-powered embedded systems, *IEEE Transactions on Very Large Scale Integration (VLSI) Systems,* Vol. 9, No. 1, pp. 15–28, 2001.

From RTL IP to Functional System-Level Models with Extra-Functional Properties

Daniel Lorenz,
Kim Grüttner
OFFIS Institute for Information Technology, Germany
{lorenz,gruettner}@offis.de

Nicola Bombieri,
Valerio Guarnieri
University of Verona, Italy
{nicola.bombieri, valerio.guarnieri}@univr.it

Sara Bocchio
STMicroelectronics, Italy
sara.bocchio@st.com

ABSTRACT

The paper presents a novel abstraction methodology for generating time- and power-annotated TLM models from synthesizable RTL descriptions. The proposed techniques allow the integration of existing RTL IP components into virtual platforms for early software development and platform design, configuration, and exploration. With the proposed approach, IP models can be natively integrated into SystemC TLM-2.0 platforms and executed 10-1000 times faster compared to state-of-the-art RTL simulators. The abstraction methodology guarantees preservation of the behaviour and timing of the RTL models. Target technology dependent power properties of IP components are represented as power state-machines and integrated into the abstracted TLM models. The experimental results show a relative error less than 10% of the abstracted model's power consumption compared to state-of-the-art RTL power simulators. The evaluation has been performed on RTL IP components with different characteristics and demonstrates the effectiveness of the presented abstraction methodology.

Categories and Subject Descriptors

B.8.2 [**Performance and Reliability**]: Performance Analysis and Design Aids; C.4 [**Performance of Systems**]: Modeling techniques

General Terms

Design, Measurement, Performance

Keywords

HW/SW Timing and Power Simulation, Virtual Prototypes, RTL to TLM Abstraction

1. INTRODUCTION

Development costs of a state-of-the-art System on Chip (SoC) can be over 80 million US$ and this cost is rising rapidly. 60% of this cost is labour and the major part of the overall development cost is verification. For the reduction of integration and verification costs, a bottom-up solution is silicon-proven IP, for example configurable processors. Well-proven IP has a high potential to significantly reduce the verification task. The technique of silicon-proven verified IP can also be extended to complete SoC subsystems.

Another emerging technology is Transaction-Level Modelling (TLM) based design and verification. To simulate complex applications on today's platforms, abstract and high performance simulation models are necessary. Today's state-of-the-art Virtual Hardware Platforms enable early software development. Component models in these platforms make use of TLM techniques [4]. For this purpose the SystemC TLM-2.0 Standard [14] allows description and simulation of inter-component communication using memory-mapped I/O (e. g. on a shared bus). TLM models can provide a number of productivity advantages: design creation is faster, golden models have less code and fewer bugs, simulation is potentially orders of magnitude faster, and silicon IP can be used without micro-architectural changes. All these advantages translate into reduced development costs.

Verification of today's SoCs is not limited to functional and timing verification. With the ever increasing complexity of hardware and software in battery-powered mobile devices, verification of the power closure becomes of significant importance. This includes the consideration of the energy consumption of all hardware components in the SoC platform (e. g. buses, memories, dedicated hardware accelerators). Usually, IP components do not provide detailed information about their power consumption. In some cases, data sheets for calculating an estimate of the power consumption in dependence of the clock frequency, supply voltage, and target technology are available. But information of these data sheets can hardly be used in functional system-level simulations, since they are not applicable to any dynamic effects. Such effects include different platform usage scenarios, which bring along different load profiles per platform component and thus different energy consumption per component over time. To enable software power management of the entire system, power properties for all components should be available during software development in the TLM platform model.

For combining the strengths of verified silicon-proven IP components with TLM-based design and verification, efficient integration of IP components (at lower levels) into a TLM verification environment becomes necessary. This integration can be performed in different ways:

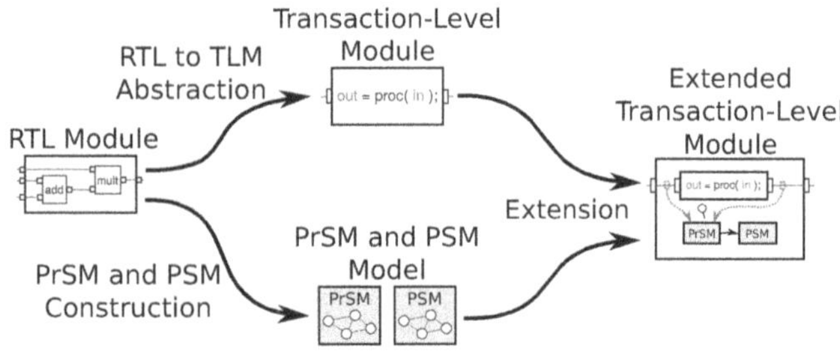

Figure 1: Overview of abstraction techniques

Top-Down: The entire SoC is specified as an executable model using a System-Level Design Language (SLDL) such as SpecC or SystemC. This model gets stepwise refined to a TLM model that represents the SoC with approximated execution times for computation and communication elements. This model enables binary compatible software development including driver and firmware development at register-level accuracy. For SoC production the platform components can either be replaced by pre-designed synthesizable IP components or need to be generated from the functional TLM model using high-level synthesis techniques. The advantage of this approach is the availability of early software and firmware development platform long before first silicon prototypes are available. The main drawback of this approach is that there is no formal proof that the synthesizable IP components match with their TLM representative regarding functionality and timing. Even with automatic synthesis from TLM to RTL the resulting RTL model needs to be verified, thus reducing the design effort but not the verification effort.

Bottom-Up: The entire SoC is built from silicon-proven verified IP components and subsystems. To enable fast and efficient software and firmware development, TLM representations of all IP components need to be available. The advantage of this approach is that the entire system is assembled from verified IP components. The drawback is that the integration and interaction with complex software cannot be handled at RTL. For this purpose a TLM model of the entire SoC platform is required. Manual component-wise abstraction from RTL to TLM is a time consuming and error-prone task. During abstraction functional and timing properties at RTL need to be represented properly in a TLM model. Without tool support this approach becomes unfeasible.

Meet-in-the-middle: In the industrial practice neither a pure top-down nor a pure bottom-up approach is applied during SoC design. Some components get realized using the top-down approach. Other components are reused from pre-existing silicon-proven IP or are extended from existing IPs. Anyhow, for software and driver integration and system verification TLM models of the entire SoC platform are state-of-the-art for all modern SoC designs.

In this paper we present a novel abstraction methodology which generates time- and power-annotated TLM models from synthesizable silicon-proven and verified RTL descriptions (see Figure 1). The proposed techniques allow the integration of existing IP components into TLM platforms for early software development, platform configuration and power profiling under realistic benchmarks considering all SoC components. With the proposed approach IP models can be executed 10-1000 times faster than at RTL while preserving functional, timing, and power properties. Regarding power properties this paper presents a concept for non-invasive simulation of energy consumption for SystemC TLM-2.0 components after automatic RTL to TLM abstraction. The term "non-invasive" describes that power annotations do not require any modifications on the functional TLM model, nor on the SystemC simulation kernel. The internal state and energy consumption of TLM components is approximated based on the observation and interpretation of the interaction with other platform components at TLM sockets. This property enables the integration of the power models with the generated TLM components and commercial SystemC simulation environments.

This paper is organized as follows. In Section 2 state-of-the-art techniques for abstracting RTL to C++ and TLM are presented. This is followed by an overview of existing work of system-level power modelling and simulation in SystemC. Section 3 describes the RTL to TLM abstraction path as shown in Figure 1. In Section 4 the RTL to TLM power abstraction and annotation path using Protocol State Machine (PrSM) and Power State Machine (PSM) construction is described. Section 5 shows the application of the RTL to TLM abstraction and power annotation on different IP components. The paper closes with a discussion of the experimental results, a summary, and an outlook on future work.

2. RELATED WORK

Some works have been proposed in the past for translating RTL VHDL and Verilog models into C/C++ descriptions, targeting verification of HW models via simulation [8, 20, 10, 17, 18, 5, 12]. In [8], a VHDL to C++ converter transforms VHDL test benches to C++ source. During the conversion, the C++ source is compiled into a small simulation kernel that runs the whole simulation with the interconnected hardware board. In [20, 10, 17], translation tools allow designers to use C++ executable files in place of VHDL models for decreasing simulation time compared to the typical acceleration process with HDL simulators. All the previous works allow designers to convert VHDL models described by a single process into C++ code, but they do not support scheduling features and synchronization among processes.

In [18], a methodology (consequently implemented in the tool VTOC) is proposed to convert synthesizable Verilog into C++. It performs a synthesis-like transformation of the input Verilog program, resolving the majority of scheduling decisions statically and resulting in a representation of the execution of the Verilog program in each clock cycle. VTOC tries to reduces the number of delta cycles by topological sorting all processes and by applying process merging. Nevertheless, all the implementation details included in the RTL descriptions and strictly related to HW models (e.g., clock accuracy, bit accuracy) are maintained during the translation to the SW domain.

Carbon Design System [5] provides commercial products that convert Verilog or VHDL RTL models into cycle accurate and register accurate SystemC models. Carbon's tools aim at creating complete virtual platforms in order to gain both a fast and accurate system validation. A method to convert clock-synchronous VHDL models into cycle-accurate C++ models is presented in [12]. It aims at the efficient integration of event-driven VHDL components into time-driven

Simulink models. Here again, HW details such as register and cycle accuracy are preserved at the model boundaries.

In contrast, the approach proposed in this article aims at generating fast C++ code to be used as SW application that does not have any detail related to the HW implementation.

The RTL-to-TLM abstraction has been addressed for the first time in [3]. In that article, the authors propose a technique to automatically abstract RTL IPs into TLM descriptions. The abstraction process converts cycle accurate RTL IPs into transaction accurate TLM descriptions, by abstracting low level implementation details typical of the RTL descriptions (e.g., the clock). A formal definition of equivalence based on events is also proposed to prove the correctness of the abstraction methodology. Nevertheless, the work does not address TLM model generation with timing annotation, which is essential for energy consumption estimation.

In [2], Power State Machines have been proposed for the first time in system-level modelling. State transitions are controlled by inputs of a power manager. Instead of a definite energy consumption, a state can have a maximal energy consumption, too. Its activity level is controlled by a power manager. Costs for state transitions are modelled by delays.

Since dynamic energy consumption emerges from activity, in [21] a concept is presented where activity is observed at the communication interfaces. A process is notified about every `default_event` of the communication channels and traces the activity. This method is very transparent and produces little overhead, but neglects the activity inside the component which can definitely behave different than the activity in the communication channels.

With *Powersim* a new approach was recently proposed in [11]. In this case the model does not have to be changed because a modified SystemC simulation kernel is used. The power model of the system is loaded at the beginning of the simulation, which does an activity estimation at every access on a SystemC data type. Due to the modified SystemC simulation kernel this approach cannot be integrated in commercial design environments, which have a proprietary SystemC kernel that usually cannot be changed. Additionally an estimation of communication, especially of abstract models (e. g. TLM), is possible only with restrictions because merely the assignment operator can be used for power annotation.

The past has shown that modelling and estimating the energy consumption through state machines with adaptation to the environment is a good possibility. In [15] this approach is used with SystemC/TLM to invoke a state transition in a state machine by calling a method at corresponding source positions in the functional model. Energy consumption can be adapted to Dynamic Voltage and Frequency Scaling (DVFS). The disadvantage of this approach is its invasiveness and thus can hardly be used for IP components. Its use with black-box IP components is not possible.

In [19] a system-level model that separates architecture and functional application model is presented. The application model is mapped on the platform model, which includes a model for the energy consumption. By using configuration files, different mappings of the application model onto the platform model can be explored. In contrast to our approach the application is an actor-based Dynamic Data Flow (DDF) Model of Computation (MoC). This approach assumes an application model described by a DDF MoC. Our proposed approach does not make any restrictions to the used MoC. It can be used with any IP component that communicates via memory-mapped I/O. For this reason our approach could be used at the platform model in [19].

3. RTL TO TLM ABSTRACTION

The process that abstracts an RTL description towards a TLM description relies on a formal model that allows us to represent designs at different abstraction levels. Among different alternatives, we select the extended finite state machine (EFSM) [6]. Given an EFSM of the RTL IP, the proposed abstraction technique is composed of the following main steps:

1. **Identification of computational phases**. An EFSM can be subdivided in three different kinds of subgraphs composing the behaviour of the RTL IP. They are: *input subgraphs*, where the IP gets data from the *Primary Inputs* (PIs), *elaboration subgraphs*, where the IP computation is carried out, and *output subgraphs*, where the computation result is put to the *Primary Outputs* (POs). Paths inside such subgraphs represent different computational phases of the design. Subgraphs and computational phases are identified as described in Section 3.1. They are used in the subsequent steps of the methodology for generating the TLM functionality and communication interface.

2. **TLM model generation**. States composing each elaboration subgraph are merged into a single macro state. We obtain a macro state per elaboration subgraph by applying merging rules described in Section 3.2. Then, the communication protocol of the TLM IP is generated by implementing an interface compliant with the IEEE 1666-2011 SystemC TLM-2.0 standard, to guarantee the generated model interoperability and reuse.

3. **TLM time annotation**. The TLM model is enriched with the time annotation (i.e., the model effective latency). As explained in detail in Section 3.3, the model delay information is extrapolated from the RTL model during the RTL-to-TLM abstraction, by mapping the computational phases identified in the first step into TLM transactions. Considering that a TLM transaction can implement one sequence of read, elaborate and write sub-phases, the cycle accurate information of such a delay is annotated in the TLM primitive that implement the transaction with the sum of clock cycles (times the clock period) involved in the RTL model during the corresponding sub-phases.

In this paper we consider RTL components to be abstracted as *target* models (i.e., slaves). Nevertheless, this is a convention, rather than a limitation as the abstraction process can be applied to whatever RTL code implementing a functionality. A component may act as both initiator and target: the initiator side is represented by code lines implementing requests to a target, while the target side is represented by code lines implementing the required IP functionality.

3.1 Identification of computational phases

Given an EFSM representing an RTL IP, we define a *computational phase* as a sequence of EFSM states that must be consistently traversed to get the input data (*input sub-phase*), elaborate them (*elaboration sub-phase*), and finally provide the related output result (*output sub-phase*). Input, elaboration and output phases belong, respectively, to input, elaboration and output subgraphs of the EFSM.

During the input sub-phase, the enabling and the update functions of the traversed transitions read input data and control lines without performing any further elaboration. Then, data are elaborated in the elaboration sub-phase without reading new values from PIs. Finally, in the output sub-phase, the update functions do not modify the computation result anymore, while they write results and control values into POs according to the communication protocol.

Definition 1. (Input Subgraph) Given an EFSM $M = \langle S, I, O, D, E, U, T\rangle$, an input subgraph M^{in} is a subgraph of M where the root is either the initial state of M or a successor of an output sub-phase, and all transitions t involved in M^{in} are in the form $((s_l, e_t, i)(s_{l+1}, u_t, \epsilon))$ for some $i \in I \setminus \{\epsilon\}$. A path inside M^{in} is called input sub-phase.

Definition 2. (Elaboration Subgraph) Given an EFSM $M = \langle S, I, O, D, E, U, T\rangle$, an elaboration subgraph M^{elab} is a subgraph of M where the root is a successor of an input sub-phase, and all transitions t involved in the M^{elab} are in the form $((s_l, e_t, \epsilon)(s_{l+1}, u_t, \epsilon))$. A path inside M^{elab} is called elaboration sub-phase.

Definition 3. (Output Subgraph) Given an EFSM $M = \langle S, I, O, D, E, U, T\rangle$, an output subgraph M^{out} is a subgraph of M where the root is a successor of an elaboration sub-phase, and all transitions t involved in M^{out} are in the form $((s_l, e_t, \epsilon)(s_{l+1}, u_t, o))$ for some $o \in O \setminus \{\epsilon\}$. A path inside M^{out} is called output sub-phase.

Definition 4. (Computational Phase) Given an EFSM $M = \langle S, I, O, D, E, U, T\rangle$, a computational phase is a path of M starting with an input sub-phase, followed by an elaboration sub-phase and finally by an output sub-phase.

At RTL, an elaboration sub-phase corresponds to a set of activities that, at TLM, can be sequentially performed in a single transaction triggered by a single event (i.e., the synchronization event which drives the model simulation), while the clock signal is abstracted away, as described in Section 3.2. Different paths, inside the same elaboration subgraph represent different alternatives which may coexist in the same TLM transaction. In contrast, I/O sub-phases implement the RTL communication protocol which can be abstracted at TLM by using the desired coding style as reported in Section 3.3.

According to the design functionality, the RTL EFSM may traverse one or more computational phases (and the related subgraph), to provide the final result. In particular, we distinguish between three different kinds of RTL designs: *single-phase, multi-phase,* and *memory-phase designs.* This distinction is relevant for the generation of the TLM communication protocols.

3.1.1 Single-phase designs

This kind of designs provides the final results by traversing a single computational phase. For example, given an IP core which computes the square root of a number. In this case, the communication protocol between such a module (let us refer to it as target) and its initiator requires that all input data (e.g., the number whose square root is required, and some control values) are collected before the computation starts. Then, during the elaboration sub-phase, the initiator is not involved and no PIs are read, until the square root result becomes available. Finally, the output sub-phase involves the communication protocol between initiator and target to provide the result before the target returns to its initial state.

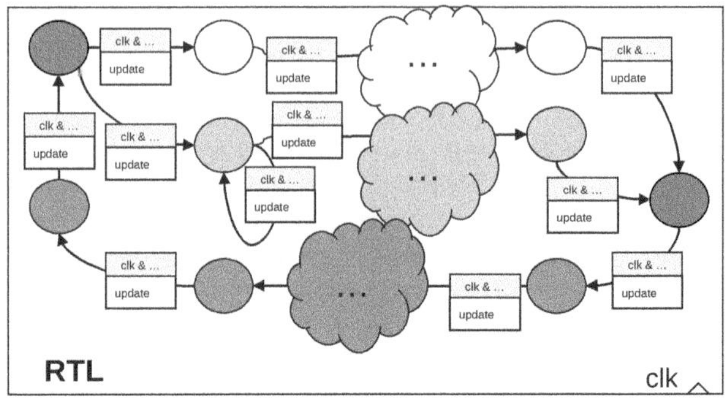

Figure 2: An RTL multi-phase design

3.1.2 Multi-phase designs

In multi-phase designs, the output result is computed by traversing more than one computational phase. At the end of each 'intermediate' computational phase, a partial result may be available or not, but the design must read new input data to proceed with the computation of the final result. Figure 2 shows the EFSM representing a cycle accurate RTL IP, where three computational phases have been highlighted by using different shades of grey. Multi-shaded states are included in more than one computational phase. The final result is available only when the EFSM reaches the last dark grey state on the left. States before the clouds belong to input sub-phases, states inside the clouds belong to elaboration sub-phases, and states after the clouds belong to output sub-phases. The identification of input, elaboration and output sub-phases on multi-phase designs is automatic, like for single-phase designs. However, as reported in Section 3.3, a more complex communication protocol for the initiator must be implemented for multi-phase designs when they are abstracted towards TLM.

3.1.3 Memory-phase designs

Memory-phase designs are similar to multi-phase designs, since they traverse more than one computational phase. However, each time a computational phase finishes, a final (non-partial) result is available for the initiator, and, moreover, the EFSM does not have to necessarily return to its initial state. Thus, such designs keep memory of the reached state after a computation has finished. As explained in Section 3.3, the communication protocol implemented for abstracting RTL memory-phase designs towards TLM is very simple, like the one for single-phase designs. A particular case of RTL memory-phase design is represented by an EFSM where the update functions of all the transitions read data, manipulate them, and compute the result, i.e., each

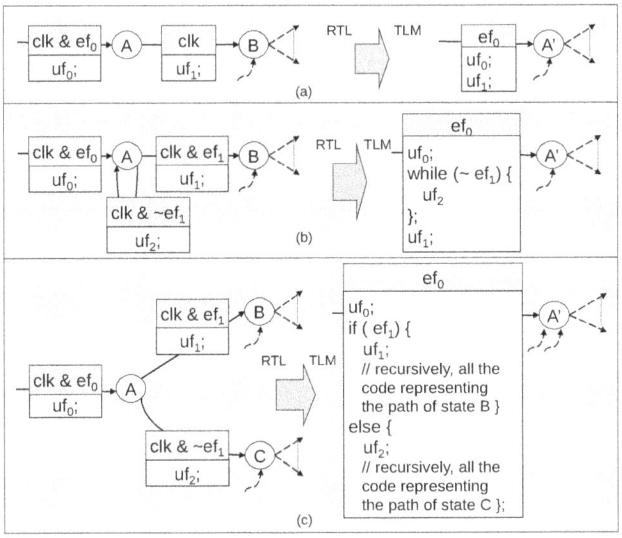

Figure 3: Merging rules

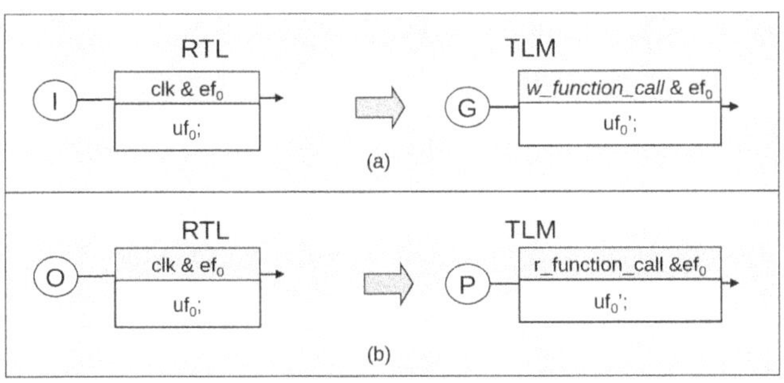

Figure 4: I/O rules

transition merges input, elaboration and output sub-phases in a single clock cycle. Such designs can be abstracted with the same strategy we use for designs where the three sub-phases are spread in several transitions.

3.2 TLM model generation

In this section we introduce the main important concepts of the abstraction process for the TLM model generation, while we refer the reader to [3] for more details on such an abstraction. The TLM model generation consists of two phases: the generation of *TLM functionality* and the generation of *TLM communication protocol*. The TLM functionality is automatically generated by abstracting the RTL IP functionality. The abstraction algorithm relies on identifying each RTL elaboration subgraph and merging it into a TLM macro state. The merging process is performed by recursively applying the three merging rules summarized in Figure 3.

As a result, each TLM macro state has a single out-going transition whose destination is the *root* of the subsequent output subgraph. The update function of such a transition contains all the code included in the original elaboration subgraph. The TLM EFSM traverses such a transition as soon as the TLM macro state is entered, since the related enabling function is always true. This means that no event

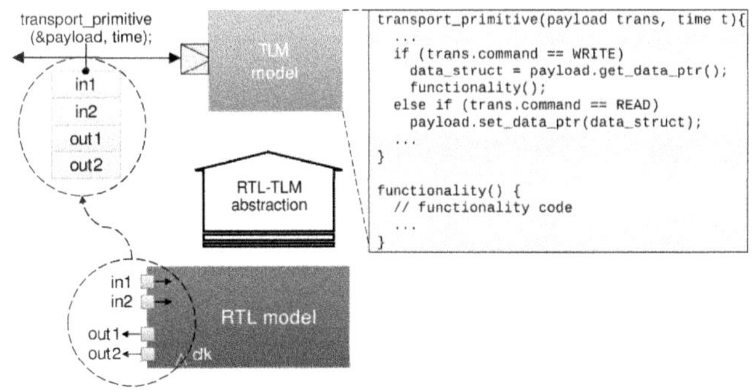

Figure 5: The TLM protocol generation

must be waited for firing the transition. During the merging of an elaboration subgraph, the clock of the RTL model is removed. This greatly improves the simulation speed as the number of TLM simulation events is extremely reduced.

Then, the TLM transaction-based communication protocol is generated by abstracting the cycle accurate RTL communication protocol. Communication in TLM is achieved through the exchange of *payload* objects between the initiator and the target (see Figure 5). The initiator provides input data to the target through a *write* transaction (i.e., write function call), so that the target can subsequently start the elaboration. Then a *read transaction* is used by the initiator to retrieve output results computed by the target. An I/O data structure is created to be stored in payload objects to allow data exchange between the initiator and the target. This data structure contains one field for each corresponding RTL I/O port. This step is performed by applying the I/O rules depicted in Figure 4, in which $w\_function\_call$ and $r\_function\_call$ represent a write and read transaction, respectively.

3.3 TLM time annotation

The TLM time annotation is automatically extrapolated during the RTL-to-TLM abstraction by mapping the computational phases identified in the first step into TLM transactions. Considering that a TLM transaction can implement one sequence of read, elaborate and write sub-phases, the main idea is to annotate the sum of clock cycles involved in the RTL model during such sub-phases.

Formally, given an input sub-phase R of the RTL model, in which the update function of the traversed transition reads data on input ports $in_{1,\dots,i}$ (i.e., $R_{in\{1,\dots,i\}}$), an elaboration sub-phase E in which data is elaborated in the update function(s) and an output sub-phase W in which the update function of the traversed transition writes the result on ports $out_{\{1,\dots,j\}}$ (i.e., $W_{out\{1,\dots,j\}}$), a TLM transaction corresponds to the RTL sequence:

$$R_{in\{1,\dots,i\}} \longrightarrow E \longrightarrow W_{out\{1,\dots,j\}} \qquad (1)$$

The RTL computational phase may be composed of one or more clock cycles. Figure 6 gives some examples. For an RTL model with a one-clock-cycle latency, i.e., the input, elaboration, and output subphases are involved in one clock cycle (Figure 6.a), one RTL computational phase is abstracted into one TLM transaction. Thus, the TLM transaction is annotated with one clock cycle times the clock period.

A TLM transaction may implement more than one RTL

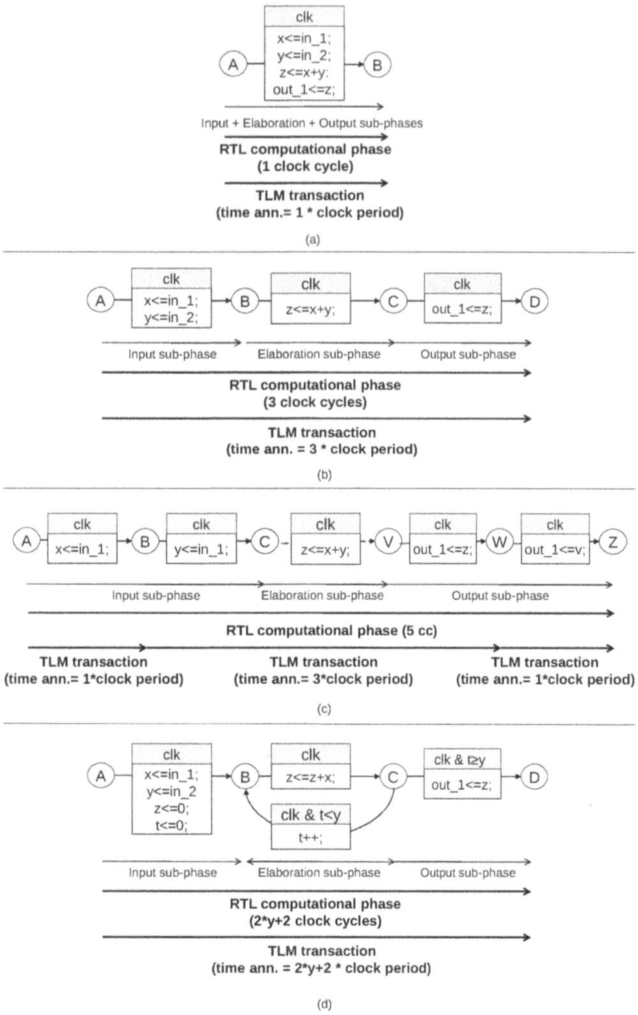

Figure 6: TLM time annotation through the mapping of RTL computational phases into TLM transactions

clock cycle when, for example the input, elaboration, and output sub-phases are triggered in more than one clock cycle (e.g., the RTL model with three clock cycle latency of Figure 6.b). In this case, the TLM transaction is annotated with three clock cycles times the clock period.

An RTL computational phase is abstracted into more TLM transactions when, for example, an input sub-phase consists of more than one consecutive transitions to read data on the same input port before moving to the elaboration sub-phase:

$$R_{in\{i\}} \longrightarrow \cdots \longrightarrow R_{in\{i\}} \longrightarrow E \longrightarrow W_{out\{j\}} \qquad (2)$$

The same concept applies to the output sub-phase:

$$R_{in\{i\}} \longrightarrow E \longrightarrow W_{out\{j\}} \longrightarrow \cdots \longrightarrow W_{out\{j\}} \qquad (3)$$

Figure 6.c shows an example of sequence (2) combined with sequence (3), which requires three computational cycles to complete the communication protocol. The input sub-phase consists of two read transitions that are mapped into two different TLM transactions, and the same happens in the output sub-phase. Thus, an RTL computational phase is mapped into three TLM transactions, each one annotated with one, three and one clock cycles times the clock period, respectively.

Other similar situations are represented by RTL computational phases in which input and elaboration sub-phases alternate before moving to the output sub-phase (or elaboration and output sub-phases alternate after an input sub-phase), as follows:

$$R_{in\{i\}} \longrightarrow E_1 \longrightarrow R_{in\{j\}} \longrightarrow E_2 \longrightarrow W_{out\{t\}} \qquad (4)$$

$$R_{in\{i\}} \longrightarrow E_1 \longrightarrow W_{out\{t\}} \longrightarrow E_2 \longrightarrow W_{out\{u\}} \qquad (5)$$

A data structure is created during the abstraction process to store information concerning (i) merging of elaboration states to generate elaboration sub-phases, and (ii) mapping of input(output) states into input(output) sub-phases. This data structure contains the following items:

- the number of merged elaboration states;
- the transitions and the input ports read in input sub-phases;
- the transitions and the output ports written in output sub-phases.

This data structure information is exploited to automatically annotate variables for timing annotation.

Finally, Figure 6.d shows an example in which the computation phase latency depends on the input data. In such a case, the two clock cycle loop of the RTL model is translated into an untimed for-loop at TLM, as explained in rule 2 of Figure 3. In the TLM model, a counter is used to count, at run-time, the number of loop iterations required to complete the sub-phase (the elaboration sub-phase in the example). At the end of the TLM transaction, the total number of iterations and the clock cycle latency of the corresponding sub-phase, which is extracted as explain previously, are used to calculate the final time to be annotated.

4. NON-INVASIVE POWER SIMULATION OF TLM COMPONENTS

Once the TLM description is generated from RTL to TLM abstraction, it is extended with power information. The power model is linked into the generated TLM at it communication socket (target or initiator). For this reason the most important part is the RTL to TLM interface abstraction because power changes are recognized by observing the component's communication on its interface. The power of the component is estimated at RTL through analysing correlations of RTL I/O operations with significant power state changes. The RTL to TLM interface abstraction function is finally used to map RTL I/O operations to TLM transactions and power model integration. The following sections describe the used Power State Machine model and its construction.

4.1 Power State Machines in SystemC

An essential requirement for the proposed approach is the estimation of black-box components. In this case the internal structure cannot be annotated or modified to record

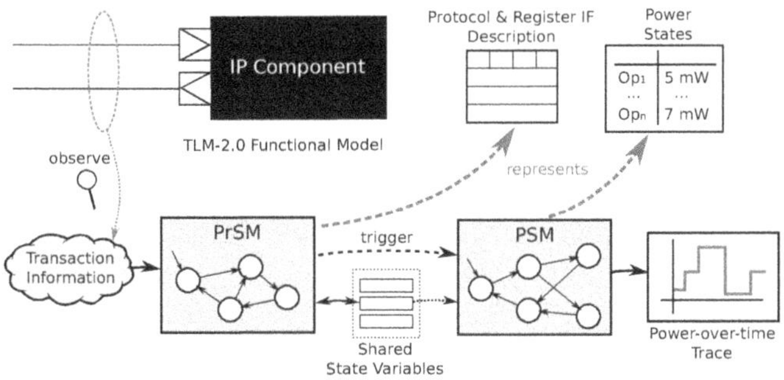

Figure 7: PSM approach overview for non-invasive simulation of energy consumption

switching activities to compute energy consumption. For this reason the internal state of an IP component is abstracted based on a correlation of its observable interaction with the estimated power consumption. The estimated energy consumption per macro states can be taken from data sheets, can be inferred from an estimation of design size or the functional complexity of the design (top-down), or can be extracted from lower level (e. g. RTL) simulations (bottom-up). With the latter approach, the most accurate model can be built, c. f. [15].

Figure 7 gives an overview of our non-invasive approach for integration of energy information with TLM IP components [16]. For using our approach the following is assumed:

- The examined IP component is either available as synthesizable functional model with TLM-2.0 interface or as a functional black-box (TLM) model and synthesizable black-box RT model.
- The register interface, i. e. the logical register organization in the global address space, and its usage has been defined.
- In addition to the various operation modes of the component an energy estimation exists (average power consumption at a given target technology or the component needs to be synthesizable for generating a power-over-time trace).

Based on the energy characteristics of the component the dynamic power model can be created. To determine the dynamic energy consumption $P(t)$ as function of time, the well-known formula

$$P(t) = \frac{1}{2} V_{\mathrm{dd}}^2 f C \cdot \alpha(t) \tag{6}$$

can be used, where C is the total switched capacitance which is always constant, V_{dd} the supply voltage, f the clock frequency, and $\alpha(t) = \{x \mid 0 \leq x \leq 1\}$ the switching activity at time t.

Since the real switching activity $\alpha(t)$ cannot be obtained at system-level, a set of macro states $S = s_1, \ldots, s_n$ is defined in the PSM to distinguish characteristic operation modes. These are time dependent, thus the time $t \in T$ can be associated with the operation modes $s \in S$ as follows:

$$\varphi : T \to S \tag{7}$$

We assume that time is already quantified into a discrete set of values. To each operation mode $s_i \in S$ an average activity, described by the arithmetic mean $\alpha_i \in A$ for the time, when s_i is active, is associated in the following way:

$$\alpha' : S \to A \quad \text{with } \alpha_i = \frac{1}{\Delta t(s_i)} \sum_{t=t_{\mathrm{beg}}(s_i)}^{t_{\mathrm{end}}(s_i)} \alpha(t) \tag{8}$$

Inserted in Equation 6 we get the average energy consumption $\overline{P}(t)$ over time:

$$\overline{P}(t) = \frac{1}{2} V_{\mathrm{dd}}^2 f C \cdot \alpha'(\varphi(t)) \tag{9}$$

Supply voltage and frequency are parameters depending on the power island and the current strategy of the power manager. For this reason we abstract from these parameters and get the average switched capacitance over time:

$$\overline{C}(t) = \frac{1}{2} C \cdot \alpha'(\varphi(t)) \tag{10}$$

In Equation 10 the output of the PSM is described. This formula is the basis for recording the average switched capacity during simulation to generate a power-over-time trace.

Since the used components are modelled with TLM-2.0, the known external register-based interfaces of a component are observed over time to approximate the internal functionality. Based on these observations, a *Protocol State Machine* (PrSM) is controlled. The main task of the PrSM is the triggering of state transitions in the PSM through observation and interpretation of the interaction between component and environment. The PrSM extracts the energetic relevant events to orthogonalize the communication and functional artefacts of the non-functional PSM model. This can lead to a reduction of complexity in the PSM because it only describes the different internal operation modes whereas the PrSM covers the protocol state of the component. Furthermore, the separation of PrSM and PSM has the advantage that components with the same access protocol and different internal implementations could use the same PrSM, only the PSM has to be changed.

The input data for the PrSM is the observed transaction information of the TLM-2.0 sockets of the component. Depending on the register interface and the semantics of read-/write operations at specific address, activities or even complex operations are triggered in the observed component. This can be modelled with transitions between states in the PrSM to abstract the functional characteristics. Such transitions can lead to notifications of the PSM.

Furthermore, there may be some functional state transitions in the IP component that cannot be detected by observing the interaction with the environment (e. g. if a target component finishes its calculation, it may not send a transaction indicating this, because target components do not initiate transactions at all). In this case the PSM is modelled as a state machine that executes state a transition after a defined delay/timeout.

It is possible to extend PrSM and PSM with shared state variables Z. These shared state variables are modified only by the PrSM and can be used to store specific configuration data, like current function choice (e. g. MD5 vs. SHA256 in a hashing module). This enables the management of context-aware information to be shared between PrSM and PSM. With this extension, the output of the PSM can also depend on these shared state variables and the computation of the average switching activity from Equation 9 and

Equation 10 has to be modified to $\alpha'(\varphi(t), Z(t))$. I.e. state transitions, delays, and output of the state machines can depend on the shared state variables. If a shared state variable describes the current clock frequency of the module, delays in the PSM can be adapted accordingly.

4.2 Protocol observation

Under the assumption that the examined component interacts with the environment via TLM-2.0 *Base Protocol* [14], several information with the following attributes are available:

- Generic Payload (R/W, base address, payload data, data length, ...)
- Current phase of transaction (TLM-2.0 LT/AT base protocol phase)
- Used interface of component (socket)
- Role of the component in the transaction (initiator, target or interconnect)

To model the PrSM, the communication with the component can be observed at multiple protocol layers. On one hand this is the mere read/write operation in the address space of a component (*transport layer*, single TLM-2.0 transaction). For a memory component this layer is mostly sufficient to describe the energetic behaviour because there is no logic relation between multiple transactions.

On the other hand for complex components like hardware accelerators, side effects inside the target component can span several transactions (*presentation layer*). In this case it is useful to partition the address space of the component semantically in control, configuration, and payload addresses. Therefore, the semantic description of the register interface is needed to abstract the functionality with the aid of suitable states and shared state variables in a PrSM.

Control data impacts the protocol flow and thus immediately the internal state of the component. An example for this is an explicit handshake register to synchronize with a hardware accelerator. Transactions at such registers ordinary lead to explicit state transitions in the PrSM. *Configuration data* influences the behaviour of a component in the following states or over a longer period of time (e. g. the choice of the algorithm for an encryption coprocessor). The values of configuration registers commonly require the introduction and observation of a state variable in the PrSM. *Payload data* is processed by the IP component, but they do not influence the communication protocol or the internal (observable) protocol flow of the component (e. g. data that should be encrypted by the above mentioned accelerator). Although the concrete used data influences the activity in a component, this is in most cases very small and can be neglected on system-level (see experiments in Section 5).

4.3 PSM Model Construction

For construction of the PSM model we assume plateaus in the power-over-time trace in which the average energy consumption keeps nearly constant over time. These plateaus are described through power states in the PSM model. That means, if a state transition in the PSM occurs, there is a change in the average energy consumption, i. e. a change between plateaus.

To generate these power values from gate-level simulations, a test bench is used that implements a use case in which preferably all operation modes are tested. During simulation the activity inside the device under test is traced and converted into a power-over-time-trace with the aid of target technology and timing information. Such a trace is shown in Section 5. This trace, overlayed with I/O events over time, provides information about periodic behaviour of energy consumption and communication dependent and independent switches of plateaus. Based on this analysis relevant power states, the average switched capacitance per power state, and transitions between power states can be extracted. Additionally, special communication attributes can be associated with power state transitions. This includes state transitions with annotated switching delays that cannot be triggered through I/O events.

The PrSM in combination with the RTL to TLM abstraction looks always the same. It has two states, *Idle* and *Write*. The PrSM is in state *Write* when a write transaction takes place, else it is in state *Idle*. The payload data are copied in the state variables when the PrSM transitions into state *Write*. This is due the fact that all read and write operations are at address 0 and all exchanged data are in the I/O data structure explained in Section 3.2. Additionally, only on write transactions the examined component processes data. Read transactions consume no time and are used for returning the output values. This PrSM is depicted in Section 5. The complete flow for creating the PrSM and PSM models is sketched in Figure 8.

5. EXPERIMENTS

The methodology presented in this paper has been applied for generating the time- and power-annotated TLM models from the following existing RTL IPs:

- an *Advanced Encryption Standard (AES)* accelerator implemented in Verilog.
- part of a *JPEG* encoder, a compression module implemented in Verilog that consists of three subcomponents: A discrete cosine transform (DCT) module, a quantization (QRN) module, and an entropy coding that implements the run-length coding (RLE) algorithm.

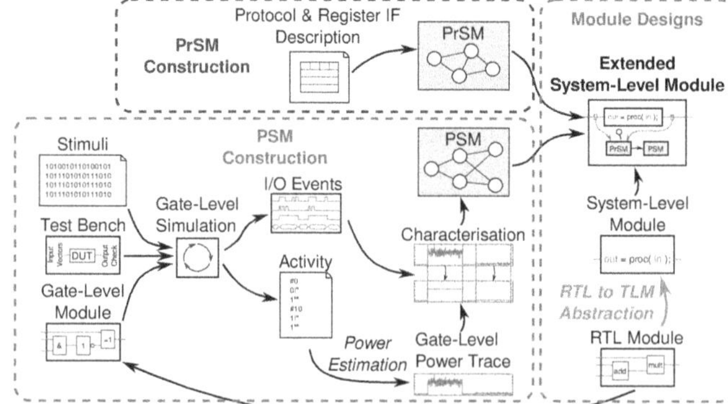

Figure 8: Flow for creating PSM and PrSM system-level models from RTL design

Table 1: Characteristic of the RTL IPs

RTL IP	PIs	POs	Gates	FFs	Latency	Th.put
AES	260	129	2751	670	505	1/505
JPEG	20	27	27714	4877	93	1
SPI	16	12	259	131	2	1/2

- a *Serial Parallel Interface (SPI)* module in Verilog.

Table 1 reports the characteristics of the test cases in terms of primary inputs (*#PIs*), primary outputs (*#POs*), number of gates (*#Gates*), number of flip-flops (*#FF*), latency, and throughput.

5.1 RTL-to-TLM abstraction

The abstraction step presented in Section 3 has been implemented in *A2T* (Automatic Abstraction Tool), a tool built on the top of HIFSuite [13]. In particular, *A2T* has been extended to automatically abstracts RTL IPs (implemented in VHDL, Verilog or SystemC) towards SystemC TLM models with timing annotation.

Table 2 reports the experimental results concerning the RTL-to-TLM abstraction. Column *Loc* reports the lines of code of the original Verilog RTL description and the automatically generated SystemC TLM implementation. Column *Comput. phase(cc)* reports the computational phase length of the RTL model (i.e., the latency) in clock cycles. Column *Trans.(#)* reports the number of TLM transactions in which the RTL computational phase is mapped (see Section 3.3). *Simul. time* reports the simulation time of both the RTL and the TLM models. The first one has been calculated by using ModelSim simulator of Mentor Graphics. The TLM model simulation time has been measured by adopting the Accellera Systems Initiative (formerly OSCI) simulation kernel [1]. These measurements are without connected PSM power model. The results on simulation of energy consumption are presented in Section 5.2.

The abstraction of AES and JPEG test cases lead to a considerable speedup. The JPEG abstraction leads to the best speedup due to the architecture complexity and finite state machine that implement the compression algorithm. In this case, the abstraction methodology allows the TLM generation process to efficiently merge RTL states into macro TLM states (see Section 3.2). The SPI speedup is lower since the finite state machine is very simple. In this case, the simulation time is spent more on data transfer rather than on data elaboration. The speedup is given by comparing the simulation time of the SystemC TLM model using Accellera Systems Initiative's proof-of-concept simulation kernel with the simulation time of the Verilog RTL model with Mentor Graphics ModelSim. The speedup of SystemC TLM versus SystemC RTL using the same simulation kernel would increase in average up to five times [9].

5.2 Experimental results on simulation of energy consumption

After the RTL design is abstracted to TLM it can be extended with the PrSM and PSM. The process for estimating the power, detecting the power states and connecting them to the corresponding I/O operations can be done in parallel. As explained in Section 4.3 the PrSM has a fixed format. The power states for the AES module are shown in Figure 9.

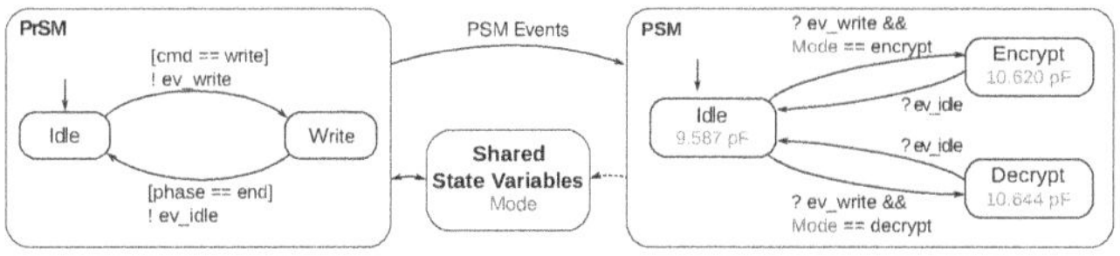

Figure 9: PrSM and PSM of the AES module

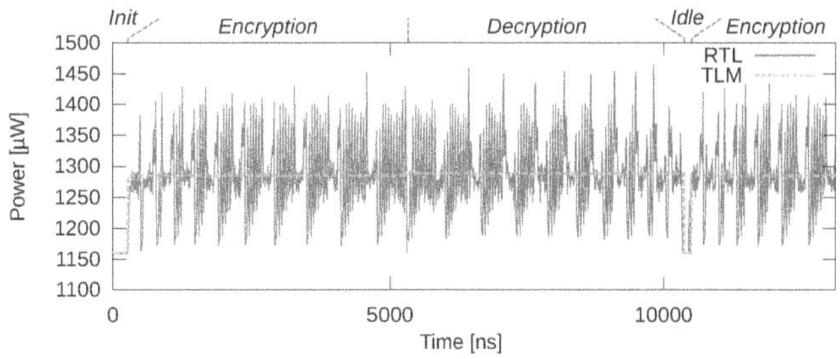

Figure 10: Comparison between gate-level and TLM power-over-time trace of the AES module

The PSM has to distinguish between encryption and decryption because these modes have different power consumptions. Since the PrSM stores payload data – in this case the operation mode of the I/O data structure – in the shared state variables, the PSM can access these and execute the correct state transitions.

Figure 10 shows power-over-time traces at gate-level which were used for extracting the relevant power states. It is overlayed with the resulting power-over-time traces of the TLM model with power properties. From this experiment it can be observed that the TLM power averages the gate-level power-over-time trace.

The shown power-over-time traces are generated with a 60 nm technology, a supply voltage of 1.1 V and a clock frequency of 100 MHz. The annotated average switched capacitances of the power states in Figure 9 are independent from the supply voltage and clock frequency. This separation enables to execute the PSM model with different supply voltages and clock frequencies during simulation. This model flexibility is required for run-time power management techniques using dynamic voltage and frequency scaling (DVFS).

To evaluate the efficiency of the PSM methodology we present the simulation run-time overhead of the TLM model extended with power properties in relation the pure TLM model. Additional, we show the accuracy of the PSM in comparison to the average gate level power consumption.

In most cases the PSM and PrSM is much simpler than the examined design. This allows an easy integration of the power model and leads to low overhead for the AES module (see Table 2). If the communication consists of many transitions containing little information the overhead increases linearly because the PrSM and PSM are triggered at every transaction several times as can be seen at the SPI module. Here every byte is transmitted in a separate transaction. As the overhead gets greater, consequently the speedup of the PSM power simulation in relation to gate level power simulation shrinks in the same manner as can be seen in column *PSM Speedup*.

PSM Err. shows the worst case error for the accuracy of the PSM power in relation to the gate-level average power.

These examples show that most components have differ-

Table 2: Experimental results of RTL-TLM abstraction

IP	RTL			TLM			RTL-TLM Speedup	PSM Overhead	PSM Err.	PSM Speedup
	Loc (#)	Comput. phase(cc)	Simul. time(s)	Loc (#)	Trans. (#)	Simul. time(s)				
AES	1,925	505	2.515	2,282	1	0.484	10.7x	3.21%	0.78%	110x
JPEG	7,105	1	32.757	14,319	1	1.792	18.3x	28.03%	0.45%	912x
SPI	456	2	2.280	1,361	1	0.404	5.6x	177.6%	0.05%	11.8x

ent operation modes in which they consume nearly the same amount of average power independent of the processed data. A component can stay in one operation mode over a span of multiple I/O transactions. This is the reason why it is important to not only observe activity, but also observe special data fields in communication to derive the correct operation mode and thus power consumption.

6. CONCLUSION AND FUTURE WORK

In this paper we have shown a strategy for abstracting existing RTL designs to TLM and annotate them with timing and power properties. We showed how to abstract the RTL design to retain equivalent functionality and how to convert the RTL I/O interface in a TLM-2.0 interface. Additionally we presented the extension with abstract timing properties and with a high accurate and efficient power model. Currently the PSM/PrSM characterisation is done manually. In the future this should be automated as far as possible to reduce the effort to a minimum. Moreover, the RTL to TLM power abstraction should also be applied to initiator components, which have not been in the scope of this work.

7. ACKNOWLEDGMENTS

This work has been partially supported by the COMPLEX FP7 European Integrated Project [7], funded by the European Commission under Grant Agreement 247999, and by the EnerSave Project, funded by the German BMBF under Grant Agreement 01BE1102.

8. REFERENCES

[1] Accellera Systems Initiative. *SystemC*. `http://www.accellera.org`.

[2] L. Benini, R. Hodgson, and P. Siegel. System-level power estimation and optimization. In *International Symposium on Low Power Electronics and Design*, ISLPED'98, pages 173–178, Monterey, CA, USA, Aug. 1998. ACM.

[3] N. Bombieri, F. Fummi, and G. Pravadelli. Automatic Abstraction of RTL IPs into Equivalent TLM Descriptions. *IEEE Transactions on Computers*, 60(12):1730–1743, 2011.

[4] L. Cai and D. Gajski. Transaction level modeling: an overview. In *Proceedings of the 1st IEEE/ACM/IFIP international conference on Hardware/software codesign and system synthesis*, CODES+ISSS '03, pages 19–24, New York, NY, USA, 2003. ACM.

[5] Carbon Model Studio. `http://carbondesignsystems.com/`.

[6] K.-T. Cheng and A. Krishnakumar. Automatic generation of functional vectors using the extended finite state machine model. In *ACM TODAES*, volume 1, pages 57–79, 1996.

[7] COMPLEX (ICT FP7 247999). COdesign and power Management in PLatform-based design space EXploration. `http://complex.offis.de`.

[8] DVM. `http://aldec.com`.

[9] W. Ecker, V. Esen, L. Schonberg, T. Steininger, M. Velten, and M. Hull. Impact of description language, abstraction layer, and value representation on simulation performance. In *Proc. of ACM/IEEE DATE*, pages 1–6, 2007.

[10] FreeHDL-V2CC. `http://linux.die.net/man/1/freehdl-v2cc`.

[11] M. Giammarini, S. Orcioni, and M. Conti. Powersim: Power Estimation with SystemC. In *Solutions on Embedded Systems*, volume 81 of *Lecture Notes in Electrical Engineering*, pages 285–300. 2011.

[12] R. Görgen, J.-H. Oetjens, and W. Nebel. Transformation of Event-Driven HDL Blocks for Native Integration into Time-Driven System Models. In *Proceedings of the Forum on specification and Design Languages (FDL'2012)*, Sept. 2012.

[13] HIFSuite. `http://hifsuite.edalab.it`.

[14] IEEE Computer Society. IEEE Standard SystemC Language Reference Manual. IEEE Std 1666–2011, Sept. 2011. ISBN 978-0-7381-6802-9.

[15] H. Lebreton and P. Vivet. Power Modeling in SystemC at Transaction Level, Application to a DVFS Architecture. In *IEEE Annual Symposium on VLSI*, ISVLSI'08, pages 463–466, Apr. 2008.

[16] D. Lorenz, P. A. Hartmann, K. Grüttner, and W. Nebel. Non-invasive Simulation of Power Consumption with SystemC. In *Power And Timing Modeling, Optimization and Simulation - 22nd International Workshop (PATMOS'2012)*, Lecture Notes in Computer Science. Springer, Sept. 2012.

[17] W. Snyder, P. Wasson, and D. Galbi. Verilator - Convert Verilog code to C++/SystemC. `http://www.veripool.org/wiki/verilator`.

[18] W. Stoye, D. Greaves, N. Richards, and J. Green. Using RTL-to-C++ translation for large SoC concurrent engineering: A case study. *IEEE Electronics Systems and Software*, 1(1):20–25, 2003.

[19] M. Streubühr, R. Rosales, R. Hasholzner, C. Haubelt, and J. Teich. ESL Power and Performance Estimation for Heterogeneous MPSoCs Using SystemC. In *Forum on specification and Design Languages (FDL'2011)*, Oldenburg, Germany, Sept. 2011.

[20] VHDLC. `http://ostatic.com`.

[21] C. Walravens, Y. Vanderperren, and W. Dehaene. ActivaSC: A highly efficient and non-intrusive extension for activity-based analysis of SystemC models. In *46th ACM/IEEE Design Automation Conference (DAC'2009)*, pages 172–177, July 2009.

Run-time Resource Management based on Design Space Exploration

Chantal Ykman-Couvreur
IMEC, Belgium
ykman@imec.be

Philipp A. Hartmann
OFFIS Institute, Germany
philipp.hartmann@offis.de

Gianluca Palermo
Politecnico di Milano, Italy
gpalermo@elet.polimi.it

Fabien Colas-Bigey
Thales Comm. & Sec., France
fabien.colas-bigey
@thalesgroup.com

Laurent San
Thales Comm. & Sec., France
laurent.san
@thalesgroup.com

ABSTRACT

A main challenge in today's embedded system design is to find the perfect balance between performance and power consumption. This paper presents a run-time resource management framework for embedded heterogeneous multi-core platforms. It allows dynamic adaptation to changing application context and transparent optimization of the platform resource usage following a distributed and hierarchical approach. A Global Resource Manager (GRM) is running in parallel with the central manager of the application on the host processor of the platform. Each IP core of the platform can execute its own Local Resource Manager (LRM), and the GRM conforms to practices of each LRM.

The operating points managed by the GRM are identified in a design-space exploration phase as a set of Pareto-optimal configurations of the application and their impacts with regards to the quality of experience, performance and energy consumption. The GRM has already been integrated in a POSIX version of an audio-driven video surveillance application in order to maximize its QoE parameters with respect to the battery duration and the energy budget of the platform, used to analyze the GRM efficiency.

Categories and Subject Descriptors

B.8.2 [**Performance and Reliability**]: Performance Analysis and Design Aids; C.4 [**Performance of Systems**]: Modeling techniques

General Terms

Design, Measurement, Performance

Keywords

Design space exploration, Run-time management, HW/SW Timing and Power Simulation, Virtual Prototypes

1. INTRODUCTION

To address the challenges introduced by future embedded computing, a generic and structured Run-time Resource Management (RRM) framework for embedded heterogeneous multi-core platforms is needed with the following features.

Firstly, the RRM has to support a variety of applications: mobile communications, networking, automotive and avionic applications, multimedia in the automobile and Internet interfaced with many embedded control systems. Such applications may run concurrently, start and stop at any time. Each application may have multiple configurations, with different constraints imposed by the external world or the user (deadlines and quality requirements, such as audio and video quality, output accuracy), different usages of various types of platform resources (processing elements, memories and communication bandwidth) and different costs (performance, power consumption). Secondly, this RRM should support a *holistic view of platform resources*. This is needed for global resource allocation decisions optimizing a utility function (also called Quality of user Experience (QoE)), given the available platform resources. This QoE will allow trade-off, negotiated with the user, between diverse requirements and costs. Thirdly, this RRM should *transparently optimize* the platform resource usage and the application mapping on the platform. This is needed to facilitate the application development and manage the QoE requirements without rewriting the application.

Next, this RRM should *dynamically adapt* to changing context. This is needed to achieve a high efficiency under changing environment conditions. QoE requirements and platform resources must be scaled dynamically (e.g., by adjusting the clock frequencies and voltages, or by switching off some functions) in order to control the energy/power consumption and the heat dissipation of the platform. Finally, this RRM should *allow different heuristics* (e.g., for platform resource allocation and task scheduling), since a single heuristic cannot be expected to fit all application domains and optimization goals.

Also, the software development productivity is very important. To facilitate the RRM implementation, a generic and structured RRM framework is required. It should be valid for any used design flow, for any target platform, and for any application domain. Moreover, since the RRM is intended for embedded platforms, only a lightweight implementation is acceptable: (a) this RRM should interface

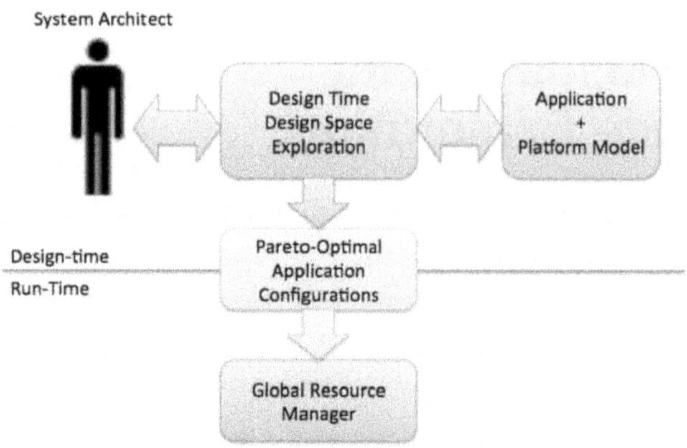

Figure 1: Two-level optimization flow

with design-time exploration to alleviate its run-time decision making; (b) the RRM implementation should be instantiated from the RRM framework, based on the target platform and the application domain.

This paper presents a RRM framework, intended for embedded heterogeneous multi-core platforms addressing these challenges, and extended from [12]. The two-level optimization flow is outlined in Figure 1. At design-time, a set of Pareto-optimal application configurations under the given QoE requirements and optimization goals are derived by an automated design-space exploration, e.g. based on the MOST tool [10]. The run-time resource management then dynamically switches between these predefined configurations at run-time.

The main contribution of this paper is the RRM instantiation for an audio-driven video surveillance application in order to maximize the QoE parameters of the application with respect to the battery duration and the energy budget of the platform. An analysis of the RRM efficiency shows a CPU processing overhead of only 1.16% on an x86 platform @800 MHz, and 0.6% on a TI OMAP 4460 platform @700 MHz.

The remainder of the paper is organized as follows. Section 2 discusses the related work. Section 3 details the proposed RRM framework. Section 4 presents the demonstrator used to illustrate our RRM instantiation in Sections 5 and 6. Section 7 describes experiments performed to analyse the efficiency of our RRM framework. Finally conclusions and future work are drawn in Section 8.

2. RELATED WORK

The Multicore Association [2] focuses on the creation of open standard APIs, specifications and guidelines that allow system programmers to adopt multi-core technology into their applications more readily. One of the Multicore projects is MRAPI, the Multicore Resource management API. The goal is to enable coordinated and concurrent access to platform resources. Nevertheless, QoE management and run-time adaptive resource management are not targeted by MRAPI.

[5] describes the challenges faced today in multi-core computing. One of them is the development of a run-time adaptive system to adapt hardware, network and applications, while optimizing the QoE. To achieve such a run-time system, the key aspect is to enable meta-programming (the programmer provides options to achieve the required application functionality) and auto-tuning (the run-time system automatically finds the best option for the current platform and generates the optimal code). This key aspect conforms to the RRM features presented in Section 1.

The European Embedded Systems Industry in cooperation with the European Union established the new European Technology Platform ARTEMIS. In its strategic research agenda [6], one of the key challenges are integrated resource management, integrated QoS, and middleware, such as the RRM presented in this paper.

Independent of ARTEMIS, some domain-specific architectures, such as NoTA [3] for mobile consumer electronics, AUTOSAR [1] for automotive electronics, and IMA [4] for avionics have been developed. They include a run-time environment layer, but with no provision yet for QoE management and adaptive resource management.

In the context of RRM, task scheduling has been investigated overwhelmingly in the last decades. The most promising approaches combine design-time exploration with run-time decision making. The task concurrency management methodology [14, 16] explores the energy-performance tradeoff at the system level. The scenario-based approach [9] is based on the concept of application scenarios identified at design time. The approach [15] allows parallel execution of tasks, while sharing the platform resources. The fast and lightweight priority-based heuristic [13] extended from [15] can be used to select near-optimal configurations for the active applications according to the available platform resources, while satisfying the QoE requirements. [17] considers statistical information about task execution profile to determine the expected energy demand based on current and subsequent tasks. [7] proposes an efficient run-time support for reconfiguration while improving the platform utilization and preserving all timing constraints. [8] proposes a dynamic resource (re)allocation mechanism for large-scale high-performance computing platforms.

3. RUN-TIME RESOURCE MANAGEMENT FRAMEWORK

The target platform for our RRM framework is an embedded heterogeneous MP-SoC platform. This platform consists of multiple IP cores, and these IP cores can be of different types (e.g., hardware accelerator, FPGA, multi-CPUs).

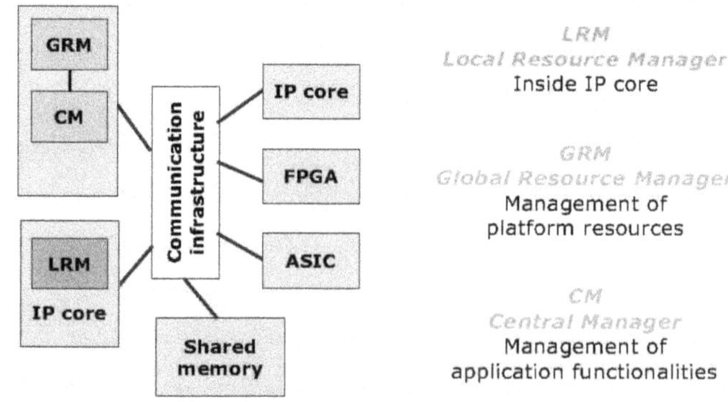

Figure 2: Distributed and hierarchical RRM approach

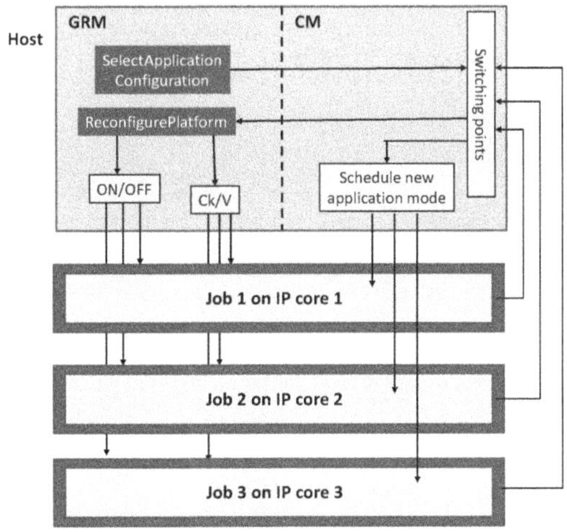

Figure 3: Communication with GRM and CM

Our RRM framework follows a distributed and hierarchical approach, illustrated in Figure 2.

On the one hand, both CM and GRM are loaded on the host processor of the platform. They are software tasks, with the same priority, and running in parallel. They are used to adapt both platform and applications at run time and to find global and optimal trade-offs in application mapping based on a given optimization goal. They conform to practices of the LRM in each IP core.

On the other hand, each IP core can execute its own resource management without any restriction, through an LRM. Such an LRM encapsulates the local policies and mechanisms used to initiate, monitor and control computation on its IP core.

As illustrated in Figure 3, the GRM manages the platform resources, whereas in parallel with the GRM, the CM manages the application functionalities:

- The platform consists of multiple IP cores, and these IP cores can be of different types, but from the GRM viewpoint, these different types are managed similarly through APIs.

- The GRM selects the application configurations (see Section 3.1) and reconfigures the IP cores accordingly. This allows the GRM to be a generic entity, being unaware of the application functionalities, and hence reusable for other embedded platforms.

- The CM informs the GRM about actions to be done, it creates the threads of the applications on the slave IP cores, and it performs some pre-processing before thread execution in parallel with the GRM. See Section 6.

3.1 Application assumptions

The target applications have to fulfil a set of assumptions, to enable the run-time management strategy based on the GRM/LRM,

Ideally, for any application, all functionalities should be accessible at any time. However, based on the user requirements, the available platform resources, the limited energy/power budget of the platform, and the target platform autonomy, it may not be possible to integrate all these functionalities on the platform at the same time. Hence the application developer has to organize the application into *application modes*, each one specifying a different subset of functionalities.

The application, within a selected mode, consists of *jobs* communicating with each other, where:

- In view of system robustness, and to make more lightweight dynamic power management, each job is mapped entirely on one IP core. Nevertheless, a job can consist of multiple tasks communicating with each other, but all of them have to run on the same IP core.

- Whereas the functional specification of a job is fixed, there may be several specific algorithms or implementations for a given job. Also a job implementation can take several forms (fixed logic, configurable logic, software) and offer different characteristics.

An *application configuration* specifies an application mapping on the platform. It is mainly characterized by: its QoS required by the user, its application mode, the job implementation, the assignment of its jobs on the IP cores of the platform, its average execution time and energy consumption, and its user benefit/value. These available application configurations are provided at design time, structured and stored in a GRM database to enable fast exploration during run-time decisions. The user benefit/value is the returned value of the utility function (see below) applied to the application configuration. It is computed at the initialization of the application (see Section 5.1).

The optimization goal, set by the user, is translated into an abstract and mathematical function, called utility function. Examples of utility functions are: performance of the application, energy/power consumption of the platform, battery life, revenue if the user has to pay for the application, fair sharing of platform resources, QoS of the application, and weighted combination of them.

4. DEMONSTRATOR

On the platform side, the hardware architecture is based on an MPSoC platform with one core acting as host processor, controlling different processing units (HW/SW). The programming model is component-based, which means that each of the processing units (PU) can be seen as co-processor. Additional hardware accelerators can be included to perform the computationally intense tasks. To enable dynamic power management, different power islands are taken into account: The host sub-system, the image acquisition pipeline, and the processing units (one power island for each PU). The overall target architecture, represented in Figure 4, consists of three ReISC DSP cores and one ReISC core acting as a host processor. The platform constraints are the battery duration (e.g., 24 hours) and the energy budget in the battery.

The application, represented in Figure 5, is from the audio-driven video surveillance domain for surveillance of critical areas. Three jobs are considered: audio activity detection on RDSP1 for environment noise detection, video processing on RDSP2 for move detection and image selection, and alarm on RDSP3. Two application modes are allowed: either audio with alarm, or audio with video.

QoE options are characterized at two levels in the application configurations. These options influence the number

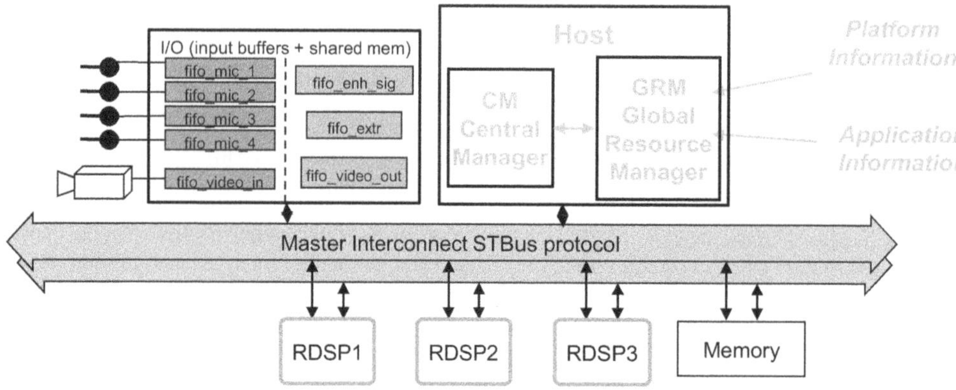

Figure 4: Platform architecture

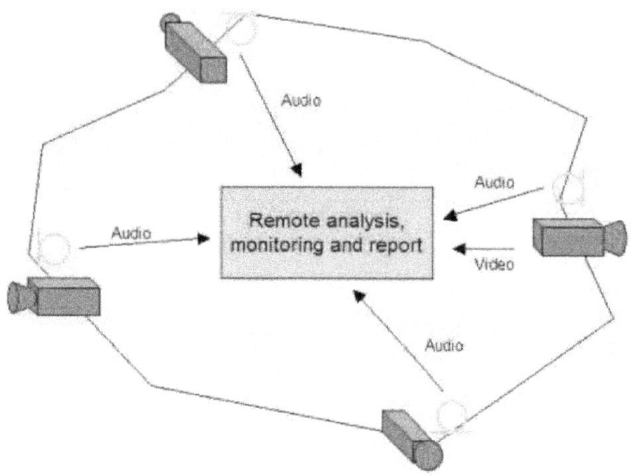

Figure 5: Audio-driven video surveillance application

of operations executed by the jobs. Hence they offer the possibility to apply dynamic voltage and frequency scaling (DVFS) to each of the IP cores to control the power consumption of the platform.

The first QoS level is related to the amount of application functionalities provided by the application configuration. This QoS should get the highest priority.

The second level is related to the QoS of the inputs and outputs of the application:

- Sampling frequency of audio inputs: two sampling frequencies can be configured: 16 bits at 8 or 16 KHz, corresponding to a bit rate of 128 or 256 Kbits/sec.
- Image resolution and rate: this depends on the camera packaged with the system. However in order to reduce the power consumption, image resolution and rate can be reduced. For video surveillance systems, it is usually not necessary to store high-definition images. An image resolution of 352x288 pixels (CIF format) or 704 x 576 pixels (4CIF format) at a rate of 16 or 25 images per second is considered.

This application being embedded, autonomy is a critical requirement, and control and reduction of energy consumption is crucial. The optimization goal is to maximize the QoS of the application, whereas the platform constraints are the energy budget and the battery duration of the platform. To that end, the utility function models the QoS of an application configuration as a weighted sum of its audio and image frequency and resolution and of the amount of application functionalities provided by its application mode.

5. GRM IMPLEMENTATION

In this paper, only one application is considered. As mentioned in Section 3, the GRM focuses on the management of the platform resources, so leaving the CM in charge of the management of the application functionalities. The GRM is implemented in C and compiled into a library `libgrm.a`, which is then linked to the application.

5.1 GRM services executed at initialization

At the initialization of the application, thus without runtime overhead, the GRM has to execute only once the following services.

`GRM_ConfigurePlatform()` loads the high-level platform specification, the platform constraints (e.g., battery duration, energy budget), and the power mode table of each IP core. A power mode of an IP core is characterized by: its supply voltage and clock frequency, its average dynamic and leakage power consumption, its available power mode transitions. A power mode transition also specifies its switching time and power consumption.

`GRM_ConfigureApplication()` loads the available application configurations derived by the design time exploration.

`GRM_DeriveUserValues()` derives the user values of the available application configurations from the selected utility function.

`GRM_SortApplicationConfigurations()` needs as input the set of Pareto-optimal application configurations in the multi-dimension space for our demonstrator. This set is derived by a design-time exploration, such as MOST [10]. This service keeps the Pareto-optimal application configurations in the two-dimension design space *user value, cost* and sorts them in ascending order according to the user value. For our demonstrator, the considered cost is the energy consumption per audio frame, and the considered two-dimension design space is illustrated in Figure 6. This service is a preprocessing to speed up the run-time execution of `GRM_SelectApplicationConfiguration()`.

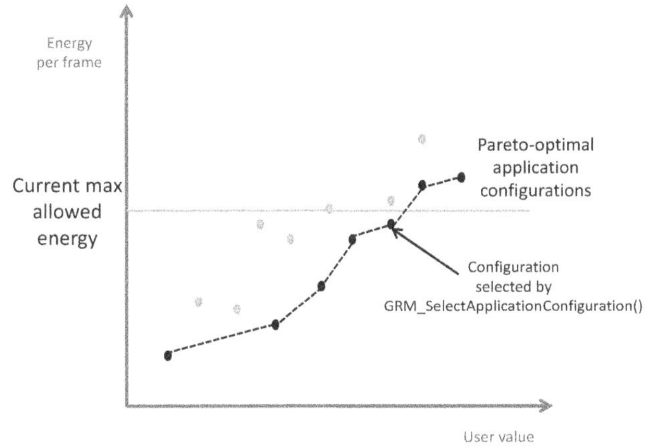

Figure 6: Two-dimension space of application configurations

5.2 GRM services executed at run time

During the run of the application, the GRM has to frequently execute the following services (more information about interrupt signals mentioned below can be found in Section 6.1):

`GRM_EstimateElapsedEnergy()` estimates the energy consumption of the platform elapsed from the application start up to this function call. Although in theory a sensor-based implementation would be possible, currently very simple energy model is used instead, where the overall platform power consumption is estimated based on the power modes of the individual IP cores:

$$\texttt{elapsed\_energy}(\texttt{platform}) = \sum_{\text{IP core}} \texttt{elapsed\_energy}(\texttt{IP core}).$$

The pseudo code of this function is as follows:

```
GRM_EstimateElapsedEnergy()
  en ← 0
  cur_time ← host_clock()
  Foreach IP core do
    Increment en by elapsed_energy(IP core)
    pm ← current_power_mode(IP core)
    Increment en by
       ( avg_leakage(pm) + avg_dyn_power(pm) )
         × (cur_time − switching_time(IP core) )
  Return en
```

where `en` denotes the estimated elapsed energy of the platform, `switching_time(IP core)` denotes `host_clock()` at the last switching point of the IP core (see Section 6.2), `elapsed_energy(IP core)` denotes the estimated energy consumption of the IP core elapsed from the system start up to the last switching point.

Whenever the GRM performs a switch between power modes of an IP core, the estimated elapsed energy of the core need to be updated during the run of the application. This update can be computed as follows:

```
cur_pm   ← current_power_mode(IP core)
new_pm   ← new_power_mode(IP core)
tm       ← power_mode_transition(cur_pm, new_pm)

Increment elapsed_energy(IP core) by
  ( avg_leakage(cur_pm) + avg_dyn_power(cur_pm) )
    × (host_clock() − switching_time(IP core) )

Increment elapsed_energy(IP core) by
    switching_power(tm) × switching_time(tm)
```

`GRM_SelectApplicationConfiguration()` selects an application configuration with the maximum user value, while meeting the platform constraints and taking the available platform resources into account. This function is frequently executed at run-time, so a lightweight implementation is mandatory. It relies on a QoS-aware optimization heuristic, providing the user with the maximum QoS according to the energy budget and the battery duration of the platform. Its pseudo code for our demonstrator is as follows, internally based on the sorted set of Pareto-solutions (see Figure 6):

```
GRM_SelectApplicationConfiguration()
  elapsed_time ← host_clock()
  remaining_time ← battery_duration(platform)
                     − elapsed_time
  call GRM_EstimateElapsedEnergy()

  remaining_energy ←
    energy_budget(platform) − elapsed_energy(platform)
  remaining_frames ←
      remaining_time / audio_frame_proc
  max_energy_per_frame ←
      remaining_energy / remaining_frames

  foreach appl_config in sorted_Pareto_set
    if energy_per_frame(appl_config)
        > max_energy_per_frame
      break
```

where it is assumed that:

- The application starts at time 0.
- `audio_frame_proc` is a QoS required by the user. It corresponds to the maximum allowed execution time to process one audio frame.
- The platform constraints are given in terms of the `platform_duration` and `energy_budget`.

`GRM_SelectApplicationConfiguration()` is executed as soon as the GRM receives the signal `sig_selection` sent by the CM. Once this service returns, the GRM sends the signal `ack_selection` to the CM. Due to the translation of the application configuration space into a two-dimension design space `[user value, cost]` and the preprocessing performed by `GRM_SortApplicationConfigurations()`, the complexity of `GRM_SelectApplicationConfiguration()` is only `O(n)`, where `n` is the size of the sorted Pareto set.

`GRM_ReconfigurePlatform()` requests each IP core of the platform to switch to the power mode specified in the newly selected application configuration. This service is executed after the execution of `GRM_SelectApplicationConfiguration()` and after the reception of the signal `sig_recrequest` sent by the CM. This service consists of the following actions performed in sequence:

- Whenever a signal sig_reconfig is received, request the reconfiguration of the corresponding IP core. This request conforms to the IP core practice and makes use of the corresponding API.
- Whenever the IP core reconfiguration is completed:
  - Confirm the CM that the corresponding IP core is ready for the next thread execution by sending the signal IPC_ready.
  - Update elapsed_energy(IP core) and switching_time(IP core).

Again, the completion of the IP core reconfiguration is acknowledged to the GRM in conformity with the IP core practice and makes use of the corresponding API. From the GRM services described above, it is worthwhile to observe that the GRM interactions with the application are done only through the CM.

6. INTERACTION FLOW BETWEEN GRM AND CENTRAL MANAGER

This section describes the interaction flow between the GRM and the CM allowing managing in parallel the platform resources and the application functionalities, as advertised in Section 3. One issue is to optimize the work repartition between the GRM and the CM in order to be as efficient and reactive as possible. A correct synchronization is required between the GRM and the CM to guarantee that the IP cores are reconfigured completely before launching the thread executions.

6.1 Communication with GRM and CM

Communications with the GRM and the CM are performed either through signals or through shared variables. As illustrated in Figure 7, two shared variables are used:

- new_AC is shared between the GRM and the CM. It is written by the GRM and read by the CM. It stores the ID of the application configuration selected by GRM_SelectApplicationConfiguration(). Whenever the CM wants to update the application configuration, it copies new_AC into current_AC.
- current_AC is shared between the CM and the slave threads. It is written by the CM and read by the slave threads. It stores the ID of the application configuration currently executed on the platform. It is through current_AC that the CM communicates the application configuration to the slave threads.

Three types of signal communication are also used:

- Communication between the GRM and the CM, whose interrupt signals are defined as follows:
  - As soon as GRM_ReconfigurationPlatform() is completed for the last selected application configuration, the GRM starts waiting for sig_selection.
  - Regularly, the CM wants to update the current application configuration. To that end, it sends sig_selection to the GRM to request the execution of GRM_SelectApplicationConfiguration().
  - ack_selection is sent by the GRM to the CM to indicate that the variable new_AC has been updated:
    * The CM can read new_AC at any time to be aware of the newly selected application mode.
    * As soon as the CM agrees to perform the reconfiguration, the CM needs to copy new_AC into the variable current_AC.
    * Before each new processing, the active slave threads need to read current_AC to be aware of the options to be executed.
  - As soon as the CM agrees to switch to the newly selected application configuration, it requests the execution of GRM_ReconfigurePlatform() by sending sig_request to the GRM.
  - As soon as sig_terminating is received, sig_reconfig(IP core) is sent by the CM to the GRM to indicate that the IP core can be reconfigured.
  - IPC_ready(IP core) is sent by the GRM to the CM to indicate that the IP core is ready to execute the thread.
- Communication between the GRM and the IP cores of the platform, whose interrupt signals are defined as follows:
  - sig_switch_pm(power_mode) is sent by the GRM to the IP core to request the switching to the given power mode.
  - ack_switch_pm is sent by the IP core to the GRM to indicate that the reconfiguration is completed with the new power mode.
- Communication between the CM and the slave threads, whose interrupt signals are defined as follows:
  - sig_wakeup is sent by the CM: either to create the thread and start its execution, or to reactivate the thread after a new power mode switching.
  - sig_terminating is sent by the slave thread to the CM as soon as a switching point (see Section 6.2) is met. This signal indicates that the thread completed its current processing, it is in a stable state and it can deal with hardware adaptations. This signal also implies that the thread reads current_AC and that it is aware whether it has to continue its execution or to enter a sleep mode before executing a new configuration.

As illustrated in Figure 8, a timeout must also be used for robustness in case of faulty IP cores or slave threads, in which case some special action must be taken by the CM. E.g., see wait(sig_terminating and ack_switch_pm for 50ms).

6.2 Dedicated switching points

Activation of new application configuration must be seamless to avoid damage and to maintain the real-time behaviour and the data integrity of the application. Obviously, this cannot be done at any time: the threads should be in a stable state (e.g., not yet started, having completed some

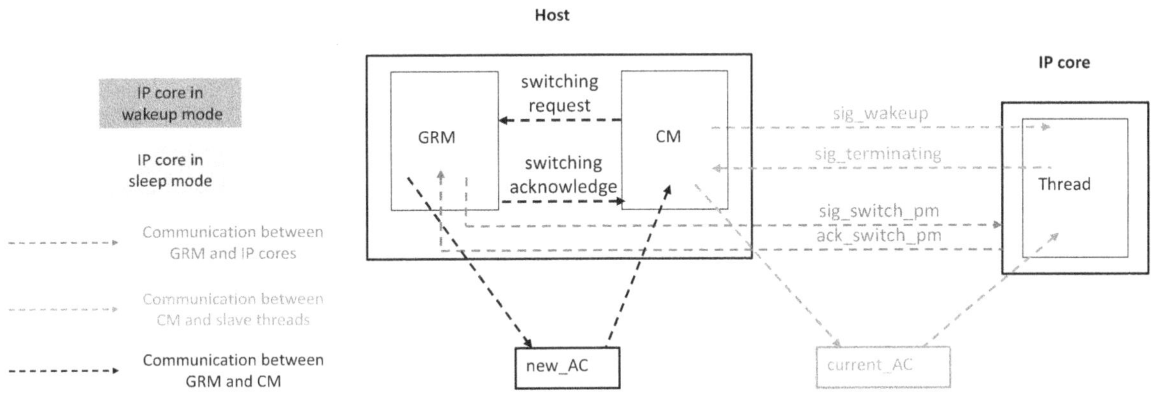

Figure 7: Communications with GRM and CM

processing, and being in a waiting state). This means that all threads will probably not switch at the same time. Hence the only robust solution is to reconfigure the IP cores and the threads one by one as soon as a thread is ready for it until the complete platform and application are reconfigured.

As a consequence, the main issue in application configuration switching is to find appropriate moments for performing such a switching. To that end, dedicated switching points must be specified by the application developer inside the source code of the job. A smooth transition from the current application configuration to the new one is illustrated in Figure 8 and performed as follows, where each thread performs the common following steps:

- Through the signal `ack_selection`, the GRM indicates the CM that an application configuration switching is required.
- Whenever a thread reaches a dedicated switching point (i.e., after some reaction time), the thread checks whether a switching is requested by reading the shared variable `current_AC`.
- If a switching is requested:
  - The thread sends a signal `sig_terminating` to the CM.
  - The thread enters a sleep mode until reception of the signal `sig_wakeup`, requesting the activation of the thread after the reconfiguration of the IP core. Both IP core reconfiguration and thread activation are not immediate. They need some freeze time due to DVFS for example. During this freeze time, the CM can perform some preprocessing before next thread activations (e.g., prepare a list of next actions for the GRM, keep sending signals `sig_reconfig`).
  - The thread starts its execution according to the newly selected configuration.

Hence the switching mechanism takes place at two levels:

- At the platform level: all IP cores, managed by the GRM, are reconfigured according to the newly selected power modes.
- At the application level: all jobs, managed by the CM, switch safely to the newly selected configuration.

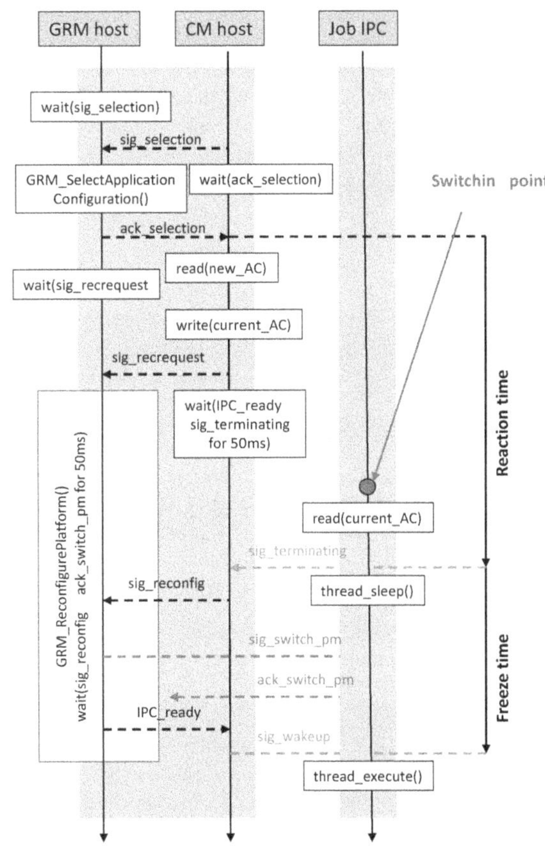

Figure 8: Application configuration switching

7. EXPERIMENTAL RESULTS

In order to perform initial experiments on the overhead and feasibility of the presented run-time management approach, both the GRM and the CM have been integrated in a POSIX-based implementation of the audio-surveillance video application. This implementation has then been deployed and tesetd on to two different platforms: an x86-based platform running at 800 MHz, and an ARM-based TI OMAP 4460 platform running at 700 MHz.

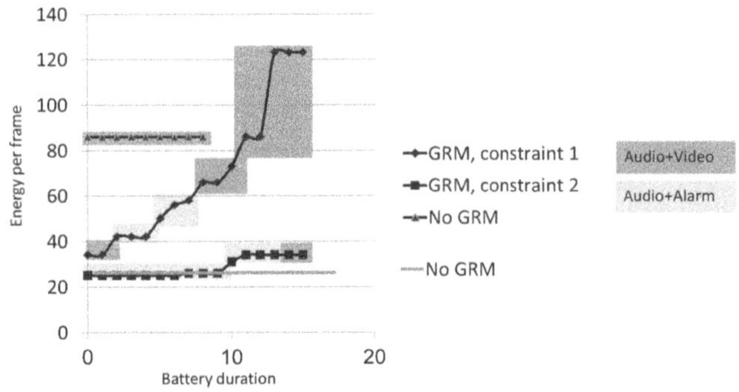

Figure 9: Energy-per-frame evolution with and without GRM

7.1 Binary size of GRM implementation

As explained in Section 5, the GRM is implemented in C and compiled into a library `libgrm.a` which is then linked to the application. The current binary size of `libgrm.a` is 107 KB on the x86 platform, without taking the GRM databases into account. Two GRM databases are also required to store the high-level specification of the platform, the IP core types, and the application configurations:

- The current binary size of the platform database is

$$\begin{aligned} 78 &+ 20 \times \texttt{ipcore\_nr} \\ &+ 54 \times \texttt{ipcore\_type\_nr} \\ &+ 20 \times \texttt{ipcore\_type\_nr} \\ &\quad\;\; \times \texttt{power\_mode\_nr} \\ &\quad\;\; \times (1 + \texttt{power\_mode\_nr}) \end{aligned}$$

  bytes, where `ipcore_nr` denotes the number of IP cores in the platform, `ipcore_type_nr` denotes the number of IP core types, and `power_mode_nr` denotes the maximum number of power modes per IP core type. E.g., in our demonstrator, where the platform consists of 4 ReISC cores, with maximum 5 available power modes, the binary size of the platform database is 1506 bytes.

- Similarly, the current binary size of the application configuration database is

$$(52 + 12 \times \texttt{job\_nr}) \times \texttt{appl\_config\_nr} \text{ bytes,}$$

  where `job_nr` denotes the number of jobs in the application and `appl_config_nr` denotes the number of application configurations. E.g., in our demonstrator, where the application consists of three jobs (i.e., alarm processing, audio activity detection, and video image processing), the binary size of an application configuration is 88 bytes.

7.2 Performance overhead and energy gain

Figure 9 illustrates the energy-per-frame evolution of our demonstrator for two platform constraints (different energy budgets, same battery duration) with and without the GRM. Due to an optimized adaptive selection of application configurations, our GRM allows optimizing the QoS of the application while keeping the platform battery alive during its whole required duration. In contrast, this cannot be ensured without such an RRM framework.

Figure 10 illustrates the CPU processing of the GRM services executed at initialization on the x86 platform. Both

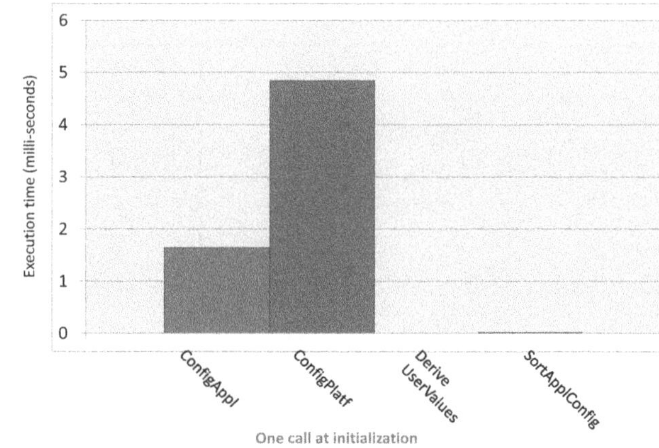

Figure 10: Performance of GRM initialization

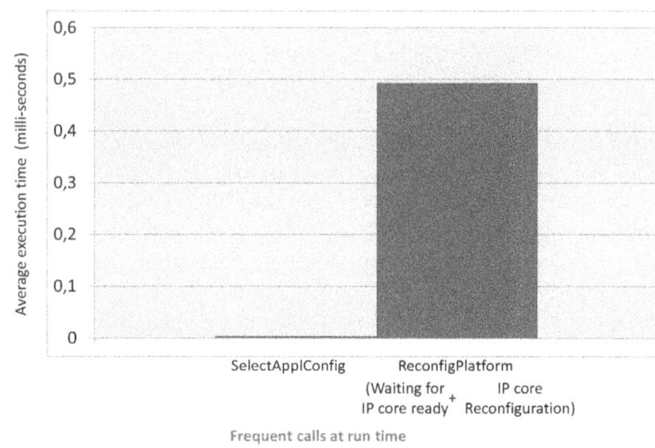

Figure 11: Performance of GRM run-time services

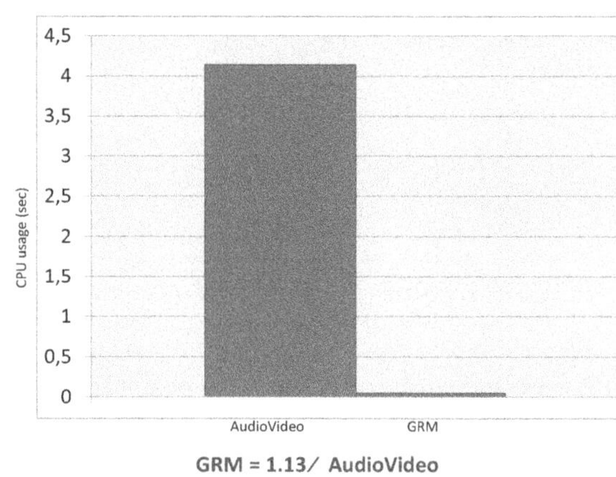

Figure 12: GRM processing overhead on x86

`GRM_ConfigurePlatform()` and `GRM_ConfigureApplication()` require more processing due to parsing of high-level platform specification and available application configurations. Nevertheless, these services are executed only once without any run-time overhead.

Figure 11 illustrates the CPU processing of the GRM services executed at run time on the x86 platform. The performance of `GRM_SelectApplicationConfiguration()` includes the one of `GRM_EstimateElapsedEnergy()`. The performance of `GRM_ReconfigurePlatform()` includes all waiting times for IP cores being ready and for IP core reconfiguration. Nevertheless the average execution time on on the x86 platform is still < 0.5 ms.

Finally, a global analysis of the GRM CPU processing overhead compared to the application processing shows an overhead of only 1.16% on an x86 platform @800 MHz (see Figure 12), and 0.6% on a TI OMAP 4460 platform running at 700 MHz. This shows that the overhead of the proposed run-time energy management mechanism is negligible and there is no significant impact on the application.

In combination, the experiments show that the proposed combined approach of design-time optimization of application configurations and their dynamic run-time management improves the overall QoE of the system.

8. CONCLUSION AND FUTURE WORK

In this paper, the run-time implementation and analysis of a two-level performance and power-optimization approach has been presented. Based on a design-time exploration, a set of Pareto-optimal application configurations are selected and dynamically managed during run-time to maximize the overall quality-of user experience under changing platform conditions.

More specifically, the main contribution of this paper is two-fold. First, the details of the run-time resource management framework addressing the challenges of future embedded computing have been presented. Secondly, this RRM framework is instantiated for an audio-driven video surveillance application in order to maximize the QoE parameters of the application with respect to the platform constraints. By using the run-time manager, the energy consumption can be reduced significantly, such that the application+platform combination can fulfil the QoE constraints. A preliminary analysis of the efficiency of the RRM framework shows a very low CPU processing and a reasonable memory overhead. Future work will focus on the integration into the real embedded platforms.

9. ACKNOWLEDGEMENTS

This work has been partially supported by the COMPLEX FP7 European Integrated Project [11], funded by the European Commission under Grant Agreement 247999.

10. REFERENCES

[1] *AUTOSAR - AUTomotive Open System ARchitecture.* http://www.autosar.org.

[2] *Multicore Association.* http://www.multicore-association.org.

[3] *NoTA world.* http://www.notaworld.org.

[4] *ARINC 653 - An avionics standard for aafe, partitioned systems*, Aug. 2008. IEEE seminar.

[5] S. Adve, V. Adve, G. Agha, M. Frank, M. Garzarán, J. Hart, W. Hwu, R. Johnson, L. Kale, R. Kumar, D. Marinov, K. Nahrstedt, D. Padua, M. Parthasarathy, S. Patel, G. Rosu, D. Roth, M. Snir, J. Torrellas, and C. Zilles. Parallel computing research at illinois - the UPCRC agenda. Technical report, University of Illinois, Urbana-Champaign, November 2008.

[6] ARTEMIS. *Strategic research agenda*, 2011. http://www.artemis.eu.

[7] M. Bassiri and H. S. Shahhoseini. Mitigating reconfiguration overhead in on-line task scheduling for reconfigurable computing systems. In *International Conference on Computer Engineering and Technology*, 2010.

[8] J. Brandt, F. Chen, V. D. Sapio, A. Gentile, J. Mayo, P. Pebay, D. Roe, D. Thompson, and M. Wong. Combining virtualization, resource characterization, and resource management to enable efficient high performance compute platforms through intelligent dynamic resource allocation. In *International Symposium on Parallel and Distributed Processing*, 2010.

[9] S. Gheorghita, M. Palkovic, J. Hamers, A.Vandecappelle, S. Mamagkakis, T. Basten, L. Eeckhout, H. Corporaal, F. Catthoor, F. Vandeputte, and K. D. Bosschere. System scenario based design of dynamic embedded systems. *ACM Transactions On Design Automation of Electronic Systems*, 14(1), January 2009.

[10] G. Palermo, C. Silvano, and V. Zaccaria. ReSPIR: A response surface-based pareto iterative refinement for application-specific design space exploration. *IEEE Transactions on Computer-Aided Design of Integrated Circuits and Systems*, 28(12):1816–1829, 2009.

[11] The COMPLEX project (247999). Codesign and power management in platform-based design space exploration. http://complex.offis.de.

[12] C. Ykman-Couvreur. Exploration framework for run-time resource management of embedded multi-core platforms. In *International Conference on Embedded Computer Systems: Architectures, MOdeling, and Simulation*, Samos, Greece, July 2010.

[13] C. Ykman-Couvreur, P. Avasare, G. Mariani, G. Palermo, C. Silvano, and V. Zaccaria. Linking run-time resource management of embedded multi-core platforms with automated design-time exploration. *Computers Digital Techniques, IET*, 5(2):123–135, March 2011.

[14] C. Ykman-Couvreur, F. Catthoor, J. Vounckx, A. Folens, and F. Louagie. Energy-aware dynamic task scheduling applied to a real-time multimedia application on an Xscale board. *Journal of Low Power Electronics (JOLPE)*, 1(3):226–237, December 2005.

[15] C. Ykman-Couvreur, V. Nollet, F. Catthoor, and H. Corporaal. Fast multidimension multichoice knapsack heuristic for MP-SoC run-time management. *ACM Transactions on Embedded Computing Systems*, 10(3):35:1–35:16, April 2011.

[16] C. Ykman-Couvreur, V. Nollet, T. Marescaux, E. Brockmeyer, F. Catthoor, and H. Corporaal. Design-time application mapping and platform exploration for MP-SoC customized run-time management. *Computers Digital Techniques, IET*, 1(2):120–128, March 2007.

[17] T. Zitterell and C. Scholl. A probabilistic and energy-efficient scheduling approach for online application in real-time systems. In *Design Automation Conference*, June 2010.

Network-aware Design-Space Exploration of a Power-Efficient Embedded Application

Parinaz Sayyah
Politecnico di Torino, Italy
parinaz.sayyah@polito.it

Mihai T. Lazarescu
Politecnico di Torino, Italy
mihai.lazarescu@polito.it

Davide Quaglia
EDALab, Italy
davide.quaglia@edalab.it

Emad Ebeid
University of Verona, Italy
emad.ebeid@univr.it

Sara Bocchio
STMicroelectronics, Italy
sara.bocchio@st.com

Alberto Rosti
STMicroelectronics, Italy
alberto.rosti@st.com

ABSTRACT

The paper presents the design and multi-parameter optimization of a networked embedded application for the health-care domain. Several hardware, software, and application parameters, such as clock frequency, sensor sampling rate, data packet rate, are tuned at design- and run-time according to application specifications and operating conditions to optimize hardware requirements, packet loss, power consumption. Experimental results show that further power efficiency can be achieved by considering also communication aspects during design space exploration.

Categories and Subject Descriptors

B.8.2 [**Performance and Reliability**]: Performance Analysis and Design Aids; C.4 [**Performance of Systems**]: Modeling techniques

General Terms

Design, Measurement, Performance

Keywords

HW/SW Timing and Power Simulation, Virtual Platform, Network Simulation, Wireless Sensor Network, Body Sensor Network

1. INTRODUCTION

The design of embedded systems is becoming increasingly complex in case of distributed applications made of several nodes consisting of hardware and software components interacting over a network. A realistic example of this kind of application is the health care wireless sensor network presented in Figure 1.

Each monitored person wears a number of wireless nodes that capture and process different kinds of body-related information; they exchange data and commands with a base station over a radio channel which is shared among different unrelated data flows.

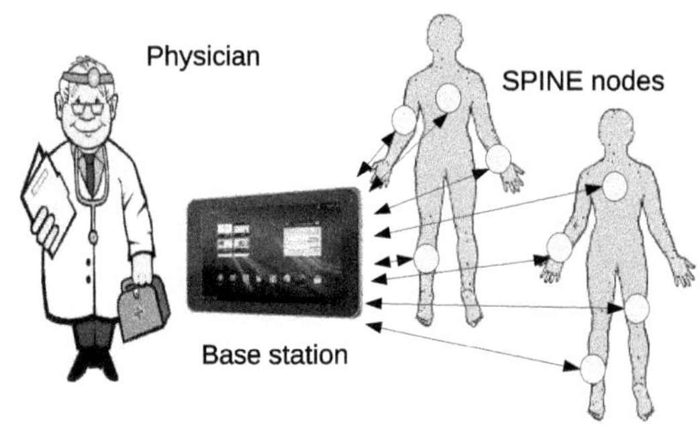

Figure 1: Example of distributed application based on networked embedded systems.

The wireless nodes are based on the open source Signal Processing in Node Environment (SPINE [8]) framework specification. It supports flexible and distributed signal processing for Wireless Body Sensor Network applications through a set of customizable functions for data acquisition, processing and communication.

The European project COMPLEX [3] uses SPINE-based software running on a 32-bit system-on-chip architecture from ST-Microelectronics as a case study for HW/SW design-space exploration (DSE) of the sensor node. Power consumption is key aspect in a mobile health care application to ensure long-time unattended operation of the sensor node. As described in Section 3.3, the ReISC SoC is highly configurable to save power when some components are not used. For each component, the definition of low-power or power-off periods usually depends on application timing constraints such as system promptness to asynchronous events or sampling rate of continuous values. In the specific case of wireless nodes transmitting on a shared channel, the network behavior plays a crucial role in determining the time behavior of the nodes with potential impact on their power consumption. Such network behavior depends on several causes and mainly by the number of concurrent data sources; an analytical approach to this study can become complex as the number of nodes increases. Therefore, network simulation is the most viable approach to make this timing analysis. Hence simulation must take into account the following aspects:

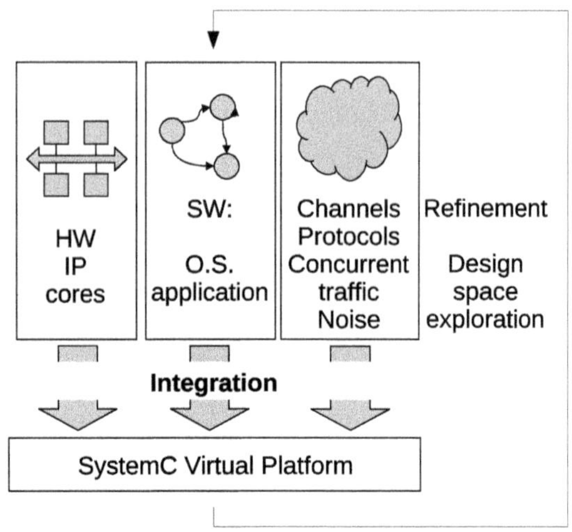

Figure 2: Generation of SystemC models from different domains: hardware, software and network.

- *software components*, such as the operating system and the application;
- *hardware components*, such as the CPU, memory, and peripherals;
- *networking scenarios* that, for instance, consist of channel behavior (e.g., path loss, collisions), communication protocols (e.g., IEEE 802.15.4), concurrent traffic and noise.

One approach for this kind of holistic simulation is the co-simulation [1] that combines and synchronizes the execution of several simulation tools, such as an instruction set simulator for software components, a VHDL simulator for hardware components, and a network simulator (e.g., NS-2 [5]) for the network. In [6] a co-simulation approach has been used to show that power optimization can be achieved by scaling CPU frequency according to the number of packets waiting to be transmitted because of network congestion.

With respect to past literature, the novel contributions of this work are:

- an industrial-level virtual platform written in SystemC [7] by STMicroelectronics is extended to simulate the wireless node in a full network scenario without using co-simulation;
- the hardware components and the network are modeled in detail, in order to enable the tuning of the power management strategy based on network timing constraints.

The resulting simulation flow is shown in Figure 2. The hardware blocks of the wireless node are modeled in SystemC at the Transaction Level (TLM) to capture their functional behavior at a high level. One of these blocks represents the CPU that executes the actual software components with machine-instruction accuracy. The hardware blocks are included in the SystemC model, together with network elements (protocol and channel). The resulting simulation models a full network scenario in which several wireless nodes interact in a realistic way.

The rest of the paper is organized as follows. Section 2 introduces the health care application. Section 3 describes the hardware platform of the wireless sensor node to be designed. Section 4 explains how all the aspects of the designed system and its operating environment can be modeled in SystemC. Section 5 describes experimentally how timing constraints derived from network simulation can be used to refine some system parameters to save power. Finally, conclusions are presented in Section 6.

2. APPLICATION

The COMPLEX project proposes a use case based on a complete and realistic Wireless Sensor Network (WSN) scenario. Its architecture, presented in Figure 1, consists of several nodes, namely *SPINE Nodes* and the *Base Station* (BS). It couples all major aspects of WSNs (sensing, processing, radio data transmission) with a non-trivial amount of local computation on the node. The raw sensed data are processed directly on the node, in order to reduce the energy consumed by the radio, which is the major limiting factor for the battery lifetime of WSN nodes.

The application is a virtual machine for health monitoring that conforms to the open specification of the SPINE [8] virtual machine for Wireless Body Sensor Network (WBSN) applications. It provides the user with a customizable set of functions that includes:

1. acquisition of various types of data (e.g., temperature, acceleration, blood oxygenation level, hearth pulse rate) and their storage in local circular buffers;
2. signal processing, including a variety of filtering, threshold detection, and other mathematical functions over the data in buffers;
3. communication via data packets with a base station either regularly or when events of interest are detected (e.g., emergency events).

The detailed application functionality is defined by the Base Station (BS) node at run time by means of configuration packets sent to each SPINE Node. The configuration can include the sampling period of individual sensors, buffer sizes, processing functions (e.g., max, mean, median) to be applied on raw sensed data, window size (i.e., the number of samples needed to compute a feature for the first time), shift size (i.e., the number of samples needed to compute the feature after the first time). The various configured tasks (e.g., sampling, feature computation, radio packet dispatch) can be selectively activated or deactivated at run time, depending on application demands.

One prominent application in the WBSN domain is fall detection by monitoring the body movements of elderly patients. In this paper, this is achieved by configuring the SPINE Node to collect and filter 3-axis acceleration samples and transmit these data over the wireless channel to the Base Station. The Base Station further processes the sensor data and detects falls based on the changes in the acceleration data over a timed window. The operator (physician or other health care professional) can monitor the patient condition by examining on the server the processed acceleration data from several sensor nodes.

To this end, the application should be configured by the operator. The first step is to connect the base station with the SPINE sensor node of interest. The operator selects those SPINE capabilities which are needed to define the

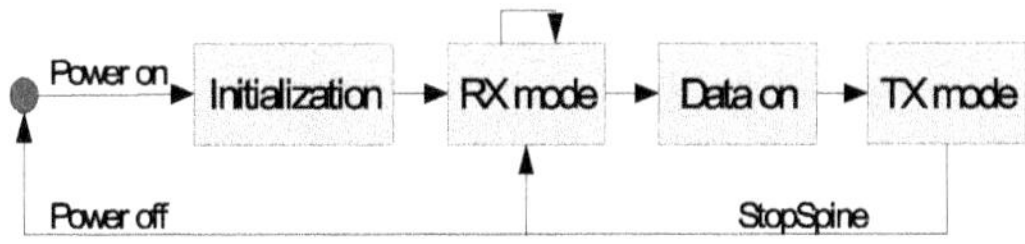

Figure 3: Behavior of the SPINE sensor node.

monitoring of interest, e.g., 3D acceleration. These decisions are then translated by the base station into configuration packets for the SPINE sensor node, which starts the requested measurements.

Specific menu items on the application user interface allow the operator to stop and resume the measurements at any time, or exit the sensor viewer altogether.

The base station can autonomously detect critical situations (e.g., the system detects that the monitored person falls when the average acceleration over a short interval of time exceeds a given threshold).

Figure 3 shows the behavior of the sensor node. After the *Initialization* phase it enters the *Receive mode* where it waits for configuration packets from the *Base Station* node.

The configuration packets are processed as received and the configuration sequence ends with a *StartSpine* command that changes the sensor node state to *Data On*. In this state, the tasks requested by the Base Station are executed.

Then the SPINE Node briefly enters the *TX mode* in which it samples and processes the sensor data and periodically sends packets with aggregated data to the Base Station.

Any incoming packets from the Base Station continue to be processed. These commands can change the set of tasks or their configuration, or can stop the processing altogether (*StopSpine* command).

3. HARDWARE PLATFORM

The hardware platform of the SPINE Node consists of:

- the *ReISC* System-on-Chip that performs sensing and data processing;
- the *RF Module* that provides wireless communications.

3.1 ReISC System-on-Chip

The ReISC SoC is the outcome of the design of a system on chip by STMicroelectronics, resulting in a real silicon chip which was taped-out at the end of 2009 using a 90 nm technology. The ReISC SoC is the first system on chip which drives a new family of ultra low power products.

The ReISC SoC encompasses the proprietary ReISC 3 core (Reduced energy Instruction Set Computer). It provides hardware support for 8/16/20/32 data sizes, variable 16 bit-based instruction length and secure data. ReISC 3 is targeted at ultra-low power applications. It operates up to 50 MHz frequency, contains embedded memories (1 Mbytes Flash memory and 32 Kbytes SRAM) and an extensive range of enhanced I/Os and peripherals.

It offers one 12-bit ADC, three general purpose 16-bit timers plus one internal timer, as well as standard and advanced communication interfaces: one I2C, two GPIOs, two SPIs, one USART, and one USB. A comprehensive set of power-saving modes allows the design of low-power applications.

The peripherals that are significant for the optimization of the SPINE Node are:

- the Serial Peripheral Interface (SPI), which handles the communication between the ReISC SoC and the RF Module;
- the General Purpose Input/Output (GPIO);
- the timers, which are used for synchronization purposes;
- the Analog-to-Digital Converter (ADC), which collects samples from the sensors;
- the Reset and Clock Control Unit (RCCU);
- the Power Manager, which is used to manage the power states of the ReISC SoC (CPU and peripherals).

The Serial Peripheral Interface (SPI) consists of a synchronous serial communication interface with a 4-pin protocol. It allows half/full-duplex, synchronous, serial communication with external devices. There are separate buffers for reception and transmission and the peripheral can operate in full-duplex mode. When the interface is configured as master it provides the communication clock to the external slave device. The interface is also capable of operating in multi-master configuration. It may be used for a variety of purposes, including simplex synchronous transfers on two lines with a possible bidirectional data line or reliable communication with CRC checking.

The General Purpose Input/Output (GPIO) is a set of pins whose behavior can be programmed through software.

There are up to four timers in the ReISC Soc platform, which may be used for a variety of purposes, including measuring the pulse length of input signals (input capture) or generating output waveforms or counting events. The internal timer is the simplest one, having only simple down-counting functionality.

The Analog-to-Digital Converter (ADC) converts a continuous signal (voltage or current) into a sequence of numbers proportional to the magnitude of the voltage or current. Its main feature is resolution, i.e., the number of discrete values it can produce over the range of analog values. ReISC ADC provides 16 multiplexed channels, with 12 bit resolution, interrupt generation at the end of conversion, and DMA request generation during conversion.

The Reset and Clock Control Unit (RCCU) manages the power-on reset for the ReISC SoC system, as well as generating the system clocks via PLLs. It allows also to enable/disable the peripherals and their clocks.

The Power Manager activates clock gating for each individual peripheral which is not used, selects the power-down state for analog hard macro when they are not required by the application, and selects the appropriate system clock frequency. In order to reduce power consumption to the minimum value, the core can also shut off the power domains for each ADC PLL and for the FLASH memory.

3.2 RF Module

The RF Module is connected through an SPI interface to the ReISC SoC, in order to provide its networking capability. The role and architecture of the RF Module inside the SPINE Node is presented in Figure 4. It consists of three components: the front-end, the network processor and the back-end.

The front-end component manages the SPI protocol to communicate with the ReISC SoC. It receives data from the

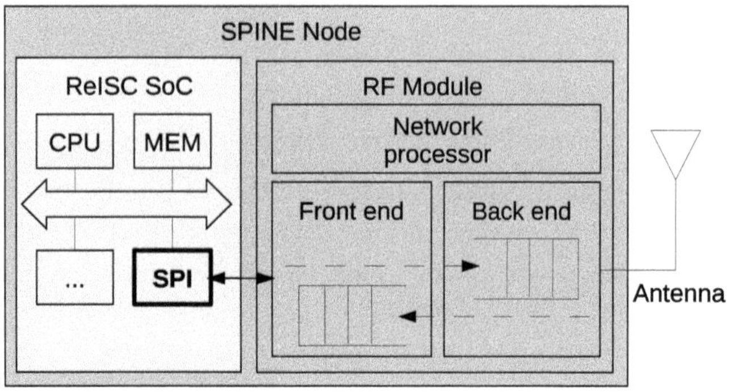

Figure 4: Architecture of the RF Module and interconnection with the ReISC SoC.

ReISC SoC to be sent to the network and those from the network, through the back-end component, to be sent to the ReISC SoC.

The SPI transmission uses simplex mode. The decision about setting the SPI controller in master or slave mode is made by the software running on the ReISC SoC. When the ReISC SoC SPI controller is in slave mode, it waits to receive data from the RF Module. When it enters the master mode it cannot be interrupted by the RF Module. Therefore, the RF module uses a local FIFO queue to temporally store the data to be transmitted to the ReISC SoC.

The network processor implements the medium access control according to the IEEE 802.15.4 [4] standard.

The back-end component addresses all the low-level details to send/receive bits on the radio channel. The transmission time of a packet is not constant since the 802.15.4 protocol provides a statistical access approach based on random wait with multiple re-transmissions in case of failure; therefore, the back-end component also contains a FIFO queue to store packets when the production rate of the ReISC SoC is higher than the transmission rate over the air.

3.3 Power consumption

To improve power consumption, the ReISC SoC can apply different power reduction techniques such as clock gating and power gating. The architecture is in fact hierarchically organized in power islands that can be switched off under the control of the power manager; finer control on the consumption can also be obtained by the RCCU that allows to set the enabling status of the peripherals and to enable or disable their clock.

The organization of the power islands is summarized here:

- An ALWAYS ON power island includes the ReISC core, the RCCU, the Power Manager, Timers, all the other components that must be kept always enabled.
- A FUNCTIONAL STATE power island (with retention flip-flops) contains the other peripherals that can be switched on/off, e.g., the SPI and the GPIOs.
- An ANALOG power island includes the ADC.

Table 1 reports the power consumption values of SPI and ADC peripherals as a function of the power mode.

Table 1: Power consumption values (in μW) of SPI and ADC peripherals as a function of the power mode.

Power mode	SPI	ADC
OFF	0	0
NO CLOCK	20	n/a
IDLE	40	30
WORKING	100	150

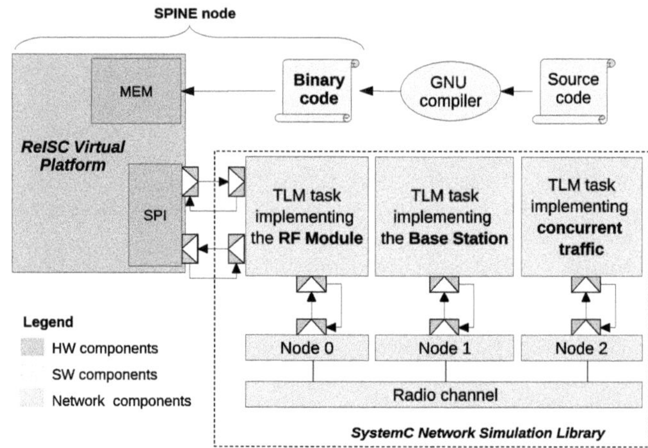

Figure 5: Modeling approach.

4. MODELING APPROACH

Figure 5 presents the whole simulation scenario, modeled completely in SystemC. The model of the SPINE Node consists of the ReISC SoC virtual platform provided by STMicroelectronics and the model of the RF Module. The former is an accurate model of the hardware components of the ReISC SoC, while the latter is modeled at the pure functional level by using the blocks provided by the SystemC Network Simulation Library (SCNSL) [2]. Software components (i.e., application and system code) are compiled for the target platform and then loaded into the memory module of the virtual platform to be executed by the CPU module. The network components, modeled by using SCNSL, consist of:

- an SCNSL task to represent the functional model of the RF Module of the SPINE Node;
- an SCNSL task to represent the functional model of the SPINE base station;
- an SCNSL task to represent the functional model of a source of concurrent traffic;
- the hosting nodes of the three previous tasks;
- the radio channel.

The simulation is performed at the TLM level; the ReISC SoC virtual platform is connected to the RF Module through two TLM sockets and each SCNSL task is connected to the corresponding SCNSL node by using a TLM socket.

It is worth remembering that we aim at optimizing the power consumption of the ReISC SoC and therefore we are interested in modeling accurately its hardware components and the software components while transmission components are not part of the design goal.

4.1 ReISC Virtual Platform

The ReISC SoC platform is provided with a virtual platform simulation framework, shown in Figure 6. It consists of an ISS of the ReISC 3 processor which communicates with the hardware models of the peripherals through a bus model. A SystemC wrapper implements the interface among the instruction-set simulator (ISS) and the rest of the system, i.e. the peripherals, that are mostly modeled in SystemC. Only the components that are more closely linked to the ISS or to the memory, have been left under the direct control of the ISS, rather than in SystemC. In Figure 6 the SystemC peripherals are shown in orange, while the parts in yellow are modeled in C within the ISS.

4.2 Network simulation

The simulation of the health care application involves three network nodes:

- one Base Station (BS), with two main purposes:
  1. to broadcast configuration packets to the SPINE Node at initialization time;
  2. to listen for incoming data packets from SPINE Node;
- SPINE Node with three main purposes:
  1. receive and process the configuration packets from the BS;
  2. perform the configured computations;
  3. transmit the sample data to the BS;
- A traffic generation node which broadcasts packets on the shared channel by using the same channel access protocol of the first two nodes (i.e., IEEE 802.15.4). Since the channel models collisions, this node is used to evaluate the effect of concurrent traffic of the communication between the SPINE Node and the Base Station.

```
01    #include <systemc>
02    #include <tlm.h>
03    #include <scnsl.hh>
04    #include "Spine_t.hh"
05    #include "Base_Station_t.hh"
06    #include "Concurrent_t.hh"

07    int sc_main( int argc, char * argv[] )
08    {
09      ...
10      Scnsl::Setup::Scnsl_t * scnsl =
                  Scnsl::Setup::Scnsl_t::get_instance();

11      // Creation of nodes:
12      Scnsl::Core::Node_t * n0 = scnsl->createNode();
13      Scnsl::Core::Node_t * n1 = scnsl->createNode();
14      Scnsl::Core::Node_t * n2 = scnsl->createNode();

15      // Creation of the wireless channel:
16      ccs.channel_type = CoreChannelSetup_t::SHARED;
17      Scnsl::Core::Channel_if_t * ch =
                  scnsl->createChannel( ccs );

18      // node-channel binding:
19      scnsl->bind( n0, ch, bsb0 );
20      scnsl->bind( n1, ch, bsb1 );
21      scnsl->bind( n2, ch, bsb1 );

22      // Mapping of task instances on to nodes:
23      Spine_t t0( "SPINE", n0);
24      Base_Station_t t1( "BS", n1);
25      Concurrent_t t2( "CBR", n2);
26      ...
```

Figure 7: Network scenario described in SystemC by using SCNSL primitives.

Figure 7 represents the network scenario described in SystemC by using SCNSL primitives to create the nodes (lines 12–14), the channel (line 17) and the tasks (lines 23–25). Node instances are also connected to the shared radio channel (lines 19–21).

In both BS and SPINE Node models, the interface to the channel is implemented by inheriting the SCNSL `TlmTask_if_t` interface and by using the corresponding transmit and receive methods, i.e., `Send()` and `b_transport()`, respectively.

Figure 8 shows the architecture of the `Base_Station_t` class. It includes two main member functions, namely `sendConfigPacket` and `receiveDataPacket`. The model of the BS includes a SystemC `SC_THREAD` which periodically calls `sendConfigPacket` with an application-specific sequence of node configuration packets for the SPINE Node.

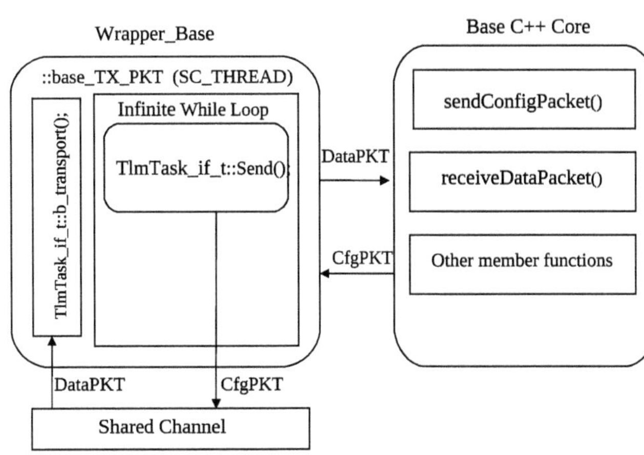

Figure 8: Architecture of the SystemC model of the Base Station.

4.3 Simulation of the software components

The simulation of the application is performed by running the system software and the SPINE code on the ISS of the ReISC SoC virtual platform. In this experiment, the ReISC

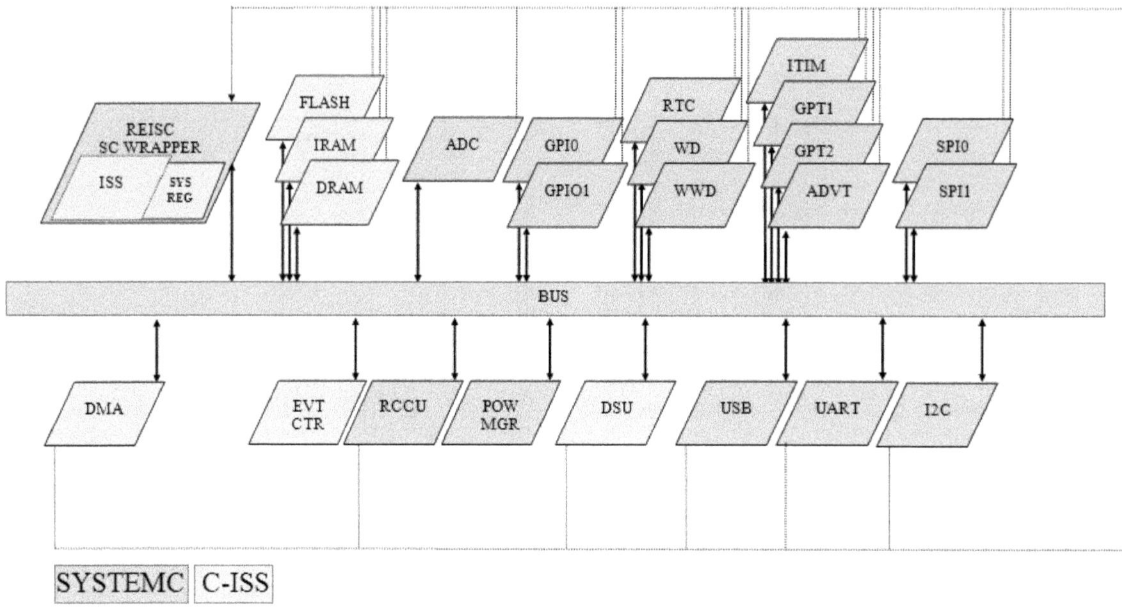

Figure 6: Architecture of the ReISC SoC virtual platform.

SoC is running at 50 MHz, with a timer configured to generate a periodic event for the SPINE application. After the initialization phase, the SPINE Node listens to receive four configuration 16-byte packets from the BS. The BS is configured to send packets every 200 ms. After receiving each packet, the radio sends it to the SPI controller which is configured to work in slave mode to raise an interrupt. The SPI interrupt handler copies the payload of the received packet into the packet buffer of the SPINE, application allowing the node to be customized and configured properly.

Upon receiving the *StartSpine* command from the BS, the SPINE Node engine starts by setting the SPI controller in master mode and initializing the timer to schedule a periodic task using the packet transmission interval defined at configuration time by the BS. Then the ADC is activated and configured to sample acceleration data over three channels. At every sampled value, the ADC interrupt is raised and the value is placed in the SPINE circular buffer. A window of samples is then processed and filtered and the result is sent to the SPI controller which sends it to the RF Module.

Note that the accelerometer sampling rate and the packet transmission rate are independent. The former can be much higher than the latter, in order to save radio power, possibly at the expense of the quality of fall detection.

5. CASE STUDY

We simulated 2 seconds of the application scenario:

- from 0 s to 0.4 s the Base Station sends four configuration packets;
- from 0.4 s to 2.0 s the SPINE Node sends sample packets to the Base Station;
- from 1.0 s to 2.0 s a third node transmits concurrent traffic which tries to saturate the channel (such concurrent traffic could represent the resulting effect of several SPINE Nodes of the WBSN).

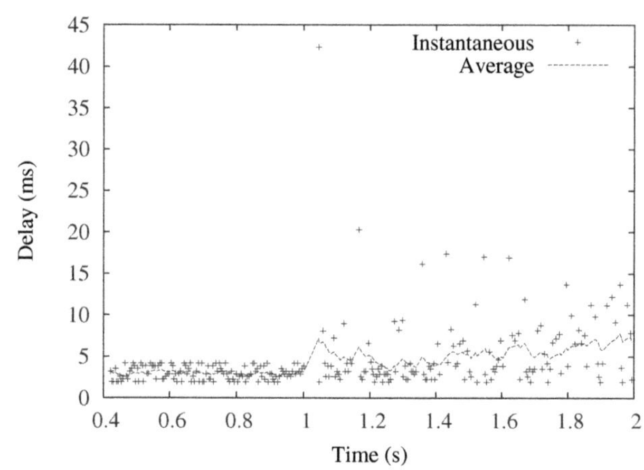

Figure 9: Instantaneous and average time spent by the SPINE Node to send a packet on the channel as a function of simulation time.

Figure 9 shows the instantaneous and average time spent by the SPINE Node to send sample packets on the channel as a function of simulation time. The value ranges from 1.9 ms to 42 ms according to the congestion level of the channel; the higher busy time during congestions is due to backoff retries and retransmissions. In this test case, the trasmission delay causes the loss of 76 packets during congested periods since the production rate of the ReISC SoC is higher that the transmission rate of the RF Module so that its output queue becomes full.

This result suggests that in some cases the optimal output rate is not determined only by application constraints but also by channel condition and the knowledge of channel statistics can allow to improve the scheduling of node activities thus decreasing energy consumption. In this section we

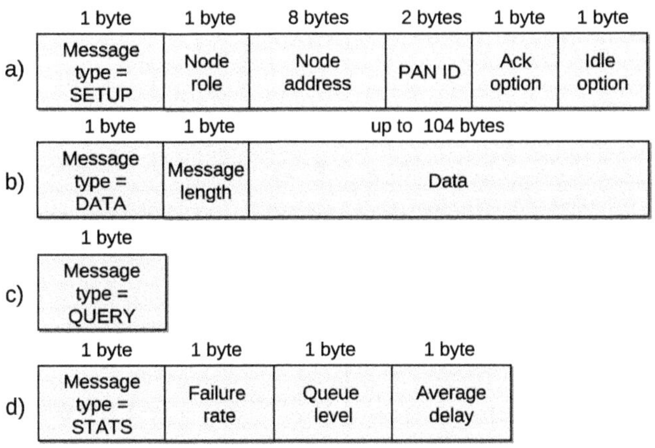

Figure 10: SPI message structure between the ReISC SoC and the RF Module: configuration command (a), data message (b), statistics request (c), and statistics response (d).

assume that the application requirements can be satisfied with a range of network transmission delays, and examine how an adaptive packet transmission scheduling strategy can reduce contention on the channel and reduce overall energy. In particular, we observed that transmission delays of up to 50 ms do not have a noticeable effect on the quality of fall detection (percentage of correct detection over percentage of false positives and false negatives). In order to use the knowledge of channel statistics to improve energy consumption, we need both a way to communicate network statistics to the ReISC SoC and an algorithm to adapt the scheduling of activities.

The SPI channel is not only used to send and receive data on the radio channel but also to configure the RF Module and to ask for transmission statistics. For this purpose, the data transmitted on the SPI channel are organized in messages structured as depicted in Figure 10. The first byte of the message determines its type. The first message is sent by the application to the RF Module to configure 802.15.4 parameters, i.e., node role (coordinator, router, end device), 64-bit MAC address, network identifier, acknowledge transmission, and behavior when it is not transmitting (idle or listening). The second message is used to carry packets to/from the network. The third message is sent by the application to the RF Module to ask for statistics about packets transmission. The fourth message is the reply which reports the number of transmission failures over 255 requests, the number of packets waiting in the output queue, and the average delay to complete a transmission (the metric shown in Figure 9. Failures happen when either the channel is found busy after a maximum number of attempts or when the maximum number of re-transmissions is reached. All these statistics can be used to estimate the channel condition.

Regarding the adaptive scheduling, in this work we assume to delay the transmission of a data message by the ReISC SoC according to the value of the variable named *Delay* which changes its value based on the following algorithm:

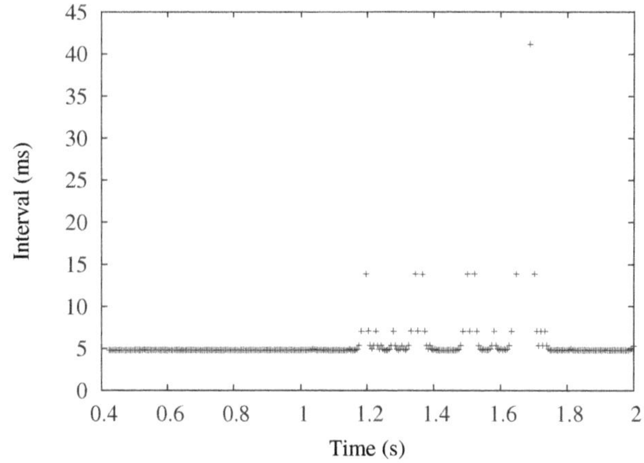

Figure 11: Time interval between two SPI data messages as a function of simulation time.

Table 2: Transmission performance and energy consumption of SPI and ADC peripherals as a function of the transmission policy.

Transmission policy	TX attempts	Received packets	PLR	Energy (μJ)
Non-adaptive	332	256	23%	400
k=1	300	233	22%	369
k=4	216	189	12%	297
k=5	205	182	11%	287
k=6	186	173	7%	271

1. Initialize *Delay* to 1 ms.

2. If the last SPI transmission failed for buffer overflow then $Delay = Delay * 2^k$ (up to a maximum, in order to preserve application functionality).

3. If the last SPI transmission was successful then $Delay = Delay/2$.

Figure 11 depicts the time interval between two SPI data messages as a function of simulation time by using the adaptive transmission scheduling with k=1. The plot shows that during channel congestion the SPINE Node sends less data.

Table 2 reports transmission performance and energy consumption of SPI and ADC peripherals as a function of the transmission policy. The second column reports the number of transmission attempts made by the SPI controller of the ReISC SoC. The third column reports the number of sample packets actually received by the Base Station. The fourth column reports the resulting packet loss rate (PLR). The fifth column reports the energy consumption of the ADC and SPI peripherals (the only components affected by the delay since the ReISC core is always running at 50 MHz). In fact, for each transmission attempt they are both working for 4.7 ms and idle until the next transmission attempt (power values are taken from Table 1). The results show that trasmission reliability increases by using a more aggressive adaptive policy while energy is saved by avoiding to send packets with a high loss probability.

Each scenario has been simulated in about 590 s on a 3 GHz Intel processor running Linus operating system.

6. CONCLUSIONS

We have presented a holistic approach to the simulation of an application based on networked embedded system. The simulation scenario has been written in SystemC/TLM and included a detailed representation of a system-on-chip running actual software components and connected to a functional representation of a wireless channel with interacting nodes. This virtual platform has been used to evaluate different application design solutions to optimize energy consumption of the SoC. In particular we adapted the transmission rate of a sensor node according to the congestion level of the channel due to the presence of concurrent traffic. The simulation approach allowed a fast exploration of different adaptation policies which increased the transmission reliability and reduced the energy consumption.

7. ACKNOWLEDGMENTS

This work has been partially supported by the COMPLEX FP7 European Integrated Project,funded by the European Commission under Grant Agreement 247999.

8. REFERENCES

[1] M. Chung and C.-M. Kyung. Enhancing performance of HW/SW cosimulation and coemulation by reducing communication overhead. *IEEE Transactions on Computers*, 55(2):125–136, Feb. 2006.

[2] SystemC Network Simulation Library – version 2, 2012. URL: http://sourceforge.net/projects/scnsl.

[3] European Commission. COdesign and power Management in PLatform-based design space EXploration - COMPLEX. URL: https://complex.offis.de/, (FP7-IST-247999), 2009.

[4] LAN/MAN Standards Committee of the IEEE Computer Society. IEEE Standard for Information technology - Telecommunications and information exchange between systems - Local and metropolitan area networks - Specific requirements - Part 15.4: Wireless Medium Access Control (MAC) and Physical Layer (PHY) Specifications for Low Rate Wireless Personal Area Networks (LR-WPANs). Sept. 2006.

[5] S. McCanne and S. Floyd. NS Network Simulator – version 2. URL: http://www.isi.edu/nsnam/ns.

[6] F. Mulas, A. Acquaviva, S. Carta, G. Fenu, D. Quaglia, and F. F. Network-adaptive management of computation energy in wireless sensor networks. In *Proc. of ACM Symposium on Applied Computing (SAC)*, pages 756–763, Mar. 2010.

[7] OSCI and IEEE. IEEE Std 1666 - 2005 IEEE Standard SystemC Language Reference Manual. *IEEE Std 1666-2005*, pages 1–423, 2006.

[8] Signal Processing In Node Environment (SPINE). URL: http://spine.tilab.com/.

Hands-On Tutorial

Coarse-Grained Reconfigurable Architectures - Compilation and Exploration

Tom Vander Aa
imec
Kapeldreef 75,
Leuven, Belgium
vanderaa@imec.be

Panagiotis Theocharis
Ghent University
Sint Pietersnieuwstraat 41,
Ghent, Belgium
Panagiotis.Theocharis@elis.ugent.be

ABSTRACT

CGRAs consist of an array of a large number of functional units (FUs) interconnected by a mesh style network. Register files are distributed throughout the CGRAs to hold temporary values and are accessible only by a subset of FUs. The FUs can execute common word-level operations, including addition, subtraction, and multiplication. CGRA processors accelerate inner loops of applications by exploiting instruction level parallelism (ILP) and in some cases also data-level and task-level parallelism (DLP & TLP).

The aim of this tutorial is to give insight in CGRA architectures, their compilation techniques, and to experience first hand how to do source code mapping on a CGRA. Therefore the tutorial consists of presentations as well as a hands-on session.

Categories and Subject Descriptors

C.1.4 **[Computer Systems Organization]**: Processor Architectures – parallel architectures.

General Terms: Performance, Design.

Keywords: CGRA, reconfigurable architecture, compiler, source code mapping.

1. SPEAKERS' BIOGRAPHY

Tom Vander Aa is a senior researcher in the Wireless Communication group of IMEC working on low energy high performance architectures and compilation techniques. Since 2005 he has been working on the ADRES coarse-grain array processor. In 2005, Tom Vander Aa obtained a PhD in electrical engineering from KULeuven, Leuven, Belgium on energy optimization for instruction memory of embedded processors. He has a master in computer science degree, also from KULeuven and is a member of the IEEE.

Panagiotis Theocharis is a doctoral researcher in the Computer Systems Lab of Ghent University working on split compilation for accelerator-based multicores. He holds a diploma in electrical and computer engineering from the National Technical University of Athens and is a member of the ACM and the IEEE.

2. TOPICS

Below is a list of topics covered during the tutorial:

- **Presentation**: Introduction to CGRAs and their compilation techniques, taking the ADRES CGRA as an example (45')
- **Presentation + demo**: Introduction to the DRESC tool chain (15')
- **Guided hands-on**: The audience can have a first try of compilation and simulation. (30')
- **Presentation**: How to optimize your source code for CGRAs (30')
- **Hands-on**: The audience will try to optimize a prepared example for the CGRA. (30')
- **Presentation**: Current research in CGRA compilation: building optimizing compilers using machine learning. (30')

CODES+ISSS'12, October 7–12, 2012, Tampere, Finland.
ACM 978-1-4503-1426-8/12/09.

Soft Errors: The Hardware-Software Interface

Kyoungwoo Lee
Yonsei University
Seoul, South Korea
kyoungwoo.lee@yonsei.ac.kr

Aviral Shrivastava
Arizona State University
Phoenix, USA
aviral.shrivastava@asu.edu

Reiley Jeyapaul
Arizona State University
Phoenix, USA
reiley@asu.edu

ABSTRACT
A recent report from the ITRS identifies soft errors, as one of the most important reliability challenges for the coming decades. Soft errors are transient errors caused by several effects e.g., voltage fluctuations, wire-cross talks, and cosmic particle strikes; and manifest as a temporary switch of the logic value of a transistor. While it is not possible to prove nor disprove that a certain error happened due to soft errors, several fiscal disasters e.g., Sun server crashes in 2000, and HP server crashes in 2005, have been attributed to soft errors. Industry has moved from the position of ignoring soft errors to adding design efforts for protection from them. For instance, in the recently announced nVIDIA's Fermi GPUs, the L1 cache, L2 cache and register files are ECC protected. Although the soft error rate is about once-per year today, it is expected to reach alarming levels of once-per-day in about a decade or two. Researchers are busy finding cost-effective solutions to protect computing devices from soft errors.

This tutorial will attempt to cover the entire gamut of soft error protection techniques, but will particularly focus on the soft error mitigation techniques at the hardware/software interface. Much time will be spent on microarchitectural, compiler, and hybrid compiler-microarchitectural techniques for soft error mitigation. This tutorial will be particularly useful for budding researchers who are fascinated by soft errors, and want to explore this as their research direction. For such researchers, this tutorial will be a one-stop-shop to acquire knowledge of and analyze seminal research work in the field of soft error mitigation, at several design layers. For developers who have been working on soft errors at different levels, this will give them a picture of what can be done at other levels, so that they can provide complementary cross-layer protection. Finally, researchers and developers working on other aspects of system design can learn how soft errors are going to affect them.

Categories and Subject Descriptors
B.7.3 [**Integrated Circuits**]: Reliability and testing
D.3.4 [**Programming Languages**]: Processors

Keywords
Soft error mitigation, compiler, microarchitectural techniques.

1. SPEAKERS AT THE TUTORIAL
Prof. Aviral Shrivastava is Associate Professor in the School of Computing Informatics, and Decision Systems Engineering at the Arizona State University, USA. He received his Masters and Ph.D. in Computer Science from University of California, Irvine, and Bachelors in Computer Science from Indian Institute of Technology, Delhi. Prof. Shrivastava received the prestigious 2010 NSF CAREER award for his research and education on Soft Errors.

Prof. Kyoungwoo Lee is Assistant Professor in the Department of Computer Science and Engineering at Yonsei University, Seoul, South Korea. His research is in the area of embedded systems, with a specific focus on cross-layer design and optimization for error-aware and energy-efficient embedded systems.

Dr. Reiley Jeyapaul is a Post-Doctoral Researcher at the Compiler Microarchitecture Lab (CML), Arizona State University, USA. His research focuses on developing methods to ensure reliability in modern and future computing systems. His recent paper on Cache Vulnerability Equations (CVE), was the second highest rated paper in LCTES 2010..

2. TOPICS COVERED
- Soft Errors, Trends, and Challenges
- Low-level and Microarchitectural Techniques
- Compiler Based Techniques for Soft Error Mitigation
- System and Program Level Techniques
- Conclusion and Future Directions

This research was partially supported by funding from National Science Foundation grant CCF-1055094 (CAREER) and the MKE (Ministry of Knowledge Economy), Korea, under the Global Collaborative R&D program supervised by the KIAT (M002300089).

Author Index

www.ingramcontent.com/pod-product-compliance
Ingram Content Group UK Ltd.
Pitfield, Milton Keynes, MK11 3LW, UK
UKHW051417290926
15471UKWH00009B/1647

9 781450 314268